*B*uy one today and you won't be waiting in line tomorrow.

Get the card that's better than cash...
The Mobil *GO* Card, a prepaid gas card that
you can use for gas, service, or snack
purchases at your neighborhood Mobil
station...a Great Gift Idea!

Call toll free...1-800-730-TO-GO to order.

*G*et one today for *ALL* your motoring needs nationwide.

The Mobil Card, a credit card that you can
apply for free with no annual fees for gas,
service, or snack purchases at Mobil stations
nationwide.

Mobil

883 821 422 01 001

MODERN TRAVELER

Call toll free...1-800-266-6624 to apply.

Introducing Mobil prepaid gas cards.

They're not credit cards.
Mobil GO Cards are prepaid gas cards that you can buy for $25, $50, or $100 and use to pay for Mobil gas, service, or Mobil Mart purchases.

They're better than cash.
With Mobil GO Cards you can pay right at the pump or at the register, so they're faster to use and more convenient than cash. Every time you use your card, the purchase amount is deducted from your card and the remaining value is printed on your receipt.

They're great for business and pleasure.
Whether you need to control business expenses or budget personal expenses, Mobil GO Cards make it easier with their preset dollar values. And they make great gifts for family, friends, and employees.

They're always there when you need them.
With Mobil GO Cards in your wallet, purse, or glove compartment, you always know you have money for gas, munchies, or unexpected repairs.

Call 1-800-730-TO-GO to order.
You may charge your order to your Mobil card or any major credit card. OR simply visit your neighborhood Mobil station and buy a card!

Mobil Oil Corporation
3225 Gallows Road, Faifax, VA 22037

Introducing the Mobil Credit Card.

It's FREE.
There's no annual fee or membership charge. No finance charge either, on balances paid on your bill within the 25-day grace period.

It's EQUAL.
Price-wise— to paying cash. We don't charge extra for credit as some do. At most Mobil locations you can quickly and conveniently "Pay at the Pump," a real time saver.

It's CONVENIENT.
Use your Mobil Credit Card locally or at 9,000 Mobil dealers in the U.S.... or at participating dealers at Canada.

It BUYS THE BEST.
Isn't your car worth it? A gas that gives you quick starts and truly cleans your engine while you drive. A motor oil that helps keep your engine like new. And more importantly, YOU the customer, a clean and safe place and friendly service.

Call 1-800-266-6624 today to apply for your Mobil Card.

MCFC National Bank
P. O. Box 419010, Kansas City, MO 64141-6010

1996

Mobil
Travel
Guide®

Southwest and South Central

Arkansas

Colorado

Kansas

Louisiana

Missouri

New Mexico

Oklahoma

Texas

Fodor's Travel Publications, Inc.

Guide Staff

General Manager: Diane Connolly
Inspection Coordinators: Thomas W. Grant,
  Kristin Schiller
Inspection Assistant: Adam Blieberg
Editorial Consultants: Andrea Lehman, J. Walman
Creative Director: Fabrizio La Rocca
Cover Design: John Olenyik
Cover Photograph: Lindsay Hebbard/Woodfin Camp

Acknowledgments

We gratefully acknowledge the help of our 100 field representatives for their efficient and perceptive inspection of every lodging and dining establishment listed; the establishments' proprietors for their cooperation in showing their facilities and providing information about them; the many users of previous editions of the the *Mobil Travel Guide* who have taken the time to share their experiences; and, for their time and information, the thousands of chambers of commerce, convention and visitors' bureaus, city, state, and provincial tourism offices, and government agencies who assisted in our research.

Mobil

Copyright

Published in 1996 by Fodor's Travel Publications, Inc.
201 E. 50th St.
New York, NY 10022

Southwest and South Central
ISBN 0-679-03049-2
ISSN 0076-9843

Printed in the United States of America
10 9 8 7 6 5 4 3 2 1

Contents

Southwest and South Central

Maps

Larger, more detailed maps are available at many Mobil service stations.

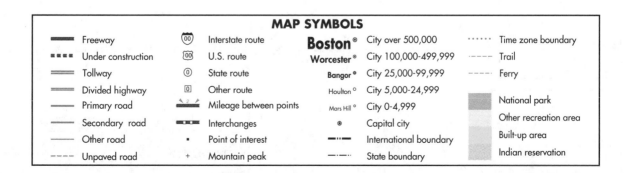

MAP SYMBOLS

▬▬ Freeway	🛡 Interstate route	**Boston**® City over 500,000
■■■■ Under construction	⬡ U.S. route	**Worcester**® City 100,000-499,999
═══ Tollway	⓪ State route	**Bangor** ● City 25,000-99,999
▬▬ Divided highway	⓪ Other route	Houlton ○ City 5,000-24,999
── Primary road	Mileage between points	Mars Hill ○ City 0-4,999
── Secondary road	■■■ Interchanges	⊛ Capital city
── Other road	· Point of interest	▬··▬ International boundary
---- Unpaved road	+ Mountain peak	▬·▬·· State boundary

······ Time zone boundary	
----- Trail	
----- Ferry	
▨ National park	
▨ Other recreation area	
▨ Built-up area	
▨ Indian reservation	

CANADA

BRITISH COLUMBIA
ALBERTA
SASKATCHEWAN
MAN

Vancouver
Victoria
Bellingham
Kamloops
Calgary
Saskatoon
Regina
Medicine Hat
Lethbridge

WASHINGTON
Seattle
Tacoma
Olympia
Yakima
Spokane
Lewiston

Portland
Salem
Eugene
Medford

OREGON

MONTANA
Great Falls
Missoula
Butte
Billings

NORTH DAKOTA
Minot
Bismarck

SOUTH DAKOTA
Pierre
Rapid City

IDAHO
Boise
Idaho Falls
Twin Falls
Pocatello

WYOMING
Casper
Cheyenne
Laramie

NEBRASKA

PACIFIC OCEAN

Eureka
Redding
Chico
Reno
Carson City
Sacramento
Stockton
San Francisco
Oakland
San Jose
Salinas
Fresno
NEVADA
Las Vegas

Logan
Ogden
Salt Lake City
Provo
UTAH
Grand Junction
St. George

COLORADO
Denver
Colorado Springs
Pueblo

KANSAS

CALIFORNIA
San Luis Obispo
Bakersfield
Santa Barbara
Los Angeles
Long Beach
San Bernardino
Riverside
Indio
San Diego

Flagstaff
Phoenix
Tucson
Yuma
ARIZONA

Santa Fe
Albuquerque
NEW MEXICO
Las Cruces
Roswell
Alamogordo

Amarillo
Lubbock
Clovis
Lawton
Wichita Falls
Abilene
TEXAS
Odessa
San Angelo
San Antonio

Tijuana
BAJA CALIFORNIA
El Centro
SONORA
El Paso
Juárez
Nuevo Casas Grandes
CHIHUAHUA
Chihuahua

MEXICO

COAHUILA
Del Rio
Piedras Negras
Monclova
Gomez Palacio
Nuevo Laredo
Laredo
McAllen
DURANGO
Durango
Monterrey
Saltillo
NUEVO LEON
ZACATECAS
SINALOA
Mazatlán
TAMAULIPAS
Ciudad Victor

HAWAII
Wailua
Honolulu
Hilo
PACIFIC OCEAN
0 100 Miles
0 200 Kilometers
© 1996 GeoSystems Global Corp.

0 250 500 Miles
0 250 500 750 Kilometers

R.U.S.
U.S.
CAN.
U.S.
ALASKA
Nome
Fairbanks
Anchorage
Valdez
Kodiak
YUKON
Dawson
Whitehorse
Juneau
B.C.
BERING SEA
ALEUTIAN ISLANDS
PACIFIC OCEAN

© 1996 GeoSystems Global Corp.

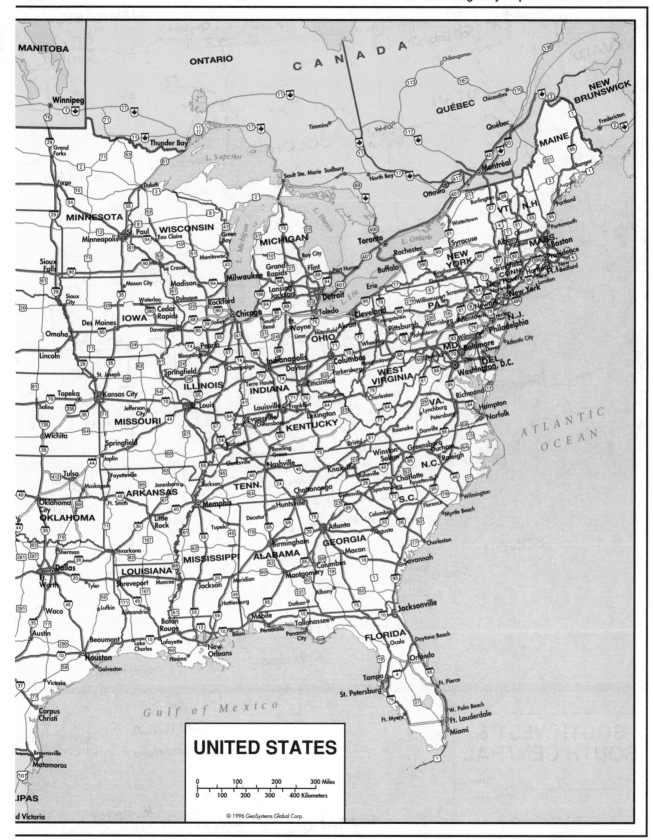

UNITED STATES

0   100   200   300 Miles
0   100   200   300   400 Kilometers

NEVADA

NEBRASKA

Laramie   Cheyenne

80   Salt Lake City
Provo   191   25   76
UTAH   40   385   83
40
6   15   70   40   25   70   385
50   70   285   Denver   70
93   15   Grand   COLORADO   24   KANSAS
Junction   50   Colorado   287
St. George   666   Springs
Los   89   160   285   Pueblo   50
Vegas   93   160   160   50
93   666   87   287
Flagstaff   285   25   83
93   40   Santa Fe   54
ARIZONA   40   Albuquerque   40   Amarillo
17   NEW   60   287
60   MEXICO   Clovis   27
95   Phoenix   191   285   70   Lubbock
8   25   83
Alamogordo   Roswell   87
Tucson   70   Abilene
19   10   Las Cruces   TEXAS
El Paso   20   Odessa
2   SONORA   Juárez   10   San Angelo
2   2   45   285   10
Nuevo   10   90   87
Casas Grandes   45
CHIHUAHUA   Del Rio   90
277   35
Chihuahua   Piedras Negras
M E X I C O
57   Nuevo   Lared
COAHUILA   Laredo
Monclova   83
57
45   49   Monterrey   57
Gomez   40
DURANGO   Palacio

SOUTHWEST &
SOUTH CENTRAL

0   100   200 Miles
0   100   200   300 Kilometers

© 1996 GeoSystems Global Corp.

IOWA
MISSOURI
ILLINOIS
INDIANA
OHIO
KENTUCKY
TENN.
ARKANSAS
OKLAHOMA
LOUISIANA
MISSISSIPPI
ALABAMA

Gulf of Mexico

Omaha • Lincoln • Des Moines • Davenport • Joliet • South Bend • Ft. Wayne • Lima • Columbus • Peoria • Bloomington • Springfield • Indianapolis • Dayton • Cincinnati • Terre Haute • Topeka • Salina • Kansas City • St. Joseph • Jefferson City • St. Louis • Louisville • Frankfort • Lexington • Wichita • Springfield • Evansville • Owensboro • Joplin • Paducah • Bowling Green • Nashville • Knoxville • Tulsa • Fayetteville • Jonesboro • Clarksville • Chattanooga • Muskogee • Jackson • Huntsville • Oklahoma City • Ft. Smith • Little Rock • Memphis • Decatur • Atlanta • Lawton • Tupelo • Birmingham • Wichita Falls • Sherman • Texarkana • Columbus • Montgomery • Dallas • Shreveport • Monroe • Jackson • Meridian • Albany • Ft. Worth • Tyler • Dothan • Waco • Lufkin • Alexandria • Hattiesburg • Austin • Beaumont • Lake Charles • Lafayette • Baton Rouge • Mobile • Tallahassee • San Antonio • Houston • Galveston • Houma • New Orleans • Biloxi • Pensacola • Panama City • Victoria • Corpus Christi • Laredo • McAllen • Brownsville • Matamoros

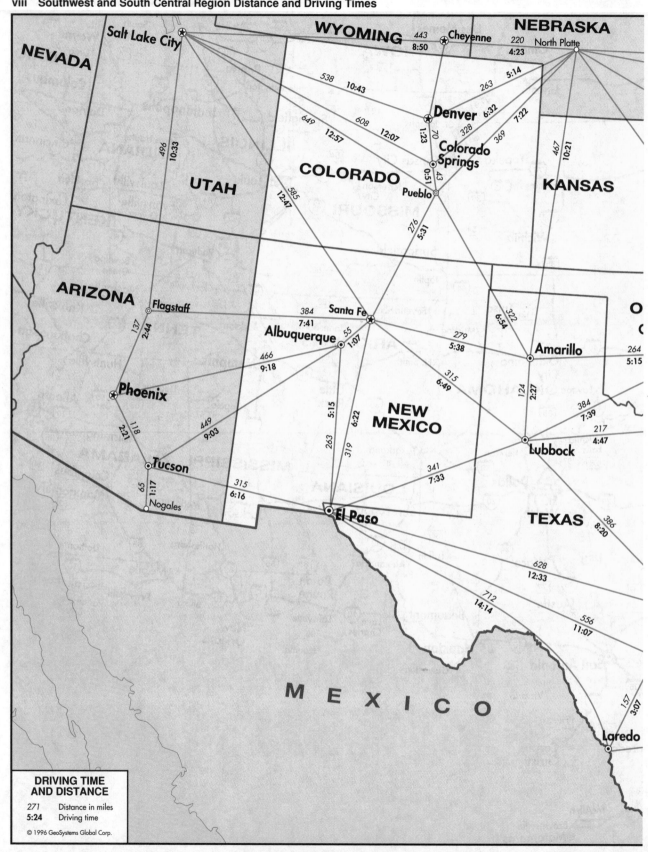

**DRIVING TIME
AND DISTANCE**

271   Distance in miles
5:24 Driving time

© 1996 GeoSystems Global Corp.

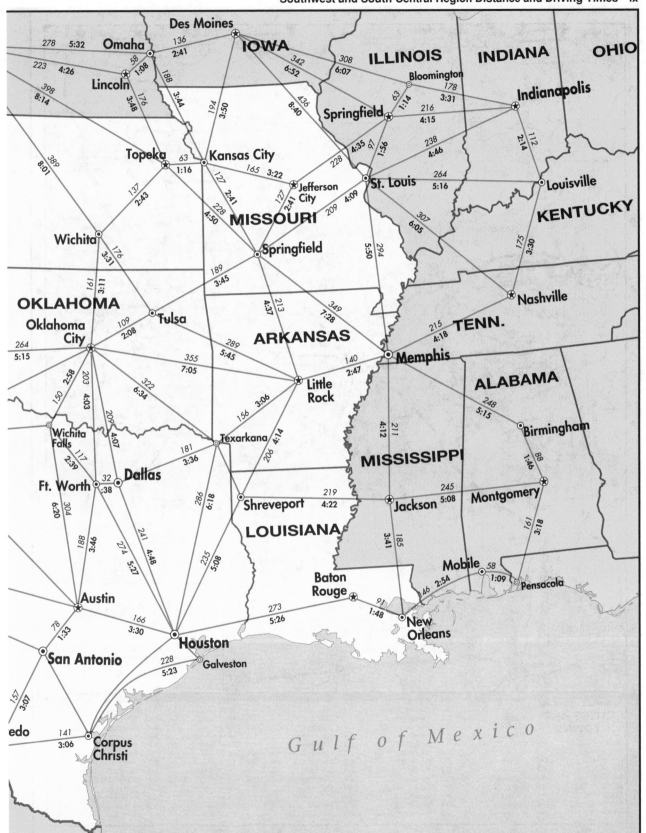

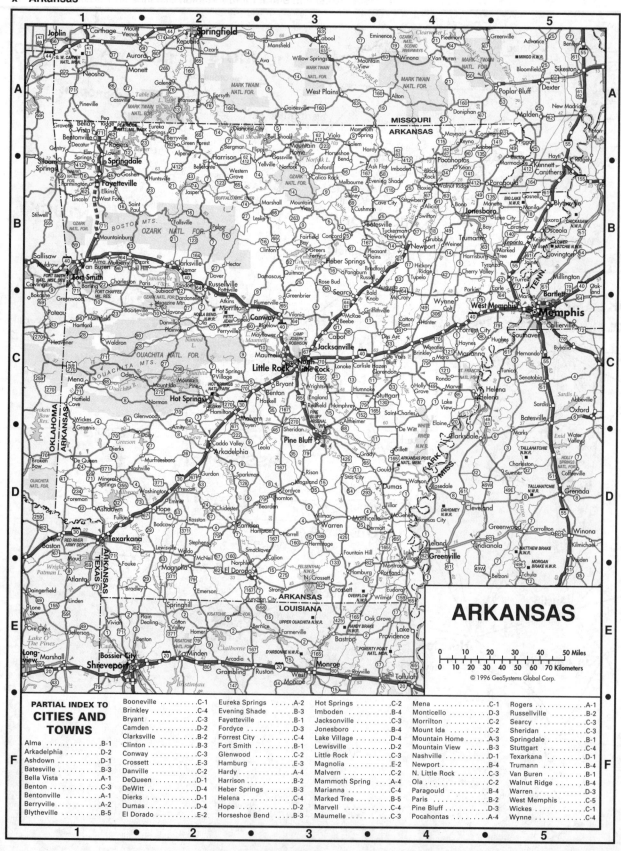

ARKANSAS

0   10   20   30   40   50 Miles
0 10 20 30 40 50 60 70 Kilometers

© 1996 GeoSystems Global Corp.

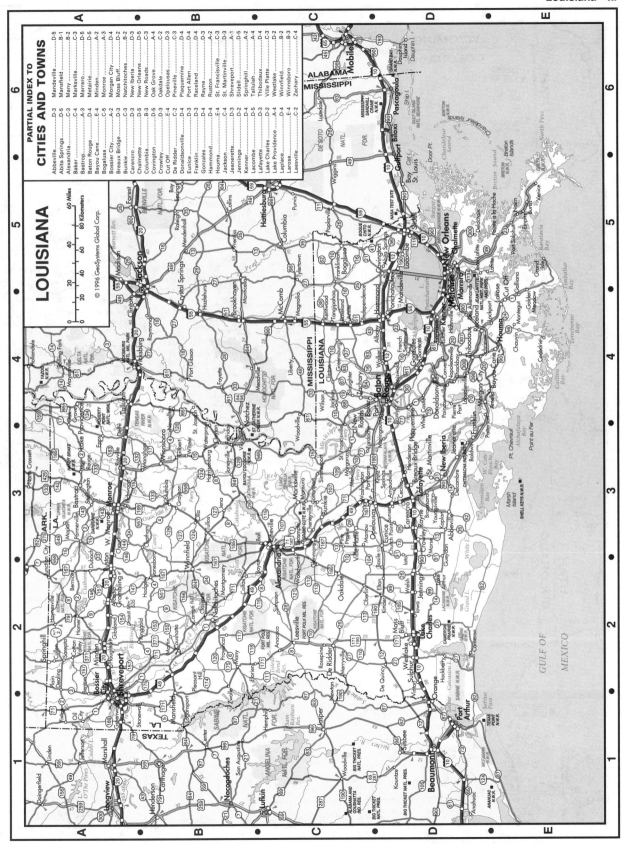

LOUISIANA

© 1996 GeoSystems Global Corp.

0   20   40   60 Miles
0   20   40   60   80 Kilometers

PARTIAL INDEX TO CITIES AND TOWNS

Abbeville	D-3
Abita Springs	D-5
Alexandria	C-3
Baker	C-4
Bastrop	A-3
Baton Rouge	D-4
Bayou Cane	E-4
Bogalusa	C-5
Bossier City	A-2
Breaux Bridge	D-3
Bunkie	C-3
Carencro	D-3
Chalmette	D-5
Columbia	B-3
Covington	D-5
Crowley	D-3
Cut Off	E-4
De Ridder	C-2
Donaldsonville	D-4
Eunice	D-3
Franklin	D-4
Gonzales	D-4
Hammond	D-4
Houma	E-4
Jackson	C-4
Jeanerette	D-3
Jennings	D-3
Kenner	D-5
Lacombe	D-5
Lafayette	D-3
Lake Charles	D-2
Lake Providence	A-4
Laplace	D-5
Larose	E-4
Leesville	C-2

Mandeville	D-5
Mansfield	B-1
Many	B-2
Marksville	C-3
Marrero	D-5
Metairie	D-5
Minden	A-2
Monroe	A-3
Morgan City	D-4
Moss Bluff	D-2
Natchitoches	B-2
New Iberia	D-3
New Orleans	D-5
New Roads	C-3
Oak Grove	A-4
Opelousas	D-3
Pineville	C-3
Plaquemine	D-4
Port Allen	D-4
Raceland	D-4
Rayne	D-3
Ruston	A-2
St. Francisville	C-4
St. Martinville	D-3
Shreveport	A-1
Slidell	D-5
Springhill	A-2
Tallulah	A-4
Thibodaux	D-4
Ville Platte	C-3
Westlake	D-2
Winnfield	B-2
Winnsboro	B-3
Zachary	C-4

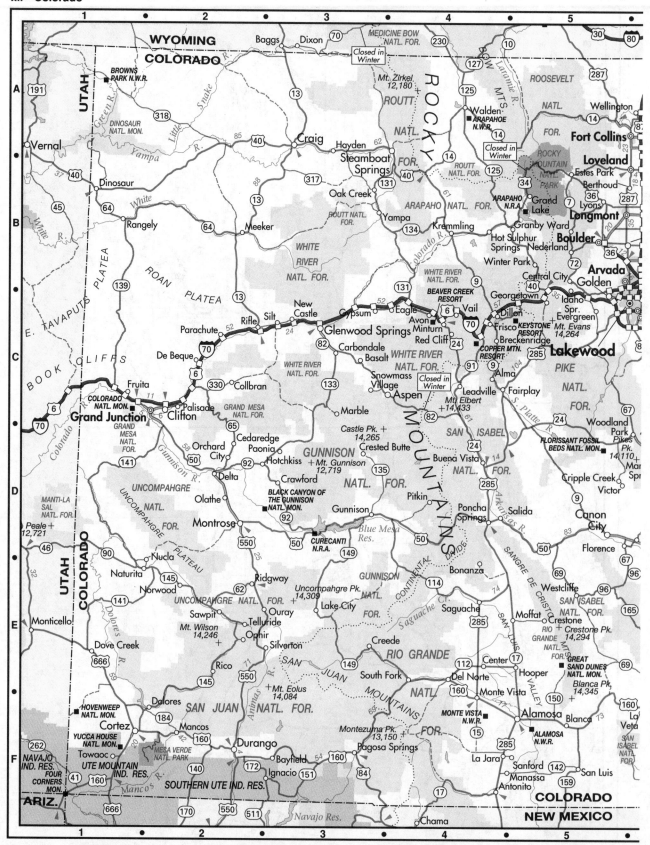

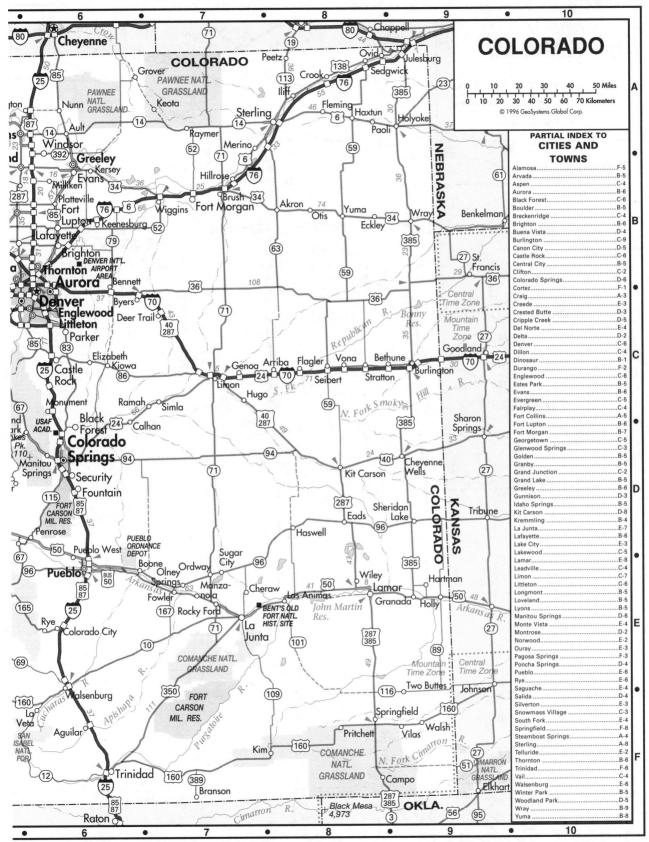

COLORADO

© 1996 GeoSystems Global Corp.

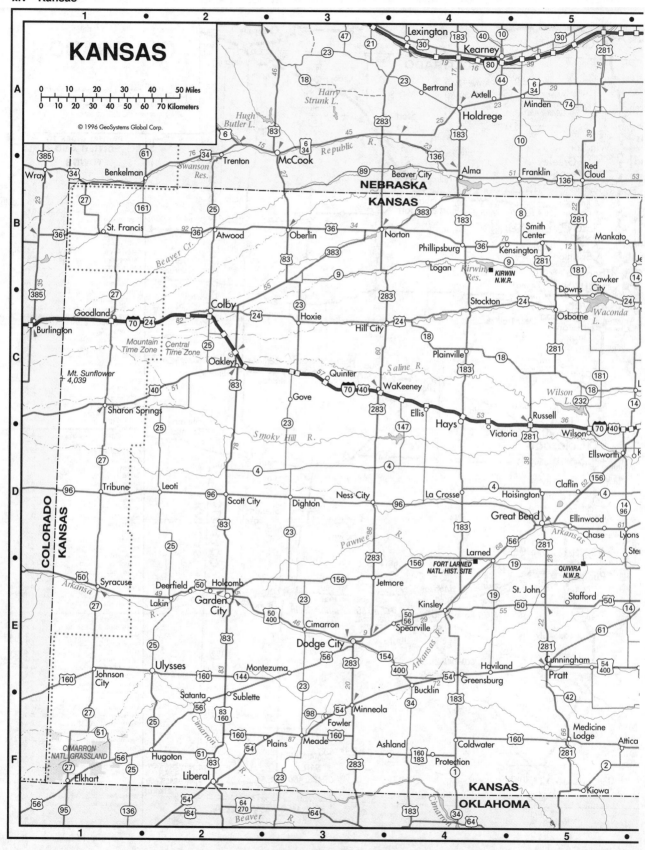

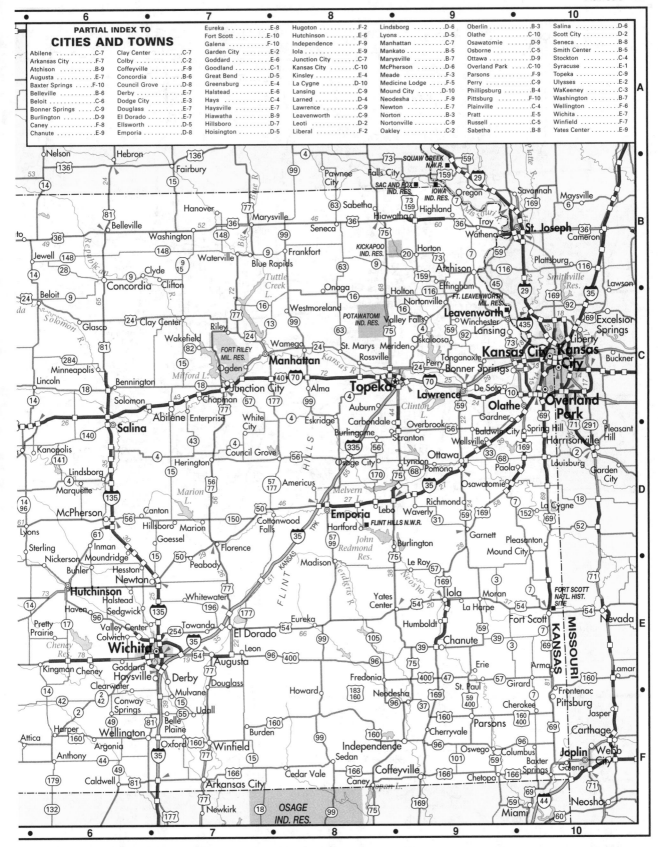

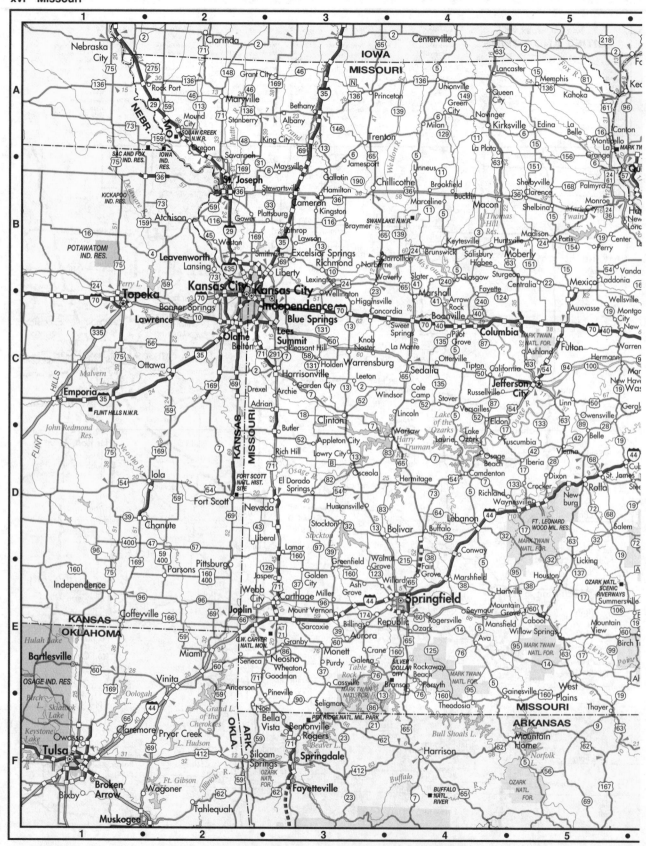

MISSOURI

0   10   20   30   40   50 Miles
0 10 20 30 40 50 60 70 Kilometers

© 1996 GeoSystems Global Corp.

PARTIAL INDEX TO
CITIES AND TOWNS

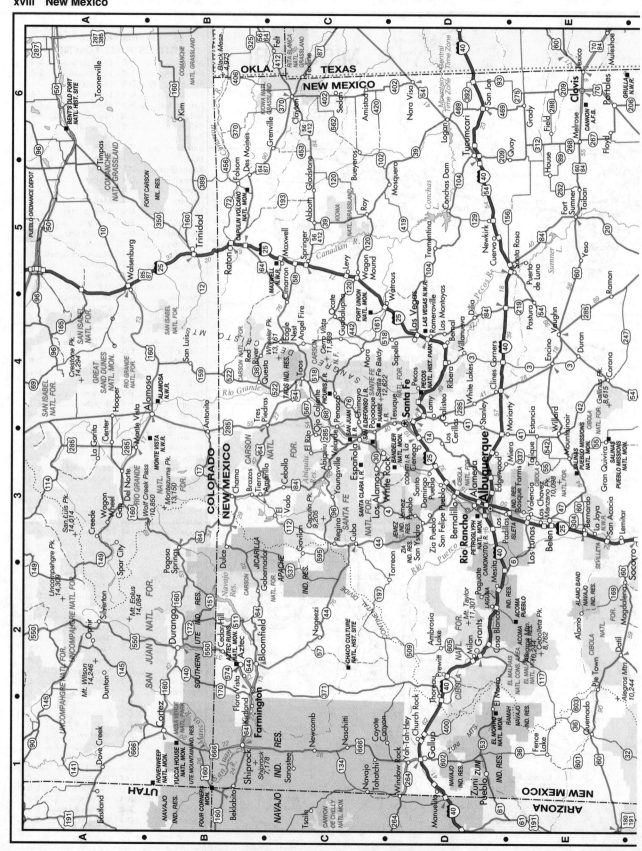

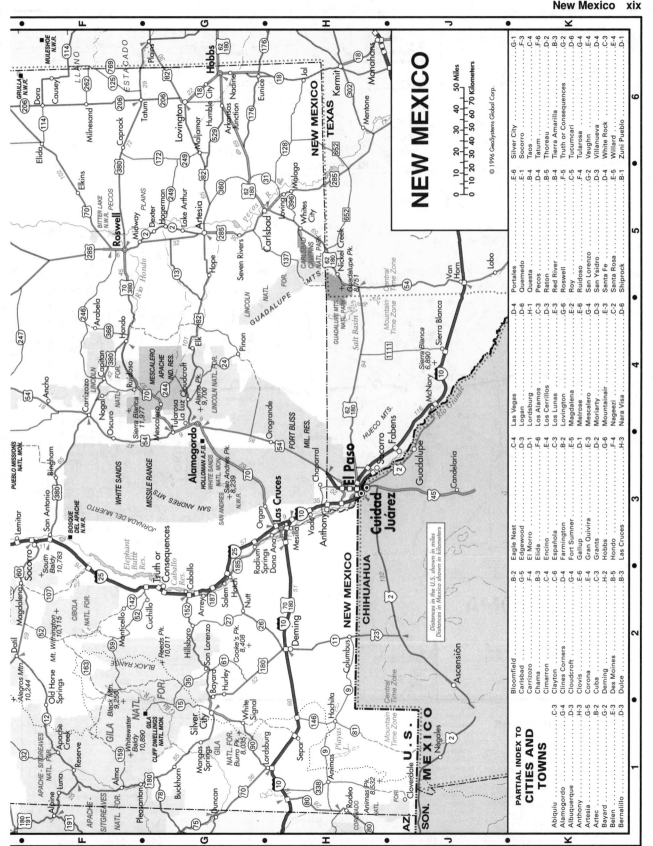

NEW MEXICO

© 1996 GeoSystems Global Corp.

0 10 20 30 40 50 Miles
0 10 20 30 40 50 60 70 Kilometers

Distances in the U.S. shown in miles
Distances in Mexico shown in kilometers

PARTIAL INDEX TO CITIES AND TOWNS

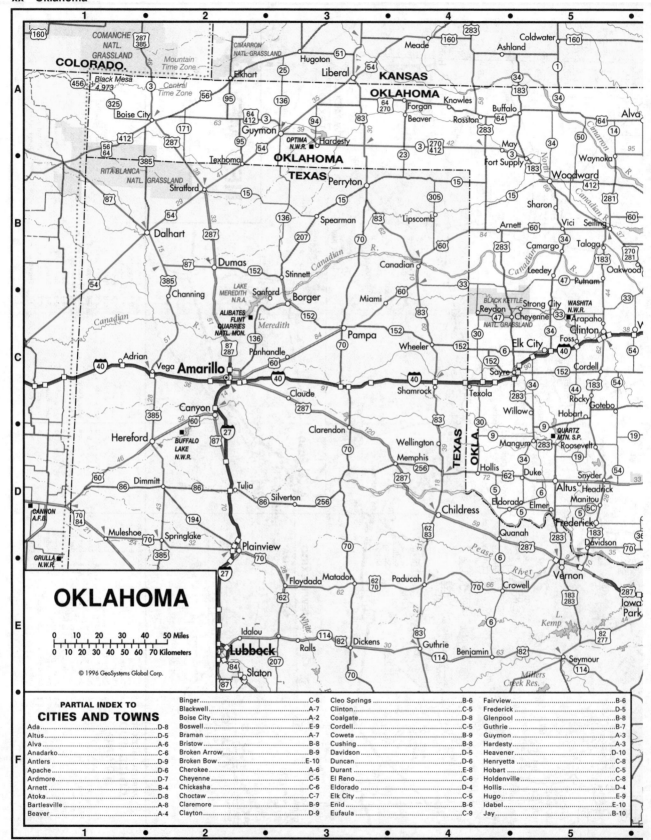

OKLAHOMA

0 10 20 30 40 50 Miles
0 10 20 30 40 50 60 70 Kilometers

© 1996 GeoSystems Global Corp.

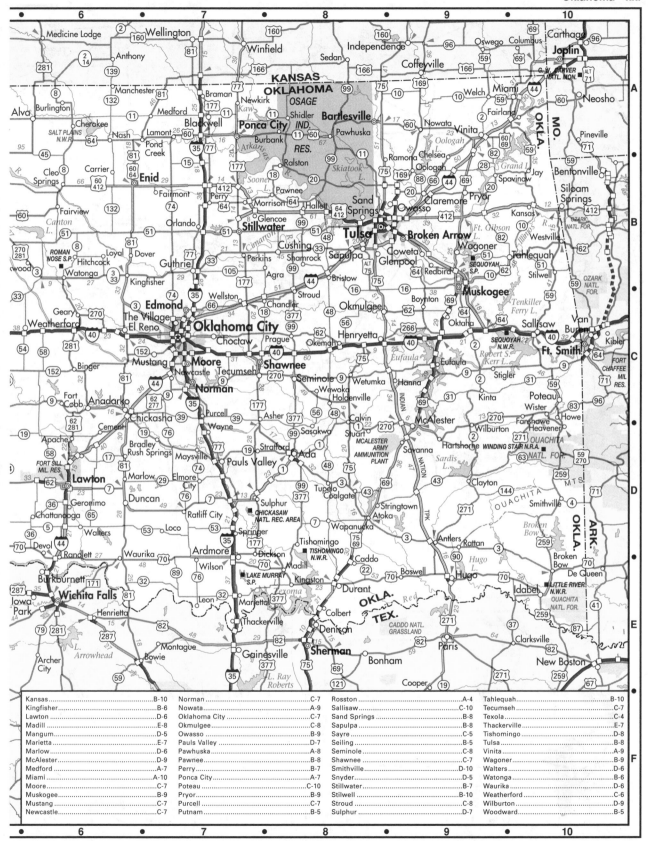

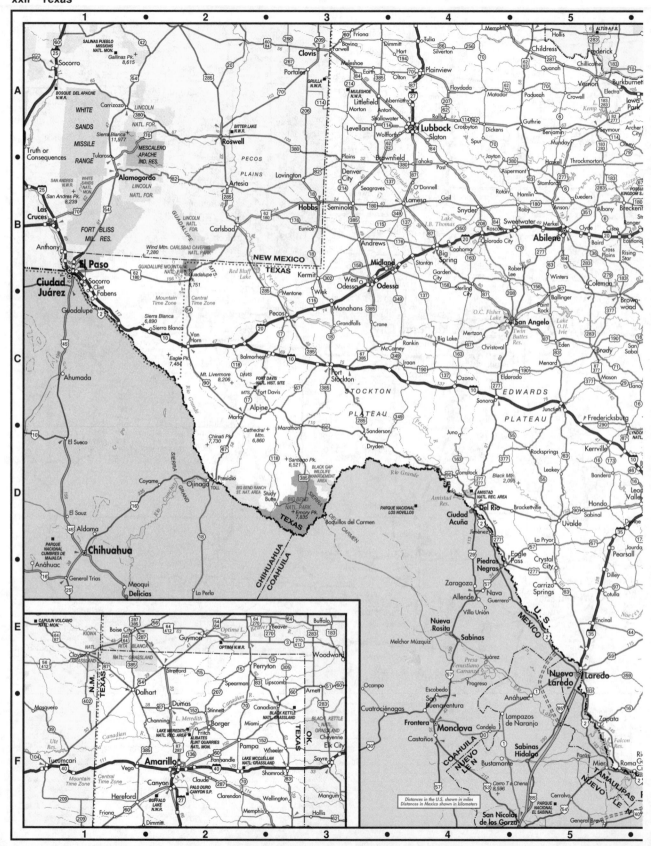

Distances in the U.S. shown in miles
Distances in Mexico shown in kilometers

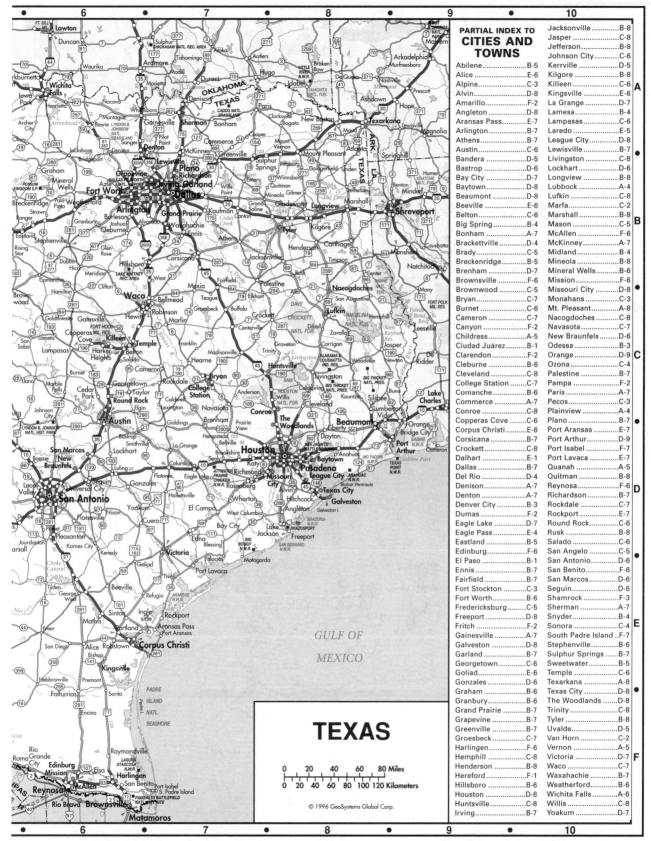

TEXAS

0   20   40   60   80 Miles

0 20 40 60 80 100 120 Kilometers

© 1996 GeoSystems Global Corp.

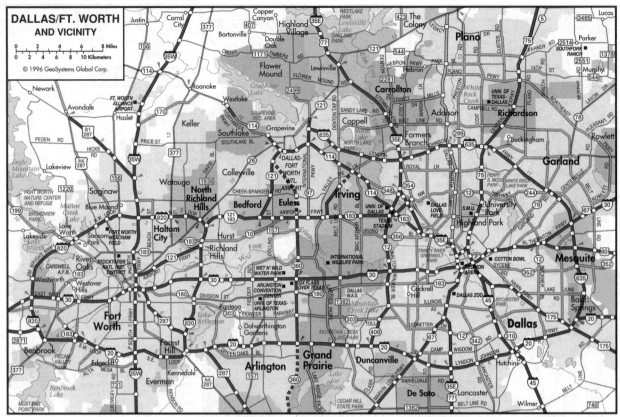

DALLAS/FT. WORTH
AND VICINITY

0 2 4 6 8 Miles
0 2 4 6 8 10 Kilometers
© 1996 GeoSystems Global Corp.

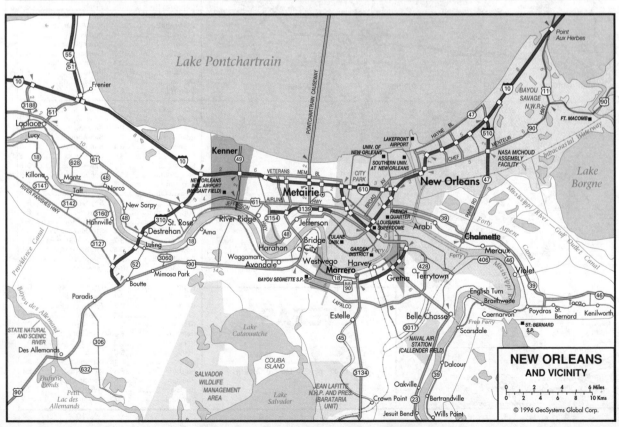

NEW ORLEANS
AND VICINITY

0 2 4 6 Miles
0 2 4 6 8 10 Kms
© 1996 GeoSystems Global Corp.

Welcome to the Mobil Travel Guide

Whether you're going on an extended family vacation, a weekend getaway, or a business trip, you need good, solid information on where to stay and eat and what to see and do. It would be nice if you could take a corps of well-seasoned travelers with you to suggest lodgings and activities, or ask a local restaurant critic for advice on dining spots, but since these options are rarely practical, the *Mobil Travel Guide* is the next best thing. It puts a huge database of information at your disposal and provides the value judgments and advice you need to use that information to its fullest.

Published by Fodor's Travel Publications, Inc., in collaboration with Mobil Corporation, the sponsor since 1958, these books contain the most comprehensive, up-to-date information possible on each region. In fact, listings are revised and ratings reviewed annually, based on inspection reports from our field representatives, evaluation by senior staff, and comments from more than 100,000 readers. These incredible data are then used to develop the *Mobil Travel Guide's* impartial quality ratings, indicated by stars, which Americans have trusted for decades.

Space limitations make it impossible for us to include every fine hotel and restaurant, so we have picked a representative group, all above-average for their type. There's no charge to any establishment for inclusion, and only places that meet our standards are chosen. Because travelers' needs differ, we make every effort to select a variety of establishments and provide the information to decide what's right for you. If you're looking for a lodging at a certain price or location, or even one that offers 24-hour room service, you'll find the answers you need at your fingertips. Take a minute to read the next section, How to Use This Book; it'll make finding the information you want a breeze.

Also look at Making the Most of Your Trip, the section that follows. It's full of tips from savvy travelers that can help you save money, stay safe, and get around more easily—the keys to making any trip a success.

Though the *Mobil Travel Guide* staff has scoured the United States to come up with an extensive and well-balanced list of the best places to stay, you don't have to beat the bushes to come up with a reservation. Now we've teamed up with an established hotel-booking service to make it easy for you to secure a room at the property of your choice. It's fast, it's free, and confirmation is guaranteed. If your first choice is booked, the operators can line up your second right away. Just call 1-800-44-MOBIL.

Of course, the passage of time means that some establishments will close, change hands, remodel, improve, or go downhill. Though every effort has been made to ensure the accuracy of all information when it was printed, change is inevitable. Always call and confirm that a place is open and that it has the features you want. Whatever your experiences at any of the establishments we list—and we hope they're terrific—or if you have general comments about our guide, we'd love to hear from you. Use the convenient postage-paid card near the end of this book, or drop us a line at the *Mobil Travel Guide,* Fodor's Travel Publications, Inc., 4709 W. Golf Road, Suite 803, Skokie, IL 60076.

So pack this book in your suitcase or toss it next to you on the front seat. If it gets dog-eared, so much the better. We here at the *Mobil Travel Guide* wish you a safe and successful trip.

Bon voyage and happy driving,

THE EDITORS

How to Use This Book

The *Mobil Travel Guide* is easy to use. At the beginning of each state chapter is a general introduction that both provides a general geographical and historical orientation to the state and covers basic statewide tourist information, from state recreation areas to seat-belt laws. The balance of each chapter is devoted to the travel destinations within the state—cities and towns, state and national parks, and tourist regions—which, like the states themselves, are arranged alphabetically.

What follows is an explanation of the wealth of information you'll find within those travel destinations—information on the area, on things to see and do there, and on where to stay and eat.

Maps and Map Coordinates

The first thing you'll notice is that next to each destination is a set of map coordinates. These refer to the appropriate state map in the front of this book. In addition, there are maps of selected larger cities in the front section as well as maps of key neighborhoods and airports within the sections on the cities themselves.

Destination Information

Because many travel destinations are so close to other cities and towns where visitors might find additional attractions, accommodations, and restaurants, cross-references to those places are included whenever possible. Also listed are addresses and phone numbers for travel-information resources—usually the local chamber of commerce or office of tourism—as well as pertinent vital statistics and a brief introduction to the area.

What to See and Do

More than 11,000 museums, art galleries, amusement parks, universities, historic sites and houses, plantations, churches, state parks, ski areas, and other attractions are described in the *Mobil Travel Guide*. A white star on a black background ★ signals that the attraction is one of the best in the city or town. Since municipal parks, public tennis courts, swimming pools, golf courses, and small educational institutions are common to most towns, they are generally excluded.

Following the attraction's description are the months and days it's open, address/location and phone number, and admission costs (see the inside front cover for an explanation of the cost symbols). Note that directions are given from the center of the town under which the attraction is listed, which may not necessarily be the town in which the attraction is located. Zip codes are listed only if they differ from those given for the town.

Events

Events—categorized as annual, seasonal, or special—are highlighted. An annual event is one that's held every year for a period of usually no longer than a week to 10 days; festivals and fairs are typical entries. A seasonal event is one that may or may not be annual and that is held for a number of weeks or months in the year, such as horse racing, summer theater, concert or opera festivals, and professional sports. Special event listings occur infrequently and mark a certain date or event, such as a centennial or other commemorative celebration.

Major Cities

Additional information on airports and transportation, suburbs, and neighborhoods, including a list of restaurants by neighborhood, may be included for large cities.

Lodging and Restaurant Listings

Organization

For both lodgings and restaurants, when a property is in a town that does not have its own heading, the listing appears under the town nearest its location with the address and town in parentheses immediately after the establishment name. In large cities, lodgings located within 5 miles of major, commercial airports are listed under a separate "Airport" heading, following the city listings.

Lodging Classifications

Each property is classified by type according to the characteristics below. Because the following features and services are found at most motels, lodges, motor hotels, and hotels, they are not shown in those listings:

- Year-round operation with a single rate structure unless otherwise quoted
- European plan (meals not included in room rate)
- Bathroom with tub and/or shower in each room
- Air-conditioned/heated, often with individual room control
- Cots
- Daily maid service
- Phones in rooms
- Elevators

Motels and Lodges. Accommodations are in low-rise structures with rooms easily accessible to parking (usually free). Properties have outdoor room entry and small, functional lobbies. Service is often limited, and dining may not be offered in lower-rated motels and lodges. Shops and businesses are found only in higher-rated properties, as are bellhops, room service, and restaurants serving three meals daily.

Lodges differ from motels primarily in their emphasis on outdoor recreational activities and in location. They are often found in resort and rural areas rather than in major cities or along highways.

Motor Hotels. Offering the convenience of motels along with many of the features of hotels, motor hotels range from low-rise structures offering limited services to multistory buildings with a wide range of services and facilities. Multiple building entrances, elevators, inside hallways, and parking areas (generally free) near access doors are some of the features of a motor hotel. Lobbies offer sitting areas and 24-hour desk and switchboard services. Often bellhop and valet services as well as restaurants serving three meals a day are found. Expanded recreational facilities and more than one restaurant are available in higher-rated properties.

The distinction between motor hotels and hotels in metropolitan areas is minor.

Hotels. To be categorized as a hotel, an establishment must have most of the following facilities and services: multiple floors, a restaurant and/or coffee shop, elevators, room service, bellhops, a spacious lobby, and recreational facilities. In addition, the following features and services not shown in listings are also found:

- Valet service (one-day laundry/cleaning service)
- Room service during hours restaurant is open
- Bellhops
- Some oversize beds

Resorts. These specialize in stays of three days or more and usually offer American Plan and/or housekeeping accommodations. Their emphasis is on recreational facilities, and a social director is often available. Food services are of primary importance, and guests must be able to eat three meals a day on the premises, either in restaurants or by having access to an on-site grocery store and preparing their own meals.

Inns. Frequently thought of as a small hotel, an inn is a place of homelike comfort and warm hospitality. It is often a structure of historic significance, with an equally interesting setting. Meals are a special occasion, and tea and drinks are frequently served in late afternoon. Rooms are usually individually decorated, often with antiques or furnishings representative of the locale. Phones, bathrooms, and TVs may not be available in every room.

Guest Ranches. Like resorts, guest ranches specialize in stays of three days or more. Guest ranches also offer meal plans and extensive outdoor activities. Horseback riding is usually a feature; there are stables and trails on the ranch property, and trail rides and daily instruction is part of the program. Many guest ranches are working ranches, ranging from casual to rustic, and guests are encouraged to participate in ranch life. Eating is often family style and may also include cookouts. Western saddles are assumed; phone ahead to inquire about English saddle availability.

Cottage Colonies. These are housekeeping cottages and cabins that are usually found in recreational areas. Any dining or recreational facilities are noted in our listing.

Dining Classifications

Restaurants. Most dining establishments fall into this category. All have a full kitchen and offer table service and a complete menu.

Unrated Dining Spots. These places, listed after Restaurants in many cities, are chosen for their unique atmosphere, specialized menu, or local flavor. They include delis, ice-cream parlors, cafeterias, tearooms, and pizzerias. Because they may not have a full kitchen or table service, they are not given a *Mobil Travel Guide* rating. Often they offer extraordinary value and quick service.

Quality Ratings

The *Mobil Travel Guide* has been rating lodgings and restaurants on a national basis since the first edition was published in 1958. For years the guide was the only source of such ratings, and it remains among the few guidebooks to rate restaurants across the country.

All listed establishments were inspected by experienced field representatives or evaluated by a senior staff member. Ratings are based upon their detailed inspection reports of the individual properties, on written evaluations of staff members who stay and dine anonymously, and on an extensive review of comments from our readers.

You'll find a key to the rating categories, ★ through ★★★★★, on the inside front cover. All establishments in the book are recommended. Even a ★ place is above average, usually providing a basic, informal experience. Rating categories reflect both the features the property offers and its quality in relation to similar establishments.

For example, lodging ratings take into account the number and quality of facilities and services, the luxury of appointments, and the attitude and professionalism of staff and management. A ★ establishment provides a comfortable night's lodging. A ★★ property offers more than a facility that rates merely one star, and the decor is well planned and integrated. Establishments that rate ★★★ are professionally managed and staffed and often beautifully appointed; the lodging experience is truly excellent and the range of facilities is extensive. Properties that have been given ★★★★ not only offer many services but also have their own style and personality; they are luxurious, creatively decorated, and superbly maintained. The ★★★★★ properties are among the best in the United States, superb in every respect and entirely memorable, year in and year out.

Restaurant evaluations reflect the quality of the food and the ingredients, preparation, and presentation as well as the property's decor and ambience. A restaurant that has fairly simple goals for menu and decor but that achieves those goals superbly might receive the same number of stars as a restaurant with somewhat loftier ambitions but whose execution falls somewhat short of the mark.

In general, ★ indicates a restaurant that's a good choice in its area, usually fairly simple and perhaps catering to a clientele of locals and families; ★★ denotes restaurants that are more highly recommended in their area; ★★★ restaurants are of national caliber, with professional and attentive service and a skilled chef in the kitchen; ★★★★ reflects superb dining choices, where remarkable food is served in equally remarkable surroundings; and ★★★★★ represents that rarefied group of the best restaurants in the country, where in addition to near perfection in every detail, there's that special something extra that makes for an unforgettable dining experience. A list of the four-star and five-star establishments in this region is located just before the state listings.

Each rating is reviewed annually and each establishment must work to maintain its rating (or improve it). Every effort is made to assure that ratings are fair and accurate; the designated ratings are published purely as an aid to travelers.

In general, only properties that are simply too new to fairly assign a rating are listed without one.

Good Value Check Mark. In all locales, you'll find a wide range of lodging and dining establishments with a ✔ in front of a star rating. This indicates an unusually good value at economical prices as follows:

In Major Cities and Resort Areas

Lodging: average $95–$115 per night for singles; average $110–$135 per night for doubles
Restaurants: average $20 for a complete lunch; average $35 for a complete dinner, exclusive of beverages and gratuities

Local Area Listings

Lodging: average $45–$55 per night for singles; average $55–$70 per night for doubles
Restaurants: average $9 for a complete lunch; average $18 for a complete dinner, exclusive of beverages and gratuities

Lodgings

Each listing gives the name, address, directions (when there is no street address), neighborhood and/or directions from downtown (in major cities), phone number (local and 800), fax number, number and type of rooms available, room rates, and seasons open (if not year-round). Also included are details on recreational and dining facilities on property or nearby, the presence of a luxury level, and credit-card information. A key to the symbols at the end of each listing is on the inside front cover. (Note that Mobil Corporation credit cards cannot be used for payment of meals and room charges.)

All prices quoted in the *Mobil Travel Guide* publications are expected to be in effect at the time of publication and during the entire year; however, prices cannot be guaranteed. In some localities there may be short-term price variations because of special events or holidays. Whenever possible, these price changes are noted. Certain resorts have complicated rate structures that vary with the time of year; always confirm listed rates when you make your plans.

Restaurants

Listings give the name, address, directions (when there is no street address), neighborhood and/or directions from downtown (in major cities), phone number, hours and days of operation (if not open daily year-round), reservation policy, cuisine (if other than American), price range for each meal served, children's meals (if offered), specialties, and credit card information. Additionally, special features such as chef ownership, ambience, and entertainment are noted. By carefully reading the detailed restaurant information and comparing prices, you can easily determine whether the restaurant is formal and elegant or informal and comfortable for families.

Terms and Abbreviations in Listings

A la carte entrees With a price, refers to the cost of entrees/ main dishes only that are not accompanied by side dishes.
AP American plan (lodging plus all meals).
Bar Liquor, wine, and beer are served in a bar or cocktail lounge and usually with meals unless otherwise indicated (e.g., "wine, beer").
Business center The property has a designated area accessible to all guests with business services.
Business servs avail The property can perform/arrange at least two of the following services for a guest: audiovisual equipment rental, binding, computer rental, faxing, messenger services, modem availability, notary service, obtaining office supplies, photocopying, shipping, and typing.
Cable Standard cable service; "premium" indicates that HBO, Disney, Showtime, or similar services are available.
Ck-in, ck-out Check-in time, check-out time.
Coin lndry Self-service laundry.
Complete meal Soup and/or salad, entree, and dessert, plus nonalcoholic beverage.
Continental bkfst Usually coffee and a roll or doughnut.
Cr cds: A, American Express; C, Carte Blanche; D, Diners Club; DS, Discover; ER, En Route; JCB, Japanese Credit Bureau; MC, MasterCard; V, Visa.
D Followed by a price, indicates room rate for a "double"— two people in one room in one or two beds (the charge may be higher for two double beds).
Each addl Extra charge for each additional person beyond the stated number of persons at a reduced price.
Early-bird dinner A meal served at specified hours, typically around 4:30–6:30 pm.
Exc Except.
Exercise equipt Two or more pieces of exercise equipment on the premises.
Exercise rm Both exercise equipment and room, with an instructor on the premises.
Fax Facsimile machines available to all guests.
Golf privileges Privileges at a course within 10 miles

Hols   Holidays

In-rm modem link   Every guest room has a connection for a modem that's separate from the phone line.

Kit. or kits.   A kitchen or kitchenette that contains stove or microwave, sink, and refrigerator and that is either part of the room or a separate room. If the kitchen is not fully equipped, the listing will indicate "no equipt" or "some equipt".

Luxury level   A special section of a hotel, covering at least an entire floor, that offers increased luxury accommodations. Management must provide no less than three of these four services: separate check-in and check-out, concierge, private lounge, and private elevator service (key access). Complimentary breakfast and snacks are commonly offered.

MAP   Modified American plan (lodging plus two meals).

Movies avail   Prerecorded videos are available for rental.

No cr cds accepted   No credit cards are accepted.

No elvtr   In hotels with more than two stories, it's assumed there are elevators; only their absence is noted.

No phones   Phones, too, are assumed; only their absence is noted.

Parking   There is a parking lot on the premises.

Private club   A cocktail lounge or bar available to members and their guests. In motels and hotels where these clubs exist, registered guests can usually use the club as guests of the management; the same is frequently true of restaurants.

Prix fixe   A full meal for a stated price; usually one price is quoted.

Res   Reservations.

S   Followed by a price, indicates room rate for a "single," i.e., one person.

Semi-a la carte   Meals include vegetable, salad, soup, appetizer, or other accompaniments to the main dish.

Serv bar   A service bar, where drinks are prepared for dining patrons only.

Serv charge   Service charge is the amount added to the restaurant check in lieu of a tip.

Snow skiing downhill/x-country   Downhill and/or cross-country skiing within 20 miles of property.

Table d'hôte   A full meal for a stated price, dependent upon entree selection; no a la carte options are available.

Tennis privileges   Privileges at tennis courts within 5 miles.

TV   Indicates color television; B/W indicates black-and-white television.

Under certain age free   Children under that age are not charged for if staying in room with a parent.

Valet parking   An attendant is available to park and retrieve a car.

VCR   VCRs in all guest rooms.

VCR avail   VCRs are available for hookup in guest rooms.

Special Information for Travelers with Disabilities

The *Mobil Travel Guide* symbol Ⓓ shown in accommodation and restaurant listings indicates establishments that are at least partially accessible to people with mobility problems. Facilities providing for the needs of travelers with disabilities are noted in the listings.

The *Mobil Travel Guide* criteria for accessibility are unique to our publication. Please do not confuse them with the universal symbol for wheelchair accessibility. When the Ⓓ symbol appears following a listing, the establishment is equipped with facilities to accommodate people using wheelchairs or crutches or otherwise needing easy access to doorways and rest rooms. Travelers with severe mobility problems or with hearing or visual impairments may or may not find facilities they need. Always phone ahead to make sure that an establishment can meet your needs.

All lodgings bearing our Ⓓ symbol have the following facilities:

- ISA-designated parking near access ramps
- Level or ramped entryways to building
- Swinging building entryway doors minimum 3'0"
- Public rest rooms on main level with space to operate a wheelchair; handrails at commode areas
- Elevators equipped with grab bars and lowered control buttons
- Restaurants with accessible doorways; rest rooms with space to operate wheelchair; handrails at commode areas
- Minimum 3'0" width entryway to guest rooms
- Low-pile carpet in rooms
- Telephone at bedside and in bathroom
- Bed placed at wheelchair height
- Minimum 3'0" width doorway to bathroom
- Bath with open sink—no cabinet; room to operate wheelchair
- Handrails at commode areas; tub handrails
- Wheelchair accessible peephole in room entry door
- Wheelchair accessible closet rods and shelves

All restaurants bearing our Ⓓ symbol offer the following facilities:

- ISA-designated parking beside access ramps
- Level or ramped front entryways to building
- Tables to accommodate wheelchairs
- Main-floor rest rooms; minimum 3'0" width entryway
- Rest rooms with space to operate wheelchair; handrails at commode areas

In general, the newest properties are apt to impose the fewest barriers.

To get the kind of service you need and have a right to expect, do not hesitate when making a reservation to question the management in detail about the availability of accessible rooms, parking, entrances, restaurants, lounges, or any other facilities that are important to you, and confirm what is meant by "accessible." Some guests with mobility impairments report that lodging establishments' housekeeping and maintenance departments are most helpful in describing barriers. Also inquire about any special equipment, transportation, or services you may need.

Making the Most of Your Trip

A few diehard souls might fondly remember the trip where the car broke down and they were stranded for a week, or the vacation that cost twice what it was supposed to. For most travelers, though, the best trips are those that are safe, smooth, and within their budget. To help you make your trip the best it can be, we've assembled a few tips and resources.

Saving Money

On Lodging

After you've seen the published rates, it's time to look for discounts. Many hotels and motels offer them—for senior citizens, business travelers, families, you name it. It never hurts to ask—politely, that is. Sometimes, especially in late afternoon, desk clerks are instructed to fill beds, and you might be offered a lower rate, or a nicer room, to entice you to stay. Look for bargains on stays over multiple nights, in the off-season, and on weekdays or weekends (depending on location). Many hotels in major metropolitan areas, for example, have special weekend package plans, which offer considerable savings on rooms and may include breakfast, cocktails, and meal discounts. Prices change frequently throughout the year, so phone ahead.

Another way to save money is to choose accommodations that give you more than just a standard room. Rooms with kitchen facilities enable you to cook some meals for yourself, reducing restaurant costs. A suite might save money for two couples traveling together. Even hotel luxury levels can provide good value, as many include breakfast or cocktails in the price of the room.

State and city sales taxes as well as special room taxes can increase your room rates as much as 25% per day. We are unable to bring this specific information into the listings, but we strongly urge that you ask about these taxes when placing reservations in order to understand the total price to you.

Watch out for telephone-usage charges that hotels frequently impose on long-distance calls, credit-card calls, and other phone calls—even those that go unanswered. Before phoning from your room, read the information given to you at check-in, and then be sure to read your bill carefully before checking out. You won't be expected to pay for charges that weren't spelled out. (On the other hand, it's not unusual for a hotel to bill you for your calls after you return home.) Consider using public telephones in hotel lobbies; the savings may outweigh the inconvenience.

On Dining

There are several ways to get a less-expensive meal at a more-expensive restaurant. Early-bird dinners are popular in many parts of the country and offer considerable savings. If you're interested in sampling a ★★★★ or ★★★★★ establishment, consider going at lunchtime. While the prices then are probably relatively high, they may be half of those at dinner and come with the same ambience, service, and cuisine.

Park Passes

While many national parks, monuments, seashores, historic sites, and recreation areas may be used free of charge, others charge an entrance fee (ranging from $1 to $4 per person to $3 to $10 per carload) and/or a "use fee" for special services and facilities. If you plan to make several visits to federal recreation areas, consider one of the following National Park Service money-saving programs:

Park Pass. This is an annual entrance permit to a specific unit in the National Park Service system that normally charges an entrance fee. The pass admits the permit holder and any accompanying passengers in a private noncommercial vehicle or, in the case of walk-in facilities, the holder's spouse, children, and parents. It is valid for entrance fees only. A Park Pass may be purchased in person or by mail from the National Park Service unit at which the pass will be honored. The cost is $10 to $15, depending upon the area.

Golden Eagle Passport. This pass, available to people who are between 17 and 61, entitles the purchaser and accompanying passengers in a private noncommercial vehicle to enter any outdoor NPS unit that charges an entrance fee and admits the purchaser and family to most walk-in fee-charging areas. Like the Park Pass, it is good for one year and does not cover use fees. It may be purchased from the National Park Service, Office of Public Inquiries, Room 1013, US Department of the Interior, 18th and C Sts NW, Washington, DC 20240, phone 202/208–4747; at any of the 10 regional offices throughout the country; and at any NPS area that charges a fee. The cost is $25.

Golden Age Passport. Available to citizens and permanent residents of the United States 62 years or older, this is a lifetime entrance permit to fee-charging recreation areas. The fee exemption extends to those accompanying the permit holder in a private noncommercial vehicle or, in the case of walk-in facilities, to the holder's spouse and children. The passport also entitles the holder to a 50% discount on use fees charged in park areas but not to fees charged by concessionaires. Golden Age Passports must be obtained in person. The applicant must show proof of age, i.e., a driver's license, birth certificate, or signed affidavit attesting to age (Medicare cards are not acceptable proof). Passports are available at most park service units where they're used, at National Park Service headquarters (see above), at park system regional offices, at National Forest Supervisors' offices, and at most Ranger Station offices (see NATIONAL PARK SERVICE AREAS and NATIONAL FORESTS in the state introductions). The cost is $10.

Golden Access Passport. Issued to citizens and permanent residents of the United States who are physically disabled or visually impaired, this passport is a free lifetime entrance permit to fee-charging recreation areas. The fee exemption extends to those accompanying the permit holder in a private noncommercial vehicle or, in the case of walk-in facilities, to the holder's spouse and children. The passport also entitles the holder to a 50% discount on use fees charged in park areas but not to fees charged by concessionaires. Golden Access Passports must be obtained in person. Proof of eligibility to receive federal benefits is required (under programs such as Disability Retirement, Compensation for Military Service-Connected Disability, Coal Mine Safety and Health Act, etc.), or an affidavit must be signed attesting to eligibility. These passports are available at the same outlets as Golden Age Passports.

For Senior Citizens

Look for the senior-citizen discount symbol in the lodging and restaurant listings. Always call ahead to confirm that the discount is being offered, and be sure to carry proof of age. At places not listed in the book, it never hurts to ask if a senior-citizen discount is offered. Two organizations provide additional information for mature travelers: the American Association of Retired Persons (AARP), 601 E St NW, Washington, DC 20049, phone 202/434–2277, and the National Council of Senior Citizens, 1331 F St NW, Washington, DC 20004, phone 202/347–8800.

Tipping

Tipping is an expression of appreciation for good service, and often service workers rely on tips as a significant part of their income. However, you never need to tip if service is poor.

In Hotels

Doormen in major city hotels are usually given $1 for getting you a cab. Bellhops expect $1 per bag, usually $2 if you have only one bag. Concierges are tipped according to the service they perform. It's not mandatory to tip when you've asked for suggestions on sightseeing or restaurants or help in making reservations for dining. However, when a concierge books you a table at a restaurant known to be difficult to get into, a gratuity of $5 is appropriate. For obtaining theater or sporting event tickets, $5–$10 is expected. Maids, often overlooked by guests, may be tipped $1–$2 per day of stay.

At Restaurants

Coffee shop and counter service wait staff are usually given 8%–10% of the bill. In full-service restaurants, tip 15% of the bill, before sales tax. In fine restaurants, where the staff is large and shares the gratuity, 18%–20% for the waiter is appropriate. In most cases, tip the maitre d' only if service has been extraordinary and only on the way out; $20 is the minimum in upscale properties in major metropolitan areas. If there is a wine steward, tip him or her at least $5 a bottle, more if the wine was decanted or if the bottle was very expensive. If your busboy has been unusually attentive, $2 pressed into his hand on departure is a nice gesture. An increasing number of restaurants automatically add a service charge to the bill in lieu of a gratuity. Before tipping, carefully review your check.

At Airports

Curbside luggage handlers expect $1 per bag. Car-rental shuttle drivers who help with your luggage appreciate a $1 or $2 tip.

Staying Safe

The best way to deal with emergencies is to be prepared enough to avoid them. However, unforeseen situations do crop up, and you can prepare for them.

In Your Car

Before your trip, make sure your car has been serviced and is in good working order. Change the oil, check the battery and belts, and make sure tires are inflated properly (this can also improve gas mileage). Other inspections recommended by the car's manufacturer should be made, too.

Next, be sure you have the tools and equipment to deal with a routine breakdown: jack, spare tire, lug wrench, repair kit, emergency tools, jumper cables, spare fan belt, auto fuses, flares and/or reflectors, flashlights, first-aid kit, and, in winter, a windshield scraper and shovel.

Bring all appropriate and up-to-date documentation—licenses, registration, and insurance cards—and know what's covered by your insurance. Also bring an extra set of keys, just in case.

En route, always buckle up!

If your car does break down, get out of traffic as soon as possible—pull well off the road. Raise the hood and turn on your emergency flashers or tie a white cloth to the roadside door handle or antenna. Stay near your car. Use flares or reflectors to keep your car from being hit.

In Your Lodging

Chances are slim that you will encounter a hotel or motel fire. The ☒ in a listing indicates that there were smoke detectors and/or sprinkler systems in the rooms we inspected. Once you've checked in, make sure that any smoke detector in your room is working properly. Ascertain the locations of fire extinguishers and at least two fire exits. Never use an elevator in a fire.

For personal security, use the peephole in your room's door.

Protecting Against Theft

To guard against theft wherever you go, don't bring any more of value than you need. If you do bring valuables, leave them at your hotel rather than in your car, and if you have something very expensive, lock it in a safe. Many hotels have one in each room; others will store your valuables in the hotel's safe. And of course, don't carry more money than you need; use traveler's checks and credit cards, or visit cash machines.

For Travelers with Disabilities

A number of publications can provide assistance. Fodor's *Great American Vacations for Travelers with Disabilities* ($18) covers 38 top U.S. travel destinations, including parks, cities, and popular tourist regions. It's available from bookstores or by calling 800/533–6478. The most complete listing of published material for travelers with disabilities is available from *The Disability Bookshop,* Twin Peaks Press, Box 129, Vancouver, WA 98666, phone 206/694–2462. A comprehensive guidebook to the national parks is *Easy Access to National Parks: The Sierra Club Guide for People with Disabilities* ($16), distributed by Random House.

The Reference Section of the National Library Service for the Blind and Physically Handicapped (Library of Congress, Washington, DC 20542, phone 202/707–9275 or 202/707–5100) provides information and resources for persons with mobility problems and hearing and vision impairments, as well as information about the NLS talking-book program.

Traveling to Mexico

Proof of citizenship—passport or certified birth certificate—is required for travel into Mexico. Aliens must carry their alien registration cards, and naturalized citizens should carry their naturalization certificates. If you are planning to stay more than 24 hours or if you are a naturalized citizen or resident alien, get a copy of current border regulations from the nearest Mexican consulate or tourism office before crossing, and make sure you understand them. A helpful booklet, "Know Before You Go," may be obtained free of charge from the nearest office of the U.S. Customs Service.

If you take your car for the day, you may find it more convenient to unload all baggage before crossing than to go through a thorough customs inspection upon your return. You will not be permitted to bring any plants, fruits, or vegetables into the United States. Federal regulations permit each U.S. citizen, 21 years of age or older, to bring back one quart of alcoholic beverage, duty-free. However, state regulations vary and may be more strict; check locally before entering Mexico. New regulations may be issued at any time, so check further if you have any questions.

Your automobile insurance is not valid in Mexico; for short visits, get a one-day policy before crossing. U.S. currency is accepted in all border cities. Mexico does not observe Daylight Saving Time.

Important Toll-Free Numbers

Hotels and Motels

Adam's Mark (800/444–2326)
Best Western (800/528–1234, TDD 800/528–2222)
Budgetel Inns (800/428–3438)
Budget Host (800/283–4678)
Clarion (800/252–7466)
Comfort (800/228–5150)
Courtyard by Marriott (800/321–2211)
Days Inn (800/325–2525)
Doubletree (800/528–0444)
Drury Inns (800/325–8300)
Econo Lodge (800/446–6900)
Embassy Suites (800/362–2779)
Exel Inns of America (800/356–8013)
Fairfield Inn by Marriott (800/228–2800)
Fairmont Hotels (800/527–4727)
Forte (800/225–5843)
Four Seasons (800/332–3442)
Friendship Inns (800/453–4511)
Guest Quarters Suites (800/424–2900)
Hampton Inn (800/426–7866)
Hilton (800/445–8667, TDD 800/368–1133)
Holiday Inn (800/465–4329, TDD 800/238–5544)
Howard Johnson (800/654–4656, TDD 800/654–8442)
Hyatt & Resorts (800/233–1234)]
Inns of America (800/826–0778)
Inter-Continental (800/327–0200)
La Quinta (800/531–5900, TDD 800/426–3101)
Loews (800/223–0888)
Marriott (800/228–9290)
Master Hosts Inns (800/251–1962)
Meridien (800/225–5843)
Motel 6 (800/437–7486)
Nikko International (800/645–5687)
Omni (800/843–6664)
Park Inn (800/437–7375)
Quality Inn (800/228–5151)
Radisson (800/333–3333)
Ramada (800/228–2828, TDD 800/228–3232)
Red Carpet/Scottish Inns (800/251–1962)
Red Lion (800/547–8010)
Red Roof Inn (800/843–7663)
Residence Inn by Marriott (800/331–3131)
Ritz-Carlton (800/241–3333)
Rodeway (800/228–2000)
Sheraton (800/325–3535)
Shilo Inn (800/222–2244)
Signature Inns (800/822–5252)
Sleep Inn (800/221–2222)
Stouffer (800/468–3571)
Super 8 (800/848–8888)
Susse Chalet (800/258–1980)
Travelodge/Viscount (800/255–3050)
Vagabond (800/522–1555)

Westin Hotels & Resorts (800/228–3000)
Wyndham Hotels & Resorts (800/822–4200)

Airlines

Air Canada (800/776–3000
Alaska (800/426–0333)
Aloha (800/367–5250)
American (800/433–7300)
America West (800/235–9292)
British Airways (800/247–9297)
Canadian (800/426–7000)
Continental (800/525–0280)
Delta (800/221–1212)
Hawaiian (800/367–5320)
IslandAir (800/323–3345)
MarkAir (800/627–5247)
Mesa (800/637–2247)
Northwest (800/225–2525)
SkyWest (800/453–9417)
Southwest (800/435–9792)
TWA (800/221–2000)
United (800/241–6522)
USAir (800/428–4322)

Trains

Amtrak (800/872–7245)

Buses

Greyhound (800/231–2222)

Car Rentals

Advantage (800/777–5500)
Alamo (800/327–9633)
Allstate (800/634–6186)
Avis (800/331–1212)
Budget (800/527–0700)
Courtesy (800/252–9756)
Dollar (800/800–4000)
Enterprise (800/325–8007)
Hertz (800/654–3131)
National (800/328–4567)
Payless (800/237–2804)
Rent-A-Wreck (800/522–5436)
Sears (800/527–0770)
Thrifty (800/367–2277)
Ugly Duckling (800/843–3825)
U-Save (800/272–8728)
Value (800/327–2501)

Four-Star and Five-Star Establishments in the Southwest and South Central

COLORADO

★★★★★

Lodgings
The Broadmoor, Colorado Springs
C Lazy U Ranch, Granby
Little Nell, Aspen
Tall Timber, Durango

★★★★

Lodgings
Brown Palace, Denver
Home Ranch, Steamboat Springs
Hotel Jerome, Aspen
Hyatt Regency-Beaver Creek, Vail
Lodge at Cordillera, Vail
Loews Giorgio, Denver
The Ritz-Carlton, Aspen
Sardy House, Aspen
Vista Verde, Steamboat Springs

Restaurants
Palace Arms (Brown Palace), Denver
Piñon's, Aspen
Renaissance, Aspen
Restaurant at Little Nell, Aspen
Zenith American Grill, Denver

LOUISIANA

★★★★

Lodgings
Inter-Continental, New Orleans
Omni Royal Orleans, New Orleans
Windsor Court, New Orleans

Restaurants
Chalet Brandt, Baton Rouge
Grill Room (Windsor Court), New Orleans
La Provence, Covington

MISSOURI

★★★★

Lodgings
The Ritz-Carlton, Kansas City
The Ritz-Carlton, St. Louis
Southmoreland, Kansas City

Restaurant
Tony's, St. Louis

NEW MEXICO

★★★★

Lodgings
Eldorado, Santa Fe
Inn of the Anasazi, Santa Fe

Restaurant
The Anasazi (Inn of the Anasazi), Santa Fe

TEXAS

★★★★★

Lodgings
Mansion on Turtle Creek, Dallas

Restaurant
The Restaurant at the Mansion on Turtle Creek, Dallas

★★★★

Lodgings
The Adolphus, Dallas
Barton Creek Resort, Austin
Crescent Court, Dallas
Four Seasons, Austin
Four Seasons Hotel-Houston Center, Houston
Four Seasons Resort & Club, Dallas
Hotel St. Germain, Dallas
Hyatt Regency Hill Country, San Antonio
La Colombe d'Or, Houston
La Mansion del Rio, San Antonio
Lancaster, Houston

Omni Mandalay at Las Colinas, Dallas
Omni Houston Hotel, Houston
Plaza San Antonio, San Antonio
The Ritz-Carlton, Houston
Tremont House, Galveston
Worthington, Fort Worth

Restaurants

The Bar and Grill (The Ritz-Carlton, Houston), Houston
French Room (The Adolphus), Dallas
La Reserve (Omni Houston Hotel), Houston

Arkansas

Population: 2,350,725	
Land area: 53,187 square miles	
Elevation: 54-2,753 feet	
Highest point: Magazine Mt (Logan County)	
Entered Union: June 15, 1836 (25th state)	
Capital: Little Rock	
Motto: The people rule	
Nickname: Land of Opportunity, The Natural State	
State flower: Apple blossom	
State bird: Mockingbird	
State tree: Pine	
State fair: Early-mid-October, 1996, in Little Rock	
Time zone: Central	

Arkansas's areas of forested wilderness are much the same as those De Soto discovered in 1541. In the lovely Ozark and Ouachita mountain ranges, separated by the Arkansas River, there are splendid hardwood forests and streams. Pine and hardwood trees shade streams with enough black bass, bream and trout to restore any angler's faith. There are deer, geese, ducks and quail to shoot and feast on in season. Ducks fly over eastern Arkansas, and such towns as Stuttgart make a big event of hunting them. The White River National Wildlife Refuge east of here is a wilderness area. Caves, springs, meadows, valleys, bayous, rice and cotton fields, magnificent lakes and rivers dot the state. For an enjoyable backwoods vacation, the visitor can hardly do better, with a choice of either a quiet rustic resort or cosmopolitan Hot Springs National Park, the renowned spa dedicated to the sophisticated pleasures as well as the therapeutic treatment of the visitor.

In contrast is the Arkansas that is one of the major producers of bromine brine in the United States. In addition, a large amount of crude oil and bauxite (aluminum ore) come from Arkansas every year. Sixty useful tree varieties grow here, and timber is big business. In fact, practically every crop except citrus fruits is cultivated on its acres, including rice, strawberries, peaches, grapes, apples, cotton, soybeans and sorghum. Arkansas is also a state plentiful in raw materials, even to the extent of having the only diamond field in North America open to the public. Preserved as Crater of Diamonds State Park (see NASHVILLE), visitors may dig for diamonds on a "finders keepers" basis.

Because Arkansas was remote, of rugged terrain and slightly off the track of the western surge of the frontier, the area was slow to develop. After the Spaniards came the French—Marquette and Joliet visited the territory in 1673 and LaSalle took possession for France in 1682. The first permanent settlement was made by Henri de Tonty in 1686 at Arkansas Post, which today is a national memorial (see). It was not until 1804, a year after Arkansas and the rest of the Louisiana Purchase had become United States property, that the government paid any attention to the area. A United States headquarters was established at Arkansas Post; in 1819 the Arkansas Territory was organized and two years later the capital was moved to Little Rock.

National Park Service Areas

Arkansas has Arkansas Post National Memorial, Buffalo National River (see both), Fort Smith National Historic Site (see FORT SMITH), Hot Springs National Park (see) and Pea Ridge National Military Park (see ROGERS).

National Forests

The following is an alphabetical list of National Forests and towns they are listed under.

Ouachita National Forest (see HOT SPRINGS & HOT SPRINGS NATIONAL PARK): Forest Supervisor in Hot Springs; Ranger offices in Booneville*, Danville*, Glenwood*, Heavener, OK*, Hot Springs, Idabel, OK, Mena, Mt Ida*, Oden*, Perryville*, Talihina, OK* and Waldron*.

Ozark National Forest (see RUSSELLVILLE): Forest Supervisor in Russellville; Ranger offices in Clarksville*, Hector*, Jasper*, Mountain View, Ozark*, Paris.

St Francis National Forest (see HELENA): Forest Supervisor in Russellville; Ranger office in Marianna*.

*Not described in text

State Recreation Areas

The following towns list state recreation areas in their vicinity under What to See and Do; refer to the individual town for directions and park information.

Listed under **Alma:** see Lake Fort Smith State Park.

Listed under **Arkadelphia:** see DeGray State Park.

Listed under **Ashdown:** see Millwood State Park.

Listed under **Bull Shoals Lake Area:** see Bull Shoals State Park.

Listed under **Camden:** see White Oak Lake State Park.

Listed under **Conway:** see Woolly Hollow State Park.

Listed under **Dumas:** see Lake Chicot State Park.

Listed under **El Dorado:** see Moro Bay State Park.

Listed under **Eureka Springs:** see Withrow Springs State Park.

Listed under **Fayetteville:** see Devil's Den State Park.

Listed under **Forrest City:** see Village Creek State Park.

Listed under **Hot Springs:** see Lake Ouachita State Park.

Listed under **Jonesboro:** see Crowley's Ridge and Lake Frierson state parks.

Listed under **Little Rock:** see Pinnacle Mountain State Park.

Listed under **Magnolia:** see Logoly State Park.

Listed under **Malvern:** see Jenkins' Ferry State Historic Monument and Lake Catherine State Park.

Listed under **Mena:** see Queen Wilhelmina State Park.

Listed under **Nashville:** see Crater of Diamonds State Park.

Listed under **Newport:** see Jacksonport State Park.

Listed under **Petit Jean State Park:** see Petit Jean State Park.

Listed under **Pocahontas:** see Old Davidsonville State Park.

Listed under **Russellville:** see Mount Nebo and Lake Dardanelle state parks.

Listed under **Walnut Ridge:** see Lake Charles State Park.

Water-related activities, hiking, various other sports, picnicking and visitor centers, camping, as well as cabins and lodges are available in many of these areas. Camping: $6.50-$15/day. Swimming: $1.75-$2; under 5 free. Pets on leash only. Campers must register at the park office before occupying a site; all sites assigned, reservations available. Parks open all year; some facilities closed December-February or March. Brochures on state parks may be obtained from the Dept of Parks and Tourism, Parks Div, One Capitol Mall, Little Rock 72201; 501/682-1191.

Fishing & Hunting

Nonresident fishing license: annual, $30; 14-day, $20; 3-day, $10. Trout permit, $7.50. Largemouth bass can be found in all big lakes; trout in the White, Little Red, Spring and Little Missouri rivers; and bluegill in most Arkansas lakes. Annual nonresident hunting license: basic (for small game), $65; annual nonresident all game hunting license: $185. Nonresident short trip license (5 days for small game) for anything in season except deer, turkey, and bear, $40. Nonresident all game license 5 days, $125; 3 days, $95. Licenses may be ordered by phone, 800/364-GAME (credit card only). Arkansas fishing and hunting regulations are available from the Game and Fish Commission, #2 Natural Resources Dr, Little Rock 72205; 501/223-6300.

Safety Belt Information

Safety belts are mandatory for all persons in front seat of vehicle. Every driver who regularly transports a child under the age of 5 years in a motor vehicle registered in this state, except one operated for hire, shall provide for the protection of such child by properly placing, maintaining and securing such child in a child passenger safety seat meeting federal standards. With any child 3-5 years of age, a safety belt shall be sufficient. For further information phone 501/569-2000.

Interstate Highway System

The following alphabetical listing of Arkansas towns in *Mobil Travel Guide* shows that these cities are within 10 miles of the indicated interstate highways. A highway map, however, should be checked for the nearest exit.

INTERSTATE 30: Arkadelphia, Benton, Hope, Little Rock, Malvern.

INTERSTATE 40: Alma, Conway, Forrest City, Fort Smith, Little Rock, Morrilton, Russellville.

INTERSTATE 55: Blytheville.

Additional Visitor Information

A variety of pamphlets and maps is distributed by the Arkansas Department of Parks and Tourism, 1 Capitol Mall, Little Rock 72201; 501/682-7777 or 800/NATURAL.

There are tourist information centers at several points of entry into Arkansas; travel consultants provide suggested tour routes, a state tour guide and literature on places of interest. The centers are open daily and located in the following cities: Bentonville, US 71S; Blytheville, I-55S; Corning, US 67S; Fort Smith/Van Buren (Dora), I-40E; El Dorado, US 167N; Harrison, US 65S; Helena, US 49E; Lake Village, jct US 65, 82 & AR 144; Mammoth Spring, US 63; Red River, US 71N; Siloam Springs, US 412E; Texarkana, I-30E and West Memphis, I-40W. Inquire locally for exact locations.

Alma (B-1)

(For accommodations see Fort Smith)

Pop 2,959 **Elev** 430 ft **Area code** 501 **Zip** 72921

What to See and Do

Lake Fort Smith State Park. This 125-acre park is surrounded by the Boston Mountains and Fort Smith and Shepherd Springs lakes. The western end of the 140-mile Ozark Highlands Trail begins here and, for a few miles, runs in conjunction with the 7-mile Evan's Point Loop Trail, offering excellent views of waterfalls, box canyons and towering bluffs. Swimming pool, bathhouse, lifeguard; fishing; boating (rentals). Hiking trails; tennis. Picnicking, playground. Limited camping (hookups), cabins. Visitor center, interpretive programs (summer). Standard fees. (Daily) 13 mi N on US 71. Contact Superintendent, PO Box 4, Mountainburg 72946; 501/369-2469. Per vehicle ¢

White Rock Mountain Recreation Area. A 94-acre primitive area at summit of 2,287-ft White Rock peak with panoramic views. Nature trails. Picnicking. Camping Apr-Sept. ¢¢¢ Eight miles from the summit on Forest Service Road 1505 is 82-acre Shores Lake with water sports, boating (ramp), picnicking, camping. Fees charged at recreation sites. (Daily) 13 mi NE on AR 215, forest roads, in Boston Mountains of Ozark National Forest. Phone 501/968-2354. **Free.**

Wiederkehr Wine Cellars. Guided wine-tasting tour (persons under 21 may not taste wines); self-guided tour of vineyards; observation tower; restaurant; gift shop. Tours. (Daily; closed some major hols) 4 mi S of I-40 exit 41, near Altus. Phone 501/468-WINE. **Free.**

Restaurant

★ ★ ★ **WIEDERKEHR'S WEIN KELLER.** *(Rte 1, Box 14, Altus 72821)* On AR 186, 4¹/₂ mi S of I-40 exit 41. 501/468-3551. Hrs: 11 am-3 pm, 5-10 pm; Sun 11 am-9 pm. Closed some major hols. Res accepted. Continental menu. Semi-a la carte: lunch $4.15-$6.25, dinner $7.25-$23.75. Child's meals. Specialties: beef and cheese fondues, quiche Lorraine, Matterhorn schnitzel. Own baking. Parking. In converted wine cellar; fireplace, beamed ceilings. Family-owned. Cr cds: A, C, D, DS, MC, V.

D

Arkadelphia (D-2)

(See Hot Springs, Malvern)

Settled 1809 **Pop** 10,014 **Elev** 245 ft **Area code** 501 **Zip** 71923

Information Chamber of Commerce, 107 N 6th St, PO Box 38; 501/246-5542.

On a bluff overlooking the Ouachita River and once an important landing for steamboats, this community is now an agricultural and industrial center producing boats, wood products, jeans, commercial roofing, brake shoes and fiberglass vaults. It is the home of Henderson State University (1890) and Ouachita Baptist University.

What to See and Do

DeGray Lake. DeGray Dam impounds the waters of the Caddo River to form this more than 13,000-acre lake with 207 miles of shoreline. Waterskiing; fishing; boating. Swimming beach. Picnicking. Visitors center. Camping (fee). (Daily) 1 mi NW off AR 7. Phone 501/246-5501. Per vehicle ¢ On the NE shore is

DeGray State Park. A 938-acre resort park. Swimming; fishing; boating (houseboat & sailboat rentals, marina, launch). Nature trail; 18-hole golf & pro shop, tennis. Picnicking, playground, store, laundry, restaurant, lodge (see). Camping (many water, electric hookups; dump station; reservations avail Apr-Oct). Visitor center; interpretive programs. Guided hikes, lake cruises, square dances, hay rides, live animal demonstrations, evening slides and films. Standard fees. 6 mi N of I-30, on AR 7. Contact Superintendent, Rte 3, PO Box 490, Bismarck 71929; 501/865-4501 or -2851.

Henderson State University Museum. Victorian house (1893) of C.C. Henderson, with displays of Caddo Indian artifacts and items of historic interest. (Mon, Wed, Fri afternoons) 10th and Henderson Sts. Phone 501/246-7311 or -5511. **Free.**

Hot Springs National Park (see). 32 mi N via AR 7.

Ouachita Baptist University (1886). (1,350 students) On the banks of the Ouachita River, surrounded by the foothills of the Ouachita Mountains. McClellan Hall contains the official papers and memorabilia of US Senator John L. McClellan. Campus tours. Phone 501/245-5206.

Annual Events

Festival of the Two Rivers. Arts & crafts, juried art show, contests, games, food. Phone 501/246-5542 for date.

Clark County Fair. Sept.

Motels

★★ **HOLIDAY INN.** *Box 450, At jct AR 7, I-30. 501/246-5831; FAX 501/246-5831, ext. 172.* 100 rms, 2 story. S, D $64.95; each addl $8; under 19 free. Crib free. Pet accepted. TV; cable (premium). Pool; poolside serv. Restaurant 6 am-10 pm. Rm serv. Ck-out noon. Meeting rms. Valet service. Cr cds: A, C, D, DS, ER, JCB, MC, V.

🅓 🐾 💤 ✕ 🐾 SC

✔★ **QUALITY INN.** *Box 420, Jct AR 7, I-30. 501/246-5855; FAX 501/246-8552.* 63 rms, 2 story. S $40-$59; D $40-$59; under 16 free. Crib $1. Pet accepted. TV; cable (premium). Pool. Coffee in lobby. Restaurant adj 24 hrs. Ck-out noon. Business servs avail. Coin lndry. Some in-rm whirlpools. Cr cds: A, C, D, DS, ER, JCB, MC, V.

🐾 💤 💤 ✕ 🐾 SC

Restaurants

✔★ **BOWEN'S.** *At jct I-30, AR 7. 501/246-8661.* Hrs: 6 am-10 pm. Closed Dec 25. Res accepted. Semi-a la carte: bkfst $1.75-$5.75, lunch, dinner $1.50-$10. Buffet: bkfst $4.35, lunch $4.65, dinner $6.25. Fri seafood buffet $8.95. Child's meals. Salad bar. Parking. Cr cds: A, DS, MC, V.

🅓

✔★ **KREG'S CATFISH.** *2805 W Pine St. 501/246-5327.* Hrs: 11 am-9 pm. Closed major hols. Semi-a la carte: lunch, dinner $3.50-$8.50. Specializes in catfish, chicken. Parking. No cr cds accepted.

🅓

Arkansas Post National Memorial (D-4)

(For accommodations see Dumas, Pine Bluff)

(40 mi SE of Pine Bluff on US 65, 17 mi N on US 165, 2 mi E on AR 169)

Arkansas Post was established in 1686 as a trading post by Henri de Tonty, lieutenant to La Salle during the latter's pioneer explorations. Although the post was never a major French settlement, by 1759 it had grown to an impressive 40-man garrison. Ownership abruptly changed hands following the British victory in the French and Indian War. France ceded Louisiana, including the Arkansas territory, to Spain in 1762. Spanish interests, however, were not long served. The Spaniards joined the American patriots during the American Revolution, not out of sympathy but as a matter of self-interest. The resulting skirmishes between Spain and Britain over the territory came to an end less than two years after Yorktown. Unable to cope with raids and aggressive frontiersmen, Spain ceded the territory back to France.

The Post was bought by the United States as part of the Louisiana Purchase in 1803. In 1819 it became the capitol of the new Arkansas Territory and the home of Arkansas' first newspaper, the Arkansas *Gazette*. In 1821 the capital and the *Gazette* both moved to Little Rock. The Post continued as a river port until the Civil War, when battles and numerous floods finally destroyed the little town.

Arkansas Post was made a state park in 1929 and a national memorial in 1964. Fishing, boating, picnicking and a view of Dam No 2, part of the Arkansas River Navigation Project, are found on its 389 acres. Personnel and exhibits, including a partial replica of a 1783 Spanish fort, tell the story of the post. Visitor center (daily; closed Dec 25). Contact Superintendent, Rte 1, Box 16, Gillett 72055; 501/548-2207.

What to See and Do

Arkansas County Museum. Museum and five buildings housing artifacts of Arkansas' first settlers; colonial kitchen; 1877 log house with period furnishings; Civil War memorabilia; child's 3-room furnished playhouse. (Mar-mid-Dec, Wed-Sat, also Sun afternoons; closed rest of yr; also closed major hols) 5 mi S of Gillett on US 165 (Great River Rd). Phone 501/548-2634. **Free.**

Ashdown (D-1)

(For accommodations see Texarkana, TX)

Founded 1892 **Pop** 5,150 **Elev** 327 ft **Area code** 501 **Zip** 71822

What to See and Do

Millwood Dam and Reservoir. This dam impounds a more than 29,500-acre lake. Swimming; fishing. Playgrounds. Camping (14-day limit, electric hookups, no hookups winter; fee at 3 areas, remaining areas free). (Daily) 9 mi E on AR 32. Phone 501/898-3343. **Free.** Adj is

Millwood State Park. Approx 800 acres. Fishing; boating (rentals, marina). Hiking trails. Picnicking, playground, rest rms, store. Camping (hookups, dump station). Standard fees. Visitor center. Contact Superintendent, Rte 1, PO Box 37AB; 501/898-2800.

Batesville (B-3)

(See Greers Ferry Lake Area, Mountain View, Newport)

Pop 9,187 **Elev** 364 ft **Area code** 501 **Zip** 72501
Information Batesville Area Chamber of Commerce, 409 Vine St; 501/793-2378.

Annual Events

White River Water Carnival. Parade, arts & crafts, beauty pageant. Late July-early Aug.

National Invitational Explorer Canoe Race. White River, from Cotter to Batesville. Phone 501/793-2378. Early Aug.

Motels

✔ ★ ★ **BEST WESTERN SCENIC.** *773 Batesville Blvd, 2 mi S at jct US 167, AR 25.* 501/698-1855. 40 rms, 2 story. S $37-$45; D $47-$52; each addl $4; under 12 free. TV; cable (premium), VCR avail. Pool. Playground. Restaurant 6 am-9 pm. Ck-out noon. Valet serv. Sundries. Refrigerators. Picnic tables. Cr cds: A, C, D, DS, MC, V.

⬛ 🏊 ⊠ 🐾 🔥 SC

★ ★ **RAMADA INN.** *1325 N St Louis.* 501/698-1800; FAX 501/698-1800, ext. 273. 124 units, 2 story. S, D $47; each addl $6; suites $90-$120; under 18 free. Crib free. TV; cable (premium). Pool; whirlpool. Coffee in rms. Restaurant 6-10 am, 5-10 pm; Sun 6 am-2 pm, 5-10 pm. Rm serv. Private club 4 pm-midnight; entertainment, dancing exc Sun. Ck-out noon. Coin lndry. Meeting rms. Refrigerator in suites. Cr cds: A, C, D, DS, ER, JCB, MC, V.

⬛ 🐾 🏊 ⊠ 🔥 SC

Benton (C-3)

(See Hot Springs, Little Rock, Malvern)

Founded 1836 **Pop** 18,177 **Elev** 416 ft **Area code** 501 **Zip** 72015
Information Benton Chamber of Commerce, 607 N Market St; 501/778-8272.

Benton, the seat of Saline County, is a center of American aluminum production with a major amount of bauxite mined in the United States coming from this area. The city also has important wood products factories.

What to See and Do

Gann Museum. Originally a medical office built in 1893 by patients who could not afford to pay the doctor, this is the only known building made of bauxite; dug from a nearby farm, hand-sawed into blocks and allowed to harden. Contains furniture and artifacts reflecting local pioneer, Niloak pottery, Native American and church history. Genealogy library. (Tues-Thurs, Sat & Sun; closed Jan 1, Thanksgiving, Dec 25) 218 S Market St. Phone 501/778-5513. **Free.**

Hot Springs National Park (see). 27 mi W via US 70.

Motels

✔ ★ **BEST WESTERN.** *17036 I-30, exit 117.* 501/778-9695; FAX 501/776-1699. 66 rms, 2 story. S $32-$42; D $44-$55; suites $40-$57; under 12 free. Crib $5. Pet accepted, some restrictions. TV; cable (premium). Pool. Playground. Restaurant 6 am-10 pm. Ck-out noon. Coin lndry. Business servs avail. Game rm. Cr cds: A, C, D, DS, MC, V.

⬛ 🐾 🏊 ⊠ 🔥 SC

★ **DAYS INN.** *1501 I-30, exit 118.* 501/776-3200; FAX 501/776-0906. 120 rms, 2 story. S $40; D $47; each addl $5; under 18 free. Crib free. Pet accepted; $5. TV; cable (premium), VCR avail. Pool. Complimentary coffee in lobby. Restaurant adj 6-1 am. Ck-out 11 am. Meeting rms. Business servs avail. Valet serv. Sundries. Cr cds: A, C, D, DS, MC, V.

⬛ 🐾 🏊 ⊠ 🔥 SC

Unrated Dining Spot

BROWN'S. *18718 I-30, exit 118.* 501/778-5033; FAX 501/798-0825. Hrs: 6:30 am-9 pm. Closed Thanksgiving, Dec 25. Buffet: bkfst $4.99, lunch $5.99, dinner $7.99. Child's meals. Specializes in seafood, catfish, chicken, roast beef. Salad bar. Parking. Country decor. Country store adj. Cr cds: DS, MC, V.

⬛

Bentonville (A-1)

(See Fayetteville, Rogers, Springdale)

Founded 1837 **Pop** 11,257 **Elev** 1,305 ft **Area code** 501 **Zip** 72712
Information Bentonville-Bella Vista Chamber of Commerce, 412 S Main St; 501/273-2841.

Bentonville was named for Thomas Hart Benton, the first senator from Missouri and a militant champion of pioneers. The town square maintains a turn-of-the-century character.

Annual Event

Sugar Creek Days. Historic re-enactments, vintage fashions, antique cars, events, music, parade. Early-mid-May.

Motels

★ **BEST WESTERN.** *2307 SE Walton Blvd.* 501/273-9727; FAX 501/273-1763. 54 rms, 2 story. S $43-$47; D $47; each addl $5; suite $85; under 12 free; higher rates special events. Crib $5. Pet accepted, some restrictions; $5. TV; cable (premium). Pool. Complimentary coffee in lobby. Restaurant adj 6 am-10 pm. Ck-out 11 am. Business servs avail. In-rm modem link. Some refrigerators. Cr cds: A, C, D, DS, MC, V.

🐾 🏊 ⊠ 🔥 SC

★ ★ **RAMADA INN.** *1209 N Walton Blvd.* 501/273-2451; FAX 501/273-7611. 152 rms, 2 story. S, D $51-$70; each addl $8; under 18 free; higher rates special events. Crib avail. TV; cable (premium). Indoor pool; poolside serv. Restaurant 6 am-2 pm, 5-10 pm. Exercise equipt; weights, treadmill. Rec rm. Cr cds: A, D, DS, MC, V.

⬛ 🏊 🏋 ⊠ 🔥 SC

★ **SUPERIOR INN.** *2301 SE Walton Blvd.* 501/273-1818; FAX 501/273-5529. 52 rms, 2 story. S $40; D $45; suite $65; higher rates special events. Crib avail. Pet accepted. TV; cable (premium). Pool. Complimentary continental bkfst. Restaurant adj 6 am-11:30 pm.

Ck-out 11 am. Free airport transportation. Picnic tables. Cr cds: A, DS, MC, V.

D ⊮ ≈ ⋈ ⋈ SC

Restaurant

★ ★ **FRED'S HICKORY INN.** *1502 N Walton Blvd. 501/273-3303.* Hrs: 11 am-2 pm, 5:30-10 pm; Sat from 5:30 pm. Closed some major hols. Res accepted. Bar. Semi-a la carte: lunch $4-$17, dinner $8-$18. Child's meals. Specializes in barbecue, spaghetti, steak. Parking. Five dining rms in log cabin. Family-owned. Cr cds: A, C, MC, V.

Berryville (A-2)

(For accommodations see Eureka Springs, Harrison)

Founded 1850 **Pop** 3,212 **Elev** 1,200 ft **Area code** 501 **Zip** 72616
Information Tourist Information Center, PO Box 402; 501/423-3704.

This area is known for poultry raising and dairy farming. There is also good fishing. Berryville is the southern gateway to the Table Rock Lake Area in Missouri (see).

What to See and Do

Carroll County Heritage Center. Local historical exhibits and genealogical material housed in old courthouse (1880). (Mon-Fri; closed major hols) 403 Public Sq. Phone 501/423-6312. ¢

Cosmic Cavern. Cavern below mountain features Ozark's largest underground lake; electrically lighted; constant 58°F. Visitor center, picnic area. 1-hour guided tours (daily). 7 mi N on AR 21. Phone 501/749-2298. ¢¢¢

Saunders Memorial Museum. Revolvers, pistols and small arms, some originally owned by Pancho Villa, Jesse James and Wild Bill Hickok; antiques, handcrafts; silver, china; rugs and furniture. (Mar-Oct, daily exc Sun) 115 E Madison, on AR 21. Phone 501/423-2563. ¢¢

Annual Events

Carroll County Fair. Wk of Labor Day.

Saunders Memorial Muzzleloading and Frontier Gun Shoot. Costumed contestants; gun show. Late Sept.

Blytheville (B-5)

Settled 1880 **Pop** 22,906 **Elev** 255 ft **Area code** 501 **Zip** 72315
Information Chamber of Commerce, PO Box 485, 72316; 501/762-2012.

Blytheville is one of two seats of Mississippi County, and a leading agricultural area. It is also an industrial and retail trade center for northeast Arkansas. Duck hunting is good here, especially on the Mississippi Flyway. Mallard Lake, 12 miles west on AR 18, has good bass, bream and crappie fishing. Big Lake Wildlife Refuge, 12 miles west on AR 18, is a winter nesting area for migratory waterfowl.

Motels

★ **BEST WESTERN COTTON INN.** *Box 1229, 1½ mi NE of jct AR 18, I-55 exit 67. 501/763-5220.* 87 rms, 2 story. S $37; D $43; each addl $4; under 12 free. Crib free. Pets accepted. TV; cable

(premium). Pool. Restaurant 5 am-9 pm. Rm serv 6 am-8 pm. Bar; dancing exc Sun. Ck-out noon. Cr cds: A, C, D, DS, MC, V.

⊮ ≈ ⋈ ⋈ SC

✔ ★ ★ **COMFORT INN.** *Jct I-55 & AR 18. 501/763-7081.* 105 rms, 2 story. S $37-$40; D $42-$45; each addl $6; under 18 free. Crib free. TV; cable (premium). Pool. Complimentary continental bkfst. Restaurant 11 am-11 pm. Private club. Ck-out noon. Meeting rms. Business servs avail. Health club privileges. Cr cds: A, C, D, DS, ER, MC, V.

D ⊮ ≈ ⋈ ⋈ SC

✔ ★ **DAYS INN.** *I-55 & AR 18. 501/763-1241.* 122 units, 2 story. June-Sept: S $29-$40; D $34-$47; each addl $5; wkly rates; higher rates special events; lower rates rest of yr. Crib free. TV; cable (premium). Pool. Ck-out noon. Coin lndry. Business servs avail. Valet serv. Sundries. Cr cds: A, C, D, DS, ER, JCB, MC, V.

⊮ ≈ ⋈ ⋈ SC

★ ★ **HOLIDAY INN.** *Box 1408, E Main St. 501/763-5800; FAX 501/763-1326.* 153 rms, 2 story. Mar-mid-Sept: S $48; D $58; each addl $7; under 19 free; wkend rates; lower rates rest of yr. Crib free. Pet accepted. TV; cable (premium). 2 pools, 1 indoor; steam rm; poolside serv. Restaurant 6 am-10 pm. Rm serv. Bar 4 pm-1 am, closed Sun; entertainment, dancing. Ck-out noon. Coin lndry. Meeting rms. Bellhops. Valet serv. Gift shop. Free airport transportation. Holidome. Cr cds: A, C, D, DS, MC, V.

D ⊮ ≈ ⋈ ⋈ SC

Buffalo National River (B-2)

(Buffalo Point Main Visitor Center, 17 mi S of Yellville via AR 14, 268; Tyler Bend Main Visitor Center, 9 mi N of Marshall via US 65)

Buffalo National River, preserving 135 miles of the free-flowing river in the scenic Ozarks of northwestern Arkansas, is known for its diversity. In the spring, whitewater enthusiasts float the upper river from Ponca to Pruitt, stopping at primitive campgrounds at Steel Creek, Kyles Landing, Erbie and Ozark. These areas also provide river access. Springs, waterfalls, streams and woods along the river attract hikers; Lost Valley features interpreter-guided hikes. River levels fluctuate, contact park headquarters for information on floatable areas. Primitive campgrounds on lower and middle stretches include Hasty, Carver, Mt Hersey, Woolum, Maumee and Rush.

The two main visitor centers are located at Buffalo Point and at Tyler Bend. Both offer swimming; fishing; canoe rentals. Self-guided trails and hikes. Picnicking. Camping (fee). Programs and demonstrations led by interpreters. Evening programs blend natural and historic interpretation with folklore and, at Buffalo Point, a weekly Ozark Folk Music Program presented by local musicians. The interpreters also lead float trips for novices and for those desiring a guided trip.

Housekeeping cabins are available from April through November. For information concerning cabin reservations contact the Buffalo Point Concessioner, HCR #66, Box 388, Yellville 72678; 501/449-6206. For general information contact the Superintendent, Buffalo National River, Box 1173, Harrison 72602; 501/741-5443.

Bull Shoals Lake Area (A-3)

(See Harrison, Mountain Home)

Area code 501

(11 mi W of Mountain Home via AR 5, 178)

Bull Shoals Lake, on the White River in the Ozarks, was created by the US Army Corps of Engineers as a flood control and hydroelectric project in 1952. The lake has a 1,000-mile shoreline, with recreation areas and boat docks at many points. Fishing is excellent both in the lake and in the White River below the dam, and other recreational activities abound. Fees charged at most recreation areas. Phone 501/425-2700.

What to See and Do

Bull Shoals State Park. More than 680 acres at SE corner of lake below dam. Fishing for trout; boating (ramp, rentals, dock). Hiking trails. Picnicking, playground, store. Camping (hookups, dump station; daily). Visitor center (camping equipment rentals); interpretive programs (Apr-Oct). Standard fees. Golden Age Passport (see INTRODUCTION). 6 mi N of Mountain Home on AR 5, then 7 mi W on AR 178. For further information contact the Superintendent, PO Box 205, Bull Shoals 72619; 501/431-5521.

Note: Since Bull Shoals Dam serves as a hydroelectric plant, the water level in the river may rise and fall suddenly. A horn sounds when water levels are changing; however, due to weather conditions, the horn cannot always be heard.

Inn

★ ★ **RED RAVEN.** *(Box 1217, Yellville 72687)* US 62 & AR 14S. 501/449-5168. 7 units, 3 story. No rm phones. S, D $49-$69. Children over 7 yrs only. TV in sitting rm. Complimentary full bkfst. Restaurant nearby. Ck-out 11 am, ck-in 2 pm. Lawn games. Picnic tables. On river. Restored Queen Anne/Victorian mansion; high ceilings, antiques, oak woodwork. Library; art gallery. Totally nonsmoking. Cr cds: DS, MC, V.

Resorts

★ ★ **CHASTAIN'S.** *(Box 290, Bull Shoals 72619)* 1 mi S, just off AR 178, 3 mi W of dam. 501/445-4242; res: 800/423-5253; FAX 501/495-7123. 60 units, 23 kits. S, D $45-$160; each addl $10; kit. units $55-$95; under 16 free. Crib free. TV; cable, VCR avail. Pool. Playground. Complimentary continental bkfst. Coffee in rms. Dining rms 5 pm-9 pm. Box lunches. Picnics. Rm serv. Private club. Ck-out 11 am. Coin lndry. Grocery 1/2 mi. Package store 3 mi. Meeting rms. Business servs avail. In-rm modem link. Free airport transportaion. Tennis. 18-hole golf, greens fee $10, pro. Lawn games. Rec rm. Exercise equipt; weights, bicycles, sauna. Fish storage. Some refrigerators. Some private patios, balconies. Picnic tables, grills. Cr cds: A, DS, MC, V.

★ ★ ★ **GASTON'S WHITE RIVER RESORT.** *(PO, Lakeview 72642)* 3 mi SE of dam, 2 mi off AR 178. 501/431-5202. 73 cottages (1-10 bedrm), 1-2 story, 47 kits. (with boat). S, D $64-$78; each addl $12.50; suites $90-$135; cottages $78-$750; kits. $78-$200; under 6 free; fishing rates. Crib free. Pet accepted. TV; cable. Pool. Playground. Dining rm 6:30 am-10 pm. Box lunches, shore lunches, picnics, cookouts. Bar. Ck-out 11 am. Grocery. Meeting rms. Gift shop. Airport, bus depot transportation. Tennis. 9 & 18-hole golf privileges, greens fee $9

& $12.50. Boats, motors. Dock. Lawn games. Rec rm. Fishing guides; clean & store area. Hiking trail; riverside walk. 3,200-ft private landing strip. Refrigerators; fireplaces. Private patios, balconies. Picnic tables. On river. Cr cds: MC, V.

Cottage Colony

✔ ★ **SHADY OAKS.** *(Rte A, Box 128, Flippin 72634)* 5 mi S on AR 178, on Jimmie Creek arm of Bull Shoals Lake. 501/453-8420; res: 800/467-OAKS; FAX 501/453-7813. 11 kit. cottages (1, 2 & 4 bedrm). Cottages $60-$75. Crib free. Pet accepted. TV, VCR avail. Pool. Playground. Restaurant 4 1/2 mi, 6 am-10 pm. Ck-out 10 am, ck-in 3 pm. Coin lndry. Grocery 5 mi. Package store 7 mi. Airport transportation. Boats, motors; lighted dock. Game rm. Rec rm. Lawn games. Fishing guides; clean & store. Refrigerators. Private patios. Picnic tables, grills. Lake swimming, waterskiing, scuba diving. Nature walks. Cr cds: DS, MC, V.

Restaurants

★ ★ **CLUB 178.** *(Box 453, Bull Shoals 72619)* 1/2 mi S on AR 178. 501/445-4949. Hrs: 10:30 am-10 pm; Sun brunch to 1 pm. Closed Mon; Jan 1, Dec 25. Res accepted Fri, Sat. Bar to 2 am. Semi-a la carte: lunch $1.95-$5, dinner $2.25-$17.95. Sun brunch $6.50. Child's meals. Specializes in seafood. Parking. Cr cds: A, MC, V.

★ **VILLAGE WHEEL.** *(Box 82, Bull Shoals 72619)* Center of town, on AR 178. 501/445-4414. Hrs: 6 am-10 pm. Closed Thanksgiving, Dec 25. Semi-a la carte: bkfst $1.65-$5.50, lunch $2.30-$5.45, dinner $4.50-$19.95. Child's meals. Specializes in omelets, broasted chicken. Salad bar. Parking. Cr cds: MC, V.

Camden (D-2)

(See El Dorado, Magnolia)

Founded 1824 **Pop** 14,380 **Elev** 198 ft **Area code** 501 **Zip** 71701

Information Camden Area Chamber of Commerce, 141 Jackson SW, PO Box 99; 501/836-6426.

Camden, home to many large industries, is situated on the Ouachita River, which is navigable throughout the year.

What to See and Do

Confederate Cemetery. More than 200 veterans of the Civil War and many unknown soldiers are buried here. Adams Ave & Pearl St.

Fort Lookout. Rifle trenches and cannon pits are still evident on the site of the old fort overlooking Ouachita River. It was one of several forts constructed to guard the town. End of Monroe St.

McCollum-Chidester House (1847). Once a stage coach headquarters, this historic house was used as headquarters at various times by Confederate General Sterling Price and Union General Frederick Steele. Contains original furnishings; mementos of the Civil War period. Setting for segments of the TV mini-series *North and South.* 926 Washington St NW. Phone 501/836-9243. ¢¢ Tours (Apr-Oct, Wed-Sat) also include

Leake-Ingham Building (1850). Used as a law office before the Civil War and as a freedmen's bureau during Reconstruction; now houses books and other memorabilia of the antebellum South.

Poison Spring Battleground Historical Monument. Site of Union defeat during Steele's Red River Campaign into southwest Arkansas. Exhibits and diorama tracing troop movement; trail to small spring; picnic area. 7 mi NW on AR 24, then 2 mi W on AR 76. **Free.**

White Oak Lake State Park. Swimming; fishing for bass, crappie and bream on 2,765-acre lake; boating (rentals). Hiking trails. Picnicking, store. Camping (hookups, dump station). Visitor center; interpretive programs (Memorial Day-Labor Day, daily). Standard fees. (Daily) 20 mi NW on AR 24, then 3 mi SE on AR 387. Contact the Superintendent, Rte 2, Box 28, Bluff City 71722; 501/685-2748. Per vehicle ¢

Annual Event

County Fair and Livestock Show. Sept.

Motor Hotel

★ ★ **HOLIDAY INN.** *950 S California Ave, 2 mi S on US 79N Bypass.* 501/836-8822; FAX 501/836-8822, ext. 707. 112 rms, 4 story. S $46.50-$50.50; D $50-$54; each addl $5; under 18 free. Crib free. TV; cable (premium). Indoor pool; wading pool. Restaurant 6 am-2 pm, 5-10 pm. Rm serv. Bar 5 pm-midnight; entertainment, dancing exc Sun. Ck-out noon. Coin lndry. Meeting rms. Valet serv. Sundries. Health club privileges. Some refrigerators. Cr cds: A, C, D, DS, ER, JCB, MC, V.

Restaurant

✔ ★ ★ **HUSH PUPPY.** *1285 Washington Ave.* 501/836-4124. Hrs: 11 am-2 pm, 5-9 pm; Sat from 5 pm. Closed Sun; July 4, Thanksgiving, Dec 25. Wine, beer. Semi-a la carte: lunch $3-$6.50, dinner $6-$13. Child's meals. Specializes in catfish, seafood, steak. Parking. Near historic district. Cr cds: A, DS, MC, V.

Conway (C-3)

(See Morrilton)

Founded 1871 **Pop** 26,481 **Elev** 316 ft **Area code** 501 **Zip** 72032
Information Chamber of Commerce, PO Box 1492; 501/327-7788.

Among the many products manufactured here are school furniture and buses, automotive testing equipment, vending machines, agricultural machinery, shoes, folding cartons, boats and pianos. Conway also is home to the University of Central Arkansas and Central Baptist College.

What to See and Do

Cadron Settlement Park. Replica of blockhouse built by early settlers in the 1770s. Also within this day-use park is Tollantusky Trail, which contains much historical information and beautiful scenery. (Daily) About 5 mi W via US 64, then S on AR 319. Phone 501/329-2986. **Free.**

Hendrix College (1876). (1,000 students) Mills Center houses Congressional office contents and some personal papers of former Congressman Wilbur D. Mills, chairman of House Ways and Means Committee and graduate of Hendrix College (Mon-Fri; closed some major hols & wk of Dec 25). Front & Washington Sts, N side of town on US 64, 65. Phone 501/450-1349 or 501/329-6811.

Petit Jean State Park (see). W via AR 60, 113, 154.

Toad Suck Ferry Lock and Dam. Site of 1820 river crossing; public viewing platform; historical markers. Adj park offers fishing; boating; picnicking; camping (fee; electric & water avail). (All yr) 5 mi W on AR 60, on the Arkansas River. Phone 501/329-2986. **Free.**

Woolly Hollow State Park. In approximately 400-acre wooded park surrounding 40-acre Lake Bennett is the Woolly Cabin, a restored one-room log structure built 1882, and many historical markers. Swimming beach; fishing; boating (rentals). Hiking trails. Picnicking, playground, snack bar. Camping (hookups). Interpretive programs (Memorial Day-Labor Day, daily). Standard fees. 12 mi N on US 65, 6 mi E on AR 285. Contact the Superintendent, 82 Woolly Hollow Rd, Greenbrier 72058; 501/679-2098.

Annual Events

Toad Suck Daze. Regional celebration featuring toad jumping; bluegrass, country and gospel music; carnival rides; arts & crafts. Phone 501/327-7788. First wkend May.

Faulkner County Fair. Sept 18-21.

Motels

✔ ★ ★ **BEST WESTERN.** *Box 1619, Jct I-40, US 64E.* 501/329-9855; FAX 501/327-6110. 70 rms, 2 story. S $36-$46; D $44-$54; each addl $4; suites $66-$72; under 12 free. Crib $5. Pet accepted, some restrictions. TV; cable (premium). Pool. Restaurant 6 am-10 pm. Ck-out noon. Business center. In-rm modem link. Coin lndry. Valet serv. Cr cds: A, C, D, DS, MC, V.

★ **COMFORT INN.** *PO Box 88, US 65N, exit 125.* 501/329-0300; FAX 501/329-8367. 60 rms, 2 story. May-Oct: S $47-$52; D $59-$69; each addl $5; suites $59; under 12 free; lower rates rest of yr. Crib $5. Pet accepted, some restrictions. TV; cable (premium). Pool. Complimentary continental bkfst. Restaurant opp 11 am-10 pm. Ck-out 11 am. Meeting rm. Business servs avail. Cr cds: A, C, D, DS, ER, JCB, MC, V.

★ ★ **DAYS INN.** *1002 E Oak St, I-40, exit 127.* 501/450-7575; FAX 501/450-7001. 51 rms, 2 story. S $40-$55; D $49-$66; each addl $5; suites $85-$94; under 12 free. Crib free. TV; cable (premium). Pool. Complimentary continental bkfst. Restaurant nearby. Ck-out 11 am. Meeting rms. Business servs avail. In-rm modem link. Cr cds: A, C, D, DS, ER, JCB, MC, V.

★ ★ **RAMADA INN.** *815 E Oak St (72033), US 64 at I-40.* 501/329-8392; FAX 501/329-0430. 78 rms, 2 story. S $46-$62; D $52-$64; each addl $8; suites $58; under 18 free. Crib free. Pet accepted, some restrictions. TV; cable (premium). Heated pool. Playground. Restaurant 6 am-10 pm. Rm serv. Ck-out noon. Meeting rms. Business servs avail. Valet serv. Sundries. Some refrigerators. Cr cds: A, C, D, DS, ER, JCB, MC, V.

Restaurant

✔ ★ **FU LIN.** *195 Farris Rd.* 501/329-1415. Hrs: 11 am-2 pm, 5-9 pm; Fri to 10 pm; Sat 5-10 pm; Sun 11:30 am-2:30 pm. Closed Dec 25. Chinese menu. Semi-a la carte: lunch $3.95-$5.75, dinner $3-$13.95. Complete meal: lunch, dinner $6.95. Sun buffet: $3.99. Specializes in beef dishes. Parking. Near Univ of Central Arkansas. No cr cds accepted.

Unrated Dining Spot

HART'S SEAFOOD. *Jct US 64 & 65.* 501/327-7041. Hrs: 4-9 pm; Fri, Sat to 9:30 pm; Sun 11:30 am-9 pm. Closed Mon, Tues;

some major hols. Res accepted. Buffet: lunch, dinner $7.95. Child's meals. Specializes in catfish, shrimp. Parking. No cr cds accepted.

[D]

Dumas (D-4)

Pop 5,520 **Elev** 163 ft **Area code** 501 **Zip** 71639
Information Chamber of Commerce, 165 S Main, PO Box 431; 501/382-5447.

What to See and Do

Arkansas Post National Memorial (see). 17 mi NE via US 165, then E on AR 169.

Desha County Museum. Artifacts depicting history of area; agricultural display, arrowhead collection. Log house farmstead. (Tues, Thurs, Sun; closed some hols) 1 mi on US 165E. Phone 501/382-4222. **Free.**

Lake Chicot State Park. Surrounding Arkansas' largest natural lake (formed centuries ago when the Mississippi changed its course); famous for its bream, crappie, catfish and bass fishing. Swimming pool, lifeguard; boating (rentals, ramp, marina). Picnicking, playground. Camping (hookups, dump station), cabins, store, coin laundry. Visitor center; exhibits; interpretive programs. Archery lessons (summer; phone for details). Standard fees. (Daily) 42 mi S on US 65 to Lake Village, 8 mi NE on AR 144. Phone 501/265-5480. Per vehicle ¢

Norrell and No 2 Locks & Dams. Major recreation areas: **Wild Goose Bayou**, N of Norrell Lock; **Merrisach Lake**, W of Lock No 2; **Pendleton Bend**, W of Dam No 2; **Moore Bayou**, S of Gillet on US 165; **Notrebes Bend**, E of Dam No 2. All areas offer fishing; boating; picnicking, playground. Camping only at Merrisach Lake, Notrebes Bend & Pendleton Bend (electric hookups, dump stations) and Moore Bayou. Fees charged at some areas. (Daily) About 11 mi E & N via US 165, 1; E on 44, then S on unnumbered roads before crossing river. Phone 501/548-2291. **Free.**

White River National Wildlife Refuge. 30 mi NE via US 165, AR 1 NE to St Charles. (See STUTTGART)

Motel

✔★ **RAMADA LIMITED.** 722 Hwy 65S, 1 mi S on US 65. 501/382-2707. 53 rms, 2 story. S $32-$38; D $39-$44; each addl $4; suites $45-$51. Crib $2. TV; cable. Pool. Complimentary coffee. Ck-out noon. Coin lndry. Some refrigerators. Cr cds: A, C, D, DS, MC, V.

[≈] [✕] [🔥] [SC]

El Dorado (E-2)

(See Camden, Magnolia)

Pop 23,146 **Elev** 286 ft **Area code** 501 **Zip** 71730
Information Chamber of Commerce, 201 N Jackson, PO Box 1271, 71731; 501/863-6113.

Legend has it that when Matthew F. Rainey's wagon broke down one day in a forest of hardwood and pine, he was so discouraged he offered all his worldly goods for sale. The farmers roundabout were such eager customers that Rainey decided to open a store on the spot and call the place El Dorado. The town led a quiet existence until oil was discovered in 1921. Soon it was inundated with drillers, speculators, engineers and merchants. Before the year was out there were 460 producing wells, and the name El Dorado had a significant ring. Today this flourishing community is the location of an oil refinery, chemical plants and many other industries.

What to See and Do

Arkansas Oil and Brine Museum. Ten-acre outdoor exhibit depicts working examples of oil production from 1920s to present. Museum exhibits; research center. Gift shop. Picnic area. (Daily; closed some major hols) 15 mi N via AR 7, at 3853 Smackover bypass. Phone 501/725-2877. **Free.**

Moro Bay State Park. Fishing; boating. Hiking. Picnicking, playground, store. Camping (hookups, dump station). Visitor center. Standard fees. (Daily) 20 mi NE via AR 15, at the confluence of Moro Bay, Raymond Lake and the Ouachita River. Phone 501/463-8555. Per vehicle ¢

Annual Event

Union County Fair. Mid-Sept.

Motel

✔★★ **COMFORT INN.** 2303 Junction City Rd. 501/863-6677; FAX 501/863-8611. 70 units, 2 story. S, D $53-$59; each addl $6; under 12 free. Crib free. Pet accepted. TV; cable (premium). Pool; whirlpool. Complimentary continental bkfst. Ck-out noon. Coin lndry. Free airport, bus depot transportation. Balconies. Cr cds: A, C, D, DS, MC, V.

[D] [🐾] [≈] [✕] [🔥] [SC]

Motor Hotel

★★★ **BEST WESTERN KINGS INN CONFERENCE CENTER.** 1920 Junction City Rd. 501/862-5191; FAX 501/863-7511. 131 rms, 2 story. S $59-$65; D $58-$64; each addl $6; suites $65-$71; kit units $55; family, wkend rates. Crib free. Pet accepted. TV; cable (premium), VCR avail. 2 pools, 1 indoor; wading pool, whirlpool, sauna. Playground. Restaurant 6 am-2 pm, 5-9 pm. Rm serv from 7 am. Private club 4-11 pm. Ck-out noon. Coin lndry. Meeting rms. Valet serv. Sundries. Airport transportation. Lighted tennis. Putting green. Miniature golf. Refrigerators. Balconies. Picnic tables. On 8 wooded acres. Cr cds: A, C, D, DS, ER, JCB, MC, V.

[🐾] [🏃] [≈] [✕] [🔥] [SC]

Eureka Springs (A-2)

(See Berryville, Harrison, Rogers)

Founded 1879 **Pop** 1,900 **Elev** 1,329 ft **Area code** 501 **Zip** 72632
Information Chamber of Commerce, PO Box 551; 501/253-8737 or 800/6-EUREKA.

Eureka Springs is a lovely Victorian city that clings to the sides of the Ozark Mountains. In the 19th century this was a well-known health spa; its springs, which gushed from limestone crevices, gained a reputation for having curative powers, and thousands of people, with every possible affliction, flocked to the city. Visitors continue to come to this community, drawn by the charm of the area, the scenery and the fishing.

What to See and Do

Eureka Springs Gardens. Specialty gardens and natural garden settings project changing panorama of color, shadow and form from sunrise to sunset. (Late May-Thanksgiving, daily) 5 mi W off US 62. Color Hot Line 501/253-9256. Phone 501/253-9244. ¢¢¢

Eureka Springs Historical Museum. Nineteenth-century area artifacts including household items, tools and photographs. (Daily exc Mon) 95 S Main St. Phone 501/253-9417. ¢¢

Frog Fantasies. Museum display featuring thousands of man-made frogs. Gift shop. (Daily) 151 Spring St. Phone 501/253-7227. ¢

Hammond Museum of Bells. More than 30 lighted exhibits trace the history and structure of bells from 800 B.C. to the present; more than 1,000 primitive, antique and fine art bells. Narrated tape tour. (Apr-mid-Nov, daily) Sr citizen rate. 2 Pine St. Phone 501/253-7411. ¢¢

Miles Musical Museum. Nickelodeons, music boxes, band organs, stringed instruments; miniature animated mechanical circus, Christmas & toy animations; musical art chapel; clocks; button mosaic pictures, paintings, wood carvings; handmade storybook dolls; Native American artifacts; mineral and rock displays. Guided tours (May-Oct, daily). 1½ mi W on US 62. Phone 501/253-8961. ¢¢¢

Onyx Cave Park. Unusual onyx formations in 57°F cave; blind cave fish display; museum of Gay 90s costumes, dolls; antique button collection; gift shop, picnicking. Continuous tours (daily). 3 mi E on US 62, 3½ mi N on county road. Phone 501/253-9321. Cave tours ¢¢

Pivot Rock and Natural Bridge. The top of Pivot Rock is 15 times as wide as the bottom; yet it is all perfectly balanced. A natural bridge and caves said to be hiding places of Jesse James are nearby. (Apr-mid-Nov) ½ mi W on US 62, 2½ mi N on Pivot Rock Rd. Phone 501/253-8982. ¢¢

Sightseeing.

Eureka Springs & North Arkansas Railway. Powered by restored 1906 steam engines; dining car. (Apr-Oct, daily exc Sun) 299 N Main St (AR 23). Phone 501/253-9623. ¢¢¢

Eureka Springs Trolley. Regularly scheduled trips through the city, historic district and many points of interest. (Apr-Nov) ¢¢

The Great Passion Play. Portrayal of life of Jesus from Palm Sunday through Ascension; evening performances. (Late Apr-late Oct, Tues-Wed & Fri-Sun) Mt Oberammergau. For reservations contact PO Box 471. Phone 501/253-9200 or 800/882-PLAY. ¢¢¢¢

Sacred Arts Center. More than 1,000 works of Christian art. (Daily) Phone 501/253-9200. ¢¢

Bible Museum. Rare bibles, artifacts and more than 6,000 volumes in 625 languages, including works on papyrus, parchment and clay cylinders and cones dating from 2000 B.C. (Daily) Phone 501/253-9200. ¢¢

New Holy Land. Re-creation of Holy Land as it was when Jesus was alive; Dead Sea; Jordan River; Sea of Galilee; Last Supper re-creation; Nativity scene. ¢¢

Christ of the Ozarks. A seven-story-tall statue of Jesus, more than one million pounds in weight and with an armspread of 65 feet.

The Rosalie House (1883). Built of handmade brick with gingerbread trim; original interior, gold leaf molding, ceiling frescoes, handmade woodwork; period furnishings. (Mid-Apr-Oct, daily; rest of yr, some wkends) 282 Spring St. Phone 501/253-7377. ¢¢

Withrow Springs State Park. This more than 700-acre recreation area stretches across mountains and valleys along the bluffs of War Eagle River. The waters of a large spring gush from a shallow cave at the foot of a towering bluff. Heated swimming pool (Memorial Day-mid-Aug, Wed-Sun; also Labor Day wkend) lifeguard; canoeing (rentals). Hiking, tennis. Picnicking, snack bar, concession, playground. Camping (hookups; dump station). Visitor center. Standard fees. (Daily) 20 mi S on AR 23. Contact Superintendent, Rte 3, Huntsville 72740. Phone 501/559-2593. Per vehicle ¢

Annual Events

Spring Tour of Historic Homes. Early Apr.

Ozark Folk Festival. Old-time music, square dancing, Gay 90s costume parade, other events. Early Oct.

Seasonal Event

Country Music Shows. Various productions with country music, comedy skits and other family entertainment. For schedules contact Chamber of Commerce. Most shows Apr-Oct.

Motels

★ ★ **1876 INN.** Rte 1, Box 247, US 62E & AR 23S. 501/253-7183; res: 800/643-3030; FAX 501/253-7183. 72 rms, 3 story. Mid-June-Sept: S $59.50-$62; D $60-$65; Oct: S $65-$69.50; D $69.50-$71.50; each addl $6; under 15 free; lower rates Mar-mid-June. Closed rest of yr. Crib free. Pet accepted; some restrictions, $10. TV; cable. Heated pool; whirlpool. Complimentary morning coffee. Restaurant 6:30-11 am, 5-8 pm. Ck-out 11 am. Business servs avail. Gift shop. Balconies. Cr cds: A, DS, MC, V.

🅳 🐾 ≋ ⋈ 🔥 SC

★ ★ **ALPEN-DORF.** Rte 4, Box 580, 3½ mi E on US 62. 501/253-9475. 30 rms, 2 story. Mid-May-late Oct: S $48; D $59; each addl $5; suites $79-$89; kit. units $69; under 18 free; lower rates rest of yr. TV; cable. Heated pool. Playground. Restaurant nearby. Ck-out 11 am. Cr cds: A, C, D, DS, MC, V.

🐾 ≋ ⋈ 🐾 SC

🗸 ★ ★ **BEST WESTERN INN OF THE OZARKS.** Box 431, 1 mi W on US 62. 501/253-9768; FAX 501/253-9768, ext. 349. 122 rms, 2 story. S $32-$69; D $38-$73; each addl $5; suites $85-$125; under 18 free; higher rates some hol wkends, War Eagle festival. Crib free. Pet accepted. TV; cable (premium), VCR avail. Heated pool. Restaurant 6:30 am-9 pm. Serv bar. Ck-out 11 am. Coin lndry. Meeting rms. Business servs avail. Lighted tennis. Golf privileges, greens fee $20. Rec rm. Some bathrm phones; wet bar in suites. Some balconies. Picnic tables. Cr cds: A, C, D, DS, MC, V.

🐾 🏃 ⛷ ≋ ⋈ 🔥 🐾

★ ★ **COLONIAL MANSION INN.** PO Box 527, AR 23 S. 501/253-7300; res: 800/638-2622; FAX 501/523-7149. 30 rms, 2 story. Apr-Nov: S, D $42-$72; each addl $6-$8; suites (up to 6 persons) $95-$120; honeymoon plan; higher rates special events; lower rates rest of yr. Crib $5. TV; cable. Pool. Complimentary continental bkfst. Restaurant nearby. Ck-out 11 am. Cr cds: A, DS, MC, V.

≋ ⋈ 🐾 SC

★ **DOGWOOD INN.** Rte 6, Box 20, AR 23, ¼ mi S of US 62. 501/253-7200; res: 800/544-1884. 33 rms, 2 story. June-Oct: S $42-$48; D $48-$56; each addl $5; lower rates rest of yr. Crib $5. TV; cable (premium). Pool. Playground. Complimentary continental bkfst. Restaurant nearby. Ck-out 11 am. In-rm modem link. Cr cds: A, DS, MC, V.

🐾 ≋ ⋈ 🔥 SC

★ **FOUR RUNNERS INN.** Rte 4, Box 306, 2 mi E on US 62, opp entrance to Passion Play. 501/253-6000; res: 800/844-6835; FAX 501/253-8654. 90 rms, 3 story. S $42-$79; D $55-$70; each addl $5; suites $66-$93; under 16 free. Crib $5. TV; cable (premium), VCR avail. Heated pool; wading pool, whirlpool. Restaurant 7am-2 pm, 5-9 pm. Bar 5 pm-1 am. Rm serv. Ck-out 11 am. Meeting rms. Business servs avail. Sundries. Game rm. Rec rm. Balconies. Cr cds: A, DS, MC, V.

🅳 🐾 ≋ ⋈ 🐾 SC

🗸 ★ **JOY.** Box 270, 1 mi W on US 62. 501/253-9568; FAX 501/253-5757. 45 rms, 2-3 story. No elvtr. June-Oct: S, D $48; each addl $4; suites $72; higher rates special events; lower rates Mar-May & Nov. Closed rest of yr. Crib free. TV; cable. Heated pool. Restaurant adj 7 am-9 pm. Ck-out 11 am. Business servs avail. Poolside rms. Balconies. On wooded grounds. Cr cds: A, DS, MC, V.

≋ 🔥

★ ★ **MATTERHORN TOWERS.** 98 Kings Hwy, on US 62. 501/253-9602; res: 800/426-0838 (exc AR). 35 units, 4 story. May-Oct:

S, D $58-$74.50; each addl $10; suites $107.50-$110; under 16 free; higher rates: some hol wkends, special events; lower rates rest of yr. Crib free. TV; cable (premium). Heated pool. Complimentary continental bkfst. Restaurant nearby. Ck-out 11 am. Sundries. In-rm whirlpools; some refrigerators. Cr cds: A, MC, V.

★★ **SWISS VILLAGE.** *Rte 6, Box 5, 1/2 mi SE on US 62. 501/253-9541; res: 800/447-6525; FAX 501/253-9541.* 55 rms, 2 story. Mid-May-Aug, Oct: S, D $54-$70; suites $74-$150; lower rates Marmid-May, Sept & Nov. Closed rest of yr. Crib free. TV; cable (premium), VCR avail. Heated pool; whirlpool. Complimentary continental bkfst. Restaurant nearby. Ck-out 11 am. Business servs avail. Some in-rm whirlpools. Balconies. Sun decks. Picnic tables. Cr cds: A, DS, MC, V.

★★ **TALL PINES.** *Rte 4, Box 58, W on US 62, at Pivot Rock Rd. 501/253-8096.* 19 cabins. June-Oct: S, D $55-$85; each addl $6; under 12 free; lower rates Mar-May, Nov-Dec. Closed rest of yr. Crib $3. TV; cable (premium). Heated pool. Complimentary coffee in rms. Restaurant nearby. Ck-out 11 am. Some in-rm whirlpools. Picnic tables, grills. In pine grove. Cr cds: A, DS, MC, V.

✔ **TRADEWINDS.** *77 Kings Hwy, on US 62. 501/253-9774.* 17 units, 1 kit. Apr-Nov: S $24-$52; D $28-$56; each addl $6; suites $45-$80; higher rates special events. Closed rest of yr. Crib $4. Pet accepted. TV; cable. Pool. Complimentary coffee. Restaurant nearby. Ck-out 11 am. Picnic tables. Cr cds: A, DS, MC, V.

Hotels

✔ **BASIN PARK.** *12 Spring St. 501/253-7837; res: 800/643-4972; FAX 501/253-6985.* 55 rms, 6 story. S, D $45-$65; under 12 free; higher rates: Jazz Fest, Blues Fest. Crib free. TV; cable, VCR avail (movies avail). Restaurant 11 am-3 pm, 5-9 pm. Bar. Ck-out 11 am. Meeting rms. Business servs avail. Historic hotel built 1905. Overlooks Basin Park and Spring. Cr cds: A, DS, MC, V.

★★ **NEW ORLEANS.** *63 Spring St. 501/253-8630; res: 800/243-8630; FAX 501/253-5949.* 22 suites, 6 story. No elvtr. S, D $80-$125; each addl $10; higher rates Oct. TV; cable. Restaurant 5-10 pm. Bar. Ck-out noon. Business servs avail. Free valet parking. Refrigerators. Balconies. In-rm whirlpools. Restored hotel, built in 1892; antique furnishings, Victorian decor. Located in historic downtown district. Cr cds: A, C, D, DS, MC, V.

Inns

★★ **ARSENIC & OLD LACE.** *60 Hillside Ave. 501/253-5454; res: 800/243-5223; FAX 501/253-2246.* 5 rms (1 with shower only), 3 story. No rm phones. Apr-Oct: S, D $90-$150; wkend rates; lower rates rest of yr. Children over 14 yrs only. TV; cable, VCR (movies avail). Complimentary full bkfst; afternoon tea/sherry. Restaurant nearby. Ck-out 11 am, ck-in 3-6 pm. Business servs avail. Free airport transportation. Balconies. Built 1992 in Victorian style of neighborhood; many antiques. Totally nonsmoking. Cr cds: A, DS, MC, V.

★★ **BRIDGEFORD HOUSE.** *263 Spring St. 501/253-7853; FAX 501/253-5497.* 4 rms, 2 story. No rm phones. S $85-$95; each addl $20; 2-day minimum wkends. TV; cable, VCR avail. Complimentary full bkfst. Complimentary coffee in rms. Ck-out 11 am, ck-in 3 pm. Refrigerator avail. Built 1884; antiques. Totally nonsmoking. Cr cds: MC, V.

★★ **CRESCENT COTTAGE.** *211 Spring St. 501/253-6022.* 3 rms, 3 story, 1 suite. D $70-$115; suite $90. Children over 13 yrs only. TV; cable, VCR avail (movies avail). Complimentary full bkfst. Restaurant nearby. Ck-out 11 am, ck-in 2:30 pm. Business servs avail. Refrigerators. Balconies. Built 1881; antiques. Totally nonsmoking. Cr cds: DS, MC, V.

★★ **DAIRY HOLLOW HOUSE.** *515 Spring St. 501/253-7444; FAX 501/253-7223.* 6 rms, 2 story. Rm phones avail. S, D $125-$165; higher rates hols & festivals. Complimentary coffee in rms. Restaurant (by res), 1 sitting: 7 pm. Rm serv. Ck-out 11 am, ck-in 4 pm. Whirlpool. Balconies. Restored farmhouse (1880) furnished with antiques. Totally nonsmoking. Cr cds: A, D, DS, MC, V.

★★★ **HEARTSTONE INN AND COTTAGES.** *35 Kings Hwy. 501/253-8916.* 12 units, 2 story, 2 kit. cottages. No rm phones. Feb 15th-Dec 15: S, D $63-$118; each addl $15; kit. cottages $95-$115; wkly rates; lower rates rest of yr. TV; cable. Complimentary full bkfst, tea. Restaurant nearby. Ck-out 11 am, ck-in 4 pm. Bellhops. Valet serv. Gift shop. Restored Victorian house (1882); antique furnishings; garden. Totally nonsmoking. Cr cds: A, DS, MC, V.

★★★ **PALACE HOTEL & BATH HOUSE.** *135 Spring St. 501/253-7474.* 8 rms, 2 story. S, D $113-$131. TV; cable. Complimentary continental bkfst, evening refreshments. Ck-out noon. Refrigerators, wet bars. Small, elegant Victorian-era hotel, completely restored; all rms have antique furnishings. Full bathhouse with massage personnel. Cr cds: A, DS, MC, V.

★★ **SCANDIA BED & BREAKFAST.** *33 Avo St, 1 mi W on US 62. 501/253-8922; res: 800/523-8922.* 7 rms. No rm phones. S, D $65-$85; suite $95-$105. TV; cable (premium), VCR avail. Complimentary full bkfst, coffee and tea/sherry. Restaurant nearby. Ck-out 11 am, ck-in 1 pm. Business servs avail. Whirlpool. Health club, golf privileges. Cr cds: A, DS, MC, V.

Cottage Colony

★★ **RED BUD VALLEY RESORT.** *Rte 1, Box 500, 2 mi E on US 62, 1 mi S on Rockhouse Rd. 501/253-9028.* 17 kit. cottages, 1-2 story. No rm phones. Apr-Nov (2 night min): kit. cottages $79-$135; under 7 free; honeymoon packages; 3 day min hols; lower rates rest of yr. TV; VCR avail (movies avail $3). Playground. Restaurant nearby. Ck-out 11 am, ck-in 3 pm. Maid serv twice wkly. Gift shop. Horseback riding. Swimming. Hiking. Fishing guides, clean & store. Balconies. Picnic tables, grills. Located in 200-acre valley with private park, roaming wildlife and spring-fed, stocked lake. Cr cds: MC, V.

Restaurants

★ **BUBBA'S.** *US 62 & Kings Hwy. 501/253-7706.* Hrs: 11:30 am-9 pm. Closed Sun; some major hols. Beer. Semi-a la carte: lunch, dinner $2.95-$14.50. Specializes in barbecue meats. Parking. Eclectic decor. No cr cds accepted.

✔ **HYLANDER STEAK & RIB.** *1 1/2 mi W on US 62. 501/253-7360.* Hrs: 4-10 pm; Fri & Sat to 11 pm. Closed Thanksgiving, Dec 25. Res accepted. Bar. Semi-a la carte: dinner $5.95-$14.95. Specializes in barbecue dishes, prime rib. Parking. Casual atmosphere. Antiques, Elvis memorabilia. Cr cds: A, DS, MC, V.

★ ★ **PLAZA.** *55 S Main. 501/253-8866.* Hrs: 11:30 am-2:30 pm, 5:30-9 pm. Continental menu. Serv bar. Semi-a la carte: lunch $3.50-$6.50, dinner $7-$22.50. Specializes in filet mignon, lobster tail. Wine-rack wall, art collection. Cr cds: A, DS, MC, V.

D

✔ ★ ★ **VICTORIAN SAMPLER.** *33 Prospect St. 501/253-8374.* Hrs: 11:30 am-3 pm, 5-8:30 pm; Sat to 9 pm. Closed Thanksgiving; also Dec-mid-Mar. Res accepted. Serv bar. Semi-a la carte: lunch $6.95-$10, dinner $10.95-$15.95. Specialties: chilled soup, desserts. Parking. Restored Victorian mansion; antiques. Gift shop on premises. Cr cds: DS, MC, V.

Fayetteville (B-1)

(See Rogers, Springdale)

Pop 42,099 **Elev** 1,400 ft **Area code** 501
Information Chamber of Commerce, 123 W Mountain St, PO Box 4216, 72702; 501/521-1710 or 800/766-4626.

This is a resort center in the Ozark Mountains. The countryside is famous for its scenery, spring and fall. There are many lakes and streams nearby for fishing. Fayetteville is the home of the University of Arkansas.

What to See and Do

Arkansas Air Museum. Exhibit spanning the history of manned flight; features collection of open cockpit biplanes. (Daily; closed Jan 1, Thanksgiving, Dec 25) 5 mi S on US 71, at Drake Field. Phone 501/521-4947. **Free.**

Devil's Den State Park. Situated in a scenic valley in the Boston Mountains, this more than 2,000-acre park in the heart of rugged Ozark terrain includes unusual sandstone formations; Devil's Den Cave; and the Devil's Icebox, where the temperature never goes above 60°F. Swimming pool (summer; lifeguard); fishing; canoeing (rentals). Nature, hiking, bridle, mountain biking trails. Picnicking, playground, restaurant (summer), snack bar, store. Camping (electric hookups, dump station; standard fees); horse camp; cabins, coin laundry. Visitor center has exhibits, camping & backpack equipment rentals. Interpretive programs. (Daily) 8 mi S on US 71, then 18 mi SW of West Fork on AR 170. For reservations contact Superintendent, Devil's Den State Park, 11333 AR 74W, West Fork 72774. Phone 501/761-3325. Per vehicle ¢

Headquarters House (1853). Greek-revival house, residence of wealthy Union sympathizer Judge Jonas Tebbetts, was used as headquarters for both Union and Confederate forces during the Civil War; period furnishings, local historical artifacts, Civil War relics. (Tues-Sat) Donation. 118 E Dickson St. Phone 501/521-2970.

Prairie Grove Battlefield State Park. Park covers approximately 130 acres of the 3.5-square-mile site where more than 18,000 Union and Confederate forces fought on Dec 7, 1862; the armies suffered a combined loss of 2,500 dead, wounded or missing. Hindman Hall Museum houses visitor center with exhibits, battle diorama, artifacts, audiovisual presentation. Historic structures in the park include Battle Monument, a chimney from Rhea's Mill; Borden House, scene of the heaviest fighting of the battle; a spring house, smokehouse, detached kitchen, schoolhouse, church, blacksmith shop and sorghum mill. Guided tours through structures (summer, daily; rest of yr by request). Picnicking, playground. 10 mi W on US 62 in Prairie Grove. Contact Superintendent, PO Box 306, Prairie Grove 72753. Phone 501/846-2990. **Free.**

University of Arkansas (1871). (14,700 students) In center of town. Phone 501/575-2000. On campus are

University Museum. Houses science, natural history and ethnological exhibits; films. (Daily; closed major hols, also Dec 24-Jan 1) Donation. Garland St. Phone 501/575-3466.

Fine Arts Center. Includes a theater, concert hall, library and exhibition gallery. (Daily; closed hols). Garland St. For concert and theater schedule phone 501/575-4752.

Walton Arts Center. Musicals, opera, plays, symphonies. Dickson & Springs Sts. For ticket information phone 501/443-5600.

Special Event

Battle Re-enactment. Prairie Grove Battlefield State Park. Costumed volunteers re-enact the historic battle and demonstrate war tactics and the life of a Civil War soldier. 1st full wkend Dec.

Motels

(Prices are generally higher on football wkends)

★ ★ **CLARION INN.** *1255 S Shiloh Dr (72701), jct US 71 & 62. 501/521-1166; FAX 501/521-1204.* 197 units, 2 story. S, D $62-$76; each addl $4; suites $95; higher rates wkends, special events; under 17 free. Crib free. TV; cable (premium). Indoor pool. Restaurant 6 am-10 pm. Rm serv from 7 am. Private club 4:30 pm-1 am; dancing. Ck-out noon. Coin lndry. Business center. In-rm modem link. Bellhops. Valet serv. Airport, bus depot transportation. Exercise equipt; weights, bicycles, whirlpool, sauna. Game rm. Some refrigerators. Cr cds: A, C, D, DS, ER, JCB, MC, V.

D ⊠ ✗ ⊠ ⌕ SC 🏃

★ ★ ★ **CLARION INN AT THE MILL.** *(3906 Greathouse Springs Rd, PO Box 409, Johnson 72741) 7 mi N on US 71, exit 50. 501/443-1800; FAX 501/443-3879.* 48 rms, 2 story. S, D $82-$88; each addl $5; suites $110-$175; under 18 free. Crib free. TV; cable. Complimentary continental bkfst. Restaurant 11 am-3 pm, 5:30-10 pm, Sat & Sun from 5:30 pm. Ck-out noon. Meeting rm. Whirlpool in suites. Historic water mill built 1835. Cr cds: A, C, D, DS, JCB, MC, V.

D ⊠ ⌕ SC

✔ ★ **DAYS INN.** *2402 N College Ave (72703). 501/443-4323; FAX 501/443-4323, ext. 470.* 150 rms, 2 story, 6 suites. S, D $45-$72; each addl $5; suites $80-$115. Crib free. Pet accepted; some restrictions, $50 deposit. TV; cable (premium), VCR avail. Pool. Complimentary continental bkfst. Ck-out noon. Coin lndry. Meeting rms. Business servs avail. Cr cds: A, C, D, DS, MC, V.

🐾 ⊠ ⊠ ⌕ SC

✔ ★ **INN OF FAYETTEVILLE.** *1000 US 71 (72701). 501/442-3041; FAX 501/442-0744.* 105 units, 2 story. S, D $40-$44; each addl $4; suites $59; under 16 free; wkly rates. Pet accepted; $10. TV; cable (premium). Pool. Complimentary continental bkfst, coffee in rms. Restaurant opp open 24 hrs. Ck-out noon. Refrigerator in suites. Cr cds: A, C, D, DS, MC, V.

D 🐾 ⊠ ✗ ⌕ ⊠ ⌕ SC

★ ★ **RAMADA INN.** *3901 N College Ave (72703). 501/443-3431; FAX 501/443-1927.* 120 rms, 2 story. S $53-$60; D $60-$66; each addl $6; under 18 free. Crib free. Pet accepted. TV; cable (premium). Pool. Playground. Restaurant 6 am-9 pm. Rm serv. Private club 5 pm-1 am. Ck-out noon. Meeting rms. Business servs avail. Valet serv. Tennis. Cr cds: A, C, D, DS, MC, V.

🐾 🏃 ⊠ ⊠ ⌕ SC

Hotel

★ ★ ★ **HILTON.** *70 N East Ave (72701). 501/442-5555; FAX 501/442-2105.* 235 rms, 15 story. S $58-$72; D $66-$82; each addl $8. Crib free. Pet accepted. TV; cable (premium), VCR avail. Indoor/outdoor pool. Restaurant 6:30 am-9 pm. Bar noon-midnight. Meeting rms. Gift shop. Free parking. Free airport, bus depot transportation. Exercise equipt; weights, bicycles. Cr cds: A, C, D, DS, ER, MC, V.

D 🐾 ⊠ ✗ ⊠ ⌕ SC

Restaurants

★ **COY'S PLACE.** *2908 N College Ave. 501/442-9664.* Hrs: 11 am-9:30 pm; Fri, Sat to 10:30 pm; Sun 4:30-9:30 pm. Closed Thanksgiving, Dec 24 & 25. Res accepted. Bar. Semi-a la carte: lunch $5-$8, dinner $7.95-$16.95. Specializes in steak, prime rib, seafood. Parking. Rustic atmosphere. Cr cds: A, D, DS, MC, V.

D

★ ★ **OLD POST OFFICE.** *1 Center Sq. 501/443-5588.* Hrs: 11 am-2 pm, 5-9 pm; Fri & Sat to 10 pm. Closed July 4, Dec 25. Res accepted. Private club. Semi-a la carte: lunch $4.50-$7.95, dinner $8.95-$17.95. Child's meals. Specializes in seafood, prime rib. Own baking. Parking. In old post office (1909); lamp posts, brass rails. Cr cds: A, C, D, MC, V.

Forrest City (C-4)

(For accommodations see Helena)

Founded 1866 **Pop** 13,364 **Elev** 276 ft **Area code** 501 **Zip** 72335
Information Chamber of Commerce, 203 N Izard; 501/633-1651.

This town is named for Confederate General Nathan Bedford Forrest, who contracted to put a railroad across Crowley's Ridge, on which the city stands. The ridge, 100 feet high and composed of loess, roughly parallels the Mississippi from Missouri to Helena, Arkansas. (Loess is windblown fine, yellowish loam that generally stands in vertical cliffs.)

What to See and Do

Village Creek State Park. Approx 7,000-acre park with two lakes situated entirely upon the unusual geologic formation of Crowley's Ridge. Swimming; fishing; boating (rentals). Hiking trails; tennis. Picnicking, playground, store. Camping (hookups, dump station); 10 fully equipped cabins. Visitor center with history, geology and botany exhibits; audiovisual presentations; interpretive programs (summer). (Daily) Standard fees. E on I-40 exit 242, then 13 mi N on AR 284. Contact Superintendent, Rte 3, Box 49-B, Wynne 72396. Phone 501/238-9406. Per vehicle ¢

Annual Event

Harvest Festival. Hot air balloon races; 5-km run. Late Sept-early Oct.

Fort Smith (B-1)

(See Alma)

Pop 72,798 **Elev** 450 ft **Area code** 501
Information Chamber of Commerce, 612 Garrison Ave, PO Box 1668, 72902; 501/783-6118.

The original fort was built on the Arkansas River in 1817 to stand between the Osages upstream and the Cherokees downstream. It also gave protection to traders, trappers and explorers and encouraged settlement in the area. Captain John Rogers became the first settler in 1821; by 1842 the town had a population of nearly 500.

In 1848, when gold was discovered in California, Fort Smith immediately became a thriving supply center and starting point for gold-rush wagons heading south across the plains. Bandits, robbers, gamblers and cutthroats moved in. Without peace officers, the territory was wild and tough until 1875, when Judge Isaac C. Parker, known later as "the hanging judge," was sent in to clean it up. He was judge of the Federal District Court at Fort Smith for 21 years; during his first 14 years there was no appeal of his decisions. Under Parker's rule, 151 men were sentenced to die and about 79 hanged, sometimes as many as six at a

time. Parker was a strict judge with a reputation for knowing and respecting the rules of evidence.

Today, Fort Smith is a leading manufacturing center in Arkansas, with more than 200 manufacturing plants and major corporations. Boston Mountain to the north is a good hunting area.

What to See and Do

Fort Smith Art Center. Built in 1879 as a residence. Changing exhibits monthly; guided tours. (Daily exc Mon; closed hols, Dec 24-Jan 1) 423 N 6th St. Phone 501/784-ARTS or 501/782-1156. **Free.**

Fort Smith National Historic Site. Park contains foundations of first Fort Smith; the original commissary from the second Fort Smith; the famous Judge Parker's courtroom; jail and reconstructed gallows. (Daily; closed Jan 1, Thanksgiving, Dec 25) Rogers Ave and 3rd Sts. Phone 501/783-3961. ¢

Old Fort Museum. Regional history, period pharmacy with working soda fountain, transportation exhibit with 1899 steam fire pumper. Changing exhibits. (Daily; closed Jan 1, Thanksgiving, Dec 24-25) 320 Rogers Ave. Phone 501/783-7841. ¢¢

Annual Events

Old Fort Days Rodeo. Memorial Day.

Old Fort River Festival. Arts & crafts, entertainment, sporting events. Mid-June.

Arkansas-Oklahoma State Fair. Late Sept.

Motels

✔ ★ ★ **BEST WESTERN TRADE WINDS INN.** *101 N 11th St (72901). 501/785-4121; FAX 501/785-0316.* 131 rms, 2 story. S $39-$48; D $43-$55; each addl $4; suites $63-$100; under 12 free. Crib free. Pet accepted. TV; cable (premium). Pool. Restaurant 4 am-10 pm; Sun 7 am-8 pm. Rm serv. Private club 3 pm-5 am, closed Sun; entertainment, dancing. Ck-out noon. Meeting rms. Business servs avail. Free airport, bus depot transportation. Wet bar in suites. Cr cds: A, C, D, DS, ER, JCB, MC, V.

D ✔ ≈ ⋈ ⋈ SC

★ ★ **SHERATON INN.** *5711 Rogers Ave (72901), near Municipal Airport. 501/452-4110; FAX 501/452-4891.* 151 rms, 2 story. S $56-$66; D $62-$77; each addl $10; suites $160; under 18 free. Crib free. Pet accepted. TV; cable (premium). Pool; wading pool. Coffee in rms. Restaurant 6 am-2 pm, 5-10 pm. Rm serv. Private club 5 pm-2 am. Ck-out noon. Meeting rms. Business servs avail. In-rm modem link. Airport transportation. Cr cds: A, C, D, DS, MC, V.

D ✔ ≈ ✈ ⋈ ⋈ SC

★ **SUPER 8.** *3810 Towson Ave (72901). 501/646-3411; FAX 501/646-3197.* 57 rms, 2 story. S $31.88-$35.88; D $39.88-$45.88; each addl $5; under 12 free. Crib free. TV; cable (premium). Complimentary coffee in rms. Restaurant adj 11 am-9:30 pm. Private club 5 pm-5 am. Ck-out 11 am. Free airport, bus depot transportation. Near Municipal Airport. Cr cds: A, C, D, DS, MC, V.

D ⋈ ⋈ SC

Hotel

★ ★ **HOLIDAY INN CIVIC CENTER.** *700 Rogers Ave (72901). 501/783-1000; FAX 501/783-0312.* 255 units, 9 story. S $72.50; D $82.50; each addl $10; suites $97-$235; under 18 free; wkend rates. Crib free. Pet accepted, some restrictions. TV; cable (premium), VCR avail. Indoor pool. Restaurant 6 am-2 pm, 5-10 pm. Private club 3 pm-1 am; entertainment, dancing. Ck-out noon. Convention facilities. Business servs avail. In-rm modem link. Gift shop. Valet parking. Free airport, bus depot transportation. Exercise equipt;

weights, bicycles, whirlpool, sauna. Some refrigerators. Cr cds: A, C, D, DS, JCB, MC, V.

[D] [🚣] [≋] [🏃] [🍳] [🔥] [SC]

Inn

★ ★ **THOMAS QUINN GUEST HOUSE.** *815 North B St (72901).* 501/782-0499. 9 kit. suites, 2 story. S $59; D $79. Crib $3. TV; cable (premium). Complimentary coffee in rms. Restaurant nearby. Ck-out noon. Concierge. Free airport transportation. Whirlpool. Restored 1863 house; 2nd floor added 1916. Corinthian columns. Near historic attractions. Cr cds: A, C, D, DS, MC, V.

[🔥] [SC]

Restaurants

✔ ★ **CALICO COUNTY.** *2401 S 56th St.* 501/452-3299. Hrs: 6 am-10 pm. Closed Thanksgiving, Dec 25. Semi-a la carte: bkfst $4, lunch, dinner $4.50-$8. Child's meals. Specializes in chicken fried steak, catfish. Country atmosphere, antique kitchen tools. Cr cds: A, C, D, DS, MC, V.

[D] [SC]

★ ★ **RED BARN.** *3716 Newlon Rd, 4 mi N on US 71/64, 1 mi W on Newlon Rd.* 501/783-4075. Hrs: 5-11 pm. Closed Sun, Mon; major hols. Res accepted. Private club. Semi-a la carte: dinner $9.50-$24.95. Child's meals. Specializes in quail, prime rib. Parking. Originally a barn, horse stalls form partitions between tables. Cr cds: A, D, DS, MC, V.

[D]

★ ★ **TALIANO'S.** *201 N 14th St.* 501/785-2292. Hrs: 11 am-1:30 pm, 5:30-9:45 pm; Sat-Mon from 5:30 pm. Closed Sun; major hols. Res accepted. Italian, Amer menu. Wine, beer. Semi-a la carte: lunch, dinner $5.75-$20. Child's meals. Specializes in veal, chicken, fish, fettuccine Alfredo. Own pasta. In historic Queen Anne/Victorian mansion; fireplaces; stained-glass windows. Family-owned. Cr cds: A, C, D, DS, MC, V.

[D] [SC]

Unrated Dining Spot

FURRS CAFETERIA. *110 Phoenix Village Mall, 4 mi S on US 71.* 501/646-4374. Hrs: 11 am-2 pm, 4:30-8 pm; Sat 11 am-8 pm; Sun to 7 pm; major hols to 6 pm. Avg ck: lunch, dinner $4.50. Specializes in steak, seafood. Cr cds: MC, V.

Greers Ferry Lake Area (B-3)

(See Batesville, Mountain View)

Area code 501

(The dam is approx 64 mi N of Little Rock via US 67/167, AR 5, 25, near Heber Springs)

This 50-mile-long lake, impounded by a dam built by the US Army Corps of Engineers, was dedicated by President John F. Kennedy shortly before his assassination in November, 1963. Since then, the area has developed rapidly, now offering 15 public recreation areas on more than 31,000 acres. Swimming, waterskiing, scuba diving; hunting; boating (rentals, marina, ramps). Nature trail up Sugar Loaf Mountain. Picnicking. Camping. Fee charged for some recreation areas. For fur-

ther information contact Heber Springs Chamber of Commerce, 1001 W Main, Heber Springs 72543. Phone 501/362-2444.

What to See and Do

Greers Ferry National Fish Hatchery. Produces 100 tons of rainbow trout annually for stocking in public fishing waters. (Daily) 3 mi N of Heber Springs on AR 25. Phone 501/362-3615. **Free.**

Little Red River. One of the finest trout streams in the area is stocked weekly. Trout of more than 15 pounds have been caught. Five commercial docks.

William Carl Gardner Visitor Center. Provides tourist information and houses exhibits interpreting history and culture of the southern Ozark region; displays relate history of the Corps of Engineers and their projects in Arkansas; interpretive slide/tape programs; guided tours of Greers Ferry Dam and Powerhouse depart from visitor center (Memorial Day-Labor Day, Mon-Fri). Nature trail with access for the disabled (guided tours in summer by request). Visitor center (Mar-Oct, daily; Feb, Nov, Dec, Sat & Sun; closed Jan 1, Thanksgiving, Dec 25). 3 mi NE of Heber Springs on AR 25. Phone 501/362-9067. **Free.**

Annual Event

Water Festival. Around Greers Ferry Lake. Ski shows, jet ski races, arts & crafts shows. 1st wkend Aug.

Motels

(Distances given are from Heber Springs unless otherwise stated)

✔ ★ **BUDGET INN.** *(616 W Main St, Heber Springs 72543)* At jct AR 25, 110. 501/362-8111. 25 rms. S $36; D $42; each addl $5; suites, studio rms $47. Crib $5. Pet accepted. TV; cable. Pool. Complimentary coffee. Restaurant nearby. Ck-out 11 am. Cr cds: A, DS, MC, V.

[🚣] [≋] [🔥] [SC]

★ **LAKESHORE RESORT.** *(801 Case Ford Rd, Heber Springs 72543)* 1½ mi N off AR 25 on AR 210W. 501/362-2315; FAX 501/362-2315. 7 kit. units. May-Oct: S, D $48; each addl $6; wkly, monthly rates; lower rates rest of yr. Crib free. TV; cable. Restaurant nearby. Ck-out 11 am. Airport transportation. Private dock; boat stall $5. Refrigerators. Picnic tables, grills. On lake; 4 acres of hilly, wooded grounds. Cr cds: A, DS, MC, V.

[🚣] [🚤] [≋] [🔥] [SC]

Resort

★ ★ **FAIRFIELD BAY RESORT.** *(Box 1008, Fairfield Bay 72088)* AR 16 E. 501/884-3333; res: 800/643-9790 (exc AR), 800/482-9826 (AR). 220 units, 1-3 story, 82 kits. S, D $59-$90; under 18 free; golf plan. Crib free. TV; cable (premium), VCR avail. 4 pools; wading pool. Playground. Supervised child's activities (June-Sept). Five restaurants, hrs vary. Ck-out 10 am, ck-in 4 pm. Grocery. Coin lndry. Business center. Sports dir. Tennis, 12 outdoor courts, 6 lighted, pro. 18-hole golf, pro, putting green, driving range. Miniature golf. Waterskiing. Marina; boat rentals. Horse stables. Bowling alley. Summer theater. Rec rm. Game rm. Refrigerators; some fireplaces. Some balconies. Picnic tables, grills. Occupies 14,000 wooded acres and borders lake. Cr cds: A, DS, MC, V.

[D] [🚤] [🏄] [🏃] [⛷] [≋] [🚣] [🔥]

Restaurants

★ ★ **CAPTAINS' HOUSE.** *(603 W Quitman, Heber Springs)* 501/362-3963. Hrs: 11 am-2 pm, 5-8 pm. Res accepted. Semi-a la carte: lunch $5-$9, dinner $7-$18. Child's meals. Specializes in char-broiled steak, chicken, seafood. Salad bar. Parking. In old home (1914). Cr cds: A, DS, MC, V.

[SC]

✔★ **CHINA DELIGHT.** *(1632 AR 25N, Heber Springs)* *501/362-7054.* Hrs: 11 am-10 pm. Closed Thanksgiving, Dec 25. Chinese menu. Semi-a la carte: lunch $3.25-$3.95, dinner $5.50-$9. Buffet: lunch $4.75, dinner $16.95. Specializes in Cantonese dishes. Parking. Chinese decor. Cr cds: A, DS, MC, V.

[D]

★ **MR B'S CATFISH.** *(1120 AR 25N, Heber Springs)* *501/362-7692.* Hrs: 11 am-10 pm. Closed Mon; Thanksgiving, Dec 25. Semi-a la carte: lunch $3.90-$7.95, dinner $4.00-$19.95. Child's meals. Specializes in catfish, steak. Parking. No cr cds accepted.

[SC]

✔★ **RED APPLE DINING ROOM.** *(1000 Country Club Rd, Heber Springs 72543) 5 mi W on AR 110, on Eden Isle. 501/362-3111.* Hrs: 6 am-10 pm. Res accepted. Continental menu. Bar 5 pm-midnight. Wine list. Semi-a la carte: bkfst $5.95-$8.95, lunch $4.75-$10.95, dinner $10.50-$25. Sun brunch $14.95. Child's meals. Specializes in soufflés, prime rib. Own baking. Combo Fri, Sat. Parking. Mediterranean decor; fountains, Spanish gates, gardens. Jacket (dinner). Cr cds: A, C, D, DS, MC, V.

[D]

Harrison (B-2)

(See Berryville, Bull Shoals Lake Area, Eureka Springs)

Pop 9,922 **Elev** 1,182 ft **Area code** 501 **Zip** 72601
Information Chamber of Commerce, PO Box 939; 501/741-2659.

Harrison, headquarters for a rustic resort area in the wild and beautiful Ozarks, is excellent for vacationing. The entire region is scenic, especially along AR 7.

What to See and Do

Dogpatch, USA. Al Capp's comic strip characters and village; railroad; variety shows; gravity house, rides. (June-Aug & Oct, daily; Sept, Thurs-Mon) 8 mi S on AR 7. Phone 501/743-1111. Fee for each attraction.

Float trips. Down the Buffalo River through the Ozark Mountains and the forested hill country. For information contact Buffalo National River (Float Trips), National Park Service, Dept of the Interior, PO Box 1173, 72602; 501/741-5443.

Mystic Caverns. Two caves with large formations; 35-foot pipe organ, eight-story crystal dome. One-hour guided tours cover 3/8 mile of lighted walks (may be strenuous). (Mar-Nov; closed Thanksgiving) 8 mi S on AR 7. Phone 501/743-1739. ¢¢¢

Annual Events

Northwest Arkansas Bluegrass Music Festival. Aug.

Northwest Arkansas District Fair. 2 mi S off US 65. Livestock show, rodeo. Sept.

Motels

★★ **HOLIDAY INN.** *816 N Main St. 501/741-2391; FAX 501/741-1181.* 120 rms, 2 story. S $48.50; D $60.50; each addl $10; under 18 free. Crib free. TV; cable (premium), VCR avail. Indoor pool; sauna. Restaurant 6:30 am-9 pm. Rm serv. Private club 5 pm-midnight. Ck-out noon. Coin lndry. Meeting rms. Business center. In-rm modem

link. Sundries. Airport transportation. Exercise equipt; weights, bicycles, whirlpool, sauna. Game rm. Cr cds: A, C, D, DS, MC, V.

[D] [≈] [✗] [⇘] [⋏] [SC] [↟]

✔★★ **RAMADA INN.** *1222 N Main St. 501/741-7611; FAX 501/741-7610.* 100 rms, 2 story. June-Oct: S $49-$55; D $56-$58; each addl $7; under 18 free; higher rates: some hol wknds, War Eagle wkend; lower rates rest of yr. Crib free. Pet accepted. TV; cable (premium). Heated pool; wading pool. Playground. Restaurant 7 am-9:30 pm. Ck-out noon. Meeting rms. Business servs avail. Valet serv. Sundries. Lighted tennis. Game rm. Cr cds: A, C, D, DS, MC, V.

[⋏] [⇘] [≈] [⇘] [⋏] [SC]

★★ **SUPER 8.** *1330 US 62/65N. 501/741-1741; FAX 501/741-8858.* 52 units, 2 story. June-Oct: S $50; D $55; under 12 free; lower rates rest of yr. Crib free. Pet accepted (deposit required). TV; cable (premium), VCR avail (movies avail). Pool. Continental bkfst. Coffee in lobby. Restaurant nearby. Ck-out 11 am. Business servs avail. Game rm. Some in-rm whirlpools. Cr cds: A, C, D, DS, MC, V.

[D] [⇘] [≈] [⇘] [⋏] [SC]

Restaurant

✔★ **BAMBOO GARDENS.** *1409 US 62/65N. 501/741-8880.* Hrs: 11 am-9 pm. Res accepted. Chinese menu. Semi-a la carte: lunch $3.25-$8.95, dinner $5.95-$9.95. Specializes in Cantonese dishes. Parking. Oriental decor. Cr cds: A, MC, V.

Heber Springs (B-3)

(see Greers Ferry Lake Area)

Helena (C-4)

(See Forrest City)

Pop 7,491 **Elev** 195 ft **Area code** 501 **Zip** 72342
Information Phillips County Chamber of Commerce, PO Box 447; 501/338-8327.

Helena, a river barge port of call since 1880, was once described by Samuel Clemens as occupying "one of the prettiest situations on the Mississippi." This broad, flat section of the Mississippi River valley is part of the cotton country known as "the Delta" and is the southern end of Crowley's Ridge, a stretch of wind-deposited yellowish loess hills that runs north to the Missouri border.

What to See and Do

Antebellum, Victorian and Edwardian Houses. An assortment of restored historic houses. To arrange for guided tours contact Beauchamp By The River Tours, 804 Columbia St, phone 501/338-3607. ¢¢¢¢

Delta Cultural Center. Housed in 1912 Missouri Pacific rail depot, center has exhibits on history of "the Delta." (Mon-Sat, also Sun and hol afternoons; closed Jan 1, Thanksgiving, Dec 25) 95 Missouri St. Phone 501/338-8919. **Free.**

Phillips County Museum. Native American artifacts, Civil War relics; local history collection; glass, china; paintings, costumes. (Tues-Sat, limited hrs; closed major hols & Dec 25-31) 623 Pecan St, adj to public library. Phone 501/338-3537. **Free.**

St Francis National Forest. Almost 21,000 acres, including 510-acre Storm Creek Lake, 520-acre Bear Creek Lake. Swimming; fishing, hunting for small game; boating. Picnicking. Camping. Fees may be charged at recreation sites. (Daily) 2 mi N on forest service road.

Contact Supervisor, 605 W Main, PO Box 1008, Russellville 72801. Phone 501/968-2354. **Free.**

Annual Event

King Biscuit Blues Festival. Phone 501/338-9144. 2nd wkend Oct.

Seasonal Event

Warfield Concert Series. Series of productions by internationally known artists. Tickets at Chamber of Commerce. Sept-May.

Motel

✔ ★ **DELTA INN.** *(1207 US 49N, West Helena 72390) 3 mi N on US 49. 501/572-7915; res: 800/748-8802; FAX 501/572-3757.* 100 rms. S $35; D $39; each addl $5; kit. units $48; under 16 free. Crib $5. TV; cable (premium). Pool. Complimentary continental bkfst. Restaurant nearby. Ck-out 11 am. Business servs avail. Cr cds: A, D, DS, MC, V.

Inn

★ ★ **EDWARDIAN.** *317 Biscoe St. 501/338-9155; res: 800/598-4749.* 12 rms, 3 story. S $44-$56; D $59-$85; each addl $10; under 10 free. Crib free. TV; cable. Complimentary continental bkfst. Ck-out 11 am, ck-in 2 pm. Balconies. Grills. Near Mississippi River. Restored historic mansion; built 1904. Many antiques. Cr cds: A, C, D, MC, V.

Hope (D-2)

(See Nashville; also see Texarkana, TX)

Founded 1852 **Pop** 9,643 **Elev** 348 ft **Area code** 501 **Zip** 71801
Information Chamber of Commerce, 108 W 3rd; 501/777-3640.

Hope is the birthplace of the 42nd President of the United States, William Jefferson Clinton. The annual Watermelon Festival regularly has winners in the 150-200 pound range. The all-time winner weighed in at 260 pounds.

What to See and Do

Old Washington Historic State Park. During the early 19th century, Washington was a convenient stop on the Southwest Trail, visited by such men as Stephen Austin, Sam Houston and Davy Crockett. Washington became the Confederate capital for the state after Little Rock was captured in 1863. The park preserves and interprets the town's past from 1824-1875. 9 mi NW on AR 4. Many historic structures remain:

Old Tavern (ca 1840) with detached kitchen, taproom; blacksmith shop where, between 1826 and 1831, James Black designed the bowie knife for James Bowie; **1874 Courthouse** now serving as park information center; **Confederate state capitol** from 1863-65; **Royston House,** restored residence of Arkansas Militia General Grandison D. Royston, president of Arkansas Constitutional Convention of 1874; **Sanders House** (1845), restored Greek-revival house; **Purdom House,** which served as medical offices of Dr James Purdom; **gun museum** with more than 600 antique weapons; and **Goodlett cotton gin.**

Guided tours of park include historical buildings (daily; closed Jan 1, Thanksgiving, Dec 24-25). Contact Park Superintendent, PO Box 98, Washington 71862; phone 501/983-2733 or -2684. **¢¢¢**

Annual Events

Jonquil Festival. Old Washington Historic State Park (see). Coincides with blooming of jonquils planted by early settlers. Craft demonstrations, bluegrass music. Mid-Mar.

Watermelon Festival. Street dances, games, contests, arts & crafts. 3rd wkend Aug.

Frontier Days. Old Washington Historic State Park (see). Pioneer activity demonstrations: knife-making and throwing, lye soap-making, lard rendering, turkey shoot. 3rd wkend Oct.

Motels

★ **BEST WESTERN.** *I-30 & AR 4, exit 30. 501/777-9222; FAX 501/777-9077.* 75 rms, 2 story. S $38-$42; D $48-$52; under 12 free. Crib $5. Pet accepted. TV; cable (premium). Pool. Playground. Complimentary coffee in lobby. Restaurant adj 6 am-10 pm. Ck-out noon. Coin lndry. Bathrm phones, refrigerators. Cr cds: A, C, D, DS, ER, MC, V.

★ ✔ ★ **HOLIDAY INN.** *I-30 & AR 4. 501/777-8601; FAX 501/777-3142.* 100 rms, 2 story. S, D $30.95-$39; each addl $7; under 18 free. Crib free. Pet accepted. TV; cable (premium). Pool; wading pool. Playground. Coffee in rms. Restaurant 6 am-10 pm. Rm serv. Private club 5 pm-2 am. Ck-out noon. Coin lndry. Meeting rms. Tennis. Lawn games. Landscaped grounds; bridges, gazebo. Cr cds: A, C, D, DS, MC, V.

Hot Springs & Hot Springs National Park (C-2)

TOWN OF HOT SPRINGS: : **Settled** 1807 **Pop** 32,462 **Elev** 632 ft **Area code** 501
Information Convention & Visitors Bureau, 134 Convention Blvd, PO Box K, 71902; 501/321-2277 or 800/772-2489.

One of the most popular spas and resorts in the United States, the colorful city of Hot Springs surrounds portions of the nearly 4,700-acre Hot Springs National Park. Approximately 1 million gallons of thermal water flow daily from the 47 springs within the park. The springs have been administered by the federal government since 1832.

The water, at an average temperature of 143°F, flows to a reservoir under the headquarters building; here it is distributed to the bathhouses through insulated pipes. Some of it is cooled to 90°F without being exposed to air or mixed with other water. The bathhouses mix the cooled and hot thermal water to regulate bath temperatures. The only differences among bathhouses are in the appointments and service.

The Libbey Memorial Physical Medicine Center specializes in hydrotherapy treatments given under the supervision of a registered physical therapist. Patients may be referred to this center by registered physicians or may get a standard bath without a referral.

Hot Springs, however, is more than a spa. It is a cosmopolitan city visited by travelers from all over the world; it is also a delightful vacation spot in the midst of beautiful wooded hills, valleys and lakes of the Ouachita region. Swimming, boating and water sports are available at nearby Catherine, Hamilton and Ouachita lakes. All three offer good year-round fishing for bream, crappie, bass and rainbow trout. The 42nd President of the United States, William Jefferson Clinton, grew up here. A Ranger District office of the Ouachita National Forest is located in Hot Springs.

What to See and Do

Arkansas Alligator Farm & Petting Zoo. Houses alligators, rhesus monkeys, mountain lions, bobcats, llamas, pygmy goats, ducks and other animals. (Daily) 847 Whittington Ave. Phone 501/623-6172. ¢¢

Auto tours. Just north of Bathhouse Row, drive from the end of Fountain Street up Hot Springs Mountain Dr to scenic overlooks at Hot Springs Mountain Tower and a picnic area on the mountaintop. West Mountain Dr, starting from either Prospect Ave (on the south) or from Whittington Ave (on the north) also provides excellent vistas of the city and surrounding countryside.

Bath House Show. Two-hour show of music and comedy acts derivative of 1930s-present; musical anthologies, reenactments of radio shows. (Summer, 1 show nightly exc Mon; rest of yr, wkends) 701 Central Ave. For reservations phone 501/623-1415. ¢¢¢

Coleman's Crystal Mine. Visitors may dig for quartz crystals; tools supplied. Shop. (Daily; closed Dec 24-25) 15 mi N on AR 7N. Phone 501/984-5328. ¢¢¢

Dryden Potteries. Pottery making demonstrations. (Mon-Fri; closed Jan 1, Thanksgiving, Dec 25) 341 Whittington Ave. Phone 501/623-4201. **Free.**

Hot Springs Arts Center. Concerts, dance and theater productions. Exhibitions of regional and national art. (Tues-Sun) Donation. 514 Central Ave. Phone 501/624-0489.

Hot Springs Mountain Tower. Tower rises 216 feet above Hot Springs National Park; glass-enclosed elevator rides 1,256 feet above sea level for spectacular view of Ouachita Mountains; fully enclosed viewing area and, higher up, open-air deck. (Daily; closed Jan 1, Thanksgiving, Dec 25) Fountain St & Hot Springs Mountain Dr, atop Hot Springs Mountain. Phone 501/623-6035. ¢¢

Josephine Tussaud Wax Museum. Over 100 figures displayed. (Daily) 250 Central Ave. Phone 501/623-5836. ¢¢

Lake Catherine State Park. S & E via AR 128, 171. (See MALVERN)

Magic Springs Family Theme Park. On 75 acres, park features more than 30 amusement rides, including Arkansas Twister wooden roller coaster; stage shows; 3,000-seat outdoor amphitheater; shops, restaurants, arcades; picnic areas. (Memorial Day-Labor Day, daily) Admission includes most entertainment and attractions. 1701 E Grand Ave. Phone 501/624-5411. ¢¢¢¢

Mid-America Museum. Exhibits focus on life, energy, matter, perception, state of Arkansas. Museum features 35,000-gallon freshwater aquarium; erosion table; laser theater; ham radio station. Restaurant, gift shop. (Memorial Day-Labor Day, daily; rest of yr, daily exc Mon; closed Jan 1, Thanksgiving, Dec 25) 500 Mid-America Blvd. Phone 501/767-3461. ¢¢

Ouachita National Forest. The Ouachita (WASH-i-taw), located in 15 counties in west-central Arkansas and southeast Oklahoma, covers approximately 1.6 million acres and includes 7 wilderness areas, 33 developed recreation areas, 7 equestrian trails, 9 navigable rivers and 8 lakes suitable for boating. Some recreation areas charge fees. (Daily) 12 mi W on US 270 or 20 mi N on AR 7. For information contact Forest Supervisor, PO Box 1270, 71902. Phone 501/321-5202. On Lake Ouachita is

Lake Ouachita State Park. Approximately 400 acres. Swimming; fishing; boating (rentals, marina). Hiking trails. Picnicking. Camping (hookups, dump station), cabins. Interpretive programs, exhibits. Standard fees. (Daily) 3 mi W on US 270, 12 mi N on AR 227. For reservations phone 501/767-9366.

Sightseeing tours.

National Park Tours. For information and reservations contact 406 Central Ave, Hot Springs 71901; 501/623-1111. (June-Aug) ¢¢¢

Belle of Hot Springs. Sightseeing, lunch and dinner cruises along Lake Hamilton on 400-passenger vessel (Feb-Nov, daily). Pirate cruise during summer months; also charter cruises. 5200 Central Ave (AR 7S). Phone 501/525-4438. ¢¢¢

White and Yellow Duck Tours. The "Amphibious Duck" travels on land and water. Board in the heart of Hot Springs and proceed on to Lake Hamilton around St John's Island. (Daily) 406 Central Ave. Phone 501/623-1111. ¢¢¢

Tiny Town. Indoor mechanical village; handmade miniatures. (Apr-Nov, daily) 374 Whittington Ave. Phone 501/624-4742. ¢¢

★ **Walking tour.** Start at

Park Headquarters and Visitor Center. Visitors see exhibit on workings and origin of the hot springs. Outside fountains bubble hot spring water. A self-guided nature trail starts here and follows the Grand Promenade. Visitor center has exhibits on the geology, Indians and history of the Hot Springs area; auditorium with slide program (daily; closed Jan 1, Dec 25). Gulpha Gorge Campground is available for stays limited to 14 days April-October, and to 30 days in a calendar year (fee). Naturalist gives evening campfire programs in summer. Inquire at visitor center. Reserve and Central Aves. Walk a few yards east to the

Grand Promenade, which leads through a nicely landscaped park above and behind Bathhouse Row, offering pleasant vistas of the city. Follow the Grand Promenade to Fountain St, where it ends. Turn left down the hill to Central Ave and find

Bathhouse Row. Tours of the Fordyce Bathhouse are offered in summer months; inquire at visitor center. (Daily; closed July 4, Thanksgiving, Dec 25). Behind Maurice Bathhouse are the

Two Open Hot Springs. At the south end of Bathhouse Row return to starting point.

Seasonal Event

Thoroughbred racing. Oaklawn Jockey Club, 2705 Central Ave. Daily. Under 10 yrs not admitted. Phone 501/623-4411 or 800/RACE-OJC. Feb-Apr.

Motels

(All prices are considerably higher during the Thoroughbred racing season, Feb-Apr)

★ ★ **AVANELLE MOTOR LODGE.** *1204 Central Ave (71902). 501/321-1332; res: 800/225-1360.* 88 rms, 2 story, 16 kits. S $44-$50; D $49-$54; each addl $5; suites from $62; kit. units $54-$58; under 18 free. Crib $2. Pet accepted. TV; cable (premium). Heated pool. Restaurant 6 am-2 pm, 5-10 pm. Rm serv. Bar from 5 pm. Ck-out noon. Meeting rms. Business servs avail. Valet serv. 36-hole golf privileges, greens fee $35. Cr cds: A, C, D, DS, MC, V.

🏊 🎿 ⊠ ⊠ 🐾 SC

★ **BRADY MOUNTAIN RESORT.** *(PO, Royal 71968) 11 mi W on US 270, then 6 mi N. 501/767-3422; FAX 501/767-3801.* 29 units, 15 kits. S, D $43-$48; each addl $3; kit. units $49-$175; apt $49-$54; lower rates Oct-Mar; 2 night min. on wkends. TV. Pool. Restaurant 7 am-8 pm. Ck-out 11 am. Fishing boats, equipt, guide; ski boat, skis; boat dock, ramps. Party barge. Rec rm. Game rm. Refrigerators. Private patios. Picnic tables, grills. On Lake Ouachita, surrounded by forest. Cr cds: A, DS, MC, V.

⊠ ⊠ 🔥

★ **HAMILTON INN RESORT.** *106 Lookout Point (71913), 6 mi S on US 7. 501/525-5666; res: 800/945-9559 (ex AR).* 58 rms, 2 story. Feb-Aug: S, D $45-$58; each addl $5; under 12 free; wkly rates; 2-day min wkends; lower rates rest of yr. TV; cable (premium), VCR avail. Pool; whirlpool. Playground. Complimentary coffee in lobby. Restaurant nearby. Ck-out 11 am. Meeting rms. Game rm. Lawn games. Balconies. Picnic tables. Cr cds: A, C, D, DS, MC, V.

D ⊠ ⊠ ⊠ 🐾 SC

★ **HOT SPRINGS RESORT.** *1871 E Grand Ave (71901), 2 mi E on US 70. 501/624-4436; res: 800/238-4891; FAX 501/624-5199.* 51 rms, 2 story. S, D $39.95; family, wkend rates. Pet accepted; $15.

TV; cable (premium). Pool. Playground. Restaurant 7 am-1 pm, 5-9 pm. Rm serv. Ck-out 11 am. Business servs avail. 9-hole golf; greens fee $3; putting green. Many refrigerators. Picnic tables. Cr cds: A, C, D, DS, MC, V.

★ **QUALITY INN.** 1125 E Grand Ave (71901). 501/624-3321; FAX 501/624-5814. 138 rms, 2 story. S, D $45-$65; each addl $5; under 18 free. Crib $4. Pet accepted. TV; cable, VCR avail. Pool. Playground. Restaurant 6 am-2 pm, 5-9 pm; Sun to 2 pm. Rm serv. Bar. Ck-out noon. Meeting rm. Business center. In-rm modem link. Game rm. Refrigerators avail. Cr cds: A, C, D, DS, MC, V.

★ **SUPER 8.** 4726 Central Ave (71913). 501/525-0188. 63 rms, 3 story. S $39.88; D $39.88-$53.88; suites $53.88; under 12 free. Crib free. TV; cable. Complimentary coffee in lobby. Restaurant opp open 24 hrs. Ck-out 11 am. Business servs avail. Cr cds: A, C, D, DS, MC, V.

Motor Hotel

★ ★ **HOLIDAY INN LAKE HAMILTON.** (71913). 5¹/2 mi S on AR 7. 501/525-1391; FAX 501/525-0813. 151 rms, 7 story. S $60-$100; D $65-$105; each addl $10; under 19 free. Crib free. Pet accepted. TV; cable (premium). Pool. Restaurant 6:30 am-2 pm, 5:30-10 pm. Rm serv. Bar 5 pm-1 am; dancing. Ck-out noon. Coin lndry. Meeting rms. Business servs avail. Bellhops. Gift shop. Lighted tennis. 18-hole golf privileges, greens fee $35. Balconies. On lake; scenic view. Dock, ramp. Cr cds: A, C, D, DS, ER, JCB, MC, V.

Hotels

★ ★ ★ **ARLINGTON RESORT HOTEL & SPA.** 239 Central Ave (71901). 501/623-7771; res: 800/643-1502 (exc AR); FAX 501/623-7771. 485 rms, 11 story. S $44-$80; D $54-$94; each addl $16; suites $110-$350; under 18 free; package rates. Crib free. Valet parking $6. TV; cable. 2 heated pools; poolside serv (Memorial Day-Labor Day). Supervised childs activities (Memorial Day-Labor Day); ages 4-12. 3 restaurants 7 am-9 pm; Fri & Sat to 10 pm. Bar; entertainment (combos), dancing. Ck-out 11 am. Coin lndry. Convention facilities. Business servs avail. Concierge. Shopping arcade. Barber, beauty shop, facial salon. Tennis. 45-hole golf privileges, greens fee $39-$55, pro, putting green, driving range. Exercise equipt; treadmill, bicycles, hot tub. Game rm. Bathhouse; massages. Refrigerators avail. Grand old hotel (ca 1925); overlooks park. Luxury level. Cr cds: A, D, DS, MC, V.

★ ★ **HILTON.** 305 Malvern Ave (71901). 501/623-6600; FAX 501/623-6600, ext. 266. 200 rms, 14 story. S, D $49-$119; each addl $10; suites $169-$349; under 18 free. Crib free. TV; cable (premium), VCR avail. Indoor/outdoor pool, whirlpool. Restaurant 7 am-2 pm, 5-9 pm. Bar 4 pm-2 am; entertainment, dancing. Ck-out 11 am. Convention facilities. Business servs avail. Concierge. Valet parking $4. Golf privileges. Cr cds: A, D, DS, MC, V.

★ ★ **RAMADA INN TOWER.** 218 Park Ave (71901). 501/623-3311; FAX 501/623-8871. 191 rms, 9 story. S $58-$68; D $68-$78; each addl $10; suites $85-$180; under 18 free. Crib free. Pet accepted. TV; cable (premium). Heated pool; wading pool. Restaurant 6 am-2 pm, 5-10 pm. Bar 4:30 pm-2 am; entertainment, dancing. Ck-out noon. Meeting rms. Business servs avail. Airport transportation. Balconies. Cr cds: A, C, D, DS, MC, V.

Inn

★ ★ **VINTAGE COMFORT INN.** 303 Quapaw Ave (79101). 501/623-3258; FAX 501/623-3258. 4 rms. S, D $60-$85; child $10. Children over 5 yrs only. TV in lobby; cable. Complimentary full bkfst, beverages. Restaurant nearby. Ck-out 11 am, ck-in 3 pm. Airport transportation. Balconies. Antiques; sitting rm. Cr cds: A, C, D, MC, V.

Resort

★ ★ **LAKE HAMILTON RESORT.** PO Box 2070 (71913), 2803 Albert Pike, 3 mi W on US 270. 501/767-5511; FAX 501/767-8576. 104 suites, 3 story. Feb-Oct: suites $75-$89; under 18 free; lower rates rest of yr. Crib free. Pet accepted. TV; cable. 2 pools, 1 indoor; whirlpool, sauna. Playground. Restaurant 7 am-9 pm. Box lunches. Picnics. Rm serv. Bar 4 pm-1 am. Ck-out noon, ck-in 2 pm. Coin lndry. Business servs avail. In-rm modem link. Grocery, package store 1/2 mi. Convention facilities. Airport transportation. Lighted tennis. Private swimming beach. Boat dock, launching ramp, rentals; motorboats; waterskiing, jetskiing. Entertainment, dancing. Game rm. Fishing guides. Refrigerators. Balconies. Picnic tables, grills. Scenic view from all rms. 10 acres on Lake Hamilton; elaborate landscaping. Fountain; duck pond; lakeside gazebo. Cr cds: A, C, D, DS, MC, V.

Cottage Colonies

★ ★ **BUENA VISTA RESORT.** 201 Aberina St (71913), 4 mi S on AR 7, then 1/2 mi SE. 501/525-1321; res: 800/255-9030 (exc AR). 40 kit. units, 1-2 story. June-Aug: S, D $69-$101; each addl $5; suites $120; under 5 free. Crib $5. Pet accepted, some restrictions. TV; cable. Pool. Playground. Ck-out 11 am, ck-in 3 pm. Coin lndry. Package store 1¹/2 mi. Conference center. Business servs avail. Lighted tennis. Miniature golf. Waterskiing. Lawn games. Rec rm. Game rm. Fishing; clean, store area. Refrigerators. Balconies. Picnic tables, grills. 10 acres on Lake Hamilton. Cr cds: MC, V.

★ **SHORECREST RESORT.** 360 Lakeland Dr (71913). 501/525-8113; res: 800/447-9914. 25 kit. cottages. Feb-early Sept: S $41; D $41-$52; each addl $4; lower rates rest of yr. Crib free. Pet accepted. TV; cable. Pool. Ck-out 11 am, ck-in 2 pm. Grocery 1¹/2 blks; package store 1/4 mi. Private beach. Complete marina nearby. Lawn games. Fishing guides; clean, store area. Refrigerators. Private patios. Picnic tables; grills. Scenic, wooded location on Lake Hamilton. Cr cds: DS, MC, V.

Restaurants

★ ★ **BOHEMIA.** 517 Park Ave. 501/623-9661. Hrs: 4-9:30 pm; also 11 am-1 pm Tues & Thurs. Closed Sun; major hols; also part of Dec & Jan. Res accepted. Czech, German menu. Serv bar. Semi-a la carte: lunch $3.50-$4.95, dinner $4.95-$13.25. Child's meals. Specialties: roast duck, Wienerschnitzel. Parking. Original paintings; extensive plate collection. Cr cds: A, DS, MC, V.

★ **CAFE NEW ORLEANS.** 210 Central Ave (71901). 501/624-3200. Hrs: 7 am-9 pm; Fri & Sat to 10 pm. Closed Dec 25. Semi-a la carte: lunch, dinner $2.75-$7.95. Specializes in creole cooking. Parking. In former hotel (1889). Art deco decor. Cr cds: A, DS, MC, V.

★ **CAJUN BOILERS.** *2806 Albert Pike Hwy (71913). 501/767-5695.* Hrs: 4-10 pm. Closed Sun; Jan 1, Thanksgiving. Cajun menu. Beer, wine. Semi-a la carte: dinner $4.50-$21.95. Child's meals. Specializes in seafood, chicken. Parking. Cr cds: A, C, D, DS, MC, V.

[D]

★ ★ **COY'S STEAK HOUSE.** *300 Coy St, off Hwy 70 E. 501/321-1414.* Hrs: 5-10 pm; Fri, Sat to 11 pm. Closed Thanksgiving, Dec 24-25. Bar. Semi-a la carte: dinner $8.95-$27.95. Child's meals. Specializes in steak, seafood. Entertainment nightly. Valet parking. Old English atmosphere; antiques, paintings. Family-owned. Cr cds: A, C, D, DS, MC, V.

[D] [SC]

★ ★ **HAMILTON HOUSE.** *130 Van Lyell Tr, 6 mi S on AR 7. 501/525-2727.* Hrs: 5:30-10 pm. Closed Jan 1, Thanksgiving, Dec 25; Easter. Res accepted Mon-Sat. Continental menu. Bar. Wine list. Semi-a la carte: dinner $10-$36.90. Child's meals. Specializes in fresh seafood, Diana torte, mushrooms Marshall. Own baking. Pianist. Valet parking. 1929 mansion with elaborate decor, many antiques; underground tunnel connects house to Lake Hamilton. Outdoor dining. Cr cds: A, D, DS, MC, V.

[D]

★ **MAGEE'S CAFE.** *362 Central Ave (71901). 501/623-4091.* Hrs: 8 am-8 pm. Closed Jan 1. Res accepted. Semi-a la carte: bkfst $3.50-$4.50, lunch, dinner $4-$6. Child's meals. Specialties: chicken-fried steak, shrimp Creole, Mississippi Mud pie. Parking. Renovated Victorian auction house (1871). Cr cds: A, MC, V.

[D]

★ **McCLARD'S BAR-B-Q.** *505 Albert Pike (71913), 2 mi W on US 270. 501/624-9586.* Hrs: 11 am-8 pm. Closed Sun & Mon; Thanksgiving, Dec 25. Beer. Semi-a la carte: lunch, dinner $2.90-$7.10. Child's meals. Specializes in barbecue ribs, hot tamale spread. Parking. Casual, 1940s atmosphere. Family-owned. No cr cds accepted.

[D]

★ **MOLLIE'S.** *538 W Grand Ave. 501/623-6582.* Hrs: 11 am-10 pm. Closed Sun; Jan 1, Thanksgiving, Dec 25. Bar. Semi-a la carte: lunch $4-$5, dinner $6.25-$14.50. Child's meals. Specializes in kosher foods. Parking. Outdoor dining. Family-owned. Cr cds: A, C, D, DS, MC, V.

[D] [SC]

★ ★ **MRS. MILLER'S CHICKEN & STEAK HOUSE.** *4723 Central Ave, 5 mi S on AR 7. 501/525-8861.* Hrs: 5-10 pm. Closed Mon; also Dec-mid-Jan. Res accepted. Bar. Semi-a la carte: dinner $8.25-$25.95. Child's meals. Specializes in fried chicken, catfish. Parking. Family-owned. Cr cds: DS, MC, V.

[D]

Jonesboro (B-4)

(See Walnut Ridge)

Founded 1859 **Pop** 46,535 **Elev** 320 ft **Area code** 501 **Zip** 72401

Information Greater Jonesboro Chamber of Commerce, 593 S Madison, PO Box 789; 501/932-6691.

Largest city in northeast Arkansas, Jonesboro is on Crowley's Ridge, the long, narrow ridge of loess (fine, windblown, yellowish loam) that stretches 150 miles from the Missouri line to Helena more or less parallel to the Mississippi River. Rice, cotton, soybean, wheat and livestock processing, manufacturing and shipping are the principal businesses of this community. Hunting and fishing are popular in this area.

What to See and Do

Arkansas State University (1909). (10,155 students) Eight colleges and a graduate school on 800-acre campus. Tours of campus. NE edge of town on US 49. Phone 501/972-2100. Also here is

Ellis Library, Convocation Center and Museum. Houses natural and state history displays. (Daily) **Free.**

Craighead Forest Park. Approx 600 acres with swimming; fishing; pedal boats. Picnicking, playground. Camping (hookups, showers, dump station). Fee for most activities. Sr citizen rate. (Daily exc Jan1, Dec 25, Thanksgiving) 2 mi S on AR 141. Phone 501/933-4604. **Free.**

Crowley's Ridge State Park. This 271-acre rolling area, once a campground for the Quapaw, has two lakes, miles of wooded hills, and is colorful with dogwood in season. The ridge is named for Benjamin Crowley, whose homestead and burial place are here. Swimming (lifeguard); fishing; boating (pedal boat rentals). Hiking trails. Picnicking, playground, restaurant, store, coin laundry nearby. Camping (many hookups, dump station), cabins. Interpretive programs (summer). Standard fees. (Daily) 15 mi N on AR 141. Phone 501/573-6751. Per vehicle ¢

Lake Frierson State Park. Famous for its brilliant array of dogwood blossoms in spring, this 135-acre park is located on the eastern shore of 350-acre Lake Frierson, which fronts the western edge of Crowley's Ridge. Fishing; boating (rentals, ramp). Hiking trails. Picnicking, playground. Camping. (Daily) 10 mi N on AR 141. Phone 501/932-2615. Per vehicle ¢

Motels

✔ ★ **AUTUMN INN.** *2406 Phillips Dr. 501/932-9339; res: 800/227-9345.* 27 rms. S $31.95; D $36.95; each addl $5; suites $37.95-$40.95; under 12 free. Crib free. TV; cable (premium). Complimentary continental bkfst, coffee. Restaurant opp 6 am-10 pm. Ck-out 11 am. Sundries. Cr cds: A, DS, MC, V.

[icons]

★ ★ **HOLIDAY INN.** *3006 S Caraway Rd, N off US 63 Bypass. 501/935-2030.* 179 rms, 2 story. S, D $50.50; each addl $7; suites $55.50-$100. Crib free. Pet accepted. TV; cable (premium). Indoor pool. Restaurant 6 am-10 pm. Rm serv. Bar 4 pm-midnight, Sat from 5 pm; entertainment exc Sun. Ck-out noon. Coin lndry. Meeting rms. Business servs avail. Airport transportation. Exercise equipt; weights, bicycles, whirlpool, sauna. Game rm. Rec rm. Cr cds: A, C, D, DS, JCB, MC, V.

[icons]

★ ★ **PARK INN.** *1421 S Caraway Rd, near Municipal Airport. 501/935-8400; FAX 501/935-7644.* 135 rms, 2 story. S $42.50; D $49.50; suites $65; under 18 free. Crib free. Pets accepted. TV; cable (premium). Pool. Restaurant 11 am-10 pm. Rm serv. Private club 5 pm-2 am; entertainment, dancing Fri, Sat. Ck-out noon. Coin lndry. Meeting rms. Sundries. Free airport transportation. Minibar in suites. Cr cds: A, C, D, DS, JCB, MC, V.

[icons]

✔ ★ **SCOTTISH INNS.** *US 63 Bypass. 501/972-8300.* 49 rms. S $29.95; D $34.95; each addl $5; under 12 free. Crib free. TV; cable (premium). Complimentary continental bkfst. Sundries. Miniature golf. Cr cds: A, C, D, DS, MC, V.

[icons]

Motor Hotel

★ ★ **WILSON INN.** *2911 Gilmore Dr. 501/972-9000; FAX 501/972-9000, ext. 110.* 108 rms, 5 story, 31 suites, 59 kits. S $34.95-$39.95; D, kits. $39.95-$44.95; each addl $5; suites $44.95-$49.95; under 19 free. Pets accepted. Crib free. TV; cable (premium). VCR avail. Whirlpool. Complimentary full bkfst, coffee. Restaurant adj 11 am-10 pm. Ck-out noon. Meeting rms. Business servs avail. Refrigerators. Wet bar in suites. Cr cds: A, C, D, DS, MC, V.

`D` `☞` `≋` `⊿` `⚐` `SC`

Restaurants

★ **FRONT PAGE CAFE.** *1101 S Caraway Rd. 501/932-6343.* Hrs: 7 am-2 pm, 4-8:30 pm; Fri & Sat to 9:30 pm, Sun 7 am-9 pm. Closed July 4, Thanksgiving, Dec 24 & 25. Semi-a carte: bkfst $2-$5, lunch & dinner $4-$10. Specializes in country foods, flying rolls. Casual country dining. Cr cds: A, D, DS, MC, V.

`D`

✔ ★ ★ **PIERO & COMPANY.** *314 S Union St. 501/933-0034.* Hrs: 11 am-2 pm, 6-10 pm; Sat from 6 pm. Closed Sun; major hols. Res accepted. Italian, Mediterranean menu. A la carte entrees: lunch, dinner from $6.95. Child's meals. Specializes in veal, pasta, pizza. Upstairs dining area features specialty pasta dishes; downstairs offers pizza and traditional cuisine. Totally nonsmoking. Cr cds: A, DS, MC, V.

Little Rock & North Little Rock (C-3)

Settled Little Rock: 1812 **Pop** Little Rock: 175,795; North Little Rock: 61,741 **Elev** 291 ft **Area code** 501

These two separate cities on opposite sides of the Arkansas River are closely allied in every way and, from the standpoint of the tourist, are one community. Little Rock, the state capital, is a regional center for transportation, entertainment, culture, medicine, education, commerce and industry. More than a "city of roses," it is known for its warm hospitality and recreational facilities. Little Rock is an unusually clean, modern, forward-looking, Southwestern capital.

Little Rock apparently got its name from French explorers who called this site on the Arkansas River "La Petite Roche" to distinguish it from larger rock outcroppings up the river. The first shack probably was built on the site in 1812, and by 1819 a townsite had been staked. The community became the territorial capital in 1821, when the seat of government was moved here from Arkansas Post (see). The first steamboat, the *Eagle,* came up the Arkansas River in 1822.

What to See and Do

Arkansas Arts Center. Exhibits include paintings, drawings, prints, sculpture and ceramics; public classes in visual and performing arts; library, restaurant, theater. Performances by the Arkansas Arts Center Children's Theater; community events. (Daily; closed Dec 25) MacArthur Park. Phone 501/372-4000.   **Free.**

Arkansas Repertory Theatre. Professional theatrical productions. 6th and Main Sts. Phone 501/378-0405.

Arkansas Symphony Orchestra. (Sept-May) Robinson Center Music Hall. For schedule contact Arkansas Symphony Orchestra Society, PO Box 7328, Little Rock 72217. Phone 501/666-1761.

Burns Park. More than 1,500 acres with fishing; boating. Wildlife trail; 27-hole golf, miniature golf, tennis. Camping (10-day max). Amusement rides, water slide (spring-fall); 9-hole Frisbee golf course. Fee for some activities. (Daily) Off I-40 in North Little Rock. Phone 501/758-2400. **Free.**

Decorative Arts Museum. Restored Greek-revival mansion (1839) houses decorative art objects ranging from Greek and Roman period to contemporary American; ceramics, glass, textiles, crafts, Oriental works of art. (Daily) 7th & Rock Sts. Phone 501/372-4000.   **Free.**

Pinnacle Mountain State Park. A cone-shaped mountain juts 1,000 feet above this heavily forested, 1,772-acre park; bordered on the west by 9,000-acre Lake Maumelle. Fishing; boating (ramps). Hiking, backpacking. Picnicking, playground. Visitor center with natural history exhibits; interpretive programs. Standard fees. (Daily) 7 mi W via AR 10, 2 mi N via AR 300. Contact Superintendent, 11901 Pinnacle Valley Rd, Roland 72135. Phone 501/868-5806. Per vehicle   ¢

⭐ **Quapaw Quarter Historic Neighborhoods.** Encompassing the original town of Little Rock and its early additions through the turn of the century, this area contains 3 National Register historic districts and 135 buildings listed on the National Register of Historic Places. Named for Arkansas' native Quapaw Indians, the area includes sites and structures associated with the history of Arkansas' capital city from the 1820s to the present. A tour of historic houses in the area is held the first weekend of May. Contact the Quapaw Quarter Assn, PO Box 165023, 72216; 501/371-0075. Restored sites in the area include

The Old State House. Originally designed by Kentucky architect Gideon Shryock, this beautiful Greek-revival building was the capitol from 1836 to 1911; now houses a museum of Arkansas history. Features include restored governor's office and legislative chambers; Granny's Attic, a hands-on exhibit; and an interpretive display of Arkansas' First Ladies' gowns. Self-guided tours. (Daily) Sr citizen rate. 300 W Markham St. Phone 501/324-9685.   ¢

Arkansas Territorial Restoration. Built in the 1820s-50s, the restoration includes four houses, outbuildings and a log house arranged to give a realistic picture of pre-Civil War Arkansas. Reception center houses exhibits, crafts shop. Guided tours. (Daily exc hols) Sr citizen rate. 3rd and Scott Sts. Phone 501/324-9351.   ¢

Arkansas Museum of Science and History. Collections pertaining to the cultural and natural history of the state are housed in only remaining building of the Little Rock Arsenal. Built between 1836 and 1840, this barrack is where General Douglas MacArthur was born; audiovisual program on Arkansas (20 min); nature gallery; geology room with life-size model of Arkansas dinosaur; Native American exhibit. (Mon-Sat, also Sun afternoons; closed Jan 1, Thanksgiving, Dec 25) Sr citizen rate. 501 E 9th St, on grounds of 15-acre MacArthur Park. Phone 501/324-9231.   ¢

Villa Marre (1881). Restored Italianate-style mansion reflects exuberance of period with ornate parquet floors, walnut woodwork and highly decorated stenciled ceilings; antique furnishings are mainly Victorian with some American empire and Edwardian pieces. House featured in opening credits of TV series *Designing Women.* Tours (Mon-Fri mornings & Sun afternoons). Sr citizen rate. 1321 Scott St. Phone 501/374-9979.   ¢¢

River Cruises. Excursions aboard sternwheeler *Spirit.* (June-Aug, Tues-Sat) Also dinner, moonlight & charter cruises. 409 W Riverfront Park. Phone 501/376-4150.

State Capitol. A scaled-down replica of the nation's capitol, the building is constructed of Batesville (AR) limestone. On south lawn is 1,600-bush rose garden comprised of 150 varieties. The legislature meets the second Monday in January of odd-numbered years for 60 days. Self-guided and guided tours (Mon-Fri). W end of Capitol Ave. Phone 501/682-5080.   **Free.**

The Old Mill (1828). Old waterwheel, gristmill. Two stones on the road to the mill are original milestones laid out by Jefferson Davis. This scenic city park is famous for its appearance in the opening scene of *Gone with the Wind.* (Daily). Fairway at Lakeshore in North Little Rock. **Free.**

Toltec Mounds Archeological State Park. This 182-acre park is the site of one of the largest and most complex prehistoric Native American settlements in the Lower Mississippi Valley; several mounds and a remnant of the embankment are visible. Guided on-site tours; paved trail is accessible to the disabled. Tours depart from the visitor center, which has exhibits explaining how archaeologists work and the history of the site; audiovisual programs; archaeological laboratory. (Tues-Sat & Sun afternoon; closed Jan 1, Thanksgiving, Dec 24 eve & Dec 25) 15 mi SE of North Little Rock, off US 165 on AR 386. Phone 501/961-9442. **Free.** Tours   ¢¢

War Memorial Park. On approximately 200 acres are rides and amusements. Golf, tennis. Picnicking. (Daily) W Markham and Fair Park Blvd. Phone 501/663-4733. Also here is

Little Rock Zoo. More than 500 animals on 40 acres. (Daily; closed Jan 1, Thanksgiving, Dec 25) Phone 501/666-2406. ¢¢

Wild River Country. Jct I-40 and I-430, Crystal Hill Rd. A 23-acre water theme park with 9 different water attractions. (June-Labor Day, daily; May, wkends only) Phone 501/753-8600. ¢¢¢¢

Annual Events

Arkansas All Arabian Horse Show. Barton Coliseum. 2nd full wkend Apr.

Riverfest. Little Rock area. Visual & performing arts festival includes exhibits by 60 artists; ballet, symphony, opera, theater, jazz, bluegrass and rock groups; children's area; bike race, 5-mile run; concessions. Memorial Day wkend.

Summerset. North Little Rock Area. Farewell to summer festival; visual & performing arts, concessions, 5-km run, sporting tournaments, entertainers, child's activities, fireworks. Labor Day wkend.

Arkansas State Fair and Livestock Show. 2300 W Roosevelt Rd. Rodeo and other events. Phone 501/372-8341. Early-mid-Oct.

Additional Visitor Information

Travelers may stop at the Visitor Information Centers (daily) at the Statehouse Convention Center, and Little Rock Regional Airport to get more information. Telefun, 501/372-3399, is a 24-hour pre-recorded entertainment hot line with a bi-weekly update on events in the Little Rock area. For any additional information contact the Little Rock Convention & Visitors Bureau, Statehouse Plaza, PO Box 3232, Little Rock 72203; 501/376-4781.

Motels

★ ★ **AMERISUITES.** *10920 Financial Center Pkwy (72211). 501/225-1075; res: 800/833-1516; FAX 501/225-2209.* 130 kit. suites, 4 story. S, D $83-$125; under 18 free; wkly rates. Crib free. TV; cable (premium), VCR (movies avail). Heated pool. Complimentary continental bkfst. Complimentary coffee in rms. Restaurant nearby. Ck-out noon. Coin lndry. Meeting rms. Business servs avail. In-rm modem link. Free airport transportation. Health club privileges. Cr cds: A, C, D, DS, ER, MC, V.

D ≈ ⌦ ⌦ ⌦ SC

★ ★ **BEST WESTERN GOVERNORS INN.** *1501 Merrill Dr (72211). 501/224-8051; FAX 501/224-8051, ext. 130.* 49 suites, 3 story. Suites $74-$105; under 12 free; wkend packages. Crib free. TV; cable (premium), VCR avail. Pool; whirlpool. Complimentary full bkfst. Complimentary coffee in rms. Ck-out noon. Meeting rms. Business servs avail. In-rm modem link. Bellhops. Sundries. Health club privileges. Some refrigerators, wet bars. Cr cds: A, C, D, DS, ER, JCB, MC, V.

D ≈ ⌦ ⌦ ⌦ SC

★ ★ **COMFORT INN.** *3200 Bankhead Dr (72206), 8 mi E on I-440, near Little Rock Airport. 501/490-2010; FAX 501/490-2229.* 119 rms, 2 story, 12 kits. S $47-$48; D $50-$52; each addl $5; kits. $55-$60; under 18 free. Crib free. Pet accepted. TV; cable (premium), VCR avail. Pool. Complimentary continental bkfst. Coffee in rms. Restaurant adj open 24 hrs. Ck-out noon. Coin lndry. Business center. Sundries. Free airport transportation. Some refrigerators. Cr cds: A, C, D, DS, MC, V.

D ⌦ ⌦ ≈ ⌦ ⌦ ⌦ SC ⌦

★ ★ **COURTYARD BY MARRIOTT.** *10900 Financial Ctr Pkwy (72211). 501/227-6000; FAX 501/227-6912.* 149 rms, 3 story, 12 suites. S $54-$72; D $62-$82; suites $92; wkly plan avail. Crib free. TV; cable (premium). Heated pool. Complimentary coffee in rms. Restaurant 6:30-10 am. Bar 4-11 pm. Ck-out 1 pm. Coin lndry. Meeting rms. Business servs avail. In-rm modem link. Valet serv. Sundries. Excercise

equipt; weights, bicycles, whirlpool, sauna. Some refrigerators. Balconies. Cr cds: A, C, D, DS, MC, V.

D ≈ ⌦ ⌦ ⌦ SC

★ ★ **HAMPTON INN I-30.** *6100 Mitchell Dr (72209), I 30 - Exit 133. 501/562-6667; FAX 501/568-6832.* 122 rms, 4 story. S $47-$52; D $55-$60; under 18 free. Crib free. Pet accepted, some restrictions. TV; cable (premium). Pool. Complimentary continental bkfst. Ck-out noon. In-rm modem link. Cr cds: A, C, D, DS, MC, V.

D ⌦ ⌦ ≈ ⌦ ⌦ ⌦ SC

★ ★ **LA QUINTA.** *11701 I-30 & I-430 (72209). 501/455-2300; FAX 501/455-5876.* 144 rms, 3 story. S $51-$58; D $59-$66; each addl $6; suites $85-$140; under 18 free. Crib free. Pet accepted, some restrictions. TV; cable (premium), VCR avail. Pool; whirlpool. Free continental bkfst. Restaurant 11 am-2 pm, 5-10 pm. Rm serv. Bar 11:30 am-midnight. Ck-out noon. Coin lndry. Meeting rms. Business servs avail. In-rm modem link. Valet serv. Cr cds: A, C, D, DS, JCB, MC, V.

D ⌦ ⌦ ≈ ⌦ ⌦ ⌦ SC

★ **LA QUINTA.** *2401 W 65th St (72209), I-30 exit 135. 501/568-1030; FAX 501/568-5713.* 112 rms, 2 story. S $47-$54; D $54-$61; each addl $7; suites $69; under 18 free. Crib free. Pet accepted, some restrictions. TV; cable (premium), VCR avail. Pool. Complimentary continental bkfst. Restaurant adj open 24 hrs. Ck-out noon. Business servs avail. In-rm modem link. Airport transportation. Cr cds: A, C, D, DS, ER, JCB, MC, V.

⌦ ≈ ⌦ ⌦ SC

★ **MOTEL 6.** *7501 I-30 (72209), exit 134. 501/568-8888; FAX 501/568-8355.* 130 units, 3 story. S $30, D $36-$41; each addl $3; suites $30-$36; under 17 free. Crib free. TV; cable (premium). Pool. Restaurant adj open 24 hrs. Ck-out noon. Business servs avail. Patios. Cr cds: A, D, DS, MC, V.

D ≈ ⌦ ⌦ SC

★ **RED ROOF INN.** *7900 Scott Hamilton Dr (72209), I-30 exit 134. 501/562-2694; FAX 501/562-1723.* 108 rms, 2 story. S $30-$35; D $36-$46; under 18 free. Crib free. Pet accepted. TV; cable (premium). Restaurant adj open 24 hrs. Ck-out noon. Business servs avail. In-rm modem link. Cr cds: A, C, D, DS, MC, V.

D ⌦ ⌦ ≈ ⌦ ⌦ SC

Motor Hotels

★ ★ ★ **HILTON INN RIVERFRONT.** *2 Riverfront Place (72114). 501/371-9000; FAX 501/371-9000, ext. 2074.* 221 units, 2 story. S $69; D $79-$84; each addl $10; suites $95-$175; wkend rates. Crib free. TV; cable (premium), VCR avail. Pool. Restaurant 6:30 am-10 pm. Rm serv. Bar 11-2 am; entertainment exc Sun. Ck-out 1 pm. Meeting rms. Business servs avail. In-rm modem link. Free valet parking. Airport transportation. Greenhouse atrium. On riverfront. Cr cds: A, C, D, DS, MC, V.

D ≈ ⌦ ⌦ ⌦ ⌦ SC

★ ★ **HOLIDAY INN WEST.** *201 S Shackelford Rd (72211), jct I-430 & I-630. 501/223-3000; FAX 501/223-2833.* 261 rms, 5 story. S $80-$90; D $88-$98; each addl $8; suites $135-$295; under 18 free; wkly, wkend rates. Crib avail. Pet accepted. TV; cable (premium). Indoor/outdoor pool; poolside serv. Complimentary coffee in rms. Restaurant 6 am-10 pm. Rm serv 5 pm-midnight. Bar 5 pm-midnight; entertainment. Ck-out noon. Meeting rms. Business servs avail. Bellhops. Valet serv. Concierge. Gift shop. Coin lndry. Free airport, RR station transportation. Exercise equipt; weights, treadmill, sauna. Cr cds: A, C, D, DS, MC, V.

D ⌦ ⌦ ≈ ⌦ ⌦ ⌦ SC

★ **MASTER'S ECONOMY INN.** *707 I-30 (72202), 9th St exit. 501/372-4392; FAX 501/372-1732.* 170 rms, 8 story. S $27.95; D $31.95; each addl $4; studio rms $49.95; under 18 free. Crib $6. TV;

cable (premium). Pool. Restaurant 6 am-2 pm, 5-10 pm. Rm serv. Ck-out noon. Meeting rms. Business servs avail. Valet serv. Free garage parking. Exercise equipt; weights, bicycles. Cr cds: A, C, D, DS, MC, V.

D ⚟ 🏃 ⊠ 🔥 SC

★ ★ **RAMADA INN.** *(200 US 67N, Jacksonville 72076) 13 mi NE on US 67, James St exit. 501/982-2183; FAX 501/985-2276.* 97 rms, 2 story. S, D $45-$52; each addl $6; under 18 free. Crib free. TV; cable, VCR avail. Pool. Playground. Restaurant 6:30 am-1:30 pm, 5-9 pm. Private club 5 pm-midnight, Sat to 2 am, Sun 2-8 pm. Ck-out noon. Coin lndry. Meeting rms. Business servs avail. Valet serv. Sundries. Cr cds: A, C, D, DS, MC, V.

D ⚟ ≈ ⊠ 🔥 SC

★ **WILSON INN.** *4301 E Roosevelt (72206), I-440 exit 3, near Little Rock Airport. 501/376-2466; FAX 501/376-2466, ext. -158.* 110 units, 5 story, 13 suites, 18 kit. units. S $35.95-$54.95; D $40.95-$50.95, each addl $5; suites $49.95; kit. units $40.95-$45.95; under 18 free. Crib free. Pet accepted, some restrictions. TV; cable (premium). Whirlpool. Complimentary continental bkfst, coffee. Ck-out noon. Meeting rm. Business servs avail. Bellhops. Free airport transportation. Refrigerators. Cr cds: A, D, DS, MC, V.

D ⚟ ✈ ⊠ 🔥 SC

Hotels

★ ★ **BEST WESTERN INN TOWNE.** *600 I-30 (72202). 501/375-2100; FAX 501/374-9045.* 134 units, 8 story, 25 kit. suites. S, D $52-$59; each addl $7; kit. suites $89; under 12 free. Crib free. TV; cable (premium), VCR avail (movies avail). Heated pool; whirlpool. Coffee in rms. Restaurant 6 am-2 pm, 5-10 pm. Bar 4 pm-midnight. Ck-out noon. Coin lndry. Meeting rms. Business center. Free airport transportation. Exercise equipt; bicycles, weights. Refrigerator in suites. Cr cds: A, C, D, DS, MC, V.

D ≈ 🏃 ⊠ 🔥 SC 🚶

★ ★ **CAPITAL.** *111 W Markham (72201). 501/374-7474; res: 800/766-7666 (exc AR), 800/482-5624 (AR); FAX 501/370-7091.* 123 rms, 4 story. S $129-$139; D $129-$149; each addl $10; suites $270-$360; under 18 free; wkend rates, honeymoon package. Valet parking $5. TV; cable, VCR avail (movies avail). Restaurant 6:30 am-2 pm, 6-11 pm. Rm serv 24 hrs. Bar 11 am-midnight. Ck-out 1 pm. Meeting rms. Business servs avail. In-rm modem link. Gift shop. Historic bldg (1877); turn-of-the-century ambience. Cr cds: A, C, D, DS, MC, V.

D 🔥 SC

★ ★ **EXCELSIOR.** *3 Statehouse Plaza (72201). 501/375-5000; res: 800/527-1745; FAX 501/375-4721.* 417 units, 19 story, 22 suites. S $89-$95; D $99-$109; each addl $10; suites $190-$550; under 18 free; wkend rates. Crib free. TV; cable (premium), VCR avail (movies avail). Restaurant 6:30 am-11 pm; 3 dining rms. Bar 11-midnight, Sun to 10 pm; entertainment. Ck-out 11 am. Convention facilities. Business servs avail. In-rm modem link. Concierge. Shopping arcade. Valet parking. Free airport transportation. Exercise equipt; weights, bicycles. 18-story glass atrium in lobby. Luxury level. Cr cds: A, C, D, DS, ER, MC, V.

D 🏃 ✈ ⊠ 🔥 SC

★ ★ **HILTON INN.** *925 S University Ave (72204). 501/664-5020; FAX 501/664-3104.* 264 units, 3 story. S $76-$86; D $86; each addl $10; suites $160-$225; under 18 free; wkend rates. Crib free. TV; cable (premium). Pool; poolside serv. Restaurant 6:30 am-10 pm. Rm serv 24 hrs. Bar 4 pm-midnight, Sun to 10 pm. Ck-out noon. Convention facilities. Business servs avail. In-rm modem link. Airport, RR station, bus depot transportation. Exercise equipt; weights, bicycle. Balconies. Cr cds: A, C, D, DS, ER, JCB, MC, V.

D ≈ 🏃 ✈ ⊠ 🔥 SC

★ **LEGACY.** *625 W Capitol (72201). 501/374-0100; FAX 501/374-0100, ext. 132.* 116 units, 6 story. S $45-$95; D $50-$95; each addl $7; suites $99-$129; studio rms $65-$75. Crib free. TV; cable. Pool. Restaurant 7 am-1:30 pm; Sat, Sun 7:30-10 am. Bar. Ck-out noon. Meeting rms. Business servs avail. Airport transportation. Many bathrm phones. Balconies. Landmark building; restored turn-of-the-century decor; garden. Cr cds: A, C, D, DS, MC, V.

D ≈ ⊠ 🔥 SC

Restaurants

★ ★ ★ **ALOUETTE'S.** *11401 N Rodney Parham. 501/225-4152.* Hrs: 11 am-1:30 pm (Fri only), 5:30-9 pm. Closed Sun & Mon; most major hols. French menu. Bar. Wine cellar. Semi-a la carte: lunch $6-$10, dinner $18-$28. Specialties: smoked duck salad, Dover sole, lobster bisque. Parking. Romantic atmosphere. Cr cds: A, C, D, DS, MC, V.

D

★ ★ **ANDRE'S HILLCREST.** *605 N Beechwood (72205). 501/666-9191.* Hrs: 11 am-2 pm, 6-9:30 pm; Sun brunch 10 am-2 pm. Closed Mon; Jan 1, Thanksgiving, Dec 25. Res accepted. Continental menu. Bar. Semi-a la carte: lunch $5.25-$6.95, dinner $6.50-$15.95. Sun brunch $4.25-$9.50. Specializes in heart healthy dishes, beef peppercorn. Own pastries. Parking. Outdoor dining overlooking landscaped grounds with pond. Converted old house decorated with artwork. Cr cds: A, C, D, DS, MC, V.

D

★ **BROWNING'S MEXICAN FOOD.** *5805 Kavanaugh Blvd, in Pulaski Heights Shopping Ctr. 501/663-9956.* Hrs: 11 am-9 pm; Fri, Sat to 10 pm. Closed Sun; major hols. Mexican, Amer menu. Beer, wine. Semi-a la carte: lunch $3.15-$5.50, dinner $4.75-$9.25. Child's meals. Parking. Mexican decor; murals. Cr cds: A, DS, MC, V.

D

★ **BRUNO'S LITTLE ITALY.** *315 N Bowman. 501/224-4700.* Hrs: 5-10 pm. Closed Sun; some hols. Italian menu. Semi-a la carte: dinner $5.95-$14.95. Child's meals. Specialties: saltimbocca, Neapolitan pizza. Own pasta, veal, shrimp. Parking. Family-owned since 1949. Cr cds: A, D, DS, MC, V.

D

★ ★ **CAFE ST MORITZ.** *225 E Markham. 501/372-0411.* Hrs: 11 am-2 pm, 6-9:30 pm; Sun 11 am-2:30 pm. Closed Mon; some major hols. Res accepted. Continental menu. Bar 5-9:30 pm. Semi-a la carte: lunch $6-$10, dinner $7-$22. Sat, Sun brunch $10. Child's meals. Specializes in soufflé, seafood, lamb, filet of beef. Parking. French country decor. Cr cds: A, C, D, DS, MC, V.

D

★ **CHIP'S BARBECUE.** *9801 Markham St (72015), in Markham Plaza. 501/225-4346.* Hrs: 10 am-9 pm. Closed Sun. A la carte entrees: lunch $3-$7.95. Semi-a la carte: dinner $6.75-$8.50. Child's meals. Specializes in barbecued ribs, chicken. Parking. Family-owned since 1961. Cr cds: A, DS, MC, V.

★ **FADED ROSE.** *1615 Rebsamen Park Rd (72207), 2 mi W on Cantrell Rd. 501/663-9734.* Hrs: 11 am-11 pm; Sun noon-9:30 pm. Closed Jan 1, Thanksgiving, Dec 25. Creole menu. Bar. Semi-a la carte: lunch $3.50-$7, dinner $4-$17. Child's meals. Specializes in seafood, steak. Parking. Rustic atmosphere. Cr cds: A, C, D, DS, MC, V.

D

★ **HUNAN.** *2924 S University, in Broadmoor Shopping Ctr. 501/562-4320.* Hrs: 11 am-10 pm; Fri to 11 pm; Sat noon-11 pm; Sun noon-9 pm. Closed Thanksgiving. Chinese menu. Bar. Semi-a la carte: lunch $3.75-$5, dinner $6-$9. Specialties: mandarin combination, Hunan beef. Cr cds: A, MC, V.

D

★★ **JUANITA'S AT THE MESA.** *1719 Merrill Dr. 501/221-7777.* Hrs: 11 am-2 pm, 5:30-10 pm; Fri to 10:30 pm, Sat 11:30 am-2:30 pm, 5:30-10:30 pm; Sun 11:30 am-2:30 pm, 5-9 pm. Closed Mon; Dec 24 & 25. Southwestern menu. Bar. Semi-a la carte: lunch $5.45-$9.95, dinner $7.95-$16.95. Sun brunch $5.50-$6.50. Specializes in fresh seafood, pork & mushroom fajitas, cheese dip. Entertainment Thurs-Sat. Parking. Southwestern decor. Cr cds: A, D, DS, MC, V.

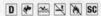

★★ **LA SCALA.** *2721 Kavanaugh Blvd. 501/663-1196.* Hrs: 11 am-1:30 pm, 6-10 pm; Sat from 6 pm. Closed Sun; Jan 1, Easter, Thanksgiving, Dec 24 & 25. Res accepted. Italian menu. Bar 4:30 pm-1 am. Extensive wine list. Semi-a la carte: lunch $6-$10, dinner $10-$25. Specialties: Pesto shrimp, tortellini. Parking. Secluded restaurant in historic district. Totally nonsmoking. Cr cds: A, C, D, DS, MC, V.

★★ **LANDRY'S CAJUN WHARF.** *2400 Cantrell Rd. 501/375-5351.* Hrs: 11 am-10:15 pm; Sat to 11:15 pm, Sun to 9:15 pm. Closed Dec 25. Res accepted. Bar. Semi-a la carte: dinner $8.95-$28.95. Child's meals. Specializes in fresh fish, seafood, steak. Entertainment. Valet parking (wkends). Patio dining. Old shipping warehouse overlooking Arkansas River. Cr cds: A, C, DS, MC, V.

★★ **SIR LOIN'S INN.** *(801 W 29th St, N Little Rock)* 3 mi N on I-30, exit 107. *501/753-1361.* Hrs: 5:30-10:30 pm; Fri, Sat from 5 pm. Closed Sun; major hols. Bar from 4 pm. Semi-a la carte: dinner $11.95-$23.95. Specializes in prime rib, teriyaki chicken. Salad bar. Parking. Family-owned. Cr cds: A, C, D, DS, MC, V.

Unrated Dining Spots

ANDRE'S WEST. *11121 N Rodney Parham Rd, in shopping center. 501/224-7880.* Hrs: 9 am-9 pm; Tues to 5 pm; Sun to 2 pm. Closed Mon; July 4, Thanksgiving, Dec 25. French, continental menu. Serv bar. Semi-a la carte: bkfst $3.30-$6.80; lunch, dinner $4.95-$18. Specializes in French breads, pastries, sandwiches. Swiss tearoom atmosphere, dining. Totally nonsmoking. Cr cds: A, C, D, DS, MC, V.

BUFFALO GRILL. *1611 Rebsamen Park Rd, 2 mi W on Cantrell Rd. 501/663-2158.* Hrs: 11 am-10 pm. Closed Sun; Thanksgiving, Dec 25. Semi-a la carte: lunch $3-$3.50, dinner $5.25-$11.95. Child's meals. Specializes in hamburgers. Parking. Cr cds: A, MC, V.

DELICIOUS TEMPTATIONS. *11220 N Rodney Parham Rd, in Pleasant Valley Plaza. 501/225-6893.* Hrs: 8 am-8 pm; Sat & Sun to 2 pm. Wine, beer. Semi-a la carte: bkfst, lunch, dinner $2.50-$7.50. Child's meals. Specializes in pita sandwiches, homemade desserts. Parking. Totally nonsmoking. Cr cds: A, DS, MC, V.

FRANKE'S CAFETERIA. *300 S University, in University Mall Shopping Ctr. 501/666-1941.* Hrs: 10:45 am-8 pm. Closed Jan 1, July 4, Thanksgiving, Dec 25. Avg ck: lunch $4, dinner $5. Specialties: scalloped eggplant, egg custard pie. Family-owned. Cr cds: DS, MC, V.

Magnolia (E-2)

(See Camden, El Dorado)

Founded 1852 **Pop** 11,151 **Elev** 325 ft **Area code** 501 **Zip** 71753
Information Magnolia-Columbia County Chamber of Commerce, 202 N Pine, PO Box 866; 501/234-4352.

Created to serve as the seat of Columbia County, Magnolia was largely dependent on cotton for many years. The town boomed with the discovery of oil in 1937. Today there are many wells in the vicinity, as well as chemical, aluminum, plastic, steel, lumber and structural wood plants.

What to See and Do

Logoly State Park. Situated on 345 acres of forested coastal plain, this park is the first in Arkansas' system to be set aside for environmental education. Formerly a Boy Scout camp, Logoly represents southern Arkansas before commercial logging operations began. Most of the park has been designated a Natural Area because of its unique plant life and 11 natural springs. Well-marked hiking trails, observation stands and photo blinds. Picnicking. Tent camping. Visitor center displays flora, fauna and history of the area; interpretive programs, exhibits. Standard fees. (Daily) 6 mi N on US 79, on County 47 (Logoly Rd). Phone 501/695-3561. Per vehicle ¢

Southern Arkansas University (1909). (2,800 students) On 781-acre campus is Greek theater and model farm; Ozmer House, an original dog-trot style farmhouse; Carl White Caddo Native American Collection is on permanent display in the Magale Library, 501/235-4170. Campus tours. N on N Jackson St, off US 79. Phone 501/235-4000.

Motel

✔★★ **BEST WESTERN COACHMAN'S INN.** *420 E Main St. 501/234-6122; FAX 501/234-1254.* 84 rms, 2 story. S $40-$50; D $40-$65; each addl $5. Crib free. Pet accepted; some restrictions. TV; cable (premium), VCR avail. Pool. Complimentary coffee & newspaper in lobby. Restaurant 11 am-9 pm. Ck-out noon. Meeting rms. Business servs avail. Refrigerators. Balconies. Cr cds: A, C, D, DS, MC, V.

Inn

★★ **MAGNOLIA PLACE.** *510 E Main St. 501/234-6122; res: 800/237-6122.* 5 rms (4 with shower only), 2 story, 1 suite. S, D $79; suite $149. Children over 14 yrs only. TV; cable. Pool privileges. Complimentary full bkfst; coffee, tea in library. Restaurant adj 11 am-9 pm, closed Sun. Ck-out noon. Built 1910 and furnished with many antiques; wrap-around porch with rocking chairs. Totally nonsmoking. Cr cds: A, C, D, DS, MC, V.

Malvern (C-2)

(See Arkadelphia, Benton, Hot Springs)

Pop 9,256 **Elev** 312 ft **Area code** 501 **Zip** 72104
Information Chamber of Commerce, 213 W 3rd St, PO Box 266; 501/332-2721.

Although dubbed "the brick capital of the world," Malvern also manufactures lumber and aluminum. The city also has small mining operations, mostly in barium and rare minerals.

What to See and Do

Hot Springs National Park (see). 20 mi NW via US 270.

Jenkins' Ferry State Historic Monument. Civil War battleground site. Swimming; fishing. Picnicking. Exhibits. 16 mi E on US 270, 6 mi S on AR 291, 2 mi SW on AR 46.

Lake Catherine State Park. Approx 2,200 acres with swimming, water sports; fishing; boating (rentals, ramp, dock). Hiking. Picnicking in pine groves. Camping (hookups, dump station; standard fees), cabins, coin laundry, store. Visitor center; nature programs (summer). SW on I-30 exit 97, 12 mi NW on AR 171. Contact Superintendent, 1200 Lake Catherine Rd, Hot Springs 71913. Phone 501/844-4176. Per vehicle ¢

Annual Events

Brickfest. Courthouse grounds. Town festival with bands, singing groups, arts & crafts, contests, concession stands. Late June.

County Fair and Livestock Show. Wkend after Labor Day.

Motel

★ **ECONOMY INN.** *1901 AR 270.* 510/332-2487. 71 rms, 2 story. May-Aug: S $32-$38; D $35-$45; each addl $3.25; family rates. Crib $5. Pet accepted, some restrictions; $5. TV; cable. Pool. Complimentary coffee in lobby. Restaurant nearby. Ck-out 11 am. Picnic tables. Cr cds: A, D, DS, MC, V.

🐾 ⛱ 🚫 🔥 **SC**

Mena (C-1)

Founded 1896 **Pop** 5,475 **Elev** 1,150 ft **Area code** 501 **Zip** 71953

Information Mena/Polk County Chamber of Commerce, 524 Sherwood St; 501/394-2912.

This town was named after the wife of a Dutch coffee broker who provided financial assistance needed for the construction of the Kansas City, Pittsburg and Gulf Railroad (now Kansas City Southern Railroad). A Ranger District office of the Ouachita National Forest (see HOT SPRINGS & HOT SPRINGS NATIONAL PARK) is located here.

What to See and Do

Janssen Park. Historic park contains a log cabin built in 1851; two small lakes, spring, small deer park and picnic areas. Opp post office.

Queen Wilhelmina State Park This 640-acre park atop Rich Mountain boasts magnificent scenery and more than 100 species of flowers, mosses and ferns. A miniature railroad takes visitors on a 1¹/₂-mile circuit of the mountaintop in the summer (fee). The original inn (1898) was built by the Kansas City Railroad as a luxury retreat; financed by Dutch investors, the inn was named for the reigning queen of the Netherlands. The current building (see INN) is a reconstruction of the original. The park also offers hiking trails, miniature golf; picnicking, playground; store, restaurant; coin laundry. Camping (electric & water hookups), shower facilities. Interpretive programs, exhibits. Animal park. Standard fees. (Daily) 13 mi NW on AR 88. Contact the Superintendant, HC-7, PO Box 53A; 501/394-2863 or 800/264-2477. Per vehicle ¢ Also here is

Talimena Scenic Drive. This 55-mile roller-coaster drive through the Ouachita National Forest to Talihina, OK, passes through the park and other areas rich in botanical and geological interest. In addition to campgrounds in the park, there are other camping locations along the drive (fees may be charged). Drive may be difficult in winter. Follow AR 88 N and W, OK 1.

Annual Event

Lum & Abner Days. Janssen Park. Festival in honor of famed radio personalities features arts & crafts, fiddlers' contest, entertainment. June.

Inn

★ ★ **QUEEN WILHELMINA LODGE.** *HC 7, Box 53A, 13 mi NW on AR 88 in Queen Wilhelmina State Park.* 501/394-2863; res: 800/264-2477; FAX 501/394-0061. 38 units, 2 story. No rm phones. Mar-Nov: D $65-$85; each addl $5; suites $85; under 12 free; lower rates rest of yr. Crib free. Supervised child's activities (memorial day-labor day; ages 7-14). Dining rm 7 am-9 pm. Ck-out 11 am. Meeting rms. Business servs avail. Airport transportation. Miniature golf. Picnic tables, grills. Modern design; native stone; windmill garden. Cr cds: A, DS, MC, V.

🚫 🔥

Morrilton (C-2)

(See Conway, Russellville)

Founded 1870 **Pop** 6,551 **Elev** 389 ft **Area code** 501 **Zip** 72110

Information Chamber of Commerce, 118 N Moose; 501/354-2393.

What to See and Do

Museum of Automobiles. Founded by former Arkansas governor Winthrop Rockefeller, the museum features an attractive display of antique and classic cars. There are autos from Rockefeller's personal collection, as well as changing exhibits of privately owned cars. (Daily; closed Dec 25) Rte 3, Petit Jean Mt. Phone 501/727-5427. ¢¢

Petit Jean State Park (see). 9 mi S on AR 9, 12 mi W on AR 154.

Motel

★ ★ **BEST WESTERN.** *AR 95 & I-40, exit 107.* 501/354-0181; FAX 501/354-1458. 54 rms, 2 story. S, D $36-$50; each addl $5; under 12 free; higher rates special events. Crib $3. Pet accepted, some restrictions. TV; cable (premium). Pool. Complimentary coffee in lobby. Complimentary continental bkfst. Restaurant adj 10:30 am-10 pm. Ck-out noon. Meeting rms. Business servs avail. Some refrigerators. Cr cds: A, C, D, DS, ER, JCB, MC, V.

🐾 ⛱ 🚫 🔥 **SC**

Mountain Home (A-3)

(See Bull Shoals Lake Area)

Pop 9,027 **Elev** 820 ft **Area code** 501 **Zip** 72653

Information Chamber of Commerce, PO Box 488; 501/425-5111 or 800/822-3536.

This is a vacation town situated midway between Arkansas' two big Ozark lakes: Bull Shoals (see) and Norfork. Fishing in lakes and rivers is very good; all varieties of water sports are available on both lakes. There are many resorts in this popular area.

What to See and Do

Norfork Lake. This 40-mile lake, impounded by a dam on the North Fork of the White River, is one of Arkansas' most attractive water vacation areas. Water sports; fishing for largemouth, striped and white bass, walleye, crappie, bream, bluegill and catfish; rainbow and brown trout are found in the North Fork River below the dam; hunting; boating (ramps, rentals, ten marinas). Picnicking, lodges. Camping (seasonal, electric hookups; fee). Toll-free state bridges cross the lake. Fees charged at some areas. (Daily) 9 mi NE on US 62. Phone 501/425-2700.

Norfork National Fish Hatchery. Largest federal trout hatchery in the country; annually distributes more than two million rainbow, brown, cut throat, brook and lake trout. (Daily) 12 mi SE on AR 5, E on AR 177. Phone 501/499-5255. **Free.**

Annual Event

Baxter County Fair. Fairgrounds. Midway, arts & crafts. Mid-Sept.

Motels

✔★★ **BEST WESTERN CARRIAGE INN.** *963 US 62E, 1 mi E.* 501/425-6001; FAX 501/425-6001, ext. -100. 82 rms, 2 story. S $43-$57; D $50-$62; each addl $6; under 12 free. Pet accepted. TV; cable (premium). Pool. Restaurant (see CHELSEA'S). Rm serv. Private club from 4:30 pm, closed Sun. Ck-out noon. Meeting rms. Cr cds: A, C, D, DS, JCB, MC, V.

★ **HOLIDAY INN.** *1 mi SW on US 62.* 501/425-5101; FAX 501/425-5101, ext. -300. 100 rms, 2 story. S $46.50-$50; D $56.50-$66.50; each addl $10; under 18 free. Crib free. Pet accepted. TV; cable (premium), VCR avail. Pool. Restaurant 6 am-10 pm. Rm serv. Private club 5 pm-1 am, closed Sun; entertainment. Ck-out noon. Coin lndry. Meeting rms. Business servs avail. In-rm modem link. Airport transportation. Cr cds: A, C, D, DS, JCB, MC, V.

✔★★ **RAMADA INN.** *1127 US 62NE.* 501/425-9191; FAX 501/424-5192. 80 rms, 2 story. S $38-$42; D $45-$49; each addl $7; under 18 free. Crib free. TV; cable (premium), VCR avail. Indoor pool. Coffee in rms. Restaurant 6 am-10 pm. Rm serv. Ck-out noon. Meeting rms. Business servs avail. In-rm modem link. Sundries. Beauty shop. Cr cds: A, C, D, DS, JCB, MC, V.

Cottage Colonies

★ **BLUE PARADISE.** *Rte 6, Box 379, Tealpoint Rd, 6 mi E on US 62, then 1/2 mi N.* 501/492-5113. 17 (1-3 bedrm) kit. cottages (boat incl). Mar-Nov: kit. cottages $38-$96; each addl $5; wkly & monthly rates; lower rates rest of yr. TV; cable. Pool. Playground. Ck-out 9 am, ck-in 3 pm. Grocery. Coin lndry. Gift shop. Boats, motors, rowboats, pontoon boats. Float trips, guides. Lawn games. Rec rm. Lighted dock. Fish clean station. Picnic tables, grills. On Norfork Lake. No cr cds accepted.

★ **TEAL POINT.** *Rte 6, Box 369, 6 mi E on US 62, then 1/2 mi N on AR 406.* 501/492-5145. 16 kit. cottages. No rm phones. June-Sept: cottages $55-$120; each addl $5; family rates; lower rates rest of yr. Crib free. Pet accepted; $5 per day. TV; cable. Pool. Playground. Restaurant 1 mi. Ck-out 9 am, ck-in 3 pm. Grocery. Coin lndry. Package store 5 mi. Boats, rentals. Game rm. Lawn games. Fishing guides. Private patios. Picnic tables, grills. On Lake Norfork. No cr cds accepted.

Restaurants

★★ **CHELSEA'S.** *(See Best Western Carriage Inn Motel)* 501/425-6001. Hrs: 5-9 pm. Closed Sun; major hols. Continental menu. Bar from 4:30 pm. Semi-a la carte: dinner $5.95-$34.95. Child's meals. Specializes in seafood, steak. Parking. Extensive wine selection. Casual elegance. Queen Anne chairs. Cr cds: A, C, D, DS, JCB, MC, V.

✔★ **FRED'S FISH HOUSE.** *6 mi E on US 62.* 501/492-5958. Hrs: 11 am-9 pm; Sun noon-6 pm. Closed Thanksgiving, Dec 25.

Semi-a la carte: lunch $3.95-$10.95, dinner $5.95-$11.95. Child's meals. Specializes in catfish, hush puppies. Parking. Overlooks Lake Norfork. Cr cds: MC, V.

Mountain View (B-3)

(See Batesville, Greers Ferry Lake Area)

Pop 2,439 **Elev** 768 ft **Area code** 501 **Zip** 72560
Information Mountain View Area Chamber of Commerce, PO Box 133; 501/269-8098.

The folk music heritage brought to these mountains by the early settlers is still an important part of the community today. Each Saturday night, if the weather is nice, folks head for the courthouse square with chairs and instruments to hear and play music. A Ranger District office of the Ozark National Forest (see RUSSELLVILLE) also is here.

What to See and Do

Blanchard Springs Caverns. Spectacular "living" caverns feature crystalline formations, an underground river and huge chambers. Guided tours depart from Visitor Information Center, which has exhibit hall and free movie; 1-hour tour of 1/2-mile Dripstone Trail and 1 3/4-hour tour of more strenuous 1 1/4-mile Discovery Trail. (Apr-Oct, daily; Nov-Mar, Wed-Sun; closed Jan 1, Thanksgiving, Dec 25) Sr citizen rate. 15 mi NW on AR 14, in Ozark National Forest. For reservations phone 501/757-2211. ¢¢¢

Ozark Folk Center State Park. This 915-acre site has an 80-acre, 50-building living museum complex dedicated to Ozark folk heritage, crafts and music. Using skills, tools and materials of the period 1820-1920, artisans demonstrate basketry, quiltmaking, woodcarving and re-create informal gatherings. Lodge, restaurant, 1,000-seat music auditorium, outdoor stage with 300 covered seats; special events all yr (see ANNUAL EVENTS). Crafts area (May-Oct, daily); music shows (nightly exc Sun); park (all yr). 2 mi N. For ticket prices phone 501/269-3851 or 800/264-FOLK. Per vehicle ¢

Annual Events

Arkansas Folk Festival. Citywide. 3rd wkend Apr.

Merle Travis Tribute. Ozark Folk Center. May.

Arkansas State Fiddler's Contest. Ozark Folk Center. Sept.

Harvest Festival. Ozark Folk Center. Concerts, crafts demonstrations, races, fiddlers' jamboree, contests. Oct.

Bean Fest and Great Arkansas Championship Outhouse Race. Homemade "outhouses" race around courthouse square. Music, tall-tale contest, games. Last Sat Oct.

Motels

✔★ **BEST WESTERN FIDDLER'S INN.** *PO Box 1438, 1 mi N on AR 14, at jct AR 9.* 501/269-2828. 48 rms, 2 story. Apr-Nov: S, D $44-$49; each addl $5; under 12 free. Crib $4. Pets accepted, $10 fee. TV; cable. Heated pool. Complimentary continental bkfst. Restaurant opp 6:30 am-8:30 pm Thur-Sun; till 2 pm Mon-Wed. Ck-out 11 am. Free local airport transportation. Cr cds: A, C, D, DS, MC, V.

★ **DOGWOOD.** *AR 14 E, 1 mi E of downtown.* 501/269-3847. 30 rms (some with shower only). Apr-Oct: S, D $48; lower rates rest of yr. Pet accepted, some restrictions. TV; cable. Pool. Complimentary coffee in lobby. Ck-out 11 am. Gift shop. Cr cds: A, DS, MC, V.

★ **OZARK FOLK CENTER LODGE.** *Box 500, 1 mi N on AR 14, 1 mi W on AR 382. 501/269-3871; res: 800/264-3655; FAX 501/269-2909.* 60 rms. Apr-Nov: S, D $45-$50; each addl $5; under 13 free; lower rates rest of yr. Crib free. TV; cable. Pool. Restaurant 7 am-8 pm. Ck-out 11 am. Meeting rms. Business servs avail. Free airport transportation. Rec rm. Private patios. Overlooks Ozark woods. In Ozark Folk Center State Park; operated by AR Dept of Parks & Tourism. Cr cds: A, DS, MC, V.

D ⊠ ⊠ ⊠

Inns

★ ★ **INN AT MOUNTAIN VIEW.** *PO Box 812, 1 mi N on Washington St. 501/269-4200; res: 800/535-1301.* 10 rms, 2 story. No rm phones. Mar-Jan 1: S $45; D $59; each addl $17; kit unit $95. Adults only. Complimentary 7-course bkfst. Restaurant nearby. Ck-out 11 am, ck-in 1 pm. Free local airport transportation. Inn built 1886, furnished with antiques. Totally nonsmoking. Cr cds: DS, MC, V.

D ⊠ ⊠

✔ ★ **WILDFLOWER BED & BREAKFAST.** *PO Box 72, Court Square. 501/269-4383; res: 800/591-4879.* 8 rms, 6 with bath, 2 story. No rm phones. S $37-$71; D $42-$72; each addl $6. Crib free. Complimentary continental bkfst. Dining rm 7 am-5 pm. Ck-out 11 am. Restored country inn (1918). Antiques. Flower and herb gardens. Totally nonsmoking. Cr cds: A, DS, MC, V.

⊠ ⊠

Nashville (D-1)

(For accommodations see Hope)

Pop 4,639 **Elev** 383 ft **Area code** 501 **Zip** 71852

What to See and Do

Crater of Diamonds State Park. This more than 850-acre pine-covered area along the banks of the Little Missouri River contains the only North American diamond mine open to the public (fee; assessment and certification free). Worked commercially from 1906 to 1949, this rare 35-acre field is open to amateur diamond hunters. More than 70,000 diamonds have been found here, including such notables as Uncle Sam (40.23 carats), Amarillo Starlight (16.37 carats) and Star of Arkansas (15.33 carats). Other stones found here include amethyst, agate, jasper, quartz. Swimming; fishing. Hiking trail. Picnicking, playground, coin laundry, restaurant (seasonal). Camping (hookups, dump station; standard fees). Visitor center; exhibits; interpretive programs. (Daily) 13 mi NE on AR 27 to Murfreesboro, 2 mi SE on AR 301. Contact the Superintendent, Rte 1, Box 364, Murfreesboro 71958; 501/285-3113. ¢¢

The Ka-Do-Ha Indian Village. Excavated ancient Native American ceremonial site; prehistoric mound-builder village; trading post; museum; arrowhead hunting; tours of excavations. (Daily; closed Dec 25) 15 mi N off AR 27, follow signs. Phone 501/285-3736. ¢¢

Newport (B-4)

(See Batesville)

Founded 1875 **Pop** 7,459 **Elev** 224 ft **Area code** 501 **Zip** 72112
Information Newport Area Chamber of Commerce, 210 Elm, PO Box 518; 501/523-3618.

The town was named Newport because in 1873 it was a new port on the White River. The seat of Jackson County, it is in an agricultural area with farming as the basic industry. Hunting, boating and fishing are the major recreational activities. The White River, Black River and 35 lakes are nearby.

What to See and Do

Jacksonport State Park. Swimming; fishing. Picnicking; coin laundry. Camping (hookups, dump station). Standard fees. (Daily) 3 mi NW on AR 69 in Jacksonport. Contact Park Superintendent, PO Box 8, Jacksonport 72075. 501/523-2143. Per vehicle ¢ Also here are

Courthouse Museum. Restored courthouse (1869); furniture represents various periods of Delta life. Indian Room; War Memorial Room with uniforms and relics; original papers. (Daily exc Mon; closed Jan 1, Thanksgiving, Dec 24, 25) ¢

Carriage House. Houses a buckboard, buggy, surrey and a sulky used in racing Thoroughbred horses from the surrounding plantations. **Free.**

Mary Woods II. Refurbished White River steamboat, berthed at Jacksonport Landing, houses maritime museum. (May-early Sept, daily exc Mon; Sept & Oct, wkends only) ¢

Annual Event

Portfest & State Catfish Cooking Contest. In Jacksonport State Park (see). Catfish dinners, arts & crafts show, footraces, concerts, stage entertainment, waterski show. First wkend June.

Motel

✔ ★ ★ **PARK INN INTERNATIONAL.** *901 US 67N. 501/523-5851; FAX 501/523-9890.* 58 rms. S $40-$44; D $44-$52; each addl $3; under 18 free. Crib free. Pet accepted. TV; cable (premium), VCR avail. Pool. Coffee in lobby. Restaurant 5 am-9 pm. Bar 4-11 pm. Ck-out noon. Coin lndry. Meeting rms. Valet serv. Sundries. Some rms with cathedral ceiling. Cr cds: A, C, D, DS, JCB, MC, V.

✦ ⊠ ⊠ ⊠ SC

North Little Rock (C-3)

(see Little Rock)

Paris (B-2)

(For accommodations see Fort Smith, Russellville)

Pop 3,674 **Elev** 432 ft **Area code** 501 **Zip** 72855
Information North Logan County Chamber of Commerce, 301 W Walnut; 501/963-2244.

A Ranger District office of the Ozark National Forest (see RUSSELLVILLE) is located here.

What to See and Do

Blue Mountain Lake. Swimming, waterskiing; fishing, hunting; boating. Picnicking. Camping. Fees charged at some areas. (Daily) 15 mi S on AR 109 to Magazine, then 11 mi E on AR 10 to Waveland. Phone 501/947-2372. **Free.**

Cove Lake Recreation Area. Near Magazine Mountain, the highest point in the state, with 160-acre lake. Swimming (fee); fishing; boating (ramps). Picnicking. Camping (fee). (May-Oct, daily) 9 mi S via AR 309. Phone 501/963-3076. Per vehicle ¢

Logan County Museum. Historical information and artifacts regarding Paris and Logan County. (Tues-Sat afternoons; closed major hols) 202 N Vine. Phone 501/963-3936. **Free.**

Petit Jean State Park (C-2)

(See Morrilton, Russellville)

(I-40 exit 108 at Morrilton, 9 mi S on AR 9, 12 mi W on AR 154)

This almost 3,500-acre rugged area is the oldest and one of the most beautiful of the Arkansas parks. Both the park and forested Petit Jean Mountain, 1,100 feet high, are named for a French girl who is said to have disguised herself as a boy to accompany her sailor sweetheart to America. While in the New World, the girl contracted an unknown disease and died, never having returned to France. Legend says she was buried on the mountain by friendly Native Americans.

Adjoining the park is the Museum of Automobiles (see MORRILTON) and Winrock Farm, former governor Winthrop Rockefeller's experimental demonstration farm, where he raised Santa Gertrudis cattle. The park also offers a swimming pool (lifeguard); boating (pedalboat, fishing boat rentals Memorial Day-Labor Day). Hiking trails, tennis. Picnicking, playgrounds, restaurant, snack bar. Camping (hookups, rent-a-camp, dump station), trailer sites, cabins, lodge. Interpretive programs, exhibits. Standard fees. Contact the Superintendent, Rte 3, Box 340, Morrilton 72110; phone 501/727-5441.

Motel

★★ **MATHER LODGE.** *(Rte 3, Box 346, Morrilton 72110) 20 mi SW of Morrilton on AR 154, in park.* 501/727-5431; res: 800/264-2462. 56 units, 1-2 story, 19 kits. S $40; D $45; each addl $5; kit. units $70; cabins $45; under 12 free. Pool. Playground. Restaurant 7 am-8 pm; late Nov-mid-Mar closed Mon-Thur. Ck-out 11 am. Meeting rm. Gift shop. Tennis. Paddleboats. State-owned. Naturalist programs daily Memorial Day-Labor Day. Scenic view overlooking valley & Arkansas River. Cr cds: A, DS, MC, V.

Cottage Colony

★★ **TANYARD SPRINGS.** *Rte 3, Box 335, AR 154, on Petit Jean Mt.* 501/727-5200; FAX 501/727-5228. 15 kit. cottages. No rm phones. S, D $125-$150; under 16 free; Crib free. Playground. Ck-out 11 am, ck-in 3 pm. Meeting rms. Business servs avail. Gift shop. Tennis privileges. Golf privileges 20 mi. Miniature golf. Lawn games. Fireplaces. Private picnic tables, grills. Individually themed, hand-crafted cabins; each named for historic personality; many antiques. On 187 wooded acres with lake. Cr cds: A, DS, MC, V.

⊡ 🏖️ 🏃 ⛷️ 🔥 SC

Pine Bluff (D-3)

Founded 1819 **Pop** 57,140 **Elev** 230 ft **Area code** 501
Information Pine Bluff Convention & Tourism Bureau, 1 Convention Center Plaza, 71601; 501/536-7600.

Any loyal citizen of Pine Bluff will tell you that, contrary to rumors, the Civil War began right here. In April, 1861, several days before Fort Sumter, a musket shot was fired across the bow of a federal gunboat in the Arkansas River. The vessel hove to and its supplies were confiscated. On October 25, 1863, Pine Bluff was occupied by Union troops, who held it against a Confederate attack. It remained in Union hands until the end of the Civil War.

This is an old town, having been founded as a trading post by Joseph Bonne, who dealt with the Quapaw with unusual success—partly because he was half Quapaw.

Today, cotton, rice, soybeans, wood processing, transformers, chemicals and paper manufacturing are the main industries. The "Mu-

rals on Main" project plans to create 22 murals on downtown buildings. To date 8 have been completed. The surrounding area offers excellent hunting and fishing. North of town, on US 79, is the local branch of the University of Arkansas.

What to See and Do

Arkansas Post National Memorial (see). 40 mi SE on US 65, then 17 mi N on US 165, then 2 mi E on AR 169.

Arts & Science Center for Southeast Arkansas. Houses visual arts and science exhibits. (Daily exc Sun; closed major hols) 220 Martin St. Phone 501/536-3375. **Free.**

Dexter Harding House. A tourist information center is located in this 1850s house. (Daily) US 65 & Pine St.

Jefferson County Historical Museum. Features exhibits on history of Pine Bluff and Jefferson County, development of area transportation, including river, roads and rail; displays of Victorian artifacts and clothing used by early settlers. (Mon-Fri; closed major hols) 201 E 4th St. Phone 501/541-5402. **Free.**

Navigation Pool (Lock) No 3. Part of the Arkansas River multiple purpose project; Huffs Island, Rising Star (fee) and Trulock. Fishing; boat launching facilities. Picnicking (fee for group picnicking in Rising Star and Trulock). Camping (Rising Star has electrical hookups, showers and dump station; fee). Some facilities closed during winter months. (Daily) 15 mi SE via US 65, AR 11. Phone 501/534-0451. Per vehicle **Free.**

Navigation Pool (Lock) No 4. Ste Marie and Sheppard Island have fishing, boat launching facilities, picnicking. Ste Marie also has a fishing dock designed for use by the disabled. Some facilities closed during winter months. Group picnicking (fee). 5 mi E via AR 81, US 65, US 79. Phone 501/534-0451. **Free.**

Pioneer Village. Re-created pioneer village with several historic structures, including a log cabin, mercantile store, blacksmith shop, barn, physician's Victorian home and a church. (Mid-June-mid-Aug, Wed-Sun) 25 mi SW via US 79 in Rison. Phone 501/325-7289. **Free.**

Motels

✔★ **ADMIRAL BENBOW.** *Box 5009 (71611), US 65S.* 501/535-8300; FAX 501/536-9247. 104 rms. S $35-$43; D $41-$48; each addl $5; under 12 free. Crib free. Pet accepted. TV; cable. Pool. Restaurant open 24 hrs. Rm serv. Ck-out noon. Meeting rms. Bellhops. Valet serv. Sundries. Refrigerators. Cr cds: A, C, D, DS, MC, V.

🐾 🏖️ 🔥 SC

★★ **THE INN.** *210 N Blake (71601).* 501/534-7222; FAX 501/534-5705. 90 units, 2 story. S $39-$40; D $42-$47; each addl $5; suites from $48; under 18 free. TV; cable. Pool. Complimentary continental bkfst. Restaurant adj 6 am-midnight. Ck-out noon. Meeting rms. Exercise equipt; weights, bicycles. Picnic tables, grills. Cr cds: A, C, D, DS, ER, JCB, MC, V.

⊡ 🐾 🏖️ 🏃 🖐️ 🔥 SC

Hotel

★★★ **HOLIDAY INN.** *2 Convention Center Plaza (71601).* 501/535-3111; FAX 501/534-5083. 200 units, 5 story, 84 suites. S $69; D $74; each addl $5; suites $79; under 18 free. Crib free. TV; cable. Indoor pool; whirlpool, sauna. Restaurant 6:30 am-10 pm. Bar 4 pm-midnight. Ck-out 11 am. Exercise equipt; weights, bicycles. Indoor putting green. Refrigerators; wet bar in suites. Atrium, balconies. Cr cds: A, C, D, DS, JCB, MC, V.

⊡ 🏖️ 🖐️ 🔥 SC

Inn

★★ **MARGLAND II, III, IV.** *703 W 2nd St (71601). 501/536-6000; res: 800/545-5383; FAX 501/536-7941.* 17 rms, 2 story. S, D $65-$95.50; under 12 free. Crib free. TV: cable (premium), VCR avail. Pool. Complimentary full bkfst. Ck-out, ck-in noon. Business servs avail. Picnic tables; grills. Three turn-of-the-century houses, porches, leaded glass; Victorian decor, antiques, old wicker. Cr cds: A, D, DS, MC, V.

Restaurant

★ **FUH MEI'S.** *303 W 31st Ave. 501/536-4500.* Hrs: 11:30 am-2 pm, 5-10 pm; Fri to 11 pm; Sat 5-11 pm. Closed Sun; some major hols. Chinese, Amer menu. Bar. Semi-a la carte: lunch $4.50-$6.95, dinner $6.50-$18.95. Buffet: lunch $5.25. Specialties: chicken & shrimp Hunan, house chicken, steak. Entertainment Fri, Sat; piano bar. Parking. Oriental decor. Cr cds: A, D, DS, MC, V.

Pocahontas (A-4)

(For accommodations see Jonesboro, Walnut Ridge)

Pop 6,151 **Elev** 310 ft **Area code** 501 **Zip** 72455
Information Chamber of Commerce, 121 E Everett St, PO Box 466; 501/892-3956.

What to See and Do

Maynard Pioneer Museum & Park. Log cabin museum; displays of antique farm equipment. Park; picnic areas. (June-Sept, daily exc Mon). Donation. 13 mi N via AR 115 in Maynard. Phone 501/647-2701.

Old Davidsonville State Park. This 163-acre park on the Black River was the site of historic Davidsonville, a small town established by French settlers in 1815; the first post office and courthouse in the state were located here. Fishing; boating (no motors; rentals). Hiking trails. Picnicking, playground; snack bar, coin laundry nearby. Camping (tent sites, hookups, dump station). Visitor center (exhibits of local artifacts). Standard fees. (Daily) 2 mi W on US 62, 9 mi S on AR 166. Phone 501/892-4708. Per vehicle ¢

Annual Event

Randolph County Fair. Fairgrounds. Late Aug-early Sept.

Rogers (A-1)

(See Bentonville, Eureka Springs, Fayetteville, Springdale)

Founded 1881 **Pop** 24,692 **Elev** 1,371 ft **Area code** 501 **Zip** 72756
Information Chamber of Commerce, 113 N 4th St, PO Box 428, 72757; 501/636-1240.

This pleasant town in the Ozark area has diversified industries, including the manufacture of air rifles, electric motors, pumps, tools, stereo speakers and office furniture and the processing of poultry.

What to See and Do

Beaver Lake. Variety of water sports on 30,000-acre reservoir with 483-mile shoreline. Swimming, waterskiing; fishing, hunting; boating (ramp, marine station, rental boats, motors). Picnicking, playground. Camping (hookups, dump station). Fee for some activities. (Daily) 4 mi E on AR 12. Phone 501/636-1210. ¢¢¢

Daisy International Air Gun Museum. Large display of non-powdered guns, some dating to late 18th century. (Mon-Fri; closed major hols) 2111 S 8th St. Phone 501/636-1200. **Free.**

Pea Ridge National Military Park. A decisive battle was fought here March 7-8, 1862, saving Missouri for the Union and resulting in the deaths of three Confederate generals: McCulloch, McIntosh and Slack. Auto tour through historic area; the Elkhorn Tavern has been restored. Visitor center (daily; closed Jan 1, Thanksgiving, Dec 25). 10 mi NE on US 62. Phone 501/451-8122. Per vehicle ¢¢

Rogers Historical Museum (Hawkins House). Exhibits on local history; recreated turn-of-the-century businesses; Victorian-era furnishings; hands-on children's discovery room. (Tues-Sat; closed most major hols) 322 S 2nd St. Phone 501/621-1154. **Free.**

War Eagle Mill. This picturesque little community is the site of one of the state's largest and most popular arts & crafts shows (May & Oct). Tours of working, water-powered gristmill (all yr). AR 12E. Phone 501/789-5343. Nearby is

War Eagle Cavern. Spectacular natural entrance. Guided tours. (May-Labor Day, daily; after Labor Day-Oct, wkends) AR 12E. Phone 501/789-2909.

Motels

★ **BEAVER LAKE LODGE.** *RR 7, 100 Dutchman Dr, 4 mi E on AR 12, then 1/4 mi N. 501/925-2313; res: 800/367-4513; FAX 501/925-1406.* 23 kit. units in motel, 3 duplex kit. cottages. Apr-Oct: S $49-$54; D $54-$59; under 12 free; wkly, monthly rates Dec-Mar; golf package; lower rates rest of yr. Crib free. Pet accepted, some restrictions; $5. TV; cable (premium). Pool. Complimentary coffee. Restaurant nearby. Ck-out 11 am. 18-hole golf privileges. Picnic tables, grills. Cr cds: A, MC, V.

✔ ★ **RAMADA INN.** *1919 US 71 B, 2 mi S on US 71. 501/636-5850.* 127 rms, 2 story. S $44-$52; D $49-$55; each addl $6; under 18 free. Crib free. Pet accepted. TV; cable (premium). Pool. Complimentary continental bkfst. Restaurant 6 am-10 pm. Private club 11-2 am. Ck-out 11 am. Meeting rms. Airport transportation. Cr cds: A, C, D, DS, JCB, MC, V.

Restaurants

★★ **PLAZA.** *200 S 1st St. 501/636-9191.* Hrs: 11 am-10 pm; Sat from 5 pm; Sun 10 am-2 pm. Closed most major hols. Bar. Semi-a la carte: lunch $5-$8, dinner $10-$18. Specializes in prime rib, fresh fish. Parking. Patio dining. In remodeled bakery. Cr cds: A, DS, MC, V.

★★ **TALE OF THE TROUT.** *4611 W New Hope Rd. 501/636-0508.* Hrs: 11:30 am-2 pm, 5-9:30 pm; Sat from 5 pm. Closed Sun; major hols. Private club. Semi-a la carte: dinner $14.95-$22.40. Specializes in trout, quail. Parking. Outdoor dining. Overlooks trout stream. Cr cds: A, C, D, DS, MC, V.

Unrated Dining Spot

WAR EAGLE MILL. *12 mi E on AR 12, then 11/2 mi on County Rd 98; follow signs. 501/789-5343.* Hrs: 8:30 am-5 pm. Closed Thanksgiving, Dec 25. Semi-a la carte: bkfst $1.50-$4.25, lunch $1.75-$4.50. Child's meals. Specializes in biscuits & gravy, buckwheat waffles, beans & cornbread, taco salad. Parking. Reproduction of 1873 mill. Mill products and gift shop. Cr cds: DS, MC, V.

Russellville (B-2)

(See Morrilton, Paris)

Founded 1842 **Pop** 21,260 **Elev** 354 ft **Area code** 501 **Zip** 72801
Information Chamber of Commerce, 708 W Main St; 501/968-2530.

Russellville is the seat of Pope County, a region producing soybeans, peaches and truck crops. The town has several types of manufacturing industries, including shoes, chemicals and rubber products, frozen foods and paper containers. The town is the home of Arkansas Tech University and is also the headquarters for the Ozark and St Francis National Forests.

What to See and Do

Holla Bend National Wildlife Refuge. Late Nov-Feb is best time for viewing ducks and geese; other species include golden and bald eagles, herons, egrets, sandpipers and scissor-tailed flycatchers. Fishing (Mar-Oct). Self-guided auto tour. (Daily) 14 mi SE via AR 7, 155. Phone 501/229-4300. Per vehicle ¢¢

Lake Dardanelle. More than 300-mile shoreline on lake formed by Dardanelle Dam, the largest in Arkansas River Navigation System. NW edge of town on AR 326. On lake is

  Lake Dardanelle State Park. Swimming; fishing; boating (rentals, marina). Bicycling. Hiking and nature trails, miniature golf. Picnicking. Camping (hookups, dump station). Seasonal interpretive programs. Standard fees. (Daily) Phone 501/967-5516. Per vehicle ¢

Mount Nebo State Park. Approx 3,400 acres atop 1,800-ft Mt Nebo, with panoramic view of Arkansas River Valley. The approach to the summit winds up the eastern side of the mountain with several scenic overlooks along the road. From base to top are a series of tight hairpin turns; not recommended for trailers over 15 ft. Swimming pool; fishing (nearby). Bicycling (rentals). Hiking trails, tennis. Picnicking, playground, store. Camping (electric hookups), cabins. Visitor center; museum; exhibits; interpretive programs. Standard fees. (Daily) 4 mi S on AR 7, 7 mi W on AR 155. Phone 800/264-2458. Per vehicle ¢

Nimrod Lake. Reservoir formed by dam on Fourche LaFave River. Swimming, waterskiing; fishing, hunting; boating. Picnicking. Tent & trailer camping (electric hookups, dump station; fee). Quarry Cove, County Line and Sunlight Bay Parks have showers; free camping at Carden Point Park (all yr). (Daily) 28 mi S on AR 7 at Fourche Junction. Phone 501/272-4324. **Free.**

Ozark National Forest. Sparkling waterfalls, lakes, underground caverns, unusual rock formations, oak forests, natural bridges and 500-1,400-foot-deep gorges are features of this 1.1 million-acre forest. Mt Magazine, the highest point in the state at 2,753 feet, is in the southern part of the forest. Swimming; fishing, hunting for deer, turkey & small game; boating. Fees may be charged at recreation sites. (Daily) 20 mi N on AR 7. Contact the Forest Supervisor, 605 W Main, PO Box 1008. Phone 501/968-2354.

Petit Jean State Park (see). 12 mi S on AR 7, then 14 mi E on AR 154.

Potts Tavern/Museum (1850). Former stagecoach stop on the Butterfield Overland mail route between Memphis and Ft Smith. Restored; museum, ladies' hats display. (Sat & Sun) 6 mi SE via I-40, exit 88. ¢

Annual Events

Pope County Fair. Mid-Sept.

Global Fest. Arkansas Tech University. International celebration; performing arts, crafts, concessions. 2nd wkend Oct.

Motel

   ★ ★ **HOLIDAY INN.** *Box 460, Jct AR 7, I-40. 501/968-4300; FAX 501/968-4300, ext. 5018.* 149 units, 2 story. S $51-$61; D $53-$63; each addl $10; under 18 free. Crib free. Pet accepted, some restrictions. TV; cable (premium). Pool. Complimentary coffee in rms. Restaurant 6 am-2 pm, 4-10 pm, Sun from 7 am. Rm serv. Private club 4:30 pm-midnight, closed Sun. Ck-out noon. Meeting rms. Business servs avail. In-rm modem link. Airport transportation. Cr cds: A, C, D, DS, ER, JCB, MC, V.

Searcy (C-3)

(See Greers Ferry Lake Area, Little Rock)

Founded 1860 **Pop** 15,180 **Elev** 264 ft **Area code** 501 **Zip** 72143

Motels

   ✔ ★ **COMFORT INN.** *107 S Rand St. 501/279-9100.* 60 rms, 2 story. S $34-$45; D $38-$45; under 14 free. Crib $5. Pet accepted. TV; cable (premium). Pool. Complimentary continental bkfst, coffee. Restaurant nearby. Ck-out 11 am. Cr cds: A, C, D, DS, ER, JCB, MC, V.

   ★ ★ **HAMPTON INN.** *3204 E Race St. 501/268-0654; res: 800/222-2222; FAX 501/268-0654, ext. 101.* 106 units, 2 story. S $60-$70; D $60-$70; each addl $6; suites $75-$100; under 18 free. Crib free. Pet accepted. TV; cable (premium), VCR avail. Indoor/outdoor pool. Restaurant 6 am-midnight. Rm serv 7 am-10 pm. Ck-out noon. Coin lndry. Meeting rm. Business center. Valet serv. Sundries. Free bus depot transportation. Exercise equipt; weights, bicycles, whirlpool, sauna. Refrigerators. Balconies. Cr cds: A, C, D, DS, ER, MC, V.

Springdale (B-1)

(See Bentonville, Fayetteville, Rogers)

Pop 29,941 **Elev** 1,329 ft **Area code** 501
Information Chamber of Commerce, 700 W Emma Ave, PO Box 166, 72765; 501/751-4694.

Poultry processing is the main industry, but there are colorful and interesting vineyards in the area around this Ozark town. The best are a few miles west on AR 68 near Tontitown, a community settled by Italian immigrants in 1897.

What to See and Do

Arts Center of the Ozarks. Visual and performing arts center. Art gallery (Mon-Fri); concerts; theater productions (fee). 216 W Grove. Phone 501/751-5441.

Shiloh Historic District. Here are the Shiloh Museum, Shiloh Church (1871), Shiloh Memorial Park and early residences. Markers in park show locations of historic Springdale buildings, streets and sites. Johnson and Spring Sts.

Shiloh Museum. The name is derived from original name of settlement and church established in 1840. Native American artifacts, antique photographic equipment, photographs and historic items of northwest Arkansas; log cabin (ca 1855); post office/general store (1871); country doctor's office (ca 1870); farm machinery. (June-Oct, daily exc Mon; rest of yr, Tues-Sat; closed hols) 118 W Johnson Ave. Phone 501/750-8165. **Free.**

Annual Event

Rodeo of the Ozarks. Held in the Arena at Emma Ave & Old Missouri Rd. July 1-4.

Motels

★★**BEST WESTERN HERITAGE INN.** *1394 W Sunset (72764). 501/751-3100.* 100 rms, 2 story. S $45-$56; D $50-$58; each addl $4; suites $68-$78; under 12 free. Crib $6. TV; cable (premium), VCR avail. Indoor pool. Complimentary coffee in lobby. Restaurant adj. Ck-out 11 am. Business servs avail. In-rm modem link. Some in-rm whirlpools. Cr cds: A, C, D, DS, MC, V.

✔★★**EXECUTIVE INN.** *2005 S Hwy 71B (72764). 501/756-6101; res: 800/544-6086; FAX 501/756-6101, ext. 295.* 101 rms, 2 story. S, D $44-$50; each addl $6; under 18 free; higher rates football wkends. Crib free. Pet accepted. TV; cable. Pool. Complimentary coffee in rms. Restaurant 10 am-10 pm. Bar 4 pm-1 am. Ck-out 11 am. Coin lndry. Meeting rms. Cr cds: A, C, D, DS, MC, V.

Hotel

★★★**HOLIDAY INN.** *1500 S 48th St (72762). 501/751-8300; FAX 501/751-4640.* 206 units, 8 story, 22 suites. S, D $82-$99; suites $99-$250; under 18 free; higher rates: U of A football, War Eagle craft show. Crib free. Pet accepted. TV; cable (premium), VCR avail. Indoor pool. Complimentary coffee. Restaurant 6 am-2 pm, 5-10 pm. Bar. Ck-out noon. Coin lndry. Business center. In-rm modem link. Gift shop. Free airport transportation. Exercise equipt; weights, bicycles, whirlpool, sauna. Cr cds: A, C, D, DS, JCB, MC, V.

Restaurants

✔★★**A. Q. CHICKEN HOUSE.** *1 mi N on US 71B. 501/751-4633.* Hrs: 11 am-9 pm. Closed Dec 25. Beer, wine. Semi-a la carte: lunch, dinner $3-$7.95. Child's meals. Specializes in Southern panfried chicken, hickory-smoked steak and ribs. Parking. Fireplaces. Cr cds: A, DS, MC, V.

SC

★★**MARY MAESTRI'S.** *(Hwy 412W, Tontitown 72770) 2 mi W on AR 412. 501/361-2536.* Hrs: 5:30-9:30 pm. Closed major hols. Res accepted. Italian, Amer menu. Beer and Wine. Semi-a la carte: dinner $7.95-$16.95. Child's meals. Own baking, pasta, spumoni. Parking. Antique furniture, oil paintings. Family-owned. Cr cds: A, C, D, DS, MC, V.

D SC

Stuttgart (C-4)

(See Pine Bluff)

Settled 1878 **Pop** 10,420 **Elev** 217 ft **Area code** 501 **Zip** 72160
Information Chamber of Commerce, 507 S Main, PO Box 932; 501/673-1602.

Founded by German immigrants led by Rev Adam Buerkle, Stuttgart is situated on the Mississippi Flyway. Stuttgart is a lively town from November through January, when it is invaded by duck hunters.

What to See and Do

Agricultural Museum of Stuttgart. Displays depict pioneer life and prairie farming; wildlife exhibit; farm equipment, including 25,000-lb steam engine; replica prairie village; scale model of early newspaper office with working printing press; toy collection; scale model of first church in Stuttgart; simulated duck hunt. Agricultural aviation presentation; rice milling exhibit. Slide presentation on modern rice, soybean & fish farming. (Daily exc Mon; closed hols) Under 16 only with adult. 921 E 4th St. Phone 501/673-7001. **Free.**

White River National Wildlife Refuge. More than 113,000-acre bottomland with 165 small lakes. Fishing, hunting for duck, deer, turkey, squirrel, raccoon; boat access. Picnicking. Primitive camping. (Mar-Oct, daily) 25 mi SE on US 165 to De Witt, then 16 mi NE on AR 1 to St Charles. Inquire locally for road conditions. Contact Refuge Manager, PO Box 308, De Witt 72042; 501/946-1468. **Free.**

Annual Event

Wings Over The Prairie Festival. Includes world championship duck calling contest, midway, exhibits, other contests. Thanksgiving wk.

Motel

✔★**TOWN HOUSE.** *701 W Michigan, 6 blks W on US 79. 501/673-2611.* 58 rms, 2 story. S, D $25-$30; higher rates: duck hunting season, golf tournament. Pet accepted. TV; cable. Pool. Restaurant 5 am-8 pm. Ck-out 11 am. Coin lndry. Sundries. Some refrigerators. Cr cds: A, C, D, DS, MC, V.

Texarkana (D-1)

(see Texarkana, TX)

Walnut Ridge (B-4)

(See Jonesboro, Pocahontas)

Pop 4,388 **Elev** 270 ft **Area code** 501 **Zip** 72476
Information Walnut Ridge Area Chamber of Commerce, PO Box 842; 501/886-3232.

What to See and Do

Lake Charles State Park. In the northeastern foothills of the Arkansas Ozarks, this 645-acre lake offers swimming beach; bass, crappie, catfish and bream fishing. Nature trail. Camping (hookups, bathhouse, dump station). Visitor center; interpretive programs (Memorial Day-Labor Day, daily). Standard fees. 2 mi S on US 67, 8 mi W on US 63, 4 mi SW on AR 25. Phone 501/878-6595. Per vehicle ¢

Motel

✔★**ALAMO COURT.** *Box 306, On US 67, 1 mi N of jct US 63, 67. 501/886-2441; res: 800/541-5590; FAX 501/886-6007.* 35 rms. S $30-$34; D $28-$41; each addl $4; under 12 free. Crib $4. Pet accepted. TV; cable. Pool. Playground. Coffee in lobby. Restaurant 6 am-9 pm. Ck-out noon. Meeting rms. Sundries. RV parking, electric hookups. Cr cds: A, C, D, DS, MC, V.

Colorado

Population: 3,294,394

Land area: 103,598 square miles

Elevation: 3,350-14,433 feet

Highest point: Mt Elbert (Lake County)

Entered Union: August 1, 1876 (38th state)

Capital: Denver

Motto: Nothing without Providence

Nickname: Centennial State, Silver State

State flower: Rocky Mountain columbine

State bird: Lark bunting

State tree: Colorado blue spruce

State fair: August 18-September 3, 1996, in Pueblo

Time zone: Mountain

From the eastern plains westward through the highest Rockies, Colorado's terrain is diverse, fascinating and spectacularly beautiful. Highest state in the Union, with an average elevation of 6,800 feet and with 53 peaks above 14,000 feet, the state has attracted sportsmen and vacationers as well as high-technology research and business.

When gold was discovered near present-day Denver in 1858, an avalanche of settlers poured into the state; when silver was discovered soon afterward, a new flood came. Mining camps, usually crude tent cities clinging to the rugged slopes of the Rockies, contributed to Colorado's colorful, robust history. Some of these mines still operate, but most of the early mining camps are ghost towns today. Thousands of newcomers arrive yearly, drawn to Colorado's Rockies by the skiing, hunting, fishing and magnificent scenery.

There are throughout the state deep gorges, rainbow-colored canyons, mysterious mesas and other strange and beautiful landmass variations carved by ancient glaciers and eons of erosion by wind, rain and water. Great mountains of shifting sand lie trapped by the Sangre de Cristo Mountains in Great Sand Dunes National Monument (see); fossils 140 million years old lie in the quarries of Dinosaur National Monument (see).

Spaniards penetrated the area by the mid-1500s. American exploration of the area first took place in 1806, three years after a good portion of the region became American property through the Louisiana Purchase. Leader of the party was Lieutenant Zebulon M. Pike, for whom Pikes Peak is named. Pike pronounced the 14,110-foot mountain unclimbable. Today one may drive to the top on a good gravel highway (first five miles paved). Colorado became a territory in 1861 and earned its "Centennial State" nickname by becoming a state in 1876, 100 years after the signing of the Declaration of Independence.

Colorado produces more tin, molybdenum, uranium, granite, sandstone and basalt than any other state. The mountain area also ranks high in production of coal, gold and silver; the state as a whole has vast deposits of brick clay and oil. Its extensively irrigated plateaus and plains are good grazing lands for stock and rich producers of potatoes, wheat, corn, sugar beets, cauliflower, fruit and flowers.

National Park Service Areas

National monuments include Black Canyon of the Gunnison, Colorado, Dinosaur, Florissant Fossil Beds and Great Sand Dunes (see all), as well as Hovenweep (see CORTEZ). There are also the Curecanti (see GUNNISON) and Arapaho (see GRANBY) national recreation areas. Mesa Verde and Rocky Mountain national parks (see both) and Bent's Old Fort National Historic Site (see LA JUNTA) are also here.

National Forests

The following is an alphabetical listing of National Forests and towns they are listed under.

Arapaho National Forest (see DILLON): Forest Supervisor in Fort Collins; Ranger offices in Denver, Dillon, Granby, Idaho Springs, Kremmling, Morrison*, Silverthorne*.

Grand Mesa National Forest (see GRAND JUNCTION): Forest Supervisor in Delta; Ranger offices in Collbran*, Grand Junction.

Gunnison National Forest (see GUNNISON): Forest Supervisor in Delta; Ranger offices in Gunnison, Paonia*.

Pike National Forest (see COLORADO SPRINGS): Forest Supervisor in Pueblo; Ranger offices in Colorado Springs, Fairplay, Lakewood*.

Rio Grande National Forest (see SOUTH FORK): Forest Supervisor in Monte Vista; Ranger offices in Creede*, Del Norte*, La Jara*, Saguache*.

Roosevelt National Forest (see ESTES PARK): Forest Supervisor in Fort Collins; Ranger offices in Boulder, Fort Collins, Greeley, Pawnee Natl Grassland*.

Routt National Forest (see STEAMBOAT SPRINGS): Forest Supervisor in Steamboat Springs; Ranger offices in Craig, Steamboat Springs, Walden*, Yampa*.

San Isabel National Forest (see PUEBLO): Forest Supervisor in Pueblo; Ranger offices in Cañon City, Leadville.

San Juan National Forest (see DURANGO): Forest Supervisor in Durango; Ranger offices in Bayfield*, Dolores*, Durango, Mancos*, Pagosa Springs.

Uncompahgre National Forest (see NORWOOD): Forest Supervisor in Delta; Ranger offices in Grand Junction, Montrose, Norwood.

White River National Forest (see GLENWOOD SPRINGS): Forest Supervisor in Glenwood Springs; Ranger offices in Aspen, Carbondale*, Dillon, Eagle*, Meeker*, Minturn*, Rifle*, Silverthorne*.

*Not described in text

State Recreation Areas

The following towns list state recreation areas in their vicinity under What to See and Do; refer to the individual town for directions and park information.

Listed under **Burlington:** see Bonny Lake State Park.

Listed under **Delta:** see Crawford and Sweitzer state parks.

Listed under **Denver:** see Chatfield and Cherry Creek state parks.

Listed under **Fort Collins:** see Lory State Park.

Listed under **Fort Morgan:** see Jackson Lake State Park.

Listed under **Golden:** see Golden Gate Canyon State Park.

Listed under **Grand Junction:** see Highline Lake and Island Acres state parks.

Listed under **Loveland:** see Boyd Lake State Park.

Listed under **Montrose:** see Ridgway State Park.

Listed under **Pagosa Springs:** see Navajo State Park.

Listed under **Pueblo:** see Lake Pueblo State Park.

Listed under **Salida:** see Arkansas Headwaters State Recreation Area.

Listed under **Steamboat Springs:** see Steamboat Lake State Park.

Listed under **Trinidad:** see Trinidad Lake State Park.

Listed under **Walsenburg:** see Lathrop State Park.

Water-related activities, hiking, riding, various other sports, picnicking and visitor centers, as well as camping, are available in many of these areas. Interpretive and watchable wildlife programs are available as well. A parks pass is required, good for driver and passengers; annual pass, $30; one-day pass, $3/car. Passes are available at self-service dispensers at all state parks and park offices. Camping is available in most parks. Reservations can be made by phoning 800/678-2267 from 8 am to 5 pm, Monday through Friday. Reservations cost $6.75 and a campground fee of $6-$12 is charged, depending on service offered. Electrical hookups are $3 per night.

Fishing, camping and picnicking are possible in most parks. For further information, or a free *Colorado State Parks Guide,* contact Colorado State Parks, 1313 Sherman #618, Denver 80203; phone 303/866-3437.

Fishing & Hunting

Nonresident fishing licenses: annual $40.25; 5-day, $18.25; 1-day, $5.25; additional one-day stamp, $5; second-rod stamp, $4. Many varieties of trout can be found in Colorado: rainbow and brown in most streams, lakes and in western Colorado River, brook in all mountain streams, and cutthroat in most mountain lakes. Mackinaw can be found in many lakes and reservoirs. Kokanee salmon are also found in many reservoirs.

Nonresident hunting licenses: elk, $250.25; deer, $150.25; small game, $40.25. For information on regulations write the Division of Wildlife, 6060 Broadway, Denver 80216; or phone 303/297-1192.

Skiing

The following towns list ski areas in their vicinity under What to See and Do; refer to the individual town for directions and information.

Listed under **Aspen:** see Aspen Highlands†, Aspen Mountain† and Tiehack/Buttermilk ski areas.

Listed under **Boulder:** see Eldora Mountain Resort†.

Listed under **Breckenridge:** see Breckenridge Ski Area†.

Listed under **Crested Butte:** see Crested Butte Mountain Resort Ski Area†.

Listed under **Dillon:** see Copper Mt Resort† and Keystone Resort† ski areas.

Listed under **Durango:** see Purgatory-Durango Ski Resort†.

Listed under **Georgetown:** see Loveland Ski Area.

Listed under **Glenwood Springs:** see Ski Sunlight Ski Area†.

Listed under **Granby:** see SilverCreek Ski Area.

Listed under **Grand Junction:** see Powderhorn Ski Resort†.

Listed under **Leadville:** see Ski Cooper Ski Area†.

Listed under **Pagosa Springs:** see Wolf Creek Ski Area.

Listed under **Salida:** see Monarch Ski Resort†.

Listed under **Snowmass Village:** see Snowmass Ski Area†.

Listed under **Steamboat Springs:** see Howelsen Hill and Steamboat† ski areas.

Listed under **Telluride:** see Telluride Ski Resort†.

Listed under **Vail:** see Arrowhead at Vail, Beaver Creek† and Vail† ski areas.

Listed under **Winter Park:** see Winter Park Resort.

† Also cross-country trails

For skiing information contact Colorado Ski Country USA, 1560 Broadway, Suite 1440, Denver 80202; phone 303/837-0793.

Safety Belt Information

Safety belts are mandatory for all persons in front seat of vehicle. Children under 4 years and under 40 pounds in weight must be in an approved safety seat anywhere in vehicle. For further information phone 303/239-4500.

Interstate Highway System

The following alphabetical listing of Colorado towns in *Mobil Travel Guide* shows that these cities are within 10 miles of the indicated Interstate highways. A highway map should, however, be checked for the nearest exit.

INTERSTATE 25: Colorado Springs, Denver, Englewood, Fort Collins, Lakewood, Longmont, Loveland, Manitou Springs, Pueblo, Trinidad, Walsenburg.

INTERSTATE 70: Breckenridge, Burlington, Central City, Denver, Dillon, Evergreen, Georgetown, Glenwood Springs, Golden, Grand Junction, Idaho Springs, Lakewood, Limon, Vail.

INTERSTATE 76: Denver, Fort Morgan, Sterling.

Additional Visitor Information

Colorado Outdoors magazine is published 6 times annually by State Department of Wildlife, 6060 Broadway, Denver 80216; phone 303/297-1192. *Colorado, Official State Vacation Guide* is available from

Colorado Tourism Board, 1625 Broadway, Suite 1700, Denver 80202; phone 800/433-2656. A pamphlet on guest ranches is available from the Colorado Dude & Guest Ranch Association, PO Box 300, Tabernash 80478; phone 303/887-3128 or 800/441-6060 (outside CO).

There are six welcome centers in Colorado providing brochures and travel information. Their locations are as follows: I-70 westbound in Burlington; I-70 eastbound in Fruita; US 40 eastbound in Dinosaur; I-25 northbound in Trinidad; US 160/666 northbound in Cortez; US 50 westbound in Lamar.

Gold mining towns abound in Colorado, as they do in many western states. Though not all towns can be reached by passenger cars, Colorado has developed the jeep tour to great advantage. Some information on ghost towns and jeep trips is listed under Breckenridge, Gunnison, Ouray, Salida and Silverton.

Alamosa (F-5)

(See Monte Vista)

Founded 1878 **Pop** 7,579 **Elev** 7,544 ft **Area code** 719 **Zip** 81101

Information Alamosa County Chamber of Commerce, Cole Park; 719/589-3681 or 800/BLU-SKYS.

The settlers who came to the center of the vast San Luis Valley were pleased to find a protected area on the Rio Grande shaded by cottonwood trees and named their new home Alamosa, Spanish for "cottonwood." The little town quickly became a rail, agricultural, mining and educational center. A Ranger District office of the Rio Grande National Forest (see SOUTH FORK) is located in La Jara, 14 mi S on US 285.

What to See and Do

Cole Park. Old Denver and Rio Grande Western narrow-gauge train on display. Chamber of Commerce located in old train station. Tennis. Ice-skating. Picnicking, playgrounds. 425 4th St, on Rio Grande River. **Free.**

Cumbres & Toltec Scenic Railroad, Colorado Limited. Round-trip excursion to Osier, CO, on 1880s narrow-gauge steam railroad. Route passes through backwoods country and mountain scenery; includes the Phantom Canyon and the Toltec Gorge. Warm clothing advised due to sudden weather changes. (Memorial Day-mid-Oct, daily) Also through trips to Chama, NM, via the **New Mexico Express** with van return. Reservations advised. 28 mi S in Antonito. Contact Box 789, Chama, NM 87520, 505/756-2151; or Box 668, Antonito, CO 81120, 719/376-5483. ¢¢¢¢¢

Fort Garland Museum. Army post (1858-83) where Kit Carson held his last command. Restored officer's quarters; collection of Hispanic folk art. (Apr-Oct, daily; rest of yr, Thurs-Mon) Sr citizen rate. 25 mi E on US 160 at Ft Garland. Phone 719/379-3512. ¢

Great Sand Dunes National Monument (see). 35 mi NE via US 160, CO 150.

Annual Events

Sunshine Festival. Cole Park. Arts, crafts, food booths, bands, horse rides, parade, pancake breakfast, contests. Wkend early June.

Alamosa Roundup Rodeo. Late June.

Motels

✔ ★ **BEST WESTERN ALAMOSA INN.** *1919 Main St.* 719/589-2567; FAX 719/589-0767. 121 rms, 2 story. Mid-May-mid-Sept: S $52-$78; D $66-$88; each addl $8; suites $85-$125; under 12 free; lower rates rest of yr. Crib $8. TV; cable. Indoor pool. Restaurant 6 am-10 pm. Bar 4 pm-midnight. Ck-out 11 am. Meeting rms. Business

servs avail. In-rm modem link. Free airport, bus depot transportation. Cr cds: A, C, D, DS, MC, V.

⊠ ⊠ ⚒ SC

★ ★ **HOLIDAY INN.** *333 Santa Fe Ave, just E on US 160.* 719/589-5833; FAX 719/589-4412. 127 rms, 2 story. June-Aug: S $61-$70; D $68-$70; each addl $10; suites $115; under 18 free; lower rates rest of yr. Crib free. TV; cable, VCR avail. Indoor pool; whirlpool, sauna. Restaurant 6 am-10 pm. Rm serv. Bar 5 pm-2 am, Sun to midnight; dancing. Ck-out noon. Coin lndry. Meeting rms. Business servs avail. Gift shop. Free airport, bus depot transportation. Holidome. Game rm. Rec rm. Cr cds: A, C, D, DS, MC, V.

D ⊠ ⊠ ⚒ SC

Inns

★ ★ **COTTONWOOD.** *123 San Juan Ave.* 719/589-3882; res: 800/955-2623; FAX 719/589-6437. 7 air-cooled rms in 2 buildings, 5 with bath, 2 share bath, 2 story, 3 kit. suites. Some rm phones. S $58-$79; D $62-$83; each addl $10-15; kit. units $83. Crib free. TV in sitting rm. Complimentary full bkfst, tea, coffee. Restaurant nearby. Ck-out 11 am, ck-in 4-7 pm. Each rm individually decorated; artwork by area artists. Some antiques. Totally nonsmoking. Cr cds: A, C, D, DS, MC, V.

⊠ ⚒

★ ★ **GREAT SAND DUNES COUNTRY CLUB & INN.** *(5303 Hwy 150, Mosca 81146) 14 mi E on US 160, then 12 mi N on Hwy 150.* 719/378-2356; res: 800/284-9213; FAX 719/378-2428. 15 rms, 1 suite. No rm phones. July-mid-Sept: S, D $180; suite $250; golf plan; lower rates mid-Sept-May; closed Nov. Crib free. TV in sitting rm. Heated pool. Complimentary full bkfst. Dining rm 7:30-10 am, 11:30 am-3 pm, 6-9 pm. Ck-out 11 am, ck-in 3 pm. 18-hole golf privileges; greens fee $65-$85, pro, putting green, driving range. Exercise equipt; weight machine, stair machine, whirlpool, sauna. Massages. Picnic tables. Ranch house built 1889; rustic decor, hand-made furniture. Bison on grounds. Totally nonsmoking. Cr cds: A, DS, MC, V.

D ⚓ ⛷ ⊠ ⛷ ⚒

Restaurant

★ **TRUE GRITS.** *100 Santa Fe Ave, jct US 160 & CO 17.* 719/589-9954. Hrs: 11 am-10 pm. Closed Sun; Dec 25. Res accepted. Bar. Semi-a la carte: lunch $3.29-$8.95, dinner $5.79-$15.99. Child's meals. Specializes in steak. Salad bar. Parking. John Wayne memorabilia. Casual dining. Cr cds: D, MC, V.

Aspen (C-4)

(See Snowmass Village)

Settled 1879 **Pop** 5,049 **Elev** 7,908 ft **Area code** 970 **Zip** 81611

Information Aspen Chamber Resort Association, 425 Rio Grande Place; 800/26-ASPEN.

Seven great silver mines made Aspen a booming camp of 15,000 in 1887. From the Smuggler Mine came a nugget of 93 percent pure silver that weighed 1,840 pounds. The boom ended with the collapse of silver prices in the early 1890s. Aspen nearly became a ghost town when the population at one time dropped to about 700. Largely through the efforts of Walter P. Paepcke, a Chicago industrialist, the city experienced a rebirth as a recreational and cultural center in the late 1940s. Today's resident population is reinforced by thousands of visitors each year. A Ranger District office of the White River National Forest (see GLENWOOD SPRINGS) is located in Aspen.

What to See and Do

Ashcroft Mining Camp. Partially restored ghost town and mining camp features 1880s buildings, hotel. (June-Sept, daily) 10 mi S. Phone 970/925-3721. **Free.**

Aspen Historical Society Museum. Exhibits depict Aspen area history. Historical walking tours (June-Sept). (Early June-Sept & mid-Dec-mid-Apr, Tues-Fri; rest of yr by appt; closed Dec 25) 620 W Bleeker St. Phone 970/925-3721. ¢¢; tours ¢¢¢¢

Recreation. Swimming, fishing, hunting (deer, elk), hiking, climbing, horseback riding, golf, tennis, ice-skating, camping, pack trips, river rafting, kayaking, hang gliding, paragliding, sailplaning, ballooning. There are 1,000 miles of trout streams and 25 lakes within a 20-mile radius of Aspen, plus many more in the surrounding mountains. More than 10 public campgrounds. Contact the Aspen Chamber Resort Association for details.

River rafting. Reservations necessary.

River Rats, Inc. Scenic river, fishing, float, whitewater and extended wilderness trips on the Roaring Fork, Arkansas, Colorado, Dolores, Gunnison and Green rivers. (Mid-May-mid-Sept) Transportation to site. Phone 970/925-7648. ¢¢¢¢¢

Blazing Paddles. Half-day, full-day and overnight trips on the Arkansas, Roaring Fork, Colorado, Gunnison and Dolores rivers. Trips range from scenic floats for beginners to exciting runs for experienced rafters. (May-Sept) Transportation to site. Phone 970/925-5651. ¢¢¢¢¢

Scenic drive to Independence Pass. A 12,095-ft pass in magnificent mountain scenery. (June-Oct; road closed rest of yr) SE on CO 82.

Skiing. Four of five and six of seven multi-day tickets purchased at any Aspen ski area are interchangeable at the four areas. For information on cross-country trails, phone the Aspen Cross-Country Center, 970/925-2145 or the Snowmass Club Touring Center, 970/923-3148.

Aspen Mountain. Gondola, 3 quad, 4 double chairlifts; patrol, school; snowmaking; restaurants, bars. 76 runs; longest run 3 mi; vertical drop 3,267 ft. (Late Nov-early Apr, daily) Cross-country skiing, ice-skating (all yr), snowmobiling, sleigh rides. Shuttle bus service to Buttermilk, Aspen Highlands and Snowmass. Racquetball, squash, swimming, tennis. In town. Phone 970/925-1220 or 800/525-6200; snow conditions 970/925-1221. ¢¢¢¢¢

Buttermilk. 1 quad, 5 double chairlifts, Mitey-mite, surface lift; patrol, school, rentals; snowmaking; cafeteria, restaurants, bar; nursery. 45 runs; longest run 3 mi; vertical drop 2,030 ft. (Late Nov-early Apr, daily) Shuttle bus service from Aspen and Snowmass. 2 mi W on CO 82. Phone 800/525-6200; snow conditions 970/925-1221. ¢¢¢¢¢

Snowmass. 12 mi NW (see SNOWMASS VILLAGE).

Aspen Highlands. 2 quads, 5 double chairlifts, 2 Pomalifts; patrol, school, rentals; snowmaking; 2 restaurants, bar. 78 runs; longest run 3.5 mi; vertical drop 3,600 ft. (Late Nov-mid-Apr, daily) Cross-country skiing, snow boarding. Shuttle bus service to and from Aspen. Half-day rates. 1½ mi SW on Maroon Creek Rd in White River National Forest (see GLENWOOD SPRINGS). Phone 970/925-1220 or 800/356-8811. ¢¢¢¢¢

Annual Events

Winterskol Carnival. Jan 10-14.

Fall Fling. Sept 15-17.

Seasonal Events

Aspen Music Festival. Aspen Music Tent, Wheeler Opera House and Harris Concert Hall. Symphonies, chamber music concerts, opera, jazz. Phone 970/925-9042. Late June-late Aug.

DanceAspen. Performances Thurs-Sat evenings. Phone 970/925-7718. July-mid-Aug.

Motels

(Because of the altitude, air conditioning is rarely necessary. Hours and dates open may vary during off-season, making it advisable to call ahead.)

★ **ASPEN BED & BREAKFAST.** *311 W Main St.* 970/925-7650; FAX 970/925-5744. 38 rms, 4 story. No elvtr. Late Nov-mid-Apr: S, D $144-$189; under 12 free; ski plan; lower rates rest of yr. Closed mid-Apr-late May. Crib $5. TV; cable (premium), VCR avail. Heated pool; whirlpool. Complimentary coffee in rms. Complimentary buffet bkfst. Restaurant nearby. Ck-out 11 am. Free ski area transportation. Downhill/x-country ski 6 blks. Refrigerators, wet bars. 4-story river rock fireplace. Some balconies. Cr cds: A, D, DS, MC, V.

⊠ ≊ 🔥 SC

★ **ASPEN MANOR.** *411 S Monarch St.* 970/925-3001; res: 800/925-6343. 22 rms. No A/C. S, D $75-$160; each addl $5-$15; under 12 free. Crib free. TV; cable. Heated pool; whirlpool, sauna (winter only). Complimentary continental bkfst. Restaurant nearby. Ck-out 10 am. Downhill/x-country ski 2 blks. Refrigerators. Park opp. Cr cds: A, MC, V.

⊠ ≊ 🔽 🔥

★★ **BOOMERANG LODGE.** *500 W Hopkins.* 970/925-3416; res: 800/992-8852; FAX 970/925-3314. 35 units, 2-3 story, 11 kits. No elvtr. No A/C. S, D $168-$236; each addl $10; studio rms $197-$222; 2-3-bedrm apts $388-$502; under 12 free (summer); higher rates Dec 25. Crib $4. TV; cable, VCR avail. Heated pool; whirlpool, sauna. Complimentary continental bkfst, tea in winter. Restaurant nearby. Ck-out 11 am. Guest lndry. Business servs avail. Free downtown transportation. Downhill/x-country ski 5 blks. Some refrigerators, fireplaces. Private patios, balconies. Garden picnic area. Cr cds: A, D, MC, V.

D ⊠ ≊ 🔽 🔥

★★★ **INN AT ASPEN.** *38750 W CO 82, near Sardy Field.* 970/925-1500; res: 800/952-1515; FAX 970/925-9037. 118 studio units with kit., 2 story. S, D $130-$220; each addl $10; suites $210-$425; under 13 free; higher rates Christmas hols. TV; cable (premium). Heated pool; poolside serv. Restaurant 7 am-9:30 pm (in season). Rm serv. Bar 11 am-11 pm. Ck-out 11 am. Meeting rms. Business servs avail. In-rm modem link. Bellhops. Valet serv. Free airport transportation. Downhill/x-country ski on site. Exercise rm; instructor, weights, bicycles, whirlpool, sauna. Massage therapy. Hiking, bicycle trails. Game rm. Refrigerators. Private patios, balconies. Picnic tables. Cr cds: A, C, D, DS, MC, V.

D ⊠ ≊ ✈ ✕ 🔽 🔥 SC

★★ **INNSBRUCK INN.** *233 W Main, 5 blks W on CO 82.* 970/925-2980; FAX 970/925-6960. 31 rms, some A/C, 2 story. Late Nov-mid-Apr: S, D $90-$175; each addl $15; suites (to 4 persons) $225; under 16, $7; higher rates Christmas hols; lower rates rest of yr. Closed mid-Apr-early June. Crib free. TV; cable. Heated pool; whirlpool, sauna. Complimentary buffet bkfst. Restaurant nearby. Ck-out 11 am. Downhill/x-country ski ½ mi. Some refrigerators. Cr cds: A, C, D, DS, MC, V.

⊠ ≊ 🔽 🔥

✔★ **LIMELITE LODGE.** *228 E Cooper.* 970/925-3025; res: 800/433-0832; FAX 970/925-5120. 63 rms, 34 A/C, 29 air-cooled, 1-3 story. No elvtr. Dec-Mar: S, D $68-$168; each addl $10; under 12 free; ski package; varied lower rates rest of yr. Pet accepted. TV; cable (premium), VCR avail. 2 heated pools; whirlpool, sauna. Playground opp. Complimentary continental bkfst. Restaurant nearby. Ck-out 10:30 am, noon in summer. Coin lndry. Downhill ski 3 blks. Refrigerators. Cr cds: A, C, D, DS, MC, V.

D ✔ ⊠ ≊ 🔽 🔥 SC

★★ **MOLLY GIBSON LODGE.** *101 W Main St.* 970/925-3434; res: 800/356-6559; FAX 970/925-2582. 50 rms, 2 story, 7 kits. Early Jan-early Apr: S, D $139-$349; each addl $10; suites $239-$349; lower rates rest of yr. Crib free. TV; cable, VCR (movies avail $3). 2

heated pools; 2 whirlpools. Complimentary continental bkfst. Restaurant nearby. Bar 4-9 pm in winter. Ck-out 10 am. Meeting rm. Business servs avail. Bellhops. Valet serv. Free airport transportation. Downhill/x-country ski 6 blks. Bicycle rentals. Refrigerators; some in-rm whirlpools. Cr cds: A, C, D, DS, MC, V.

⊠ ⊠ 🐾 SC

Motor Hotels

★ ★ ★ **ASPEN MEADOWS.** *845 Meadows Rd, on grounds of Aspen Institute, near Sardy Field. 970/925-4240; res: 800/452-4240; FAX 970/925-7790.* 98 units in 6 bldgs (58 with shower only), 58 suites. No A/C. Jan-Mar: S, D $195-$235; each addl $20; suites $265-$395; under 16 free; lower rates rest of yr. Crib $20. Garage parking $4. TV; cable (premium), VCR. Complimentary coffee in rms. Restaurant 7-9 am, noon-2 pm, 6-9 pm. Rm serv. Bar 3-10 pm. Ck-out 11 am. Meeting rms. Business servs avail. In-rm modem link. Bellhops. Sundries. Valet serv. Free airport, ski area transportation. Tennis. 18-hole golf privileges. Downhill/x-country ski 1 mi. Exercise rm; instructor, weight machine, treadmill, whirlpool, steam rm. Masseur, Mountain bike rentals. Wet bars. Balconies. Picnic tables. On 40-acres; Bauhaus-style architecture. Cr cds: A, C, D, DS, MC, V.

D 🐾 ⊠ 🎿 🏂 ⊠ ✈ ⊠ ⊠ 🐾 SC

★ ★ **ASPEN SQUARE.** *617 E Cooper. 970/925-1000; res: 800/862-7736; FAX 970/925-1017.* 105 air-cooled condo apts with kit., 3-4 story. Feb-Mar: D $259-$411; each addl (after 4th person) $15; higher rates Christmas; lower rates rest of yr. Crib free. TV; cable (premium), VCR. Heated pool. Restaurant adj 7:30 am-3:30 pm. Ck-out 10 am. Coin lndry. Meeting rms. Business servs avail. In-rm modem link. Bellhops. Concierge. Free garage parking. Downhill ski adj; x-country ski 1 mi. Exercise equipt; bicycles, stair machines, whirlpool. Balconies. Cr cds: A, MC, V.

⊠ ⊠ 🏂 ✈ ⊠ 🐾

★ ★ **HOTEL ASPEN.** *110 W Main St. 970/925-3441; res: 800/527-7369; FAX 970/920-1379.* 45 rms, 2-3 story. No elvtr. Feb 11-Mar 26: D $169-$249; each addl $20; under 13 free; higher rates hols; lower rates rest of yr. Crib free. TV; cable, VCR avail. Heated pool; whirlpool. Complimentary continental bkfst. Ck-out 11 am. Free ski shuttle. Downhill ski 8 blks. Refrigerators, wet bars. Cr cds: A, C, D, DS, MC, V.

⊠ ⊠ ⊠ 🐾 SC

★ **SNOWFLAKE INN.** *221 E Hyman Ave. 970/925-3221; res: 800/247-2069; FAX 970/925-8740.* 38 air-cooled kit. units, 3 story, 28 suites. No elvtr. Late Nov-mid-Apr: S, D $139-$189; each addl $20; suites $159-$525; under 18 free; summer wkly rates; lower rates rest of yr. Crib free. TV; cable (premium), VCR avail. Heated pool; whirlpool, sauna. Complimentary continental bkfst in winter. Complimentary coffee in rms. Restaurant nearby. Ck-out 10 am. Coin lndry. Business servs avail. Bellhops. Valet serv. Airport transportation in winter. Downhill ski 2½ blks; x-country ski 3½ blks. Some fireplaces. Grills. Cr cds: A, C, D, DS, MC, V.

⊠ ⊠ ⊠ 🐾 SC

Hotels

★ ★ ★ **HOTEL JEROME.** *330 E Main St. 970/920-1000; res: 800/331-7213; FAX 970/925-2784.* One of Colorado's grand hotels since 1889, the Jerome is grandly Victorian. The sumptuous public areas sport five kinds of wallpapers; guest rooms are individually decorated with period pieces. 93 rms, 3-4 story. Mid-Nov-mid-Mar: S, D $245-$450; suites $395-$1,650; lower rates rest of yr. Garage $10. TV; cable (premium), VCR (movies avail $6). Heated pool; poolside serv. Restaurant 7 am-10 pm (also see JEROME). Rm serv 24 hrs. Bar noon-2 am (bar menu to midnight). Ck-out 11 am. Meeting rms. Business servs avail. In-rm modem link. Concierge. Gift shop. Free airport transportation; also ski transportation. Downhill/x-country ski 4 blks.

Exercise equipt; weight machines, treadmill, whirlpools. Bathrm phones, refrigerators. Cr cds: A, C, D, MC, V.

D ⊠ ⊠ 🎿 ⊠ 🐾 SC

★ ★ ★ ★ **LITTLE NELL.** *675 E Durant Ave. 970/920-4600; res: 800/525-6200; FAX 970/920-4670.* Aspen's only true ski-in, ski-out hotel has upscale, rustic mountain lodge decor: exposed beams, stripped pine gate leg table and oatmeal carpet in the guest rooms, and luxurious bathrooms. Atmosphere is noticeably warm thanks to an unusually helpful, friendly staff. 92 rms, 4 story, 13 suites. S, D $240-$485; suites $475-$2,300; higher rates winter. Crib free. Pet accepted. Garage; valet parking $12. TV; cable (premium), VCR avail (movies avail $4.95). Heated pool; poolside serv. Restaurant (see RESTAURANT AT LITTLE NELL). Bar 3 pm-midnight; entertainment Thurs-Sat. Ck-out noon. Meeting rms. Business servs avail. In-rm modem link. Concierge. Shopping arcade. Free airport transportation. Ski shuttle to other mountains. Downhill ski on site. Exercise rm; instructor, weights, bicycles, whirlpool, steam rm. Massage. Bathrm phones, refrigerators, minibars, gas fireplaces. Cr cds: A, C, D, DS, JCB, MC, V.

D 🐾 ⊠ ⊠ 🎿 ⊠ 🐾

★ ★ ★ ★ **THE RITZ-CARLTON, ASPEN.** *315 E Dean St. 970/920-3300; FAX 970/925-8998.* The reception area of this imposing red-brick hotel at the base of Aspen Mountain hosts antique clocks, crystal chandeliers, and a $5 million art collection. Guest quarters are more casual but still posh. 257 rms, 6 story. Early Jan-late Mar & early June-early Oct: S, D $295-$525; each addl $25; suites $595; under 18 free; ski plans; lower rates rest of yr. Crib free. Pet accepted. Valet parking $17. TV; cable (premium), VCR avail (movies avail). Heated pool; poolside serv (summer). Supervised child's activities (Nov-mid-Apr); ages 3-16. Restaurants 6:30 am-11 pm. Rm serv 24 hrs. Bar 11-1 am; entertainment. Ck-out noon. Convention facilities. Business center. Concierge. Gift shop. Beauty shop. Free airport transportation. Golf privileges. Downhill ski 2 blks, x-country ski 2 mi; rental equipt. Hiking. Bicycles (rentals). Exercise rm; instructor, weight machine, bicycles, whirlpools, saunas, steam rms. Masseuse. Bathrm phones, minibars. Some balconies. Luxury level. Cr cds: A, C, D, DS, ER, JCB, MC, V.

D 🐾 ⊠ ⊠ 🎿 🏂 ⊠ ✈ ⊠ ⊠ 🐾

Inns

★ ★ **CRESTAHAUS.** *1301 E Cooper Ave. 970/925-7081; res: 800/344-3853; FAX 970/925-1610.* 31 rms, 2 story. No A/C. Late Nov-early Apr: S, D $125-$175; each addl $20; higher rates winter hols; lower rates rest of yr. Crib free. Pet accepted, some restrictions; $10 per day. TV; cable, VCR avail. Pool; whirlpool, sauna. Complimentary continental bkfst. Restaurant nearby. Ck-out 11 am, ck-in 3 pm. Coin lndry. Meeting rm. Business servs avail. Local airport transportation. Downhill/x-country ski 7 blks. Health club privileges. Lounge with fireplace. Cr cds: D, MC, V.

D 🐾 ⊠ ⊠ ✈ 🐾

★ ★ **HOTEL LENADO.** *200 S Aspen St. 970/925-6246; res: 800/321-3457; FAX 970/925-3840.* 19 rms, 2 story. Mid-Dec-mid-Apr: S, D $219-$329; higher rates winter hols; lower rates rest of yr. TV; cable (premium), VCR avail. Complimentary full bkfst, afternoon refreshments. Bar 4 pm-midnight. Ck-out noon, ck-in 4 pm. Meeting rms. Business servs avail. Bellhops. Valet serv. Concierge. Downhill/x-country ski 6 blks. Hot tub. Some refrigerators, in-rm whirlpools, wet bars. Balconies. Library. Cr cds: A, D, MC, V.

⊠ 🐾

★ ★ ★ ★ **SARDY HOUSE.** *128 E Main St. 970/920-2525; res: 800/321-3457; FAX 970/920-4478.* A winding staircase with a magnificent oak balustrade leads to the beautifully appointed guest rooms of this 1892 house, which offer panoramic views of the mountains. 20 units, 3 story. Mid-Nov-mid-Apr: D $240-$300; suites $375-$550; higher rates winter hols; lower rates rest of yr. TV; cable (premium), VCR avail. Pool; whirlpool, sauna, poolside serv. Free full bkfst. Dining rm 7:30-10:30 am, 6-9:30 pm. Rm serv. Bar 3:30 pm-midnight. Ck-out noon, ck-in 4 pm. Business servs avail. Concierge. Downhill/x-country ski 5 blks. Health club privileges. Some refrigerators, bathrm phones, in-rm steam baths. Cr cds: A, D, MC, V.

✒ ★ **ULLR LODGE.** *520 W Main St. 970/925-7696; FAX 970/920-4339.* 24 units, 2 story, 13 kits. No A/C. Mid-Nov-early Apr: S, D $110-$230; each addl $10; higher rates hols; lower rates rest of yr. Crib $6. TV; cable (premium). Pool; whirlpools. Complimentary continental bkfst in summer, full bkfst in winter. Restaurant nearby. Ck-out 10 am, ck-in 3 pm. Coin lndry. Downhill/x-country ski 1 mi. Rec rm. Some refrigerators. Cr cds: A, D, MC, V.

Restaurants

(A city ordinance bans smoking in all restaurants within the city limits of Aspen.)

★ ★ ★ **ABETONE.** *620 E Hyman. 970/925-9022.* Hrs: 6-10:30 pm. Closed Sun, Mon; also mid-Apr-June & Oct-Thanksgiving. Res accepted Tues-Sat. Northern Italian menu. Bar. Wine cellar. Semi-a la carte: dinner $9.75-$30. Specializes in lobster, pasta, veal. Outdoor dining. Casual elegance. Cr cds: A, MC, V.

D

★ **ASPEN GROVE.** *525 E Cooper. 970/925-6162.* Hrs: 7:30 am-10 pm. No A/C. Continental menu. Bar. Semi-a la carte: bkfst, lunch $3.75-$8, dinner $10-$19. Child's meals. Specializes in egg dishes, pasta, seafood. Outdoor dining. Casual. Cr cds: MC, V.

D

★ ★ **CACHE CACHE.** *205 S Mill St. 970/925-3835.* Hrs: 5:30-10 pm. Closed mid-Apr-May, Oct-Nov. Res accepted. No A/C. French menu. Bar. Semi-a la carte: dinner $14-$24. Specialties: osso bucco on risotto cake with Marsala sauce, salmon. Patio dining. Casual dining. Cr cds: A, MC, V.

✒ ★ **CANTINA.** *411 E Main St. 970/925-3663.* Hrs: 11 am-10:30 pm. Mexican, Amer menu. Bar to 1 am. Semi-a la carte: lunch, dinner $4.95-$15.95. Child's meals. Specialties: quesadilla vegetarian, cantina camarones, chimichanga, chile rellenos. Outdoor dining. Mexican decor. Cr cds: A, MC, V.

D

★ ★ **THE CHART HOUSE.** *219 E Durant Ave. 970/925-3525.* Hrs: 5:30-10 pm. Res accepted. Bar. Semi-a la carte: dinner $12.95-$30. Child's meals. Specializes in prime rib, seafood, steak, mud pie. Salad bar. Parking. Cr cds: A, D, DS, MC, V.

★ ★ **THE GRILL ON THE PARK.** *307 S Mill St. 970/920-3700.* Hrs: 11:30 am-11 pm. Bar. Semi-a la carte: lunch $6.95-$10.50, dinner $6.95-$23.50. Specializes in Southwestern & Oriental cuisine. Outdoor dining. On mall; overlooks Wagner Park. Cr cds: A, MC, V.

D

★ **GUIDO'S.** *Cooper & Galena. 970/925-7222.* Hrs: 10 am-3 pm, 5:30-10 pm. Winter months from 5:30 pm. Closed mid-Apr-mid-June & Oct-Thanksgiving. Res accepted. Swiss, French menu. Bar. Semi-a la carte: lunch $5.75-$11, dinner $16-$26. Child's meals. Specialties: Wienerschnitzel, filet mignon, fondues. Outdoor dining. European chalet decor; scenic view of mountains. Family-owned. Cr cds: A, DS, MC, V.

D SC

★ ★ **JEROME.** *(See Hotel Jerome) 970/920-1000.* Hrs: 7 am-10 pm. Res accepted. Bar noon-2 am. Semi-a la carte: bkfst $4-$14.50, lunch $6.95-$14, dinner $18.50-$29.50. Specializes in fresh fish, rack of lamb. Classical music in summer, jazz in winter. Valet parking. Outdoor dining. Antiques. Cr cds: A, C, D, MC, V.

D

✒ ★ ★ **LA COCINA.** *308 E Hopkins. 970/925-9714.* Hrs: 5-10 pm. Closed Dec 25; also mid-Apr-May, Nov. No A/C. Mexican menu. Bar. Semi-a la carte: dinner $6.50-$10.75. Child's meals. Specializes in posole, blue corn tortillas. Outdoor dining. No cr cds accepted.

★ **MAIN STREET BAKERY & CAFE.** *201 E Main St. 970/925-6446.* Hrs: 7 am-9:30 pm; wkend hrs vary. Closed Thanksgiving, Dec 25. No A/C. Wine, beer. Semi-a la carte: bkfst $4.75-$8.95, lunch $3.75-$10.95, dinner $8.95-$16.95. Child's meals. Specializes in cinnamon raisin french toast, grilled chicken with artichoke garlic sauce. Own breads, desserts. Parking. Outdoor dining in shaded courtyard. Totally nonsmoking. Cr cds: A, MC, V.

D SC

★ ★ **MOTHERLODE.** *314 E Hyman. 970/925-7700.* Hrs: 5:30-10:30 pm. Closed Thanksgiving, Dec 25; also mid-Apr-May, mid-Oct-Thanksgiving. Italian menu. Bar to 1:30 am. Semi-a la carte: dinner $11-$22. Specializes in pasta, seafood. Outdoor dining. Casual dining. Family-owned. Cr cds: A, DS, MC, V.

D

★ ★ ★ **PIÑON'S.** *105 S Mill St. 970/920-2021.* Exotic food is right at home in the outstanding atmosphere of this restaurant with mountain views. The ranch decor consists of a leather bar, columns of stripped timbers, a pressed tin ceiling, and unfinished pine millwork. Hrs: 6-10 pm. Closed mid-Apr-mid-June, Oct-mid-Nov. Res required. Bar. A la carte entrees: dinner $22-$35. Specialties: lobster strudel, ahi sautéed with macadamia nut breading and lime butter, elk tournedos sautéed with ginger and a pink peppercorn sauce. Own baking. Cr cds: A, MC, V.

★ ★ **PINE CREEK COOKHOUSE.** *Aspen mailing address: 310 AABC, 2 mi W on CO 82, then continue 12 mi on Castle Creek Rd, in old abandoned mining town of Ashcroft. 970/925-1044.* Sittings: noon & 1:30 pm, 6 & 8:30 pm. Winter hrs vary. Closed May & Oct-mid-Nov. Res required. No A/C. Continental menu. Bar. Semi-a la carte: lunch $8.95-$14.95, dinner $19-$32. Specialties: rainbow trout, cold cherry soup, rack of lamb, Hungarian dishes. Salad bar (lunch). Parking. Outdoor dining. Unique dining in cabin located in a scenic valley in the Elk Mountains (elev 9,800 ft); overlooks Castle Creek. Arrive via x-country ski trail or horse-drawn sleigh in winter ($20 per person). Totally nonsmoking. Cr cds: A, MC, V.

★ ★ ★ **POPPIES BISTRO CAFE.** *834 W Hallam. 970/925-2333.* Hrs: 6-10:30 pm. Closed mid-Apr-mid-June & late Oct-mid-Nov. Res accepted. No A/C. Continental menu. Bar. Wine cellar. Semi-a la carte: dinner $22-$35. Specialties: shrimp remoulade, steak au poivre, lamb chops, sautéed soft shell crabs. Own baking, pasta. Parking. Intimate dining in Victorian house (1889). Period furnishings; antiques. Cr cds: A, MC, V.

★ ★ ★ **RENAISSANCE.** *304 E Hopkins. 970/925-2402.* The American cuisine here has French and Oriental accents and is served in a cozy, white-walled room with southwestern decor, pink tablecloths, and abstract sculpture. The wine room has 1,000 bottles of wine. Hrs: 6-10:30 pm. Res accepted. Modern French menu. Bar. Extensive wine list. A la carte entrees: dinner $24-$32. Child's meals. Specialties: escargot, caesar ravioli, fresh sautéed foie gras. Menu changes nightly. Own baking. Valet parking. Outdoor dining. Cr cds: A, MC, V.

D

★ ★ ★ **RESTAURANT AT LITTLE NELL.** *(See Little Nell Hotel) 970/920-4600.* An elegant bilevel room overlooks a snowscape of the Aspen mountain gondolas during the winter season. Diners are seated in cushioned armchairs in this romantic, wood-trimmed restaurant. Hrs: 7-10:30 am, 11:30 am-2:30 pm, 6-10 pm; Fri & Sat to 10:30 pm; afternoon tea 3-6 pm; Sun brunch 11:30 am-2:30 pm. Res accepted. Oriental-influenced cuisine. Bar 3 pm-2 am. Extensive wine cellar. A la carte entrees: bkfst $7-$12.50, lunch $9-$19, dinner $19-$33. 3-course dinner $33. Sun brunch $19-$24. Specialties: charred tuna steak, rack of lamb. Valet parking. Outdoor dining (seasonal). Cr cds: A, C, D, DS, JCB, MC, V.

D

★ ★ ★ **SYZYGY.** *520 E Hyman Ave, 2nd fl.* 970/925-3700. Hrs: 6-10 pm. Closed mid-Apr-May. Res accepted. Bar. A la carte entrees: dinner $22-$34. Specializes in fresh fish, rack of lamb, pasta. Own pastries. Blues/Jazz band Wed-Sun. Art deco decor; water wall fountains. Cr cds: A, D, DS, MC, V.

D

✔ ★ ★ **WIENERSTUBE.** *633 E Hyman.* 970/925-3357. Hrs: 7 am-2:30 pm. Closed Mon. Continental menu. Bar. Semi-a la carte: bkfst $1.75-$9.95, lunch $2-$18.95. Child's meals. Daily European specialties. Outdoor dining. Cr cds: A, D, DS, MC, V.

D

Unrated Dining Spots

BOOGIES. *534 E Cooper Ave.* 970/925-6610. Hrs: 8 am-10 pm. Closed mid-Apr-mid-June. Bar 11 am-closing. Semi-a la carte: bkfst $3.75-$5.95, lunch, dinner $1.95-$6.95. Child's meals. Specializes in meat loaf. Diner. Cr cds: MC, V.

D

CRYSTAL PALACE DINNER THEATER. *300 E Hyman.* 970/925-1455; FAX 970/920-9664. Hrs: 5:30 pm-12:30 am (winter); 7:30-11:30 pm (summer); wkends 5:30 pm-12:30 am. Closed Sun & Mon (summer); also mid-Apr-mid-Jun & Sept-Nov. Res required. Continental menu. Bar. Complete meals: dinner $45. Serv charge 18%. Child's meals. Specializes in prime rib, salmon Béarnaise, rack of lamb. Dinner theater. Victorian decor. Cr cds: A, C, D, DS, MC, V.

Aurora (B-6)

(see Denver International Airport Area)

Beaver Creek (C-4)

(see Vail)

Black Canyon of the Gunnison National Monument (D-3)

(For accommodations see Montrose)

(12 mi NE of Montrose via US 50, CO 347)

Within this monument 12 of the most spectacular miles of the rugged gorge of the Gunnison River slice down to a maximum depth of 2,700 feet. At one point the river channel is only 40 feet wide. Narrowest width between north and south rims at the top is 1,100 feet. The combination of dark, weathered rock and lack of sunlight due to the narrowness of the canyon give the monument its name.

Piñon trees, some more than 500 years old, add to the spectacular scenery, along with numerous mule deer. There are scenic drives along South Rim (road plowed to Gunnison Point in winter) and North Rim (approx May-Oct). There are also hiking areas and concessions (June-Labor Day). The visitor center (spring-fall) is located at Gunnison Point on the South Rim. A descent into the canyon requires a free hiking permit from visitor center. Cross-country skiing is open in winter from Gunnison Point to High Point. Interpretive programs are offered

(summer only). For information contact Superintendent, 2233 E Main St, Suite A, Montrose 81401; 970/249-1915. Per car ¢¢

Boulder (B-5)

(See Denver, Longmont, Lyons)

Settled 1858 **Pop** 83,312 **Elev** 5,344 ft **Area code** 303
Information Convention & Visitors Bureau, 2440 Pearl St, 80302; 303/442-2911 or 800/444-0447.

This is the only city in the US that obtains part of its water supply from a city-owned glacier, Arapaho Glacier, 28 miles west. Boulder's location at the head of a rich agricultural valley and the base of the Rocky Mountains gives it an ideal year-round climate. The city's unique greenbelt system serves as both a buffer to preserve its picturesque setting and as an extensive park system for outdoor enthusiasts.

Considered the technical and scientific center of Colorado, Boulder is home to the laboratories of the National Institute of Standards and Technology, the National Center for Atmospheric Research and many private high-technology companies.

Like many cities in Colorado, Boulder enjoys a wealth of cultural activity, including a symphony, music and dance festivals, and outdoor performances of Shakespeare on summer evenings.

A Ranger District office of the Roosevelt National Forest (see ESTES PARK) is located in Boulder.

What to See and Do

Boulder Art Center. Exhibits of contemporary and regional painting, sculpture, other media; emphasis on cutting edge Colorado art. Lectures, workshops and special events. (Daily exc Mon; closed some hols) Donation. 1750 13th St. Phone 303/443-2122.

Boulder Laboratories of the National Institute of Standards and Technology, National Oceanic and Atmospheric Administration and National Telecommunications & Information Administration. Offices (Mon-Fri; closed hols). Self-guided tours during office hours. Guided tours include video, demonstration of low-temperature phenomena; visit to NIST atomic clock, NOAA solar forecast center. Tours (June-Aug, Tues & Thurs; rest of yr, Thurs) 325 Broadway. Phone 303/497-3244. **Free.**

Boulder Museum of History. Collections of Boulder history from 1858 to the present; permanent and rotating interpretive exhibits; educational programs. (Tues-Sat afternoons) Harbeck House (1899), 1206 Euclid Ave. Phone 303/449-3464. ¢

Boulder Reservoir. Swimming (Memorial Day-Labor Day, daily), waterskiing; fishing; boating (daily; get permit for power boat at main gate), rentals. Picnicking. (Daily) 2 mi N on CO 119. Phone 303/441-3461 or -3468. ¢¢

Downtown Mall. Pedestrian shopping mall offers fine shops and restaurants, acrobatic shows, mime performances, strolling musicians; periodic art and cultural festivals. Pearl St between 11th & 15th Sts.

National Center for Atmospheric Research. Designed by I.M. Pei. Exhibits on global warming, weather, the sun, aviation hazards, and supercomputing. Also 400-acre nature preserve on site. Guided tours (summer, Mon-Sat afternoons; rest of yr, Wed only). (Daily) 1850 Table Mesa Dr. Phone 303/497-1174 (recording). **Free.**

Skiing. Eldora Mountain Resort. 5 chairlifts, 2 surface lifts; patrol, school, rentals; snowmaking; cafeteria, bar; nursery. 43 runs; longest run 2 mi; vertical drop 1,400 ft. (Mid-Nov-early Apr) Cross-country skiing (27 mi), night skiing (Jan-mid-Mar, Thurs-Sat). 21 mi W on CO 119 near Nederland. Phone 303/440-8700. ¢¢¢¢¢

University of Colorado (1876). (25,000 students) Tours of campus. Phone 303/492-1411. On the 786-acre campus, the distinctive native sandstone and red-tile buildings include Old Main, Norlin Library and

University of Colorado Museum. Displays relics and artifacts of early human life in the area, plus regional geological, zoological and botanical collections. Changing exhibits. (Daily; closed university hols) Broadway and 15th St, in Henderson Bldg. Phone 303/492-6892. **Free.**

Fiske Planetarium and Science Center. Programs using a new computerized control system giving a three-dimensional effect; science classes for all ages, special events (fees). Lobby exhibits. Phone 303/492-5001. Planetarium **¢¢**

Sommers-Bausch Observatory. Star gazing. (Weather permitting, school yr exc university hols) Reservations necessary Fri. Phone 303/492-5001. **Free.**

Macky Auditorium Concert Hall. Artist Series, guest artists, Boulder Philharmonic Orchestra. Concerts during school yr. 17th St and University Ave. For ticket information phone 303/492-6309.

Annual Events

Kinetic Conveyance Sculpture Challenge. People-powered sculpture race across land and water. Early May.

Bolder Boulder. 10 km race. Includes citizens race and world class heats. Phone 303/444-7223. Memorial Day.

Seasonal Events

Colorado Music Festival. Chautauqua Park, 900 Baseline Rd. Entertainment, lectures. Phone 303/449-1397. 8 wks, June-Aug.

Colorado Shakespeare Festival. Mary Rippon Outdoor Theater, University of Colorado. Three Shakespeare plays in repertory. Phone 303/492-1527 (information) or -8181 (tickets). July-Aug.

Motels

★ ★ ★ **COURTYARD BY MARRIOTT.** *4710 Pearl East Circle (80301).* 303/440-4700; FAX 303/440-8975. 149 rms, 3 story. May-Oct: S, D $94-$104; suites $144-$154; under 12 free; wkly rates; lower rates rest of yr. Crib free. TV; cable (premium), VCR avail. Indoor pool. Complimentary coffee in rms. Restaurant 6:30-11 am, 6-10 pm. Bar 4-11 pm. Ck-out 1 pm. Coin lndry. Meeting rms. Business servs avail. In-rm modem link. Valet serv. Airport transportation. Exercise equipt; weight machine, stair machine, whirlpool. Refrigerator in suites. Cr cds: A, C, D, DS, MC, V.

D ⚡ 🏊 🧖 🍴 🚭 🐾 SC

★ ★ **RESIDENCE INN BY MARRIOTT.** *3030 Center Green Dr (80301), Foothills Pkwy at Valmont.* 303/449-5545; FAX 303/449-2452. 128 kit. suites, 2 story. Kit. suites $115-$179; wkly rates. Pet accepted; $5 per night, $50 minimum. TV; cable (premium), VCR avail (movies avail). Heated pool; whirlpool. Complimentary continental bkfst. Ck-out noon. Coin lndry. Meeting rms. Business servs avail. Valet serv. Health club privileges. Picnic tables, grills. Cr cds: A, C, D, DS, MC, V.

D ⚡ 🐾 🏊 🚭 🐾 SC

Motor Hotel

★ ★ **BROKER INN.** *555 30th St (80303).* 303/444-3330; res: 800/338-5407; FAX 303/444-6444. 116 rms, 4 story. May-Sept: S, D $98-$108; each addl $6; suites $160-$185; under 18 free; wkend rates; lower rates rest of yr. Crib free. Pet accepted. TV; cable (premium). Heated pool; whirlpool, poolside serv. Complimentary bkfst. Restaurant 6:30-10:30 am, 11 am-2 pm, 5-10 pm. Rm serv. Bar 11-2 am, Sun to midnight; entertainment. Ck-out noon. Meeting rms. Business center. In-rm modem link. Bellhops. Valet serv. Health club privileges. Airport, bus depot transportation. Some bathrm phones, in-rm steam baths. Cr cds: A, C, D, MC, V.

D ⚡ 🐾 🏊 🚭 🐾 SC 🏃

Hotels

★ ★ ★ **BOULDERADO.** *2115 13th St (80302).* 303/442-4344; res: 800/433-4344; FAX 303/442-4378. 160 rms, 5 story. S $119-$139; D $139-$151; each addl $12; suites $159-$171; under 12 free. Crib free. TV; cable (premium), VCR avail. Restaurant 6:30 am-10 pm. Bars 10:30-1 am; entertainment. Ck-out 11 am. Meeting rms. In-rm modem link. Airport transportation. Health club privileges. Some refrigerators. Balconies. Restored historic hotel (1908); authentic Victorian furnishings. Cr cds: A, C, D, DS, JCB, MC, V.

D 🚭 🐾 SC

★ ★ **CLARION HARVEST HOUSE.** *1345 28th St (80302).* 303/443-3850; FAX 303/443-1480. 270 rms, 4-5 story. S $144-$158; D $164-$168; suites $225-$550; family rates. Crib free. TV; cable (premium), VCR avail. 2 heated pools, 1 indoor; wading pool, poolside serv. Playground. Restaurant 6:30 am-10 pm. Bar 4 pm-2 am, Sat from 11 am, Sun 11 am-midnight. Ck-out 11 am. Coin lndry. Meeting rms. Business center. In-rm modem link. Gift shop. Tennis, pro. Exercise rm; weight machine, bicycles, whirlpool. Lawn games. Some refrigerators. Some private patios, balconies. Cr cds: A, C, D, DS, ER, JCB, MC, V.

D ⚡ 🎾 🏊 🏃 🧖 🚭 🐾 SC 🏃

Inns

✔ ★ ★ ★ **THE ALPS.** *38619 Boulder Canyon Dr (80303), 3 mi W on CO 119.* 303/444-5445; FAX 303/444-5522. 12 rms, 2 story. No A/C. S $75-$170; D $90-$185; each $20; wkly rates; higher rates UC events. Children over 12 only. TV in sitting rm; cable (premium). Complimentary full bkfst. Complimentary refreshments in sitting rm. Restaurant nearby. Ck-out 11 am, ck-in 4 pm. Business servs avail. In-rm modem link. Bellhop. Downhill/x-country ski 18 mi. Game rm. Some balconies. Picnic tables. Rms individually furnished. Fireplaces, many antiques. Entrance to inn is original log cabin (1870s) which served as both stagecoach stop and bordello. Totally nonsmoking. Cr cds: A, C, D, DS, MC, V.

⚡ 🚭 🐾

✔ ★ ★ **BRIAR ROSE.** *2151 Arapahoe Ave (80302).* 303/442-3007. 9 rms, 7 A/C, 2 story. May-Sept: S $85-$120; D $100-$135; each addl $15; lower rates rest of yr. Complimentary continental bkfst, tea. Ck-out noon, ck-in 3 pm. Business servs avail. Airport transportation. Health club privileges. English country-style home (1897); antiques. Totally nonsmoking. Cr cds: A, D, MC, V.

🚭 🐾

Restaurants

★ ★ ★ **FLAGSTAFF HOUSE.** *3¹/₂ mi W of US 36 Baseline Rd exit.* 303/442-4640. Hrs: 6-10 pm. Closed Jan 1, July 4, Dec 24 & 25. Res accepted. Innovative Amer menu. Bar 5 pm-midnight. Wine cellar. Semi-a la carte: dinner $22-$39. Specializes in Colorado beef, fresh seafood, game. Own baking. Valet parking. Tableside serv. Chef-owned. Cr cds: A, C, D, DS, JCB, MC, V.

D

★ ★ **GREENBRIAR.** *8537 N Foothills Hwy (US 36).* 303/440-7979. Hrs: 5-10 pm; Sun brunch 11 am-2:30 pm. Closed Jan 1. Res accepted. Continental menu. Bar to 2 am. Semi-a la carte: dinner $16-$37. Sun brunch $18. Specialties: rack of Colorado lamb, venison. Parking. Patio dining. Old World atmosphere; book-lined walls; native stone fireplace. Cr cds: A, D, MC, V.

D

★ ★ ★ **JOHN'S.** *2328 Pearl St.* 303/444-5232. Hrs: 5:30-10 pm. Closed July 4, Thanksgiving, Dec 25. Res accepted. Varied menu. Serv bar. Semi-a la carte: dinner $15.50-$22. Specialties: filet mignon au poivre, salmon Brettonne, breast of duck. Own sauces, ice cream. Located in cottage. Totally nonsmoking. Cr cds: A, C, D, DS, MC, V.

✔★ **PASTA JAY'S.** 925 Pearl St. 303/444-5800. Hrs: 11 am-11 pm. Closed Thanksgiving, Dec 25. Italian menu. Wine, beer. Semi-a la carte: lunch, dinner $3.75-$12.25. Child's meals. Specializes in manicotti. Parking. Outdoor dining. Bistro-style dining. Totally non-smoking. Cr cds: D, DS, MC, V.

D

★★ **ROYAL PEACOCK.** 5290 Arapahoe Ave. 303/447-1409. Hrs: 11:30 am-2:30 pm, 5:30-10:30 pm. Res accepted. East Indian menu. Bar. Semi-a la carte: lunch $6.25-$11, dinner $7-$22. Specializes in curry, tandoori, wild game. Parking. Outdoor dining. East Indian decor. Cr cds: A, MC, V.

Breckenridge (C-4)

(See Dillon, Fairplay)

Settled 1859 **Pop** 1,285 **Elev** 9,602 ft **Area code** 970 **Zip** 80424

Information Breckenridge Resort Chamber, 309 N Main St, PO Box 1909, phone 970/453-6018; or Guest Services and Activities Center, 201 S Main St, phone 970/453-5579.

Gold was first panned in the Blue River in 1859; by the following year Breckenridge was a booming gold rush town. More recently, it has become a thriving resort area, with skiing, summer activities and ghost towns to explore.

What to See and Do

Breckenridge Ski Area. 4 high-speed quads, 1 triple, 8 double chair-lifts, 1 T-bar, 2 ponylifts; school, rentals; snowmaking; 3 cafeterias, 2 restaurants on mountain, picnic area; 4 nurseries (from 2 mo). 112 runs on 3 interconnected mountains; longest run 3 mi; vertical drop 3,398 ft. (Mid-Nov-early May, daily) Cross-country skiing (23 km), heliskiing, ice-skating, snowboarding, sleigh rides. Shuttle bus service. Multi-day, half-day & off-season rates. Chairlift and alpine slide operate in summer (mid-June-mid-Sept). Ski Hill Rd, 1 mi W off CO 9. Phone 970/453-5000; for lodging information and reservations phone 800/221-1091. ¢¢¢¢¢

Ghost towns. Lincoln City, Swandyke, Dyersville, others. Some can be reached only by jeep or on horseback; inquire locally.

Walking tours through historic district; also tours to abandoned mines, gold panning and assay demonstrations. Led by Summit Historical Society. (Wed-Sat) Phone 970/453-9022. ¢¢

Annual Events

Ullr Fest & World Cup Freestyle. Honoring Norse god of snow. Parades, fireworks, Nordic night and ski competition. 7 days mid-Jan.

No Man's Land Day Celebration. Celebrates time when Colorado became a state of the Union, while the Breckenridge area was mistakenly forgotten in historic treaties. This area became part of Colorado and the United States at a later date. Celebration features emphasis on Breckenridge life in the 1880s; parade, dance, games. 2nd wkend Aug.

Seasonal Events

Breckenridge Music Festival. Classical music performances and workshops. Phone 970/453-9142. June-Aug.

Backstage Theatre. Downtown. Melodramas, musicals, comedies. Contact PO Box 297; phone 970/453-0199. July-Labor Day, mid-Dec-Mar.

Hotels

★★ **BEAVER RUN.** 620 Village Rd. 970/453-6000; res: 800/525-2253; FAX 970/453-7234. 438 air-cooled kit. suites, 8 story.

Mid-Nov-mid-Apr: kit. suites $180-$650; lower rates rest of yr. Crib free. TV; cable (premium). 2 pools, 1 heated, 1 indoor/outdoor; poolside serv in winter. Complimentary coffee in rms. Restaurant 7 am-10 pm. No rm serv. Bar 11-2 am; seasonal entertainment. Ck-out 11 am. Coin lndry. Convention facilities. Business servs avail. Concierge. Shopping arcade. Tennis. Downhill ski on site/x-country ski 1 mi. Exercise equipt; weight machine, bicycles, whirlpool, sauna. Rec rm. Fireplaces. Some in-rm whirlpools. Balconies. Cr cds: A, C, DS, MC, V.

⊠ ⚲ ⌲ ✕ ⚲ SC

★★★ **HILTON.** PO Box 8059, 550 Village Rd. 970/453-4500; FAX 970/453-0212. 208 air-cooled rms, 10 story. Mid-Dec-mid-Apr: S, D $145-$225; suites $290-$390; children free; ski plans; higher rates special events; lower rates rest of yr. TV; cable (premium). Indoor pool; whirlpool. Coffee in rms. Restaurant 7-11:30 am, 5:30-10 pm. Bar 11-2 am, Sun to midnight. Ck-out 10 am. Meeting rms. Business center. Valet serv. Concierge. Sports shop. Garage. Airport, bus depot transportation. Downhill/x-country ski ½ blk. Exercise equipt; stair machine, bicycles, sauna. Massage. Refrigerators, wet bars. Balconies. Cr cds: A, C, D, DS, ER, JCB, MC, V.

D ⚲ ⌲ ✕ ⊠ ⚲ SC ⚶

★★ **RIVER MOUNTAIN LODGE.** 100 S Park St. 970/453-4711; res: 800/627-3766; FAX 970/453-1763. 175 kit. condo units, 3-4 story. S, D $89-$599. TV; cable (premium), VCR avail. Pool; whirlpool. Ck-out 10 am. Coffee in lobby. Guest lndry. Meeting rms. Business servs avail. Concierge. Covered parking. Airport, bus depot transportation. Downhill/x-country ski ½ mi. Exercise equipt; weights, bicycles, sauna. Refrigerators; some fireplaces. Cr cds: A, D, DS, MC, V.

D ⚲ ⌲ ✕ ⊠ ⚲

Inns

★★★ **ALLAIRE TIMBERS INN.** 9511 CO 9. 970/453-7530; res: 800/624-4904; FAX 970/453-8699. 10 rms, 2 story, 2 suites. Mid-Feb-Mar: S, D $145; suites $205-$215; ski, golf, honeymoon plans; lower rates rest of yr. Children over 13 yrs only. Cable TV upon request. Complimentary coffee in library, full bkfst. Complimentary tea/sherry in afternoon. Restaurant nearby. Ck-out 11 am, ck-in 3-7 pm. Concierge. In-rm modem link. Downhill/x-country ski 2 mi. Balconies. Totally non-smoking. Cr cds: A, DS, MC, V.

D ⚲ ⊠ ⚲

★ **COTTEN HOUSE.** 102 S French St. 970/453-5509. 4 rms (2 with shower only), 2 story. No A/C. No rm phones. Dec-Mar: S, D $80-$95; under 2 free; 3-day min winter, 2-day min summer; lower rates rest of yr. Crib $5. Cable TV with VCR in common rm. Complimentary full bkfst; tea/sherry in afternoon. Restaurant nearby. Ck-out 10 am, ck-in 4-6 pm. Luggage handling. Downhill/x-country ski 1 mi. Picnic table. House built 1886. Two blocks from Main St. Totally nonsmoking. No cr cds accepted.

⚲ ⊠ ⚲

★★★ **WILLIAMS HOUSE.** 303 N Main St. 970/453-2970; res: 800/795-2975. 6 rms, 1 cottage. No A/C. Rm phone in cottage. Feb-Mar: S, D $120; cottage $175; higher rates Dec 25-Jan 1; lower rates rest of yr. Closed 3 wks May, 3 wks Oct. Adults only. Cable TV in cottage and parlor, VCR avail. Whirlpools. Complimentary full bkfst. Complimentary cider and tea in afternoon. Restaurant nearby. Ck-out 10 am, ck-in by appt. Concierge. Downhill/x-country ski 1 mi. Health club privileges. Refrigerator in cottage. Picnic tables. Built in 1885; antiques, fireplaces. Totally nonsmoking. Cr cds: A.

D ⚲ ⊠ ⚲

Restaurants

★ **BRECKENRIDGE BREWERY.** 600 S Main St. 970/453-1550. Hrs: 11 am-midnight. Closed Dec 25. Bar. Semi-a la carte: lunch $4.95-$6.95, dinner $5.95-$14.95. Child's meals. Specializes in baby-back ribs, fish 'n chips, fajitas. Local bands Tues. Parking. Outdoor dining. Microbrewery; tours wkends. Second-story dining arranged around brew kettles. Cr cds: A, DS, MC, V.

SC

★ **BRIAR ROSE.** *109 E Lincoln St. 970/453-9948.* Hrs: 5-10 pm. Res accepted. Continental menu. Bar 4:30 pm-2 am. Semi-a la carte: dinner $10-$50. Child's meals. Specializes in prime rib, game, steak. Entertainment (ski season). Parking. 1890s Victorian decor; on site of old mining boarding house. Cr cds: A, DS, MC, V.

★ ★ **CAFE ALPINE.** *106 Adams. 970/453-8218.* Hrs: 11 am-9 pm. Res accepted. Continental menu. Bar. Semi-a la carte: lunch $4.95-$9.95, dinner $15.95-$25.95. Child's meals. Specialties: spanek-opeta, Viet-Thai peanut stir-fry. Outdoor dining. Cozy, informal dining in 3 rms. Totally nonsmoking. Cr cds: A, MC, V.

D

★ ★ **HEARTHSTONE.** *130 S Ridge St. 970/453-1148.* Hrs: 11:30 am-10 pm. Res accepted. No A/C. Bar. Semi-a la carte: lunch $3.95-$7.95 (summer only), dinner $10.50-$19.95. Child's meals. Specializes in prime rib, fresh seafood. Parking. Outdoor dining. In Victorian house (1886). View of mountains and ski area. Totally nonsmoking. Cr cds: A, MC, V.

D

✔ ★ **HORSESHOE II.** *115 Main St (CO 9). 970/453-7463.* Hrs: 7:30 am-10 pm. No A/C. Bar to midnight. Semi-a la carte: bkfst $3.50-$6, lunch $4-$6.50, dinner $3.95-$17.50. Child's meals. Outdoor dining. Former miners' supply store (1880). Cr cds: A, MC, V.

D

✔ ★ ★ **MI CASA.** *600 Park Ave. 970/453-2071.* Hrs: 4 pm-closing; summer from 5 pm. No A/C. Mexican, Amer menu. Bar from 3 pm. Semi-a la carte: dinner $5.95-$9.95. Child's meals. Specialties: chimichanga, fajitas, fresh seafood, deep-fried ice cream. Parking. Mexican decor. Outdoor dining. Totally nonsmoking. Cr cds: A, MC, V.

D

★ ★ **PIERRE'S.** *111 S Main St. 970/453-0989.* Hrs: 11:30 am-2:30 pm (summer), 5:30-10 pm. Closed Mon; Dec 25; also May and 1st 2 wks Nov. Res accepted. French, Amer menu. Bar. Semi-a la carte: lunch $6.25-$9, dinner $15-$26. Specialties: Rocky Mountain trout, rack of lamb. Parking. Outdoor dining. Chef-owned. Cr cds: MC, V.

D

★ **POIRRIER'S CAJUN CAFE.** *224 S Main. 970/453-1877.* Hrs: 11:30 am-2 pm, 5-10 pm. No A/C. Cajun-Creole menu. Bar. Semi-a la carte: lunch $4.95-$9, dinner $8.95-$19.95. Child's meals. Specializes in catfish, seafood platter. Outdoor dining. Totally nonsmoking. Cr cds: A, D, DS, MC, V.

D

★ ★ **ST BERNARD INN.** *103 S Main St. 970/453-2572.* Hrs: 5-10 pm. Closed May. Res accepted. No A/C. Italian menu. Bar. Semi-a la carte: dinner $9.25-$18.75. Child's meals. Specialties: fettucine verde Alfredo, cannelloni di mare. Parking. In historic mercantile building. Old mining memorabilia. Cr cds: A, D, DS, MC, V.

★ ★ **SWAN MOUNTAIN INN.** *16172 CO 9, at Swan Mountain Rd. 970/453-7903.* Hrs: 7:30-10:30 am, 11:30 am-2:30 pm, 5:30-9:30 pm; winter hrs vary. Res accepted. No A/C. Continental menu. Bar. Semi-a la carte: bkfst $6.50-$8.50, lunch $6.95-$7.95, dinner $12.95-$18.95. Child's meals. Specialties: marinated pork tenderloin, black raspberry roast duckling. Parking. Outdoor dining. Log structure; view of mountains. Totally nonsmoking. Cr cds: DS, MC, V.

D SC

Buena Vista (D-4)

(See Leadville, Salida)

Founded 1879 **Pop** 1,752 **Elev** 7,955 ft **Area code** 719 **Zip** 81211
Information Chamber of Commerce, 343 S US 24, Box 2021; 719/395-6612.

Lying at the eastern edge of the Collegiate Range and the central-Colorado mountain region, Buena Vista is a natural point of departure for treks into the mountains. Within 20 miles are 12 peaks with elevations above 14,000 feet, 4 rivers and more than 500 mountain lakes and streams.

What to See and Do

Hiking, camping, mountain biking and cross-country skiing. Equipment rentals, supplies, maps and information on trails and routes may be obtained from Trailhead Ventures; phone 719/395-8001.

River rafting.

Arkansas River Tours. Quarter-day to three-day, mild to wild white-water rafting and fishing trips on the Arkansas River. (May-Aug) Contact Box 1032-M; phone 800/321-4352. ¢¢¢¢

Bill Dvorak's Kayak & Rafting Expeditions. Half-day to twelve-day trips on the Arkansas, Colorado, Dolores, Green, Gunnison, North Platte, Rio Chama and Rio Grande rivers. (Mid-Apr-early Oct) Phone 719/539-6851 or 800/824-3795. ¢¢¢¢¢

Noah's Ark Whitewater Rafting Company. Half-day to three-day trips on the Arkansas River. (Mid-May-late Aug) Phone 719/395-2158. ¢¢¢¢¢

Wilderness Aware. Half-day to ten-day river rafting trips on the Arkansas, Colorado, Dolores, North Platte, Gunnison, Animas and Piedra rivers. (May-Sept) Phone 719/395-2112 or 800/462-7238. ¢¢¢¢¢

Motels

★ **GREAT WESTERN SUMAC LODGE.** *Box 747, 428 S US 24. 719/395-8111.* 30 rms, 2 story. Mid-May-Sept: S, D $56-$68; each addl $5; lower rates rest of yr. TV; cable (premium). Complimentary coffee in lobby. Restaurant nearby. Ck-out 10 am. X-country ski 7 mi. Picnic tables, grill. Mountain view; shaded lawn, stream. Cr cds: A, C, D, DS, MC, V.

 SC

✔ ★ **TOPAZ LODGE.** *Box 596, 115 N US 24, 1/4 blk N of jct US 24, CO 306. 719/395-2427.* 18 rms (fans in each unit). No A/C. Mid-May-mid-Sept: S $40-$55; D $55-$76; each addl $4; wkly rates off-season; lower rates rest of yr. Crib $4. Pet accepted; some restrictions, $5. TV; cable. Playground opp. Complimentary coffee in rms. Restaurant nearby. Ck-out 10 am. Tennis opp. X-country ski 7 mi. Cr cds: A, C, D, DS, MC, V.

Inn

★ ★ **ADOBE.** *PO Box 1560, 303 N US 24. 719/395-6340.* 5 air-cooled rms, 2 suites. No rm phones. May-Sept: S, D $69-$89; each addl $10; suites $79-$89; lower rates rest of yr. TV; cable. Complimentary full bkfst. Restaurant adj 11:30 am-3 pm, 4:30-9:30 pm. Ck-out 11 am, ck-in 3 pm. Street parking. Restored house built 1880; Southwest decor. Fireplaces, solarium. Totally nonsmoking. Cr cds: MC, V.

Guest Ranch

★ ★ **DEER VALLEY RANCH.** *(16825 County 162, Nathrop 81236) S on US 24, 6 mi W on County 162.* 719/395-2353. 10 rms in lodges, 19 kit. cottages. No A/C. AP, June-Aug: S $105; D $210; 6-12 yrs $65; 3-5 yrs $45; EP cottages 1-4, $225-$280; each addl $40; lower rates rest of yr. TV; VCR avail (movies avail). 2 pools; whirlpools, sauna. Free supervised child's activities (June-Aug); ages 4-12. Dining rm 8-9 am, noon-1 pm, 6-7 pm. Box lunches. Ck-out 11 am, ck-in 3 pm. Meeting rms. Business servs avail. Free bus depot transportation. Tennis. Golf privileges. X-country ski 9 mi. Rec rm. 4-wheel-drive vehicle for rent. Hiking trails. River rafting. Fishing lake. Gold panning. Square dancing in summer. Lawn games. Guides. Refrigerators; fireplaces. Private patios. No alcoholic beverages. No cr cds accepted.

Restaurants

✔ ★ **CASA DEL SOL.** *333 N US 24.* 719/395-8810. Hrs: 11:30 am-3 pm, 4:30-9:30 pm; winter hrs vary. Closed Nov-mid-Dec & Apr. Res accepted. Mexican menu. Semi-a la carte: lunch $1.90-$6, dinner $8.50-$12.50. Child's meals. Specialties: pechuga Suiza, homemade desserts. Parking. Outdoor dining. In 1880 miner's cabin. Cr cds: MC, V.

✔ ★ **DELANEY'S DEPOT.** *605 S US 24.* 719/395-8854. Hrs: 6:30 am-9 pm; Sun from 7:30 am. Closed Thanksgiving, Dec 25; also mid-Apr-mid-May. Semi-a la carte: bkfst $2.95-$5.95, lunch $2.70-$5.95, dinner $5.95-$12.95. Sun buffet: $7.50. Child's meals. Specializes in spare ribs, chicken. Salad bar. Parking. Model trains. No cr cds accepted.

[SC]

Burlington (C-9)

Pop 2,941 **Elev** 4,160 ft **Area code** 719 **Zip** 80807
Information Chamber of Commerce, 415 15th St, PO Box 62; 719/346-8070.

What to See and Do

Bonny Lake State Park. A 2,000-acre lake has swimming, waterskiing; fishing; boating (ramps). Picnicking, concession. Camping. Standard fees. (Daily) 23 mi N on US 385, near Idalia. Phone 303/354-7306. Per vehicle ¢¢

Kit Carson County Carousel. Built in 1905, this restored carousel houses a 1912 Wurlitzer Monster Military Band organ. (Memorial Day-Labor Day, daily, afternoon-mid-evening) Fairgrounds, Colorado Ave and 15th St. Fee for 20-min tour and 4-min ride ¢

Old Town. Historical village with 20 buildings reflects Colorado prairie heritage. Also cancan shows, gunfights & melodramas (summer); 2-day hoedown (Labor Day wkend). (Daily; closed Jan 1, Easter, Thanksgiving,Dec 25) 420 S 14th St. Phone 719/346-7382 or 800/288-1334. ¢¢

Annual Events

Little Britches Rodeo. Fairgrounds. Early June.

Kit Carson County Fair & Rodeo. Fairgrounds. Phone 719/346-8133. Early Aug.

Motels

✔ ★ **BUDGET HOST CHAPARRAL MOTOR INN.** *405 S Lincoln, I-70 exit 437 & US 385.* 719/346-5361; res: 800/456-6206; FAX

719/346-8502. 39 rms. June-Sept: S $33-$43; D $34-$44; each addl $4; under 12 free; lower rates rest of yr. Crib $5. Pet accepted, some restrictions. TV; cable (premium). Heated pool; whirlpool. Restaurant adj 6 am-11 pm. Ck-out 11 am. In-rm modem link. Cr cds: A, C, D, DS, MC, V.

★ **SLOAN'S.** *1901 Rose Ave.* 719/346-5333. 27 rms, 1-2 story. S $22-$28; D $28-$40; each addl $3. Crib $4. TV; cable. Pool. Restaurant nearby. Ck-out 10:30 am. In-rm modem link. Free airport, bus depot transportation. Cr cds: A, C, D, DS, MC, V.

Cañon City (D-5)

(See Colorado Springs, Cripple Creek, Pueblo)

Founded 1859 **Pop** 12,687 **Elev** 5,332 ft **Area code** 719 **Zip** 81212
Information Chamber of Commerce, 403 Royal Gorge Blvd, PO Box 749; 719/275-2331 or 800/876-7922.

Lieutenant Zebulon Pike, in 1807, was one of the first white men to camp on this site, which was long a favored spot of the Ute Indians. Cañon (pronounced Canyon) City is located at the mouth of the Grand Canyon of the Arkansas River, ringed by mountains. The poet Joaquin Miller, as town judge, mayor and minister during the early gold-mining days, once proposed renaming the town Oreodelphia, but the horrified miners protested that they could neither spell nor pronounce it. Legend has it that the same earthy logic prevailed when, in 1868, Cañon City was offered either the state penitentiary or the state university. The miners chose the former, pointing out that it was likely to be the better attended institution. A Ranger District office of the San Isabel National Forest (see PUEBLO) is located in Cañon City, phone 719/275-4119.

What to See and Do

Cañon City Fine Arts Center. Community art center; features visual art exhibits, cultural programs. (Tues-Sun; closed hols) 505 Macon Ave. Phone 719/275-2790. **Free.**

Cañon City Municipal Museum. Complex includes outdoor buildings; Rudd Cabin, a pioneer log cabin constructed in 1860, and Stone House built in 1881. Second floor Municipal Bldg galleries display a mineral and rock collection, artifacts from settlement of the Fremont County region and a gun collection. (Early May-Labor Day, daily exc Mon; rest of yr, Tues-Sat; closed major hols) 612 Royal Gorge Blvd (US 50). Phone 719/269-9018. ¢

Colorado Territorial Prison Museum and Park. Housed in the women's prison facility (1935), this museum and resource center displays exhibits and memorabilia of the Colorado prison system. Picnicking is permitted on the grounds. Adj is an active medium-security prison. (Daily; closed some hols) 1st & Macon Aves. Phone 719/269-3015. ¢¢

Rafting. There are many rafting companies in the area. For information contact the Cañon City Chamber of Commerce, phone 800/876-7922.

Royal Gorge Country's Buckskin Joe Park and Railway. Old West theme park includes old Western town with 30 authentic buildings; antique steam train and car museum; restaurant and saloon. Other activities here are daily gunfights, horse-drawn trolley ride, magic shows and entertainment. Also 3-mile, 30-min train ride to rim of Royal Gorge. Railway (Mar-mid-Nov, daily). Park (May-Sept, daily). 8 mi W via US 50, 1 mi S on rd to Royal Gorge. Phone 719/275-5149 or -5485. All activities included in admission ¢¢¢¢

★ **Royal Gorge.** Magnificent canyon with cliffs rising more than 1,000 feet above Arkansas River. Royal Gorge Suspension Bridge, 1,053 feet above river, is highest in the world (recreational vehicles larger than small van or small camper not permitted on bridge). Royal Gorge Incline Railway, the world's steepest, takes passengers 1,550 feet to bottom of canyon. A 2,200-foot aerial tramway glides across the spectacular canyon. Theater; entertainment gazebo; restaurants; gift shops. (Daily) 8 mi W on US 50, then 4 mi SW. Phone 719/275-7507. ¢¢¢

Annual Events

Blossom & Music Festival. First wkend May.

Royal Gorge Rodeo. First wkend May.

Motels

★ ★ **BEST WESTERN ROYAL GORGE.** *1925 Fremont Dr.* 719/275-3377; res: 800/231-7317; FAX 719/275-3931. 67 rms, 2 story. May-Sept: S $60; D $70-$84; each addl $5; lower rates rest rest of yr. Crib free. Pet accepted, some restrictions; $10. TV; cable (premium), VCR avail. Heated pool; whirlpool, poolside serv. Playground. Restaurant 6 am-9 pm. Bar noon-2 am. Ck-out 11 am. Coin lndry. In-rm modem link. Picnic tables. Cr cds: A, C, D, DS, JCB, MC, V.

[D] [✦] [≋] [⊠] [🐾] [SC]

★ ★ **CAÑON INN.** *3075 E US 50.* 719/275-8676; res: 800/525-7727 (CO); FAX 719/275-8675. 152 rms, 2 story. May-Sept: S $60-$90; D $70-$90; each addl $7; under 16 free; lower rates rest of yr. Crib free. Pet accepted; $20. TV; cable (premium). Heated pool; 6 indoor spas. Restaurant 6 am-10 pm. Rm serv. Bar 4 pm-2 am. Ck-out 11 am. Coin lndry. Meeting rms. Business servs avail. Valet serv. Free local airport, bus depot transportation. Some bathrm phones, refrigerators. Cr cds: A, C, D, DS, MC, V.

[D] [✦] [≋] [⊠] [🐾] [SC]

Restaurant

✔ ★ ★ **MERLINO'S BELVEDERE.** *1330 Elm Ave.* 719/275-5558. Hrs: 5-10 pm; Fri & Sat 4:30-10:30 pm; Sun noon-9 pm; winter: 5-9:30 pm; Fri & Sat to 10 pm; Sun noon-8 pm. Closed Thanksgiving, Dec 25. Italian, Amer menu. Bars. Semi-a la carte: dinner $7.25-$16.50. Child's meals. Specializes in homemade pasta, steak. Own soups. Parking. Mediterranean decor. Bakery on premises. Family-owned. Cr cds: A, C, D, DS, MC, V.

[D]

Central City (B-5)

(For accommodations see Denver, Georgetown, Golden, also see Idaho Springs)

Settled 1859 **Pop** 335 **Elev** 8,496 ft **Area code** 303 **Zip** 80427
Information Gilpin County Chamber of Commerce, PO Box 343, Blackhawk, 80422; 303/582-5077.

Perched along steep Gregory Gulch, Central City's precarious location did not prevent it from becoming known as "the richest square mile on earth" when the first important discovery of gold in Colorado was made here in 1859. More than $75 million worth of metals and minerals have come from Central City and neighboring settlements.

What to See and Do

Gilpin County Historical Society Museum. Exhibits, housed in an early schoolhouse (1870) under continuing restoration, re-create early gold-mining life in Gilpin County; replicas of a Victorian house and period shops with authentic furnishings; collection of antique dolls; personal effects of sheriff gunned down in 1896. (Memorial Day wkend-Labor Day, daily; other times by appt) 228 E High St. Phone 303/582-5283. ¢¢ Also maintained by the Historical Society is the

The Thomas House Museum (1874). On display are the belongings of one family who lived in this house. (Memorial Day wkend-Labor

Day, Thurs-Sun; rest of yr, by appt) 209 Eureka St. Phone 303/582-5283. ¢¢

Lace House (1863). An outstanding example of carpenter-Gothic architecture. Period furnishings. (Late May-early Sept, daily; rest of yr, by appt) Donation. 1 mi E on Main St in Black Hawk. Phone 303/582-5221.

Site of First Gold Lode Discovery in Colorado. Granite monument marks spot where John H. Gregory first found gold May 6, 1859. Boundary of Central City and Black Hawk.

Teller House (1872). A restored Victorian casino with a museum made of U.S. Grant and Baby Doe Tabor suites and a complete collection of Belter furniture; house bar is site of the "Face on the Bar Room Floor." Tours (fee). (Daily) 120 Eureka St. Phone 303/582-3200. **Free.**

Annual Event

Central City Jazz Festival. 3 days of Dixieland jazz. Late Aug.

Restaurant

★ ★ **BLACK FOREST INN.** *(CO 279, Black Hawk 80422)* 1 mi E, 2 blks W off CO 119. 303/279-2333. Hrs: 11 am-9:30 pm; Sun to 8 pm. Res accepted. German, Amer menu. Bars. Semi-a la carte: lunch $4-$8.75, dinner $10.95-$22.95. Specializes in wild game (varies according to season). Own ice cream. Entertainment Fri-Sun. Bavarian decor. No cr cds accepted.

[D] [SC]

Colorado National Monument (C-1)

(For accommodations see Grand Junction)

(5 mi W of Grand Junction, off CO 340)

Wind, water, a 10-mile fault and untold eons have combined to produce spectacular erosional forms. In the 32-square-mile monument, deep canyons with sheer walls form amphitheaters for towering monoliths, rounded domes and other geological features. Wildlife includes deer, foxes, coyotes, porcupines and a growing herd of desert bighorn sheep. Rim Rock Drive, accessible from either Fruita or Grand Junction, is a spectacular 22-mile road along the canyon rims. There are picnicking and camping facilities within the monument (all yr; fee for camping). The Saddlehorn Visitor Center has geology and natural history exhibits (daily). Daily interpretive programs are offered in summer. Hiking and cross-country skiing trails are open in season. For detailed information contact Chief Ranger, Fruita, CO 81521; phone 970/858-3617. Per private vehicle ¢¢

Colorado Springs (D-6)

(See Cañon City, Cripple Creek, Manitou Springs)

Founded 1871 **Pop** 281,140 **Elev** 6,008 ft **Area code** 719
Information Convention & Visitor Bureau, 104 S Cascade, Ste 104, 80903; 719/635-7506 or 800/888-4748.

Colorado Springs, at the foot of Pikes Peak, is surrounded by areas containing fantastic rock formations. It was founded by by General William J. Palmer and the Denver and Rio Grande Railroad as a summer playground and health resort. The headquarters of Pike National Forest is in Colorado Springs.

What to See and Do

Broadmoor-Cheyenne Mountain Area. 4 mi S on Nevada Ave, then W on Lake Ave to Broadmoor Hotel. Opp hotel is

El Pomar Carriage House Museum. Lake Ave & Lake Circle. Collection of fine carriages, vehicles, Western articles of 1890s. (Daily exc Mon; closed hols) **Free.** Around hotel grounds and golf course is start of

Broadmoor-Cheyenne Mountain Highway. Zigzags up east face of Cheyenne Mt; view of plains to east. Round trip to Shrine of the Sun (see) is 6 miles. (Daily; weather permitting) Toll (includes zoo, Shrine of the Sun) ¢¢¢ 2 miles up highway is

Cheyenne Mountain Zoological Park. Approx 500 animals including primate, penguin, giraffe, feline and birds of prey collections. (Daily) Sr citizen rate. Phone 719/475-9555 (recording). ¢¢¢ Admission includes

Shrine of the Sun. Memorial to Will Rogers. Built of Colorado pink granite and steel. Contains Rogers memorabilia. (Daily)

Colorado Springs Fine Arts Center. Permanent collections include Native American and Hispanic art, Guatamalan textiles, 19th and 20th-century American Western paintings, graphics and sculpture by Charles M. Russell and other American artists. Changing exhibits; painting and sculpture classes; repertory theater performances; films. (Daily exc Mon; closed hols) 30 W Dale St. Phone 719/634-5581. ¢¢

Colorado Springs Pioneers Museum. Exhibits portray the history of Pikes Peak region. (Tues-Sat; May-Sept, also Sun afternoons; closed some hols) 215 S Tejon St. Phone 719/578-6650. **Free.**

Flying W Ranch. A working cattle and horse ranch with chuckwagon suppers and Western stage show. More than 12 restored buildings with period furniture. (Mid-May-Sept, daily; rest of yr, Fri & Sat; closed Dec 25-Feb) 3330 Chuckwagon Rd, 8 mi NW on 30th St, 2 mi W of I-25 on Garden of the Gods Rd. Reservations required; phone 719/598-4000 or 800/232-FLYW. Meal & show (summer) ¢¢¢¢; (winter) ¢¢¢¢¢

⚜ **Garden of the Gods.** Outstanding geological formations, including famous Balanced Rock and Kissing Camels. Dramatic views at sunrise and sunset. Visitor center on Ridge Rd at southeast edge of park (daily; closed Dec 24-Jan 1). Guided nature walks. Park (all yr). 3 mi NW on US 24, then right on 30th St. Phone 719/578-6640. **Free.** In the park is

Garden of the Gods Trading Post. Established in 1900. Southwestern art gallery displays contemporary Native American jewelry, Santa Clarapottery, Hopi kachinas. Gift shop. Near Balanced Rock, at S end of park. Phone 719/685-9045 or 800/874-4515. **Free.**

Gray Line bus tours. Contact 3704 W Colorado Ave, 80904; 719/633-1747 or 800/345-8197.

Hall of Presidents. Wax museum featuring all US presidents in 23 room-size sets. More than 100 wax figures created by the studios of Mme Josephine Tussaud of London. Fairyland of characters from children's stories. (Daily; winter hrs vary) 1050 S 21st St. Phone 719/635-3553. ¢¢

Industrial Tour. Van Briggle Art Pottery Co. Exhibitions of "throwing on the potter's wheel"; self-guided tours. (Daily exc Sun; closed Jan 1, Thanksgiving, Dec 25) 600 S 21st St at W US 24. Phone 719/633-7729. **Free.**

Magic Town. Theatrical sculpture, created by sculptor Michael Garman, is a combination of miniature cityscapes and characters together with theatre techniques. Gift shop. (Daily) 2418 W Colorado Ave. Phone 719/471-9391. ¢¢

May Natural History Museum. Collection of more than 7,000 invertebrates from the tropics. Also here is **Museum of Space Exploration** with hundreds of models and NASA space photos and movies. (May-Sept, daily) Campground (fee). 9 mi SW on CO 115. Phone 719/576-0450 or 800/666-3841. Both museums. ¢¢

McAllister House Museum (1873). Six-room Gothic-style cottage; Victorian furnishings. Carriage house. Guided tours. (May-Aug, Wed-Sun; rest of yr, Thurs-Sat) 423 N Cascade Ave. Phone 719/635-7925. ¢

Museum of the American Numismatic Association. Displays and research collections of coins, tokens, medals, paper money; library. (Memorial Day-Labor Day, daily exc Sun; rest of yr, Mon-Fri; closed hols) 818 N Cascade Ave. Phone 719/632-2646. **Free.**

Old Colorado City. Renovated historic district features more than 100 quaint shops and restaurants. (Daily) 3 mi W on US 24. Phone 719/577-4112. **Free.**

Palmer Park. Magnificent views from scenic roads and trails among its 710 acres on Austin Bluffs. Picnic areas. On Maizeland Rd off N Academy Blvd. **Free.**

Pike National Forest. The more than 1,100,000 acres north & west of town via US 24 includes world-famous Pikes Peak; picnic grounds, campgrounds (fee); Wilkerson Pass (9,507 ft), 45 miles west on US 24, with visitor information center (Memorial Day-Labor Day); Lost Creek Wilderness, northwest of Lake George, Mt Evans Wilderness, northwest of Bailey. Contact the Supervisor, 1920 Valley Dr, Pueblo 81008; 719/545-8737. There is also a Ranger District office in Colorado Springs at 601 S Weber; 719/636-1602. **Free.**

⚜ **Pikes Peak** (14,110 ft). Toll road climbs 7,309 feet. (May-Oct, daily; weather permitting) Closed during annual Hill Climb in July (see ANNUAL EVENTS). 10 mi W on US 24 to Cascade, then 19 mi on toll road to summit. Phone 719/684-9383. Toll ¢¢

Cog railway Up to eight trips daily (May-Oct, inquire for schedule). Reservations required. 515 Ruxton Ave in Manitou Springs, 5 mi W on US 24. Phone 719/685-5401. Round trip ¢¢¢¢

Pikes Peak Ghost Town. Authentic Old West town under one roof in an 1899 railroad building. Includes antique-furnished buildings such as general store, livery, jail, saloon and re-created Victorian home. Also horseless carriages and buggies and a 1903 Cadillac. Old-time nickelodeons, player pianos, arcade "movies" and shooting gallery. (Daily) Sr citizen rate. US 24 W at 400 S 21st St. Phone 719/634-0696. ¢¢

Pro Rodeo Hall of Fame and American Cowboy Museum. Traces the rodeo lifestyle and its development over more than 100 yrs. Multimedia presentation documents rodeo's evolution from its origins in 19th-century ranch work to its present status as a major spectator sport. More than 90 exhibits of historic and modern cowboy and rodeo gear; changing Western art exhibits. The outdoor exhibits include live rodeo animals and a replica rodeo arena. (Daily; closed Jan 1 and 2, Easter, Thanksgiving, Dec 25) 101 Pro Rodeo Drive (I-25 exit 147 Rockrimmon Blvd). Phone 719/528-4764. ¢¢¢

Seven Falls. Only completely lighted canyon and waterfall in the world. Best seen from Eagle's Nest, reached by mountain elevator. Native American dance interpretations (summer, daily). Night lighting (summer). 7 mi SW on Cheyenne Blvd in S Cheyenne Cañon. Phone 719/632-0765. ¢¢¢

US Air Force Academy (1955). (4,200 cadets) On 18,000 acres at foot of Rampart Range of Rocky Mts where cadets undergo four-year academic, military and physical training. Striking, modern cadet chapel (daily; closed for private services); Sunday service open to public. Cadet Wing marches to lunch may be watched from wall near Chapel (academic yr). Planetarium programs for public (free). Visitor center has self-guided tour brochures, theater and exhibits on cadet life and academy history (daily; closed Jan 1, Thanksgiving, Dec 25). N on I-25 exit 150B (South Gate) or 156B (North Gate). Phone 719/472-2555. Visitor center **Free.**

US Olympic Complex. National headquarters of the US Olympic Committee, 15 national sports governing bodies and Olympic Training Center where more than 15,000 athletes train each year. Guided tours include film and walking tour of training center. (Daily) One Olympic Plaza, 2 blks N of Platte Ave (US 24 E), at Union Blvd. Phone 719/578-4618 or -4644 (recording). **Free.**

White House Ranch Historic Site. A living history program demonstrating everyday life in the region; 1868 homestead, 1895 working ranch, 1907 Orchard House. Braille nature trail. (June-Labor Day, Wed-Sun; after Labor Day-Dec 25, wkends; closed rest of yr) 3202 Chambers Way, 4 mi W via I-25, Garden of Gods exit to 30th St, S to Gateway Rd at E entrance of Garden of the Gods. Phone 719/578-6777. ¢¢

World Figure Skating Hall of Fame and Museum. Exhibits on history of figure skating; art, memorabilia, library; skate gallery; video collection. (May-Sept, daily exc Sun; rest of yr, Mon-Fri; closed hols) 20 First St, off Lake Ave. Phone 719/635-5200. **Free.**

Annual Events

Pikes Peak Auto Hill Climb. Pikes Peak Toll Rd. July 4.

Pikes Peak or Bust Rodeo. Spencer Penrose Stadium. Phone 719/635-3547. 1st full wk Aug.

Pikes Peak Marathon. Footrace from cog depot to summit and back. Aug.

Seasonal Event

Greyhound racing. Rocky Mountain Greyhound Park. 1 mi N on Nevada Ave. For schedule phone 719/632-1391. Apr-late Sept.

Motels

★ **CASCADE HILLS.** (7885 US 24 W, Cascade 80809) 10 mi NW on US 24. 719/684-9977. 14 rms (shower only), 2 story, 2 kit. units, 2 cottages. 6 units A/C, 8 air-cooled. Memorial Day-Sept: S $49; D $55; each addl $4; kit. units $85-$105; cottages $150-$200; wkly rates; lower rates rest of yr. TV; cable (premium). Whirlpool. Complimentary coffee in lobby, continental bkfst. Ck-out 10 am. Some refrigerators. Picnic tables. Cr cds: DS, MC, V.

★ **COMFORT INN.** 8280 CO 83 (80920), off I-25 exit 150A. 719/598-6700; FAX 719/598-3443. 110 units, 4 story. S, D $45-$125; under 18 free. Crib free. TV; cable (premium). Pool. Continental bkfst. Restaurant nearby. Ck-out 11 am. Meeting rms. Business servs avail. In-rm modem link. Valet serv. Some refrigerators. Near USAF Academy. Cr cds: A, D, DS, JCB, MC, V.

★ ★ **DRURY INN.** 8155 N Academy Blvd (80920), I-25 exit 150A. 719/598-2500. 118 rms, 4 story. May-early Sept: S, D $74-$109; each addl $10; under 18 free; lower rates rest of yr. Crib free. Pet accepted, some restrictions. TV; cable (premium). Heated pool. Complimentary bkfst. Restaurant adj open 24 hrs. Ck-out noon. Coin lndry. Meeting rms. Business servs avail. In-rm modem link. Valet serv. Exercise equipt; weight machine, stair machine, whirlpool. Some refrigerators. Cr cds: A, C, D, DS, MC, V.

✔ ★ **GARDEN OF THE GODS.** 2922 West Colorado Avenue (80904). 719/636-5271. 32 rms, 1-2 story, 2 cottages. Mid-May-mid-Sept: S, D $46.50-$69.50; each addl $5; cottages $89.50-$120; lower rates rest of yr. Crib $3. TV; cable (premium). Indoor pool; sauna. Coffee in lobby. Restaurant nearby. Ck-out 11 am. Cr cds: A, C, D, DS, MC, V.

★ ★ **HAMPTON INN-NORTH.** 7245 Commerce Center Dr (80919), I-25 exit 149. 719/593-9700; FAX 719/598-0563. 128 rms, 4 story. Late May-Sept: S $85; D $95; under 18 free; lower rates rest of yr. Crib free. Pet accepted; $25 refundable. TV; cable (premium), VCR avail. Indoor pool. Complimentary continental bkfst. Restaurant nearby. Meeting rm. Business servs avail. In-rm modem link. Valet serv. Cr cds: A, C, D, DS, MC, V.

✔ ★ **MEL-HAVEN LODGE.** 3715 W Colorado Ave (80904). 719/633-9435; res: 800/762-5832. 21 rms, 2 story, 14 kits. Mid-May-mid-Sept: S $45-$60; D $60-$95; each addl $5; suites $90-$135; kit. units $5 addl; lower rates May 1-mid-May, mid-Sept-Oct. Closed rest of yr. Crib $4. TV; cable (premium). Heated pool; whirlpool. Playground.

Complimentary coffee in lobby. Restaurant nearby. Ck-out 11 am. Coin lndry. Sundries. Many refrigerators. Picnic tables, grill. Cr cds: A, C, D, DS, MC, V.

★ ★ **RESIDENCE INN BY MARRIOTT.** 3880 N Academy Blvd (80917). 719/574-0370; FAX 719/574-7821. 96 kit. suites, 2 story. S, D $115-$149; each addl $10; under 18 free. Crib $5. Pet accepted; $15 per day. TV; cable (premium), VCR avail. Heated pool; whirlpool. Complimentary continental bkfst. Ck-out noon. Meeting rms. Business servs avail. In-rm modem link. Coin lndry. Valet serv. Free airport transportation. Refrigerators. Some fireplaces. Balconies. Grills. Cr cds: A, D, DS, JCB, MC, V.

★ ★ **RODEWAY INN.** 2409 E Pikes Peak Ave (80909). 719/471-0990; FAX 719/471-0990. 113 rms, 2 story. May-early Sept: S $50-$60; D $58-$68; each addl $6; kit. units $95; under 18 free; lower rates rest of yr. Crib free. Pet accepted. TV; cable (premium). Heated pool. Complimentary coffee in lobby. Restaurant adj 6 am-10 pm. Bar to midnight. Ck-out noon. Meeting rms. Business servs avail. Some fireplaces. Cr cds: A, C, D, DS, JCB, MC, V.

Motor Hotels

★ ★ ★ **BEST WESTERN LE BARON.** 314 W Bijou (80905), I-25 Bijou exit 142. 719/471-8680; res: 800/477-8610; FAX 719/471-0894. 206 rms, 3 story, 15 suites. Mid-May-mid-Oct: S $79-$89; D $89-$99; each addl $10; suites $179-$229; lower rates rest of yr. Crib free. TV; cable, VCR avail. Heated pool; poolside serv. Complimentary coffee in rms. Restaurant 6 am-9 pm. Rm serv. Bar 11 am-midnight. Ck-out 11 am. Meeting rms. Business servs avail. In-rm modem link. Bellhops. Free airport transportation. Exercise equipt; weight machine, bicycles. Refrigerator in suites. Balconies. Cr cds: A, C, D, DS, MC, V.

★ ★ ★ **EMBASSY SUITES.** 7290 Commerce Center Dr (80919), I-25 exit 149. 719/599-9100; FAX 719/599-4644. 207 suites, 4 story. Mid-Apr-mid-Sept: S $115-$125; D $120-$130; each addl $10; under 12 free; package plans; wkend rates; lower rates rest of yr. TV; cable (premium). Indoor pool; hot tub. Complimentary full bkfst. Coffee in rms. Restaurant 11:30 am-2:30 pm, 6-10 pm. Rm serv. Bar to midnight. Ck-out noon. Coin lndry. Meeting rms. Business servs avail. In-rm modem link. Bellhops. Gift shop. Tennis, golf privileges. Exercise equipt; weights, bicycles, whirlpool, sauna. Game rm. Refrigerators. Balconies. Atrium; glass elevators. Cr cds: A, C, D, DS, JCB, MC, V.

✔ ★ ★ **QUALITY INN.** 555 W Garden of the Gods Rd (80907), off I-25 exit 146. 719/593-9119; FAX 719/260-0381. 157 rms, 4 story. Mid-May-mid-Sept: S $90-$120; D $95-$125; each addl $10; under 18 free; lower rates rest of yr. Crib free. Pet accepted; $20. TV; cable. Heated pool. Complimentary continental bkfst. Restaurant adj open 24 hrs. Ck-out 11 am. Coin lndry. Meeting rms. Business servs avail. In-rm modem link. Valet serv. Cr cds: A, C, D, DS, JCB, MC, V.

★ ★ **RADISSON AIRPORT.** 1645 Newport Dr (80916), near airport. 719/597-7000; FAX 719/597-4308. 145 rms, 2 story. S $85; D $95; each addl $12.50; suites $134; under 18 free; wkly rates. Crib free. Pet accepted, some restrictions; $50. TV; cable (premium). Indoor pool; poolside serv. Complimentary coffee in rms. Complimentary bkfst. Restaurant 11 am-10 pm. Rm serv 24 hrs. Bar. Ck-out noon. Coin lndry. Meeting rms. Business servs avail. Bellhops. Concierge. Gift shop. Free airport transportation. Exercise equipt; weight machine, rowers, whirlpool. Game rm. Cr cds: A, C, D, DS, ER, JCB, MC, V.

★ ★ ★ **RADISSON INN.** *8110 N Academy Blvd (80920), I-25 exit 150A.* 719/598-5770; FAX 719/598-3434. 200 rms, 2-4 story. May-Sept: S, D $75-$105; each addl $10; suites $129-$229; under 18 free; wkend rates; lower rates rest of yr. Crib free. Pet accepted, some restrictions. TV; cable, VCR avail. Indoor pool; whirlpool, sauna. Coffee in rms. Restaurants 6:30 am-10 pm. Rm serv. Bar from 11 am. Ck-out noon. Meeting rms. Business servs avail. In-rm modem link. Gift shop. Coin lndry. Free airport transportation. Health club privileges. Near USAF Academy. Cr cds: A, C, D, DS, ER, JCB, MC, V.

[D] [icons] [SC]

★ ★ ★ **RED LION.** *1775 E Cheyenne Mountain Blvd (80906), I-25 exit 138.* 719/576-8900; FAX 719/576-4450. 299 rms, 5 story. S $106-$146; D $121-$161; each addl $15; suites $325-$525; under 18 free; wkend, honeymoon · rates. Crib free. Pet accepted. TV; cable (premium), VCR avail. Indoor pool; hot tub. Coffee in rms. Restaurant 6 am-11 pm. Rm serv. Bar 11-2 am; entertainment, dancing Tues-Sat. Ck-out noon. Convention facilities. Business servs avail. In-rm modem link. Bellhops. Valet serv. Gift shop. Free airport transportation. Exercise equipt; weights, bicycles, whirlpool, sauna. Some bathrm phones. Private patios, balconies. Cr cds: A, C, D, DS, ER, MC, V.

[D] [icons] [SC]

★ ★ ★ **SHERATON.** *2886 S Circle Dr (80906), off I-25 exit 138.* 719/576-5900; FAX 719/576-5900, ext. 2424. 502 rms, 2-4 story. Mid-May-mid-Sept: S, D $95-$145; suites $175-$325; under 18 free; wkend rates; some lower rates rest of yr. Crib $5. Pet accepted. TV; cable (premium), VCR avail. 2 pools, 1 indoor; wading pool. Playground. Coffee in rms. Restaurant 6 am-10 pm. Rm serv. Bars 2 pm-midnight; entertainment Fri-Sat. Ck-out 11 am. Convention facilities. Business servs avail. In-rm modem link. Bellhops. Concierge. Free airport, bus depot transportation. Lighted tennis. Putting green. Exercise equipt; weight machine, bicycles, whirlpool, steam rm, sauna. Game rm. Some refrigerators. Private patios, balconies. Cr cds: A, C, D, DS, JCB, MC, V.

[D] [icons] [SC]

Hotels

✔ ★ ★ ★ **DOUBLETREE ANTLERS.** *4 S Cascade Ave (80903), Pikes Peak Ave & Cascade Ave; I-25 Bijou exit.* 719/473-5600; FAX 719/389-0259. 290 rms (some with shower only), 13 story. S $70-$155; D $85-$170; each addl $15; suites $125-$825; under 18 free; wkend rates. Crib free. Pet accepted, some restrictions. Garage $5. TV; cable (premium), VCR avail. Indoor pool; poolside serv. Complimentary coffee in rms. Restaurants 6:30 am-midnight; Fri & Sat to 1 am. Bars 11-1 am, Sun to midnight. Ck-out noon. Convention facilities. Business servs avail. In-rm modem link. Concierge. Gift shop. Free airport, bus depot transportation. Exercise equipt; weights, treadmill, bicycles, whirlpool. Cr cds: A, C, D, DS, ER, JCB, MC, V.

[D] [icons] [SC]

★ ★ ★ **MARRIOTT.** *5580 Tech Center Dr (80919), off I-25 exit 147.* 719/260-1800; FAX 719/260-1492. 310 rms, 9 story. S $120; D $130; suites $235-$300; under 18 free. Crib free. TV; cable (premium), VCR avail. 2 pools, 1 indoor. Restaurant 6:30 am-11 pm. Bar 11-midnight. Ck-out noon. Lndry facilities. Convention facilities. Business servs avail. Gift shop. Exercise equipt; weight machine, bicycles, sauna. Cr cds: A, C, D, DS, JCB, MC, V.

[D] [icons] [SC]

Inns

★ ★ ★ **HEARTHSTONE.** *506 N Cascade Ave (80903), I-25 to exit 143, then 3 blks E, then 1 mi S.* 719/473-4413; res: 800/521-1885; FAX 719/473-1322. 25 rms, 23 with bath, 3 story. No rm phones. S $70-$140; D $80-$150; each addl $15; under 4 free. Crib free. Complimentary full bkfst. Ck-out 11 am, ck-in 2-10 pm. Meeting rm. Gift shop. Some private patios, fireplaces. Restored Victorian mansion (1885);

brass fixtures, carved beds, many antique furnishings. Some rms with view of Pikes Peak. Totally nonsmoking. Cr cds: A, MC, V.

[D] [icons]

★ ★ ★ **HOLDEN HOUSE.** *1102 W Pikes Peak (80904).* 719/471-3980. 6 rms, 2 story. S, D $70-$105. Adults preferred. TV in sitting rm. Complimentary full bkfst, coffee (24 hrs), tea & cookies. Restaurant nearby. Ck-out 11 am, ck-in 4-6 pm. Victorian house (1902); some fireplaces, antique furnishings. Totally nonsmoking. Cr cds: A, D, DS, MC, V.

[icons]

★ ★ ★ **ROOM AT THE INN.** *618 N Nevada Ave (80903).* 719/442-1896; FAX 719/442-6802. 7 rms (1 with shower only), 3 story. S, D $85-$110; each addl $10. Children over 12 yrs only. Whirlpool. Complimentary full bkfst. Complimentary tea and coffee in afternoon. Restaurant nearby. Ck-out 11 am, ck-in 4-6 pm. Concierge serv. Luggage handling. Queen Anne Victorian home built in 1896; 3-story turret, wraparound porch. Totally nonsmoking. Cr cds: A, DS, MC, V.

[D] [icons]

Resort

★ ★ ★ ★ ★ **THE BROADMOOR.** *Box 1439 (80901), Lake Ave at Lake Circle, I-25 exit 138.* 719/634-7711; res: 800/634-7711; FAX 719/577-5700. This famous 3,500-acre resort resembles a small city set around a private lake; a spa, several restaurants, world-class golf courses, and a tennis center are among the facilities. Guest rooms vary greatly in size, decor, and aspect; the newest have a European style and oversized white-marble bathrooms. 700 rms. Mid-May-mid-Oct: S, D $225-$375; suites $280-$1,600; package plans; lower rates rest of yr. Crib free. TV; cable (premium), VCR avail. 4 pools, heated, 1 indoor; wading pool, poolside serv, lifeguard. Supervised child's activities (June-Labor Day & Dec 25 hols); ages 3-12. Dining rm open 24 hrs (also see PENROSE ROOM). Rm serv 24 hrs. Box lunches, snack bar. Bars noon-1 am; Sun to midnight. Ck-out noon, ck-in 4 pm. Convention facilities. Business servs avail. In-rm modem link. Concierge. Airport, RR station, bus depot transportation. Tennis (indoor in winter), pro. Recreational facilities (all extra) include: 3 18-hole golf courses, greens fee, pro, putting green, driving range. Boats. Bicycles. Skeet, trap and sporting clay shooting. Horseback riding. Hot-air ballooning. Entertainment, dancing, movie theater. Exercise rm; instructor, weight machine, bicycles, whirlpool, sauna. Masseuse. Fishing/hunting guide service. Minibars; some refrigerators. Balconies. Center for large convention groups. Cr cds: A, C, D, DS, MC, V.

[D] [icons]

Guest Ranch

★ ★ ★ **LOST VALLEY GUEST RANCH.** *(29555 Goose Creek Rd, Sedalia 80135) 18 mi W on US 24, then 24 mi N on CO 67, 3 mi NW on County 126, then 9 mi SW on dirt road (follow ranch signs).* 303/647-2311; FAX 303/647-2315. 24 cabins (1-3 bedrm). No A/C. No rm phones. AP, Mid-June-Labor Day, wkly: $1,425 each; family rates; lower daily rates rest of yr. Pool; whirlpools. Playground. Free supervised child's activities (Memorial Day-Labor Day); ages 3-18. Coffee in cabins. Box lunches, picnics, cookouts. Ck-out Sun 10 am, ck-in Sun 2 pm. Coin lndry. Meeting rms. Business servs avail. Tennis. Trap shooting. Hayrides, wagon rides. Spring and fall cattle round-ups. Lawn games. Soc dir, entertainment, square dancing. Rec rm. Fishing school; fish cleaning, storage, cooking. Refrigerators, fireplaces. Private porches, balconies. Beautiful view of mountains. Authentic working ranch. Homesteaded in 1883. No cr cds accepted.

[icons]

Restaurants

★ ★ **BECKETT'S.** *128 S Tejon, 2 blks S off Pikes Peak Ave. 719/635-3535.* Hrs: 11 am-10 pm; Sun from 5 pm. Closed Thanksgiving, Dec 25. Res accepted. Bar. Semi-a la carte: lunch $4.25-$8, dinner $5.50-$15.95. Child's meals. Specializes in spit-roasted chicken, barbecued ribs. Entertainment Thurs-Sat evenings. Outdoor dining in season. In basement of historic hotel. Cr cds: A, MC, V.

[D]

★ ★ **EDELWEISS.** *34 E Ramona Ave. 719/633-2220.* Hrs: 11:30 am-2 pm, 5-9 pm; Fri & Sat to 9:30 pm; Sun from 5 pm. German, Amer menu. Bar. Semi-a la carte: lunch $3.95-$6.95, dinner $7.25-$15.95. Specialties: Wienerschnitzel, Sauerbraten. Own soups. German music & entertainment Fri, Sat. Parking. Outdoor dining. Former schoolhouse (1890). Family-owned. Cr cds: A, D, DS, MC, V.

✔ ★ **GIUSEPPE'S OLD DEPOT.** *10 S Sierra Madre. 719/635-3111.* Hrs: 11 am-10 pm; Fri & Sat to 11:45 pm. Closed Thanksgiving, Dec 25. Res accepted. Italian, Amer menu. Bar. Semi-a la carte: lunch, dinner $5.95-$14.95. Child's meals. Specializes in lasagne, pizza, prime rib, Reuben sandwich. Salad bar. Parking. Large main dining rm with several different size dining areas. In historic railroad depot (1887); railroad memorabilia on display. Cr cds: A, C, D, DS, MC, V.

[D]

★ ★ **HATCH COVER.** *252 E Cheyenne Mountain Blvd. 719/576-5223.* Hrs: 11 am-2 pm, 5-10 pm; Sat & Sun from 5 pm; Sun brunch 10:30 am-2 pm. Res accepted. Bar to 2 am. Semi-a la carte: lunch $4.50-$8.95, dinner $10-$25. Sun brunch $4.95-$9.95. Specializes in fresh seafood, prime rib. Parking. Aquariums. Cr cds: A, D, DS, MC, V.

[SC]

★ ★ **LA PETITE MAISON.** *1015 W Colorado Ave. 719/632-4887.* Hrs: 5-10 pm; early-bird dinner 5-6:30 pm. Res accepted. Closed Sun & Mon; Jan 1, July 4, Dec 24 & 25. Serv bar. Semi-a la carte: dinner $7.95-$20.75. Specializes in duck, lamb, seasonal fresh fish. Parking. In renovated house (1894). Totally nonsmoking. Cr cds: A, C, D, DS, MC, V.

[D]

✔ ★ **MAGGIE MAE'S.** *2405 E Pikes Peak Ave. 719/475-1623.* Hrs: 6 am-10 pm; Sat & Sun to 9 pm. Closed Dec 25. Mexican, Amer menu. Bar to midnight. Semi-a la carte: bkfst $4-$7, lunch $4.25-$7, dinner $6-$11. Child's meals. Specializes in omelettes, green chili, soups, steak. Parking. Cr cds: A, DS, MC, V.

✔ ★ ★ **MASON JAR.** *5050 N Academy Blvd. 719/598-1101.* Hrs: 11 am-10 pm; to 9 pm in winter. Closed Thanksgiving, Dec 25. Bar. Semi-a la carte: lunch $3.50-$5.25, dinner $5-$11. Child's meals. Specializes in chicken-fried steak, prime rib. Own desserts. Parking. Cr cds: DS, MC, V.

[D]

★ ★ ★ **PENROSE ROOM.** *(See The Broadmoor Resort) 719/634-7711.* Hrs: 6:30-9:30 pm; Sat to 10 pm. Res accepted. Continental menu. Bar. Semi-a la carte: dinner $23-$32. Specialties: whole roasted Amish duck bigarade, poached filet of Atlantic salmon "Dieppoise," peppered tenderloin of beef carpaccio, classic steak tartar. Own baking. Band trio. Jacket, tie. Cr cds: A, C, D, DS, MC, V.

[D]

Unrated Dining Spots

FURRS CAFETERIA. *2206 E Pikes Peak Ave, in Central Bank Plaza. 719/632-3515.* Hrs: 11 am-8 pm. Closed Dec 25. Avg ck: lunch, dinner $4.90-$6.75. Specializes in roast beef, chicken-fried steak. Cr cds: MC, V.

LA CRÊPERIE. *204 N Tejon. 719/632-0984.* Hrs: 10 am-9 pm; Mon to 3 pm, Sun 11 am-3 pm. Closed most major hols. Res accepted. Continental menu. Wine, beer. Semi-a la carte: lunch $5-$8, dinner $7.50-$15. Specializes in crêpes, country French cuisine. Former streetcar horse stable (1892). Country French decor. Cr cds: A, D, MC, V.

OLD CHICAGO. *7115 Commerce Center Dr, I-25 exit 149. 719/593-7678.* Hrs: 11-2 am; Sun to midnight. Closed Thanksgiving, Dec 25. Bar. Italian, Amer menu. Semi-a la carte: lunch $4.95-$7.95, dinner $5.95-$15.95. Child's meals. Specializes in deep-dish pizza, pasta. Parking. Sports bar atmosphere. Cr cds: A, MC, V.

[D] [SC]

OLD CHICAGO PASTA & PIZZA. *118 N Tejon. 719/634-8812.* Hrs: 11 am-midnight; Sun from noon. Closed Thanksgiving, Dec 25. Res accepted. Italian menu. Bar to 2 am, Sun to midnight. Semi-a la carte: lunch $3.95-$6.50, dinner $5.95-$10.95. Child's meals. Specializes in pizza, pasta bar. Own pasta. Outdoor dining. Cr cds: A, MC, V.

[D] [SC]

Copper Mountain (C-4)

(see Dillon)

Cortez (F-1)

Settled 1890 **Pop** 7,284 **Elev** 6,201 ft **Area code** 303 **Zip** 81321
Information Cortez/Mesa Verde Visitor Info Bureau, PO Box HH; 303/565-8227 or 800/253-1616.

Originally a trading center for sheep and cattle ranchers whose spreads dot the plains to the south, Cortez now accommodates travelers visiting Mesa Verde National Park (see) and oilmen whose business takes them to the nearby Aneth Oil Field. In the semidesert area 38 miles southwest of Cortez is the only spot in the nation where one can stand in four states (Colorado, Utah, Arizona, New Mexico) and two Native American nations (Navajo and Ute) at one time; a simple marker located approximately 100 yards from the Four Corners Highway (US 160) indicates the exact place where these areas meet. There are many opportunities for hunting and fishing in the Dolores River Valley.

What to See and Do

Anasazi Heritage Center and Escalante Ruins. Museum of exhibits, artifacts and documents from excavations on public lands in southwest Colorado, including the Dolores Archaeological Program. Represents the Northern San Juan Anasazi Tradition (ca A.D. 1 to 1300). Within a half-mile of the center are the Dominguez and Escalante ruins—the latter discovered by a Franciscan friar in 1776. Excavations revealed kivas and other structures, pottery and ceremonial artifacts. (Daily; closed Jan 1, Thanksgiving, Dec 25) 8 mi N on CO 145, then 2 mi NW on CO 184. Phone 303/882-4811. **Free.**

Hovenweep National Monument. Monument consists of six units of prehistoric ruins; the best preserved is at Square Tower, which includes the remains of pueblos and towers. Self-guided trail, park ranger on duty; visitor area (daily); camping (daily; limited facilities in winter). 20 mi NW on US 666 to Pleasant View and follow signs 5 mi W on County BB, then 20 mi S on County 10. Phone 303/529-4461. **Free.** Camping ¢¢¢

Lowry Pueblo Ruins. Constructed by Anasazi Indians (ca 1075). Forty excavated rooms include one great and seven smaller kivas. Picnic facilities. No camping. (Daily, weather & road conditions permitting) 21 mi NW on US 666 to Pleasant View, then 9 mi W on county road. Phone 303/247-4082. **Free.**

Mesa Verde National Park (see). 10 mi E on US 160.

Ute Mountain Tribal Park. The Ute Mountain Tribe is developing this 125,000-acre park on their tribal lands, opening hundreds of largely unexplored 800-year-old Anasazi ruins to the public. Tours begin at the Ute Mountain Visitor Center/Museum, 19 miles south via US 666 (daily); reservations required. Backpacking trips in summer. Primitive camping available. For further information, reservations phone 303/565-3751, ext 282 or 800/847-5485. Tours ¢¢¢¢¢

Annual Events

Ute Mountain Rodeo. Early June.

Montezuma County Fair. 1st wk Aug.

Motels

★ **ANASAZI.** 640 S Broadway. 970/565-3773; res: 800/972-6232 (exc CO); FAX 970/565-1027. 87 rms, 1-2 story. June-Sept: S $57; D $69-$71; each addl $6; under 18 free; lower rates rest of yr. Crib free. Pet accepted. TV; cable, VCR avail. Heated pool; whirlpool. Restaurant 5:30 am-10 pm. Rm serv 7 am-9 pm. Bar; entertainment, dancing Fri & Sat. Ck-out noon. Meeting rms. Business servs avail. In-rm modem link. Gift shop. Free airport transportation. Cr cds: A, D, DS, MC, V.

D ⮐ ⩩ ⊠ 🔥 SC

★ ★ **BEST WESTERN TURQUOISE.** 535 E Main St. 970/565-3778; FAX 970/565-3439. 46 rms, 2 story. June-Sept: S $73-$92; D $92-$115; each addl $5; lower rates rest of yr. Crib free. Pet accepted, some restrictions. TV; cable. Heated pool. Ck-out 11 am. Coin lndry. Business servs avail. In-rm modem link. Free airport transportation. Cr cds: A, C, D, DS, MC, V.

⮐ ⩩ ⊠ 🔥 SC

✔ ★ ★ **HOLIDAY INN EXPRESS.** 2121 E Main St. 970/565-6000; FAX 970/565-3438. 100 rms, 3 story. S $48-$90; D $55-$96; each addl $6; under 18 free. Crib free. Pet accepted, some restrictions. TV; cable (premium). Indoor pool. Complimentary continental bkfst, coffee. Restaurant nearby. Ck-out 11 am. Business servs avail. In-rm modem link. Valet serv. Free airport transportation. Exercise equipt; weight machines, ski machine, whirlpool. Cr cds: A, C, D, DS, JCB, MC, V.

D ⮐ ⩩ 🏋 ⊠ 🔥 SC

Restaurant

★ ★ **HOMESTEADERS.** 45 E Main. 970/565-6253. Hrs: 7 am-3 pm, 5-9 pm. Closed major hols; also Sun Nov-Apr. Res accepted. Serv bar. Semi-a la carte: bkfst $2.65-$5.79, lunch $2.49-$5.25, dinner $4.45-$12. Child's meals. Specializes in Southwestern cuisine. Rustic Western decor. Cr cds: A, DS, MC, V.

SC

Craig (A-3)

(See Steamboat Springs)

Pop 8,091 **Elev** 6,186 ft **Area code** 970 **Zip** 81625
Information Greater Craig Area Chamber of Commerce, 360 E Victory Way, 81625; 970/824-5689 or 800/864-4405.

Craig is known for excellent big game hunting for elk, deer and antelope and bass fishing in Elkhead Reservoir. The Yampa River area draws float-boaters, hikers and wildlife photographers in summer and cross-country skiiers and snowmobilers in winter. A Ranger District office of the Routt National Forest (see STEAMBOAT SPRINGS) is located in Craig.

What to See and Do

Dinosaur National Monument (see). 88 mi W on US 40 to monument headquarters.

Marcia. Private luxury Pullman railroad car of David Moffat. Tours avail through Moffat County Visitors Center. City Park, US 40. Phone 970/824-5689. **Free.**

Museum of Northwest Colorado. Local history, Native American artifacts; wildlife photography. Cowboy and gunfighter collection. Also the Edwin C. Johnson Collection (Johnson was governor of Colorado & US senator). (May-Dec, daily exc Sun; rest of yr, Mon-Fri) Donation. 590 Yampa Ave, Old State Armory, center of town. Phone 970/824-6360.

Save Our Sandrocks Nature Trail. This sloped three-quarter-mile trail provides a view of Native American petroglyphs on the sandrocks. Trailguide available at the Cooperative Extension Office, 200 W Victory Way. (May-Nov) On the 900 block of Alta Vista Drive. Phone 970/824-6673. **Free.**

Motels

★ **A BAR Z MOTEL.** 2690 W US 40. 970/824-7066; res: 800/458-7228; FAX 970/824-3641. 42 rms, 2 story. S $38; D $43-$75; each addl $4; under 12 free; wkly rates. Pet accepted; $4. TV; cable (premium). Complimentary continental bkfst, coffee in rms. Restaurant adj. Ck-out 11 am. Coin lndry. Business servs avail. Whirlpool. Game rm. Picnic tables, grills. Cr cds: A, D, DS, MC, V.

⮐ ⊠ 🔥 SC

★ ★ **HOLIDAY INN.** 300 S CO 13, 1 mi SW. 970/824-4000; FAX 970/824-3950. 169 rms, 2 story. S $56-$62; D $62-$68; each addl $6; suites $76-$82; under 19 free. Crib free. Pet accepted. TV; cable (premium), VCR avail. Indoor pool; whirlpool, poolside serv. Restaurant 6 am-9:30 am, 5:30-9:30 pm. Rm serv. Bar 4 pm-midnight; dancing Fri, Sat. Coin lndry. Meeting rms. Business servs avail. In-rm modem link. Valet serv. Holidome. Exercise equipt: stair machine, bicycle, weights. Game rm. Cr cds: A, C, D, DS, JCB, MC, V.

D ⮐ ⩩ 🏋 ⊠ 🔥 SC

Crested Butte (D-3)

(See Gunnison)

Founded 1880 **Pop** 878 **Elev** 8,908 ft **Area code** 970 **Zip** 81224
Information Crested Butte Vacations, 12 Snowmass Road, PO Box A, Mount Crested Butte 81225; 800/544-8448.

Crested Butte is a remarkably picturesque mining town in the midst of magnificent mountain country. Inquire locally for information on horseback pack trips to Aspen (see) through the West Elk Wilderness. Guided fishing trips are available on the more than 1,000 miles of streams and rivers within a two-hour drive of Crested Butte.

What to See and Do

Crested Butte Mountain Resort Ski Area. 3 triple, 5 double chairlifts, 4 surface lifts, 1 high speed quad; patrol, school, rentals; snowmaking; cafeteria, restaurant, bar; nursery. 85 runs; longest run 2.6 mi; vertical drop 3,062 ft. (Late Nov-mid-Apr, daily) Multi-day, half-day rates. 19 mi of groomed cross-country trails, 100 mi of wilderness trails; snowmobiling, sleigh rides. 3 mi N on county road in Gunnison National Forest (see GUNNISON). Phone 970/349-2333 or -2323 for snow conditions. ¢¢¢¢

Motel

(Hours and dates open may vary during off-season, making it advisable to call ahead)

✔ ★ **OLD TOWN INN.** *Box 990, 201 N 6th St.* 970/349-6184. 33 rms, 2 story. S $45-$80; D $50-$95; each addl $8; higher rates: spring break, week of Dec 25. Pet accepted, some restrictions; $8. TV; cable (premium). Complimentary continental bkfst. Restaurant nearby. Ck-out 11 am. Coin lndry. Free ski area transportation. Downhill/x-country ski 3 mi. Hot tub. Picnic tables. Cr cds: A, C, D, DS, MC, V.

[D] [icons] [SC]

Lodges

★ ★ **ELK MOUNTAIN.** *129 Gothic Ave.* 970/349-7533; res: 800/374-6521; FAX 970/349-5114. 16 air-cooled rms, 3 story. Mid-Nov-Mar: S, D $98-$108; lower rates rest of yr. Children over 12 yrs only. TV; cable (premium), VCR avail (movies avail). Complimentary bkfst buffet. Restaurant nearby. Ck-out 10 am. Business servs avail. Valet serv. Downhill/x-country ski 2 mi. Whirlpool. Some balconies. Totally nonsmoking. Cr cds: A, D, DS, MC, V.

[icons]

★ ★ **NORDIC BED & BREAKFAST INN.** *Box 939, On Treasury Rd.* 970/349-5542; FAX 970/349-6487. 28 rms, 2 story, 3 kits. No A/C. Thanksgiving-Mar: S, D $80-$103; each addl $10; kit. units $142-$186; family, wkly rates (summer); ski, golf plans; varied lower rates rest of yr. Crib $5. TV; cable (premium), VCR avail. Complimentary continental bkfst. Restaurant nearby. Ck-out 11 am. Meeting rm. Business servs avail. In-rm modem link. Downhill ski 1 blk. Hot tub. Fireplace in lobby. Cr cds: A, MC, V.

[D] [icons] [SC]

Motor Hotel

★ ★ **MOUNTAIN LAIR.** *500 Gothic Rd (81225).* 970/349-8000; res: 800/642-4422; FAX 970/349-8050. 125 rms, 5 story. Mid-Nov-mid-Apr: S, D $70-$145; each addl $10; under 13 free; ski, golf rates; lower rates rest of yr. Closed May & Oct. Crib free. TV; cable, VCR avail. Complimentary coffee in rms. Restaurant adj 7:30 am-10 pm. Ck-out 11 am. Bellhops. Gift shop. Downhill/x-country ski 1 block. Refrigerators. Cr cds: A, D, DS, MC, V.

[D] [icons] [SC]

Hotel

★ ★ ★ **GRANDE BUTTE.** *Box A (81225), 500 Gothic Rd.* 970/349-4000; res: 800/642-4422; FAX 970/349-4466. 261 rms, 6 story. Mid-Nov-early Apr: S, D $87-$180; suites $140-$265; under 12 free; ski, golf plans; lower rates rest of yr. Crib free. TV; cable, VCR avail. Indoor pool. Coffee in rms. Restaurant 5-10 pm. Bar 11 am-midnight; entertainment, dancing (winter). Ck-out 11 am. Convention facilities. Business center. In-rm modem link. Concierge. Free covered parking. Downhill/x-country ski on site. Exercise equipt; weight machine, treadmill, whirlpools, sauna. Refrigerators, wet bars, in-rm whirlpools; some fireplaces. Balconies. Picnic tables. Luxury level. Cr cds: A, D, DS, MC, V.

[D] [icons] [SC]

Inn

★ ★ **CRESTED BUTTE CLUB.** *512 2nd St.* 970/349-6655; res: 800/815-2582; FAX 970/349-7580. 7 air-cooled rms, 2 story. Mid-Nov-mid-Apr (2-day min): S, D $150-$225; each addl $35; ski, golf plans; lower rates rest of yr. TV; cable (premium). Indoor pool. Complimentary bkfst buffet. Restaurant opp 5-10 pm. Ck-out 11 am, ck-in 3 pm. Concierge serv. Luggage handling. Business servs avail. Golf privileges, greens fee $35, putting green, driving range. Downhill ski 2 mi; x-country 1 blk. Health club privileges. Built in 1886; many family heirlooms, fireplaces. Totally nonsmoking. Cr cds: A, DS, MC, V.

[icons]

Restaurants

✔ ★ **DONITA'S CANTINA.** *332 Elk Ave.* 970/349-6674. Hrs: 5:30-9:30 pm. No A/C. Mexican menu. Semi-a la carte: dinner $7.50-$17.95. Child's meals. Specializes in Tex-Mex cuisine. Own desserts. Mexican decor. Former hotel (1881) with original pressed tin ceiling. Cr cds: A, DS, MC, V.

★ ★ **GOURMET NOODLE.** *411 3rd St.* 970/349-7401. Hrs: 6-10 pm. Closed mid-Apr-mid-June & last wk Sept-Thanksgiving. Res accepted. No A/C. Italian menu. Bar. Semi-a la carte: dinner $9.95-$23.95. Child's meals. Specializes in elk, seafood, pasta. Totally nonsmoking. Cr cds: A, MC, V.

★ ★ **LE BOSQUET.** *201 Elk Ave.* 970/349-5808. Hrs: 11:30 am-2 pm, 6-10 pm; winter from 5:30 pm. Closed mid-Apr-mid-May. Res accepted. No A/C. French menu. Bar. Semi-a la carte: lunch $3.50-$7.95, dinner $9.95-$25.95. Specializes in lamb, fresh seafood, chicken. Own desserts. Outdoor dining (lunch). French decor. Totally nonsmoking. Cr cds: A, DS, MC, V.

★ ★ **PENELOPE'S.** *120 Elk Ave.* 970/349-5178. Hrs: 5:30-10 pm; Sun 8:30 am-1 pm, 5:30-10 pm. Closed mid-Apr-mid-June & mid-Oct-mid-Nov. Res accepted. No A/C. Semi-a la carte: bkfst, brunch $3.50-$8, dinner $9.95-$25.95. Child's meals. Specializes in fresh seafood, steak, lamb. Parking. Outdoor dining. Located in 1879 bldg; greenhouse. Family-owned. Cr cds: A, MC, V.

Unrated Dining Spot

BAKERY CAFE. *302 Elk Ave.* 970/349-7280. Hrs: 7 am-9 pm. Closed Dec 25. No A/C. European menu. Wine, beer. A la carte entrees: bkfst, lunch $2-$5, dinner $3-$6. Specializes in soups & sandwiches, pizza, salad bar. Outdoor dining. Cr cds: MC, V.

Cripple Creek (D-5)

(See Cañon City, Colorado Springs, Manitou Springs)

Settled 1891 **Pop** 584 **Elev** 9,508 ft **Area code** 719 **Zip** 80813
Information Chamber of Commerce, PO Box 650; 719/689-2169 or 800/526-8777.

Long considered worthless by mining experts despite frequent reports of gold, the "$300 million cow pasture" was finally developed by tenderfeet, who did their prospecting with pitchforks.

At its height, Cripple Creek and the surrounding area produced as much as $25 million in gold in a single year (at $20 per ounce). Few "Wild West" towns experienced a more colorful past. Jack Johnson and Jack Dempsey both worked here, the latter once fighting a long, bloody battle for $50. Texas Guinan, the speak-easy hostess, started her career here. In 1900, the town had a population of more than 25,000 with more than 500 gold mines in operation. Today only a handful of people live in the shadow of 10,400-foot Mt Pisgah. The town has been designated a National Historic Mining District. The present buildings were built after a great fire in 1896 destroyed the old town. Much restoration of the historic structures is in progress.

What to See and Do

Cripple Creek District Museum. Artifacts of Cripple Creek's glory; pioneer relics, mining and railroad displays; Victorian furnishings. Heritage Art Gallery and Assay Office (summer only; free). (Memorial Day-mid-Oct, daily; winter, early spring, wkends only). On CO 67. Phone 719/689-2634. ¢¢

Cripple Creek-Victor Narrow Gauge Railroad. An authentic locomotive and coaches depart from Cripple Creek District Museum. Four-mile round trip past many historic mines. (Late May-early Oct, daily, departs every 45 min) On CO 67. Phone 719/689-2640. ¢¢¢

Imperial Hotel (1896) (see INN). This hotel was constructed shortly after the town's great fire. The Imperial Players perform Victorian melodramas in the Gold Bar Room Theatre (mid-June-Dec, daily exc Mon). Phone 719/689-7777 or 800/235-2922. For reservations phone 719/689-2922. ¢¢¢

Mollie Kathleen Gold Mine. Descend 1,000 feet on a 40-minute guided tour through a gold mine. (May-Oct, daily) 1 mi N on CO 67. Phone 719/689-2465. ¢¢¢

Old Homestead (1896). Opulent brothel that flourished during the gold rush; original furnishings. (Memorial Day-Oct, daily) 353 E Myers Ave. Phone 719/689-3090. ¢¢

Victor. Victor, the "city of mines," actually does have streets paved with gold (low-grade ore was used to surface streets in the early days). 7 mi S on CO 67.

Annual Event

Donkey Derby Days. Last wkend June.

Hotel

✔★ **INDEPENDENCE.** *153 Bennett Ave. 719/689-2744.* 7 air-cooled rms, 2 story. S, D $55-$79.50. TV; cable. Restaurant 11:30 am-midnight. Bar. Ck-out 10 am. Rms & lobby on second floor. Cr cds: A, DS, MC, V.

Inns

★ **IMPERIAL HOTEL.** *Box 869, 123 N 3rd St. 719/689-7777; res: 800/235-2922; FAX 719/689-0416.* 29 rms, 3 story, 11 baths, 18 share baths. No A/C. S, D $65-$95; each addl $15. Restaurant (see IMPERIAL DINING ROOM). Bars 10-2 am; entertainment exc Mon. Ck-out 11 am. Meeting rms. Built 1896. Victorian decor; antiques. Gold Bar Room Theatre. Cr cds: A, DS, MC, V.

★★ **VICTOR HOTEL.** *(4th St & Victor Ave, Victor 80860) 6 mi S on CO 67. 719/689-3553; res: 800/748-0870; FAX 719/689-3979.* 30 air-cooled rms, 4 story. Mid-May-mid-Oct: S $89; D $99; under 12 free; lower rates rest of yr. Pet accepted. TV; cable (premium). Complimentary continental bkfst. Restaurant 11:30 am-2 pm, 5-9 pm; closed Mon. Rm serv. Ck-out 11 am. Former bank; bird-cage elevator. Cr cds: A, DS, MC, V.

D ✔ ⊠ ⊠ SC

Restaurants

★ **COLORADO GRANDE-MAGGIE'S.** *300 E Bennett. 719/689-3517.* Hrs: 7 am-2:30 pm. Bar 8-2 am. Semi-a la carte: bkfst .99¢-$5.40, lunch $3.25-$5.25, dinner $5.95-$13.95. Child's meals. Specializes in prime rib. Victorian decor; brocade chairs, lace curtains, restored pressed tin ceiling. Cr cds: MC, V.

D

✔★★ **IMPERIAL DINING ROOM.** *(See Imperial Hotel Inn) 719/689-7777.* Hrs: 11 am-2:30 pm, 5-9 pm; Sun brunch 10 am-3 pm. Res accepted. Bars 8-2 am. Buffet: lunch $6.95, dinner $12.95. Parking. Authentic Old West Victorian decor. Buffet/show combination avail. Cr cds: A, DS, MC, V.

Delta (D-2)

(See Montrose)

Settled 1880 **Pop** 3,789 **Elev** 4,953 ft **Area code** 970 **Zip** 81416
Information Chamber of Commerce, 301 Main St; 970/874-8616.

Situated in Colorado's largest fruit-growing area, Delta annually produces millions of dollars worth of apples, peaches and cherries. For information on Gunnison National Forest (see GUNNISON), Uncompahgre National Forest (see NORWOOD) and Grand Mesa National Forest (see GRAND JUNCTION), write the Supervisor, 2250 US 50 in Delta.

What to See and Do

Black Canyon of the Gunnison National Monument (see). Approx 40 mi SE via US 50 & CO 347.

Crawford State Park. Swimming, waterskiing; fishing; boating (ramps). Winter sports. Picnicking. Camping. Standard fees. (Daily) 20 mi E to Hotchkiss, then 11 mi S on CO 92. Phone 970/921-5721. Per vehicle ¢¢

Sweitzer State Park. Swimming, waterskiing; fishing; boating (ramps). Picnicking, birdwatching. Standard fees. (Daily) 3 mi SE off US 50. Phone 970/874-4258. Per vehicle ¢¢

Annual Event

Deltarado Days. Delta Round-up Club, 4 mi E. Parade, barbecue, craft booths, games, square dancing, PRCA Rodeo. Last wkend July.

Seasonal Event

Thunder Mountain Lives Tonight! Confluence Park. Outdoor pageant dramatizing the history of Thunder Mountain (Grand Mesa). Native American ceremonies; rodeo, shoot-out. Phone 970/874-8616. Tues-Sat nightly. Early July-Labor Day.

Motel

✔★★ **BEST WESTERN SUNDANCE.** *903 Main St, 5 blks S on US 50. 970/874-9781; FAX 970/874-5440.* 41 rms, 2 story. June-Sept: S $40-$50; D $45-$53; each addl $5; under 12 free; lower rates rest of yr. Pet accepted. TV; cable (premium). Heated pool; whirlpool. Complimentary coffee. Complimentary full bkfst. Restaurant 6:30 am-9 pm. Rm serv. Bar 11-2 am. Ck-out 11 am. Coin lndry. Meeting rm. In-rm modem link. Exercise equipt; weights, treadmill. Cr cds: A, C, D, DS, MC, V.

✔ ⊠ ⊀ ⊠ ⊠ SC

Denver (C-6)

Settled 1858 **Pop** 467,610 **Elev** 5,280 ft **Area code** 303
Information Denver Metro Convention & Visitors Bureau, 1555 California St, Ste 300, 80202; 303/892-1505 or 303/892-1112.

The "mile high city," capital of Colorado, began as a settlement of gold seekers, many of them unsuccessful. Denver almost lost out to several booming mountain mining centers. In 1858 the community (together with Auraria—the two were consolidated in 1860) consisted of some 60 raffish cabins, plus Colorado's first saloon. With the opening of silver mines in the 1870s Denver came into its own. By 1890 the population had topped 100,000. Nourished by the wealth that poured in from the silver districts, Denver rapidly became the most important city in the state. Today, with the Great Plains sweeping away to the east, the foothills and the Front Range of the Rocky Mountains immediately to the west and a dry, mild climate, Denver is a thriving transportation, industrial, commercial, cultural and vacation center. It has also become a headquarters for energy research and production.

The Denver Mountain Park System is unique in the Rocky Mountain foothills. It covers 13,448 acres, scattered over 380 square miles. The chain begins 15 miles west of the city and extends to Summit Lake (12,740 feet), 60 miles west. A Ranger District office of the Arapaho National Forest (see DILLON) is located in Denver.

Transportation

Airport: See DENVER INTL AIRPORT AREA.

Car Rental Agencies: See toll-free numbers under Introduction.

Public Transportation: Buses (Regional Transportation District), phone 303/299-6000.

Rail Passenger Service: Amtrak 800/872-7245.

What to See and Do

Arvada Center for the Arts & Humanities. Performing arts center with concerts, plays, classes, demonstrations, art galleries, banquet hall. New amphitheater seats 1,200 (June-early Sept). Historical museum with old cabin and pioneer artifacts. (Daily) 6901 Wadsworth Blvd, NW in Arvada. Phone 303/431-3939 for ticket information. Museum and gallery **Free.**

Byers-Evans House/Denver History Museum. Restored Victorian-house featuring the history of two noted Colorado pioneer families. Interactive video programs tell the story of the Queen City of the West. Guided tours avail. (Daily exc Mon; closed hols) Sr citizen rate. 1310 Bannock St. Phone 303/620-4933. **¢¢**

Chatfield State Park. Swimming beach, bathhouse, waterskiing; fishing; boating (rentals, dock), marina; hiking, biking, bridle trails. Picnicking. Snack bar. Nature center; interpretive programs. Camping (electrical hookups, dump station). Standard fees. (Daily) 1 mi S on Wadsworth St, at C-470, near Littleton. Phone 303/791-7275. Per vehicle **¢¢**

Cherry Creek State Park. Swimming, bathhouse, waterskiing; fishing; boating (ramps, rentals). Horseback riding. Picnicking (shelters), concession. Camping. Model airplane field, shooting range. Standard fees. (Daily) 1 mi S of I-225 on Parker Rd (CO 83), near south Denver. Phone 303/690-1166. Per vehicle **¢¢**

Civic Center. W of Capitol Complex. Includes

Denver Public Library. First phase of new library opened in 1995; it encompasses the old library. Largest public library in Rocky Mountain region with nearly 4 million items; outstanding Western History collection, Patent Depository Library, genealogy collections and branch library system. Programs, exhibits. (Daily; closed most hols) 1357 Broadway. Phone 303/640-6200. **Free.**

Denver Art Museum. Houses collection of art objects representing almost every culture and period, including a fine collection of Native American arts; changing exhibits. (Daily exc Mon; closed major hols) Sr citizen rate. Sat **free.** 100 W 14th Ave Pkwy, south side of Center. Phone 303/640-2793. **¢¢**

Denver City and County Building. Courts, municipal council and administrative offices. W side of Center.

Greek Theater. Outdoor amphitheater, summer folk dancing. S side of Center.

Comanche Crossing Museum. Memorabilia of the completion of the transcontinental railway, artifacts pertaining to area history; seven buildings with period rooms; restored schoolhouse (1891); Strasburg Union Pacific Depot; caboose, wood-vaned windmill (1880), and homestead on landscaped grounds. (June-Aug, daily) Donation. 30 mi E in Strasburg. Phone 303/622-4322.

Denver Botanic Gardens. Outdoor areas with herb, rose, and Japanese gardens; rock alpine garden and alpine house; landscape demonstration gardens; Boettcher Memorial Conservatory, which houses more than 850 tropical and subtropical plants; orchid and bromeliad pavilion; education building with library. (Daily; closed Jan 1, Dec 25) Sr citizen rate. 1005 York St. Phone 303/331-4000. **¢¢**

Denver Firefighters Museum. Housed in Fire House No. 1; maintains atmosphere of working firehouse; firefighting equipment from mid-1800s. (Mon-Fri, late morning-early afternoon) Fire house restaurant on 2nd floor. 1326 Tremont Place. Phone 303/892-1436. **¢**

Denver Museum of Natural History. 90 habitat exhibits from four continents displayed against natural backgrounds; Prehistoric Journey exhibit displays dinosaurs in re-created environments; earth sciences lab; gems and minerals; Native American collection. (Daily; closed Dec 25) Sr citizen rate. 2001 Colorado Blvd, in City Park. Phone 303/322-7009. **¢¢** Combination tickets available for

Charles C. Gates Planetarium. Contains a Minolta Series IV star projector; presents a variety of star and laser light shows daily; phone 303/370-6351 for schedule and fees. The **Phipps IMAX Theater** has an immense motion picture system projecting images on screen 4½ stories tall and 6½ stories wide. Daily showings. Phone 303/370-6300. **¢¢**

Hall of Life. Health education center has permanent exhibits on genetics, fitness, nutrition and the five senses. Classes and workshops (fee). (Daily) Phone 303/322-7009.

Denver Performing Arts Complex. One of the most innovative and comprehensive performing arts centers in the country. With the recent addition of the Temple Hoyne Buell Theatre, the complex is the second largest in the nation. The complex also contains shops and restaurants. Speer & Arapahoe Sts. Included are

The Galleria, a walkway covered by an 80-foot-high arched glass canopy. It connects all of the theatres in the complex.

Temple Hoyne Buell Theatre, the most recent addition to the complex. The 2,800-seat theatre has a glass facade and Colorado sandstone walls. It is host to Opera Colorado and Broadway plays and home of the Colorado Ballet. Phone 303/640-2862.

The Helen Bonfils Theatre Complex, home of the Denver Center Theatre Company. Contains three theaters: the Stage, seating 547 in a three-quarter circle around a thrust platform; the Space, a theater-in-the-round seating 450; and the Source, a small theater presenting new plays by American playwrights. Also contains the **Frank Ricketson Theatre**, a 195-seat theater available for rental for community activities, classes and festivals. Phone 303/893-4100 (ticket office) or 303/893-4000 for tours.

Boettcher Concert Hall, the first fully "surround" symphonic hall in the US; all of its 2,630 seats are within 75 feet of the stage. Home of the Colorado Symphony Orchestra (Sept-early June) and Opera Colorado with performances "in the round" (May). For schedule phone 303/640-2862.

Auditorium Theatre (1908). Past host to grand opera, political conventions, minstrel shows, revivalist meetings and military maneuvers; now hosts touring Broadway productions and the Colorado Ballet. Home of Colorado Contemporary Dance. Phone 303/640-2862.

Elitch Gardens. Relocated into downtown area in 1995. Amusement park with over 23 major rides. Observation tower, 100-foot high Ferris wheel. Flower gardens, lakes and waterfalls. (Memorial Day-Labor Day, daily) Platte River Valley. Phone 303/595-4386. **¢¢¢¢**

Forney Transportation Museum. Collection of more than 300 antique cars, carriages, cycles, sleighs, steam locomotives and coaches; 60 costumed figures. (Daily; closed Jan 1, Thanksgiving, Dec 25) 1416 Platte St, I-25 exit 211. Phone 303/433-3643 or -5896. **¢¢**

Molly Brown House Museum (ca 1889). House of "the unsinkable" Molly Brown, famous socialite and heroine of the *Titanic* disaster (1912); period furnishings. Carriage house has displays on Denver history, the Brown family and the *Titanic*. Guided tours by costumed docents. (Memorial Day-Labor Day, daily; rest of yr, daily exc Mon; closed major hols) Sr citizen rate. 1340 Pennsylvania St. Phone 303/832-4092. **¢¢**

Museum of Western Art. International showcase for the art of Western America. Collection includes works by Bierstadt, Moran, Farny, Russell,

Remington, Blumenschein, O'Keefe and 50 other artists who lived or traveled extensively in the West between the Civil War and World War II. Permanent and changing exhibits are housed in historic landmark Old Navarre Building (1880), which has served as a collegiate institute, bordello and gambling hall in its colorful past. Guided tours (by appt). (Tues-Sat; closed major hols) Sr citizen rate. 1727 Tremont Pl. Phone 303/296-1880. ¢¢

Park system. More than 200 parks within city provide approximately 4,400 acres of facilities for boating, fishing and other sports. The system includes 6 golf courses. There are also 27 mountain parks within 72 miles of the city covering 13,448 acres of land in the Rocky Mountain foothills. Phone 303/964-2500. Parks of special interest include

City Park. Contains the Denver Museum of Natural History, an 18-hole golf course and the **Denver Zoo.** Animals in natural habitats; primates, felines and giraffes; aviary, children's zoo, miniature railroad. (Daily) Children under 16 must be accompanied by adult at zoo. Sr citizen rate. Runs between 17th & 26th Aves, York St & Colorado Blvd. Phone 303/331-4110. ¢¢¢

Cheesman Park. Park has excellent views of nearby mountain peaks with aid of dial and pointers. Congress Park swimming pool (fee) is adj. Located between Cheesman & Congress Parks is the Denver Botanic Gardens (fee), with the Boettcher Memorial Conservatory. E 8th Ave & Franklin St.

Washington Park. Large recreation center with indoor pool (fee). Floral displays include replica of George Washington's gardens at Mount Vernon. Park runs between S Downing & S Franklin Sts, E Louisiana & E Virginia Aves.

★ Red Rocks Park. Amphitheater (9,500-seat) in natural setting of huge red rocks. Site of Easter sunrise service and summer concerts (fee). 12 mi SW, off CO 26 between I-70 and US 285.

(Mountain park usage is sometimes restricted. No camping exc at Chief Hosa Lodge; shelters (fee) by reservation only. For hours and detailed information regarding Denver Mountain Park trips, contact the Denver Parks & Recreation Dept, 303/964-2500.)

Pearce-McAllister Cottage (1899). Dutch Colonial-revival house contains original furnishings. Guided tours give insight into upper middle-class lifestyle of the 1920s. Second floor houses Denver Museum of Dolls, Toys and Miniatures. (Tues-Sat, also Sun afternoons) Sr citizen rate. 1880 N Gaylord St. Phone 303/322-3704. ¢¢

Sakura Square. Denver's Japanese Cultural and Trade Center features Oriental restaurants, shops, businesses; authentic Japanese gardens. Site of famed Buddhist Temple. Lawrence to Larimer Sts on 19th St. Phone 303/295-0305.

Sightseeing tours.

Gray Line bus tours. Contact PO Box 17527, 80217; 303/289-2841.

Colorado History Tours. Two-hour guided walking tours; three-hour guided step-on bus tours. Reservations required; 10 people minimum. Prices and schedules vary. Phone 303/866-4686.

16th Street Mall. This tree-lined, pedestrian promenade of red and gray granite runs through the center of Denver's downtown shopping district; outdoor cafes, shops, restaurants, hotels, fountains and plazas line its mile-long walk. European-built shuttle buses offer transportation from either end of the promenade. 16th St, between Market St and Broadway. Along the mall are

Shops at Tabor Center. A multi-level, glass-encased center housing more than 60 specialty shops, pushcarts, artisans and food vendors; 34-ft computer-controlled fountain, cast iron antique clock (1900). Named after famed developer Horace A.W. Tabor, who made his millions in silver mining and built Denver's first skyscraper on this block. (Daily) On Mall, between Larimer & Arapahoe Sts. Phone 303/572-6868.

Larimer Square. Restoration of the first street in Denver, this collection of shops, galleries, nightclubs and restaurants is set among Victorian courtyards, gaslights, arcades and buildings; carriage rides around square. (Daily) Larimer St between 14th & 15th Sts. Phone 303/534-2367.

State Capitol Complex. Includes

State Capitol. Colorado granite; dome (covered with gold leaf from Colorado mines) offers panoramic view. (Mon-Fri) E Colfax Ave & Sherman St. Phone 303/866-2604. Tours **Free.**

Colorado History Museum. Permanent and rotating exhibits on people and history of Colorado. Dioramas, full-scale mining equipment, Anasazi artifacts, photographs; sodhouse. Headquarters of Colorado Historical Society. (Daily; closed Jan 1, Thanksgiving, Dec 25) Sr citizen rate. 1300 Broadway. Phone 303/866-3682. ¢¢

The Children's Museum of Denver. Hands-on environment allows children to learn and explore the world around them. Exhibits include a room with thousands of plastic balls; Kidslope, a year-round ski slope; science center; grocery store. (June-Aug, daily; rest of yr, daily exc Mon; closed some major hols) Children's Museum Theater (wkends) and special events. 2121 Children's Museum Dr, off I-25 exit 211. Phone 303/433-7444. ¢¢

Turner Museum. Large collection of works by 19th-century painter J.M.W. Turner; also features works by landscape artist Thomas Moran. Tours. (Daily) 773 Downing St. Phone 303/832-0924. With guided tour ¢¢¢

United States Mint. Established in 1862. Tours (Mon-Fri; closed major hols). Children under 14 only with adult. No photography permitted in building. 320 W Colfax Ave, W of Civic Center; use Cherokee St entrance. Phone 303/844-5588. **Free.**

University of Denver (1864). (8,000 students) Handsome 125-acre main campus with Penrose Library, Harper Humanities Gardens, Shwayder Art Building, Seely G. Mudd Building (science), William T. Driscoll University Center and historic buildings dating from the 1800s. The 33-acre Park Hill campus at Montview Blvd & Quebec St is the site of the University of Denver Law School (Lowell Thomas Law Building) and the Lamont School of Music (Houston Fine Arts Center; for schedule phone 303/871-6400). Campus tours. S University Blvd & E Evans Ave. Phone 303/871-2711. The university maintains

Chamberlin Observatory. Houses large telescope in use since 1894; lectures. Tours (Tues & Thurs; closed hols, Christmas wk; reservations necessary). Observatory Park, 2930 E Warren Ave. Phone 303/871-3222. ¢

Annual Events

National Western Livestock Show, Horse Show and Rodeo. National Western Complex and Coliseum. Phone 303/297-1166. 2 wks Jan.

Cherry Blossom Festival. Sakura Square. 2nd wkend June.

Seasonal Events

Greyhound racing. Mile High Greyhound Park. 7 mi NE at jct I-270 & Vasquez Blvd; 6200 Dahlia St. Parimutuels. Mid-June-mid-Feb, nightly exc Sun; matinee racing Mon, Wed & Sat. Satellite "off-track" betting all yr. Phone 303/288-1591.

Professional sports. Broncos (football), Mile High Stadium, W 19th & Eliot Sts, phone 303/433-7466; also Colorado Rockies (baseball) at Coors Field, phone ROCKIES. Adj to Stadium is McNichols Arena, home of Nuggets (basketball), phone 303/893-6700.

Denver Area Suburbs

The following suburbs and towns in the Denver area are included in the *Mobil Travel Guide.* For information on any one of them, see the individual alphabetical listing. Boulder, Central City, Englewood, Evergreen, Golden, Idaho Springs, Lakewood.

Denver International Airport Area

For additional accommodations, see DENVER INTERNATIONAL AIRPORT AREA, which follows DENVER.

City Neighborhoods

Many of the restaurants, unrated dining establishments and some lodgings listed under Denver include neighborhoods as well as exact street addresses. Geographic descriptions of the Downtown and 16th St Mall are given, followed by a table of restaurants arranged by neighborhood.

Downtown: Southeast of Wynkoop St, west of Grant St, north of 14th St and east of Speer Blvd. **North of Downtown:** North of Wynkoop St. **South of Downtown:** South of 14th Ave. **East of Downtown:** East of Grant St. **West of Downtown:** West of Cherry Creek.

16th St Mall: 16th St from Market St on the NW to Broadway on the SE.

DENVER RESTAURANTS BY NEIGHBORHOOD AREAS

(For full description, see alphabetical listings under Restaurants)

DOWNTOWN

Al Fresco. 1515-23 Market St

The Broker. 821 17th St

European Cafe. 1515-23 Market St

Le Central. 112 E 8th Ave

Mccormick's Fish House. 1659 Wazee St

Old Spaghetti Factory. 1215 18th St

Palace Arms (Brown Palace Hotel). 321 17th St

Rocky Mountain Diner. 800 18th St

Trinity Grille. 1801 Broadway

Wynkoop Brewing Company. 1634 18th St

Zenith American Grill. 1750 Lawrence St

NORTH OF DOWNTOWN

Brittany Hill. 9350 Grant

Morton's Of Chicago. 1710 Wynkoop

SOUTH OF DOWNTOWN

Buckhorn Exchange. 1000 Osage St

Chives American Bistro. 1120 E 6th Ave

Fresh Fish Co. 7800 E Hampden Ave

Pour La France. 730 S University Blvd

Soren's. 315 Detroit St

Tuscany (Loews Giorgio Hotel). 4150 E Mississippi Ave

Wellshire Inn. 3333 S Colorado Blvd

EAST OF DOWNTOWN

Cliff Young. 700 E 17th Ave

Normandy French Restaurant. 1515 Madison

Strings. 1700 Humbolt St

Tante Louise. 4900 E Colfax Ave

WEST OF DOWNTOWN

Baby Doe's Matchless Mine. 2520 W 23rd Ave

Furrs Cafeteria. 4900 Kipling

Imperial Chinese. 431 S Broadway

Note: When a listing is located in a town that does not have its own city heading, it will appear under the city nearest to its location. In these cases, the address and town appear in parenthesis immediately following the name of the establishment.

Motels

★ ★ **COURTYARD BY MARRIOTT.** *7415 E 41st Ave (80216), I-70 exit 278, east of downtown.* 303/333-3303; FAX 303/399-7356. 145 rms, 3 story. S, D $85-$95; each addl $10; suites $99-$109; under 18 free; wkend rates. Crib free. TV; cable (premium). Indoor pool. Complimentary coffee in rms. Restaurant 6:30-10 am, 5-10 pm; Sat, Sun from 7 am. Bar 4-11 pm. Ck-out 1 pm. Coin lndry. Meeting rms. Business servs avail. In-rm modem link. Valet serv. Exercise equipt; weight machine, bicycles, whirlpool. Refrigerator in suites. Balconies. Cr cds: A, C, D, DS, MC, V.

D ≈ ✕ ⊠ ⛵ SC

★ ★ **LA QUINTA AIRPORT.** *3975 Peoria St (80239), I-70 exit 281, east of downtown.* 303/371-5640; FAX 303/371-7015. 112 rms, 2 story. S, D $69-$89; each addl $10; under 18 free. Crib free. Pet accepted, some restrictions. TV; cable (premium). Heated pool. Complimentary continental bkfst in lobby. Restaurant adj open 24 hrs. Ck-out noon. Coin lndry. Business servs avail. In-rm modem link. Valet serv. Free airport transportation. Some refrigerators. Cr cds: A, C, D, DS, MC, V.

D ⛵ ≈ ⊠ ⛵ SC

✔ ★ ★ **LA QUINTA CENTRAL.** *3500 Park Ave W (80216), I-25 exit 213, west of downtown.* 303/458-1222; FAX 303/433-2246. 105 rms, 3 story. S, D $51-$64; each addl $6; under 18 free. Crib free. Pet accepted. TV; cable (premium), VCR avail. Pool. Complimentary bkfst. Complimentary coffee in lobby. Restaurant adj open 24 hrs. Ck-out noon. Meeting rms. Business servs avail. Valet serv. Cr cds: A, C, D, DS, MC, V.

D ⛵ ≈ ⊠ ⛵ SC

★ ★ **QUALITY INN SOUTH.** *6300 E Hampden Ave (80222), I-25 exit 201, east of downtown.* 303/758-2211; FAX 303/753-0156. 185 rms, 1-2 story. S, D $65-$80; each addl $8; under 18 free; wkend rates. Crib free. Pet accepted; $5 per day. TV; cable (premium). Pool; whirlpool, sauna, poolside serv. Complimentary coffee in rms. Restaurant 6 am-11 pm. Rm serv. Bar 4-11 pm. Ck-out noon. Coin lndry. Meeting rms. Business servs avail. In-rm modem link. Lawn games. Some refrigerators. Private patios, balconies. Picnic tables. Cr cds: A, C, D, DS, ER, JCB, MC, V.

D ⛵ ≈ ⊠ ⛵ SC

★ ★ **RESIDENCE INN BY MARRIOTT-DOWNTOWN.** *2777 Zuni (80211), jct Speer Blvd N, I-25 exit 212B, west of downtown.* 303/458-5318. 156 kit. suites, 2 story. S $89-$109; D $109-$139; under 16 free; wkend rates. Crib free. TV; cable (premium), VCR avail. Heated pool. Complimentary continental bkfst. Restaurant nearby. Ck-out noon. Meeting rms. Business servs avail. Valet serv. Free grocery shopping serv. RR station, bus depot transportation. Exercise equipt; weights, bicycles, whirlpool. Health club privileges. Refrigerators; many fireplaces. Private patios, balconies. Cr cds: A, C, D, DS, JCB, MC, V.

D ≈ ✕ ⊠ ⛵ SC

Motor Hotels

✔ ★ **DAYS HOTEL-AIRPORT.** *4590 Quebec St (80216), just N of I-70 exit 278, east of downtown.* 303/320-0260; FAX 303/320-7595. 195 rms, 5 story. S $52-$69; D $57-$74; each addl $7; suite $110; under 17 free. Crib free. Pet accepted; $25. TV; cable (premium), VCR avail. Pool. Complimentary coffee in rms. Restaurant 6 am-2 pm, 5:30-10 pm; Sat & Sun 6 am-1 pm, 5:30-10 pm. Rm serv. Bar 4 pm-midnight, Sat & Sun from 5 pm. Ck-out noon. Coin lndry. Meeting rms. Business servs avail. In-rm modem link. Bellhops. Valet serv. Gift shop. Free airport transportation. Exercise equipt; weight machine, bicycles, whirlpool. Cr cds: A, C, D, DS, MC, V.

⛵ ≈ ✕ ⊠ ⛵ SC

★ ★ **MANY MANSIONS.** *1313 Steele St (80206), east of downtown.* 303/355-1313; res: 800/225-7829; FAX 303/355-1313, ext.

200. 36 kit. suites, 8 story. S $90; D $105-$145; each addl $15; under 12 free; wkly, monthly rates. Crib free. TV; cable, VCR avail. Complimentary coffee in rms. Complimentary full bkfst wkdays (continental bkfst, wkends). Restaurant nearby. Ck-out noon. Coin Indry. Meeting rms. Business servs avail. Free garage parking. Balconies. Picnic tables, grills. Cr cds: A, C, D, DS, ER, JCB, MC, V.

⊠ ⋈ SC

★ **RAMADA INN-AIRPORT.** *3737 Quebec St (80207), east of downtown.* 303/388-6161; FAX 303/388-0426. 148 rms, 4 story. S, D $71-$95; each addl $10; under 18 free; wkend rates. Crib free. Pet accepted. TV; cable. Heated pool. Complimentary coffee in rms. Restaurant 6 am-11 pm. Rm serv. Bar 11-2 am, Sun to midnight. Ck-out noon. Meeting rms. Busienss servs avail. In-rm modem link. Bellhops. Valet serv. Gift shop. Free airport transportation. Health club privileges. Some refrigerators. Cr cds: A, C, D, DS, ER, JCB, MC, V.

D ⊡ ⋈ ⊠ ⋈ SC

★★ **SHERATON-DENVER AIRPORT.** *3535 Quebec St (80207), east of downtown.* 303/333-7711; FAX 303/322-2262. 195 rms, 8 story. S $85-$105; D $95-$115; each addl $15; under 17 free; wkend plans. Crib free. TV; cable (premium), VCR avail. Indoor pool. Restaurant 6 am-midnight; Sun from 7 am. Rm serv. Bar 11-2 am, Sun to midnight. Ck-out noon. Coin Indry. Meeting rms. Business center. Bellhops. Valet serv. Gift shop. Free airport transportation. Exercise equipt; weight machine, stair machine, whirlpool. Lawn games. Some private patios, balconies. Cr cds: A, C, D, DS, JCB, MC, V.

D ⊡ ⫞ ⋈ ⊠ ⋈ SC ⫟

Hotels

★★ **ADAM'S MARK.** *1550 Court Place (80202), on 16th St Mall.* 303/893-3333; FAX 303/623-0303. 744 rms, 22 story. S $140; D $160; each addl $10; suites $260-$850; under 18 free; wkend rates. Crib free. Garage $10 daily; in/out privileges. Pet accepted, some restrictions. TV; cable (premium). 5th floor pool; poolside serv. Restaurant 6:30 am-11 pm. Bar 11-1 am; entertainment. Rm serv 24 hrs. Ck-out noon. Coin Indry. Convention facilities. Business center. In-rm modem link. Concierge. Shopping arcade. Barber, beauty shops. Exercise equipt; stair machine, bicycles, steam rm, sauna. Health club privileges. Luxury level. Cr cds: A, C, D, DS, ER, JCB, MC, V.

D ⊡ ⫞ ⋈ ⫟ ⊠ ⋈ SC ⫟

★★★★ **BROWN PALACE.** *321 17th St (80202), downtown.* 303/297-3111; res: 800/321-2599 (exc CO), 800/228-2917 (CO); FAX 303/293-9204. Opened in 1892, this grand dame of Colorado hotels has lodged luminaries from President Eisenhower to the Beatles. A dramatic stained-glass window tops the nine-story lobby; rooms are decorated with Victorian flair. 230 rms, 9 story. S $179; D $184-$199; each addl $15; suites $245-$675; under 12 free; wkend package plan. Garage in/out $14. Crib free. TV; cable (premium), VCR avail. Restaurants (see PALACE ARMS). Afternoon tea 2-4:30 pm. Rm serv 24 hrs. Bar 10:30 am-midnight; entertainment exc Sun. Ck-out noon. Meeting rms. Business center. In-rm modem link. Concierge. Gift shop. Barber. Valet parking. Exercise equipt; bicycles, rowing machine. Some refrigerators. Cr cds: A, C, D, DS, JCB, MC, V.

⫟ ⊠ ⋈ SC ⫟

★★★ **BURNSLEY.** *1000 Grant St (80203), downtown.* 303/830-1000; res: 800/231-3915 (exc CO); FAX 303/830-7676. 82 kit. suites, 16 story. Suites $89-$155; each addl $10. Pet accepted, some restrictions. $50. TV; cable (premium), VCR avail (movies avail $7). Pool. Complimentary coffee in rms. Complimentary bkfst. Restaurant 6:30 am-2 pm, 6-9 pm. Rm serv to 11 pm. Bar from 11 am. Ck-out noon. Meeting rms. Business center. Garage parking. Health club privileges. Balconies. Converted apartment building in residential area, near State Capitol. Cr cds: A, C, D, MC, V.

⊡ ⫞ ⊠ ⋈ SC ⫟

⫞★ **COMFORT INN.** *401 17th St (80202), downtown.* 303/296-0400; FAX 303/297-0774. 229 rms, 22 story. S $60-$84; D

$65-$94; each addl $10; suites $89-$150; under 18 free; wkend rates. Covered valet parking $9. TV; cable (premium), VCR avail. Complimentary continental bkfst. Restaurant adj wkdays 6:30 am-9 pm. Rm serv 24 hrs. Bar 10:30 am-midnight. Ck-out noon. Meeting rms. Business servs avail. In-rm modem link. Shopping arcade. Barber, beauty shop. Health club privileges. Cr cds: A, C, D, DS, JCB, MC, V.

D ⋈ ⊠ ⋈ SC

★★ **EMBASSY SUITES.** *7525 E Hampden Ave (80231), off I-25E exit 201, south of downtown.* 303/696-6644; FAX 303/337-6202. 206 suites, 7 story. S $145; D $155; each addl $10; under 12 free; wkend rates. Crib free. TV; cable (premium), VCR avail. Indoor pool. Coffee in rms. Complimentary bkfst. Restaurant 11:30 am-2:30 pm, 5-10 pm. Bar 11:30-2 am, Sun to midnight. Ck-out 1 pm. Coin Indry. Meeting rms. Business servs avail. In-rm modem link. Gift shop. Exercise equipt; bicycles, stair machine, whirlpool, sauna, steam rm. Refrigerators, minibars. Balconies. Cr cds: A, C, D, DS, JCB, MC, V.

D ⫞ ⫞ ⋈ ⊠ ⋈ SC

★★★ **EMBASSY SUITES-AIRPORT.** *4444 N Havana St (80239), I-70 exit 280, east of downtown.* 303/375-0400; FAX 303/371-4634. 212 suites, 7 story. Suites $125-$135; each addl $12; under 12 free; ski plans, wkend package. Crib free. Pet accepted, some restrictions. TV; cable (premium), VCR avail. Indoor pool; poolside serv. Complimentary full bkfst. Coffee in rms. Restaurant 6 am-11 pm. Bar to 2 am. Ck-out 1 pm. Coin Indry. Meeting rms. Business servs avail. In-rm modem link. Gift shop. Free airport transportation. Exercise equipt; weights, bicycles, whirlpool, steam rm, sauna. Refrigerators; some minibars. Cr cds: A, C, D, DS, JCB, MC, V.

D ⫞ ⫞ ⫞ ⋈ ⊠ ⋈ SC

★★ **EXECUTIVE TOWER INN.** *1405 Curtis St (80202), downtown.* 303/571-0300; res: 800/525-6651; FAX 303/825-4301. 337 rms, 16 story. S $147-$174; D $157-$182; each addl $10; suites $180-$340; under 16 free; wkend rates. Crib free. Pet accepted, some restrictions. TV; cable (premium), VCR avail (movies avail $2). Indoor pool. Restaurants 6:30 am-10 pm. Bar 11-2 am, Sun to midnight. Ck-out noon. Coin Indry. Meeting rms. Business center. In-rm modem link. Garage. Valet serv. Tennis. Exercise rm; instructor, weights, stair machine, whirlpool, sauna, steam rm. Rec rm. Cr cds: A, C, D, ER, JCB, MC, V.

D ⫞ ⫟ ⫞ ⫟ ⫟ ⋈ ⋈ SC ⫟

★★ **HOLIDAY INN.** *(10 E 120th Ave, Northglenn 80233) 6 mi N on I-25, exit 223.* 303/452-4100; FAX 303/457-1741. 236 rms, 6 story. Apr-Sept: S, D $80-$125; each addl $10; suites $150-$175; under 17 free; wkend rates; lower rates rest of yr. Crib avail. TV; cable (premium), VCR avail. Indoor pool; poolside serv, whirlpool. Restaurant 6 am-10 pm. Bar noon-2 am; entertainment Wed-Sat. Ck-out noon. Convention facilities. Business servs avail. In-rm modem link. Gift shop. Free airport transportation. Exercise equipt; bicycle, treadmill. Cr cds: A, D, DS, MC, V.

D ⋈ ⫟ ⋈ ⋈ SC

★★★ **HYATT REGENCY DENVER.** *1750 Welton St (80202), downtown.* 303/295-1234; FAX 303/292-2472. 511 rms, 26 story. S $89-$170; D $89-$185; each addl $15; suites $350-$1,000; under 18 free. Crib free. Garage, valet parking $12. TV; cable (premium), VCR avail. Pool; poolside serv. Complimentary coffee in rms. Restaurant 6 am-midnight. Bar 10:30-2 am. Ck-out noon. Meeting rms. Business center. In-rm modem link. Concierge. Airport transportation. Tennis. Health club privileges. Bathrm phones, minibars; some refrigerators. Luxury level. Cr cds: A, C, D, DS, ER, JCB, MC, V.

D ⫟ ⫞ ⫟ ⋈ ⋈ SC ⫟

★★★ **HYATT REGENCY TECH CENTER.** *7800 Tufts Ave (80237), at jct I-25, I-225, south of downtown.* 303/779-1234; FAX 303/850-7164. 448 rms, 11 story. S $117-$145; D $132-$160; each addl $15; suites $250-$400; under 18 free; wkend plans. Crib free. TV; cable (premium), VCR avail. Indoor pool; poolside serv. Supervised child's activities (Fri, Sat evenings); ages 3-16. Complimentary coffee in rms. Restaurant 6:30 am-11 pm. Bar 3 pm-2 am. Ck-out noon.

Convention facilities. Business center. In-rm modem link. Concierge. Gift shop. Valet parking. Airport transportation. Lighted tennis. Exercise equipt; weights, bicycles, whirlpool, sauna. Some refrigerators, bathrm phones. Luxury level. Cr cds: A, C, D, DS, ER, JCB, MC, V.

[D] [icons] [SC] [icon]

★★★★ **LOEWS GIORGIO.** *4150 E Mississippi Ave (80222), south of downtown.* 303/782-9300; FAX 303/758-6542. A modern steel-and-glass facade conceals an Italian Renaissance-style interior distinguished by magnificent frescoes. Guest rooms are spacious and elegant. 197 rms, 11 story. S $180-$195; D $200-$230; each addl $20; suites $215-$500; under 14 free; wkend packages. Pet accepted, some restrictions. TV; cable (premium), VCR avail (movies avail $3). Coffee in rms. Restaurant (see TUSCANY). Bar 10 am-midnight. Ck-out 11 am. Meeting rms. Business center. In-rm modem link. Concierge. Gift shop. Valet parking. Exercise equipt; treadmills, stair machines. Bathrm phones, minibars; some refrigerators. Complimentary newspaper. Library. Cr cds: A, C, D, DS, JCB, MC, V.

[D] [icons] [SC] [icon]

✓★★ **MARRIOTT DENVER TECH CENTER.** *4900 DTC Pkwy (80237), off I-25 exit 199, south of downtown.* 303/779-1100; FAX 303/740-2523. 626 rms, 2-10 story. S, D $87-$135; suites $260-$335; under 17 free; wkend plans. Crib free. Pet accepted. TV; cable (premium), VCR avail. 2 pools, 1 indoor. Restaurant open 24 hrs. Bar 11 am-midnight; entertainment. Ck-out noon. Convention facilities. Business servs avail. Shopping arcade. Valet parking. Exercise rm; instructor, weights, bicycles, whirlpool, steam rm, sauna. Rec rm. Refrigerators. Some balconies. Cr cds: A, C, D, DS, JCB, MC, V.

[D] [icons] [SC]

★★ **MARRIOTT-CITY CENTER.** *1701 California St (80202), downtown.* 303/297-1300; FAX 303/298-7474. 612 rms, 19 story. S $160-$170; D $180-$195; each addl $10; suites $225-$825; under 12 free; wkend plans. Crib free. Valet parking; fee. Pet accepted, some restrictions. TV; cable (premium), VCR avail. Indoor pool; poolside serv. Restaurant 6:30 am-10 pm. Rm serv to midnight. Bar 11-2 am. Ck-out noon. Convention facilities. Business center. Concierge. Valet servs. Shopping arcade. Exercise rm; instructor, weight machine, stair machines, whirlpool, sauna. Game rm. Some bathrm phones, refrigerators. Luxury level. Cr cds: A, C, D, DS, ER, JCB, MC, V.

[D] [icons] [SC] [icon]

★★ **MARRIOTT-SOUTHEAST.** *6363 E Hampden Ave (80222), I-25 exit 201, south of downtown.* 303/758-7000; FAX 303/691-3418. 595 rms, 11 story. S, D $82-$130; suites $150-$350; under 18 free; wkend package plan. Crib free. TV; cable (premium), VCR avail. 2 pools, 1 indoor; poolside serv. Restaurant 6 am-11 pm. Bar 11 to midnight. Ck-out 1 pm. Complimentary coffee. Coin lndry. Convention facilities. Concierge. Shopping arcade. Barber, beauty shop. Covered parking. Airport transportation. Exercise rm; weight machine, bicycles, whirlpool. Game rm. Some bathrm phones, refrigerators; some private patios. Luxury level. Cr cds: A, C, D, DS, ER, JCB, MC, V.

[D] [icons] [SC]

★★★ **OXFORD.** *1600 17th St (80202), downtown.* 303/628-5400; res: 800/228-5838 (exc CO); FAX 303/628-5413. 81 rms, 5 story. S $135-$160; D $145-$170; each addl $10; suites from $275; under 12 free. Crib free. Valet parking $12. TV; cable, VCR avail. Restaurant 6:30-10 am, 11 am-2 pm, 5-10 pm; Fri, Sat to 11 pm; Sun 7 am-10 pm. Rm serv 24 hrs. Bar. Ck-out 1 pm. Meeting rms. Business servs avail. In-rm modem link. Concierge. Valet serv. Barber, beauty shop. Exercise rm; instructor, weight machine, stair machine, whirlpool, steam rm. Elegant, European-style; many antiques. Minibars. First luxury hotel built in Denver (1891). Cr cds: A, C, D, DS, MC, V.

[D] [icons] [SC]

★★ **STAPLETON PLAZA.** *3333 Quebec St (80207), east of downtown.* 303/321-3500; res: 800/950-6070; FAX 303/322-7343. 300 rms, 11 story. S, D $125-$135; each addl $10; suites $205-$395; under 12 free; wkly, wkend package plans. Crib free. TV; cable (premium).

Pool; poolside serv. Complimentary coffee. Restaurant 6 am-11 pm. Rm serv 24 hrs. Bars 11-2 am; Sun to midnight. Ck-out noon. Convention facilities. Business center. Shopping arcade. Free garage parking. Free airport transportation. Exercise rm; instructor, weight machines, stair machine, whirlpool, sauna, steam rm. Balconies. Built around 11-story atrium; glass-enclosed elvtrs. Cr cds: A, C, D, DS, ER, JCB, MC, V.

[D] [icons] [SC] [icon]

★★★ **STOUFFER RENAISSANCE.** *3801 Quebec St (80207), east of downtown.* 303/399-7500; FAX 303/321-1783. 400 rms, 12 story. S $140-$150; D $150-$160; each addl $10; suites $250; under 18 free; wkend ski plans. Covered parking $4 overnight; valet $6. TV; cable (premium), VCR avail. 2 heated pools, 1 indoor. Complimentary coffee in rms. Restaurant 6:30 am-11 pm. Rm serv 24 hrs. Bar 11-1 am; entertainment. Ck-out 1 pm. Convention facilities. Business center. In-rm modem link. Concierge. Gift shop. Free airport transportation. Exercise equipt; weight machines, bicycles, whirlpool, steam rm. Refrigerators; minibar, some bathrm phones. Balconies. Dramatic 10-story central atrium. Luxury level. Cr cds: A, C, D, DS, ER, JCB, MC, V.

[D] [icons] [SC] [icon]

★★★ **THE WARWICK.** *1776 Grant St (80203), downtown.* 303/861-2000; res: 800/525-2888; FAX 303/839-8504. 194 rms, 15 story. S, D $155-$165; each addl $10; suites $200-$800; under 18 free; wkend package plan. Crib free. Garage $5. Pet accepted. TV; cable (premium). Rooftop pool (in season); poolside serv. Complimentary continental bkfst. Restaurant 6:30 am-2 pm, 6-10 pm. Rm serv 24 hrs. Bar 11 am-midnight. Ck-out 1 pm. Meeting rms. Business servs avail. In-rm modem link. Concierge. Valet servs. Airport transportation. Free railroad station, bus depot transportation. Health club privileges. Many wet bars. Bathrm phones, refrigerators. Some balconies. Cr cds: A, C, D, DS, JCB, MC, V.

[D] [icons] [SC]

★★★ **WESTIN HOTEL TABOR CENTER.** *1672 Lawrence St (80202), in Tabor Center, downtown.* 303/572-9100; FAX 303/572-7288. 420 rms, 19 story. S $169; D $184; each addl $15; suites $309-$499; under 18 free; wkly rates. Crib free. Pet accepted, some restrictions. Garage $6-$12. TV; cable (premium), VCR avail. Indoor/outdoor pool; poolside serv, hot tub. Restaurant 6-11 am; dining rm 11 am-2 pm, 5-10 pm, Sat to 11 pm. Rm serv 24 hrs. Bar 5 pm-1:30 am; pianist Tues-Sat. Ck-out 1 pm. Convention facilities. Business center. In-rm modem link. Shopping arcade. Exercise equipt; weight machine, stair machine, whirlpool, sauna, steam rm. Refrigerators, honor bars; some bathrm phones. Some balconies. Luxury level. Cr cds: A, C, D, DS, ER, JCB, MC, V.

[D] [icons] [SC] [icon]

Inns

★ **THE CAMBRIDGE.** *1560 Sherman St (80203), downtown.* 303/831-1252; res: 800/877-1252; FAX 303/831-4724. 27 suites, 3 story. S, D $109-$129; each addl $10; under 12 free. Crib free. Pet accepted; $30. Valet parking $7. TV; cable (premium). Complimentary coffee in rms. Complimentary continental bkfst. Restaurant 11 am-10 pm, Sat 5-11 pm, closed Sun. Rm serv. Ck-out noon, ck-in after 3 pm. Business servs avail. In-rm modem link. Bellhops. Valet serv. Concierge. Airport, downtown transportation. Refrigerators. Antique furnishings, oil paintings, original prints; no two suites alike. Cr cds: A, D, DS, ER, MC, V.

[icons] [SC]

✓★★ **CASTLE MARNE.** *1572 Race St (80206), east of downtown.* 303/331-0621; res: 800/926-2763; FAX 303/331-0623. 9 air-cooled rms, 3 story. No elvtr. S $70-$185; D $85-$185. Children over 10 yrs only. Complimentary full bkfst, afternoon tea. Restaurant nearby. Ck-out 11 am, ck-in 4 pm. Business center. Bellhops. Valet serv. Concierge. Some street parking. Game rm. Some balconies, in-rm whirlpools. Antiques. Library/sitting rm. Built 1889; Romanesque mansion was residence of museum curator. Cheesman Park 3 blks. Totally nonsmoking. Cr cds: A, C, D, DS, MC, V.

✓ ★ ★ **HOLIDAY CHALET.** 1820 E Colfax Ave (80218), east of downtown. 303/321-9975; res: 800/626-4497; FAX 303/377-6556. 10 kit. suites, 3 story. S, D $49-$67.50; each addl $5; under 12 free; wkly rates. Crib free. Pet accepted; $50. TV; VCR avail. Garage parking $3. Complimentary bkfst. Complimentary coffee in rms. Restaurant nearby. Ck-out noon. Meeting rm. Concierge. Restored brownstone built in 1896. Library; 1880 salt water fish prints. Totally nonsmoking. Cr cds: A, C, D, DS, MC, V.

★ ★ ★ **QUEEN ANNE.** 2147 Tremont Pl (80205), downtown. 303/296-6666; res: 800/432-4667; FAX 303/296-2151. 14 rms, 3 story. No elvtr. S, D $75-$125; each addl $15; suites $135-$155. Children over 12 yrs only. Complimentary bkfst & refreshments. Ck-out noon, ck-in 3 pm. Business servs avail. In-rm modem link. Health club privileges. Built 1879. Antiques; garden. In the Clements Historic District. Totally nonsmoking. Cr cds: A, D, DS, MC, V.

✓ ★ ★ **VICTORIA OAKS.** 1575 Race St (80206), east of downtown. 303/355-1818; res: 800/662-6257. 9 rms (2 share bath), 3 story. No elvtr. S $45-$75; D $55-$85; each addl $15. Pet accepted, some restrictions. TV in sitting rm; VCR. Complimentary continental bkfst, refreshments. Ck-out noon, ck-in 3 pm. In-rm modem link. Kitchen, lndry privileges. 1897 rooming house, Victorian antiques. Cr cds: A, C, D, DS, ER, MC, V.

Restaurants

★ **AL FRESCO.** 1515-23 Market St (80202), downtown. 303/534-0404. Hrs: 11 am-2 pm, 5-10 pm; Fri & Sat to 11 pm. Res accepted. Northern Italian menu. A la carte entrees: lunch $5.95-$10.95, dinner $8.95-$16.95. Specializes in pizza, zitti Al Fresco. Outdoor dining. Casual dining on 3 levels. Cr cds: A, C, D, DS, MC, V.

★ ★ **BABY DOE'S MATCHLESS MINE.** 2520 W 23rd Ave, west of downtown. 303/433-3386. Hrs: 11 am-2:30 pm, 4:30-10 pm; Fri, Sat to midnight; Sun 4-10 pm; Sun brunch 9 am-2:30 pm. Res accepted. Semi-a la carte: lunch $4.95-$12.95, dinner $12.95-$32. Buffet: lunch $7.95. Sun brunch $15.95. Child's meals. Specializes in seafood, steak. Parking. Replica of Matchless Mine in Leadville; memorabilia of era. Cr cds: A, C, D, DS, MC, V.

★ ★ **BRITTANY HILL.** 9350 Grant, I-25 exit 220, north of downtown. 303/451-5151. Hrs: 11 am-10 pm; Fri, Sat to 11 pm; Sun 4-10 pm; Sun brunch 9 am-2:30 pm. Res accepted. Continental menu. Bar to midnight. Wine list. Semi-a la carte: lunch $5.95-$7.95, dinner $12.95-$25.95. Sun brunch $15.95. Specializes in prime rib, fresh seafood. Patio deck. Scenic view of city, mountains. Cr cds: A, D, DS, MC, V.

★ ★ ★ **THE BROKER.** 821 17th St, downtown. 303/292-5065. Hrs: 11 am-2:30 pm, 5-11 pm. Closed Dec 25. Res accepted. Continental menu. Bar. Semi-a la carte: lunch $5-$11, dinner $19-$35. Specialties: prime rib, filet Wellington. In vault & board rms of converted bank (1903). Cr cds: A, D, DS, MC, V.

★ **BUCKHORN EXCHANGE.** 1000 Osage St, south of downtown. 303/534-9505. Hrs: 11 am-2 pm, 5:30-9:30 pm; Fri & Sat 5-10 pm; Sun 4-9 pm. Closed major hols. Bar. Semi-a la carte: lunch $2.95-$14, dinner $17-$36. Specializes in steak, buffalo, elk. Entertain-

ment Wed-Sat. Roof garden dining. Historical landmark & museum, built 1893. Cr cds: A, C, D, DS, MC, V.

✓ ★ ★ **CHIVES AMERICAN BISTRO.** 1120 E 6th Ave, south of downtown. 303/722-3800. Hrs: 4 pm-1 am. Closed Thanksgiving, Dec 25. Res accepted. Varied menu. Bar. Semi-a la carte: dinner $6.95-$17.95. Specializes in grilled fresh seafood, pasta. New American cuisine. Parking. Cr cds: D, DS, MC, V.

★ ★ **CLIFF YOUNG.** 700 E 17th Ave, east of downtown. 303/831-8900. Hrs: 11:30 am-2 pm, 5-11 pm; Sun 5-10 pm. Closed major hols. Bar. Wine list. Semi-a la carte: lunch $7-$14, dinner $15-$33. Specialty: herb-crusted Colorado rack of lamb. Own baking. Entertainment (evenings). Valet parking. In renovated Victorian storefront and office building (1890). Cr cds: A, C, D, DS, JCB, MC, V.

★ ★ **EUROPEAN CAFE.** 1515-23 Market St (80202), downtown. 303/825-6555. Hrs: 11 am-2 pm, 5-10 pm; Fri & Sat to 11 pm. Res accepted. Continental menu. Bar. A la carte entrees: lunch $5.95-$10.95, dinner $8.95-$26.95. Specialties: rack of lamb, spicy tuna. Valet parking. Intimate dining. Victorian decor. Cr cds: A, C, D, DS, MC, V.

★ ★ **FRESH FISH CO.** 7800 E Hampden Ave (80237), south of downtown. 303/740-9556. Hrs: 11:30 am-2:30 pm, 5-11 pm; Sat from 5 pm; Sun 10 am-2 pm (brunch), 5-10 pm. Closed Dec 25. Bar. Semi-a la carte: lunch $5.95-$9.95, dinner $13.95-$25.95. Sun brunch $14.95. Child's meals. Specializes in calamari, salmon. Parking. Many large aquariums throughout restaurant. Cr cds: A, C, D, DS, MC, V.

★ ★ ★ **IMPERIAL CHINESE.** 431 S Broadway (80209), west of downtown. 303/698-2800. Hrs: 11 am-10 pm; wkends to 10:30 pm. Closed July 4, Thanksgiving, Dec 25. Chinese menu. Bar. Wine list. Semi-a la carte: lunch $5.95-$8.95, dinner $7.95-$15.95. Specialties: sesame chicken, whole steamed bass. Parking. Contemporary Chinese decor with many artifacts. Cr cds: A, D, MC, V.

✓ ★ **LE CENTRAL.** 112 E 8th Ave, at Lincoln St, downtown. 303/863-8094. Hrs: 11:30 am-2 pm, 5:30-10 pm; Sun 5-9 pm; Sun brunch 11 am-2 pm. Closed Dec 25. French menu. Serv bar. Semi-a la carte: lunch $5.95-$7.95, dinner $8-$13.50. Sun brunch $5-$8. Specializes in country French dishes. Cr cds: MC, V.

★ ★ **McCORMICK'S FISH HOUSE.** 1659 Wazee St, downtown. 303/825-1107. Hrs: 6:30-10 am, 11 am-2 pm, 5-10 pm; Fri to 11 pm; Sat 7 am-2 pm, 5-11 pm; Sun 7 am-2 pm, 5-10 pm; Sun brunch 7 am-2 pm. Closed Dec 25. Res accepted. Bar. Semi-a la carte: bkfst $4-$8, lunch, dinner $5-$20. Sun brunch $4-$10. Sterling silver chandeliers. Cr cds: A, C, D, DS, MC, V.

★ ★ ★ **MORTON'S OF CHICAGO.** 1710 Wynkoop, downtown. 303/825-3353. Hrs: 5:30-11 pm; Sun 5-10 pm. Closed major hols. Bar from 5 pm. Wine list. A la carte entrees: dinner $16.95-$29.95. Specializes in steak, lobster. Valet parking. Menu recited. Cr cds: A, C, D, JCB, MC, V.

★ ★ ★ **NORMANDY FRENCH RESTAURANT.** 1515 Madison, at E Colfax Ave, east of downtown. 303/321-3311. Hrs: 11:30 am-2 pm, 5-10 pm; Sat from 5 pm; Sun 5-9 pm. Closed Mon. Res accepted; required hols. French menu. Bar. Wine cellar. A la carte entrees: lunch $7.75-$10.50, dinner $9.95-$23.25. Child's meals. Specializes in osso bucco, rack of lamb. Parking. Family-owned. Cr cds: A, C, D, DS, MC, V.

[D] [≞]

✔★ **OLD SPAGHETTI FACTORY.** *1215 18th St, at Lawrence St, downtown.* 303/295-1864. Hrs: 11:30 am-2 pm, 5-10 pm; Fri to 11 pm; Sat 4:30-11 pm; Sun 4-10 pm. Closed Thanksgiving, Dec 24, 25. Italian menu. Bar. Semi-a la carte: lunch $3.25-$5.45, dinner $4.25-$9.25. Specialties: homemade lasagne, chicken Parmesan. Located on ground floor of Tramway Cable Bldg (1889). Trolley car, antique display. Cr cds: DS, MC, V.

[D] [≞]

★★★ **PALACE ARMS.** *(See Brown Palace Hotel)* 303/297-3111. Artifacts from the Napoleonic era—among them dueling pistols believed to have belonged to Bonaparte and Josephine—are displayed near the red leather booths of this intimate dining room, which also features a mirrored ceiling and huge chandelier. Hrs: 11:30 am-2 pm, 6-10 pm; Sat, Sun from 6 pm. Res accepted. Continental, regional Amer menu. Bar to 1 am. Extensive wine list. Semi-a la carte: lunch $8.50-$16, dinner $19.50-$34. Specializes in rack of lamb, fresh seafood. Own baking. Valet parking. Jacket, tie. Cr cds: A, C, D, DS, JCB, MC, V.

[D] [≞]

✔★ **POUR LA FRANCE.** *730 S University Blvd, south of downtown.* 303/744-1888. Hrs: 7 am-10 pm; Fri, Sat to midnight. Closed Thanksgiving, Dec 25. French, Amer menu. Bar. Semi-a la carte: bkfst $2-$6.95, lunch $2.95-$7.95, dinner $6.95-$12.75. Child's meals. Specializes in desserts, pastries. Outdoor dining. Near Univ of Denver. Cr cds: A, DS, MC, V.

[D] [SC] [≞]

✔★ **ROCKY MOUNTAIN DINER.** *800 18th St, at Stout, downtown.* 303/293-8383. Hrs: 11 am-11 pm; Sun 10 am-9 pm. Closed Jan 1, July 4, Thanksgiving, Dec 25. Res accepted. Bar to midnight. Semi-a la carte: lunch, dinner $4.95-$14.95. Child's meals. Specialties: buffalo meatloaf, duck enchiladas. Outdoor dining. Saloon-style decor, western motif. Cr cds: A, D, DS, MC, V.

[D] [≞]

★★ **SOREN'S.** *315 Detroit St, 3½ blks N of Cherry Creek Shopping Center, south of downtown.* 303/322-8155. Hrs: 11 am-9:30 pm; Fri & Sat to 10 pm; Sun 10:30 am-2:30 pm. Closed Jan 1, Thanksgiving, Dec 25. Res accepted. Bar. Semi-a la carte: lunch $5.75-$10.50, dinner $5.75-$18; Sun brunch $6-$10.50. Child's meals. Specialties: baked salmon in horseradish crust, Maryland crab cakes. Classical guitarist Fri-Sun. Outdoor dining. 4 dining areas. Cr cds: A, DS, MC, V.

[D] [≞]

★★★ **STRINGS.** *1700 Humbolt St (80218), east of downtown.* 303/831-7310. Hrs: 11 am-11 pm; Sat to midnight; Sun 5-10 pm. Closed major hols. Res accepted. Bar. Extensive wine list. Semi-a la carte: lunch $10-$17, dinner $18-$30. Child's meals. Specializes in penne bagutta, roast loin of Colorado lamb. Valet parking. Outdoor dining. Six dining areas, each with its own decor and ambience. Chef-owned. Cr cds: A, C, D, DS, MC, V.

[D] [≞]

★★★ **TANTE LOUISE.** *4900 E Colfax Ave, east of downtown.* 303/355-4488. Hrs: 5:30-10 pm. Closed Sun. Res accepted. Continental menu. Bar. Wine cellar. Semi-a la carte: dinner $15.95-$32.95. Child's meals. Specializes in duck, roast rack of lamb. Own pastries, dressings. Valet parking. Outdoor dining. French decor. Cr cds: A, C, D, DS, MC, V.

[D] [≞]

★ **TRINITY GRILLE.** *1801 Broadway, downtown.* 303/293-2288. Hrs: 11 am-10:30 pm; Fri, Sat to 11 pm. Closed Sun; most major hols. Res accepted. Bar. Semi-a la carte: lunch $4.50-$12.95, dinner

$5.95-$28.95. Specializes in Maryland crab cakes, fresh seafood. Casual dining. Cr cds: A, D, DS, MC, V.

[D] [≞]

★★★ **TUSCANY.** *(See Loews Giorgio Hotel)* 303/782-9300. Hrs: 6 am-10 pm; Sun brunch 11 am-2 pm. Res accepted; required Sun, hols. Northern Italian menu. Bar noon-midnight. Wine cellar. Semi-a la carte: bkfst $2.50-$12.50, lunch $8.25-$15.25, dinner $12.50-$25. Sun brunch $22.95. Child's meals. Specializes in pasta, seafood. Pianist, harpist Fri-Sun. Valet parking. Quiet, elegant dining rm; fireplace, frescoes. Outdoor dining. Cr cds: A, C, D, DS, JCB, MC, V.

[D] [≞]

★★★ **WELLSHIRE INN.** *3333 S Colorado Blvd, south of downtown.* 303/759-3333. Hrs: 7-10 am, 11:30 am-2:30 pm, 4:30-10 pm; Fri, Sat to 11 pm; Sun 10 am-2 pm, 4:30-9 pm; Sun brunch to 2 pm. Closed Jan 1, Memorial Day, Labor Day. Res accepted. Bar. Semi-a la carte: bkfst $4.75-$9.75, lunch $7.50-$12, dinner $14-$29. Sun brunch $5.25-$12. Specializes in salmon, rack of lamb, steak. Pianist evenings. Parking. Outdoor dining. Tudor-style inn. Totally nonsmoking. Cr cds: A, D, MC, V.

[D]

✔★★ **WYNKOOP BREWING COMPANY.** *1634 18th St, downtown.* 303/297-2700. Hrs: 11-2 am; Sun to midnight; Sun brunch 10 am-2 pm. Closed Thanksgiving, Dec 25. Bar. Semi-a la carte: lunch $4.95-$7.50, dinner $4.95-$15.95. Sun brunch $8.95. Specialties: shepherd's pie, bangers & mash. Entertainment Thurs-Sat. In J.S. Brown Mercantile Bldg (1899). Brewery kettles displayed; beer brewed on premises. Cr cds: A, C, D, DS, JCB, MC, V.

[D] [≞]

★★★ **ZENITH AMERICAN GRILL.** *1750 Lawrence St (80202), downtown.* 303/820-2800. This attractive space sports a cool high-tech look—track lighting, striking artwork, and black-and-white tables—in addition to courtyard dining. The kitchen produces creative southwestern variations and lighter versions of traditional Colorado meat-and-potatoes cuisine. Hrs: 11 am-10 pm; Sat from 5 pm; Sun 5-9 pm. Closed some major hols. Res accepted. Bar. Wine list. Semi-a la carte: lunch $7-$12, dinner $15-$30. A la carte entrees: $5-$10.50, dinner $13-$24. Specialties: fresh game & seafood. Valet parking. Cr cds: A, D, MC, V.

[D]

Unrated Dining Spot

FURRS CAFETERIA. *4900 Kipling, west of downtown.* 303/423-4602. Hrs: 11 am-8 pm; Fri & Sat to 8:30 pm. Avg ck: lunch $4.50, dinner $5.50. Cr cds: A, MC, V.

[D] [≞]

Denver International Airport Area (B-6)

(See Denver)

Services and Information

Information: 800/AIR-2-DEN.

Weather: 303/337-2500.

Lost and found: 303/342-4062.

Club Lounges: Admirals Club (American), Concourse C; Crown Room (Delta), Concourse C; Presidents Club (Continental), Concourse A; Red Carpet Clubs East and West (United), Concourse B.

Motel

★ ★ **HAMPTON INN AURORA.** *(1500 S Abilene St, Aurora 80012) I-70 W to I-225, S to exit 7.* 303/369-8400; FAX 303/369-0324. 132 rms, 4 story. S $67-$75; D $75-$83; under 18 free. Crib free. TV; cable (premium), VCR avail. Heated pool. Coffee in rms. Complimentary buffet bkfst. Ck-out noon. Coin lndry. Meeting rms. Business servs avail. Valet serv. Health club privileges. Some refrigerators. Cr cds: A, C, D, DS, JCB, MC, V.

Motor Hotel

★ ★ **BEST WESTERN EXECUTIVE.** *(4411 Peoria St, Denver 80239) N of I-70.* 303/373-5730; FAX 303/371-1401. 197 rms, 2-3 story. Apr-Sept: S $105; D $115; each addl $10; suites $135; under 18 free; lower rates rest of yr. Crib avail. Pet accepted; $75 deposit. TV; cable (premium), VCR avail. Heated pool. Complimentary coffee in rms. Restaurant 6 am-10 pm. Rm serv. Bar. Ck-out noon. Coin lndry. Meeting rms. Business servs avail. In-rm modem link. Bellhops. Concierge. Free airport transportation. Exercise equipt; weight machine, treadmill. Balconies. Picnic tables. Cr cds: A, D, DS, MC, V.

Hotels

★ ★ **DOUBLETREE.** *(13696 East Iliff Place, Aurora 80014) I-70 W to I-225, S to exit 5.* 303/337-2800; FAX 303/752-0296. 254 rms, 6 story. S $130; D $140; each addl $10; suites $175-$225; under 18 free; wkend rates. Crib free. TV; cable (premium), VCR avail (movies avail $8). Indoor pool; poolside serv. Restaurant 6:30 am-10 pm. Bar 11-2 am. Ck-out noon. Business center. In-rm modem link. Gift shop. Tennis & golf privileges. Exercise equipt; bicycles, stair machine. Some bathrm phones, in-rm whirlpools. Cr cds: A, C, D, DS, ER, JCB, MC, V.

★ ★ **RED LION.** *(3203 Quebec St, Denver 80207)* 303/321-3333; FAX 303/329-5233. 573 rms, 9 story. S $124-$129; D $134-$139; suites $200-$350; each addl $10; under 18 free; wkend rates. Crib free. Pet accepted. TV; cable (premium), VCR avail. Indoor pool. Complimentary coffee. Restaurant 6 am-11 pm. Rm serv 24 hrs. Bar 11-2 am, Sun to midnight. Ck-out noon. Convention facilities. Business center. In-rm modem link. Valet. Free airport transportation. Exercise equipt; weight machine, stair machine, whirlpool, sauna. Some bathrm phones, refrigerators. Balconies. Sun deck. Cr cds: A, C, D, DS, ER, MC, V.

Dillon (C-4)

(See Breckenridge, Georgetown, Leadville, Vail)

Pop 553 **Elev** 8,858 ft **Area code** 970 **Zip** 80435
Information Summit County Chamber of Commerce, PO Box 214, Frisco 80443; 800/530-3099.

The entire town was moved in the early 1960s to make way for Dillon Lake, a reservoir for the Denver water system. The new Dillon, a modern, planned community, has become a popular resort area in the midst of wonderful mountain scenery. Ranger District offices of the Green Mountain Reservoir (see KREMMLING) and the White River National Forest, Arapaho division, (see GLENWOOD SPRINGS) are located in Dillon.

What to See and Do

Arapaho National Forest. Campgrounds, picnic grounds and winter sports areas on more than one million acres. Of special interest are Lake Dillon, Arapaho National Recreation Area with 5 reservoirs and Mt Evans Wilderness Area with the 14,264-foot-high Mt Evans, which has the highest auto road in the US. N, S & E via US 6, CO 9. For information contact the Visitor Center, Arapaho and Roosevelt National Forests, 1311 S College, Fort Collins 80526; 970/498-1100. (Daily) Camping ¢¢¢

Copper Mt Resort Ski Area. 2 high-speed quad, 6 triple, 8 double chairlifts, 4 surface lifts; patrol, school, rentals; snowmaking; cafeteria, restaurants, bar; nursery. 96 runs; longest run 2.8 mi; vertical drop 2,760 ft. (Nov-Apr, daily) Cross-country skiing. Half-day rates. (See RESORT) Athletic club. Summer activities include boating, sailing, rafting; hiking, bicycling, horseback riding, golf, tennis; jeep tours. Chairlift also operates to summit of mountain (late June-Sept, daily). 12 mi SW at jct I-70 & CO 91. Phone 970/968-2882 or 800/458-8386. ¢¢¢¢¢

Keystone Resort Ski Area. Four ski mountains. Patrol, school, rentals. Snowmaking at Keystone, North Peak and The Outback. Cafeteria, restaurant, bar; nursery; lodge. (Late Oct-early May) Cross-country skiing, night skiing, ice-skating, snowmobiling, sleigh rides. Shuttle bus service. Combination, half-day and sr citizen ski rates; package plans. Summer activities include golf, tennis, boating and rafting; horseback riding, bicycling, jeep riding and gondola rides. 6 mi E on US 6. Phone 800/222-0188. ¢¢¢¢¢

Keystone Mt. Gondola, 2 triple, 8 double, 4 quad, 2 high-speed chairlifts, 4 surface lifts. 53 runs; longest run 3 mi; vertical drop 2,340 ft. (Late Oct-early May) Night skiing on 13 runs (mid-Nov-early Apr). ¢¢¢¢¢

North Peak. 1 high-speed gondola, 1 quad and 1 triple chairlifts. 19 runs; longest run 2 1/2 mi; vertical drop 1,620 ft. (Mid-Nov-late Apr) ¢¢¢¢¢

Arapahoe Basin. 1 triple, 4 double chairlifts. 61 runs; longest run 1 1/2 mi; vertical drop 1,670 ft. (Mid-Nov-June) ¢¢¢¢¢

The Outback. 1 high-speed quad chairlift. 17 runs; longest run 2 1/2 mi, vertical drop 1,520 ft. (Mid-Nov-late Apr) ¢¢¢¢¢

Lake Dillon. Fishing; boating, rafting (ramps, rentals, marinas). Hiking. Picnicking. Camping. Jeep tours (fee). (Daily) Just S of town in Arapaho National Foreston 3,300 acres. Phone 970/468-5400. **Free.**

Silverthorne Factory Stores. Mall contains over 45 outlet stores. Snack bars. (Daily) 2 mi N to I-70, exit 205, in Silverthorne. Phone 970/468-9440.

Annual Event

Mountain Community Fair. 2nd wkend July.

Motels

(Because of the altitude, air conditioning is rarely necessary)

★ ★ **BEST WESTERN PTARMIGAN LODGE.** *PO Box 218, 3 blks S of US 6, on Lake Dillon Dr.* 970/468-2341; FAX 970/468-6465. 69 rms, 1-2 story, 3 kits. No A/C. Late Dec-early Apr: S, D $110-$130; each addl $5-$10; kit. units $10 addl; lower rates rest of yr. Crib free. Pet accepted, $15. TV; cable (premium). Whirlpool. Sauna. Complimentary continental bkfst. Restaurant adj 7 am-10 pm. Ck-out 11 am. Meeting rms. Business servs avail. Free ski area transportation. Downhill/x-country ski 5 1/2 mi. Boating. Some balconies. On lake. Cr cds: A, C, D, DS, JCB, MC, V.

✔ ★ **DAYS INN.** *580 Silverthorne Lane, jct US 6, CO 9, I-70 exit 205.* 970/468-8661; FAX 970/468-5583. 73 air-cooled rms, 3 story, 30 kits. Nov-Apr: S $70-$150; D $80-$150; suites, kit. units $150-$200; under 18 free; lower rates rest of yr. Crib free. Pet accepted. TV; cable, VCR avail. Wading pool, whirlpool, sauna. Complimentary continental bkfst, coffee. Restaurant nearby. Ck-out 10 am. Coin lndry. Business servs avail. Downhill/x-country ski 6 mi. Many fireplaces. Cr cds: A, C, D, DS, MC, V.

⌨ 🦎 🏊 ⊠ 🔥 SC

✔ ★ **SNOWSHOE.** *(Box 400, Frisco 80443) 1¹/₂ mi S on US 6 off I-70 Business exit 203. 303/668-3444; res: 800/445-8658; FAX 970/668-3883.* 37 rms, 2 story, 9 kits. No A/C. Late Dec-Mar: S, D $75; kit. units $3-$6 addl; lower rates rest of yr. TV; cable (premium), VCR avail. Complimentary continental bkfst, coffee. Whirlpool, sauna. Restaurant nearby. Ck-out 10 am. Downhill ski 6 mi; x-country ski 1 mi. Some refrigerators. Cr cds: A, D, DS, MC, V.

🏊 ⊠ 🔥 SC

Motor Hotel

★ **HOLIDAY INN SUMMIT COUNTY.** *Box 4310, Off I-70 exit 203. 970/668-5000; FAX 970/668-0718.* 216 rms, 3-6 story. Late Dec-Mar: S, D $79-$175; lower rates rest of yr. TV; cable (premium), VCR avail. Indoor pool. Restaurant 6 am-2 pm, 5-10 pm. Rm serv. Bar 11-2 am, Sun to midnight; entertainment Fri, Sat in season. Ck-out noon. Coin lndry. Meeting rms. Business servs avail. In-rm modem link. Bellhops. Valet serv. Gift shop. Ski area transportation. Downhill/x-country ski 10 mi. Holidome. Exercise equipt; treadmill, bicycles, whirlpool, sauna. Game rm. Rec rm. Some refrigerators. Balconies. Cr cds: A, C, D, DS, JCB, MC, V.

⌨ 🦎 🏊 🏃 ⊠ 🔥 SC

Resort

★ ★ ★ **COPPER MOUNTAIN.** *(Box 3001, I-70 & CO 91, Copper Mountain 80443) I-70 exit 195. 970/968-2882; res: 800/458-8386; FAX 970/968-2308.* 525 units in 15 bldgs, 1-7 story. S, D $79-$199; each addl $15; full condo units $172-$585; under 14 free; higher rates late Dec; AP, MAP avail; ski, biking, golf, tennis, honeymoon plans. Crib free. TV; cable (premium), VCR avail (movies avail $3). Indoor pool. Playground. Supervised child's activities; ages 3-12. Complimentary coffee in rms. Dining rm (see PESCE FRESCO). Rm serv. Box lunches. Picnics. Bar 11-2 am. Ck-out 11 am, ck-in 4 pm. Grocery. Coin lndry. Package store. Convention facilities. Business servs avail. In-rm modem link. Some services limited in summer. Valet serv. Concierge. Sports dir. Indoor tennis, pro. 18-hole golf, pro, putting green, driving range. Paddleboats. Downhill/x-country ski on site. Ice-skating, ski rentals; sleigh rides. Bicycle rentals. Lawn games. Guides. Entertainment. Rec rm. Game rm. Exercise rm; instructor, weights, bicycles, whirlpool, steam rm, sauna. Massage therapy. Many refrigerators, fireplaces. Many balconies. Picnic tables, grills. For all seasons; extensive grounds on 250 acres. Cr cds: A, C, DS, MC, V.

⌨ 🦎 ⛷ 🏊 🏃 🏇 🏊 🏃 ⊠ 🔥 SC

Restaurants

★ ★ ★ **ALPENGLOW STUBE.** *(Keystone Resort, Keystone) access by gondola only (allow 40 min each way). 970/468-2316.* Hrs: 5-8:30 pm. Closed Sun; also mid-Apr-late June & early Sept-late Nov. Res accepted. Continental menu. Bar. Extensive wine list. Complete 6-course meal $72. Specializes in game dishes, rack of lamb. Outdoor dining. Alpine atmosphere in large log structure, native stone fireplace. Cr cds: A, C, D, DS, MC, V.

⌨

★ ★ **BLUE SPRUCE.** *I-70 at exit 201, ¹/₂ mi E of I-70. 970/668-5900.* Hrs: 5-10 pm; also Sun 9 am-1:30 pm. Res accepted. No A/C. Continental menu. Bar. Semi-a la carte: dinner $12.95-$31.95; Sun brunch $6.95-$12.95. Specializes in lamb, fresh fish, prime rib. Own desserts. Parking. Cr cds: A, DS, MC, V.

⌨

★ ★ **KEYSTONE RANCH.** *(Keystone Rd, Keystone) 7 mi E on US 6, 1¹/₂ mi S on Keystone Rd. 970/468-4161.* Hrs: 5:45-8:45 pm. Closed Sun summer months. Res required. No A/C. Bar. Wine list. Complete meals: dinner $62. Child's meals. Specializes in wild game, elk medallion. Valet parking. Log ranch house with view of mountains; fireplace. Cr cds: A, C, D, DS, MC, V.

★ ★ **PESCE FRESCO.** *(See Copper Mountain Resort) 970/968-2882.* Hrs: 7 am-10 pm. Res accepted. Northern Italian menu. Bar. Semi-a la carte: bkfst $4.95-$7.50, lunch $4.50-$7.95, dinner $12.95-$21.95. Child's meals. Specializes in seafood, North American elk. Parking. Outdoor dining. Colorful decor. Deck faces ski runs. Cr cds: A, C, D, DS, MC, V.

⌨

★ ★ ★ **SKI TIP LODGE.** *(Montezuma Rd, Keystone) 970/468-4202.* Hrs: 5:45-9 pm. Closed Thurs summer months. Res accepted; required wkends. Bar. Complete meal: dinner $46. Child's meals. Specialties: venison chop, champagne-poached salmon. Parking. Former stagecoach stop; Western decor. View of lake & mountains. Totally nonsmoking. Cr cds: A, C, D, DS, MC, V.

Dinosaur National Monument (A-1)

(88 mi W of Craig on US 40 to monument headquarters)

About two-thirds of the 325-square-mile monument is in Colorado. Access to this backcountry section, a land of fantastic, deeply eroded canyons of the Green and Yampa rivers, is via the Harpers Corner Road, starting at monument headquarters on US 40, 2 miles east of Dinosaur, Colorado. At Harpers Corner, the end of this 32-mile surfaced road, a one-mile foot trail leads to a promontory overlooking the Green and Yampa rivers.

The entrance to the Dinosaur Quarry section in Utah is at the junction of US 40 and UT 149 in Jensen, Utah, 13 miles east of Vernal. Seven miles north on UT 149 is the Dinosaur Quarry; 4 to 5 miles farther is the Green River campground. No lodgings are available other than campgrounds.

Visitor centers and one quarry section campground are open all year. The remainder are often closed by snow approximately mid-Nov-mid-Apr. For detailed information contact Superintendent, 4545 Hwy 40, Dinosaur 81610; 970/374-3000.

What to See and Do

Camping, picnicking. Green River campground near Dinosaur Quarry in Utah (Memorial Day-Labor Day; fee); Lodore, Deerlodge, and Echo Park campgrounds in Colorado; Harpers Corner has picnic facilities.

Dinosaur Quarry. Remarkable fossil deposit; exhibit of 150-million-year-old dinosaur remains; preparation laboratory on display. (Daily; extended hrs in summer; closed Jan 1, Thanksgiving, Dec 25) Per vehicle 7 mi N of Jensen, Utah, on UT 149. ¢¢

Fishing. Utah or Colorado license required.

Monument Headquarters and Information Center. At park entrance in Colorado. Display panels; audiovisual program, talks. (June-Labor Day, daily; rest of yr, Mon-Fri exc hols) **Free.**

Other activities. Self-guided nature trails (all yr), evening campfire programs, guided nature walks, children's programs, dinosaur talks (summer). Backpacking on marked trails; obtain permit at visitor centers.

River rafting. Permit must be obtained in advance from National Park Service. Guided trips from various concessionaires. Obtain list at visitor centers or from the superintendent.

Durango (F-2)

(See Cortez)

Founded 1880 **Pop** 12,430 **Elev** 6,523 ft **Area code** 970 **Zip** 81301
Information Chamber Resort Assn, 111 S Camino Del Rio, PO Box 2587; 970/247-0312 or 800/525-8855.

Will Rogers once said of Durango, "It's out of the way and glad of it." For more than 100 years this small Western city has profited from its "out of the way" location at the base of the San Juan Mountains. Durango has been the gateway to Colorado's riches for Indians, fur traders, miners, prospectors, ranchers and engineers.

Founded by the Denver & Rio Grande Railroad, Durango was a rowdy community during its early days. The notorious Stockton-Esk-ridge gang once engaged local vigilantes in an hour-long gun battle in the main street. A local expedition to New Mexico to "dig up Aztecs" in 1885 was supplied with "5 cases of chewing tobacco, 3 cases of beer, 10 gallons of heavy liquids, 4 burro-loads of the stuff that busted Parliament, 7 reels of fuse, a box of soap, 2 boxes of cigars, a fish line, 20 pairs of rubber boots, 200 loaves of bread, a can of lard, and one pound of bacon." In the 1890s the Durango *Herald-Democrat* was noted for the stinging, often profane, wit of pioneer editor "Dave" Day, who once had 42 libel suits pending against him. Headquarters of San Juan National Forest is in Durango, as well as a District Ranger office for the forest.

What to See and Do

Big-game hunting in season. Vallecito Lake Resort Area. San Juan National Forest. Also on Bureau of Land Mangement.

Carriage Works Theatre. Year-round productions from Shakespeare and contemporary playwrights performed by The Company. (Thurs-Sat) 1160 Main St. Phone 970/247-0136. ¢¢¢

Diamond Circle Theatre. Professional turn-of-the-century melodrama and vaudeville performances (June-Sept, nightly; closed Sun). Advance reservations advised. In Strater Hotel (see HOTEL). Phone 970/247-4431 or -3400. ¢¢¢¢

Fishing. Lemon Dam, 12 mi NE on Florida Rd. Vallecito Lake, 18 mi NE on Florida Rd. Also Pine, Animas, Dolores rivers.

Mesa Verde National Park (see). 37 mi W on US 160.

Purgatory-Durango Ski Resort. 4 triple, 5 double chairlifts; patrol, school, rentals; 5 restaurants, 5 bars; nursery, lodge; specialty stores. 70 runs; longest run 2 mi; vertical drop 2,029 ft. (Late Nov-early Apr) Cross-country skiing. Multiday, half-day rates. Chairlift and alpine slide also operate mid-June-Labor Day (daily; fee); other summer activities. 25 mi N on US 550, in San Juan National Forest: Phone 970/247-9000 or 800/525-0892. ¢¢¢¢¢

Rocky Mountain High Jeep Tours. All-day, 1/2-day, 2- & 3-hr guided tours of ghost towns, historic mine tours and scenic tours. Jeep rentals also avail. Tours depart from 46825 US 550N; also departures from Silverton (see). For details contact PO Box 3337, Durango 81302 or phone 800/530-2022. ¢¢¢¢

San Juan National Forest. This forest of nearly two million acres includes the Weminuche Wilderness, Colorado's largest designated wilderness, with several peaks topping 14,000 feet, as well as the South San Juanand Lizard Head wildernesses. The Colorado Trail begins in Durango and traverses the backcountry all the way to Denver. Recreation includes fishing in high mountain lakes and streams; boating, whitewater rafting; hiking, biking, camping and four-wheel driving. The San Juan Skyway is a 236-mile auto loop through many of these scenic areas. (Daily) N on US 550; E & W on US 160. For information contact the Supervisor, 701 Camino del Rio; 970/247-4874.

Southern Ute Indian Cultural Museum. Historical museum contains archival photos, turn-of-the-century Ute Indian clothing and tools and accessories. Multimedia presentation. Gift shop. (Daily exc Sun; closed major hols) 23 mi SE via US 160 & CO 172 in Ignacio. Phone 970/563-9583. ¢

⭐ **The Silverton (Durango & Silverton Narrow Gauge Railroad).** America's last regularly scheduled narrow-gauge passenger train, in service since 1882, runs between Durango and Silverton, using original passenger coaches and steam engines. The 3½-hr trip each way passes over spectacular southwest Colorado rocky mountain scenery and through the Canyon of Rio de Las Animas. (Daily) Under 5 free if not occupying seat. A winter holiday train excursion is also in operation (day before Thanksgiving-Jan 1; closed Dec 24 & 25). Depot, 479 Main Ave. For details, check with the passenger agent, Durango, phone 970/247-2733. Ticket window (daily). Advance reservations required. ¢¢¢¢

In San Juan National Forest is Tall Timber Resort (see RESORT), accessible only by the Silverton Railroad or by helicopter.

Annual Events

Snowdown Winter Carnival. Last wk Jan.

Iron Horse Bicycle Classic. Memorial Day wkend.

Durango Cowboy Gathering. 1st wkend Oct.

Motels

⭐ **ADOBE INN.** 2178 Main Ave. 970/247-2743; res: 800/251-8773; FAX 970/247-5345. 25 rms, 2 story, 5 kit. units. Mid-May-mid-Aug: S $78-$88; D $88-$98; kit. units $100-$120; under 12 free; ski plan; lower rates rest of yr. Pet accepted, some restrictions. TV; cable (premium). Heated pool; whirlpool. Complimentary coffee in lobby. Ck-out 11 am. Coin lndry. Cr cds: A, DS, MC, V.

🔲 🏊 🚫 🐾 **SC**

✔ ⭐ **ALPINE.** 3515 N Main Ave, 2½ mi N on US 550. 970/247-4042; res: 800/818-4042; FAX 970/385-4489. 25 rms, 1 & 2 story. Mid-May-mid-Oct: S $68-$74; D $78-$84; each addl $4; ski rates; lower rates rest of yr. Crib free. Pet accepted, some restrictions. TV; cable (premium). Restaurant nearby. Ck-out 11 am. Cr cds: A, D, DS, MC, V.

D 🐾 🚫 🔥

⭐ ⭐ **BEST WESTERN DURANGO INN.** Box 3099 (81302), 21382 US 160W. 970/247-3251; FAX 970/385-4835. 72 rms, 2 story. Memorial Day-Sept: S, D $89-$95; suites $119; under 12 free; ski plans; higher rates Christmas hols; lower rates rest of yr. Crib $4. TV; cable, VCR avail. Heated pool; whirlpool, sauna. Playground. Restaurant 6:30 am-10 pm. Bar from 4 pm. Ck-out 11 am. Business servs avail. In-rm modem link. Game rm. Cr cds: A, C, D, DS, JCB, MC, V.

D 🏊 🚫 🔥

⭐ **BEST WESTERN PURGATORY.** 49617 US 550. 970/247-9669; FAX 970/247-9681. 31 air-cooled kit. units, 2 story, 21 suites. Late Nov-Mar: S $85-$120; D $90-$140; suites $120-$198; under 13 free (summer); higher rates Christmas hols; lower rates rest of yr. Crib free. Pet accepted; $6 per day. TV; cable (premium), VCR avail. Indoor pool; whirlpool. Complimentary continental bkfst. Restaurant 5-9 pm. Bar. Ck-out 11 am. Meeting rms. Business servs avail. In-rm modem link. Downhill/x-country ski adj. Picnic tables. Cr cds: A, C, D, DS, MC, V.

D 🐾 🚶 🏊 🚫 🔥

⭐ ⭐ **DAYS INN.** 1700 Animas View Dr, 4 mi N on US 550. 970/259-1430; FAX 970/259-5741. 95 rms, 3 story. Late June-Aug: S, D $70-$92; each addl $6; under 18 free; higher rates Christmas hols; lower rates rest of yr. Crib free. TV; cable (premium). Indoor pool. Ck-out 11 am. Business servs avail. In-rm modem link. Exercise equipt; bicycles, weight machines, whirlpools, saunas. Cr cds: A, C, D, DS, JCB, MC, V.

🏊 🚫 🔥 **SC**

★★ **DURANGO LODGE.** *150 E 5th St. 970/247-0955; FAX 970/385-1882.* 39 rms, 2 story. May-Oct: S $57-$79; D $59-$91; each addl $5; under 17 free; ski rates; lower rates rest of yr. Crib free. TV; cable. Heated pool; whirlpool. Complimentary coffee in rms. Restaurant nearby. Ck-out noon. Some refrigerators. Balconies. Cr cds: A, C, D, DS, ER, MC, V.

⊠ ⊠ ⚒

★ **ECONO LODGE.** *2002 Main Ave. 970/247-4242; FAX 970/385-4713.* 41 rms, 2 story. Late May-Sept: S $74-$95; D $82-$105; each addl $4; suites $105; under 18 free; ski plans; higher rates Dec 25; lower rates rest of yr. Crib free. TV; cable, VCR avail. Heated pool; wading pool, whirlpool. Complimentary coffee in lobby. Restaurant nearby. Ck-out 11 am. Cr cds: A, D, DS, MC, V.

⊠ ⊠ ⚒ SC

★★ **HAMPTON INN.** *3777 N Main. 970/247-2600.* 76 rms, 3 story. Mid-May-late Oct: S $75-$90; D $85-$110; suites $135; under 18 free; lower rates rest of yr. TV; cable (premium). Indoor pool; whirlpool. Complimentary continental bkfst. Complimentary coffee in lobby. Restaurant opp 11 am-10 pm. Ck-out 11 am. Coin lndry. Meeting rms. Business servs avail. In-rm modem link. Cr cds: A, C, D, DS, MC, V.

D ⊠ ⊠ ⚒ SC

✔★★ **IRON HORSE INN.** *5800 N Main Ave, 4 mi N on US 550. 970/259-1010; res: 800/748-2990; FAX 970/385-4791.* 141 bi-level rms. S $65-$95; D $75-$115; each addl $5; suites $90-$115; under 12 free; ski packages. Crib $6. Pet accepted. TV; cable (premium). Indoor pool; sauna, whirlpool. Restaurant 6:30-10 am, 5:30-9 pm. Ck-out 11 am. Coin lndry. Meeting rms. Business servs avail. Free airport transportation. Game rm. Lawn games. Fireplaces. Cr cds: A, C, D, DS, MC, V.

⚓ ⚡ ⊠ ⚒ SC

★★ **JARVIS SUITE.** *125 W 10th St. 970/259-6190; res: 800/824-1024; FAX 970/259-6190.* 22 kit. suites, 3 story. May-Oct: S $89-$143; D $99-$143; each addl $10; under 12 free; ski plans; higher rates late Dec; lower rates rest of yr. Pet accepted. TV; cable, VCR avail. Complimentary coffee. Restaurant opp 7 am-11 pm. Ck-out noon. Coin lndry. Meeting rms. Business servs avail. In-rm modem link. Restored historic hotel (1888). Cr cds: A, D, DS, MC, V.

D ⚓ ⊠ ⚒ SC

✔★★ **LANDMARK.** *3030 N Main Ave. 970/259-1333; res: 800/252-8853; FAX 970/247-3854.* 48 rms, 2 story. No elvtr. Mid-May-mid-Oct, mid-Dec-early Jan: S $69-$89; D $75-$89; each addl $5; suites $120; ski plan; lower rates rest of yr. Crib $5. TV; cable (premium). Heated pool; whirlpool, sauna. Complimentary coffee in lobby. Restaurant nearby. Ck-out 11 am. Business servs avail. Cr cds: A, C, D, DS, MC, V.

D ⊠ ⊠ ⚒ SC

✔★ **RODEWAY INN.** *2701 N Main Ave. 970/259-2540; res: 800/752-6072; FAX 970/247-9642.* 31 rms, 2 story. Mid-May-Sept: S $58-$98; D $68-$98; each addl $5; under 17 free; lower rates rest of yr. Pet accepted, some restrictions. TV; cable (premium), VCR avail (movies $5.99). Indoor pool; whirlpool. Complimentary continental bkfst. Restaurant nearby. Ck-out 11 am. Coin lndry. Business servs avail. Cr cds: A, D, DS, ER, JCB, MC, V.

⚓ ⊠ ⊠ ⚒ SC

Motor Hotel

★★★ **RED LION INN.** *501 Camino Del Rio. 970/259-6580; FAX 970/259-4398.* 159 rms, 4 story. Mid-May-mid-Oct: S, D $129-$164; each addl $15; suites $300; under 18 free; ski plans; higher rates late Dec; lower rates rest of yr. Crib free. Pet accepted. TV; cable. Indoor pool; whirlpool, poolside serv. Restaurant 6 am-10 pm. Rm serv. Bar 11:30 am-midnight. Ck-out noon. Coin lndry. Meeting rms. Business servs avail. Bellhops. Valet serv. Gift shop. Beauty shop. Free airport

transportation. Exercise equipt; weight machines, bicycles, sauna. Private patios, balconies. Cr cds: A, C, D, DS, ER, JCB, MC, V.

D ⚓ ⚓ ⊠ ✗ ⊠ ⊠ ⚒ SC

Hotel

★★★ **STRATER.** *699 Main Ave. 970/247-4431; res: 800/247-4431; FAX 970/259-2208.* 93 rms, 4 story. May-mid-Oct, Washington's birthday, late Dec: S $95-$150; D $115-$170; lower rates rest of yr. TV; cable. Restaurant 6-11 am, 5:30-10 pm. Bar 11-2 am; entertainment. Ck-out noon. Meeting rms. Business servs avail. In-rm modem link. Concierge. Valet parking. Whirlpool. Built 1887; Victorian decor, many antiques. Unusual 1890 Diamond Belle Bar. Summer theater. Shopping center within hotel complex. Totally nonsmoking. Cr cds: A, C, D, DS, JCB, MC, V.

⊠ ⚒

Inns

★★ **COUNTRY SUNSHINE.** *35130 US 550N, 14 mi N, follow signs. 970/247-2853; res: 800/383-2853.* 7 air-cooled rms, 2 story. No rm phones. Mid-May-mid-Oct: S, D $85; each addl $15; lower rates rest of yr. Complimentary full bkfst, tea. Ck-out 10:30 am, ck-in 4-6 pm. Downhill ski 12 mi; x-country ski on site. Whirlpool. Picnic tables, grills. Antiques. Library/sitting rm. Totally nonsmoking. Cr cds: A, DS, MC, V.

⚓ ⊠ ⚒

★★ **LELAND HOUSE.** *721 E 2nd Ave. 970/385-1920; res: 800/664-1920; FAX 970/385-1967.* 10 air-cooled rms, 2 story, 10 kits. S $85-$95; D $95-$105; each addl $15; suites $125-$145; ski plan. Crib $15. TV; cable (premium). Complimentary coffee in rms. Complimentary full bkfst, afternoon tea/sherry. Restaurant adj 11:30 am-2:30 pm, 5-10:30 pm. Ck-out 11 am, ck-in 3 pm. Concierge serv. Luggage handling. Refrigerators. Picnic tables. Restored apartment building (1927); many antiques. Totally nonsmoking. Cr cds: A, DS, MC, V.

⊠ ⚒ SC

★★★ **LIGHTNER CREEK.** *999 C.R. 207, Approx 3 mi W on US 160, 1 mi on Lightner Creek Rd. 970/259-1226; FAX 970/259-0732.* 8 rms (3 share bath), 2 story. No A/C. No rm phones. May-Oct: S, D $95-$150; each addl $35; lower rates rest of yr. Children over 9 yrs only. Cable TV in some rms. Complimentary full bkfst. Complimentary coffee in library, afternoon tea/sherry. Ck-out 11 am, ck-in 4-6 pm. Business servs avail. Country French house built 1903; many antiques, baby grand piano. Gazebo. Cr cds: DS, MC, V.

D ⚓ ⊠ ⚒

★★ **ROCHESTER HOTEL.** *726 N 2nd Ave. 970/385-1920; res: 800/664-1920; FAX 970/385-1967.* 15 rms, 2 story, 2 suites, 1 kit. unit. No A/C. June-Oct: S, D $125-$185; each addl $15; suites $165-$185; kit. unit $165; ski plans; lower rates rest of yr. Children over 14 yrs only. Pet accepted, some restrictions; $15. TV; cable (premium), VCR avail. Complimentary full bkfst. Restaurant opp 11:30 am-2:30 pm, 5-10:30 pm. Ck-out 11 am. Meeting rms. Business servs avail. Luggage handling. Some refrigerators. Restored hotel originally built in 1892. Each room is named and decorated for a movie that was filmed in the area. Totally nonsmoking. Cr cds: A, DS, MC, V.

D ⚓ ⊠ ⚒ SC

Resort

★★★★ **TALL TIMBER.** *(Box 90M, Silverton Star Rte) 25 mi N, accessible only by Silverton train or helicopter. 970/259-4813.* This family-run luxury resort is set in 180 secluded acres of high-altitude desert and offers an individualized wilderness vacation. Many of the luxury log cabin-style, duplex apartments, which feature stone fireplaces and lush carpeting have whirlpool baths. The absence of phones, TVs, and radios guarantees absolute peace and quiet. 10

suites, 2 story. No A/C. No rm phones. AP, July 2-Sept & mid-Dec-early Jan, wkly: 7 days, 6 nights: S $3,500; D $1,900/person; each addl $1,900; 4 days, 3 nights: S $2,500; D $1,400/person; each addl $1,400; 3-12 yrs 50% less; under 3 yrs $300; transfer from Durango included; lower rates mid-May-July 1, Oct. Closed rest of yr. Crib free. Indoor/outdoor pool; whirlpools, sauna. Coffee in rms. Dining rm 7:30-9:30 am, 12:30-1:30 pm, 6:30-7:30 pm (continental menu). Box lunches, helicopter picnics. Ck-out 10:30 am, ck-in 3:30 pm. Gift shop. Tennis. 9-hole par 3 golf, putting green, driving range. Stocked pond for children. Downhill ski 3 min by air; x-country ski on site. Hiking trails. Horseshoes. Refrigerators, wet bars. Balconies. Library. Totally nonsmoking. No cr cds accepted.

Guest Ranches

★ ★ **COLORADO TRAILS RANCH.** *PO Box 848, 12 mi NE on County 240 (15th St).* 970/247-5055; res: 800/323-3833; FAX 970/385-7372. 33 air-cooled rms in 12 cabins. No rm phones. AP, wkly: $1,000-$1,300/person; family rates. Closed Oct-May. Children over 5 yrs only. Heated pool; whirlpool, lifeguard. Free supervised child's activities from 5 yrs. Teen club. Dining rm (3 sittings): 7:30-9 am, 12:30 pm, 6:30 pm. Box lunches, snack bar, picnics. Ck-out 10 am, ck-in 2 pm. Lndry facilities. Meeting rms. Business servs avail. Gift shop. Free airport transportation. Sports dir. Tennis. Waterskiing. Hiking. Trap shooting. Hayrides. Archery. Lawn games. Entertainment. Game rm. Fish guides. On 525 acres; adj to San Juan National Forest. Cr cds: A, D, DS, MC, V.

★ ★ **LAKE MANCOS.** *Box 2061 M (81302), W on US 160 to Mancos, then ⅓ mi N via CO 184, then 5 mi NE on County 42.* 970/533-7900; res: 800/325-9462. 13 cabins, 4 rms in lodge. No A/C. No rm phones. Early July-Aug, AP, wkly (from Sun): S, D $1,025/person; family rates; lower rates Sept & June. Closed rest of yr. Crib free. Heated pool; whirlpool. Free supervised child's activities (mid-June-late Aug); from 4 yrs. Dining rm. Box lunches; snacks. Ck-out 10 am, ck-in 2 pm. Coin lndry. Airport, bus depot transportation. Sports dir. Lawn games. Soc dir; entertainment. Jeep tours, hayrides. Rec rm. Refrigerators. Private patios. Secluded mountain location. Established in 1956. Cr cds: DS, MC, V.

★ ★ ★ **WILDERNESS TRAILS RANCH.** *(23486 County Road 501, Bayfield 81122) 26 mi NE of Bayfield off US 160 on Vallecito Rd.* 970/247-0722; FAX 970/247-1006. 20 rms in 10 cabins. No A/C. No rm phones. AP, Mid-June-late Aug, wkly: S $1,680; D $1,380/person; family rates; lower rates early-mid-June & Sept. Closed rest of yr. Heated pool; whirlpool. Playground. Free supervised child's activities from age 3. Dining rm: bkfst 7:30-9 am, lunch from noon, dinner from 6 pm. Setups. Box lunches, picnics, cookouts. Ck-out 10 am, ck-in 3 pm. Coin lndry. Meeting rms. Gift shop. Airport, bus depot transportation. Waterskiing, windsurfing, rafting, boats, motor boats. Overnight camping. Hayrides. 4-wheel driving trips. Lawn games. Entertainment; square dancing; movies. Rec rm. Game rm. Fishing guide. Picnic tables, grills. Fireplace in lounge. Porches, patios. Mountain resort. Totally nonsmoking. Cr cds: DS, MC, V.

★ ★ ★ **WIT'S END.** *(254 County Rd 500, Vallecita 81122) 20 mi E on US 160 to Bayfield, 18 mi N on County Rd 501, then ¾ mi N on County Rd 500.* 970/884-4113; FAX 970/884-3261. 21 kit. cabins, 1-2 story. No A/C. AP, Memorial Day-Labor Day (7-day min): D, cabins $2,940-$3,380; each addl $1,470; 4-12 yrs $1,085; under 3 free; lower rates rest of yr. Crib free. TV; VCR (movies avail). Heated pool; whirlpool. Free supervised child's activities (Mid-June-Labor Day); from 3 yrs. Dining rm 7 am-3 pm, 5-9 pm. Rm serv. Box lunches. Bar; entertainment. Ck-out 9 am, ck-in 4 pm. Grocery, coin lndry, package store. Meeting rms. Gift shop. Airport, bus depot transportation. Tennis. X-country ski on site. Horse stables. Hay rides. Snowmobiles, sleighing. Mountain bikes. Soc dir. Fishing/hunting guides, clean & store.

Picnic tables, grills. In valley on 361 acres; all cabins are adj to a river or pond. Stone fireplaces, knotty pine interiors. Totally nonsmoking. Cr cds: A, DS, MC, V.

Restaurants

★ ★ **ARIANO'S.** *150 E 6th St.* 970/247-8146. Hrs: 5-10 pm. Closed Sun Oct-mid-May; Thanksgiving, Dec 25. Northern Italian menu. Bar from 5 pm. Semi-a la carte: dinner $9.95-$21. Child's meals. Specialties: chicken Vincent, veal Marsala, fettucine Napolitano. Own pasta. Turn-of-the-century building originally a saloon and brothel. Totally nonsmoking. Cr cds: A, MC, V.

D

★ ★ **FRANCISCO'S.** *619 Main Ave.* 970/247-4098. Hrs: 11 am-10 pm. Mexican, Amer menu. Bar. Semi-a la carte: lunch $5.50-$9.50, dinner $7.25-$19.75. Child's meals. Specializes in steak, fresh seafood, chicken. Own desserts. Mexican decor. Family-owned. Cr cds: A, C, D, DS, MC, V.

D   SC

✔ ★ **GRANDMA CHUNG'S.** *937 Main Ave.* 970/247-8673. Hrs: 11 am-9 pm; summer Sun from 5 pm. Asian menu. Beer. Semi-a la carte: lunch, dinner $3.50-$8.95. Specializes in vegetarian & homestyle Korean dishes. Outdoor dining. Totally nonsmoking. Cr cds: MC, V.

★ ★ **LOLA'S PLACE.** *725 E 2nd.* 970/385-5880. Hrs: 11 am-2:30 pm, 5-10 pm; Mon to 2:30 pm; Sat from 5 pm. Closed Sun; major hols. Res accepted. Bar. Semi-a la carte: lunch $6-$20, dinner $6-$25. Specialties: venison, Thai curry noodles. Parking. Outdoor dining. Totally nonsmoking. Cr cds: A, MC, V.

✔ ★ **LORI'S FAMILY DINING.** *2653 Main Ave.* 970/247-1224. Hrs: 6 am-9 pm; summer to 10 pm. Closed Thanksgiving, Dec 25. Semi-a la carte: bkfst $2.75-$7.95, lunch, dinner $4.95-$11.95. Salad bar. Child's meals. Specializes in barbecued ribs, shrimp, Mexican dishes. Parking. Cr cds: MC, V.

SC

★ ★ **PALACE GRILL.** *1 Depot Place.* 970/247-2018. Hrs: 11:30 am-3 pm, 5:30-10 pm. Closed Thanksgiving, Dec 25. Continental menu. Wine cellar. Semi-a la carte: lunch $5.90-$11.50, dinner $13.50-$22.50. Child's meals. Specializes in duck, mesquite-grilled steak, trout. Own pastries. Parking. Outdoor dining. In restored 1893 building; Victorian decor, Tiffany lamps. Smoking at bar only. Cr cds: A, D, DS, MC, V.

★ ★ **RED SNAPPER.** *144 E 9th St.* 970/259-3417. Hrs: 5-10 pm. Closed Thanksgiving, Dec 25. Bar. Semi-a la carte: dinner $8.95-$38. Child's meals. Specializes in grilled fresh seafood, steaks, prime rib. Salad bar. Own desserts. Parking. Fish tanks. Turn-of-the-century building (1904). Totally nonsmoking. Cr cds: A, MC, V.

D

Unrated Dining Spot

CARVERS BAKERY CAFE/BREWERY. *1022 Main Ave.* 970/259-2545. Hrs: 6:30 am-10 pm; Sun to 1 pm. Closed Jan 1, Thanksgiving, Dec 25. Southwestern menu. Bar from 4 pm; brew pub. Semi-a la carte: bkfst $3.25-$5.95, lunch $4.75-$6.75, dinner $4.75-$6.75. Cr cds: MC, V.

D

Englewood (C-6)

(See Denver, Lakewood)

Pop 29,387 **Elev** 5,369 ft **Area code** 303

Information Chamber of Commerce, 701 W Hampden Ave, Suite G-34, 80154, phone 303/789-4473; or the South Metro Denver Chamber of Commerce, 7901 S Park Plaza #110, Littleton 80120, phone 303/795-0142.

Englewood is located in Denver's south metro area, which is home to the Denver Technological Center.

What to See and Do

Castle Rock Factory Shops. More than 40 outlet stores; food court. (Daily) Approx 24 mi S on I-25, exit 184, in Castle Rock. Phone 303/688-4494.

The Museum of Outdoor Arts. Outdoor sculpture garden on 400 acres. Guided tours avail (fee). Lunchtime summer performance series (Wed). (Daily; closed some major hols) 1 mi S on S Broadway, then 4 mi E on E Arapahoe Rd, then N on Greenwood Plaza Blvd. Phone 303/741-3609. **Free.** The museum includes

Fiddlers Green Amphitheatre. Host to summer concerts. Phone 303/220-7000.

Motels

★ ★ **COURTYARD BY MARRIOTT.** *6565 S Boston St (80111). 303/721-0300; FAX 303/721-0037.* 155 rms, 2 story. S $69-$100; D $88-$100; each addl $10; suites $83-$105; wkly rates. Crib free. TV; cable (premium), VCR avail. Indoor pool. Complimentary coffee in rms. Bkfst avail. Bar. Ck-out 1 pm. Coin lndry. Meeting rms. Business servs avail. In-rm modem link. Valet serv. Sundries. Exercise equipt; weight machine, bicycles, whirlpool. Game rm. Refrigerator in suites. Balconies. Picnic tables. Cr cds: A, D, DS, MC, V.

D ≊ 🛉 ⊠ 🔥 **SC**

✔ ★ ★ **HAMPTON INN-SOUTHEAST.** *9231 E Arapahoe Rd (80112), just E of I-25 exit 197. 303/792-9999; FAX 303/790-4360.* 152 rms, 5 story. S $64-$75; D $74-$85; under 18 free; wkly rates. Crib free. TV; cable (premium), VCR avail. Heated pool. Complimentary coffee in rms. Complimentary continental bkfst buffet. Restaurant nearby. Ck-out noon. Coin lndry. Meeting rms. Business servs avail. In-rm modem link. Valet serv. Exercise equipt; weight machine, bicycles. Health club privileges. Cr cds: A, C, D, DS, MC, V.

D 🛏 ≊ 🛉 ⊠ 🔥 **SC**

★ ★ **RESIDENCE INN BY MARRIOTT-SOUTH.** *6565 S Yosemite (80111), just W of I-25 exit 197. 303/740-7177; FAX 303/740-7177, ext. 129.* 128 kit. suites, 1-2 story. S, D $115-$150; each addl free; wkend, wkly, monthly rates. Crib free. Pet accepted; $10 fee. TV; cable (premium). Heated pool; whirlpool. Complimentary continental bkfst. Complimentary refreshments 5-7 pm Mon-Fri. Restaurant nearby. Ck-out noon. Coin lndry. Business servs avail. In-rm modem link. Valet serv. Health club privileges. Refrigerators; many fireplaces. Private patios, balconies. Picnic tables, grills. Cr cds: A, C, D, DS, JCB, MC, V.

🛏 ≊ ⊠ 🔥 **SC**

Motor Hotels

★ ★ ★ **EMBASSY SUITES-TECH CENTER.** *10250 E Costilla Ave (80112), 1 mi E of I-25 exit 197. 303/792-0433; FAX 303/792-0432.* 236 suites, 9 story. Suites $89-$139; each addl $10; under 12 free; wkly, wkend rates. Crib free. Pet accepted. TV; cable (premium), VCR avail. Indoor pool. Complimentary full bkfst. Complimentary coffee in rms. Restaurant 11 am-11 pm. Rm serv. Bar. Ck-out noon. Meeting rms. Business servs avail. In-rm modem link. Bellhops. Valet serv. Gift shop. Exercise equipt; weight machine, bicycles, whirlpool. Health club privileges. Game rm. Refrigerators. Cr cds: A, C, D, DS, JCB, MC, V.

D 🛏 ≊ 🛉 🛉 ⊠ ⊠ 🔥 **SC**

✔ ★ **HILTON-DENVER SOUTH.** *7801 E Orchard Rd (80111), I-25 exit 198, 1 blk W on Orchard Rd. 303/779-6161; FAX 303/689-7080.* 301 rms, 6 story. S $78-$133; D $88-$143; each addl $10; suites $195-$275; under 18 free. Crib free. Pet accepted. TV; cable (premium), VCR avail. Indoor/outdoor pool. Coffee in rms. Restaurant 6:30 am-10 pm. Rm serv 24 hrs. Bars 11-midnight. Ck-out noon. Convention facilities. Business servs avail. In-rm modem link. Bellhops. Valet serv. Gift shop. Exercise equipt; weight machine, bicycles, sauna. Balconies. Cr cds: A, C, D, DS, ER, JCB, MC, V.

D 🛏 ≊ 🛉 ⊠ ⊠ 🔥 **SC**

Hotels

★ ★ ★ **INVERNESS.** *200 Inverness Dr W (80112), off I-25 exit 195. 303/799-5800; FAX 303/799-5873.* 302 rms, 5 story. S, D $69-$129; each addl $10; suites $169-$288; under 12 free; golf plans. Crib free. TV; cable (premium), VCR avail. 2 pools, 1 indoor; poolside serv. Restaurant (see THE SWAN). Bar 11-1 am. Ck-out noon. Convention facilities. Business center. In-rm modem link. Concierge. Gift shop. Valet parking. Airport, RR station, bus depot transportation. Lighted tennis. 18-hole golf, greens fee $60, putting green, driving range. Pro shop. Exercise rm; instructor, weight machine, bicycles, whirlpool, sauna. Rec rm. Minibars. Some balconies. Near Centennial Airport. Luxury level. Cr cds: A, C, D, DS, ER, JCB, MC, V.

D 🛏 🛉 🛉 ≊ 🛉 ⊠ ⊠ 🔥

★ ★ **RADISSON-SOUTH.** *7007 S Clinton St (80112), off I-25 exit 197. 303/799-6200; FAX 303/799-4828.* 263 rms, 10 story. S, D $130; each addl $10; under 12 free; wkly rates. Crib free. TV; cable. Heated pool; whirlpool; poolside serv. Complimentary coffee in rms. Restaurant 6:30 am-10:30 pm. Bar 11:30-2 am. Ck-out noon. Convention facilities. Business servs avail. Concierge. Gift shop. Health club privileges. Some bathrm phones. Luxury level. Cr cds: A, C, D, DS, ER, MC, V.

D 🛏 ≊ ⊠ ⊠ 🔥 **SC**

Restaurants

★ ★ ★ **CHATEAU PYRENEES.** *6538 S Yosemite Circle, off I-25 exit 197, Arapahoe Rd. 303/770-6660.* Hrs: 11:30 am-2 pm, 5:30-10 pm. Closed Sun. Res accepted. French, continental menu. Bar. Wine cellar. Semi-a la carte: lunch $6.50-$13.50, dinner $15.50-$26. Specialties: carré d'agneau, sweetbreads, fresh seafood. Valet parking. Elegant decor; antique grand piano; art collection; replica of crystal chandelier from 19th-century Spanish mansion. Jacket. Cr cds: A, C, D, DS, JCB, MC, V.

D

✔ ★ **COUNTY LINE BARBEQUE.** *(8351 Southpark Lane, Littleton 80120) 303/797-3727.* Hrs: 11 am-2 pm, 5-9 pm; Sat & Sun to 10 pm. Closed Thanksgiving, Dec 24 & 25. Bar. Semi-a la carte: lunch $4.95-$8.50, dinner $7.95-$14.95. Child's meals. Specializes in baby back ribs, mixed barbecue platter, homemade ice cream. Parking. Covered deck dining with view of mountains and Chatfield Lake. Rustic decor; 40s and 50s memorabilia. Totally non-smoking. Cr cds: A, D, DS, MC, V.

D

✔ ★ **FRATELLI'S.** *1200 E Hampden Ave (80110). 303/761-4771.* Hrs: 6:30 am-10 pm; Fri & Sat to 11 pm; Sun 8 am-9 pm. Closed Thanksgiving, Dec 25. Res accepted. Italian menu. Bar. Semi-a la carte: bkfst $3-$7, lunch $5-$12, dinner $7-$15. Child's meals. Specialities: pollo Fratelli, lasagne. Parking. Four dining areas. Antique bar built for Grand Tabor Hotel in Leadville. Family-owned. Cr cds: A, C, D, DS, MC, V.

D **SC**

✔★ ★ **GRADY'S AMERICAN GRILL.** *(5140 S Wadsworth Blvd, Littleton 80123)* 303/973-5140. Hrs: 11 am-10:30 pm; Fri & Sat to 11:30 pm; Sun to 10 pm. Closed Thanksgiving, Dec 25. Res accepted. Bar. Semi-a la carte: lunch, dinner $5.50-$14. Child's meals. Specializes in prime rib, mesquite grilled salmon. Parking. Outdoor dining. Three dining areas on two levels. Cr cds: A, D, DS, MC, V.

D

✔★ **SAFFRON.** 6600 S Quebec (80111). 303/290-9705. Hrs: 11:30 am-2 pm, 5:30-9 pm; Fri to 10 pm; Sat 5:30-10 pm. Closed Sun; some major hols. Res accepted. Continental menu. Bar. Semi-a la carte: lunch $5.95-$9.95, dinner $9.95-$16.95. Specializes in Mediterranean dishes. Parking. Three dining rms. Contemporary decor. Cr cds: A, C, D, DS, MC, V.

D

★ **SAMURAI.** 9625 E Arapahoe Rd (80112). 303/799-9991. Hrs: 11 am-2 pm, 5-10 pm; Sat & Sun from 5 pm. Closed July 4, Dec 25. Res accepted. Japanese menu. Bar. Semi-a la carte: lunch $4.95-$11.95, dinner $8.50-$30. Child's meals. Specializes in shabu-shabu, sushi. Parking. Japanese art & artifacts. Private, traditional Japanese dining experience avail. Cr cds: A, D, DS, MC, V.

D

★ ★ ★ **THE SWAN.** *(See Inverness Hotel)* 303/799-5800. Hrs: 6-10 pm. Closed Sun, Mon; Jan 1, Easter. Res accepted. Continental menu. Bar. Extensive wine list. Semi-a la carte: dinner $17-$32. Child's meals. Specializes in rack of lamb, smoked salmon and prawns. Classical guitarist, harpist Tues-Sat. Valet parking. Fine dining in contemporary, relaxing atmosphere. Cr cds: A, C, D, DS, ER, JCB, MC, V.

D

Estes Park (B-5)

(See Fort Collins, Granby, Grand Lake, Loveland, Lyons)

Settled 1875 **Pop** 3,184 **Elev** 7,522 ft **Area code** 970 **Zip** 80517
Information Information Center at the Chamber of Commerce, 500 Big Thompson Ave, PO Box 3050; 970/586-4431 or 800/443-7837.

Rimmed by snow-capped mountains, Estes Park is the gateway to Rocky Mountain National Park and a resort area that offers a wide variety of activities throughout the year.

What to See and Do

✪ **Aerial Tramway.** Two cabins, suspended from steel cables, move up or down Prospect Mt at 1,400 feet per minute. Superb view of Continental Divide during trip; picnic facilities at 8,896-foot summit; panoramic dome shelter; snack bar. (Mid-May-mid-Sept, daily) 420 Riverside Dr, 2 blks S of Elkhorn St. Phone 970/586-3675 or 970/756-6921. ¢¢¢

Barleen Family Theater. Country music/comedy and dinner concerts. (May-Oct) Phone 970/586-5749 or -5741. ¢¢¢¢

Big Thompson Canyon. One of the most beautiful canyon drives in the state. E on US 34.

Colorado-Big Thompson Project, Estes Power Plant. Vast Bureau of Reclamation project. Power plant, gallery tours. (Mon-Fri) 1 mi E on US 36, edge of Lake Estes. Phone 970/586-4151. **Free.**

Enos Mills Original Cabin (1885). On this family-owned 200-acre nature preserve stands the cabin of Enos Mills, regarded as the "Father of Rocky Mountain National Park." In the shadow of Longs Peak, the cabin contains photos, notes and documents of the famed naturalist.

Nature guide (fee) and self-guided nature trails. (May-Oct, daily; rest of yr, by appt) 8 mi S on CO 7. Phone 970/586-4706. **Free.**

Estes Park Area Historical Museum. Three facilities include a building that served as headquarters of Rocky Mountain National Park from 1915 to 1923. Exhibits on history of the park, the town and surrounding area. (Apr-Sept, daily; Oct & Dec, wkends) 200 Fourth St, across from lake. Phone 970/586-6256. ¢

Estes Park Ride-a-Kart. Go-karts, bumper boats & cars, mini-golf and mini-train in miniature Western town. Separate fees. (May-Sept, daily) 2250 Big Thompson Hwy, 2 mi E on US 34. Phone 970/586-6495.

Fishing, boating, hiking, horseback riding, mountain climbing. Fishing for trout in local lakes and streams. Fishing license needed at Estes Park. Boating on Lake Estes; motors, boats for rent; permit required for private boats; docks (mid-May-early Sept, daily). More than 1,500 mountain-trained horses and ponies are used for breakfast rides, pack trips. National Park Service conducts guided hikes in Rocky Mountain National Park (see); climbers attempt Longs Peak (14,255 ft). Certified guides also available in town.

Fun City Amusement Park. Bumper cars (fee); 15-lane giant slide and spiral slide (fee); arcade; miniature golf. (Mid-May-mid-Sept, daily) 375 Moraine Ave. Phone 970/586-2070.

Rocky Mountain National Park (see). 3 mi W on US 34, 36.

Roosevelt National Forest. More than 780,000 acres of icy streams, mountains and beautiful scenery. Trout fishing. Hiking trails. Winter sports area. Picnicking. Camping. Of special interest are the Cache la Poudre River, five wilderness areas and the Peak to Peak Scenic Byway. Surrounds town on N, E & S. For information contact the Visitor Center, 1311 S College, Fort Collins 80526; 970/498-1100. (Daily) Camping **Free.**

Annual Events

Rooftop Rodeo. Rodeo parade, nightly dances, kids jamboree. 5 days mid-July.

Scottish-Irish Highland Festival. Athletic and dance competitions, arts and crafts shows, magic shows, folk dancing. Wkend after Labor Day.

Seasonal Events

Estes Park Music Festival. Rocky Ridge Music Center. Chamber, symphonic and choral concerts. Early June-late Aug.

Horse shows. Wkends June-Sept.

Motels

(Because of the altitude, air conditioning is rarely necessary)

✔★ **ALPINE TRAIL RIDGE INN.** *Moraine Rte, 927 Moraine Ave.* 970/586-4585; res: 800/233-5023; FAX 970/586-6249. 48 rms. No A/C. June-early Sept: S $58-$78; D $63-$85; each addl $5; golf plans; lower rates May-mid-June & early Sept-mid-Oct. Closed rest of yr. Crib $5. TV; cable. Pool. Coffee in lobby. Restaurant 7 am-9 pm. Bar. Ck-out 10:30 am. Business servs avail. Airport transportation. Some refrigerators. Some balconies. Mountain views. Cr cds: A, C, D, DS, MC, V.

D 〰 ⊠ 🎿

★ ★ **BEST WESTERN LAKE ESTES RESORT.** *1650 Thompson Hwy, 1 1/2 mi E on US 34.* 970/586-3386; FAX 970/586-9000. 58 rms. No A/C. Late June-late Aug: S $85-$100; D $95-$110; suites $120-$200; ski, rafting plans; lower rates rest of yr. Crib $5.50. TV; cable (premium), VCR avail (movies avail $6.99). Heated pool; wading pool, whirlpool, sauna. Playground. Coffee in lobby. Restaurant nearby. Ck-out 11 am. Coin lndry. Meeting rms. Business servs avail. X-country ski 10 mi. Rec rm. Lawn games. Refrigerators; some bathrm phones, in-rm whirlpools, fireplaces. Picnic tables. On lake. Cr cds: A, C, D, DS, ER, JCB, MC, V.

★ **BIG THOMPSON TIMBERLANE LODGE.** *Box 387, 740 Moraine Ave, US 36W.* 970/586-3137; FAX 970/586-4373. 34 rms, 28 kits. June-early Sept: S, D, cottages $98-$275; each addl $10; 1-3-bedrm cabins $108-$275; wkly rates; lower rates rest of yr. TV; cable (premium), VCR avail. Pool; wading pool, whirlpool. Playground. Complimentary coffee. Restaurant adj 7 am-10 pm. Ck-out 10 am. Coin lndry. Business servs avail. Refrigerators. Picnic tables, grills. On Big Thompson River. Cr cds: MC, V.

★★ **COMFORT INN.** *1450 Big Thompson Ave.* 970/586-2358. 75 rms, 1-2 story. June-Aug: S, D $65-$140; each addl $7; under 18 free; 2-day min stay wkends; lower rates rest of yr. Crib $3. TV; cable. Heated pool; whirlpool. Playground. Complimentary coffee in lobby, continental bkfst. Restaurant adj 7 am-9 pm. Ck-out 10:30 am. Business servs avail. X-country ski 8 mi. Lawn games. Some refrigerators. Some balconies. Picnic tables. Cr cds: A, C, D, DS, MC, V.

★★ **DEER CREST.** *1200 Fall River Rd.* 970/586-2324; res: 800/331-2324. 26 air-cooled rms, 2 story, 8 suites, 7 kit. units. June-Sept: S, D, suites, kit. units $74-$95; each addl $10; lower rates rest of yr. Children over 12 yrs only. TV; cable (premium). Heated pool; whirlpool. Complimentary coffee in lobby. Restaurant nearby. Ck-out 10 am. Airport transportation. X-country ski 7 mi. Refrigerators. Balconies. Picnic tables, grills. On Fall River. Totally nonsmoking. Cr cds: MC, V.

★ **FAWN VALLEY INN & CHALETS.** *Box 4365, 2760 Fall River Rd, 3 1/2 mi W on US 34, 1 mi E of park entrance.* 970/586-2388; res: 800/525-2961; FAX 970/586-0394. 25 condos (1-2 bedrms), 1-2 story. No A/C. S, D $110-$140; each addl $10; 3-day min in season. TV; cable (premium), VCR avail. Pool; whirlpool. Restaurant (see DARK HORSE). Bar to 2 am. Ck-out 11 am. Coin lndry. Meeting rms. Business servs avail. X-country ski 4 mi. Refrigerators; many fireplaces. Many balconies. Picnic tables, grills. 8 acres on Fall River. Cr cds: DS, MC, V.

✔★ **OLYMPUS LODGE.** *Box 547, 2365 Big Thompson Ave.* 970/586-8141; res: 800/248-8141. 22 rms, 8 A/C. Memorial Day-mid-Sept: S, D $62-$85; each addl $8; wkly rates; lower rates rest of yr. Crib $5. TV; cable. Complimentary coffee, continental bkfst in summer. Restaurant nearby. Ck-out 10 am. Meeting rms. Airport transportation. X-country ski 13 mi. Rec rm. Lawn games. Guest lounge. Some refrigerators. Picnic tables. Cr cds: A, D, DS, MC, V.

★ **PONDEROSA LODGE.** *1820 Fall River Rd.* 970/586-4233; res: 800/628-0512. 19 rms, 2 story. No A/C. No rm phones. Mid-May-Oct (2-day min): S $65-$105; D $70-$115; each addl $5; kits. $110-$175; under 6 free; lower rates rest of yr. Crib free. TV; cable (premium). Complimentary coffee in lobby. Restaurant nearby. Ck-out 10 am. X-country ski 2 mi. Some refrigerators. Balconies. Picnic tables. Cr cds: DS, MC, V.

★ **SILVER SADDLE.** *Box 1747-MT, 1260 Big Thompson Ave.* 970/586-4476; FAX 970/586-4476. 55 rms, 42 A/C, 1-2 story. Late June-late Aug: S, D $68-$106; suites $116-$144; kit. units $106-$144; wkly rates; lower rates May-late June, late Aug-Oct. Jan-Mar by reservation only. Crib $4. TV; cable (premium), VCR avail. Heated pool; whirlpool. Playground. Complimentary continental bkfst. Complimentary coffee in lobby. Restaurant nearby. Ck-out 11 am. Coin lndry. Meeting rm. Business servs avail. In-rm modem link. Lawn games. Refrigerators; some bathrm phones. Some balconies. Picnic tables, grills. Totally nonsmoking. Cr cds: A, C, D, DS, MC, V.

✔★ **TRAPPER'S MOTOR INN.** *Box 487, 553 W Elkhorn, 1/2 mi W on US 34 Business.* 970/586-2833; res: 800/552-2833. 19 rms, 2 story. 3 A/C. No rm phones. Mid-June-early Sept: S, D $46-$66; lower rates rest of yr. TV; cable (premium). Playground. Complimentary coffee in lobby. Restaurant nearby. Ck-out 10 am. X-country ski 8 mi. Lawn games. Whirlpool. Some refrigerators. Picnic tables. Cr cds: A, MC, V.

Lodge

★★★ **BOULDER BROOK.** *1900 Fall River Rd.* 970/586-0910; res: 800/238-0910; FAX 970/586-8067. 16 air-cooled kit. suites, 1-2 story. May-Oct (2-night min): suites $125-$179; wkly rates; lower rates rest of yr. Crib free. TV; cable (premium), VCR (movies $1). Complimentary coffee in rms. Ck-out 11. Business servs avail. In-rm modem link. Airport transportation. Whirlpool. X-country ski 7 mi. Minibars. Some in-rm whirlpools. Balconies. Picnic tables, grills. On banks of Fall River. Cr cds: A, DS, MC, V.

Motor Hotel

✔★ **HOLIDAY INN RESORT.** *Box 1468, 101 S St Vrain Hwy.* 970/586-2332; FAX 970/586-2332, ext. 299. 150 rms, 3-4 story, 5 suites. Late June-late Aug: S, D $86-$97; each addl $8; suites $159; under 18 free; lower rates rest of yr. Crib free. TV; cable (premium). Indoor pool. Restaurant 6:30 am-2 pm, 4:30-10 pm. Rm serv. Bar noon-2 am; Sun to midnight. Ck-out 11 am. Coin lndry. Meeting rms. Business servs avail. Bellhops. Valet serv. Airport transportation. X-country ski 7 mi. Exercise equipt; weights, treadmill. Holidome. Game rm. Cr cds: A, C, D, DS, JCB, MC, V.

Inn

★★★ **RIVER SONG.** *Box 1910, 1765 Lower Broadview, 1 mi W on US 36, left at light on Mary's Lake Rd, 1/4 mi across Bridge, right on Country Rd to end.* 970/586-4666. 9 rms, 1-2 story, 5 suites. No A/C. No rm phones. S, D $135-$150; each addl $50, suites $170-$205. Children over 12 yrs only. Complimentary full bkfst, tea, coffee & cookies. Dinner with advance reservation. Ck-out noon, ck-in 4-7 pm. Airport transportation. X-country ski 7 mi. Refrigerators. Many in-rm whirlpools. Balconies. Picnic tables. Located on 30 acres, adj to Rocky Mountain National Park; serene setting with scenic views. Many ponds & trails. Built 1918; decorated with a blend of antique and modern country furnishings. Totally nonsmoking. Cr cds: MC, V.

Guest Ranches

★★ **ASPEN LODGE AT ESTES PARK.** *6120 S St Vrain Hwy, 7 mi S on CO 7.* 970/586-8133; res: 800/332-6867. 59 units, 36 rms in lodge, 23 cottage units. No A/C. S, D $194-$400 (3-, 4-, and 7-day min); family rates; AP June-Aug. Crib free. TV in lobby. Pool. Playground. Free supervised child's activities (June-Sept); ages 5-12. Dining rm (public by res) 7-10 am, noon-2 pm, 6-9 pm. Box lunches, barbecue, bkfst rides. Bar. Ck-out 11 am, ck-in 3 pm. Meeting rms. Business servs avail. Concierge. Gift shop. Airport transportation. Sports dir. Tennis. X-country ski on site. Ice skating, snowshoeing. Hayrides, overnight cookouts. Mountain bike rentals. Lawn games. Handball. Entertainment, dancing; movies. Game rm. Rec rm. Exercise rm; instructor, weights, rowing machine, whirlpool, sauna. Picnic tables, grills. Petting zoo (summer months). Cr cds: A, D, DS, MC, V.

★ ★ **WIND RIVER RANCH.** *Box 3410M, 7 mi S on CO 7.* 970/586-4212; res: 800/523-4212; FAX 970/586-2255. 4 air-cooled units in lodge, 11 cottages (1-3-bedrm). No rm phones. Early June-Sept, AP (3-day min): D $1,125-$1,185/person/wk; 3-12, $340-$1,125/wk; 13-18, $960-$1,125/wk; under 3, $100/wk; daily rates. Closed rest of yr. Heated pool; whirlpool. Playground. Free supervised child's activities (June-Sept), ages 4-12. Dining rm: 7:30-9 am, 12:30-1:30 pm, 6:30-7:30 pm. Box lunches. Wine, beer. Ck-out 10 am, ck-in 3 pm. Grocery, coin lndry, package store 7 mi. Meeting rms. Business servs avail. Airport, bus depot transportation. Hiking, rafting. Many fireplaces. Many private porches. Cr cds: DS, MC, V.

Cottage Colonies

✔ ★ **COLORADO COTTAGES.** *Moraine Rte, 1241 High Dr.* 970/586-4637; res: 800/468-1236. 11 units, 1-2 story. Mid-June-Labor Day: kit. cottages $62-$105; each addl $5; wkly rates; honeymoon plans; lower rates rest of yr. TV; cable (premium). Restaurant opp 7 am-9:30 pm. Ck-out 10 am, ck-in 3 pm. Airport transportation. X-country ski 8 mi. Fireplaces. Picnic tables, grills. Cr cds: A, DS, MC, V.

★ **IDLEWILDE.** *3030 Moraine Rte, 3 mi W on CO 66.* 970/586-3864. 13 kit. cottages. No A/C. No rm phones. Mid-May-mid-Oct: 1-3-bedrm cottages $69-$212; each addl $10. Closed rest of yr. Crib free. TV; cable. Playground. Restaurant nearby. Ck-out 10 am, ck-in 3 pm. Grocery, coin lndry, package store 1¼ mi. Hot tub. Lawn games. Refrigerators. Library. Screened porches. Picnic tables, grill. Knotty pine interiors. No cr cds accepted.

★ ★ **MACHIN'S COTTAGES IN THE PINES.** *Box 2687, 2450 Eagle Cliff Rd, 2 mi W on US 36, ½ mi S on CO 66, then follow signs.* 970/586-4276. 17 kit. cottages, 4 one-bedrm, 9 two-bedrm, 4 three-bedrm. Kit. cottages $70-$160; each addl $10; wkly rates. Closed Oct-late May. Crib $3. Pet accepted, some restrictions. TV; cable (premium). Playground. Ck-out 10 am, ck-in 2 pm. Grocery, coin lndry, package store 1½ mi. Gift shop. Hiking trails. Patios. Picnic tables, grills. On 14 hilly acres. Cr cds: A, MC, V.

★ ★ **McGREGOR MOUNTAIN LODGE.** *2815 Fall River Rd, 3½ mi W on US 34.* 970/586-3457; FAX 970/586-4040. 36 units, 3 motel rms, 10 condos (1-2 bedrms), 16 cottages. No A/C. No rm phones. June-Sept: S, D $70-$105; each addl $8; kit. cottages $110-$249; wkly rates; lower rates rest of yr. Crib $5. TV; cable, VCR. Playground. Complimentary coffee in lobby. Restaurant nearby. Ck-out 11 am, ck-in 3 pm. Grocery, coin lndry ½ mi. Airport transportation. Hot tub. Lawn games. Many refrigerators, fireplaces. Private patios. Covered barbecue area; picnic tables, grills. On 10 acres overlooking Fall River Canyon. Rocky Mt Natl Park adj. Cr cds: DS, MC, V.

★ ★ **STREAMSIDE CABINS.** *1260 Fall River Rd.* 970/586-6464; res: 800/321-3303; FAX 970/586-6272. 19 air-cooled kit. cabins & cabin suites. Summer: cabins $115-$240; cabin suites $120-$165; $12 each addl; some special package plans; lower rates rest of yr. Crib free. TV; cable (premium), VCR (movies avail). Playground. Complimentary coffee in rms. Restaurant adj. Ck-out 10:30 am, ck-in 3 pm. Grocery, coin lndry, package store ½ mi. Business servs avail. X-country ski 6 mi. Hiking. Lawn games. Fireplaces. Porches, decks. Picnic tables, grills. On 17 acres on Fall River. Cr cds: A, DS, MC, V.

★ ★ **SUNNYSIDE KNOLL.** *1675 Fall River Rd.* 970/586-5759. 8 rms, 7 kit. units. No A/C. No rm phones. June-Sept: S, D $89-$179; each addl $10; kit. units $99-$179 (4-day min); wkly rates; lower rates rest of yr. Children over 12 yrs only. TV; VCR avail. Heated pool. Complimentary coffee in rms. Restaurant nearby. Ck-out 11 am.

X-country ski 8 mi. Lawn games. Rec rm. Exercise equipt; stair machine, bicycles. Refrigerators, fireplaces; some in-rm whirlpools. Private patios. Picnic tables, grills. Cr cds: DS, MC, V.

Restaurants

★ ★ **BLACK CANYON INN.** *800 MacGregor Ave.* 970/586-9344. Hrs: 11:30 am-2 pm, 5-9 pm. Closed Mon. Res accepted. Continental menu. Bar. Semi-a la carte: lunch $5.95-$9.95, dinner $12.95-$19.95. Child's meals. Specializes in seafood, wild game. Parking. Built in 1927 of rough-cut logs. Two-story moss & rock fireplace. Cr cds: A, DS, MC, V.

★ **DARK HORSE.** *(See Fawn Valley Inn & Chalets Motel)* 970/586-5654. Hrs: 11 am-3 pm, 5-10 pm; Sun brunch 11 am-2 pm. Res accepted. Bar to 2 am. Semi-a la carte: lunch $5.95-$9, dinner $14-$20. Child's meals. Specializes in wild game, seafood. Parking. Outdoor dining. River view. Cr cds: DS, MC, V.

★ ★ ★ **FAWN BROOK INN.** *(PO Box 387, Allenspark 80510) 16 mi S on CO 7.* 303/747-2556. Hrs: 5-8:30 pm. Closed Mon; also 3 wks Jan. Res accepted. No A/C. Continental menu. Bar. Semi-a la carte: dinner $22-$39. Child's meals. Specializes in roast duckling, venison. Parking. Intimate dining areas. Rustic Austrian decor. Cr cds: A, MC, V.

★ ★ **FRIAR'S.** *157 W Elkhorn Ave, in Old Church Shops.* 970/586-2806. Hrs: 11:30 am-9 pm; early Oct-late May to 5 pm. Closed Thanksgiving, Dec 25. Res accepted. Bar. Semi-a la carte: lunch $3-$7.25, dinner $10.75-$13. Child's meals. Specializes in roast pork loin, cajun chicken. Salad bar. Outdoor dining. Cr cds: A, C, D, DS, MC, V.

✔ ★ **MAMA ROSE'S.** *338 E Elkhorn Ave.* 970/586-3330. Hrs: 11 am-9 pm; winter from 4:30 pm. Closed Thanksgiving, Dec 24 & 25; Jan & Feb; also Mon & Tues (winter). Italian menu. Bar. Semi-a la carte: lunch $4.95-$8.95, dinner $5.95-$13.95. Specializes in veal Parmesan, chicken Parmesan, fettucine Alfredo. Outdoor dining. Victorian decor; large fireplace. Totally nonsmoking. Cr cds: A, DS, MC, V.

Evergreen (C-5)

(See Central City, Denver, Golden, Idaho Springs)

Pop 7,582 **Elev** 7,040 ft **Area code** 303 **Zip** 80439

Information Evergreen Area Chamber of Commerce, 29015 Upper Bear Creek Rd, PO Box 97; 303/674-3412.

What to See and Do

Hiwan Homestead Museum. Restored 17-room log lodge (1880); Native American artifacts, changing exhibits. Tours (daily exc Mon; closed 1st wk Jan, major hols). 4208 S Timbervale Dr. Phone 303/674-6262. **Free.**

International Bell Museum. More than 5,000 bells of widely varying size and age, many historic, artistic or unusual. (Memorial Day-Labor-Day, daily exc Mon) 30213 Upper Bear Creek Rd, off CO 74. Phone 303/674-3422. **¢¢**

Annual Events

Rodeo Weekend. Rodeo, parade. Phone 303/670-6062. Wkend late June.

Mountain Rendezvous. At Hiwan Homestead Museum. Craft and trapping demonstrations by mountain men, food, entertainment, old-fashioned games. 1st Sat Aug.

Inn

★★**HIGHLAND HAVEN.** *4395 Independence Trail. 303/674-3577; FAX 303/674-9088.* 16 rms (10 with showers only), 1-2 story, 6 suites, 6 kit. cottages. No A/C. S, D $60-$70; suites $110-$160; kit. cottages $110-$130; under 6 free; wkly plans. TV; cable. Complimentary continental bkfst. Restaurant nearby. Ck-out 11 am, ck-in 2-3 pm. In-rm modem link. Balconies. On Bear Creek. Cr cds: A, DS, MC, V.

Fairplay (C-4)

(For accommodations see Breckenridge, Buena Vista)

Settled 1859 **Pop** 387 **Elev** 9,920 ft **Area code** 719 **Zip** 80440
Information Town Clerk, 400 Front St, PO Box 267; 719/836-2622.

This broad valley, known for many years as South Park, was called "Bayou Salado" or "Salt Creek" by early French trappers. The Ute Indians prized the valley for summer trapping and as a hunting ground. In 1859, gold was discovered, and several towns, including Fairplay, sprang up overnight. Now the county seat, Fairplay was founded with the slogan, "In this camp we will have fair play; no man can have more ground than he can work." Within the valley, which is larger than the state of Rhode Island, nearly every kind of recreational opportunity is available to the visitor.

What to See and Do

Monument to Prunes, a Burro. In memory of a faithful burro named Prunes who packed supplies to every mine in Fairplay for more than 60 years. Front Street.

Pike National Forest (see COLORADO SPRINGS). Camping. A Ranger District office is located at junction of US 285 & CO 9. (Daily) Phone 719/836-2031. **Free.**

South Park City Museum. Restoration of mining town includes 30 original buildings, 60,000 artifacts (ca 1860-1900); exhibits on trading, mining, social aspects of era. (Mid-May-mid-Oct, daily; rest of yr, by appt) Sr citizen rate. 100 4th St. Phone 719/836-2387. ¢¢

Annual Event

World's Championship Pack Burro Race. Commemorating the burros who packed supplies for the miners; 28-mile course uphill to Mosquito Pass and return. Phone 719/836-2427. Last full wkend July.

Florissant Fossil Beds National Monument (D-5)

(For accommodations see Colorado Springs, Cripple Creek, Manitou Springs)

(22 mi W of Manitou Springs on US 24)

Florissant Fossil Beds National Monument consists of 6,000 acres once partially covered by a prehistoric lake. Thirty-five million years ago, ash and lava flows from volcanoes in the area filled the lake, fossilizing its living organisms. Insects, seeds and leaves of the Oligocene Epoch are preserved in perfect detail as well as remarkable samples of standing petrified Sequoia stumps. On the grounds are nature trails, picnic areas and a restored 19th-century homestead. Guided tours are available. The visitor center is 2 miles south on County Road 1 (daily; closed Jan 1, Thanksgiving, Dec 25). For information contact the Superintendent, PO Box 185, Florissant 80816; 719/748-3253. Per family ¢¢; Per person ¢

Fort Collins (A-5)

(See Greeley, Loveland)

Settled 1864 **Pop** 87,758 **Elev** 5,003 ft **Area code** 970
Information Fort Collins Convention & Visitors Bureau, 420 S Howes St, PO Box 1998, 80522-1998; phone 970/482-5821 or 800/274-3678.

A favorite camping ground for pioneers, Fort Collins is now an educational, recreational and industrial community. Headquarters for the Roosevelt National Forest (see ESTES PARK) and the Arapaho National Forest (see DILLON) are located in Fort Collins.

What to See and Do

Colorado State University (1870). (22,000 students) Land-grant institution with an 833-acre campus. Pingree Park at 9,500 ft, adj to Rocky Mt National Park, is the summer campus for natural resource science education and forestry. Main entrance at W Laurel & Howes Sts, W of College Ave. Phone 970/491-1101.

Fort Collins Museum. Exhibits include a model of the city's namesake, the army post Fort Collins; fine collection of Folsom points and Native American beadwork; display of historic household, farm and business items; three historic cabins; changing exhibits. (Daily exc Mon; closed major hols) 200 Mathews St. Phone 970/221-6738. **Free.**

Lincoln Center. Includes theater for the performing arts, concert hall, sculpture garden, art gallery and display areas with changing exhibits. (Daily) 417 W Magnolia. Phone 970/221-6735. **Free.**

Lory State Park. Approx 2,500 acres. Nearby is Horsetooth Reservoir. Waterskiing; boating (ramps, rentals). Nature trails, hiking, stables. Picnicking. (Daily) 9 mi NW in Bellvue. Phone 970/493-1623. Per vehicle ¢¢

Scenic circle drives. Eleven colorful drives, from 50 to 200 miles, including trip through beautiful Poudre Canyon and Cameron Pass (10,285 ft) in Roosevelt National Forest (see ESTES PARK). Inquire at Fort Collins Convention & Visitors Bureau.

Motels

✔★**BEST WESTERN UNIVERSITY INN.** *914 S College (80524), 6 blks S on US 287. 970/484-1984; FAX 970/484-1987.* 74 rms, 2 story. May-Sept: S $44-$48, D $48-$56; under 12 free; lower rates rest of yr. Crib free. TV; cable, VCR avail. Pool. Complimentary continental bkfst. Restaurant nearby. Ck-out noon. Valet serv. In-rm modem link. Cr cds: A, C, D, DS, MC, V.

⊠ ⊠ ⊠ SC ⚐

★ ★ COMFORT INN. *1638 E Mulberry St (80524), 1¹/₂ mi E on CO 14. 970/484-2444; FAX 970/221-0967.* 43 rms, 1-2 story. May-Aug: S, D $54.50-$69.50; each addl $5; suites $75.50-$85.50; under 18 free; higher rates special events; lower rates rest of yr. Crib free. TV; cable. Pool. Complimentary coffee in rms. Complimentary continental bkfst. Restaurant adj 7 am-midnight. Ck-out 11 am. Sundries. Transportation to Denver avail. Some in-rm steam baths. Private patios. Cr cds: A, D, DS, MC, V.

D ⊠ ⊠ ⊠ SC

Motor Hotel

✔ ★ HOLIDAY INN. *3836 E Mulberry St (80524), 1 mi E on CO 14 at I-25. 970/484-4660; FAX 970/484-2363.* 180 rms, 2-4 story. Mid-May-mid-Sept: S, D $69-$89; each addl $5; under 18 free; higher rates: graduation, special events; lower rates rest of yr. Crib free. Pet accepted. TV; cable, VCR avail. Indoor pool; wading pool, whirlpool, saunas. Restaurant 6 am-2 pm, 5:30-10 pm. Rm serv. Bar 11-2 am; Sun to 10 pm. Ck-out noon. Coin lndry. Meeting rms. In-rm modem link. Gift shop. Airport, bus depot transportation. Exercise equipt; weight machines, bicycles. Holidome. Rec rm. Game rm. Sun deck. Some balconies. Cr cds: A, C, D, DS, JCB, MC, V.

D ⚐ ⊠ ⊠ ⊠ SC

Hotel

★ ★ ★ MARRIOTT. *350 E Horsetooth Rd (80525). 970/226-5200; FAX 970/282-0561.* 229 rms, 6 story. S, D $65-$97; each addl $10; suites $110-$150; under 14 free; wkly rates. TV; cable. Indoor/outdoor pool. Restaurant 6 am-2:30 pm, 5-9 pm. Bar 4:30-11 pm, Fri & Sat to 2 am; entertainment, dancing Fri & Sat. Ck-out noon. Coin lndry. Meeting rms. Concierge. Gift shop. Airport transportation. X-country ski 15 mi. Exercise equipt; weight machines, bicycles, whirlpool. Luxury level. Cr cds: A, C, D, DS, JCB, MC, V.

D ⚐ ⊠ ⊠ ⊠ ⊠ SC

Inn

✔ ★ HELMSHIRE INN. *1204 S College Ave (80524). 970/493-4683.* 25 rms, 3 story. S, D $79; each addl $10. Crib free. TV; cable. Complimentary full bkfst at 24-hr restaurant nearby. Ck-out 11 am, ck-in after 3 pm. Health club privileges. Each rm individually decorated. Totally nonsmoking. Cr cds: A, D, MC, V.

⊠ ⊠ SC

Fort Morgan (B-7)

(See Sterling)

Pop 9,068 **Elev** 4,330 ft **Area code** 970 **Zip** 80701
Information Fort Morgan Area Chamber of Commerce, 300 Main St, PO Box 971; 970/867-6702.

What to See and Do

Fort Morgan Museum. Permanent and changing exhibits depicting history of northeast Colorado. Pamphlet for self-guided walking tour of historic downtown. (Daily exc Sun) 414 Main St. Phone 970/867-6331. **Free.**

Jackson Lake State Park. Swimming, waterskiing; fishing; boating (rentals, ramps). Picnicking (shelters), concession, groceries. Camping. Standard fees. (Daily) I-76W to CO 39, 7¹/₄ mi N to County Y5, then 2¹/₂ mi W to County 3. Phone 970/645-2551. Per vehicle ¢¢

Annual Event

Rodeo. 10 mi E in Brush. World's largest amateur rodeo. Wkend early July.

Motels

★ ★ BEST WESTERN PARK TERRACE. *725 Main St, I-76 exit 80. 970/867-8256.* 24 rms, 2 story. Mid-May-Sept: S $46-$52; D $56-$59; each addl $3; lower rates rest of yr. Crib $2. Pet accepted; $25. TV; cable (premium). Pool; whirlpool. Coffee in rms. Restaurant adj 5:30 am-9 pm. Ck-out 11 am. Business servs avail. In-rm modem link. Picnic tables. Cr cds: A, C, D, DS, MC, V.

⚐ ⊠ ⊠ ⊠ SC

✔ ★ CENTRAL. *201 W Platte Ave, I-76 exit 80. 970/867-2401.* 19 rms. May-Sept: S $33.95-$39.95; D $39.95-$46.95; each addl $5; suites from $49; under 10 free; lower rates rest of yr. Pet accepted, some restrictions. TV; cable (premium), VCR avail (movies avail $2). Complimentary coffee. Restaurant nearby. Ck-out 11 am. Business servs avail. In-rm modem link. Refrigerator all units. Cr cds: A, C, D, DS, MC, V.

D ⚐ ⊠ ⊠ SC

Georgetown (C-5)

(See Central City, Dillon, Golden, Idaho Springs, Winter Park)

Founded 1859 **Pop** 891 **Elev** 8,512 ft **Area code** 303 **Zip** 80444
Information Town of Georgetown Visitor Information, PO Box 426; 303/569-2555.

Georgetown is named for George Griffith, who discovered gold in this valley in 1859 and opened up the area to other gold seekers. The area around Georgetown has produced almost $200 million worth of gold, silver, copper, lead and zinc. Numerous 19th-century structures remain standing. Georgetown's famous Hotel de Paris was run by a Frenchman, Louis Dupuy, who, though charming, was very cavalier to any guest who did not please him.

What to See and Do

Georgetown Loop Historic Mining and Railroad Park. Park features mine, crushing mill and reconstructed mine buildings. Also here is the reconstructed Georgetown Loop Railroad that carries visitors on a scenic 6¹/₂-mile round trip, which includes the reconstructed Devil's Gate Viaduct. This railroad was used in the late 1800s for shipping of ore and it was hailed as an engineering marvel. Crossing itself once, turning nearly three-and-one-half circles and crossing four bridges, it connected Georgetown with Silver Plume during the boomtown era. A scheduled stop is made at the mine area for tours. The train leaves from Devil's Gate Viaduct (W on I-70 to exit 228, then ¹/₂ mi S on Old US 6) or Silver Plume (I-70, exit 226). Five or six round trips/day. (Late May-early Oct, daily) Phone 303/670-1686 or 303/569-2403. ¢¢¢¢

Hamill House Museum (1867). Early Gothic-revival house acquired by William A. Hamill, Colorado silver magnate and state senator; period furnishings. Partially restored carriage house and office. (June-Sept, daily; rest of yr, Sat & Sun) Sr citizen rate. 305 Argentine St. Phone 303/569-2840. ¢¢

Hotel de Paris Museum (1875). Internationally known hostelry built and operated by Louis Dupuy; elaborately decorated; original furnishings; courtyard. (May-Sept, daily; rest of yr, daily exc Mon) Sr citizen rate. 409 6th St. Phone 303/569-2311. ¢¢

Loveland Ski Area. 2 triple,1 quad, 5 double chairlifts, 1 Pomalift, 1 Mighty-mite; patrol, school, rentals; snowmaking; cafeteria, restaurants, bars; nursery. 60 runs; longest run 1.5 mi; vertical drop 1,680 ft. (Mid-Oct-mid-May, daily) 12 mi W on I-70, exit 216. Phone 303/569-3203 or 303/571-5580 (Denver direct). ¢¢¢¢¢

Inn

★ **MAD CREEK.** *(167 Park Ave, Empire 80438) E on I-70, 2 mi N on US 40.* 303/569-2003. 3 rms, 2 share bath, 2 story. No A/C. No rm phones. S $39-$59; D $49-$69; each addl $10. Children over 10 yrs only. TV in main rm, VCR. Whirlpool. Complimentary full bkfst. Complimentary coffee, tea/sherry in afternoon. Ck-out 10:30 am, ck-in 4:30 pm. Downhill/x-country ski 20 mi. Victorian cottage built in 1881; rock fireplace. Totally nonsmoking. Cr cds: MC, V.

Guest Ranch

★★ **NORTH FORK.** *(PO Box B, Shawnee 80475) 30 mi S on County Rd 16, over Guanella Pass (gravel road), 6 mi E on US 285 to sign, 1¹/₂ mi to ranch.* 970/838-9873; res: 800/843-7895; FAX 970/838-1549. 7 rms, 3 cottages. No A/C. No rm phones. AP, July-Aug, wkly: S $1,195; 6-12 yrs, $995; 2-6 yrs, $300-$795; lower rates late May-June & early-mid-Sept. Closed rest of yr. Crib free. Heated pool; whirlpool. Free supervised child's activities (June-Aug); ages 1-6. Complimentary coffee in rms. Dining rm 7:30-8:30 am, 12:30 pm & 6:30 pm sittings. Box lunches. Picnics. Ck-out 10 am, ck-in 3 pm. Grocery, package store 6 mi. Meeting rms. Gift shop. Free guest lndry. Airport transportation. Horse stables. Hiking. Lawn games. Game rm. Fishing guides, clean and store. Refrigerator in cottages. Some porches. Picnic tables, grills. On South Platte River. No cr cds accepted.

Glenwood Springs (C-3)

(See Aspen, Snowmass Village)

Settled 1885 **Pop** 6,561 **Elev** 5,763 ft **Area code** 970 **Zip** 81601

Information Chamber of Commerce, 1102 Grand Ave; 970/945-6589 or 800/221-0098.

Doc Holliday, the famous gunman, died here in 1887. His marker bears the wry inscription, "He died in bed."

Today, Glenwood Springs is a popular year-round health spa resort where the visitor may both ski and swim in a single day. The town is the gateway to White River National Forest. Aspen and Vail (see both) are less than an hour's drive. Excellent game and fishing country surrounds Glenwood Springs, and camping areas sprinkle the region.

What to See and Do

Mineral pools & baths.

Glenwood Hot Springs Pool. Two outdoor pools, one two blocks long, are fed by warm mineral water and open year round; the recreational pool is 90°F, the thermal 104°F; also children's pool, miniature golf, water slide (summers). Lifeguards, athletic club, bathhouse, lodge, restaurant. (Daily) On US 6, 24 off I-70 exit 116. Phone 970/945-6571 or 800/537-7946 (CO). ¢¢¢

River rafting, hunting, fishing, camping, horseback riding, pack trips. For details and locations, inquire at the Chamber of Commerce.

Scenic drives. Beautiful Hanging Lake and Bridal Veil Falls are a two-mile hike from the road. The marble quarries in the Crystal River Valley are the source of stones for the Lincoln Memorial in Washington, DC, and the Tomb of the Unknown Soldier in Arlington National Cemetery. On CO 133, to Lookout Mountain, Redstone, Marble, Maroon Peaks, Glenwood Canyon.

Ski Sunlight. Triple chairlift, two double chairlifts, surface tow; patrol, school, rentals; cafeteria, bar; nursery. 40 runs; longest run 2¹/₂ mi; vertical drop 2,010 ft. (Late Nov-early Apr, daily) Half-day rates. Also cross-country touring center, 15 mi; fee. 10 mi SW via County 117. Phone 970/945-7491, 800/445-7931. ¢¢¢¢¢

White River National Forest. More than 2,500,000 acres in the heart of the Colorado Rocky Mountains. Recreation at 70 developed sites with boat ramps, picnicking, campgrounds and observation points; Holy Cross, Flat Tops, Eagles Nest, Maroon Bells-Snowmass, Raggeds, Collegiate Peaks and Hunter-Frying Pan wildernesses (check with local ranger for information before entering wildernesses or any backcountry areas). Many streams and lakes with trout fishing; large deer and elk populations; Dillon, Green Mountain and Ruedi reservoirs. Winter sports at 11 ski areas. N, W, E & S of town. For information contact the Supervisor's Office, Old Federal Bldg, 9th & Grand, PO Box 948; 970/945-2521. Camping ¢¢¢

Annual Events

Strawberry Days Festival. Arts & crafts fair, rodeo. 3rd wkend June.

Garfield County Fair & Rodeo. 27 mi W in Rifle. Late Aug.

Motels

★★ **BEST WESTERN ANTLERS.** *171 W 6th St, 1 blk W of I-70 exit 116.* 970/945-8535; FAX 970/945-9388. 101 units, 1-2 story, 13 2-rm units. Mid-May-Sept: S $59-$88; D $75-$118; each addl $8; suites $110-$170; lower rates rest of yr. Crib $5. TV; cable (premium). Heated pool; wading pool, whirlpool. Playground. Coffee in lobby. Restaurant nearby. Ck-out 11 am. Coin lndry. Free RR station transportation. Downhill/x-country ski 10 mi. Lawn games. Cr cds: A, C, D, DS, ER, JCB, MC, V.

★ **CEDAR LODGE.** *2102 Grand Ave.* 970/945-6579; res: 800/854-3761; FAX 970/945-4420. 50 rms, 2 story, 5 suites. May-Sept: S $43; D $60.50; each addl $5; suites $84.50; kits. $100; higher rates: Strawberry Days & hols. Crib $5. TV; cable (premium). Heated pool; whirlpool, sauna. Complimentary coffee in lobby. Restaurant nearby. Ck-out 11 am. Coin lndry. Free RR station transportation. Downhill/x-country ski 10 mi. Some refrigerators. Cr cds: A, C, D, DS, MC, V.

★ **CRYSTAL VALLEY MANOR.** *(0215 Redstone Blvd, Redstone 81623) 15 mi S on CO 82, then 15 mi S on CO 133.* 970/963-2365. 12 kits. units, 2 story. No A/C. No rm phones. Late May-Oct: S, D $70; each addl $7; wkly rates; lower rates rest of yr. TV. Complimentary coffee in rms. Restaurant nearby. Ck-out 11 am. X-country ski 1 blk. Picnic tables, grills. On river. Totally nonsmoking. No cr cds accepted.

✔★ **GLENWOOD MOTOR INN.** *141 W 6th St.* 970/945-5438; res: 800/543-5906. 45 rms (3 with shower only, 32 with A/C), 2 story. June-mid-Sept: S $38-$45; D $45-$54; each addl $4; wkly rates; higher rates hols (2-day min); lower rates rest of yr. Crib free. Pet accepted, some restrictions; $20. TV; cable (premium). Complimentary coffee in lobby. Restaurant opp 7 am-2 pm. Ck-out 11 am. Coin lndry. Free RR station transportation. Downhill/x-country ski 10 mi. Whirlpool, sauna. Balconies. Cr cds: A, D, DS, MC, V.

★ **NATIONAL 9 HOMESTEAD INN.** *52039 US 6/24.* 970/945-8817; res: 800/456-6685. 35 rms, 2 story. Mid-May-Sept: S, D $40-$70; each addl $8; ski packages; lower rates rest of yr. Crib $5. Pet accepted, some restrictions; $25. TV; cable (premium). Complimentary coffee in lobby. Restaurant nearby. Ck-out 11 am. Downhill/x-country ski 12 mi. Whirlpool. Some refrigerators. Sun deck. Picnic tables. Cr cds: A, C, D, DS, MC, V.

[D] [icons] SC

✔★ **RUSTY CANNON.** *(701 Taughenbaugh, Rifle 81650)* 28 mi W off I-70 exit 90. 970/625-4004; res: 800/341-8000; FAX 970/625-3604. 88 rms, 2 story. S $32; D $45-$48; each addl $8. Crib free. Pet accepted, some restrictions. TV; cable. Heated pool; sauna. Complimentary coffee in lobby. Restaurant adj 6:30 am-10 pm. Ck-out 11 am. Coin lndry. Valet serv. Cr cds: A, C, D, DS, MC, V.

[D] [icons] SC

Motor Hotels

★★ **HOT SPRINGS LODGE.** *415 6th St, I-70 exit 116.* 970/945-6571; res: 800/537-7946 (CO); FAX 970/945-6683. 107 units, 5 story. Mar-Sept: S $65-$84; D $70-$89; each addl $5; ski plans; lower rates rest of yr. TV; cable. Pool. Complimentary coffee in rms. Restaurant 7 am-8 pm; winter to 3 pm. Bar 2-10 pm. Ck-out noon. Coin lndry. Meeting rms. Business servs avail. In-rm modem link. Bellhops. Covered parking. Airport, RR station, bus depot transportation. Miniature golf. Downhill/x-country ski 10 mi. Exercise rm; instructor, weights, bicycles, whirlpool, steam rm, sauna. Game rm. Some refrigerators. Private patios, balconies. Picnic tables. Cr cds: A, C, D, DS, MC, V.

[D] [icons]

✔★★ **REDSTONE INN.** *(82 Redstone Blvd, Redstone 81623)* 10 mi SE on CO 82 to Carbondale, then 18 mi S on CO 133. 970/963-2526; res: 800/748-2524. 35 air-cooled rms, 3 story, 3 suites. No elvtr. S, D $42-$135; suites $90-$135; Crib $5. TV. Heated pool. Restaurant 7 am-10 pm. Bar. Ck-out 11 am. Meeting rms. Beauty shop. Street parking. Tennis. X-country ski 1/4 mi. Exercise equipt; rowing machine, bicycles, whirlpool. Game rm. Built 1902; antiques, fireplaces, clock-tower. Cr cds: A, MC, V.

[icons]

Inns

★★★ **CLEVEHOLM MANOR.** *(58 Redstone Blvd, Redstone 81623)* 10 mi S on CO 82 to Carbondale, then 18 mi S on CO 133. 970/963-3463; res: 800/643-4837 (exc CO); FAX 970/963-3463. 16 air-cooled rms, 8 with bath, 8 share bath, 2-3 story, 3 suites. No rm phones; central phone 24 hrs. S, D $95-$125; each addl $20; suites $155-$180. Pet accepted; $200. TV in lounge. Complimentary continental bkfst, refreshments. Dining rm Fri, Sat 6-8:30 pm. Restaurant nearby. Ck-out 11 am, ck-in 3 pm. X-country ski on site. Lawn games. Bicycles. Turreted mansion (1889) built by turn-of-the-century coal baron as Redstone Castle; European-executed stonework, woodwork; gold-leafed ceilings; Tiffany light fixtures; antiques, original furnishings. Totally nonsmoking. Cr cds: A, MC, V.

[icons]

★★★ **MT. SOPRIS.** *(0165 Mt Sopris Ranch Rd, Carbondale 81623)* 15 mi S on CO 82 to jct CO 82 & CO 133, 3 mi SW (follow signs). 970/963-2209; res: 800/437-8675; FAX 970/963-8975. 15 rms, 2 story, 1 kit. unit. A/C in lounge. S, D $85-$250; each addl $10; kit. unit $175. Children over 12 yrs only. TV; VCR in lounge. Heated pool; whirlpool. Complimentary coffee in lounge. Complimentary full bkfst. Meeting rm. Business servs avail. In-rm modem link. Downhill/x-country ski 20 mi. Rec rm. Balconies. Western log complex of 3 bldgs on 14 acres; llama pasture. Totally nonsmoking. Cr cds: MC, V.

[D] [icons]

Cottage Colony

★★ **AVALANCHE RANCH.** *(12863 CO 133, Redstone 81623)* 15 mi S on CO 82, 15 mi S on CO 133. 970/963-2846; FAX 970/963-3141. 11 kit. cabins, 4 rms in farmhouse (2 share baths). No A/C. No rm phones. S, D, cabins $85-$135; under 8 free; min stay hols, wkends. Adults only in farmhouse. Crib free. Pet accepted, some restrictions; $10. TV in main rm, VCR avail. Playground. Complimentary coffee, tea in rms. Complimentary continental bkfst. Ck-out 11 am, ck-in 3 pm. Rec rm. Lawn games. Picnic tables, grills. On Crystal River. Renovated 1913 farmhouse with antiques; rustic log cabins. Totally nonsmoking. Cr cds: DS, MC, V.

[icons]

Restaurants

★ **CRYSTAL CLUB CAFE.** *(0467 Redstone Blvd, Redstone 81623)* 15 mi S on CO 82, then 15 mi S on CO 133. 970/963-9515. Hrs: 11:30 am-10 pm. Closed Mon-Fri, Nov-Apr. No A/C. Italian, Amer menu. Bar. Semi-a la carte: lunch $5.50-$8, dinner $5.50-$15.75. Child's meals. Specializes in chicken Marsala. Parking. Outdoor dining. Country Western decor; stone fireplace. No cr cds accepted.

✔★ **THE FIRESIDE.** *51701 US 6/24, 1/2 mi E of I-70 exit 114.* 970/945-6613. Hrs: 11 am-10 pm; Sun brunch 9 am-3 pm. Bar. Semi-a la carte: lunch $3.95-$7.95, dinner $6.95-$16.95. Buffet (Mon-Thurs): lunch $5.95. Sun bkfst buffet: $5.95. Sun brunch $9.95. Child's meals. Specializes in prime rib, steak, chicken. Salad bar. Parking. Cr cds: A, D, DS, MC, V.

[D] SC

★★ **FLORINDO'S.** *721 Grand Ave.* 970/945-1245. Hrs: 11:30 am-3 pm, 5-10:30 pm; Sat from 5 pm. Closed Sun; Easter, Memorial Day, Thanksgiving, Dec 25. Italian menu. Serv bar. Semi-a la carte: lunch $6.95-$7.95, dinner $9.95-$17.95. Child's meals. Specializes in salmon in parchment paper, pasta, veal chops. Art deco-style decor. Totally nonsmoking. Cr cds: MC, V.

[D]

★ **LOS DESPERADOS.** *0055 Mel Rey Rd.* 970/945-6878. Hrs: 11:30 am-10 pm; Sun from 11 am. Closed some major hols. Res accepted. Mexican menu. Bar. Semi-a la carte: lunch $5.50-$9, dinner $5.75-$10.50. Child's meals. Specializes in enchiladas, fajitas. Parking. Outdoor dining. Colorful Mexican decor. Family-owned. Cr cds: A, DS, MC, V.

[D]

★★ **RIVERS.** *2525 S Grand Ave.* 970/928-8813. Hrs: 11 am-10 pm. Closed Dec 25. Res accepted. Bar. Semi-a la carte: lunch $3.25-$7.95, dinner $6.95-$22.95. Child's meals. Specialties: smoked trout paté, elk medallions. Parking. Outdoor dining. Many windows for view of Fork River. Cr cds: A, MC, V.

[D]

★★★ **SOPRIS.** *7215 CO 82, 6 mi S on CO 82.* 970/945-7771. Hrs: 5-10 pm. Res accepted. Continental menu. Bar to midnight. Semi-a la carte: dinner $9-$27. Child's meals. Specializes in veal, lamb, fresh seafood. Parking. Cr cds: A, DS, MC, V.

[D] SC

Golden (B-5)

(See Central City, Denver, Evergreen, Idaho Springs)

Founded 1859 **Pop** 13,116 **Elev** 5,674 ft **Area code** 303 **Zip** 80401

Information Greater Golden Chamber of Commerce, 507 14th St, PO Box 1035, 80402; 303/279-3113.

Once a rival of Denver, Golden was capital of the Colorado Territory from 1862 to 1867.

What to See and Do

Astor House Hotel Museum (1867). First stone hotel west of the Mississippi. Period furnishings. Self-guided and guided tours. Victorian gift shop. (Tues-Sat; closed hols) 822 12th St. Phone 303/278-3557. ¢

Colorado Railroad Museum. An 1880-style railroad depot houses memorabilia and operating model railroad. More than 50 historic locomotives and cars from Colorado railroads displayed outside. (Daily; closed Thanksgiving, Dec 25) 17155 W 44th Ave (10th St E of Golden). Phone 303/279-4591 or 800/365-6263. ¢¢

Colorado School of Mines (1874). (2,950 students) World-renowned institution devoted exclusively to education of mineral, energy and material engineers and applied scientists. Tours of campus. Main entrance at 19th & Elm Sts. Phone 303/273-3000 or 800/446-9488 (exc CO). On campus are

> **USGS National Earthquake Information Center.** (Mon-Fri, by appt; closed hols) Illinois & 17th Sts. Phone 303/273-8500. **Free.**

> **Geology Museum.** Mineral and mining history exhibits. (Daily exc Sun) 16th & Maple Sts. Phone 303/273-3815. **Free.** Off campus is

> **Edgar Mine.** Experimental mine operated by Colorado School of Mines, federal government and by manufacturers for equipment testing. (Tues-Sat, by appt) Located in Idaho Springs (see). 303/567-2911 ¢¢

DAR Pioneer Museum. Houses more than 4,000 items dating from Golden's territorial capital days; includes household articles, clothing, furniture; mining, military and ranching equipment; unique Indian doll collection. (Daily exc Sun; winter hrs limited; closed hols) Wheelchair accessible. Donation. 911 10th St (City Hall). Phone 303/278-7151.

Golden Gate Canyon State Park. On 10,020 acres. Nature and hiking trails. Cross-country skiing. Picnicking. Camping (dump station). Visitor center. Panorama Point Overlook provides 100-mile view of the Continental Divide. Standard fees. (Daily) 2 mi N via CO 93, then left on Golden Gate Canyon Rd and continue W for 15 mi. Phone 303/592-1502. Per vehicle ¢¢

Heritage Square. Old-fashioned shopping area with 1880s atmosphere. Includes more than 40 unique craft and gift shops, cafes, bumper cars and alpine slide (rides, early May-late Sept). (Daily; closed Jan 1, Thanksgiving, Dec 25) Jct CO 40, 93. Phone 303/279-2789.

Historic buildings.

> **Territorial Capitol** (1861). Legislative sessions were held here, on the upper floor, from 1862 to 1867. 12th & Washington Sts (Loveland Building).

> **Largest cobblestone building** in the US. Approx 3,000 wagonloads of cobblestones were used in the construction. The rocks are from Clear Creek and the quartz from Golden Gate Canyon. 13th & Arapahoe Sts.

⭐ **Industrial tour. Coors Brewing Company.** Tours of Coors brewing and malting processes. Tours for hearing impaired and foreign guests may be arranged. Children welcome when accompanied by an adult. (Mon-Sat) 13th & Ford Sts. For tour schedule phone 303/277-BEER. **Free.**

Lariat Trail. Leads to Denver Mountain Parks. Lookout Mountain, 5 miles west off US 6, is the nearest peak. At summit is

> **Buffalo Bill Memorial Museum and Grave.** Comprehensive history of one of the American West's most famous characters, Buffalo Bill Cody. (May-Oct, daily; rest of yr, daily exc Mon; closed Dec 25) Picnic area. Phone 303/526-0747. ¢

Annual Event

Buffalo Bill Days. Parade, golf tournament. July.

Motel

✔ ★ ★ **LA QUINTA.** 3301 Youngfield Service Rd, I-70 exit 264. 303/279-5565; FAX 303/279-5841. 129 rms, 3 story. S, D $59-$79; under 18 free. Crib free. TV; cable (premium), VCR avail. Pool. Compli-

mentary continental bkfst. Restaurant nearby. Ck-out noon. Coin lndry. Meeting rms. Business servs avail. In-rm modem link. Valet serv. Cr cds: A, C, D, DS, MC, V.

D ✋ ☲ ⊠ ⚒ SC

Motor Hotels

★ ★ ★ **MARRIOTT DENVER WEST.** 1717 Denver West Mariott Blvd, I-70 exit 263. 303/279-9100; FAX 303/271-0205. 307 rms, 6 story. S, D $80-$120; suites $200-$400; under 18 free; wkend rates. Crib free. TV; cable (premium). 2 pools, 1 indoor; poolside serv. Restaurant 6:30 am-11 pm. Rm serv. Bar 11:30-2 am, Sun to midnight. Ck-out noon. Coin lndry. Convention facilities. Business servs avail. In-rm modem link. Bellhops. Valet serv. Gift shop. Airport transportation. Exercise equipt; weights, bicycles, whirlpool, sauna. Health club privileges. Game rm. Some refrigerators. Some private patios, balconies. View of foothills. Cr cds: A, C, D, DS, ER, JCB, MC, V.

D ☲ ✗ ⊠ ⚒ SC

★ ★ ★ **TABLE MOUNTAIN INN.** 1310 Washington Ave. 303/277-9898; res: 800/762-9898; FAX 303/271-0298. 32 rms, 2 story, 3 suites. S, D $87-$105; each addl $5; suites $130-$145; under 12 free; wkend rates. Crib free. TV; cable (premium), VCR avail. Complimentary coffee in rms. Restaurant 7-2 am. Rm serv. Bar from 11 am. Ck-out 11 am. Meeting rms. Business servs avail. In-rm modem link. Valet serv. Airport transportation. Some refrigerators. Balconies. Southwestern decor. Cr cds: A, D, DS, JCB, MC, V.

D ⊠ ⚒

Restaurants

★ ★ **CHART HOUSE.** 25908 Genesee Trail. 303/526-9813. Hrs: 5-10 pm; Sun 4:30-9 pm. Res accepted. Bar to 11 pm; wkends to midnight. Semi-a la carte: dinner $15-$36.95. Child's meals. Specializes in prime rib, seafood. Salad bar. Parking. Nautical decor. View of mountains & city. Cr cds: A, C, D, DS, MC, V.

D SC

✔ ★ **HAMPTON'S.** 1518 Washington Ave. 303/279-8151. Hrs: 9 am-3 pm; Sat to 2 pm. Closed Sun. Res accepted. Homestyle, Amer menu. Semi-a la carte: lunch $4.95-$5.99. Child's meals. Specializes in quiche, adobe chicken. Salad bar. Parking. 4 dining areas in converted house. Totally nonsmoking. Cr cds: MC, V.

Granby (B-5)

(See Grand Lake, Kremmling, Winter Park)

Pop 966 **Elev** 7,939 ft **Area code** 303 **Zip** 80446
Information Chamber of Commerce, PO Box 35; 303/887-2311.

Immediately northeast of Granby is the Arapaho National Recreation Area developed by the Department of Interior as part of the Colorado-Big Thompson Reclamation Project. There is swimming and mineral bathing at Hot Sulphur Springs. Several national forests, lakes and big-game hunting grounds are within easy reach. Two ski areas are nearby (also see WINTER PARK) and a Ranger District Office of the Arapaho National Forest (see DILLION) is located in Granby.

What to See and Do

Arapaho National Recreation Area. Includes Shadow Mountain, Willow Creek, Monarch, Grand and Granby lakes. Boating, fishing, hunting, camping (fee), picnicking, horseback riding. (Daily) 6 mi NE on US 34. Contact US Forest Service, PO Box 10; 303/887-3331. **Free.**

Grand County Historical Association. Museum exhibits depict the history of skiing, ranching and Rocky Mountain railroads; archaeological finds; reconstructed old buildings, wagons and tools. (Memorial Day-Labor Day, daily; winter, Wed-Sat) 10 mi W via US 40 in Hot Sulphur Springs. Phone 303/725-3939. ¢

Rocky Mountain National Park (see). Entrance 15 mi N via US 34 at Grand Lake.

Skiing. SilverCreek Ski Area. 2 triple chairlifts, 1 double chairlift, 1 Pomalift; patrol, school, rentals; snowmaking; concession, cafeteria, bar; nursery, day-lodge. 22 runs; longest run 6,100 ft; vertical drop 1,000 ft. (Dec-mid-Apr) Snowboarding, sleigh rides. Health club. 3 mi SE on US 40. Phone 303/887-3384, 303/629-1020 (Denver) or 800/448-9458. ¢¢¢¢¢

Motel

✔★ **BROKEN ARROW.** *Box 143, 1 mi W on US 40.* 970/887-3532. 12 rms. No A/C. S $26; D $32-$38; each addl $4. Crib free. TV; cable (premium). Playground. Restaurant nearby. Ck-out 10 am. Free RR station, bus depot transportation. Downhill/x-country ski 3 mi. Refrigerators. Picnic tables. Cr cds: A, DS, MC, V.

Resort

★★ **INN AT SILVER CREEK.** *(Box 4222, Silver Creek) 2 mi S on US 40.* 970/887-2131; res: 800/926-4386; FAX 970/887-2350. 342 rms, 3 story, 252 kits. No A/C. Feb-Mar: S, D $90; each addl $10; kit. units $106-$256; ski plan; higher rates late Dec; lower rates rest of yr. Crib free. Pet accepted; $12 per day. TV; cable (premium), VCR avail. Pool. Restaurant 7 am-10 pm. Bar 5 pm-2 am. Ck-out 10 am, ck-in 4 pm. Coin lndry. Convention facilities. Business servs avail. Shopping arcade. Free RR station, bus depot transportation. Lighted tennis. Downhill ski 1 mi. Ski rentals. Sleigh rides. Racquetball. Whitewater rafting. Mountain bikes. Hot-air balloon rides. Exercise equipt; weight machine, bicycles, whirlpool, sauna. In-rm whirlpools; many refrigerators, fireplaces. Private patios, balconies. Cr cds: A, C, D, DS, MC, V.

Guest Ranches

★★★★★ **C LAZY U RANCH.** *Box 379, 3 mi W on US 40, then 4 mi NW on CO 125.* 970/887-3344; FAX 970/887-3917. This luxury dude ranch, family owned and run, has comfortable wood cabins containing log fires, lounge areas, and tea/coffee makers. Recreational choices include exploring 5,000 acres of spectacular trails on horseback, fly fishing, complimentary tennis instruction, hiking, rafting, and cross-country or downhill skiing and telemarking in winter. 4 rms in lodge, 41 1-5 rm units in cottages. No A/C. No rm phones. AP (7-day min), Jun-Aug, wkly: S, D $1,550-$3,200/person; ski package plan; lower rates early June, Sept & mid-Dec-Mar. Closed rest of yr. TV in game rm; VCR avail. Heated pool; poolside serv, whirlpool, sauna. Playground. Free supervised child's activities; ages 3-18. In-rm coffee. Dining rm (guests only). Barbecues, outdoor buffets. Bars 11-12:30 am. Ck-out 10 am, ck-in 3 pm. Complimentary lndry facilities. Meeting rms. Business servs avail. Valet serv. Gift shop. Tennis, pro. Paddle boats. Stocked lake. Downhill ski 20 mi; x-country ski on site. Sleighing, tobogganing, ice-skating. Racquetball. Skeet, trap range. Trail rides. Hayrides. Petting zoo. Lawn games. Rec rm. Library. Entertainment, dancing. Exercise equipt; bicycles, stair machine. Fishing guides; cleaning and storage. Some fireplaces. No cr cds accepted.

★★ **DROWSY WATER RANCH.** *Box 147M, 6 mi W on US 40.* 970/725-3456; res: 800/845-2292. 8 rms in lodge, 9 cottages. No A/C. AP, June-Sept, wkly: S $1,020; D $955/person; each addl $830; under 5, $435; daily rates avail. Closed rest of yr. Crib free. Heated pool; whirlpool. Playground. Free supervised child's activities (June-Sept); ages 1-5. Family-style meals in lodge; also trail bkfst, buffets, cookouts, picnicking. Ck-out 11 am, ck-in 2 pm. Coin lndry 7 mi.

Meeting rms. Gift shop. Free local RR station, bus depot transportation. Soc dir. Lawn games. Fishing & hunting guides. Riding & hiking trails. Hayrides. Rodeo events. Staff show. Square dancing. Optional white water rafting ($40/person) & pack ($30/person) trips. Some private porches. Picnic tables, grills. No cr cds accepted.

Grand Junction (C-2)

Settled 1881 **Pop** 29,034 **Elev** 4,597 ft **Area code** 970

Information Visitor & Convention Bureau, 740 Horizon Dr, 81506; 970/244-1480, 800/962-2547.

Grand Junction's name stems from its location at the junction of the Colorado (formerly the Grand) and Gunnison rivers. The altitude and warm climate combine to provide a rich agricultural area, which produces peaches, pears and grapes for the local wine industry. The city serves as a trade and tourist center for western Colorado and eastern Utah as well as a gateway to 2 national parks, 6 national forests and 7 million acres of public land. Fishing, hunting, boating and hiking may all be enjoyed in the nearby lakes and mountain streams.

What to See and Do

Colorado National Monument (see). 10 mi W, off CO 340.

Cross Orchards Historic Site. Operated from 1896 to 1923 by owners of Red Cross shoe company. Living history farm with historically costumed guides interprets the social and agricultural heritage of western Colorado. Restored buildings and equipment on display; narrow gauge railroad exhibit and country store. Demonstrations, special events. (Tues-Sat) Sr citizen rate. 3073 Patterson/F Rd. Phone 970/434-9814. ¢¢

Dinosaur Hill. Self-guided walking trail interprets quarry of paleontological excavations. (Daily) 5 mi W, 1½ mi S of Fruita on CO 340. Phone 970/241-9210. **Free.**

Dinosaur Valley Museum. Half-scale animated dinosaurs, full-scale skeletal exhibits, and related displays show the paleontology of western Colorado. Working laboratory prepares fossils excavated from local quarries. (May-Sept, daily; rest of yr, Tues-Sat) 4th St at 362 Main. Phone 970/241-9210. ¢¢

★ **Grand Mesa National Forest.** This 346,221-acre alpine forest includes a flat-top, basalt-capped tableland at 10,500 feet. There are more than 300 alpine lakes and reservoirs, many with trout; boat rentals are available. The mesa is also a big-game hunting area, with horses available for rent. There are excellent areas for cross-country skiing, snowmobiling, picnicking and camping (fee at some campgrounds); there is also a lodge and housekeeping cabins. From the rim of Lands End, western most spot on Grand Mesa, there is a spectacular view of much of western Colorado. Also located within the forest is Powderhorn Ski Resort and the Crag Crest National Recreational Trail. Approx 40 mi E via I-70 & CO 65. For information contact the Forest Supervisor, 2250 US 50, Delta 81416; 970/874-7691. Ranger District offices are located in Grand Junction & Collbran and for Uncompaghre Forest to the southwest as well.

Museum of Western Colorado. Features exhibits on regional, social and natural history of the Western Slope; collection of small weapons; wildlife exhibits. (Daily exc Sun) Tours by appt. 468 S 4th St. Phone 970/242-0971. ¢

Powderhorn Ski Resort. Quad chairlift, 2 double chairlifts, 1 surface lift; patrol, school, rentals; snowmaking; snack bar, restaurants, bar; day-lodge. 29 runs; longest run 2.2 mi; vertical drop 1,650 ft. (Mid-Dec-mid-Apr, daily) Cross-country trails (7 mi), snowboarding, snowmobiling, sleigh rides. Half-day rates. Summer activities include fishing, rafting trips, biking, horseback riding, western cookouts. 20 mi E via I-70, exit 49. E on CO 65. Phone 970/268-5700 or 800/241-6997. ¢¢¢¢¢

Rabbit Valley Trail Through Time. 1 1/2-mi self-guided walking trail through a paleontologically significant area. Fossilized flora and fauna from the Jurassic Age. No pets allowed. (Daily) 30 mi W on I-70, 2 mi from UT border. Phone 970/241-9210. **Free.**

Riggs Hill. Three-quarter-mile self-guided walking trail in an area where bones of the *Brachiosauras* dinosaur were discovered in 1900. (Daily) Intersection of S Broadway and Meadows Way. Phone 970/241-9210. **Free.**

River Rafting. On the Colorado, Green and Yampa rivers. Two-day to five-day whitewater raft trips. Contact Adventure Bound, Inc., 2392 H Road, 81505; 970/241-5633 or 800/423-4668. **¢¢¢¢¢**

State Parks.

Island Acres. Swimming; fishing. Picnicking. Grocery store nearby. Camping. Standard fees. 15 mi E, off I-70 exit 47. Phone 970/464-0548 or 970/434-3388.

Highline Lake. Swimming, waterskiing; fishing, waterfowl hunting; boat ramps, shelters. Picnicking. Camping. Standard fees. 18 mi NW on I-70 to Loma, then 6 mi N on CO 139. Phone 970/858-7208.

Annual Events

Colorado Stampede. Rodeo. 3rd wk June.

Colorado Mountain Winefest. Wine tastings, outdoor events. Late Sept.

Motels

★ ★ **BEST WESTERN SANDMAN.** 708 Horizon Dr (81506), 1/2 mi S at I-70 Airport exit 31. 970/243-4150; FAX 970/243-1828. 79 rms, 2 story. Mid-May-mid-Oct: S $40-$48; D $44-$52; each addl $4-$6; under 12 free; lower rates rest of yr. Crib free. Pet accepted, some restrictions. TV; cable. Heated pool. Complimentary coffee in lobby. Restaurant adj open 24 hrs. Ck-out 11 am. Coin lndry. Meeting rm. Business servs avail. In-rm modem link. Free airport transportation. Some refrigerators. Cr cds: A, C, D, DS, MC, V.

[D] [symbols] SC

✔ ★ **BUDGET HOST INN.** 721 Horizon Dr (81506), I-70 Airport exit 31. 970/243-6050; res: 800/888-5736. 54 rms, 2 story. Mid-May-mid-Oct: S $38-$43; D $45-$50; each addl $5; under 12 free; lower rates rest of yr. Crib free. TV; cable (premium). Heated pool. Playground. Complimentary coffee in lobby. Restaurant adj 6 am-10 pm. Ck-out 11 am. Coin lndry. Cr cds: A, C, D, DS, MC, V.

[symbols] SC

★ ★ **HOWARD JOHNSON LODGE.** 752 Horizon Dr (81506), near Walker Field Airport. 970/243-5150. 100 rms, 2 story. S, D $40-$69; each addl $5; under 18 free. Crib free. Pet accepted; $10. TV; cable. Heated pool. Restaurant 6 am-10 pm. Ck-out noon. Coin lndry. Meeting rms. Business servs avail. Bellhops. Free airport, RR station, bus depot transportation. Tennis. Private patios, balconies. Cr cds: A, C, D, DS, MC, V.

[D] [symbols] SC

✔ ★ **WEST GATE INN.** 2210 US 6 & 50 (81505), I-70 exit 26. 970/241-3020; res: 800/453-9253; FAX 970/243-4516. 100 rms, 2 story. S $35-$50; D $42-$68; each addl $6; under 11 free. Crib free. Pet accepted. TV; cable (premium). Heated pool. Restaurant 6 am-10 pm. Bar 3 pm-2 am. Ck-out 11 am. Coin lndry. Meeting rms. Business servs avail. Cr cds: A, C, D, DS, MC, V.

[D] [symbols] SC

Motor Hotels

★ ★ **HOLIDAY INN.** Box 1725 (81502), 755 Horizon Dr, N off I-70 airport exit 31, near Walker Field Airport. 970/243-6790; FAX 970/243-6790. 291 rms, 2 story. S $53-$63; D $59-$69; each addl $6;

suites $73-$79; under 20 free. Crib free. Pet accepted. TV; cable (premium), VCR avail. 2 pools, 1 indoor; whirlpool. Restaurant 6 am-10 pm. Rm serv. Bar 11-1:30 am, Sun to midnight; entertainment, dancing exc Sun. Ck-out 11 am. Coin lndry. Meeting rms. Business servs avail. In-rm modem link. Bellhops. Gift shop. Free airport, RR station, bus depot transportation. Putting green. Exercise equipt; weight machine, bicycles, sauna. Holidome. Game rm. Cr cds: A, C, D, DS, JCB, MC, V.

[D] [symbols] SC

★ ★ **RAMADA INN.** 2790 Crossroads Blvd (81506), 1/2 mi NE from I-70 exit 31, near Walker Field Airport. 970/241-8411; FAX 970/241-1077. 158 rms, 6 story. S $72; D $79; each addl $7; suites $85-$210; under 18 free; wkend rates. Pet accepted. TV; cable (premium). Indoor pool; whirlpool. Complimentary coffee 6-10 am. Restaurant 6 am-2 pm, 5-10 pm. Rm serv. Bar 11-1 am, Sun to midnight; dancing. Ck-out noon. Business servs avail. In-rm modem link. Gift shop. Free airport, RR station, bus depot transportation. Cr cds: A, C, D, DS, MC, V.

[D] [symbols] SC

Hotel

★ ★ ★ **HILTON.** 743 Horizon Dr (81506), near Walker Field Airport. 970/241-8888; FAX 970/242-7266. 264 units, 8 story. May-Oct: S $69-$120; D $79-$140; each addl $10; suites $104-$265; family, wkend rates; golf, ski plans; lower rates rest of yr. Crib free. Pet accepted; $50. TV; cable (premium). Heated pool; poolside serv. Playground. Restaurant 6 am-11 pm. Bar 11-2 am; entertainment (summer), dancing exc Sun. Ck-out 11 am. Convention facilities. Business servs avail. Gift shop. Free airport, RR station, bus depot transportation. Lighted tennis. Exercise equipt; weight machine, bicycles, whirlpool. Game rm. Lawn games. Bathrm phones. Luxury level. Cr cds: A, C, D, DS, ER, MC, V.

[D] [symbols] SC

Restaurants

★ ★ **FAR EAST.** 1530 North Ave (US 6). 970/242-8131. Hrs: 11 am-9:30 pm. Closed major hols. Res accepted. Chinese, Amer menu. Bar. Semi-a la carte: lunch $4-$10, dinner $5-$17. Child's meals. Specializes in Szechwan, Cantonese dishes. Parking. Fountain. Family-owned. Cr cds: A, C, D, DS, MC, V.

[D]

✔ ★ **STARVIN' ARVIN'S.** 754 Horizon Dr. 970/241-0430. Hrs: 6 am-10 pm. Closed Thanksgiving, Dec 25. Semi-a la carte: bkfst $1.99-$4.95, lunch $2.99-$4.99, dinner $3.99-$9.99. Child's meals. Specializes in chicken-fried steak, beef. Own pastries. Parking. Casual atmosphere; antique photographs. Cr cds: DS, MC, V.

[D]

★ ★ **THE WINERY.** 642 Main St. 970/242-4100. Hrs: 5:30-10 pm. Closed Dec 25. Bar from 4:30 pm. Semi-a la carte: dinner $7.50-$26.90. Specializes in steak, seafood. Salad bar. Restored 1890s building. Totally nonsmoking. Cr cds: A, C, D, DS, MC, V.

Grand Lake (B-5)

(See Estes Park, Granby)

Pop 259 **Elev** 8,380 ft **Area code** 970 **Zip** 80447

Information Grand Lake Area Chamber of Commerce, US 34 & CO 278, PO Box 57; 970/627-3402 or 800/531-1019.

Grand Lake is on the northern shore of the largest glacial lake in Colorado, source of the Colorado River. Ute Indians shunned the vicinity because, according to legend, mists rising from the lake were the spirits of women and children killed when Cheyenne and Arapahoe attacked a Ute village on the shore.

As the state's oldest resort village, Grand Lake boasts the world's highest yacht club, a full range of water recreation and horseback riding and pack trips on mountain trails. Grand Lake is at the terminus of Trail Ridge Road at the west entrance to Rocky Mountain National Park.

What to See and Do

National Park Service lectures, field trips. (Summer) **Free.**

Rocky Mountain National Park (see). Just N on US 34.

Snowmobiling and cross-country skiing. Back areas of Arapaho National Forest (see DILLON), portion of Trail Ridge Rd and local trails around Grand Lake, Shadow Mt and Granby Lakes. (Nov-May) Inquire locally for details.

Annual Events

Winter Carnival. Ice-skating, snowmobiling, ice sculptures, parade. Early Feb.

Buffalo Barbecue & Western Days Celebration. Street and boat parades, events, food. 3rd wk July.

Lipton Cup Sailing Regatta. Early Aug.

Rocky Mountain Repertory Theatre. Community Building, Town Square. Four musicals change nightly, Tues-Sun. Reservations advised. For schedule contact PO Box 1682 or phone Chamber of Commerce. Late June-late Aug.

Motels

(Because of the altitude, air conditioning is rarely necessary)

★ **BIGHORN LODGE.** *Box 1260, 613 Grand Ave.* 970/627-8101; res: 800/341-8000. 20 rms, 2 story. Mid-Dec-mid-Mar, mid-May-mid-Sept: S, D $60-$65; family rates; higher rates special events. Crib $5. TV; cable (premium). Whirlpool. Restaurant nearby. Ck-out 10 am. Downhill ski 18 mi; x-country ski 1 mi. Cr cds: A, C, D, DS, MC, V.

D ⚡ ≋ ⊠ 🔥

✔ ★ ★ **DRIFTWOOD LODGE.** *Box 609, 12255 US 34, 3 mi S on US 34.* 970/627-3654. 17 units, 9 kits. No A/C. Mid-May-Sept, mid-Dec-early Jan: S $55-$70; D $59-$80; each addl $5; 2-rm units $65-$75; kit. units $5 addl; lower rates rest of yr. Crib free. TV; cable (premium). Heated pool; wading pool, whirlpool, sauna. Playground. Ck-out 10 am. In-rm modem link. Local airport, RR station, bus depot transportation. Downhill ski 16 mi; x-country ski 4 mi. Snowmobiling. Lawn games. Some refrigerators. Picnic tables, grills. Overlooks lake. Cr cds: A, D, MC, V.

⚡ ≋ ⊠ 🔥

★ ★ **WESTERN RIVIERA.** *419 Garfield Ave, 419 Garfield Ave, 3/4 mi E of US 34.* 970/627-3580. 19 rms, 2 story, 6 kit. cabins. No rm phones. Mid-May-Sept: S, D $57-$70; each addl $7; family units $80-$94 cabins $80-$94; lower rates mid-Dec-Mar, Oct. Closed rest of yr. Crib $5. TV; cable, VCR avail. Whirlpool. Complimentary coffee in lobby. Restaurant adj. Ck-out 10 am. Downhill ski 18 mi; x-country ski 1 mi. Some refrigerators. Fireplace in lobby. On lakefront; scenic view. Cr cds: D, MC, V.

D ⚡ ⊠ 🔥

Lodge

★ **GRAND LAKE LODGE.** *15500 Hwy 34, US 34, 1/2 mi S of Rocky Mountain National Park entrance.* 970/627-3967. 56 air-cooled units, 1-2 story, 24 kit. units, 32 cottages. No rm phones. June-mid-Sept: S, D, kit. units, cottages $60-$100; family rates. Closed rest of yr. Crib $5. Heated pool. Playground. Dining rm 7:30-10

am, 11:30 am-2:30 pm, 5:30-9:30 pm; Sun 9:30 am-1:30 pm. Bar 11 am-11 pm; entertainment Thurs-Sun, dancing wkends. Ck-out 10 am. Coin lndry. Meeting rms. Concierge. Gift shop. Free RR station, bus depot transportation. Game rm. Rec rm. Lawn games. Balconies. Picnic tables, grills. Overlooks Grand Lake and Shadow Mountain Reservoir; surrounded by national park. Cr cds: A, DS, MC, V.

D ⚡ ≋ ⊠ 🔥

Inn

★ ★ **HUMMINGBIRD.** *132 Lakeview Dr.* 970/627-3417. 3 rms, 2 story. No A/C. No rm phones. June-Oct: S, D $65; higher rates hols (2-day min). Closed rest of yr. Children over 10 yrs only. TV in lobby; cable. Complimentary full bkfst. Ck-out 10 am, ck-in 4-6 pm. Guest lndry. X-country ski 3 mi. View of lake & mountains. Totally nonsmoking. Cr cds: MC, V.

≋ ⊠ 🔥

Restaurants

★ ★ **CAROLINES CUISINE.** *9921 US 34 #27, at Soda Springs Ranch.* 970/627-9404. Hrs: 5-9:30 pm. Sun brunch 10 am-1:30 pm. Closed Mon; 2 wks Apr & 2 wks Nov. Res accepted. French, Amer menu. Bar. Semi-a la carte: dinner $12.95-$17.75. Sun brunch $8-$12. Child's meals. Specialties: steak Diane, escargot Provencale. Pianist Sat. Parking. Outdoor dining. 3 dining rms; European decor. Smoking at bar only. Cr cds: A, C, D, DS, MC, V.

D SC

★ ★ **RED FOX.** *411 W Portal Rd.* 970/627-3418. Hrs: 5-11 pm. No A/C. Bar. Semi-a la carte: dinner $4.95-$32. Specializes in steak, cajun shrimp. Jazz combo Sun. Parking. Outdoor dining. Stone fireplace. View of mountains and lake. Cr cds: D, DS, MC, V.

D

Great Sand Dunes National Monument (E-5)

(For accommodations see Alamosa)

Elev 8,000-9,000 ft

(35 mi E & N of Alamosa via US 160, CO 150)

The Great Sand Dunes, tallest in North America, lie along the base of the Sangre de Cristo Mountains, on the floor of the San Luis Valley. The dunes, some of which reach a height of over 700 feet, are trapped here by the mountains, providing endless changes in color and mood. Warm and inviting by day, yet eerie and forbidding by moonlight, they have inspired strange legends of wild, web-footed horses, mysteriously disappearing wagon trains and herds of sheep. During the late spring and early summer a stream flows along the edge of the dunes. A self-guided nature trail and picnic areas are nearby. A campground is open all yr (fee). The visitor center is open daily; closed winter hols. Interpretive programs are offered Memorial Day-Labor Day. For further information contact the Superintendent, 11500 Hwy 150, Mosca 81146; 719/378-2312. Per car ¢¢

What to See and Do

Great Sand Dunes 4-Wheel Drive Tour. A twelve-mile, three-hour round trip tour through Great Sand Dunes National Monument; spectacular scenery; stops for short hikes on dunes. (May-Oct, daily) Six-person minimum. For information contact Great Sand Dunes Oasis, Mosca 81146; 719/378-2222. ¢¢¢¢

Greeley (B-6)

(See Fort Collins, Loveland)

Founded 1870 **Pop** 60,536 **Elev** 4,664 ft **Area code** 970 **Zip** 80631

Information Greeley Convention & Visitors Bureau, 1407 8th Ave; 970/352-3566 or 800/449-3866.

Horace Greeley conceived of "Union Colony" as a Utopian agricultural settlement similar to the successful experiment at Oneida, New York. The town was founded by Nathan Meeker, agricultural editor of Greeley's *New York Tribune*. Thanks to irrigation, the region today is rich and fertile and sustains a thriving community. Greeley is the seat of Weld County. A Ranger District office of the Roosevelt National Forest (see ESTES PARK) is located in Greeley.

What to See and Do

Centennial Village. Restored buildings show the growth of Greeley and Weld County from 1860-1920; period furnishings; tours, lectures, special events. (May-Oct, daily exc Mon) Sr citizen rate. N 14th Ave & A St. Phone 970/350-9220 or -9224. ¢¢

Fort Vasquez. Reconstructed adobe fur trading post of the 1830s contains exhibits of Colorado's fur trading and trapping industries, the Plains Indians, and archaeology of the fort. (Memorial Day-Labor Day, daily; rest of yr, by appt) 18 mi S on US 85 near Platteville. Phone 970/785-2832. **Free.**

Meeker Home (1870). The house of city founder Nathan Meeker contains many of his belongings, as well as other historical mementos. (May-Oct, Tues-Sat; closed hols) Sr citizen rate. 1324 9th Ave. Phone 970/350-9220. ¢¢

Municipal Museum. County history archives, pioneer life exhibits; library; tours. (Tues-Sat; closedhols) 919 7th St. Phone 970/350-9220. **Free.**

University of Northern Colorado (1889). (10,500 students) 11th Ave between 20th & 24th Sts, 16th to 20th St between 8th & 11th Aves. Phone 970/351-1890 or -1889. On the 236-acre campus are

Mariani Art Gallery. Features faculty, student and special exhibitions. Multipurpose University Center. **Free.**

James A. Michener Library. Colorado's largest university library. Collection includes materials owned by Michener while writing his book *Centennial*.

Annual Events

Independence Stampede Greeley Rodeo. Late June-July 4.

Weld County Fair. 1st wk Aug.

Motor Hotel

★ ★ **BEST WESTERN RAMKOTA INN.** 701 8th St. 970/353-8444; FAX 970/353-4269. 148 rms, 3 story. S $55-$63; D $63-$71; each addl $8; suites $120-$150; under 18 free. Crib free. Pet accepted. TV; cable. Indoor pool; poolside serv. Complimentary coffee in rms. Restaurant 6 am-10 pm. Rm serv. Bar 11 am-12 am. Ck-out noon. Meeting rms. Valet serv. Airport transportation. Health club privileges. Game rm. Balconies. Cr cds: A, C, D, DS, MC, V.

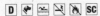

Restaurant

✔ ★ ★ **THE EAT'N PLACE.** *(101 2nd St, Eaton) 7 mi N on US 85.* 970/454-3636. Hrs: 6 am-9 pm. Closed Sun. Res accepted. Continental menu. Bar from 4:30 pm. Semi-a la carte: bkfst 95¢-$8.25, lunch

$1.65-$10.45, dinner $4.25-$15.95. Specializes in prime rib, shrimp, steak. Parking. Garden decor. Cr cds: A, DS, MC, V.

Gunnison (D-3)

(See Crested Butte)

Settled 1874 **Pop** 4,636 **Elev** 7,703 ft **Area code** 970 **Zip** 81230

Information Gunnison Country Chamber of Commerce, 500 E Tomichi Ave, Box 36; 970/641-1501.

With 2,000 miles of trout-fishing streams and Colorado's largest lake within easy driving range, Gunnison has long been noted as an excellent fishing center.

What to See and Do

Alpine Tunnel. Completed by Denver, South Park & Pacific Railroad in 1881 and abandoned in 1910, this railroad tunnel, 11,523 feet above sea level, is 1,771 feet long. (July-Oct) 36 mi NE via US 50, County 765, 3 mi E of Pitkin on dirt road.

Cumberland Pass (12,200 ft). Gravel road linking towns of Pitkin and Tincup. (July-Oct) 36 mi NE via US 50, County 765.

Curecanti National Recreation Area. Named for the Ute Chief Curicata, who roamed and hunted in this territory. This area along the Gunnison River drainage includes Blue Mesa, Morrow Point and Crystal lakes. Elk Creek Marinas, Inc offers boat tours on Morrow Point Lake (Memorial Day-Labor Day, daily); phone 970/641-0402 for reservations. Blue Mesa Lake has waterskiing, windsurfing; fishing; boating (ramps, rentals). Picnicking. Camping (fee). The Elk Creek Visitor Center is 16 miles west (mid-Apr-Oct, daily). 5 mi W on US 50. For information contact Superintendent, 102 Elk Creek; 970/641-0406 or -2337. (Daily) **Free.**

Gunnison National Forest. Forest contains 27 peaks more than 12,000 feet high within 1,662,839 acres of magnificent mountain scenery. Activities include fishing, hiking, picnicking and camping. A four-wheeling and a winter sports area is nearby (see CRESTED BUTTE). Also within the forest are West Elk Wilderness and portions of the Maroon Bells-Snowmass, Collegiate Peaks, La Garita and Raggeds wilderness areas. N, E and S on US 50. For information phone 970/641-0471. A Ranger District office is located in Gunnison.

Gunnison Pioneer Museum. County and area history; pioneer items, narrow-gauge railroad, 1905 schoolhouse. (Memorial Day-Labor Day, daily) E edge of town on US 50. Phone 970/641-4530 or -0740. ¢¢

Old mining town of Tincup. Inquire locally about other mining towns; "20-Circle Tour" ghost town maps provided free at the Visitor Center, 500 E Tomichi Ave (US 50). 40 mi NE on County road 765.

Taylor Park Reservoir. Road runs through 20-mile canyon of Taylor River. Fishing, hunting; boating. Camping. (Memorial Day-Labor Day, daily) 10 mi N on CO 135 to Almont, then 22 mi NE on County Road 742 (CO 59) in Gunnison National Forest. Phone Ranger District Office at 970/641-0471. Camping ¢¢¢ **Free.**

Western State College of Colorado (1901). (2,500 students) In the college library is the **Jensen Western Colorado Room** containing a collection of books and materials relating to Western history and culture. Escalante Dr between N Adams & N Colorado Sts. Phone 970/943-3035 or -2103.

Annual Event

Cattlemen's Days, Rodeo & County Fair. Mid-July.

Motels

★ ★ **BEST WESTERN TOMICHI VILLAGE.** *Box 763, US 50 E. 970/641-1131; FAX 970/641-9954.* 50 rms, 2 story. May-Sept: S $56-$64; D $60-$84; each addl $4; higher rates late Dec; lower rates rest of yr. Crib $3. TV; cable, VCR avail (movies avail $5). Indoor pool; whirlpool. Complimentary continental bkfst. Restaurant 6:30-9:30 am, 11 am-2 pm, 5-9 pm. Ck-out 11 am. Meeting rms. Free airport transportation. Exercise equipt; bicycle, stair machine. Corral facilities in hunting season. Cr cds: A, C, D, DS, JCB, MC, V.

★ ★ **HOLIDAY INN EXPRESS.** *400 E Tomichi Ave. 970/641-1288; FAX 970/641-1332.* 52 rms, 1-2 story. Mid-May-mid-Sept: S $48-$80; D $48-$85; each addl $5; suites $60-$95; under 19 free; rafting, ski plans; higher rates hols; lower rates rest of yr. Crib $2. TV; cable. Indoor pool. Complimentary bkfst. Restaurant nearby. Ck-out noon. Coin lndry. Meeting rm. Business servs avail. In-rm modem link. Free airport, bus depot transportation. Exercise equipt; stair machine, bicycles, whirlpool. Cr cds: A, C, D, DS, MC, V.

★ **RAMADA LIMITED.** *1011 W Rio Grande Ave. 970/641-2804; FAX 970/641-1420.* 36 rms, 2 story. Mid-May-mid-Dec: S $58; D $58-$68; each addl $6; under 19 free; lower rates rest of yr. Crib free. TV; cable. Indoor pool; whirlpool. Complimentary continental bkfst. Ck-out noon. Cr cds: A, C, D, DS, MC, V.

✔ ★ **SUPER 8.** *411 E Tomichi Ave, near County Airport. 970/641-3068; FAX 970/641-1323.* 49 rms, 2 story. S $35.88-$55.88; D $39.88-$71.88; each addl $5; ski plan. Crib $2. TV; cable (premium). Complimentary coffee in lobby. Restaurant adj 6 am-9 pm. Ck-out 11 am. Free airport transportation. Cr cds: A, C, D, DS, MC, V.

★ ★ **WATER WHEEL INN.** *Box 882, 2 mi W on US 50. 970/641-1650; res: 800/642-1650; FAX 970/641-1650.* 53 rms. Mid-June-Aug: S, D $70-$80; each addl $5; suites $80; lower rates rest of yr. TV; cable (premium). Whirlpool. Complimentary continental bkfst, coffee in lobby. Restaurant adj. Ck-out 11 am. Meeting rm. Business servs avail. Free airport, bus depot transportation. 18-hole golf adj. Cr cds: A, C, D, DS, MC, V.

Inn

★ ★ **MARY LAWRENCE.** *601 N Taylor St, near County Airport. 970/641-3343.* 5 rms, 2 story, 2 suites. No A/C. No rm phones. S, D $69; each addl $15-$25; suites $85; ski plan. Children over 6 yrs only. TV in suites. Complimentary full bkfst. Ck-out 11 am, ck-in 4-6 pm. Free airport transportation. Italianate inn built 1885 was womens boarding house. Many antiques. Totally nonsmoking. Cr cds: MC, V.

Guest Ranches

★ ★ **HARMEL'S.** *Box 944M, 10 mi N on CO 135, then 7 mi NE on Taylor River Rd (County 742). 970/641-1740.* 8 lodge rms, 19 kit. cottages, 11 suites. No A/C. No rm phones. Mid-June-Aug, AP: S $100-110; D $200-$220; each addl $100-$110; lower rates mid-May-mid-June, Sept. Closed rest of yr. Crib free. TV in rec rm. Heated pool. Playground. Free supervised child's activities. Complimentary coffee in rms. Dining rm 7:30-10 am, 6-9 pm. Box lunches, cookouts. Bar 4:30-10 pm; dancing. Ck-out 10 am, ck-in 2 pm. Grocery. Coin lndry. Meeting rms. Tackle store. Gift shop. Free airport, bus depot transportation. Whitewater rafting. Trap shooting. Hayrides. Bicycles (rentals).

Lawn games. Rec rm. Game rm. Refrigerators. Picnic tables. 300 acres on Taylor River. Cr cds: DS, MC, V.

★ ★ **POWDERHORN.** *Powderhorn (81243), 9 mi W on US 50, 16 mi S on CO 149, 10 mi SW on County Rd 27. 970/641-0220; res: 800/786-1220.* 13 air-cooled cabins (1-2-bedrm). AP, June-late Sept, wkly: cabins $990/person. Closed rest of yr. Crib free. Heated pool; whirlpool. Playground, children's fishing pond. Complimentary coffee in rms. Box lunches. Snack bar. Ck-out 10 am, ck-in 4 pm. Coin lndry. Free airport transportation. Horse trail rides. Hiking. Lawn games. Rec rm. Refrigerators. Picnic tables, grills. Family-oriented ranch in remote area along Cebolla Creek. No cr cds accepted.

★ ★ **WAUNITA HOT SPRINGS.** *8007 County Rd 887, 19 mi E on US 50, then 8 mi N. 970/641-1266.* 22 rms, 1-2 story. AP, wkly, June-mid-Sept: S $1,060; D $1,980; each addl $650-$900; groups only Dec-Mar; lower rates mid-Sept-Mar. Closed rest of yr. TV in lobby. Hot spring-fed pool; whirlpool. Dining rm 7:30-9 am; lunch (1 sitting) 12:30 pm, dinner (1 sitting) 6:30 pm. Box lunches. Ck-out 11 am, ck-in 3 pm. Coin lndry. Free local airport, bus depot transportation. Square dancing. Game rm. Hayrides, jeep trips, snowmobiles. Overnight camping. Raft trips avail. Petting zoo. Fishing/hunting guides; fish cleaning and storage. No cr cds accepted.

★ ★ **WHITE PINE RANCH.** *7500 Country Rd 887, 19 mi E on US 50, then 7 mi N on CR 887. 970/641-6410.* 4 rms. No A/C. No rm phones. AP, June-Sept, 6 days: $1,050; under 5 free; family rates; 3-day min stay; lower rates rest of yr. Crib free. TV; VCR. Whirlpool. Complimentary full bkfst. Box lunches, snacks, picnics. Bar; entertainment Sat. Ck-out 11:30 am, ck-in 1 pm. Lndry serv. Free airport transportation. Horse stables. Hiking. Fishing/hunting guide, fish/game clean & store. Rafting. Bicycles. On 938 acres surrounded by Gunnison National Forest. Totally nonsmoking. Cr cds: MC, V.

Cottage Colony

✔ ★ **CHAR-B RESORT.** *(Box 279MG, Almont 81210) 10 mi N on CO 135, 7 mi NE on Taylor River Rd (County 742), then 2 mi N on Spring Creek Rd (County 744). 970/641-0751; res: 817/937-3245 (winter).* 16 kit. cottages (1-5 bedrm). No A/C. May-Nov: cottages $60-$105; each addl $6; wkly rates. Closed rest of yr. Crib $4. TV in rec rm. Hot tub. Playground. Restaurant nearby. Ck-out 10 am, ck-in 2 pm. Grocery. Coin lndry. Airport, bus depot transportation. Lawn games. Rec rm. Refrigerators; some fireplaces. Picnic tables, grills. Rustic decor. Scenic location on Spring Creek. Cr cds: MC, V.

Restaurant

★ ★ **THE TROUGH.** *2 mi W on US 50. 970/641-3724.* Hrs: 5:30-10 pm; Fri & Sat to 10:30 pm. Closed Jan-Apr. Res accepted. No A/C. Bar 4:30 pm-2 am. Semi-a la carte: dinner $8.45-$24.45. Child's meals. Specializes in steak, prime rib, fresh seafood, wild game. Parking. Cr cds: A, DS, MC, V.

Idaho Springs (B-5)

(See Central City, Denver, Dillon, Georgetown, Golden)

Settled 1859 **Pop** 1,834 **Elev** 7,524 ft **Area code** 303 **Zip** 80452
Information Visitors Center, PO Box 97; 303/567-4382 or 800/685-7785.

Idaho Springs, the site of Colorado's earliest gold strikes (1859), is today a tourist resort as well as the urban center for more than 200 mines, from which uranium, molybdenum, tungsten, zinc, lead and gold are pulled from the earth. The town is named for the famous radium hot springs, first known and used by Ute Indians; bathing in the springs is still considered beneficial. The world's longest mining tunnel, five miles, once ran from Idaho Springs through a mountain to Central City (see); only a portion remains (not open to visitors). The road to Mt Evans (elevation 14,260 feet) is the highest paved road in North America. A Ranger District office of the Arapaho National Forest (see DILLON) is located in Idaho Springs.

What to See and Do

Argo Town, USA. Reproduction of Western mining town; includes shops and **Argo Gold Mill.** This mill was first operated in 1913 to support mines intersected by the "mighty Argo" Tunnel; today it offers guided tours that unfold the history of the mill and the story of mining. **Clear Creek Mining and Milling Museum.** Illustrates the role of mining in the past. **Double Eagle Gold Mine.** Authentic and truly representative gold mine has direct access from the Argo Gold Mill. (Daily) 23rd Ave-Riverside Dr. Phone 303/567-2421. ¢¢¢

Colorado School of Mines—Edgar Mine. Experimental mine operated by students, also by government for training and by manufacturers for equipment testing; 1-hr guided tour hourly (mid-June-mid-Aug, Tues-Sat; rest of yr, by appt). Colorado Ave & 8th St, ½ mi N on 8th St. Contact Mining Dept, Colorado School of Mines, Golden 80401; 303/567-2911. Wear boots or old shoes and sweater or coat. ¢¢

Phoenix Gold Mine. The only working gold mine in the state that is open to the public. (Daily; closed Dec 25) Approx 2½ mi SW via Stanley Road to Trail Creek Rd. Phone 303/567-0422 or 800/685-7785. ¢¢¢

Saint Mary's Glacier. Park car approximately one mile northwest of Alice, then proceed a half-mile on foot. 12 mi NW via I-70, Fall River Rd to Alice, a ghost town.

Annual Event

Gold Rush Days. Parades, picnic, foot races and mining contests, arts and crafts. Mid-July.

Inn

★ ★ **ST MARY'S GLACIER.** *336 Crest Dr, exit 238 off I-70, 10 mi N on Fall River Rd, follow signs.* 303/567-4084. 7 rms, 3 story. No A/C. S, D $79-$129; theme wkend rates. Children over 14 yrs only. Cable TV in sitting rm, VCR. Whirlpool. Complimentary full bkfst. Complimentary coffee, tea, sherry in afternoon. Ck-out 11 am, ck-in 4-7 pm. X-country ski on premises. Many balconies. Picnic tables. Hand-hewn log inn with majestic mountain views from every window. At 10,500 feet, this is one of the highest inns in North America. Totally nonsmoking. Cr cds: A, MC, V.

Keystone (C-5)

(see Dillon)

Kremmling (B-4)

(See Granby)

Pop 1,166 **Elev** 7,360 ft **Area code** 970 **Zip** 80459

A Ranger District office of the Arapaho National Forest (see DILLON) is located in Kremmling.

What to See and Do

Green Mountain Reservoir. Waterskiing; fishing; boating (ramps). Picnicking, groceries. Camping (fee). (Daily) 16 mi S on CO 9. Contact Dillon Ranger District, Box 620, Silverthorne 80498; 970/468-5400 or -5434 (recording).

Guest Ranch

★ ★ **LATIGO RANCH.** *PO Box 237, 201 County Rd 1911.* 970/724-9008; res: 800/227-9655. 10 air-cooled cottages. AP, June-Aug, wkly: cottages $1,365/person; family rates; lower rates Sept-mid-Nov, mid-Dec-Mar. Closed rest of yr. Crib free. TV in lobby. Heated pool; whirlpool. Playground. Free supervised child's activities (June-Sept); ages 3-14. Complimentary coffee in rms. Dining rm 7:30-9 am, 12:30-1:30 pm, 6:30-8 pm. Box lunches. Picnics. Entertainment nightly; dancing Tues, Thurs. Ck-out 4 pm, ck-in 2 pm. Coin lndry. Meeting rms. Business servs avail. Bellhops. Valet serv. Concierge. Gift shop. Airport, RR station transportation. X-country ski on site. Tobogganing. Horse stables. Hiking. Lawn games. Soc dir. Rec rm. Game rm. Fishing/hunting guides, clean & store. Refrigerators. Porches. Picnic tables. On lake. Cr cds: A, MC, V.

La Junta (E-7)

Settled 1875 **Pop** 7,637 **Elev** 4,066 ft **Area code** 719 **Zip** 81050
Information Chamber of Commerce, 110 Santa Fe Ave; 719/384-7411.

La Junta (la HUN-ta, Spanish for "the Junction") is at a junction of the old Navajo and Santa Fe Trails. The town is known for its Koshare Indian Dancers, a group of Explorer Scouts who perform authentic Native American dances here and throughout the country.

This is the center of an irrigated farming area, producing melons and commercial vegetables. Cattle auctions are held throughout the year. The Holbrook Lake area has become a popular recreational center.

What to See and Do

Bent's Old Fort National Historic Site. The fort has been reconstructed as accurately as possible to its appearance in 1845-46; the furnishings are antique and reproductions. The original structure, located on the Mountain Branch of the Santa Fe Trail, was built as as a privately owned frontier trading post (ca 1833). Due to its existence and location, the old fort played a central role in the "opening of the west." For 16 years, until its abandonment in 1849, the fort was an important frontier hub of American trade and served as a rendezvous for trappers, Native Americans and Hispanic traders on the Santa Fe Trail. It also served as the center of Army operations to protect the traders using the Santa Fe Trail. Self-guided tour. Summer "living history" programs. (Daily; closed Jan 1, Thanksgiving, Dec 25) 8 mi NE on CO 109 & 194 E. Phone 719/384-2596. ¢

⭐ **Koshare Indian Kiva Museum.** Housed in a domed building, a copy of ceremonial kivas in the Southwest, the museum features Native American baskets, arrowheads, paintings and carvings, as well as paintings by Southwestern artists. (June-Aug, daily; rest of yr, Tues-Sun afternoons; closed Jan 1, Easter, Thanksgiving, Dec 25) 115 W 18th St. Phone 719/384-4411. ¢

Otero Museum. History of Otero County and surrounding areas. Santa Fe Railroad history; artifacts. (June-Sept, daily) 2nd and Anderson Sts. Phone 719/384-7500. Free.

Annual Events

Arkansas Valley Fair and Exposition. Rocky Ford. Fairgrounds, grandstand. Colorado's oldest continuous fair. Highlight is "watermelon day," when every visitor receives free watermelon. Phone 719/254-7483. 1 wk late Aug.

Early Settlers Day. Fiddlers contest, crafts, parade. Sat after Labor Day.

Koshare Winter Night Ceremonial. In Kiva Museum. Nightly performances. Wk of Dec 25 and 1st wkend Jan.

Seasonal Event

Koshare Indian Dances. In Kiva Museum. Dances by nationally famous Boy Scout troop. Sat eves. Late June-early Aug.

Motels

✔★★ **BEST WESTERN BENT'S FORT INN.** *(E US 50, Las Animas 81054) 20 mi E on US 50 at jct CO 194. 719/456-0011; FAX 719/456-2550.* 38 rms, 2 story. S $38; D $52; each addl $6; under 12 free. Pet accepted, some restrictions. TV; cable. Pool. Restaurant 6 am-8 pm. Rm serv. Bar 5-10 pm. Ck-out noon. Meeting rms. Business servs avail. Free airport, bus depot transportation. Cr cds: A, C, D, DS, MC, V.

 SC

★★ **QUALITY INN.** *1325 E 3rd St. 719/384-2571; FAX 719/384-5655.* 60 rms, 2 story. S $40-$49; D $45-$54; each addl $2; suites $65; under 19 free. Crib $5. Pet accepted, some restrictions. TV; cable (premium), VCR avail (movies avail). Heated pool; whirlpool, poolside serv. Coffee in rms. Restaurant 5:30 am-10 pm. Rm serv. Bar. Meeting rms. Business servs avail. In-rm modem link. Free airport transportation. Refrigerator in suites. Cr cds: A, C, D, DS, ER, JCB, MC, V.

 SC

✔★ **STAGECOACH INN.** *905 W 3rd St, 1 mi W on US 50. 719/384-5476; FAX 719/384-9091.* 30 rms, 2 story. S $35-$40; D $42-$46; each addl $4. Crib $4. Pet accepted; $10 refundable. TV; cable (premium). Pool. Complimentary continental bkfst, Mon-Fri. Restaurant nearby. Ck-out 11 am. Cr cds: A, C, D, DS, MC, V.

 SC

Restaurant

✔★ **CHIARAMONTE'S.** *208 Santa Fe, 1¹/₂ blks S of US 50. 719/384-8909.* Hrs: 11 am-2 pm, 5-9 pm. Closed major hols. Res accepted. Continental menu. Bar. Semi-a la carte: lunch $4.35-$7.95, dinner $8.50-$13.75. Specializes in steak, seafood. Own soups. Cr cds: DS, MC, V.

Lake City (E-3)

Pop 223 **Elev** 8,658 ft **Area code** 970 **Zip** 81235
Information Chamber of Commerce, PO Box 430; 970/944-2527 or 800/569-1874.

Lake City teemed with gold seekers in the 1870s. Now empty cabins and entire ghost towns dot the hills above the town. Among Lake City's 75 historic homes and buildings are the first church and bank on the Western Slope. Lake San Cristobal and the Lake Fork of the Gunnison River offer excellent fishing.

In the winter of 1873-74, Alferd Packer led a group of gold prospectors into the San Juan Mountains above Lake City. Emerging from the mountains in the spring, only Packer survived, claiming his companions had abandoned him. For the next 10 years, Packer was a fugitive. However, in 1883, he was convicted of murder and cannibalism. The victims' grave sites are located on the south edge of town.

What to See and Do

Alpine Triangle Recreation Area. Approx 250,000 acres administered by Bureau of Land Management and the US Forest Service for primitive and motorized recreation, mining, grazing and watershed protection. The area has 5 peaks that are more than 14,000 ft high; excellent backpacking and fishing; habitat for deer, elk, mountain sheep, black bear. Many historical mining tramways, stamp mills and ghost towns are scattered throughout the area. Mill Creek Campground (14 mi SW) has a picnic area and 22 tent & trailer sites with water (Memorial Day-Oct, daily, weather permitting; fee for camping). Lake San Cristobal (3 mi S of town), the second largest natural lake in the state, was formed by the Slumgullion earthflow 700 years ago. Williams Creek (10 mi SW) has picnic areas and 21 tent and trailer sites with water (Memorial Day-Oct, daily; fee for camping). Southeast of town is the site where Alferd Packer murdered and mutilated five prospectors in the winter of 1873-1874. S & W of town; access by the Alpine Loop National Backcountry Byway (4-wheel drive necessary in some places). Phone 970/641-0471. Camping fee: Mill Creek ¢¢; Williams Creek ¢¢¢

Annual Event

Alferd Packer Barbeque Cookoff. Late May.

Lodge

★★ **CRYSTAL LODGE.** *CO 149, 2 mi S on CO 149. 970/944-2201; res: 800/984-1234; FAX 970/944-2504.* 18 rms, 1-2 story, 5 suites, 4 cottages. No A/C. No rm phones. Memorial Day-Sept (2-day min): S, D $55; each addl $10; suites, cottages $85-$95; under 2 free; ski rates; lower rates rest of yr. Crib free. Pet accepted, some restrictions; $25. TV; VCR avail. Heated pool; poolside serv, whirlpool. Restaurant 8-10:30 am, 11:30 am-1:30 pm, 5:30-8:30 pm. Bar. Ck-out 11 am. Meeting rms. Business servs avail. X-country ski 1 mi. Many refrigerators. Surrounded by San Juan Mountains. Totally nonsmoking. Cr cds: MC, V.

Inn

★ **CINNAMON.** *426 Gunnison Ave. 970/944-2641; res: 800/337-2335.* 5 air-cooled rms, 3 share bath, 2 story, 1 suite. No rm phones. S, D $75-$105; ski plan. Crib free. Complimentary full bkfst. Restaurant nearby. Ck-out 11 am, ck-in 4-6 pm. Country inn built 1878. Totally nonsmoking. Cr cds: MC, V.

Restaurant

★ **LAKE CITY CAFE.** *310 Gunnison Ave. 970/944-2733.* Hrs: 7 am-9 pm. No A/C. Italian, Amer menu. Bar 11 am-10 pm. Semi-a la carte: bkfst $3.75-$5.75, lunch $3.95-$5.95, dinner $7.95-$14.95. Child's meals. Specialties: pizza, pasta, chicken-fried steak. Parking. Outdoor dining. Built 1877. Former cigar factory. Cr cds: MC, V.

Lakewood (C-5)

(See Denver, Englewood, Golden)

Pop 126,481 **Elev** 5,450 ft **Area code** 303
Information West Chamber Serving Jefferson County, 10140 West Colfax Ave, Ste 1, 80215-3910; 303/233-5555.

This suburban community west of Denver was once dotted with farms and fruit orchards and with the summer houses of wealthy Denver residents.

What to See and Do

Bear Creek Lake Park. Approx 2,600 acres. Waterskiing school; fishing; boating (10 hp limit, rentals, marina). Hiking, bicycle trails. Picnicking. Camping (no electricity). Archery. View of downtown Denver from Mt Carbon. (Daily; closed Jan 1, Thanksgiving, Dec 25) Sr citizen rate. 1/4 mi E of C-470 on Morrison Rd. Phone 303/697-6159. Per vehicle ¢

Crown Hill Park. This 168-acre nature preserve includes Crown Hill Lake and a wildlife pond. Fishing. Hiking, bicycle, bridle trails. (Daily) W 26th Ave at Kipling St (CO 391). Phone 303/271-5925. **Free.**

Historical Belmar Village. Nature, art and historical exhibits in 127-acre park. Turn-of-the-century farm; one-room schoolhouse; vintage farm machinery; Barn Gallery with permanent and changing exhibits, interpretive displays. Lectures, workshops; visitor center. (Daily) 797 S Wadsworth Blvd (CO 121), just S of Alameda Blvd (CO 26). Phone 303/987-7850. **Free.**

Motels

✔★★ **COMFORT INN-SOUTHWEST.** *3440 S Vance St (80227), near jct Hampden Ave (US 285) & Wadsworth Blvd (CO 121). 303/989-5500; FAX 303/989-2981.* 120 rms, 2 story, 8 suites. S $60; D $68; each addl $8; suites $85; under 18 free; wkly, wkend rates. Crib free. Pet accepted. TV; cable (premium). Heated pool; whirlpool. Complimentary continental bkfst, refreshments. Restaurant opp open 24 hrs. Ck-out noon. Coin lndry. Meeting rm. Business servs avail. Bellhops. Valet serv. Airport transportation. Exercise equipt; bicycles, rower. Some refrigerators. Cr cds: A, C, D, DS, ER, MC, V.

D ♥ ≋ ⨯ ⊠ ⚲ SC

★★ **HAMPTON INN-DENVER SOUTHWEST.** *3605 S Wadsworth Blvd (80235). 303/989-6900; FAX 303/985-4730.* 148 rms, 4 story. S $57-$61; D $65-$69; each addl $8; under 18 free. TV; cable (premium). Heated pool. Complimentary continental bkfst, coffee. Restaurant adj 11-1. Ck-out noon. Coin lndry. Meeting rms. Business servs avail. In-rm modem link. Bellhops. Valet serv. Exercise equipt; weights, bicycles. Health club privileges. Some refrigerators. Cr cds: A, C, D, DS, MC, V.

D ≋ ⨯ ⊠ ⚲ SC

Motor Hotel

★★ **HOLIDAY INN-LAKEWOOD.** *7390 W Hampden Ave (80227), near jct Hampden Ave (US 285) & Wadsworth Blvd (CO 121). 303/980-9200; FAX 303/980-6423.* 190 rms, 6 story. S, D $79-$89; each addl $10; suites $125; under 19 free; wkend rates. Crib free. TV; cable (premium), VCR avail. Heated pool. Complimentary coffee in rms. Restaurant 6 am-2 pm, 5-10 pm. Rm serv. Bar 4 pm-midnight. Ck-out noon. Coin lndry. Meeting rms. Business servs avail. In-rm modem link. Bellhops. Valet serv. Gift shop. Exercise equipt; weight machine, bicycles, whirlpool, sauna. Some refrigerators. Cr cds: A, C, D, DS, ER, JCB, MC, V.

D ≋ ⨯ ⊠ ⚲ SC

Hotels

★ **DOUBLETREE.** *137 Union Blvd (80228). 303/969-9900; FAX 303/989-9847.* 170 rms, 6 story. S, D $54-$130; each addl $5-$10; under 18 free; wkend rates. Crib free. Pet accepted, some restrictions; $10. TV; cable (premium), VCR avail. Heated pool. Complimentary coffee in rms. Restaurant 6-9 am, 5-10 pm. Bar. Ck-out noon. Meeting rms. Business servs avail. No bellhops. Denver airport transportation.

Exercise equipt; bicycle, stair machine, whirlpool, sauna. Health club privileges. Some refrigerators. Cr cds: A, C, D, DS, ER, JCB, MC, V.

D ♥ ≋ ⨯ ⊠ ⚲ SC

★★★ **SHERATON DENVER WEST.** *360 Union Blvd (80228), at Simms St, near Denver Federal Center. 303/987-2000; FAX 303/969-0263.* 242 rms, 12 story. S, D $115-$145; each addl $10; under 18 free; honeymoon package; wkend rates. Crib free. Pet accepted; some restrictions, $50 deposit. TV; cable (premium). Indoor pool; hot tub. Coffee in rms. Restaurant 6:30 am-9:30 pm. Bar 11-2 am, Sun to midnight. Ck-out 1 pm. Convention facilities. Business center. In-rm modem link. Concierge. Valet serv. Gift shop. Barber, beauty shop. Exercise rm; instructor, weight machine, bicycles, whirlpool, steam rm, sauna. Massage therapy. Some refrigerators, bathrm phones. Luxury level. Cr cds: A, C, D, DS, JCB, MC, V.

D ♥ ≋ ⨯ ⊰ ⊠ ⚲ SC ♿

Restaurants

★★ **THE FORT.** *(19192 CO 8, Morrison) 5 mi W on CO 8. 303/697-4771.* Hrs: 5:30-10 pm; Sat from 5 pm; Sun 4-9 pm. Closed Dec 24 & 25. Res accepted. Bar. Semi-a la carte: dinner $13.95-$29.95. Child's meals. Specializes in Southwestern cuisine, game. Outdoor dining. Multiple dining areas in adobe building patterned after Bent's Fort. Southwestern artifacts; kiva fireplaces. View of Denver. Cr cds: A, C, D, DS, JCB, MC, V.

D

★ **SIMMS LANDING.** *11911 W 6th Ave, at Simms St. 303/237-0465.* Hrs: 11 am-10 pm; Fri to 11 pm; Sat 10 am-11 pm; Sun brunch 8 am-2:30 pm. Closed Dec 25. Bar to midnight. Semi-a la carte: lunch $4.95-$8.95; dinner $8.95-$17.95. Buffet: lunch $7.95, Sun brunch $12.95. Child's meals. Specializes in prime rib, steak, fresh seafood. Entertainment Wed-Sat. Valet parking. Outdoor dining. Panoramic view of Denver; nautical setting. Cr cds: A, C, D, DS, MC, V.

D

Unrated Dining Spot

CASA BONITA OF DENVER. *6715 W Colfax Ave. 970/232-5115.* Hrs: 11 am-9:30 pm; Fri, Sat to 10 pm. Closed Thanksgiving, Dec 25. Mexican, Amer menu. Serv bar. Semi-a la carte, cafeteria-style: lunch, dinner $5.49-$8.49. Entertainment: musicians, divers, gunfights, magician, puppet show, dancing monkeys in costume. Parking. Carnival atmosphere, Mexican decor; 30-ft waterfall. Cr cds: A, MC, V.

Lamar (E-8)

Pop 8,343 **Elev** 3,622 ft **Area code** 719 **Zip** 81052
Information Chamber of Commerce, 109 E Beech St; 719/336-4379.

What to See and Do

Big Timbers Museum. Named for the giant cottonwoods on the banks of the Arkansas River. Museum with newspapers, art, drawings, artifacts of area history. (Daily, afternoons; closed Jan 1, Good Friday, Thanksgiving, Dec 25) 7517 US 50. Phone 719/336-2472. **Free.**

Motels

★★★ **BEST WESTERN COW PALACE INN.** *1301 N Main St. 719/336-7753; FAX 719/336-9598.* 102 rms, 2 story. June-Aug: S $65-$75; D $70-$80; each addl $5; lower rates rest of yr. Crib $10. Pet accepted. TV; cable (premium), VCR avail. Indoor pool; poolside serv, hot tub. Coffee & tea in rms. Restaurant 5 am-10 pm. Rm serv. Bar 11-2 am, Sun to midnight. Ck-out 11 am. Meeting rms. Business servs avail. Gift shop. Barber, beauty shop. Free airport, RR station, bus depot transportation. Golf privileges, greens fee $3, driving range. Balconies. Enclosed courtyard; tropical gardens. Cr cds: A, C, D, DS, MC, V.

✔ ★ **BLUE SPRUCE.** *1801 S Main St, 1 mi S on US 287, 385.* *719/336-7454; FAX 719/336-4729.* 29 rms. S $28-$32; D $34-$38; each addl $4. Crib $1. TV; cable (premium). Pool. Restaurant nearby. Ck-out 11 am. In-rm modem link. Free airport, RR station, bus depot transportation. Some refrigerators. Cr cds: A, C, D, DS, MC, V.

Leadville (C-4)

(See Buena Vista, Dillon, Vail)

Settled 1860 **Pop** 2,629 **Elev** 10,152 ft **Area code** 719 **Zip** 80461

Information Greater Leadville Area Chamber of Commerce, 809 Harrison Ave, PO Box 861; 719/486-3900 or 800/933-3901.

Located just below the timberline, Leadville's high altitude contributes to its reputation for excellent skiing, cool summers and beautiful fall colors. First a rich gold camp, then an even richer silver camp, the town boasts a lusty, brawling past in which millionaires were made and destroyed in a single day; a barrel of whiskey could net $1,500; tents pitched on Main Street were advertised as "the best hotel in town"; and thousands of dollars could be and were lost on the turn of a card in the town's iniquitous saloons and smoky gambling halls.

Leadville's lively history is intertwined with the lives of Horace Tabor and his two wives, Augusta and Elizabeth Doe, whose rags-to-riches-to-rags story is the basis of the American opera *The Ballad of Baby Doe*. The famed "unsinkable" Molly Brown made her fortune here, as did David May, Charles Boettcher, Charles Dow and Meyer Guggenheim.

Until 1950, Leadville was a decaying mining town. However, a burst of civic enthusiasm rejuvenated it in the following years. With new schools, a hospital, medical clinic and recreational facilities, Leadville again began to grow. Victorian architecture in the downtown area has been preserved.

A Ranger District office of the San Isabel National Forest (see PUEBLO) is located in Leadville.

What to See and Do

Healy House-Dexter Cabin. The restored Healy House, built in 1878, contains many fine Victorian-era furnishings. Dexter Cabin, built by early mining millionaire James V. Dexter, appears on the outside to be an ordinary two-room miner's cabin; built as a place to entertain wealthy gentlemen, the cabin's interior is surprisingly luxurious. (Memorial Day-Labor Day, daily) Sr citizen rate. 912 Harrison Ave. Phone 719/486-0487. ¢¢

Heritage Museum and Gallery. Diorama and displays depict local history; scale model replica of Ice Palace, Victorian costumes, memorabilia of mining days. Changing exhibits of American art. (Memorial Day-Sept, daily) Sr citizen rate. 9th St & Harrison Ave. Phone 719/486-1878. ¢¢

Leadville National Fish Hatchery. The original building of hatchery constructed in 1889 is still in use. Approx 45 tons of rainbow, lake, brown and cutthroat trout are produced here annually. Hiking and ski-touring trails are nearby. (Daily) 7 mi SW via US 24, 2844 CO 300. Phone 719/486-0189. **Free.**

Leadville, Colorado & Southern Railroad Train Tour. Departs from old depot at 326 E 7th St for 23-mile round trip scenic ride following the headwaters of the Arkansas River through the Rocky Mountains. Res-

ervations recommended. (Memorial Day-Oct, daily) Phone 719/486-3936. ¢¢¢¢

National Mining Hall of Fame and Museum. History and technology exhibits of the mining industry. Hall of Fame dedicated to those who have made significant contributions to the industry. (May-Oct, daily; rest of yr, Mon-Fri; closed major hols) 120 W 9th St. Phone 719/486-1229. ¢¢

Sightseeing. Historic tour of Leadville aboard a horse-drawn surrey. Departs from Chamber of Commerce. (June-Labor Day, daily) ¢¢

Ski Cooper. Triple, double chairlifts; Pomalift, T-bar; patrol, school, rentals; snowcat tours; cafeteria; nursery. 26 runs; longest run 1½ mi; vertical drop 1,200 ft. (Late Nov-early Apr, daily) Groomed cross-country skiing (15 mi). Summit of Tennessee Pass, 10 mi N on US 24. Phone 719/486-3684. ¢¢¢¢¢

⭐ **Tabor Opera House** (1879). Now a museum, this theater was elegantly furnished at the time of construction. At the time Leadville had a population of 30,000. The theater was host to the Metropolitan Opera, the Chicago Symphony and most of the famous actors and actresses of the period. Their pictures line the corridors. Many of the original furnishings, much of the scenery and the dressing areas are still in use and on display. The Tabor box, where many dignitaries were Tabor's guests, is part of the theater tour. Summer shows (inquire locally). Self-guided tours (Memorial Day-Sept, daily exc Sat). 308 Harrison Ave. Phone 719/486-1147. ¢¢

The Matchless Mine. When H.A.W. Tabor died in 1899, his last words to his wife, Baby Doe, were "Hold on to the Matchless," which had produced as much as $100,000 a month in its bonanza days. Faithful to his wish and ever hopeful, the once fabulously rich Baby Doe lived on in poverty in the little cabin next to the mine for 36 years; in it, she was found frozen to death in 1935. The cabin is now a museum. (June-Labor Day, daily) 2 mi E on E 7th St. Phone 719/486-0371. ¢

Annual Events

Boom Days & Burro Race. 1st full wkend Aug.

Victorian Christmas & Home Tour. First Sat Dec.

Seasonal Event

Oro City: Rebirth of a Miners' Camp. Re-created 1860s tent city featuring gold panning, gunsmithing, dancing, beer making; entertainment; storytelling. Phone 719/486-2015 or -3900. First 2 wkends July.

Motels

★ ★ **DELAWARE HOTEL.** *700 Harrison Ave. 719/486-1418; res: 800/748-2004; FAX 719/486-2214.* 36 air-cooled rms, 32 with shower only, 3 story, 4 suites. No elvtr. No rm phones. S $60-$70; D $65-$75; each addl $5; suites $90-$100; ski plan. Crib $10. TV. Complimentary full bkfst. Restaurant 7 am-2 pm, 5-9 pm. Bar; dancing Fri & Sat. Ck-out 11 am. Meeting rms. Whirlpool. Historic hotel (1886); Victorian lobby. Cr cds: A, C, D, DS, MC, V.

★ **LEADVILLE INN.** *25 Jacktown Pl, ¼ mi S on US 24. 719/486-3637.* 56 rms, 3 story. No A/C. No elvtr. S $40; D $50. Pet accepted; $20 refundable. TV; cable (premium). Coffee in lobby. Ck-out 11 am. Sauna. Game rm. Cr cds: A, C, D, DS, MC, V.

Inns

✔ ★ ★ **APPLEBLOSSOM.** *120 W 4th St. 719/486-2141; res: 800/982-9279.* 6 air-cooled rms, 4 share bath, 2 story. No rm phones. S $49-$79; D $59-$79; each addl $8-$15; higher rates hols (3-night min). Complimentary full bkfst. Restaurant opp 7 am-3 pm, 5-9 pm. Ck-out 11 am, ck-in 4-8 pm. Bellhop. Downhill ski 8 mi; x-country ski 1 mi. Health club privileges. Sitting rm. Built 1879; many antiques. Totally nonsmoking. Cr cds: A, MC, V.

★ ★ **LEADVILLE COUNTRY INN.** *PO Box 1989, 127 E 8th St. 719/486-2354; res: 800/748-2354.* 9 air-cooled rms, 2 story. Some rm phones. S $52-$102; D $67-$127; each addl $15. Children over 7 yrs only. TV in some rms. Complimentary full bkfst, coffee & tea. Restaurant nearby. Ck-out 11 am, ck-in 4-6 pm. Downhill/x-country ski 10 mi. Hot tub. Built 1892; furnished with antiques. Totally nonsmoking. Cr cds: A, D, DS, MC, V.

✔ ★ ★ **WOOD HAVEN MANOR.** *807 Spruce St. 719/486-0109; res: 800/748-2570.* 8 air-cooled rms (7 with bath), 3 story. Some rm phones. S $49-$85; D $59-$95; each addl $10. Children over 3 yrs only. TV in sitting rm. Complimentary full bkfst, coffee. Restaurant nearby. Ck-out 11 am, ck-in 4 pm. Downhill/x-country ski 15 mi. Built 1895; antiques. Totally nonsmoking. Cr cds: A, DS, MC, V.

Restaurants

✔ ★ **HI COUNTRY.** *115 Harrison Ave. 719/486-3992.* Hrs: 7 am-10 pm; off season 11 am-9 pm. Closed some major hols. Semi-a la carte: bkfst $3.50-$5.50, lunch $3.50-$6, dinner $4.50-$10.50. Child's meals. Specializes in prime rib. Parking. Three dining areas. Mounted wildlife. No cr cds accepted.

✔ ★ **LEADVILLE DINER.** *115 W 4th St. 719/486-3812.* Hrs: 6:30-9:30 pm. Closed Thanksgiving, Dec 25. Wine, beer. Semi-a la carte: bkfst $2.50-$6.50, lunch $3-$7, dinner $6-$13. Parking. Cr cds: MC, V.

★ **PROSPECTOR.** *2798 CO 91, 3 mi N on CO 91. 719/486-3955.* Hrs: 10 am-3 pm, 5-9 pm. Sun brunch 11 am- 3 pm. Closed Mon; Easter, Memorial Day, Dec 25; also Apr-mid-May & mid-Oct-mid-Nov. Res accepted. Bar. Semi-a la carte: lunch $5.95-$12.50, dinner $12.50-$24.95. Sun brunch $13.95. Child's meals. Specializes in steak, seafood. Salad bar. Parking. Old pictures of Wild West outlaws. Cr cds: MC, V.

Limon (C-7)

Pop 1,831 **Elev** 5,365 ft **Area code** 719 **Zip** 80828

Motels

★ **PREFERRED MOTOR INN.** *158 E Main St. 719/775-2385.* 42 rms. S $34-$48; D $46-$62; each addl $4; suites $75-$100. Crib $4. TV; cable (premium). Indoor pool; whirlpools, hot tub. Restaurant nearby. Ck-out 10 am. Meeting rms. In-rm modem link. Free airport, bus depot transportation. Game rm. some in-rm steam baths. Balconies. Cr cds: A, D, DS, MC, V.

✔ ★ **SAFARI.** *637 Main St. 719/775-2363.* 28 rms, 1-2 story. June-Sept: S $40-$42; D $48; each addl $4; suites $52; lower rates rest of yr. Pet accepted. TV; cable (premium). Pool. Playground. Complimentary coffee in rms. Restaurant opp. Ck-out 10 am. Coin lndry. In-rm modem link. Private patios. Cr cds: A, D, DS, MC, V.

★ **SILVER SPUR.** *514 Main St. 719/775-2807; FAX 719/775-9071.* 25 rms. Memorial Day-Labor Day: S $39-$43; D $47; each addl $4; lower rates rest of yr. Pet accepted; $5. TV; cable

(premium), VCR avail. Complimentary coffee in lobby. Restaurant opp 6 am-2 pm, 5-7:30 pm. Ck-out 10 am. Cr cds: A, DS, MC, V.

Inn

★ ★ **MIDWEST COUNTRY INN.** *Box 550, 795 Main, on US 24, 40. 719/775-2373.* 32 rms, 2 story. June-Aug: S $34-$36; D $38-$42; each addl $4; suites $50; lower rates rest of yr. TV; cable. Coffee in lobby. Restaurant nearby. Ck-out 10 am, ck-in 2 pm. Gift shop. Garden. Cr cds: A, C, D, DS, MC, V.

Restaurant

✔ ★ **FIRESIDE JUNCTION.** *2295 9th St, US 24 & I-70, exit 359. 719/775-2396.* Hrs: 6 am-10 pm. Closed Dec 24-25. Res accepted. Mexican, Amer menu. Serv bar. Semi-a la carte: bkfst $3.69-$6.30, lunch $5-$7, dinner $5.50-$13.99. Child's meals. Specializes in chicken fried steak. Salad bar. Parking. Cr cds: A, DS, MC, V.

Longmont (B-5)

(See Boulder, Denver, Loveland, Lyons)

Founded 1870 **Pop** 51,555 **Elev** 4,979 ft **Area code** 303
Information Chamber of Commerce, 528 N Main St, 80501; 303/776-5295.

What to See and Do

Longmont Museum. Changing and special exhibits on art, history, space and science; permanent exhibits on the history of Longmont and the St Vrain Valley. (Daily exc Sun; closed hols) 375 Kimbark St. Phone 303/651-8374. **Free.**

Annual Event

Boulder County Fair and Rodeo. Fairgrounds. 9 days early Aug.

Motor Hotel

★ ★ **RAINTREE PLAZA.** *1900 Ken Pratt Blvd (80501). 303/776-2000; res: 800/843-8240; FAX 303/776-2000.* 210 rms, 2 story. S $91; D $101; each addl $10; suites $130-$185; under 18 free. Crib free. Pet accepted. TV; cable. Heated pool. Complimentary bkfst buffet. Coffee in rms. Restaurant 6 am-2 pm, 5 pm-midnight; Sat 6-10 am, 5-10 pm; Sun 6 am-3 pm, 5-10 pm. Rm serv. Bar. Ck-out noon. Free lndry facilities. Meeting rms. Bellhops. Valet serv. Airport transportation. Exercise equipt; weight machine, bicycles, whirlpool, sauna. Wet bars, refrigerators. Cr cds: A, C, D, MC, V.

Loveland (B-5)

(See Estes Park, Fort Collins, Greeley, Longmont, Lyons)

Founded 1877 **Pop** 37,352 **Elev** 4,982 ft **Area code** 970
Information Chamber of Commerce, Jct US 34 & I-25, 80537; 970/667-6311.

In recent years more than 300,000 valentines have been remailed annually by the Loveland post office, stamped in red with the "Sweetheart Town's" cachet, a different valentine verse each year.

What to See and Do

Boyd Lake State Park. Swimming, waterskiing; fishing; boating (ramps, rentals). Picnicking (shelters, showers). Camping (dump station). Standard fees. (Daily) 1 mi E on US 34, then 2 mi N. Phone 970/663-2797. Per vehicle ¢

Annual Event

Larimer County Fair and Rodeo. Mid-Aug.

Seasonal Event

Dog racing. Cloverleaf Kennel Club. 4 mi E at jct US 34, I-25. Races nightly. Matinees Mon, Wed, Sat & Sun. Parimutuel betting. No minors. Phone 970/667-6211. Mar-June.

Inn

★ ★ **LOVELANDER.** *217 W 4th St (80537). 970/669-0798; res: 800/459-6694; FAX 970/669-0797.* 11 rms, 2 story. Rm phones avail. S $69-$115; D $79-$125; each addl $20. Children over 10 yrs only. TV in sitting rm. Pool. Complimentary full bkfst, coffee & tea/sherry. Restaurants nearby. Ck-out 11 am, ck-in 3 pm. Business servs avail. Concierge. Street parking. Airport transportation. Some balconies. Picnic tables. Built 1902; antiques, sitting room with fireplace. Totally nonsmoking. Cr cds: A, DS, MC, V.

Guest Ranch

★ ★ ★ **SYLVAN DALE GUEST RANCH.** *2939 N County Rd 31D (80538), 7 mi W on US 34. 970/667-3915; FAX 970/635-9336.* 9 cabins (1-3-bedrm units), "wagon wheel barn," 1-2 story. No A/C. Mid-June-early Sept, 6 days: $725/person; family rates; lower rates rest of yr. Crib free. Pool. Playground. Free supervised child's activities (mid-June-Labor Day). Dining rm (public by res). Box lunches, cookouts, bkfst rides, overnight pack trips. Ck-out 11 am, ck-in 3 pm. Grocery ¼ mi. Meeting rms. Business servs avail. Free local airport, bus depot transportation. Tennis. Lawn games. Rec rm. Entertainment, square dancing. Trout-stocked lake. Some fireplaces. Working ranch on 3,000 acres bordered by Roosevelt National Forest. Totally nonsmoking. No cr cds accepted.

Restaurants

✔ ★ **THE BORDER.** *281-A E 29th St (80538). 970/663-1550.* Hrs: 11 am-11 pm. Closed Dec 25. Res accepted. Mexican, Amer menu. Bar. Semi-a la carte: lunch, dinner $3.75-$14.95. Child's meals. Specialities: chicken enchiladas, tacos al carbon. Parking. Outdoor dining. 5 dining areas. Hand-painted Mexican scenes on walls. Cr cds: A, DS, MC, V.

★ ★ **SUMMIT.** *3208 W Eisenhower, 7 mi W of I-25, 2½ mi W of Lake Loveland on US 34. 970/669-6648.* Hrs: 11:30 am-2 pm, 4:30-9:30 pm; Mon from 4:30 pm, Fri, Sat to 10:30 pm; Sun brunch 10 am-2 pm; Easter & Mother's Day 9 am-10 pm. Closed Dec 25. Res accepted. Bar 4 pm-midnight. Semi-a la carte: lunch, dinner $8.95-$14.95. Child's meals. Specializes in prime rib, steak, seafood. Salad bar. Parking. Outdoor dining. Mountain view. Cr cds: A, D, MC, V.

Lyons (B-5)

(See Boulder, Estes Park, Longmont, Loveland)

Pop 1,227 **Elev** 5,360 ft **Area code** 303 **Zip** 80540
Information Chamber of Commerce, PO Box 426; 303/823-5215, Town Hall. The Visitors Center at 4th & Broadway is staffed Memorial Day-Labor Day, daily; 303/823-6640.

Annual Event

Good Old Days Celebration. Midway, parade, flea market, craft fair, food. Phone 303/823-6692. Last wkend June.

Guest Ranch

★ ★ **PEACEFUL VALLEY LODGE & GUEST RANCH.** *475 Peaceful Valley Rd, 18 mi SW on CO 72 via CO 7. 303/747-2881; FAX 303/747-2167.* 45 rms in 3 lodges, 6 share baths; 10 cabins. No A/C. Many rm phones. AP, Memorial Day-Labor Day: S $1,190-$1,447; D $1,100-$1,355/person/week; family rates; lower rates rest of yr. TV in lounge. Indoor pool; wading pool, whirlpool, sauna. Playground. Supervised child's activities (Memorial Day-Labor Day); ages 3-18. Dining rm (public by res) 8-9 am, 1 pm, 6:30 pm. Box lunches, picnics, barbecues. Serv bar. Ck-out 10 am, ck-in 2-4 pm. Coin lndry. Business center. Gift shop. Denver airport, RR station, bus depot transportation. Tennis. X-country ski ½ mi. Backcountry tours; overnight pack trips. Soc dir; entertainment, square dancing (summer), campfires. Llama trekking. Sleigh rides. Rec rm. Varied social program. Some fireplaces. Beautiful mountain setting on 300 acres. Cr cds: A, C, D, DS, MC, V.

Restaurants

★ **ANDREA'S.** *216 E Main St. 303/823-5000.* Hrs: 8 am-9 pm. Closed Wed; Dec 25. Res accepted. German menu. Bar. Semi-a la carte: bkfst $2.95-$7.95, lunch $3.95-$11.95, dinner $6.95-$18.95. Specialities: pepper steak, sauerbraten. Bavarian folk music Fri & Sat. Parking. Bavarian decor. Cr cds: A, DS, MC, V.

★ ★ **BLACK BEAR INN.** *42 E Main St, ½ mi E on US 36. 970/823-6812.* Hrs: 11 am-2:30 pm, 5:30-10 pm; Sat from 5:30 pm, Sun noon-9 pm. Closed Mon & Tues; also Jan-mid-Feb. Res accepted; required wkends. Continental menu. Bar. Wine list. Semi-a la carte: lunch $6.25-$11.75, dinner $11-$24. Specializes in veal, châteaubriand, fresh seafood. Own apple strudel. Parking. Patio dining. Swiss, Bavarian decor; fireplace; many European antiques. Cr cds: A, C, D, DS, MC, V.

★ ★ **LA CHAUMIERE.** *12311 N St Vrain Drive. 303/823-6521.* Hrs: 5:30-10 pm; Sun 2-9 pm. Closed Mon. Res accepted. Continental menu. Serv bar. A la carte entrees: dinner $11.50-$17.50. Child's meals. Specializes in sweetbreads, seafood. Own ice cream. Parking. Fireplace. View of mountains. Cr cds: A, MC, V.

Manitou Springs (D-6)

(See Colorado Springs)

Founded 1872 **Pop** 4,535 **Elev** 6,320 ft **Area code** 719 **Zip** 80829
Information Chamber of Commerce, 354 Manitou Ave; 719/685-5089 or 800/642-2567.

Manitou Springs' many mineral springs, familiar to the Native Americans, gave nearby Colorado Springs its name. The natives, attributing supernatural powers to the waters (Manitou is a Native American word for "Great Spirit"), once marked off the surrounding area as a sanctuary. The town today is a popular tourist resort.

What to See and Do

Cave of the Winds. Fascinating 45-minute guided tour through underground passageways filled with beautiful stalactites, stalagmites and flowstone formations created millions of years ago. Tours leave every 15 min (daily). Light jacket and comfortable shoes recommended. Laser light show in canyon is 15 stories high and is accompanied by music (May-Sept, evenings). (May-Sept, daily) From Manitou Ave & US 24, go 6 mi W on US 24 to Cave of the Winds Rd; turn right and continue 1/2 mi to visitors center. Phone 719/685-5444. Cave tour ¢¢¢; Laser show ¢¢

Iron Springs Chateau. Melodrama dinner theater featuring a traditional "olio" show. Named for the mineral-rich water beneath the ground. (Daily exc Sun) 444 Ruxton Ave. Phone 719/685-5104. ¢¢¢¢¢

Manitou Cliff Dwellings Museum. Outdoor southwestern Native American preserve; architecture of the cliff-dwelling natives, ca A.D. 1100-1300. Native American dancing (June-Aug). Museum (Mar-Nov, daily). W on US 24. Phone 719/685-5242. ¢¢

Miramont Castle Museum (ca 1895). A 28-room, 4-story Victorian house featuring nine styles of architecture, miniatures and doll collection, railroad museum, tea room, soda fountain, gardens. (Daily; closed Easter, Thanksgiving, Dec 25) 9 Capitol Hill Ave. Phone 719/685-1011. ¢¢

Motels

✔★**RED WING.** 56 El Paso Blvd. 719/685-5656; res: 800/733-9547. 27 rms, 2 story, 11 kits. S $34-$49; D $36-$59; kit. units $10 addl. Crib free. TV; cable. Heated pool. Playground. Complimentary coffee in rms. Restaurant nearby. Ck-out 10 am. Refrigerators. Cr cds: A, C, D, DS, MC, V.

🏊 🚫 🔥 SC

★**SILVER SADDLE.** 215 Manitou Ave. 719/685-5611. 54 rms, 1-2 story. Mid-May-mid-Sept: S $69.50; D $74.50-$79.50; under 18 free; each addl $6; suites $104.50-$109.50; varied lower rates rest of yr. Crib free. TV; cable (premium), VCR avail. Pool; whirlpool. Complimentary coffee. Restaurant nearby. Ck-out 10:30 am. Some in-rm whirlpools. Cr cds: A, C, D, DS, MC, V.

🏊 🚫 🔥 SC

★**VILLA.** 481 Manitou Ave. 719/685-5492; res: 800/341-8000. 47 rms, 2 story, 7 kits. Memorial Day-Labor Day: S $72; D $72-$77; kits. $86-$90; lower rates rest of yr. Crib free. TV; cable (premium). Heated pool; whirlpool. Complimentary coffee in lobby. Restaurant opp 7 am-10 pm. Ck-out 11 am. Coin lndry. Business servs avail. Picnic tables. Cr cds: A, C, D, DS, MC, V.

🏊 🚫 🔥

Inns

★★**EASTHOLME IN THE ROCKIES.** (4445 Haggerman, Cascade 80809) 5 mi N on US 24. 719/684-9901. 6 rms (4 with shower only), 2 share bath, 3 story. No A/C. No rm phones. S $49; each addl $8. Children over 9 yrs only. Complimentary full bkfst. Restaurant nearby. Ck-out 11 am, ck-in 3 pm. Originally a hotel built in 1885; many antiques. Totally nonsmoking. No cr cds accepted.

🚫

★★**ONALEDGE.** 336 El Paso Blvd. 719/685-4265; res: 800/530-8253. 5 rms, 3 story, 2 suites. No rm phones. May-Oct: S, D $80-$130; each addl $10; suites $120-$130; lower rates rest of yr.

Children over 12 yrs only. TV; cable (premium), VCR avail. Complimentary full bkfst. Complimentary coffee, tea, sherry in sitting rm. Restaurant adj 5-10 pm. Ck-out 11 am, ck-in 4-10 pm. Free airport transportation. English Tudor home built in 1912; beautiful views of Pikes Peak. Totally nonsmoking. Cr cds: A, DS, MC, V.

🚫 SC

★★**RED CRAGS.** 302 El Paso Blvd. 719/685-1920; res: 800/721-2248. 7 air-cooled rms, 4 story. No rm phones. S, D $75-$150; each addl $20. Children over 10 yrs only. Complimentary full bkfst, coffee, tea & wine. Restaurant nearby. Ck-out 11 am, ck-in 4-6 pm. Mansion (1870) originally built as a hospital. On bluff with view of Pikes Peak, Garden of Gods. Antiques, fireplaces. Totally nonsmoking. Cr cds: A, DS, MC, V.

🚫 🔥

Restaurants

★★★**BRIARHURST MANOR.** 404 Manitou Ave. 719/685-1864. Hrs: 6 pm-midnight; Sun (summer only) 11 am-7 pm (brunch). Res accepted. Continental menu. Bar. Wine cellar. Semi-a la carte: dinner $10.50-$29.95; Wed night buffet $16.95. Complete meals: dinner $17. Sun brunch $12.50. Child's meals. Specialties: Rocky Mountain rainbow trout, châteaubriand, rack of lamb. Own baking. Parking. Outdoor dining. Homegrown fresh vegetables & herbs. Tudor manor (1876); originally residence of founder of Manitou Springs. Cr cds: A, D, MC, V.

D SC

★★★**CRAFTWOOD INN.** 404 El Paso Blvd. 719/685-9000. Hrs: 5-10 pm. Closed Jan 1, Dec 25. Res accepted. Bar. Wine cellar. Semi-a la carte: dinner $10-$25. Specializes in Colorado cuisine, wild game, seafood. Parking. Outdoor dining. Built in 1912 on 1 1/2 acres of landscaped gardens; view of Pikes Peak. Casual country setting. Totally nonsmoking. Cr cds: DS, MC, V.

D

✔★★**MISSION BELL INN.** 178 Crystal Park Rd, 1 3/4 mi S of US 24 Business. 719/685-9089. Hrs: 5-9:30 pm. Closed Jan 1, Thanksgiving, Dec 25; also Mon from Oct-May. Res accepted. Mexican menu. Serv bar. Semi-a la carte: dinner $7.50-$10. Specializes in stuffed pepper, stuffed sopapilla, fried ice cream. Parking. Outdoor dining. Cr cds: MC, V.

★★**STAGE COACH.** 702 Manitou Ave. 719/685-9400. Hrs: 11:30 am-3 pm, 4:30-9:30 pm. Closed Mon; Jan 1, Dec 25. Res accepted. Bar. Semi-a la carte: lunch $4.50-$8.95, dinner $7.95-$19.95. Child's meals. Specializes in prime rib, buffalo steak. Parking. Outdoor dining. Rustic log structure built 1881. Fireplace. Cr cds: MC, V.

D

Mesa Verde National Park (F-1 - F-2)

(See Cortez, Durango)

Elev 6,929 ft at park headquarters

Information Superintendent, PO Box 8, 81330; phone 970/529-4465 or 719/529-4475.

(8 mi E of Cortez, 36 mi W of Durango, on US 160 to park entrance, then 15 mi S to Visitor Center)

Mesa Verde, Spanish for "green table," is a large plateau towering 1,500 to 2,000 feet above the surrounding valleys. The home of farming Pueblo Indians for more than eight centuries, it is famous for well-preserved, pre-Columbian cliff dwellings in the shallow alcoves of its many canyon walls.

Public campgrounds, including trailer sites (15 hookups), 4 miles from park entrance, are open in nonfreezing weather (May-Oct; fee). Speed limit within park is 35 mph or as posted. The park is open year-round. Golden Eagle Passport accepted (see INTRODUCTION). Per vehicle (wkly) ¢¢

Because of the fragile nature of the cliff dwellings, one regulation is rigidly enforced: the cliff dwellings are entered *only* while rangers are on duty (year-round, weather permitting).

What to See and Do

Campfire program. Short talks by rangers on Pueblo Indians and natural history of area. (Memorial Day-Labor Day, nightly, weather permitting)

✪ **Far View Visitor Center.** All visitors are recommended to stop at center first. (May-Sept, daily) 15 mi S of park entrance.

Museum. Exhibits tell story of Mesa Verde people: their arts, crafts, industries. (Daily) Park headquarters, 21 mi S of park entrance.   **Free.**

Park Point Fire Lookout (elevation, 8,572 ft). Spectacular views of entire Four Corners area of Colorado, Arizona, New Mexico and Utah. Access road closed in winter. Halfway between park entrance and headquarters.

Picnic areas. One at headquarters and one on each loop of Ruins Rd.

Ruins Road Drive. Two 6-mile, self-guided loops afford visits to 10 excavated mesa-top ruins illustrating 700 years of architectural development; views of 20 to 30 cliff dwellings from canyon rim vantage points. (Daily; closed during heavy snowfalls) Enter at crossroads near museum.

Ruins trips. The cliff dwellings are entered *only* while rangers are on duty. During the summer, five cliff dwellings may be visited at specific hours; during the winter there are trips to Spruce Tree House only, weather permitting. Obtain daily schedule sheet and tickets for Cliff Palace and Balcony House tours at Far View Visitor Center in summer, entrance station or museum in winter. Balcony House tours are limited to 50 persons; Cliff Palace tours are limited to the first 60. The cliff dwellings that are open to the public are

Spruce Tree House. Best preserved in Mesa Verde; contains 114 living rooms and 8 ceremonial rooms, called kivas. Self-guided to site in summer; ranger-guided rest of yr. In canyon behind museum.

Cliff Palace. First major dwelling to be discovered (1888). More than 200 living rooms, 23 kivas, numerous storage rooms. Guided tours in summer, fall and spring; closed winter. On the Ruins Rd, 20-minute drive from Visitor Center.   ¢

Balcony House. Noted for ladder and tunnel features; accessible only by 32-foot-long ladder. Ranger-guided mid-Oct. On Ruins Rd, 25-minute drive from Visitor Center.   ¢

Long and Step Houses and Badger House Community. Ranger-conducted (Long) and self-guided (Step) trips (Memorial Day-Labor Day); inquire at Visitor Center or museum for details. On Wetherill Mesa, 12 mi from Visitor Center.

Motel

★ ★ **FAR VIEW LODGE.** *(Box 277, Mancos 81328) At Navajo Hill, in park 15 mi from entrance (check here for rms available).* 970/529-4421. 150 rms, 1-2 levels. No A/C. No rm phones. Late Apr-late Oct: D $73-$89; each addl $6; under 13 free. Closed rest of yr. Crib $4. Pet accepted, some restrictions. Restaurant 6:30 am-9 pm; dining rm 5-9:30 pm. Bar 4-11 pm. Ck-out 11 am. Coin lndry. Gift shop. Private balconies. Picnic tables. Hiking trails. Mesa Verde tours avail. Educational programs. Magnificent view of canyon, Shiprock. Camping sites, trailer facilities. Park concession. General store, take-out serv, coin showers. Cr cds: A, D, DS, MC, V.

D 🐾 🎿 🐾

Monte Vista (E-4)

(See Alamosa)

Pop 4,324 **Elev** 7,663 ft **Area code** 719 **Zip** 81144
Information Chamber of Commerce, 1035 Park Ave; 719/852-2731.

Located in the heart of the high-altitude San Luis Valley, Monte Vista was named for the Spanish "mountain view."

What to See and Do

Historical Society Headquarters. In 1875 library; information about history of Monte Vista. (Apr-Dec, Mon-Fri afternoons) 110 Jefferson St. Phone 719/852-4396.   **Free.**

Monte Vista National Wildlife Refuge. Created as a nesting, migration, and wintering habitat for waterfowl and other migratory birds. Marked visitor tour road. 6 mi S via CO 15. Contact the Refuge Manager, 9383 El Rancho Lane, Alamosa 81101; 719/589-4021 (Mon-Fri).   **Free.**

Annual Events

Ski-Hi Stampede. Ski-Hi Park. Rodeo, carnival, arts & crafts show, street parade, barbecue, Western dances. Phone 719/852-2055. Last wkend July.

San Luis Valley Fair. Ski-Hi Park. Phone 719/589-2271. Mid-Aug.

Motels

★ ★ **BEST WESTERN MOVIE MANOR.** *2830 US 160, 3 mi W.* 719/852-5921; res: 800/771-9468; FAX 719/852-0122. 60 rms, 2 story. May-Labor Day: S $72-$76; D $76-$82; each addl $5; lower rates rest of yr. Pet accepted. TV; cable (premium), VCR avail. Playground. Restaurant 6 am-2 pm, 5-10 pm. Bar from 5 pm. Ck-out 11 am. Business servs avail. In-rm modem link. Exercise equipt; weight machines, bicycle. Drive-in movies visible from rms; speakers in most rm. Cr cds: A, C, D, DS, ER, MC, V.

D 🐾 ✈ 🛏 🐾 SC

★ ★ **COMFORT INN.** *1519 Grande Ave.* 719/852-0612. 43 rms, 2 story. May-mid-Oct: S $60-$65; D $75-$80; each addl $5; under 12 free; lower rates rest of yr. Crib free. Pet accepted. TV; cable (premium), VCR avail. Indoor pool; whirlpool. Complimentary continental bkfst. Restaurant nearby. Ck-out 11 am. Business servs avail. In-rm modem link. Cr cds: A, C, D, DS, ER, JCB, MC, V.

D 🐾 🏊 🛏 🐾 SC

✔ ★ ★ **MONTE VILLA INN.** *925 1st Ave.* 719/852-5166; res: 800/527-5168. 39 units, 3 story. S $40-$50; D $60; each addl $5; under 10 free; wkly rates; ski plan. Crib $5. TV; cable. Restaurant 6 am-10 pm; winter to 9 pm. Rm serv. Bar 4:30 pm-2 am. Ck-out 11 am. Cr cds: A, C, D, DS, MC, V.

🛏 🐾 SC

Montrose (D-2)

(See Delta, Ouray)

Founded 1882 **Pop** 8,854 **Elev** 5,806 ft **Area code** 970 **Zip** 81401
Information Chamber of Commerce, 1519 E Main St; 970/249-5515 or 800/873-0244.

Montrose is a trading center for a rich mining, agricultural and recreational area in the Uncompahgre Valley, irrigated by diversion of the waters of the Gunnison River to the Uncompahgre. It is headquarters for the operation and maintenance of all generating and transmission facilities of the Colorado River Storage Project stemming from the Power Operations Center. Several fishing areas are nearby including the Gunnison River east of town and Buckhorn Lakes southeast. A Ranger District office of the Uncompahgre National Forest (see NORWOOD) is located in Montrose.

What to See and Do

Black Canyon of the Gunnison National Monument (see). 12 mi NE via US 50, CO 347.

Montrose County Historical Museum. Collections of antique farm machinery; archaeological artifacts; pioneer cabin with family items; tool collection; early electrical equipment; Montrose newspapers 1896-1940. (May-Sept, daily) Main St & Rio Grande, in Depot Building. Phone 970/249-2085. ¢

Ridgway State Park. This 2,320-acre park includes four recreational areas and a reservoir. Swimming, waterskiing, scuba diving, sailing, sailboarding; boating (marina). Hiking, bicycling. Cross-country skiing, sledding. Picnicking, playground. Improved camping, laundry, concession. Standard fees. (Daily) 20 mi S on US 550. Phone 970/626-5822. Per vehicle ¢¢

Scenic Drive. Owl Creek Pass. Drive 23 miles south on US 550 to the left-hand turnoff for Owl Creek Pass, marked by a US Forest Service sign, then east 7 miles along Cow Creek to Debbie's Park. In this meadow, Debbie Reynolds was filmed in the wild west breakfast scene in *How The West Was Won.* The next 8 miles climb to the crest of Owl Creek Pass at 10,114 feet. Fifteen miles from the pass is **Silver Jack Reservoir**, an area with good fishing and scenic hiking trails. About 20 miles north, the road joins US 50 at Cimarron. The road is not recommended for large trucks or RVs and may be impassable in inclement weather.

Ute Indian Museum and Ouray Memorial Park. On home grounds of Chief Ouray and his wife, Chipeta. History of Utes in artifacts and objects of 19th- and early 20th-century Ute craftsmanship, clothing, dioramas, photographs. Self-guided tours. (May-Sept, daily) Sr citizen rate. 17253 Chipeta Dr, 3 mi S on US 550. Phone 970/249-3098. ¢

Motels

★ ★ ★ **BEST WESTERN RED ARROW MOTOR INN.** *Box 236, 1702 E Main.* 970/249-9641; FAX 970/249-8380. 60 rms, 2 story. July-Aug: S, D $99-$109; suites $109-$125; children free; varied lower rates rest of yr. Crib $8. TV; cable (premium), VCR avail. Heated pool; whirlpool. Playground. Complimentary coffee in rms. Restaurant 7 am-9 pm. Ck-out noon. Coin lndry. Meeting rms. Business servs avail. Free airport, bus depot transportation. Lawn games. Bathrm phones, refrigerators; some in-rm whirlpools. Many private patios, balconies. Cr cds: A, C, D, DS, MC, V.

D ⓧ ⓧ ⓧ SC

★ **BLACK CANYON.** *1605 E Main.* 970/249-3495. 49 rms, 1-2 story. May-Sept: S, D $45-$75; each addl $4; suites $95; under 13 free; lower rates rest of yr. Crib $4. Pet accepted, some restrictions. TV; cable (premium). Heated pool. Complimentary continental bkfst (winter). Complimentary coffee in lobby. Restaurant nearby. Ck-out 11 am. Meeting rms. Business servs avail. In-rm modem link. Cr cds: A, C, D, DS, MC, V.

D ⓧ ⓧ ⓧ ⓧ SC

★ ★ **COUNTRY LODGE.** *1624 E Main (US 50).* 970/249-4567. 22 rms. June-mid-Nov: S $56-$65; D $72-$88; each addl $5; kit. units $10 extra; lower rates rest of yr. Crib free. TV; cable. Heated pool. Playground. Complimentary coffee in lobby. Restaurant nearby. Ck-out 11 am. Some refrigerators. Cr cds: A, D, DS, MC, V.

D ⓧ ⓧ ⓧ

★ **SAN JUAN INN.** *1480 US 550 S.* 970/249-6644; FAX 970/249-9314. 50 rms, 2 story. June-mid-Nov: S $48-$53; D $56-$61;

each addl $5; under 13 free; lower rates rest of yr. Crib free. Pet accepted. TV; cable, VCR avail. Indoor pool; whirlpool. Complimentary coffee in lobby. Restaurant adj 6 am-10 pm. Ck-out 11 am. Free airport transportation. Cr cds: A, C, D, DS, MC, V.

 ⓧ ⓧ ⓧ

★ **TRAPPER.** *1225 E Main St.* 970/249-3426; res: 800/858-5911. 27 rms. Memorial Day-Labor Day: S $40-$45; D $50-$56; each addl $3; lower rates rest of yr. Crib $3. TV; cable (premium), VCR avail. Complimentary continental bkfst (winter). Complimentary coffee in lobby. Restaurant nearby. Ck-out 11 am. Cr cds: A, C, D, DS, MC, V.

 ⓧ

✔ ★ **WESTERN.** *1200 E Main St, 8 blks E on US 50, near Municipal Airport.* 970/249-3481; res: 800/445-7301. 28 rms, 1-2 story. June-Labor Day: S $38-$44; D $48-$58; each addl $4; suites $65-$90; lower rates rest of yr. Crib $4. TV; cable (premium), VCR avail. Heated pool. Complimentary coffee in lobby. Restaurant nearby. Ck-out 10 am. Sun deck. Cr cds: A, D, DS, MC, V.

ⓧ ⓧ ⓧ

Restaurants

★ ★ **GLENN EYRIE.** *2351 S US 550, 18 blks S on US 550.* 970/249-9263. Hrs: 5-9 pm; Res accepted. Serv bar. Semi-a la carte: dinner $8.50-$22. Child's meals. Specializes in fish, seafood, beef. Parking. Outdoor dining. Cr cds: A, C, D, DS, MC, V.

✔ ★ **THE WHOLE ENCHILADA.** *44 S Grand Ave, 3 blks W of Townsend Ave.* 970/249-1881. Hrs: 11 am-10 pm. Closed major hols. Res accepted. Bar to 10:30 pm. Semi-a la carte: lunch, dinner $3.95-$9.95. Specializes in Mexican dishes. Outdoor dining. Cr cds: A, DS, MC, V.

Norwood (E-2)

(For accommodations see Telluride)

Pop 429 **Elev** 7,006 ft **Area code** 970 **Zip** 81423
Information Chamber of Commerce, PO Box 116; 970/327-4707.

Near the edge of the Uncompahgre National Forest, this ranching community sits atop Wright's Mesa. This mesa and surrounding national forests contain a wide variety of wildlife that make this one of the most popular hunting areas in Colorado.

What to See and Do

Miramonte Lake. Fishing, boating, windsurfing. Fishing also in San Miguel River, Gurley Lake, Ground Hog Reservoir and nearby streams and mountain lakes. Inquire locally for information, permits. 18 mi SW.

Uncompahgre National Forest. More than 940,000 acres of alpine forest ranging in elevation from 7,500 to 14,000 feet, with many peaks higher than 13,000 feet. Fishing, hunting. Hiking. Picnicking. Camping (fee at some campgrounds). Four-wheel drive areas. Snowmobiling, cross-country skiing. Also within the forest is a portion of the San Juan Skyway. N, E & S of town. For information contact the Forest Service, 1760 Grand Ave; phone 970/327-4261. Within the forest are Big Blue and Mt Sneffles wilderness areas and portions of Lizard Head Wilderness Area.

Annual Event

San Miguel Basin Fair and Rodeo. Fairgrounds. 4-H fair and rodeo. Phone 970/327-4393. Last full wkend July.

Ouray (E-3)

(See Montrose, Silverton)

Settled 1875 **Pop** 644 **Elev** 7,811 ft **Area code** 970 **Zip** 81427
Information Ouray Chamber Resort Assn, PO Box 145; 970/325-4746 or 800/228-1876.

The average 19th-century traveler found the gold and silver mines around Ouray of greater interest than the town's setting. In the 20th century, with the mining boom days over, Ouray's location in a natural basin surrounded by majestic 12,000- to 14,000-foot peaks of the San Juan Mountains has finally gained the appreciation of the visitor. Ouray, named for a Ute chief, is reached by the magnificent Million Dollar Highway (US 550), which was blasted from sheer cliff walls high above the Uncompahgre River.

What to See and Do

"San Juan Odyssey." A 35-minute audio-visual journey through awe-inspiring San Juan Mountains. (June-Sept, daily) For details contact the Ouray Chamber Resort Assn. Main St.

Bachelor-Syracuse Mine Tour. Mine in continuous operation since 1884. Guided tour aboard a mine train, advances 3,350 feet horizontally into Gold Hill (mine temperature 47° F). Within the mine, visitors see mining equipment, visit work areas and learn how explosives are used. Gold panning. Outdoor cafe. (Late May-Sept, daily; closed July 4) County 14, 1 mi N via US 550, Dexter Creek Rd exit. Phone 970/325-4500. ¢¢¢

Bear Creek Falls. Road crosses bridge over 227-foot falls; an observation point is nearby. 3 mi S on US 550.

Box Cañon Park. Canyon Creek has cut a natural canyon 20 feet wide, 400 feet deep. View of thundering falls from floor of canyon is reached by stairs and suspended bridge. Some trails to the falls are not easily accessible for novice hikers. Picnic tables are available in beautiful settings. Children must be accompanied by an adult. (May-mid-Oct, daily) ½ mi S on US 550. Phone 970/325-4323. ¢

Jeep trips. Guides take visitors to ghost towns, mountain passes and mines, many above the timberline; some full-day trips. (Mid-May-mid-Oct, daily) Also jeep rentals. Phone 970/325-4444. Trips ¢¢¢¢

Ouray County Historical Museum. Former hospital constructed in 1887 now houses artifacts; mining, ranching and Ute relics. (Daily) 420 6th Ave. Phone 970/325-4576. ¢¢

Recreation.

Hot Springs Pool. Outdoor oval pool fed by natural mineral hot springs; sulphur-free. Bathhouse. (Daily) Ouray City Park, US 550 N. Phone 970/325-4638 ¢¢

Fishing in lakes and streams. **Hunting, riding** in surrounding mountains. **Ski** course with rope tow at edge of town; designed for children and beginners (free).

Annual Events

Music In Ouray. Series of chamber music concerts. 2nd wk June.

Artists' Alpine Holiday & Festival. National exhibit, competition in all media. 1 wk mid-Aug.

Ouray County Fair & Rodeo. 12 mi N in Ridgway. Labor Day wkend.

Imogene Pass Mountain Marathon. The 18-mile course starts at Ouray's 7,800-foot elevation, crosses over Imogene Pass (13,114 ft), and ends at Main St, Telluride (8,800 ft). Race route follows old mining trail. Phone 970/728-1299. Sat after Labor Day.

Motels

★ **ALPINE.** *Box 603, 645 Main. 970/325-4546.* 12 rms. No A/C. No rm phones. Mid-June-Sept: S, D $58; each addl $5; kit. unit $68; lower rates rest of yr. Crib free. TV, some B/W; cable. Complimentary coffee in rms. Restaurant opp 6:30 am-9 pm. Ck-out 11 am. Gift shop. X-country ski 8 mi. Totally nonsmoking. Cr cds: DS, MC, V.

★ ★ **BOX CANYON LODGE & HOT SPRINGS.** *Box 439, 45 3rd Ave, 2 blks W of US 550. 970/325-4981; res: 800/327-5080; FAX 970/325-0223.* 38 rms, 2 story. No A/C. June-Sept: S $75; D $75-$82; each addl $6; suites $98-$130; higher rates Christmas hols; lower rates rest of yr. Crib $5. TV; cable (premium), VCR avail. Complimentary coffee in lobby. Restaurant nearby. Ck-out 11 am. Outdoor whirlpools fed from mineral hot springs. Fireplace in suites. Balconies. Sun decks. At mouth of canyon; scenic view. Near river. Cr cds: A, C, D, DS, MC, V.

✔★ ★ **CASCADE FALLS LODGE.** *191 5th Ave. 970/325-7203; res: 800/438-5713; FAX 970/325-4840.* 33 rms, 2 story. S, D $92; each addl $3-$6; under 6 free; lower rates rest of yr. Crib free. TV; cable (premium). Complimentary continental bkfst. Restaurant nearby. Ck-out 11 am. Whirlpool. Cr cds: D, DS, MC, V.

✔★ **CIRCLE M.** *Box 126M, 1 blk W of US 550. 970/325-4394; res: 800/523-2589 (CO).* 19 rms, 1-2 story. No A/C. Mid-June-Sept: S $55; D $60-$68; each addl $4; lower rates mid-Apr-early June, Oct. Closed rest of yr. Crib free. TV; cable (premium). Playground. Complimentary coffee in rms. Restaurant nearby. Ck-out 10:30 am. Balconies. Picnic tables. Sun deck. Cr cds: A, C, D, DS, MC, V.

★ **MATTERHORN.** *201 6th Ave. 970/325-4938; res: 800/334-9425.* 25 air-cooled rms, 2 story, 3 suites. Mid-June-Sept: S $72-$76; D $79-$83; each addl $5; suites $98; lower rates May-early June & Oct. Closed rest of yr. TV; cable (premium). Heated pool; whirlpool. Complimentary coffee in rms. Restaurant nearby. Ck-out 11 am. Cr cds: D, DS, MC, V.

★ ★ **OURAY CHALET.** *Box 544, 510 Main. 970/325-4331; res: 800/924-2538.* 30 rms, 2 story. Mid-June-late Sept: S, D $65-$75; each addl $3; lower rates rest of yr. Closed mid-Oct-mid May. Crib $3. TV; cable (premium). Complimentary coffee in rms. Restaurant adj 6 am-9 pm. Ck-out 11 am. Free bus depot transportation. Whirlpool. Cr cds: A, DS, MC, V.

★ ★ **OURAY VICTORIAN INN.** *PO Box 1812, 50 3rd Ave. 970/325-7222; res: 800/443-7361; FAX 970/325-7225.* 38 rms, 2 story, 4 suites. No A/C. Mid-June-Sept: S, D $75-$81; each addl $6; suites $90; under 6 free; ski plans; lower rates rest of yr. TV; cable (premium). Playground. Complimentary continental bkfst (Nov-Mar). Complimentary coffee in rms. Restaurant nearby. Ck-out 11 am. Meeting rms. Whirlpool. Picnic tables. On river. Cr cds: A, C, D, DS, MC, V.

★ ★ **SUPER 8.** *(373 Palomino Trail, Ridgway 81432) 970/626-5444; FAX 970/626-5898.* 52 rms, 2 story. Mid-June-Labor Day: S, D $69.88-$76.88; each addl $7; suites $99.88; under 13 free; ski plan; higher rates some hols; lower rates rest of yr. Crib $5. TV; cable (premium). Indoor pool; whirlpool, sauna. Complimentary continental bkfst. Restaurant nearby. Ck-out 11 am. Coin lndry. Meeting rms. X-country ski on site. Game rm. Cr cds: A, C, D, DS, MC, V.

Inns

★ ★ **DAMN YANKEE.** *PO Box 709, 100 6th Ave. 970/325-4219; res: 800/845-7512; FAX 970/325-0502.* 9 air-cooled rms, 3 story, 1 suite. Mid-June-Sept: S, D $92-$125; each addl $10; suite $145-$165; special rates (winter); ski plans; lower rates rest of yr. Children over 11 yrs only. TV; cable (premium). Complimentary full bkfst, coffee. Restaurant nearby. Ck-out 11 am, ck-in 3-6 pm. Street parking. Balconies. Surrounded by San Juan Mountains. Whirlpool in gazebo. Totally nonsmoking. Cr cds: A, D, DS, MC, V.

⬛ ✕ 🔥

★ ★ **ST ELMO.** *426 Main St. 970/325-4951; FAX 970/325-0348.* 9 rms, 2 story. S, D $88-$98; each addl $10; suites $95-$98; lower rates rest of yr. TV in sitting rm; cable (premium). Full bkfst. Restaurant (see BON TON). Bar. Ck-out 11 am, ck-in 1 pm. Whirlpool, sauna. Restored 1898 hotel; antiques. Totally nonsmoking. Cr cds: A, DS, MC, V.

⬛ ✕ 🔥

Restaurants

★ ★ **BON TON.** *(See St Elmo Inn) 970/325-4951.* Hrs: 5-10 pm; winter 5:30-9 pm; Sun brunch 9:30 am-1 pm. Closed Dec 25. Res accepted. Italian menu. Bar. Wine list. Semi-a la carte: dinner $9.50-$22. Sun brunch $8.95. Child's meals. Specializes in pasta, seafood, steak. Parking. Built 1898. Outdoor dining. Casual dining. Totally nonsmoking. Cr cds: A, DS, MC, V.

★ **BUEN TIEMPO.** *206 7th Ave. 970/325-4544.* Hrs: 5-10 pm. Closed Mon & Tues during winter; Dec 25. Res accepted. No A/C. Mexican menu. Bar. Semi-a la carte: dinner $5-$12. Specialties: carne adovada, carne asada. Parking. Outdoor dining. Casual dining. In 1891 bldg, originally a hotel. Totally nonsmoking. Cr cds: MC, V.

✔ ★ **CECILIA'S.** *630 Main St. 970/325-4223.* Hrs: 6:30 am-9 pm. Closed Nov-Apr. Semi-a la carte: bkfst $3.15-$6.50, lunch $2.75-$10, dinner $6.35-$12.95. Child's meals. Specializes in soup, homemade pastries. In movie theater. No cr cds accepted.

🄳

★ ★ **COACHLIGHT.** *118 W 7th Ave, 1½ blks W of US 550. 970/325-4361.* Hrs: 5-9:30 pm. Closed mid-Oct-Apr. Res accepted. Continental menu. Serv bar. Semi-a la carte: dinner $7.95-$17.95. Child's meals. Specialties: miner's marinated filet, spinach fandango, chocolate French silk pie. Parking. Located in former hotel built in 1888. Cr cds: MC, V.

🄳

Pagosa Springs (F-3)

Founded 1880 **Pop** 1,207 **Elev** 7,105 ft **Area code** 970 **Zip** 81147
Information Chamber of Commerce, 402 San Juan St, PO Box 787; 970/264-2360 or 800/252-2204.

These remarkable mineral springs (153°F) are used for bathing and to heat houses and buildings. Deer and elk hunting are popular activities. The town is surrounded by the San Juan National Forest (see DURANGO). A Ranger District office of the forest is located in Pagosa Springs.

What to See and Do

Fred Harman Art Museum. Displays of original paintings by Fred Harman, Western artist and comic illustrator best remembered for his famous Red Ryder and Little Beaver comic strip. Also rodeo, movie and Western memorabilia. (Late May-early Oct, daily; rest of yr, Mon-Fri;

closed July 4) 2 mi W on US 160, across from jct Piedra Rd. Phone 970/731-5785. ¢

Navajo State Park. Waterskiing; fishing; boating (ramps, rentals). Picnicking (shelters), groceries, restaurant. Camping (dump station). Visitor center. Airstrip. Standard fees. (Daily) 17 mi W on US 160, then 18 mi S on CO 151 near Arboles. Phone 970/883-2208. Per vehicle ¢¢

Rocky Mountain Wildlife Park. Zoo exhibits animals indigenous to the area; wildlife museum; wildlife photography displays. (May-Oct, afternoons) 5 mi S on US 84. Phone 970/264-4515. ¢¢

Wolf Creek Pass (10,857 ft). Scenic drive across the Continental Divide. The east approach is through the Rio Grande National Forest (see SOUTH FORK), the west approach through the San Juan National Forest (see DURANGO). Best time to drive through is September; spectacular views of aspens changing color. Drive takes approximately one hour. 20 mi NE via US 160. Nearby is

Wolf Creek Ski Area. 2 triple chairlifts, 2 double chairlifts, Pomalift; patrol, school, rentals; cafeteria, restaurant, bar; day-lodge. 50 runs; longest run 2 mi; vertical drop 1,425 ft. (Early Nov-Apr, daily) Shuttle bus service. Phone 970/264-5629 (snow conditions & off-season). ¢¢¢¢¢

Treasure Mountain. Begin at top of Wolf Creek Pass, just E of summit marked where Continental Divide Trail winds southward and connects with Treasure Mountain Trail. Legend states that in 1790, 300 men mined $5 million in gold and melted it into bars, but were forced to leave it behind. The gold has never been found.

Annual Event

Winter Fest. Winter carnival, more than 30 individual and team events for all ages. Early Feb.

Motels

✔ ★ **HI COUNTRY LODGE.** *PO Box 485, 3821 US 160 E. 970/264-4181; res: 800/862-3707.* 29 units, 19 A/C, 2 story, 4 kit. cottages. S $37-$42; D $42-$47; each addl $5; kit. cottages $57-$62; under 12 free; wkly rates; ski plans. Crib free. TV; cable. Complimentary continental bkfst. Restaurant adj 5:30-9 pm. Ck-out 11 am. Coin lndry. Meeting rms. Downhill ski 20 mi; x-country ski 3 mi. Tubing hill (winter). Whirlpool. Cr cds: A, C, D, DS, MC, V.

🄳 ✕ 🔥 SC

★ **SPRING INN.** *165 Hot Springs Blvd. 970/264-4168; res: 800/225-0934; FAX 970/264-4707.* 23 rms. S, D $54-$74; each addl $5; ski plan. TV; cable (premium), VCR (movies avail $2.50). Complimentary coffee in lobby. Restaurant opp 6 am-10 pm. Ck-out noon. Gift shop. Whirlpools. Game rm. Hot springs; unlimited use to guests. Cr cds: D, DS, MC, V.

🄳 ✕ 🔥 SC

Resort

★ **PAGOSA LODGE.** *Box 4400 (81157), 3½ mi W on US 160. 970/731-4141; res: 800/523-7704 (exc CO); FAX 970/731-4343.* 100 rms, 2-3 story. Late May-Oct: S, D $65-$145; under 18 free; ski, golf plans; some lower rates rest of yr. TV; cable, VCR (movies avail $4). Indoor pool; steam rm, sauna. Playground. Supervised child's activities (June-Oct); ages 4-12. Restaurants 6:30 am-10 pm. Box lunches, snacks. Bar 4 pm-2 am. Ck-out 11 am, ck-in 4 pm. Meeting rms. Business servs avail. Airport transportation. Tennis, pro. 18-hole & 9-hole golf, greens fee, pro, putting green, driving range. Canoes, rowboats. Whitewater rafting. X-country ski on site. Sleigh rides. Hot-air balloon rides. Jeep tours. Bicycle rentals. Lawn games. Rec rm. 6,500-ft private airstrip. Private patios. Picnic tables. On lake. Cr cds: A, D, DS, MC, V.

🄳 🚤 🎿 🏇 ⛷ ⊠ ✕ 🔥 SC

Restaurant

★ **ELKHORN CAFE.** *438 C Pagosa St. 970/264-2146.* Hrs: 6 am-9 pm. Closed some major hols. Res accepted. Mexican, Amer menu. Semi-a la carte: bkfst $1.85-$6.25, lunch $4.65-$6.05, dinner $6.25-$13.50. Child's meals. Specialties: bkfst burrito, stuffed sopapilla. Casual dining. Family-owned. Cr cds: A, DS, MC, V.

Pueblo (E-6)

(See Cañon City, Colorado Springs)

Settled 1842 **Pop** 98,640 **Elev** 4,662 ft **Area code** 719

Information Chamber of Commerce, PO Box 697, 81002, phone 719/542-1704; or the Pueblo Visitors Information Center, 3417 N Elizabeth St, 81008, phone 719/543-1742. The Visitors Information Center is open daily.

Pueblo began as a crossroad for Native Americans, Spaniards and fur traders. When the Rio Grande Railroad reached here in 1872, Pueblo was the leading center for steel and coal production west of the Mississippi. Today Pueblo is a major transportation and industrial center; more than half of all goods manufactured in Colorado are produced in Pueblo.

What to See and Do

City parks. Approx 700 acres of parks within city. Two of the largest are

City Park. Swimming pool (Memorial Day-Labor Day, daily; fee); children's fishing. 9-hole, 18-hole golf and driving range (fee), tennis. Picnicking. Zoo (fee); herds of wildlife, children's farm, Eco Center, Rainforest. Historical carousel area (Memorial Day-Labor Day, daily; fee). 17-mile river trail system. Park (daily). Goodnight Ave. **Free.**

Mineral Palace Park. Swimming pool (fee); children's fishing. Picnicking. Rose garden, greenhouse. Pueblo Art Guild Gallery with local artists exhibits (Sat & Sun; closed Dec-Feb) Main St. **Free.** Phone 719/566-1745 or 719/542-1704. **Free.**

El Pueblo Museum. Full-sized replica of Old Fort Pueblo, which served as a base for fur traders and other settlers from 1842 to 1855. Exhibits on Anasazi Indians, steel and ore production and narrow-gauge railroads. (Daily exc Thanksgiving and Dec 25) Sr citizen rate. 324 W First St. Phone 719/583-0453. **¢¢**

Fred E. Weisbrod Aircraft Museum. Outdoor museum features static aircraft display. Adj is the **B-24 Aircraft Memorial Museum**, with indoor displays of the history of the B-24 bomber. Guided tours. (Mon-Sat, also Sun afternoons; closed hols) Pueblo Memorial Airport. Phone 719/948-3355 or -9219. **Free.**

Lake Pueblo State Park. Swimming, waterskiing; boating. Hiking. Camping (dump station). Standard fees. (Daily) 6 mi W via CO 96 or US 50W. Phone 719/561-9320. Per vehicle **¢**

Pueblo Symphony. Performances at Memorial Hall, S Union & Grand Aves and at Hoag Hall, USC campus. (Oct-May) Sr citizen rate. Phone 719/546-0333. **¢¢¢¢**

Rosemount Victorian House Museum. This 37-room mansion contains original Victorian furnishings and the McClelland Collection of world curiosities. (Daily exc Mon; closed most major hols; also closed Jan) Sr citizen rate. 419 W 14th St. Phone 719/545-5290. **¢¢**

San Isabel National Forest. On 1,109,782 acres. Three sections of forest lie adjacent to this highway with picnicking, camping and two winter sports areas: Monarch and Ski Cooper. In the southern part of the forest is the Spanish Peaks National Natural Landmark. Collegiate Peaks, Mt Massive and Holy Cross Wilderness areas are also within the forest, as well as four wilderness study areas. Colorado's highest peak, Mt Elbert (14,433 ft), is within the forest south of Leadville (see). NW and W via US 50. For information contact the Supervisor, 1920 Valley Dr, 81008; 719/545-8737. Also in forest is

Lake Isabel. A 310-acre recreation area. Fishing; boating (no motors). Picnicking. Camping. No swimming. 43 mi SW via I-25, CO 165 or 32 mi SW on CO 76.

Sangre de Cristo Arts and Conference Center. Four art galleries including the Francis King Collection of Western Arton permanent display; changing art exhibits; children's museum, workshops, dance studios, theater; gift shop. Gallery (daily exc Sun; closed hols). 210 N Santa Fe Ave. Phone 719/543-0130; central box office, phone 719/542-1211. Galleries **free;** Children's Museum **¢**

The Greenway and Nature Center of Pueblo. Small reptile exhibit and Raptor Center, special nature programs (by appt). Also 36 miles of hiking and biking trails (rentals). Cafe. (Daily; closed Jan 1, Thanksgiving, Dec 25) 5200 Nature Center Rd, 5 mi W via US 50. Phone 719/545-9114. **Free.**

University of Southern Colorado (1975). (4,000 students) Developed from Pueblo Junior College established in 1933. Chemistry Building has Geological Museum with mineral, rock and fossil exhibits, maps (academic yr, Mon-Fri; closed most hols; free). 2200 Bonforte Blvd. Campus tours (Mon-Fri, by appt), contact Admissions Office, Administration Building; 719/549-2461.

Annual Event

Colorado State Fair. Fairgrounds, Prairie Ave. PRCA rodeo, grandstand and amphitheater entertainment, livestock and agricultural displays, industrial and high technology displays, home arts, fine arts and crafts, carnival. Phone 719/561-8484. Aug 18-Sept 3.

Seasonal Event

Pueblo Greyhound Park. 3215 Lake Ave, S on I-25. Parimutuel betting. Phone 719/566-0370. Satellite betting Apr-Sept. Live racing Oct-Mar.

Motels

★ ★ **BEST WESTERN INN AT PUEBLO WEST.** *Box 7414 (81007), 201 McCulloch Blvd, 8¹/2 mi W on US 50W. 719/547-2111; FAX 719/547-0385.* 80 rms, 2 story. June-Sept: S $64-$89; D $69-$97; each addl $5; under 12 free; lower rates rest of yr. Crib free. TV; cable (premium). Pool. Restaurant 6 am-10 pm. Ck-out noon. Business servs avail. In-rm modem link. Private patios. Cr cds: A, D, DS, MC, V.

⏹ 🏊 🚫 🔥 SC

★ ★ **COMFORT INN.** *4645 I-25 N (81008). 719/542-6868; FAX 719/542-6868.* 60 rms, 2 story. Memorial Day-Aug: S, D $60-$80; each addl $5; lower rates rest of yr. TV; cable (premium). Indoor pool; whirlpool. Complimentary continental bkfst. Restaurant nearby. Ck-out 11 am. Cr cds: A, C, D, DS, MC, V.

⏹ 🏊 🚫 🔥 SC

✔ ★ **DAYS INN.** *4201 N Elizabeth (81008). 719/543-8031; FAX 719/546-1317.* 37 rms, 2 story. S $46-$75; D $59-$85; each addl $6; suites $75-$135; under 13 free. Crib free. TV; cable (premium). Indoor pool. Complimentary continental bkfst. Restaurant nearby. Ck-out 10 am. Business servs avail. In-rm modem link. Exercise equipt; bicycles, treadmill, whirlpool. Refrigerator in suites. Cr cds: A, C, D, DS, JCB, MC, V.

⏹ 🏊 🏋 🚫 🔥 SC

★ ★ **HAMPTON INN.** *4703 N Freeway (81008), just off I-25 N at Eagleridge, exit 102. 719/544-4700.* 112 rms, 2 story. S $54-$69; D $58-$89; under 19 free; golf plans. Pet accepted, $10 fee. TV; cable (premium), VCR avail. Heated pool. Coffee in rms. Complimentary continental bkfst. Ck-out noon. Coin lndry. Meeting rm. Business servs avail. In-rm modem link. Valet serv. Health club privileges. Cr cds: A, C, D, DS, MC, V.

Motor Hotel

★ ★ HOLIDAY INN. *4001 N Elizabeth St (81008), at jct US 50W, I-25 exit 101.* 719/543-8050; FAX 719/543-8050, ext. 260. 193 rms, 2 story. S $65; D $75; each addl $10; suites $100-$150; under 17 free. Crib free. TV, VCR avail (movies $7.95). Indoor pool. Complimentary continental bkfst. Restaurant 6 am-2 pm, 5-10 pm. Rm serv. Bar 4 pm-2 am, Sun to midnight. Ck-out noon. Coin lndry. Meeting rms. Business servs avail. In-rm modem link. Bellhops. Free airport, bus depot transportation. Health club privileges. Game rm. Cr cds: A, C, D, DS, JCB, MC, V.

Inn

✔ ★ ★ ABRIENDO. *300 W Abriendo Ave (81004).* 719/544-2703; FAX 719/542-6544. 10 rms, 3 story, 1 suite. S $49-$84; D $54-$89; each addl $10; suite $83. Children over 6 yrs only. TV; VCR avail. Complimentary full bkfst. Restaurant nearby. Ck-out 11 am, ck-in 3:30-7 pm. Business servs avail. In-rm modem link. Built 1906; antiques. Totally nonsmoking. Cr cds: A, D, MC, V.

Restaurants

★ CACTUS FLOWER. *2149 Jerry Murphy Rd (81001).* 719/545-8218. Hrs: 11 am-10 pm; Sat from 4 pm. Closed Sun; most major hols. Res accepted. Mexican menu. Bar. Semi-a la carte: lunch $3.95-$6.95, dinner $5.95-$12.95. Child's meals. Specializes in fajitas, Southwestern cuisine. Parking. Cr cds: A, D, DS, MC, V.

✔ ★ CAFE DEL RIO. *5200 Nature Center Rd, at the Greenway and Nature Center.* 719/545-1009. Hrs: 11 am-9 pm; Sun brunch 10 am-2 pm. Closed Mon. Res accepted. Serv bar. Semi-a la carte: lunch $4.25-$5.95, dinner $9.95-$16.95. Child's meals. Specializes in regional American dishes. Own soups. Parking. Outdoor dining. On river bank; adobe building built by volunteers. Cr cds: A, DS, MC, V.

★ ★ GAETANO'S. *910 US 50 W.* 719/546-0949. Hrs: 11 am-10 pm; Sat from 4 pm; early-bird dinner 4-6 pm. Closed Sun; Jan 1, Dec 25. Res accepted. Italian, Amer menu. Bar. Semi-a la carte: lunch $3.95-$8.95. Complete meals: dinner $6.95-$17.95. Child's meals. Specializes in steak, seafood, lasagne. Parking. Casual dining. Family-owned. Cr cds: A, D, DS, MC, V.

★ ★ ★ LA RENAISSANCE. *217 E Routt Ave.* 719/543-6367. Hrs: 11 am-2 pm, 5-9 pm; Sat from 5 pm. Closed Sun; most major hols. Res accepted. Continental menu. Bar. Wine list. Complete meals: lunch $4.95-$9.50, dinner $9.95-$24. Specializes in baby back ribs, prime rib. Parking. Church built in 1888; garden room. Cr cds: A, C, D, DS, MC, V.

Unrated Dining Spot

FURRS CAFETERIA. *1101 Bonforte Blvd, 1/2 mi E of I-25 exit 100A.* 719/544-9473. Hrs: 11 am-8 pm. Closed Dec 25. Avg ck: lunch $4.50, dinner $5.50. Pianist evenings. Cr cds: MC, V.

Rocky Mountain National Park (B-5)

(For accommodations see Estes Park, Granby, Grand Lake, Loveland, Lyons)

Elev 7,800-14,255 ft

(Park headquarters is 3 mi W of Estes Park on US 36; western entrance at Grand Lake)

More than 100 years ago Joel Estes built a cabin on Fish Creek, one of the higher sections of north-central Colorado. Although the Estes family moved away, more settlers soon followed, and the area became known as Estes Park. Described by Albert Bierstadt, one of the great 19th-century landscape artists of the West, as America's finest composition for the painter, the land west of where Estes settled was set aside as Rocky Mountain National Park in 1915.

Straddling the Continental Divide, with valleys 8,000 feet in elevation and 111 named peaks more than 10,000 feet high, the 415-square-mile park contains a staggering profusion of peaks, upland meadows, sheer canyons, glacial streams and lakes. Dominating the scene is Longs Peak, with its east face towering 14,255 feet above sea level. The park's forests and meadows provide sanctuary for more than 750 varieties of wildflowers; more than 260 species of birds; for such indigenous mammals as deer, wapiti (American elk), bighorn sheep, beaver and other animals. There are five campgrounds, two of which take reservations from May-early September (fee; write Mistix, PO Box 9029, Clearwater, FL 34618; 800/365-2267.) Some attractions are not accessible during winter months. $5/car/wk; Golden Eagle Passport accepted (see INTRODUCTION). For further information contact Superintendent, Rocky Mountain Natl Park, Estes Park 80517-8397; 970/586-1333.

What to See and Do

Bear Lake Road. Scenic drive (plowed in winter months) into high mountain basin is rimmed with precipitous 12,000- to 14,000-foot peaks. At end of road self-guided nature trail circles Bear Lake. Other trails lead to higher lakes, gorges, glaciers. Bus service (summer).

 Headquarters Building. Information (publications sales, maps); program on park (daily); guided walks and illustrated evening programs (summer only; daily). Just outside E entrance station on US 36 approach.

Moraine Park Museum. Exhibits, information, publications sales, maps. (Apr-Sept, daily) 1 mi inside park from Beaver Meadows entrance.

Never Summer Ranch. Historic pioneer homestead and preserved 1920s dude ranch. (Weather permitting, mid-June-Labor Day, daily) 10 miles N of Grand Lake entrance on Trail Ridge Rd. Phone 970/627-3471.

Trail Ridge Road. Above-the-treeline road roughly parallels a trail once used by Utes and Arapahos; 8 miles of full 48-mile length is above 11,000 feet; entire drive provides views of Rocky Mountain grandeur and, far to the east, the Great Plains; overlooks provide stopping places for views of Longs Peak and Forest Canyon. Self-guided tour brochure can be obtained at park HQ and visitor centers; Alpine Visitor Center at Fall River Pass has exhibits on alpine tundra ecology (summer, daily). Road closed to transmountain travel mid-Oct-late May. W of Estes Park to Grand Lake, crossing Continental Divide.

Salida (D-4)

(See Buena Vista)

Founded 1880 **Pop** 4,737 **Elev** 7,036 ft **Area code** 719 **Zip** 81201
Information Heart of the Rockies Chamber of Commerce, 406 W US 50; 719/539-2068.

On the eastern slope of the Rocky Mountains, Salida is a town surrounded by San Isabel National Forest (see PUEBLO). A pleasant climate (thus Salida's nickname "the banana belt") and good recreational facilities make Salida popular with visitors, especially during the annual FIBArk Whitewater Boat Race (see ANNUAL EVENTS).

What to See and Do

Arkansas Headwaters State Recreation Area. Area of 5,000 acres, with an outstanding waterway that cuts its way through rugged canyons for 148 miles, from Leadville to Pueblo. Fishing; boating (ramps). One of the world's premier waterways for kayaking & whitewater rafting. Hiking, bridle trails. Picnicking. Interpretive programs. Camping. (Daily) US 24, 285 & 50. Phone 719/539-7289. Per vehicle ¢

Fishing, hunting. Fishing in Arkansas River, O'Haver, North Fork, Franzhurst, Sand lakes, mountain lakes and streams. Excellent big-game hunting from October to December.

Jeep tours to mountainous areas inaccessible by car, over trails, old railroad beds. Outfitters offer half-hour, half-day and full-day trail rides, fishing, hunting, photography and pack trips. Contact Chamber of Commerce for details.

Monarch Ski Resort. 4 double chairlifts; patrol, school, rentals; cafeteria, restaurant, bar; nursery. 54 runs; longest run 2 mi; vertical drop 1,160 ft. (Mid-Nov-mid-Apr, daily) Multiday, half-day rates. Cross-country skiing. 18 mi W on US 50 at Monarch Pass (11,312 ft). Phone 719/539-3573 (ski administration) or -2581 (hotel); 800/332-3668 (reservations and information). ¢¢¢¢

Mt Shavano Fish Hatchery. 1/2 mi W on CO 291. (Daily) State-operated hatchery. US 50 at I Street. Phone 719/539-6877. **Free.**

River rafting. There are many rafting companies that offer half- to four-day trips on the Arkansas River from Browns Canyon through the Royal Gorge (mid-May-Sept). For prices and information call the Chamber of Commerce, 719/539-2068.

Salida Museum. Museum features mineral display, Indian artifacts, early pioneer household display, mining and railroad display. (Late May-earlySept, daily) **Free.**

Tenderfoot Drive. Spiral drive encircling Mt Tenderfoot. Views of surrounding mountain area and upper Arkansas Valley. W on CO 291.

The Angel of Shavano. Every spring the snow melts on the 14,239-foot slopes of Mt Shavano leaving an outline called "The Angel."

Annual Events

FIBArk River International Whitewater Boat Race. International experts compete in a 26-mile kayak race. Other events include slalom, raft, foot and bicycle races. Father's Day wkend.

Chaffee County Fair. 5 days last wkend July.

Christmas Mountain USA. 3-day season opener; more than 3,500 lights outline a 700-ft Christmas tree on Tenderfoot Mountain; parade. Late Nov.

Motel

★ ★ **BEST WESTERN COLORADO LODGE.** *352 W Rainbow Blvd, 3 blks W on US 50. 719/539-2514; res: 800/777-7947; FAX 719/539-4316.* 35 rms. May-Oct: S $57; D $61-$89; each addl $3; higher rates March, Christmas hols; lower rates rest of yr. Crib $3. TV; cable (premium). Indoor pool; 2 whirlpools, sauna. Complimentary

continental bkfst. Restaurant opp 6 am-9 pm. Ck-out 10 am. Business servs avail. Coin lndry. Free local airport, bus depot transportation. Downhill ski 16 mi; x-country ski 12 mi. Cr cds: A, C, D, DS, ER, MC, V.

Restaurants

✔ ★ ★ **COUNTRY BOUNTY.** *413 W Rainbow Blvd. 719/539-3546.* Hrs: 6:30 am-9 pm. Closed Thanksgiving, Dec 24-25. Res accepted. Amer menu. Semi-a la carte: bkfst $2.25-$5.75, lunch $2.65-$6.95, dinner $5-$12. Child's meals. Specializes in desserts, almond chicken Shanghai. Parking. Dining rm overlooking garden and mountains. Totally nonsmoking. Cr cds: DS, MC, V.

SC

★ ★ **MT SHAVANO INN.** *1220 E Rainbow Blvd. 719/539-4561.* Hrs: 11 am-2 pm, 4-10 pm. Closed Wed. Res accepted. Italian, Amer menu. Bar. Semi-a la carte: lunch $6.49, dinner $7.95-$19.95. Specializes in prime rib, beer-battered shrimp. Parking. Outdoor dining. Attractive, informal dining rm. Cr cds: MC, V.

D

Silverton (E-3)

(See Durango, Ouray)

Settled 1874 **Pop** 716 **Elev** 9,318 ft **Area code** 970 **Zip** 81433
Information Chamber of Commerce, PO Box 565; 970/387-5654 or 800/752-4494.

"The mining town that never quit" sits in the San Juan Mountains with other communities that were also once known for mining; the last mine in Silverton closed in 1991. Both Silverton and the ghost towns provide reminders of Colorado's mining history. Tourists have now discovered the beauty and recreational opportunities of the area.

What to See and Do

Circle Jeep Tour. Mapped jeep route with historical information to many mines and ghost towns. Contact the Chamber of Commerce. Map ¢

Old Hundred Gold Mine Tour. Guided 1-hr tour of underground mine offers view of mining equipment, crystal pockets, veins; learn about methods of hardrock mining. (Memorial Day-Sept, daily) Sr citizen rate. 5 mi E via CO 110, on County Rd 4A. Phone 970/387-5444 or 800/872-3009. ¢¢¢

Rocky Mountain High Jeep Tours. All-day, 1/2-day, 2- & 3-hr guided tours of ghost towns, historic mine tours & scenic tours. Jeep rentals also avail. For details contact PO Box 3337, Durango 81302 or phone 800/530-2022. ¢¢¢¢¢

San Juan County Historical Society Museum. Located in old three-story jail. Mining and railroad artifacts from Silverton's early days. (Memorial Day-mid-Oct, daily) Main St. Phone 970/387-5838 ¢

The Silverton. Narrow-gauge train (see DURANGO).

Annual Events

Iron Horse Bicycle Classic. Bicycles race the Silverton narrow-gauge train. Late May.

Hardrockers Holiday. Mining skills competition. Mid-Aug.

Brass Band Festival. Mid-Aug.

Inns

★ **ALMA HOUSE.** *Box 780, 220 E 10th St. 970/387-5336.* 10 air-cooled rms, 2¹/₂ story, 2 with bath, 8 share bath. No rm phones. May-Sept: S, D $55; suites $85. Closed Nov-Apr. Pet accepted, some restrictions. TV; cable (premium). Restaurant adj 7-9 am, 11:30 am-2 pm, 6:30-10 pm. Ck-out, ck-in noon. Free bus depot transportation. Built 1898. Victorian furnishings. Cr cds: A, DS, MC, V.

⊷ ⊠ 🕯 SC

★ **WYMAN.** *Box 780, 1371 Greene St, across from Town Hall. 970/387-5372; FAX 970/387-5745.* 19 air-cooled rms, 2 story. Mid-May-mid-Oct: S, D $68-$82; each addl $5; lower rates rest of yr. TV; cable, VCR (movies avail). Complimentary coffee (continental bkfst in season). Restaurant nearby. Ck-out 10 am, ck-in anytime. Business servs avail. Street parking. Built 1902. Victorian furnishings. Totally nonsmoking. Cr cds: A, DS, MC, V.

⊠ 🕯 SC

Restaurant

★ **HANDLEBARS.** *117 E 13th St. 970/387-5395.* Hrs: 10:30 am-10 pm. Closed Nov-Apr. No A/C. Bar to 2 am. Semi-a la carte: lunch $3.75-$8.95, dinner $3.45-$17.95. Child's meals. Specializes in baby back ribs, homemade chili & soup. Entertainment Tues-Sat. Built in 1881; display of antique mining and ranching artifacts. Cr cds: DS, MC, V.

Unrated Dining Spot

FRENCH BAKERY. *1250 Greene St. 970/387-5423.* Hrs: 7 am-3 pm. Closed Jan 1; also Nov-Apr. Bar. Semi-a la carte: bkfst $3-$5.50, lunch $4.25-$5.95. Specializes in soup, sandwiches. Originally a saloon, built 1896. Full service bakery. Cr cds: A, D, DS, ER, MC, V.

Snowmass Village (C-3)

(See Aspen, Glenwood Springs)

Pop 1,449 **Elev** 8,604 ft **Area code** 970 **Zip** 81615
Information Snowmass Resort Association, 38 Village Square, PO Box 5566; 970/923-2000 or 800/766-9627.

All facilities of Snowmass Village are available to guests of the accommodations listed below. **Year-round:** Nearly 50 outdoor heated pools and hot tubs, saunas. Child's and teen programs; sitter list. Convention facilities. More than 20 restaurants in village; bars. Free shuttle bus throughout village; local airport transportation. **Summer:** Fishing (license, equipt avail). Rafting, hiking, horseback riding, 18-hole golf, tennis (fees for all); jeep & bicycle tours; hot-air balloon rides. **Winter:** Skiing (beginner-to-expert runs), instruction; cross-country skiing, barbecue sleigh rides, dogsled tours, guided snowshoe tours; swimming, indoor tennis.

What to See and Do

Bicycle trips and jeep trips throughout the Snowmass/Aspen area. Transportation and equipment provided. (June-Sept) Contact Blazing Adventures, Box 5929; phone 970/923-4544. ¢¢¢¢¢

Krabloonik Husky Kennels. Half-day dog-sled trips by reservation (Dec-Apr). Kennel tours (Mid-June-Sept, daily exc Mon). 5 mi SW of CO 82 on Divide Rd. Contact PO Box 5517; 970/923-3953. Trips ¢¢¢¢; Kennel tours ¢¢

River rafting. Snowmass Whitewater. Half-day, full-day and overnight trips on the Arkansas, Roaring Fork, Colorado, Gunnison and Dolores rivers. Trips range from scenic floats for beginners to exciting runs for experienced rafters. (May-Oct daily, depending on snow melt) Transportation to site. 70 Snowmass Village Mall. Phone 970/923-4544 or 800/282-7238. ¢¢¢¢

Skiing. Snowmass Ski Area. 3 quad, 2 triple, 9 double chairlifts, 2 platter pulls; patrol, school, rentals; restaurants, bar; nursery. 72 runs; longest run 4.2 mi, vertical drop 4,087 ft. (Late Nov-mid-Apr, daily) Cross-country skiing (50 mi). Shuttle bus service from Aspen. Phone 800/525-6200; central reservations phone 800/332-3245. ¢¢¢¢¢

Motor Hotels

(Hours and dates open may vary during off-season, making it advisable to call ahead)

★★ **CRESTWOOD.** *Box 5460, 400 Wood Rd. 970/923-2450; res: 800/356-5949; FAX 970/923-5018.* 122 air-cooled kit. condos (1-3 bedrm), 3 story. No elvtr. Feb-Mar: S, D $264-$642; each addl $25; under 13 free in summer (2 max); ski plans; higher rates Christmas hols; lower rates rest of yr. Crib $5. TV; cable (premium), VCR (movies avail $4). Heated pool. Complimentary coffee. Ck-out 10 am. Guest lndry. Meeting rms. Business servs avail. In-rm modem link. Bellhops. Valet serv. Aspen airport transportation. Downhill/x-country ski on site. Exercise equipt; treadmill, stair machine, whirlpool, sauna. Refrigerators, fireplaces. Balconies. Grills. Cr cds: A, D, DS, MC, V.

D ⊷ ≋ 🕴 ⊠ 🕯

★★ **HOTEL WILDWOOD.** *Box 5037, 40 Elbert Ln, overlooks Snowmass Village Mall. 970/923-3550; res: 800/445-1642; FAX 970/923-4844.* 148 rms, 3-4 story. Nov-Mar: S, D $88-$225; each addl $25; suites $175-$600; under 12 free; ski plans; lower rates rest of yr. Crib free. TV; cable (premium), VCR avail. Heated pool; whirlpool, poolside serv. Supervised child's activities. Complimentary continental bkfst (winter). Restaurant 5-10 pm. Rm serv. Bar. Ck-out 10 am. Coin lndry. Meeting rms. Business servs avail. Bellhops. Valet serv. Concierge. Free airport transportation. Downhill/x-country ski 1 blk. Health club privileges. Refrigerators. Patios, balconies. Cr cds: A, C, D, DS, MC, V.

D ⊷ ≋ ⊠ 🕯 SC

★★★ **SILVERTREE.** *Box 5009, 100 Elbert Lane, on Snowmass Village Mall. 970/923-3520; res: 800/525-9402; FAX 970/923-5192.* 261 rms, 2-7 story. No A/C. Late Nov-early Apr: S, D $130-$375; each addl $25; suites $295-$1,400; under 12 free; family rates in summer; higher rates mid-late Dec; varied lower rates rest of yr. Crib free. TV; cable. 2 heated pools; whirlpool, poolside serv. Playground. Supervised child's activities. Coffee in rms. Restaurant 7 am-10 pm. Rm serv. Bar 11:30-1 am; entertainment, dancing. Ck-out 10 am. Coin lndry. Meeting rms. Business center. Valet serv. Concierge. Shopping arcade. Free local airport transportation. Downhill/x-country ski on site. Ski rentals. Exercise equipt; weight machine, bicycles, steam rm. Masseuse. Bicycle rentals. Lawn games. Refrigerators. Private patios, balconies. Cr cds: A, C, D, DS, MC, V.

D ⊷ ⊷ ≋ 🕴 ⊠ 🕯 SC 🏃

Resort

★★★ **SNOWMASS LODGE AND CLUB.** *PO Drawer G-2, 0239 Snowmass Club Circle. 970/923-5600; res: 800/525-6200; FAX 970/923-6944.* 76 hotel rms, 4 story, 62 villas. Mid-Nov-mid-Apr: S, D $125-$395; each addl $20; villas $185-$730; under 12 free; wkly, ski, golf plans; higher rates hols; lower rates rest of yr. TV; cable (premium), VCR avail. 2 heated pools; wading pool, whirlpool, poolside serv. Supervised child's activities; ages 6 months-8 yrs. Complimentary coffee in rms. Restaurant 7 am-10:30 pm. Box lunches. Rm serv. Bar 11-2 am. Ck-out noon, villas 10 am, ck-in 4 pm. Grocery, package store 1 mi. Coin lndry. Meeting rms. Business servs avail. In-rm modem link. Gift shop. Free valet parking. Free airport, ski area transportation. Sports dir. Lighted & indoor tennis, pro. 18-hole golf, pro, putting green, driving range. Downhill ski 1 mi; x-country ski on site. Ski rentals.

Snowmobiling, sleighing, tobogganing, avail. Entertainment. Exercise rm; instructor, weights, bicycles, steam rm, sauna. Refrigerators. Private patios, balconies. Cr cds: A, C, D, DS, JCB, MC, V.

Restaurants

★ ★ **KRABLOONIK.** *5 mi SW of CO 82 on Brush Creek Rd, then right 1 mi on Divide Rd.* 970/923-3953. Hrs: summer 6-10 pm (closed Tues); winter 11 am-2 pm, 5:30-10 pm. Closed mid-Apr-May & Oct-Thanksgiving. Res accepted. No A/C. French, Amer menu. A la carte entrees: lunch $8-$25, dinner $22.50-$49.50. Specializes in fresh seafood and wild game, elk, caribou, quail, wild boar. Parking. Rustic atmosphere. Dogsled rides in winter; kennel tours in summer. Totally nonsmoking. Cr cds: MC, V.

★ ★ **LA BOHEME.** *315 Gateway Bldg, in Snowmass Village Mall.* 970/923-6804. Hrs: 11 am-2 pm, 5:30-10:30 pm. Closed mid-Apr-June 1 & Oct-Thanksgiving. Res accepted. French, continental menu. Bar. Wine list. Semi-a la carte: lunch $7-$10.50, dinner $24-$32. Child's meals. Specializes in wild game, seafood. Pianist, jazz combo wkends. Outdoor dining. Relaxing atmosphere with view of Roaring Fork Valley. Totally nonsmoking. Cr cds: A, DS, MC, V.

✔ ★ **STEW POT.** *62 Snowmass Village Mall.* 970/923-2263. Hrs: 11:30 am-9 pm. Closed mid-Apr-May, Oct-Thanksgiving. No A/C. Bar. Semi-a la carte: lunch, dinner $3.75-$8.50. Child's meals. Specializes in homemade stews, soup, country cooking. Outdoor dining. Totally nonsmoking. Cr cds: MC, V.

South Fork (E-4)

(See Monte Vista)

Pop 250 (est) **Elev** 8,200 ft **Area code** 719 **Zip** 81154
Information Chamber of Commerce, PO Box 116; 719/873-5512.

Located at Wolf Creek Pass along US 160 in the heart of the San Juan Mountains, this resort community is popular for skiing, snowmobiling, fishing and rafting and for the jeep trails in the surrounding area.

What to See and Do

Rio Grande National Forest. This rugged forest surrounding the San Luis Valley includes Wolf Creek Pass (10,850 ft) (see PAGOSA SPRINGS). Within the forest is the rugged Sangre de Cristo back country and parts of Weminuche, South San Juan and La Garita wildernesses. Fishing; hunting; boating. Hiking. Downhill & cross-country skiing, snowmobiling. Picnicking. Camping, N, S & W of town. Contact forest headquarters, 1803 W US 160, Monte Vista 81144; 719/852-5941. In forest are

Creede (pop 653). Frontier mining town. 22 mi NW on CO 149.

Skiing. Wolf Creek Ski Area. (See PAGOSA SPRINGS) 18 mi SW on US 160.

Annual Event

Rio Grande Raft Races. 13-mile course. Usually 2nd wkend June.

Seasonal Event

Creede Repertory Theater. 21 mi NW on CO 149 in Creede. Classic and modern comedies, drama, musicals. Advance reservations suggested. Nightly exc Mon; also Wed & Fri afternoons; children's matinee Sat in Aug. Contact PO Box 269, Creede 81130. Phone 719/658-2540. Early June-Labor Day.

Lodge

✔ ★ **WOLF CREEK SKI.** *Box 283, 31042 US 160W.* 719/873-5547; res: 800/874-0416. 49 air-cooled rms, 1-2 story, 18 kit. units. S $40-$48; D $47-$55; kit. units $55-$65; ski plans; wkly rates. Crib free. Pet accepted. TV; cable. Playground. Dining rm 6-10:30 am, 5-9 pm. Bar. Ck-out 10 am. Meeting rms. Business servs avail. In-rm modem link. Free local airport transportation. Downhill ski 18 mi; x-country ski 3 mi. Snowmobiling. Hiking. Fishing. Whirlpool. Cr cds: A, C, D, DS, MC, V.

Restaurant

★ **HUNGRY LOGGER.** *US 160.* 719/873-5504. Hrs: 6 am-10 pm; winter to 8 pm. Semi-a la carte: bkfst $1.25-$7.25, lunch $2.75-$6.25, dinner $6.95-$25. Child's meals. Specializes in bbq ribs, pastries. Salad bar. Parking. Casual atmosphere. Cr cds: A, DS, MC, V.

Steamboat Springs (A-4)

Settled 1875 **Pop** 6,695 **Elev** 6,728 ft **Area code** 970 **Zip** 80477
Information Steamboat Springs Chamber Resort Association, PO Box 774408; 970/879-0880.

Before the Ute Indians retreated into Utah, Steamboat Springs was originally their summer home. The area's first white settlers were ranchers. Coal mining also became a very viable industry.

Skiing and Norwegian-style ski-jumping came to this area with the arrival of the Norseman Carl Howelsen in 1913, making it one of the most popular winter sports in the area. Ten national ski-jumping records have been set on Steamboat Springs' Howelsen Hill; the area has produced 34 winter Olympians, which has helped earn it the name of "Ski Town USA." Summer activities include hot-air ballooning, horseback riding, hiking, bicycling, river rafting, canoeing and llama trekking. One of the largest elk herds in North America ranges near the town. There are over 100 natural hot springs in the area. The headquarters and access routes to Routt National Forest are in or near Steamboat Springs.

What to See and Do

Routt National Forest. More than one and one-third million acres including the 139,898-acre Mt Zirkel Wilderness and 38,870 acres of the 235,230-acre Flat Tops Wilderness. Fishing, hunting. Winter sports area. Hiking. Picnicking. Camping. N, E, S and SW of town. Contact the Supervisor, 29587 W US 40, Suite 20, 80487; 970/879-1722. A Ranger District office is also located in town.

Scenic drives. The following drives are accessible in summer and are well-maintained paved and gravel-surfaced roads. Impressive view of valley and Howelsen Ski Complex. **Fish Creek Falls** (283 ft). 3 mi E. Picnic area. **Buffalo Pass** (10,180 ft). 15 mi NE. Impressive road atop Continental Divide leading to formerly inaccessible trout-filled lakes. **Rabbit Ears Pass** (9,680 ft). 22 mi SE. Additional information available at information centers.

Skiing.

Howelsen Hill Ski Complex. International ski/jump complex includes one double chairlift, Pomalift, rope tow, 5 ski jumping hills; patrol; ice-skating, bobsledding, snowboarding. (Dec-Mar, daily) Also summer activities. Off US 40 on River Rd via 5th St bridge. Phone 970/879-4300. ¢¢¢

Steamboat. Gondola, 2 high-speed quads, 6 triple, 7 double chairlifts, 2 surface tows; patrol, school, rentals; cafeterias, restaurants, bars; nursery. 106 runs; longest run 3 mi; vertical drop 3,600 ft. (Late

Nov-early Apr, daily) Cross-country skiing (14 mi). Multi-day, half-day rates. Gondola also operates mid-June-Labor Day (daily; fee). 3 mi E on US 40. Phone 800/922-2722. ¢¢¢¢¢

Steamboat Health & Recreation Assn. Three hot pools fed by 103°F mineral water; lap pool; saunas; exercise classes; massage; weight room; tennis courts (summer). (Daily) 136 Lincoln Ave, E end of town. Phone 970/879-1828. ¢¢; Also here is

Hot Slide Hydrotube. Tube slide with 350 feet of hot water. (Daily) ¢¢

Steamboat Lake State Park. Swimming, waterskiing; fishing; boating (ramps). Picnicking. Camping. Standard fees. (Daily) 26 mi N on County 129. Phone 970/879-3922. Per vehicle ¢¢

Strawberry Park Natural Hot Springs. Mineral springs feed four pools; water cooled from 160°F to 105°F. Changing area; picnicking; camping, cabins. (Daily) 7 mi NE at 44200 County 36. Phone 970/879-0342. ¢¢

Tread of Pioneers Museum. Pioneer and cattle ranching artifacts, Indian displays, antique ski equipment. (Daily) 8th and Oak Sts. Phone 970/879-2214. ¢¢

Annual Events

Winter Carnival. Snow & ski competitions, parade. Early Feb.

Cowboy Roundup Days. Rodeos, parade, entertainment. July 4th wkend.

Rainbow Weekend. Balloon rally, concerts, rodeo. Mid-July.

Vintage Auto Race and Concours d'Elegance. Labor Day wkend.

Motel

(Rates may be higher during Winter Carnival. Hours and dates open may vary during off-season, making it advisable to call ahead.)

✔ ★ **ALPINER.** PO Box 770054, 424 Lincoln Ave. 970/879-1430; res: 800/538-7519; FAX 970/879-0054. 32 rms, 2 story. Mid-Nov-Mar: S, D $70-$95; each addl $10; under 12 free; lower rates rest of yr. Crib free. Pet accepted. TV; cable (premium). Complimentary coffee in rms. Restaurant opp 6 am-10 pm. Bar. Ck-out 10 am. Downhill ski 1 mi; x-country ski ½ mi. Free shuttle to ski area. Cr cds: A, C, D, DS, MC, V.

Lodges

★ **GLEN EDEN RESORT.** (PO Box 908, Clark 80428) 18 mi N on CO 129. 970/879-3907; res: 800/882-0854; FAX 970/870-0858. 28 kit. cottages, 1-2 story. Jan-Sept: cottages $110-$125; each addl $20; under 12 free; higher rates: mid-Dec-early Jan, hunting season; lower rates rest of yr. Crib free. TV; VCR avail (movies avail $5). Heated pool; whirlpools. Playground. Dining rm 11 am-9 pm. Bar. Ck-out 10 am, ck-in 4 pm. Coin lndry. Grocery ½ mi. Meeting rms. Business servs avail. Free ski transportation. Tennis. Downhill ski 20 mi; x-country ski on site. Bicycles avail. Some balconies. Picnic tables, grills. Cr cds: MC, V.

★ ★ **SKY VALLEY.** PO Box 3132, E US 40, 8 mi S. 970/879-7749; res: 800/538-7519; FAX 970/879-7752. 24 rms, 3 story. No A/C. No elvtr. Late Nov-mid-Apr: S, D $85-$150; each addl $10; under 12 free; higher rates Christmas; lower rates rest of yr. Crib free. Pet accepted, some restrictions; $50. TV; cable, VCR avail. Complimentary bkfst. Dining rm 7-10 am, noon-2 pm, 5-8 pm. Bar 3-11 pm. Ck-out 11 pm. Meeting rms. Business servs avail. Free ski area, downtown transportation. Downhill ski 7 mi; x-country ski 5 mi. Whirlpool, sauna. Totally nonsmoking. Cr cds: A, C, D, DS, MC, V.

Motor Hotels

★ ★ **BEST WESTERN PTARMIGAN INN.** Box 773240, 2304 Apres Ski Way; 2 mi E, 1 mi NE of US 40. 970/879-1730; res: 800/538-7519; FAX 970/879-6044. 77 rms, 47 A/C, 3-4 story. Late Nov-mid-Apr: S, D $89-$209; each addl $10; under 12 free; higher rates late Dec; ski, tour package plans; varied lower rates rest of yr. Closed early Apr-late May. Crib free. Pet accepted. TV; cable. Heated pool; whirlpool, sauna. Complimentary coffee. Restaurant 7 am-noon, 5-10 pm. Rm serv. Bar 4 pm-midnight. Ck-out 10 am. Coin lndry. Meeting rm. Valet serv. Downhill/x-country ski on site. Ski rentals, storage. Many refrigerators. Balconies. Mountain bike rentals. View of Mt Werner, valley. Cr cds: A, C, D, DS, ER, JCB, MC, V.

★ ★ **HOLIDAY INN.** Box 775007, 3190 S Lincoln Ave, 2 mi E on US 40. 970/879-2250; FAX 970/879-0251. 82 rms, 2 story. Late Jan-Mar: S, D $99-$159; each addl $10; under 19 free; higher rates late Dec-early Jan; varied lower rates rest of yr. Crib free. Pet accepted; some restrictions; $50 deposit. TV; cable (premium), VCR avail. Heated pool; wading pool; whirlpool. Complimentary continental bkfst. Restaurant 6 am-2 pm, 5-10 pm. Rm serv. Bar 4 pm-midnight. Ck-out 11 am. Coin lndry. Meeting rm. Business servs avail. In-rm modem link. Valet serv. Downhill/x-country ski 1 mi. Game rm. Lawn games. Some refrigerators. Cr cds: A, C, D, DS, JCB, MC, V.

★ ★ **RANCH AT STEAMBOAT SPRINGS.** 1 Ranch Rd (80487), SE via US 40, E on Mt Werner Rd, then NE on Steamboat Blvd to Clubhouse Dr, then E on River Queen, left on Natches Way, 1st right to ranch. 970/879-3000; res: 800/525-2002; FAX 970/879-5409. 88 1-4-bedrm kit. condos, 2 story. No A/C. Feb-Mar & Dec: S, D $250-$420; lower rates rest of yr. TV; cable (premium), VCR avail (movies avail $3.50). Heated pool; whirlpool, sauna. Supervised childs activities (Nov-Apr); ages 3-13. Ck-out 10 am. Free lndry facilities. Meeting rms. Business servs avail. Concierge. Garage. Tennis. Downhill/x-country ski ½ mi. Balconies. Picnic tables, grills. On 35 acres. Cr cds: A, MC, V.

Inn

✔ ★ **INN AT STEAMBOAT.** 3070 Columbine Dr, off US 40 Walton Creek Rd exit. 970/879-2600; res: 800/872-2601; FAX 970/879-9270. 32 rms, 2-3 story. No A/C. No elvtr. Mid-Nov-mid-Apr: S, D $75-$128; each addl $10; under 12 free; ski plans; lower rates rest of yr. Crib free. TV; cable (premium), VCR avail. Heated pool; sauna. Complimentary bkfst. Coffee in lobby. Serv bar 3-11 pm. Ck-out 11 am, ck-in 3 pm. Coin lndry. Free ski area transportation. Downhill/x-country ski ½ mi. Game rm. Many balconies. Totally nonsmoking. Cr cds: A, DS, MC, V.

Resort

★ ★ ★ **SHERATON STEAMBOAT RESORT.** PO Box 774808, 2200 Village Inn Court. 970/879-2220; FAX 970/879-7686. 311 rms, 8 story. S, D $99-$259; each addl $15; suites $249-$649; kit. units $139-$580; under 17 free; ski, golf plans; varied lower rates June-mid-Sept, Thanksgiving-mid-Dec, Jan. Closed mid-Apr-mid-May, mid-Oct-mid-Nov. TV; cable (premium). Heated pool; whirlpool. Supervised child's activities (June-Sept); ages 4-12. Complimentary coffee in rms. Dining rm 6:30 am-2 pm, 5:30-10 pm. Rm serv. Bar 2 pm-1 am. Ck-out 11 am, ck-in 3 pm. Coin lndry. Convention facilities. Business servs avail. Bellhops. Concierge. Shopping arcade. Tennis privileges. 18-hole golf privileges, pro. Downhill/x-country ski on site; rentals. Exercise equipt; weights, stair machine, sauna. Health club privileges. Game rm.

Refrigerators. Private patios. Picnic tables. Cr cds: A, C, D, DS, ER, JCB, MC, V.

D ⊠ ⚞ ⚟ ≈ ⚟ ⊠ ⚞ SC

Guest Ranches

★ ★ ★ **HOME RANCH.** *(Box 822, Clark 80428) 20 mi N on CO 129, then follow signs.* 970/879-1780; FAX 970/879-1795. This ranch occupies 1,500 evergreen- and aspen-dotted acres in the Elk River Valley. Innovative Southwestern cuisine is served in the vaulted-ceiling lodge house, and guest cabins are furnished with genuine Stickley pieces. 6 rms in lodge, 8 cottages. No rm phones. AP, Memorial Day-mid-Oct & mid-Dec-Apr 1, wkly: D $2,975-$3,500; each addl $200/day. Closed rest of yr. TV in lounge; VCR avail. Heated pool; sauna. Hot tub. Playground. Supervised child's activities; ages 6-16. Complimentary coffee in rms. Dining rm 8-9 am, noon-1 pm, dinner (1 sitting) 7 pm; children's dinner 5:30 pm. Box lunches, snacks, picnics. Ck-out 10 am, ck-in 4 pm. Complimentary lndry facilities. Meeting rms. Business servs avail. Free local airport, bus depot, ski transportation. Sports dir. Tennis privileges. Downhill ski 20 mi; x-country ski on site. Sleighing, tobogganing. Guided hiking. Horse riding instruction avail. Lawn games. Soc dir; entertainment, movies. Rec rm. Fishing guides; cleaning & storage. Fly fishing instruction avail. Petting zoo for children. Refrigerators, wood stoves. Private hot tub at each cabin. Private porches. Ranch rodeo, barbecue. Library. Cr cds: A, DS, MC, V.

D ⊠ ⚞ ⚟ ⚞ ≈ ⚟ ⚞

★ ★ ★ **VISTA VERDE.** *Box 465, 20 mi N on CO 129, then 5 mi E on Seed House Rd.* 970/879-3858; res: 800/526-7433; FAX 970/879-1413. Luxurious accommodations and gourmet dining could make you forget that you're on a guest ranch, but a step outside onto the 540-acres of this property will remind you why you came here in the first place. 8 cabins, 1-2 story, 3 lodge rms. No A/C. Early June-late Sept, AP (7-day min): S, D $1,495/person/wk; under 12, $995/wk; lower rates mid-Dec-Mar. Playground. Free supervised child's activities (late May-mid-Sept). Coffee in rms. Dining rm. Box lunches; snack bar; picnics. Meeting rms. Business servs avail. Free guest lndry. Gift shop. Free local airport, bus depot transportation. Lake swimming. X-country ski on site. Sleighing, tobogganing. Mountain bikes. Guided hiking trips. Float & backpack trips; gold-panning expeditions. Rock climbing with guide. Hot-air ballooning. Hayrides. Cattle drives. Dog sledding. Rec rm. Game rm. Lawn games. Entertainment, dancing, movies in lodge. Exercise equipt; rowing machine, bicycles, whirlpool, sauna. Fish/hunt guides. Refrigerators. Wood stoves. Private porches. Totally nonsmoking. No cr cds accepted.

D ⊠ ⚞ ⚟ ⚞ ≈ ⚟ ⚞

Restaurants

★ ★ **GIOVANNI'S.** *127 11th St.* 970/879-4141. Hrs: 5:30-10 pm; off season 6-9 pm. Res accepted. Italian menu. Bar. Semi-a la carte: dinner $10.95-$23.95. Child's meals. Specializes in lamb, veal saltimbocca. Four dining areas. Old World Italian charm. Totally nonsmoking. Cr cds: A, C, D, DS, JCB, MC, V.

D

★ ★ **L'APOGÉE.** *911 Lincoln Ave.* 970/879-1919. Hrs: 5:30-10:30 pm. Res accepted. Bar. Wine cellar. French menu. Semi-a la carte: dinner $15.95-$26. Child's meals. Specialties: oysters Rockefeller, wild mushrooms, filet mignon, rack of lamb. Menu changes every 3 months. 1886 building. Patio dining. Totally nonsmoking. Cr cds: A, MC, V.

★ ★ **LA MONTAÑA.** *2500 Village Dr, in Village Center.* 970/879-5800. Hrs: 5-10 pm. Closed Thanksgiving. Res accepted. Mexican, Southwestern menu. Bar 5-10 pm. Semi-a la carte: dinner $8.95-$24. Child's meals. Specializes in elk loin with pecans, fajitas, red chili pasta. Parking. Outdoor dining. Totally nonsmoking. Cr cds: A, DS, MC, V.

★ ★ **ORE HOUSE AT THE PINE GROVE.** *1465 Pine Grove Rd, 1 1/2 mi E, off US 40.* 970/879-1190. Hrs: 5-10 pm. Res accepted. Bar. Semi-a la carte: dinner $11.95-$29.50. Child's meals. Specializes steak, prime rib, fresh seafood, game. Salad bars. Parking. Outdoor dining. Old ranch decor. Fireplaces; ranch antiques. Cr cds: A, DS, MC, V.

D SC

★ ★ **STEAMBOAT YACHT CLUB.** *811 Yampa Ave.* 970/879-4774. Hrs: 11:30 am-2:30 pm, 5:30-10 pm. Res accepted. Bar. Semi-a la carte: lunch $5.50-$7.50, dinner $9.95-$21.95. Child's meals. Specializes in fresh seafood, tournedos. Parking. Outdoor dining overlooking river and ski slopes. Totally nonsmoking. Cr cds: A, MC, V.

D

✔ ★ **WINONA'S.** *617 Lincoln Ave.* 970/879-2483. Hrs: 7 am-3 pm; also 4:30-9:30 pm summer only. Closed Thanksgiving, Dec 25. Wine, beer. Semi-a la carte: bkfst $1.95-$5.95, lunch $1.50-$6, dinner $6-$10. Specializes in deli sandwiches, pastries. Parking. Outdoor dining. Totally nonsmoking. Cr cds: MC, V.

Sterling (A-8)

Pop 10,362 **Elev** 3,939 ft **Area code** 970 **Zip** 80751
Information Logan County Chamber of Commerce, 109 N Front, PO Box 1683; 970/522-5070.

What to See and Do

Outdoor sculptures. Sterling is known as the "City of Living Trees" because of the unique carved trees found throughout town. A self-guided tour map shows where to find the 16 sculpted trees created by a local sculptor. Call the Logan County Chamber of Commerce for more information.

Overland Trail Museum. Collections of Native American artifacts, cattlebrands, farm machinery; archaeological, paleontological exhibits, one-room schoolhouse, fire engine, children's displays; local historical items; park and picnic area. (Apr-Nov, daily) 21053 County 26 1/2, just off I-76. Phone 970/522-3895. **Free.**

Motels

★ ★ ★ **BEST WESTERN SUNDOWNER.** *Rte 1, Overland Trail St, 1 blk W of I-76 exit 125B.* 970/522-6265. 29 rms. S $64; D $72; each addl $8; under 12 free. Crib $5. Pet accepted. TV; cable (premium). VCR avail. Heated pool. Complimentary continental bkfst. Restaurant nearby. Ck-out 11 am. Coin lndry. Business servs avail. In-rm modem link. Exercise equipt; weight machine, bicycles, whirlpool. Balconies. Picnic tables, grills. Cr cds: A, C, D, DS, MC, V.

⚞ ≈ ⚟ ⚞ ⚟ SC

★ ★ **COLONIAL.** *915 S Division Ave.* 970/522-3382. 14 rms. May-Oct: S $24-$26; D $28-$38; each addl $2; under 6 free; wkly rates; lower rates rest of yr. Crib avail. Pet accepted, some restrictions. TV; cable (premium). Playground. Ck-out 11 am. Some refrigerators. Cr cds: A, DS, MC, V.

D ⚞ ⚟ ⚞

✔ ★ ★ **RAMADA INN.** *I-76 exit 125A & US 6, 1/2 mi E on US 6.* 970/522-2625; FAX 970/522-1321. 100 rms, 2 story. S $45-$68; D $57-$74; each addl $7; under 18 free. Crib free. Pet accepted; $25. TV; cable (premium). VCR avail. Indoor pool. Complimentary coffee in rms. Restaurant 6 am-10 pm. Bar 3:30-10 pm. Ck-out noon. Meeting rms. Business servs avail. Exercise equipt; bicycle, treadmill, whirlpool, sauna. Game rm. Cr cds: A, C, D, DS, ER, JCB, MC, V.

D ⚞ ⚟ ≈ ⚟ ⚞ ⚟ SC

Restaurant

✔ ★ **GOLDEN CORRAL FAMILY STEAK HOUSE.** *102 Hays. 970/522-9483.* Hrs: 11 am-10 pm; Fri & Sat to 11 pm. Closed Thanksgiving, Dec 25. Res accepted. Semi-a la carte: lunch $3.99-$7.50, dinner $4.99-$7.99. Child's meals. Specializes in steak, chicken. Salad bar. Parking. Cr cds: MC, V.

D SC

Telluride (E-2)

(See Norwood)

Settled 1878 **Pop** 1,309 **Elev** 8,800 ft **Area code** 970 **Zip** 81435
Information Telluride Visitor Services, 666 W Colorado Ave, Box 653; 800/525-3455.

Gray granite and red sandstone mountains surround this mining town named for the tellurium ore containing precious metals found in the area. Telluride, proud of its bonanza past, has not changed its facade. Because of its remoteness and small size, Telluride remains uncrowded and retains its history. Summer activities include fly fishing, mountain biking, river rafting, hiking, jeep trips, horseback riding and camping as well as 30 annual events from May to October.

What to See and Do

Bear Creek Trail. A two-mile canyon walk with view of tiered waterfall. (May-Oct) S end of Pine St.

Bridal Veil Falls. Highest waterfall in Colorado. Structure at top of falls was once a hydro-electric power plant, which served the Smuggler-Union Mine operations. It has been recently renovated, and now provides auxiliary electric power to Telluride. 2¹/₂ mi E on CO 145.

Skiing. Telluride Ski Resort. 2 Quad chairlifts, 2 triple, 5 double chairlifts, 1 surface lift; patrol, school, rentals; restaurants; nursery. 64 runs; longest run 2.8 mi; vertical drop 3,155 ft. (Thanksgiving-early Apr, daily) Cross-country skiing, heliskiing, ice-skating, snowmobiling, sleigh rides. Shuttle bus service and 2 in-town chairlifts. Contact PO Box 653; 800/525-3455. ¢¢¢¢-¢¢¢¢¢

Annual Events

Mountain Film Festival. Memorial Day wkend.

Balloon Rally. Early June.

Bluegrass Festival. Town Park. Mid-June.

Jazz Festival. Town Park. Early Aug.

Chamber Music Festival. Mid-Aug.

Telluride Hang Gliding Festival. Mid-June.

Motor Hotel

★ ★ **ICE HOUSE.** *PO Box 2909, 310 S Fir St. 970/728-6300; res: 800/544-3436; FAX 970/728-6358.* 42 air-cooled rms, 4 story, 7 suites. S, D $125-$160; each addl $15; suites $190-$235; under 13 free; higher rates: music & film festivals, Christmas hols, special events. Crib free. TV; cable (premium), VCR avail. Pool; sauna. Complimentary continental bkfst. Restaurant nearby. Ck-out 10 am. Meeting rms. Business servs avail. Bellhops. Valet serv. Concierge. Free covered parking. Downhill ski ¹/₂ blk; x-country ski adj. Whirlpool. Minibars. Balconies. Cr cds: A, C, D, DS, JCB, MC, V.

D ✖ ✖ ✖ ✖

Inns

★ **MANITOU HOTEL.** *333 S Fir St. 970/728-4011.* 12 rms, 2 story. No A/C. Mid-Feb-Mar: S, D $125-$195; higher rates: festivals, hols; lower rates rest of yr. TV; cable (premium). Complimentary continental bkfst, coffee. Restaurant nearby. Ck-out 10 am, ck-in 4 pm. Downhill ski 1 blk; x-country ski on site. Whirlpool. Refrigerators. Antiques. Cr cds: A, DS, MC, V.

✖ ✖ ✖ ✖

★ ★ ★ **PENNINGTON'S MOUNTAIN VILLAGE INN.** *Mailing address: PO Box 2428, 100 Pennington Court, 1¹/₂ mi S on CO 145 in Telluride Mountain Village. 970/728-5337; res: 800/543-1437.* 12 suites, 3 story. No A/C. Nov-Mar: S, D $140-$250; higher rates hols; closed 2 wks in Nov, 3 wks in May; lower rates rest of yr. TV; cable (premium). Complimentary full bkfst, refreshments. Ck-out noon, ck-in 3 pm. Lndry facilities. Whirlpool, steam rm. Downhill ski 1¹/₂ mi; x-country ski on site. Library. Game rm. Minibars. Balconies. French-country decor; rms with mountain view. Located on golf course. Totally nonsmoking. Cr cds: A, DS, MC, V.

D ✖ ✖ ✖

★ ★ ★ **SAN SOPHIA.** *PO Box 1825, 330 W Pacific Ave, just off Main St, downtown. 970/728-3001; res: 800/537-4781; FAX 970/728-6226.* 16 air-cooled rms, 2 story. S, D $100-$140; each addl $25; higher rates: music & film festivals & Dec-Mar. Closed Apr, Nov. Children over 10 yrs only. TV; cable (premium). Complimentary full bkfst. Restaurant nearby. Ck-out 11 am, ck-in 3 pm. Business servs avail. In-rm modem link. Downhill ski 1 blk; x-country ski on site. Whirlpool. Some balconies. Modern frame structure built in Victorian style with octagon tower observatory; bay windows; library, sitting rm. Interiors blend Victorian and modern Southwest design; stained and etched glass, period furnishings. Spectacular mountain views from all guest rms. Totally nonsmoking. Cr cds: A, MC, V.

✖ ✖ ✖

✔ ★ **VICTORIAN.** *401 W Pacific, 1 blk S off CO 45. 970/728-6601.* 26 rms, 6 share bath, 2 story, 2 kits. No A/C. Late Nov-early Apr: S $55-$112; D $63-$121; each addl $6; under 7 free; higher rates: mid-Dec-early Jan, Washington's birthday, special events; lower rates rest of yr. Crib $6. TV. Complimentary continental bkfst. Restaurant nearby. Ck-out 10 am, ck-in 4 pm. Downhill/x-country ski. Whirlpool, sauna. Refrigerators. Cr cds: A, C, D, DS, MC, V.

D ✖ ✖ ✖ SC

Resort

★ ★ ★ **THE PEAKS AT TELLURIDE.** *134 Country Club Dr, S on CO 145 to Mtn Village Blvd, then ¹/₂ mi E to Country Club Dr, near Municipal Airport. 970/728-6800; res: 800/789-2220; FAX 970/728-6175.* 181 air-cooled units, 8 story, 28 suites. Jan-Mar: S, D $350-$440; suites $475-$550; under 18 free; golf & ski plans; higher rates Dec hols; lower rates rest of yr. Crib free. Pet accepted, some restrictions. TV; cable (premium), VCR (movies avail $6). 2 pools, 1 indoor and 1 indoor/outdoor; poolside serv. Supervised child's activities. Complimentary coffee in lobby. Dining rm 7 am-11 pm. Box lunches. Rm serv 7 am-10:30 pm. Bar. Ck-out noon, ck-in 4 pm. Meeting rms. Business servs avail. In-rm modem link. Bellhops. Valet serv. Maid serv twice daily. Concierge. Gift shop. Covered valet parking. Free airport transportation. Sports dir. Tennis, pro. 18-hole golf, greens fee $75-$95 (incl cart), pro, putting green, driving range. Downhill/x-country ski on site; rentals. Snowmobiles, sleighing. Hiking. Exercise rm; instructor, weight machine, bicycles, whirlpools, sauna. Extensive 4-level spa facility (43,000 sq ft) includes 44 treatment rms, 2 pools, diverse selection of services and activities. Refrigerators, minibars. Some balconies. Every rm has spectacular view of the mountains. Luxurious 4-season resort located mid-mountain, within Telluride Mountain Village; situated in the San Juan Mountains of Southwest Colorado. Cr cds: A, D, MC, V.

D ✖ ✖ ✖ ✖ ✖ ✖ ✖ ✖ ✖

Guest Ranch

★ **SKYLINE.** *7214 CO 145. 970/728-3757; FAX 970/728-6728.* 10 air-cooled rms in lodge (1 story), 6 air-cooled kit. cottages (1-3 story). AP, June-Sept, wkly: $1,100/person; lower rates rest of yr. Crib free. Complimentary full bkfst. Box lunches, picnics. Ck-out 10 am, ck-in 3 pm. Gift shop. Coin lndry. Downhill ski 5 mi; x-country ski on site. Hiking. Fish/hunt guides. Totally nonsmoking. Cr cds: A, DS, MC, V.

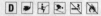

Restaurants

✔ ★ **FLORADORA.** *103 W Colorado Ave. 970/728-3888.* Hrs: 11 am-10 pm. Southwestern menu. Bar to 2 am. Semi-a la carte: lunch $5-$9, dinner $6-$15. Child's meals. Specializes in steak, pasta, fajitas. Salad bar. Stained-glass windows, Tiffany-style lamps. Totally nonsmoking. Cr cds: A, DS, MC, V.

★ **LEIMGRUBER'S BIERSTUBE.** *573 W Pacific Ave. 970/728-4663.* Hrs: 11:30 am-10 pm, Sat from 4 pm; winter months from 4 pm. Closed Sun (summer months); also July 4, Apr-Memorial Day. Res accepted. German, Amer menu. Bar from 4 pm. Semi-a la carte: lunch $2.50-$9, dinner $8.50-$19.95. Specialties: Wienerschnitzel, Jaegerschnitzel, pasta & chicken. Own pastries. Outdoor dining. Bavarian decor; mountain view. Totally nonsmoking. Cr cds: A, MC, V.

★ **SOFIO'S.** *110 E Colorado Ave. 970/728-4882.* Hrs: 7-11:30 am, 5:30-10 pm; Sun 7:30 am-noon, 5:30-10 pm. Closed Thanksgiving evening; also 2-3 wks Apr-May & 2 wks Nov. Mexican, Amer menu. Bar. Semi-a la carte: bkfst $2.95-$7.50, dinner $3.95-$15.95. Child's meals. Specializes in chiles rellenos, huachinango ala Veracruzana, fajitas. 1889 building. Totally nonsmoking. Cr cds: A, MC, V.

Trinidad (F-6)

(See Walsenburg; also see Raton, NM)

Settled 1859 **Pop** 8,580 **Elev** 6,025 ft **Area code** 719 **Zip** 81082
Information Trinidad-Las Animas County Chamber of Commerce, 309 Nevada Ave; 719/846-9285.

Bat Masterson was sheriff and Kit Carson was a frequent visitor to Trinidad when it was a busy trading post along the Santa Fe Trail. Today the town specializes in coal mining, ranching, farming and tourism. It is the seat of Las Animas County.

What to See and Do

A.R. Mitchell Memorial Museum of Western Art. Features Western paintings by Arthur Roy Mitchell, Harvey Dunn, Harold von Schmidt and other famous artists; Western and Native American artifacts; Hispanic religious folk art. Housed in a 1906 former department store with original tin ceiling, wood floors, horseshoe-shaped mezzanine. (Apr-Sept, daily exc Sun; also by appt; closed hols) 150 E Main St. Phone 719/846-4224. **Free.**

Baca House, Bloom House and Pioneer Museum. Colorado Historical Society administers this museum complex. The Baca House (1869) is a restored nine-room, two-story adobe house built by a wealthy, Hispanic sheep rancher. The Bloom House (1882) is a restored Victorian mansion and garden built by cattleman and banker George C. Bloom. The Pioneer Museum, in adobe outbuildings, has exhibits relating to the Santa Fe Trail, southern Colorado and open-range cattle days. Guided tours (Memorial Day-Sept, daily; rest of yr, by appt). Sr citizen rate. 300 E Main St, on the historic Santa Fe Trail. Phone 719/846-7217. ¢¢

Trinidad Lake State Park. A 2,300-acre park with a 500-acre lake. Waterskiing; fishing; boating (ramps). Nature trails; mountain biking. Picnicking, playground. Camping (electrical hookups, showers, dump station). Interpretive programs (Memorial Day-Labor Day, Fri, Sat, hols). Standard fees. (Daily) 3 mi W on CO 12. Phone 719/846-6951. Per vehicle ¢¢

Motels

✔ ★ **BUDGET HOST.** *10301 Santa Fe Trail Dr, off I-25 exit 11. 719/846-3307.* 16 rms. June-mid-Sept: S $29.95-$59.95; D $39.95-$69.95; wkly rates; lower rates rest of yr. Crib $3. Pet accepted; $3. TV. Complimentary coffee in lobby. Restaurant nearby. Ck-out 11 am. Free airport, RR station, bus depot transportation. Lawn games. Picnic tables, grills. Features 107-ft oil derrick. Located along the Mountain Branch of the Santa Fe Trail. Cr cds: A, C, D, DS, MC, V.

★ **BUDGET SUMMIT INN.** *9800 Santa Fe Trail Dr. 719/846-2251; FAX 719/846-2254.* 39 rms (21 with shower only), 2 story. Memorial Day-Labor Day: S $40-$80; D $50-$80; each addl $6; lower rates rest of yr. Pet accepted; $3. TV; cable. Whirlpool. Complimentary coffee in lobby. Complimentary continental bkfst. Restaurant adj open 24 hrs. Ck-out 11 am. Coin lndry. Business servs avail. In-rm modem link. Rec rm. Lawn games. Some refrigerators. Cr cds: A, C, D, DS, MC, V.

Motor Hotel

✔ ★ ★ **HOLIDAY INN.** *Rte 1, I-25, I-25 exit 11. 719/846-4491; FAX 719/846-2440.* 113 rms, 2 story. June-Sept: S $59-$69; D $69-$79; each addl $10; under 18 free; lower rates rest of yr. Crib free. Pet accepted, some restrictions. TV; cable, VCR avail. Indoor pool; poolside serv. Restaurant 6 am-10 pm. Rm serv from 7 am. Bar 4 pm-midnight. Ck-out noon. Coin lndry. Meeting rms. Business servs avail. Gift shop. Exercise equipt; treadmill, bicycles, whirlpool. Game rm. Lawn games. Some bathrm phones, refrigerators. Cr cds: A, C, D, DS, JCB, MC, V.

Restaurant

★ ★ **CHEF LIU'S.** *1423 Country Club Dr. 719/846-3333.* Hrs: 11 am-9:15 pm; Fri & Sat to 9:45 pm. Closed Thanksgiving; also Mon from Thanksgiving-Mar. Res accepted. Chinese menu. Bar. Semi-a la carte: lunch $3.75-$4.50, dinner $6.50-$16.95. Specialties: sweet & sour volcano shrimp, Peking beef, pepper steak. Parking. Chinese decor. Cr cds: A, DS, MC, V.

Vail (C-4)

(See Dillon, Leadville)

Pop 3,659 **Elev** 8,160 ft **Area code** 970 **Zip** 81657
Information Vail Valley Tourism & Convention Bureau, 100 E Meadow Dr; 970/476-5677 or 800/525-3875.

A resort community in White River National Forest (see GLENWOOD SPRINGS), Vail offers activities including golf, tennis, bicycling, swimming, jeep trips; river rafting, scenic gondola rides; hunting and fishing in season, and, of course, skiing in winter.

What to See and Do

Colorado Ski Heritage Museum & Ski Hall of Fame. Skiing artifacts and photographs tracing the history of skiing in Colorado for more than 120 years. Exhibits include an historical timeline of skiing, 10th Mountain Division, Colorado Ski Hall of Fame, World Alpine Ski Championships; nordic skiing, the evolution of skiing; boot and pole exhibits; video presentations. (Memorial Day-late Sept, late Nov-mid Apr, daily exc Mon; closed Jan 1, Easter, Thanksgiving, Dec 25) 231 S Frontage, in Vail Village Transportation Center. Phone 970/476-1876. **Free.**

Skiing.

Vail Ski Resort. 7 high-speed quads, 2 fixed-grip quads, 3 triple, 6 double chairlifts, 5 surface lifts, 1 gondola; patrol, school, rentals; snowmaking; cafeterias, restaurants, bars; nursery. Longest run 4.5 mi; vertical drop 3,250 ft. (Late Nov-mid-Apr, daily) Cross-country trails, rentals (Nov-Apr; fee); ice-skating, snowmobiling, sleigh rides. Gondola and Vista Bahn (May-Aug, daily; Sept, wkends; fee). In town on I-70, exit 176. Phone 970/476-5601. Summer ¢¢¢; Winter ¢¢¢¢¢

Beaver Creek Resort. 3 quad chairlifts, 4 triple, 4 double chairlifts; patrol, school, rentals; snowmaking; cafeteria, restaurants, bar; nursery. Longest run 2.75 mi; vertical drop 3,340 ft. (Late Nov-mid-Apr, daily) Cross-country trails and rentals (Nov-Apr), ice-skating, snowmobiling, sleigh rides. Chairlift rides (May-Aug, daily; Sept, wkends; fee). 10 mi W on I-70, exit 167, then 3 mi S. Phone 970/949-5750. Snowphone for both areas 970/476-4888 or -4889. Summer ¢¢¢; Winter ¢¢¢¢¢

Arrowhead at Vail. Quad chairlift, 1 rope tow; patrol, school, rentals; snowmaking; cafeteria, bar. 13 runs; longest run 2.5 mi; vertical drop 1,700 ft. (Late Dec-Apr). 10 mi W on I-70, exit 167, then 2 mi W on US 6. Phone 970/926-3029; snow conditions 970/926-3909. ¢¢¢¢¢

Annual Events

Gerald Ford Invitational Golf Tournament & Concert. Mid-Aug.

Vailfest. Special events, activities and scenic tours. Mid-Sept.

Lodges

(Hours and dates open may vary during off-season, making it advisable to call ahead)

★ ★ **LION SQUARE.** *660 W Lionshead Place. 970/476-2281; res: 800/525-5788; FAX 970/476-7423.* 108 units, 3-7 story, 83 townhouses. No A/C. Nov-Apr: S, D $115-$225; townhouses $160-$760; under 17 free; lower rates rest of yr. Crib free. Free garage parking. TV; cable (premium), VCR avail. Heated pool; whirlpool, sauna. Supervised child's activities (Nov-Apr); ages 5-12. Coffee in rms. Complimentary continental bkfst. Restaurant 5-10 pm. Bar. Ck-out 10 am. Coin lndry. Meeting rms. Business servs avail. Valet serv. Concierge. Ski shop. Downhill ski adj; x-country ski on site. Health club privileges. Lawn games. Refrigerators. Balconies. Picnic tables, grills. On creek; adj to gondola. Cr cds: A, C, D, DS, MC, V.

D ★ ★ ★ ★ ★ ★ SC

★ ★ ★ **LODGE AT CORDILLERA.** *(Box 1110, Edwards 81632) W on I-70 to Edwards, exit 163, 2 mi W on US 6 to Squaw Creek Rd, then 2 mi S. 970/926-2200; res: 800/548-2721; FAX 970/926-2486.* Hand-carved Spanish pine woodwork and furnishings create rustic luxury at this palatial mountaintop retreat with sweeping vistas of a pristine wilderness area. 28 rms, 3 story. S, D $240-$295; suites $240-$595; under 16 free; golf & spa plans. Crib free. Pet accepted. TV; cable (premium), VCR avail. 2 pools, 1 indoor. Restaurant (see PICASSO). Box lunches. Rm serv 6:30 am-11pm. Bar; entertainment wkends. Ck-out noon, ck-in 4 pm. Meeting rms. Business servs avail. Valet serv. Concierge. Gift shop. Tennis, pro. 18-hole golf, pro, greens fee $100 (inclusive). Downhill ski 8 mi; x-country ski on site; rentals. Hiking. Bicycle rentals. Exercise rm; instructor, weight machine, treadmill, whirlpool, sauna, steam rm. Health/spa facilities. Many fireplaces,

sleeping lofts. Many balconies, private decks. Totally nonsmoking. Cr cds: A, C, D, DS, MC, V.

D ★ ★ ★ ★ ★ ★ ★ ★ ★ ★ SC

Motor Hotels

★ ★ ★ **BEST WESTERN VAILGLO LODGE.** *Box 189, 701 W Lionshead Circle, 5 blks W of I-70 Vail exit 176. 970/476-5506; FAX 970/476-3926.* 34 air-cooled rms, 4 story. Feb-Mar, Dec: S, D $189-$195; each addl $15; under 6 free; higher rates Dec 25; lower rates rest of yr. Crib free. TV; cable (premium). Heated pool; whirlpool. Complimentary continental bkfst. Restaurant adj 7-3 am. Ck-out noon. Business center. In-rm modem link. Valet serv. Downhill/x-country ski 1 blk. Refrigerators. Balconies. Cr cds: A, C, D, DS, MC, V.

★ ★ ★ ★ SC ★

★ ★ **GASTHOF GRAMSHAMMER.** *231 E Gore Creek Drive, 3 blks S of I-70 exit 176. 970/476-5626; FAX 970/476-8816.* 28 units, 4 story. No A/C. Thanksgiving-Easter: S, D $195-$595; each addl $40; under 12 free in summer; lower rates mid-Nov. Closed mid-Apr-May. Crib avail. TV; cable, VCR avail. Complimentary continental bkfst. Restaurant 11:30 am-3 pm, 5:45-10 pm. Bar 11:30-2 am, Sun to midnight. Ck-out 11:30 am. Meeting rms. Business servs avail. Valet serv. Shopping arcade. Downhill ski 1 blk. Ski rental; ski shop. Health club privileges. Some kit. units, refrigerators, fireplaces. Some balconies. Austrian decor. Cr cds: A, D, MC, V.

★ ★ ★

★ ★ ★ **INN AT BEAVER CREEK.** *(Box 36, Avon 81620) 10 Elk Track Lane, 4 mi S of I-70 exit 167. 970/845-7800; FAX 970/949-2308.* 45 air-cooled rms, 4 story. Late Jan-Mar: S, D $250-$300; each addl $15; suites $500; higher rates late Dec; lower rates rest of yr. Closed mid-Apr-mid-May. Crib free. TV; cable (premium), VCR avail. Heated pool; whirlpool, sauna, steam rm. Complimentary continental bkfst. Coffee in rms. Restaurant nearby. Bar 3-10 pm. Ck-out 10 am. Free lndry. Meeting rms. Business servs avail. In-rm modem link. Bellhops. Valet serv. Concierge. Downhill/x-country ski on site. Refrigerators. Cr cds: A, MC, V.

D ★ ★ ★ ★

★ ★ **SITZMARK LODGE.** *183 Gore Creek Dr. 970/476-5001; FAX 970/476-8702.* 35 rms, 3 story, 1 kit. No A/C. Late Feb-late Apr: S $160-$195; D $170-$230; each addl $15; under 12 free in summer; lower rates rest of yr. Crib $5. TV; cable (premium). Pool; whirlpool, sauna. Complimentary continental bkfst (winter). Restaurant 6-10 pm. Bar. Ck-out 11 am. Coin lndry. Business servs avail. Shopping arcade. Covered parking. Downhill/x-country ski ½ blk. Refrigerators; some fireplaces. Balconies. Cr cds: DS, MC, V.

★ ★ ★ ★

★ ★ **VAIL ATHLETIC CLUB.** *352 E Meadow Dr. 970/476-0700; res: 800/822-4754; FAX 970/476-6451.* 38 air-cooled rms, 3 story, 7 suites, 7 kit. units. Feb-Mar: S, D $295-$330; suites $610-$1,140; kit. units $360; under 12 free; higher rates Dec 25; lower rates rest of yr. Crib free. TV; cable (premium), VCR avail. Indoor pool. Supervised child's activities; ages 2-16. Complimentary coffee in rms. Complimentary continental bkfst. Restaurant 7-10 am, 5:30-10 pm. Rm serv. Bar 3:30 pm-closing. Ck-out 11 am. Coin lndry. Meeting rms. Business servs avail. Bellhops. Valet serv. Concierge. Free garage parking. Tennis privileges. Golf privileges, greens fee $75, pro, putting green, driving range. Downhill/x-country ski 3 blks. Exercise rm; instructor, weights, bicycles, whirlpool, sauna, steam rm. Refrigerators; some wet bars. Balconies. Cr cds: A, MC, V.

D ★ ★ ★ ★ ★ ★ ★ ★ SC

Hotels

★ ★ **BEAVER CREEK LODGE.** *(26 Avondale Ln, Beaver Creek 81620) Approx 7 mi W on I-70, N on Avon Rd. 970/845-9800; res:*

800/732-6777; FAX 970/845-8242. 71 air-cooled suites, 4 story. Feb-Mar: S, D $240-$1,100; each addl $25; under 16 free; 7-night min Dec 25; lower rates rest of yr. Crib free. TV; cable (premium), VCR (movies avail $7.95). Indoor/outdoor pool; whirlpool. Complimentary coffee in rms. Restaurant 7 am-10 pm. Bar. Ck-out 11 am. Coin lndry. Meeting rms. Business servs avail. Concierge. Barber, beauty shops. Free valet parking. Downhill/x-country ski ½ blk. Exercise equipt; weights, bicycles, sauna. Minibars, fireplaces. Some balconies. Cr cds: A, C, D, DS, MC, V.

D 📞 🏊 🏋 🎿 🚭 🔥 SC

★ ★ ★ THE PINES LODGE. (PO Box 36, 141 Scott Hill Rd, Beaver Creek 81620) 7 mi W on I-70, exit 167. 970/845-7900; res: 800/688-2411; FAX 970/845-7809. 60 air-cooled rms, 4 story, 4 suites, 12 kit. units. Early-Jan-Mar: S, D $275-$375; each addl $25; suites $500-$1,400; under 12 free; ski, golf packages; higher rates Christmas hols; lower rates rest of yr. Crib free. TV; cable (premium), VCR (movies avail). Heated pool; whirlpool, poolside serv. Coffee in rms. Restaurant 7 am-10 pm. Bar 4-11 pm; entertainment. Ck-out 11 am. Meeting rms. Business servs avail. Concierge. Beauty shop. Free airport transportation. Downhill/x-country ski adj. Exercise equipt; bicycles, treadmill. Game rm. Refrigerators. Many balconies. Traditional Alpine structure; high-pitched roofs, dormers, towers. Modern Southwestern interior; stone fireplaces, adobe walls, pine furnishings. Cr cds: A, MC, V.

D 🏊 🏊 🎿 🚭 🔥

★ ★ THE WESTIN HOTEL. 1300 Westhaven Dr, 1½ mi W of I-70, Vail exit 176. 970/476-7111; FAX 970/479-7020. 290 rms, 4 story. Late Nov-mid-Apr: S, D $309-$429; suites $500-$995; under 18 free; ski, honeymoon plans; lower rates rest of yr. Crib free. Valet parking $14. Pet accepted; $50. TV; cable (premium), VCR avail. Heated pool; whirlpool, poolside serv. Coffee in rms. Restaurants 7 am-10 pm. Rm serv 24 hrs. Bars 3:30 pm-1:30 am; entertainment. Ck-out noon. Meeting rms. Business center. Concierge. Shopping arcade. Tennis. Downhill/x-country ski on site. Exercise rm; instructor, weights, bicycles, sauna, steam rm. Spa services. Ski rentals. Mountain bike rentals. Refrigerators, minibars. Private patios, balconies. On river. Cr cds: A, C, D, DS, ER, JCB, MC, V.

D 🏊 📞 🏋 🎾 🏊 🎿 🚭 🔥 SC 🛶

Inns

✔ ★ ★ BLACK BEAR. 2405 Elliott Rd. 970/476-1304; FAX 970/476-0433. 12 air-cooled rms, 2 story. Mid-Nov-mid-Apr: S, D $110-$170; each addl $25; higher rates Dec 25; lower rates mid-May-mid-Nov. Closed rest of yr. TV in sitting rm; cable (premium). Complimentary full bkfst, coffee & tea/sherry. Restaurant opp 7 am-11 pm. Ck-out 11 am, ck-in 3-7 pm. Meeting rm. Business servs avail. In-rm modem link. Downhill/x-country ski 1½ mi. Game rm. Lawn games. Antiques; on banks of Gore Creek. Totally nonsmoking. Cr cds: DS, MC, V.

D 📞 🏊 🚭 🔥

★ ★ ★ CHRISTIANIA AT VAIL. 356 E Hanson Ranch Rd. 970/476-5641; FAX 970/476-0470. 11 air-cooled rms, 3 story, 6 suites. Jan-Mar: S, D $200-$315; suites $320; kit. suite $420; each addl $25; Dec, Feb & Mar (7-night min); lower rates rest of yr. Crib avail. Parking $5. TV; cable, VCR avail. Heated pool; sauna. Complimentary continental bkfst. Restaurant adj 8 am-10 pm. Ck-out 11 am, ck-in 4 pm. Business servs avail. Bellhops. Downhill/x-country ski adj. Rec rm. Minibars. Bavarian-style inn. Destinctive decor in each rm. Some antiques, hand-carved furnishings. Totally nonsmoking. Cr cds: MC, V.

D 🏊 🚭 🔥

✔ ★ ★ EAGLE RIVER. (145 N Main St, Minturn 81645) 7 mi W on I-70, exit 171. 970/827-5761; res: 800/344-1750; FAX 970/827-4020. 12 rms, 3 story. No elvtr. Nov-Mar: S, D $119-$180; each addl $20; higher rates late Dec; lower rates rest of yr. Children over 12 yrs preferred. TV; cable, VCR avail. Complimentary full bkfst. Restaurant opp open 24 hrs. Ck-out 11 am, ck-in 3-10 pm. Meeting rm. Business servs avail. Downhill/x-country ski 7 mi. Mountain bikes avail. Whirl-

pool. Built as inn in 1894; renovated adobe structure. Santa Fe furnishings, decor. Totally nonsmoking. Cr cds: A, MC, V.

📞 🏊 🚭 🔥 SC

Resorts

★ ★ CHARTER AT BEAVER CREEK. (Box 5310, Beaver Creek 81620) 3 mi S of I-70 exit 167. 970/949-6660; res: 800/525-6660; FAX 970/949-6709. 64 lodge rms, 4-6 story, 105 condos. Late Nov-mid-Apr: S, D $150-$255; suites $210-$1,160; ski, golf plans; higher rates late Dec; lower rates rest of yr. Crib $6. TV; cable (premium), VCR. 2 pools, 1 indoor; wading pool. Supervised child's activities (Jan-Apr); ages 3-11. Coffee in rms. Dining rm 7-11:30 am, 5:30-9:30 pm; summer 7 am-2 pm, 5-10 pm. Box lunches. Bar 4-10 pm; summer 6-10 pm. Ck-out 11 am, ck-in 4 pm. Meeting rms. Business servs avail. In-rm modem link. Bellhops. Concierge. Beauty shop. Valet parking. Ski shop. Tennis privileges, pro. 18-hole golf privileges opp, pro. Downhill/x-country ski on site. Sleighing. Snowmobiles. Exercise equipt; weights, bicycles, whirlpool, sauna, steam rm. Refrigerators. Fireplace in condos. Balconies. Luxurious resort lodge. Cr cds: A, MC, V.

D 🏊 🏋 🎾 🏊 🎿 🚭 🔥 🛶

★ ★ ★ HYATT REGENCY—BEAVER CREEK. (136 E Thomas Pl, Beaver Creek 81620) 2 mi S off I-70 exit 167. 970/949-1234; FAX 970/949-4164. This multi-gabled slopeside resort in a traditional mountain setting offers contemporary amenities. The lobby sports an imposing antler chandelier, while guest rooms are decorated in country pine style. 295 air-cooled rms, 6 story, 31 suites. Dec-Mar: S, D $390-$565; each addl $25; suites $925-$2,220; under 18 free; ski, golf plans; lower rates rest of yr. Crib free. Valet parking $10. Pet accepted, some restrictions. TV; cable (premium), VCR avail. Heated pool; indoor step-in, poolside serv. Playground. Supervised child's activities; ages 5-12. Complimentary coffee in rms. Dining rm 7 am-10 pm. Box lunches, picnics. Rm serv 6 am-midnight. Bar 11:30-1:30 am; entertainment. Ck-out noon, ck-in 4 pm. Deli. Coin lndry. Convention facilities. Business center. In-rm modem link. Bellhops. Valet serv. Concierge. Shopping arcade. Barber, beauty shop. Recreation dir. Tennis, pro. 18-hole golf privileges, greens fee $100, pro, putting green, driving range. Downhill/x-country ski on site. Hiking. Bicycles (rentals). Lawn games. Exercise rm; instructor, bicycles, stair machine, treadmill, whirlpool, sauna, steam rm. Massage. Spa facilities. Fishing/hunting guides. Minibars. Balconies. Cr cds: A, C, D, DS, ER, JCB, MC, V.

D 📞 📞 🏊 🏋 🎾 🏊 🎿 🚭 🔥 SC 🛶

★ ★ MARRIOTT MOUNTAIN RESORT-VAIL. 715 W Lionshead Circle, off S Frontage Rd, 5 blks W of I-70 exit 176. 970/476-4444; FAX 970/476-1647. 350 units, 6 story, 54 kits. Some A/C. Jan-Mar: S, D $236-$263; each addl $20; kit. units, suites $300-$825; under 18 free; ski, package plans; higher rates Christmas hols; varied lower rates rest of yr. Crib free. TV; cable (premium). 2 pools, 1 indoor; poolside serv (summer). Coffee in rms. Restaurants 7 am-midnight. Rm serv 7:30 am-10:30 pm. Bars noon-2 am. Ck-out 11 am, ck-in 4 pm. Coin lndry. Convention facilities. Valet serv. Concierge. Gift shop. Beauty shop. Tennis. Downhill/x-country ski ¼ mi. Ski rentals. Exercise rm; instructor, weights, bicycles, whirlpool, sauna, steam rm. Refrigerators; many fireplaces. Balconies. Cr cds: A, C, DS, MC, V.

D 🏊 🎾 🏊 🎿 🚭 🔥 SC

★ ★ ★ SONNENALP. 20 Vail Rd. 970/476-5656; res: 800/654-8312; FAX 970/476-1639. 186 rms, 3 villas (3-4 story). Some A/C. Early Jan-early Apr: S, D $290-$318; each addl $25; suite $330-$1,150; under 5 free; sports activities packages; higher rates Christmas season; lower rates rest of yr. TV; cable (premium), VCR avail. 2 indoor/outdoor pools. Supervised child's activities (winter months); infant-6 yrs. Complimentary full bkfst. Restaurant 7 am-10 pm. Rm serv. Bar. Ck-out 11 am. Meeting rms. Business center. In-rm modem link. Bellhops. Valet serv. Concierge. Free valet parking. Tennis privileges. 18-hole golf privileges, pro, putting green, driving range. Downhill/x-country ski ¼ mi. Exercise equipt; weights, bicycles, whirlpool, sauna, steam rm. Game rm. Some balconies. Cr cds: A, D, MC, V.

Restaurants

★ ★ **ALPENROSE.** *100 E Meadow Dr. 970/476-3194.* Hrs: 11:30 am-10 pm; summer from 9 am; Mon to 6 pm. Closed Tues; also mid-Apr-late-May & mid-Oct-mid-Nov. Res accepted. No A/C. German, continental menu. Bar. Semi-a la carte: bkfst $4.75-$7.50, lunch $7-$9, dinner $18-$24. Specializes in veal, fresh fish, European pastries. Outdoor dining, two terraces. Exceptional view. Cr cds: MC, V.

★ ★ **BEANO'S CABIN.** *(PO Box 915, Avon 81620) 7 mi W on I-70 to exit 167, then 4 mi S, in Beaver Creek. 970/845-5770.* Hrs: 5-10 pm. Closed mid-Apr-mid-June. Res required. Bar. Complete meals: dinner $69. Child's meals. Specializes in seafood, venison filet. Guitarist. Outdoor dining. Access by horse-drawn wagon, van or on horseback; winter months by sleigh or ski. Rustic mountain cabin on challenging slope. Totally nonsmoking. Cr cds: A, MC, V.

★ **BLU'S.** *193 E Gore Creek Dr, downstairs from the children's fountain. 970/476-3113.* Hrs: 9 am-11 pm. Closed May. Bar. Semi-a la carte: bkfst $4.75-$6.95, lunch $4.50-$10.50, dinner $6-$19. Child's meals. Outdoor dining. Cr cds: A, C, D, DS, MC, V.

★ **CHILI WILLY'S.** *(101 Main St, Minturn) 7 mi W on I-70, exit 171. 970/827-5887.* Hrs: 11 am-2:30 pm, 5-10 pm; summer from 5:30 pm. Closed Thanksgiving, Dec 25. Bar. Semi-a la carte: lunch $4.95-$11.95, dinner $8.95-$16.95. Child's meals. Specializes in Tex-Mex dishes. Parking. Outdoor dining. Rustic decor; casual atmosphere. Totally nonsmoking. Cr cds: DS, MC, V.

★ ★ **GOLDEN EAGLE INN.** *118 Beaver Creek Plaza. 970/949-1940.* Hrs: 11:30 am-10 pm. Res accepted. Bar. Semi-a la carte: lunch $6-$9, dinner $13-$25. Child's meal's. Specializes in wild game, salmon. Parking. Outdoor dining. 3 dining areas. Contemporary decor. Cr cds: A, MC, V.

★ ★ **LANCELOT INN.** *205 E Gore Creek Dr, 3 blks S of I-70 exit 176. 970/476-5828.* Hrs: 6-10 pm. Closed May. Res accepted. No A/C. Bar 5 pm-closing. Semi-a la carte: dinner $12.95-$26.95. Child's meals. Specializes in prime rib, Colorado beef, fresh seafood, boneless chicken breast. Outdoor dining in summer. Overlooks landscaped creek. Totally nonsmoking. Cr cds: A, MC, V.

★ ★ **MIRABELLE AT BEAVER CREEK.** *(55 Village Rd, Beaver Creek) ³/₄ mi S of I-70 exit 167. 970/949-7728.* Hrs: 6-10 pm. Closed Mon; May; also mid-Oct-mid-Nov. Res accepted. French menu. Semi-a la carte: dinner $17-$25. Specializes in elk loin, lobster with creamy polenta. Own pastries, ice cream. Parking. Outdoor dining. Built 1898; believed to be on site of first house in valley of Beaver Creek. Totally nonsmoking. Cr cds: DS, MC, V.

★ ★ **MONTAUK.** *549 W Lionshead Mall. 970/476-2601.* Hrs: 3-10 pm; summer months 5-9:30 pm. Closed Thanksgiving. Res accepted. Bar. Semi-a la carte: dinner $14.95-$21.95. Specializes in fresh grilled seafood. Outdoor dining. Grill theme. Totally nonsmoking. Cr cds: A, MC, V.

★ ★ **PICASSO.** *(See Lodge At Cordillera) 970/926-2200.* Hrs: 7-10 am, noon-2 pm, 6-10 pm; Sun brunch noon-2 pm. Res accepted. French menu. Bar. Wine cellar. A la carte entrees: lunch $5.95-$12.95. Complete meals: dinner $24-$50. Sun brunch $20. Guitarist Thurs-Sat. Valet parking. Outdoor dining. Overlooks mountain range. Original Picasso paintings. Totally nonsmoking. Cr cds: A, C, D, DS, MC, V.

★ ★ **SWEET BASIL.** *193 E Gore Creek Dr. 970/476-0125.* Hrs: 11:30 am-2:30 pm, 5:30-10 pm. Res accepted. No A/C. Bar. Semi-a la carte: lunch $4.95-$8.95, dinner $18-$28. Specializes in fresh fish, homemade pasta. Outdoor dining. Totally nonsmoking. Cr cds: A, MC, V.

★ ★ **TYROLEAN INN.** *400 E Meadow Dr. 970/476-2204.* Hrs: 6-10 pm. Closed Tues (summer). Res accepted. Continental menu. Bar. Semi-a la carte: dinner $14-$26. Child's meals. Specializes in wild game, fresh seafood. Outdoor dining. 3 level dining area. Large logging sled suspended from ceiling. Austrian atmosphere. Cr cds: A, MC, V.

Walsenburg (E-6)

(See Trinidad)

Founded 1873 **Pop** 3,300 **Elev** 6,182 ft **Area code** 719 **Zip** 81089
Information Chamber of Commerce, 400 Main St, Railroad Depot; 719/738-1065.

Named after a German pioneer merchant, the present town was originally the small Spanish village of La Plaza de los Leones.

What to See and Do

Fort Francisco Museum. Original adobe trading fort (1862) now contains exhibits of pioneer cattle ranching and commercial mining. The site also has a saloon, blacksmith shop, one-room schoolhouse and collection of Indian artifacts. (Late May-early Sept, daily) 16 mi SW on US 160 & CO 12 in La Veta. Phone 719/742-3638. ¢

Lathrop State Park. Swimming, waterskiing; fishing; boating (ramps). Golf. Picnicking (shelters). Camping (dump station). Visitor Center. Standard fees. (Daily) 3 mi W on US 160. Phone 719/738-2376. Per vehicle ¢¢

Walsenburg Mining Museum. Exhibits on the history of coal mining in Huerfano County, the Trinidad coal fields and Raton basin. (May-Oct, Mon-Fri; rest of yr, by appt) W 5th St, Old County Jail Bldg. Phone 719/738-1107. ¢

Motel

✔ ★ ★ **BEST WESTERN RAMBLER.** *Box 48, 1¹/₂ mi N of Walsenburg I-25 exit 52. 719/738-1121; FAX 719/738-1093.* 32 rms. Mid-May-early Sept: S $59-$75; D $75; under 18 free; lower rates rest of yr. Crib free. Pet accepted, some restrictions. TV; cable (premium), VCR avail. Heated pool. Ck-out 11 am. Free bus depot transportation. Cr cds: A, C, D, DS, MC, V.

Restaurant

✔ ★ ★ **IRON HORSE.** *503 W 7th St. 719/738-9966.* Hrs: 11 am-2 pm, 4:30-10 pm; Sat & Sun from 4:30 pm. Winter hrs vary. Closed Thanksgiving, Dec 24 & 25; 3 wks Feb. Bar. Semi-a la carte: lunch $3.95-$6.75, dinner $7.95-$14.95. Specializes in steak, ribs, chicken, Italian dishes. Parking. 3 dining rms in turn-of-the-century armory. Cr cds: A, DS, MC, V.

Winter Park (B-5)

(See Central City, Georgetown, Granby, Idaho Springs)

Pop 528 **Elev** 9,040 ft **Area code** 303 **Zip** 80482
Information Winter Park/Fraser Valley Chamber of Commerce, PO Box 3236; 303/726-4118.

Winter Park is part of the unique Denver Mountain Park System, located on the western slope of Berthoud Pass in the Arapaho National Forest (see DILLON).

What to See and Do

Skiing. Winter Park Resort. 4 high-speed quad, 4 triple, 12 double chairlifts; patrol, school, rentals; snowmaking; cafeterias, restaurants, bars. NASTAR and coin-operated race courses. (Mid-Nov-mid-Apr, daily) The three interconnected mountain areas include **Winter Park**, **Mary Jane** and **Vasquez Ridge**. 112 runs; longest run 5.1 mi; vertical drop 3,060 ft. Half-day rates. Chairlift and alpine slide also operate late June-mid-Sept (daily). Bicycle rentals, miniature golf (summer, fee). 1 mi SE off US 40. Phone 303/726-5514. ¢¢¢¢¢

The Children's Center within the Winter Park Resort is an all-inclusive ski center for children (inquire about ages) with children's ski slopes, rentals, school and day care. Phone 303/726-5514. ¢¢¢¢¢

Motel

(Hours and dates open may vary during off-season, making it advisable to call ahead)

★ **HI COUNTRY HAUS RESORT CONDOMINIUMS.** *Box 3095, 1 blk E on US 40; rental office in Park Place Shopping Center. 970/726-9421; res: 800/228-1025; FAX 970/726-8004.* 306 kit. condos, 3 story. 1-bedrm $88-$180; 2-bedrm $108-$306; 3-bedrm $144-$408; studio $84-$176; ski, golf plans; summer package. Crib $7.50. TV; cable. Indoor pool; whirlpool, sauna. Playground. Ck-out 10 am. Coin lndry. Meeting rms. Business servs avail. RR station transportation. Downhill ski 2 mi. Game rm. Lawn games. Refrigerators, fireplaces. Balconies. Picnic tables, grills. Stocked trout pond. Cr cds: A, DS, MC, V.

Lodge

★ ★ **IRON HORSE RESORT.** *PO Box 1286, 257 Winter Park Dr. 970/826-8851; res: 800/621-8190; FAX 970/726-2321.* 126 air-cooled kit. condos, 6 story. Nov-Apr: condos $85-$410; lower rates

rest of yr. Crib $5. TV; cable. Indoor/outdoor pool. Complimentary coffee in rms. Restaurant 7-10 am, 11:30 am-2:30 pm, 5-9:30 pm. Bar 3 pm-midnight; entertainment Fri, Sat. Ck-out 10 am, ck-in 4 pm. Grocery 4 mi. Coin lndry. Package store 2 mi. Meeting rms. Business center. Bellhops. Concierge. Free RR station, bus depot transportation. Downhill/x-country ski on site. Hiking. Lawn games. Game rm. Exercise equipt; weights, bicycles, steam rms, whirlpool. Balconies. Picnic tables, grills. On river. Cr cds: A, MC, V.

Hotel

★ ★ **VINTAGE RESORT.** *PO Box 1369, 100 Winter Park Dr. 970/726-8801; res: 800/472-7017; FAX 970/726-9230.* 118 air-cooled rms, 5 story, 90 kit. units. Mid-Nov-mid-Apr: S, D $85-$190; suites $225-$450; higher rates Dec 15-Jan 4; lower rates rest of yr. Crib free. TV; cable (premium). Heated pool. Complimentary coffee in rms. Restaurant 7 am-9:30 pm. Rm serv (seasonal). Bar 3 pm-midnight; entertainment some wkends, winter. Ck-out 11 am. Coin lndry. Meeting rms. Business servs avail. In-rm modem link. Gift shop. Free RR station, bus depot transportation. Downhill/x-country ski on site. Exercise equipt; weights, bicycles, whirlpool, sauna. Game rm. Picnic tables. Cr cds: A, C, D, DS, MC, V.

Restaurant

★ ★ **CHALET LUCERNE.** *78521 US 40. 970/726-5402.* Hrs: 8 am-2:30 pm, 5-9:30 pm; winter from 5 pm. Closed Mon; Easter; also May, mid-Oct-mid-Nov. Res accepted. No A/C. Swiss, Amer menu. Bar. Semi-a la carte: bkfst $3.95-$6.95, lunch $4.25-$8.25, dinner $8-$18.90. Child's meals. Specialties: beef fondue, veal Zurich. Parking. Outdoor dining. Authentic Swiss decor. Cr cds: DS, MC, V.

Ⓓ

Woodland Park (D-6)

(see Colorado Springs)

Kansas

Population: 2,477,574

Land area: 82,280 square miles

Elevation: 680-4,039 feet

Highest point: Mount Sunflower (Wallace County)

Entered Union: January 29, 1861 (34th state)

Capital: Topeka

Motto: To the stars through difficulties

Nickname: The Sunflower State, The Jayhawker State

State flower: Sunflower

State bird: Meadowlark

State tree: Cottonwood

State fair: September 6-15, 1996, in Hutchinson

Time zone: Central and Mountain

Native Americans inhabited Kansas thousands of years before Spanish conquistador Francisco Vasquez de Coronado explored the territory in 1541. Though looking for gold and the fabled Land of Quivira, Coronado instead found what he called "the best country I have ever seen for producing all the products of Spain." Other early explorers of Kansas were partners Meriwether Lewis and William Clark. Army Captain Zebulon Pike also explored the area, continuing westward to discover what is now Pike's Peak in Colorado.

By the 1840s, traders and immigrants had established the Santa Fe and Chisholm Trails across the region. Kansas pre-Civil War activity included the exploits of John Brown, who operated the Underground Railway for runaway slaves escaping through Kansas. Many clashes occurred between antislavery and proslavery forces as Kansas was being admitted to the Union. As railroads expanded westward, the era of cattle drives made such towns as Abilene, Hays, Wichita and Dodge City centers of the legendary Old West, as did such men as Bat Masterson, Wyatt Earp, Wild Bill Hickok and the Dalton Gang.

Eastern Kansas is green, fertile and hilly, with woods, streams and lakes. Western Kansas is a part of the Great Plains, once the grass-covered haunt of the buffalo. In 1874, Mennonite immigrants from Russia introduced their Turkey Red wheat seed to Kansas soil, helping to establish Kansas as the "breadbasket of the nation." Today agriculture has expanded to include a wide range of crops, cattle and other livestock. Other leading industries include the manufacturing of airplanes and farm equipment, salt mining and oil refining.

Crappie, walleye, bass and channel catfish abound in many lakes and streams to lure the fisherman. Deer, quail, pheasant, ducks, geese and many other species of game attract the hunter.

National Park Service Areas

Kansas has Fort Larned National Historic Site (see LARNED) and Fort Scott National Historic Site (see FORT SCOTT).

State Recreation Areas

The following towns list state recreation areas in their vicinity under What to See and Do; refer to the individual town for directions and park information.

Listed under **Beloit:** see Glen Elder State Park.

Listed under **El Dorado:** see El Dorado State Park.

Listed under **Emporia:** see Eisenhower State Park.

Listed under **Eureka:** see Fall River State Park.

Listed under **Independence:** see Elk City State Park.

Listed under **Junction City:** see Milford State Park.

Listed under **Lawrence:** see Clinton State Park.

Listed under **Lindsborg:** see Kanopolis State Park.

Listed under **Manhattan:** see Tuttle Creek State Park.

Listed under **Mankato:** see Lovewell State Park.

Listed under **Meade:** see Meade State Park.

Listed under **Norton:** see Prairie Dog State Park.

Listed under **Ottawa:** see Pomona State Park.

Listed under **Pittsburg:** see Crawford State Park.

Listed under **Russell:** see Wilson State Park.

Listed under **Scott City:** see Lake Scott State Park.

Listed under **Stockton:** see Webster State Park.

Listed under **Topeka:** see Perry State Park.

Listed under **WaKeeney:** see Cedar Bluff State Park.

Listed under **Wichita:** see Cheney State Park.

Listed under **Yates Center:** see Toronto State Park.

Water-related activities, hiking, riding, various other sports, picnicking and visitor centers, as well as camping, are available in many of these areas. Annual vehicle permit $23; daily vehicle permit $4. There is camping at most areas (2-wk max). Annual camping permit $38; daily camping permit $4; electricity, water, trailer utility hookup $6. Pets on hand-held leash or in cage only; no pets on bathing beaches. A camping guide is published by the Kansas Department of Wildlife and Parks, Public Information, 512 SE 25th Ave, Pratt 67124; 316/672-5911.

Fishing & Hunting

The state maintains more than 35 state fishing lakes and 48 wildlife management and public hunting areas.

Nonresident fishing license: annual $30; 5-day $15; 24-hour $4. Nonresident hunting license: annual $60; 48-hour nonresident waterfowl license $20; Kansas migratory habitat stamp $3; handling fee on all licenses $1. Hunters born on or after July 1, 1957 must have a hunter's safety course certificate card in order to purchase a license.

For digests of hunting and fishing regulations, contact Kansas Department of Wildlife and Parks, Public Information, 512 SE 25th Ave, Pratt 67124; 316/672-5911. The department also publishes hunting and fishing guides.

Safety Belt Information

Safety belts are mandatory for all persons in front seat of vehicle. Children under the age of 4 must be in an approved safety seat anywhere in vehicle. Children ages 4-13 must wear a safety belt anywhere in vehicle. For further information phone 913/532-5780.

Interstate Highway System

The following alphabetical listing of Kansas towns in *Mobil Travel Guide* shows that these cities are within 10 miles of the indicated Interstate highways. A highway map should, however, be checked for the nearest exit.

INTERSTATE 35: El Dorado, Emporia, Kansas City, Ottawa and Wichita.

INTERSTATE 70: Abilene, Colby, Goodland, Hays, Junction City, Kansas City, Lawrence, Manhattan, Oakley, Russell, Salina, Topeka and WaKeeney.

INTERSTATE 135: Lindsborg, McPherson, Newton, Salina and Wichita.

Important Note

Areas of Kansas along the Missouri River and its tributaries that were affected by record flooding in 1993 may still be recovering from damage sustained as a result. Bridges, roads and highways in particular may require repairs. Contact the Kansas Travel and Tourism Division or inquire locally before planning to travel in these areas.

Additional Visitor Information

The Travel and Tourism Division, Department of Commerce & Housing, 700 SW Harrison St, Suite 1300, Topeka 66603, phone 913/296-2009 or 800/2-KANSAS, distributes the *Kansas Attractions Guide, Kansas Transportation Map* and *Calendar of Events.*

Visitors to Kansas will find welcome centers on I-70W, just west of Goodland; at the Kansas City exit on I-70E (milepost 415); at the southern entrance into Kansas on the turnpike in South Haven; at 229 E Pancake Blvd in Liberal; at 231 E Wall St in Fort Scott; at the Civic Center Depot in Abilene; at the Santa Fe Depot/Chamber in Atchison; at the Brown Mansion on US 169 in Coffeeville; on US 81 near North Belleville; and at the State Capitol in Topeka. Visitors will find information and brochures helpful in planning stops at points of interest.

Abilene (C-7)

(See Junction City, Salina)

Founded 1858 **Pop** 6,242 **Elev** 1,153 ft **Area code** 913 **Zip** 67410

Information Convention & Visitors Bureau, 201 NW 2nd, Box 146; 913/263-1770 or 800/569-5915.

Once famous as a Kansas "cow town," Abilene in 1867 was the terminal point of the Kansas Pacific (later Union Pacific) Railroad and the nearest railhead for the shipment of cattle brought north over the Chisholm Trail. The number shipped east from here between 1867 and 1871 has been estimated at more than a million, and often 500 cowboys were paid off at a time. City marshals Tom Smith and Wild Bill Hickok brought in law and order in the 1870s. Today Abilene is a wheat center, perhaps best known as the boyhood home of Dwight D. Eisenhower.

What to See and Do

Dickinson County Historical Museum. Exhibits depict life of early pioneer days, the Native Americans and the buffalo; antique toys and household items used at the turn of the century; cowboys and cattle trails; Heritage Center, carousel, log cabin. Teaching tours for children by appt. (Early Apr-late Oct, daily; rest of yr, by appt) 412 S Campbell St. Phone 913/263-2681. ¢ Admission includes

Museum of Independent Telephony. More than a century of telephone history; large collection of telephones from 1876 to present; insulators, cables, pay stations. Exhibits include old switchboard and crank-type phones. (Same days as Dickinson County Historical Museum) Guided tours by appt. Phone 913/263-2681.

⊠ **Eisenhower Center.** This house (1887), where Dwight Eisenhower and his five brothers were raised, was purchased by the family in 1898. Interior and most furnishings are original. Museum houses changing exhibits of mementos, souvenirs and gifts received during Dwight D. Eisenhower's career; murals in lobby depict his life. 30-min orientation film shown in Visitor Center. Library contains presidential papers. President and Mrs. Eisenhower are buried in the Meditation Chapel. (Daily; closed Jan 1, Thanksgiving, Dec 25) Museum ¢; chapel, library (free). There are wheelchair lifts to entrances. 200 SE 4th St, E of KS 15. Phone 913/263-4751. **Free.**

Greyhound Hall of Fame. Exhibits, 10-min film on breeding and racing of greyhounds. (Daily; closed Jan 1, Thanksgiving, Dec 25) 407 S Buckeye St. Phone 913/263-3000. **Free.**

Hall of Generals. Wax museum featuring famous army, navy, marine and air force generals who served under Eisenhower during World War II. (Daily; closed Jan 1, Thanksgiving, Dec 25) 100 SE 5th St. Phone 913/263-4194. ¢

Lebold-Vahsholtz Mansion. Restored Victorian mansion with period furnishings. (All yr, by appt; closed Thanksgiving, Dec 25) 106 N Vine. Phone 913/263-4356. ¢¢

"Old Abilene Town." Replica of Abilene during cattle boom includes original buildings of era; stagecoach rides. (Daily; closed Thanksgiving, Dec 25) Hours may vary. Stagecoach rides avail (May-Aug; fee); museum by donation. 201 SE 6th at Kuney St. Phone 913/263-4612. **Free.**

Annual Events

National Greyhound Meet. 1½ mi W on US 40 at the Greyhound Association. Greyhound racing in the hometown of the National Greyhound Assn. Last wk Apr & second wk Oct.

Central Kansas Free Fair and PRCA Wild Bill Hickok Rodeo. 3rd wk Aug.

Motels

★ ★ **BEST WESTERN ABILENE'S PRIDE.** *1709 N Buckeye (KS 15), I-70 exit 275. 913/263-2800; FAX 913/263-3285.* 80 rms, 1-2 story. S $39-$55; D $42-$60; each addl $4. Crib free. TV; cable. Heated pool. Complimentary continental bkfst. Restaurant 11 am-9 pm; Fri & Sat to 10 pm, Sun to 8 pm. Bar. Ck-out 11 am. Meeting rm. Exercise equipt; weights, bicycles, whirlpool. Cr cds: A, C, D, DS, JCB, MC, V.

✔ **DIAMOND.** *1407 NW 3rd St, I-70 exit 275. 913/263-2360.* 30 rms. S $20-$25; D $21-$40; each addl $2. TV; cable (premium). Complimentary coffee in lobby. Ck-out 11 am. Refrigerators. Cr cds: MC, V.

★ **SUPER 8.** *2207 N Buckeye, I-70 exit 275. 913/263-4545; FAX 913/263-7448.* 62 rms, 3 story. No elvtr. S $34.88-$39.88; D $42.88-$50.88; each addl $4; suites $47.88-$59.88; under 12 free. Crib free. Pet accepted, some restrictions; $10. TV; cable (premium). Complimentary coffee in lobby. Restaurant adj 6:30 am-midnight. Ck-out 11 am. Meeting rms. Business servs avail. Cr cds: A, D, DS, MC, V.

Restaurant

✔ ★ ★ ★ **KIRBY HOUSE.** *3rd & Kirby. 913/263-7336.* Hrs: 11 am-2 pm, 5-9 pm; Sun to 3 pm. Closed Jan 1, Dec 25. Res accepted. Bar. Semi-a la carte: lunch $2.95-$5.95, dinner $4.95-$15.95. Child's meals. Specialties: chicken Marco Polo, country-fried steak, peppercorn steak. Parking. Ten dining rms in Victorian house (1885). Totally nonsmoking. Cr cds: DS, MC, V.

Arkansas City (F-7)

(See Winfield; also see Ponca City, OK)

Founded 1870 **Pop** 12,762 **Elev** 1,120 ft **Area code** 316 **Zip** 67005
Information Chamber of Commerce, 126 E Washington; 316/442-0230.

Arkansas City, situated near the Oklahoma border, is home to meat packing, oil refining and aircraft-related industries. Approximately 45,000 homesteaders started the run for the Cherokee Strip on September 16, 1893, from here. The run was a race held by the US government as a means to give away land for settlement in what was then the Oklahoma Territory.

What to See and Do

Chaplin Nature Center. More than 200 acres of woodland, prairie and streams along the Arkansas River; nature center, self-guided trails. (Daily; guided tours by appt) 3 mi W on US 166, then 2 mi N on gravel road (follow signs). Phone 316/442-4133. **Free.**

Cherokee Strip Land Rush Museum. Articles related to the Cherokee Strip Run; reference library on Run, Native Americans, geneology. (Daily exc Mon; closed major hols) 1 mi S on US 77. Phone 316/442-6750. **¢¢**

Annual Events

River Valley Art Festival. Wilson Park. More than 80 juried artists display and sell their works. Entertainment, international foods. First wkend June.

Arkalalah Celebration. Last wkend Oct.

Motels

★ **BEST WESTERN HALLMARK MOTOR INN.** *1617 N Summit (US 77). 316/442-1400; FAX 316/442-4729.* 47 rms. S $38.95; D $42.95; each addl $6; under 12 free. Crib free. Pet accepted. TV; cable (premium). Pool. Complimentary coffee in rms. Complimentary continental bkfst. Ck-out 11 am. Business servs avail. Cr cds: A, C, D, DS, MC, V.

★ ★ **REGENCY COURT INN.** *3232 N Summit (US 77). 316/442-7700; res: 800/325-9151; FAX 316/442-1218.* 86 rms. S, D, studio rms $38.95-$44.95; each addl $6; suites $98.80; under 12 free. Crib free. Pet accepted; $5. TV; cable. Indoor pool; whirlpool. Restaurant 7 am-1:30 pm, 5-8:30 pm; Fri, Sat to 9 pm; Sun 7 am-1:30 pm. Private club 4 pm-midnight, closed Sun. Ck-out 11 am. Meeting rms. Business servs avail. In-rm modem link. Game rm. Cr cds: A, D, DS, MC, V.

Atchison (B-9)

(See Hiawatha, Leavenworth; also see St Joseph, MO)

Founded 1854 **Pop** 10,656 **Elev** 810 ft **Area code** 913 **Zip** 66002
Information Atchison Area Chamber of Commerce, 200 S 10th St, Box 126; 913/367-2427.

Atchison grew up around a desirable landing site on the Missouri River—an important factor in its crowded history. Lewis and Clark camped here in 1804; so did Major Stephen Longstreet's Yellowstone Expedition in 1819; French explorers from the colony of Louisiana preceded both. In the 1850s and 1860s steamboat and wagon traffic to the west was bustling; mail coaches left daily on the 17-day round trip to Denver. A railroad from St Joseph, Missouri, established in 1859 by means of an Atchison city bond issue, was the first direct rail connection eastward from a point this far west. Another Atchison bond issue the same year made the Atchison, Topeka and Santa Fe railroad possible, although the first lines were not opened until 1872. The town's position in the Missouri-Kansas border struggles of the 1850s caused it to be named for US Senator David Rice Atchison of Missouri (who, it is claimed, was president of the United States from noon, March 4 to noon, March 5, 1849). Today Atchison is a manufacturing and wholesale center, producing flour, feeds, alcohol and steel castings. It is also the birthplace of aviatrix Amelia Earhart.

What to See and Do

Amelia Earhart Birthplace. House built in 1861 by Judge Alfred Otis, Amelia Earhart's grandfather. Earhart was born here July 24, 1897 and lived her early years here. Includes exhibits of her childhood and some of her flying memorabilia. (May-Sept, Mon-Sat, also Sun afternoons; rest of yr, by appt) 223 N Terrace. Phone 913/367-4217. **¢**

Atchison County Museum. Amelia Earhart exhibit; World War I collection; gun, barbed wire collection; pictures, local historical items. Tours. (Daily) 200 S 10th St. Phone 913/367-6238. **¢**

City Parks.

Jackson Park. Covers 115 acres with iris-bordered drives; scenic view of the Missouri River valley from Guerrier Hill. Pavilion (fee), picnicking (May-Oct, daily). 1500 S 6th St. **Free.**

Independence Park. Five-acre park with boat landing on Missouri River; near downtown. **Free.**

Warnock Lake Recreation Area. Camping (fee), fishing, swimming, beach; picnicking. (Daily) 2 mi SW. Phone 913/367-4179. **Free.**

Evah C. Cray Historical Home Museum. 19th-century period rooms, country store, children's display. (May-Aug, daily; Mar-Apr & Sept-Oct,

Fri-Mon; rest of yr, by appt) Children only with adult. 805 N 5th St. Phone 913/367-3046. ¢

International Forest of Friendship. A Bicentennial gift to the United States from the city and the International Organization of Women Pilots, the Ninety Nines Inc. The forest includes trees from all 50 states and from 33 countries. A concrete walkway (wheelchair accessible) winds through the forest; embedded in the walkway are granite plaques honoring those people who have contributed to the advancement of aviation; statue of Amelia Earhart; NASA astronaut memorial. (Daily) 2 mi SW, just S of Warnock Lake. Phone 913/367-2427. **Free.**

Annual Event

Atchison County Fair. Mid-Aug.

Motel

★ **COMFORT INN.** 509 S 9th St. 913/367-7666; FAX 913/367-7566. 45 rms, 3 story, 10 suites. No elvtr. S $42; D $46; each addl $4; suites $54; under 18 free. Crib $4. Pet accepted. TV; cable. Complimentary continental bkfst, coffee. Restaurant nearby. Bar 5 pm-2 am, closed Sun. Ck-out 11 am. Meeting rms. Picnic tables. Cr cds: A, C, D, DS, MC, V.

D ✸ ⊠ ⊠ SC

Restaurant

✔★ **TIME OUT.** 337 S 10th St. 913/367-3372. Hrs: 6 am-9 pm; Fri & Sat to 2:30 am; Sun 7 am-9 pm. Closed most major hols. Semi-a la carte: bkfst $1.95-$5.95, lunch & dinner $1.95-$7.95. Child's meals. Salad bar. Parking. No cr cds accepted.

D SC

Belleville (B-6)

(See Concordia, Mankato)

Pop 2,517 **Elev** 1,550 ft **Area code** 913 **Zip** 66935
Information Chamber of Commerce, 1812 L St; 913/527-2310.

Belleville's Rocky Pond was used in early railroad days to provide water for steam engines and supply ice for refrigerated cars. Fishing, picnicking and camping are allowed in Rocky Pond Park.

A Sandzen mural from WPA days hangs in the Post Office, 18th and L Sts.

What to See and Do

Crossroads of Yesteryear Museum. Log cabin (1870), rural school, church (1900) and museum on 5 acres. Exhibits feature artifacts of the county, the history of agriculture, and the Bertil Olson Tool Collection. (Daily; closed most major hols) 2726 US 36. Phone 913/527-5971. **Free.**

Pawnee Indian Village Museum. Built on site of a Pawnee village (ca 1820); excavated earth lodge floor; displays depicting Pawnee culture. (Daily exc Mon; closed hols) 13 mi W on US 36, then 8 mi N on KS 266. Phone 913/361-2255. **Free.**

Annual Event

North Central Kansas Free Fair. Features Midget Nationals car races. Phone 913/527-2488. 1st wkend Aug.

Motel

✔★★ **BEST WESTERN BEL VILLA.** 215 US 36, at jct US 81. 913/527-2231. 38 rms. S $34; D $38-$54; each addl $4; higher rates: Memorial Day wkend, racing events, hunting season. Crib free. Pet accepted, some restrictions. TV; cable (premium). Pool. Playground. Restaurant 6 am-10 pm. Bar. Ck-out 11 am. Meeting rms. Business servs avail. In-rm modem link. Sundries. Free airport transportation. Golf privileges. Lawn games. Cr cds: A, C, D, DS, MC, V.

✸ 🏋 ⊠ ⊠ 🔥 SC

Beloit (C-6)

(See Concordia, Mankato)

Pop 4,066 **Elev** 1,386 ft **Area code** 913 **Zip** 67420

What to See and Do

Glen Elder State Park. A 1,250-acre park on 12,600-acre lake. An early Native American historical site. It was here that Margaret Hill McCarter wrote some of her well-loved tales of Kansas. Swimming beach; fishing; boating (ramp, marina). Picnicking. More than 300 primitive and improved campsites (dump station). Amphitheater. Standard fees. (Daily) 12 mi W on US 24. Phone 913/545-3345. Per Vehicle ¢¢

Motel

✔★ **MAINLINER INN.** RFD 1, Box 47 A, at jct US 24 & KS 9. 913/738-3531; res: 800/794-8514. 26 rms, 2 story. S $28-$43; D $40-$60; each addl $5; higher rates pheasant hunting season. Crib $5. Pet accepted. TV; cable (premium). Complimentary coffee in lobby 7-11 am. Restaurant adj 11:30 am-2 pm, 5-9 pm; closed Mon. Ck-out 11 am. In-rm modem link. Cr cds: A, C, D, DS, MC, V.

D ✸ ⊠ 🔥

Chanute (E-9)

(See Iola, Parsons, Yates Center)

Founded 1873 **Pop** 9,488 **Elev** 943 ft **Area code** 316 **Zip** 66720
Information Chamber of Commerce, 21 N Lincoln, PO Box 747; 316/431-3350.

What to See and Do

Martin and Osa Johnson Safari Museum. Contains artifacts and photographs of the South Seas, Borneo and African trips of photo-explorers Martin and Osa Johnson (she was born in Chanute); exhibits illustrating West African village life include ceremonial artifacts and musical instruments; 10-min film shown at regular intervals. Wildlife paintings and sketches, other art objects displayed in the Selsor Gallery. Stott Explorers Library houses expedition journals, monographs, books on exploration. (Daily; closed major hols) 111 N Lincoln Ave, located in a renovated Santa Fe train depot. Phone 316/431-2730. ¢¢

Annual Events

Mexican Fiesta. Celebration of Mexican independence from Spain. 2nd wkend Sept.

Artist Alley & Fall Festival. Includes parade, art booths. 4th wkend Sept.

Coffeyville (F-9)

(See Independence, Parsons)

Founded 1869 **Pop** 12,917 **Elev** 736 ft **Area code** 316 **Zip** 67337

Information Convention & Visitors Bureau, 807 Walnut, PO Box 457; 316/251-1194 or 800/626-3357.

Named for Colonel James A. Coffey, who in 1869 built a house and store near the Verdigris River, Coffeyville, with the coming of the railroad shortly after its settlement, followed the usual pattern of cow towns. The famous Dalton raid occurred here October 5, 1892, when the three Dalton brothers and two confederates attempted to rob two banks at once and fought a running battle with armed citizens. Several of the defenders were killed or wounded; of the gang, only Emmett Dalton survived.

The town prospered with the development of natural gas and oil fields in 1903. Today its chief industries are oil refineries, smelters, oil field equipment, games and puzzles, power transmissions and foundries. Wendell Willkie, the Republican presidential candidate in 1940, lived and taught school here.

What to See and Do

Brown Mansion (1904). Designed by proteges of Stanford White; original furniture, hand-painted canvas wall coverings; Tiffany chandelier in dining room. (Mar-Dec, daily; closed most major hols) 2019 Walnut St. Phone 316/251-0431. ¢¢

Dalton Museum. Dalton raid souvenirs; mementos of Wendell Willkie and Walter Johnson. (Daily) 113 E 8th St. Phone 316/251-5944. ¢

Annual Events

Inter-State Fair and Rodeo. 2nd full wk Aug.

Dalton Defenders Day. Commemorates the Dalton raid on Coffeyville. 1st wkend Oct.

Motel

★★ **APPLE TREE INN.** *820 E 11th St. 316/251-0002; FAX 316/251-1615.* 43 rms, 2 story. S $42.50, D $50.50; charge for each addl. Crib $2. Pet accepted; $3. TV; cable (premium). Indoor pool; whirlpool. Complimentary continental bkfst 6-9 am, coffee in lobby. Restaurant nearby. Ck-out noon. Business servs avail. In-rm modem link. Cr cds: A, D, DS, MC, V.

D ✉ ≋ ⊠ 🔥

Colby (C-2)

(See Goodland, Oakley)

Founded 1885 **Pop** 5,396 **Elev** 3,160 ft **Area code** 913 **Zip** 67701

Information Convention & Visitors Bureau, 265 E 5th, PO Box 572; 913/462-7643.

This town is located in the center of the wheat belt.

What to See and Do

Northwest Research Extension Center. Branch of Kansas State University. Crop, soil, irrigation, sheep and horticulture research. (Mon-Fri) W of city, ¼ mi S of US 24. 105 Experiment Farm Rd. Phone 913/462-7575. **Free.**

Prairie Museum of Art & History. Museum complex is located on a 24-acre site, adj to I-70 between exits 53 and 54. On exhibit are rare bisque and china dolls; Meissen, Tiffany, Sèvres, Capo de Monte, Royal Vienna, Satsuma, Ridgway, Wedgwood and Limoges; glass and crystal, such as Redford, Stiegel, Steuben, Gallé; Chinese and Japanese artifacts; textiles; furniture. On the museum site are a sod house, restored 1930s farmstead, one-room schoolhouse, a country church and one of the largest barns in Kansas. (Daily exc Mon; closed hols) 1905 S Franklin St. Phone 913/462-4590. ¢¢

Annual Event

Thomas County Free Fair. Aug.

Motels

★ **BEST WESTERN CROWN.** *2320 S Range (KS 25) at jct I-70. 913/462-3943.* 29 rms. June-Sept: S $39-$49; D $43-$56; each addl $6; lower rates rest of yr. Crib free. Pet accepted. TV; cable (premium). Heated pool. Complimentary coffee in rms. Restaurant nearby. Ck-out 11 am. Business servs avail. In-rm modem link. Airport transportation. Cr cds: A, C, D, DS, MC, V.

✉ ≋ ⊠ 🔥 SC

★★ **RAMADA INN.** *Box 487, 1950 S Range (KS 25) at jct I-70. 913/462-3933; FAX 913/462-7255.* 117 rms, 2 story. S $39-$62; D $46-$70; each addl $5; under 18 free. Crib free. TV; cable (premium). Heated pool. Restaurant 6:30 am-10 pm. Rm serv. Bar 5-midnight. Ck-out noon. Meeting rms. Business servs avail. In-rm modem link. Valet serv. Sundries. Cr cds: A, C, D, DS, JCB, MC, V.

D ≋ ⊠ 🔥 SC

Concordia (B-6)

(See Belleville, Beloit)

Pop 6,167 **Elev** 1,369 ft **Area code** 913 **Zip** 66901

Information Chamber of Commerce, 205 W 6th St; 913/243-4290.

What to See and Do

🎭 **The Brown Grand Theatre.** Built in 1907 by Colonel Napoleon Bonaparte Brown at a cost of $40,000, the restored 650-seat theatre has two balconies and features a grand drape, which is a reproduction of a Horace Vernet painting entitled "Napoleon at Austerlitz." Theatre currently hosts plays, concerts and shows. Guided tours (daily, limited hrs; fee). 310 W 6th St. Phone 913/243-2553.

Annual Event

North Central Kansas Rodeo. Early July.

Motel

★ **BEST WESTERN THUNDERBIRD MOTOR INN.** *Box 673, N on US 81. 913/243-4545; FAX 913/243-5058.* 50 rms. S $39; D $46; each addl $5; under 12 free. Crib $5. Pet accepted, some restrictions. TV; cable (premium). Pool; whirlpool. Restaurant 6 am-9 pm; wkend hrs vary. Private club 5 pm-midnight; closed Sun. Ck-out 11 am. Coin lndry. Meeting rms. Business servs avail. Sundries. Cr cds: A, C, D, DS, MC, V.

✉ ≋ ⊠ 🔥 SC

Council Grove (D-8)

(See Emporia, Junction City)

Founded 1858 **Pop** 2,228 **Elev** 1,233 ft **Area code** 316 **Zip** 66846

Information Convention & Visitors Bureau, 200 W Main St; 800/732-9211.

As the last outfitting place on the Santa Fe Trail between the Missouri River and Santa Fe, Council Grove, now a National Historic Landmark, holds historic significance in the development of the West. The town grew up around a Native American campground in a grove of oaks near the Neosho River. It is an agricultural and merchandising center. The town also has many lovely turn-of-the-century buildings, several parks and two lakes.

What to See and Do

Council Grove Federal Lake. Covers 3,200 acres. Fishing, hunting; boating, marina (seasonal). Camping (some fees/night). (Daily) 1 mi N on KS 177. Phone 316/767-5195. Per Vehicle ¢

Council Oak Shrine. Here the treaty of 1825 was signed between US government commissioners and the Osage. 210 E Main St.

Custer's Elm Shrine. Elm trunk stands as a shrine to the tree that was 100 feet tall, 16 feet in circumference and reputedly sheltered the camp of General George Custer in 1867 when he was leading an expedition in western Kansas. Neosho St, 6 blks S of Main St.

Kaw Mission State Historic Site. Stone building (1851) where members of the Methodist Church once taught Native Americans; also one of the first Kansas schools for children of settlers. (Daily exc Mon; closed hols) 500 N Mission St. Phone 316/767-5410. **Free.**

Old Calaboose. (1849). Only pioneer jail on Santa Fe Trail in early days. 502 E Main St, on US 56.

Post Office Oak. Mammoth oak tree with a cache at its base served as an unofficial post office for pack trains and caravans on the Santa Fe Trail 1825-1847. E Main St between Union & Liberty Sts.

The Madonna of the Trail Monument. One of 12 statues erected in each of the states through which the National Old Trails Roads passed. The Madonna pays tribute to pioneer mothers and commemorates the trails that opened the West. Union & Main Sts.

Annual Event

Wah-Shun-Gah Days. Kaw Inter-tribal Pow-wow, Santa Fe trail ride and supper, antique tractor pull, street dance. 2nd wkend June.

Motel

✔★★ **COTTAGE HOUSE.** *25 N Neosho, 1/2 blk N of US 56.* 316/767-6828; res: 800/727-7903. 36 rms, 1-2 story. S $30-$52; D $38-$68; each addl $8; suites $85-$90; under 12 free. Crib $8. Pet accepted, some restrictions; $8. TV; cable, VCR avail. Continental bkfst 6:30-11 am. Restaurant nearby. Ck-out 11 am. Meeting rm. Business servs avail. In-rm modem link. Gift shop. Whirlpool, sauna. Some refrigerators, in-rm whirlpools. Built in 1867 as a cottage and blacksmith shop; some antiques; gazebo. Cr cds: A, C, D, DS, MC, V.

Restaurant

✔★★ **HAYS HOUSE 1857.** *112 W Main St (US 56).* 316/767-5911. Hrs: 6 am-9 pm; Fri & Sat to 10 pm; winter to 8:30 pm; Sun buffet 11 am-2 pm. Closed Jan 1, Dec 25. Res accepted. Bar from 5 pm. Semi-a la carte: bkfst, lunch $2.95-$8.50, dinner $5.50-$13.75. Sun brunch $9.50. Child's meals. Specializes in aged beef, skillet-fried chicken. Salad bar. Own desserts. Building erected 1857; Old West atmosphere. Cr cds: DS, MC, V.

Dodge City (E-3)

Settled 1872 **Pop** 21,129 **Elev** 2,530 ft **Area code** 316 **Zip** 67801

Information Convention & Visitors Bureau, 4th and Spruce, PO Box 1474; 316/225-8186.

Memorable for buffalo hunts, longhorn cattle and frontier marshals, Dodge City was laid out by construction crews of the Santa Fe Railroad and named for nearby Fort Dodge. Vast herds of buffalo—estimated at 24 million or more—which then covered the surrounding plains, had been hunted for years. But the railroad provided transportation to make the hides commercially profitable. A skilled hunter could earn $100 in a day at the industry's height; by 1875 the herds were nearly exterminated. Cattle drives, also stimulated by the railroad, took the buffalo's place in the town's economy. In 1882 Dodge City became the cowboy capital of the Southwest. Among its notable peace officers were Bat Masterson and Wyatt Earp. The prevalence of sudden and violent death resulted in the establishment of Boot Hill cemetery. In the mid-1880s the era of the cattle drives ended; by 1890 much of the grazing land had been plowed for crops. Dodge City is now the hub of one of the nation's greatest wheat-producing areas and a growing production and marketing center for cattle.

What to See and Do

★ **Historic Front Street.** Reconstruction of two blocks of main street of 1870s: Long Branch Saloon, Saratoga Saloon, general store, blacksmith, saddle shop, drugstore, many other businesses. Beeson Gallery contains exhibits, many objects of historical significance from the Southwest and Dodge City; Hardesty House, home of an early cattle baron, has been restored and furnished with original pieces; exhibits of early banking.

Boot Hill Museum. Museum and cemetery are on site of original Boot Hill Cemetery; depot, locomotive, "Boot Hill Special." Old Fort Dodge Jail; gun collection. Stagecoach rides in summer. (Daily; closed Jan 1, Thanksgiving, Dec 25) Sr citizen rate. Front St. Phone 316/227-8188. ¢¢¢

Home of Stone (1879). Preserved Victorian home with many original furnishings; occupied until 1964. Guided tours (June-Aug, daily; rest of yr, by appt). Donation. 112 E Vine St. Phone 316/227-6791 or 316/225-4926.

Annual Event

Dodge City Days. Parades; PRCA rodeo features cowboy competition in several events. Last wk July-1st wkend Aug.

Seasonal Event

Long Branch Saloon. Chuck wagon dinner, nightly (fee). Variety show, nightly (fee). Stagecoach rides; reenacted gunfights, nightly; medicine shows, daily. Front St. Phone 316/227-8188. Late May-late Aug.

Motels

(Rates may be higher during hunting season, special events)

★★ **BEST WESTERN SILVER SPUR LODGE.** *Box 119, 1510 W Wyatt Earp Blvd (US 50).* 316/227-2125; FAX 316/227-2030. 121 rms, 1-2 story. S $44-$54; D $52-$62; each addl $5; suites $60-$70. Crib $2. Pet accepted, some restrictions; $5. TV; cable (premium), VCR avail. Heated pool. Restaurant 6 am-9 pm. Rm serv. Bar 4 pm-midnight; entertainment, dancing. Ck-out noon. Meeting rms. Business servs avail. Valet serv exc Sun. Free airport transportation. Cr cds: A, C, D, DS, MC, V.

D 🏃 ≈ ⊠ 🐾 SC

✔★★ **DAYS INN-DODGE HOUSE.** *2408 W Wyatt Earp Blvd (US 50).* 316/225-9900. 131 rms, 2 story. S $35-$60; D $40-$60; each addl $6; suites $75-$120; under 12 free. Crib free. TV; cable (premium), VCR avail. 2 pools, 1 indoor; sauna. Restaurant 6 am-9 pm; Fri & Sat to 10 pm; Sun from 6:30 am. Bar 11 am-midnight; closed Sun. Ck-out noon. Meeting rms. Business center. Valet serv exc Sat & Sun. Free airport transportation. Game rm. Cr cds: A, C, D, DS, JCB, MC, V.

D 🏃 ≈ ⊠ 🐾 SC

★ **SUPER 8.** *1708 W Wyatt Earp Blvd (US 50).* 316/225-3924; FAX 316/225-5793. 64 rms, 3 story. S $34.88-$40.88; D $42.88-$54.88; under 12 free; higher rates special events. Crib free. Pet accepted. TV; cable (premium), VCR avail. Pool. Complimentary continental bkfst. Complimentary coffee in rms. Restaurant adj 6 am-10 pm. Ck-out noon. Cr cds: A, C, D, DS, MC, V.

D 🏃 ≈ ⊠ 🐾 SC

El Dorado (E-7)

(See Eureka, Newton, Wichita)

Pop 11,504 **Elev** 1,291 ft **Area code** 316 **Zip** 67042
Information Chamber of Commerce, 383 E Central, PO Box 509; 316/321-3150.

El Dorado, the seat of Butler County, is located on the western edge of the Flint Hills. The city's growth can be attributed to oil; two refineries are here. Stapleton No. 1, the area's first gusher (1915), is commemorated by a marker at the northwestern edge of the town.

What to See and Do

El Dorado State Park. The largest of Kansas' state parks, El Dorado is made up of 4 areas totalling 4,000 acres. Rolling hills, wooded valleys and open prairie make up the natural environment of the park. El Dorado Lake, 8,000 acres, is also within the park. Swimming beaches; fishing (with license); boating (ramps, marina). Hiking trails. Picnicking, concession. More than 1,100 primitive and improved campsites (hook-ups, dump stations). Standard fees. (Daily) 5 mi NE on KS 177. Phone 316/321-7180. Per vehicle ¢¢

Kansas Oil Museum and Butler County Historical Museum. Interpretive displays depicting oil, ranching and agricultural history, includes a model rotary drilling rig; outdoor historic oil field exhibits include restored cable-tool drilling rig, shotgun lease house, antique engines. Library, archives. Gift shop. Walking tour, nature trail. (Daily, afternoons; closed hols) 383 E Central Ave. Phone 316/321-9333.   **Free.**

Motel

✔★★ **BEST WESTERN RED COACH INN.** *2525 W Central St (US 254).* 316/321-6900; FAX 316/321-6900, ext. -208. 73 rms, 2 story, 1 kit. unit. S $38-$58; D $42-$62; each addl $5. Crib $4. TV; cable (premium). Indoor pool; whirlpool, sauna. Restaurant 6 am-11 pm. Rm serv. Ck-out 11 am. Business servs avail. Exercise equipt; treadmill, bicycle. Game rm. Some in-rm whirlpools. Cr cds: A, C, D, DS, JCB, MC, V.

🏃 ≈ 🍴 ⊠ 🐾 SC

Emporia (D-8)

(See Council Grove)

Founded 1857 **Pop** 25,512 **Elev** 1,150 ft **Area code** 316 **Zip** 66801
Information Convention & Visitors Bureau, 427 Commercial St, PO Box 417; 316/342-1600 or 800/279-3730.

This was the home of one of America's most famous editors, William Allen White. His Emporia *Gazette* attracted nationwide attention. The seat of Lyon County and gateway to the Flint Hills, Emporia is a center of industry, agriculture and education.

What to See and Do

Eisenhower State Park. A 1,785-acre park on 6,900-acre lake. Crappie, walleye, catfish and bass. Beach, bathhouse; fishing; boating (ramp). Picnicking; walking trail. Camping (electricity, dump station). Standard fees. (Daily) 20 mi E on I-35, 7 mi N on US 75. Phone 316/528-4102. Per vehicle ¢¢

Emporia *Gazette* Building. Houses White's widely quoted newspaper; small one-room museum displays newspaper machinery used in White's time. (Daily exc Sun; closed hols) 517 Merchant St. Phone 316/342-4805.   **Free.**

Flint Hills National Wildlife Refuge. Hiking, camping. Wild food gathering permitted. Bald eagles present in fall and winter. Fishing and hunting in legal seasons. (Daily; some portions closed during fall migration of waterfowl) 10 mi E on I-35, then 8 mi S on KS 130. Phone 316/392-5553.   **Free.**

Lyon County Historical Society and Museum. Valuable collection of city directories, newspapers dating from 1857 on microfilm; a complete file of the *Gazette;* genealogy collection for Lyon County, including marriage and cemetery records; gift gallery. (Daily; closed most hols) 118 E 6th Ave, at Mechanic St. Phone 316/342-0933.   **Free.**

National Teachers Hall of Fame. Galleries and tributes to some of the best teachers in America. (Mon-Fri; closed hols) Donation. 1320 C of E Dr. Phone 316/341-5660 or 800/968-3224.

Peter Pan Park. Approx 50 acres given to the city by the White family; bust of William Allen White by Jo Davidson. Swimming pool, wading pool (June-Aug, daily); lake (children under age 14 and senior citizens may fish here). Softball fields. Picnic grounds. (Daily) Kansas Ave & Neosho St. Phone 316/342-5105.   **Free.**

Red Rocks, the William Allen White Residence. Three-story house of Colorado sandstone; unusual Victorian-Gothic design. Private. 927 Exchange St.

Soden's Grove Park. Approx 30 acres bordered on S by Cottonwood River; baseball field, picnic area; miniature train (seasonal, evenings). S Commercial & Soden's Rd. Located in park is

Emporia Zoo. More than 73 species of native and exotic wildlife. Drive or walk through. (Daily) Phone 316/342-5105.   **Free.**

Annual Events

Twin Rivers Festival. Emporia State University Campus. Celebration of the arts featuring arts & crafts; children's section; recreational activities; concessions. Mid-June.

Lyon County Free Fair. Fairgrounds, W US 50. Exhibits, entertainment, rodeos. 1st full wk Aug.

Seasonal Event

Summer Theater. Karl C. Bruder Theatre at Emporia State University . Phone 316/341-5256. Early June-late July.

Motels

✔★ **DAYS INN.** *3032 W US 50 Business.* 316/342-1787; FAX 316/342-2292. 39 rms, 1-2 story. S $36-$48; D $48-$58; each addl $6. Crib free. Pet accepted, some restrictions. TV; cable (premium). Indoor pool; whirlpool. Complimentary continental bkfst 6-10 am. Restaurant opp 6 am-9 pm. Ck-out 11 am. Business servs avail. In-rm modem link. Bus depot transportation. Game rm. Cr cds: A, C, D, DS, MC, V.

★★★ **HOLIDAY INN-HOLIDOME.** *2700 W 18th Ave.* 316/343-2200; FAX 316/343-2200, ext. 333. 133 rms, 2 story. S, D $49-$65; suites $60-$140; under 19 free. Crib free. TV; cable (premium), VCR avail. Indoor/outdoor pool; whirlpool, sauna. Restaurant 6 am-10 pm. Rm serv. Bar 4 pm-1 am; entertainment Fri evenings, dancing. Ck-out noon. Coin lndry. Meeting rms. Business servs avail. Bellhops. Holidome. Game rm. Cr cds: A, C, D, DS, ER, JCB, MC, V.

★★ **QUALITY INN.** *3021 W US 50.* 316/342-3770; FAX 316/342-3770. 56 rms. S $36-$50; D $44-$60; each addl $7; suites $75; under 18 free. Crib free. Pet accepted. TV; cable (premium). Indoor pool. Restaurant 6 am-9 pm. Rm serv. Ck-out 11 am. Meeting rm. Business servs avail. In-rm modem link. Exercise equipt; weights, bicycle, whirlpool. Game rm. Cr cds: A, C, D, DS, ER, JCB, MC, V.

✔★ **RAMADA INN.** *1839 Merchant St (KS 99), just off I-35.* 316/342-8850; FAX 316/343-6366. 60 rms, 2 story. S, D $40-$85; under 18 free. Crib free. TV; cable (premium), VCR avail. Pool. Restaurant 6 am-10 pm. Lounge 4 pm-midnight. Ck-out noon. Meeting rms. Business servs avail. In-rm modem link. Cr cds: A, C, D, DS, MC, V.

Eureka (E-8)

(See El Dorado, Yates Center)

Pop 2,974 **Elev** 1,084 ft **Area code** 316 **Zip** 67045

What to See and Do

Fall River State Park. Park encompasses 917 acres that overlook a 2,500-acre reservoir. Rolling uplands forested by native oak adjoining native tallgrass prairies. Beach, bathhouse; fishing; boating (ramps, docks). Trails. Picnicking. Tent & trailer camping (electricity, dump station). Standard fees. (Daily) 17 mi SE, just off KS 96. Phone 316/637-2213. Per vehicle ¢¢

Greenwood County Historical Society & Museum. Collection of historical artifacts; 19th-century kitchen and farm display; county newspapers from 1868 to 1986; genealogy section. (Mon-Fri; closed major hols) 120 W 4th St. Phone 316/583-6682. **Free.**

Motel

✔★ **BLUE STEM LODGE.** *1314 E River St (US 54).* 316/583-5531. 27 rms. S $28-$32; D $32-$38; each addl $4. Pet accepted, some restrictions. Crib $2. Pool. Complimentary coffee in rms. Restaurant nearby. Ck-out 11 am. Golf privileges. Cr cds: A, C, D, DS, MC, V.

Fort Scott (E-10)

(See Pittsburg; also see Nevada, MO)

Founded 1842 **Pop** 8,362 **Elev** 846 ft **Area code** 316 **Zip** 66701

Information Fort Scott Area Visitor Information Center, 231 E Wall St, PO Box 205; 800/245-FORT.

Named for General Winfield Scott and established as a military post between Fort Leavenworth and lands designated for the displaced Cherokee, Fort Scott was manned by troops in 1842. Although the fort was abandoned in 1853 and its buildings sold at auction in 1855, the town survived. Located only five miles from the Missouri border, it became a center for pre-Civil War agitation by those for, as well as those against slavery. Rival groups had headquarters on the Plaza—the former parade ground—in the Free State Hotel and Western Hotel. John Brown and James Montgomery were among the antislavery leaders who met here. During the Civil War the fort was again active as a supply center for Union troops. In more recent times the town has been a grain and livestock center, with manufacturing becoming increasingly important.

What to See and Do

Fort Scott National Historic Site. Established in 1842, the fort was the base for infantry and dragoons protecting the frontier. The buildings have been restored and reconstructed to represent the fort (ca 1845-55). Visitor center located in restored post hospital; officers' quarters, powder magazine, dragoon stable, guardhouse, bakery, quartermaster's storehouse, post headquarters and barracks; museum exhibits, audiovisual programs (daily). Some special events. Living history & interpretive programs (June-Aug, wkends). (Daily; closed Jan 1, Thanksgiving, Dec 25) Old Fort Blvd, at business jct US 69 & 54. Phone 316/223-0310. ¢

Gunn Park. Along the Marmaton River. Covers 135 acres, 2 lakes. Fishing (fee). Picnicking, playground. Camping (fee). (Daily) W edge of town. Phone 316/223-0550. **Free.**

Historic Trolley Tour. Narrated trolley tours pass the historic 1840s fort, one of the country's oldest national cemeteries, and several blocks of Victorian architecture. (Apr-Nov, daily) 231 E Wall. Contact Visitor Information Center for schedule. ¢¢

Annual Events

Good Ol' Days Celebration. Early June.

Bourbon County Fair. Fairgrounds. Late July.

Pioneer Harvest Fiesta. Fairgrounds. Steam, gas engine and tractor show; demonstrations of farm activities. Early Oct.

Motel

✔★★ **BEST WESTERN FORT SCOTT INN.** *101 State St, at 1st St.* 316/223-0100; FAX 316/223-1746. 78 rms, 1-2 story. S $42-$45; D $44-$50; under 12 free. Crib free. Pet accepted; $5. TV; cable (premium), VCR avail. Pool. Complimentary continental bkfst 5:30-10 am. Restaurant open 24 hrs. Ck-out noon. Coin lndry. Meeting rms. Business servs avail. In-rm modem link. Exercise equipt; weight machine, bicycle, whirlpool, sauna. Picnic tables. Cr cds: A, C, D, DS, MC, V.

Garden City (E-2)

Founded 1878 **Pop** 24,097 **Elev** 2,839 ft **Area code** 316 **Zip** 67846
Information Chamber of Commerce, 1511 E Fulton Terrace; 316/276-3264.

This is the center for raising and processing much of the state's beef for shipment throughout the world. The city is also the heart of the state's irrigation operations, which are important to wheat, alfalfa and corn crops in the area.

What to See and Do

Finnup Park & Lee Richardson Zoo. More than 300 mammals and birds can be found in the zoo. Picnic area, playgrounds; food and gift shop (fee for vehicles; closed Jan 1, Thanksgiving, Dec 25). Swimming pool (Mar-Nov, daily). Museum with memorabilia of early settlers (daily). S city limits, on US 83. Phone 316/276-1250 (zoo) or 316/272-3664 (museum). **Free.**

Annual Events

Beef Empire Days. Early June.

Finney County Fair. Mid-Aug.

Mexican Fiesta. 2nd wkend Sept.

Motels

✔ ★ ★ **BEST WESTERN WHEAT LANDS MOTOR INN.** 1311 E Fulton. 316/276-2387; FAX 316/276-4252. 86 units, 1-2 story. S $39-$47; D $47-$56; each addl $4; suites $58-$68; under 12 free; wkly rates. Crib $3. Pet accepted. TV; cable (premium), VCR avail. Heated pool. Complimentary coffee in lobby. Restaurant adj 6 am-9 pm. Bar 4 pm-2 am, closed Sun; entertainment, dancing. Ck-out 1 pm. Coin lndry. Meeting rms. Business servs avail. In-rm modem link. Valet serv. Gift shop. Barber, beauty shop. Airport, RR station, bus depot transportation. Golf privileges. Some bathrm phones; refrigerator in suites. Cr cds: A, C, D, DS, JCB, MC, V.

[icons]

★ ★ **PLAZA INN.** 1911 E Kansas Ave (US 156). 316/275-7471; res: 800/875-5201; FAX 316/275-4028. 109 rms, 2 story. S $48-$54; D $58-$64; each addl $10; suites $80-$90. Crib free. Pet accepted. TV; cable (premium), VCR avail. Indoor pool; whirlpool, sauna. Restaurant 6 am-10 pm; Sun 7 am-8 pm. Rm serv. Bar 4 pm-1 am; entertainment, dancing exc Sun. Ck-out noon. Meeting rms. Business servs avail. Bellhops. Free airport transportation. Golf privileges. Game rm. Cr cds: A, C, D, DS, MC, V.

[icons]

Goodland (C-1)

(See Colby)

Pop 4,983 **Elev** 3,683 ft **Area code** 913 **Zip** 67735
Information Convention and Visitors Bureau, 104 W 11th, PO Box 628; 913/899-3515.

What to See and Do

High Plains Museum. Houses replica of the first patented American helicopter (built 1910). Also display of Native American artifacts; farm implements, 19th-century clothing and household goods; miniature local history dioramas. (Mon-Sat, also Sunday afternoons; closed major hols) 17th & Cherry Sts. Phone 913/899-4595. **Free.**

Annual Event

Northwest Kansas District Free Fair. Early Aug.

Motels

✔ ★ ★ **BEST WESTERN BUFFALO INN.** 830 W US 24, I-70 exit 19, near Municipal Airport. 913/899-3621; FAX 913/899-5072. 93 rms, 2 story. June-Sept: S $40; D $55-$65; each addl $5-$8; lower rates rest of yr. Crib $5. Pet accepted; some restrictions. TV; cable (premium), VCR avail. Indoor pool; wading pool, whirlpool. Playground. Restaurant 6 am-9 pm; summer to 10 pm. Bar 5-10 pm. Ck-out 11 am. Guest lndry. Meeting rm. Business servs avail. In-rm modem link. Airport transportation. Cr cds: A, C, D, DS, MC, V.

[icons]

★ ★ **HOLIDAY INN.** 2218 Commerce Rd, I-70 exit 17. 913/899-3644; FAX 913/899-3646. 79 rms, 2 story. S $49-$70; D $54-$75. Crib free. Pet accepted. TV; cable (premium), VCR avail. Indoor pool. Playground. Restaurant 6 am-2 pm, 5-10 pm. Rm serv. Bar 5 pm-midnight. Ck-out noon. Guest lndry. Meeting rms. Business servs avail. Airport, bus depot transportation. Miniature golf. Exercise equipt; bicycles, whirlpool, sauna. Holidome. Game rm. Cr cds: A, C, D, DS, JCB, MC, V.

[icons]

Great Bend (D-5)

(See Larned)

Founded 1871 **Pop** 15,427 **Elev** 1,849 ft **Area code** 316 **Zip** 67530
Information Convention and Visitors Bureau, 1307 Williams, PO Box 400; 316/792-2401.

Great Bend, named for its location on the Arkansas River, was an early railhead on the Santa Fe Trail.

What to See and Do

Barton County Historical Society Museum and Village. Village contains church (ca 1895), schoolhouse (ca 1915), agricultural buildings, native stone blacksmith shop, Dodge homestead, depot and post office. Museum exhibits include local Indian history, furniture, clothing, antique doll collection, farm machinery, fire truck. (Apr-mid-Nov, daily exc Mon; rest of yr by appt) Donation. S Main St. Phone 316/793-5125.

Brit Spaugh Park and Zoo. Swimming pool (fee). Zoo. Picnicking, playground. (Daily) N Main St. Phone 316/793-4160. **Free.**

Cheyenne Bottoms. Migratory waterfowl refuge, public hunting area and bird-watching area. Water area about 13,000 acres. Fishing from shoreline in all pools (catfish, bullheads, carp). (Daily) 5 mi N on US 281, then 2 mi E. Phone 316/793-7730. **Free.**

Quivira National Wildlife Refuge. This 21,820-acre refuge includes 5,000 acres of managed wetlands and 15,000 acres of tall grass prairie. It was established in 1955 to provide a feeding and resting area for migratory waterfowl during spring and fall migrations. Auto tour route and wildlife drive (daily). Hunting and fishing permitted some seasons. 34 mi SE via US 281 & County Rd 636. Phone 316/486-2393. **Free.**

Annual Event

Barton County Fair. Early Aug.

Motel

★ ★ **BEST WESTERN ANGUS INN.** 2920 10th St (US 56, KS 96). 316/792-3541; FAX 316/792-8621. 90 units, 2 story. S $44-$54; D

$51-$71; studio rm $49-$59; each addl $4; under 18 free. Crib $3. Pet accepted; some restrictions. TV; cable (premium), VCR avail (movies avail $4). Indoor pool; whirlpool, sauna. Restaurant 6 am-11 pm. Rm serv from 5 pm. Ck-out 11 am. Meeting rms. Business servs avail. Airport transportation. Exercise equipt; bicycles, step machine. Game rm. Rec rm. Cr cds: A, C, D, DS, MC, V.

Motor Hotel

✔ ★ ★ HOLIDAY INN. 3017 W 10th St (US 56). 316/792-2431; FAX 316/792-5561. 173 rms, 2 story. S, D $50-$55; under 18 free. Crib free. Pet accepted. TV; cable (premium). Indoor pool; whirlpool, sauna. Restaurant 6 am-10:30 pm. Rm serv. Bar 5 pm-1 am. Ck-out noon. Coin lndry. Meeting rms. Business servs avail. In-rm modem link. Airport transportation. Holidome. Cr cds: A, C, D, DS, JCB, MC, V.

Restaurant

✔ ★ K-BOB'S STEAKHOUSE. 4812 10th St (US 56). 316/792-7326. Hrs: Mon-Thur 11 am-9 pm; Fri & Sat to 10 pm; Sunday 9:30 am-9 pm. Closed Dec 25. A la carte entrees: lunch, dinner $3.49-$10.99. Buffet (Fri, Sat): lunch $5.49, dinner $7.99 & $12.99. Sun brunch $6.99. Specializes in steak, chicken-fried steak, catfish. Salad bar. Parking. Southwestern decor. Cr cds: A, MC, V.

D

Greensburg (E-4)

(See Pratt)

Pop 1,792 Elev 2,230 ft Area code 316 Zip 67054
Information Chamber of Commerce, 315 S Sycamore; 316/723-2261.

Incorporated in 1886, Greensburg is named for pioneer stagecoach driver "Cannonball" Green. This community came to life in 1884 when two railroads extended their lines here and brought settlers. In 1885, the railroads began construction of what has been called the world's largest hand-dug well; it is still in good condition today.

What to See and Do

Big Well. The well is 32 feet wide and 109 feet deep; steps lead downward to water level (fee). Gift shop contains 1,000-lb pallasite meteorite found on a nearby farm and said to be largest of its type ever discovered. (Daily; closed Thanksgiving, Dec 25) 315 S Sycamore St, 3 blks S of US 54. Phone 316/723-2261. ¢

Motel

✔ ★ ★ BEST WESTERN J-HAWK. 515 W Kansas Ave (US 54). 316/723-2121; FAX 316/723-2650. 30 rms. S $34-$41; D $48-$52; each addl $5; under 12 free. Crib $5. TV; cable (premium). Indoor pool; whirlpool. Complimentary continental bkfst. Ck-out 11 am. Meeting rms. In-rm modem link. Free airport transportation. Cr cds: A, C, D, DS, MC, V.

Hays (C-4)

(See Russell, WaKeeney)

Founded 1867 Pop 17,767 Elev 1,997 ft Area code 913 Zip 67601
Information Convention & Visitors Bureau, 1301 Pine, Suite B; 913/628-8202.

Fort Hays, military post on the old frontier, gave this railroad town its name. Oil, grain, cattle, educational and medical facilities, tourism and light industry are important to the area.

What to See and Do

Ellis County Historical Society and Museum. More than 26,000 items on display in museum; includes antique toys and games, musical instruments; rotating exhibits include quilts from the 1800s to present (selected days Apr-June). Also here are one-room schoolhouse and oldest structure in Ellis County. (June-Aug, Tues-Fri; also Sat & Sun afternoons; rest of yr, Tues-Fri; closed major hols) Donation. 100 W 7th St. Phone 913/628-2624.

Historic Fort Hays. Parade grounds, small buffalo herd. Museums in original guardhouse, officers' quarters and blockhouse; visitor center. (Daily; closed Jan 1, Easter, Thanksgiving, Dec 24 & 25) Donation. Frontier Historical Park. SW edge of town; 4 mi S of I-70 at exit 157. Phone 913/625-6812.

Sternberg Museum of Natural History. Natural history, paleontological and geological collections. (Tues-Sat, also Sun & Mon afternoons; closed Jan 1, Thanksgiving, Dec 25) 2911 Canterbury Dr. Phone 913/628-4286. ¢¢

Annual Events

Ellis County Fair. Ellis County Fairground. Entertainment, activities, tractor pull, arts & crafts. Late July.

Pioneer Days. 2 full days of living history at Historic Ft Hays includes demonstrations of butter churning, tatting, ropemaking, rug weaving, whittling, stonepost cutting. Contact Convention & Visitors Bureau. Sept.

Oktoberfest. Arts & crafts, entertainment. Oct 5.

Motels

(Rates may be higher during hunting season, special events)

★ ★ BEST WESTERN VAGABOND. 2524 Vine St (US 183). 913/625-2511; FAX 913/625-8879. 92 rms, 1-2 story. S $44-$60; D $52-$70; each addl $4; suites $70-$125; under 12 free. Crib $4. Pet accepted. TV; cable (premium). Complimentary coffee in rms. Restaurant 7 am-9 pm. Bar 5 pm-midnight. Ck-out noon. Meeting rms. Business servs avail. Valet serv. Free airport transportation. Cr cds: A, C, D, DS, MC, V.

✔ ★ BUDGET HOST VILLA INN. 810 E 8th St. 913/625-2563; FAX 913/625-3967. 49 rms, 1-2 story. S $25-$40; D $30-$50; each addl $3; suites $49-$65. Crib $5. Pet accepted; some restrictions. TV; cable. Pool. Coffee in rms. Restaurant nearby. Ck-out noon. Business servs avail. Free airport transportation. Picnic tables. Cr cds: A, C, D, DS, MC, V.

D

★ ★ DAYS INN. 3205 N Vine St (US 183), I-70 exit 159. 913/628-8261; FAX 913/628-8261, ext. -303. 104 rms, 2 story. S $40-$52; D $52-$62; each addl $5; suites $75-$85; under 17 free. Crib free. TV; cable (premium), VCR avail. Heated pool. Playground. Continental bkfst in lobby. Complimentary coffee in rms. Restaurant adj 6 am-11 pm. Ck-out noon. Meeting rms. Business servs avail. In-rm modem link. Bathrm phones. Cr cds: A, C, D, DS, MC, V.

✔ ★ ★ **HAMPTON INN.** *3801 Vine St (US 183), at jct I-70.* *913/625-8103; FAX 913/625-3006.* 116 rms, 2 story. S, D $47-$60; suites $90. Crib free. Pet accepted. TV; cable (premium). Pool privileges adj. Complimentary continental bkfst 6-10 am. Restaurant adj. Ck-out noon. Business servs avail. In-rm modem link. Free airport transportation. Cr cds: A, C, D, DS, MC, V.

★ ★ **HOLIDAY INN.** *3603 Vine St (US 183), at jct I-70.* *913/625-7371; FAX 913/625-7250.* 190 rms, 2 story. S, D $60-$75; suites $75-$100; under 19 free. Crib free. Pet accepted. TV; cable (premium). Indoor pool; whirlpool, sauna, steam rm. Restaurant 6:30 am-2 pm, 5-10 pm. Rm serv. Ck-out noon. Business servs avail. In-rm modem link. Valet serv. Gift shop. Airport transportation. Holidome. Rec rm. Cr cds: A, C, D, DS, JCB, MC, V.

Restaurant

✔ ★ **GUTIERREZ.** *1106 E 27th.* *913/625-4402.* Hrs: 11 am-10 pm; Fri, Sat to 10 pm; Sun to 9 pm. Closed some major hols. Res accepted. Mexican, Amer menu. Bar. Semi-a la carte: lunch $2.75-$8, dinner $5-$9. Child's meals. Specializes in fajitas, quesadillas, chimichangas. Own chips. Parking. Cr cds: MC, V.

Hiawatha (B-9)

(See Atchison, Seneca; also see St Joseph, MO)

Pop 3,603 **Elev** 1,136 ft **Area code** 913 **Zip** 66434
Information Chamber of Commerce, 413 Oregon St; 913/742-7136.

What to See and Do

Davis Memorial. Eccentric half-million-dollar tomb features 11 life-sized Italian marble statues depicting John Davis and his wife in various periods of their lives. Completed in 1937. 1/2 mi E in Mount Hope Cemetery.

Annual Event

Halloween Parade. Afternoon and evening parade held every year since 1914. Oct 31.

Motel

✔ ★ ★ **HIAWATHA INN.** *1100 S 1st St, at jct US 36 & US 73.* *913/742-7401; FAX 913/742-3334.* 40 rms, 2 story. S $36; D $40; each addl $4; under 12 free. TV; cable, VCR avail. Heated pool. Restaurant (see HEARTLAND). Supper club 5 pm-midnight. Ck-out 11 am. Meeting rms. Business servs avail. Free airport transportation. Private patios, balconies. Cr cds: A, C, D, DS, MC, V.

Restaurant

✔ ★ **HEARTLAND.** *(See Hiawatha Inn) 913/742-7401.* Hrs: 6 am-9 pm. Res accepted. Bar 5 pm-midnight. Semi-a la carte: bkfst $1.50-$5.25, lunch $3.75-$5.75, dinner $4.99-$14.99. Buffet $5.95.

Child's meals. Specializes in seafood, steak. Salad bar. Parking. Cr cds: A, C, D, DS, MC, V.

Hutchinson (E-6)

(See McPherson, Newton, Wichita)

Founded 1872 **Pop** 39,308 **Elev** 1,538 ft **Area code** 316
Information Greater Hutchinson Convention & Visitors Bureau, 117 N Walnut, PO Box 519, 67504; 316/662-3391.

In 1887, drillers for natural gas discovered some of the world's richest rock salt deposits under the town of Hutchinson. The industry was promptly established; today the town is a major producing center, with a mine and processing plants. Oil fields surround Hutchinson; wheat storage (50 million bushels) and shipping is also an important industry. The first settlers, concerned with learning and culture, established schools and founded literary and musical societies. An opera house was built by public subscription in 1882.

What to See and Do

Dillon Nature Center. More than 150 species of birds, along with deer, coyote and other animals, can be spotted at the center, which includes nature trails, a discovery building and two ponds for fishing & canoeing. Guided nature tours (by appt), discovery building (Mon-Fri). Grounds (daily; days vary for canoe rentals and fishing). 3002 E 30th St. Phone 316/663-7411. **Free.**

Kansas Cosmosphere and Space Center. Major Space Science Center for Midwest, featuring Hall of Space Museum exhibits with extensive NASA collection. Cosmosphere with planetarium (fee) and Omnimax (70 mm) projectors. Cosmosphere shows (daily). (Daily; closed Dec 25) Sr citizen rate. 1100 N Plum. Phone 316/662-2305. Omnimax theater ¢¢

Reno County Museum. Features permanent exhibit "Reno County: the First Fifty Years," along with several temporary exhibits. Educational program offers lectures, classes and workshops. (Daily exc Sun, Mon; closed most major hols) 100 S Walnut St. Phone 316/662-1184. **Free.**

Annual Events

National Junior College Basketball Tournament. Sports Arena. Mid-Mar.

Kansas State Fair. Fairgrounds, 2000 N Poplar. Phone 316/669-3600. Sept 6-15.

Motels

✔ ★ ★ **COMFORT INN.** *KS 61 & 17th St (67501).* *316/663-7822; FAX 316/663-6636.* 64 rms, 3 story. S $45.95-$58.95; D $47.95-$60.95; under 18 free. Crib free. TV; cable (premium), VCR avail (movies avail). Pool; whirlpool, sauna. Complimentary continental bkfst. Restaurant nearby. Ck-out noon. Business servs avail. In-rm modem link. Valet serv. Cr cds: A, C, D, DS, ER, JCB, MC, V.

★ **QUALITY INN CITY CENTER.** *15 W 4th St (67501), at Main St.* *316/663-1211; FAX 316/663-6636.* 98 rms, 2 story. S $40.95-$48.95; D $48.95-$58.95; suites $48.95-$130; under 18 free; wkly rates; higher rates: state fair, college basketball tournament. Crib free. Pet accepted, some restrictions. TV; cable (premium), VCR avail. Pool. Restaurant 6:30 am-9 pm; Sun 7 am-2 pm. Rm serv. Bar 4 pm-midnight. Ck-out noon. Meeting rms. Business servs avail. In-rm modem link. Sundries. Golf privileges. Balconies. Cr cds: A, C, D, DS, ER, JCB, MC, V.

★ ★ **RAMADA INN.** *1400 N Lorraine St (67501). 316/669-9311; FAX 316/669-9830.* 220 rms, 2 story. S, D $66-$72; each addl $6; suites $175-$250; under 18 free; higher rates state fair, special events. Crib free. TV; cable (premium), VCR avail. Heated pool; whirlpool, sauna. Restaurants 6 am-2 pm, 5-10 pm. Rm serv. Bar. Ck-out noon. Coin lndry. Meeting rms. Business servs avail. In-rm modem link. Free local airport transportation. Lighted tennis. Rec rm. Picnic tables. Cr cds: A, C, D, DS, ER, JCB, MC, V.

D ⚷ ⌘ ⊠ ⚒ ⚲ SC

Restaurants

★ ★ **PRIME THYME.** *2803 N Main (67502). 316/663-8037.* Hrs: 11 am-10 pm; Sun to 9 pm. Closed some major hols. Bar. A la carte entrees: lunch $4.25-$7.25, dinner $6.99-$20. Child's meals. Specializes in prime rib, steak, teriyaki chicken, seafood. Parking. Cr cds: A, DS, MC, V.

D SC

★ **TOMMASSI.** *17 E 2nd (67501), in Towers Bldg. 316/663-9633.* Hrs: 5-10 pm; Fri & Sat to 11 pm. Closed Sun; Thanksgiving, Dec 24 & 25. Res accepted. Italian, Amer menu. Bar. Semi-a la carte: dinner $7.25-$21.95. Specializes in seafood, prime rib, pasta. Cr cds: MC, V.

D

Independence (F-9)

(See Coffeyville, Parsons)

Founded 1870 **Pop** 9,942 **Elev** 826 ft **Area code** 316 **Zip** 67301
Information Convention & Visitors Bureau, 322 N Penn, PO Box 386; 316/331-1890.

Montgomery County, of which Independence is the seat, was part of the Osage Indian Reservation. In 1869 the Independent Town Company from Oswego, Kansas, obtained 640 acres from the tribe. When the Osage moved to Oklahoma following a treaty in 1870, the entire reservation was opened to settlement. The discovery of natural gas in 1881 and of oil in 1903 caused temporary booms. Today leading industrial products are cement, electrical and electronic parts and equipment, wood products, truck bodies and gas heaters. Farming in the area produces beef cattle, dairy products, hogs, wheat, beans, alfalfa, corn and grain sorghums.

Alfred M. Landon, presidential candidate in 1936, playwright William Inge, author Laura Ingalls Wilder, oilman Harry F. Sinclair and actress Vivian Vance lived here.

What to See and Do

Independence Museum. Miscellaneous collections on display; period rooms and monthly exhibits. (Thurs-Sat) 8th & Myrtle Sts. Phone 316/331-3515. ¢

"Little House on the Prairie." Reproduction of log cabin occupied by Laura Ingalls Wilder's family from 1869-1870. Also one-room schoolhouse (ca 1870) and old post office. (Mid-May-Aug, daily) Donation. 13 mi SW on US 75. Phone 316/331-1890.

Recreation areas. Elk City State Park. An 857-acre park on 4,500-acre lake. Nearby is Table Mound, overlooking Elk River Valley, site of one of the last Osage villages. Arrowheads and other artifacts are still found. Beach; fishing; boating (ramp, dock). Hiking, nature trails. Picnicking. Camping (electricity, dump station). Standard fees. (Daily) 7 mi NW off US 160. **Montgomery State Fishing Lake.** Fishing; boating. Picnicking. Primitive camping. 4 mi S via 10th St Rd, then 1 mi E. Phone 316/331-6295. Per Vehicle ¢¢

Riverside Park. Covers 124 acres. Ralph Mitchell Zoo, Kiddy Land, miniature train (fee), merry-go-round (fee), and miniature golf (fee) (May-Labor Day, daily; rest of yr, phone for hrs). Swimming pool (Memorial Day-Labor Day, daily; fee). Tennis courts; playground; picnic grounds, shelter houses. Park (daily). Oak St & Park Blvd. Phone 316/332-2513 or -2512. **Free.**

Annual Event

"Neewollah." Week-long Halloween festival. Musical entertainment. Last full wk Oct.

Motels

★ ★ **APPLE TREE INN.** *201 N 8th St. 316/331-5500; FAX 316/331-0641.* 64 rms, 2 story. S $45-$48; D $51.45-$55.45; each addl $4; suites $55-$90.50; higher rates "Neewollah." Crib avail. Pet accepted. TV, cable (premium). Indoor pool; whirlpool. Complimentary continental bkfst 6:30-9:30 am, coffee in lobby. Restaurant opp 11 am-10 pm. Ck-out noon. Business servs avail. In-rm modem link. Health club privileges. Some refrigerators. Cr cds: A, C, D, DS, MC, V.

D ⚷ ⌂ ⌘ ⊠ ⚲

✔ ★ **BEST WESTERN PRAIRIE INN.** *Box 26, Jct US 160W & US 75. 316/331-7300; FAX 316/331-8740.* 40 rms. S $36-$44; D $44-$50; each addl $4; wkend rates. Crib free. Pet accepted, some restrictions. TV; cable (premium), VCR avail (movies avail $5). Pool. Complimentary continental bkfst. Restaurant nearby. Private club 5-11 pm. Ck-out 11 am. Business servs avail. In-rm modem link. Cr cds: A, C, D, DS, MC, V.

 ⌘ ⊠ ⚲ SC

Iola (E-9)

(See Chanute, Yates Center)

Pop 6,351 **Elev** 960 ft **Area code** 316 **Zip** 66749
Information Chamber of Commerce, 208 W Madison, PO Box 722; 316/365-5252.

What to See and Do

Allen County Historical Museum Gallery. Display of historical artifacts and memorabilia. (May-Sept, Tues-Sat or by appt) 207 N Jefferson. Phone 316/365-3051. **Free.** Next door is

Old Jail Museum. Historic building; downstairs is solitary confinement cell (1869) and cell cage (1891); upper floor is re-creation of sheriff's living quarters (1869-1904). (Days same as Museum Gallery) 207 N Jefferson. **Free.**

Bowlus Fine Arts Center. Hosts a number of cultural attractions in the 750-seat capacity auditorium. 205 E Madison. Phone 316/365-4765.

Museum Room. Collection and display of historical artifacts. (Mon-Fri; closed hols) Allen County Courthouse, on Courthouse Sq. Phone 316/365-3051. **Free.**

Annual Event

Allen County Fair. Fairgrounds and Everett Shepherd Park. 2nd wk Aug.

Motels

★ ★ **BEST WESTERN INN.** *Box 169, 1315 N State, N on US 169. 316/365-5161; FAX 316/365-6808.* 53 rms. S $35-$38; D $38-$50; each addl $6; suites $39-$45. Crib $2. TV; cable (premium). Pool. Continental bkfst 6-10 am. Complimentary coffee in rms. Restaurant 6 am-9 pm; Sun 7 am-2 pm. Private club 5-11 pm. Ck-out noon. Meeting rm. Business servs avail. Refrigerators; some bathrm phones. Cr cds: A, C, D, DS, MC, V.

[D] [⚊] [⚊] [⚊] [SC]

✓★ **CROSSROADS.** *Box 713, 14 N State, at jct US 54 & US 169.* 316/365-2183; *FAX* 316/365-2183. 54 rms, 1-2 story. S $29; D $36; each addl $3; suites $35-$38. Crib $3. TV; cable (premium). Pool. Complimentary coffee in rms. Restaurant nearby. Ck-out 11 am. Cr cds: A, C, D, DS, MC, V.

[⚊] [⚊] [⚊] [SC]

Junction City (C-7)

(See Abilene, Council Grove, Manhattan)

Settled 1855 **Pop** 20,604 **Elev** 1,107 ft **Area code** 913 **Zip** 66441
Information Geary County Convention & Visitors Bureau, 425 N Washington, PO Box 1846; 913/238-2885 or 800/JCT-CITY.

Its situation at the junction of the Republican and Smoky Hill rivers gave the town its name. The seat of Geary County, it has long been a trading point for soldiers from Fort Riley.

What to See and Do

Fort Riley (1853). A 101,000-acre military reservation; once a frontier outpost and former home of the US Cavalry School. Marked tour. (Daily) N on KS 57, NE on KS 18; located along I-70. Phone 913/239-3032. Here are

First Territorial Capitol. "Permanent" capitol July 2-6, 1855, before Free Staters won legislative majority. (Daily exc Mon; closed major hols) **Free.**

St Mary's Chapel (1855). Kansas' first native limestone church; still in use.

Custer House. The George Armstrong Custers lived in quarters similar to this house. (Memorial Day-Labor Day, daily; May & Sept, Sat & Sun only) **Free.**

US Cavalry Museum. Army memorabilia and local history. (Daily; closed some major hols) **Free.**

1st Infantry Division Museum. Division history and memorabilia. (Tues-Sat; closed Jan 1, Thanksgiving, Dec 25) **Free.**

Milford Lake. A 15,700-acre reservoir with a 163-mi shoreline; arboretum, fish hatchery, nature center. Swimming; fishing, boating (marinas). Picnicking. Camping. (fee). (Daily) 4 mi NW via US 77, KS 57. Phone 913/238-5714. Per Vehicle **¢¢**

Milford State Park. A 1,084-acre park on 16,200-acre lake. Largest man-made lake in Kansas. Native red cedars border shoreline. Nearby is Fort Riley, a major military reservation. Beach, bathhouse; fishing; boating (rentals, ramps, docks, marina). Concession. Tent & trailer camping (electricity, dump station). Standard fees. (Daily) 5 mi NW on KS 57. Phone 913/238-3014.

Motels

✓★ **BEST WESTERN JAYHAWK.** *110 Flint Hills Blvd, in Grandview Plaza, I-70 exit 299.* 913/238-5188; *FAX* 913/238-7585. 48 rms, 1-2 story, 20 kits. S $35-$45; D $45-$55; each addl $4; kit. units $38-$56; under 12 free. Crib $4. Pet accepted. TV; cable (premium), VCR avail. Pool. Complimentary coffee in rms. Restaurant nearby. Ck-out noon. Some chairs. Picnic tables. Cr cds: A, C, D, DS, JCB, MC, V.

[D] [⚊] [⚊] [⚊] [⚊] [SC]

★ **DAYS INN.** *1024 S Washington, 1 blk NE of I-70 exit 296.* 913/762-2727; *FAX* 913/762-2751. 108 rms, 2 story. S $40-$58; D $47-$60; each addl $5; under 17 free. Crib free. Pet accepted, some

restrictions. TV; cable (premium). 2 pools, 1 indoor; whirlpool, sauna. Complimentary continental bkfst. Coffee in rms. Restaurant adj open 24 hrs. Bar 4 pm-midnight, closed Sun. Ck-out noon. Coin lndry. Meeting rms. Business servs avail. Valet serv. Game rm. Rec rm. Cr cds: A, C, D, DS, ER, MC, V.

[D] [⚊] [⚊] [⚊] [⚊] [SC]

★ **GOLDEN WHEAT BUDGET INN.** *820 S Washington St, I-70, exit 296.* 913/238-5106. 20 rms (6 with shower only). Mar-Oct: S $30; $D 35-$40; each addl $5; under 14 free; lower rates rest of yr. Crib $3. TV; cable (premium). Complimentary coffee in lobby. Restaurant nearby. Ck-out 11 am. Cr cds: A, DS, MC, V.

[D] [⚊] [⚊] [SC]

★ **HARVEST INN.** *1001 E 6th St, 1/4 mi NW of I-70 exit 299.* 913/238-8101; *res:* 800/762-0270; *FAX* 913/238-7470. 99 rms, 2 story. May-Sept: S $40; D $47; suites $65; under 12 free; wkly rates; lower rates rest of yr. Crib free. Pet accepted, some restrictions. TV; cable (premium). Pool. Restaurant 7 am-2 pm, 5-9 pm. Rm serv. Bar 5-10 pm. Ck-out noon. Coin lndry. Meeting rm. Business servs avail. In-rm modem link. Some refrigerators. Picnic tables. Cr cds: A, C, D, DS, MC, V.

[D] [⚊] [⚊] [⚊] [⚊] [SC]

Kansas City (C-10)

(See Lawrence, Leavenworth, Overland Park; also see Independence, MO, Kansas City, MO)

Settled 1843 **Pop** 149,767 **Elev** 744 ft **Area code** 913
Information Kansas City, Kansas Area Convention & Visitors Bureau, 753 State Ave, Ste 101, in Brotherhood Building, 66117; 913/321-5800.

Kansas City, as it is today, was formed by the consolidation of eight individual towns. The earliest of these, Wyandot City, was settled in 1843 by the Wyandot, an emigrant tribe from Ohio, who bought part of the Delaware tribes' land. This cultured group brought government, schools, churches, business and agricultural methods to the area. In 1849, alarmed at the influx of settlers on their way to seek California gold, the Wyandot took measures to dispose of their property at a good price. Their successors created a boomtown and changed the spelling to "Wyandotte." Other towns arose nearby, especially as the meat-packing industry developed. Eventually they all merged into the present city, which took the name of one of the earliest towns.

Kansas City has several grain elevators, in addition to fabricating steel mills, automobile manufacturers, soap factories, railway yards and various other industries.

What to See and Do

Community Nature Center Nature Trail. A 20-acre wildlife preserve within the city limits. Many varieties of native animals and vegetation may be seen, including the largest burr oak tree in the state. (Daily) Near 72nd & Parallel Pkwy; adj N end of Community College campus. Phone 913/334-1100. **Free.**

Grinter House (1857). Home of Moses Grinter, first European settler in Wyandotte County; period furnishings. (Tues-Sat, also Sun afternoons; closed hols) Maintained by the Kansas State Historical Society. 1420 S 78th St. Phone 913/299-0373. **Free.**

Huron Cemetery. The tribal burial ground of the Wyandots; an estimated 400 burials (1844-1855). In Huron Park, Center City Plaza, between 6th & 7th Sts, in the heart of the business district.

National Agricultural Center and Hall of Fame. National Farmer's Memorial; history and development of agriculture; library/archives, gallery of rural art; Museum of Farming; "Farm-town USA" exhibit; one-mile nature trail. (Mid-Mar-Nov, daily; closed Thanksgiving) 18 mi W on I-70, at 630 Hall of Fame Dr (N 126th St) in Bonner Springs. Phone 913/721-1075. **¢¢**

Sightseeing. River City USA. Home of the *Missouri River Queen,* a turn-of-the-century paddle-wheel steamer, and the *America,* a multi-level yacht. Both offer afternoon and evening cruises on the Missouri River. Sightseeing trips and dinner cruises avail. (Daily) 1 River City Dr. For schedule phone 913/281-5300 or 800/373-0027. **¢¢¢-¢¢¢¢¢**

The Children's Museum of Kansas City. Learning museum for children ages 4 to 12 has more than 40 hands-on interactive exhibits dealing with science, history, art and technology. Exhibits include a shadow retension wall, grocery store, a slice of city streets, a crawl around salt water aquarium, chain reaction demonstrations and simple machines. (Daily exc Mon) 4601 State Ave, in the Indian Springs Shopping Center. Phone 913/287-8888. **¢¢**

★ The Granada Theatre. Acclaimed organists accompany silent movies from the 20s on the Grande Barton theatre pipe organ, the only such organ in the Midwest. Also offered in this restored 1928 movie palace are organ concerts and movies from the 30s, 40s and 50s. 1015 Minnesota Ave. For schedule, fees phone 913/621-7177.

The Woodlands. Thoroughbred, quarter horse and greyhound racing; two grandstands. (Horse racing mid-Aug-early Nov, Wed-Sun; greyhound racing all-yr) 99th and Leavenworth Rd. Phone 913/299-9797. **¢**

Wyandotte County Historical Society and Museum. Native American artifacts, horse-drawn fire engine, pioneer furniture, costumes, county history; research library, archives. (Daily exc Mon; closed mid-Dec-Jan 2) 15 mi W on I-70, Bonner Springs exit, at 631 N 126th St in Bonner Springs. Phone 913/721-1078. **Free.**

Annual Event

Renaissance Festival. Adj to Agricultural Hall of Fame in Bonner Springs. Phone 800/373-0357. Seven wkends beginning Labor Day wkend.

Motels

✔★ AMERICAN MOTEL. *7949 Splitlog (66112), I-70 exit 414.* 913/299-2999. 158 rms, 3 story. S $29.50; D $34.50; each addl $5; under 12 free; wkly, monthly rates. Crib free. TV; cable (premium). Pool. Complimentary coffee in lobby. Restaurant nearby. Ck-out 11 am. Coin lndry. Business servs avail. In-rm modem link. Game rm. Cr cds: A, C, D, DS, MC, V.

D ⊠ ⊠ ⊠ SC

★★ BEST WESTERN INN. *501 Southwest Blvd (66103), at jct 7th St Trafficway (US 169), 1 blk S of I-35.* 913/677-3060; FAX 913/677-7065. 113 rms, 2 story. S $56-$66; D $65-$75; each addl $7; under 18 free. Crib free. TV; cable (premium), VCR avail. Heated pool; whirlpool. Complimentary continental bkfst. Complimentary coffee in rms. Restaurant adj 6 am-midnight. Bar to 1:30 am. Ck-out noon. Coin lndry. Meeting rm. Business servs avail. In-rm modem link. Valet serv. Med Center transportation. Refrigerators. Cr cds: A, C, D, DS, ER, JCB, MC, V.

D ⊠ ⊠ ⊠ ⊠ SC

Restaurants

✔★ EVERGREEN. *7648 State Ave, Wyandotte Plaza Shopping Center.* 913/334-7648. Hrs: 11 am-10 pm. Closed Thanksgiving. Chinese menu. Serv bar. Complete meals: lunch $3.95-$4.95. A la carte entrees: dinner $4.95-$8.95. Specializes in seafood Szechwan style, egg rolls, sweet & sour dishes. Oriental decor. Cr cds: A, C, D, DS, MC, V.

D ⊐

✔★ MRS. PETER'S CHICKEN DINNERS. *4960 State Ave (US 24), 3 blks W of I-635.* 913/287-7711. Hrs: 5-9 pm; Sun noon-8 pm. Closed Mon, Tues; Jan 1, Thanksgiving, Dec 25; also 1st 2 wks Jan. Complete meals: dinner $9-$16.50. Specializes in fried chicken, country-fried steak, pork chops. Parking. Gift shop. Antiques. Cr cds: DS, MC, V.

D ⊐

Larned (D-4)

(See Great Bend)

Founded 1872 **Pop** 4,490 **Elev** 2,004 ft **Area code** 316 **Zip** 67550
Information Chamber of Commerce, 502 Broadway, PO Box 240; 316/285-6916 or 800/747-6919.

What to See and Do

Fort Larned National Historic Site (1859-1878). Considered one of the best preserved frontier military posts along the Santa Fe Trail; quadrangle of nine original stone buildings plus reconstructed blockhouse. Includes officers' quarters, enlisted men's barracks, blacksmith & carpenter shops, post bakery, hospital, quartermaster and commissary storehouses. Visitor center contains museum, orientation program and bookstore. Conducted tours (Mon-Fri in summer). Living history programs, demonstrations and special events (most summer wkends). One-mile history/nature trail. Picnic area. (Daily; closed Jan 1, Thanksgiving, Dec 25) 6 mi W on KS 156. Phone 316/285-6911. **¢**

Santa Fe Trail Center. Museum and library with exhibits explaining exploration, transportation, settlement and cultural development along the Santa Fe Trail. On the grounds are a sod house, frontier schoolhouse, limestone cooling house, dugout and depot. (Memorial Day-Labor Day, daily; rest of yr, daily exc Mon; closed Jan 1, Thanksgiving, Dec 25) 2 mi W. Phone 316/285-2054. **¢¢**

Motel

★★ BEST WESTERN TOWNSMAN. *123 E 14th St, at jct US 56 & US 156.* 316/285-3114; FAX 316/285-7139. 44 rms. S $36-$46; D $40-$50; each addl $3; under 17 free. Crib $2. Pet accepted. TV; cable (premium), VCR avail. Pool. Coffee in rms. Restaurant opp 6 am-10 pm. Ck-out noon. Business servs avail. In-rm modem link. Sundries. Tennis, golf privileges. Cr cds: A, C, D, DS, MC, V.

D ⊠ ⊠ ⊠ ⊠ ⊠ ⊠ SC

Lawrence (C-9)

(See Kansas City, Leavenworth, Ottawa, Topeka)

Founded 1854 **Pop** 65,608 **Elev** 850 ft **Area code** 913
Information Convention & Visitors Bureau, 734 Vermont, PO Box 586, 66044; 913/865-4411.

Lawrence had a stormy history in the territorial years. It was founded by the New England Emigrant Aid Company and named for one of its prominent members. The center of Free State activities, the town was close to a state of war from 1855 until the Free Staters triumphed in 1859. The Confederate guerrilla leader, William Quantrill, made one of his most spectacular raids on Lawrence in 1863, burning the town and killing 150 citizens. After the Civil War, the town experienced a gradual and peaceful growth as an educational, cultural, trading and shipping point and developed a variety of industries.

What to See and Do

Baker University (1858). (850 students) Oldest university in state. Original building is now Old Castle Museum and Complex, housing pioneer relics and Native American artifacts (daily exc Mon; closed hols); Quayle Bible collection (daily), reservations required at Collins

Library. Campus tours. 13 mi S on US 59, then 5 mi E on US 56 in Baldwin City. Phone 913/594-6451.

Clinton State Park. A 1,485-acre park on 7,000-acre lake. High, heavily wooded hills and grassland on the north shore. Beach, bathhouse; fishing; boating (ramps, docks). Nature trails. Picnicking, concession. Camping (electricity, dump station). Standard fees. (Daily) 4 mi W off US 40. Phone 913/842-8562. Per Vehicle **¢¢**

Haskell Indian Nations University. (1884). (1,000 students) A 320-acre campus. More than 120 tribes are represented among the students. Campus is a registered historic landmark; cultural activities; American Indian Athletic Hall of Fame. (Mon-Fri) 155 Indian Ave. Phone 913/749-8450.

Lawrence Arts Center. Galleries featuring work of local artists and craftsmen; performance hall for theater, dance and music; art classes and workshops for all ages. (Daily exc Sun) 200 W 9th St. Phone 913/843-ARTS. **Free.**

Outdoor Sculpture Exhibit. Downtown, on Massachusetts St. For brochure about current exhibit phone 913/865-4411.

University of Kansas (1866). (26,000 students) A 1,000-acre campus. Some of the campus attractions are the Campanile Bell Tower; Museum of Natural History (daily; phone 913/864-4540); Museum of Anthropology (daily; phone 913/864-4245); and Spencer Museum of Art (daily exc Mon; phone 913/864-4710). (All buildings closed hols) Tours of campus. Phone 913/864-3506.

Watkins Community Museum. Museum housed in 1888 bank building; Victorian era children's playhouse; 1920 Milburn Light Electric car; Quantrill Raid artifacts; permanent and changing exhibits pertaining to the history of Lawrence and Douglas County. (Daily exc Mon; closed most major hols, also Dec 24 to 1st Tues in Jan) 1047 Massachusetts St. Phone 913/841-4109. **Free.**

Annual Events

Kansas Relays. Memorial Stadium. One of the major track and field events in the country. Phone 913/864-3486. 3rd wk Apr.

Douglas County Free Fair. 2nd wk Aug.

Motels

★ ★ **BEST WESTERN HALLMARK INN.** 730 Iowa St (66044), 1 mi W on US 59. 913/841-6500; FAX 913/841-6612. 59 rms, 2 story. S $42.95-$55.95; D $46.95-$55.95; each addl $4; under 12 free; higher rates U of K events. Crib free. Pet accepted, some restrictions. TV; cable (premium). Pool. Complimentary coffee in rms, continental bkfst in lobby. Restaurant nearby. Ck-out noon. Coin lndry. Business servs avail. In-rm modem link. Cr cds: A, C, D, DS, MC, V.

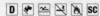

✔ ★ **BISMARCK INN.** 1130 N 3rd St (66044), I-70 exit 204. 913/749-4040; res: 800/665-7466; FAX 913/749-3016. 53 rms, 3 story. S, D $33.90-$39.90; each addl $6; under 16 free; higher rates U of K football season. Crib free. TV; cable (premium). Complimentary continental bkfst, coffee in lobby. Restaurant nearby. Ck-out 11 am. Coin lndry. Game rm. Cr cds: A, DS, MC, V.

★ **DAYS INN.** 2309 Iowa St (66046). 913/843-9100; FAX 913/843-0486. 112 rms, 2 story. S $34-$60; D $40-$65; each addl $4; suite $75; under 18 free; monthly rates. Crib free. Pet accepted. TV; cable (premium). Pool. Coffee in rms. Restaurant 6 am-9 pm; Sun to 2 pm. Rm serv. Bar 4 pm-midnight; wkend hrs vary. Ck-out noon. Coin lndry. Meeting rms. Sundries. 18-hole golf privileges, greens fee $35-$45. Some refrigerators. Cr cds: A, C, D, DS, JCB, MC, V.

✔ ★ **WESTMINSTER INN.** 2525 W 6th St (US 40) (66049). 913/841-8410; FAX 913/841-1901. 60 rms, 2 story. S $36; D $46-$50; each addl $4. Crib free. Pet accepted. TV; cable (premium); VCR avail.

Pool. Complimentary coffee in lobby. Restaurant nearby. Ck-out noon. Meeting rm. Business servs avail. Cr cds: A, C, D, DS, MC, V.

Motor Hotel

★ ★ ★ **HOLIDAY INN.** 200 McDonald Dr (66044). 913/841-7077; FAX 913/841-2799. 192 rms, 4 story. S $69-$89; D $69-$89; each addl $6; suites $125-$185; under 17 free; higher rates major college activities. Crib free. Pet accepted. TV; cable, VCR avail. Indoor pool; poolside serv. Restaurant 6 am-10 pm; Fri, Sat to 11 pm. Rm serv. Bar 4 pm-1 am. Ck-out noon. Business servs avail. In-rm modem link. Coin lndry. Exercise equipt; bicycle, stair machine, whirlpool, sauna. Holidome. Game rm. Rec rm. Cr cds: A, C, D, DS, JCB, MC, V.

Hotel

★ ★ ★ **ELDRIDGE.** 7th & Massachusetts (66044). 913/749-5011; res: 800/527-0909; FAX 913/749-4512. 48 suites, 5 story. S $66-$74; D $74-$235; under 12 free; higher rates major college events. Crib free. Valet parking. TV; cable, VCR avail. Complimentary coffee in rms. Restaurant 7 am-2 pm, 5-9 pm; Fri & Sat to 10 pm. Bar 11-10 pm. Ck-out noon. Meeting rms. Business servs avail. Gift shop. Barber, beauty shop. Transportation to Kansas City. Exercise equipt; bicycle, treadmill, whirlpool, sauna. Refrigerators, wet bars. Built in 1855 as a Free State hostelry for abolitionists; many fights during the Civil War took place here. Cr cds: A, C, D, DS, MC, V.

Inn

★ ★ **HALCYON HOUSE.** 1000 Ohio St (66044). 913/841-0314; FAX 913/843-7273. 9 rms, 4 share bath, 3 story. D $45-$85. Children over 12 yrs only. TV in some rms; cable in lobby. VCR avail (movies avail). Complimentary full bkfst. Ck-out 11 am, ck-in 1 pm. Tennis privileges. 27-hole golf privileges. Health club privileges. Balconies. Victorian inn built 1885. Cr cds: A, MC, V.

Restaurants

✔ ★ **DOS HOMBRES.** 815 New Hampshire St (66044). 913/841-7286. Hrs: 11-12:30 am. Mexican, Amer menu. Bar. Semi-a la carte: lunch, dinner $1.95-$10.95. Specializes in fajitas, chimichangas, quesadilla. Parking. Outdoor dining. Casual atmosphere. Cr cds: A, DS, MC, V.

★ ★ ★ **FIFI'S NABIL.** 925 Iowa St (US 59) (66044). 913/841-7226. Hrs: 11 am-2 pm, 5-10 pm; Sun, Mon 5-9 pm. Closed major hols. Res accepted. Continental menu. Semi-a la carte: lunch $2.95-$6.25, dinner $3.95-$13.95. Bar. Specialties: steak Diane, veal, fresh seafood. Parking. Cr cds: A, DS, MC, V.

Leavenworth (C-9)

(See Atchison, Kansas City, Lawrence; also see Kansas City, MO, St Joseph, MO)

Founded 1854 **Pop** 38,495 **Elev** 800 ft **Area code** 913 **Zip** 66048
Information Convention & Visitors Bureau, 518 Shawnee St, PO Box 44; 913/682-4113 or 800/844-4114.

Leavenworth was the first incorporated town in Kansas Territory. At first strongly pro-slavery, Leavenworth had many border conflicts, but during the Civil War it was loyal to the Union. In the years just before the war, the town was the headquarters for a huge overland transportation and supply operation sending wagons and stagecoaches northwest on the Oregon Trail and southwest on the Santa Fe Trail. Fort Leavenworth, adjoining the city, is the oldest military post in continuous operation (since 1827) west of the Mississippi River. A federal penitentiary is on the grounds adjacent to the fort. Industries in the city of Leavenworth include the Hallmark Card Company and the production of flour, milling machinery and agricultural chemicals.

What to See and Do

Fort Leavenworth. Features of interest are US Army Command and General Staff College, US Disciplinary Barracks, National Cemetery, Buffalo Soldier Monument, branches of the Oregon and Santa Fe Trails. Frontier Army Museum features artifacts of pioneer history and the Army of the West. (Daily; closed Jan 1, Easter, Thanksgiving, Dec 25) Fort (all yr). Obtain self-guided tour pamphlet at museum. 3 mi N on US 73. Phone 913/684-5604.   **Free.**

Leavenworth's Victorian Carroll Museum. 1867 Victorian home and furnishings; schoolroom, general store; local mementos. (Daily exc Mon; closed hols, also Dec 25-3rd wk Feb) 1128 5th Ave. Phone 913/682-7759.   ¢

Annual Event

Buffalo Bill Cody Days. Haymarket Square. Entertainment; dances & outhouse races; wrestling; craft show; Sat parade. Mid-late Sept.

Motels

★ ★ **BEST WESTERN HALLMARK INN.** *3211 S 4th St (US 73). 913/651-6000; FAX 913/651-7722.* 52 rms, 2 story. S $47.95; D $57.95-$61.95; each addl $6; under 12 free. Crib free. TV; cable (premium). Pool. Complimentary continental bkfst. Coffee in rms. Restaurant nearby. Ck-out noon. Business servs avail. In-rm modem link. Coin lndry. Valet serv. Sundries. Cr cds: A, C, D, DS, JCB, MC, V.

D ≈ ✕ ⊛ SC

★ **RAMADA INN.** *101 S 3rd St, 1 blk E of US 73. 913/651-5500; FAX 913/651-6981.* 97 rms, 2 story. S $40-$70; D $46-$70; each addl $6; suites $60-$70; under 18 free. Crib free. Pet accepted, some restrictions. TV; cable (premium). Pool. Restaurant 6 am-2 pm, 5 pm-9pm. Rm serv. Bar 5-11 pm. Ck-out 1 pm. Meeting rms. Business servs avail. Valet serv. Sundries. Cr cds: A, C, D, DS, JCB, MC, V.

D ⊬ ≈ ✕ ⊛ SC

Restaurant

★ ★ **SKYVIEW.** *504 Grand. 913/682-2653.* Hrs: 5:30-8:30 pm. Closed Sun, Mon; Dec 24-30; also 1st 2 wks July. Bar. Semi-a la carte: dinner $10-$30. Specializes in steak, chicken, seafood. Parking. Victorian house (1892); antique tile fireplaces, hand-woven portieres (ca 1850). Gazebo & herb garden. Cr cds: C, D, DS, MC, V.

Liberal (F-2)

Founded 1888 **Pop** 16,573 **Elev** 2,836 ft **Area code** 316 **Zip** 67901

Information Chamber of Commerce, 505 N Kansas Ave, PO Box 676; 316/624-3855.

Liberal's name comes from the generosity of one of its first settlers, Mr. S.S. Rogers. Although water was scarce in southwestern Kansas, Mr. Rogers never charged parched and weary travelers for the use of his well—a "liberal" fee.

Liberal, on the eastern edge of the Hugoton-Oklahoma-Texas Panhandle natural gas field, has many gas and oil company offices. Its agricultural products have become more diversified through irrigation. Beef processing and aircraft production are also important.

What to See and Do

Coronado Museum. Displays depict early life of town; some exhibits trace Francisco Coronado's route through Kansas. Also included are Dorothy's House from the story of *The Wizard of Oz.* (Daily exc Mon; closed hols) 567 E Cedar St. Phone 316/624-7624. Dorothy's House ¢¢¢

Liberal Air Museum. Aviation collection of more than 80 aircraft includes civilian aircraft, military aircraft from World War II and planes of the Korean and Vietnam era. Also here are NASA traveling exhibits and Liberal Army Airfield exhibit. Theater, library, special events and guest speakers. (Daily; closed Jan 1, Thanksgiving, Dec 25) Sr citizen rate. 2000 W Second St. Phone 316/624-5263.   ¢¢¢

Annual Events

International Pancake Race. Housewives compete simultaneously with women in Olney, England, running a 415-yd S-shaped course with a pancake in a skillet, flipping it en route. Shrove Tues in Feb.

Five-State Free Fair. 3rd wk Aug.

Oztoberfest. Munchkin parade, carnival. 3rd wkend Oct.

Motels

✔ ★ ★ **GATEWAY INN.** *720 E Hwy 54, 2 mi E on US 54, near Municipal Airport. 316/624-0242; res: 800/833-3391.* 101 rms, 2 story. S $36-$39; D $44-$47; each addl $3; under 12 free. Crib free. Pet accepted, some restrictions. TV; cable (premium). Pool. Restaurant 6 am-2 pm, 5-9 pm. Bar 4 pm-2 am. Ck-out noon. Coin lndry. Meeting rms. Business servs avail. In-rm modem link. Valet serv (wkdays only). Gift shop. Free airport transportation. Tennis. Picnic tables, grill. Cr cds: A, C, D, DS, MC, V.

D ⊬ ⚹ ≈ ✈ ✕ ⊛ SC

★ ★ **LIBERAL INN.** *603 E Pancake Blvd (US 54). 316/624-7254; res: 800/458-4667.* 123 rms, 2 story. S $32-$47; D $35-$54; each addl $5; suites $65-$100; under 12 free; higher rates: pheasant season, Compressor Institute. Crib free. TV; cable (premium). Indoor pool; whirlpool. Restaurant 6 am-10:30 pm; Sun from 7 am. Rm serv. Private club 5 pm-1 am. Ck-out noon. Coin lndry. Meeting rms. Bellhops. Valet serv Mon-Fri. Sundries. Free airport transportation. Picnic tables. Cr cds: A, C, D, DS, MC, V.

D ⊬ ≈ ✕ ⊛ SC

Restaurant

✔ ★ **KING'S PIT BAR-B-Q.** *355 E Pancake Blvd (US 54). 316/624-2451.* Hrs: 11 am-9 pm. Closed Sun; some major hols. Res accepted. Semi-a la carte: lunch, dinner $3.95-$11.95. Child's meals. Specializes in family-style barbecue, steak, seafood. Parking. Cr cds: D, DS, MC, V.

D SC

Lindsborg (D-6)

(See McPherson, Salina)

Founded 1869 **Pop** 3,076 **Elev** 1,333 ft **Area code** 913 **Zip** 67456

Information Chamber of Commerce, 104 E Lincoln, PO Box 191; 913/227-3706.

Lindsborg was founded by a band of Swedish immigrants who pioneered cooperative farming in Kansas. The Swedish heritage of Lindsborg is evident in the Old World motifs of its business district, Bethany College and in its cultural life, which includes many ethnic festivals.

What to See and Do

Birger Sandzen Memorial Art Gallery. Paintings and prints by Birger Sandzen and other artists; fountain by Carl Milles. (Wed-Sun afternoons; closed major hols) 401 N 1st St, on Bethany College campus. Phone 913/227-2220. ¢

Kanopolis State Park. A l,585-acre park on 3,550-acre lake. Excellent fishing for white bass, crappie, walleye, catfish and largemouth bass. Hiking, bridle trails in rugged Horsethief Canyon, site of 150 foot high Inscription Rock, with petroglyphs representing 3 Native American cultures covering the face of the cliff. North of reservoir is Mushroom Rock area, containing unique sandstone creations shaped like giant toadstools. Beach, bathhouse; fishing; boating (ramp, dock, marina). Picnicking, concession. Tent & trailer camping (electricity, dump station). Standard fees. (Daily) 19 mi W on KS 4, then N on KS 141. Phone 913/546-2565. Per vehicle ¢¢

McPherson County Old Mill Museum & Park. Museum features Native American history, natural history, collections on pioneer and Swedish culture. Smoky Valley Roller Mill and Swedish Pavilion (1904) have been restored. (Daily exc Mon; closed major hols) 120 Mill St, on the Smoky Hill River. Phone 913/227-3595. ¢

REO Auto Museum. Collection of antique autos (1906-1936) displayed in annex to 1930 service station complete with antique hand-operated gas pumps. (Mon-Sat; also Sun afternoons; closed major hols) US 81 Business (KS 4), at Lincoln. Phone 913/227-3252. ¢

Annual Events

Messiah Festival. Presser Hall, Bethany College campus. Special art shows, concerts and recitals, including oratorios of Handel and Bach; presented annually since 1882. For ticket information phone 913/227-3311. Eight days, Palm Sunday-Easter.

Midsummer's Day Festival. Swedish ethnic celebration. Folk dancing, arts & crafts. 3rd Sat June.

Lucia Fest. Christmas season ushered in according to 18th-century Swedish tradition. 2nd Sat Dec.

Motel

✔★ **VIKING.** Box 227, on I-135 Business Loop. 913/227-3336. 24 rms, 2 story. S $29-$35; D $39-$50; each addl $4; higher rates special events. Crib $4. TV; cable. Pool. Complimentary coffee. Ck-out 11 am. Rec rm. Cr cds: A, C, D, DS, MC, V.

Inn

★★ **SWEDISH COUNTRY INN.** 112 W Lincoln. 913/227-2985; res: 800/231-0266. 19 rms, 2 story. S $45-$52.50; D $55-$75; under 6 free. Crib free. TV. Complimentary buffet bkfst. Dining rm 7-11 am; Sun to 10 am. Ck-out 11 am, ck-in 1 pm. Street parking. Bicycles

avail. Sauna. Built 1901; Handmade Swedish pine furnishings. Totally nonsmoking. Cr cds: MC, V.

Restaurants

★ **BRUNSWICK HOTEL.** 202 S Main St. 913/227-2903. Hrs: 11 am-1:30 pm, 5-9 pm. Closed Sun & Mon; most major hols. Res accepted. Swedish, Amer menu. Semi-a la carte: lunch $2.65-$6, dinner $6-$11. Child's meals. Specializes in prime rib, steak, seafood. Salad bar. Parking. Dining rms in former hotel (1887). Victorian decor. Cr cds: DS, MC, V.

D SC

✔★ **CHUCK WAGON.** 435 E McPherson. 913/227-2434. Hrs: 7:30 am-8 pm. Closed Tues; Jan 1, Thanksgiving, Dec 25. Res accepted. Semi-a la carte: bkfst $1.95-$5.95, lunch $3.50-$5, dinner $3.95-$8.95. Child's meals. Specializes in chicken-fried steak, roast beef, catfish. Salad bar. Parking. Western and Native American art. Family-owned. No cr cds accepted.

D

★★ **SWEDISH CROWN.** 121 N Main St. 913/227-2076. Hrs: 11 am-9 pm; Sun 10:30 am-8 pm; winter hrs vary. Closed Jan 1, July 4, Dec 25. Res accepted. Swedish, Amer menu. Private club. Semi-a la carte: lunch $2.95-$5.75, dinner $6.95-$12.95. Child's meals. Specialties: Swedish meatballs, Swedish ham loaf. Entertainment Fri & Sat. Parking. Cr cds: A, DS, MC, V.

D

Manhattan (C-7)

(See Junction City)

Founded 1854 **Pop** 37,712 **Elev** 1,040 ft **Area code** 913 **Zip** 66502

Information Convention & Visitors Bureau, 555 Poyntz, PO Box 988; 913/776-8829 or 800/759-0134.

Several early settlements were combined to form Manhattan. Lying in a limestone bowl-shaped depression resulting from glacial action, the town developed as a trading center for farm products. Later, when the Rock Island Railroad extended a branch here, it became a shipping point. Kansas State University is in Manhattan; its forerunner, Bluemont College, opened in 1859.

What to See and Do

CiCo Park. Swimming (fee), gamefields, wheelchair path, arboretum, tennis, playground. NW edge of town on KS 113. Phone 913/536-0056. **Free.**

City Park. Picnicking, tennis, playground, games; swimming (Memorial Day-Labor Day); rose garden with 400 varieties of roses (spring-summer). Also here is a pioneer log cabin with farm and shop tools on display (Apr-Oct, Sun & by appt; phone 913/587-2757). Historic cast-iron fountain, monument to Quivera. (Daily) Poyntz Ave between 11th & 14th Sts. Park information phone 913/587-2757. **Free.**

Goodnow House Museum (ca 1860). Original limestone home of Isaac T. Goodnow, pioneer educator; period furnishings. (Daily exc Mon; closed most hols) 2301 Claflin Rd. Phone 913/539-3731. **Free.**

Hartford House (1855). Period furnishings in restored prefabricated house. One of ten buildings brought to Manhattan in 1855 on a riverboat by a group of Free Staters (those who wished to establish Kansas as antislavery territory). (Daily exc Mon; closed major hols) 2309 Claflin Rd, in Pioneer Park. Phone 913/537-2210. **Free.**

Kansas State University (1863). (21,500 students) Buildings constructed of native limestone on 668-acre campus. Geological displays in Thompson Hall (Mon-Fri). Tours, Anderson Hall (Mon-Fri). 17th & Anderson Sts, center of town. Phone 913/532-6250.

Riley County Historical Museum. Changing exhibits depict history of Riley County; lifestyle of early Kansas settlers; farm, household and Native American tools; clothing, musical instruments, furniture; archives and library. (Daily exc Mon; closed major hols) 2309 Claflin Rd, in Pioneer Park. Phone 913/537-2210. **Free.**

Sunset Zoological Park. Includes the Australian Outback, with wallabies and kangaroos, Primate Building, Asian Forest Preserve and a children's petting zoo. (Daily) Oak St & Summit Ave, SW edge of city off US 24, KS 18. Phone 913/587-APES. ¢

Tuttle Creek State Park. A 1,156-acre park on 15,800-acre lake. Special observation area with distant views of the Blue River Valley and Randolph Bridge, largest in Kansas. Beach, bathhouse; fishing; boating (marina). Picnicking, concession. Tent & trailer camping (electricity, dump station). Standard fees. 5 mi N on US 24. Phone 913/539-7941. **Free.** Vehicle permit ¢¢

Motels

✔★ **DAYS INN.** *1501 Tuttle Creek Blvd, at US 24 Bypass. 913/539-5391; FAX 913/539-0847.* 119 rms, 2 story. S $45-$65; D $50-$65; each addl $4; under 18 free. Crib free. Pet accepted. TV; cable (premium), VCR avail. Heated pool. Playground. Complimentary coffee in rms. Complimentary continental bkfst. Ck-out noon. Coin lndry. Meeting rms. Business servs avail. In-rm modem link. Valet serv. Sundries. Lawn games. Some refrigerators. Picnic tables, grills. Cr cds: A, C, D, DS, JCB, MC, V.

D 🛌 ≋ 🗙 🦯 SC

✔★ **SUPER 8.** *200 Tuttle Creek Blvd. 913/537-8468; FAX 913/537-8468.* 87 rms, 3 story. No elvtr. S $37.88-$41.88; D $45.88-$50.88; under 12 free. Crib $2. TV; cable (premium), VCR avail. Complimentary continental bkfst, coffee in lobby. Restaurant opp open 24 hrs. Ck-out 11 am. Business servs avail. In-rm modem link. Cr cds: A, D, DS, MC, V.

D 🗙 🦯 SC

Motor Hotels

★★★ **HOLIDAY INN.** *530 Richards Dr (Ft Riley Blvd). 913/539-5311; FAX 913/539-8368.* 197 rms, 3 story. S, D $73-$89; each addl $5; suites $165-$250; under 19 free; higher rates special events. Crib free. Pet accepted. TV; cable (premium). Indoor pool; wading pool; whirlpool, sauna. Restaurant 6 am-10 pm. Rm serv. Bar 4 pm-midnight. Ck-out noon. Coin lndry. Meeting rms. Business servs avail. In-rm modem link. Valet serv. Gift shop. Local airport transportation. Holidome. Game rm. Balconies. Cr cds: A, C, D, DS, JCB, MC, V.

D 🛌 ≋ 🗙 🦯 SC

★★★ **RAMADA INN.** *17th & Anderson, adj to Kansas State University. 913/539-7531; FAX 913/751-3909.* 116 rms, 6 story. S $67-$88; D $67-$88; each addl $6; under 18 free. Crib free. Pet accepted. TV; cable (premium), VCR avail. Heated pool. Restaurant 6:30 am-2 pm, 5-10 pm; Sun 6 am-2 pm, 5-10 pm. Rm serv. Bar 2 pm-10 pm, Fri & Sat to 11 pm. Ck-out noon. Meeting rms. Business servs avail. In-rm modem link. Valet serv. Sundries. Free airport transportation. Health club privileges. Some refrigerators. Cr cds: A, C, D, DS, JCB, MC, V.

D 🛌 ≋ 🗙 🗙 SC

Restaurant

★★ **HARRY'S UPTOWN SUPPER CLUB.** *418 Poyntz, in Wareham Hotel. 913/537-1300.* Hrs: 11 am-2 pm, 5-9 pm; Fri, Sat to 10 pm. Closed Sun; some major hols. Bar to midnight. Semi-a la carte:

lunch $3.95-$6.95, dinner $11.50-$23.95. Specializes in beef, chicken, fresh seafood. Cr cds: A, DS, MC, V.

D

Mankato (B-5)

(For accommodations see Belleville, Beloit, Smith Center)

Pop 1,037 **Elev** 1,776 ft **Area code** 913 **Zip** 66956

What to See and Do

Lovewell State Park. A 1,100-acre park on 3,000-acre lake shaded by dense growth of cedar and burr oak. The State Historical Society's Pawnee Indian Village and Archaeological Museum is nearby, east of Lovewell Dam. Beach, bathhouse; boating (ramps, dock, marina). Picnicking, playground, concession. Camping (electricity, dump station). Interpretive center. Standard fees. (Daily) 20 mi NE via US 36, KS 14, unnumbered road. Phone 913/753-4971. Per vehicle ¢¢

Motel

★ **CREST-VUE.** *US 36 E. 913/378-3515.* 12 rms. S $25; D $32; each addl $2; under 5 free; higher rates hunting season. Crib free. Pet accepted. TV; cable. Complimentary coffee in lobby. Restaurant adj 11 am-1:30 pm, 5-9 pm. Ck-out 11 am. Picnic tables. Cr cds: A, MC, V.

D 🛌 🦯

Restaurant

★ **BUFFALO ROAM STEAK HOUSE.** *US 36 E. 913/378-3971.* Hrs: 11 am-1:30 pm, 5-9 pm; Sat from 5 pm. Closed Sun; most major hols. Res accepted. Mexican, Amer menu. Beer. Semi-a la carte: lunch $3.95-$5.95, dinner $5.95-$21.50. Child's meals. Specializes in steak, seafood. Salad bar. Parking. Western memorabilia. Family-owned. Totally non-smoking. Cr cds: DS, MC, V.

Marysville (B-7)

(See Seneca)

Founded 1854 **Pop** 3,359 **Elev** 1,202 ft **Area code** 913 **Zip** 66508
Information Chamber of Commerce, 1016 Center St, Box 16; 913/562-3101.

This was the first home station out of St Joseph, Missouri, on the Pony Express route. Many emigrant parties camped near here in the 1840s and '50s, including the ill-fated Donner Party, for which Donner Pass in California is named.

What to See and Do

Hollenberg Pony Express Station. Built in 1857; believed to be first house in Washington County. Six-room frame structure served as a family house, neighborhood store and tavern as well as a station on the Pony Express. (Wed-Sat; closed major hols) N on KS 148, E on KS 243, near Hanover. Phone 913/337-2635. **Free.**

Koester House Museum. Restored Victorian home of 1876; original furnishings, costumes. (May-Oct, daily exc Mon; rest of yr by appt; closed major hols) 919 Broadway. Phone 913/562-2417 or -5331. ¢¢

Pony Express Barn Museum. Original Pony Express barn (1859), home station #1; houses Native American artifacts, Pony Express memorabilia; doll collection, displays of old tools and harness equipt. (Daily; afternoons; schedule may vary some months) 106 S 8th St. Phone 913/562-3825. ¢

Motels

★ **BEST WESTERN SURF.** *2005 Center St, US 36E.* 913/562-2354; FAX 913/562-2354. 52 rms. S $30-$40; D $38-$48; each addl $4-$6. Crib free. Pet accepted, some restrictions. TV; cable (premium), VCR avail. Playground. Complimentary coffee in lobby. Restaurant nearby. Ck-out 11 am. Coin lndry. Business servs avail. Exercise equipt; bicycle, stair machine, sauna. Refrigerators. Cr cds: A, C, D, DS, ER, MC, V.

D ☜ ☒ ♨ SC

✔ ★ **THUNDERBIRD.** *Rte 1, US 36 W, 1 mi W of jct US 77.* 913/562-2373; res: 800/662-2373; FAX 913/562-2373, ext. 26. 21 rms. S $28.75-$34.75; D $37.75-$42.75; each addl $4. Crib $4. Pet accepted, some restrictions. TV; cable (premium). Continental bkfst. Complimentary coffee in rms. Ck-out 11 am. In-rm modem link. Golf privileges. Refrigerators. Cr cds: A, C, D, DS, MC, V.

☜ ☆ ♨ SC

McPherson (D-6)

(See Hutchinson, Lindsborg, Newton, Salina)

Pop 12,422 **Elev** 1,504 ft **Area code** 316 **Zip** 67460

Information Chamber of Commerce or the Convention & Visitors Bureau, 306 N Main, PO Box 616; 316/241-3303 or 800/324-8022.

Both the city and the county it is in bear the name of Civil War hero General James Birdseye McPherson, who was killed in the Battle of Atlanta in 1864. Today the center of a diversified agricultural region, McPherson also has a large oil refinery and manufactures plastic pipe, RVs, pharmaceutical products, fiberglass insulation and other products.

What to See and Do

Maxwell Wildlife Refuge. A 2,500-acre prairie provides natural environment for elk, deer, buffalo. Observation tower; 46-acre fishing lake, boat ramp; nature trail. Primitive campsites. (Daily) 14 mi NE via US 56, Canton exit. Phone 316/628-4455. **Free.**

McPherson Museum. 1920s mansion contains America's first synthetic diamond, a collection of meteorites, wood carvings, bell collection, art, dolls, Oriental items, Native American artifacts, pioneer relics, mounted birds and eggs, saber-tooth tiger, giant ground sloth, fossils, rocks and minerals. (Tues-Sun afternoons; closed major hols) 1130 E Euclid. Phone 316/245-2574. **Free.**

Annual Events

Prairie Day Celebration. At Maxwell Game Refuge. 2nd wkend June.

McPherson County Fair & Rodeo. Late June.

Motels

★ ★ **BEST WESTERN HOLIDAY MANOR.** *2211 E Kansas (US 56), at jct I-135.* 316/241-5343; FAX 316/241-8086. 110 rms, 2 story. S $36-$46; D $42-$52; suites $75-$95; each addl $2; under 12 free. Crib $2. Pet accepted, some restrictions. TV; cable (premium). 2 pools, 1 indoor; whirlpool, sauna. Restaurant 6 am-10 pm. Rm serv.

Private club 5 pm-midnight. Ck-out noon. Meeting rms. Business servs avail. Valet serv. Cr cds: A, C, D, DS, MC, V.

D ☜ ☒ ☒ ♨ SC

✔ ★ **RED COACH INN.** *Box 474, 2111 E Kansas (US 56), at jct I-135.* 316/241-6960; res: 800/362-0072 (exc KS), 800/362-0072 (KS); FAX 316/241-4340. 88 rms, 1-2 story. S $34.95-$42.95; D $38.95-$48.95; each addl $4; suites $54.95-$82.95. Crib $3. Pet accepted, some restrictions. TV; cable (premium), VCR avail (movies avail $3.20). Indoor pool; whirlpool, sauna. Playground. Restaurant 6 am-11 pm. Rm serv. Ck-out noon. Meeting rms. Business servs avail. In-rm modem link. Sundries. Rec rm. Cr cds: A, C, D, DS, MC, V.

D ☜ ☒ ☒ ♨ SC

Meade (F-3)

Pop 1,526 **Elev** 2,497 ft **Area code** 316 **Zip** 67864

What to See and Do

Meade County Historical Society. History of Meade County through exhibits of furnished rooms. (Daily exc Mon; closed Dec 25) Donation. 200 E Carthage. Phone 316/873-2359 or 316/873-5168.

Meade State Park. Originally carved out of the Turkey Track Ranch, 900-acre park has varied terrain of prairie, rolling hills, bogs and a small lake. Beach, bathhouse; fishing; boating (ramps, dock). Picnicking. Camping (electricity, dump station). Standard fees. (Daily) 13 mi SW on KS 23. Phone 316/873-2572. Per Vehicle ¢¢

Medicine Lodge (F-5)

Founded 1873 **Pop** 2,453 **Elev** 1,510 ft **Area code** 316 **Zip** 67104

Information Chamber of Commerce, 209 W Fowler; 316/886-3417.

Long before settlers came to Kansas, Native Americans of all the Plains tribes peacefully shared the use of a "medicine lodge" on the Medicine River in a spot they regarded as sacred. In 1867, when the US Government planned a peace council to end the Indian wars, the site of the present town was chosen by the tribes for the meeting. Two weeks of negotiations, with 15,000 Indians and 600 government commissioners present, resulted in a treaty that fixed the Kansas southern boundary and opened the area to settlement. The town was officially chartered in 1879. Today the town of Medicine Lodge is a shipping point for cattle and wheat and has a large gypsum plant. It was the home of the hatchet-wielding temperance crusader Carry Nation.

What to See and Do

Carry A. Nation Home Memorial. WCTU shrine and museum; original furnishings. (Wed-Sun) 211 W Fowler Ave, at Oak St. Phone 316/886-3553 or -3417. ¢

Gypsum Hills. Deep canyons in hills carved by erosion. "Gyp Hills Scenic Drive" is well-marked. 4 mi W on US 160. For information about tours or the annual spring horseback trail rides and fees, phone 316/886-9815.

Medicine Lodge Stockade. Replica of 1874 stockade. Log house with authentic 1800s furnishings; house built of gypsum; museum with pioneer relics. (Daily) On US 160. Phone 316/886-3417. ¢

Motel

✔ ★ **BEST WESTERN COPA.** *401 W Fowler, ¼ mi E of jct US 160, 281.* 316/886-5673; FAX 316/886-5241. 54 rms, 2 story. S

$31-$37; D $35-$40; each addl $3. Crib $3. Pet accepted. TV; cable (premium). Pool. Complimentary continental bkfst in lobby 6-11 am. Restaurant adj 6 am-10 pm. Ck-out 11 am. Picnic tables. Lake 1 mi. Cr cds: A, C, D, DS, MC, V.

Newton (E-7)

(See El Dorado, Hutchinson, McPherson, Wichita)

Founded 1871 **Pop** 16,700 **Elev** 1,448 ft **Area code** 316 **Zip** 67114
Information Convention & Tourism Bureau, 500 N Main, PO Box 353; 316/283-7555.

When the Santa Fe Railroad extended its line to Newton in 1871, the town succeeded Abilene as the terminus of the Chisholm Cattle Trail and the meeting place of cowboys, gamblers and gunmen.

Mennonites migrating from Russia settled in this area in the 1870s, bringing the Turkey Red hard winter wheat they had developed on the steppes. This revolutionized Kansas agriculture and made it one of the world's greatest wheat areas. Newton still has a large Mennonite population, with the oldest educational institution of the sect, Bethel College. Active in historic preservation, Newton has adapted such buildings as the Old Mill, 500 Main Place, and Newton Station into interesting shopping, eating and business sites.

What to See and Do

Kansas Learning Center for Health. Exhibits on human body; transparent "talking" model. (Daily exc Sat) 10 mi W on US 50, then 2 mi S on KS 89, at 505 Main St in Halstead. Phone 316/835-2662. ¢

Kauffman Museum. A Mennonite museum devoted to the environment and people of the plains. Exhibits include prairie animals and birds, and the cultural history of the Cheyenne and the central Kansas Mennonites. Log cabin, 1880s farmhouse, barn & windmill. (Daily) 1 mi N via KS 15, in North Newton on the campus of Bethel College. Phone 316/283-1612. ¢

Warkentin House (1887). Victorian mansion with original furnishings; also carriage house and gazebo (June-Aug, Tues-Sun afternoons; Apr-May & Sept-Dec, Sat & Sun only). 211 E 1st St. For tours contact the Convention and Tourism Bureau, phone 316/283-7555. ¢¢

Annual Events

Chisholm Trail Festival. Athletic Park. July 4 wkend.

Harvey County Free Fair. Mid-Aug.

Bethel College Fall Festival. Phone 316/283-2500. 2nd wkend Oct.

Motel

★ ★ **BEST WESTERN RED COACH INN.** Box 872, 1301 E 1st St, I-135 exit 31. 316/283-9120; FAX 316/283-4105. 81 rms, 1-2 story. S $40-$64; D $46-$64; each addl $6; suites $70; under 18 free. Crib $4. Pet accepted, some restrictions. TV; cable (premium), VCR avail. Indoor pool. Restaurant 6 am-11 pm; closed Dec 25. Rm serv. Ck-out 11 am. Meeting rm. Business servs avail. Valet serv. Free airport transportation. Exercise equipt; bicycle, stair machine, whirlpool, sauna. Game rm. Rec rm. Cr cds: A, C, D, DS, ER, JCB, MC, V.

Inn

★ ★ **HAWK HOUSE.** 307 W Broadway. 316/283-2045; res: 800/500-2045. 4 rms, 1 with bath, 3 story. S $40-$50; D $50-$60. Crib free. Complimentary full bkfst, coffee & tea. Restaurant nearby. Ck-out

10 am, ck-in 5:30 pm. Picnic tables, grills. Turn-of-the-century house (1914); period antiques, original wallpaper and woodwork. Totally non-smoking. Cr cds: MC, V.

Restaurant

★ ★ **OLD MILL RESTAURANT.** 301 Main (KS 15). 316/283-3510. Hrs: 11 am-9 pm; Fri & Sat to 10 pm; Sun brunch 11 am-2 pm. Closed some major hols. Res accepted. American menu. Bar. Wine cellar. Semi-a la carte: lunch $3.95-$6, dinner $4.50-$13.95. Sun brunch $9.95. Child's meals. Specializes in steak, seafood. Salad bar. Own baking. On site of old mill warehouse. Cr cds: A, DS, MC, V.

Norton (B-3)

(See Oberlin, Phillipsburg)

Founded 1871 **Pop** 3,017 **Elev** 2,339 ft **Area code** 913 **Zip** 67654
Information Chamber of Commerce, 3 Washington Square, PO Box 97; 913/877-2501.

What to See and Do

Gallery of Also Rans. Photographs and biographies of unsuccessful presidential candidates. (Mon-Fri; closed hols) First State Bank mezzanine, 105 W Main. **Free.**

Prairie Dog State Park. A 1,000-acre park on 600-acre lake. Site of a restored sod house furnished with articles of the homestead era and an original old schoolhouse (ca 1800). Wildlife observation. Beach, bathhouse; fishing; boating (ramps, dock). Picnicking. Camping (electricity, dump station). Standard fees. (Daily) 4 mi W via US 36 to KS 261, S 1 mi. Phone 913/877-2953. Per vehicle ¢¢

Station 15. "Look in" building; 1859 stagecoach depot replica; costumed figures. (Daily) US 36, Wayside Park. **Free.**

Motels

★ **BEST WESTERN BROOKS.** 900 N State St, at jct US 36, 283. 913/877-3381; FAX 913/877-2188. 35 rms, 1-2 story. S $35-$39; D $42-$48; each addl $3. TV; cable. Pool. Coffee in rms. Restaurant nearby. Ck-out 11 am. Business servs avail. In-rm modem link. Free airport transportation. Cr cds: A, C, D, DS, MC, V.

★ **BUDGET HOST HILLCREST.** Box 249, on US 36, 1/2 mi W of jct US 283, 383. 913/877-3343. 26 rms. S $29.95-$34; D $38.95; each addl $3; higher rates special events, hols. Crib $3. TV; cable (premium). Pool. Playground. Complimentary coffee in rms. Restaurant nearby. Ck-out 11 am. Free airport transportation. City park adj. Cr cds: A, C, D, DS, MC, V.

Oakley (C-2)

(See Colby)

Pop 2,045 **Elev** 3,029 ft **Area code** 913 **Zip** 67748

What to See and Do

Fick Fossil and History Museum. Fossils, rocks, minerals; shark tooth collection (11,000 teeth); unique fossil paintings, photographs; general store, sod house, depot replica. Changing exhibits. Tours. (Daily; closed Jan 1, Dec 25) 700 W 3rd St. Phone 913/672-4839. **Free.**

Motels

★ ★ **BEST WESTERN GOLDEN PLAINS.** *RR Box 3, at jct US 40, 83. 913/672-3254; FAX 913/672-3200.* 26 rms, 2 story. S $45-$55; D $53-$63; each addl $4; suites $65-$85; higher rates pheasant season. Crib $6. TV; cable. Heated pool. Complimentary continental bkfst 7-9 am. Ck-out 11 am. Golf privileges. Some patios. Picnic table. Cr cds: A, C, D, DS, MC, V.

★ **FIRST INTERSTATE INN.** *Box 426, at I-70, US 40, E Oakley exit 76. 913/672-3203; res: 800/462-4667.* 29 rms, 1-2 story. S $31.95; D $36.95; each addl $5; under 10 free. Pet accepted. Crib free. TV; cable (premium). Restaurant opp open 24 hrs. Ck-out 11 am. Cr cds: A, C, D, DS, MC, V.

Restaurant

★ ★ **COLONIAL STEAK HOUSE.** *US 83, I-70, exit 70. 913/672-4720.* Hrs: 6 am-11 pm; Sun buffet 11 am-9 pm. Closed Thanksgiving, Dec 25. Res accepted. Semi-a la carte: bkfst $2.45-$4.65, lunch $3-$12.95, dinner $4.50-$12.95. Buffet: lunch, dinner $5.95. Child's meals. Specializes in steak, fried chicken, homemade pies and desserts. Salad bar. Parking. Many antiques. Cr cds: A, DS, MC, V.

Oberlin (B-3)

(For accommodations see Norton)

Founded 1873 **Pop** 2,197 **Elev** 2,562 ft **Area code** 913 **Zip** 67749
Information Oberlin Convention & Visitors Bureau, 132 S Penn; 913/475-3441.

What to See and Do

Decatur County Museum. Native American artifacts, tools, sod house, church, school, doctor's office, 19th-century depot, jail. (Apr-Nov, Tues-Sat; closed hols)258 S Penn Ave. Phone 913/475-2712. ¢¢

Annual Events

Decatur County Fair. 4-H exhibits, parade, carnival, theater production. Early Aug.
Mini-Sapa Days. Decatur County Museum (see). Two-day fall festival honors those killed in Northern Cheyenne Indian Raid of 1878. 1st wkend Oct.

Osawatomie (D-9)

(For accommodations see Ottawa)

Founded 1855 **Pop** 4,590 **Elev** 865 ft **Area code** 913 **Zip** 66064
Information Chamber of Commerce, 526 Main St, PO Box 338; 913/755-4114.

Osawatomie is chiefly associated with John Brown (1800-1859), most famous of the militant abolitionists. In 1856, in the Battle of Osawatomie, five of his men were killed. He was later executed in Charles Town, WV, and buried at his home in North Elba, NY.

What to See and Do

Driving tour. One-hour driving tour includes six sites on the National Register of Historic Places. Contact Chamber of Commerce for details.
Fishing. Marais des Cygnes Wildlife Refuge and Pottawatomie River. City Lake, 4 mi NW.
John Brown Memorial Park. Site of one of the first battles of the Civil War. Contains a life-size statue of Brown; also a log cabin he used (now a state museum) with period furnishings (daily exc Mon, Tues; closed Jan 1, Thanksgiving, Dec 25). Picnic facilities. Campsites (hookups; fee). Park (all yr, daily). 10th & Main Sts, W side of town. Phone 913/755-4384. **Free.**

Annual Event

John Brown Jamboree. Parade, carnival and entertainment. Wkend late June.

Ottawa (D-9)

(See Lawrence, Osawatomie)

Founded 1837 **Pop** 10,667 **Elev** 901 ft **Area code** 913 **Zip** 66067
Information Chamber of Commerce, 109 E 2nd St, PO Box 580; 913/242-1000.

In 1832, the Ottawa Indians were given land in this area in exchange for their Ohio lands. In 1837, the Reverend Jotham Meeker established the Ottawa Indian Baptist Mission. During the border warfare it was headquarters for Free State men, including John Brown. Today the town is a trading and manufacturing center.

What to See and Do

Dietrich Cabin Museum. In Pioneer log cabin (1859); restored, period furnishings. (Apr-Oct, Sat & Sun afternoons; rest of yr, by appt only) City Park, Main & 5th Sts. Phone 913/242-4097. **Free.**
Old Depot Museum. Historical museum housing relics of area; model railroad room; general store; period rooms. (Apr-Oct, Sat & Sun afternoons; rest of yr, by appt only) 135 Tecumseh St, 1/2 blk S of KS 68. Phone 913/242-4097. ¢
Ottawa Indian Burial Grounds. Jotham Meeker is buried here. NE of city.
Pomona Reservoir. A 4,000-acre reservoir; 8 developed public use areas, 1 access area. Swimming; fishing, hunting; boating (rentals). Nature trails. Picnicking. Camping, group camping (fee). (Daily) 20 mi W on KS 68, 268. Phone 913/453-2201. **Free.** Also on reservoir is
Pomona State Park. A 490-acre park on 4,000-acre lake. Beach, bathhouse; fishing; boating (rentals, ramps, docks, marina). Picnicking, shelters; cafe. Nature trail. Tent & trailer camping (hookups, dump station). Interpretive programs. Standard fees. (Daily) 15 mi W on KS 68, 5 mi W on KS 268, then N on KS 368. Phone 913/828-4933. Per vehicle ¢¢

Annual Events

Franklin County Fair. Fairgrounds. Rodeo. 3rd wk July.

Yule Feast Weekend. Ottawa University. Parade, Christmas homes tours, craft fair. Reservations required for madrigal dinner. Phone 913/242-5200 or 800/755-5200. Dec 3-5.

Motel

✔★ **BEST WESTERN HALLMARK INN.** 2209 S Princeton Rd (US 59). 913/242-7000; FAX 913/242-8572. 60 rms, 2 story. S $42-$52; D $46-$56; each addl $4; under 13 free. Crib free. Pet accepted, some restrictions. TV; cable (premium). Pool. Complimentary continental bkfst. Complimentary coffee in rms. Restaurant adj 6 am-11 pm; wkends open 24 hrs. Ck-out noon. Coin lndry. Meeting rm. Cr cds: A, C, D, DS, MC, V.

D ✦ ≋ ⊠ 🔥 SC

Overland Park (C-10)

(see Kansas City; also see Kansas City, MO)

Pop 111,790 **Elev** 950 ft **Area code** 913
Information Convention & Visitors Bureau, 10975 Benson, Ste 350, 66210; 913/491-3600 or 800/262-PARK.

The suburb Overland Park is located directly south of Kansas City.

What to See and Do

✪ **NCAA Visitors Center.** The center celebrates intercollegiate athletics through photographs, video presentations and displays covering all 21 men's and women's sports and all NCAA championships. The 12,000 square-foot area contains a multipurpose theater with presentations to match the changing athletic seasons; an awards and honors area and a 96-foot mural painted as a tribute to the NCAA's development. Two football and basketball rooms surround the viewer with a 360-degree photograph, simulating an actual game experience. (Daily; closed Jan 1, Thanksgiving, Dec 25) 6201 College Blvd. Phone 913/339-0000 or 800/735-6222. ¢

Old Shawnee Town. Re-creation of a typical Midwestern pioneer town of the 1800s-early 1900s. Collection of buildings and structures includes both originals and replicas; all are authentically furnished. (Daily exc Mon; closed major hols) N on I-35 to Johnson Dr, then W to 57th & Cody, in Shawnee. Phone 913/268-8772. **Free.** Guided tours ¢

Shawnee Methodist Mission. Established in 1839 as mission and school; 3 original buildings. (Daily exc Mon; closed major hols) 3403 W 53rd St, at Mission Rd, 1 blk N of Shawnee Mission Pkwy in Fairway. Phone 913/262-0867. **Free.**

Motels

★★ **BEST WESTERN HALLMARK INN EXECUTIVE CENTER.** 7000 W 108th St (66211). 913/383-2550; FAX 913/383-2099. 181 rms, 2 story. S $62; D $67; each addl $5; suites $75-$95; under 18 free; special wkend plans. Crib free. TV; cable (premium), VCR avail. Heated pool. Complimentary bkfst buffet. Restaurant 6:30 am-2 pm, 5-10 pm. Rm serv. Bar 5 pm-midnight. Ck-out 11 am. Coin lndry. Meeting rms. Business servs avail. In-rm modem link. Valet serv. Gift shop. Refrigerators. Picnic tables, grills. Cr cds: A, C, D, DS, MC, V.

D ≋ ⊠ 🔥 SC

★★ **CLUBHOUSE INN.** 10610 Marty (66212), I-435, N on Metcalf, W on 107th. 913/648-5555; res: 800/CLUB INN; FAX 913/648-7130. 143 rms, 3 story, 22 suites. S $75-$85; D $85-$95; each addl $10; suites $85-$99; under 16 free; wkly rates. Crib free. TV; cable (premium). Heated pool; whirlpool. Complimentary full bkfst, coffee.

Restaurant nearby. Ck-out noon. Coin lndry. Meeting rms. Valet serv. Refrigerator, wet bar in suites. Balconies. Grills. Cr cds: A, C, D, DS, MC, V.

D ≋ ⊠ 🔥 SC

★★★ **COURTYARD BY MARRIOTT.** 11301 Metcalf Ave (66210). 913/339-9900; FAX 913/339-6091. 149 rms, 3 story. S $89; D $99; each addl $10; suites $95-$105; under 16 free; wkly, wkend rates. Crib free. TV; cable (premium). Indoor pool. Complimentary coffee in rms. Bkfst avail. Bar 4:30-11 pm. Ck-out 1 pm. Coin lndry. Meeting rms. Business servs avail. In-rm modem link. Valet serv. Sundries. Exercise equipt; weights, bicycles, whirlpool. Refrigerator in suites. Balconies. Cr cds: A, C, D, DS, MC, V.

D ≋ ✗ ⊠ 🔥 SC

★★ **DRURY INN.** 10951 Metcalf Ave (66210). 913/345-1500; FAX 913/345-1500. 155 rms, 4 story. S $69-$74; D $79-$84; each addl $10; under 18 free. Crib free. Pet accepted, some restrictions. TV; cable (premium). Pool. Complimentary continental bkfst, coffee. Restaurant nearby. Ck-out noon. Meeting rms. Business servs avail. In-rm modem link. Valet serv. Health club privileges. Cr cds: A, C, D, DS, MC, V.

D ✦ ≋ ⊠ 🔥 SC

✔★ **FAIRFIELD INN BY MARRIOTT.** 4401 W 107th (66207), I-435 exit 77. 913/381-5700; FAX 913/381-5700, ext. 709. 134 rms, 3 story. S $42.95-$49.95; D $52.95-$59.95; each addl $7; under 18 free. Crib free. TV; cable (premium). Pool. Continental bkfst avail. Restaurant nearby. Ck-out noon. Meeting rm. In-rm modem link. Valet serv. Sundries. Health club privileges. Cr cds: A, C, D, DS, MC, V.

D ≋ ✗ ⊠ 🔥 SC

★★ **HAMPTON INN.** 10591 Metcalf Frontage Rd (66212). 913/341-1551; FAX 913/341-8668. 134 rms, 5 story. S $59-$74; D $70-$75; under 18 free. Crib free. TV; cable (premium). Pool; whirlpool. Complimentary continental bkfst. Complimentary coffee in rms. Restaurant nearby. Ck-out noon. Meeting rms. Business servs avail. In-rm modem link. Health club privileges. Cr cds: A, C, D, DS, MC, V.

D ≋ ⊠ 🔥 SC

★★ **RESIDENCE INN BY MARRIOTT.** 6300 W 110th St (66211), I-435, S on Metcalf, E on College, N on Lamar. 913/491-3333; FAX 913/491-1377. 112 suites, 2 story. S, D $104-$140; under 12 free; wkly, monthly rates. Crib free. Pet accepted, some restrictions. TV; cable (premium). Pool. Complimentary continental bkfst. Ck-out noon. Coin lndry. Meeting rm. Business servs avail. In-rm modem link. Valet serv. Exercise equipt; weights, bicycles, whirlpool, sauna. Sports court. Some fireplaces. Private patios, balconies. Picnic tables, grills. Landscaped courtyard. Cr cds: A, C, D, DS, JCB, MC, V.

D ✦ ≋ ✗ ⊠ 🔥 SC

✔★★ **WHITE HAVEN.** 8039 Metcalf Ave (66204). 913/649-8200; res: 800/752-2892. 78 rms, 1-2 story. 9 kit. units. S $35-$40; D $42-$46; each addl $2; suites, kit. units $58. Crib $1. Pet accepted, some restrictions. TV; cable (premium). Pool. Complimentary morning coffee. Restaurant adj 6:30 am-9 pm; Sun 7 am-3 pm. Ck-out noon. Refrigerators. Cr cds: A, C, D, DS, MC, V.

D ✦ ≋ ⊠ 🔥

Motor Hotel

★★ **RADISSON.** 8787 Reeder Rd (66214). 913/888-8440; FAX 913/888-3438. 192 rms, 8 story. S $65-$85; D $75-$85; each addl $7; suites $100; under 18 free. Crib free. TV; cable (premium), VCR avail. Heated indoor/outdoor pool; whirlpool, sauna. Complimentary coffee in rms. Restaurant 6 am-2 pm, 5-10 pm. Rm serv. Bar; entertainment, dancing. Ck-out noon. Meeting rms. Business center. In-rm modem link. Valet serv. Kansas City Airport transportation. Cr cds: A, C, D, DS, MC, V.

D ≋ ⊠ 🔥 SC ⊼

Hotels

★ ★ **DOUBLETREE.** *10100 College Blvd (66210).* 913/451-6100; FAX 913/451-3873. 357 rms, 18 story. S, D $109-$149; each addl $10; suites $175-$450; under 18 free; wkend rates. Crib free. Pet accepted, some restrictions. TV; cable, VCR avail. Indoor pool; whirlpool, sauna, poolside serv. Restaurants 6 am-11 pm (also see ROTISSERIE). Bar 4-1 am, Sun 4 pm-midnight; dancing. Ck-out noon. Convention facilities. Business center. In-rm modem link. Gift shop. Airport transportation. Some refrigerators. Cr cds: A, C, D, DS, ER, JCB, MC, V.

⊡ 🐾 ≋ 🛷 🏊 🖐 SC 🚶

★ ★ **MARRIOTT-OVERLAND PARK.** *10800 Metcalf (66210).* 913/451-8000; FAX 913/451-5914. 397 rms, 11 story. S, D $109-$129; suites $200-$350; under 18 free; wkly, wkend rates. Crib free. Pet accepted. TV; cable (premium), VCR avail. Indoor/outdoor pool; poolside serv. Complimentary coffee. Restaurant (see NIKKO). Bar 11:30-1 am. Ck-out noon. Meeting rms. Business center. In-rm modem link. Concierge. Gift shop. Airport transportation. Exercise equipt; weights, bicycles, whirlpool. Game rm. Traditional & Oriental decor. Luxury level. Cr cds: A, C, D, DS, JCB, MC, V.

⊡ 🐾 ≋ 🛩 🏊 🖐 SC 🚶

Restaurants

★ ★ **CHIEN DYNASTY.** *9921 W 87th St (66212).* 913/888-3000. Hrs: 11 am-9:30 pm; Fri & Sat to 10:30 pm; Sun to 9 pm; Sun brunch 11:30 am-2 pm. Closed Thanksgiving, Dec 25. Res accepted. Chinese menu. Bar. Semi-a la carte: lunch $4.50-$5.50, dinner $6.95-$23.75. Lunch buffet $5.45. Sun brunch $7.95. Specializes in Szechuan & Hunan dishes. Three dining areas; Chinese paintings, figurines and vases. Cr cds: A, D, DS, MC, V.

⊡ 🔧

★ ★ **COYOTE GRILL.** *(4843 Johnson Dr, Mission) N on US 169, in Mission Shopping Center.* 913/362-3333. Hrs: 11 am-10 pm; wkends to 11 pm; Sun brunch to 2 pm. Bar. Semi-a la carte: lunch $3.50-$10, dinner $3.50-$20. Sun brunch $4.50-$8. Specializes in pasta, Southwestern cuisine. Southwestern art. Cr cds: A, D, DS, MC, V.

⊡ 🔧

✔ ★ **DON CHILITO'S.** *(7017 Johnson Dr, Mission) N on US 169.* 913/432-3066. Hrs: 11 am-9 pm; Fri, Sat to 10 pm. Closed Thanksgiving, Dec 25. Mexican menu. Beer. Semi-a la carte: lunch, dinner $3-$9.99. Specializes in burritos. Parking. Family-owned. Cr cds: DS, MC, V.

⊡ 🔧

★ ★ **HOUSTON'S.** *7111 W 95th St (66212), at Metcalf St.* 913/642-0630. Hrs: 11 am-11 pm; Fri & Sat to midnight. Closed Thanksgiving, Dec 25. Bar. Semi-a la carte: lunch, dinner $5.95-$18.95. Child's meals. Specializes in steak, fresh fish. Parking. Casual elegance. Cr cds: A, MC, V.

⊡ 🔧

★ ★ **JOHNNY CASCONE'S.** *6863 W 91st St.* 913/381-6837. Hrs: 11 am-10 pm; Sun 4-9 pm. Closed major hols. Res accepted Sun-Thurs. Italian, Amer menu. Bar. Semi-a la carte: lunch $4-$8, dinner $7-$17. Child's meals. Specializes in lasagne, seafood, steak. Parking. Country decor. Cr cds: A, C, D, DS, MC, V.

⊡ 🔧

★ ★ **K.C. MASTERPIECE.** *10985 Metcalf (66210).* 913/345-1199. Hrs: 11 am-10 pm; Fri, Sat to 11 pm; Sun 11 am-9:30 pm. Closed Thanksgiving, Dec 25. Bar. Semi-a la carte: lunch $5.25-$13.95, dinner $6-$15. Child's meals. Specializes in baby back ribs, filet of pork,

turkey. Parking. Authentic 1930s decor; ornamental tile floor. Display of barbecue memorabilia. Cr cds: A, C, D, DS, MC, V.

⊡ 🔧

✔ ★ **LEONA YARBROUGH'S.** *(2800 W 53rd St, Fairway 66205) W on Shawnee Mission Pkwy.* 913/722-4800. Hrs: 11 am-8 pm; Sun to 7 pm. Closed Mon; also Dec 25 and 1 wk following. Semi-a la carte: lunch $2.95-$9.50, dinner $5.25-$10.75. Child's meals. Specializes in fried chicken, liver & onions, roast pork. Parking. Full bakery on premises. Family-owned. No cr cds accepted.

🔧

★ ★ ★ **NIKKO.** *(See Marriott-Overland Park Hotel)* 913/451-8000. Hrs: 5-10 pm; Fri & Sat to 11 pm. Closed some major hols. Res accepted. Japanese menu. Bar. Semi-a la carte: dinner $12.95-$25.95. Child's meals. Specializes in swordfish, filet mignon. Parking. Japanese decor; tepanyaki service. Cr cds: A, C, D, DS, MC, V.

⊡ SC 🔧

★ ★ ★ **ROTISSERIE.** *(See Doubletree Hotel)* 913/451-6100, ext. 1978. Hrs: 6 am-10 pm; wkends from 7 am; Sun brunch 10 am-2 pm. Res accepted. Bar 4 pm-1 am. Wine list. Semi-a la carte: bkfst $3.95-$8.95, lunch $4.75-$9.25, dinner $16.95-$21.95. Buffet: bkfst $7.95, lunch $7.50. Sun brunch $16.95. Child's meals. Specializes in prime rib, steak, seafood. Salad bar. Parking. Skylight, waterfall and many plants give the three dining areas a relaxing atmosphere. Cr cds: A, C, D, DS, ER, JCB, MC, V.

⊡ SC

Unrated Dining Spot

GATES BAR-B-QUE. *2001 W 103rd, Leawood) E on W 103rd St, at state line.* 913/383-1752. Hrs: 10 am-11 pm; Fri, Sat to midnight. Closed Thanksgiving, Dec 25. Beer. A la carte entrees: lunch, dinner $4.50-$14. Specializes in barbecue ribs, beef, chicken. Parking. No cr cds accepted.

⊡ 🔧

Parsons (F-9)

(See Chanute, Coffeyville, Independence, Pittsburg)

Founded 1871 **Pop** 11,924 **Elev** 907 ft **Area code** 316 **Zip** 67357

Information Chamber of Commerce, 1715 Corning, PO Box 737; 316/421-6500.

Parsons' economy is based on industry and agriculture. The Union Pacific railroad is here, as well as assorted industries. Dairying, beef cattle and cereal grains are important.

What to See and Do

Fishing, picnicking, boating. Neosho County State Fishing Lake. Campgrounds. 5 mi N on US 59, then 3 mi E on unnumbered road. **Lake Parsons.** 4 mi N on US 59, then 3½ mi W. Beach, bathhouses. Camping, electrical hookups (fee). **Marvel Park.** E Main St. Camping, electrical hookups. (Daily) Phone 316/421-7077. **Free.**

Pearson-Skubitz Big Hill Lake. Swimming; fishing; boating (ramps). Hiking. Picnic area. Camping (fee). (Mar-Oct, daily) 9 mi W on US 160, then 5 mi S on unnumbered road, then 3 mi W on unnumbered road. Phone 316/336-2741. **Free.**

Oakwood Cemetery. Contains Civil War graves and monuments. S Leawood.

Parsons Historical Museum. Display of items dating from 1871; memorabilia related to Missouri-Kansas-Texas Railroad. (May-Oct, Fri-Sun or by appt) 18th & Corning. **Free.**

Motels

★ **DAYS INN.** *400 E Main (US 160 E).* 316/421-5000; res: 800/835-0369; FAX 316/421-9123. 81 rms, 2 story. S $30.45-$33.20; D $36.90-$47.98; each addl $5; suites $52-$63. Crib free. TV; cable (premium). Pool. Restaurant 6:30 am-9 pm; Sun to 2 pm. Private club 5-11 pm. Ck-out 11 am. Coin lndry. Meeting rms. Business servs avail. In-rm modem link. Bathrm phones. Cr cds: A, C, D, DS, MC, V.

★ **TOWNSMAN.** *US 59 S.* 316/421-6990; res: 800/552-4408; FAX 316/421-4767. 38 rms. S $28-$30; D $33-$35; each addl $2; under 4 free. Crib free. Pet accepted, some restrictions. TV; cable (premium). Pool. Restaurant 6 am-9 pm. Ck-out 11 am. Business servs avail. Refrigerators avail. Cr cds: A, C, D, DS, MC, V.

Hotel

✔ ★ **THE PARSONIAN.** *1725 Broadway, at 18th St.* 316/421-4400. 55 rms, 8 story. S $26-$30; D $34-$45; each addl $3. Crib free. TV; cable (premium), VCR avail. Restaurant 6 am-7:30 pm. Private club 4-11 pm. Ck-out 11 am. Meeting rms. No bellhops. Cr cds: A, D, MC, V.

Phillipsburg (B-4)

(See Norton, Smith Center, Stockton)

Pop 2,828 **Elev** 1,951 ft **Area code** 913 **Zip** 67661
Information Phillipsburg Area Chamber of Commerce, 270 State St; 913/543-2321.

What to See and Do

Kirwin National Wildlife Refuge. An overlay project on a flood control reservoir. Auto tour route, nature trail, picnic facilities, primitive camping. (Daily) 5 mi S on US 183, then 6 mi E on KS 9 near Kirwin. Phone 913/543-6673. **Free.**

Old Fort Bissell. Replicas of fort and sod house; authentic log cabin; one-room schoolhouse (ca 1870); depot; store; old gun collection. (Mid-Apr-Sept, daily exc Mon) Donation. City Park, W edge of town, on US 36. Phone 913/543-6212.

Annual Events

Phillips County Fair. 4-H Fairgrounds. Phone 913/543-2722. Late July-early Aug.

Rodeo. One of the largest in the state. Early Aug.

Motel

✔ ★ **MARK V.** *320 W State St (US 36).* 913/543-5223; res: 800/219-3149; FAX 913/543-2323. 33 rms, 2 story. S $27; D $34; each addl $6. Crib free. TV; cable (premium). Pool. Complimentary coffee in lobby. Restaurant nearby. Ck-out 10 am. Picnic tables. Park adj. Cr cds: A, C, D, DS, MC, V.

Pittsburg (F-10)

(See Fort Scott, Parsons; also see Joplin, MO)

Founded 1876 **Pop** 17,775 **Elev** 944 ft **Area code** 316 **Zip** 66762
Information Convention & Visitors Bureau, 117 W 4th, PO Box 1115; 316/231-1212.

Rich in natural resources, this coal center of Kansas, which began as a mining camp, was named for Pittsburgh, Pennsylvania. Surviving depressions and strikes, today it is a prosperous consumer, industrial and educational center.

What to See and Do

Crawford County Historical Museum. Artifacts related to coal industry of area; also old schoolhouse and store. (Wed-Sun afternoons; closed hols) N of 20th St on Bypass 69. Phone 316/231-1440. **Free.**

Crawford State Park. In the heart of the strip coal mining area, here is a tiny piece of the Ozarks with redbuds and flowering trees in the spring and brilliant autumn colors in the fall. Located on small lake. Beach, bathhouse; fishing; boating (rentals, ramps, dock, marina). Picnicking, concession. Camping (electricity, dump station). Standard fees. (Daily) 7 mi N on US 69, then 7 mi W on KS 57, then 9 mi N on KS 7. Phone 316/362-3671. Per Vehicle **¢¢**

Lincoln Park. Swimming pool (late May-Aug, daily); wading pool, picnic and campgrounds, tennis courts, batting cage, playground, kiddie rides. Park (mid-Apr-mid-Oct). 18-hole golf, driving range, miniature golf (all yr). Fee for activities. (Daily) Memorial Dr & US 69 Bypass. Phone 316/231-8070.

Motel

★ ★ **HOLIDAY INN EXPRESS.** *PO Drawer 1638, 4020 Parkview Dr (US 69N).* 316/231-8700; FAX 316/231-8700, ext. -754. 100 rms, 2 story. S, D $50-$72; each addl $6; under 20 free; higher rates special events. TV; cable (premium), VCR avail. Pool; whirlpool. Complimentary bkfst buffet. Ck-out noon. Coin lndry. Meeting rms. Business servs avail. In-rm modem link. Valet serv. Exercise equipt; weights, bicycle. Picnic tables. Game rm. Cr cds: A, C, D, DS, JCB, MC, V.

Pratt (E-5)

(See Greensburg, Medicine Lodge)

Founded 1884 **Pop** 6,687 **Elev** 1,891 ft **Area code** 316 **Zip** 67124
Information Chamber of Commerce, 114 N Main, PO Box 469; 316/672-5501.

What to See and Do

Kansas State Fish Hatchery/Nature Center. Covers 187 acres and has more than 90 brood ponds, a nature center, aquarium; picnicking. One of the first channel catfish hatcheries. (Daily exc Sat, Sun) Operations headquarters of the Dept of Wildlife and Parks are located on the grounds. 2 mi E on US 54, then 1 mi S on KS 64. Phone 316/672-5911. **Free.**

Pratt County Historical Society Museum. Pioneer Room settings including complete dentist's office, 1890 kitchen, blacksmith shop, gun collection and artifacts, old-time Main Street. (Daily exc Mon; also by appt) 208 S Ninnescah. Phone 316/672-7874. **Free.**

Annual Event

Pratt County Fair. Fairgrounds, S of town. Phone 316/672-6121. Late July.

Motel

✔★★ BEST WESTERN HILLCREST. *1336 E 1st St. 316/672-6407; FAX 316/672-6707.* 42 rms. S $32-$38; D $38-$43; each addl $4; under 12 free. Crib $4. Pet accepted. TV; cable (premium), VCR avail. Pool. Complimentary continental bkfst. Restaurant nearby. Ck-out noon. Meeting rm. Refrigerators. Cr cds: A, D, DS, MC, V.

Russell (C-5)

(For accommodations see Hays)

Pop 4,781 **Elev** 1,826 ft **Area code** 913 **Zip** 67665

Russell is located in the heart of an oil district.

What to See and Do

Deines Cultural Center. Houses permanent and traveling art exhibits; collection of wood engravings by E. Hubert Deines. (Tues-Sun afternoons) 820 N Main St. Phone 913/483-3742. **Free.**

Fossil Station Museum. History of Russell County. Also houses furniture and artifacts of settlers in building made of hand-hewn post rock. (May-Sept, daily exc Mon; winter, by appt) 331 Kansas St. Phone 913/483-3637. **Free.**

Oil Patch Museum. History of the oil industry in Russell County. Outdoor displays of oil equipment are also included. (May-Labor Day, daily) Guided tours. Jct I-70 & US 281. Phone 913/483-6640. **Free.**

Wilson Dam & Reservoir. Swimming; fishing; boating. Camping (fee) (Daily). 21 mi E on I-70 to Wilson, then 8 mi N on KS 232. On southern shore is

Wilson State Park. A 927-acre park on 9,000-acre lake. An area of unique beauty with deep canyons and steep hills devoid of trees and brush. Rugged chimney rocks and arches rim the lake on Hell Creek Canyon. Home to thousands of migratory water fowl. Beach, bathhouse; fishing; boating (rentals, ramps, dock, marina). Hiking trails. Picnicking, concession. Camping (electricity, dump station). Standard fees. (Daily) 21 mi E on I-70, then 5 mi N on KS 232. Phone 913/658-2465. Per vehicle **¢¢**

Salina (D-6)

(See Abilene, Lindsborg, McPherson)

Founded 1858 **Pop** 42,303 **Elev** 1,220 ft **Area code** 913 **Zip** 67401
Information Chamber of Commerce, 120 W Ash, PO Box 586; 913/827-9301.

The Salina site was chosen by a New York newspaper correspondent who established a store to trade with Native American hunting parties. Business improved in 1860 when gold hunters stocked up on their way to Pikes Peak. The arrival of the Union Pacific Railroad in 1867 brought new growth, and the wheat crops in the 1870s established a permanent economy. Alfalfa, now one of the state's major crops, was first introduced in Kansas by a Salina resident in 1874. The city was rebuilt in 1903 after the Smoky Hill flood destroyed four-fifths of the community. Today it is a leading agricultural center; manufacturing also contributes to its economic base.

What to See and Do

Bicentennial Center. Concerts; trade shows & expositions; athletic events; special events. Kenwood Park. Phone 913/826-7200.

Central Kansas Flywheels Historical Museum. Museum features antique farm machinery and other artifacts from central Kansas. Craft show (mid-May). (Apr-Sept, daily exc Mon; closed hols) 1100 W Diamond Rd. Phone 913/825-8473. **¢**

Salina Art Center. Features art exhibits; also hands-on art laboratory for children. (Tues-Sun afternoons; closed some hols) 242 S Santa Fe. Phone 913/827-1431. **Free.**

Smoky Hill Historical Museum. Area history represented by photos and artifacts; changing exhibits; general store period room. (Daily exc Mon; closed major hols) 211 W Iron Ave. Phone 913/826-7460. **Free.**

Annual Events

Smoky Hill River Festival. 2nd wkend June.

Tri-Rivers Fair and Rodeo. Mid-Aug.

Steam Engine and Antique Farm Engine Show. At Central Kansas Flywheels Historical Museum. Antique tractor pull. Wheat threshing, log sawing and other early farming skills. Phone 913/825-8473. Mid-Aug.

Motels

★ BEST WESTERN MID-AMERICA. *Box 132, 1846 N 9th, I-70 exit 252. 913/827-0356; FAX 913/827-7688.* 108 rms, 2 story. Mid-May-mid-Oct: S $39-$46; D $46-$54; each addl $3; suites $70-$75; under 12 free; lower rates rest of yr. Crib $1. Pet accepted; some restrictions. TV; cable (premium), VCR avail. Indoor/outdoor pool; whirlpool, sauna, poolside serv. Restaurant 6 am-10 pm. Rm serv. Bar 5 pm-1 am. Ck-out noon. Meeting rms. Business servs avail. In-rm modem link. Sundries. Cr cds: A, C, D, DS, MC, V.

✔★ BUDGET HOST VAGABOND II. *217 S Broadway (US 81 Business). 913/825-7265; FAX 913/825-7003.* 45 rms, 2 story. S $26-$40; D $34-$45; each addl $4; kit. $4/day addl. Crib $1. Pet accepted. TV; cable (premium). Pool. Complimentary coffee in rms. Restaurant adj 6 am-10 pm; Sun to 2 pm. Ck-out 11 am. Business servs avail. Cr cds: A, C, D, DS, MC, V.

★ COMFORT INN. *1820 W Crawford. 913/826-1711; FAX 913/826-1711.* 60 rms. S $50-$57; D $52-$73; each addl $7; under 18 free. Crib free. Pet accepted, some restrictions. TV; cable (premium), VCR avail. Indoor pool; whirlpool. Complimentary continental bkfst. Restaurant nearby. Ck-out 11 am. Business servs avail. In-rm modem link. Some refrigerators. Cr cds: A, C, D, DS, ER, JCB, MC, V.

★★★ HOLIDAY INN. *Box 796, 1616 W Crawford. 913/823-1739; FAX 913/823-1791.* 192 rms, 3 story. S $69; D $50-$65; suites $75-$115; under 12 free. Crib free. TV; cable (premium). Indoor/outdoor pool; poolside serv. Playground. Restaurant 6 am-10 pm; Sun to 9 pm. Rm serv. Bar 4 pm-midnight; dancing exc Sun. Ck-out noon. Coin lndry. Meeting rms. Business servs avail. In-rm modem link. Bellhops. Valet serv. Sundries. Airport, bus depot transportation. Miniature golf. Exercise equipt; weight machine, bicycle, whirlpool, sauna. Game rm. Cr cds: A, C, D, DS, JCB, MC, V.

★★ RAMADA INN. *1949 N 9th St, I-70, exit 252. 913/825-8211; FAX 913/823-1048.* 103 rms, 2 story. May-Nov: S $50; D $58; each addl $6; under 18 free. Crib free. Pet accepted; $10 deposit. TV; cable (premium). Heated pool. Restaurant 6 am-9 pm. Rm serv. Bar 5

pm-midnight. Ck-out noon. Meeting rms. Business servs avail. Cr cds: A, C, D, DS, MC, V.

★ ★ **RED COACH INN.** *2020 W Crawford, I-135, exit 92. 913/825-2111; FAX 913/825-6973.* 114 rms, 2 story. S $36-$42; D $44-$50; each addl $4; suites $68-$95; under 12 free. Crib $3. Pet accepted, some restrictions. TV; cable (premium), VCR (movies avail). Indoor pool; whirlpool, sauna. Playground. Restaurant 6 am-11 pm. Rm serv. Ck-out noon. Meeting rms. Business servs avail. In-rm modem link. Sundries. Coin lndry. Lighted tennis. Miniature golf. Game rm. Refigerator in suites. Cr cds: A, C, D, DS, MC, V.

Restaurants

✔★ ★ **BROOKVILLE HOTEL DINING ROOM.** *(Box 7, Brookvillle 67425) 15 mi W on KS 140, 7 mi S of I-70 Brookville exit 238. 913/225-6666.* Hrs: 5-8:30 pm; Sun 11 am-7:30 pm. Closed Mon, Christmas, Thanksgiving. Res accepted. Serv bar. Complete meals: family-style chicken dinner $10.75. Own biscuits. Parking. In historic frontier hostelry; period decor. Cr cds: DS, MC, V.

D

★ ★ **GIORGIO'S.** *1200 E Crawford. 913/825-0200.* Hrs: 11 am-10 pm; Sun to 8 pm; Sun brunch to 2 pm. Res accepted. Italian, Amer menu. Bar. Semi-a la carte: lunch $2.95-$7.95, dinner $5.95-$13.95. Sun brunch $7.95. Child's meals. Specializes in angel hair pasta, orzo pasta, Tour of Italy platter. Italian decor. Cr cds: A, DS, MC, V.

D

✔★ **GUTIERREZ.** *1935 S Ohio. 913/825-1649.* Hrs: 11 am-10 pm. Closed Easter, Dec 25. Res accepted. Mexican, Amer menu. Bar. Semi-a la carte: lunch $5-$7, dinner $8-$12. Child's meals. Specializes in chimichangas. Parking. Cr cds: A, DS, MC, V.

D

Scott City (D-2)

Pop 3,785 Elev 2,978 ft Area code 316 Zip 67871

What to See and Do

Lake Scott State Park. A memorial marker notes the 17th-century pueblo ruins of El Cuartelejo; the old Steele home is open for viewing. Spring-fed lake is bordered by willow, cedar, elm, pine and cottonwood trees. Beach, bathhouse; boats (rentals, ramp, dock). Picnicking, concession. Camping (electricity, dump station). Standard fees. (Daily) 10 mi N on US 83, N on KS 95. Phone 316/872-2061. Per Vehicle ¢¢

Seneca (B-8)

(For accommodations see Hiawatha, Marysville)

Pop 2,027 Elev 1,131 ft Area code 913 Zip 66538

What to See and Do

Fort Markley and Indian Village. Old Western town with Victorian home (fee), museum, art gallery, antique shop; buffalo herd; boating, fishing; tent & trailer sites (fee); restaurant. (Daily) 1/2 mi W on US 36. Phone 913/336-2285. ¢

Motels

★ **SENECA.** *1106 North St, on US 36W. 913/336-6127.* 12 rms. S $24; D $30; each addl $2. Crib avail. Pet accepted, some restrictions. TV; cable. Complimentary coffee in lobby. Restaurant nearby. Ck-out 11 am. Many refrigerators. Cr cds: A, D, DS, MC, V.

★ **STARLITE.** *410 North St, on US 36. 913/336-2191.* 16 rms. S $27; D $30-$34; each addl $3; under 12 free. Crib $3. Pet accepted, some restrictions. TV; cable (premium). Complimentary coffee in lobby. Restaurant opp 11 am-9 pm. Ck-out 11 am. Cr cds: A, C, D, DS, MC, V.

Restaurant

✔★ **WIND MILL.** *604 N 4th St, 1/2 blk S of US 36. 913/336-3696.* Hrs: 11 am-1:30 pm, 5-9 pm. Closed Mondays, Jan 1, July 4, Dec 25. Res accepted. Bar. Semi-a la carte: lunch $3.75-$5, dinner $5-$10.95. Buffet: lunch (Tues-Fri, Sun) $5.65. Child's meals. Specializes in prime rib, seafood, steak. Salad bar. Parking. No cr cds accepted.

D

Smith Center (B-5)

(See Mankato, Phillipsburg)

Pop 2,016 Elev 1,804 ft Area code 913 Zip 66967

What to See and Do

Home on the Range Cabin. Restored cabin where homesteader Dr. Brewster M. Higley wrote the words to the song "Home on the Range" in 1872. (Daily) 8 mi W on US 36, then 8 mi N on KS 8, then 3/4 mi W. Phone 913/282-6258. **Free.**

Old Dutch Mill. In Wagner Park. (May-Sept, daily) **Free.**

Motels

★ **MODERN AIRE.** *117 W US 36, at jct US 281. 913/282-6644; res: 800/727-7332.* 16 rms. S $26-$36; D $38-$46; each addl $4; higher rates pheasant hunting season. Crib $4. TV; cable (premium). Pool. Complimentary coffee in lobby. Restaurant nearby. Ck-out 11 am. Local airport transportation. Cr cds: A, C, D, DS, MC, V.

✔★ **U.S. CENTER.** *116 E US 36, at jct US 281. 913/282-6611; res: 800/875-6613.* 21 rms. S $25-$30; D $30-$40; each addl $4; family units. Crib $2. TV; cable (premium). Heated pool. Playground. Restaurant adj 6 am-9 pm. Ck-out 11 am. Free airport transportation. Picnic tables. Cr cds: A, C, D, DS, MC, V.

Restaurant

✔★ ★ **INGLEBORO.** *319 N Main. 913/282-3798.* Hrs: 11 am-2 pm, 5-9 pm; Sat 5-10 pm. Closed Dec 25. Bar. Semi-a la carte: lunch $3.95-$5.95, dinner $6.50-$13.95. Child's meals. Specializes in steak, seafood, prime rib. Parking. Victorian building, furnishings. Cr cds: A, DS, MC, V.

Stockton (C-4)

(For accommodations see Phillipsburg)

Pop 1,507 **Elev** 1,792 ft **Area code** 913 **Zip** 67669
Information City of Stockton, PO Box 512; 913/425-6162.

What to See and Do

Log Hotel. Replica of first log hotel. Main St.

Rooks County Museum. Houses artifacts related to Rooks County history; records, old newspapers, photographs, family heirlooms; old-time general store display; horse-drawn buggy. (Mon-Wed; other times by appt) Fairgrounds, SE part of town, off US 183S. Phone 913/425-7217. **Free.**

Webster State Park. An 880-acre park located on Webster Reservoir on South Fork of Solomon River, with 1,400 acres of water. Walleye, catfish, bass, crappie and bullheads. Beach, bathhouse; fishing; boating (ramps, dock). Trails. Picnicking. Camping (electricity, dump station). Standard fees. (Daily) 8 mi W on US 24. Phone 913/425-6775. Per Vehicle **¢¢**

Topeka (C-9)

(See Lawrence; also see Kansas City, MO)

Founded 1854 **Pop** 119,883 **Elev** 951 ft **Area code** 913
Information Topeka Convention & Visitors Bureau, 913/234-1030 or 800/235-1030.

The capital city of Kansas was born because a young Pennsylvanian, Colonel Cyrus K. Holliday, wanted to build a railroad. The present Topeka site, on the Kansas River (familiarly the Kaw), was chosen as a suitable terminus, and a town company was formed in 1854. It flourished, becoming the Shawnee county seat in 1857, and in 1861, when Kansas became a state, Topeka was designated state capital. Colonel Holliday's railroad, the Atchison, Topeka and Santa Fe, began to build westward from Topeka in 1869; its general offices and machine shops were established there in 1878 and are still important to the city. Other industries today include tires, steel products, cellophane, printing, insurance, grain milling and meatpacking. The Menninger Foundation, world-famous psychiatric clinic and research center, is in Topeka. Herbert Hoover's vice president, Charles Curtis, who was part Kaw and a descendant of one of Topeka's earliest settlers, was born here.

What to See and Do

Combat Air Museum. Jets, cargo transports, bombers, fighters and trainers from 1917-1980 are displayed here, as well as military artifacts. Guided tours (by appt). (Daily; closed Jan 1, Thanksgiving, Dec 25) Forbes Field, Hanger 602, 5 mi S on US 75. Phone 913/862-3303. **¢¢**

Governor's Mansion (Cedar Crest). Period architecture with Loire Valley overtones on 244 acres. Built in 1928, bequeathed to state in 1955. Became governor's residence in 1962. Guided tours (Fri afternoons). Fairlawn Rd at I-70, 1 mi N. Phone 913/296-3636. **Free.**

Heartland Park Topeka. Motorsports complex featuring professional and amateur race events. (Daily) 1805 SW 71st St. For scheduled events and fees phone 913/862-4781.

Kansas Museum of History. Contains displays relating to the history of Kansas and the plains. Museum, changing exhibits, hands-on Discovery Place. (Daily; closed Jan 1, Easter, Thanksgiving, Dec 25) 6425 SW 6th St. Phone 913/272-8681. **Free.**

Kansas State Historical Society. Library of Kansas, Native American and Western history and genealogy; one of largest newspaper collections in the nation; manuscript, photograph & map collections. State Historic Preservation Office; State Archaeology Office. (Daily exc Sun;

closed major hols) Center for Historical Research, 120 W 10th St, at Jackson St. State archives. Phone 913/296-3251. **Free.**

Lake Shawnee. A 400-acre man-made lake. Swimming, waterskiing; fishing; boating. Picnicking. E 29th St & West Edge Rd.

Parks.

Ward-Meade Historical Home. Historical Ward-Meade house, restored rock barn, cabins, depot, general store, caboose and school (Tues-Fri; two tours daily). Botanical gardens (free). Gift shop. 124 NW Fillmore. Phone 913/295-3888. **¢¢**

Gage Park. Approx 160 acres; includes 3-acre rose garden, conservatory; swimming pool (Memorial Day-Labor Day); tennis courts, picnic facilities; miniature train ride & restored 1908 carousel (May-Labor Day, fee). (Daily) Gage Blvd between W 6th & W 10th Sts. **Free.** Also in park is

Topeka Zoo. Discovering Apes Bldg with orangutans and gorillas; Lions Pride exhibit; tropical rain forest under geodesic dome with plants and free-roaming animals. (Daily; closed Dec 25) 6th & 10th St entrances. Phone 913/272-5821. **¢¢**

Perry State Park. A 1,600-acre park on 12,200-acre lake. Beach, bathhouse; fishing; boating (ramps, docks). Trails. Picnicking. Camping (electricity, dump station). Standard fees. (Daily) 18 mi NE via US 24, KS 237, near Ozawkie. Phone 913/246-3449. Per Vehicle **¢¢**

✪ **Potwin Place.** Community of stately homes, towering trees & distinctive circular parks on 70 acres. Begun in 1869, the area is a landmark of Topeka's heritage. Self-conducted walking & driving tours. Between 1st & 4th Sts on Woodlawn & Greenwood Sts. Phone 913/234-2644.

State Capitol. Design based on US Capitol. On the grounds are statues of Lincoln and the Pioneer Woman, both by Topeka-born sculptor Merrell Gage; murals on 2nd floor by John Steuart Curry and Lumin Martin Winter; those on 1st floor by David H. Overmeyer; 2nd floor statuary by Pete Felten. Guide service (daily exc Sun; closed Jan 1, Thanksgiving, Dec 25). On 20-acre square in center of city. Phone 913/296-3966. **Free.**

Washburn University of Topeka (1865). (6,600 students) Liberal arts college. Tours, including Mulvane Art Center, Petro Allied Health Center, observatory and planetarium. 17th St & College Ave. Phone 913/231-1010.

Annual Events

Airshow Topeka. Combat Air Museum Airshow & Superbatics at Forbes Field. Phone 913/862-3303. Aug.

Huff 'n Puff Balloon Rally. Phillip Billard Airport. Hot air balloons. Sept.

Motels

✔ ★ ★ **BEST WESTERN MEADOW ACRES.** *2950 S Topeka Ave (66611).* 913/267-1681. 83 rms. S $36-$42; D $54-$62; each addl $6; under 12 free. Crib $4. TV; cable (premium). Indoor pool. Complimentary continental bkfst, coffee in rms. Restaurant nearby. Ck-out noon. Business servs avail. Some refrigerators. Cr cds: A, C, D, DS, MC, V.

⬜ D 🏊 ⊠ 🐾 SC

★ ★ **CLUBHOUSE INN.** *924 SW Henderson Rd (66615).* 913/273-8888; FAX 913/273-5809. 121 rms, 2 story, 17 suites. S $65; D $75; each addl $10; suites $81; under 10 free; wkly, wkend rates. Crib free. TV; cable (premium). Heated pool; whirlpool. Complimentary full bkfst, coffee. Ck-out noon. Coin lndry. Meeting rms. Business servs avail. In-rm modem link. Valet serv. Health club privileges. Refrigerator, wet bar in suites. Balconies. Grills. Cr cds: A, C, D, DS, MC, V.

⬜ D 🏊 ⊠ 🐾 SC

★ ★ **DAYS INN.** *1510 SW Wanamaker Rd (66604).* 913/272-8538. 62 rms, 2 story, 6 suites. S $42.95-$59.95; D $47.95-$69.95; each addl $5; suites $49.95-$69.95; under 12 free; higher rates Heartland auto races. Crib $5. Pet accepted. TV; cable (premium). Indoor pool; whirlpool. Complimentary continental bkfst, coffee. Restaurant nearby. Ck-out 11 am. Business servs avail. Game rm. Refrigerator in suites. Cr cds: A, D, DS, MC, V.

[D] [symbols] [SC]

✔★ **LIBERTY INN.** 3839 S Topeka Blvd (US 75) (66609). 913/266-4700; FAX 913/267-3311. 132 rms, 2 story. S $37-$48; D $41-$55; each addl $6; suites $95. Crib free. Pet accepted, some restrictions. TV; cable. Pool. Playground. Restaurant 6:30 am-2 pm. Rm serv. Bar 5 pm-2 am, closed Sun. Ck-out noon. Meeting rms. Business servs avail. Valet serv. Local airport transportation. Many refrigerators. Private patios, balconies. Cr cds: A, C, D, DS, ER, JCB, MC, V.

[D] [symbols] [SC]

Motor Hotels

★★★ **HOLIDAY INN-CITY CENTRE.** 914 Madison (66607), I-70 10th St exit. 913/232-7721; FAX 913/232-7721, ext. -290. 203 rms, 9 story. S, D $55.50; each addl $6; under 18 free. Crib free. TV; cable (premium). Pool. Restaurant 6 am-2 pm, 5-10 pm. Rm serv. Bar 11 am-midnight; Fri to 2 am, Sat to 10 pm. Ck-out noon. Coin lndry. Meeting rms. Business servs avail. In-rm modem link. Bellhops. Valet serv. Airport transportation. Health club privileges. Luxury level. Cr cds: A, C, D, DS, ER, JCB, MC, V.

[D] [symbols]

★★ **RAMADA INN.** Box 1598 (66601), 420 E 6th St, at downtown jct US 40 & I-70. 913/234-5400; FAX 913/232-0011. 422 rms, 3-11 story. S, D $48-$76; each addl $7; suites $80-$250; under 18 free; wkend rates. Crib free. Pet accepted, some restrictions; $20. TV; cable (premium), VCR avail. Pool. Restaurants 6 am-9 pm. Rm serv. Bar 4 pm-midnight; entertainment, dancing. Ck-out noon. Coin lndry. Convention facilities. Business servs avail. Bellhops. Valet serv. Sundries. Gift shop. Barber, beauty shop. Free local airport transportation. Exercise equipt; bicycles, stair machine, whirlpool, sauna. Some bathrm phones, refrigerators. Cr cds: A, C, D, DS, MC, V.

[D] [symbols] [SC]

★★ **THE SENATE LUXURY SUITES.** 900 SW Tyler St (66612). 913/233-5050; res: 800/488-3188; FAX 913/233-1614. 52 suites, 3 story. S, D $53-$150; under 12 free; higher rates Heartland races. TV; cable (premium), VCR avail. Complimentary continental bkfst. Ck-out noon. Coin lndry. Meeting rms. Business center. Valet serv. Exercise equipt; weight machine, bicycles, whirlpool. Health club privileges. Many refrigerators. Balconies. Cr cds: A, C, D, DS, MC, V.

[D] [symbols] [SC]

Inn

★★★ **HERITAGE HOUSE.** 3535 SW 6th St (66606). 913/233-3800; FAX 913/233-9793. 11 rms, 3 story. S, D $69-$159; higher rates Heartland auto races. TV; cable (premium). Complimentary full bkfst, coffee. Restaurant (see HERITAGE HOUSE). Ck-out noon, ck-in 2:30 pm. Business servs avail. In-rm modem link. Turn-of-the-century farm house; antiques, front porch. Cr cds: A, C, D, DS, MC, V.

[symbols] [SC]

Restaurants

✔★ **CARLOS O'KELLY'S.** 3425 S Kansas Ave (66611). 913/266-3457. Hrs: 11 am-10 pm; Fri & Sat to 11 pm. Closed Thanksgiving, Dec 25. Res accepted. Mexican, Amer menu. Bar. Semi-a la carte: lunch $1.95-$5.95, dinner $1.95-$10.95. Lunch buffet $4.99. Child's meals. Specializes in fajitas, enchilada de Monterey. Parking. Hacienda atmosphere. Cr cds: A, D, DS, MC, V.

[D] [SC]

★★ **GIORGIO'S.** 425 SW 30th St. 913/266-2772. Hrs: 11 am-9 pm; Fri & Sat to 10 pm; Sun to 8 pm; Sun brunch to 2 pm. Res accepted. Italian, Amer menu. Bar. A la carte entrees: lunch $4.95-$6.95, dinner $6.95-$12.95. Sun brunch $8.95. Child's meals. Specializes in Black Angus beef, veal Marsala, eggplant Parmesan. Parking. Cr cds: A, DS, MC, V.

[D]

★★★ **HERITAGE HOUSE.** (See Heritage House Inn) 913/233-3800. Hrs: 5:30-9 pm; Fri also 11:30 am-1:30 pm. Sun brunch to 1:30 pm. Closed some major hols. Res accepted. Bar. Wine cellar. A la carte: lunch $15, dinner $20-$60. Sun brunch $18. Specializes in seafood, desserts. Own baking. Parking. Cr cds: A, C, D, DS, MC, V.

[D]

★★ **KOBE STEAK HOUSE OF JAPAN.** 5331 SW 22nd Pl, in Fairlawn Plaza. 913/272-6633. Hrs: 5:30-9 pm; Fri, Sat 5-10 pm; Sun 4-8 pm. Res accepted. Japanese menu. Bar. Semi-a la carte: dinner $7.95-$22. Child's meals. Specializes in chicken, seafood, hibachi steak. Japanese art work. Cr cds: A, D, DS, MC, V.

[D]

✔★★ **McFARLAND'S.** 4133 Gage Center Dr, in Gage Shopping Ctr. 913/272-6909. Hrs: 11 am-8 pm; Fri & Sat to 8:30 pm; Sun 11 am-2:30 pm. Closed some major hols. Res accepted (groups over 6). Bar. Semi-a la carte: lunch $2.50-$8, dinner $6-$12.50. Child's meals. Family-owned. Cr cds: MC, V.

[D]

WaKeeney (C-3)

(See Hays)

Founded 1877 **Pop** 2,161 **Elev** 2,465 ft **Area code** 913 **Zip** 67672
Information Chamber of Commerce, 216 Main St; 913/743-2077.

This county seat, halfway between Denver and Kansas City, produces extra-high-protein wheat.

What to See and Do

Cedar Bluff State Park. A 1,700-acre park on 1,600-acre lake. Channel catfish, bass, crappie and walleye. Dam is 12,500 feet long and rises 134 feet above the stream bed. Sweeping view of the Smoky Hill River Valley as it winds through prehistoric, fossil-rich chalk beds. Beach, bathhouse; fishing; boating (ramps, docks). Trails. Picnicking. Tent & trailer camping (electricity, dump station). Standard fees. (Daily) 8 mi SE on I-70, then 13 mi S on KS 147. Phone 913/726-3212. Per Vehicle ¢¢

Chalk beds. Rich in fossils. In Smoky Hill River Valley. W of town.

Annual Event

Trego County Free Fair. County fairgrounds. Early Aug.

Motel

✔★ **BUDGET HOST TRAVEL INN.** RR 2, Box 2B, at I-70 exit 128 & US 283. 913/743-2121; FAX 913/743-6704. 27 rms. S $25-$30; D $35-$45; each addl $3; under 18 free. Crib free. Pet accepted. TV; cable (premium). Pool. Restaurant adj 6 am-10 pm. Ck-out 11 am. Cr cds: A, D, DS, MC, V.

[symbols] [SC]

Inn

★ ★ **THISTLE HILL.** *Rt 1, Box 93, off I-70.* 913/743-2644. 4 rms (1 with shower only), 2 story. Rm phone avail. S $45-$55; D $55-$65; each addl $10. Complimentary full bkfst. Ck-out 11 am, ck-in 4 pm. Luggage handling. Picnic tables. Covered patio overlooking gardens. On 320-acre farm with 60-acre wildflower preserve. Cr cds: MC, V.

Wichita (E-7)

(See El Dorado, Hutchinson, Newton)

Settled 1864 **Pop** 304,011 **Elev** 1,305 ft **Area code** 316
Information Wichita Convention & Visitors Bureau, 100 S Main, Suite 100, 67202; 316/265-2800.

The largest city in Kansas has a definite metropolitan flavor, with its tall buildings, wide streets and bustling tempo. Still a major marketing point for agricultural products, it is now best known as an aircraft production center. Three plants build more private aircraft than all the other combined cities of the nation. McConnell Air Force Base is here. Wichita is the petroleum capital of Kansas, with many independent oil companies represented. More wheat is milled here than anywhere in the state, and some of the nation's largest grain elevators for wheat storage are here.

The town's first settlers were the Wichita, who built a village of grass lodges on the site. The following year James R. Mead set up a trading post and in 1865 sent his assistant, Jesse Chisholm, on a trading expedition to the Southwest. His route became famous as the Chisholm Trail, over which longhorn cattle were driven through Wichita to the Union Pacific at Abilene. As the railroad advanced southwestward, Wichita had its turn as the "cow capital" in the early 1870s. By 1880, farmers, drawn by the land boom, had run their fences across the trail and the cattle drives were shifted west to Dodge City. The interrupted prosperity was restored by the wheat crops of the next two decades and the discovery of oil after the First World War.

What to See and Do

Allen-Lambe House Museum and Study Center. Designed in 1915 by Frank Lloyd Wright as a private residence, it is considered the last of Wright's prairie houses. Living and dining room surround a sunken garden; furniture designed by Wright in collaboration with interior designer George M. Niedecken. Visitor center, bookstore. Guided tours (by appt only). 255 N Roosevelt St. Phone 316/687-1027. ¢¢

Botanica, The Wichita Gardens. Display of exotic flowers as well as plants native to Kansas. Among the gardens are the Butterfly Garden, Shakespearean Garden, Aquatic Collection, and Xeriscape Demonstration Garden. (Apr-Dec, Mon-Sat, also Sun afternoons; rest of yr, Mon-Fri) 701 Amidon. Phone 316/264-9799 (recording) or -0448. ¢¢

Century II Convention Center. Circular structure houses convention & exhibition halls, meeting rooms, theater, concert hall. 225 W Douglas. Phone 316/264-9121. For ticket information phone 316/263-4717.

Cheney State Park. A 1,913-acre park at 9,537-acre lake. Popular with sailboat and windsurfing enthusiasts. Large-scale regattas are a featured part of the many lake activities. Beach, bathhouse; fishing; boating (ramps, docks, marina). Camping (electricity, dump station). Standard fees. (Daily) 20 mi W on US 54, then 4 mi N on KS 251. Phone 316/542-3664. Per Vehicle ¢¢

Clifton Square. 19th-century houses converted into shops; brick walkways and old-fashioned lampposts. (Daily) 3700 E Douglas at Clifton, in historic College Hill neighborhood. Phone 316/686-2177.

Edwin A. Ulrich Museum of Art. Exhibitions of contemporary art; also outdoor mural by Joan Miró. (Tues-Sun; closed hols) Tours by appt. On Wichita State University campus, in the McKnight Art Center. Phone 316/689-3664. **Free.** Also on campus are

Martin H. Bush Outdoor Sculpture Collection. Boasts a 53-piece representation of 20th-century sculpture by internationally known artists.

Corbin Education Center. Designed by Frank Lloyd Wright. (Mon-Fri) 1845 Fairmount, near Yale & 21st Sts. Phone 316/689-3301.

Fellow-Reeve Museum of History and Science. Collection of Native American, African and pioneer relics; North American big game animals. (School yr: Mon, Wed & Fri afternoons, Tues & Thurs mornings; rest of yr, by appt only; closed hols) On Friends University campus, Davis Building, 4th floor. Phone 316/292-5594. ¢

Indian Center Museum. Changing exhibits of past and present Native American art. (Mar-Dec, daily; rest of yr, daily exc Mon; closed major hols) 650 North Seneca. Phone 316/262-5221. ¢

Lake Afton Public Observatory. Public programs (2 hrs) offer opportunity to view a variety of celestial objects through a 16-inch reflecting telescope; astronomy computer games; exhibits and displays. Programs begin half-hour after sunset. (Sept-May, Fri & Sat; June-Aug, Fri-Sun; closed Dec 23-Jan 1) 25000 W 39th St S; 15 mi SW via US 54, Viola Rd exit. Phone 316/794-8995. ¢

O.J. Watson Park. Covers 119 acres; fishing, boats; miniature golf; pony, train and hayrack rides (fees). Picnic area, concession. (Apr-late Oct) S Lawrence Rd at Carp St, just S of Arkansas River. Phone 316/529-9940. **Free.**

Old Cowtown Museum. A 40-building historic village museum depicting Wichita life from 1865-1880; restaurant, shops. (Mar-Oct, Mon-Sat, also Sun afternoons; rest of yr, wkends only) (See ANNUAL EVENTS) 1871 Sim Park Dr. Phone 316/264-0671. ¢¢

Omnisphere and Science Center. Planetarium and hands-on science center. (Daily exc Mon; closed some hols) 220 S Main St. Phone 316/337-9178. ¢¢

Sedgwick County Zoo and Botanical Garden. Animals in their natural habitat; African veldt; herpetarium; jungle; pampas outback; boat & train rides (summer). (Daily) 5555 Zoo Blvd. Phone 316/942-2212. ¢¢¢

Wichita Art Museum. Traveling exhibits; collection of American art; paintings & sculpture by Charles M. Russell; pre-Columbian art; works by contempory and historic Kansas artists. (Daily exc Mon; closed hols) 619 Stackman Dr. Phone 316/268-4921. **Free.**

Wichita Center for the Arts. Changing and permanent exhibits. (Daily exc Mon; closed major hols) Also School of Art for adults and children, School for Children and Adults' Theatre with concerts, plays and recitals. 9112 E Central. Phone 316/634-2787. **Free.**

Wichita-Sedgwick County Historical Museum. Local history, Native American artifacts, period rooms, costume collection, 1917 Jones Auto display. (Daily exc Mon; closed hols) 204 S Main St. Phone 316/265-9314. ¢

Annual Events

Jazz Festival. Jazz clinic; professional entertainment. Phone 316/262-2351. Apr.

Wichita River Festival. Includes twilight pop concert and fireworks; antique bathtub races; hot-air balloon launch; athletic events; entertainment. Phone 316/267-2817. Mid-May.

Indian Powwow. Tribes gather from all over the country and Canada. Traditional dances; crafts; ethnic food. Phone 316/262-5221. July.

National Baseball Congress World Series (amateur). Lawrence Stadium, Maple & Sycamore Sts. Phone 316/267-3372. Aug.

Old Sedgwick County Fair. Old Cowtown Museum. Re-creation of 1870s fair; crafts, livestock, demonstrations, music, food, games. Phone 316/264-0671. 1st full wkend Oct.

Seasonal Event

Professional sports. Wichita Wings (soccer). Kansas Coliseum, I-35 at 85th St N. Phone 316/262-3545. Mid-Nov-May.

Motels

★ ★ **BEST WESTERN RED COACH INN.** *915 E 53rd St N (67219), I-135 exit 13.* 316/832-9387; FAX 316/832-9443. 152 rms, 2 story. S $40-$60; D $48-$60; each addl $4; suites $89-$119; under 12 free. Crib $3. TV; cable (premium), VCR avail (movies avail $3). Indoor pool; whirlpool, sauna. Playground. Restaurant 6 am-11 pm. Rm serv. Ck-out noon. Meeting rms. Business servs avail. Sundries. Game rm. Rec rm. Golf course opp. Cr cds: A, D, DS, MC, V.

D ⛱ 🏊 🐾 SC

★ ★ **BEST WESTERN TUDOR INN.** *9100 E Kellogg St (67207), on US 54, I-35 exit 50.* 316/685-0371; FAX 316/685-4668. 116 rms, 2 story. May-Aug: S, D $40.99-$42.99; each addl $2; suites $75; under 14 free; lower rates rest of yr. Crib $6. TV; cable (premium). Pool. Complimentary continental bkfst. Restaurant (see CHATEAU-BRIAND). Ck-out 11 am. Meeting rms. Business servs avail. Valet serv. Refrigerator in suites. Cr cds: A, C, D, DS, MC, V.

D ⛱ 🏊 🐾 SC

★ ★ **CLUBHOUSE INN.** *515 S Webb Rd (67207), Kellogg St (US 54, KS 96) at I-35.* 316/684-1111; FAX 316/684-0538. 120 rms, 2 story. S $69; D $79; each addl $5; suites $89-$110; under 16 free; wknd, wkly rates. Crib free. TV; cable (premium). Heated pool; whirlpool. Complimentary full bkfst. Restaurant nearby. Ck-out noon. Business servs avail. Refrigerator in suites. Many balconies. Cr cds: A, C, D, DS, MC, V.

D ⛱ 🏊 🐾

★ **DAYS INN.** *550 S Florence (67209), on US 54W.* 316/942-1717. 43 rms, 2 story. S $44.95; D $49.95; each addl $5; family rates. Crib free. TV; cable (premium). Complimentary continental bkfst. Restaurant adj 11 am-11 pm. Ck-out 11 am. Business servs avail. In-rm modem link. Many refrigerators. Near airport. Cr cds: A, C, D, DS, MC, V.

D 🏊 🐾 SC

★ ★ **LA QUINTA INN.** *7700 E Kellogg St (US 54, KS 96) (62707).* 316/681-2881; FAX 316/681-0568. 122 rms, 2 story. S $55-$65; D $63-$73; each addl $7; under 18 free. Crib free. Pet accepted, some restrictions. TV; cable (premium), VCR avail. Pool. Complimentary continental bkfst. Restaurant adj 11:30 am-11 pm; Fri, Sat to midnight; Sun to 10 pm. Ck-out noon. Meeting rms. Business servs avail. In-rm modem link. Cr cds: A, C, D, DS, MC, V.

D 🐾 ⛱ 🏊 🐾 SC

★ ★ **RESIDENCE INN BY MARRIOTT-DOWNTOWN.** *120 W Orme St (67213), 1 blk S of Kellogg St (US 54).* 316/263-1061; FAX 316/263-3817. 64 kit. suites, 2 story. 1 bedrm suites $94; 2 bedrm suites $114; wknd, wkly, monthly rates. Crib free. Pet accepted; $5 per day. TV; cable (premium), VCR avail. Pool; whirlpool. Complimentary continental bkfst. Ck-out noon. Coin lndry. Business servs avail. In-rm modem link. Health club privileges. Many fireplaces. Private patios, balconies. Grill. Cr cds: A, C, D, DS, JCB, MC, V.

D 🐾 ⛱ 🏊 🐾 SC

★ ★ **RESIDENCE INN BY MARRIOTT-EAST.** *411 S Webb Rd (67207).* 316/686-7331; FAX 316/686-2345. 64 kit. suites, 2 story. S $99; D $124; wknd rates. Crib free. Pet accepted; $50 refundable and $7 per day. TV; cable (premium), VCR avail. Pool; whirlpool. Complimentary continental bkfst. Ck-out noon. Coin lndry. Business servs avail. In-rm modem link. Health club privileges. Lawn games. Refrigerators. Many fireplaces. Grills. Cr cds: A, C, D, DS, MC, V.

D 🐾 ⛱ 🏊 🐾 SC

✔ ★ **SCOTSMAN INN WEST.** *5922 W Kellogg St (US 54) (67209).* 316/943-3800; res: 800/950-7268; FAX 316/943-3800. 72 rms, 3 story. S $32.95; D $37.95; each addl $2; suites $44-$59; under 17 free. Crib $3. TV; cable (premium). Complimentary coffee in lobby. Restaurant nearby. Ck-out noon. Coin lndry. Business servs avail. Refrigerators. Cr cds: A, C, D, DS, MC, V.

D 🏊 🐾

✔ ★ **STRATFORD HOUSE INN.** *5505 W Kellogg St (US 54) (67209), W of I-235.* 316/942-0900. 40 rms, 2 story. S $35.95; D $39.95-$43.95; under 12 free. Crib free. Pet accepted. TV; cable (premium). Complimentary continental bkfst. Restaurant nearby. Ck-out 11 am. Business servs avail. Cr cds: A, C, D, DS, MC, V.

D 🐾 ⛱ 🏊 🐾

✔ ★ **WICHITA INN-EAST.** *8220 E Kellogg St (US 54) (67207), 1/2 mi W of KS Tpke E Wichita exit.* 316/685-8291; FAX 316/685-0835. 96 rms, 3 story. S $33; each addl $4; under 10 free. Crib free. TV; cable (premium). Complimentary continental bkfst, coffee. Restaurant nearby. Ck-out 11 am. Coin lndry. Business servs avail. In-rm modem link. Valet serv. Cr cds: A, C, D, DS, MC, V.

D 🏊 🐾

★ ★ **WICHITA SUITES.** *5211 E Kellogg St (US 54) (67218).* 316/685-2233; res: 800/243-5953; FAX 316/685-4152. 90 suites, 4 story. S $69-$76; D $79-$86; each addl $7; under 6 free. Crib free. TV; cable (premium). Heated pool. Complimentary full bkfst, refreshments. Restaurant nearby. Ck-out noon. Coin lndry. Meeting rms. In-rm modem link. Valet serv. Sundries. Exercise equipt; weights, treadmill, whirlpool, sauna. Refrigerators. Cr cds: A, D, DS, MC, V.

D ⛱ 🏃 🏊 🐾

Motor Hotels

★ ★ **COMFORT SUITES.** *658 Westdale (67209), near Mid-Continent Airport.* 316/945-2600; FAX 316/945-5033. 50 suites, 3 story. S, D $70-$80. TV; cable (premium). Heated pool. Complimentary bkfst. Coffee in rms. Bar. Ck-out noon. Meeting rms. Business servs avail. Airport transportation. Refrigerators. Cr cds: A, C, D, DS, MC, V.

D ⛱ 🏃 🏊 🐾 SC

★ **FAMILY INN.** *221 E Kellogg (67202), on US 54.* 316/267-9281; res: 800/435-8282; FAX 316/267-3665. 150 rms, 7 story. Apr-Sept: S $44.77; D $49.77; under 18 free; wkly rates; lower rates rest of yr. Crib free. Pet accepted, some restrictions; $15. TV; cable. Pool. Restaurant 6 am-10 pm. Rm serv. Bar 10:30-2 am. Ck-out 11 am. Coin lndry. Meeting rms. Business servs avail. In-rm modem link. Game rm. Refrigerator avail. Minibars. Cr cds: A, D, DS, MC, V.

🐾 ⛱ 🐾 SC

★ ★ **HOLIDAY INN AIRPORT.** *5500 W Kellogg (67209), near Mid-Continent Airport.* 316/943-2181; FAX 316/943-6587. 152 rms, 5 story. S $73-$81; D $81-$88; each addl $9; under 12 free; wknd rates. Crib free. Pet accepted. TV; cable, VCR avail. Indoor pool; whirlpool, sauna, poolside serv. Complimentary coffee in rms; bkfst. Restaurant 6 am-10 pm. Rm serv. Bar 5 pm-1 am. Ck-out noon. Coin lndry. Meeting rms. Business servs avail. In-rm modem link. Bellhops. Valet serv. Free airport transportation. Cr cds: A, C, D, DS, ER, JCB, MC, V.

D 🐾 ⛱ 🏃 🏊 🐾 SC

★ ★ **HOLIDAY INN-EAST.** *7335 E Kellogg St (US 54) (67207), 1/2 mi W of KS Tpke, W Kellogg St exit.* 316/685-1281; FAX 316/685-8621. 192 rms, 6 story. S, D $69-$82; suites $82-$150; under 18 free. Crib free. Pet accepted. TV; cable (premium), VCR avail. Indoor pool; whirlpool. Coffee in rms. Restaurant, dining rm 6 am-10 am, 6-10 pm; wkends 7-11 am, 6-10 pm. Rm serv. Bar 5 pm-midnight. Ck-out noon. Coin lndry. Meeting rms. Business servs avail. Bellhops. Valet serv. Barber, beauty shop. Free airport transportation. Exercise equipt; weights, bicycle. Game rm. Indoor tropical garden. Cr cds: A, C, D, DS, JCB, MC, V.

D 🐾 ⛱ 🏃 🏊 🐾 SC

★★ **RAMADA INN AIRPORT.** *5805 W Kellogg St (US 54) (67209), just W of I-235, near Mid-Continent Airport.* 316/942-7911; FAX 316/942-0854. 206 rms, 2 story. S $69; D $74; each addl $5; suites $125-$195; under 18 free; wkend rates. Crib free. TV; cable (premium), VCR avail. Pool; wading pool. Restaurant 6 am-2 pm, 5-10 pm; Sat & Sun from 7 am. Rm serv. Bar noon-2 am, Sun to 1 am; entertainment, dancing exc Sun. Ck-out noon. Meeting rms. Business servs avail. In-rm modem link. Bellhops. Valet serv. Free airport transportation. Some private patios, balconies, refrigerators. Cr cds: A, C, D, DS, ER, JCB, MC, V.

Hotels

★★ **HARVEY HOTEL.** *549 S Rock Rd at E Kellogg St (US 54) (67207).* 316/686-7131; FAX 316/686-0018. 260 rms, 9 story. S, D $89-$99; suites $125-$375; wkend, family rates. Crib free. Pet accepted; $100 refundable and $25. TV; cable (premium), VCR avail. Pool. Coffee in rms. Restaurant 6:30 am-10 pm; Sun from 7 am. Bar 2 pm-midnight. Ck-out 1 pm. Meeting rms. Business servs avail. In-rm modem link. Gift shop. Free airport transportation. Cr cds: A, C, D, DS, MC, V.

★★ **MARRIOTT.** *9100 Corporate Hills Dr (67207).* 316/651-0333; FAX 316/651-0990. 294 units, 11 story. S $115-$136; D $125-$146; suites $175-$275; under 18 free; wkly, wkend rates. Crib free. Pet accepted. TV; cable (premium), VCR avail. Indoor/outdoor pool; poolside serv. Coffee in rms. Restaurant 6:30 am-11 pm. Bar noon-2 am. Ck-out noon. Business servs avail. Concierge. Gift shop. Free airport transportation. Exercise equipt; weight machine, bicycles, whirlpool, sauna. Luxury level. Cr cds: A, C, D, DS, ER, JCB, MC, V.

Inn

★★ **INN AT THE PARK.** *3751 E Douglas (67218).* 316/652-0500; FAX 316/652-0610. 12 suites, 3 story. S $79-$129; D $89-$139. TV; cable. Complimentary continental bkfst. Complimentary coffee in rms. Restaurant nearby. Ck-out 11 am, ck-in 4 pm. Whirlpool. Picnic tables. Built 1909; suites designed individually by local designers. Cr cds: A, DS, MC, V.

Restaurants

★★ **CHATEAU-BRIAND.** *(See Best Western Tudor Inn Motel)* 316/682-4212. Hrs: 5-10 pm. Closed Sun; major hols. Res accepted. Bar. Semi-a la carte: dinner $5.50-$32. Child's meals. Specialty: châteaubriand. Parking. Cr cds: A, C, D, DS, MC, V.

★★ **THE GRAPE.** *550 N Rock Rd (67206).* 316/634-0113. Hrs: 11-2 am. Closed Sun; Jan 1, Thanksgiving, Dec 25. Bar. A la carte entrees: lunch from $4, dinner $7.95-$14.95. Specializes in cheese boards, fish, char-broiled steaks. Pianist Thurs-Sat. Parking. Outdoor dining. Cr cds: A, D, DS, MC, V.

★★ **OLIVE TREE.** *2949 N Rock Rd (67226).* 316/636-1100. Hrs: 11 am-10 pm; Fri & Sat to 11 pm; Sun 5-10 pm. Closed Dec 25. Res accepted. Continental menu. A la carte entrees: lunch $6-$9, dinner $12.95-$21.95. Specializes in fresh salmon, lamb, duck. Parking. Outdoor dining. Cr cds: A, C, D, DS, MC, V.

★★★ **THE PORTOBELLO ROAD.** *504 S Bluff (67218).* 316/684-5591. Hrs: 11 am-10 pm; Sat from 5 pm; Sun noon-8 pm. Closed Easter, Dec 25. Res accepted. Continental menu. Serv bar. Wine list. Semi-a la carte: lunch $5.50-$8.50, dinner $13-$34.95. Sun

brunch $12. Specializes in fresh seafood, veal, hand-cut steak. Pianist. Valet parking. Formal dining in country inn atmosphere. Cr cds: A, D, MC, V.

Unrated Dining Spot

ROCK ISLAND CAFE. *725 E Douglas.* 316/263-1616. Hrs: 7 am-3 pm; Sat 7:30 am-2:30 pm. Closed Sun; most major hols. Semi-a la carte: bkfst $1.50-$3, lunch $2-$5. Specializes in deli sandwiches. Outdoor dining. Built 1890; former baggage building at Rock Island train depot. Parking. No cr cds accepted.

Winfield (F-7)

(See Arkansas City)

Founded 1870 **Pop** 11,931 **Elev** 1,127 ft **Area code** 316 **Zip** 67156
Information Chamber of Commerce, 205 E 9th, PO Box 640; 316/221-2420.

Settled on land leased from Osage Chief Chetopah for $6, Winfield manufactures crayons, water coolers, ice chests; it has oil and gas wells.

What to See and Do

Cowley County Historical Museum. Glass collection, period rooms, early artifacts, library, archives. (Sat & Sun afternoons) 1011 Mansfield. Phone 316/221-4811. **Free.**

Recreation.

Fairgrounds and Pecan Grove. Surrounded by Walnut River. Fishing. Picnicking, playground. (Daily) W end of North Ave. **Free.**

City Lake. A 2,400-acre recreation area includes reservoir with 21-mile shoreline. Swimming; fishing; boating (launching ramp). Tent & trailer camping. Permits required; per vehicle ¢¢. (Daily) 10 mi NE. Phone 316/221-5635 or -5500.

Motel

★ **BUDGET HOST CAMELOT.** *1710 Main St, on US 77.* 316/221-9050. 30 rms, 2 story. S $37-$39; D $40-$43; each addl $4; higher rates Walnut Valley Festival. Crib $5. TV; cable (premium). Complimentary coffee in lobby. Restaurant nearby. Ck-out 11 am. Cr cds: A, D, DS, MC, V.

Yates Center (E-9)

(For accommodations see Chanute, Eureka, Iola)

Pop 1,815 **Elev** 1,136 ft **Area code** 316 **Zip** 66783

What to See and Do

Toronto State Park. A 1,075-acre park at 2,800-acre lake. Located in the Chautauqua Hills region, the forested uplands of Black Jack and Post Oak overlook the 2,800-acre reservoir nestled in the Verdigris Valley. Beach, bathhouse; fishing; boating (ramps, docks). Trails. Picnicking, concession. Tent & trailer camping (reservations accepted; hookups, dump station). (Daily) 12 mi W on US 54, then S on KS 105. Phone 316/637-2213. Per vehicle ¢¢; Camping ¢¢

Louisiana

Population: 4,219,973	
Land area: 44,520 square miles	
Elevation: 0-535 feet	
Highest point: Driskill Mt (Bienville Parish)	
Entered Union: April 30, 1812 (18th state)	
Capital: Baton Rouge	
Motto: Union, Justice, Confidence	
Nicknames: Bayou State, Sportsman's Paradise, Pelican State	
State flower: Magnolia	
State bird: Eastern Brown pelican	
State tree: Bald Cypress	
State fair: October 17-27, 1996, in Shreveport	
Time zone: Central	

The soil of Louisiana was carried down from the central valley of the United States by the Ouachita, Mississippi, Red, Sabine and Pearl rivers. Much of the state is a flat, moist, rich-soiled delta with a distinct historic and ethnic atmosphere.

The area was discovered by Spaniards, named by the French (for Louis XIV) and settled by both. People with the blood of those French Canadians driven from Acadia (Nova Scotia) by the British in 1755 are called Acadians ("Cajuns"). Americans of English, Irish and German origin also helped settle Louisiana.

The land is semitropical, beautifully unusual, full of legend and tradition; a land of bayous with cypress and live oak overhung with Spanish moss. Some of its people live in isolation on the bayous and riverbanks, where they still fish, trap and do a little farming. Southern and southwestern Louisiana are predominantly Roman Catholic; the northern section is largely Protestant. It is the only state whose divisions are called parishes rather than counties.

The northern and southern parts of the state are quite different topographically. In the southern area are fine old mansions and sugar cane plantation estates, many of which are open to the public. (See BATON ROUGE for a plantation tour.) The north is more rural, with beautiful rivers, hills, forests and cotton plantation mansions. This is the area from which the colorful Huey Long came; he was born in Winnfield.

Petroleum and natural gas taken from far underground, shipped abroad or processed in large plants, contribute to Louisiana's thriving industrial and manufacturing economy. As these businesses expand, the service sector continually grows to meet demands.

Hernando De Soto discovered the Mississippi in 1541. La Salle claimed Louisiana for France in 1682. Pierre Le Moyne, Sieur d'Iberville, first came to the state in 1699. His brother, Jean Baptiste Le Moyne, Sieur de Bienville, founded New Orleans in 1718, three years after the founding of Natchitoches by Cavalier St Denis.

To prevent Louisiana from falling into the hands of the English, Louis XV of France gave it to his cousin, Charles III, King of Spain. In 1801 Napoleon regained it for France, though no one in Louisiana knew of this until 1803, only 20 days before the Louisiana Purchase made it US territory.

This colorful history established it as the state it is—individual, different, exciting. It remains the old Deep South at its best—gracious, cultured and hospitable.

National Park Service Area

Louisiana has Jean Lafitte National Historical Park and Preserve (see NEW ORLEANS).

National Forest

Kisatchie National Forest (see ALEXANDRIA): Forest Supervisor in Pineville*; Ranger offices in Alexandria, Homer*, Leesville*, Natchitoches, Pollock*, Winnfield*.

*Not described in text

State Recreation Areas

The following towns list state recreation areas in their vicinity under What to See and Do; refer to the individual town for directions and park information.

Listed under **Bastrop:** see Chemin-A-Haut State Park.

Listed under **Covington:** see Fontainebleau State Park.

Listed under **Franklin:** see Cypremort Point State Park.

Listed under **Lake Charles:** see Sam Houston Jones State Park.

Listed under **Minden:** see Lake Bistineau State Park.

Listed under **New Orleans:** see St Bernard State Park.

Listed under **Opelousas:** see Chicot State Park.

Water-related activities, hiking, various other sports, picnicking and visitor centers, as well as camping, are available in many of these areas. An admission fee ($2/car for up to 4 people, 50¢/each additional) is charged at most Louisiana state parks. Many parks have swimming, fishing, boating (rentals), camping (unimproved sites, $10/site/night; improved, $12/site/night; 2-wk max). Swimming pools are operated Memorial Day-Labor Day. Some parks have cabins (2-wk max reservations made at each park). Reservations for Oct-Mar are placed between July 1-3 by phone only on "first come" basis annually. After July 3 reservations will be accepted by phoning or writing the particular park. Reservations for Apr-Sept are placed between Jan 2-4 by phone only on "first come" basis annually. After Jan 4 reservations will be accepted by phoning or writing the particular park. **Note:** Reservations may only be made between 8 am-5 pm, Mon-Fri. In the event that the above dates fall on a wkend or holiday, reservations may be made the next following business day. Golden Age Passport accepted. Pets on leash only; not permitted within any state park building. For further information contact the Office of State Parks, PO Box 44426, Baton Rouge 70804; 504/342-8111.

Fishing & Hunting

Nonresident fishing license: $31; 7-day, $26; 2-day (including saltwater), $23. Nonresident saltwater fishing license: $36; 7-day, $26; 2-day (including freshwater), $23. Fishing licenses are valid from the date of purchase until June 30. Nonresident basic season hunting license: $86; 5-day, $51. Nonresident All Game Season: $161.50; 5-day, $95.50. Nonresident migratory game bird license (3-day): $45.50; nonresident waterfowl (duck) stamp: $7.50. Nonresident archery license: $25.50. For details on hunting and fishing regulations contact Louisiana Department of Wildlife and Fisheries, PO Box 98000, Baton Rouge 70898; 504/765-2887.

Safety Belt Information

Safety belts are mandatory for all persons in front seat of vehicle. Children under 5 years must be in an approved passenger restraint anywhere in vehicle: ages 3-5 may use a regulation safety belt in back seat, however, in front seat children must use an approved safety seat; age 3 and under must be in an approved safety seat. For further information phone 504/925-6991.

Interstate Highway System

The following alphabetical listing of Louisiana towns in the *Mobil Travel Guide* shows that these cities are within 10 miles of the indicated Interstate highways. A highway map should be checked, however, for the nearest exit.

INTERSTATE 10: Baton Rouge, Jennings, Kenner, Lafayette, Lake Charles, Metairie, New Orleans, Slidell.

INTERSTATE 12: Baton Rouge, Covington, Hammond, Slidell.

INTERSTATE 20: Bossier City, Minden, Monroe, Ruston, Shreveport, West Monroe.

INTERSTATE 49: Alexandria, Lafayette, Natchitoches, Opelousas, Shreveport.

INTERSTATE 55: Hammond, Kenner.

INTERSTATE 59: Slidell.

Additional Visitor Information

For detailed information on Louisiana, contact the Office of Tourism, Department of Culture, Recreation and Tourism, Inquiry Section, Box 94291, Baton Rouge 70804; 504/342-8119 or 800/33-GUMBO.

There are several tourist information centers in Louisiana; visitors will find information and brochures helpful in planning stops at points of interest. Some of the locations are as follows: in the northern part of the

state on westbound I-20 at Tallulah and on eastbound I-20 at Greenwood; in the central part of the state on the eastern border on US 84 at Vidalia; in the southern part of the state at Baton Rouge in Memorial Hall of the State Capitol, on St Ann Street in the French Quarter in New Orleans, southbound on I-59 near Pearl River, westbound on I-10 near Slidell, southbound on I-55 at Kentwood, eastbound on I-10 near Sabine River and south of the Louisiana-Mississippi state line on US 61 in St Francisville. (Daily, approx 8 am-5 pm; hours may vary)

Alexandria (C-3)

Founded 1806 **Pop** 49,188 **Elev** 82 ft **Area code** 318

Information Alexandria/Pineville Area Visitors & Convention Bureau, PO Box 8110, 71306; 318/443-7049.

In the heart of Louisiana, Alexandria became the center of the 1864 Red River Campaign of the Civil War, which resulted in the burning of the town. During World War II, Camps Beauregard, Livingston, Claiborne and Polk and Alexandria Air Force Base, all nearby, feverishly trained young Americans to fight. The largest maneuvers in US history, involving 472,000 troops, took place in this area.

Both Alexandria and Pineville, located on the Red River where it is joined by the Bayou Rapides, are centers for farming and livestock production, lumbering and light manufacturing. Water sports are popular at Fort Buhlow Lake and other nearby lakes.

What to See and Do

Alexandria Museum of Art. National and regional changing exhibits. (Tues-Sat; closed hols) Sr citizen rate. 933 Main St. Phone 318/443-3458. ¢

Bringhurst Park. Alexandria Zoo. Tennis; 9-hole golf. Picnicking, playground. (Daily) W off Masonic Dr. ¢ For zoo phone 318/473-1385. **Free.**

Cotile Recreation Area. Swimming, bathhouse, waterskiing; fishing; boating (ramp). Picnicking. Tent & trailer camping (fee). (Daily) Addl fee for boat, ski rig. Phone 318/793-8995. Per car ¢

Kent House (ca 1800). Restored French-colonial plantation house furnished with period pieces; outbuildings include milkhouse, barn, cabins, detached kitchen, carriage house. Herb and formal gardens; open-hearth cooking demonstration (Oct-Apr, Wed). Guided tours. (Daily; closed Jan 1, Thanksgiving, Dec 25) Sr citizen rate. 2 blks W on Bayou Rapides Rd off US 165/71. Phone 318/487-5998. ¢¢

Kisatchie National Forest. Louisiana's only national forest covers 600,000 acres. Dogwood and wild azalea bloom in the shadows of longleaf, loblolly and slash pine. Wild Azalea National Recreation Trail, the state's longest hiking trail (31 mi), is in the Evangeline District. Swimming, waterskiing; fishing, hunting. Hiking; off-road vehicles. Picnicking. Camping (tent & trailer sites). Fees are charged at some recreation sites. N, W and S of town. Contact Forest Supervisor, 2500 Shreveport Hwy, Pineville 71360; 318/473-7160.

National Cemetery (1867). Shamrock St in Pineville. Also in Pineville is **Rapides Cemetery** (1772), at David Street.

Motels

★ ★ **BEST WESTERN OF ALEXANDRIA.** *2720 W MacArthur Dr (71303).* 318/445-5530; FAX 318/445-8496. 154 rms, 2 story. S $49; D $56; each addl $6; suites $81-$125; under 18 free. Crib free. Pet accepted. TV; cable (premium). Pool; wading pool, poolside serv. Restaurant adj 5-10 pm. Bar 4-10 pm. Ck-out noon. Meeting rms. Business servs avail. Bellhops. Valet serv. Airport transportation. Lighted tennis. Picnic tables. Cr cds: A, C, D, DS, MC, V.

🐾 🏃 🏊 🎿 🔥 **SC**

★ ★ **HOLIDAY INN.** *2716 N MacArthur Dr (71303). 318/487-4261; FAX 318/445-0891.* 127 rms, 2 story. S $55-$60; D $58-$65; each addl $5; under 12 free; wkly, wkend & hol rates. Crib avail. Pet accepted, some restrictions. TV; cable (premium). Restaurant 6:30 am-2 pm, 5-10 pm. Rm serv. Bar; entertainment Tues-Sun. Ck-out noon. Meeting rms. Business center. In-rm modem link. Bellhops. Some refrigerators. Cr cds: A, C, D, DS, MC, V.

[icons]

✔ ★ **RAMADA INN.** *2211 N MacArthur Dr (71301). 318/443-2561; FAX 318/473-0142.* 167 rms, 2 story. S $44; D $49-$55; each addl $5; suites $95-$125; under 18 free. Pet accepted; some restrictions. TV; cable. Pool. Restaurant 6 am-2 pm, 5-10 pm. Bar 9-2 am; dancing Thurs-Sat. Coin lndry. Meeting rms. Business servs avail. Valet serv. Airport transportation. Cr cds: A, D, MC, V.

[icons]

✔ ★ **RODEWAY INN.** *742 MacArthur Dr (71301). 318/448-1611; FAX 318/473-2984.* 121 rms, 2 story. S $36-$40; D $40-$50; each addl $10; suites $57-$62; studio rms $38-$50; under 17 free. Crib free. Pet accepted; $25 deposit. TV; cable (premium). VCR avail. Pool; wading pool. Restaurant adj open 24 hrs. Ck-out noon. Business servs avail. Airport transportation. Cr cds: A, C, D, DS, MC, V.

[icons]

★ **TRAVELODGE ALEXANDRIA.** *1146 MacArthur Dr (71303). 318/443-1841; FAX 318/448-4845.* 70 rms, 2 story. S $36-$38; D $39-$49; each addl $3; under 17 free. TV; cable. Pool. Complimentary coffee in rms. Ck-out noon. Sundries. Cr cds: A, C, D, DS, ER, JCB, MC, V.

[icons]

Hotels

★ ★ ★ **HOLIDAY INN.** *4th & Jackson Sts (71301). 318/442-9000; FAX 318/442-9007.* 173 rms, 7 story. S $56-$66; D $66-$80; each addl $10; suites $86-$175; under 18 free; wkend rates. Crib free. TV; cable. Pool; whirlpool. Restaurant 6:30 am-2 pm, 5:30-10 pm. Bar 4:30-11 pm. Ck-out 11 am. Meeting rms. Business center. Free airport transportation. Tennis privileges. 18-hole golf privileges, greens fee, pro, putting green. Health club privileges. Cr cds: A, C, D, DS, MC, V.

[icons]

★ ★ **HOTEL BENTLEY.** *200 DeSoto St (71301), adj to Jackson St Bridge. 318/448-9600; res: 800/356-6835 (exc LA); FAX 318/448-0683.* 178 rms, 8 story. S $72; D $82; each addl $10; suites $100-$195; tour packages; wkend rates. Crib free. TV; cable (premium), VCR avail. Pool; poolside serv. Restaurant (see BENTLY ROOM). Bar 2:30 pm-2 am; entertainment, dancing exc Sun. Ck-out noon. Meeting rms. Business center. Concierge. Free valet parking; garage. Golf privileges. Exercise equipt; weights, bicycles, whirlpool. Some refrigerators. Opp river. Restored hotel, built 1908; on National Register of Historic Places. 18th-century period furnishings in all rms. Cr cds: A, C, D, DS, MC, V.

[icons]

Restaurants

★ ★ ★ **BENTLEY ROOM.** *(See Hotel Bentley) 318/448-9600.* Hrs: 6:30 am-10 pm; Sun brunch 11 am-2 pm. Res accepted. French, Amer menu. Bar 2:30 pm-2 am. Semi-a la carte: bkfst $3.95-$6.95, lunch $5.50-$12.95, dinner $10.95-$26.95. Sun brunch $7.50-$14.95. Child's meals. Specializes in fresh Gulf fish, steak, Louisiana-style pastas, veal chops. Pianist Tues-Sat. Valet parking. Formal, elegant atmosphere. Cr cds: A, C, D, DS, MC, V.

[icon]

★ ★ **CUCOS.** *2303 MacArthur (71301), S on I-71. 318/442-8644.* Hrs: 11 am-11 pm; Fri, Sat to midnight. Closed Thanksgiving,

Dec 25. Mexican, Amer menu. Bar. Semi-a la carte: lunch $4-$6, dinner $6.95-$18. Child's meals. Specializes in chimichangas, grilled fajitas. Parking. Cr cds: A, D, DS, MC, V.

[icon]

Bastrop (A-3)

(See Monroe and West Monroe)

Founded 1846 **Pop** 13,916 **Elev** 126 ft **Area code** 318 **Zip** 71220
Information Bastrop-Morehouse Chamber of Commerce, 512 E Jefferson, PO Box 1175, 71221; 318/281-3794.

Bastrop is one of the few industrial cities in northern Louisiana. Wood pulp and wood products are the principal output. This is a center of the Monroe Gas Field, with its more than 1,700 producing wells. Bastrop is also a cattle and agricultural area, with cotton, rice and soybeans the staple crops. Seasonal hunting for dove, quail, duck, squirrel and deer is popular.

What to See and Do

Bussey Brake Reservoir. On 2,200 acres. Fishing; boating (fee). Camping (fee). (Daily; closed Dec 25) 7 mi N on LA 599. Phone 318/281-4507. **Free.**

Chemin-A-Haut State Park. More than 500 wooded acres at the intersection of bayous Chemin-A-Haut and Bartholomew. A portion of the "high road to the South" was originally an Indian trail. Swimming, bathhouse; fishing; boating (rentals). Hiking. Picnicking. Tent and trailer sites. All-yr overnight cabins capacity of 4, max of 6. Standard fees. (Daily) 10 mi N on US 425. Contact Manager, 14656 State Park Rd; 318/283-0812. Per vehicle ¢¢

Snyder Memorial Museum. Museum covers 150 years of Morehouse Parish history; antique furniture, kitchen utensils, farm equipment, clothing and Native American artifacts. Gallery features changing art and photographic exhibits. (Daily) 1620 E Madison Ave. Phone 318/281-8760. **Free.**

Annual Event

North Louisiana Cotton Festival and Fair. Sept.

Motels

✔ ★ **BASTROP INN.** *1053 E Madison St, 1 mi N on US 165, LA 2. 318/281-3621; res: 800/BAS-TROP; FAX 318/283-1501.* 108 rms, 1-2 story. S $27-$44; D $29-$47; suites $40-$61; studio rms $42-$57; under 12 free. Crib free. TV; cable (premium). Pool. Complimentary coffee in rms. Restaurant 5 am-11 pm. Rm serv. Private club 3 pm-midnight. Ck-out noon. Coin lndry. Meeting rms. Sundries. Golf privileges. Refrigerators. Cr cds: A, C, D, DS, MC, V.

[icons]

★ **COUNTRY INN.** *1815 E Madison. 318/281-8100.* 30 rms, 2 story. S $33-$38; D $38-$43; each addl $5; under 12 free. Crib free. TV; cable (premium). Complimentary coffee in rms. Restaurant adj 11 am-midnight. Ck-out noon. Cr cds: A, C, D, DS, ER, MC, V.

[icons]

Baton Rouge (D-4)

(See Jackson, St Francisville)

Founded 1719 **Pop** 219,531 **Elev** 58 ft **Area code** 504

Information Baton Rouge Area Convention & Visitors Bureau, 730 North Blvd, PO Box 4149, 70821; 504/383-1825.

Named by its French founders for a red post that marked the boundary between the lands of two Native American tribes, Baton Rouge, the busy capital of Louisiana, is also a major Mississippi River port. Clinging to its gracious past, the area has restored antebellum mansions, gardens, tree-shaded campuses, splendid Cajun and Creole cuisine and historic attractions that reflect the culture and struggle of living under ten flags over a period of two centuries. Institutions of higher education in Baton Rouge include Louisiana State University and Southern University and Agricultural and Mechanical College.

What to See and Do

★ **Downtown Riverfront.** Along the banks of the Mississippi in downtown Baton Rouge is the

Old State Capitol. Completed in 1849, Louisiana's old state capitol may be the country's most extravagant example of the Gothic-revival style popularized by the British Houses of Parliament. The richly ornamented building was enlarged in 1881 and abandoned as the capitol in 1932. Self-guided tours. (Daily exc Mon; closed major hols) Adjacent to the Old State Capitol are the river observation deck and the

Louisiana Arts and Science Center Riverside. Originally a railroad station, this building houses fine art, sculpture; cultural and historical exhibits; Egyptian exhibition; Discovery Depot, hands-on galleries for children. Outside are a sculpture garden and restored five-car train. (Daily exc Mon; closed hols) 100 S River Rd. Phone 504/344-5272. ¢ Also here is Old Governor's Mansion. Along riverfront is

USS *Kidd*. World War II *Fletcher*-class destroyer. Visitors may roam decks and explore interior compartments. Unique dock allows ship to be exhibited completely out of water when Mississippi River is in its low stages. Adjacent museum houses ship model collection, maritime artifacts, restored P-40 Flying Tiger fighter plane. Visitor center, observation tower overlooks river; Memorial Wall dedicated to service personnel. (Daily; closed Thanksgiving, Dec 25) Sr citizen rate. 305 S River Rd. Phone 504/342-1942. ¢¢ Also along river is

***Samuel Clemens* Steamboat.** Daytime harbor tours on the Mississippi River and evening dinner cruises. (Apr-Aug, daily; rest of yr, Wed-Sun) Reservation required for dinner cruise. Departs from foot of Florida St. Phone 504/381-9606. Harbor tour ¢¢¢

Greater Baton Rouge Zoo. Walkways overlook 140 acres of enclosed habitats for more than 900 animals and birds. Sidewalk trams and miniature train tour zoo (fee). (Daily; closed Jan 1, Dec 25) 6 mi N off I-10, exit 8 then right on Thomas Rd. Phone 504/775-3877. ¢

Heritage Museum and Village. Turn-of-the-century Victorian house with period rooms, exhibits. Also rural village replicas including church, school, store and town hall. (Mon-Fri, also Sat-Sun afternoons; closed hols) 1606 Main St, 10 mi N on LA 19 in Baker. Phone 504/774-1776. **Free.**

Houmas House (1840). Large, restored sugar plantation features Greek-revival mansion with early Louisiana-crafted furnishings; spiral staircase; belvedere; hexagonal garconnieres in gardens. Used in filming of *Hush, Hush, Sweet Charlotte*. (Daily; closed Jan 1, Thanksgiving, Dec 25) 22 mi SE on I-10 to Gonzales, then right 4 mi S on LA 44 to River Rd in Burnside. Phone 504/473-7841 or 504/522-2262. ¢¢¢

Laurens Henry Cohn, Sr Memorial Plant Arboretum. This unusual 16-acre tract of rolling terrain contains more than 120 species of native and adaptable trees and shrubs; several major plant collections; herb/fragrance garden; tropical collection in greenhouse. Tours by request. (Daily; closed Jan 1, Dec 25) 12056 Foster Rd. Phone 504/775-1006. **Free.**

Louisiana State University and Agricultural and Mechanical College (1860). (26,607 students) Highland Rd, SW edge of city. Phone 504/388-3202. On campus are

Tiger Cage. Home of Mike VI, LSU Bengal Tiger mascot. (Daily feeding).

Memorial Tower. Built in 1923 as a monument to Louisianians who died in World War I. Houses LSU Museum of Art that features original 17th through mid-19th century rooms from England and America. Self-guided tours. (Daily; closed hols) Phone 504/388-4003. **Free.**

Outdoor Greek Theater. Natural amphitheater seats 3,500.

Museum of Geoscience. Exhibits pertaining to archaeology, geology and geography. (Mon-Fri) In Howe/Russell Geoscience Complex. Phone 504/388-5620. **Free.**

Indian Mounds. The mounds are believed to have served socio-religious purposes and date from 3,300-2,500 B.C. At corner of Field House Dr and Dalrymple Dr. **Free.**

Rural Life Museum. Museum complex is divided into plantation, folk architecture and exhibits building. Plantation includes blacksmith shop, open-kettle sugar mill, commissary, church. (Mar-Oct, daily; rest of yr Mon-Fri) Under 12 only with adult. Entrance at jct I-10 & Essen Lane, at Burden Research Plantation. Phone 504/765-2437. ¢¢

Union Art Gallery. (Daily) Union Building. Phone 504/388-5141. **Free.**

Museum of Natural Science. Features extensive collection of birds from around the world; wildlife scenes including Louisiana marshlands and swamps, Arizona desert, alpine regions and Honduran jungles. (Daily exc Sun) Foster Hall. Phone 504/388-2855. **Free.**

Magnolia Mound Plantation. Early 19th-century, Creole-style building restored to emphasize lifestyle of colonial Louisiana; period rooms; detached kitchen with garden; weekly demonstrations of open-hearth Creole cooking. Costumed docents. Visitor center; gift shop. (Daily exc Mon; closed hols) Sr citizen rate. 2161 Nicholson Dr. Phone 504/343-4955. ¢¢

Norfolk Tours. Two-hour guided bus tours of city. Also plantation and swamp boat tours. Phone 504/383-2215. ¢¢¢

Nottoway Plantation (ca 1860). One of the South's most imposing houses, Nottoway contains more than 50,000 square feet, including 64 rooms, 200 windows and 165 doors. In a near perfect state of "originality," the house is famous for its all-white ballroom. Restaurant; overnight accommodations avail. Tours (daily; closed Dec 25). 18 mi S via LA 1. Phone 504/545-2730. ¢¢

Old Governor's Mansion. Mansion restored to period of 1930s, when it was built for Governor Huey P. Long. Original furnishings, memorabilia of former governors. (Sat & Sun; closed hols) 502 North Blvd. Phone 504/344-9465. ¢

Parlange Plantation (1750). Owned by relatives of the builder, this working plantation is a rare example of "bousillage" architecture. Doorways and ceiling moldings are of hand-carved cypress; two octagonal, brick dovecotes flank the driveway. (Daily; closed some major hols) 19 mi W on US 190, then 8 mi N on LA 1. Phone 504/638-8410. ¢¢¢

★ **Plantations and St Francisville.** Driving tour (approx 100 mi). Drive N from Baton Rouge on US 61 approx 23 mi, then turn E on LA 965 to

Oakley (1806). While living at Oakley and working as a tutor, John James Audubon painted 32 of his *Birds of America*. Spanish-colonial Oakley is part of **Audubon State Commemorative Area,** a 100-acre tract set aside as a wildlife sanctuary. House & park (daily; closed Jan 1, Thanksgiving, Dec 25). Sr citizen rate. Phone 504/635-3739. ¢

Return to US 61, drive N approx 4 mi to St Francisville (see). Just E of town on LA 10 & US 61 is

Rosedown (1835). Magnificently restored antebellum mansion with many original furnishings; 28 acres of formal gardens include century-old camellias and azaleas, fountains, gazebos and an alley of century-old, moss-draped live oaks. (Daily; closed Dec 24 & 25) For schedule information phone 504/635-3332. ¢¢¢

Continue W to US 61, then drive N approx 2 mi to

The Myrtles Plantation (1796). Known as one of "America's most haunted mansions," this carefully restored house of French influence boasts outstanding examples of wrought iron and ornamental plasterwork; period furniture. (Daily; closed Dec 24 & 25) 7747 Hwy 61. Phone 504/635-6277. ¢¢¢

Then drive N on US 61 approx 1 mi to LA 66, then W on Highland Rd to

Greenwood (1830). Original Greek-revival plantation house survived the Civil War and post-war economic recession only to burn in 1960. A working plantation producing cattle, hay and pecans, Greenwood has been rebuilt and furnished with period antiques. (Daily; closed major hols) 6838 Highland Rd. Phone 504/655-4475. ¢¢

Return to US 61 and proceed N to

Cottage Plantation (1795-1850). The oldest part of the main house was begun during Spanish control of area. Outbuildings include smokehouse, school, slave cabins. Accomodations and breakfast available. Tours (daily; closed major hols). Phone 504/635-3674. ¢¢

Approx 19 mi N, just E of US 61 in Woodville, MS is

Rosemont Plantation (1810). The restored family residence of Jefferson Davis, president of the Confederacy, includes many Davis family furnishings. Tours available for house, grounds and family cemetery. (Mon-Fri, also wkends Mar-Apr) Phone 601/888-6809. ¢¢¢

Return to Baton Rouge via US 61.

Plaquemine Locks. The locks were built (1895-1909) to control the water level between the Bayou Plaquemine and the Mississippi. Larger locks built at Port Allen in 1961 caused the closing of these historic locks, designed by George Goethals, who later designed the Panama Canal. When built, the Plaquemine Locks had the highest freshwater lift (51 ft) in the world. Area features original lockhouse and locks; interpretive center with displays; observation tower with view of Mississippi. (Mon-Fri; closed major hols) 15 mi S on LA 1, across from Old City Hall. Phone 504/681-7158. **Free.**

Port Hudson State Commemorative Area. This 650-acre area encompasses part of a Civil War battlefield, site of the longest siege in American military history. It features viewing towers (40 ft), Civil War guns, trenches and hiking trails. Interpretive programs tell the story of how, in 1863, 6,800 Confederates held off a Union force of 30,000 to 40,000 men. (Daily; closed Jan 1, Thanksgiving, Dec 25) 15 mi N via US 61. Phone 504/654-3775. ¢

State Capitol (1932). Built during Huey P. Long's administration, the 34-story, 450-foot *moderne,* skyscraper capitol is decorated with 27 different varieties of marble. Memorial Hall floor is laid with polished lava from Mt Vesuvius; the ceiling is leafed in gold. Observation tower offers view of city; Loredo Taft sculpture groups on either side of entrance symbolize the pioneer and patriotic spirit. Tour of first floor on request at information desk; observation tower (daily; closed Jan 1, Easter, Thanksgiving, Dec 25). Third St and Spanishtown Rd. Phone 504/342-7317 or 504/664-8746. **Free.** The Capitol complex includes the

Capitol Grounds. On the south side are formal gardens that focus on a sunken garden with a monumental statue erected over the grave of Huey Long, who was buried here in 1935 after being assassinated in the Capitol. To the east more gardens surround the

Old Spanish Arsenal museum, one-time military garrison that dates from the Spanish-colonial period. Beyond, across Capitol Lake, is the

Governor's Mansion. Greek-revival/Louisiana plantation in style, the mansion was built in 1963 to replace an earlier official residence. Tours (Mon-Fri by appt only). 1001 Capitol Access Rd. Phone 504/342-5855. **Free.** To the southwest are the

Pentagon Barracks. Built in 1822 as part of a US military post, the columned, galleried buildings later became the first permanent home of Louisiana State University. Also on grounds is the

Louisiana State Library. Collection of some 350,000 books, including extensive section of Louisiana historical books, maps and photographs. (Mon-Fri; closed hols) 760 N 3rd St. Phone 504/342-4914. **Free.**

West Baton Rouge Museum. Exhibits include Louisiana duck decoys; large-scale 1904 model sugar mill; bedroom featuring American Empire furniture; sugar plantation slave cabin (ca 1850) and French Creole house (ca 1830); changing exhibits. (Tues-Sat; closed hols) 2 mi W on I-10, at 845 N Jefferson in Port Allen. Phone 504/336-2422. **Free.**

Annual Events

FestForAll. Downtown area, particularly North Blvd. Juried shows and exhibits featuring up to 120 artisans and craftspeople and 1,200 performers. Performing arts, including drama, music, dance, children's theater and street entertainment. Special events include RunForAll, gallery show, Children's Village and art demonstrations. Traditional Louisiana and international cuisine. Phone 504/383-1825. Late May.

Blues Festival. Downtown area, particularly North Blvd. Three-day event featuring blues, Cajun, zydeco and gospel music. Traditional Louisiana cuisine. Phone 504/383-1825. Oct.

Christmas on the River. Dec.

Motels

(Rates may be higher during Mardi Gras Festival & football wkends)

★ ★ **BEST WESTERN-CHATEAU LOUISIANNE SUITE HOTEL.** *710 N Lobdell (70806).* 504/927-6700; FAX 504/927-6709. 50 suites, 3 story. S $64-$79; D $69-$89; each addl $8; under 12 free. Crib free. TV; cable (premium). Pool; whirlpool, steam rm. Complimentary continental bkfst (6:30-9:30 am). Complimentary coffee in rms. Restaurant 11:30 am-2 pm, 6-10:30 pm; Sat dinner only. Rm serv. Bar 4:30-10:30 pm. Ck-out noon. Coin lndry. Meeting rm. Business servs avail. In-rm modem link. Some refrigerators. Cr cds: A, C, D, DS, MC, V.

D 🏊 🚫 🐾 SC

★ ★ **HAMPTON INN.** *4646 Constitution Ave (70808), off I-10 exit 158.* 504/926-9990; FAX 504/923-3007. 141 rms, 8 story. S $65; D $72; under 18 free. Crib free. TV; cable (premium). Pool. Complimentary continental bkfst. Ck-out noon. Meeting rms. Business servs avail. Valet serv. Cr cds: A, C, D, DS, MC, V.

D 🏊 🚫 🐾 SC

✔ ★ ★ **LA QUINTA.** *2333 S Acadian Thrwy (70808), off I-10 exit 157B.* 504/924-9600; FAX 504/924-2609. 142 rms, 2 story. S, D $57-$64; each addl $7; under 18 free. Crib free. Pet accepted; some restrictions. TV; cable (premium). Pool. Complimentary continental bkfst. Restaurant adj open 24 hrs. Ck-out noon. Meeting rms. Business servs avail. In-rm modem link. Valet serv. Airport transportation. Cr cds: A, C, D, DS, MC, V.

D 🐾 🏊 🚫 🐾 SC

✔ ★ **QUALITY INN.** *10920 Mead Frontage Rd (70816).* 504/293-9370; FAX 504/293-8889. 150 rms, 2 story. S $40-$50; D $49.50-$62.50; each addl $3; under 12 free. TV; cable (premium). Pool. Complimentary coffee in rms. Restaurant 6:30 am-noon, 5:30-9 pm. Rm serv. Bar 5 pm-midnight; entertainment, dancing Tues-Sat. Ck-out noon. Coin lndry. Meeting rms. Game rm. Refrigerators avail. Cr cds: A, C, D, DS, ER, JCB, MC, V.

🏊 🚫 🐾 SC

★ ★ **RESIDENCE INN BY MARRIOTT.** *5522 Corporate Blvd (70808), N of I-10 exit 158.* 504/927-5630; FAX 504/926-2317. 80 kit. suites, 2 story. Suites $69-$128; wkend packages. Crib free. TV; cable (premium). VCR avail. Pool; whirlpool. Complimentary bkfst buffet. Restaurant nearby. Rm serv. Ck-out noon. Coin lndry. Meeting rms. Business servs avail. Valet serv. Tennis. Fireplaces. Grills. Extensive grounds. Cr cds: A, C, D, DS, JCB, MC, V.

D 🏊 🚫 🐾 SC

✔ ★ ★ **SHONEY'S INN.** 9919 Gwenadele Dr (70816), at jct I-12, US 61; Airline Hwy exit 2B. 504/925-8399; res: 800/222-2222; FAX 504/927-1731. 194 rms, 2 story. S $60; D $66; suites $91; under 18 free; wkend rates. Crib free. Pet accepted; some restrictions. TV; cable (premium). Pool. Complimentary coffee. Restaurant 6 am-midnight; Fri-Sat to 3 am. Ck-out noon. Meeting rms. Valet serv. Cr cds: A, C, D, DS, ER, MC, V.

☐D ☐✔ ☐≈ ☐✕ ☐✕ ☐🔥 ☐SC

Motor Hotels

★ ★ **HOLIDAY INN-HOLIDOME SOUTH.** 9940 Airline Hwy (70816), at jct I-12, US 61. 504/924-7021; FAX 504/924-7021, ext. 1987. 333 rms, 6 story. S $65-$83; D $64-$78; suites $141-$276; under 18 free. TV; cable (premium). Pool; wading pool. Restaurant 6 am-10 pm. Rm serv. Bar noon-1 am. Ck-out noon. Coin lndry. Meeting rms. Business center. Airport transportation. Exercise equipt; weights, bicycles, whirlpool. Holidome. Some balconies. Luxury level. Cr cds: A, C, D, DS, JCB, MC, V.

☐D ☐≈ ☐✕ ☐✕ ☐✕ ☐🔥 ☐SC ☐🚶

★ ★ **QUALITY SUITES.** 9138 Bluebonnet Centre Blvd (70809), off I-10 Bluebonnet exit. 504/293-1199; FAX 504/296-5014. 120 rms, 3 story. S, D $76; each addl $10; suites $150; under 18 free; wkend, monthly rates. Crib free. TV; cable, VCR. Pool. Complimentary bkfst. Restaurant 6 am-10:30 pm; Sat from 7 am; Sun 7-10 am. Bar 5-11 pm. Ck-out 11 am. Meeting rms. Business servs avail. In-rm modem link. Sundries. Health club privileges. Refrigerators, minibars. Balconies. Picnic tables, grills. Cr cds: A, D, DS, MC, V.

☐D ☐≈ ☐✕ ☐🔥 ☐SC

★ **RAMADA.** 1480 Nicholson Dr (70802). 504/387-1111; FAX 504/387-1111, ext. 7647. 284 rms, 11 suites, 2 story. S, D $53-$68; each addl $7; suites $165-$320; under 12 free. Crib free. TV; cable. Pool; poolside serv. Restaurant 6 am-10 pm. Rm serv. Bar 4 pm-2 am. Ck-out noon. Meeting rms. Business servs avail. Free airport transportation. Cr cds: A, C, D, DS, MC, V.

☐D ☐≈ ☐✕ ☐🔥 ☐SC

Hotels

★ ★ **CROWN STERLING SUITES.** 4914 Constitution Ave (70808), off I-10 exit 158. 504/924-6566; FAX 504/923-3712. 224 suites, 8 story. Suites $79-$130; each addl $10; under 12 free; wkend rates. Crib free. TV; cable (premium); whirlpool, steam rm. Complimentary full bkfst, coffee in rms. Restaurant 11 am-2 pm, 5-10 pm. Bar to 10:30 pm. Ck-out 1 pm. Meeting rms. Business servs avail. Gift shop. Free airport transportation. Refrigerators. Built around large atrium featuring gazebo & courtyard; small pond with waterfalls, fish & ducks. Cr cds: A, C, D, DS, ER, JCB, MC, V.

☐D ☐≈ ☐✕ ☐🔥 ☐SC

★ ★ **HILTON.** 5500 Hilton Ave (70808), I-10 exit 158 at College Dr. 504/924-5000; FAX 504/925-1330. 297 rms, 21 story. S $90; D $95; each addl $10; suites $135-$360. Crib free. TV; cable (premium), VCR avail. Pool. Restaurant 6:30 am-11 pm; Sun brunch 11 am-2 pm. Bar 2 pm-2 am. Ck-out noon. Convention facilities. In-rm modem link. Free airport transportation. Lighted tennis. Exercise equipt; weights, bicycles, sauna. Luxury level. Cr cds: A, C, D, DS, ER, JCB, MC, V.

☐D ☐🚶 ☐≈ ☐✕ ☐✕ ☐🔥 ☐SC

Inn

★ ★ ★ **NOTTOWAY PLANTATION.** (PO Box 160, White Castle 70788) 20 mi S, on LA 1. 504/545-2730; FAX 504/545-8632. 13 rms, 3 story, 3 suites. Many rm phones. S $95-$250; D $125-$250; each addl $30; suites $200-$250. Crib free. TV. Pool. Complimentary full bkfst, tea/sherry. Complimentary coffee in rms. Restaurant (see RANDOLPH HALL). Ck-out 11 am, ck-in 2:30 pm. Bellhops. Concierge. Balconies. Antiques. Library/sitting rm. Antebellum mansion; Corinthian columns, hand-carved marble mantels, 65-ft long Grand White ballroom. Tours avail. On Mississippi River. Cr cds: A, DS, MC, V.

☐≈ ☐✕ ☐🔥

Restaurants

★ **THE CABIN.** (Box 85, Burnside 70738) I-10 S to LA 44 S, at jct LA 44 & 22. 504/473-3007. Hrs: 8 am-3 pm; Thur to 9 pm; Fri, Sat to 10 pm; Sun to 6 pm. Closed Jan 1, Thanksgiving, Dec 25. Res accepted. Bar. Cajun menu. Semi-a la carte: lunch, dinner $4.95-$15.95. Child's meals. Specializes in gumbo, red beans & rice, buttermilk pie. Former Monroe Plantation slave cabins (ca 1840); old farm tools, household antiques. Parking. Cr cds: A, DS, MC, V.

★ ★ ★ **CHALET BRANDT.** 7655 Old Hammond Hwy. 504/927-6040. Cypress beams, a 17-foot fireplace, Oriental rugs, and antique copper pots lend character to this elegant eatery. Hrs: 5:30-10 pm; Thurs also 11:30 am-2 pm. Closed Sun; some major hols; also wk of July 4 & Dec 24-Jan 1. Res accepted Memorial Day-Labor Day. Continental menu with Louisiana flair. Serv bar. Semi-a la carte: lunch $9-$15.75, dinner $9.75-$30. Child's meals. Specializes in fresh seafood, veal, duck, lamb, beef, chicken. Own pastries. Chef-owned. Parking. Jacket. Cr cds: A, C, D, MC, V.

☐D

★ ★ **DAJONEL'S.** 7327 Jefferson Hwy. 504/924-7537. Hrs: 11:30 am-2:30 pm, 5-10 pm; Sat, Sun from 5 pm; Sun brunch 11 am-2 pm. Closed most major hols. French, continental menu. Bar. Semi-a la carte: lunch $7.95-$16.95, dinner $13.95-$26.95. Specializes in steak, seafood, rack of lamb. Parking. European country inn atmosphere. Cr cds: A, D, DS, MC, V.

☐D ☐SC

✔ ★ **DON'S SEAFOOD & STEAK HOUSE.** 6823 Airline Hwy. 504/357-0601. Hrs: 11 am-10 pm; Fri, Sat to 11 pm. Closed Thanksgiving, Dec 25. Res accepted. Bar. Semi-a la carte: lunch, dinner $6.95-$15.99. Child's meals. Specializes in seafood, steak. Oyster bar. Cr cds: A, C, D, DS, MC, V.

☐D

★ ★ **JUBAN'S.** 3739 Perkins Rd, in shopping center. 504/346-8422. Hrs: 11:30 am-2, 5:30-10 pm; Sat 5:30-10 pm. Closed Sun; major hols. Res accepted. Creole menu. Bar. Semi-a la carte: lunch $5.95-$17, dinner $10.95-$23.95. Child's meals. Specializes in stuffed soft-shelled crab, crawfish stuffed shrimp, veal. Cr cds: A, MC, V.

☐D

★ ★ ★ **LAFITTE'S LANDING.** (Sunshine Bridge Access Rd (LA 70), Donaldsonville 70346) 30 mi S on I-10, exit 182 to Donaldsonville, under Sunshine Bridge. 504/473-1232. Hrs: 11 am-3 pm, 6-10 pm; Sun 11 am-8 pm. Closed Mon; Jan 1, July 4, Dec 25. Res accepted. Continental menu. Bar. Wine list. Semi-a la carte: lunch $5.95-$21.95, dinner $16.95-$24.95. Child's meals. Specialties: soft-shell crawfish, crawfish-stuffed rack of lamb. Salad bar. Parking. Raised Acadian cottage that was plantation home. Cr cds: DS, MC, V.

☐D

✔ ★ **MIKE ANDERSON'S.** 1031 W Lee Dr, 4 mi S of I-10 exit 158. 504/766-7823. Hrs: 11 am-2 pm, 5-9:30 pm; Fri, Sat 11 am-10:30 pm; Sun 11 am-9 pm. Closed major hols. Res accepted Mon-Thur (lunch only). Southern Louisiana menu. Bar. Semi-a la carte: lunch $5.95-$7.95, dinner $8.95-$16.95. Child's meals. Specializes in seafood. Oyster bar. Parking. Nautical decor. Cr cds: A, D, DS, MC, V.

☐D ☐SC

★ ★ **THE PLACE.** 5255 Florida Blvd, 3 mi W of Airline Hwy. 504/924-5069. Hrs: 11 am-2:30 pm, 5:30-10pm; Mon to 2:30 pm; Sat from 5:30; Sun 11 am-2:30 pm. Closed Dec 25. Res accepted. Continental menu. Bar. Semi-a la carte: lunch $5.95-$16, dinner $12.95-$24.95. Child's meals. Specializes in steak, fresh seafood, veal. Entertainment Fri & Sat 7-10 pm. Parking. Exposed brick walls; patio with fountain. Cr cds: A, D, DS, MC, V.

☐ D ☐ SC

★ **RALPH & KACOO'S.** *7110 Airline Hwy.* 504/356-2361. Hrs: 11:30 am-2 pm, 5-10 pm; Fri to 10:30 pm; Sat 11:30 am-10:30 pm; Sun 11:30 am-9 pm. Closed Jan 1, Thanksgiving, Dec 25. Bar. Semi-a la carte: lunch $3.95-$8.95, dinner $6.95-$17.95. Child's meals. Specializes in seafood, broiled fish, crawfish dishes (in season), steak. Parking. Nautical decor. Cr cds: A, C, D, DS, MC, V.

☐ D

★ ★ **RANDOLPH HALL.** *(See Nottoway Plantation Inn)* 504/545-2730. Hrs: 11 am-3 pm, 6-9 pm. Closed Dec 25. Res accepted. Cajun, creole menu. Bar. A la carte entrees: lunch $8-$12, dinner $15-$22. Child's meals. Specialties: gumbo, jambalaya. Parking. Pianist wkends. Plantation atmosphere. Cr cds: A, DS, MC, V.

★ ★ **RUTH'S CHRIS STEAK HOUSE.** *4836 Constitution, S off I-10 College Dr exit.* 504/925-0163. Hrs: 11:30 am-11:30 pm; Sat 4 pm-midnight. Closed Sun; major hols. Bar. A la carte entrees: lunch, dinner $8.50-$22.95. Specializes in steak, live Maine lobster. Parking. Cr cds: A, C, D, MC, V.

☐ D

Bossier City (A-2)

(See Shreveport)

Pop 52,721 **Elev** 174 ft **Area code** 318

Information Shreveport-Bossier Convention & Tourist Bureau, 629 Spring St, PO Box 1761, Shreveport 71166; 318/222-9391 or 800/551-8682.

Barksdale Air Force Base, home of the 8th Air Force and the 2nd Bombardment Wing, is located near Bossier City.

What to See and Do

Eighth Air Force Museum. Aircraft displayed include B-52 Stratofortress, P-15 Mustang and F-84 Thunderstreak. Desert Storm memorabilia. Gift shop. (Daily) Barksdale Air Force Base, north gate. Phone 318/456-3067. **Free.**

Isle of Capri Casino. 77 Isle of Capri Blvd. Phone 318/678-7777 or 800/386-4753.

Touchstone Wildlife & Art Museum. Various dioramas depict animals and birds in their natural habitats. (Daily exc Mon; closed major hols) 5 mi E on US 80. Phone 318/949-2323. ¢

Annual Event

Super Derby Festival. A month of competition, pageantry and entertainment leading to the Super Derby race at Louisiana Downs. Phone 318/425-1800. Sept.

Seasonal Event

Thoroughbred racing. Louisiana Downs. 3 mi E on US 80 at I-220. Wed-Sun; also Memorial Day, July 4 and Labor Day. Phone 318/742-5555. Late Apr-mid-Oct.

Motels

★ ★ **LA QUINTA.** *309 Preston Blvd (71111).* 318/747-4400; FAX 318/747-1516. 130 rms, 2 story. Apr-Nov: S $61; D $68; each addl $10; suites $77-$83; under 18 free; lower rates rest of yr. Crib free. TV;

cable. Pool. Complimentary continental bkfst. Restaurant adj open 24 hrs. Ck-out noon. Meeting rms. Airport, RR station, bus depot transportation. Cr cds: A, C, D, DS, MC, V.

☐ D ☐ ☐ ☐ SC

★ ★ **RESIDENCE INN BY MARRIOTT.** *1001 Gould Dr (71111), at I-20 Old Minden Rd exit.* 318/747-6220; FAX 318/747-3424. 72 kit. units, 2 story. S, D $89-$129. TV; cable (premium). Pool; whirlpool. Complimentary continental bkfst. Ck-out noon. Valet serv. Sundries. Health club privileges. Refrigerators. Private patios, balconies. Picnic tables, grills. Cr cds: A, C, D, DS, JCB, MC, V.

☐ D ☐ ☐ ☐ SC

Motor Hotels

★ **GRAND ISLE HOTEL.** *3033 Hilton Dr (71111), on I-20 at Airline Dr exit.* 318/747-2400; FAX 318/747-6822. 245 rms, 2 story. Apr-Oct: S $65-$70; D $75-$80; suites $110-$150; lower rates rest of yr. Crib free. TV; cable. Pool; poolside serv. Restaurant 6 am-2 pm, 5-10 pm. Rm serv. Bars 11-2 am; piano bar, dancing exc Sun. Ck-out noon. Meeting rms. Bellhops. Valet serv. Sundries. Gift shop. Free airport, bus depot transportation. Exercise equipt; weight machine, bicycles. Cr cds: A, C, D, DS, MC, V.

☐ D ☐ ☐ ☐ ☐ SC

★ ★ **SHERATON-BOSSIER INN.** *2015 Old Minden Rd (71111), at I-20, Old Minden Rd exit 21.* 318/742-9700; FAX 318/742-9700, ext. 340. 212 rms, 2 story. S, D $68-$125; each addl $10; suites $125-$145; under 18 free. Crib free. TV; cable. Pool; whirlpool, steam rm, poolside serv. Restaurant 6 am-2 pm, 5-10 pm; Sun from 7 am. Rm serv. Bar 4 pm-2 am; entertainment, dancing exc Sun. Ck-out noon. Meeting rms. Bellhops. Sundries. Free airport, bus depot transportation. Lawn games. Cr cds: A, C, D, DS, ER, MC, V.

☐ D ☐ ☐ SC

Restaurant

★ ★ **RALPH & KACOO'S.** *1700 Old Minden Rd, located in Bossier Cross Roads Shopping Center.* 318/747-6660. Hrs: 11:30 am-10 pm; Fri, Sat to 10:30 pm; Sun to 9 pm. Closed some hols. Cajun, Amer menu. Bar; closed Sun. Semi-a la carte: lunch, dinner $5.95-$18.95. Specializes in fresh seafood, broiled fish, hush puppies. Own desserts. Cr cds: A, D, DS, MC, V.

☐ D

Covington (D-5)

(See Hammond, Kenner, Metairie, New Orleans, Slidell)

Founded 1813 **Pop** 7,691 **Elev** 25 ft **Area code** 504 **Zip** 70433

Information St Tammany Parish Convention & Visitors Bureau, 600 N US 190, Suite 15; 504/892-0520 or 800/634-9443.

Covington is situated in a wooded area north of Lake Pontchartrain, which is crossed via the 24-mile Lake Pontchartrain Causeway from New Orleans. With mild winters and semi-tropical summers, Covington is a town of pecan, pine and oak woods, vacation houses and recreational opportunities, especially swimming, waterskiing and boating. The Delta Regional Primate Research Center of Tulane University is located on 500 acres 3 miles south of town. A number of Thoroughbred horse farms are also in the area.

What to See and Do

Fontainebleau State Park. A live oak alley forms the entrance to this 2,700-acre park on the north shore of Lake Pontchartrain; on grounds are the ruins of a plantation brickyard and sugar mill. Swimming;

fishing, boating. Picnicking. Tent and trailer sites (hookups, dump station). Standard fees. (Daily) 12 mi SE on US 190. Phone 504/624-4443. Per vehicle ¢¢

Motel

★★ **HOLIDAY INN HOLIDOME.** *501 N Hwy 190, at jct I-12.* *504/893-3580; FAX 504/893-4807.* 156 rms, 2 story. S $62-$72; D $70-$80; each addl $8; under 19 free; wkend rates. Crib free. TV; cable (premium), VCR avail. 2 pools, 1 indoor. Restaurant 6:30 am-2 pm, 5:30-10 pm. Rm serv. Bar from 4 pm. Ck-out noon. Coin lndry. Meeting rms. Business servs avail. Bellhops. Valet serv. Exercise equipt; bicycle, rowing machine, whirlpool. Game rm. Cr cds: A, C, D, DS, ER, JCB, MC, V.

D ⊠ ✗ ⋈ 🔥 SC

Restaurants

★★ **THE DAKOTA.** *629 N US 190. 504/892-3712.* Hrs: 11 am-2:30 pm, 5-10 pm; Fri to 11 pm; Sat 5-11 pm; Sun noon-8 pm. Closed some major hols. Res accepted. Contemporary Southern Louisiana cuisine. Bar. Semi-a la carte: lunch $6-$12, dinner $15-$22.50. Child's meals. Specializes in steak, lamb, fresh seafood. Parking. Local artwork on display. Cr cds: A, D, MC, V.

D

★★★ **LA PROVENCE.** *(Box 805, Lacombe 70445) 7 mi from Causeway on US 190E. 504/626-7662.* This one-story house with sitting room and authentic French furnishings evokes the experience of dining in a fine tavern in the French countryside. On the north shore of Lake Ponchartrain, it's about an hour's drive from central New Orleans. Hrs: 5-11 pm; Sun 1-9 pm. Closed Mon, Tues; Dec 25. Res required. French, regional menu. Serv bar. Wine list. Semi-a la carte: dinner $17-$28. Specialties: canard à l'ail, duck l'orange, carré d'agneau aux herbes de Provence. Own baking. Pianist Fri-Sun. Parking. Cr cds: A, MC, V.

D

✔★★★ **TREY YUEN.** *(600 N Causeway, Mandeville) ¹/₂ mi N of N end of Causeway. 504/626-4476.* Hrs: 5-10 pm; Fri, Sat to 11 pm; Sun 11:30 am-9:30 pm; also Wed-Fri 11:30 am-2 pm. Closed major hols; Mardi Gras. Chinese menu. Bar. Semi-a la carte: lunch $4.75-$7.50, dinner $8.95-$15. Specialties: crawfish in lobster sauce, Szechwan alligator, soft shell crab. Parking. Overlooks rock garden. Family-owned. Cr cds: A, C, D, DS, MC, V.

D

Franklin (D-3)

(See Morgan City, New Iberia)

Founded 1808 **Pop** 9,004 **Elev** 15 ft **Area code** 318 **Zip** 70538

Information Tourism Department, City of Franklin, 300 Iberia St, PO Box 567; 318/828-6326 or 800/962-6889.

Said to be named by founder Guinea Lewis for Benjamin Franklin, this town on the Bayou Teche is a center of salt-mining, sugar-refining and the manufacturing of carbon black, which is used in the production of rubber and ink.

What to See and Do

Chitimacha Cultural Center. Museum exhibits, crafts and 10-minute video focus on history and culture of Chitimacha Tribe of Louisiana. Walking tours. A unit of Jean Lafitte National Historical Park (see NEW ORLEANS). (Daily; closed Jan 1, Dec 25) Approx 15 mi N on LA 87 in Charenton. Phone 504/589-3882 or 318/923-4830. **Free.**

Cypremort Point State Park. The 185-acre site offers access to the Gulf of Mexico. Man-made beach in the heart of a natural marsh affords fresh and saltwater fishing and other seashore recreation opportunities. (Daily) Standard fees. 5 mi N via US 90, 16 mi W via LA 83, then 7 mi SW on LA 319. Phone 318/867-4510. Per vehicle ¢¢

Grevemberg House (ca 1850). Greek-revival house with fine collection of antique furnishings dating from the 1850s; children's toys; paintings and Civil War relics. (Thurs-Sun; closed hols) Sr citizen rate. St Mary Parish Museum. City Park on Sterling Rd. Phone 318/828-2092. ¢

Oaklawn Manor Plantation (1837). Restored in 1927, the massive Greek-revival house has walls 20 inches thick; is furnished with European antiques; and is surrounded by one of the largest groves of live oaks in the US. (Daily; closed most major hols & Dec 24) 5 mi NW off US 90, LA 182. Phone 318/828-0434. ¢¢¢

Motel

★★ **BEST WESTERN FOREST.** *Box 1069, 1909 Main St. 318/828-1810.* 77 rms, 1-2 story. S $49-$51; D $56.50-$62.50; each addl $5; under 12 free. Crib $5. TV; cable (premium). Pool. Restaurant 5:30 am-9:30 pm. Rm serv. Ck-out noon. Meeting rms. Business servs avail. In-rm modem link. Valet serv. Some refrigerators. Cr cds: A, C, D, DS, MC, V.

D ⊠ ⋈ 🔥 SC

Hammond (D-4)

(For accommodations see Baton Rouge, Covington, Kenner)

Pop 15,871 **Elev** 47 ft **Area code** 504

Restaurant

★★★ **TREY YUEN.** *2100 N Morrison Blvd. 504/345-6789.* Hrs: 11 am-2 pm, 5-10 pm; Fri to 11 pm; Sat 5-11 pm; Sun 11:30 am-9:30 pm. Closed hols. Chinese menu. Bar. A la carte entrees: lunch $4.75-$7.50, dinner $4.50-$15. Complete meals: dinner $11.50 & $15. Specializes in alligator, soft-shelled crabs & crawfish. Parking. Exotic dining rooms overlook rock garden with pagoda and bridge over pool stocked with Chinese carp. Cr cds: A, C, D, DS, MC, V.

D SC

Unrated Dining Spot

MORRISON'S CAFETERIA. *2000 SW Railroad Ave, in Hammond Square Mall. 504/542-0588.* Hrs: 11 am-3 pm, 4-8 pm; Sat 11 am-8 pm; Sun to 6:30 pm. Avg ck: lunch, dinner $5. Cr cds: A, DS, MC, V.

D

Houma (E-4)

(See Morgan City, Thibodaux)

Founded 1832 **Pop** 30,495 **Elev** 0-12 ft **Area code** 504

Information Houma-Terrebonne Tourist Commission, 1702 S St Charles St, PO Box 2792, 70361; 504/868-2732 or 800/688-2732.

Houma, on Bayou Terrebonne and the Intracoastal Waterway, has for many years been a center for fishing, shrimping and fur trapping. Known as the "Venice of America," Houma is famous for Cajun food and hospitality.

What to See and Do

Annie Miller's Swamp & Marsh Tours. Boat trips (2-3 hr) through winding waterways in swamps and wild marshlands. See birds, alligators, wild game, tropical plants and flowers. (Mar-Oct, 2 departures daily) Phone 504/879-3934. ¢¢¢¢

Fishing. Excellent fresh and saltwater angling in nearby bays and bayous. Fishing best May-Nov. Charter boats avail.

Southdown Plantation House/Terrebonne Museum (1893). The first floor, Greek-revival in style, was built in 1859; the second floor, late Victorian/Queen Anne in style, was added in 1893; 21-room house includes stained glass, Boehm and Doughty porcelain bird collection, Terreboone Parish history room, re-creation of Allen Ellender's senate office, antique furniture, mardi gras costumes. (Daily; closed major hols) Sr citizen rate. Intersection of LA 311 and St Charles St. Phone 504/851-0154. ¢¢

Annual Events

Taste of the Bayou. Food fest. Mar.

Blessing of the Shrimp Fleet. Apr.

Praline Festival. Late Apr.

Unrated Dining Spot

PICCADILLY CAFETERIA. *1704 W Park Ave, 4 mi W of US 90 on LA 24, in shopping center.* 504/879-4222. Hrs: 11 am-8:30 pm. Closed Dec 25. Avg check: lunch, dinner $6.50. Specializes in crawfish étouffée, roast beef, strawberry pie. No cr cds accepted.

Jackson (C-4)

(See Baton Rouge, St Francisville)

Pop 3,891 **Elev** 180 ft **Area code** 504 **Zip** 70748
Information Feliciana Chamber of Commerce, PO Box 667; 504/634-7155.

What to See and Do

Jackson Historic District. District includes 123 structures covering approximately 65 percent of town; structures range from storefronts and warehouses to cottages and mansions; architectural styles range from Renaissance and Greek-revival to Queen Anne and California stick-style bungalow.

Milbank Historic House (1836). Greek-revival townhouse, originally built as a banking house for the Clinton-Port Hudson Railroad, features first- and second-floor galleries supported by twelve 30-foot columns. Overnight stays avail. Tours (daily; closed hols). Sr citizen rate. 3045 Bank St. Phone 504/634-5901. ¢¢

Inns

★ ★ **ASPHODEL.** *4626 LA 68.* 504/654-6868. 18 units, 2 story, 7 suites. No rm phones. D $55-$150. Closed 3 days at Christmas, 2 wks Jan. Pool. Complimentary full bkfst. Dining rm 7:30-9 am, 11:30 am-3 pm, Wed & Thurs 5:30-7:30 pm; Fri, Sat 5:30-9 pm. Ck-out noon, ck-in 3 pm. Lawn games. Antiques. Library/sitting rm; fireplace in some rms. Antebellum house (1840); veranda. Cr cds: MC, V.

★ ★ **MILBANK.** *3045 Bank St.* 504/634-5901. 4 units, 3 with bath, 2 story, 2 kits. No rm phones. D $75. TV in some rms. Complimentary full bkfst, coffee. Restaurant nearby. Ck-out noon, ck-in 4 pm.

Balconies. Antiques. Library/sitting rm. Former bank and newspaper office (1836). Cr cds: MC, V.

Restaurant

✔ ★ ★ **MAJOR'S BEAR CORNERS.** *On LA 10, in center of town.* 504/634-2844. Hrs: 5:30-9 pm; Sun 11 am-2 pm. Closed Mon & Tues; Jan 1, Dec 25; also wk of July 4. Bar. Semi-a la carte: dinner $8.95-$14.95. Specialties: eggplant Lynnette, quail, trout. Own desserts. Parking. Originally a billiards hall (1821); solarium, fireplace, antiques. Cr cds: A, MC, V.

Jennings (D-2)

(See Lake Charles)

Founded 1888 **Pop** 11,305 **Elev** 22 ft **Area code** 318 **Zip** 70546
Information Greater Jennings Chamber of Commerce, 414 Cary Ave, PO Box 1209; 318/824-0933.

The Southern Pacific Railroad urged Midwesterners to settle in Jennings soon after its line was built in 1880. The town was chartered in 1884. On September 21, 1901, Louisiana's first oil well, five miles northeast, came in, bringing pioneer oil developers to the area. Today, Jennings remains a center of beef, soybean and rice production, while oil continues to contribute to the local economy.

What to See and Do

Zigler Museum. Museum contains galleries of wildlife and natural history, European and American art; antique handguns. (Daily exc Mon; closed major hols) Sr citizen rate. 411 Clara St. Phone 318/824-0114. ¢

Motel

✔ ★ ★ **HOLIDAY INN.** *Box 896, I-10 & LA 26.* 318/824-5280; FAX 318/824-7941. 131 rms, 2 story. S $50; D $55; each addl $5. Crib free. TV. Pool. Restaurant 6 am-2 pm, 5-10 pm. Rm serv. Bar 4 pm-2 am; Sat to midnight; closed Sun. Ck-out noon. Meeting rms. Business servs avail. In-rm modem link. Bellhops. Cr cds: A, C, D, DS, JCB, MC, V.

D ≈ ⊠ 🔥 SC

Restaurant

★ **GOLDEN DRAGON.** *Rt 2, Box 720-A, I-10 & LA 26.* 318/824-4280. Hrs: 10:30 am-9:30 pm. Closed major hols. Chinese menu. Serv bar. Lunch buffet $6.95. Semi-a la carte: dinner $4.99-$19.99. Child's meals. Specializes in Cantonese, Hunan cuisine. Parking. Aquarium. Cr cds: A, DS, MC, V.

D

Kenner (D-4)

(See Metairie, New Orleans)

Pop 72,033 **Elev** 5 ft **Area code** 504

Motor Hotels

(Rates may be higher during Mardi Gras Festival & football wkends)

★ ★ ★ **HOLIDAY INN-NEW ORLEANS AIRPORT.** *2929 Williams Blvd (70062), near New Orleans Intl Airport.* 504/467-5611; FAX 504/469-4915. 304 rms, 2 bldgs, 2-5 story. S $95; D $109; each addl $10; under 19 free; wkend rates. Crib free. TV; cable (premium). Indoor pool; poolside serv. Restaurant 6 am-10 pm. Rm serv. Bar noon-2 am; entertainment, dancing Thurs-Sun. Ck-out noon. Coin lndry. Meeting rms. Business servs avail. In-rm modem link. Bellhops. Valet serv. Sundries. Free airport transportation. Holidome. Game rm. Cr cds: A, C, D, DS, JCB, MC, V.

D 🏊 ✈ 🛏 🔥 SC

★ ★ **LA QUINTA.** *2610 Williams Blvd (70062), near New Orleans Intl Airport.* 504/466-1401; FAX 504/466-0319. 194 rms, 5 story. S $65-$85; D $71-$100; under 18 free. Crib free. TV; cable (premium). Pool. Complimentary continental bkfst. Restaurant nearby. Ck-out noon. Meeting rms. Coin lndry. Valet serv. Free airport transportation. Cr cds: A, D, DS, MC, V.

D 🏊 ✈ 🛏 🔥 SC

★ ★ **RADISSON AIRPORT.** *2150 Veterans Blvd (70062), near New Orleans Intl Airport.* 504/467-3111; FAX 504/469-4634. 247 rms, 8 story. Feb-May: S, D $59-$109; suites $275-$350; under 18 free. Crib free. Pet accepted, some restrictions. $100. TV; cable (premium), VCR avail. Pool; poolside serv. Complimentary coffee in rms. Restaurant 6:30 am-10 pm. Rm serv. Bar 3 pm-midnight. Ck-out noon. Meeting rms. Business servs avail. Bellhops. Sundries. Valet serv. Free airport transportation. Refrigerators avail. Cr cds: A, C, D, DS, ER, MC, V.

D 🐾 🏊 ✈ 🛏 🔥

Hotel

★ ★ ★ **HILTON-NEW ORLEANS AIRPORT.** *901 Airline Hwy (70063), near New Orleans Intl Airport.* 504/469-5000; FAX 504/466-5473. 317 units, 6 story. S $108-$141; D $118-$151; each addl $10; suites $295-$395; family rates; wkend rates. Crib free. TV; cable (premium), VCR avail. Pool; poolside serv. Coffee in rms. Restaurant 6 am-10:30 pm. Bar 11-1 am. Ck-out 1 pm. Convention facilities. Business servs avail. In-rm modem link. Gift shop. Free airport transportation. Lighted tennis. Golf privileges, putting green. Exercise equipt; weight machines, bicycles, whirlpool. Minibars. Cr cds: A, C, D, DS, ER, JCB, MC, V.

D 🏃 🏌 🏊 🤾 ✈ 🛏 🔥 SC

Lafayette (D-3)

(See New Iberia, Opelousas, St Martinville)

Founded 1823 **Pop** 94,440 **Elev** 41 ft **Area code** 318
Information Lafayette Convention & Visitors Commission, 1400 NW Evangeline Thrwy, PO Box 52066, 70505; 800/346-1958.

Acadians from Nova Scotia came to the Lafayette area to escape British persecution. A significant percentage of today's residents continue to speak French or a patois and continue to maintain a strong feeling of kinship with Nova Scotia and France. These descendants of the French Acadians form the nucleus of the Louisiana Cajuns, who have contributed greatly to the state's rich culture.

Today, Lafayette is a commercial city, built around retail trade, light industry, agriculture and oil. Area farmers produce soybeans, rice, sugar cane as well as beef and dairy products. Many oil companies drilling for and pumping offshore oil have regional offices in the area, with headquarters in Lafayette's Heymann Oil Center.

Despite its industrial image, Lafayette has retained its "small-town" charm. Live oaks and azaleas abound around the town, as do clumps of native iris, the city's official flower. Tours of the navigable Bayou Vermilion are now available to visitors.

What to See and Do

Acadian Village: A Museum of Acadian Heritage and Culture. This restored, 19th-century Acadian village features fine examples of unique Acadian architecture with houses, a general store and a chapel. Crafts displays and sales. (Daily; closed Mardi Gras, major hols) Sr citizen rate. 5 mi S via US 167, Johnston St S, Ridge Rd W. Phone 318/981-2364 or 800/962-9133. ¢¢

Chretien Point Plantation (1831). Restored Greek-revival mansion; site of a Civil War battle; stairway of manor copied for Tara in the 1939 movie *Gone with the Wind.* (Daily; closed major hols) 5 mi W on I-10 to LA 93, 11 mi N to LA 356, west 1 blk to Parish Rd 2-151, then 1 mi N. Phone 318/662-5876 or 318/233-7050. ¢¢¢

Lafayette Museum (1800-1849). Once residence of Alexandre Mouton, first Democratic governor of the state, the house is now a museum with antique furnishings, Civil War relics and carnival costumes. (Daily exc Mon; closed Mardi Gras, major hols) 1122 Lafayette St. Phone 318/234-2208. Sr citizen rate. ¢¢

Lafayette Natural History Museum, Planetarium and Nature Station. Planetarium programs; environmental trails and nature station; changing exhibits. (Daily; closed Mardi Gras, hols) 637 Girard Park Dr. Phone 318/268-5544. Museum ¢¢

University Art Museum. There are two locations: the permanent collection is at 101 Girard Park Drive (Mon-Fri; closed major hols); changing exhibits are staged at Fletcher Hall, East Lewis and Girard Park Circle (Mon-Fri, also Sun afternoons; closed major hols). Phone 318/482-5326. Permanent collection **Free.** Fletcher Hall exhibits ¢

University of Southwestern Louisiana (1900). (16,200 students) The tree-shaded campus serves as an arboretum with many Southern plant species. Cypress Lake, a miniature Louisiana cypress swamp, has fish, alligators and native irises. Facilities for the disabled (wheelchair access). E University Ave. Phone 318/482-1000.

Annual Events

Azalea Trail. Mid-Mar.

Festival International de Louisiane. International and Louisiana performing and visual arts and cuisine. Phone 318/232-8086. Mid-Apr.

Festivals Acadiens. Cajun music & food festival. 3rd wkend Sept.

Seasonal Event

Thoroughbred racing. Evangeline Downs. 3 mi N on US 167. Parimutuel betting. Proper attire required in clubhouse. Phone 318/896-7223. Early Apr-Labor Day, Mon & Thurs-Sat; also some Sun.

Motels

★ ★ **COMFORT INN.** *1421 SE Evangeline Thrwy (70501), near airport.* 318/232-9000; FAX 318/233-8629. 200 rms, 2 story. S $52-$58; D $57-$63; each addl $5; suites $99-$110; under 18 free; family rates; higher rates Crawfish Festival. Crib free. Pet accepted, some restrictions. TV; cable (premium). Pool. Complimentary continental bkfst. Complimentary coffee in rms. Restaurant 6 am-2 pm, 5-10 pm. Rm serv. Bar 2 pm-2 am; entertainment. Ck-out noon. Coin lndry. Meeting rms. Business center. In-rm modem link. Bellhops. Gift shop. Valet serv. Free airport, RR station, bus depot transportation. Exercise equipt; weights, bicycles. Refrigerators. Cr cds: A, C, D, DS, ER, JCB, MC, V.

⬜ 🧺 🏊 🏃 ✈ 🎿 🔥 SC 🚶

✔★ **HOLIDAY INN EXPRESS.** *2503 SE Evangeline Thrwy (70508), near Municipal Airport.* 318/234-2000; FAX 318/234-6373. 102 rms, 2 story. S, D $51-$57; each addl $6; under 18 free; higher rates Crawfish Festival. Crib free. TV; cable (premium), VCR avail. Complimentary bkfst. Restaurant adj 6 am-2 pm, 4:30-10 pm. Ck-out noon. Coin lndry. Meeting rms. Business servs avail. Valet serv. Free airport transportation. Tennis privileges. Health club privileges. Some refrigerators, wet bars. Cr cds: A, C, D, DS, JCB, MC, V.

⬜ 🏊 ✈ 🔥 SC

★★ **HOLIDAY INN NORTH.** *2716 NE Evangeline Thrwy (70507), at I-10.* 318/233-0003; FAX 318/233-0360. 196 rms, 2 story. S, D $54-$60; each addl $6; under 18 free. Crib free. TV; cable (premium). Pool; wading pool. Complimentary coffee in rms. Restaurant 6:30 am-10 pm. Rm serv. Bar 4:30 pm-2 am. Ck-out noon. Coin lndry. Meeting rms. Business center. Bellhops. Valet serv. Free airport transportation. Exercise equipt; weights, weight machine. Game rm. Cr cds: A, C, D, DS, JCB, MC, V.

⬜ 🎿 🔥 SC 🚶

★ **LA QUINTA.** *2100 NE Evangeline Thrwy (70501), at I-10.* 318/233-5610; FAX 318/235-2104. 138 rms, 2 story. S $52-$59; D $59-$69; each addl $7; under 18 free. Crib free. Pet accepted, some restrictions. TV; cable (premium). Pool. Complimentary continental bkfst. Restaurant adj open 24 hrs. Ck-out noon. Meeting rms. Business servs avail. Airport transportation. Cr cds: A, C, D, DS, MC, V.

⬜ 🧺 🎿 🔥 SC

✔★ **RED ROOF INN.** *1718 N University Ave (70507), I-10 exit 101.* 318/233-3339. 108 rms, 2 story. S $29.99; D $36.99-$39.99; each addl $7; under 18 free; higher rates special events. Crib free. Pet accepted, some restrictions. TV. Complimentary coffee in lobby. Restaurant nearby. Ck-out noon. Meeting rms. Business servs avail. Sundries. Valet serv. Free airport transportation. Cr cds: A, C, D, DS, MC, V.

⬜ 🧺 🎿 🔥 SC

✔★ **TRAVELODGE.** *1101 W Pinhook Rd (70503).* 318/234-7402; FAX 318/234-7404. 61 rms, 2 story. S $38-$40; D $43-$50; each addl $3; under 18 free; higher rates special events. Crib free. TV; cable (premium). Pool. Complimentary coffee in rms. Complimentary continental bkfst. Restaurant adj 11 am-10 pm. Ck-out noon. Valet serv. Refrigerators avail. Cr cds: A, C, D, DS, MC, V.

⬜ 🧺 🎿 🔥 SC

Motor Hotels

★★ **HOTEL ACADIANA.** *1801 W Pinhook Rd (70508), 5 mi SW of I-10 exit 103A, via Evangeline Thrwy.* 318/233-8120; res: 800/826-8386 (exc LA), 800/874-4664 (LA); FAX 318/234-9667. 290 rms, 6 story. S, D $69-$79; each addl $10; suites $175-$225; under 18 free. TV; cable (premium), VCR avail. Pool. Restaurant 6 am-10 pm. Bars 11-2 am; entertainment, dancing exc Sun, Mon. Ck-out noon. Convention facilities. Business center. In-rm modem link. Free airport transportation. Refrigerators, wet bars. Luxury level. Cr cds: A, C, D, DS, MC, V.

⬜ 🧺 🎿 🔥 SC 🚶

✔★ **RAMADA INN-AIRPORT.** *2501 SE Evangeline Thrwy (70508), near Municipal Airport.* 318/234-8521; FAX 318/232-5764. 192 rms. S $44-$48; D $52-$56; each addl $6; suites $120; under 18 free. Crib free. TV; cable (premium), VCR avail. Pool. Restaurant 6 am-2 pm, 4:30-10 pm. Rm serv. Bar 4:30 pm-midnight. Ck-out noon. Coin lndry avail. Meeting rms avail. Business center. In-rm modem link. Bellhops. Valet serv. Free airport, RR station transportation. Lighted tennis. Exer-

cise equipt; weight machine, bicycles, sauna. Wet bar in suites. Cr cds: A, C, D, DS, ER, JCB, MC, V.

⬜ 🎿 🏊 🏃 ✈ 🎿 🔥 SC 🚶

Hotel

★★★ **HILTON & TOWERS.** *1521 W Pinhook Rd (70505).* 318/235-6111; FAX 318/261-0311. 327 rms, 15 story. S $75-$85; D $80-$95; each addl $10; suites $155-$205. TV; cable (premium), VCR avail. Pool; poolside serv. Restaurant 6 am-10 pm. Bar 11:30-2 am; dancing. Ck-out noon. Business center. In-rm modem link. Airport transportation. Game rm. Some bathrm phones. Private patios. Boat dock. River walk. Luxury level. Cr cds: A, C, D, DS, MC, V.

⬜ 🧺 🎿 🔥 SC 🚶

Inn

★★ **TANTE DA'S.** *2631 SE Evangeline Thrwy (70508), I-10 exit 103A, near Regional Airport.* 318/264-1191. 4 rms. Rm phone by request. S $75-$100; D $85-$125; family rates, wkly rates; 2-day min stay for special events. TV in sitting rm. Complimentary full bkfst, afternoon tea/sherry. Restaurant adj 11 am-10 pm; wkend hrs vary. Ck-out 10 am, ck-in 4-6 pm. Free airport, RR station transportation. Queen Anne-revival cottage built 1902, reconstructed and moved to this site in 1989. Totally nonsmoking. Cr cds: A, DS, MC, V.

✈ 🎿 🔥 🚶

Restaurants

★★★ **BLAIR HOUSE.** *1316 Surrey (70501).* 318/234-0357. Hrs: 11 am-10 pm; Fri to 10:30 pm; Sat 5-10:30 pm. Closed some major hols. Res accepted. Bar. Semi-a la carte: lunch $6-$10, dinner $7.95-$19.95. Child's meals. Specializes in steak, fresh seafood, Cajun dishes. Own baking. Parking. Family-owned. Cr cds: A, D, DS, MC, V.

⬜

★★★ **CAFE VERMILIONVILLE.** *1304 W Pinhook Rd (70503).* 318/237-0100. Hrs: 11 am-2 pm, 5:30-10 pm; Sat from 5:30 pm; Sun 11 am-2 pm. Closed some major hols. Res accepted. Cajun creole menu. Bar. Semi-a la carte: lunch $6.95-$15.95, dinner $14.95-$23.95. Brunch $7.95-$17.95. Specializes in fresh seafood, grilled steaks, Acadian crawfish dishes. Own baking. Parking. Outdoor dining. Lafayette's earliest inn. Cr cds: A, D, DS, MC, V.

⬜

★★★ **CHARLEY G'S SEAFOOD GRILL.** *3809 Ambassador Caffery Pkwy (70503).* 318/981-0108. Hrs: 11 am-2 pm, 5:30-10 pm; Fri, Sat to 11 pm. Sun brunch 11 am-2 pm. Closed major hols. Res accepted. Bar to 11 pm. A la carte entrees: lunch $6.95-$17, dinner $6.95-$19. Specializes in Creole & Cajun cuisine. Entertainment Fri-Sun. Parking. Cr cds: A, MC, V.

✔★ **DON'S SEAFOOD & STEAK HOUSE.** *301 E Vermilion St (70501).* 318/235-3551. Hrs: 11 am-9:30 pm; Fri & Sat to 10:30 pm. Closed Dec 25; Mardi Gras. Res accepted. Regional menu. Bar. Semi-a la carte: lunch $5.95-$8.95, dinner $9.50-$15.95. Child's meals. Specialties: stuffed red snapper, crabmeat au gratin, oyster en brochette. Parking. Rustic decor. Cr cds: A, C, D, DS, MC, V.

⬜

★★ **I MONELLI.** *4017 Johnston St (70503).* 318/989-9291. Hrs: 11:30 am-2 pm, 5:30-10 pm. Closed Sun & Mon; some major hols; also Mardi Gras & Ash Wednesday. Res accepted. Italian menu. A la carte entrees: lunch $3.95-$9.95, dinner $7.95-$18.95. Specializes in cannelloni, spaghetti al pesto, shrimp scampi. Parking. Intimate dining. Cr cds: A, DS, MC, V.

⬜

★ ★ **LA FONDA.** *3809 Johnston St (70506).* 318/984-5630. Hrs: 11 am-10 pm. Closed Sun, Mon; also wk of July 4, Thanksgiving-following Tues. Mexican, Amer menu. Bar. Semi-a la carte: lunch, dinner $5-$13. Specializes in steak, chicken. Own tortillas. Parking. Cr cds: A, C, D, DS, MC, V.

D

★ **POOR BOY'S RIVERSIDE INN.** *(240 Tubing Rd, Broussard 70518) S on US 90, right on Southpark Rd to Tubing Rd.* 318/837-4011. Hrs: 11 am-10 pm; Fri to 11 pm; Sat 5-11 pm. Closed Sun; some major hols. Res accepted. Cajun menu. Serv bar. Complete meals: lunch $6.25. Semi-a la carte: dinner $9.50-$21.95. Specializes in flounder, shrimp, crabmeat dishes. Parking. In rural setting overlooking pond. Family-owned. Cr cds: A, C, D, DS, MC, V.

D

★ **PREJEAN'S.** *3480 US 167N (70507).* 318/896-3247. Hrs: 11 am-10 pm; Fri, Sat to 11 pm. Closed Jan 1, Dec 25. Res accepted. Cajun menu. Bar. A la carte entrees: lunch $5.95-$9.95, dinner $9.25-$16.95. Child's meals. Specializes in alligator, steak, fresh seafood. Cajun band. Parking. Cajun artifacts; mounted, stuffed wildlife on display, including a 14-ft alligator believed to have been 65 yrs old when captured. Cr cds: A, D, DS, MC, V.

D SC

★ **PRUDHOMME'S CAJUN CAFE.** *4676 NE Evangeline Thrwy (70520).* 318/896-7964. Hrs: 11 am-10 pm; Sun to 2:30 pm. Closed Mon; Jan 1, Easter, Dec 25. Cajun menu. Bar. Semi-a la carte: lunch $6.25, dinner $8.75-$19.45. Specialities: pan-fried stuffed catfish, pan-fried rabbit, eggplant pirogue. Parking. Rustic decor; antique photographs. Cr cds: A, MC, V.

D

✔ ★ ★ **ROBIN'S.** *(Box 542, Henderson 70517) I-10, exit 115, 2 mi E on LA 352.* 318/228-7594. Hrs: 10 am-10 pm; Fri, Sat to 11 pm. Closed Thanksgiving, Dec 24-26. Res accepted. Cajun, Creole menu. Serv bar. Semi-a la carte: lunch, dinner $7-$14. Child's meals. Specialties: crawfish, crabmeat au gratin, frogs' legs étouffées. Parking. Cr cds: A, C, D, DS, MC, V.

D

★ **RUTH'S CHRIS STEAK HOUSE.** *507 W Pinhook Rd (70508).* 318/237-6123. Hrs: 11 am-11:30 pm; Sat from 4 pm; Sun 3-10 pm. Closed some major hols; also Good Friday. Res accepted. Bar. A la carte entrees: lunch $12-$20, dinner $25-$40. Specializes in prime beef, Maine lobster. Parking. Cr cds: A, C, D, ER, MC, V.

Unrated Dining Spot

PICCADILLY CAFETERIA. *100 Arnould, 3 mi SW on US 167 to Johnston St, then 3 mi W.* 318/984-7876. Hrs: 11 am-8:30 pm. Closed Dec 25. Avg ck: lunch, dinner $6. Specialties: crawfish étouffée, fruit & creme pie. Parking. Cr cds: A, DS, MC, V.

RANDOL'S. *2320 Kaliste Saloom Rd.* 318/981-7080. Hrs: 5-10:30 pm. Closed some major hols. Cajun menu. Bar. Semi-a la carte: dinner $5.95-$14.95. Child's meals. Specializes in steamed crabs, crawfish. Cajun music. Located in restored 19th-century Cajun dance hall. Cr cds: MC, V.

D

Lake Charles (D-2)

Founded ca 1781 **Pop** 70,580 **Elev** 20 ft **Area code** 318

Information Southwest Louisiana Convention & Visitors Bureau, located off I-10 on North Beach, 1211 N Lakeshore Dr, PO Box 1912, 70602; 318/436-9588 or 800/456-SWLA.

In approximately 1781, a Frenchman named Charles Sallier settled on the shore of a pleasant lake, married and built a house. His property became known to travelers as "Charlie's Lake," and his hospitality became famous. However, the town grew slowly until the Southern Pacific Railroad's link between Houston and New Orleans was finished. Stimulated by railroad transportation and under the more sedate name of "Lake Charles," the town began its real growth, mainly via timber and rice culture. Captain J.B. Watkins began a tremendous penny-postcard publicity campaign in 1887. It was effective, but not so effective as the discovery of oil and sulphur early in the 20th century. In 1926, when a deepwater port was opened, the city's future was assured.

A massive reforestation project, centered around Lake Charles and begun in the 1950s, revitalized the area's lumber industry. Now oil, rubber and chemicals have joined cattle and rice to make this a vital industrial center. McNeese State University is located in Lake Charles.

What to See and Do

Brimstone Historical Society Museum. Commemorates turn-of-the-century birth of the local sulphur industry with exhibits explaining the development of the Frasch mining process; other exhibits deal with southwest Louisiana; also traveling exhibits. (Mon-Fri; closed hols) 800 Picard Rd in Frasch Park, 11 mi W via I-10, exit N onto Ruth St, then W on Logan St in Sulphur. Phone 318/527-7142. **Free.**

"Charpentier" Historical District. District includes 20 square blocks of downtown area; architectural styles range from Queen Anne, Eastlake and "Carpenter's Gothic" (known locally as "Lake Charles style") to Western stick-style bungalows. Tours (fee) and brochures describing self-guided tours may be obtained at the Convention & Visitors Bureau.

Creole Nature Trail Scenic Byway. Follow LA 27 in a circular route ending back at Lake Charles. Unique composite of wildflowers, animals, shrimp, crab, many varieties of fish plus one of the largest alligator populations in the world; winter habitat of thousands of ducks and geese; views of several bayous, Intracoastal Waterway, oil platforms, beaches, beach for wildlife refuges and a bird sanctuary. Automobile nature trail (105 mi); walking nature trail (1½ mi). (Daily) Begins 15 mi SW off I-10 via LA 27. For map contact the Convention & Visitors Bureau. **Free.**

Fishing, hunting. On and around Lake Calcasieu. Fishing in Calcasieu River; deep-sea, jetty fishing at Cameron, Gulf of Mexico.

Imperial Calcasieu Museum. Items of local historical interest. Complete rooms and shops; toy collection, rare Audubon prints. Gibson-Barham Gallery houses art exhibits. On premises is the 300-yr-old Sallier Oak tree. (Daily exc Mon; closed major hols) 204 W Sallier St. Phone 318/439-3797. ¢

Port of Lake Charles. Docks and turning basin. Ships pass down the Calcasieu ship channel and through Lake Calcasieu. W end of Shell Beach Dr.

Sam Houston Jones State Park. The approx 1,000 acres include lagoons in a densely wooded area at the confluence of the west fork of the Caslcasieu and Houston Rivers and Indian Bayou. Fishing; boating (rentals, launch). Nature trails, hiking. Picnicking. Tent and trailer sites (hookups, dump station), cabins. Standard fees. (Daily) 12 mi N, off US 171 on LA 378. Contact 107 Sutherland Rd; 70611; 318/855-2665. Per vehicle ¢

Annual Event

Contraband Days. Lake Charles Civic Center. Honors "gentleman pirate" Jean Lafitte. Boat races, midway, concerts, arts & crafts display. 2 wks early May.

Seasonal Event

Horse racing. Delta Downs. 30 mi W via I-10 in Vinton. Minimum age 18. Jacket required in Clubhouse, Skyline. Thoroughbreds Sept-Mar, Thurs-Sat evenings; Sun matinee; no racing Jan 1, Super Bowl Sun, Easter, Mother's Day and wk of Dec 25. Also quarterhorse racing

Apr-Labor Day. For schedule, reservations phone 318/589-7441 or 433-3206

Motels

✔★★ **BEST WESTERN-RICHMOND SUITES.** *920 N US 171 (70601), I-10 at US 171.* 318/433-5213; FAX 318/439-4243. 146 rms, 2 story, 30 kit. suites. S $69-$89; D $79-$99; each addl $10; kit. suites $79-$89; under 18 free. Crib free. TV; cable (premium). Pool; hot tub. Playground. Complimentary bkfst buffet. Ck-out noon. Coin lndry. Meeting rms. Business center. Airport transportation. Exercise equipt; weight machine, rowing machine. Private patios, balconies. Cr cds: A, C, D, DS, MC, V.

★ **CHATEAU CHARLES.** *(2600 US 90W, Westlake 70669)* at jct I-10. 318/882-6130; FAX 318/882-6601. 222 rms. S $64-$74; D $60-$72; each addl $8; suites $155-$205; under 12 free; wkend rates. Crib free. TV; cable (premium). Pool; poolside serv. Restaurant open 24 hrs. Rm serv. Bar 11-2 am; entertainment, dancing exc Sun. Ck-out noon. Business center. Bellhops. Coin lndry. Airport transportation. Refrigerators. Cr cds: A, C, D, DS, MC, V.

Motor Hotel

★★ **HOLIDAY INN.** *505 N Lakeshore Dr (70601), I-10 exit 29 & 30A.* 318/433-7121; FAX 318/436-8459. 269 rms, 4 story. S $66-$96; D $76-$106; each addl $10; suites $250-$350; under 18 free; wkend rates. Crib free. TV; cable (premium). Pool; poolside serv. Restaurant 6 am-midnight. Rm serv. Bar 6-2 am. Ck-out noon. Convention facilities. Business servs avail. In-rm modem link. Bellhops. Valet serv. Free local airport transportation. Some refrigerators, wet bars. On lake. Cr cds: A, C, D, DS, MC, V.

Restaurants

★★★ **CAFE MARGAUX.** *765 Bayou Pines East (70601).* 318/433-2902. Hrs: 11 am-2 pm, 6-10 pm; Sat from 6 pm. Closed Sun; Dec 25. Res accepted. French, continental menu. Bar. Wine cellar. Semi-a la carte: lunch $6.50-$12.75, dinner $18.50-$24.50. Buffet: lunch $8.45. Specializes in seafood, veal. Own pastries. Parking. Cr cds: A, C, D, DS, MC, V.

★★★ **CHÂTEAU NOUVEAU.** *815 Bayou Pines Dr (70601).* 318/439-8364. Hrs: 6-9 pm; Fri, Sat to 9:30 pm. Closed Sun; major hols. Res accepted. Continental menu. Bar. A la carte entrees: dinner $12.75-$24. Specialties: New Orleans turtle soup, filet mignon au poivre vert, fish almondine. Parking. Victorian decor; antiques. Cr cds: A, DS, MC, V.

★★ **HUNTER'S HARLEQUIN.** *1717 LA 14 (70601), at Legion St.* 318/439-2780. Hrs: 11 am-2 pm, 4-11 pm; Sat from 4 pm. Closed Sun; major hols. Res accepted. Bar. Semi-a la carte: lunch $4.25-$10.95, dinner $10.50-$20.75. Child's meals. Specializes in steak, crab dishes, tuna steak. Salad bar. Parking. Several dining rms provide intimate atmosphere; attractive landscaping. Family-owned. Cr cds: A, MC, V.

★ **JEAN LAFITTE.** *505 W College St (70605).* 318/474-2730. Hrs: 11 am-10 pm; Sat 5-11 pm. Closed Sun; major hols. Cajun, Amer menu. Bar. Semi-a la carte: lunch $5.35-$13.95, dinner $9-$19.50. Child's meals. Specializes in fresh seafood, steak, crawfish.

Parking. Acadian atmosphere; scenes & maps of Louisiana on walls, bookshelves with old books. Cr cds: A, DS, MC, V.

★ **PAT'S OF HENDERSON.** *1500 Siebarth Dr (70601).* 318/439-6618. Hrs: 11 am-10 pm; Fri & Sat to 10:30 pm; Sun to 9 pm. Closed Thanksgiving, Dec 25. Res accepted. Cajun, Amer menu. Bar. Semi-a la carte: lunch $6.50-$15, dinner $10-$15. Child's meals. Specializes in rib-eye steak, stuffed snapper, seafood. Parking. Colonial design with walnut paneling and framed portraits. Cr cds: A, C, D, MC, V.

★ **PAW PAW'S.** *300 US 171 (70601).* 318/439-5410. Hrs: 11 am-11 pm. Res accepted. Cajun menu. Bar; Sun from noon. Semi-a la carte: lunch $7.95-$12.95, dinner $7.95-$14.95. Child's meals. Specializes in crawfish & catfish dishes. Parking. Three dining rms with nautical theme; shrimp boat in pond. Family-owned. No cr cds accepted.

✔★ **PEKING GARDEN.** *2433 E Broad St (70601).* 318/436-3597. Hrs: 11 am-2 pm, 5-10 pm; Fri, Sat to 11 pm. Closed Thanksgiving. Chinese menu. Bar. Semi-a la carte: lunch $4.45-$6.95, dinner $6.95-$10.75. Child's meals. Specializes in Hunan cuisine, steak, seafood. Parking. Chinese artifacts in dining rm. Cr cds: A, MC, V.

★ **TONY'S PIZZA.** *335 E Prien Lake Rd (70601).* 318/477-1611. Hrs: 10 am-midnight. Closed Thanksgiving, Dec 25. Italian menu. Beer. A la carte entrees: lunch, dinner $4.50-$6.50. Specializes in pizza, deli sandwiches, salads. Own pasta. Parking. Popular with locals, this restaurant has a very friendly, family-oriented atmosphere. Family-owned. Cr cds: A, D, DS, MC, V.

Many (B-2)

(For accommodations see Natchitoches)

Settled 1837 **Pop** 3,112 **Elev** 321 ft **Area code** 318 **Zip** 71449
Information Sabine Parish Tourist Commission, 920 Fisher Rd, 318/256-5880; or contact the Louisiana Tourist Center, LA 6W, 318/256-4114.

What to See and Do

Fort Jesup State Commemorative Area. Fort established in 1822 by Zachary Taylor features restored 1830s army kitchen; reconstructed officers' quarters and museum (Daily; closed Jan 1, Thanksgiving, Dec 25); on 21 acres. Picnic facilities. Sr citizen rate. 6 mi E on LA 6. Phone 318/256-4117. ¢

Hodges Gardens. Has 4,700 acres of gardens, greenhouses; 225-acre lake. Wild and cultivated flowers and plants all yr. Terrazzo map commemorating Louisiana Purchase. Wildlife, fishing boat rentals, picnic facilities. Special events include Easter service, July 4 festival and Christmas lights festival. (Daily; closed Jan 1, Dec 24 & 25) Sr citizen rate. 12 mi S on US 171. Phone 318/586-3523. ¢¢¢

Toledo Bend Dam and Reservoir. W on LA 6. (See JASPER, TX)

Annual Events

Battle of Pleasant Hill Re-enactment. 18 mi N on LA 175, N of Pleasant Hill. Three-day event includes beauty pageant, Confederate ball, parade and battle re-enactment. Early Apr.

Sawmill Days. 8 mi S via US 171 in Fisher. 3rd wkend May.

Sabine Free State Festival. 10 mi S in Florien. Beauty pageant; syrup-making, basket-weaving and quilting demonstrations; arts & crafts exhibits; flea market. Phone 318/586-7286. 1st wkend Nov.

Metairie (D-5)

(See Kenner, New Orleans)

Pop 149,428 **Elev** 5 ft **Area code** 504

(Rates may be higher during Mardi Gras Festival & football wkends)

Motel

★ ★ **LA QUINTA.** *5900 Veterans Memorial Blvd (70003). 504/456-0003.* 153 rms, 3 story. S $64; D $71; suites $84; under 18 free. TV; cable (premium). Pool. Free continental bkfst. Restaurant adj open 24 hrs. Ck-out noon. Meeting rms. Business servs avail. In-rm modem link. Valet serv. Airport transportation. Cr cds: A, C, D, DS, MC, V.

[D] [≈] [⊠] [⊠] [SC]

Motor Hotels

★ ★ **HOLIDAY INN.** *3400 I-10 S Service Rd (70001). 504/833-8201; FAX 504/838-6829.* 195 rms, 4 story. S, D $65-$125; each addl $10; under 18 free. Crib free. TV; cable (premium). Pool. Complimentary coffee in rms. Restaurant 6 am-2 pm, 5:30-10 pm. Rm serv. Bar 4 pm-midnight. Ck-out noon. Coin lndry. Meeting rms. Business servs avail. In-rm modem link. Bellhops. Valet serv. Free airport transportation. Balconies. Cr cds: A, C, D, DS, JCB, MC, V.

[D] [≈] [⊠] [⊠] [SC]

★ **HOLIDAY INN I-10.** *6401 Veteran Blvd (70003), I-10 exit 225. 504/885-5700; FAX 504/454-8294.* 219 rms, 7 story. Jan-Apr & Oct-Nov: S $72-$150; D $82-$150; each addl $10; under 18 free; lower rates rest of yr. Crib free. TV; cable (premium), VCR avail. Pool; whirlpool. Restaurant 6 am-2 pm, 5-10 pm. Rm serv. Bar 4 pm-midnight. Ck-out noon. Meeting rms. Business servs avail. In-rm modem link. Bellhops. Sundries. Valet serv. Free airport, French Quarter transportation. Balconies. Cr cds: A, C, D, DS, MC, V.

[D] [≈] [⊠] [⊠] [SC]

Hotels

★ ★ **BEST WESTERN LANDMARK.** *2601 Severn Ave (70002), I-10 at Causeway. 504/888-9500; FAX 504/889-5792.* 342 rms, 17 story. S $65-$125; D $75-$145; each addl $10; suites $150-$275; higher rates Jazz Fest. Crib free. TV; cable (premium), VCR avail. Pool. Restaurant 6:30 am-10 pm. Bar to 1 am. Ck-out 11 am. Coin lndry. Meeting rms. Business servs avail. In-rm modem link. Gift shop. Free airport, French Quarter transportation. Exercise equipt; weight machine, bicycles, sauna. Balconies. Cr cds: A, C, D, DS, MC, V.

[D] [✦] [≈] [↑] [⊠] [⊠] [SC]

★ ★ **SHERATON-NORTH.** *3838 N Causeway Blvd (70002). 504/836-5253; FAX 504/846-4562.* 210 rms, 16 story. S, D $79-$165; suites $180; under 17 free; wkend rates. Crib free. TV; cable (premium). Indoor pool. Restaurant 6 am-10 pm. Rm serv to midnight. Bar noon-midnight. Ck-out noon. Meeting rms. Gift shop. Barber. Free garage parking. Free airport transportation. Lighted tennis. Exercise rm; instructor, weights, bicycles, whirlpool, sauna. Some refrigerators. View of Lake Pontchartrain. Luxury level. Cr cds: A, C, D, DS, JCB, MC, V.

[D] [✦] [≈] [↑] [✦] [⊠] [⊠] [SC]

Restaurants

★ ★ ★ **ANDREA'S.** *3100 19th St (70002). 504/834-8583.* Hrs: 11 am-10 pm; wkend hrs vary; Sun brunch 11 am-3 pm. Closed Jan 1, July 4, Labor Day. Res accepted. Northern Italian, continental menu. Bar. Wine list. Semi-a la carte: lunch, dinner $8.95-$26.50. Complete meals: dinner $29.95. Brunch $17.95. Child's meals. Specializes in pasta dishes, seafood, veal. Own baking. Cr cds: A, C, D, DS, MC, V.

[SC]

★ ★ **AUGIE'S GLASS GARDEN.** *3300 S I-10 Service Rd. 504/835-3300.* Hrs: 11 am-11 pm; Sun to 9 pm. Res accepted. Cajun, Creole menu. Bar. Semi-a la carte: lunch $6.95-$9.95, dinner $10.95-$28. Child's meals. Specializes in seafood, veal. Own bread pudding. Jazz band Wed-Sun. Parking. Waterfalls, plants. Cr cds: A, DS, MC, V.

[D] [SC]

★ ★ ★ **CROZIER'S RESTAURANT FRANCAIS.** *3216 W Esplanade N. 504/833-8108.* Hrs: 5:30-10 pm. Closed Sun, Mon; major hols. Res accepted. French provincial menu. Bar. Wine list. Semi-a la carte: dinner $20-$24. Child's meals. Own baking. Parking. French country decor. Cr cds: A, C, D, DS, MC, V.

[D]

★ ★ **IMPASTATO'S.** *3400 16th St. 504/455-1545.* Hrs: 5 pm-midnight; early-bird dinner 5-6 pm. Closed Sun, Mon; most hols; also Mardi Gras. Res accepted. Italian menu. Bar. Semi-a la carte: dinner $20-$38. Specializes in fettucine, fresh Maine lobster, fresh grilled salmon, pecan smoked filet mignon. Vocalist. Cr cds: A, MC, V.

[D] [SC]

★ ★ **LA RIVIERA.** *4506 Shores Dr, off N Clearview Pkwy, 1 blk W on Belle Dr to Shores Dr. 504/888-6238.* Hrs: 11:30 am-2 pm, 5:30-10 pm; Mon from 5:30; Fri, Sat 5:30-11 pm. Closed Sun; major hols; also wk before Labor Day. Res accepted. Italian, Amer menu. Bar. A la carte entrees: lunch, dinner $10.95-$17. Complete meals: dinner $19-$28. Child's meals. Specializes in pasta, veal dishes, seafood. Own baking. Parking. Family-owned. Cr cds: A, C, D, DS, JCB, MC, V.

[D]

✔ ★ ★ **RALPH & KACOO'S.** *601 Veterans Memorial Blvd. 504/831-3177.* Hrs: 11 am-10 pm; Fri, Sat to 11 pm; Sun to 9 pm. Closed Thanksgiving, Dec 25; also Mardi Gras. Cajun seafood menu. Bar. Semi-a la carte: lunch, dinner $4.95-$17.95. Specialties: trout Ruby, shrimp, crawfish. Valet parking. Cr cds: A, C, D, DS, MC, V.

[D]

Unrated Dining Spots

MORNING CALL. *3325 Severn Ave, at 17th St. 504/885-4068.* Open 24 hrs. Closed Jan 1, Mardi Gras, Dec 25. Specialties: beignets and New Orleans chicory coffee (cafe au lait). No cr cds accepted.

PICCADILLY CAFETERIA. *8908 Veterans Blvd. 504/467-4224.* Hrs: 11 am-8:30 pm. Closed Dec 25. Avg ck: lunch, dinner $5.75. Specializes in fresh salads, vegetables, desserts. No cr cds accepted.

[D]

Minden (A-2)

(For accommodations see Bossier City, Shreveport)

Founded 1836 **Pop** 13,661 **Elev** 259 ft **Area code** 318 **Zip** 71055

Information Chamber of Commerce, 101 Sibley Rd, PO Box 819, 71058; 318/377-4240.

What to See and Do

Germantown Museum. Museum includes three buildings completed in 1835 by Germans seeking freedom from persecution; replicas of commune smokehouse and blacksmith shop; records and artifacts used by the settlers. (Wed-Sun) 8 mi NE via I-20 and Parish Rd 114. Phone 318/377-6061. ¢¢

Lake Bistineau State Park. This 750-acre park in heart of pine forest includes a large lake. Swimming, waterskiing; fishing; boating (rentals, launch). Tent & trailer sites, cabins. Standard fees. (Daily) 9 mi SW on US 79, 80, then 13 mi S on LA 163. Phone 318/745-3503. Per vehicle ¢

Monroe and West Monroe (A-3)

(See Bastrop)

Settled 1785 **Pop** Monroe: 54,909; West Monroe: 14,096 **Elev** 74 ft **Area code** 318 **Zip** West Monroe: 71291

Information Monroe-West Monroe Convention & Visitors Bureau, 1333 State Farm Dr, Monroe 71202; 318/387-5691.

In March 1783, a swashbuckling young French adventurer named Jean Baptiste Filhiol, then in the service of the King of Spain, married the beautiful daughter of a wealthy Opelousas family. Shortly thereafter he took her in a keelboat up the Mississippi, the Red, the Black and Ouachita rivers into the wilderness to establish a great personal estate. Flooded out, Filhiol and his bride moved downstream to the site of Monroe, where he settled, calling his post Fort Miro in honor of the Spanish governor.

Filhiol was an excellent administrator, and the post prospered. In 1819 the first steamboat, the *James Monroe,* traveled up the Ouachita. After some shipboard conviviality, residents decided to rename their town for the boat.

The Monroe natural gas field, one of the world's largest, affords the city a great industrial advantage; nearby forests provide raw materials for the paper products, furniture and chemicals produced in Monroe.

What to See and Do

✪ **Emy-Lou Biedenharn Foundation.** (Daily exc Mon; closed major hols) 2006 Riverside Dr. Phone 318/387-5281. **Free.** Includes

Bible Museum. Museum-library contains early and rare Bibles, archaeological artifacts, coins, antique musical instruments and furnishings.

Biedenharn family house, (1914). Built by Joseph Biedenharn, first bottler of Coca-Cola, contains antiques, fine furnishings, silver dating from 18th century and Coca-Cola memorabilia.

ELsong Gardens & Conservatory. These formal gardens, enclosed within brick walls, were originally designed to accommodate musical events. Today, background music is triggered by lasers as visitors stroll through separate gardens linked by winding paths. There are four fountains, including a porcelain fountain from garden of Russian Empress Catherine the Great.

Fishing, water sports. Ouachita River in city; Chenière Lake (3,600 acres) 4 miles west; D'Arbonne Lake (15,000 acres) 35 miles north; Bayou DeSiard (1,200 acres) 3 miles northeast; Black Bayou (2,600 acres) 6 miles north.

Louisiana Purchase Gardens and Zoo. Formal gardens, moss-laden live oaks, waterways and winding paths surround naturalistic habitats for more than 850 exotic animals in this 80-acre zoo; boat and miniature train rides. Picnicking, concessions. (Daily; closed Thanksgiving, Dec 25; rides, concessions, Apr-Oct only). Special trail for disabled. Sr citizen rate. Bernstein Park Dr. Phone 318/329-2400. ¢¢

Masur Museum of Art. Permanent and changing exhibits. (Tues-Thurs, also Fri-Sun afternoons; closed major hols) 1400 S Grand St. Phone 318/329-2237. **Free.**

Northeast Louisiana University (1931). (11,000 students) 700 University Ave. Phone 318/342-1000. On campus are

Bry Hall Art Gallery. Art exhibits, photographs by American and foreign artists, students, faculty. (Mon-Fri; closed Easter, July 4, Thanksgiving, also mid-Aug-early Sept, mid-Dec-early Jan) Phone 318/342-1375. **Free.**

Museum of Natural History. Geological exhibits include Native American, Latin American and African artifacts. (Mon-Fri; closed Easter, July 4, Thanksgiving, also mid-Aug-early Sept, mid-Dec-early Jan) 3rd floor of Hanna Hall. Phone 318/342-1878. **Free.**

Museum of Zoology. Fishes collection is one of the largest and most complete in the nation. (Mon-Fri; closed Easter, July 4, Thanksgiving, also mid-Aug-early Sept, mid-Dec-early Jan) 1st floor of Garret Hall. Phone 318/342-1799. **Free.**

Rebecca's Doll House. Approximately 2,000 antique artist dolls; French, German, Parian, china, cloth, metal, wax, composition, primitive, peddler, pincushion dolls. Hand-carved wooden dolls portray the Last Supper. (By appt only) 4500 Bon Aire Dr. Phone 318/343-3361. ¢

Motels

★ **BEST WESTERN MONROE.** *610 Civic Center Blvd, Monroe (71201), I-20 exit Civic Center, back under I-20.* 318/323-4451; FAX 318/323-1728. 92 rms, 2 story. S $42-$47; D $42-$57; each addl $5; under 12 free. Crib free. TV; in-rm movies. Pool. Complimentary full bkfst. Restaurant 6 am-10 pm. Rm serv. Bar 4 pm-midnight. Ck-out noon. Private patios, balconies. Cr cds: A, C, D, DS, ER, MC, V.

✔ ★ **DAYS INN.** *2102 Louisville Ave, Monroe (71201).* 318/325-5851; FAX 318/323-3808. 130 rms. S $37; D $41; suites $49-$51. Pet accepted. TV; cable. Pool. Playground. Complimentary full bkfst. Restaurant 6:30-9:30 am. Bar 4 pm-2 am. Ck-out noon. Coin lndry. Meeting rms. Valet serv. Cr cds: A, C, D, DS, MC, V.

✔ ★ **HOWARD JOHNSON.** *5650 Frontage Rd, Monroe (71202).* 318/345-2220; FAX 318/343-4098. 58 rms, 2 story. S $36-$39; D $39-$44; under 16 free. Crib free. TV; cable (premium), VCR avail. Pool. Complimentary continental bkfst. Business services avail. Cr cds: A, C, D, DS, ER, MC, V.

★ ★ **LA QUINTA.** *1035 US 165 Bypass, Monroe (71203).* 318/322-3900; FAX 318/323-5537. 130 units, 2 story. S $49; D $54; each addl $5; suites $65; under 18 free. Crib free. Pet accepted. TV; cable. Pool. Complimentary continental bkfst. Restaurant adj. Meeting rms. Free airport, bus depot transportation. Cr cds: A, C, D, DS, MC, V.

★ **RED ROOF INN.** *102 Constitution Dr, West Monroe (71292).* 318/388-2420; FAX 318/388-2499. 97 rms, 3 story. S $32.99-$36.99; D $36.99-$40.99; each addl $7; under 18 free. Crib free. Pet accepted. TV; cable (premium). Complimentary coffee in lobby. Restaurant adj open 24 hrs. Ck-out noon. Business servs avail. Cr cds: A, D, DS, MC, V.

✔ ★ **STARTFORD HOUSE INN.** *(927 US 165 S, Monroe 71202)* 318/388-8868; res: 800/338-2931. 40 rms, 2 story. S $38-$39.95; D $38-$43.95. Crib free. TV; cable. Complimentary continental bkfst. Restaurant opp open 24 hrs. Ck-out 11 am. Cr cds: A, C, D, DS, MC, V.

Motor Hotel

★ ★ ★ **HOLIDAY INN HOLIDOME.** *(PO Box 7860, Monroe 71211)* *1/2 blk N of US 165 Bypass at I-20, 1/2 blk N of I-20 exit N Bastrop.* 318/387-5100. 260 rms, 2 story. S $57-$65; D $63-$70; each addl $6; suites $70-$135; under 18 free; some wknd rates. Crib free. TV; cable, in-rm movies. 2 pools, 1 indoor; wading pool, poolside serv. Restaurant 6 am-2 pm, 5-10 pm. Rm serv. Bars 4 pm-2 am; dancing exc Sun. Ck-out noon. Coin lndry. Meeting rms. Bellhops. Valet serv. Sundries. Free airport, bus depot, mall transportation. Putting green. Exercise equipt; weights, bicycles, whirlpool, steam rm, sauna. Game rm. Cr cds: A, C, D, DS, MC, V.

D 🏊 ✈ 🛏 🐾 SC

Restaurants

★ ★ **CHATEAU.** *2007 Louisville Ave Monroe, 1 mi NE on US 80.* 318/325-0384. Hrs: 11 am-midnight. Closed Sun; some major hols. Italian, Amer menu. Res accepted. Bar. Semi-a la carte: lunch $6-$7.50, dinner $9-$26. Specializes in fresh seafood, steak. Entertainment Fri, Sat. Parking. Cr cds: A, DS, MC, V.

D

★ ★ **McELROY'S LES RENDEZVOUS.** *(812 N 3rd St, Monroe 71201)* 318/325-7437. Hrs: 11 am-10 pm. Closed Sun; some major hols. Res accepted. French menu. Bar. Semi-a la carte: lunch $5-$10, dinner $8-$15. Specializes in grilled chicken, filet Rendezvous. Entertainment Wed, Fri & Sat. Parking. New Orleans-style dining. Cr cds: A, DS, MC, V.

D

✔ ★ **NEW ORLEANS CAFE.** *(300 Washington St, Monroe 71201)* 318/323-8996. Hrs: 11 am-9 pm; Fri to 10 pm; Sat 5-10 pm. Closed Sun; most major hols. Creole menu. Bar. Semi-a la carte: lunch $3.95-$7.95, dinner $8-$16. Specialties: crawfish etouffee, shrimp du ciel. Parking. Casual, French Quarter atmosphere. Cr cds: A, MC, V.

D

★ ★ **WAREHOUSE NO. 1.** *One Olive St, 2 blks S of US 80 & the Louisville Ave Bridge at the river.* 318/322-1340. Hrs: 5-9 pm; Fri, Sat to 9:30 pm. Closed Sun; major hols; also Mon after Easter. Bar. Semi-a la carte: dinner $7.95-$24.95. Child's meals. Specializes in catfish, chicken, seafood, steak. Valet parking. Outdoor deck dining. Located in old corrugated tin cotton warehouse on levee overlooking Ouachita River. Cr cds: A, C, D, DS, MC, V.

D

Unrated Dining Spots

MORRISON'S CAFETERIA. *4700 Mill Haven Rd (West), I-20 exit Garrett Rd.* 318/322-5230. Hrs: 11 am-2:30 pm, 4-8 pm; Sat 11 am-8 pm; Sun 11 am-6:30 pm. Closed Dec 25. Avg ck: lunch $5, dinner $5.50. Cr cds: A, DS, MC, V.

PICCADILLY CAFETERIA. *2203 Louisville Ave, in Twin City Shopping Center, 2 mi N on US 80W, 165 Bypass.* 318/325-5414. Hrs: 10:30 am-8:30 pm. Closed Dec 25. Avg ck: lunch $5.50, dinner $6.50. Specializes in southern Louisiana cuisine. Cr cds: A, C, D, DS, MC, V.

D 🛏

Morgan City (D-4)

(See Franklin, Houma, Thibodaux)

Founded ca 1850 **Pop** 14,531 **Elev** 5 ft **Area code** 504
Information St Mary Parish Tourist Commission, PO Box 2332, 70381; 504/395-4905 or 800/256-2931.

Originally named Brashear City for the Brashear family, upon whose plantation the town was laid out, the name was later changed to Morgan City in honor of Charles Morgan, president of the New Orleans, Opelousas and Great Western Railroad, which established its western terminus in the town. Morgan, a shipping and railroad magnate, was responsible for dredging Morgan City's first port as well operating the first steamboat on the Gulf of Mexico (1835).

Morgan City was a strategic point during the Civil War. Today it is an important inland port and commercial fishing center. In addition to its large shrimp industry, Morgan City has become a headquarters for offshore oil drilling. It is in the process of further developing its tourist industry.

What to See and Do

Brownell Memorial Park & Carillon Tower. Park preserves swamp in its natural state; on property is a 106-foot carillon tower with 61 bronze bells. (Daily) N off LA 70 on Lake Palourde. Phone 504/384-2283. **Free.**

Fishing and hunting. A vast interlocking network of bayous, rivers and lakes, with cypress, tupelo, gumwood forests and sugar cane fields, makes the whole area excellent for the hunting of small game and duck and for fishing.

Kemper Williams Park. This 290-acre park offers nature and jogging trails; tennis courts, golf driving range, baseball diamonds. Picnicking. Camping (hookups; addl fee). (Daily; closed hols) 8 mi W via US 90, Cotton Rd exit in Patterson. Phone 504/395-2298. ¢

Lake End Park. Swimming beach; fishing in lake and bayous; boating (launch, marina). Picnicking (shelter). Tent & trailer sites (hookups; fee). (Daily) On Lake Palourde along LA 70. Phone 504/380-4623. Per car ¢

Swamp Gardens and Wildlife Zoo. Outdoor exhibits depict both the history of the human settlement of the great Atchafalaya Basin and the natural flora and fauna of the swamp. Guided walking tours only. (Daily; closed Jan 1, Dec 25) 725 Myrtle St in Heritage Park. Phone 504/384-3343. ¢

Turn-of-the-Century House. Restored 1906 house with period furnishings and artifacts relating to local history; also elaborate Mardi Gras costumes. Guided tours. (Mon-Fri; closed major hols) 715 Second St. Phone 504/380-4651. ¢¢

Annual Event

Louisiana Shrimp and Petroleum Festival and Fair. Saturday: Children's Day activities, amusement rides, parade, hands-on children's village, storytelling; coronation of adult court, coronation ball. Sunday: blessing of shrimp and petroleum fleets on Berwick Bay, parade, fireworks. Also arts & crafts fair; entertainment, gospel tent, music in park; food fest. Phone 504/385-0703. Labor Day wkend.

Motel

★ **HOLIDAY INN.** *Box 2060 (70831), 520 Roderick St.* 504/385-2200; FAX 504/384-3810. 177 rms, 2 story. S, D $51-$56; each addl $10; suites $70-$125; under 18 free. Crib free. TV; cable (premium). Pool. Restaurant 5:30 am-10 pm. Rm serv. Bar 5 pm-midnight. Ck-out noon. Meeting rms. Business servs avail. In-rm modem link. Valet serv. Cr cds: A, C, D, DS, JCB, MC, V.

D 🏊 🛏 🐾 SC

Natchitoches (B-2)

(See Many)

Founded 1714 **Pop** 16,609 **Elev** 125 ft **Area code** 318 **Zip** 71457

Information Natchitoches Parish Tourist Commission, 781 Front St, PO Box 411, 71458; 318/352-8072 or 800/259-1714.

Natchitoches is the oldest permanent settlement in the Louisiana Purchase Territory. In 1714, a French expedition, led by Louis Juchereau de St Denis, established a post on the site of the present city to open trade with Indians and the Spaniards in Texas. The following year, Fort St Jean Baptiste was constructed to provide protection against the Indians and to prevent the Spaniards from extending the frontier of Texas any farther eastward. The name Natchitoches is derived from the name of a Native American tribe. The town is on the Cane River, a few miles from the Red River. A Ranger District office of the Kisatchie National Forest (see ALEXANDRIA) is in Natchitoches.

What to See and Do

Bayou Folk Museum. Displays depict history of Cane River country in restored house of writer Kate Chopin; period furniture. Also reconditioned blacksmith shop, doctor's office. (Daily; closed July 4, Thanksgiving, Dec 25, Easter) 20 mi S, just off LA 1 in Cloutierville. Phone 318/379-2233. ¢¢

Beau Fort Plantation (1790). Restored Creole cottage (1¹/₂ story) at the head of an alley of live oaks boasts an 84-foot front gallery, enclosed courtyard and landscaped gardens. (Daily; closed major hols) 10 mi S via LA 1, 119 in Bermuda. Phone 318/352-5340. ¢¢

Fort St Jean Baptiste State Commemorative Area. On this five-acre site is a replica of the fort as it was when first built to halt Spanish movement into Louisiana; restoration includes barracks, warehouse, chapel, mess hall and Native American huts. (Daily; closed Jan 1, Thanksgiving, Dec 25) Standard fees. Downtown on Cane River. Phone 318/357-3101. ¢

Melrose Plantation. Complex of eight plantation buildings includes Yucca House (ca 1795), the original cabin, the Big House and the African House. Originally the residence of Marie Therese Coincoin, a former slave whose son developed the Spanish land grant into a thriving antebellum plantation. Melrose was restored at the turn of the century by "Miss Cammie" Garrett Henry, who turned it into a repository of local arts and crafts. (Daily; closed July 4, Thanksgiving, Dec 25, Easter) 16 mi S on LA 119. Phone 318/379-0055. ¢¢

National Fish Hatchery & Aquarium. Twenty tanks of indigenous fish, turtles and alligators. (Daily; closed Jan 1, Dec 25) S on LA 1 Business. Phone 318/352-5324. **Free.**

Northwestern State University (1884). (8,412 students) The 916-acre campus is on Chaplin's Lake. On campus are the Lousiana Sports Writers Hall of Fame in Prather Coliseum, the Archives Room of Watson Memorial Library, the Folklife Center and the Williamson Archaeological Museum in Kyser Hall and the Normal Hill Historic District. College Ave at end of 2nd St. Phone 318/357-6361.

Annual Events

Melrose Plantation Arts & Crafts Festival. Jury-approved works of more than 100 artists and craftspeople. 2nd wkend June.

Natchitoches-Northwestern Folk Festival. NSU Prather Coliseum. Festival spotlights a different industry or occupation each year and works to preserve Louisiana folk art forms; music, dance, crafts, storytelling, foods. Phone 318/357-4332. 3rd wkend July.

Natchitoches Pilgrimage. City and Cane River tours of houses and plantations; also candlelight tour Sat. Phone 318/352-8072. 2nd full wkend Oct.

Christmas Festival of Lights. More than 140,000 lights are turned on after a full day of celebration to welcome the Christmas season. Phone 318/352-8072. 1st Sat Dec.

Motor Hotel

✔ ★ ★ **HOLIDAY INN.** *Box 2249, 3 mi S on LA 1 S Bypass.* 318/357-8281. 144 rms, 2 story. S $42-$48; D $46-$52; suites $85-$96; under 18 free. Crib free. TV; cable (premium). Pool. Restaurant 6 am-10 pm; Sun from 7 am. Rm serv. Bar 5 pm-midnight; dancing exc Sun. Ck-out 11 am. Coin lndry. Meeting rms. Business servs avail. In-rm modem link. Sundries. Free airport, bus depot transportation. Cr cds: A, D, DS, MC, V.

D ✔ ≋ ≍ ⋌ SC

Inn

★ ★ **FLEUR-DE-LIS.** *336 2nd St.* 318/352-6621; res: 800/489-6621. 5 rms, 2 story. No rm phones. S $60; D $70; each addl $10. TV in sitting rm; cable. Complimentary full bkfst, coffee & tea/wine. Restaurant nearby. Ck-out 11 am, ck-in 2 pm. Health club privileges. Turn-of-the-century house located in historic district of oldest settlement in Louisiana Purchase. Cr cds: A, MC, V.

D ≍ ⋌

Restaurants

✔ ★ **LASYONE'S.** *622 2nd St.* 318/352-3353. Hrs: 7 am-7 pm. Closed Sun; most hols. Res accepted. Cajun, Amer menu. Semi-a la carte: bkfst $1.95-$4, lunch, dinner $3.95-$8.95. Specializes in meat pies, red beans and sausage. Built in 1859. Family-owned. No cr cds accepted.

D

★ ★ **MARINER'S.** *Box 2479, Off LA 1S bypass, at Sibley Lake.* 318/357-1220; FAX 318/352-5529. Hrs: 4:30-10 pm; Sun 11 am-9 pm; Sun brunch to 2 pm. Closed major hols exc Easter. Res accepted. Bar. Semi-a la carte: dinner $10-15. Sun brunch $9.95. Child's meals. Specializes in steak, seafood. Salad bar. Parking. Patio dining. Nautical decor; view of lake. Cr cds: A, MC, V.

D

New Iberia (D-3)

(See Franklin, Lafayette, St Martinville)

Founded 1779 **Pop** 31,828 **Elev** 20 ft **Area code** 318 **Zip** 70560

Information Iberia Parish Tourist Commission, 2704 Hwy 14; 318/365-1540.

New Iberia was settled by French and Acadians, but named by the first Spanish settlers. The early settlers experimented with the cultivation of flax but were not successful. Many families of original settlers still reside in and around New Iberia.

Sugar cane grows in the surrounding country and raw sugar is processed in and around New Iberia. Year-round vegetable crops are important. Iberia Parish is one of the state's largest producers of oil; rock salt is mined here. New Iberia is good place from which to leisurely explore the Bayou Teche country.

What to See and Do

Avery Island. An enormous mass of rock salt underlies the area. The salt was first mined in 1862, when a Union blockade left the Confederate army and entire South in dire need of salt. Toll road onto island (fee); no bicycles or motorcycles permitted. 7 mi SW via LA 14, 329. On island are

McIlhenny Company. Tabasco brand pepper sauce is made on the island. Guided tours of factory and Tabasco Country Store. (Daily exc Sun; closed most hols). Phone 318/365-8173. **Free.**

Jungle Gardens. Avery Island's most spectacular feature was developed by the late Edward Avery McIlhenny. Camellias, azaleas, iris and tropical plants, in season, form a beautiful display. Enormous flocks of egrets, cranes and herons, among other species, are protected here and may be seen in early spring and summer; ducks and other wild fowl in winter. Chinese Garden contains a fine Buddha dating from A.D. 1000. (Daily) Phone 318/369-6243. **¢¢**

Bouligny Plaza. In park are depictions of history of the area; gazebo, historic landmarks, beautiful view along the bayou. On Main St in center of town.

Konriko Rice Mill and Company Store. Tours of the oldest rice mill in US; next door is replica of the original company store, with antique fixtures and merchandise typical of Acadiana and Louisiana. Tours; film (daily exc Sun; closed major hols). Sr citizen rate. 309 Ann St. Phone 318/367-6163 or 800/551-3245. **¢¢**

Live Oak Gardens. Twenty acres of landscaped gardens and nature preserve. Gallery of the Gradens art museum. Also on premises is Victorian residence of 19th-century actor Joseph Jefferson (tours). Restaurant. Gift shop. (Daily; closed Jan 1, Thanksgiving, Dec 24 & 25) Sr citizen rate. On Jefferson Island, 8 mi W off LA 14. Phone 318/365-3332. **¢¢¢**

★ Shadows-on-the-Teche (1834). A National Trust property. Red brick and white-pillared Greek revival house was built on the banks of the Bayou Teche by sugar-planter David Weeks. Home to four generations of his family, it served as center of antebellum plantation system. The house was restored and its celebrated gardens created in the 1920s by the builder's great-grandson, Weeks Hall, who used the estate to entertain such celebrities as D.W. Griffith, Anais Nin and Walt Disney. House is surrounded by three acres of azaleas, camellias and massive oaks draped in Spanish moss. (Daily; closed Jan 1, Thanksgiving, Dec 25) Sr citizen rate. 317 E Main St. Phone 318/369-6446. **¢¢**

Annual Events

Sugar Cane Festival and Fair. Last wkend Sept.

Christmas on the Teche. Parade & street dance. 1st Sat after Thanksgiving.

Motels

★ BEST WESTERN. 2714 Hwy 14. 318/364-3030; FAX 318/367-5311. 105 rms, 2 story. S $49; D $54; each addl $6; suites $60-$84; under 18 free. Crib free. TV; cable (premium), VCR avail. Pool; wading pool. Complimentary continental bkfst. Restaurant 5 am-9 pm; Sun 4 am-noon. Rm serv. Bar 4 pm-2 am; closed Sun. Ck-out noon. Meeting rms. Business servs avail. In-rm modem link. Sundries. Coin lndry. Cr cds: A, C, D, DS, MC, V.

D ⚏ ⊠ ⊠ SC

✔ ★★ HOLIDAY INN. 2915 Hwy 14, 1 mi W at jct US 90, LA 14. 318/367-1201; FAX 318/367-7877. 179 rms, 2 story. S $49-$54; D $54-$59; each addl $6; under 18 free. Crib free. TV; cable (premium), VCR avail. Pool. Playground. Restaurant 6 am-1:30 pm, 6-9 pm. Rm serv. Bar 4 pm-midnight. Ck-out 1 pm. Coin lndry. Meeting rms. Business servs avail. In-rm modem link. Valet serv. Sundries. Cr cds: A, C, D, DS, JCB, MC, V.

D ⚏ ⊠ ⊠ SC

Restaurant

★ LITTLE RIVER INN. 1000 Parkview Dr, Suite 16, in Bayou Landing Shopping Ctr. 318/367-7466. Hrs: 11 am-10 pm; Fri to 11 pm; Sat 5-11 pm. Closed Sun; most major hols. Res accepted. Cajun menu. Bar. Semi-a la carte: lunch, dinner $6-$16. Child's meals. Specializes in seafood. Parking. Family-owned. Cr cds: A, C, D, DS, MC, V.

D

New Orleans (D-5)

Founded 1718 **Pop** 496,938 **Elev** 5 ft **Area code** 504

New Orleans is a beguiling combination of old and new. Named for the Duc d'Orléans, Regent of France, it was founded by Jean Baptiste Le Moyne, Sieur de Bienville. From 1763 to 1801, the territory of Louisiana was under Spanish rule. In 1801 Napoleon regained it for France, though no one in Louisiana knew of this until 1803, only 20 days before the Louisiana Purchase made it US territory. The first institution of higher learning in Louisiana, the College of Orleans, opened in New Orleans in 1811. The following year the first steamboat went into service between New Orleans and Natchez. Louisiana was admitted to the Union on April 30, 1812, with New Orleans as capital. The War of 1812 was over when, on January 8, 1815, General Sir Edward Pakenham attacked New Orleans with a British force and was decisively defeated by General Andrew Jackson at Chalmette Plantation. This is now a national historical park. During the Civil War, New Orleans was captured by Union forces and held under tight military rule for the duration.

The population is extremely cosmopolitan with its Creoles (descendants of the original French and Spanish colonists), Cajuns (descendants of the Acadians who were driven from Nova Scotia by the British in 1755) and other groups whose ancestors came from Italy, Africa and the islands of the Caribbean.

Among tourists, New Orleans is famous for the old world charm of its French Quarter. Visitors come from all over the country to dine in its superb restaurants, listen to its incomparable jazz and browse in Royal Street's fine antique shops. In the world of trade, New Orleans is known as one of the busiest and most efficient international ports in the country. Over one hundred steamship lines dock here. As many as 52 vessels can be berthed at one time.

Transportation

Car Rental Agencies: See toll-free numbers under Introduction.

Public Transportation: Streetcars & buses (Regional Transit Authority), phone 242-2600.

Rail Passenger Service: Amtrak 800/872-7245.

Airport Information

New Orleans Intl Airport: Information 504/464-0831; lost and found 504/464-2672; weather 504/465-9212; Crown Room (Delta), Concourse D.

Because New Orleans is a tourist destination city, visitors should exercise caution regarding their safety and security while visiting the French Quarter, Louis Armstrong Park and other areas of the city.

What to See and Do

Auto or streetcar tour of universities and Audubon Park. Go southwest on St Charles Avenue from Canal Street; the St Charles Avenue streetcar can be picked at this same point. **¢** The first point of interest is

Lafayette Square, with statues of Franklin, Clay and McDonough. A few blocks beyond is

Lee Circle, Howard Avenue, with a statue of Robert E. Lee by Alexander Doyle.

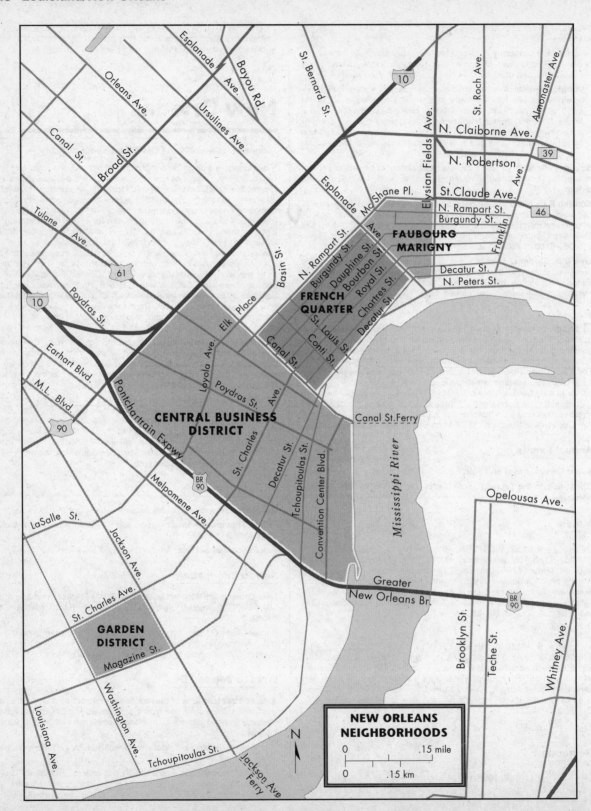

Esplanade Ave.

Bayou Rd.

Orleans Ave.

St. Bernard St.

Ursulines Ave.

Canal St.

Broad St.

I-10

St. Roch Ave.

Almonaster Ave.

N. Claiborne Ave.

N. Robertson

39

Tulane Ave.

Esplanade Ave.

McShane Pl.

Elysian Fields Ave.

St. Claude Ave.

N. Rampart St.

Burgundy St.

46

Franklin Ave.

61

Basin St.

N. Rampart St.

Burgundy St.

Dauphine St.

Bourbon St.

Royal St.

Chartres St.

FAUBOURG
MARIGNY

Decatur St.

N. Peters St.

Poydras St.

I-10

Elk Place

FRENCH
QUARTER

St. Louis St.

Conti St.

Decatur St.

Earhart Blvd.

Loyola Ave.

Canal St.

Canal St. Ferry

M.L. Blvd.

90

Pontchartrain Expwy.

Poydras St.

CENTRAL BUSINESS
DISTRICT

St. Charles Ave.

Decatur St.

Tchoupitoulas St.

Convention Center Blvd.

Mississippi River

Melpomene Ave.

BR 90

Opelousas Ave.

LaSalle St.

Jackson Ave.

Greater
New Orleans Br.

BR 90

St. Charles Ave.

GARDEN
DISTRICT

Magazine St.

Brooklyn St.

Teche St.

Whitney Ave.

Louisiana Ave.

Washington Ave.

Tchoupitoulas St.

Jackson Ave. Ferry

N

**NEW ORLEANS
NEIGHBORHOODS**

0   .15 mile

0   .15 km

The Garden District, bounded roughly by Magazine Street, St Charles, Jackson and Washington avenues, was once the social center of New Orleans American (as opposed to Creole) aristocracy. There are still beautiful Greek-revival and Victorian houses, with palms, magnolias and enormous live oaks on the spacious grounds in this area. A walking tour of the Garden District, conducted by a national park ranger, departs from the corner of 1st and St Charles (by appt only; not offered during Mardi Gras, Dec 25). Next, continue on St Charles about three miles to

Loyola University (1912). (3,500 students) The buildings on the 21-acre campus are Tudor-Gothic in style. Tours are arranged through the Office of Admissions (Mon-Fri, twice daily). 6363 St Charles Ave. Phone 504/865-3240. Just beyond Loyola is

Tulane University (1834). (11,500 students) The 110-acre main campus, located uptown, offers art galleries and other exhibits. The Tulane University Medical Center, located downtown, includes the School of Medicine, the School of Public Health and Tropical Medicine and a 300-bed private hospital. The University also operates the Delta Regional Primate Research Center (see COVINGTON). Phone 504/865-5000 (main campus), 504/588-5263 (Med Ctr). Directly across St Charles Ave is

Audubon Park and Zoological Garden. This 400-acre park, designed by the Olmstead brothers, is nestled between St Charles Ave and the Mississippi River and is surrounded by century-old live oak trees. The park features an 18-hole golf course, bicycle and jogging paths and tennis courts. The zoo displays more than 1,800 animals in naturalistic settings. Among its attractions are the Louisiana swamp exhibit, the reptile "encounter" and the tropical bird house. (Daily; closed Jan 1, Mardi Gras, Thanksgiving, Dec 25 & 1st Fri in May) Sr citizen rate. 6500 Magazine St. Phone 504/861-2537. Zoo Cruise. Zoo admission ¢¢¢ Return to Canal Street via St Charles Avenue, either by automobile or streetcar.

Auto tour to City Park and Lake Pontchartrain (allow 2 to 4 hrs). Drive northwest on Esplanade or northeast on North Carrollton Avenue to the Esplanade entrance. Proceed along Lelong Drive to the

New Orleans Museum of Art. Included among the special collections are the Peter Carl Fabergé jeweled *objets d'art;* early 19th-century Louisiana furnishings; Italian paintings from the 13th-18th centuries; 19th-century French art; ancient, European and American glass; 18th-century portrait miniatures. Also included is the art of Western Civilization from the pre-Christian era to the present. Also, the arts of Africa, the Far East and pre-Columbian America and an extensive photography collection. Special exhibits from various cultures and periods. (Daily exc Mon; closed Mardi Gras & hols) Sr citizen rate. City Park. Phone 504/488-2631. ¢¢¢ Southwest of the museum are the

Dueling Oaks, where many an affair of honor was settled in the early 18th century. Just beyond are the

Bandstand and Peristyle, the latter an attractive classical structure. North of the Peristyle is a

Rose garden, which also has azaleas, camellias and gardenias. On the middle west edge of the park are the

Recreation areas. Four 18-hole golf courses, a driving range, lighted tennis courts and lagoons for boating. (Fee) The north side of City Park is only a few blocks from

Lake Pontchartrain. Take Wisner Blvd or Marconi Drive and stop off at Robert E. Lee Blvd near Wisner Blvd to see the

Southern Regional Research Center of the US Dept of Agriculture, 1100 Robert E. Lee Blvd, which finds and develops new and improved uses for southern farm crops. Guided tours by appt. (Mon-Fri; closed hols) Phone 504/286-4200. **Free.** From the Research Center the lake is one-and-one-half miles away via Beauregard Avenue. Follow Lakeshore Drive east to the

University of New Orleans (1958). (16,084 students) On shores of Lake Pontchartrain, the 345-acre campus is the center of a residential area. Fine Arts Gallery (Mon-Fri; closed hols). Phone 504/286-6000. West along Lakeshore Drive are

City Yacht Harbor, New Orleans Yacht Club, Southern Yacht Club and a marina. About two miles west is the

Lake Pontchartrain Causeway, 24 mi long (toll). To return to the downtown area from the causeway, follow I-10.

Confederate Museum. Collection of Civil War artifacts includes uniforms, weapons, medical instruments, battle flags; main hall contains section devoted to memorabilia of Jefferson Davis. (Daily exc Sun; closed Mardi Gras, hols) Sr citizen rate. 929 Camp St. Phone 504/565-8027. ¢¢

Destrehan Plantation. Built in 1787, this is the oldest plantation house left intact in the lower Mississippi Valley; ancient live oaks. Gift shop. Guided tours. (Daily; closed major hols) Approx 17 mi W via LA 48 in Destrehan. Phone 504/764-9315. ¢¢

Gray Line bus tours. Contact 1300 World Trade Center, 70130; 504/587-0861 or 800/535-7786.

Historic New Orleans Custom House. Begun in 1848, interrupted by the Civil War and completed in 1881, the Greek-revival building with neo-Egyptian details was used in part as an office by Major General Benjamin "Spoons" Butler, during Union occupation, and in part as a prison for Confederate soldiers. A great dome was planned, but the great weight of the existing building caused the foundation to settle, and the dome was never completed. (In 1940, the building had sunk 30 inches, while the street level had been raised 3 feet.) Of particular interest is the famed Marble Hall, an architectural wonder. Self-guided tour. (Mon-Fri) Decatur and Canal Sts. Phone 504/589-2976. **Free.**

Jean Lafitte National Historical Park and Preserve. Consists of four units: the New Orleans, Chalmette, Barataria and Acadian. The Isleño, Chitimacha and Tunica-Biloxi cultural centers operate through cooperative agreements with the park. (Daily) Phone headquarters at 504/589-3882. **Free.**

New Orleans Unit. Walking tours, which leave from the center, include the "Tour du Jour," which has a different theme each day; "History of New Orleans," an exploration of the French Quarter; "Faubourg Promenade," a tour of the Garden District (by appt only) that departs from the corner of 1st and St Charles Ave (on the St Charles streetcar line). The Folklife/Visitor Center also offers exhibits and audiovisual programs; performances and demonstrations by traditional musicians, artists and craftspeople; information about the ethnic population of the delta. Unit & tours (daily; closed Mardi Gras, Dec 25). Folklife/Visitor Center, 916 N Peters in French Quarter *(may move to 419 Decatur St in French Quarter).* Phone 504/589-2636. **Free.**

Chalmette Unit. Scene of the 1815 Battle of New Orleans. Visitor Center has audiovisual presentation of battle; museum; National Cemetery; two self-guided auto tour roads; field interpretation. (Daily; closed Mardi Gras, Dec 25) 6 mi E on St Bernard Hwy (LA 46) in Chalmette (from Canal St, take Rampart St, which merges into St Claude Ave). Phone 504/589-4428. **Free.**

Barataria Preserve Unit. Visitor center has information desk, exhibits, movies. Trails through bottomland hardwood forest, swamp and marsh. Guided and self-guided walks. Canoeing and fishing. (Daily; closed Dec 25) On west bank of the Mississippi, 15 mi S on LA 45 (Barataria Blvd). Phone 504/689-2002. **Free.**

Acadian Unit. Consists of three Acadian cultural centers: Acadian Cultural Center (Lafayette), Wetlands Acadian Cultural Center (Thibodaux) and Prairie Acadian Cultural Center (Eunice). For further information phone 318/264-6862. **Free.**

Isleño Center. Interprets history and contemporary culture of Canary Islanders who were settled here by the Spanish government in the late 1700s. Interpretive exhibits, information about self-guided auto tours to Isleño communities. (Daily; closed Mardi Gras, Dec 25) Approx 14 mi SE on LA 46. Phone 504/682-0862. **Free.**

Chitimacha Cultural Center. (See FRANKLIN)

Longue Vue House & Gardens. A grand city estate furnished with original English and American antiques is located on eight acres of formal and picturesque gardens; changing exhibits in galleries and seasonal horticultural displays in gardens. (Daily; closed hols) Sr citizen rate. 7 Bamboo Rd, I-10 Metairie Rd exit. Phone 504/488-5488. ¢¢¢

Musée Conti-Wax Museum of Louisiana Legends. Costumed figures, including Jean Lafitte, Andrew Jackson and Marie Laveau with her voodoo dancers, depict the history and legends of New Orleans and the Louisiana Territory. Programs in French, German, Italian, Spanish and Japanese. (Daily; closed Mardi Gras, Dec 25) 917 Conti St, in French Quarter. Phone 504/525-2605. ¢¢¢

★ **New Orleans Historic Voodoo Museum.** Exhibits include collection of photographs, masks, musical instruments, altars and other items associated with the practice of voodoo. Gift shop. Guided tours; also walking tours (fee). (Daily) 724 Rue Dumaine, in French Quarter. Phone 504/523-7685. ¢¢

New Orleans Pharmacy Museum (*La Pharmacie Française*) (1823). Louis Dufilho, the first licensed pharmacist in the US, operated an apothecary shop here until 1867. Ground floor contains pharmaceutical memorabilia of 1800s, including apothecary jars filled with medicinal herbs and voodoo powders, surgical instruments, pharmacy fixtures and a black and rose Italian marble soda fountain (ca 1855). (Daily exc Mon; closed hols) 514 Chartres St, in French Quarter. Phone 504/565-8027. ¢

Pitot House (1799). One of the last remaining French colonial/West Indies-style plantation houses along Bayou St John. Residence of James Pitot, first elected mayor of incorporated New Orleans. Restored; furnished with antiques. (Wed-Sat; closed hols) 1440 Moss St. Phone 504/482-0312. ¢¢

Preservation Hall. Traditional New Orleans jazz concerts most evenings. 726 St Peter St. For schedule, fee information phone 504/522-2841.

Riverfront Area.

Riverfront Streetcar Line. Vintage streetcars follow a route (1½ mi) along the Mississippi riverfront from Esplanade, past the French Quarter, to the World Trade Center, Riverwalk, Convention Center and back. Exact change fare ¢ Between the streetcar line and the river, opposite Jackson Square, is the

Moonwalk. This promenade atop the levee affords scenic views of the French Quarter, downtown and river. South of the Moonwalk is

Toulouse Street Wharf. Foot of Toulouse St and the river. Sales office and departure point for riverboat cruises and bus tours of city and countryside. South of the wharf is

Woldenberg Riverfront Park. Covering 17 acres on the riverfront, Woldenberg Park offers the city its first direct access to the river in 150 years; ships and paddlewheelers dock along the park. Between Toulouse and Canal Sts. In Woldenberg Park is

Aquarium of the Americas. A branch of the Audubon Institute, which also supervises the Audubon Zoo, the Aquarium of the Americas houses some 10,000 specimens representing more than 400 species; arranged around four ecosystems—Mississippi delta, Gulf of Mexico, Caribbean reef and Amazon rain forest—the collections include such exotic creatures as lemon sharks. River cruises are available from the aquarium to Audubon Zoo. (Daily; closed Dec 25, also Mardi Gras) Sr citizen rate. Along the river between Canal and Bienville Sts. Phone 504/861-2537. ¢¢¢ Across Canal Street to the south is the

World Trade Center of New Orleans. Center houses offices of many maritime companies and foreign consulates involved in international trade. Revolving cocktail lounge on 33rd floor offers fine views of the city and river. Viewpoint observation deck on the 31st floor is accessed through an outside glass elevator located in lobby. (Daily; closed major hols) 2 Canal St at river. Phone 504/525-2185. ¢ South of the World Trade Center are

Levee and docks. From the foot of Canal Street turn right and walk along the busy docks to the coffee and general cargo wharves, which are most interesting. Smoking is forbidden in the dock area. Rides on the Canal Street Ferry are free. Along the docks are paddlewheel and other excursion boats. Continue south along riverfront to the

Riverwalk. This half-mile-long festival marketplace has more than 140 national and local shops, restaurants and cafes. The Riverwalk

structure was converted from world's fair pavilions. (Daily; closed Thanksgiving, Dec 25) 1 Poydras St. Phone 504/522-1555.

River cruises. Daily excursions depart from the riverfront.

Sternwheeler steamboat *Natchez* makes two-hour harbor cruises and evening dinner cruise. Jazz is featured on all cruises. New Orleans Steamboat Co, 1300 World Trade Center, 70130; 504/586-8777 or 800/233-2628. ¢¢¢¢-¢¢¢¢¢

The river boat *John James Audubon* provides river transportation between the Aquarium of the Americas and the Audubon Zoo seven miles upriver; round-trip or one-way, return may be made via St Charles Avenue Streetcar (addl fee). Phone 504/587-8777 or 800/233-2628. Round-trip ticket price includes admission to both Audubon Zoo and Aquarium of the Americas ¢¢¢¢¢

The sternwheelers *Delta Queen* and *Mississippi Queen* offer 3- to 12-night cruises on the Mississippi, Ohio, Cumberland and Tennessee rivers year-round. For details contact Delta Queen Steamboat Co, 30 Robin St Wharf, 70130-1890; 504/586-0631 or 800/533-1949.

Paddlewheeler Creole Queen offers sightseeing cruises to Chalmette National Historical Park, site of the Battle of New Orleans; and dinner and jazz cruises. The *Cajun Queen* offers harbor cruises from Aquarium of the Americas (1½-hr tour with narration and on-board alligators). For reservations contact New Orleans Paddlewheels, Inc, New Orleans International Cruise Ship Terminal, Poydras St Wharf, 70130; 504/524-0814 or 504/529-4567. ¢¢¢¢-¢¢¢¢¢

San Francisco Plantation (1853-56). While a remarkable example of the "steamboat-Gothic" style in detail, the structure is typical of Creole building: galleried with main living quarters on the second floor; dining room and various service rooms on ground floor. Authentically restored, the interior features five decorated ceilings (two are original). Used as the setting of Frances Parkinson Keyes' novel *Steamboat Gothic*. (Daily; closed Mardi Gras, some major hols) Approx 35 mi W via US 61 or I-10 and LA 44 in Garyville. Phone 504/535-2341. ¢¢¢

St Bernard State Park. Approximately 350 acres near the Mississippi River with many viewing points of the river; network of man-made lagoons. Swimming. Camping. Standard fees. (Daily) 18 mi SE on LA 39. Phone 504/682-2101. **Free.**

★ **St Charles Avenue Streetcar.** The 13-mile line was begun in 1835; it is the oldest continuously operating street railway in the world. The line runs on St Charles Avenue from downtown through the Garden District, near the Audubon Zoo and turns onto Carrollton Avenue, the main thoroughfare of the uptown district, an area with many shops. Phone 504/569-2700. Exact change, one-way fare ¢

The Superdome. Dominating the skyline of downtown is the world's largest enclosed stadium-arena; accommodates up to 87,500 people. Site of conventions, trade shows, concerts, the home games of the Saints football team, Tulane University football and the annual Sugar Bowl Classic. 45-minute tours (daily exc during some events; closed some hols). Sugar Bowl Drive. Phone 504/587-3808. ¢¢¢

★ **Walking tour in the Vieux Carré** (literally, "old square"), bounded by Iberville, North Rampart and Esplanade streets and the Mississippi River, usually called the **French Quarter.** Note that all street names change when they cross Canal and run into this old area of New Orleans. Entering the Quarter is to enter another world, one that seems to exist in a different time and move to a different rhythm. Begin the tour at

Jackson Square, bordered by Chartres, St Peter, Decatur and St Ann streets. The area was established as a drill field in 1721 and was called the Place d'Ármes until 1848, when it was renamed for Andrew Jackson, hero of the Battle of New Orleans. The statue of Jackson was the world's first equestrian statue with more than one hoof unsupported; the scuptor, the American Clark Mills, had never seen an equestrian statue and, therefore, did not know the pose was thought impossible. The square and surrounding plaza is one of the best places in the Quarter for watching people and listening to sidewalk jazz musicians. South of the square, at St Peter and Decatur, is

Jackson Brewery. This historic brewery was converted into a large retail, food and entertainment complex with 75 shops and restaurants, outdoor dining and a riverfront promenade. (Daily; closed Dec 25) Phone 504/587-0749.

Pontalba Building, facing across Jackson Square, was completed in 1850 and 1851 by the Baroness Pontalba, to beautify the square. Still occupied and used as intended (duplex apartments above ground-floor offices and shops), the buildings are now owned by the city and the Louisiana State Museum. **The 1850 House,** 523 St Ann Street, is furnished in the manner of the period (Tues-Sun; closed major hols). Sr citizen rate. Phone 504/524-9118. ¢¢ Across the square on Chartres Street are the Cabildo, St Louis Cathedral and the Presbytère.

St Louis Cathedral (1794), a minor basilica; this is the third church on this site and the oldest cathedral in the US (begun 1789, dedicated 1794). (Daily; closed Mardi Gras) Donation. For tour information phone 504/525-9585. Behind the cathedral, via Pirate's Alley (between the cathedral and the Cabildo) is the

Cathedral Garden. The monument in the center was erected in honor of French marines who died while nursing New Orleans' citizens during a yellow fever outbreak. Picturesque, narrow Pirate's Alley bordering the garden is a favorite spot for painters. On the Alley is the house in which William Faulkner lived when he wrote his first novel. The garden is also called St Anthony's Square in memory of a beloved priest known as Pére Antoine. Return to the front of the cathedral via Pére Antoine's Alley, the little street opposite Pirate's Alley. Next to the cathedral is the

The Presbytère (1791). Architecturally similar to the Cabildo, the building was intended to house clergy serving the parish church. A series of fires kept the Presbyteère incomplete until 1813, when it was finished by the US government. It is now a museum with changing and permanent exhibitions on Louisiana culture and history. The Presbytère, like the Cabildo, is part of the Louisiana State Museum complex. (Daily exc Mon; closed hols) Sr citizen rate. 751 Chartres St. Phone 504/568-6968. ¢¢ East of the square, at the corner of St Ann and Decatur, is the

French Market, which has been a farmers' market for nearly two centuries. The market's "Café du Monde" (see UNRATED DINING) is a popular and famous coffee stand specializing in café au lait (half coffee with chicory, half hot milk) and beignets (square-shaped doughnuts sprinkled with powdered sugar). The cafe never closes (exc Dec 25), and the café au lait and beignets are inexpensive. The downriver end of the French Market houses booths in which produce is sold. Just east of the market across Barracks Street is

The Old US Mint. Designed by William Strickland in 1835, the mint produced coins for both the US and for the Confederate States. Today, the Mint houses permanent exhibitions of jazz, Mardi Gras memorabilia and the Louisiana State Museum's Historical Center, a research facility. (Tues-Sun; historical center also Mon, Tues by appt; closed hols) Esplanade and Decatur Sts. Phone 504/568-6968. ¢¢ From the Mint stroll up Esplanade past some unusual old houses to Chartres, then turn left and walk to the corner of Chartres and Ursulines. On the left side of the street is the Ursulines Convent, which dates back to 1749; on the right is

Beauregard-Keyes House and Garden (ca 1826). Greek-revival, Louisiana raised cottage restored by its former owner, the novelist Frances Parkinson Keyes. Confederate Army General Pierre G.T. Beauregard lived here for more than a year following the Civil War. Exhibits include the main house and servant quarters, which together form a handsome, shaded courtyard. (Keyes actually lived informally in the servant quarters, which are filled with her books, antiques and family heirlooms.) To the side of the main house is a formal garden (visible from both Chartres and Ursulines streets) that is part of the guided tour conducted by costumed docents. (Daily exc Sun; closed major hols) Sr citizen rate. 1113 Chartres St. Phone 504/523-7257. ¢¢ At Ursulines turn right, away from the river, and walk one block to Royal and turn right again. Midway down the block is

Gallier House Museum. This elegant, Victorian town house by architect James Gallier, Jr has been restored to the period of his residency, 1860-68. (Mon-Sat, also Sun afternoons; closed major hols) Sr citizen rate. 1118-32 Royal St. Phone 504/523-6722. ¢¢ Next walk one-and-one-half blocks up Royal (facing the business district's

high-rise buildings) to St Philip, turn right and walk to Bourbon; on the corner is

"Lafitte's Blacksmith Shop." The origin of this structure has been lost in time, but it probably dates from 1772. By legend, it was once a blacksmith shop operated by the brothers Lafitte, infamous pirates. It is now a bar. 941 Bourbon St. Next, walk up Bourbon one block to Dumaine, turn left and go one block to

Madame John's Legacy. This is one of the oldest domestic buildings in the Mississippi Valley, built about 1727, rebuilt 1788, restored 1981 and part of Louisiana State Museum (private). Return to Royal Street, noticing throughout the French Quarter the beautiful cast-iron grillwork balconies, each with a distinctive theme in its pattern. 632 Dumaine St. Turn right on Royal, and walk to

Maison Le Monnier. Built in 1811 and sometimes called the "sky-scraper", this was the first building in the Vieux Carré more than two stories high. This house was used as the setting of George W. Cable's novel *Sieur George.* 640 Royal St (private). Notice the YLR, for Yves LeMonnier, worked into the grillwork. Across the street is

Adelina Patti's House and Courtyard. Former residence of the famous 19th-century opera prima donna. 631 Royal St.

Court of Two Sisters (see RESTAURANTS). This restaurant with a beautiful, spacious patio, is a delightful place to drop in for a drink or a cup of tea. 613 Royal Street.

Mid-19th-Century Townhouse. Headquarters of New Orleans Spring Fiesta Association (see ANNUAL EVENTS). Early 19th-century antiques, Victorian pieces; *objets d'art.* Guided tours (Mon-Fri afternoons). 826 St Ann St. Phone 504/581-1367. ¢¢

Historic New Orleans Collection (Museum and Research Center). Comprised of several historic buildings housing a museum and comprehensive research center for state and local history. Main exhibition gallery presents changing displays on Louisiana's history and culture. The 1792 Merieult House features a pictorial history of New Orleans and Louisiana; the Williams Residence shows the elegant lifestyle of the Collection's founders. There is also a touch-tour for the visually impaired. (Tues-Sat; closed major hols) No children under 12 in Williams Residence. 533 Royal St. Phone 504/523-4662. Gallery **free.** Guided tours of Merieult & Williams houses ¢

Brulatour Courtyard, 520 Royal St, is lined with interesting shops. Turn right at St Louis Street and walk one-half block to

Antoine's (see RESTAURANTS). In existence since 1840, Antoine's has been featured in novels and films and is where oysters Rockefeller was invented—"a dish so rich it was named Rockefeller." 713 St Louis St. Continue on St Louis one-and-one-half blocks, crossing Bourbon St, to the

Hermann-Grima Historic House (1831). The Georgian design reflects the post-Louisiana Purchase, American influence on traditional French and Spanish styles in the Quarter; the furnishings typify a well-to-do lifestyle during the period 1831-60. The restored house has elegant interiors, two landscaped courtyards, slave quarters, a stable and a working, period kitchen; Creole cooking demonstrations on open hearth (Oct-May, Thurs). Tour begins at 820 St Louis Street. (Daily exc Sun; closed hols) Sr citizen rate. 820 St Louis St. Phone 504/525-5661. ¢¢ Next, return to Royal and turn right to

Casa Faurie. The mansion (ca 1795) was built by an ancestor of French artist Edgar Degas. It later became headquarters of the Banque de la Louisiane; note the monogram, BL, worked into the grillwork. In 1819 the house was sold to Martin Gordon and became one of the social centers of the city; in 1828 General Andrew Jackson was honored with a banquet in the house. Today, the Casa Faurie is Brennan's, a distinctive restaurant, especially famous for its breakfasts; drinks are served on the patio (see RESTAURANTS). Across the street, the white marble building is the old US Circuit Court of Appeals. 417 Royal St. The next corner, Royal and Conti, was the city's original

Center of Banking. The old Louisiana State Bank, 403 Royal, was designed in 1821 by Benjamin Latrobe, one of the architects of the Capitol in Washington. The 343 Royal building was completed in the early 1800s for the old Bank of the United States. The old Bank of

Louisiana, 334 Royal, was built in 1826; it is now the French Quarter Police Station. At the corner of Royal and Bienville turn right, away from the river, and walk to

The Old Absinthe House, at the corner of Bienville and Bourbon. In this tavern, built shortly after 1806, Andrew Jackson and Jean Lafitte are supposed to have met to plan the defense of New Orleans in 1815. Now, continue along Bienville Street four blocks to North Rampart, turn right and walk five blocks to

Louis Armstrong Park. To the left of the entrance, which is built to resemble a Mardi Gras float, is a stand of very old live oak trees. This area was originally known as Congo Square, where slaves were permitted to congregate on Sunday afternoons; it was also the scene of voodoo rites. After the Civil War, the square was named for General P.G.T. Beauregard. The Louis Armstrong park, which includes an extensive water garden that focuses upon a larger than life-sized statue of Armstrong, was expanded from the original square and contains the municipal auditorium and the Theatre of the Performing Arts. To return to Jackson Square, walk back toward the river on St Peter Street.

For a more thorough tour of the many interesting points in the Vieux Carré and surrounding area see the "New Orleans Walking and Driving Tour" brochure, available at the Visitor Information Center of the Greater New Orleans Tourist and Convention Commission, 529 St Ann St, phone 566-5011.

Annual Events

Sugar Bowl College Football Classic. Superdome. Jan 1.

Mardi Gras (literally "Fat Tuesday," the day before Lent begins). The New Orleans Carnival, perhaps the most famous celebration in the United States, officially opens two weeks before Shrove Tuesday and includes torchlight parades, street dancing, costume balls, masquerades. It is handled by 60 secret societies called "Krewes," of which the oldest is that of Comus, organized in 1857. Mardi Gras Day, Feb 20.

French Quarter Festival. Features free musical entertainment; numerous stages throughout quarter; jazz brunch; race (5 km); children's activities. Phone 504/522-5730. Mid-Apr.

Spring Fiesta. Opening night parade; crowning of Queen and court. Tours of various New Orleans private houses and plantations. Blooming gardens; costumed hosts and hostesses. Contact 826 St Ann St, 70116; 504/581-1367. Begins 1st Fri after Easter.

New Orleans Jazz and Heritage Festival. Outdoor weekend activities at Fair Grounds Race Track with Louisiana specialty foods, crafts and 11 stages of simultaneous music, including traditional and contemporary jazz, rock, Gospel, rhythm and blues, ragtime, country and western, blues, Cajun, folk, Latin and Afro-Caribbean. Evening concerts in various concert halls and clubs. Contact PO Box 53407, 70153; 504/522-4786. Last wkend Apr-1st wkend May.

Seasonal Events

Horse racing. Fair Grounds Racetrack (1872). 1751 Gentilly Blvd, 5 mi N from French Quarter. America's third oldest racetrack. Parimutuel betting. Jackets required in clubhouse. Phone 504/944-5515; for clubhouse reservations phone 504/943-2200. Wed-Sun. Late Nov-Mar.

Sports. Saints (NFL football); Tulane University NCAA football; the Bayou Classic; the Sugar Bowl Classic; and basketball tournaments are all played in the Superdome.

Additional Visitor Information

For further information contact the Greater New Orleans Tourist & Convention Commission, 1520 Sugar Bowl Dr, 70112; 504/566-5011.

If in town for a short time, study one of the weekly visitors' guides; all the current events of interest are listed there. For young children visiting the city, the Tourist Commission offers a special guide entitled *New Orleans for Kids* ($5).

New Orleans Area Suburbs and Towns

The following suburbs and towns in the New Orleans area are listed in the *Mobil Travel Guide.* For information on any one of them, see the individual alphabetical listing. Covington, Kenner, Metairie, Slidell.

City Neighborhoods

Many of the restaurants, unrated dining establishments and some lodgings listed under New Orleans include neighborhoods as well as exact street addresses. A map showing these neighborhoods can be found immediately following the airport map. Geographic descriptions of these areas are given, followed by a table of restaurants arranged by neighborhood.

Central Business District: Fronting on the Mississippi River and bounded by Canal St, I-10 and US 90. **North of Central Business District:** North of I-10. **West of Central Business District:** West of I-10/US 90 Business.

Faubourg Marigny: Adjacent to the French Quarter across Esplanade Ave; south of McShane Pl, west of Elysian Fields and northeast of Esplanade Ave.

French Quarter (*Vieux Carré*): Fronting on the Mississippi River and bounded by Esplanade Ave, N Rampart, Canal and Decatur Sts.

Garden District: South of St Charles Ave, west of Jackson Ave, north of Magazine St and east of Washington Ave.

NEW ORLEANS RESTAURANTS
BY NEIGHBORHOOD AREAS

(For full description, see alphabetical listings under Restaurants)

CENTRAL BUSINESS DISTRICT

Bon Ton Cafe. 401 Magazine St

Emeril's. 800 Tchoupitoulas St

Grill Room (Windsor Court Hotel). 300 Gravier St

L'economie. 325 Girod St

Mike's On The Avenue. 628 St Charles Ave

Mother's. 401 Poydras St

Sazerac (Fairmont Hotel). 123 Baronne

Upperline. 1413 Upperline St

The Veranda (Inter-Continental Hotel). 444 St Charles Ave

NORTH OF CENTRAL BUSINESS DISTRICT

Christian's. 3835 Iberville St

Gabrielle. 3201 Esplanade Ave

Louisiana Pizza Kitchen. 2808 Esplanade Ave

Tavern On The Park. 900 City Park Ave

WEST OF CENTRAL BUSINESS DISTRICT

Bangkok Cuisine. 4137 S Carrollton Ave

Brigtsen's. 723 Dante St

Camellia Grill. 626 S Carrollton Ave

Casamento's. 4330 Magazine

Chez Nous Charcuterie. 5701 Magazine St

Five Happiness. 3605 S Carrollton Ave

Gautreau's. 1728 Soniat St

Mosca's. 4137 US 90W

Robear's Lighthouse Bar & Grill. 7360 W Roadway

Windjammer. 8550 Pontchartrain Blvd

FAUBOURG MARIGNY

Feelings Cafe. 2600 Chartres St

Praline Connection. 542 Frenchmen St

Snug Harbor Jazz Bistro. 626 Frenchmen St

FRENCH QUARTER (VIEUX CARRÉ)

Angelo Brocata's Italian Ice Cream Parlor. 537 St Ann St

Antoine's. 713 St Louis St

Arnaud's. 813 Rue Bienville

Bacco. 310 Chartres St

Bayona. 430 Rue Dauphine

Bella Luna. 914 N Peter

Bistro (Hotel Maison De Ville Inn). 727 Toulouse St

Brennan's. 417 Royal St

Broussard's. 819 Rue Conti

Cafe Du Monde. 800 Decatur St

Cafe Pontalba. 546 St Peter St

Central Grocery. 923 Decatur St

Clover Grill. 900 Bourbon St

Court Of Two Sisters. 613 Royal St

Desire Oyster Bar (Royal Sonesta Hotel). 300 Bourbon St

G & E Courtyard Grill. 1113 Decatur St

Galatoire's. 209 Bourbon St

La Madeleine. 547 St Ann St

Maximo's Italian Grill. 1117 Rue Decatur

Mike Anderson's. 215 Bourbon St

Mr B's Bistro. 201 Royal St

Nola. 534 St Louis St

The Original French Market. 1001 Decatur St

Pelican Club. 312 Exchange Place

Rib Room (Omni Royal Orleans). 621 St Louis St

Tony Moran's Pasta E Vino. 240 Bourbon St

Tujague's. 823 Decatur St

GARDEN DISTRICT

Caribbean Room (Pontchartrain). 2031 St Charles Ave

Commander's Palace. 1403 Washington Ave

Delmonico. 1300 St Charles Ave

Versailles. 2100 St Charles Ave

Note: When a listing is located in a town that does not have its own city heading, it will appear under the city nearest to its location. In these cases, the address and town appear in parenthesis immediately following the name of the establishment.

Motels

(Most accommodations increase their rates greatly for the Mardi Gras Festival and the Sugar Bowl Game wkend. Reservations should be made as far ahead as possible and confirmed.)

✔ ★ **CHATEAU.** *1001 Rue Chartres (70116), in French Quarter.* 504/524-9636. 45 rms, 2 story, 5 suites. S $69-$89; D $79-$99; each addl $10; suites $109-$140; under 18 free; higher rates special events. Crib free. TV; cable (premium). Pool. Restaurant 7 am-3 pm. Rm serv. Bar. Ck-out 1 pm. Bellhops. Valet serv. Valet parking. Made up of 18th-century bldgs around courtyard. Cr cds: A, C, D, ER, MC, V.

✔ ★ **NEWCOURT INN.** *10020 I-10 Service Rd at Read Blvd (70127), I-10 exit 244, north of central business district.* 504/244-9115; res: 800/821-4009. 143 rms, 2 story. S, D $60; each addl $5; suites $100; family rates; higher rates special events. Crib free. TV; cable (premium). Pool. Complimentary continental bkfst. Ck-out noon. Business servs avail. Cr cds: A, C, D, DS, MC, V.

★ **PRYTANIA PARK.** *1525 Prytania St (70130), in Garden District.* 504/524-0427; res: 800/862-1984; FAX 504/522-2977. 62 units, 2 story, 49 kits. S $79-$89; D $89-$99; suites $99-$150; each addl $10; under 12 free; summer packages. Crib free. TV; cable. Continental bkfst. Restaurant nearby. Ck-out noon. Business servs avail. Free parking. Some refrigerators. Balconies. Cr cds: A, C, D, DS, JCB, MC, V.

Motor Hotels

★ ★ **BIENVILLE HOUSE.** *320 Decatur St (70130), in French Quarter.* 504/529-2345; res: 800/535-7836; FAX 504/525-6079. 83 rms, 4 story. Sept-May: S $85-$145; D $95-$150; each addl $10; suites $175-$375; under 16 free; lower rates rest of yr. Crib free. Valet parking $10-$14. TV; cable, VCR avail. Pool. Restaurant 7 am-10 pm. Bar 11 am-11 pm. Ck-out noon. Meeting rms. Business servs avail. Bellhops. Valet serv. Health club privileges. Balconies. Courtyard surrounds pool. Cr cds: A, C, D, DS, MC, V.

★ **CLARION CARRIAGE HOUSE-FRENCH MARKET INN.** *501 Rue Decatur (70130), in French Quarter.* 504/561-5621; FAX 504/566-0160. 54 units, 4 story. Late Dec-May, Sept-Oct: S, D $129-$250; each addl $10; suites $158-$400; higher rates special events; lower rates rest of yr. TV; cable. Complimentary continental bkfst. Restaurant nearby. Bar. Ck-out 11 am. Business servs avail. In-rm modem link. Bellhops. Concierge. Built in 1753 for the Baron de Pontalba; served as residence for French governor. Cr cds: A, C, D, DS, ER, JCB, MC, V.

★ ★ **DAUPHINE ORLEANS.** *415 Dauphine St (70112), in French Quarter.* 504/586-1800; res: 800/521-7111; FAX 504/586-1409. 109 rms, 2-4 story. S $129-$179; D $149-$189; each add $15; suites $179-$359; under 12 free; higher rates special events. Crib free. Pet accepted. Garage $10. TV; cable (premium). Pool. Complimentary continental bkfst. Bar 3:30 pm-midnight; Sat, Sun from noon. Ck-out noon. Meeting rms. Business servs avail. In-rm modem link. Bellhops. Valet parking. Exercise equipt; weights, bicycles, whirlpool. Minibars. Balconies. Also patio courtyard opp with 14 rms; varied styles, sizes. Library. Cr cds: A, C, D, DS, ER, JCB, MC, V.

★ ★ ★ **HOLIDAY INN-CHATEAU LE MOYNE.** *301 Dauphine St (70112), in French Quarter.* 504/581-1303; FAX 504/523-5709. 171 rms, 5 story. S $110-$195; D $125-$210; each addl $15; suites $205-$450; under 18 free. Crib free. Garage $10. TV; cable (premium). Heated pool; poolside serv. Restaurant 6:30 am-2 pm, 5-10 pm. Rm serv. Bar 4-10:30 pm. Ck-out 11 am. Meeting rms. Business servs avail. In-rm modem link. Bellhops. Valet serv. Concierge. Some bathrm phones in suites. Balconies. Tropical courtyard. Cr cds: A, C, D, DS, JCB, MC, V.

✔ ★ ★ **LE RICHELIEU.** *1234 Chartres St (70116), in French Quarter.* 504/529-2492; res: 800/535-9653; FAX 504/524-8179. 86 rms, 4 story. S $85-$130; D $100-$140; each addl $15; suites $160-$475; higher rates special events. Crib free. TV, VCR avail. Pool; poolside serv. Restaurant 7 am-9 pm. Rm serv. Bar to 1 am. Ck-out 1 pm. Business servs avail. Bellhops. Valet serv. Concierge. Refrigerators.

Balconies. Landscaped courtyard. Cr cds: A, C, D, DS, ER, JCB, MC, V.

⌘ 🔥

★ ★ **PROVINCIAL.** *1024 Rue Chartres (70116), in French Quarter.* 504/581-4995; res: 800/535-7922; FAX 504/581-1018. 106 rms, 2-4 story. S, D $120-$160; each addl $15; suites from $225; under 18 free; summer, Creole Christmas rates; higher rates special events. Crib free. TV; cable (premium), VCR avail. Pool; poolside serv. Restaurant 7 am-2 pm. Rm serv. Bar. Ck-out noon. Meeting rm. Business servs avail. In-rm modem link. Valet serv. Balconies. Carriageway entrance; antique furnishings. Cr cds: A, C, D, DS, ER, JCB, MC, V.

D ⌘ 🔥 SC

★ ★ **SAINT ANN-MARIE ANTOINETTE.** *717 Rue Conti (70130), in French Quarter.* 504/581-1881. 66 rms, 5 story, 18 suites. S $99-$169; D $119-$189; each addl $15; suites $199-$499; summer rates. Crib free. TV; cable (premium). Pool; poolside serv. Restaurant 7-11 am; Sat, Sun to noon. Rm serv. Bar. Ck-out noon. Meeting rms. Business servs avail. Bellhops. Valet serv. Concierge. Bathrm phones; refrigerators avail. Balconies. Cr cds: A, C, D, MC, V.

D ⌘ 🔥 SC

★ ★ **THE SAINT LOUIS.** *730 Rue Bienville (70130), in French Quarter.* 504/581-7300; res: 800/535-9111; FAX 504/524-8925. 71 rms, 5 story, 32 suites. S $135-$189; D $155-$219; each addl $15; suites $229-$639; under 12 free; summer rates. Crib free. Valet parking $10.50. TV; cable (premium). Swimming privileges. Restaurant 7-11 am, 6-10:30 pm. Rm serv. Bar 5 pm-midnight; entertainment Fri, Sat. Ck-out noon. Meeting rms. Business servs avail. Bellhops. Valet serv. Concierge. Bathrm phones; refrigerators avail; minibar in suites. Some balconies. French antiques. Enclosed courtyard with fountains, tropical patio. Cr cds: A, C, D, MC, V.

D ⌘ 🔥 SC

Hotels

★ ★ ★ **BOURBON ORLEANS.** *717 Orleans St (70116), in French Quarter.* 504/523-2222; res: 800/521-5338; FAX 504/525-8166. 211 rms, 6 story, 60 suites. Mid-Sept-mid-June: S $95-$140; D $115-$160; each addl $15; suites $225-$350; under 12 free; Creole Christmas rates; higher rates special events; lower rates rest of yr. Crib free. Valet parking $12. TV; cable (premium), VCR avail. Pool; poolside serv. Coffee in rms. Restaurant 7 am-10 pm. Rm serv 24 hrs. Bar 11 am-midnight; wkends to 2 am. Ck-out noon. Meeting rms. Business servs avail. In-rm modem link. Concierge. Bathrm phones; refrigerator, minibar in suites. Some balconies. Cr cds: A, C, D, DS, MC, V.

D ⌘ 🔥 SC

★ ★ **DOUBLETREE.** *300 Canal St (70130), in central business district.* 504/581-1300; FAX 504/522-4100. 363 rms, 17 story. S, D $110-$165; each addl $10; suites $250-$1,500; under 18 free. Crib free. Valet parking $12. TV; cable (premium), VCR avail. Pool; poolside serv. Restaurant 6:30 am-10 pm; Fri, Sat to 11 pm. Rm serv. Bar from 11 am. Ck-out noon. Coin lndry. Meeting rms. Business servs avail. In-rm modem link. Exercise equipt; weights, bicycles. Adj to French Quarter, convention center and Aquarium of the Americas. Cr cds: A, C, D, DS, ER, JCB, MC, V.

D ⌘ 🏃 🔥 SC

★ ★ **FAIRMONT.** *123 Baronne (70140), 1/2 blk off Canal St between University Pl & Baronne, in central business district.* 504/529-7111; FAX 504/522-2303. 732 rms, 14 story. S $145-$190; D $170-$215; each addl $25; suites from $315; under 12 free; wkend rates, package plans avail. Crib free. Valet parking $10. TV; cable. Heated pool; poolside serv. Restaurant 6 am-midnight (also see SAZERAC). Rm serv 24 hrs. Bar. Ck-out 1 pm. Convention facilities. Concierge. Drugstore. Barber, beauty shop. Lighted tennis. Exercise equipt;

weights, treadmill. Landmark turn-of-the-century hotel. Cr cds: A, C, D, DS, JCB, MC, V.

D 🏃 ⌘ 🏃 🔥 SC

★ ★ **GRENOBLE HOUSE.** *329 Dauphine St (70112), in French Quarter.* 504/522-1331; FAX 504/524-4968. 17 kit. suites, 3 story. S $145-$265, D $275-$355; each addl $30; wkly, summer rates; higher rates special events. Crib free. TV; cable. Pool; whirlpool. Complimentary continental bkfst. Complimentary coffee in rms. Restaurant adj 6-10 pm. Ck-out noon, ck-in 3 pm. Concierge. Balconies. Restored 19th-century town house; courtyard. Antiques. Cr cds: A, MC, V.

⌘ 🔥

★ ★ ★ **HILTON RIVERSIDE.** *Poydras at the Mississippi River (70140), in central business district.* 504/561-0500; FAX 504/568-1721. 1,600 rms, 29 story. S $190-$210; D $215-$235; each addl $25; suites from $395; wkend packages. Crib free. Valet parking $11/24 hrs. TV; cable (premium), VCR avail. 2 heated pools; poolside serv. Restaurant 6-2 am. Rm serv 24 hrs. Ck-out noon. Convention facilities. Business center. In-rm modem link. Concierge. Gift shop. Barber, beauty shop. Indoor, outdoor tennis; pro. Exercise equipt; weights, bicycles, whirlpool, sauna. Minibars. Connected to riverwalk. Luxury level. Cr cds: A, C, D, DS, JCB, MC, V.

D 🏃 ⌘ 🏃 🏃 🔥 SC 🏃

✔ ★ ★ **HOLIDAY INN DOWNTOWN-SUPERDOME.** *330 Loyola Ave (70012), in central business district.* 504/581-1600; FAX 504/586-0833. 297 rms, 18 story. S $75-$150; D $90-$165; each addl $15; under 19 free. Crib free. Valet parking $15. TV; cable (premium). Heated pool. Restaurant 6 am-10 pm. Bar. Ck-out noon. Meeting rms. Business servs avail. In-rm modem link. Gift shop. Luxury level. Cr cds: A, C, D, DS, JCB, MC, V.

D ⌘ 🔥 SC

★ ★ ★ **HOLIDAY INN-CROWNE PLAZA.** *333 Poydras St (70130), in central business district.* 504/525-9444; FAX 504/581-7179. 439 units, 23 story. S, D $115-$215; each addl $15; suites $325-$645; under 18 free; higher rates special events. Crib free. Garage parking $7.50; valet $11. TV; cable (premium). Pool. Restaurant 6:30 am-10 pm. Coffee in rms. Bar noon-midnight. Ck-out noon. Convention facilites. Business servs avail. Concierge. Exercise equipt; weights, bicycles. Refrigerators avail. Luxury level. Cr cds: A, C, D, DS, ER, JCB, MC, V.

D ⌘ 🏃 🔥 SC

★ ★ **HOTEL DE LA POSTE.** *316 Rue Chartres (70130), in French Quarter.* 504/581-1200; res: 800/448-4927; FAX 504/523-2910. 100 rms, 5 story. S $110-$135; D $125-$150; each addl $25; suites $165-$200; under 16 free. Crib free. TV; cable (premium). Pool; poolside serv. Restaurant 7:30 am-10 pm. Bar. Ck-out noon. Meeting rm. Business servs avail. In-rm modem link. Valet parking. Built around landscaped courtyard. Cr cds: A, C, D, DS, MC, V.

D ⌘ 🔥 SC

★ ★ ★ **HYATT REGENCY.** *Poydras Plaza (70140), at Loyola, adj to Superdome in central business district.* 504/561-1234; FAX 504/587-4141. 1,184 rms, 32 story. S $165; D $190; each addl $25; suites $350-$850; under 18 free; wkend rates. Crib free. Valet parking $12. TV; cable (premium), VCR avail. Heated pool; poolside serv. Supervised child's activities. Restaurant 6-1 am; dining rms 10:30 am-2:30 pm, 6-10:30 pm. Bars 11-2 am; entertainment, dancing. Ck-out noon. Convention facilities. Business center. In-rm modem link. Concierge. Barber, beauty shop. Airport transportation; free local transportation. Exercise equipt; weights, treadmill. Connected to Superdome & shopping complex. Luxury level. Cr cds: A, C, D, DS, ER, JCB, MC, V.

D ⌘ 🏃 🔥 SC 🏃

★ ★ ★ **INTER-CONTINENTAL.** *444 St Charles Ave (70130), in central business district.* 504/525-5566; res: 800/327-0200; FAX 504/523-7310. Pale golden marble and lush landscaping greet guests of this modern high-rise. Most rooms are decorated in contemporary style, but some suites have antiques. 482 units, 15 story, 30 suites. S $180-$220; D $200-$240; each addl $20; suites $350-$2,000; under 14 free; wkend plans. Valet parking $12. TV; cable (premium), VCR avail. Heated pool; poolside serv. Restaurant 6 am-11 pm (also see THE VERANDA). Rm serv 24 hrs. Bars 11-1 am; entertainment. Convention facilities. Business center. In-rm modem link. Concierge. Gift shop. Beauty shop. Airport transportation. Exercise equipt; weight machine, bicycles. Massage. Bathrm phones, TVs; some refrigerators, minibars. Some balconies. Luxury level. Cr cds: A, C, D, DS, ER, JCB, MC, V.

⊡ ⩰ 🛪 ⊠ 🔥 SC ✈

★ ★ **LAFAYETTE.** 600 St Charles (70130), in central business district. 504/524-4441; res: 800/733-4754; FAX 504/523-7327. 44 rms, 5 story, 20 suites. S, D $135-$350; suites $225-$650; family rates; higher rates wkends (2-day min) & Jazz Fest. Crib free. Valet parking $10. TV; cable (premium), VCR avail. Coffee in rms. Restaurant 7 am-11 pm. Bar. Ck-out 11 am. Business servs avail. In-rm modem link. Concierge. Airport transportation. Health club privileges. Minibars. Balconies. Renovated hotel first opened 1916. Cr cds: A, C, D, DS, ER, JCB, MC, V.

⊡ ⊠ 🔥 SC

★ ★ **LE MERIDIEN.** 614 Canal St (70130), in central business district. 504/525-6500; res: 800/543-4300; FAX 504/525-8068. 494 rms, 30 story. S $170-$230; D $190-$250; each addl $20; suites $500-$1,500; under 16 free. Crib free. Garage $12; valet. TV; cable (premium), VCR avail. Heated pool; poolside serv. Restaurant 6:30 am-10:30 pm. Rm serv 24 hrs. Bar 4 pm-1:30 am; entertainment. Ck-out noon. Convention facilities. Business center. In-rm modem link. Concierge. Shopping arcade. Exercise rm; instructor, weight machines, bicycles, whirlpool, sauna. Bathrm phones, minibars. Adj to French Quarter. Cr cds: A, C, D, DS, ER, JCB, MC, V.

⊡ ⩰ 🛪 ⊠ 🔥 SC

★ ★ **LE PAVILLON.** 833 Poydras St (70140), in central business district. 504/581-3111; res: 800/535-9095; FAX 504/522-5543. 226 rms, 10 story. S, D $99-$190; suites $295-$595; under 18 free; higher rates special events. Crib free. Valet parking $11. TV; cable (premium), VCR avail. Heated pool; poolside serv. Restaurant 6:30 am-10 pm. Rm serv 24 hrs. Bar 10:30-1 am. Ck-out noon. Meeting rms. Business servs avail. In-rm modem link. Concierge. Airport transportation. Bathrm phones; refrigerators avail. Cr cds: A, C, D, DS, ER, MC, V.

⊡ ⩰ ⊠ 🔥 SC

★ ★ **MAISON DUPUY.** 1001 Toulouse St (70112), at Burgundy, in French Quarter. 504/586-8000; res: 800/535-9177; FAX 504/566-7450. 198 rms, 5 story. S, D $175-$205; each addl $25; suites $240-$1500; under 17 free. Crib free. Garage $10. TV; cable (premium), VCR avail. Heated pool; poolside serv. Restaurant 7 am-2 pm, 5-10 pm. Bar from 11 am. Ck-out noon. Meeting rms. Business servs avail. In-rm modem link. Exercise equipt; weights, bicycles. Balconies. Cr cds: A, C, D, DS, MC, V.

⊡ ⩰ 🛪 ⊠ 🔥 SC

★ ★ **MARRIOTT.** 555 Canal St (70140), at Chartres St, in central business district. 504/581-1000; FAX 504/523-6755. 1,290 units, 41 story. S, D $199; each addl $20; suites $600-$1,200; under 17 free; wkend rates. Crib free. Valet parking $12. TV; cable, VCR avail. Heated pool; wading pool, poolside serv. Restaurant 6:30 am-11 pm. Rm serv 24 hrs. Bar 10-2 am; entertainment. Ck-out noon. Coin lndry. Convention facilities. Business center. In-rm modem link. Concierge. Gift shop. Exercise equipt; weights, bicycles, sauna. Refrigerators avail. Adj to French Quarter. Luxury level. Cr cds: A, C, D, DS, ER, JCB, MC, V.

⊡ ⩰ 🛪 ⊠ 🔥 SC

★ ★ **MONTELEONE.** 214 Rue Royale (70140), in French Quarter. 504/523-3341; res: 800/535-9595; FAX 504/528-1019. 600 rms, 17 story. S $115-$165; D $145-$210; each addl $25; suites $250-$680; under 18 free; higher rates special events. Crib free. TV; cable (premium), VCR avail. Rooftop heated pool; poolside serv. Restaurant

6:30 am-11 pm. Revolving bar 11-2 am; entertainment. Ck-out noon. Meeting rms. Business center. In-rm modem link. Concierge. Shopping arcade. Barber. Valet parking $10. Exercise equipt; weights, bicycles. Some bathrm phones. Family-owned since 1886. Cr cds: A, C, D, DS, JCB, MC, V.

⊡ ⩰ 🛪 ⊠ 🔥 SC ✈

★ ★ ★ **OMNI ROYAL ORLEANS.** 621 St Louis St (70140), in French Quarter. 504/529-5333; res: 800/843-6664; FAX 504/529-7089. Built in 1960, this property re-creates a grand hotel of the 1800s. Gilt mirrors and Italian marble abound in guest rooms and public areas alike; three magnificent lobby chandeliers were imported from France. 346 rms, 7 story. S, D $140-$310; each addl $20; suites $350-$1,000; under 17 free; package plans. Crib free. Valet parking $12. TV; cable (premium), VCR avail. Rooftop heated pool; poolside serv. Restaurant (see RIB ROOM); La Riviera poolside restaurant 9 am-8 pm (Apr-Oct). Rm serv 24 hrs. Bars 11-2 am; entertainment. Ck-out noon. Meeting rms. Business center. In-rm modem link. Concierge. Barber, beauty shop. Exercise equipt; weights, bicycles. Bathrm phones, minibars; some whirlpools. Some balconies. Observation deck. Cr cds: A, C, D, DS, ER, JCB, MC, V.

⊡ ⩰ 🛪 ⊠ 🔥 SC ✈

★ ★ **PONTCHARTRAIN.** 2031 St Charles Ave (70140), in Garden District. 504/524-0581; res: 800/777-6193; FAX 504/529-1165. 102 rms, 12 story. S, D $125-$180; each addl $25; 1-2 bedrm suites $225-$800; under 12 free. Crib free. Valet parking $10. TV; cable, VCR avail. Restaurants 7 am-2:30 pm, 5:30-10 pm (also see CARIBBEAN ROOM). Rm serv 24 hrs. Bar 11-1 am; entertainment Thurs-Sat. Ck-out 1 pm. Meeting rms. Business center. Free airport transportation. Many refrigerators; some wet bars. Landmark of historic neighborhood, rms are individually decorated with an antique motif. Cr cds: A, C, D, DS, MC, V.

⊡ ⊠ 🔥 SC ⊟ ✈

✔ ★ ★ **RAMADA.** 2203 St Charles Ave (70140), in Garden District. 504/566-1200; FAX 504/581-1352. 133 units, 9 story. S $99; D $109; each addl $10; suites $139; under 17 free; higher rates special events. Crib free. TV; cable (premium), VCR avail. Restaurant 6:30 am-2 pm, 5-10 pm. Bar 4-11 pm. Ck-out noon. Meeting rms. Business servs avail. Free airport transportation. Some refrigerators. Cr cds: A, C, D, DS, ER, JCB, MC, V.

⊡ ⊠ 🔥 SC

★ ★ **ROYAL SONESTA.** 300 Bourbon St (70140), in French Quarter. 504/586-0300; res: 800/766-3782; FAX 504/586-0335. 500 rms, 7 story. S $140-$225; D $160-$270; each addl $35; suites $300-$1,000; studio rms $260; under 17 free; travel package plans; min stay required Mardi Gras, special events. Crib free. Garage $13. TV; cable, VCR avail. Heated pool; poolside serv. Restaurants 6:30 am-11:30 pm (also see DESIRE OYSTER BAR). Bars 9-3 am; entertainment. Ck-out noon. Meeting rms. Business center. In-rm modem link. Airport transportation. Exercise equipt; weight machine, bicycle. Minibars. Luxury level. Cr cds: A, C, D, DS, ER, JCB, MC, V.

⊡ ⩰ 🛪 ⊠ 🔥 SC ✈

★ ★ **SHERATON.** 500 Canal St (70130), in central business district. 504/525-2500; FAX 504/595-5550. 1,100 rms, 49 story. S $130-$215; D $155-$239; each addl $25; suites from $250; under 18 free. Crib free. Valet parking $12. TV; cable (premium), VCR avail. Pool; poolside serv. Complimentary coffee in rms. Restaurant 6:30-11 pm. Rm serv 24 hrs. Bar from 11 am; entertainment. Ck-out noon. Convention facilities. Business center. In-rm modem link. Concierge. Shopping arcade. Exercise equipt; weight machine, bicycles. Game rm. Adj to French Quarter. Luxury level. Cr cds: A, C, D, DS, ER, JCB, MC, V.

⊡ ⩰ 🛪 ⊠ 🔥 SC ✈

★ ★ **THE WESTIN CANAL PLACE.** 100 Rue Iberville (70130), in Canal Place Shopping Ctr, in French Quarter. 504/566-7006; FAX 504/553-5120. 438 rms, 29 story. S $165-$180; D $180-$195; each addl $25; suites $245-$1,500; under 19 free; wkend, honeymoon, local attraction packages. Crib free. Garage $12; valet. TV; cable (premium).

Heated pool; poolside serv. Restaurant 6:30 am-10 pm. Rm serv 24 hrs. Bar 11-2 am. Ck-out 1 pm. Convention facilities. Business servs avail. Concierge. Shopping arcade. Barber, beauty shop. 18-hole golf privileges, pro, putting green, driving range. Health club privileges. Bathrm phones, minibars. Outstanding views of Mississippi River. Luxury level. Cr cds: A, C, D, DS, ER, JCB, MC, V.

★ ★ ★ ★ **WINDSOR COURT.** *300 Gravier St (70140), in central business district.* 504/523-6000; res: 800/262-2662; FAX 504/596-4513. This gracious hotel is full of notable art and antiques (art tours are Saturday at 4 pm), yet features exceptionally friendly service. The famous Grill Room is one of the city's best restaurants, and guest rooms feature a muted, elegant decor, with parquet floors and travertine and marble bathrooms. 315 units, 23 story, 275 suites. S, D $235-$290; suites $310-$525, each addl $25; under 18 free. Crib free. Valet parking $15. TV; cable (premium), VCR avail. Heated pool; poolside serv. Restaurant (see GRILL ROOM). British high tea daily (2-6 pm), Sat & Sun brunch. Rm serv 24 hrs. 2 bars from 9 am; entertainment. Ck-out 1 pm. Convention facilities. Business servs avail. In-rm modem link. Concierge. Gift shop. Airport transportation. Indoor tennis privileges adj, pro. 18-hole golf privileges, greens fee $35, pro, putting green, driving range. Exercise rm; instructor, weights, bicycles, whirlpool, sauna, steam rm. Massage. Bathrm phones, refrigerators, minibars; wet bar in suites. Balconies. Cr cds: A, C, D, DS, MC, V.

Inns

★ **THE FRENCHMEN.** *417 Frenchmen St (70116), in Faubourg Marigny.* 504/948-2166; res: 800/831-1781; FAX 504/948-2258. 27 rms, 2 story. S, D $84-$135; each addl $20; summer rates. Indoor parking $5. TV; cable (premium). Pool; whirlpool. Complimentary continental bkfst. Serv bar 24 hrs. Ck-out 1 pm, ck-in 3 pm. Concierge serv 24 hrs. Balconies. Two town houses built 1860; individually decorated rms; antiques. Rms overlook courtyard, pool & patio. Cr cds: A, MC, V.

★ ★ ★ **HOTEL MAISON DE VILLE.** *727 Toulouse St (70130), in French Quarter.* 504/561-5858; res: 800/634-1600; FAX 504/5289939. 23 rms, 1-3 story, 5 cottages. S, D $175-$305; each addl $30; suites $270; kit. cottages $425-$525. Children over 12 yrs only. Valet parking (fee). TV; cable (premium), VCR. Pool at cottages. Complimentary continental bkfst, tea/sherry. Restaurant (see BISTRO). Rm serv. Ck-out noon, ck-in 3 pm. Business servs avail. In-rm modem link. Bellhops. Valet serv. Private patios, balconies. Overlooks courtyard with fountain and garden. Cr cds: A, C, D, DS, MC, V.

★ **HOTEL ST PIERRE.** *911 Rue Burgundy (70116), in French Quarter.* 504/524-4401; FAX 504/524-6800. 75 rms, 2 story. S $99; D $119; each addl $10; under 12 free; wknds (2-night min); higher rates special events; lower rates rest of yr. Crib free. Pet accepted. TV; cable, VCR. 2 pools. Complimentary continental bkfst. Restaurant nearby. Ck-out 11 am. Business servs avail. Bellhops. Concierge. Valet serv. Refrigerators avail. Cr cds: A, C, D, DS, MC, V.

★ ★ ★ **HOUSE ON BAYOU.** *2275 Bayou Rd (70119), in Faubourg Marigny.* 504/945-0992; res: 800/88-BAYOU. 8 rms (1 with shower only), 2 story. Oct-May: S $105; D $105-$245; kit. $105-$135; lower rates rest of yr. Children over 12 yrs only. TV; VCR avail. Pool; whirlpool. Complimentary full bkfst; afternoon refreshments. Ck-out noon, ck-in 3 pm. Concierge serv. Luggage handling. Indigo plantation house built 1798 and furnished with antiques. Dining rm overlooks tropical courtyard. Totally nonsmoking. Cr cds: A, MC, V.

✔ ★ ★ **LAMOTHE HOUSE.** *621 Esplanade Ave (70116), in Faubourg Marigny.* 504/947-1161; res: 800/367-5858; FAX 504/943-6536. 20 rms, 3 story. S, D $95-$195; suites $140-$250. Crib free. TV; cable

(premium), VCR avail. Complimentary continental bkfst. Restaurant nearby. Ck-out 11 am, ck-in 2 pm. Business servs avail. Parking. Airport transportation. Restored town house built around patio; antique furnishings. Adj to French Quarter. Cr cds: A, MC, V.

★ ★ ★ **MELROSE MANSION.** *937 Esplanade Ave (70116), in Faubourg Marigny.* 504/944-2255. 8 rms, 2 story, 4 suites. D $225-$250; suites $325-$425. TV; cable, VCR avail. Heated pool. Complimentary full bkfst, coffee & tea. Restaurant nearby. Rm serv. Ck-out noon, ck-in 1 pm. Business servs avail. Free airport, RR station, bus depot transportation. Some in-rm marble whirlpools. Balconies. Antiques. Library. Historic Victorian-Gothic mansion (1884); pillared verandas, tropical patio. Overlooks French Quarter. Cr cds: A, DS, MC, V.

★ ★ ★ **SONIAT HOUSE.** *1133 Chartres St (70116), in French Quarter.* 504/522-0570; res: 800/544-8808; FAX 504/522-7208. 31 rms, 3 story, 14 suites. S, D $145-$185; each addl $25; suites $235-$600. Adults only. Valet parking $12. TV. Continental bkfst avail. Ck-out 1 pm, ck-in 3 pm. Bellhops. Concierge. Bathrm phones; whirlpool in suites. 1830s town house with carriage entrance and sweeping stairways. Hand-carved four-poster beds; antiques. Private courtyard with fountain and tropical plants. Cr cds: A, MC, V.

Restaurants

★ ★ ★ **ANTOINE'S.** *713 St Louis St, in French Quarter.* 504/581-4422. Hrs: 11:30 am-2 pm, 5:30-9:30 pm. Closed Sun; Mardi Gras; major hols. Res required. French, Creole menu. Serv bar. A la carte entrees: lunch $12-$24, dinner $20-$50. Specialties: oysters Rockefeller, pompano en papillote, souffléed potatoes. Many world-famous dishes have been created & served by Antoine's; one of the great wine cellars of the US. Established 1840. Family-owned. Jacket (dinner). Cr cds: A, C, D, MC, V.

★ ★ ★ **ARNAUD'S.** *813 Rue Bienville, in French Quarter.* 504/523-5433. Hrs: 11:30 am-2:30 pm, 6-10 pm; Fri to 10:30 pm; Sat 6-10:30 pm; Sun 6-10 pm; Sun jazz brunch 10 am-2:30 pm. Closed major hols. Res accepted. French, Creole menu. Bars. Wine cellar. A la carte entrees: lunch $9-$15, dinner $25-$50. Complete meals: lunch $9-$15. Sun brunch $16-$26. Specialties: shrimp Arnaud, pompano en croute, filet mignon Charlemond. Own desserts. Built in 1790; opened in 1918 and restored to original design. Jacket (dinner). Cr cds: A, C, D, MC, V.

★ ★ **BACCO.** *310 Chartres St, in French Quarter.* 504/522-2426. Hrs: 7-10 am, 11:30 am-2:30 pm, 6-10 pm; Sat 8:30-10 am, 11:30 am-2:30 pm, 5:30-10:30 pm; Sun 8:30-10 am, 10:30 am-2:30 pm (brunch), 6-10 pm. Closed Mardi Gras, Dec 24-25. Res accepted. Italian cuisine with Creole accents. Bar. Semi-a la carte: bkfst $4-$7, lunch $7.75-$12, dinner $10.50-$22.50. Sun brunch $7-$12. Specializes in wood-fired pizza, grilled seafood. Parking. Cr cds: A, C, D, MC, V.

★ **BANGKOK CUISINE.** *4137 S Carrollton Ave, west of central business district.* 504/482-3606. Hrs: 11 am-3 pm, 5-10 pm; Fri to 11 pm; Sat 5-11 pm; Sun 5-10 pm. Closed July 4, Thanksgiving, Dec 25. Res accepted. Thai menu. Semi-a la carte: lunch $4.50-$6.95, dinner $6.95-$16.95. Specializes in seafood. Parking. Candlelight dining. Cr cds: A, MC, V.

★ ★ **BAYONA.** *430 Rue Dauphine, in French Quarter.* 504/525-4455. Hrs: 11:30 am-2 pm, 6-10 pm; Fri to 11 pm; Sat 6-11 pm. Closed Sun; Mardi Gras, Easter, Dec 25. Res accepted. Mediterranean menu. Bar. Semi-a la carte: lunch $8-$12, dinner $11-$19. Specializes in grilled duck, fresh fish. Outdoor dining in courtyard with fountain. Located in a century-old Creole cottage. Cr cds: A, D, DS, MC, V.

D

★ ★ ★ **BELLA LUNA.** *914 N Peter, Decatur at Dumaine, in French Quarter.* 504/529-1583. Hrs: 6-10:30 pm. Closed Dec 24; Mardi Gras. Res accepted. Continental menu. Bar. A la carte entrees: dinner $15-$23. Specializes in homemade fettucine, quesadillas, crab cakes. Located in French Market; exceptional view of Mississippi River. Cr cds: A, D, DS, MC, V.

D ⬛

★ ★ **BISTRO.** *(See Hotel Maison De Ville Inn)* 504/528-9206. Hrs: 11:30 am-2 pm, 6-10:30 pm; Sun from 6 pm. Res accepted. Serv bar. Wine list. Semi-a la carte: lunch $10-$13, dinner $17-$25. Specializes in pork, game, local seafood. Own desserts. Outdoor dining. Bistro setting, in 18th-century house. Cr cds: A, D, MC, V.

D ⬛

★ ★ **BON TON CAFE.** *401 Magazine St, in central business district.* 504/524-3386. Hrs: 11 am-2 pm, 5-9:30 pm. Closed Sat, Sun; major hols. Cajun menu. A la carte entrees: lunch $8.50-$19.50, dinner $17.50-$24.25. Child's meals. Specialties: red fish Bon Ton, crawfish dishes. Wrought iron chandelier, shuttered windows, wildlife prints on exposed brick walls. Cr cds: A, D, MC, V.

D ⬛

★ ★ ★ **BRENNAN'S.** *417 Royal St, in French Quarter.* 504/525-9711. Hrs: 8 am-2:30 pm, 6-10 pm. Closed Dec 24 (evening), 25. Res required. French, Creole menu. Bar. Wine cellar. Complete meals: bkfst $18-$37, dinner $28.50-$36. Own desserts. Best known for unusual bkfsts. Cocktails served in courtyard. Located in 1795 mansion where Andrew Jackson was a frequent guest. Family-owned. Cr cds: A, C, D, DS, JCB, MC, V.

D ⬛

★ ★ ★ **BRIGTSEN'S.** *723 Dante St, west of central business district.* 504/861-7610. Hrs: 5:30-10 pm. Closed Sun, Mon; most major hols & Dec 24. Res accepted. Cajun, Creole menu. Serv bar. A la carte entrees: dinner $14-$24. Specializes in rabbit, duck, seafood. Parking. In restored 1900s house built from river barge timbers. French-country decor. Menu changes daily. Cr cds: A, D, MC, V.

★ ★ ★ **BROUSSARD'S.** *819 Rue Conti, in French Quarter.* 504/581-3866. Hrs: 5:30 pm-10 pm. Closed Dec 25. Res accepted. French, Creole menu. Bar. A la carte entrees: dinner $19-$32.50. Specialties: veal Broussard, Pompano Napoleon, bananas Foster. Outdoor dining. Courtyard patio. Jacket. Cr cds: A, C, D, DS, MC, V.

D ⬛

★ **CAFE PONTALBA.** *546 St Peter St (70116), in French Quarter.* 504/522-1180. Hrs: 10:30 am-10 pm; wkends 10 am-11 pm. Closed Dec 25. Cajun, Creole menu. Bar. Semi-a la carte: lunch, dinner $3.95-$15.95. Specializes in gumbo, jambalaya, etouffee. Open restaurant overlooking busy Jackson Square; great for people watching. Family-owned. Cr cds: DS, MC, V.

⬛

★ ★ **CARIBBEAN ROOM.** *(See Pontchartrain Hotel)* 504/524-0581. Hrs: 6-10 pm; Sun 11 am-2:30 pm. Closed Mon. Creole menu. Bar. Wine cellar. A la carte entrees: dinner $4.25-$39.95. Sun brunch $19.95. Child's meals. Specialties: trout Eugene, crab Remick, Creole classic gumbo. Valet parking. Formal dining in romantic setting. In business since 1927. Totally nonsmoking. Cr cds: A, C, D, DS, MC, V.

D

✔ ★ **CASAMENTO'S.** *4330 Magazine, west of central business district.* 504/895-9761. Hrs: 11:30 am-1:30 pm, 5:30-9 pm. Closed Mon; some major hols; June-Aug. Beer. Semi-a la carte: lunch, dinner

$5-$15. Child's meals. Specializes in oyster loaves, seafood gumbo, soft shell crab. Family-owned. No cr cds accepted.

D

★ ★ ★ **CHRISTIAN'S.** *3835 Iberville St, north of central business district.* 504/482-4924. Hrs: 11:30 am-2 pm, 5:30-10 pm; Sat from 5:30 pm. Closed Sun & Mon; Dec 25. Res accepted. French, Creole menu. Bar. Wine cellar. Complete meals: lunch $9.75-$15.50. A la carte entrees: dinner $12.50-$20. Specialties: oysters Roland, baby veal Christian, bouillabaisse. Homemade ices, ice cream. Parking. In renovated former church (1904). Cr cds: A, C, D, MC, V.

D ⬛

★ ★ ★ **COMMANDER'S PALACE.** *1403 Washington Ave, in Garden District.* 504/899-8221. Hrs: 11:30 am-2 pm, 6-10 pm; Sat brunch 11:30 am-1 pm; Sun brunch 10 am-1 pm. Closed Mardi Gras, Dec 24, 25. Res accepted. Haute Creole menu. Bar. Wine cellar. Semi-a la carte: lunch $12-$24, dinner $19-$26. Complete meals: lunch $10.50-$14, dinner $27-$35. Brunch $19-$26. Specialties: turtle soup, trout with roasted pecans, bread pudding soufflé. Dixieland band at brunch. Valet parking. Outdoor dining. Located in Queen Anne/Victorian building in residential area. Family-owned. Jacket (dinner & Sun brunch). Cr cds: A, C, D, DS, MC, V.

D ⬛

★ ★ **COURT OF TWO SISTERS.** *613 Royal St, in French Quarter.* 504/522-7261. Hrs: 5:30-10 pm; brunch 9 am-3 pm. Closed Dec 25. Res accepted. French, Creole menu. Bar. A la carte entrees: dinner $5.50-$30. Complete meals: dinner $35, brunch $21. Child's meals. Specialties: shrimp Toulouse, lobster étouffée. Jazz trio at brunch. Outdoor dining. Built in 1832; spacious patio; courtyard. Family-owned. Cr cds: A, D, DS, MC, V.

D ⬛

★ ★ **DELMONICO.** *1300 St Charles Ave (70130), in Garden District.* 504/525-4937. Hrs: 11:30 am-9 pm; Fri & Sat to 9:30 pm. Closed some major hols. Res accepted. Creole menu. Bar. Semi-a la carte: lunch $8.50-$16.50, dinner $12.50-$22. Specialties: stuffed shrimp, seafood kebab, blackened catfish. Parking. Although the decor is formal, the atmosphere is decisively friendly; original works by local artist John McRady hang on the walls. Family-owned since 1911. Cr cds: A, C, D, DS, MC, V.

D ⬛

✔ ★ **DESIRE OYSTER BAR.** *(See Royal Sonesta Hotel)* 504/586-0300. Hrs: 11:30 am-11:30 pm; Fri, Sat to 12:30 am. Bar. Semi-a la carte: lunch, dinner $7-$15.25. Child's meals. Specializes in Creole cuisine. Own baking. Parking. Bistro doors & windows offer view of French Quarter streets. Cr cds: A, C, D, DS, ER, JCB, MC, V.

D ⬛

★ ★ ★ **EMERIL'S.** *800 Tchoupitoulas St, in central business district.* 504/528-9393. Hrs: 11:30 am-2 pm, 6-10 pm; Sat from 6 pm. Closed Sun; Mardi Gras, most major hols. Res accepted. Creole, Amer menu. Bar. Wine list. A la carte entrees: lunch $6-$15, dinner $14-$28. Menu changes seasonally. Located in renovated warehouse. Near convention center. Cr cds: A, C, D, DS, MC, V.

D ⬛

★ ★ **FEELINGS CAFE.** *2600 Chartres St, in Faubourg Marigny.* 504/945-2222. Hrs: 6-10 pm; Fri 11 am-2 pm, 6-11 pm; Sat 6-11 pm; Sun 5-9 pm; Sun brunch 11 am-2:30 pm. Closed Thanksgiving, Dec 25; also Mardi Gras. Creole menu. Bar. Semi-a la carte: lunch $8.75-$14.75, dinner $9.75-$16.75. Sun brunch $14-$18.50. Specializes in seafood, veal, baked duck with orange glaze. Own desserts. Pianist Fri-Sat. Outdoor dining. Located in out-building of 18th-century plantation; antiques, original artwork. Cr cds: A, C, D, DS, MC, V.

D ⬛

✔ ★ **FIVE HAPPINESS.** *3605 S Carrollton Ave, west of central business district.* 504/488-6468. Hrs: 11:30 am-10:30 pm; Fri, Sat to 11:30 pm; Sun noon-10:30 pm. Closed Thanksgiving. Chinese menu. Bar. Semi-a la carte: lunch from $5.20, dinner from $6.95. Specializes in mandarin & Szechwan dishes. Parking. Cr cds: A, C, D, DS, MC, V.

D ⌂

★ ★ **G & E COURTYARD GRILL.** 1113 Decatur St, in French Quarter. 504/528-9376. Hrs: 11:30 am-2:30 pm, 6-10 pm; Fri, Sat to 11 pm; Sun 6-10 pm. Closed Mon; Thanksgiving, Dec 25. Res accepted. Continental menu. Bar. A la carte entrees: lunch $9-$15, dinner $11-$23. Specializing in grilled loin chops, grilled salmon filet. Patio dining in canopied courtyard. European cafe atmosphere. Cr cds: A, C, D, DS, MC, V.

⌂

★ ★ **GABRIELLE.** 3201 Esplanade Ave (70119), north of central business district. 504/948-6233. Hrs: 5:30-10 pm; Fri 11:30 am-2 pm, 5:30-10 pm. Closed Sun & Mon; major hols; also closed Mardi Gras. Res accepted. Bar. Semi-a la carte: dinner $13-$21. Specializes in contemporary Creole cuisine. Own sausage, desserts. Parking. Outdoor dining. Bistro atmosphere. Cr cds: A, C, D, DS, MC, V.

★ ★ **GALATOIRE'S.** 209 Bourbon St, in French Quarter. 504/525-2021. Hrs: 11:30 am-9 pm; Sun from noon. Closed Mon; major hols; also Mardi Gras. French, Creole menu. Serv bar. A la carte entrees: lunch, dinner $13-$24. Specialties: trout Marguery, oysters en bronchette. Family-owned. Jacket (after 5 pm). Cr cds: A, MC, V.

D ⌂

★ ★ ★ **GAUTREAU'S.** 1728 Soniat St (70115), west of central business district. 504/899-7397. Hrs: 6-10 pm. Closed Sun; most major hols; also 1st 2 wks July. Res accepted. New American cuisine. Wine. A la carte entrees: dinner $11-$21.95. Specializes in seafood, Contemporary Louisiana cooking. Menu changes seasonally. Valet parking. Former drug store from early 1900s; original medicine cabinets, pressed-tin ceiling. Totally non-smoking. Cr cds: A, C, D, DS, MC, V.

★ ★ ★ ★ **GRILL ROOM.** (See Windsor Court Hotel) 504/522-1992. Rejuvenated Creole classics are elegantly served on the covered terrace or in the deep-carpeted, dining rooms outfitted with British furnishings and paintings spanning several centuries. Hrs: 7-10:30 am, 11:30 am-2:30 pm, 6:30-10:30 pm; Sat, Sun from 10:30 am, brunch to 2:30 pm. Res accepted. Continental, regional cuisine. Bar 11 am-midnight. Wine cellar. A la carte entrees: bkfst $8-$13, lunch $9.75-$19.75, dinner $19.50-$45. Sat & Sun brunch $16-$27. Specialties: oysters polo, rack of lamb, mandarin coffee glazed duck, fresh seafood. Own baking. Valet parking. Jacket. Cr cds: A, C, D, DS, MC, V.

D ⌂

★ ★ **L'ECONOMIE.** 325 Girod St, in central business district. 504/524-7405. Hrs: 11 am-2 pm, 6-9:30 pm; Fri to 10:30 pm; Sat 6-10:30 pm. Closed Sun; Mardi Gras, major hols. Res accepted. French menu. Bar. A la carte entrees: lunch $6-$13, dinner $12-$24. Specialties: seared ostrich with port wine, poached salmon with mango buerre blanc, par-baked oysters with Danish blue cheese. Bistro atmosphere. Cr cds: A, C, D, DS, MC, V.

D ⌂

✔ ★ **LOUISIANA PIZZA KITCHEN.** 2808 Esplanade Ave, north of central business district. 504/488-2800. Hrs: 5:30-11 pm. Closed Dec 25. Mediterranean menu. Bar. A la carte entrees: dinner $6-$10. Specializes in wood-fired gourmet pizza. Local artwork on display. Cr cds: A, C, D, DS, MC, V.

⌂

★ ★ **MAXIMO'S ITALIAN GRILL.** 1117 Rue Decatur, in French Quarter. 504/586-8883. Hrs: 6 pm-midnight. Northern Italian menu. Bar. Semi-a la carte: dinner $8.95-$24.95. Specializes in pasta, veal, grilled fish. Own desserts, ice cream. Outdoor balcony dining. Contemporary decor with antique light fixtures. Cr cds: A, C, D, DS, MC, V.

D ⌂

★ **MIKE ANDERSON'S.** 215 Bourbon St (70130), in French Quarter. 504/524-3884. Hrs: 11:30 am-10 pm; Fri & Sat to 11 pm. Closed Thanksgiving, Dec 25. Bar. Semi-a la carte: lunch, dinner $7.95-$15.95. Specializes in broiled seafood, Po-Boys, guitreau. Oyster bar. Nautical decor utilizing much brass. Cr cds: A, D, DS, MC, V.

D ⌂

★ ★ ★ **MIKE'S ON THE AVENUE.** 628 St Charles Ave, in the Lafayette Hotel, in central business district. 504/523-1709. Hrs: 11:30 am-2 pm, 6-10 pm; Sat & Sun from 6 pm. Closed some major hols. Res accepted. Bar. Wine list. Asian/Southwest fusion menu. Semi-a la carte: lunch $4.75-$14, dinner $32-$50. Specializes in Chinese dumplings, crayfish cakes, grilled lamb chops. Cr cds: A, C, D, DS, MC, V.

D ⌂

★ ★ **MOSCA'S.** 4137 US 90W, 4¹/₂ mi W of Huey Long Bridge, west of central business district. 504/436-9942. Hrs: 5:30-9:30 pm. Closed Sun, Mon; Dec 25; also Aug. Res accepted. Italian menu. Bar. A la carte entrees: dinner $23-$28. Specializes in shrimp, chicken, oysters. Own pasta. Parking. Family-owned. No cr cds accepted.

⌂

★ ★ ★ **MR B'S BISTRO.** 201 Royal St, in French Quarter. 504/523-2078. Hrs: 11:30 am-3 pm, 5:30-10 pm; Sun jazz brunch 10:30 am-3 pm. Closed Mardi Gras, Dec 24-25. Res accepted. Creole menu. Bar. Wine list. Complete meals: lunch $10-$15, dinner $18-$26. Semi-a la carte: lunch $9-$11, dinner $10-$22. Sun brunch $7.50-$12.75. Specializes in pasta, hickory-grilled food, seafood. Entertainment. Bistro decor with mahogany bar, etched-glass walls, white marble-topped tables. Cr cds: A, D, MC, V.

D ⌂

★ ★ **NOLA.** 534 St Louis St (70130), in French Quarter. 504/522-6652. Hrs: 11:30 am-2 pm, 6-10 pm; Fri & Sat to midnight; Sun from 6 pm. Closed Jan 1, Thanksgiving, Dec 25. Res accepted. Creole menu. Bar. Semi-a la carte: lunch $8-$15, dinner $10-$20. Specialties: Lafayette Boudin stewed with beer, onions, cane syrup and Creole mustard, cedar plank roasted Gulf fish. In renovated warehouse. Original artwork. Cr cds: A, C, D, DS, MC, V.

D ⌂

★ **THE ORIGINAL FRENCH MARKET.** 1001 Decatur St, in French Quarter. 504/581-9855. Hrs: 11 am-11 pm; Fri to midnight; Sat to 1 am. Closed Thanksgiving, Dec 25. Creole, Cajun menu, oyster bar. Bar. Semi-a la carte: lunch, dinner $6-$20. Child's meals. Specializes in fresh seafood. Entertainment; Fri, Sat evenings. Balcony dining. Beamed ceiling, gaslight sconces, brick bar. Cr cds: A, C, D, DS, MC, V.

D ⌂

★ ★ ★ **PELICAN CLUB.** 312 Exchange Place (70130), in French Quarter. 504/523-1504. Hrs: 5:30-10 pm; Fri & Sat to 11 pm. Closed Easter, Thanksgiving, Dec 25; also Mardi Gras. Res accepted. Continental menu. Bar. Wine cellar. Semi-a la carte: $5.50-$21.50. Specialties: claypot seafood with glass noodles, pecan-crusted fish with Louisiana oysters, broiled Atlantic salmon. Piano bar. Three dining rms in a converted townhouse. Understated, casual elegance. Cr cds: A, C, D, DS, MC, V.

D ⌂

✔ ★ **PRALINE CONNECTION.** 542 Frenchmen St, in Faubourg Marigny. 504/943-3934. Hrs: 11 am-10:30 pm; Fri, Sat to midnight. Closed Dec 25. Southern Creole menu. Bar. Semi-a la carte: lunch $3-$5.95, dinner $4-$12.95. Child's meals. Specializes in fried chicken, pork chops, bread pudding with praline sauce. Candy room features praline confections. Cr cds: A, C, D, DS, MC, V.

D ⌂

★ ★ ★ **RIB ROOM.** (See Omni Royal Orleans Hotel) 504/529-7045. Hrs: 6:30 am-3 pm, 6-11 pm; Sat & Sun brunch 11:30 am-3 pm. Res accepted. Bar. Wine cellar. Semi-a la carte: lunch $12-$17, dinner

$20-$26. Sat & Sun brunch $8.50-$15.50. Specializes in rotisserie prime rib, seafood, traditional dishes with Creole flair. Own pastries. Parking. Cr cds: A, C, D, DS, MC, V.

SC ⌐⌐

✔★ **ROBEAR'S LIGHTHOUSE BAR & GRILL.** 7360 W Roadway, West End Park, west of central business district. 504/282-3415. Hrs: 11 am-10 pm; Fri, Sat to 11 pm. Bar to 2 am. Semi-a la carte: lunch, dinner $4.95-$12.95. Child's meals. Specializes in seafood. Parking. Patio dining. Cr cds: A, MC, V.

D ⌐⌐

★★ **SAZERAC.** (See Fairmont Hotel) 504/529-7111. Hrs: 11:30 am-2 pm, 6-10 pm; Sat from 10 am. Res accepted. French Creole menu. A la carte entrees: lunch $10-$15, dinner $17-$32. Complete meals: lunch $14.95. Specialties: roast Louisiana duckling, grilled pompano, grilled veal chops. Own pastries, desserts. Pianist 6-10 pm and Sun brunch. Valet parking. Formal decor; original art. Cr cds: A, C, D, DS, JCB, MC, V.

⌐⌐

★ **SNUG HARBOR JAZZ BISTRO.** 626 Frenchmen St (70116), in Faubourg Marigny. 504/949-0696. Hrs: 5-11:30 pm; Fri & Sat to 12:30 am. Closed Easter, Dec 25. Bar to 1:30 am. Semi-a la carte: dinner $5.50-$18. Child's meals. Specializes in hamburgers, shrimp. Modern jazz nightly. Casual dining. Cr cds: A, MC, V.

D ⌐⌐

★★ **TAVERN ON THE PARK.** 900 City Park Ave, north of central business district. 504/486-3333. Hrs: 11:30 am-2:30 pm, 5-10 pm; Sat from 5 pm. Closed Sun & Mon; Mardi Gras, Thanksgiving, Dec 25. Res accepted. Creole menu. Bar. Semi-a la carte: lunch $7-$11, dinner $20-$25. Complete meals: lunch $10.95, dinner $24.95. Child's meals. Specialties: Australian lobster tail, stuffed soft shell crab, trout Martha. Parking. Outdoor dining. Overlooks park. Cr cds: A, C, D, DS, JCB, MC, V.

D ⌐⌐

★ **TONY MORAN'S PASTA E VINO.** 240 Bourbon St, at Old Absinthe House, in French Quarter. 504/523-3181. Hrs: 5:30 pm-midnight. Closed Mon; Dec 25. Res accepted. Italian menu. Bar. A la carte entrees: dinner $7-$16. Specializes in Northern Italian cuisine, fresh pasta. Family-owned. Cr cds: A, C, D, MC, V.

D ⌐⌐

★★ **TUJAGUE'S.** 823 Decatur St, in French Quarter. 504/525-8676. Hrs: 11 am-3 pm, 5-10:30 pm; Sat to 11 pm. Res accepted. French, Creole menu. Bar 10 am-11 pm. Complete meals: lunch $6.95-$13.95, dinner $23.95-$28.95. Child's meals. Specialties: shrimp Creole, crawfish, crab & spinach bisque. Established in 1856 in old Spanish armory (1750); original tile, authentic beams. Oldest standing bar in city. Cr cds: A, C, D, DS, JCB, MC, V.

D ⌐⌐

★★★ **UPPERLINE.** 1413 Upperline St (70115), in central business district. 504/891-9822. Hrs: 5:30-9:30 pm. Closed Tues; July 4, Thanksgiving, Dec 25. Res required. Bar. Wine cellar. A la carte entrees: dinner $5.50-$18.50. Complete meals $25-$35. Child's meals. Specialties: roast duck with garlic port, fried green tomatoes with remoulade sauce. Parking. Famous for the artwork displayed, this restaurant is a favorite for romantic dinners. French windows afford view of garden. Cr cds: A, D, MC, V.

D ⌐⌐

★★★ **THE VERANDA.** (See Inter-Continental Hotel) 504/525-5566. Hrs: 6:30 am-2 pm, 5:30-10 pm; Sun jazz brunch 11 am-2:30 pm. Res accepted. Continental menu. Bar 11-1 am. A la carte entrees: bkfst $8.95-$13, lunch $7-$14, dinner $8.95-$21.95. Buffet: bkfst $12.95, lunch $11.95. Sun brunch $24. Specializes in regional American dishes,

seafood. Valet parking. Garden-like setting. Cr cds: A, C, D, DS, JCB, MC, V.

D ⌐⌐

★★ **VERSAILLES.** 2100 St Charles Ave, in Garden District. 504/524-2535. Hrs: 6-10 pm. Closed Sun; Mardi Gras, major hols; also 2 wks in summer. Res accepted. French, Creole menu. Bar. Wine cellar. A la carte entrees: dinner $18-$28. Specialties: bouillabaisse Marseillaise, veal Farci Versailles, chocolate pava. Own baking. Free valet parking. Cr cds: A, C, D, MC, V.

D ⌐⌐

★★ **WINDJAMMER.** 8550 Pontchartrain Blvd, west of central business district. 504/283-8301. Hrs: 11 am-11 pm; Fri to midnight; Sat 5 pm-midnight; Sun 5-11 pm. Closed Mardi Gras, July 4, Labor Day, Dec 25. Res accepted. Cajun, Amer menu. Bar. Semi-a la carte: lunch $7.95-$11.95, dinner $7.95-$24.95. Specializes in seafood, steak. Family-owned. Cr cds: A, C, D, DS, MC, V.

D ⌐⌐

Unrated Dining Spots

ANGELO BROCATA'S ITALIAN ICE CREAM PARLOR. 537 St Ann St, on Jackson Square, in French Quarter. 504/525-9676. Hrs: 10 am-6 pm; Fri to 10 pm; Sat to 11 pm; Sun 9 am-8 pm. Closed Thanksgiving, Dec 25. Specializes in Italian ice creams, ices & baked goods. Est 1905. In Lower Portalbo Apartments on Jackson Square. No cr cds accepted.

⌐⌐

CAFE DU MONDE. 800 Decatur St, at St Ann St in French Quarter. 504/525-4544. Open 24 hrs. Closed Dec 25. Specializes in beignets (hot doughnuts sprinkled with powdered sugar), New Orleans chicory coffee, cafe au lait. Covered outdoor dining. In French Market. No cr cds accepted.

⌐⌐

CAMELLIA GRILL. 626 S Carrollton Ave, west of central business district. 504/866-9573. Hrs: 9-1 am; Fri to 3 am; Sat 8-3 am; Sun 8-1 am. Closed most hols. Semi-a la carte: bkfst, lunch, dinner $1.50-$7. Specializes in omelettes, gourmet sandwiches, pecan pie. Popular night spot; unique place. Family-owned. No cr cds accepted.

CENTRAL GROCERY. 923 Decatur St, in French Quarter. 504/523-1620. Hrs: 8 am-5:30 pm; Sun from 9 am. A la carte entrees: bkfst, lunch, dinner $3.75-$6.95. Specialty: muffuletta sandwich. French, Greek & Syrian foods. Sandwich bar in Italian grocery. Near Jackson Square. Family-owned. No cr cds accepted.

CHEZ NOUS CHARCUTERIE. 5701 Magazine St, west of central business district. 504/899-7303. Hrs: 11 am-6:30 pm; Sat to 5 pm. Closed Sun; most major hols. Creole menu. A la carte entrees: lunch $1.65-$6.50. Specialties: grillades, jambalaya. Outdoor dining. Gourmet delicatessen in grocery store. Cr cds: MC, V.

CLOVER GRILL. 900 Bourbon St (70116), in French Quarter. 504/523-0904. Open 24 hrs. A la carte entrees: bkfst $2-$5, lunch, dinner $3-$7. Specializes in hamburgers, club sandwiches. Open kitchen. No cr cds accepted.

⌐⌐

LA MADELEINE. 547 St Ann St, in French Quarter. 504/568-9950. Hrs: 7 am-9 pm. Closed Jan 1. French menu. Wine, beer. Avg ck: bkfst $5, lunch, dinner $7.50. Specializes in croissants, quiche, pastries. Own baking. Located in one of the famous Pontalba Bldgs (1851) on Jackson Sq. No cr cds accepted.

SC

MOTHER'S. 401 Poydras St, in central business district. 504/523-9656. Hrs: 5 am-10 pm; Sun from 7 am. Cajun, Creole menu. A la carte entrees: bkfst $4.75-$7.50, lunch, dinner $3.75-$8. Specializes in New Orleans plate lunches, po' boys sandwiches, Mother's "ferdi special" (mix of ham & beef). Former residence (1830); extensive collection of US Marine memorabilia. Cafeteria-style service. No cr cds accepted.

Opelousas (D-3)

(See Lafayette)

Founded ca 1720 **Pop** 18,151 **Elev** 70 ft **Area code** 318 **Zip** 70570

Information Tourist Information Ctr, 220 Academy St; 800/424-5442; or contact the Tourism & Activities Committee, 441 E Grolee, PO Box 712; 318/948-4731.)

French is spoken as often as English in this charming old town, the third oldest in the state. Opelousas was a trading post from the early 1700s until 1774, when St Landry's church was established. Farm specialties are yams, cotton, corn, rice and soybeans. These crops, along with beef, pork and dairy products, bring millions into the parish annually.

What to See and Do

Chicot State Park. Nearly 6,000 acres of rolling woodland surround a 2,000-acre artificial lake stocked with bream, bass and crappie. Swimming, fishing; boating (launch, rentals). Hiking. Camping, cabins. Standard fees. (Daily) 36 mi NW via US 167, LA 3042 near Ville Platte. Phone 318/363-2503. Per vehicle ¢ Also here is

Louisiana State Arboretum. The 300-acre arboretum on Lake Chicot includes more than 150 species of plant life indigenous to Louisiana; nature trails. (Daily) Phone 318/363-2403. **Free.**

Jim Bowie Museum. Bowie memorabilia. Local historical items; 18th-century colonial house built by a woman named Venus. (Daily; closed major hols) Donation. E end of US 190 and Academy St. Phone 318/948-6263 or 800/424-5442.

Washington. Built between 1780 and 1835, the antebellum buildings in this historic river port include Hinckley House (1803), House of History (1820), Camellia Cove (1825), De La Morandiere (1830). Many houses are open for tours (fee). 6 mi N via I-49 at LA 103. Check locally for hours and fees or phone 826-3627 or -3906.

Annual Event

Louisiana Yambilee. Yambilee Fairgrounds, US 190W. Held in honor of the yam; although often confused, the yam and the sweet potato are, technically, two distinct species. Last full wkend Oct.

Motel

★ **QUALITY INN.** 4501 I-49 S, I-49 exit 15. 318/948-9500; FAX 318/942-5035. 67 rms, 2 story. S $56-$58; D $62-$68; each addl $6; suites $92; under 18 free. Crib $5. TV; cable (premium). Pool; whirlpool, sauna, poolside serv. Restaurant 6:30-9:30 am, 11 am-1:30 pm, 6-10 pm; Sat, Sun 7-11 am. Rm serv. Bar from 4 pm, closed Sun; dancing Mon-Sat. Ck-out noon. Meeting rms. Business center. In-rm modem link. Balconies. Cr cds: A, C, D, DS, ER, JCB, MC, V.

Restaurant

★ ★ **STEAMBOAT WAREHOUSE.** *(Main St, Washington 70589)* 6 mi N via I-49, exit 25. 318/826-7227. Hrs: 5-10 pm; Sun 11 am-2 pm. Closed Dec 25. Cajun menu. Bar. Semi-a la carte: lunch, dinner $12-$15. Specialties: crawfish etouffee, crawfish palmetto, cat-

fish Lizzy. Parking. Restored historic building in charming town filled with antebellum buildings. Cr cds: A, DS, MC, V.

Ruston (A-2)

Founded 1884 **Pop** 20,027 **Elev** 319 ft **Area code** 318 **Zip** 71270

Information Ruston/Lincoln Convention and Visitors Bureau, 900 N Trenton, Box 150, 71273-0150; 318/255-2031.

What to See and Do

Lincoln Parish Museum. Restored house (1886) with items of local history. (Mon-Fri; closed hols) 609 N Vienna St. Phone 318/251-0018. **Free.**

Louisiana Tech University (1894). (10,150 students) The campus, which is wooded and hilly, is on the west side of Ruston; the Horticture Center with more than 500 species of native and exotic plants is south of town, off US 80W (Mon-Fri; free); also the Louisiana Tech Equine Center (daily; free). Phone 318/257-0221 or -4427.

Annual Event

Louisiana Peach Festival. 2nd wkend June.

Seasonal Event

Louisiana Passion Play. For reservations phone 318/255-6277 or 800/204-2101. June-Sept.

Motels

✔ ★ ★ **BEST WESTERN KINGS INN.** 1111 N Trenton, I-20 at US 167 exit 85. 318/251-0000; FAX 318/251-1453. 52 rms, 2 story. S $40-$48; D $50-$60; each addl $3; higher rates special events. Crib $2. TV; cable (premium). Pool. Complimentary continental bkfst. Restaurant adj 11 am-midnight. Ck-out noon. Coin lndry. Business servs avail. In-rm modem link. Some refrigerators. Cr cds: A, C, D, DS, MC, V.

★ **COMFORT INN.** 1801 N Service Rd E, I-20 exit 86. 318/251-2360; FAX 318/251-2370. 50 rms, 2 story. S $45-$50; D $50-$55; each addl $5; under 18 free. Crib $5. TV; cable. Pool. Complimentary continental bkfst 6:30-9:30 am. Ck-out noon. Free airport transportation. Cr cds: A, C, D, DS, ER, JCB, MC, V.

★ ★ **HOLIDAY INN.** Box 1189, 3/4 mi E at jct US 167, I-20. 318/255-5901; FAX 318/255-3729. 231 rms, 1-2 story. S $44-$62; D $46-$64; each addl $6; suites $105-$120; under 19 free. Crib free. Pet accepted. TV; cable. 2 pools; wading pool. Playground. Restaurant 6 am-10 pm. Rm serv. Ck-out noon. Coin lndry. Meeting rms. Valet serv. Lawn games. Cr cds: A, C, D, DS, JCB, MC, V.

St Francisville (C-3)

(See Baton Rouge, Jackson)

Pop 1,700 **Elev** 115 ft **Area code** 504 **Zip** 70775

Information West Feliciana Historical Society, 11757 Ferdinand St, PO Box 338; 504/635-6330.

This picturesque old town, chartered under Spanish dominion, has been called "two miles long and two yards wide" because it was built on a narrow ridge. St Francisville is listed on the National Register of Historic Places.

What to See and Do

 Plantations and historic buildings. (For details see What to See and Do under BATON ROUGE; the following directions are from St Francisville.) **Catalpa,** 4 mi N on US 61; **Oakley,** 1 mi S via US 61, then 3 mi E on LA 965; **Cottage,** 5 mi N on US 61; **Butler Greenwood,** 3 mi N on US 61; **Greenwood,** 3 mi N on US 61, then 4 1/2 mi W on LA 66 to Highland Rd; **Rosedown,** E of town on LA 10; **Rosemont,** 24 mi N on US 61. Also of interest are **Grace Episcopal Church** (1858), in town on LA 10; **Afton Villa Gardens,** 4 mi N on US 61; and the **Myrtles Plantation,** 1 mi N on US 61.

Annual Event

Audubon Pilgrimage. Tour of historic plantation houses, two gardens and rural homestead. 3rd wkend Mar.

Inns

★ ★ **BARROW HOUSE.** *9779 Royal St.* 504/635-4791. 5 rms, 3 suites. 2 rm phones. S $75; D $95; each addl $20; suites $115-$135. Closed Dec 22-25. TV, VCR. Complimentary tea/sherry. Dinner by advance res. Ck-out 11 am, ck-in 3-7 pm. Business servs avail. Library/sitting rm. Built in 1809; antiques. Cr cds: MC, V.

★ **WOLF SCHLESINGER HOUSE - ST FRANCISVILLE INN.** *5720 N Commerce St.* 504/635-6502; *res:* 800/488-6502. 9 rms, 1-2 story. S $55-$60; D $65-$70; each addl $8; under 6 free. Crib free. TV; cable. Pool. Complimentary full bkfst. Restaurant (see ST FRANCISVILLE INN). Ck-out 11 am, ck-in noon. Library/sitting rm. Built in 1880; Victorian architecture. Ceiling medallion decorated with Mardi Gras masks. Cr cds: A, C, D, DS, MC, V.

Restaurant

★ ★ **ST FRANCISVILLE INN.** *(See Wolf Schlesinger House - St Francisville Inn)* 504/635-6502. Hrs: 11 am-2 pm, 5:30-8:30 pm; Sun to 2 pm. Closed Mon & Tues, also major hols. Southern Louisiana, Cajun menu. Bar. Semi-a la carte: lunch $2.95-$8.45, dinner $5.95-$16.95. Specializes in seafood, steak. Own desserts. Parking. Restored Victorian mansion (1880); New Orleans-style courtyard; large oak trees with Spanish moss. Cr cds: A, C, D, DS, MC, V.

St Martinville (D-3)

(See Lafayette, New Iberia)

Settled ca 1760 **Pop** 7,137 **Elev** 19 ft **Area code** 318 **Zip** 70582
Information Chamber of Commerce, Box 436; phone 318/394-7578.

Few towns in Louisiana have a more colorful history than St Martinville. On the winding, peaceful Bayou Teche, St Martinville was first settled about 1760. In the years thereafter, Acadians, driven out of Nova Scotia by the British, drifted into St Martinville with the hope of finding religious tolerance. The town is the setting for part of Henry Wadsworth Longfellow's "Evangeline." Although based on an actual romance between Emmeline Labiche and Louis Arceneaux, Longfellow took considerable liberty with the facts.

During the French Revolution, many Royalist refugees came to St Martinville, and for a time, barons, marquises and counts, with their elegantly gowned ladies, attended luxurious balls and operas, which led to the town being called *Le Petit Paris.* Members of the colony steadfastly believed they would one day return to France and rule again.

In quick succession, yellow fever, a terrible fire, a hurricane and the end of steamboat travel on the bayou triggered the decline of the town at about the time of the Civil War. Today, St Martinville is a quiet, old-fashioned hamlet.

What to See and Do

Evangeline Oak. This ancient, moss-draped live oak is said to be the meeting place of the real Evangeline and her Gabriel. On the bayou at end of Port St.

Longfellow-Evangeline State Commemorative Area. This 157-acre park, on the banks of the Bayou Teche, is a reconstruction of a typical 19th-century plantation. The restored Olivier plantation was begun in approximately 1810 by Pierre Olivier du Clozel, a French Creole. The structure employs wooden pegs; walls are made of Spanish moss-mixed bousillage and cypress; period furnishings; replica of 1840s kitchen and kitchen garden. Fishing; boating (launch). Picnicking. (Daily; closed Jan 1, Thanksgiving, Dec 25) Standard fees. Just N of town on LA 31. Phone 318/394-3754. ¢

St Martin of Tours Catholic Church (1837). Established in 1765 as mother church of the exiled Acadians, the present, restored building contains stained glass windows; an exquisitely carved baptismal font, which was a gift of Louis XVI of France; a gold and silver sanctuary light; a painting of St Martin de Tours by Jean Francois Mouchet; and other religious artifacts. Guided tours (by appt only). Sr citizen rate. 103 S Main St. Phone 318/394-7334. Tours ¢¢ Behind the church's left wing is

Evangeline Monument. Monument marks the spot where Emmeline Labiche, "Evangeline," is believed to be buried. Monument was erected by Dolores Del Rio, who portrayed Evangeline in a 1929 silent movie filmed in St Martinsville. On church square is

Petit Paris Museum. Museum contains a collection of elaborate carnival costumes, local memorabilia and gift shop. (Daily) Phone 318/394-7334. ¢¢ Also on square is

Presbytère. The priest's residence, Greek revival in style, was constructed in 1856. By legend, it was built in such a grand manor in the hope that St Martinville would be designated as seat of the diocese. (Daily) Phone 318/394-7334. Tours ¢¢

Inn

✔ ★ ★ **OLD CASTILLO HOTEL.** *220 Evangeline Blvd.* 318/394-4010; *res:* 800/621-3017; *FAX* 318/394-7983. 5 rms, 2 story. No rm phones. S, D $50-$80. Complimentary full bkfst. Restaurant (see LA PLACE D'EVANGELINE). Ck-out, ck-in 1 pm (flexible). Street parking. Library/sitting rm. Historic hotel, built early 1800s. Located on the banks of Bayou Teche, beneath the Evangeline Oak; near Evangeline Oak Park. Cr cds: A, MC, V.

Restaurant

★ **LA PLACE D'EVANGELINE.** *(See Old Castillo Hotel Inn)* 318/394-4010. Hrs: 8 am-9 pm; Mon & Tues to 5 pm; Sun to 2 pm. Closed Jan 1, Thanksgiving, Dec 25. Res accepted Fri, Sat. French, Cajun menu. Bar. Semi-a la carte: bkfst $1.50-$5, lunch, dinner $4.95-$22. Child's meals. Specializes in seafood. Casual dining; overlooks Bayou Teche. Cr cds: A, MC, V.

Shreveport (A-1)

(See Bossier City)

Founded 1839 **Pop** 198,525 **Elev** 204 ft **Area code** 318

Information Shreveport-Bossier Convention & Tourist Bureau, 629 Spring St, PO Box 1761, 71166; 318/222-9391 or 800/551-8682.

The Red River was, until 1835, jammed for nearly 165 miles of its course with driftwood, snags and tree trunks; then Henry Miller Shreve, river captain and steamboat inventor, bulled his way through this "Great Raft" to cut a channel. He founded Shreveport, which thrived as a river town until the river silted up and steamboats could no longer navigate it. The river is in the process of being rehabilitated to allow barge traffic to travel from the Gulf to Shreveport. Oil and gas were discovered in the area in 1905. Now Shreveport is a heavily industrialized city and lumber-producing center.

What to See and Do

American Rose Center. Center consists of 60 individually designed rose gardens, which were donated by rose societies from across the US; 20,000 rosebushes, 500 azaleas and other flowering plants and shrubs. (Mid-Apr-Oct, daily) 14 mi W via I-20 to exit 5, then N to 8877 Jefferson-Paige Rd. Phone 318/938-5402. ¢¢

C. Bickham Dickson Park. Shreveport's largest park (585 acres) contains a 200-acre oxbow lake with pier. Fishing. Hayrides. Picnicking, playground. (Daily exc Mon; closed some major hols) Jct 70th St & Bert Kouns. Phone 318/673-7808. Some fees.

Hamel's Amusement Park. Thirty-acre park with a variety of rides and games. (Summer, Wed-Sun; spring & fall, Sat & Sun) 3232 E 70th St. 318/869-3566.

Louisiana State Exhibit Museum. Remarkable dioramas and murals of prehistory and resources of Louisiana area; exhibits of antique and modern items; historical gallery. (Daily exc Sun, Mon; closed hols) 3015 Greenwood Rd, I-20, fairgrounds exit. Phone 318/632-2020. ¢

R.S. Barnwell Memorial Garden and Art Center. Combination art and horticulture facility has permanent and changing exhibits. Flower displays include seasonal and native plantings of the area; sculpture garden with a walk-through bronze sculpture; fragrance garden for the visually impaired. (Mon-Fri, also Sat-Sun afternoons; closed hols) 601 Clyde Fant Pkwy. Phone 318/673-7703. **Free.**

R.W. Norton Art Gallery. American and European paintings, sculpture, decorative arts and manuscripts from the 15th to the 20th centuries; includes large collection of western art by Frederic Remington and Charles M. Russell. (Tues-Fri, also wkend afternoons; closed most hols) 4747 Creswell Ave. Phone 318/865-4201. **Free.**

The Strand Theatre. Restored ornate theater built 1925. 619 Louisiana Ave. For schedule phone 318/226-8555 or 318/226-1481.

Water Town. Twenty-acre water activity theme park features speed slides, adventure slides, wave pool, plus two other pools; restaurant & concessions. (May, Sat & Sun; June-late Aug, daily; also Labor Day wkend) I-20 W, Industrial Loop exit. Phone 318/938-5473. ¢¢¢-¢¢¢¢¢

Annual Events

Red River Revel Arts Festival. Riverfront area. National festival featuring fine arts, crafts, pottery, jewelery; music and performing arts; films; creative writing, poetry; ethnic foods. Phone 318/424-4000. Early Oct.

Louisiana State Fair. Fairgrounds. One of the largest fairs in the country, annually draws more than 600,000 people. Entertainment, agriculture & livestock competition. Phone 318/635-1361. Oct 17-27.

Motels

★ ★ **BEST WESTERN RICHMOND SUITES.** 5101 Monkhouse Dr (71109), I-20 Airport exit, near Regional Airport. 318/635-6431; FAX 318/635-6040. 121 rms, 2 story. S $59-$89; D $69-$99; each addl $10; under 18 free. Crib free. TV; cable (premium), VCR avail. Pool; wading pool, whirlpool, sauna. Complimentary coffee in rms; evening refreshments. Complimentary bkfst buffet. Restaurant adj open 24 hrs. Ck-out noon. Coin lndry. Meeting rms. Business servs avail. In-rm modem link. Free airport transportation. Cr cds: A, C, D, DS, MC, V.

D ⮥ ✈ ⊠ 🔥 SC

✔ ★ **DAYS INN.** 4935 W Monkhouse Dr (71109). 318/636-0080; FAX 318/635-4517. 148 rms, 3 story. Apr-Nov: S $35-$45; D $47-$52; each addl $5; family rates; higher rates racing season; lower rates rest of yr. Crib free. TV; cable. Pool. Restaurant 5-10 am. Ck-out noon. Sundries. Free airport, RR station, bus depot transportation. Cr cds: A, C, D, DS, MC, V.

D ⮥ ⊠ 🔥 SC

✔ ★ **ECONO LODGE.** 4911 Monkhouse Dr (71109), I-20 exit 13, near Regional Airport. 318/636-0771. 65 rms, 2 story. May-Sept: S $32.95-$44.95; D $44.95-$49.95; each addl $6; under 18 free; higher rates special events. Pet accepted, some restrictions; deposit required. TV. Pool. Complimentary coffee in lobby. Restaurant adj open 24 hrs. Ck-out noon. Business center. Cr cds: A, DS, MC, V.

D 🐾 ⮥ 🔥 SC

Motor Hotels

★ ★ **BEST WESTERN CHATEAU SUITE.** 201 Lake St (71101), I-20 exit 19A (Spring St). 318/222-7620; res: 800/845-9334. 79 units, 42 kit. suites, 5 story. S $64-$94; D $75-$95; each addl $10; kit. suites $79-$99; under 12 free. Crib free. TV. Pool. Restaurant 6-10:30 am. Bar from 2 pm. Ck-out 1 pm. Meeting rms. Bellhops. Free airport transportation. Cr cds: A, C, D, DS, MC, V.

D ⮥ ⊠ 🔥

★ ★ ★ **HOLIDAY INN-FINANCIAL PLAZA.** 5555 Financial Plaza (71129), I-20 at Buncomb or Pines Rd exit. 318/688-3000; FAX 318/687-4462. 230 rms, 6 story. S, D $62-$72; each addl $10; suites $120-$150; under 18 free. Crib free. TV; cable (premium), VCR. Indoor/outdoor pool; wading pool, poolside serv. Restaurant 6 am-10 pm. Bar 11-1 am; entertainment. Ck-out noon. Business center. In-rm modem link. Coin lndry. Bellhops. Valet serv. Free airport transportation. Exercise equipt; weights, bicycle, whirlpool, saunas. Holidome. Private patios, balconies. Cr cds: A, C, D, DS, MC, V.

D ⮥ 🏋 ⊠ 🔥 SC 🚶

✔ ★ **HOWARD JOHNSON- NORTH MARKET.** 1906 N Market St (71107). 318/424-6621; FAX 318/221-1028. 140 rms, 2 story. S $38-$48; D $48-$58; each addl $6; under 12 free. Crib free. TV; cable (premium). Pool. Bar 1 pm-midnight. Ck-out noon. Meeting rms. Business servs avail. Free airport transportation. Cr cds: A, D, DS, MC, V.

D ⮥ ⊠ 🔥 SC

★ ★ **RAMADA INN.** 5116 Monkhouse Dr (71109). 318/635-7531; FAX 318/635-1600. 255 rms, 2-4 story. S $59-$69; each addl $10; suites $125-$150; under 18 free. Crib avail. TV; cable. Pool. Restaurant 6 am-10 pm. Rm serv. Bar 11-2 am; entertainment, dancing. Ck-out noon. Convention facilities. Bellhops. Valet serv. Gift shop. Free valet parking. Free airport, RR station, bus depot transportation. Exercise equipt; weight machine, bicycles, whirlpool. Game rm. Cr cds: A, C, D, DS, JCB, MC, V.

D 🐾 ⮥ 🏋 ⊠ 🔥 SC

Hotel

★ ★ ★ **SHERATON SHREVEPORT.** 1419 E 70th St (71105). 318/797-9900; FAX 318/798-2923. 270 rms, 6 story. S $79-$109; D $89-$107; each addl $10; suites $199-$299; under 18 free. Crib free. TV. Pool; whirlpool. Restaurant 6:30 am-10:30 pm. Rm serv. Bar 11-2 am; closed Sun; dancing. Ck-out noon. Convention facilities. Concierge. Free airport transportation. Bathrm phones, refrigerators. Luxury level. Cr cds: A, C, D, DS, MC, V.

D ☒ ☒ ☒ SC

Inns

★★**FAIRFIELD PLACE.** *2221 Fairfield Ave (71104).* 318/222-0048; FAX 318/226-0631. 6 rms, 2 story. S $95-$105; D $95-$145; each addl $14; suites $145. TV; cable, VCR avail (movies avail). Complimentary full bkfst, coffee & tea/sherry. Restaurant nearby. Ck-out 11 am, ck-in 2 pm. Private parking. Built in 1880 for a Louisiana Supreme Court Justice. Totally nonsmoking. Cr cds: A, MC, V.

☒ ☒ ☒

★★**TWENTY-FOUR THIRTY-NINE FAIRFIELD.** *2439 Fairfield Ave (71104).* 318/424-2424; FAX 318/226-9382. 4 rms, 3 story. S,D $85-$125. Children over 13 yrs only. TV; cable. Complimentary full bkfst, tea/sherry. Ck-out 11 am, ck-in by appt. Antiques. Library/sitting rm. Victorian mansion (ca 1905); landscaped gardens, carved oak staircase, crystal chandeliers. Totally nonsmoking. Cr cds: A, D, MC, V.

☒

Restaurants

★★**DON'S SEAFOOD.** *3100 Highland (71104).* 318/865-4291. Hrs: 11 am-10 pm; Fri, Sat to 11 pm. Closed Thanksgiving, Dec 25. Res accepted. Cajun, Creole menu. Bar. Semi-a la carte: lunch, dinner $6-$17.95. Child's meals. Specializes in seafood, steak, crawfish in season. Parking. Family-owned. Cr cds: A, C, D, DS, MC, V.

D

★★★**MONSIEUR PATOU.** *855 Pierremont Rd #135 (71106).* 318/868-9822. Hrs: 11:30 am-2 pm, 6-11 pm; Mon & Sat from 6 pm. Closed Sun; some major hols. Res accepted. French menu. Bar. Wine cellar. A la carte entrees: lunch $32.95. Complete meals: dinner from $50. Specialties: roasted duck with coriander, lobster bisque, grilled fish with champagne sauce. Parking. Formal dining. Louis XV decor; antiques. Cr cds: A, C, D, DS, MC, V.

D

★★**SMITH'S CROSS LAKE INN.** *5301 S Lakeshore Dr (71109).* 318/631-0919. Hrs: 5-10 pm. Closed Sun; Jan 1, Thanksgiving, Dec 25. Res accepted. Bar. Semi-a la carte: dinner $9-$29.50. Child's meals. Specializes in charcoal-broiled steak, seafood, catfish. Valet parking. View of lake. Family-owned. Cr cds: A, C, D, DS, MC, V.

D

✔★**SUPERIOR GRILL.** *6123 Line Ave (71106).* 318/869-3243. Hrs: 11 am-10 pm; Fri, Sat to 11 pm. Closed Dec 25. Mexican menu. Bar. Semi-a la carte: lunch $5-$9, dinner $7.50-$14.95. Specialty: mesquite-grilled fajitas. Mexican cantina-style decor. Cr cds: A, C, D, DS, MC, V.

D

✔★**T. S. STATION.** *750 Shreveport Hwy (71105), 3 mi SE.* 318/865-3594. Hrs: 11 am-10 pm; Fri, Sat to 11 pm. Closed Thanksgiving, Dec 25. Bar. Semi-a la carte: lunch $4.75-$7.75, dinner $6.95-$12.95. Child's meals. Specializes in prime rib, steak, seafood. Salad bar. Parking. Antiques, stained glass. Cr cds: A, D, DS, MC, V.

Slidell (D-5)

(See Covington, New Orleans)

Pop 24,124 **Elev** 9 ft **Area code** 504
Information St Tammany Parish Convention & Visitors Bureau, Hwy 190 N, Suite 15, Covington 70433; 504/892-0520 or 800/634-9443.

What to See and Do

Ft Pike State Commemorative Area. Fort was constructed shortly after the War of 1812 to defend navigational channels leading to New Orleans. Visitors can stroll through authentic brick archways and stand overlooking the Rigolets as sentries once did. (Daily; closed Jan 1, Thanksgiving, Dec 25) Standard fees. 8 mi E via US 190, then 6 mi SW on US 90. Phone 504/662-5703. **Free.**

✖ **John C. Stennis Space Center.** Visitor Center has indoor and outdoor exhibits, displays, demonstrations and movies built around "Space-Oceans-Earth" theme. Space Shuttle Test Complex is on site. 45-minute bus tour. (Daily; closed Easter, Thanksgiving, Dec 25) 12 mi NE via I-10 exit 2, in Mississippi. Phone 601/688-2370. **Free.**

Motels

✔★**BUDGET HOST.** *1662 Gause Blvd (70458), I-10 at US 190, exit 266.* 504/641-8800. 96 rms, 2 story. S $28-$39; D $40-$60; each addl $5; under 12 free; higher rates: Sugar Bowl, Mardi Gras, special events. Crib free. TV; cable. Pool. Complimentary coffee in lobby. Restaurant adj open 24 hrs. Ck-out noon. Cr cds: A, C, D, DS, ER, MC, V.

D ☒ ☒ ☒ SC

★★**LA QUINTA.** *794 E I-10 Service Rd (70461), exit 266.* 504/643-9770. 173 rms, 2 story. Feb-Mar: $56; D $62-$68; each addl $6; under 18 free; higher rates special events; lower rates rest of yr. Crib free. Pet accepted. TV; cable (premium), VCR avail. Pool; whirlpool. Complimentary continental bkfst. Restaurant adj 6 am-11 pm. Ck-out noon. Coin lndry. Meeting rms. Business servs avail. Cr cds: A, C, D, DS, MC, V.

D ☒ ☒ ☒ ☒ SC

★★**RAMADA INN.** *I-10 & Gause Blvd (70461), I-10 exit 266.* 504/643-9960; FAX 504/643-3508. 143 rms, 2 story. May-Aug: S $45-$70; D $50-$80; each addl $8; under 18 free; higher rates: Mardi Gras, Sugar Bowl, other special events; lower rates rest of yr. Crib free. TV; cable. Pool; wading pool, poolside serv. Restaurant 6 am-2 pm, 4-10 pm. Bar 2 pm-2 am; entertainment, dancing Tues-Sat. Ck-out noon. Meeting rms. Cr cds: A, C, D, DS, JCB, MC, V.

D ☒ ☒ ☒ SC

Inn

★★★**SALMEN-FRITCHIE HOUSE.** *127 Cleveland Ave (70458).* 504/643-1405; res: 800/235-4168. 6 units, 2 story, 3 suites. S $75-$85; D $85-$95; each addl $15; suites $115-$125. Children over 10 yrs only. TV in sitting rm, also in all rms. Complimentary full bkfst, tea. Complimentary coffee in rms. Restaurant nearby. Ck-out 11 am, ck-in 3-7 pm. Antiques. Library/sitting rm. Former mayor's house (1895); porches, gazebo. Tours. Totally nonsmoking. Cr cds: A, MC, V.

☒ ☒

Thibodaux (D-4)

(See Houma, Morgan City)

Pop 14,035 **Elev** 15 ft **Area code** 504 **Zip** 70301
Information Chamber of Commerce, 1048 Canal Blvd, PO Box 467, 70302; 504/446-1187.

What to See and Do

Laurel Valley Village. Village consists of the remains of a turn-of-the-century sugar cane plantation, including the sugar mill (1845), schoolhouse, two-story boarding house, country store, blacksmith shop and more than 50 other support buildings; also museum. (Daily; closed hols). 2 mi S on LA 308. Phone 504/446-7456. **Free.**

Madewood Plantation House (1846). Refined example of domestic Greek-revival is furnished with period antiques and houses an extensive art collection. House served as setting for the movie *A Woman called Moses*. On the grounds are family cemetery and other historic buildings. (Daily; closed Jan 1, Thanksgiving, Dec 25) Sr citizen rate. NW on LA 308 in Napoleonville. Phone 504/369-7151. ¢¢

Oak Alley Plantation (1839). Quintessential antebellum, Greek-revival plantation house: alley of 300-year-old live oaks lead to mansion surrounded by first- and second-floor galleries supported by massive columns; interior remodeled in 1930s with antiques and modern furnishings of day. Featured in many films. Extensive grounds with many old trees. Picnicking, restaurant. (Daily; closed Jan 1, Thanksgiving, Dec 25) 25 mi N on LA 20 (or via I-10 & US 90 from New Orleans), then left on Great River Rd, about 3 mi N of Vacherie. Phone 504/265-2151 or 504/523-4351 (from New Orleans). ¢¢¢

Missouri

Population: 5,117,073

Land area: 68,945 square miles

Elevation: 230-1,772 feet

Highest point: Taum Sauk Mountain (Iron County)

Entered Union: August 10, 1821 (24th state)

Capital: Jefferson City

Motto: Let the welfare of the people be the supreme law

Nickname: The Show Me State

State flower: Hawthorn

State bird: Bluebird

State tree: Dogwood

State fair: August 16-25, 1996, in Sedalia

Time zone: Central

Since the migration and settlement of Missouri followed the Mississippi and Missouri rivers, the eastern border and the northern and central areas have much more historic interest than the south. When the first French explorers came down the Mississippi in the late 17th century, Missouri was included in the vast territory claimed for the French king and named Louisiana in his honor. The transfer to Spanish dominion in 1770 made little lasting impression; French names and traditions have remained throughout the state, especially south of St Louis along the Mississippi. When the United States purchased all of Louisiana in 1803, Missouri, with its strategic waterways and the already thriving town of St Louis, became a gateway to the West and remained one throughout the entire westward expansion period. The Pony Express began in St Joseph in the northwestern corner of the state. The extreme northeast, along the Mississippi, is the land of Mark Twain. The central area, north of the Missouri River, was the stomping ground of Daniel Boone, and to the west the Santa Fe, Oregon and California trails crossed the land. Missouri's southeastern section contains some of the oldest settlements in the state. Settlers came here from the South and New England; later Germans and other Europeans arrived. Consequently, traditions are as varied as the state's topography. Missouri's admission to the Union in 1821 resulted from a famous compromise between free and slave-holding states; in the Civil War its people were sharply divided.

Topographically, Missouri is divided into four regions: the northeastern glacial terrain, the central and northwestern prairie, the Ozark highlands in most of the southern portion and the southeastern alluvial plain. Indicative of the northeastern section are picturesque river scenery, souvenirs of steamboat days, prosperous farmlands and fine saddle horses. Westward along the Iowa border is rich, prairie farm country. Long-staple cotton is an important crop in the fertile alluvial plain of the Mississippi River. Southwest of St Louis is Meramec Valley, a forested rural area. It stretches to the northern edge of the Ozarks, which extend south and west to the state borders and affords varied and beautiful mountain scenery. Lakes of all sizes, including Lake of the Ozarks, one of the largest man-made lakes in the United States, and swift-flowing streams, where fish are plentiful, abound in this area. The southeastern section of the state has large springs and caves.

Misssouri's diverse farm economy includes the production of corn, wheat, fruit, cotton, tobacco and livestock. Missouri's lead mines provide more than three-quarters of the nation's supply. Other mineral products include zinc, coal, limestone, iron ores and clays. The variety of manufactured products is almost endless; shoes, clothing, beer, transportation equipment, foundry and machine shop products are among the most important. St Louis, on Missouri's eastern border, and Kansas City, on the western side, provide the state's metropolitian areas.

National Park Service Areas

Missouri offers visitors Jefferson National Expansion Memorial (see ST LOUIS), Ozark National Scenic Riverways (see VAN BUREN), Wilson's Creek National Battlefield (see SPRINGFIELD), George Washington Carver National Monument (see) Harry S Truman National Historic Site (see INDEPENDENCE) and Ulysses S. Grant National Historic Site, near St Louis.

National Forest

Mark Twain National Forest (see BONNE TERRE, CASSVILLE, POPLAR BLUFF and ROLLA): Forest supervisor in Rolla; Ranger offices in Ava*, Cassville, Doniphan*, Fredericktown*, Fulton, Houston*, Poplar Bluff, Potosi*, Rolla, Salem*, Van Buren, Willow Springs*, Winona*.

*Not described in text

Mark Twain National Forest offers swimming, float trips, fishing, hunting, hiking, horseback riding and picnicking. Camping (regular season, Apr-Sept; some areas open year round; $5-$10/site/night). Trailer sites at many campgrounds (no hookups). For further information contact the Forest Supervisor, 401 Fairgrounds Rd, Rolla 65401; 314/364-4621.

State Recreation Areas

The following towns list state recreation areas in their vicinity under What to See and Do; refer to the individual town for directions and park information.

Listed under **Arrow Rock:** see Arrow Rock State Historic Site and Van Meter State Park.

Listed under **Bonne Terre:** see St Francois and Washington state parks.

Listed under **Branson/Table Rock Lake Area:** see Table Rock State Park.

Listed under **Camdenton:** see Pomme de Terre State Park.

Listed under **Cameron:** see Wallace State Park.

Listed under **Cape Girardeau:** see Trail of Tears State Park.

Listed under **Cassville:** see Roaring River State Park.

Listed under **Chillicothe:** see Pershing State Park.

Listed under **Clinton:** see Harry S Truman State Park.

Listed under **Excelsior Springs:** see Watkins Woolen Mill State Historic Site.

Listed under **Hermann:** see Graham Cave State Park.

Listed under **Kirksville:** see Thousand Hills State Park.

Listed under **Lake of the Ozarks:** see Lake of the Ozarks State Park.

Listed under **Lebanon:** see Bennett Spring State Park.

Listed under **Macon:** see Long Branch State Park.

Listed under **Monroe City:** see Mark Twain State Park.

Listed under **Mound City:** see Big Lake State Park.

Listed under **Pilot Knob:** see Johnson's Shut-Ins and Sam A. Baker state parks.

Listed under **Poplar Bluff:** see Lake Wappapello State Park.

Listed under **Rolla:** see Montauk State Park.

Listed under **St Louis:** see Mastodon and Dr. Edmund A. Babler Memorial state parks.

Listed under **Sedalia:** see Knob Noster State Park.

Listed under **Stockton:** see Stockton State Park.

Listed under **Sullivan:** see Meramec and Onondaga Cave state parks.

Listed under **Wentzville:** see Cuivre River State Park.

Listed under **Weston:** see Lewis & Clark State Park.

Water-related activities, hiking, riding, various other sports, picnicking and visitor centers, as well as camping, are available in many of these areas. Tent, trailer sites: Apr-Oct, $6/day/basic, $12-$15/day/improved; Nov-Mar, $5/day/basic, $10-$11/day/improved; limit 15 consecutive days; water and sanitary facilities Apr-Oct only in most parks; reservations accepted at some parks. Lodging reservation: 1-day deposit (2-day minimum Memorial Day-Labor Day), contact concessionaire in park. Most cabins, dining lodges are open mid-Apr-Oct. Parks are open daily, year round. Senior citizen discounts. Pets on leash only. For further information contact the Missouri Department of Natural Resources, PO Box 176, Jefferson City 65102; 314/751-2479 or 800/334-6946.

Fishing & Hunting

Float trips combine scenic river floating with fishing. Trips vary from half-day to one week. Anglers can bring their own canoes, rent canoes or hire professional guides to manipulate johnboats (flat-bottomed boats suited to shallow waters). Some outfitters provide equipment and food. About 25 Ozark rivers have black bass, goggle-eye, walleye, sunfish and trout. *Missouri Ozark Waterways* provides information on float fishing and may be purchased from the Missouri Dept of Conservation, PO Box 180, Jefferson City 65102-0180; 314/751-4115.

Squirrel, rabbit and quail hunting are fair to good in most areas. Deer, doves and wild turkeys are relatively plentiful. The larger lakes and rivers are used by migrating ducks, geese and other waterfowl. Contact the Dept of Conservation for free outdoor maps.

Nonresident fishing permit: $30; 1-day $3; trout stamp $6. Nonresident hunting permit: turkey $75; small game $60; nonresident archer's hunting permit $75; deer $110. Nonresident furbearer hunting and trapping permit: $75. To purchase permits and obtain regulations contact MO Dept of Conservation, PO Box 180, Jefferson City 65102-0180;314/751-4115.

Skiing

The following towns list ski areas in their vicinity under What to See and Do; refer to the individual town for directions and information.

Listed under **St Louis:** see Hidden Valley Ski Area.

Listed under **Springfield:** see Snow Bluff Ski Area.

Safety Belt Information

Safety belts are mandatory for all persons in front seat of passenger vehicle. Children under 4 years must be in an approved child passenger restraint system. For further information phone 314/526-6115.

Interstate Highway System

The following alphabetical listing of Missouri towns in *Mobil Travel Guide* shows that these cities are within 10 miles of the indicated interstate highways. A highway map should be checked, however, for the nearest exit.

INTERSTATE 29: Kansas City, Mound City, St Joseph, Weston.

INTERSTATE 35: Bethany, Cameron, Excelsior Springs, Kansas City.

INTERSTATE 44: Carthage, Clayton, Joplin, Lebanon, Mount Vernon, Rolla, St Louis, Springfield, Sullivan, Waynesville.

INTERSTATE 55: Cape Girardeau, Rolla, Sainte Genevieve, St Louis, Sikeston.

INTERSTATE 70: Blue Springs, Columbia, Fulton, Independence, Kansas City, St Charles, St Louis, Wentzville.

Additional Visitor Information

For general information contact the Missouri Division of Tourism, 301 W High St, Box 1055, Jefferson City 65102; 314/751-4133. For a Missouri travel information packet, phone 800/877-1234. An official state highway map may be obtained from Highway Maps, Highway & Transportation Dept, Box 270, Jefferson City 65102. Another good source of information on Missouri is *The Ozarks Mountaineer,* bimonthly, HCR 3, Box 868, Kirbyville 65679.

Visitor centers are located in St Louis, I-270 at Dunn Rd; Joplin, I-44 at state line; Kansas City, I-70 at the Truman Sports Complex; Hannibal, US 61, 2 mi S of jct with US 36; Rock Port, I-29, just S of jct with US 136; and Marston, I-55, S of New Madrid. They are open all year; the hours vary.

Arrow Rock (C-4)

(For accommodations see Columbia)

Pop 70 **Elev** 700 ft **Area code** 816 **Zip** 65320
Information Historic Site Administrator, Box 1; 816/837-3330.

What to See and Do

Arrow Rock State Historic Site. A 200-acre plot with many restored buildings and historical landmarks of the Old Santa Fe Trail. Picnicking, concession. Camping (dump station; standard fees). Interpretive center. Phone 816/837-3330. In town. Park includes

Old Tavern (ca 1834). Restored; period furnishings, historical exhibits and general store; restaurant. (May-Sept, daily exc Mon) Phone 816/837-3200. On guided walking tour.

George Caleb Bingham House (1837). Restored house built by the artist; period furnishings. (June-Aug, daily) On guided walking tour.

Van Meter State Park. More than 900 acres. Remains found at this archaeological site date from 10,000 B.C.; Old Fort, only known earthworks of its kind west of the Mississippi. Visitor Center explains history of area. Fishing. Picnicking, playground. Camping. Standard fees. (Daily) 22 mi NW on MO 41, then W & N on MO 122. Phone 816/886-7537.

Walking tour. Guided tour includes restored log courthouse (1839), gunshop and house (ca 1844), printshop (1868), stone jail (1870), medical museums and Arrow Rock State Historic Site. Tour begins at Information Center. (Memorial Day-Labor Day, daily; spring & fall, wkends; other times by appt) Phone 816/837-3231. ¢¢

Seasonal Event

Arrow Rock Lyceum Theater. In town on MO 41. Missouri's oldest professional regional theater. Wed-Sat evenings; matinees Wed & Sun. Phone 816/837-3311. June-Aug.

Bethany (A-3)

(See Cameron)

Settled 1840 **Pop** 3,005 **Elev** 904 ft **Area code** 816 **Zip** 64424
Information Chamber of Commerce, 116 N 16th St, PO Box 202; 816/425-6358.

Motel

✔★ ★ **BEST WESTERN I-35 INN.** Jct I-35 & US 136 exit 92. 816/425-7915; FAX 816/425-3697. 78 rms. S $45-$51; D $51-$61; each addl $5. Crib $4. TV; cable. Complimentary continental bkfst. Restaurant adj 6 am-11 pm. Ck-out 11 am. In-rm modem link. Coin lndry. Whirlpool. Picnic tables. Cr cds: A, C, D, DS, MC, V.

D ✔ ⊠ ⊠ SC

Blue Springs (C-3)

(For accommodations see Independence, Kansas City; also see Kansas City, KS)

Pop 40,153 **Elev** 950 ft **Area code** 816
Information Chamber of Commerce, 1000 Main St, 64015; 816/229-8558.

What to See and Do

Civil War Museum of Jackson County. Exhibits, historic battlefield and soldiers' cemetery. (Apr-Sept, Mon-Sat & Sun afternoons; rest of yr, Wed-Sat & Sun afternoons; closed Jan 1, Thanksgiving, Dec 25) S on MO 7 to US 50, then 7 mi E, in Lone Jack. Phone 816/566-2272. ¢¢

Fleming Park. This more than 4,400-acre park includes 970-acre Lake Jacomo and 960-acre Blue Springs Lake. Swimming, beach, water slide; fishing; boating (rentals, marina). Camping. Wildlife exhibit, special activities (fee). Park (daily). S on MO 7, then 2 mi W on US 40 to Woods Chapel Rd S. **Free.** In park is

Missouri Town 1855. More than 30 original western Missouri buildings from 1820-1860 brought to the site and restored. Mercantile store, blacksmith and cabinetmaker's shop. Furnishings, gardens, livestock and site interpreters in period attire. Special events; candlelight tours (fee). (Mid-Apr-mid-Nov, Wed-Sun; rest of yr, Sat & Sun; closed Jan 1, Thanksgiving, Dec 25) Sr citizen rate. 8010 E Park Rd. E side of Lake Jacomo. Phone 816/795-8200 or 816/524-8770. ¢¢

Restaurant

★ ★ ★ **MARINA GROG & GALLEY.** (22 A North Lake Shore Dr, Lake Lotawana 64806) 10 mi S on MO 7, Colborn Rd to Gate 1. 816/578-5511. Hrs: 11:30 am-2:30 pm, 5-9 pm; Mon & Tues from 5 pm; wknd hrs vary. Closed Jan 1, Dec 25. Res accepted. Bar. Wine list. Semi-a la carte: lunch $4.95-$12.95, dinner $10.95-$27.95. Sun brunch $12.95. Child's meals. Specializes in seafood, steak. Parking. Outdoor dining overlooking lake. Nautical theme includes 1,500-gallon aquarium that separates dining area from bar. Cr cds: A, D, DS, MC, V.

 D

Bonne Terre (D-6)

(For accommodations see Sainte Genevieve)

Pop 3,871 **Elev** 830 ft **Area code** 314 **Zip** 63628

What to See and Do

Bonne Terre Mine Tours. One-hour walking tours through lead and silver mines that operated from 1864 to 1962; historic mining tools, ore cars, ore samples, underground lake (boat tour), flower garden; museum exhibits. (Apr-Sept, daily; rest of yr, daily, limited hrs) On MO 47, at Park & Allen Sts. Phone 314/358-2148. ¢¢¢

Mark Twain National Forest (Potosi Ranger District). Swimming beach; boat launching at Council Bluff Recreation Area. Nature trails. Camping. Standard fees. (Daily) W via MO 47, S via MO 21, E via MO 8. Contact Ranger District office 314/438-5427 or Forest Supervisor 314/364-4621. **Free.**

St Francois State Park. A 2,700-acre park with fishing; canoeing. Hiking. Picnicking. Improved camping. Naturalists. Standard fees. (Daily) 4 mi N on US 67. Phone 314/358-2173. **Free.**

Washington State Park. More than 1,400-acre park containing petroglyphs (interpretations available). Swimming pool; fishing; canoeing in Big River. Hiking trails. Playground; dining lodge, cabins. Improved camping. Standard fees. (Daily) 15 mi NW via MO 47, 21. Phone 314/586-2995. **Free.**

Branson/Table Rock Lake Area (E-4)

(See Cassville, Rockaway Beach, Springfield; also see Bull Shoals Lake Area, AR)

Pop 3,706 **Elev** 722 ft **Area code** 417 **Zip** 65616
Information Branson/Lakes Area Chamber of Commerce, US 65 & MO 248, PO Box 1897; 417/334-4136.

The resort town of Branson, situated in the Ozarks, is in the region that provided the setting for Harold Bell Wright's novel *The Shepherd of the Hills*. Both Lake Taneycomo and Table Rock Lake have excellent fishing for trout, bass and crappie. In recent years Branson has become a mecca for fans of country music.

What to See and Do

College of the Ozarks (1906). (1,500 students) Liberal arts college where students work, rather than pay, for their education. 3 mi S on US 65, exit County V. Phone 417/334-6411. On campus are

Edwards Mill. Working reproduction of an 1880s water-powered gristmill. Weaving studio on second floor; store. (Daily; closed mid-Dec-Jan) **Free.**

Ralph Foster Museum. Ozark-area Indian artifacts; Ozark relics; apothecary, cameo, gun, coin collections; mounted game animals; Ozarks Hall of Fame. (Daily; closed Thanksgiving; also mid-Dec-Jan) Sr citizen rate. Phone 417/334-6411. ¢¢

★ **Entertainment shows.**

Baldknobbers Hillbilly Jamboree. Mar-mid-Apr, Fri & Sat; mid-Apr-mid-Dec, daily exc Sun. 3 mi W on MO 76. Phone 417/334-4528.

Presleys' Jubilee. Mar-mid-Dec. 4 mi W on MO 76. Phone 417/334-4874.

Mel Tillis Theater. Mar-Dec. 2527 N MO 248 (Shepherd of the Hills Expy). Phone 417/335-6635.

Shoji Tabuchi Theatre. Mar-Dec. 3260 MO 248 (Shepherd of the Hills Expy). Phone 417/334-7469.

Foggy River Boys Music Show. Quartet harmony. Daily exc Fri. Apr-Dec. 2 mi W on MO 76. Phone 417/334-2563.

Jim Stafford Theatre. 3440 W MO 76. Phone 417/335-8080.

Roy Clark Celebrity Theatre. Apr-Dec. 3425 W MO 76. Phone 417/334-0076.

76 Music Hall. 1919 W MO 76. Phone 417/335-2484.

Moe Bandy Americana Theater. Featuring Moe Bandy most shows. Mid-Apr-Oct; also Nov & Dec. 4 mi W via MO 76. Phone 417/335-8176.

The Grand Palace. Late Apr-Dec. 2700 W MO 76. Phone 417/33-GRAND.

Andy Williams Moon River Theatre. Apr-Dec. 2500 W MO 76. Phone 417/334-4500.

Sons of the Pioneers. Early May-Oct. W MO 76 at Gretna Rd. Phone 417/334-4363.

Al Brumley's Memory Valley Show. Mar-Dec. W MO 76. Phone 417/334-0023 or 417/334-3499.

BoxCar Willie Theater. Apr-Dec. 3454 W MO 76. Phone 417/334-8696 or 800/942-4626.

Tony Orlando Yellow Ribbon Music Theater. Mar-Dec. MO 165. Phone 417/335-TONY.

Wayne Newton Theatre. May-mid-Dec. 3701 MO 76. Phone 417/339-2963.

Blackwood Quartet. W MO 76. Phone 417/336-5863 or 800/477-5183.

Lawrence Welk Show. Welk Resort Center, 1984 MO 165. Phone 417/336-3575.

Glen Campbell/Will Rogers Theatre. Featuring John Davidson. MO 248 (Shepherd of the Hills Expy). Phone 417/337-5900.

Osmond Family Theater. Apr-Dec. 3216 W MO 76. Phone 417/336-6100.

Charley Pride Theatre. Apr-Dec. 755 Gretna Rd. Phone 417/337-7433.

Cristy Lane Theatre. 3600 W MO 76. Phone 417/335-5111.

Blackwood Family Music Show. Mar-Dec. W MO 76, across from Wal-Mart. Phone 417/336-5863.

Van Burch & Wellford. Shenandoah South Theatre. Apr-Dec. MO 248 (Shepherd of the Hills Expy). Phone 417/336-3986.

Mutton Hollow Craft & Entertainment Village. Ozark craftsmen at work. Musical entertainment; carnival rides. Restaurants. (Late Apr-Oct, daily) 5 mi W on MO 76. Phone 417/334-4947. ¢¢¢

Ripley's Believe It Or Not! Museum. Hundreds of exhibits in eight galleries. Allow at least 1 hr. Phone 417/337-5300. ¢¢¢

Shepherd of the Hills Trout Hatchery. Largest trout hatchery in state. Visitor Center has aquariums, exhibits, slide presentation. Guided tours (Memorial Day-Labor Day). Hiking trails; picnicking. (Daily; closed Jan 1, Thanksgiving, Dec 25) W on MO 76 to MO 165, then 6 mi S. Phone 417/334-4865. **Free.**

★ **Shepherd of the Hills.** Jeep-drawn conveyance tours (70 min) include authentically furnished Old Matt's Cabin, home of the prominent characters in Harold Bell Wright's Ozark novel *The Shepherd of the Hills;* Old Matt's Mill, an operating steam-powered saw and gristmill; 230-foot Inspiration Tower; craft demonstrations, horseback riding and music shows. (Late Apr-late Oct, daily) 5586 W MO 76. Phone 417/334-4191. Tours ¢¢¢¢   On grounds is

Outdoor Theater. Outdoor, historical pageant adapted from Harold Bell Wright's best-selling novel. (May-late Oct, nightly) Phone 417/334-4191 for ticket information.

Sightseeing.

Sammy Lane Pirate Cruise Water Pageant. Narrated folklore cruise (70 min) on Lake Taneycomo leaves several times a day. (Apr-Oct, daily) Departs from foot of Main St. Phone 417/334-3015. ¢¢¢

Lake Queen **Cruises.** A 1¼-hour narrated cruise of scenic Lake Taneycomo aboard 149-passenger *Lake Queen;* also dinner and breakfast cruises. (Early Apr-Dec, daily) Departs from foot of Main St. Phone 417/334-3015. ¢¢¢

"Ride the Ducks." Scenic 70-min land and water tour on amphibious vehicles. (Mar-Nov, daily) 2½ mi W on MO 76. For rates phone 417/334-3825.

Table Rock Helicopters. Scenic tours of lakes area. (Mar-Nov, daily) Phone 417/334-6102.

Showboat Branson Belle. Bkfst, lunch & dinner cruises. (Mid-Apr-mid-Dec, daily) Departs from MO 165 near Table Rock Dam. Phone 417/336-7171. ¢¢¢¢¢

Polynesian Princess. Sightseeing, bkfst & dinner cruises. Departs from Gages Long Creek Marina, on MO 86. For schedule phone 417/337-8366. ¢¢¢¢-¢¢¢¢¢

Silver Dollar City. Amusement park with Ozark Mountain theme; craftsfolk demonstrate frontier skills; comedy skits presented throughout park; country, bluegrass, gospel and Dixieland bands; 10 thrill rides including raft ride, water boggan, railway, roller coasters. Also tours of Marvel Cave with 20-story-high entrance "room." (Mid-May-Oct, daily; late Apr-mid-May, Wed-Sun) (See ANNUAL EVENTS) Sr citizen rate. 9 mi W on MO 76. Phone 417/338-2611 or 417/338-8100. ¢¢¢¢

Stone Hill Winery. Guided tours and bottling demonstrations. Gift shop. (Mon-Sat, also Sun afternoons; closed Jan 1, Thanksgiving, Dec 25) 5 mi W on MO 76, then 2 blks S on MO 165. Phone 417/334-1897. **Free.**

Table Rock Dam & Lake. This 43,100-acre reservoir, formed by impounding waters of White River, offers swimming, waterskiing and scuba diving; fishing for bass, crappie & walleye; boating (rentals; commercial docks; marine dump station). Hunting for deer, turkey, rabbit & waterfowl. Picnicking, playgrounds. Camping (15 parks, fee charged in most areas; showers, trailer dump stations). (Daily) 4 mi W on MO 76, then 6 mi S on MO 165. Phone 417/334-4101. Per vehicle ¢

Table Rock State Park. More than 350 acres. Fishing; sailing (docks, ramp), boating (marina, rentals), scuba service. Picnicking. Improved camping (dump station). Standard fees. (Daily) 5 mi W on MO 165, off US 65. Phone 417/334-4704 or -3069 (marina). **Free.**

Waltzing Waters. Colored fountains set to music create a display more than 20 feet high and 60 feet wide. Indoor performances hourly. Also stage shows. (Daily) 4¹/2 mi W on MO 76. Phone 417/334-4144. Fountains ¢¢; Stage show ¢¢¢

White Water. Family water park; streams, slides, flumes, wave pool. (Late May-early Sept, daily) Sr citizen rate. 4 mi W on MO 76. Phone 417/334-7487. ¢¢¢¢¢

Annual Events

Branson Jam/Branson Fest. Mid-Mar.

International Festival. In Silver Dollar City. Late Apr-mid-May.

National Festival of Craftsmen. In Silver Dollar City. Fiddle making, mule-powered sorghum molasses making, wood carving, barrel making and dozens of other crafts. Mid-Sept-late Oct.

Motels

★★ **BEST WESTERN MOUNTAIN OAK LODGE.** *Box 1106 (65615), 5 mi W on MO 76.* 417/338-2141; FAX 417/338-8320. 150 rms, 3 story. Apr-early Dec: S, D $59-$69; each addl $5; suites $80; under 18 free. Closed rest of yr. Crib $3. TV; cable (premium). Pool; wading pool. Restaurant 6:30 am-2 pm, 4:30-8 pm. Rm serv. Bar 2 pm-1 am. Ck-out noon. Coin lndry. Meeting rms. Business servs avail. Sundries. Gift shop. Free Silver Dollar City transportation. Tennis. Game rm. Balconies. Cr cds: A, C, D, DS, ER, JCB, MC, V.

⊠ 🎿 ☄ 🏊 🚫 🔥 SC

★★ **BEST WESTERN TRAVEL INN.** *448 MO 248, at US 65.* 417/334-5121; FAX 417/334-6039. 272 rms, 2-4 story. Sept-Dec: S $45-$68; D $49-$72; each addl $5; suites $125-$135; under 17 free; lower rates rest of yr. Crib $5. TV; cable. Pool; wading pool, whirlpool. Complimentary coffee in rms. Restaurant nearby. Ck-out 11 am. Business servs avail. In-rm modem link. Bellhops. Shopping arcade. Game rm. Picnic tables. Cr cds: A, C, D, DS, MC, V.

D ☄ 🏊 🚫 🔥 SC

★★ **CLARION AT FALL CREEK RESORT.** *1 Fall Creek Dr, 2¹/2 mi S on MO 165.* 417/334-6404; res: 800/562-6636; FAX 417/335-4652. 290 kit. units, (1, 2 & 3-bedrms), 20 studio rms. 1-bedrm condos $89; 2-bedrm condos $119-$139; 3-bedrm condos $189; studio rms $72. TV; cable (premium), VCR avail (movies avail $3.49). 4 pools, 1 indoor. Playground. Restaurant 7 am-4 pm. Ck-out 10:30 am. Coin lndry. Business center. Tennis. Miniature golf. Exercise equipt; weight machines, treadmill. Marina, boat rentals. Lawn games. Patio tables, grills. Cr cds: A, D, DS, JCB, MC, V.

D 🏄 🎿 🏊 🏃 🚫 ☄ 🔥 SC 🎣

✔★ **DAYS INN.** *3524 Keeter St.* 417/334-5544; FAX 417/334-2935. 425 rms, 4 story. Mid-Apr-Oct: S, D $42-$92; each addl $6; under 12 free; lower rates rest of yr. Pet accepted; $8.50 per day. TV. Pool; wading pool, whirlpool. Playground. Complimentary continental bkfst, coffee. Restaurant 7 am-8 pm. Ck-out 11 am. Business servs avail. Sundries. Cr cds: A, D, DS, MC, V.

D 🐾 🏊 🚫 🔥 SC

✔★ **EDGEWOOD.** *1800 MO 76 W.* 417/334-1000; res: 800/641-4106; FAX 417/334-0476. 296 rms, 2-6 story. S, D $30-$71.50; each addl $5 after 4th person. Crib $5. TV. Pool. Complimentary coffee in lobby. Restaurant adj 6:30 am-8 pm. Ck-out 11 am. Coin lndry. Meeting rm. Business servs avail. In-rm modem link. Picnic tables, grills. Cr cds: A, DS, MC, V.

D 🏊 🚫 🔥 SC

★★ **FOXBOROUGH INN.** *589 Shepherd of the Hills Expwy (MO 248).* 417/335-4369; res: 800/335-4369; FAX 417/335-5043. 175 rms, 3 story. May-Oct: S, D $52.95-$62.95; each addl $5; under 18 free; lower rates rest of yr. Crib free. TV; cable, VCR avail. Pool. Complimentary continental bkfst. Complimentary coffee in lobby. Snack bar. Restaurant nearby. Ck-out 11 am. Coin lndry. Meeting rms. Business servs avail. Gift shop. Cr cds: A, C, D, DS, MC, V.

D 🏊 🚫 🔥 SC

✔★★ **GAZEBO INN.** *2424 MO 76.* 417/335-3826; res: 800/873-7990; FAX 417/335-3889. 73 rms, 3 story, 14 suites. S, D $39.95-$69.95; suites $79.95-$130. Crib free. TV; cable. Pool. Free continental bkfst. Restaurant adj 7 am-9 pm. Ck-out 11 am. Totally nonsmoking. Cr cds: A, DS, MC, V.

🏊 🚫 🔥 SC

★★ **HAMPTON INN.** *3695 MO 76.* 417/337-5762; FAX 417/337-8733. 110 rms, 5 story. S, D $65-$85; under 17 free. Closed mid-Dec-mid-Apr. Crib free. TV; cable (premium). Indoor pool; whirlpool. Complimentary continental bkfst. Restaurant nearby. Ck-out noon. Valet serv. Cr cds: A, D, DS, MC, V.

D 🐾 🏊 🚫 🔥 SC

★ **HOLIDAY INN.** *Box 340, 1 mi W of jct MO 65, MO 76.* 417/334-5101; FAX 417/334-0789. 220 rms, 1-3 story. No elvtr. Apr-Dec: S, D $70-$99; each addl $6; suites $100-$125; under 19 free; lower rates rest of yr. Crib $10. TV; cable (premium). Pool; wading pool, whirlpool. Complimentary coffee in rms. Restaurant 7 am-2 pm, 5-8 pm. Rm serv. Bar 5 pm-midnight; entertainment. Ck-out 11 am. Coin lndry. Meeting rms. Business servs avail. In-rm modem link. Game rm. Cr cds: A, C, D, DS, JCB, MC, V.

D 🏊 🚫 🔥 SC

★ **HOLIDAY INN EXPRESS.** *1000 W Main St on MO 76.* 417/334-1985; FAX 417/334-1984. 90 rms, 5 story. July-Oct: S, D $62.50-$69.50; lower rates rest of yr. TV; cable (premium). Indoor pool; whirlpool. Complimentary continental bkfst. Restaurant opp 6 am-9 pm. Ck-out 11 am. Business servs avail. In-rm modem link. Valet serv. Rec rm. Cr cds: A, C, D, DS, JCB, MC, V.

D 🏊 🚫 🔥 SC

★ **MAGNOLIA INN.** *3311 Shepherd of the Hills Expwy (MO 248).* 417/334-2300; res: 800/222-7239; FAX 417/336-4165. 152 rms, 2 story. May-Oct: S, D $62-$80; each addl $4; under 12 free; lower rest of yr. Crib free. TV; cable. Pool; whirlpool. Complimentary coffee in lobby. Restaurant opp 6-2 am. Ck-out 11 am. Coin lndry. Gift shop. Barber, beauty shop. Game rm. Cr cds: A, DS, MC, V.

D 🏊 🚫 🔥 SC

✔★ **MELODY LANE INN.** *Box 637 (65615), 2¹/2 mi W on MO 76.* 417/334-8598; res: 800/338-8598; FAX 417/334-3799. 140 rms, 2-3 story. No elvtr. Mar-Dec: S, D $39.50-$62; each addl $5. Closed rest of year. Crib $5. TV; VCR avail. Pool; whirlpool. Continental bkfst avail 7-11 am. Ck-out 11 am. Business servs avail. Coin lndry. Cr cds: A, MC, V.

D 🏊 🚫 🔥 SC

★★ **SETTLE INN.** *3050 Green Mt Dr* 417/335-4700; res: 800/677-6906; FAX 417/335-3906. 300 rms, 3-4 story. Sept-Oct: S $45-$72; suites $99-$129; under 5 free; lower rates rest of yr. Crib free. Pet accepted; $5. TV; cable (premium). Indoor pool; whirlpool, sauna. Complimentary bkfst. Restaurant 11 am-midnight. Rm serv. Bar; entertainment. Ck-out 2 pm. Coin lndry. Meeting rms. Business servs avail.

Concierge. Gift shop. Valet serv. Game rm. Balconies. Cr cds: A, DS, MC, V.

⬚ ⬚ ⬚ ⬚ ⬚ SC

★ **SHADOWBROOK.** *Box 1127, 2 mi W on MO 76.* 417/334-4173; res: 800/641-4600. 60 rms, 2-3 story. June-Oct: S, D $52-$78; each addl $5; lower rates rest of yr. Crib $5. TV. Heated pool. Restaurant adj 6:30 am-9 pm. Ck-out 11 am. Cr cds: A, DS, MC, V.

⬚ ⬚ SC

★★ **SOUTHERN OAKS INN.** *3295 Shepherd of the Hills Expy (MO 248).* 417/335-8108; res: 800/324-8752; FAX 417/335-8861. 150 rms, 2 story. May-Oct: S, D $57.95; suites $95; under 17 free; lower rates rest of yr. Crib free. TV; cable (premium), VCR avail. 2 pools, 1 indoor; whirlpool. Complimentary bkfst, coffee in lobby. Restaurant opp 6 am-10 pm. Ck-out 11 am. Coin lndry. Meeting rms. Business servs avail. Refrigerator in suites. Some balconies. Cr cds: A, DS, MC, V.

⬚ ⬚ ⬚ ⬚ SC

★ **TRAVELODGE.** *3102 Falls Pkwy* 417/334-7523; FAX 417/336-2495. 81 rms, 2 story. May-Oct: S, D $45-$73; each addl $5; under 17 free; lower rates rest of yr. Crib $3. TV; cable (premium). Pool. Complimentary continental bkfst. Ck-out 11 am. Meeting rm. Business servs avail. Gift shop. Picnic table. Cr cds: A, D, DS, MC, V.

⬚ ⬚ ⬚ ⬚ SC

Lodge

★★★ **BIG CEDAR.** *(612 Devil's Pool Rd, Ridgedale 65739) 9 mi S on US 65, W on MO 86 to Devil's Pool Rd.* 417/335-2777; FAX 417/335-2340. 208 rms in 2 bldgs, 11 suites, 48 cottages. May-Oct: S, D $115-$125; suites $189-$240; cottages $155-$272; log cabins $249-$549; lower rates rest of yr. Crib free. TV; cable (premium). Heated pool; poolside serv. Playground. Supervised child's activities (Memorial Day-Labor Day); ages 4-12. Dining rm 6 am-10 pm. Rm serv. Bar noon-1 am; entertainment. Ck-out 11 am. Coin lndry. Meeting rms. Business servs avail. Sundries. Gift shop. Lighted tennis. Miniature golf. Exercise equipt; weights, bicycles, sauna. Lawn games. Water sports. Some balconies. Elegant, rustic atmosphere, wooded grounds, stone pathways. On lake; marina. Cr cds: A, DS, MC, V.

⬚ ⬚ ⬚ ⬚ ⬚ ⬚ ⬚ ⬚ SC

Motor Hotels

★★★ **LODGE OF THE OZARKS.** *3431 W MO 76.* 417/334-7535; FAX 417/334-6861. 191 rms, 4 story. Apr-Dec: S, D $80-$95; lower rates rest of yr. Crib $5. TV; cable. Indoor pool; whirlpool. Restaurants 7 am-8 pm. Bar noon-1 am; entertainment, dancing. Ck-out 11 am. Meeting rms. Business servs avail. Bellhops. Valet serv. Concierge. Barber, beauty shop. Game rm. Some refrigerators, wet bars. Cr cds: A, DS, MC, V.

⬚ ⬚ ⬚ ⬚

★★ **PALACE INN.** *2820 MO 76 W, 2¹/₂ mi W on MO 76, adj to Grand Palace.* 417/334-7666; res: 800/PALACE-N; FAX 417/334-7720. 166 rms, 7 story. Late May-Oct: S, D $70-$140; each addl $5; suites $95-$140; lower rates rest of yr. Crib $5. TV; cable. Heated pool; whirlpool, sauna. Restaurant 7-11 am, 4:30-9 pm. Bar 1-11 pm. Ck-out 11 am. Coin lndry. Business servs avail. In-rm modem link. Beauty shop. Free local airport transportation. Some refrigerators. Many balconies. Cr cds: A, DS, MC, V.

⬚ ⬚ ⬚ ⬚

Hotel

★★★ **CROWNE PLAZA.** *120 Wildwood Dr S adj to Grand Palace.* 417/335-5767; FAX 417/335-7979. 500 rms, 10 story. S, D

$79-$105; each addl $10; suites $150; under 19 free. Crib free. TV; cable (premium). Indoor/outdoor pool; poolside serv. Complimentary coffee in rms. Restaurant 6 am-10 pm. Bar 4 pm-1 am. Ck-out 11 am. Meeting rms. Business center. In-rm modem link. Concierge. Gift shop. Barber, beauty shop. Exercise equipt; weight machine, treadmill, whirlpool, sauna. Cr cds: A, C, D, DS, JCB, MC, V.

⬚ ⬚ ⬚ ⬚ ⬚ SC ⬚

Inn

★★ **THE BRANSON HOTEL.** *214 W Main.* 417/335-6104. 9 rms, 2 story. S, D $95-$105. Closed Jan & Feb. Children 9 & over. TV; cable. Complimentary full bkfst; afternoon tea, sherry. Restaurant opp 5 am-11 pm. Ck-out 11 am, ck-in 4-8 pm. 3 blks from lake. Built 1903. Victorian decor, antiques. Refrigerators. Author Harold Bell Wright stayed here while writing *Shepherd of the Hills*. Totally nonsmoking. No cr cds accepted.

⬚ ⬚

Resort

★★ **POINTE ROYALE RESORT.** *4 Pointe Royale Dr.* 417/334-5614; res: 800/962-4710; FAX 417/334-5620. 275 kit. condos, 3 story. May-Oct: S, D $76-$275; lower rates rest of yr. Crib $3. TV; cable, VCR avail. Pool; sauna. Restaurants 8 am-midnight. Bar. Ck-out 10 am. Meeting rms. Business servs avail. Lndry facilities. Maid serv wkly. Lighted tennis. 18-hole golf, greens fee $40, putting green. Picnic tables, grills. On Lake Taneycomo. Cr cds: A, D, DS, MC, V.

⬚ ⬚ ⬚ ⬚ ⬚ ⬚

Cottage Colonies

★ **BRIARWOOD.** *Box 506, E on MO 76, 2¹/₂ mi N of MO 76 bridge on Lakeshore Dr.* 417/334-3929. 16 kit. cottages. May 15-Oct 31: 1-bedrm $44-$54; 2-bedrm $59-$78; 3-bedrm $110-$120; each addl $5; wkly rates; lower rates Mar-mid-May & Nov. Closed rest of yr. Crib free. TV; cable. Pool. Playground. Ck-out 10 am. Sundries. Game rm. Lawn games. Grills. On Lake Taneycomo; boats, motors, dock, fish storage. No cr cds accepted.

⬚ ⬚ ⬚

★ **TURKEY CREEK RANCH.** *(HC 3, Box 3180, Theodosia 65761) Lake Rd; 47 mi E on US 160, then 3 mi S on County P, then 1³/₄ mi SE on County NN 7; follow signs.* 417/273-4362. 24 (1-3 bedrm) kit. cottages. Memorial Day-Labor Day (1-wk min): kit. cottages $77-$122; each addl $6; lower rates Mar-May & Sept-Nov. Closed rest of yr. Crib free. TV. 2 pools, 1 indoor; wading pool, whirlpool. Playground. Restaurant 7-10:30 am, 3-8 pm. Ck-out 11 am, ck-in 3 pm. Grocery 9 mi. Coin lndry. Putting green. Tennis. Sailboats, paddleboats, canoes avail; bass boats, pontoons for rent. 3 docks. Bridle trails. Lawn games. Rec rm. 400 acres on lake. No cr cds accepted.

⬚ ⬚ ⬚ ⬚ ⬚ ⬚ ⬚

Restaurants

★★ **CANDLESTICK INN.** *Box 680, 1¹/₂ mi E on MO 76, on Mt Branson.* 417/334-3633. Hrs: 5-9 pm; Fri & Sat to 10 pm. Closed Thanksgiving, Dec 25. Res accepted. Bar 4-10 pm. Semi-a la carte: dinner $10.95-$31.50. Child's meals. Specializes in steak and seafood. Parking. Overlooks Lake Taneycomo. Cr cds: A, D, DS, MC, V.

✔★ **FRIENDSHIP HOUSE.** *(College of the Ozarks, Point Lookout) 2 mi S on US 65.* 417/334-6411. Hrs: 7 am-7:30 pm; Sun to 3 pm. Res accepted. Semi-a la carte: bkfst $1-$3.65, lunch $2.95-$4.25, dinner $5.95-$7.95. Buffet: bkfst $4.50, lunch $7.75, dinner $7.95; Sun $8.50. Child's meals. Specializes in Ozark country-style cooking. Salad bar. Parking. Overlooks college campus. Student operated. Totally nonsmoking. Cr cds: A, DS, MC, V.

[D]

★ **HOME CANNERY.** *1810 W Hwy 76.* 417/334-6965. Hrs: 6:30 am-7:30 pm. Closed late-Dec-Mar. Serv bar. Semi-a la carte: bkfst $4.99, lunch $6.99, dinner $9.99. Child's meals. Parking. Totally nonsmoking. Cr cds: A, MC, V.

[D]

★ **MR G'S.** *202 N Commercial Dr.* 417/335-8156. Hrs: 11 am-11 pm. Closed major hols. Res accepted. Italian menu. Bar. Semi-a la carte: lunch, dinner $3.95-$9.95. Specializes in Chicago-style pizza, pasta. Parking. Popular family-run establishment. Cr cds: MC, V.

✔ ★ **UNCLE JOE'S BAR-B-Q.** *3½ mi W on MO 76, adj to Grand Palace.* 417/334-4548. Hrs: 11 am-10 pm; Apr to 8 pm. Closed mid-Dec-late Jan. Semi-a la carte: lunch $4.95-$6.40, dinner $7.20-$14.60. Child's meals. Specializes in hickory-smoked ribs, ham. Salad bar. Parking. Totally nonsmoking. Cr cds: DS, MC, V.

[D] [SC]

Camdenton (D-4)

(For accommodations see Lake Ozark, Osage Beach)

Pop 2,561 **Elev** 1,043 ft **Area code** 314 **Zip** 65020
Information Chamber of Commerce, PO Box 1375; 314/346-2227 or 800/769-1004.

Camdenton is near the Niangua Arm of the Lake of the Ozarks (see).

What to See and Do

Bridal Cave. Tour (1 hr) includes colorful onyx formations, underground lake; temperature constant 60°F; lighted concrete walks. Nature trails. Visitors center, picnic area, gift shop. (Daily; closed Thanksgiving, Dec 25) 2 mi N on MO 5, then 1½ mi on Lake Rd 5-88. Phone 314/346-2676. ¢¢¢

Ha Ha Tonka State Park. More than 2,500 acres on the Niangua Arm of the Lake of the Ozarks; classic example of "karst" topography characterized by sinks, caves, underground streams, large springs and natural bridges, all remnants of an immense ancient cavern system. Features include the Colosseum, a natural theater-like pit; Whispering Dell, 150-foot sink basin that transmits sound along its entire length; Natural Bridge, 70 feet wide, 100 feet high and spanning 60 feet; remains of burned castle (ca 1910). Fishing. Hiking. Picnicking. Standard fees. (Daily) 5 mi SW via US 54. Phone 314/346-2986. **Free.**

Pomme de Terre State Park. On the shore of 7,800-acre Pomme de Terre Resevoir; a favorite for water activities, inluding muskie fishing. Swimming; beaches; fishing; boating (rentals, marina). Hiking trails. Picnicking. Camping (hookups, dump station). Standard fees. (Daily) 30 mi W via US 54, then S on County D, near Nemo. Phone 314/852-4291. **Free.**

Annual Event

Dogwood Festival. Entertainment, crafts, food, carnival. 3rd wkend Apr.

Cameron (B-3)

(See Excelsior Springs, St Joseph)

Established 1855 **Pop** 4,831 **Elev** 1,036 ft **Area code** 816 **Zip** 64429
Information Chamber of Commerce, PO Box 252; 816/632-2005.

Cameron was laid out by Samuel McCorkle, who named the town after his wife, Malinda Cameron. The completion of the railroad in 1858 spurred population and economic growth, making Cameron an agricultural trade center.

What to See and Do

Wallace State Park. More than 500 acres. Swimming; fishing; canoeing. Hiking trails. Picnicking, playground. Improved camping (dump station). Standard fees. (Daily) 7 mi S on US 69, I-35, then E on MO 121. Phone 816/632-3745. **Free.**

Motel

✔ ★ **BEST WESTERN RAMBLER.** *PO Box 469, ½ mi N on US 69, I-35 Business Loop at jct US 36.* 816/632-6571. 36 rms, 1-2 story. S $32-$40; D $35-$46; each addl $4. Pet accepted. TV; cable. Pool. Complimentary continental bkfst. Restaurant opp 11 am-10 pm. Ck-out 11 am. Cr cds: A, C, D, DS, ER, MC, V.

[🗐] [⚡] [≋] [⊗] [🐾] [SC]

Restaurant

★ **PRINGLE'S.** *US 69 & Grand Ave, 3 blks S of jct US 36 & US 69 on Business Loop I-35.* 816/632-6110. Hrs: 11 am-10 pm; Sun noon-8 pm. Closed Tues, Wed; some major hols; also 1st 2 wks Oct. Res accepted. Bar. Semi-a la carte: lunch $4.25-$6.95, dinner $4.95-$15. Child's meals. Specializes in fried chicken, steak, seafood. Salad bar. Parking. Early Amer decor, antiques. Family-owned. No cr cds accepted.

Cape Girardeau (E-7)

(See Sainte Genevieve, Sikeston)

Settled 1793 **Pop** 34,438 **Elev** 400 ft **Area code** 314 **Zip** 63701
Information Convention & Visitors Bureau, 1707 Mt Auburn Rd, PO Box 617; 314/335-1631 or 800/777-0068.

On early maps, a rocky promontory on the Mississippi River 125 miles below St Louis was labeled "Cape Girardot" (or "Girardeau"), named for a French ensign believed to have settled there about 1720. In 1792, an Indian agent for the Spanish government, Louis Lorimier, set up a trading post at the site of the present city and encouraged settlement through the Spanish policy of offering tax-exempt land at nominal cost.

Cape Girardeau's location assured a flourishing river traffic before the Civil War; sawmills, flour mills and packing houses contributed to the prosperity. The war, however, ended river trade, and the earliest railroads bypassed the town, triggering further decline; but the arrival, in the late 1880s, of new railroads, and the completion, in 1928, of a bridge across the Mississippi contributed to industrial growth and the widening of Cape Girardeau's economic base. St Vincent's Academy (1843) and Southeast Missouri State University (1873), which has a mural in its library depicting the history of the area, are located in the town.

What to See and Do

Bollinger Mill State Historic Site. Day-use park features historic 19th-century gristmill. Also oldest covered bridge in the state (1868). (Daily; closed some hols) 20 mi NW via US 61, MO 72W & MO 34S in Burfordville. Phone 314/243-4591. Tour ¢

Cape River Heritage Museum. Exhibits on Cape Girardeau's early heritage, 19th-century industry, education and culture. Gift shop. (Mar-Dec, Wed, Sat & Sun; also by appt; closed Thanksgiving, Dec 25) 538 Independence. Phone 314/334-0405 or 314/335-6333. ¢

Cape Rock. Site of original trading post. Reached by Cape Rock Dr, circling the city.

Court of Common Pleas Building. Central portion built about 1854 to replace previous log structure. During the Civil War, cells in the basement housed prisoners. Outstanding view of Mississippi River from park. Spanish & Themis Sts.

Glenn House (ca 1885). Victorian house with period furnishings, memorabilia of Mississippi River and steamboat era; tours. (Apr-Dec, Fri-Sun; closed Thanksgiving, Dec 25) 325 S Spanish St. Phone 314/334-1177. ¢¢

Old St Vincent's Church (1853). English Gothic-revival church showing Roman influences. More than 100 medieval-design plaster masks. Hand-carved doors. Spanish & Main Sts.

Rose Display Garden. Test garden (approx 300 plants) for new roses; blooming season May-Sept. Garden (daily). Perry Ave & Parkview Dr in Capaha Park. **Free.**

St Louis Iron Mountain & Southern Railway. A 1946 steam locomotive pulls vintage 1920s cars through scenic woodlands; trips range from 80 minutes to 5 hours. (Apr-Oct, Sat & Sun; also by charter) NW via I-55 exit 99, then 4 mi W on US 61 (MO 72) at jct MO 25 in Jackson. Phone 314/243-1688. ¢¢¢

Trail of Tears State Park. More than 3,000-acre park on limestone bluffs overlooking Mississippi River. Commemorates forced migration of Cherokee Nation over Trail of Tears from their homeland to Oklahoma. Fishing; boating. Hiking, equestrian trails. Picnicking. Primitive & improved camping (showers, trailer hookups). Nature center. Standard fees. (Daily) 10 mi N on MO 177. Phone 314/334-1711. **Free.**

Annual Events

Riverfest. Water & Main Sts, downtown. Festival along the Mississippi River includes arts & crafts, food, entertainment. 1 wkend early June.

Semo District Fair. Arena Park. Agricultural products, crops, animals; entertainment, carnival, food. 1 wk mid-Sept.

Motels

★ ★ **DRURY LODGE.** *PO Box 910, at jct I-55 & County K exit 96.* 314/334-7151. 140 rms, 2 story. S $55-$60; D $63-$68; each addl $8; under 18 free. Crib free. TV; cable (premium), VCR avail. Pool; wading pool. Playground. Complimentary bkfst buffet. Restaurant 6 am-10 pm. Rm serv. Bars 4 pm-1:30 am. Ck-out noon. Meeting rms. Business servs avail. In-rm modem link. Valet serv. Sundries. Game rm. Cr cds: A, C, D, DS, MC, V.

⊠ ⊠ 🐾 **SC**

★ ★ **HOLIDAY INN WEST PARK.** *PO Box 1570, I-55 & William St.* 314/334-4491; FAX 314/334-7459. 186 rms, 2 story. S, D $75-$85; each addl after 1, $10; under 18 free. Pet accepted. TV; cable (premium). Indoor/outdoor pool; wading pool. Restaurant 6 am-2 pm, 5 pm- 10 pm; Sun to 9 pm. Rm serv. Bar 4 pm-1 am; Sun 5-9 pm. Ck-out 11 am. Coin lndry. Meeting rms. Business servs avail. In-rm modem link. Valet serv. Free airport, bus depot transportation. Health club privileges. Rec rm. Holidome. Bathrm phones. Cr cds: A, C, D, DS, JCB, MC, V.

D 🐾 ⊠ ⊠ 🐾 **SC**

Restaurants

✔ ★ **BG'S OLDE TYME DELI & SALOON.** *205 S Plaza Way.* 314/335-8860. Hrs: 11 am-10 pm; Fri, Sat to 11 pm. Closed major hols. Bar. Semi-a la carte: lunch, dinner $4.29-$5.79. Child's meals. Specializes in deli sandwiches, fried chicken, cajun catfish. Salad bar. Continuous showings of contemporary movies. Cr cds: A, C, D, DS, MC, V.

★ **BROUSSARD'S CAJUN CUISINE.** *120 N Main St.* 314/334-7235. Hrs: 10 am-10 pm; Fri & Sat to 11 pm; Sun from 11 am. Closed Thanksgiving, Dec 25. Res accepted. Cajun menu. Bar. Semi-a la carte: lunch, dinner $2.95-$16.95. Specializes in crawfish étouffée, seafood. Blues band Thurs-Sat. Cr cds: A, DS, MC, V.

Carthage (E-3)

(See Joplin, Lamar, Mount Vernon)

Founded 1842 **Pop** 10,747 **Elev** 1,002 ft **Area code** 417 **Zip** 64836
Information Chamber of Commerce, 107 E 3rd St; 417/358-2373.

Carthage was founded as the seat of Jasper County in 1842. The first major Civil War battle west of the Mississippi River was fought here July 5, 1861. Among early residents were Belle Star, Confederate spy and outlaw, who lived here as a girl; Annie Baxter, the first woman in the US to hold elective office, who was elected County Clerk here in 1890; and James Scott, ragtime musician and composer, who began his career here in 1906. Many interesting Victorian houses can still be found in Carthage.

What to See and Do

Courthouse (1894). Built of Carthage marble, with mural by Lowell Davis depicting local history. (Mon-Fri; closed hols) Courthouse Square, downtown.

George Washington Carver National Memorial (see). Approx 14 mi S on US 71A.

Powers Museum. Museum devoted to local history and arts. Rotating exhibits on late 19th-early 20th-century clothing, furniture, holiday celebrations. Research library; gift shop. (Feb-Dec, daily exc Mon; closed most major hols) 1617 Oak St. Phone 417/358-2667. **Free.**

Precious Moments Chapel. Structure houses murals by Samuel J. Butcher. Also museum; gardens; gift shops; cafes. (Mar-Dec, daily; limited hrs Jan & Feb) 480 Chapel Rd. S on US 71A to Hwy HH, then W to Chapel Rd. Phone 417/358-7599 or 800/543-7975. ¢

Red Oak II. Restored boyhood hometown of artist Lowell Davis. 1930s village includes visitor center, general store, Belle Starr museum (fee), country school, church, feed & seed store, saw mill and gas station. (Daily; closed hols) 3 mi NE via MO 96, then follow sign N. Phone 417/358-9018. **Free.**

Annual Event

Maple Leaf Festival. Parade, marching band competition, arts & crafts, house tours. 3rd wkend Oct.

Motels

★ **DAYS INN.** *2244 Grand Ave.* 417/358-2499. 40 rms. S $34; D $40-$44; each addl $5; under 12 free. Crib free. TV; cable (premium). Complimentary continental bkfst. Restaurant nearby. Ck-out 11 am. Business servs avail. In-rm modem link. Cr cds: A, D, DS, MC, V.

D ⊠ 🐾 **SC**

✔ ★ **ECONO LODGE.** *1441 W Central.* 417/358-3900. 82 rms, 2 story. S $42.95-$45.95; D $49.95-$59.95; each addl $5; under

18 free. Crib $3. TV; cable (premium). Indoor pool. Complimentary continental bkfst. Ck-out 11 am. Meeting rm. Whirlpool. Cr cds: A, D, DS, JCB, MC, V.

D ⚮ ⃠ ⃠ SC

Inn

★ ★ **GRAND AVENUE.** *1615 Grand Ave. 417/358-7265.* 5 rms, 4 with shower only, 2 story. No rm phones. Apr-Dec: D $69-$79; each addl $20; wkly rates; lower rates rest of yr. Children over 9 yrs only. TV in library. Complimentary full bkfst, refreshments. Dinner by arrangement. Ck-out 11 am, ck-in 4-6 pm. Parking. Queen Anne-style, Victorian house (1890); antiques. Smoking on porch only. Cr cds: MC, V.

⃠ ⃠ ⃠

Restaurant

★ **BAM-BOO GARDENS.** *102 N Garrison, jct US 71, 96. 417/358-1611.* Hrs: 11 am-9 pm; Fri to 10 pm. Closed Sun; Jan 1, Thanksgiving, Dec 25; also 1st wk Aug. Res accepted Mon-Thurs. Chinese menu. Buffet: lunch $5.49, dinner $6.49. Specializes in cashew chicken, sweet & sour chicken. Parking. Cr cds: MC, V.

D

Cassville (E-3)

(For accommodations see Branson/Table Rock Lake Area)

Pop 2,371 **Elev** 1,324 ft **Area code** 417 **Zip** 65625
Information Chamber of Commerce, 504 Main St; 417/847-2814.

What to See and Do

Mark Twain National Forest (Cassville Ranger District). Approx 70,300 acres. Fishing; boat launching; camping at Big Bay Campground (standard fees). Picnicking at Piney Creek Wilderness Area. (Daily) E via MO 76 or MO 86; S via MO 112. Contact Ranger District office 417/847-2144 or Forest Supervisor 314/364-4621.

Ozark Wonder Cave. Seven rooms with multicolored onyx, stalactites and stalagmites; 45-min tour. (Daily) 45 mi W via MO 76, then 5 mi S on MO 59, near Noel. Phone 417/475-3579. ¢¢

Roaring River State Park. Approximately 3,300 acres of spectacular hill country. Trout fishing. Hiking. Picnicking; dining lodge, general store. Improved camping (dump station), cabins, motel. Naturalist program & nature center; fish hatchery. (Mar-Oct) (Daily) Standard fees. 7 mi S on MO 112. Phone 417/847-2539 or 417/847-2330 (cabins). **Free.**

Chillicothe (B-3)

Settled 1837 **Pop** 8,804 **Elev** 798 ft **Area code** 816 **Zip** 64601
Information Chamber of Commerce, 715 Washington St, 2nd Floor, PO Box 407; 816/646-4050.

Chillicothe, seat of Livingston County, is a Shawnee word meaning "our big town." Named for Chillicothe, Ohio, the city is located in a rich farming, livestock and dairy region. Sloan's Liniment was developed here about 1870 by Earl Sloan. An Amish community located approximately 25 miles northwest of town, near Jamesport, has many interesting shops.

What to See and Do

General John J. Pershing Boyhood Home State Historic Site. This 11-room house, built in 1858, has been restored to and furnished in the 1860s-1880s period; museum; guided tours. Also here is statue of "Black Jack" Pershing, Wall of Honor and relocated Prairie Mound School, one-room schoolhouse where Pershing taught before entering West Point. (Daily; closed some major hols) 20 mi E on US 36, then 1 mi N on MO 5 in Laclede. Phone 816/963-2525. ¢

Pershing State Park. This 2,759-acre memorial to Gen John J. Pershing offers fishing; canoeing. Hiking trails. Picnicking. Improved camping (dump station). North of the park is the Locust Creek covered bridge, the longest of four remaining covered bridges in the state. Standard fees. (Daily) 18 mi E on US 36, then S on MO 130. Phone 816/963-2299. **Free.**

Swan Lake National Wildlife Refuge. This 10,670-acre resting and feeding area attracts one of the largest concentrations of Canada geese in North America. Fishing; hunting. Observation tower (daily), visitor center with exhibits, specimens and wildlife movies (Mon-Fri). Refuge and fishing (Mar-mid-Oct, Mon-Fri). Self-guided interpretive trail. 19 mi E on US 36 to Laclede Jct, then 13 mi S on MO 139 to Sumner; main entrance 1 mi S. Phone 816/856-3323. **Free.**

Motel

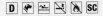

✔ ★ ★ **BEST WESTERN INN.** *1020 S Washington, at jct US 36 & 65. 816/646-0572; FAX 816/646-1274.* 60 rms, 1-2 story. S $38-$48; D $42-$52; each addl $5. Crib $5. Pet accepted. TV; cable. Pool. Continental bkfst. Restaurants nearby. Ck-out noon. Meeting rm. Refrigerators. Cr cds: A, C, D, DS, MC, V.

D ✔ ⚮ ⃠ ⃠ SC

Clayton (C-6)

(See St Louis)

Settled 1820 **Pop** 13,874 **Elev** 550 ft **Area code** 314 **Zip** 63105
Information Chamber of Commerce, 7730 Bonhomme, Suite 100; 314/726-3033.

Clayton, a western suburb of St Louis, was first settled by Virginia-born Ralph Clayton, for whom the city is named. In 1877, the budding town became the seat of St Louis County when Clayton and another early settler, Martin Hanley, donated part of their land for a new courthouse. Today Clayton is a major suburban St Louis residential and business center.

What to See and Do

Craft Alliance Gallery. Contemporary ceramic, fiber, metal, glass and wood exhibits. (Tues-Sat; closed hols) N on Hanley Rd to Delmar Blvd, E to 6640 Delmar Blvd in University City. Phone 314/725-1177. **Free.**

Forest Park. (See ST LOUIS) Approx 2 mi E via Clayton Rd or Forsyth Blvd.

Washington University (1853). (11,000 students) On campus are Graham Chapel, Edison Theatre and Francis Field, site of first Olympic Games in US (1904). E on Forsyth Blvd, hilltop campus entrance at Hoyt Dr. Phone 314/935-5000. Also here is

    Washington University Gallery of Art. Established in 1888, this was the first art museum west of the Mississippi River; a branch of the museum later became the St Louis Art Museum. Collections of 19th- and 20th-century American and European paintings; sculpture and old and modern prints. (Mon-Fri, also Sat & Sun afternoons; closed hols) Steinberg Hall. Phone 314/935-5490. **Free.**

Motor Hotel

★ ★ ★ **CHESHIRE INN & LODGE.** *(6300 Clayton Rd, St. Louis 63117)* S on Brentwood Blvd to Clayton Rd. 314/647-7300; res: 800/325-7378; FAX 314/647-0442. 106 rms, 4 story. S $99-$113; D $113-$119; each addl $6; suites $130-$250; under 12 free; wkend rates. Crib free. TV; cable (premium), VCR avail. Indoor/outdoor pool; poolside serv. Complimentary continental bkfst Mon-Fri. Restaurant (see CHESHIRE INN). Rm serv. Bar 11-1:30 am; entertainment exc Sun. Ck-out 2 pm. Meeting rms. Business servs avail. In-rm modem link. Bellhops. Valet serv Mon-Fri. Sundries. Free garage. Exercise rm; instructor, weights, bicycles, whirlpool, steam rm, sauna. Some refrigerators. Some balconies. Elegant Tudor decor. English garden. Cr cds: A, C, D, DS, MC, V.

D ⊠ ✗ ⊠ ⊠ SC

Hotels

★ ★ ★ **DANIELE.** 216 N Meramac. 314/721-0101; FAX 314/721-0609. 82 rms, 4 story. S, D $99; suites $150-$375; under 18 free; wkly, wkend rates. Pet accepted. TV; cable (premium), VCR avail. Pool. Restaurant (see DANIELE). Bar. Ck-out noon. Meeting rms. Business servs avail. In-rm modem link. Free covered parking. Free airport transportation. Health club privileges. Some refrigerators, wet bars. Cr cds: A, C, D, DS, ER, MC, V.

✔ ⊠ ⊠ ⊠

★ ★ ★ **RADISSON.** 7750 Carondelet Ave. 314/726-5400; FAX 314/726-6105. 189 rms, 2-8 story. S $99-$109; D $109-$115; each addl $10; suites $119-$185; under 18 free; wkly rates, wkend package plan. Crib free. TV; cable. 2 pools, 1 indoor. Complimentary continental bkfst 6:30-9 am. Coffee in rms. Restaurant 6 am-11 pm. Bar 11-1 am. Ck-out noon. Meeting rms. Business servs avail. In-rm modem link. Barber. Free garage parking; valet. Airport transportation. Exercise equipt; weights, bicycles, whirlpool, sauna. Game rm. Refrigerators; some wet bars. Cr cds: A, C, D, DS, ER, JCB, MC, V.

D ⊠ ✗ ⊠ ⊠ SC

Inn

★ ★ ★ **SEVEN GABLES.** 26 N Meramec. 314/863-8400; FAX 314/863-8846. 32 rms, 3 story. No elvtr. S, D $99-$139; suites $159-$260; each addl $20; wkend rates. Pet accepted, some restrictions; $20. Valet parking $6. TV; cable (premium). Restaurant 6:30 am-11 pm. Rm serv. Bar 11-12:30 am. Ck-out 1 pm, ck-in 3 pm. Meeting rm. Business servs avail. In-rm modem link. Bellhops. Valet serv. Health club privileges. Designed in early 1900s; inspired by sketches in Hawthorne's novel House of Seven Gables. Renovated inn; European country-style furnishings. Cr cds: A, C, D, DS, MC, V.

✔ ⊠ SC

Restaurants

★ ★ **ANNIE GUNN'S.** *(16806 Chesterfield Airport Rd, Chesterfield 63005)* W on I-64 (US 40), exit 19. 314/532-7684. Hrs: 11 am-10 pm; Fri, Sat to 11 pm; Sun noon-8 pm. Closed Mon; some major hols. Res accepted. Bar. Semi-a la carte: lunch $5.95-$10.95, dinner $5.95-$23.95. Specializes in steak, seafood. Parking. Outdoor dining; view of gardens. Originally built in 1935 as a meat market and smokehouse. Cr cds: A, D, MC, V.

D ⊟

★ ★ ★ **BENEDETTO'S.** *(10411 Clayton Rd, Frontenac 63131)* 6 mi W on I-64, in Le Chateau Village. 314/432-8585. Hrs: 11:30 am-2 pm, 5-11 pm; Sun 4:30-9 pm. Closed some major hols. Res accepted. Italian menu. Bar. Wine cellars. A la carte entrees: lunch $3.95-$9.95, dinner $7.50-$19. Sun brunch $25-$30. Specializes in veal, fresh fish,

beef. Parking. Formal dining in elegant surroundings. Tableside preparation. Cr cds: A, C, D, DS, MC, V.

D

★ ★ ★ **BOFINGER.** 200 S Brentwood Blvd. 314/721-0100. Hrs: 11:30 am-3 pm, 5:30-10:30 pm; Sat from 5:30 pm. Closed Sun; major hols. Res accepted. Continental menu. Bar. Semi-a la carte: lunch $5.95-$11.95, dinner $9-$15. Specializes in magret de canard, pheasant, venison, Dover sole. Own baking. Pianist. Valet parking. Cr cds: A, C, D, MC, V.

D ⊟

★ **CANDICCI'S.** 7910 Bonhomme. 314/725-3350. Hrs: 11:30 am-11 pm; Fri, Sat to midnight; Sun 4:30-9:30 pm. Closed major hols. Res accepted. Italian menu. Bar. Semi-a la carte: lunch $4-$7, dinner $7.25-$18.50. Outdoor dining. In restored apartment building. Cr cds: A, C, D, DS, ER, MC, V.

D

★ ★ **CHESHIRE INN.** *(See Cheshire Inn & Lodge Motor Hotel)* 314/647-7300. Hrs: 6:30 am-10 pm; Sat 7:30 am-11 pm; Sun 9 am-2 pm, 5-9:30 pm; Sun brunch to 2 pm. Res accepted. Bar 11-1:30 am; Sun to midnight. Semi-a la carte: lunch $5.95-$8.95, dinner $10.95-$21.95. Sun brunch $10.95. Child's meals. Specializes in prime rib, steak, fresh seafood. Pianist. Valet parking. Spit roasting in view. Old English architecture, decor. Carriage ride with dinner Fri, Sat (weather permitting; res one wk in advance suggested; fee). Transportation to Muni Opera. Cr cds: A, C, D, DS, MC, V.

D ⊟

★ ★ **DANIELE.** *(See Daniele)* 314/721-0101. Hrs: 6 am-2 pm, 5-10 pm; Sun to 10 am. Closed most major hols. Res accepted. Continental menu. Bar. Semi-a la carte: bkfst $4.95-$7.95, lunch $6.95-$10.95. Complete meals: dinner $15. Specializes in steak, veal, prime rib. Valet parking. Elegant dining. No smoking at dinner. Cr cds: A, C, D, DS, MC, V.

D

✔ ★ ★ ★ **FIO'S LA FOURCHETTE.** 7515 Forsyth Ave. 314/863-6866. Hrs: 6-11 pm. Closed Sun & Mon; major hols. Res accepted. French menu. Bar. Semi-a la carte: dinner $18-$24. Complete meals: dinner $42 & $47. Specializes in fresh seasonal dishes, soufflé. Valet parking. Intimate dining in two dining rms. Cr cds: A, C, D, MC, V.

D

★ ★ ★ **NANTUCKET COVE.** 101 S Hanley St, at Carondolet Ave. 314/726-4900. Hrs: 11 am-2 pm, 5-9:30 pm; Fri to 10:30 pm; Sat 5-10:30 pm; Sun 5-8:30 pm. Closed Jan 1, Dec 25. Res accepted. Bar. Wine list. Semi-a la carte: lunch $2-$14, dinner $4-$44. Specializes in fresh seafood, lobster. Parking. Outdoor dining. Famous St Louis seafood restaurant that recently moved to this location. Family-owned. Cr cds: A, D, DS, MC, V.

D ⊟

Unrated Dining Spot

ANDRÉ'S SWISS CONFISERIE. *(1026 S Brentwood Blvd, Richmond Heights)* S on Brentwood Blvd. 314/727-9928. Hrs: 7:30 am-5:30 pm; Fri to 9 pm. Closed Sun; major hols. Res accepted. Swiss menu. Wine, beer. Semi-a la carte: bkfst $2.95-$5.25, lunch, dinner $6-$12.50. Specialties: cheese fondue, vol au vent, quiche Lorraine. Parking. Tea rm/candy/pastry shop. Swiss decor. Family-owned. Cr cds: DS, MC, V.

D

Clinton (C-3)

(See Harrisonville, Sedalia)

Pop 8,703 **Elev** 803 ft **Area code** 816 **Zip** 64735

Information Tourism Association, 200 S Main St; 816/885-8166.

Selected as the county seat in 1837, Clinton was called "the model town of the prairies." It has a large and attractive shopping square and is situated near Harry S Truman Lake.

What to See and Do

Harry S Truman State Park. Swimming, beach; fishing; boating (ramp, rentals, marina). Hiking. Picnicking. Camping (hookups, dump station). Standard fees. (Mar-Nov, daily) Approx 20 mi E on MO 7, then 2 mi N on County UU, on Truman Lake. Phone 816/438-7711. **Free.**

Henry County Museum. Built in 1886 by Anheuser-Busch as a distributing point, restored structure now houses historical documents, cemetery records, war relics, Native American artifacts, antique dolls, glass, china; Victorian parlor and old-fashioned kitchen; stable. **Adair Annex** has turn-of-the-century village; art gallery. (Apr-Dec, Tues-Sat, limited hrs; also by appt) Donation. 203 W Franklin St. Phone 816/885-8414.

Kumberland Gap Pioneer Settlement. Re-creation of a typical 1870s village featuring general store, trading post, blacksmith shop, schoolhouse and a reconstructed log cabin. (Mid-May-Oct, wkends only) 9 mi E on MO 7 to County C, continue E to County T, then S to County TT, then W, near Truman Lake. Phone 816/547-3899. **¢¢**

Motel

✔★ COLONIAL INN. *On MO 13 Bypass, at MO 7 (E Franklin St).* 816/885-2206; FAX 816/885-2833. 32 rms, 1-2 story. S $26-$35; D $33-$43; each addl $6; higher rates state fair. Crib $6. TV; cable. Pool. Playground. Complimentary coffee in rms. Restaurant adj 6 am-midnight. Ck-out 11 am. Picnic tables. Cr cds: A, C, D, DS, MC, V.

Restaurants

★ UCHIE'S. *127 W Franklin, N side of square.* 816/885-3262. Hrs: 5 am-8 pm. Closed Sun; major hols; also 1st 2 wks Jan. Semi-a la carte: bkfst $1.30-$6.45, lunch, dinner $1.90-$9.25. Specializes in biscuits & gravy, Missouri cured country ham. Salad bar. Parking. Located in pre-1865 building. No cr cds accepted.

★ WIN-MILL. *219 MO 7.* 816/885-8434. Hrs: 6 am-9 pm. Closed Wed; also late Dec-Feb. Res accepted. Semi-a la carte: bkfst $2.65-$6.30, lunch $5.25-$6.45, dinner $5.25-$11.95. Buffet: bkfst $4.59, lunch, dinner $6.50. Child's meals. Soup & Salad bar. Parking. 3 dining rms. Family-owned. No cr cds accepted.

D SC

Columbia (C-5)

(See Fulton, Hermann, Jefferson City)

Settled 1819 **Pop** 69,101 **Elev** 758 ft **Area code** 314

Information Convention & Visitors Bureau, 300 S Providence Rd, PO Box N, 65205; 314/875-1231.

An educational center from its earliest years, Columbia is the home of Columbia College, Stephens College and the University of Missouri, the oldest state university west of the Mississippi. Established as Smithton, the town was moved a short distance to ensure a better water supply and renamed Columbia. In 1822 the Boone's Lick Trail was rerouted to pass through the town. The University of Missouri was established in 1839, and the citizens of Boone County raised $117,900—in hard times and often with personal hardship—to secure the designation of state university. Classes began in 1841, and the town has revolved around the institution ever since. The School of Journalism, founded in 1908, was the first degree-granting journalism school in the world.

What to See and Do

Nifong Park. Park includes visitor center, restored 1877 Maplewood house (Apr-Oct, Sun, limited hrs), Maplewood Barn Theater (summer; fee), Boone County Historical Society Museum; petting zoo, lake, picnicking. Park (daily). Nifong Blvd at Ponderosa Dr, off US 63. Phone 314/443-8936. **Free.**

Shelter Gardens. Miniature mid-American environment with a pool and stream, domestic and wild flowers, more than 300 varieties of trees and shrubs, rose garden, garden for visually impaired; replica schoolhouse, gazebo. Concerts in summer. (Daily; closed Dec 25) On grounds of Shelter Insurance Co, 1817 W Broadway; S at I-70 Stadium Blvd exit. Phone 314/445-8441. **Free.**

Stephens College (1833). (800 women) On 240-acre campus is the Firestone Baars Chapel on Walnut St (Mon-Fri), designed in 1956 by Eero Saarinen; art gallery (Sept-May, daily), solar-heated visitors center. E Broadway & College Ave. Phone 314/442-2211 or 314/876-7111.

University of Missouri-Columbia (1839). (22,140 students) This 1,334-acre campus contains numerous collections, exhibits, galleries and attractions. Campus tours (Mon-Fri). Campus map/guide at the Visitor Relations office, Reynolds Alumni & Visitor Center, Conley Ave. Phone 314/882-6333 or 314/882-2121. Of special interest are

Ellis Library. One of the largest libraries in the Midwest. Exhibits; rare book room contains page from a Gutenberg Bible. **State Historical Society of Missouri,** east ground wing, has early newspapers & works by Missouri artists (phone 314/882-7083); Western Historical Manuscripts, includes holdings from Great Plains region (phone 314/882-6028 for schedule). Main library (daily; closed hols; schedule may vary between terms and in summer). Lowry Mall between Memorial Union & Jesse Hall. Phone 314/882-4391.

Museum of Art and Archaeology. Comprehensive collection includes more than 13,000 objects from around the world, from paleolithic period to the present. Cast gallery has casts made from original Greek and Roman sculpture. Gift shop. (Daily exc Mon; closed hols) Pickard Hall on Francis Quadrangle. Phone 314/882-3591. **Free.**

Museum of Anthropology. Artifacts from 9000 B.C. to present. Gift shop. (Mon-Fri; closed hols) Swallow Hall on Francis Quadrangle. Phone 314/882-3764. **Free.**

Research Reactor Facility. Guided tours include displays and a view of the reactor core. (Tues-Fri; appt required) S of Memorial Stadium on Providence Rd in University Research Park. Phone 314/882-4211. **Free.**

Edison Electric Dynamo. The recently restored dynamo, given to the university in 1882 by its inventor, Thomas Alva Edison, was used on campus in 1883 for the first demonstration of incandescent lighting west of the Mississippi. (Mon-Fri) Lobby of Engineering Bldg, E 6th St between Stewart Rd & Elm St.

Botany Greenhouses & Herbarium. Greenhouse has tropical and desert rooms displaying cacti, yucca, orchids, palms and climbing bougainvillea. (Mon-Fri, by appt) Tucker Hall, off Hitt St, E of McKee Gymnasium. Phone 314/882-6888. **Free.**

Annual Events

Show-Me State Games. Missouri's largest amateur athletic event with approximately 20,000 participants in 30 different events. Late July.

Boone County Fair. First held in 1835, earliest fair west of the Mississippi; includes exhibits, horse show. Late July-early Aug.

National Hot Air Balloon Championships. Aug 16-25.

Boone County Heritage Festival and Old-Time Fiddling Contest. Mid-Sept.

Motels

(Rates may be higher during special college events)

✔★ **BUDGET HOST.** *900 Vandiver Dr (65202), I-70 exit 127.* 314/449-1065; FAX 314/442-6266. 156 rms, 2 story. S $25.95-$34.95; D $39.95-$49.95; each addl $5; under 12 free; wkly rates; higher rates special events. Crib $5. Pet accepted, some restrictions; $3. TV; cable, in-rm movies avail. Heated pool. Complimentary continental bkfst. Restaurant nearby. Ck-out 11 am. Coin lndry. Sundries. Some refrigerators. Picnic tables. Cr cds: A, C, D, DS, MC, V.

★ **CAMPUS INN.** *1112 Stadium Blvd (65201).* 314/449-2731; FAX 314/449-6691. 98 rms, 2 story. S $40; D $48; suites $65; wkly rates; higher rates wkends. Crib free. TV; cable (premium). Pool. Restaurant 7 am-1 pm. Bar. Rm serv. Ck-out noon. Meeting rms. Business servs avail. Cr cds: A, C, D, DS, MC, V.

★★ **HOLIDAY INN-EAST.** *1412 N Providence Rd (65202).* 314/449-2491; FAX 314/874-6720. 142 rms, 2 story. S $59-$75; D $60-$75; suites $175; under 18 free. Crib free. TV; cable. Heated pool. Restaurant 6 am-2 pm, 5-10 pm. Rm serv. Bar 5 pm-midnight. Ck-out noon. Meeting rms. Sundries. Exercise equipt; bicycle, stair machine, whirlpool, sauna. Holidome. Cr cds: A, C, D, DS, JCB, MC, V.

★ **SUPER 8.** *3216 Clark Ln (65202), I-70 exit 128A.* 314/474-8488; FAX 314/474-4180. 75 rms, 3 story. S $37.88-$56.88; D $45.88-$56.88; each addl $5; suites $65.88-$96.88; under 12 free; higher rates special events. Crib avail. TV; cable (premium), VCR avail. Complimentary continental bkfst. Restaurant adj 6 am-10 pm. Ck-out 11 am. Business servs avail. Cr cds: A, C, D, DS, MC, V.

Motor Hotel

★★★ **HOLIDAY INN EXECUTIVE CENTER.** *2200 I-70 Dr SW (65203), I-70 exit 124.* 314/445-8531; FAX 314/445-7607. 315 rms, 6 story. S $65.75-$93.75; D $75.75-$103.75; each addl $10; suites $175-$300. Crib free. Pet accepted. TV; cable, VCR avail. 2 pools, 1 indoor; poolside serv. Restaurant open 24 hrs. Rm serv. Bar 11 am-1:30 am, Sun noon-midnight. Ck-out 11 am. Meeting rms. Business servs avail. In-rm modem link. Bellhops. Concierge. Gift shop. Beauty shop. Exercise equipt; weights, bicycles, whirlpool, sauna. Adj Exposition Center. Luxury level. Cr cds: A, C, D, DS, MC, V.

Restaurants

★★ **BOONE TAVERN.** *811 E Walnut St (65201).* 314/442-5123. Hrs: 11 am-midnight; Sun from 10 am. Closed Thanksgiving, Dec 25. Bar. Semi-a la carte: lunch $4.95-$8.95, dinner $9.95-$18.95. Sun brunch $8.95. Child's meals. Specializes in prime rib, seafood. Outdoor dining. Turn-of-the-century memorabilia. Cr cds: A, C, D, DS, MC, V.

★★ **HADEN HOUSE.** *4515 MO 763N (65202).* 314/443-6212. Hrs: 5 pm-10 pm; Sun 11:30 am-9 pm. Closed Mon. Res accepted. Bar. Semi-a la carte: dinner $9.95-$18.95. Child's meals. Specializes in smoked meats, prime rib, southern cuisine. Parking.

Early Southern decor, antiques. Built in 1830s. Cr cds: A, C, D, DS, MC, V.

★★ **KATY STATION.** *402 E Broadway.* 314/449-0835. Hrs: 11 am-10 pm; Fri, Sat to 11 pm. Closed Dec 25. Bar. Semi-a la carte: lunch $3.95-$7.95, dinner $7.95-$16.95. Child's meals. Specializes in prime rib. Salad bar. Own desserts. Parking. Outdoor dining. Dining in restored railroad car built in 1909. Cr cds: A, D, DS, MC, V.

Excelsior Springs (B-3)

(See Independence, Kansas City; also see Kansas City, KS)

Pop 10,354 **Elev** 900 ft **Area code** 816 **Zip** 64024
Information Chamber of Commerce, 101 E Broadway; 816/630-6161.

Excelsior Springs was established in 1880 when two settlers, Anthony W. Wyman and J.V.D Flack, discovered various natural springs on Wyman's property. Today, the city is a health resort, offering the visitor bottled water from the springs and medicinal baths in the city-operated bathhouse.

What to See and Do

Excelsior Springs Historical Museum. Includes murals, bank, antiques, antique bedroom, doctor's office, dental equipment. (Daily) 101 E Broadway. Phone 816/630-3712 or -6161. **Free.**

Hall of Waters. Samples of mineral water may be purchased. Mineral baths for both men and women (by appt). 201 E Broadway. Phone 816/630-0753. Baths ¢¢¢¢

⭐ **Jesse James' Farm.** House where outlaw James was born and raised with brother Frank; original furnishings; guided tours. Theater production of *The Life & Times of Jesse James* (Aug, Fri-Sun; fee). Visitor center; slide program, historical museum. (Mon-Sat, also Sun afternoons) Approx 12 mi W on MO 92 to Kearney, then follow signs 3 mi on Jesse James Farm Rd. Phone 816/628-6065. ¢¢ Opp is

Historic Claybrook Plantation. Restored pre-Civil War house, which later was residence of James' daughter. Guided tours (fee). (Mid-May-Aug, daily) Phone 816/628-6065.

Watkins Woolen Mill State Historic Site. Woolen factory and gristmill built and equipped in 1860; contains original machinery. Original owner's house, summer kitchen, ice house, smokehouse, fruit dryhouse, family cemetery, church and school. Guided tours. (Daily; closed some hols) Recreation area adjoining site has swimming; fishing. Bicycle & hiking trail. Camping (dump station). Standard fees. (Daily) 6½ mi N on US 69, then 1½ mi W on County MM. Phone 816/296-3357 (site) or -3387 (camping). Tour ¢

Inn

★ **CRESCENT LAKE MANOR.** *1261 St Louis Ave.* 816/637-2958; res: 800/897-2958. 4 rms, share 2 baths, 2 story. No rm phones. S, D $55-$70. Adults preferred. TV avail. Pool. Complimentary full bkfst. Ck-out 11 am, ck-in after 3 pm. KC airport transportation. Turn-of-the-century mansion surrounded by moat. Cr cds: MC, V.

Fulton (C-5)

(For accommodations see Columbia, Jefferson City)

Pop 10,033 **Elev** 770 ft **Area code** 314 **Zip** 65251
Information Chamber of Commerce, 409 Court St; 314/642-3055 or 800/257-3554.

Named in honor of Robert Fulton, inventor of the steamboat, this town was home to both architect Gen M.F. Bell, who designed many of Fulton's historic buildings, and Henry Bellaman, author of the best selling novel *Kings Row,* which depicted life in Fulton at the turn of the century. The town is home to Westminster College (1851), William Woods University (1870) and the Missouri School for the Deaf. A Ranger District office of the Mark Twain National Forest is located here.

What to See and Do

Little Dixie Lake Conservation Area. More than 600 acres with 205-acre lake; fishing (permit required); boating (ramp, 10 hp limit), rowboat rentals (Apr-Oct); hiking; picnicking. (Daily) 10 mi NW via County F or I-70, in Millersburg. Phone 314/592-4080. **Free.**

Westminster College (1851). (750 students) Winston Churchill delivered his "Iron Curtain" address here on March 5, 1946. 7th St & Westminster Ave. Phone 314/642-3361. On campus is

> **Winston Churchill Memorial and Library.** To memorialize Churchill's "Iron Curtain" speech, the bombed ruins of Sir Christopher Wren's 17th-century Church of St Mary, Aldermanbury, were dismantled, shipped from London to Westminster College, reassembled and, finally, restored. The church was rehallowed in 1969 with Lord Mountbatten of Burma and Churchill's daughter, Lady Mary Soames, in attendance. The undercroft of the church houses a museum, gallery and research library with letters, manuscripts, published works, photos, memorabilia; five original Churchill oil paintings; philatelic collections; antique maps; clerical vestments; slide show. (Daily; closed Jan 1, Thanksgiving, Dec 25) Phone 314/592-1369. ¢¢ Adjacent to the memorial is

> **Breakthrough.** This 32-foot sculpture, by Churchill's granddaughter, was created to memorialize the Berlin Wall. The piece uses eight concrete sections of the actual wall; two human silhouettes cut through the concrete represent "freedom passing through."

Annual Event

Kingdom Days. Three-day festival celebrating the Civil War incident that residents claim made the county a sovereign entity; entertainment, concessions, events. Last full wkend June.

George Washington Carver National Monument (E-3)

(For accommodations see Joplin)

(2 mi W of Diamond on County V, then 1/2 mi S)

Born a slave on the farm of Moses Carver, George Washington Carver (1864?-1943) rose to become an eminent teacher, humanitarian, botanist, agronomist and pioneer conservationist. Carver was the first African-American to graduate from Iowa State University. He received both a bachelor's and a master's degree in science. He then headed the Department of Agriculture at Booker T. Washington's Tuskegee Institute in Alabama.

Authorized as a national monument in 1943, this memorial to Carver perpetuates a vital part of the American historical heritage. The visitor center contains a museum and audiovisual presentation depicting Carver's life and work. A three-quarter-mile, self-guided trail passes the birthplace site, the statue of Carver by Robert Amendola, the restored 1881 Moses Carver house, the family cemetery and the woods and streams where Carver spent his boyhood. (Daily; closed Jan 1, Thanksgiving, Dec 25). Contact Superintendent, PO Box 38, Diamond 64840-0038; 417/325-4151. Museum **Free.**

Hannibal (B-6)

(See Monroe City)

Settled 1818 **Pop** 18,004 **Elev** 491 ft **Area code** 314 **Zip** 63401
Information Visitors & Convention Bureau, 505 N 3rd, PO Box 624; 314/221-2477.

Hannibal is world-famous as the home town of the great novelist Samuel Clemens (Mark Twain) as well as the setting of *The Adventures of Tom Sawyer,* which records many actual events of Clemens' boyhood. Here, he served his printer's apprenticeship and gained a fascination for "steamboating" in the days when the river was the source of the town's prosperity.

What to See and Do

Adventures of Tom Sawyer Diorama Museum. *The Adventures of Tom Sawyer* in three-dimensional miniature scenes carved by Art Sieving. (Daily; closed Jan 1, Easter, Thanksgiving, Dec 25) 323 N Main St. Phone 314/221-3525. ¢

Becky Thatcher House. House where Laura Hawkins (Becky Thatcher) lived during Samuel Clemens' boyhood; upstairs rooms have authentic furnishings. (Daily; closed Jan 1, Thanksgiving, Dec 25) 209-211 Hill St. Phone 314/221-0822. **Free.**

Hannibal Trolley. Narrated tour aboard trolley. Open air summer months, enclosed rest of season. (Mid-Apr-Oct, daily; rest of yr by appt) 301 N Main St. Phone 314/221-1161. ¢¢¢

Haunted House on Hill Street. Life-size wax figures of Mark Twain, his family and his famous characters; gift shop. (Mar-Nov, daily) 215 Hill St. Phone 314/221-2220. ¢

Mark Twain Cave. This is the cave in *The Adventures of Tom Sawyer* in which Tom and Becky Thatcher were lost and where Injun Joe died; 52°F temperature. One-hour guided tours (daily; closed Thanksgiving, Dec 25). Lantern tours to nearby Cameron Cave (Memorial Day-Labor Day, daily; ¢¢¢). Campground adj. Sr citizen rate. 1 mi S, off MO 79. Phone 314/221-1656. ¢¢¢

⭐ **Mark Twain Museum and Boyhood Home.** Museum houses Mark Twain memorabilia, including books, letters, photographs and family items. Two-story white frame house in which the Clemens family lived in the 1840s and 1850s, restored and furnished with period pieces and relics. (Daily; closed Jan 1, Thanksgiving, Dec 25) 208 Hill St. Phone 314/221-9010. ¢¢ Admission includes

> **Pilaster House & Grant's Drugstore** (1846-47). The Clemens family lived in this Greek-revival house, which contains a restored old-time drugstore, pioneer kitchen, doctor's office and living quarters where John Clemens, Twain's father, died. Hill & Main Sts.

> **John M. Clemens Law Office.** Restored courtroom and law office where Twain's father presided as justice of the peace. Hill St.

> **Museum Annex.** Audiovisual presentations on Mark Twain & Hannibal; displays. (Mid-Apr-mid-Oct, daily) 415 N Main. Phone 314/221-9603.

Mark Twain River Excursions. One-hour cruises on the Mississippi River; also two-hour dinner cruises. (Early May-Oct, daily) Departs from foot of Center St. Phone 314/221-3222 or 800/621-2322. ¢¢¢

Riverview Park. This 400-acre park on bluffs overlooking the Mississippi River contains a statue of Samuel Clemens at Inspiration Point. Nature trails. Picnicking; playground. (Mon-Fri) Phone 314/221-0154. **Free.**

Rockcliffe Mansion. Restored, beaux-arts mansion overlooking river; 30 rooms, many original furnishings. Samuel Clemens addressed a gathering here in 1902. Guided tours. (Daily; closed Jan 1, Thanksgiving, Dec 25) 1000 Bird St. Phone 314/221-4140. **¢¢**

Tom and Huck Statue. Life-size bronze figures of Huck Finn and Tom Sawyer by F.C. Hibbard. Main & North Sts, at the foot of the hill that was their playground.

Twainland Express. Narrated tours past points of interest in historic Hannibal, some aboard open-air, train-style trams. (Apr-Oct, daily) 400 N 3rd St. Phone 314/221-5593. **¢¢¢**

Annual Events

Mississippi River Art Fair. Memorial Day wkend.

Tom Sawyer Days. National fence painting contest, frog jumping, entertainment. 4 days early July.

Autumn Historic Folklife Festival. Mid-1800s crafts, food, entertainment. 3rd wkend Oct.

Seasonal Events

Mark Twain Outdoor Theater. 4 mi S on US 61 at Clemens Landing. Performances based on the books of Mark Twain. Stage setting is a reconstruction of mid-1800s Hill St, where Twain lived. Phone 314/221-2945. June-Aug.

Molly Brown Dinner Theater. 200 N Main St. Professional musicals, including *Twain and Company* and Christmas holiday show. Reservations required for dinner show. Phone 314/221-8940. May-Dec.

Motels

✔★ **ECONO LODGE.** *612 Mark Twain Ave. 314/221-1490; res: 800/424-4777.* 49 rms, 2 story. June-Aug: S $39-$48; D $55-$65; each addl $5; higher rates for special events; lower rates rest of yr. TV; cable. Pool; wading pool. Restaurant adj 6:30 am-11 pm. Ck-out 11 am. Cr cds: A, D, DS, MC, V.

🏊 🚱 🔥 SC

★★★ **HOLIDAY INN.** *4141 Market St, at jct US 61. 314/221-6610; FAX 314/221-3840.* 241 rms, 2 story. Memorial Day-Labor Day: S $70-$95; D $80-$95; each addl $7; under 19 free; lower rates rest of year. Crib free. TV; cable (premium). Indoor pool; whirlpool, sauna, poolside serv. Restaurant 6 am-10 pm. Rm serv 7 am-2 pm, 5-9 pm. Bar 11-1 am. Ck-out 11 am. Coin lndry. Meeting rms. Business servs avail. In-rm modem link. Bellhops. Gift shop. Beauty shop. Holidome. Cr cds: A, C, D, DS, JCB, MC, V.

D 🐾 🏊 🚱 🔥 SC

★ **SUPER 8.** *US 61 S. 314/221-5863; FAX 314/221-5478.* 59 rms, 3 story. No elvtr. Late May-early Sept: S $60.88-$70.88; D $68.88-$87.88; each addl $5; suites $90.88; higher rates special events; lower rates rest of yr. Crib $5. TV; cable. Pool. Complimentary coffee in lobby. Ck-out 1 am. Meeting rms. City park adj. Cr cds: A, C, D, DS, MC, V.

D 🏊 🚱 🔥 SC

Motor Hotel

✔★★ **BEST WESTERN HOTEL CLEMENS.** *401 N 3rd St, opp Mark Twain Home & Museum. 314/248-1150; FAX 314/248-1155.* 78 rms, 3 story. Mid-May-mid-Sept: S $55-$75; D $68-$95; each addl $6; higher rates: Memorial Day, July 4, Labor Day; lower rates rest of yr. Crib $5. TV; cable (premium), VCR avail. Indoor pool; whirlpool. Complimentary continental bkfst, coffee. Restaurant opp 6 am-10 pm. Ck-out 11 am. Coin lndry. Meeting rms. Business servs avail. Free airport, bus depot transportation. Game rm. In historic district near the Mississippi River. Cr cds: A, C, D, DS, ER, JCB, MC, V.

D 🐾 🏊 🚱 🔥 SC

Inns

★★ **FIFTH STREET MANSION.** *213 S 5th St. 314/221-0445; res: 800/874-5661.* 7 rms, 3 story. Rm phones avail. S, D $60-$90; each addl $15. Crib free. Complimentary full bkfst. Restaurant nearby. Ck-out 11 am, ck-in 3 pm. Italianate house (1858) where Samuel Clemens dined in 1902. Original Tiffany stained-glass windows, light fixtures, fireplaces; walnut-paneled library; antiques. In historic district near river. Cr cds: A, DS, MC, V.

🚱 🔥

★★★ **GARTH WOODSIDE MANSION.** *RR 1, S on US 61 to Warren Barrett Dr, follow signs. 314/221-2789.* 8 rms, 3 story. No rm phones. S, D $65-$105; each addl $20. Complimentary full bkfst, tea. Restaurant nearby. Ck-out 11 am, ck-in 4 pm. Lawn games. Some balconies. Second-empire/Victorian mansion (1871), where Samuel Clemens was often a guest. On 39 acres with pond, woods. Many antiques original to house; 3-story "flying" staircase. Totally nonsmoking. Cr cds: MC, V.

🐾 🚱 🔥

Restaurants

★ **CARRIAGE HOUSE.** *421 Clinic Rd. 314/248-3343.* Hrs: 4 pm-10 pm. Closed Sun; most major hols. Res accepted. Continental menu. Bar. A la carte entrees: dinner $7.95-$15.95. Child's meals. Specializes in seafood, chicken, pasta. Parking. Nostalgic atmosphere; antiques. Cr cds: A, C, D, DS, MC, V.

D

✔★ **LOGUE'S.** *121 Huckleberry Hts Dr (US 61S). 314/248-1854.* Hrs: 5:30 am-9 pm. Closed Jan 1, Thanksgiving, Dec 25. Semi-a la carte: bkfst $1.50-$4.95, lunch $2-$5, dinner $3.50-$6.50. Child's meals. Specializes in fried chicken, homemade tenderloin. Parking. No cr cds accepted.

D

★★ **MISSOURI TERRITORY.** *600 Broadway. 314/248-1440.* Hrs: 4-9 pm; Sun brunch 11 am-2 pm. Bar to 1:30 am. Dinner $7.95-$14.95. Sun brunch $7.95. Child's meals. Specializes in seafood, steaks, prime rib. Parking. Located in old, Italianate-style federal building (1888). Cr cds: DS, MC, V.

D SC

Harrisonville (C-3)

(See Independence, Kansas City; also see Kansas City, KS)

Pop 7,683 **Elev** 904 ft **Area code** 816 **Zip** 64701

Information Chamber of Commerce, 400 E Mechanic; phone 816/884-5352.

Harrisonville, the retail and government center of Cass County, was named for Albert Harrison, a Missouri congressman.

Annual Event

Log Cabin Festival. 1st wkend Oct.

Motel

✔ ★ **BEST WESTERN.** *2201 Rockhaven Rd, at jct US 71 & MO 291. 816/884-3200; FAX 816/884-3200, ext. 100.* 30 rms. S $37-$45; D $45-$55; each addl $5; under 12 free. Crib $4. TV; cable (premium). Pool. Playground. Complimentary coffee in lobby. Ck-out 11 am. Some refrigerators. Cr cds: A, C, D, DS, ER, JCB, MC, V.

Hermann (C-5)

(See Columbia)

Founded 1836 **Pop** 2,754 **Elev** 519 ft **Area code** 314 **Zip** 65041
Information Historic Hermann Information Center, German School Bldg, 4th & Schiller Sts, PO Box 88; phone 314/486-2781.

German immigrants, unhappy with the English atmosphere of Philadelphia, bought this land and founded the town with the purpose of maintaining their German culture. The cultivation of grapes and the making of wine started early and was a thriving business until Prohibition. Today winemaking has been revived in the area, and German culture is still in evidence.

What to See and Do

Deutsche Schule Arts & Crafts. Exhibits from more than 100 craftspeople, including handmade quilting, china painting, basketmaking, toll painting, woodcutting. Demonstrations by crafters during festival wkends. (Daily; closed Easter, Thanksgiving; also Dec 25-mid-Jan) German School Bldg, 4th & Schiller Sts. Phone 314/486-3313. **Free.**

Deutschheim State Historic Site. Dedicated to Missouri's German immigrants and German-American folk art and material culture, 1830-1920. Includes authentically furnished Pommer-Gentner House (1840) on Market St and Strehly House and Winery (ca 1840-1867) on W 2nd St. Kitchen, herb & flower gardens; special events. (Daily; closed some major hols) 109 W 2nd St. Phone 314/486-2200. ¢

Graham Cave State Park. Native Americans occupied this cave approximately 10,000 years ago. About 350 acres with fishing, nature trails, playground, improved camping (dump station). Visitor center. (Daily) Standard fees. 13 mi N on MO 19, then 5 mi W, off I-70. Phone 314/564-3476. **Free.**

Historic Hermann Museum. Heritage Museum in 1871 building, with artifacts of early settlers; River Room depicts history of early river men; children's museum has toys, furniture of 1890s; handmade German bedroom set; 1886 pump organ. Mechanism of town clock may be seen. (Apr-mid-Nov, daily; rest of yr, by appt) German School Building, 4th & Schiller Sts. Phone 314/486-2017 or -2781. ¢

White House (late 1860s). Restored hotel; tours; doll collection, mineral collection. (Apr-mid-Nov, days vary) 232 Wharf St. Phone 314/486-3200. ¢

Wineries.

Stone Hill Winery. Guided tour of wine cellars; wine tasting. Restaurant. Gift shop. (See ANNUAL EVENTS) (Daily) S via MO 19 then W via MO 100, on Stone Hill Hwy (follow signs). Phone 314/486-2120. ¢

Hermannhof Winery. This 150-year-old winery includes 10 wine cellars. Sausage making; cheeses. Sampling. Tours ¢ (Apr-Nov, daily; rest of yr, Sat & Sun). 330 E 1st St. Phone 314/486-5959. **Free.**

Annual Events

Maifest. Dancing, parades; crafts; house tour. 3rd full wkend May.

Great Stone Hill Grape Stomp. Stone Hill Winery. 2nd Sat Aug.

Winefest, Octoberfest. Area wineries. Wine cellar tours, wine samples; craft demonstrations; German music, food. First four wkends in Oct.

Motel

✔ ★ **HERMANN.** *112 E 10th St. 314/486-3131.* 24 rms. S $35-$41; D $39-$43; each addl $2. Crib $5. TV; cable (premium). Restaurant adj 6 am-7 pm. Ck-out 11 am. Cr cds: A, DS, MC, V.

Inn

★ ★ **WILLIAM KLINGER.** *108 E Second St. 314/486-5930.* 7 rms, 3 story. No rm phones. D $90-$127. TV. Complimentary full bkfst. Ck-out 11 am, ck-in 3-5 pm. Street parking. Meeting rm. Victorian town house built 1878; period furnishings. Totally nonsmoking. Cr cds: MC, V.

Restaurant

★ ★ **VINTAGE 1847.** *S on MO 19 to MO 100, then W to Stone Hill Winery. 314/486-3479.* Hrs: 11 am-8:30 pm; Fri to 9 pm; Sat to 10 pm. Closed Thanksgiving, Dec 25. Res accepted; required Sat. Continental menu. Wine. Semi-a la carte: lunch $7-$12, dinner $15-$25. Child's meals. Specializes in schnitzel, fresh seafood, French onion soup. Parking. In former stable and carriage house of working winery. Cr cds: A, DS, MC, V.

Independence (C-3)

(See Blue Springs, Kansas City; also see Kansas City, KS)

Founded 1827 **Pop** 112,301 **Elev** 900 ft **Area code** 816
Information Tourism Division, 111 E Maple, 64050; 816/325-7111.

Independence was an outfitting point for westbound wagon trains from 1830 to 1850. The scene of much of the "Mormon Wars" of the early 1830s, it was ravaged by raiders and occupied by Union and Confederate troops during the Civil War. Today it is best known as the hometown of President Harry S Truman.

What to See and Do

1859 Marshal's Home and Jail Museum. Restored building contains dungeon-like cells, marshal's living quarters, regional history museum. One-room schoolhouse (1870). (Daily; closed Jan-Feb) Sr citizen rate. 217 N Main St. Phone 816/252-1892. ¢¢

Bingham-Waggoner Estate. Famous Missouri artist George Caleb Bingham lived here from 1864-1870; also the homestead of the Waggoner family, millers of "Queen of the Pantry" flour. (Apr-Oct, daily) Sr citizen rate. 313 W Pacific. Phone 816/461-3491. ¢¢

Brady Cabin and Spring. (1827). Cabin furnished with items typical of those brought westward by the pioneers; spring was meeting place of Native Americans and settlers. (May-Oct, daily exc Thurs, limited hrs) Truman & Noland Rds. Phone 816/325-7111. **Free.**

Fort Osage. Restoration of one of the first US outposts in the Louisiana Territory following the purchase from France. Built in 1808 by William Clark of the Lewis and Clark expedition, fort includes officers' quarters, soldiers' barracks, trading post, factor's house, museum; costumed guides. Visitor center contains dioramas, exhibits, gift shop. Special events; candlelight tours (fee). (Mid-Apr-mid-Nov, Wed-Sun; rest of yr, Sat & Sun; closed Jan 1, Thanksgiving, Dec 25) 10 mi E of MO 291 on

US 24 to Buckner, then 3 mi N to Sibley, then 1 mi N following signs. Phone 816/795-8200 or 816/249-5737. ¢¢

Harry S Truman Courtroom and Office Museum. Restored office and courtroom where Truman began his political career as presiding county judge; 30-minute audiovisual show on Truman's boyhood and early career. Tours. Sr citizen rate. (Apr-Nov, Wed-Sun, rest of yr, Sat-Sun) Jackson County Courthouse, 22807 Woods Chapel Rd. For hrs phone 816/795-8200 or 816/881-4467. ¢¢

 Harry S Truman National Historic Site (Truman House). Truman's residence from the time of his marriage to Bess Wallace in 1919 until his death in 1972; an excellent example of late 19th-century, Victorian architecture, the house, built by Bess Truman's grandfather, was the birthplace of Margaret Truman and served as the summer White House from 1945 to 1953. Guided tours. Ticket Center at Truman Rd & Main St. (Memorial Day-Labor Day, daily; rest of yr, daily exc Mon; closed Jan 1, Thanksgiving, Dec 25) Sr citizen rate. 219 N Delaware St. Phone 816/254-9929 or -7199. ¢

National Frontier Trails Center. Partially restored flour mill, at site of Santa Fe, California and Oregon trails, serves as museum, interpretive center, library and archive of westward pioneer expansion; film (17 min), exhibits. (Daily; closed Jan 1, Nov 11, Thanksgiving, Dec 25). 318 W Pacific, at Osage St. Phone 816/325-7575. ¢¢

The Harry S Truman Library & Museum. Includes presidential papers; mementos of public life; reproduction of President Truman's White House office; Thomas Hart Benton mural. Graves of President and Mrs Truman in courtyard. Museum (daily; closed Jan 1, Thanksgiving, Dec 25). Library (Mon-Fri). US 24 & Delaware St. Phone 816/833-1225 (museum) or -1400 (library). ¢¢

Truman Farm Home. Truman lived in this two-story, white frame house in the decade preceding World War I; during these years—"the best years," according to Truman—he farmed the surrounding 600 acres, worked as a mason and postmaster, served as a soldier and courted Bess Wallace. Interior features period furnishings, including original family pieces; outbuildings include garage, outhouse, chicken coop and smokehouse. Special events in May & Dec. (Mid-Apr-mid-Nov, Thurs-Sat; rest of yr, by appt) 19 mi S via I-435 to US 71, S on US 71 to 12301 Blue Ridge Blvd in Grandview. Phone 816/795-8200. ¢¢

Vaile Mansion (1881). House, designed for local entrepreneur Colonel Harvey Vaile, has 30 rooms and is an example of Second Empire architecture; ceiling murals. (Apr-Oct, daily) Sr citizen rate. 1500 N Liberty. Phone 816/325-7430 or 816/325-7111. ¢¢

World Headquarters Complex, Reorganized Church of Jesus Christ of Latter Day Saints. Auditorium, museum and art gallery; 6,300-pipe organ; recitals (June-Aug, daily; rest of yr, Sun only). Japanese meditation garden. Guided tours (daily; closed Jan 1, Thanksgiving, Dec 25). River & Walnut Sts. Phone 816/833-1000.

Annual Events

Truman Celebration. Tribute to President Truman. Early May.

Santa-Cali-Gon. Celebration commemorating the Santa Fe, California and Oregon trails; melodrama, contests, arts & crafts, square dancing. Phone 816/252-4745. Labor Day wkend.

Motels

★ ★ **HOWARD JOHNSON EAST.** 4200 S Noland Rd (64055). 816/373-8856; FAX 816/373-3312. 171 rms, 2 story. S $47-$57; D $57-$67; suites $85; under 18 free. Crib free. TV; cable (premium), VCR avail. 2 pools, 1 indoor; saunas, whirlpool. Restaurant adj open 24 hrs. Bar 4 pm-1 am. Ck-out noon. Meeting rms. Business servs avail. Valet serv. Some refrigerators. Private patios, balconies. Cr cds: A, C, D, DS, ER, JCB, MC, V.

🅓 🖼 🌊 🏊 🐾 SC

✔ ★ **RED ROOF INN.** 13712 E 42nd Terrace (64055). 816/373-2800; FAX 816/373-0067. 108 rms, 2 story. S $28-$37; D $38-$47; each addl $8; under 18 free. Crib free. Pet accepted. TV; cable. Complimentary coffee. Restaurant nearby. Ck-out noon. Health club privileges. Cr cds: A, C, D, DS, MC, V.

🅓 🖼 🌊 🏊

★ **SHONEY'S INN.** 4048 S Lynn Court Dr (64055). 816/254-0100; res: 800/222-2222; FAX 816/254-6796. 114 rms, 2 story. S $42-$47; D $48-$60; each addl $6; under 18 free. Crib free. TV; cable (premium). Pool. Restaurant 6 am-midnight; Fri, Sat to 3 am. Ck-out noon. Meeting rm. Business servs avail. Cr cds: A, C, D, DS, ER, MC, V.

🅓 🌊 🏊 🐾 SC

Inn

✔ ★ **WOODSTOCK.** 1212 W Lexington (64050). 816/833-2233. 11 rms, 2 story. S $40-$65; D $45-$70; each addl $7.50; suites $70. Crib $3. TV in some rms, lobby; cable. Complimentary full bkfst, coffee and tea. Restaurant nearby. Ck-out 11 am, ck-in 4 pm. Airport, bus depot transportation. In historic area of town near Truman house and library and World Headquarters of Reorganized Church of Jesus Christ of Latter Day Saints. Totally nonsmoking. Cr cds: A, DS, MC, V.

🅓 🏊 🐾 SC

Restaurants

★ **GAROZZO'S DUE.** 12801 E US 40 (64055). 816/737-2400. Hrs: 11 am-10 pm; Fri to 11 pm; Sat 4-11 pm; Sun 3-9 pm. Closed most major hols. Italian menu. Bar. Semi-a la carte: lunch $6.95-$14, dinner $7.95-$22. Child's meals. Specialties: vitello Marion, bistecca Modiga, pork neckbones. Parking. Outdoor dining. Cr cds: A, DS, MC, V.

🅓

✔ ★ **STEPHENSON'S RED MULE PUB & GRILL.** 16506 E US 40. 816/478-1810. Hrs: 11:30 am-10 pm; Sun to 9 pm. Closed Dec 24, 25. Bar. Semi-a la carte: lunch $4.25-$5.95, dinner $5.25-$13.95. Child's meals. Specialties: pan-fried chicken, chicken-fried steak, catfish. Western decor. Cr cds: A, DS, MC, V.

🅓

✔ ★ **TIPPIN'S.** 2931 S Noland Rd. 816/252-8890. Hrs: 7 am-10 pm; Fri, Sat to midnight. Closed Dec 25. Semi-a la carte: bkfst $2.25-$6.25, lunch $4-$7, dinner $6-$10.95. Child's meals. Specializes in soups, salads, homemade pies. Cr cds: A, D, DS, MC, V.

🅓

★ ★ **V'S ITALIANO RISTORANTE.** 10819 E US 40. 816/353-1241. Hrs: 11:30 am-10 pm; Fri, Sat to 11 pm; Sun 10 am-8 pm; Sun brunch 10 am-2 pm. Closed some major hols. Res accepted. Italian, Amer menu. Bar. Semi-a la carte: lunch $4.50-$8.45, dinner $7.95-$16.95. Child's meals. Specialties: lasagne, veal parmesan, rum cake. Parking. Family-owned. Cr cds: A, C, D, DS, MC, V.

SC

Jefferson City (C-5)

(See Columbia, Fulton)

Settled ca 1825 **Pop** 35,481 **Elev** 702 ft **Area code** 314

Information Jefferson City Convention & Visitors Bureau, 213 Adams St, PO Box 776, 65102; 314/634-3616 or 800/769-4183.

Jefferson City was chosen for the state capital in 1826. Near a river landing, it consisted of a foundry, a shop and a mission. Its growth was not steady, and as late as 1895 efforts were being made to move the seat of government. Since 1900, however, the city has prospered. The present capitol, completed in 1917, confirmed its status. Named for Thomas Jefferson, it is known locally as "Jeff City."

What to See and Do

Cole County Historical Society Museum (ca 1870). One of three four-story row houses built in the Federal style, the museum features Victorian furnishings and household items; inaugural gowns from Missouri's first ladies dating from 1877; research library. Guided tours (Tues-Sat). 109 Madison St. Phone 314/635-1850. ¢

Governor's Mansion (1871). Renaissance-revival architecture by George Ingham Barnett; period furnishings, stenciled ceilings, period wall coverings and late 19th-century chandeliers. Tours (Tues & Thurs; closed Aug & Dec). 100 Madison St. Phone 314/751-4141. **Free.**

Lake of the Ozarks (see). Approx 42 mi SW on US 54.

State Capitol (1918). On a bluff overlooking the Missouri River, this building, of Carthage stone, is the third state capitol in Jefferson City; both predecessors burned. A Thomas Hart Benton mural is in the House Lounge, third floor, west wing; also paintings by N.C. Wyeth and Frank Brangwyn. Tours (30 min). (Daily; closed some major hols) High St & Broadway. Phone 314/751-4127. **Free.**   Also here is

Missouri State Museum. Offers two permanent exhibits; History Hall, with several themes of Missouri history, and Resources Hall. (Daily; closed major hols) Phone 314/751-4127. **Free.**   Near here is

Jefferson Landing State Historic Site. Restored mid-1800s riverboat landing. Lohman Bldg (1839) features exhibits and audiovisual presentation on history of Jefferson City and Missouri Capitol. Union Hotel (1855) contains gallery of exhibits by local artists. (Daily; closed major hols) 100 blk of Jefferson St. Phone 314/751-3475. **Free.**

Motor Hotels

✔ ★ ★ **BEST WESTERN INN.** *1937 Christy Lane (65101).* 314/635-4175; FAX 314/635-6769. 79 rms, 1-2 story. S $45-$53; D $54-$57; suites $60-$70; under 12 free. Crib $2. TV; cable (premium). Indoor pool. Restaurant 6 am-2 pm, 4:30-9 pm; Sun 7 am-3 pm. Rm serv. Bar 3 pm-1 am; entertainment, dancing exc Sun. Ck-out noon. Guest lndry. Meeting rms. Business servs avail. In-rm modem link. Valet serv. Sundries. Cr cds: A, C, D, DS, MC, V.

D ⊗ ⊗ ⊗ SC

✔ ★ ★ **HOTEL DE VILLE.** *319 W Miller St (65101), 2 blks S of Capitol Building.* 314/636-5231; FAX 314/636-5260. 98 rms, 3 story. S, D $56; each addl $7; suites $68; under 17 free. Crib free. Pet accepted. TV; cable (premium), VCR avail. Pool. Restaurant 6 am-10 pm. Rm serv. Bar 11-1 am, closed Sun. Ck-out noon. Meeting rms. Business servs avail. Valet serv. Cr cds: A, C, D, DS, ER, JCB, MC, V.

D ⊗ ⊗ ⊗ ⊗ SC

★ ★ **RAMADA INN.** *1510 Jefferson St (65109).* 314/635-7171; FAX 314/635-8006. 235 rms, 2 story. S $55-$60; D $60-$65; each addl $5; suites $125; under 18 free. Crib free. TV; cable (premium). Pool. Coffee in rms. Restaurant 6:30 am-2 pm, 5-10 pm; Sun from 7 am. Rm serv. Bar 5 pm-1:30 am, Sun noon-8 pm; entertainment exc Sun. Ck-out 11 am. Meeting rms. Business center. Sundries. Free RR station, bus depot transportation. Airport transportation. Exercise equipt; weights, bicycles. Game rm. Refrigerator in suites. Cr cds: A, C, D, DS, MC, V.

D ⊗ ⊗ ⊗ ⊗ SC ⊗

Hotel

★ ★ ★ **CAPITOL PLAZA.** *415 W McCarty (65101).* 314/635-1234; res: 800/338-5088; FAX 314/635-4565. 255 rms, 9 story, 40 suites. S $80.50-$93.50; D $90.50-$103.50; each addl $10; suites $99.50-$250; under 18 free; wkend rates. Crib free. TV; cable (premium). Indoor pool; poolside serv. Restaurant 6 am-10 pm (also see CARNEGIE'S). Bar 11-2 am, Sun to 10 pm; entertainment, dancing exc

Sun. Ck-out noon. Convention facilities. Business center. Gift shop. Covered parking. Refrigerator, wet bar, coffee in suites. Cr cds: A, C, D, DS, MC, V.

D ⊗ ⊗ ⊗ SC ⊗

Restaurants

★ ★ ★ **CARNEGIE'S.** *(See Capitol Plaza)* 314/635-1234. Hrs: 5-10 pm. Closed Sun; most major hols. Res accepted. Continental menu. Bar. Wine list. Semi-a la carte: dinner $16.95-$29.95. Specializes in nouvelle cuisine, filet mignon, pasta. Tableside preparation. Parking. Formal dining. Cr cds: A, C, D, DS, MC, V.

D

✔ ★ **PIZZARIA NAPOLITANA.** *2336 Missouri Blvd.* 314/636-5221. Hrs: 11 am-10 pm; Fri to 11 pm, Sat 4-11 pm. Closed some major hols. Res accepted Sun-Thurs. Italian, Greek, Amer menu. Bar. Semi-a la carte: lunch $1.95-$4.25, dinner $5.75-$12.95. Buffet: $4.25. Child's meals. Specializes in steak, lasagne, pizza. Salad bar. Parking. Contemporary decor. Cr cds: MC, V.

D SC

Joplin (E-2)

(See Carthage, Mount Vernon)

Settled 1838 **Pop** 40,961 **Elev** 972 ft **Area code** 417
Information Convention & Visitors Bureau, 222 W 3rd St, 64802; 417/625-4789 or 800/657-2534.

The discovery of lead here convinced an early settler to establish a town and name it after another settler, Rev Harris G. Joplin. As the mining boom continued, another community, Murphysburg, grew up on the west side of Joplin Creek. The two towns were rivals until 1873 when both agreed to incorporate into one city. Today, Joplin, one of Missouri's larger cities, is home to many manufacturing industries.

What to See and Do

George Washington Carver National Monument (see). Approx 2 mi E via US 66, 5 mi S via US 71, 8 mi E on County V, then 1/2 mi S.

Missouri Southern State College (1937). (6,000 students) This 332-acre campus includes Taylor Performing Arts Center, Mission Hills estate and Spiva Art Center (phone 417/623-0183) with changing exhibits (daily exc Mon; closed hols; also early Aug). Tours. Newman & Duquesne Rds. Phone 417/625-9300. **Free.**

Museum Complex. Schifferdecker Park. W edge of city on US 66. Here are

Tri-State Mineral Museum. Models of lead and zinc-mining equipment, mineral and history displays. (May-Sept, daily; rest of yr, Wed-Sun afternoons; closed hols) Phone 417/623-2341. **Free.**

Dorothea B. Hoover Historical Museum. Period rooms with late 19th-century furnishing; miniatures, including a circus, photographs, musical instruments, Victorian doll house and playhouse; antique toys; dolls; Native American artifacts; cut glass. (Wed-Sun, afternoons; closed hols; late Dec-early Jan) Under 12 only with adult. Phone 417/623-1180. **Free.**

Post Memorial Art Reference Library. Art research facility resembling 16th-century English hall. Furniture and artwork date to 13th century. (Daily exc Sun; closed major hols) 300 Main St. Phone 417/782-7678. **Free.**

Thomas Hart Benton Exhibit. Includes mural, "Joplin at the Turn of the Century, 1896-1906," as well as photographs, clay models, personal letters and other paintings by Benton. (Mon-Fri; closed hols) In Municipal Building, 303 E 3rd St. **Free.**

Motels

✔★ **BEST WESTERN HALLMARK INN.** *3600 Range Line Rd (64804), jct I-44 & US 71.* 417/624-8400; FAX 417/781-5625. 96 rms, 2 story. S $42-$52; D $50-$60; each addl $6; suites $85; under 12 free. TV; cable (premium), VCR avail. Pool. Playground. Coffee in rms. Restaurant nearby. Ck-out noon. Business servs avail. In-rm modem link. Valet serv. Airport transportation. Refrigerators avail. Cr cds: A, C, D, DS, ER, JCB, MC, V.

🅳 ⊠ ⊠ ⊠ SC

★★ **DRURY INN.** *3601 Range Line (64804), I-44 exit 8B.* 417/781-8000. 109 rms, 4 story. Memorial Day-Labor Day: S $58; D $64-$80; each addl $5; under 18 free; lower rates rest of yr. Crib free. Pet accepted, some restrictions. TV; cable (premium), VCR avail. Indoor pool; whirlpool. Complimentary continental bkfst. Restaurant adj 6 am-10 pm. Ck-out noon. Meeting rms. Business servs avail. In-rm modem link. Health club privileges. Some refrigerators. Cr cds: A, C, D, DS, MC, V.

🅳 ⊠ ⊠ ⊠ ⊠ SC

✔★ **THUNDERBIRD.** *2121 Range Line (64804), N of I-44 exit 8B.* 417/624-7600. 30 rms. S $32-$38; D $36-$42; each addl $3. Crib $2. TV; cable (premium). Pool. Playground. Restaurant adj 6 am-midnight. Ck-out 11 am. Cr cds: A, C, D, MC, V.

⊠ ⊠ ⊠

★ **WESTWOOD.** *1700 W 30th St (64804).* 417/782-7212; FAX 417/624-0265. 33 rms, 2 story. S $35-$65; D $39-$76; each addl $4; kits. $44-$74; under 12 free; wkly rates. Crib $5. Pet accepted; $25. TV; cable (premium). Pool. Complimentary coffee in lobby. Ck-out 11 am. Coin lndry. Cr cds: A, DS, MC, V.

🅳 ⊠ ⊠ ⊠ ⊠ SC

Motor Hotels

★★★ **HOLIDAY INN HOTEL & CONVENTION CENTER.** *3615 Range Line (64804).* 417/782-1000; FAX 417/623-4093. 264 rms, 2-5 story. S $67-$74.50; D $67-$74.50; each addl $10; suites $89.50-$175.50; under 18 free. Crib free. Pet accepted, some restrictions. TV; cable (premium), VCR avail. 2 pools, 1 indoor. Restaurant 6 am-10 pm. Rm serv. Bar; entertainment. Ck-out noon. Meeting rms. Business servs avail. In-rm modem link. Bellhops. Valet serv. Free airport, bus depot transportation. Exercise equipt; weights, bicycles, whirlpool, steam rm, sauna. Atrium. Cr cds: A, C, D, DS, JCB, MC, V.

🅳 ⊠ ⊠ ⊠ 🎿 ⊠ ⊠ SC

★ **RAMADA INN.** *3320 Range Line Rd (64804), jct I-44 & US 71.* 417/781-0500; FAX 417/781-9388. 171 rms, 2-3 story. S $50-$62; D $58-$72; each addl $8; suites $95-$130; under 18 free. Crib free. Pet accepted. TV; cable (premium). 2 pools, 1 indoor; whirlpool, sauna. Playground. Restaurant 6:30 am-10 pm. Rm serv. Bar. Ck-out noon. Meeting rms. Business servs avail. In-rm modem link. Bellhops. Valet serv. Free airport transportation. Lighted tennis. Cr cds: A, C, D, DS, ER, MC, V.

🅳 ⊠ ⊠ ⊠ ⊠ ⊠ SC

Restaurants

✔★ **KITCHEN PASS.** *1212 Main St.* 417/624-9095. Hrs: 11 am-10 pm; wkends to 11 pm. Closed Sun; major hols. Res accepted. Bar to 1:30 am; entertainment Fri & Sat. Semi-a la carte: lunch $3.25-$5.75, dinner $7.75-$12.95. Child's meals. Specializes in seafood, steak, chicken. Parking. Cr cds: A, DS, MC, V.

★ **WILDER'S.** *1216 Main St.* 417/623-7230. Hrs: 11 am-9 pm; Fri & Sat to 10 pm. Closed Sun; most major hols. Res accepted. Bar. Semi-a la carte: lunch, dinner $2.65-$14.95. Child's meals. Spe-

cializes in mesquite wood cooking. Parking. Operating since 1929; nostalgic decor. Cr cds: A, MC, V.

Unrated Dining Spot

WYATT'S CAFETERIA. *3132 Range Line Rd.* 417/623-3325. Hrs: 11 am-8 pm; Fri, Sat to 8:30 pm. Closed Dec 25. Avg ck: lunch $4.40, dinner $5.50. Specializes in roast beef, baked eggplant casserole, desserts. Parking. Cr cds: A, D, DS, MC, V.

🅳

Kansas City (C-2)

Settled 1838 **Pop** 435,146 **Elev** 800 ft **Area code** 816

Kansas City is the distributing point for a huge agricultural region. It is one of the country's leading grain and livestock markets and is famous for its steak and barbecue. The city is also a great industrial center, with food processing, milling, petroleum refining and vehicle assembling high in importance. Kansas City, Kansas, across the Missouri River, is politically separate, but the two cities, constituting the Greater Kansas City area, form an economic unit.

Kansas City, Missouri, developed as a steamboat landing for the town of Westport, four miles south on the Santa Fe Trail, and a competitor of Independence as the trail's eastern terminus and outfitting point. The buildings that sprang up along this landing soon eclipsed Westport, which was eventually incorporated into the new city. Kansas City's roaring overland trade was disturbed by the border warfare of the 1850s and the Civil War, but peace and the railroads brought new growth and prosperity. A network of railway lines, following the natural water-level routes that converge at the mouth of the Kansas River, made Kansas City a great terminus.

Its citizens, famous for their "booster" spirit, were aroused to the need for civic improvement in the 1890s by the crusade of William Rockhill Nelson, *Kansas City Star* publisher. As a result, today's Kansas City boasts 52 boulevards, totaling 155 miles, and more fountains than any city except for Rome.

Transportation

Car Rental Agencies: See toll-free numbers under Introduction.

Public Transportation: Area Transit Authority, phone 816/221-0660.

Rail Passenger Service: Amtrak phone 800/872-7245 or 816/421-4725.

Airport Information

Kansas City Intl Airport: Information phone 816/243-5237; lost and found phone 816/243-5215; weather phone 816/540-6021; cash machines, Terminals A, B, C; Admirals Club (American), Terminal A; Presidents Club (Continental), Terminal C.

What to See and Do

Antiques, Art and Design Center. More than twenty shops and galleries located in old historic area. 45th & State Line.

⭐ **Arabia Steamboat Museum.** Excavated pioneer artifacts from steamboat *Arabia*, which went down in 1856. The boat, discovered in 1988, carried 200 tons of cargo. Replica of main deck; hands-on displays. (Mon-Sat & Sun afternoons; closed some hols) 400 Grand Ave. Phone 816/471-4030. ¢¢¢

Benjamin Ranch. Re-creation of early Western town; horseback and pony rides, sleigh rides, hayrides; chuckwagon food, western equipment and livestock. Picnic facilities. (Apr-Nov, daily) Fees vary by

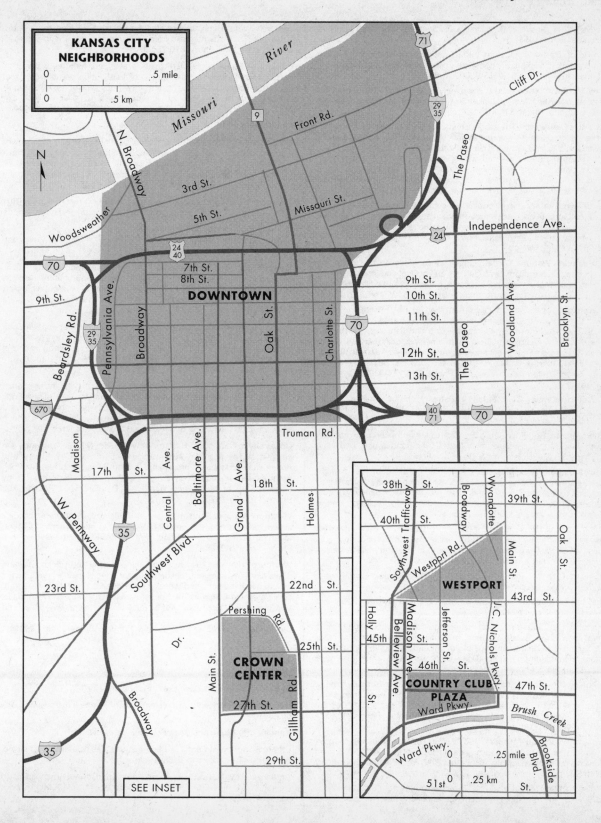

KANSAS CITY NEIGHBORHOODS

0 — .5 mile
0 — .5 km

N

Missouri River

N. Broadway

Woodsweather

3rd St.

5th St.

Front Rd.

Missouri St.

9

29 35

Cliff Dr.

The Paseo

Independence Ave.

24

70

24 40

70

9th St.

Beardsley Rd.

Pennsylvania Ave.

Broadway

Oak St.

Charlotte St.

7th St.
8th St.

DOWNTOWN

9th St.
10th St.
11th St.
12th St.
13th St.

The Paseo

Woodland Ave.

Brooklyn St.

29 35

670

40 71

70

Truman Rd.

Madison

17th St.

Central Ave.

Baltimore Ave.

Grand Ave.

18th St.

Holmes

W. Pennway

35

Southwest Blvd.

23rd St.

22nd St.

Dr.

Pershing Rd.

Main St.

Gillham Rd.

25th St.

CROWN CENTER

27th St.

Broadway

35

29th St.

SEE INSET

38th St.

Southwest Trafficway

40th St.

Westport Rd.

Broadway

Wyandotte

39th St.

Main St.

Oak St.

WESTPORT

43rd St.

Holly St.

45th St.

Belleview Ave.

Madison Ave.

Jefferson St.

J.C. Nichols Pkwy.

46th St.

COUNTRY CLUB PLAZA

Ward Pkwy.

47th St.

Brush Creek

Brookside Blvd.

Ward Pkwy.

51st St.

0 — .25 mile
0 — .25 km

activity. (See ANNUAL EVENTS) On the Old Santa Fe Trail, I-435 & E 87th. Phone 816/761-5055.

Board of Trade. Stock index trading and world's largest hard winter wheat market. Visitors may observe trading from third floor. (Mon-Fri) 4800 Main St. Phone 816/753-7500. **Free.**

City Market. Outdoor market since early 1800s (daily). Indoor farmers' market (Apr-Sept, Mon-Sat, also Sun afternoons). Main to Grand Sts, 3rd to 5th Sts. Phone 816/842-1271.

Country Club Plaza. The nation's first planned shopping center (1922) consists of 55 acres encompassing more than 180 shops and 25 restaurants in and around Spanish/Moorish-style, arcaded buildings. The plaza features tree-lined walks, statues, fountains and murals; re-creations of Spain's Seville light and Giralda tower; horse-drawn carriage rides; free entertainment. Shops (daily). 47th between Nichols Pkwy & Madison Ave, S of downtown. Phone 816/753-0100.

★ Crown Center. This entertainment complex offers shopping, theaters, restaurants and hotels around a landscaped central square; free concerts (mid-June-Aug, Fri evenings), exhibits and ice-skating (mid-Nov-Mar). Shops (daily). Pershing & Grand Ave. Phone 816/274-8444. In Crown Center are

Hallmark Visitors Center. Exhibit areas focus on history of the greeting card industry. Included are audiovisual and interactive displays; die-making and manufacturing demonstrations; film presentation. (Daily exc Sun; closed some hols) Phone 816/274-5672. **Free.**

Kaleidoscope. Participatory creative art exhibit for children ages 5-12 only; Discovery Room features a hands-on creative area where children explore art by touching, doing and listening; studio with specially designed art projects. (Mid-June-Aug, daily exc Sun; rest of yr, Sat or Mon-Fri with advance res) Adults may view activity through one-way mirrors. Three 90-minute sessions per day; tickets avail half-hour before each session. Phone 816/274-8300 or -8301. **Free.**

Coterie-Kansas City's Family Theatre. Nonprofit professional children's theater. (Early Feb-late Dec, daily exc Mon) 2450 Grand Ave. Phone 816/474-6552. ¢¢

Government Buildings. Includes City Hall with observation roof on 30th floor (Mon-Fri; closed hols); federal, state and county buildings. 11th to 13th Sts, Holmes to McGee Sts. **Free.**

Jesse James Bank Museum (1858). Restored site of first daylight bank robbery by James gang (1866). Jesse James memorabilia; handscribed bank ledger books and other relics of early banking. (Daily; closed Jan 1, Thanksgiving, Dec 25) 15 mi N via I-35, in Liberty, on Old Town Square. Phone 816/781-4458. ¢¢

John Wornall House Museum (1858). Restored farmhouse interprets lives of prosperous Missouri farm families from 1830-1865; herb garden; gift shop. (Tues-Sat, also Sun afternoons; closed hols) Sr citizen rate. 61st Terrace and Wornall. Phone 816/444-1858. ¢¢

Kansas City Art Institute (ca 1885). 4415 Warwick Blvd. Phone 816/561-4852. On campus is

Kemper Museum of Contemporary Art and Design. (Daily exc Mon; closed some hols)

Kansas City Museum. Science, history and technology exhibits housed in former estate of lumber millionaire Robert A. Long; re-creation of 1821 trading post, 1860 storefront and functioning 1910 drugstore; planetarium; gift shop. (Daily exc Mon; closed major hols) 3218 Gladstone Blvd. Phone 816/483-8300. ¢¢

Kansas City Zoological Gardens. Zoo includes a tropical habitat, Australian walkabout, cat walk and ape house; miniature train, pony and camel rides; interpretive programs. (Daily; closed Jan 1, Dec 25) Swope Park, Meyer Blvd & Swope Pkwy, just off I-435. Phone 816/871-5700. ¢¢

Liberty Memorial Museum. World War I military museum houses weapons, uniforms; full-scale replica of military trench. A 217-foot-high tower provides view of city ¢. (Wed-Sun; closed some hols) 100 W 26th St, opp Union Station. Phone 816/221-1918. ¢

Nelson-Atkins Museum of Art. Collections range from Sumerian art of 3000 B.C. to contemporary paintings and sculpture; period rooms; decorative arts; Henry Moore sculpture garden. Guided tours (free). (Tues-Sat & Sun afternoons; closed some major hols) Free on Sat. 4525 Oak St, at 47th St. Phone 816/751-1ART. ¢¢

Oceans of Fun. This 60-acre family water park features wave pool, several twisting water slides, boats, children's pools and playgrounds. (Late May-Labor Day, daily) One- and two-day passports; also combination Worlds of Fun/Oceans of Fun passports. 10 mi NE via I-435 exit 54, between Parvin Rd & NE 48th St. Phone 816/454-4545. ¢¢¢¢

Sightseeing.

Kansas City Trolley. Trolley makes continuous circuit from downtown through Crown Center to Westport Square, Country Club Plaza and the River Market; 17 stops include museums, hotels, restaurants. (Early Mar-late Dec, daily; closed Thanksgiving) Phone 816/221-3399. ¢¢

Kansas City Sightseeing. Tours to points of interest in Kansas City, Independence and surrounding area; six-person minimum. Phone 816/833-4083.

Gray Line bus tours. Contact PO Box 414475, 64141; phone 913/268-5252.

Thomas Hart Benton Home and Studio State Historic Site (1903-04). Eclectic-style residence of the artist from 1939 until his death in 1975; studio contains many of Benton's tools and equipment; changing exhibits. (Daily; closed some major hols) 3616 Belleview. Phone 816/931-5722. ¢

Toy & Miniature Museum of Kansas City. Miniatures, antique doll houses and furnishings from 1840s to mid-20th century. (Wed-Sat, also Sun afternoons; closed major hols; also 1st 2 wks Sept) Sr citizen rate. 5235 Oak St at 52nd St, on University of Missouri-Kansas City campus. Phone 816/333-2055. ¢¢

Union Cemetery (1857). Some notables buried here include artist George Caleb Bingham and Alexander Majors, founder of the Pony Express; graves of more than 1,000 Civil War soldiers. Self-guided walking tours. 227 E 28th St Terrace. For further information phone 816/221-4373 (cemetery) or 816/561-6630 (park district).

University of Missouri-Kansas City (1933). (11,500 students) On campus is Toy and Miniature Museum of Kansas City, library with Americana and local historical exhibits, Marr Sound Archives, Jazz Film Archives, Geosciences Museum and Gallery of Art. Performances by Conservatory of Music and Academic Theater. 5100 Rockhill Rd. Phone 816/235-1576.

Westport Square. Renovation of the 1830s square includes specialty shops, galleries and restaurants; Pioneer Park traces Westport's role in founding of Kansas City. Shops (daily). Broadway at Westport Rd. Phone 816/756-2789.

Worlds of Fun. A 170-acre entertainment complex with amusement rides, live entertainment, children's area, special events, restaurants; includes looping steel and wooden roller coasters and whitewater raft, spill water, log flume and hydroflume rides. (Late May-late Aug, daily; Apr-late May & Sept-Oct, Sat & Sun; closed Labor Day) One- and two-day passports; also combination Worlds of Fun/Oceans of Fun passports. 10 mi NE via I-435 exit 54. Phone 816/454-4545. ¢¢¢¢

Annual Events

St Patrick's Parade. Downtown. Sun before Mar 17.

Kansas City Pro Rodeo. Benjamin Ranch. Phone 816/761-5055. Wk of July 4.

Kansas City Blues and Jazz Festival. Late July.

Ethnic Enrichment Festival. Many nationalities celebrate with music, dance, cuisine and crafts. 3 days Aug.

American Royal Livestock, Horse Show and Rodeo. American Royal Center, 1701 American Royal Court. Phone 816/221-9800. 18 days early-mid-Nov.

Seasonal Events

Missouri Repertory Theatre. Center for the Performing Arts, 50th & Cherry Sts. Professional equity theater company; classic and contemporary productions. Annual performance of *A Christmas Carol*. Daily exc Mon. Phone 816/235-2700. Sept-May.

Lyric Opera. 11th St & Central. Opera productions in English. Mon, Wed, Fri & Sat. Phone 816/471-7344. Apr-May & mid-Sept-mid-Oct; holiday production in Dec.

Starlight Theater. Near 63rd & Swope Pkwy in Swope Park. Outdoor amphitheater featuring Broadway musicals and contemporary concerts. Performances nightly. Phone 816/363-STAR. Early June-Aug.

Kansas City Symphony. 1020 Central. Concert series of symphonic and pop music. Fri-Sun, some Wed. Phone 816/471-0400. Sept-May.

Professional sports. Harry S Truman Sports Complex, I-435 & I-70. Royals (baseball), Royals Stadium, phone 816/921-8000. Chiefs (football), Arrowhead Stadium, phone 816/924-9300. Kemper Memorial Arena, 1800 Genessee: Attack (indoor soccer), phone 816/474-2255; Blades (hockey), phone 816/931-3330.

Additional Visitor Information

The Kansas City Convention & Visitors Bureau has a free visitor guide, calendar of events and information on industrial tours in the area; 1100 Main St, Suite 2550, 64105; phone 816/221-5242 or 800/767-7700. The Friday and Sunday editions of the *Kansas City Star* also provide listings of current activities.

Kansas City Area Suburbs and Towns

The following suburbs and towns in the Kansas City area are included in the *Mobil Travel Guide*. For information on any one of them, see the individual alphabetical listing. In Missouri: Blue Springs, Excelsior Springs, Independence. In Kansas: Kansas City, Overland Park.

City Neighborhoods

Many of the restaurants, unrated dining establishments and some lodgings listed under Kansas City include neighborhoods as well as exact street addresses. A map showing these neighborhoods can be found immediately following the airport map. Geographic descriptions of these areas are given, followed by a table of restaurants arranged by neighborhood.

Country Club Plaza: South of Downtown; south of 46th St, west of Nichols Pkwy, north of Ward Pkwy and east of Madison Ave.

Crown Center: South of Pershing Rd, west of Gillham Rd, north of 27th St and east of Main St.

Downtown: South of the Missouri River, west of I-70, north of Truman Rd and east of I-29/I-35. **North of downtown:** North of Missouri River. **South of Downtown:** South of US 40. **East of Downtown:** East of US 70.

Westport: Area north of Country Club Plaza; south of Westport Rd, west of Main St, north of 43rd St and east of Southwest Trafficway.

KANSAS CITY RESTAURANTS
BY NEIGHBORHOOD AREAS

(For full description, see alphabetical listings under Restaurants)

COUNTRY CLUB PLAZA

Emile's. 302 Nichols Rd

Fedora Cafe & Bar. 210 W 47th St

Figlio. 209 W 46th Terrace

Harry Starker's. 200 Nichols Rd

K.C. Masterpiece. 4747 Wyandotte St

Parkway 600. 600 Ward Pkwy

Plaza III The Steakhouse. 4749 Pennsylvania

Raphael Dining Room (Raphael). 325 Ward Pkwy

The Rooftop (The Ritz-Carlton, Kansas City Hotel). 401 Ward Pkwy

CROWN CENTER

The American Restaurant. 25th & Grand Ave

Milano. 2450 Grand Ave

DOWNTOWN

Italian Gardens. 1110 Baltimore

Jennie's. 511 Cherry St

Savoy Grill (Savoy Bed & Breakfast Hotel). 219 W 9th St

NORTH OF DOWNTOWN

Cascone's. 3733 N Oak

Paradise Grill. 5225 NW 64th St

Stroud's. 5410 NE Oak Ridge Dr

SOUTH OF DOWNTOWN

André's Confiserie Suisse. 5018 Main St

Cafe Allegro. 1815 W 39th St

Casa De Fajitas. 423 Southwest Blvd

Charlie's Lodge. 7953 State Line Rd

Costello's Greenhouse. 1414 W 85th St

EBT. 1310 Carondelet Dr

Golden Ox. 1600 Genessee

Grand Street Cafe. 4740 Grand Ave

Hereford House. 2 E 20th St

Jasper's. 405 W 75th St

Jess & Jim's Steak House. 517 E 135th St

Le Picnique. 301 E 55th St

Smoke Stack Bar-B-Q Of Martin City. 13441 Holmes St

Stephenson's Apple Farm. 16401 E US 40

Stroud's. 1015 E 85th St

Trattoria Marco Polo. 7514 Wornall Rd

EAST OF DOWNTOWN

Smuggler's. 1650 Universal Plaza Dr

WESTPORT

Californos. 4124 Pennsylvania

Classic Cup. 4130 Pennsylvania

Metropolis American Grill. 303 Westport Rd

Note: When a listing is located in a town that does not have its own city heading, it will appear under the city nearest to its location. In these cases, the address and town appear in parenthesis immediately following the name of the establishment.

Motels

★ ★ **BEST WESTERN COUNTRY INN.** *7100 NE Parvin Rd (64117), northeast of downtown.* 816/453-3355; FAX 816/453-0242. 86 rms, 2 story. May-Sept: S $69-$74; D $79-$84; each addl $5; under 12 free; lower rates rest of yr. Crib free. TV; cable (premium). Pool. Complimentary continental bkfst, coffee. Restaurant nearby. Ck-out 11 am. Business servs avail. Cr cds: A, C, D, DS, MC, V.

D ⊠ ⊠ ⊠ SC

★ ★ **BEST WESTERN COUNTRY INN.** *11900 Plaza Circle (64153), north of downtown.* 816/464-2002. 43 rms, 2 story. S $54.95-$60.95; D $58.95-$68.95; each addl $4; under 12 free; higher rates special events. Crib free. TV; VCR avail. Complimentary continental bkfst. Restaurant adj 6 am-11 pm. Ck-out noon. Meeting rm. Business servs avail. Free airport transportation. Near airport. Cr cds: A, C, D, DS, MC, V.

D ⊠ ⊠ SC

★ **BEST WESTERN SEVILLE PLAZA.** *4309 Main St (69111), in Country Club Plaza.* 816/561-9600; FAX 816/561-9600. 77 rms, 4 story. S $69-$85; D $69-$85; each addl $5; under 18 free; higher rates hols, Plaza Lights Festival. Crib free. TV; cable (premium), VCR avail. Complimentary continental bkfst. Restaurant nearby. Ck-out noon. Meeting rms. In-rm modem links. Bellhops. Valet serv. Whirlpool. Some refrigerators. Cr cds: A, C, D, DS, MC, V.

D ⊠ ⊠ SC

✔ ★ **BUDGETEL INN.** *2214 Taney (64116), I-435 exit 210, north of downtown.* 816/221-1200; FAX 816/471-6207. 100 rms, 3 story. S $42.95-$46.95; D $44.95-$62.95; each addl $7; under 18 free. Pet accepted, some restrictions. TV; cable (premium). Complimentary continental bkfst, coffee. Restaurant adj 7 am-midnight. Ck-out noon. Business servs avail. Sundries. Cr cds: A, C, D, DS, MC, V.

D ✉ ⊠ ⊠

★ ★ **HAMPTON INN.** *11212 N Newark Circle (64153), I-29 exit 112th St, north of downtown.* 816/464-5454; FAX 816/464-5416. 120 rms, 4 story. S $53-$59; D $59-$65. Crib free. TV; cable (premium). Pool. Complimentary continental bkfst, coffee in lobby. Ck-out noon. Coin lndry. Meeting rms. Business servs avail. In-rm modem link. Valet serv. Free airport transportation. Some refrigerators. Cr cds: A, C, D, DS, MC, V.

D ⊠ ⊠ ⊠ SC

★ ★ **HOLIDAY INN NORTHEAST.** *7333 NE Parvin Rd (64117), I-435 exit 54, north of downtown.* 816/455-1060; FAX 816/455-0250. 167 rms, 3 story. S, D $75-$98; under 18 free. Crib free. TV; cable (premium). Indoor pool; whirlpool, sauna. Restaurant 6:30-11 am, 5-10 pm. Rm serv. Bar 4 pm-midnight. Ck-out noon. Coin lndry. Meeting rms. Business servs avail. In-rm modem link. Bellhops. Valet serv. Sundries. Free airport transportation (by res). Holidome. Game rm. Near Worlds of Fun. Cr cds: A, C, D, DS, JCB, MC, V.

D ⊠ ⊠ ⊠ SC

★ ★ **RESIDENCE INN BY MARRIOTT.** *9900 NW Prairie View Rd (64153), north of downtown.* 816/891-9009; FAX 816/891-9009, ext. 3113. 110 kit. suites, 2 story. S, D $105-$125; wkly, monthly rates. Crib free. Pet accepted, some restrictions; $100. TV; cable (premium), VCR avail (movies avail). Heated pool; wading pool, whirlpool. Complimentary continental bkfst. Ck-out noon. Coin lndry. Meeting rms. Business servs avail. In-rm modem link. Valet serv. Sundries. Free airport transportation. Lawn games. Exercise equipt; stair machine, bicycles, whirlpool. Private patios, balconies. Gazebo area with grills. Cr cds: A, C, D, DS, JCB, MC, V.

D ✉ ⊠ ⊼ ⊠ ⊠ SC

Motor Hotels

✔ ★ ★ **CLUBHOUSE INN.** *11828 NW Plaza Circle (64153), I-29 exit 13, near Intl Airport, north of downtown.* 816/464-2423; res: 800/CLUB-INN; FAX 816/464-2560. 138 rms, 7 story. S $70-$80; D $80-$90; each addl $10; suites $115-$125; under 10 free. Crib free. TV; cable (premium). Indoor pool. Complimentary bkfst buffet. Ck-out noon. Coin lndry. Meeting rms. Business servs avail. Valet serv. Free airport transportation. Downhill ski 15 mi. Exercise equipt; treadmill,

bicycles, whirlpool. Some refrigerators. Wet bar in suites. Balconies. Cr cds: A, C, D, DS, MC, V.

D ⊠ ⊠ ⊼ ⊼ ⊠ ⊠

★ ★ **DOUBLETREE AIRPORT HOTEL.** *8801 NW 112th St (64195), north of downtown.* 816/891-8900; FAX 816/891-8030. 350 rms, 11 story. S, D $89-$109; each addl $10; family rates; wkend plans. Crib free. TV; cable (premium). 2 pools, 1 indoor; poolside serv. Restaurant 6 am-11 pm. Rm serv. Bar to 1 am, Sun 11 am-midnight. Ck-out 1 pm. Meeting rms. Business servs avail. In-rm modem link. Bellhops. Valet serv. Sundries. Free airport transportation. Lighted tennis. Exercise rm; instructor, weights, bicycles, whirlpool, sauna. Picnic tables. Gazebo near pool & tennis areas. Cr cds: A, C, D, DS, ER, JCB, MC, V.

D ⊼ ⊠ ⊼ ⊠ ⊠ SC

★ ★ ★ **HOLIDAY INN AIRPORT.** *11832 Plaza Circle (64153), I-29 exit 13, near Intl Airport.* 816/464-2345; FAX 816/464-2543. 196 rms, 5 story. S, D $85-$95; family, wkend & hol rates. Crib free. Pet accepted. TV; cable (premium), VCR avail. Pool. Restaurant 6 am-11 pm. Rm serv. Bar 3:30 pm-1 am. Ck-out noon. Coin lndry. Meeting rms. Business center. In-rm modem link. Gift shop. Valet serv. Free airport transportation. Exercise equipt; weight machine, sauna. Game rm. Lawn games. Some refrigerators. Cr cds: A, C, D, DS, ER, JCB, MC, V.

D ⊠ ⊠ ⊼ ⊼ ⊠ ⊠ SC ⊼

★ ★ ★ **HOLIDAY INN-SPORTS COMPLEX.** *4011 Blue Ridge Cutoff (64133), east of downtown.* 816/353-5300; FAX 816/353-1199. 163 rms, 6 story. S $74-$86; D $82-$94; each addl $8; under 18 free. Crib free. TV; cable (premium), VCR avail. Indoor pool. Restaurant 6 am-10 pm. Rm serv. Bar 4 pm-midnight. Ck-out noon. Coin lndry. Meeting rms. Business center. In-rm modem link. Bellhops. Valet serv. Gift shop. Sundries. Underground parking. Exercise equipt; bicycles, treadmill, whirlpool, sauna. Game rm. Overlooks Harry S Truman Sports Complex. Cr cds: A, C, D, DS, JCB, MC, V.

D ⊠ ⊼ ⊠ ⊠ SC ⊼

★ ★ ★ **MARRIOTT KANSAS CITY AIRPORT.** *775 Brasilia (64153), 15 mi NW on I-29, at Intl Airport, north of downtown.* 816/464-2200; FAX 816/464-5915. 382 rms, 9 story. S, D, studio rms $69-$150; suites $250-$450; under 18 free; wkend plan. Crib free. Pet accepted. TV; cable (premium). Indoor pool. Restaurant 6 am-11 pm. Rm serv. Bar 11:30-1 am, Sun 12:30 pm-midnight. Ck-out noon. Coin lndry. Meeting rms. Business center. In-rm modem link. Bellhops. Valet serv. Gift shop. Free airport transportation. Downhill ski 15 mi. Excercise equipt; weights, bicycles, whirlpool, sauna. Rec rm. Lawn games. Private patios, picnic tables. On lake. Luxury level. Cr cds: A, C, D, DS, JCB, MC, V.

D ✉ ⊠ ⊠ ⊼ ⊼ ⊠ ⊠ SC ⊼

★ ★ **QUARTERAGE HOTEL.** *560 Westport Rd (64111), in Westport.* 816/931-0001; res: 800/942-4233; FAX 816/931-8891. 123 rms, 4 story. S $79-$90; D $89-$100; each addl $10; suites $90-$140; under 16 free; higher rates special events; wkend rates. Crib free. TV; cable (premium), VCR avail. Complimentary bkfst buffet, coffee. Restaurant adj 11 am-11 pm. Ck-out noon. Meeting rms. Business servs avail. Exercise equipt; weight machine, bicycles, whirlpool, sauna. Health club privileges. Some bathrm phones, wet bars. Refrigerator, whirlpool in suites. Some balconies. Cr cds: A, D, DS, MC, V.

D ⊼ ⊠ ⊠

✔ ★ ★ **RAMADA INN AT HISTORIC BENJAMIN RANCH.** *6101 E 87th St (64138), south of downtown, off of I-435.* 816/765-4331; FAX 816/765-7395. 250 rms, 3-4 story. S $55-$65; D $60-$70; each addl $6; suites $100-$175; studio rms $75; under 18 free; wkend rates. Crib free. TV; cable (premium), VCR avail. Heated pool. Restaurant 6:30 am-2 pm, 5-10 pm; Fri & Sat to 11 pm; Sun 7 am-2 pm, 5-10 pm. Rm serv 7 am-10 pm. Bar 1 pm-1 am, Sun 1 pm-midnight; entertainment, dancing. Ck-out noon. Convention facilities. Business servs avail. In-rm modem link. Bellhops. Valet serv. Free airport transportation. Health club privileges. Private patios, balconies. Cr cds: A, C, D, DS, JCB, MC, V.

D ≈ ⊠ 🔥 SC

Hotels

✔★★★ **ADAM'S MARK.** *9103 E 39th St (64133), south of downtown.* 816/737-0200; res: 800/444-2326; FAX 816/737-4713. 374 rms, 15 story. S $79-$109; D $79-$139; each addl $10; suites $150-$565; studio rms $150; under 18 free; wkend rates. Crib free. TV; cable. 2 heated pools, 1 indoor. Restaurant 6 am-11 pm. Bars 11-3 am, Sun noon-midnight; entertainment. Ck-out noon. Coin lndry. Convention facilities. Business servs avail. In-rm modem link. Gift shop. Tennis. Exercise rm; instructor, weights, bicycles, whirlpool, sauna. Rec rm. Some bathrm phones. Adj to Truman Sports Complex. Cr cds: A, C, D, DS, MC, V.

D 🏃 ≈ 🎿 ⊠ 🔥 SC

★★★ **CROWNE PLAZA.** *4445 Main St (64111), in Country Club Plaza.* 816/531-3000; FAX 816/531-3007. 296 rms, 19 story. S $119-$134; D $129-$159; each addl $10; suites $350-$450; under 18 free. Crib free. Pet accepted, $50 deposit. Garage free; valet parking $5. TV; cable. Indoor pool. Restaurant 6:30 am-10 pm. Bar 3 pm-1 am. Ck-out noon. Convention facilities. In-rm modem link. Gift shop. Concierge. Exercise rm; instructor, weight machines, bicycles, whirlpool. Some refrigerators. Luxury level. Cr cds: A, C, D, DS, JCB, MC, V.

D 🐾 ≈ 🎿 ⊠ 🔥 SC

★★★ **EMBASSY SUITES.** *7640 NW Tiffany Springs Pkwy (64153), I-29 Tiffany Springs exit, near Intl Airport, north of downtown.* 816/891-7788; FAX 816/891-7513. 236 suites, 8 story. Suites $82-$144; under 18 free. Crib free. TV; cable (premium), VCR avail. Indoor pool. Complimentary full bkfst. Complimentary coffee in rms. Restaurant 11 am-2 pm, 5-10 pm; wkends from 7 am. Bar 11-1 am, wkends to 3 am; entertainment, dancing. Ck-out noon. Coin lndry. Convention facilites. Business servs avail. Concierge. Gift shop. Free airport transportation. Exercise equipt; rowing machine, bicycles, whirlpool, sauna. Refrigerators, wet bars. Cr cds: A, C, D, DS, JCB, MC, V.

D ≈ 🎿 🎿 ⊠ 🔥 SC

★★ **HISTORIC SUITES.** *612 Central (64105), downtown.* 816/842-6544; res: 800/733-0612; FAX 816/842-0656. 100 suites, 5 story. S, D $110-$180; under 18 free; wkly rates; lower rates hol wkends. Crib free. Pets accepted, some restrictions. TV; cable (premium), VCR avail (movies avail $5.99). Pool. Complimentary continental bkfst. Complimentary coffee in rms. Restaurant nearby. No rm serv. Coin lndry. Meeting rms. Business servs avail. In-rm modem link. No bellhops. Garage parking. Exercise equipt; weight machine, bicycles, whirlpool, sauna. Turn-of-the-century design. Cr cds: A, C, D, DS, MC, V.

D ≈ 🎿 ⊠ 🔥 SC

★★ **HOLIDAY INN.** *1215 Wyandotte (64105), downtown.* 816/471-1333; FAX 816/283-0541. 190 rms, 16 story. S, D $73-$99; each addl $8; suites $99-$125; under 13 free; wkend rates. Crib free. TV; cable (premium), VCR avail. Rm serv. Ck-out noon. Meeting rms. Business center. Covered parking. Health club privileges. Cr cds: A, C, D, DS, MC, V.

D ⊠ 🔥 SC 🏌

★★★ **HYATT REGENCY CROWN CENTER.** *2345 McGee St (64108), in Crown Center.* 816/421-1234; FAX 816/435-4190. 731 rms, 42 story. S $120-$150; D $145-$175; each addl $25; suites $195-$800; under 18 free; wkend rates. Crib free. Valet parking $10.75, garage $8.75. TV; cable (premium), VCR avail. Heated pool; poolside serv. Restaurants 6:30 am-midnight. Bars 11-1 am; entertainment. Ck-out noon. Convention facilities. Business servs avail. In-rm modem link. Concierge. Gift shop. Lighted tennis. Exercise rm; weights, bicycles,

whirlpool, steam rm, sauna. Minibars. Luxury level. Cr cds: A, C, D, DS, JCB, MC, V.

D 🏃 ≈ 🎿 ⊠ 🔥 SC

★★★ **MARRIOTT DOWNTOWN.** *200 W 12th St (64105), downtown.* 816/421-6800; FAX 816/421-6800, ext. 4418. 573 rms, 22 story. S $140; D $160; each addl $15; suites $250-$500; wkend rates. Crib free. TV; cable (premium), VCR avail. Indoor pool. Restaurant 6 am-midnight. Bar 11:30-1:30 am; entertainment, dancing. Ck-out noon. Convention facilities. Business center. Concierge. Gift shop. Exercise rm; instructor, weights, bicycles, sauna. Some refrigerators. Luxury level. Cr cds: A, C, D, DS, MC, V.

D ≈ 🎿 ⊠ 🔥 🏃

✔★★ **PARK PLACE.** *1601 N Universal Ave (64120), I-435 Front St exit, north of downtown.* 816/483-9900; res: 800/821-8532; FAX 816/231-1418. 330 rms, 9 story. S, D $62-$79; each addl $10; suites $79-$109; under 18 free; wkend rates; package plans. Crib free. Pet accepted; deposit required. TV; cable (premium). Indoor/outdoor pool. Complimentary coffee in rms. Restaurant 6:30 am-10 pm; Fri, Sat to 11 pm. Bar 11-1:30 am; entertainment, dancing exc Sun. Ck-out noon. Meeting rms. Business center. Gift shop. Free airport transportation. Lighted tennis. Exercise equipt; weights, bicycles, sauna. Some bathrm phones, refrigerators. Private patios, some balconies. Cr cds: A, C, D, DS, ER, MC, V.

D 🐾 🏃 ≈ 🎿 🎿 ⊠ 🔥 🏃

★★ **RADISSON SUITES.** *106 W 12th St (64105), downtown.* 816/221-7000; FAX 816/221-8902. 214 rms, 20 story, 181 suites, 16 kit. units. S, D $89-$109; each addl $10; suites $99-$250; under 18 free; wkend rates. Crib free. TV; cable (premium), VCR avail. Complimentary continental bkfst. Restaurants 6:30 am-11 pm. Bar 10:30 am-midnight; wkends 11-3 am. Ck-out noon. Meeting rms. Business center. In-rm modem link. Valet parking. Free airport transportation. Exercise equipt; weight machines, bicycles. Cr cds: A, C, D, DS, ER, MC, V.

D 🎿 ⊠ 🔥 SC

★★★ **RAPHAEL.** *325 Ward Pkwy (64112), in Country Club Plaza.* 816/756-3800; res: 800/821-5343; FAX 816/756-3800, ext. 2199. 123 rms, 9 story. S $95-$135; D $115-$155; each addl $20; under 18 free; hol, wkend plans. Crib free. TV; cable (premium). Complimentary continental bkfst in rms. Restaurant (see RAPHAEL DINING ROOM). Rm serv 24 hrs. Bar to 1 am, closed Sun. Ck-out 1 pm. Business servs avail. In-rm modem link. Free garage, valet parking. Refrigerators, minibars. Cr cds: A, C, D, DS, MC, V.

⊠ 🔥 SC

★★★★ **THE RITZ-CARLTON, KANSAS CITY.** *401 Ward Pkwy (64112), at Wornall Rd, Country Club Plaza.* 816/756-1500; res: 800/241-3333; FAX 816/756-1635. Crystal chandeliers, imported marble, and original art create an air of luxury. Some guest rooms have balconies with views of Country Club Plaza. 373 rms, 12 story. S, D $149-$179; suites $225-$1,200; under 17 free; wkend rates; higher rates Thanksgiving. Crib free. Garage: free self-park, valet $9. TV; cable (premium), VCR avail. Heated pool; wading pool, poolside serv. Supervised child's activities (June-Aug). Restaurant 6:30 am-2:30 pm, 5:30-10 pm (also see THE ROOFTOP). Rm serv 24 hrs. Bar 5 pm-midnight; entertainment, dancing. Ck-out noon. Convention facilities. Business center. In-rm modem link. Concierge. Airport transportation. Exercise equipt; weights, bicycles, sauna, steam rm. Massage. Bathrm phones, refrigerators, minibars. Private patios, balconies. Luxury level. Cr cds: A, C, D, DS, ER, JCB, MC, V.

D ≈ 🎿 ⊠ 🔥 SC 🏃

★★ **SAVOY BED & BREAKFAST.** *219 W 9th St (64105), downtown.* 816/842-3575. 100 suites, 6 story. S, D $79-$120; each addl $20; under 16 free. TV; cable (premium), VCR avail. Complimentary full bkfst. Complimentary coffee in rms. Restaurant (see SAVOY GRILL). Bar. Ck-out 1 pm. Coin lndry. Business servs avail. Concierge. Wet bars. Restored 1888 landmark building with original architectural detail; stained & leaded glass, tile floors, tin ceilings. Cr cds: A, C, D, DS, MC, V.

★ ★ ★ **SHERATON SUITES.** *770 W 47th St (64112), in Country Club Plaza.* 816/931-4400; FAX 816/516-7330. 258 suites, 18 story. S $149; D $169; each addl $20; under 16 free; wkend rates. Crib free. Valet parking $6. TV; cable (premium), VCR avail. Indoor/outdoor pool; poolside serv. Complimentary buffet bkfst. Complimentary coffee in rms. Restaurant 6 am-11 pm. Bar from 11 am. Ck-out noon. Coin lndry. Meeting rms. Business servs avail. In-rm modem link. Exercise equipt; weight machine, rower, whirlpool. Refrigerators; some wet bars. Some balconies. Cr cds: A, C, D, DS, ER, JCB, MC, V.

★ ★ ★ **THE WESTIN CROWN CENTER.** *1 Pershing Rd (64108), at Main St, in Crown Center.* 816/474-4400; res: 800/228-3000; FAX 816/391-4438. 725 rms, 18 story. S $140-$160; D $165-$185; each addl $25; suites $300-$1,000; under 18 free; wkend package. Crib free. Pet accepted. TV; cable, VCR avail. Heated pool; poolside serv. Supervised childs activities (ages 6-12). Restaurants 6 am-midnight. Bars 11:30-1 am; entertainment. Ck-out noon. Convention facilities. Business center. In-rm modem link. Barber, beauty shop. Airport transportation. Lighted tennis. Putting green. Exercise rm; instructor, weights, bicycles, whirlpool, sauna, steam rm. Rec rm. Lawn games. Refrigerators, wet bars. Private patios, balconies. Indoor tropical waterfall and garden. Luxury level. Cr cds: A, C, D, DS, ER, JCB, MC, V.

Inns

★ ★ **DOANLEIGH WALLAGH.** *217 E 37th St (64111), south of downtown.* 816/753-2667; FAX 816/753-2408. 5 rms, 3 story. S, D $90-$135; each addl $10. TV; cable (premium), VCR avail. Complimentary full bkfst. Restaurant nearby. Ck-out 11 am, ck-in 3 pm. Private parking. Library; grand piano, organ. Built in 1907; many antiques. Cr cds: A, MC, V.

★ ★ ★ **SOUTHMORELAND.** *116 E 46th St (64112), in Country Club Plaza.* 816/531-7979; FAX 816/531-2407. Accommodations in this 1913 Colonial revival-style mansion honor notable Kansans. The Thomas Hart Benton Room has the Misson oak furniture favored by the artist, while the Satchel Paige Room resembles a sportsman's lodge. 12 rms, 3 story. S $90-$135; D $100-$145. Adults preferred. TV in sitting rm; cable (premium), VCR avail. Complimentary full bkfst; afternoon wine & cheese. Restaurants nearby. Ck-out 11 am, ck-in 4:30 pm. Business servs avail. In-rm modem link. Airport transportation. Solarium. Totally nonsmoking. Cr cds: A, MC, V.

Restaurants

★ ★ ★ **THE AMERICAN RESTAURANT.** *25th & Grand Ave, top floor of Hall's, in Crown Center.* 816/426-1133. Hrs: 11:15 am-2 pm, 6-10 pm; Fri & Sat 6-11 pm. Closed Sun; major hols. Res accepted. Bar. Wine cellar. A la carte entrees: lunch $8-$14, dinner $18-$32. Dinner tasting menu avail. Specializes in contemporary American cuisine with ethnic influences and traditional American cuisine. Own baking, ice cream. Pianist. Valet parking. Jacket. Cr cds: A, C, D, DS, MC, V.

★ ★ **CAFE ALLEGRO.** *1815 W 39th St (64111), south of downtown.* 816/561-3663. Hrs: 11:30 am-2 pm, 6-10 pm. Closed Sun; major hols; also 1 wk Jan. Res accepted. Continental menu. Bar. Wine list. Semi-a la carte: lunch $6-$11, dinner $16-$25. Specialties: grilled salmon with Chinese mustard glaze, veal chop with roasted garlic

mashed potatoes. Parking. Intimate dining rm with original art. Totally nonsmoking. Cr cds: A, D, MC, V.

★ ★ **CALIFORNOS.** *4124 Pennsylvania (64111), in Westport.* 816/531-7878. Hrs: 11 am-3 pm, 5-10 pm; Fri, Sat to 11 pm; Sun noon-9 pm. Closed some major hols. Res accepted. Bar to midnight. Semi-a la carte: lunch, dinner $5-$20. Specializes in California-style grilled cuisine. Pianist Fri & Sat evenings. Valet parking. Outdoor dining. Casual atmosphere. Cr cds: A, MC, V.

★ **CASA DE FAJITAS.** *423 Southwest Blvd (64108), south of downtown.* 816/471-7788. Hrs: 11 am-9 pm; Fri & Sat to 11 pm. Closed major hols. Mexican menu. Bar. Semi-a la carte: lunch, dinner $4.95-$11.95. Child's meals. Specializes in fajitas, sampler plates. Parking. Casual atmosphere. Cr cds: A, C, D, DS, MC, V.

★ ★ **CASCONE'S.** *3733 N Oak, north of downtown.* 816/454-7977. Hrs: 11 am-10 pm; Fri, Sat to 11 pm; Sun 4-9 pm. Closed July 4, Dec 25. Res accepted. Italian, Amer menu. Bar. Semi-a la carte: lunch $6.50-$9, dinner $12-$24. Child's meals. Specializes in chicken, steak, seafood. Parking. Cr cds: A, C, D, DS, MC, V.

✔ ★ **CHAPPELL'S.** *(323 Armour Rd, North Kansas City) N on MO 35 to Armour Rd exit.* 816/421-0002. Hrs: 11 am-10 pm; Fri, Sat to 11 pm. Closed Sun; most major hols. Bar. Semi-a la carte: lunch $4.95-$6.25, dinner $4.95-$14.95. Child's meals. Specializes in steak, prime rib, hamburgers. Extensive collection of sports memorabilia. Cr cds: A, C, D, DS, MC, V.

★ ★ **CHARLIE'S LODGE.** *7953 State Line Rd (64114), south of downtown.* 816/333-6363. Hrs: 11:30 am-10:30 pm; Fri & Sat to 11:30 pm; Sun 4-9:30 pm; early-bird dinner 4-6 pm. Closed some major hols. Res accepted. Bar. Semi-a la carte: lunch $5-$9, dinner $8-$17. Child's meals. Specializes in steak, fresh seafood. Parking. Six dining rooms. Sportsman's lodge atmosphere; hunting and fishing decor. Cr cds: A, DS, MC, V.

✔ ★ ★ **COSTELLO'S GREENHOUSE.** *1414 W 85th St, at Ward Parkway, south of downtown.* 816/333-5470. Hrs: 11 am-10 pm; Sat & Sun to 11 pm; Sun brunch 10 am-2:30 pm. Closed most major hols. Res accepted. Bar. Semi-a la carte: lunch $5.95-$14.95, dinner $6.95-$16.95. Sun brunch $9.95. Child's meals. Specializes in prime rib, chicken, pasta. Salad bar. Entertainment Wed. Parking. Greenhouse atmosphere; many plants, flowers in bloom. Cr cds: A, C, D, DS, MC, V.

★ ★ ★ **EBT.** *1310 Carondelet Dr, in United Missouri Bank Building, south of downtown.* 816/942-8870. Hrs: 11 am-2:30 pm, 5-9:30 pm; Fri to 10 pm; Sat 5-10 pm. Closed Sun; major hols. Res accepted. Bar. Wine cellar. Semi-a la carte: lunch $6.50-$11.95, dinner $11.95-$29.95. Specializes in seafood, steak, chicken. Tableside preparation. Own baking. Jazz pianist Tues-Sat. Decorated with palm trees, fountain; antiques, gilded iron elevator. Jacket. Cr cds: A, D, DS, MC, V.

✔ ★ **EMILE'S.** *302 Nichols Rd (64112), in Country Club Plaza.* 816/753-2771. Hrs: 9 am-10:30 pm; Mon to 5 pm; Fri & Sat to 11:30 pm; Sun 11 am-5 pm. Closed Jan 1, Thanksgiving, Dec 25. Res accepted. German, Amer menu. Bar. Semi-a la carte: lunch, dinner $4.95-$13.95. Specialties: beef rouladen, Wienerschnitzel, Kasseler rippchen. Accordionist Fri, Sat. Parking. Outdoor dining. Cr cds: A, DS, MC, V.

★ ★ **FEDORA CAFE & BAR.** *210 W 47th St, in Country Club Plaza. 816/561-6565.* Hrs: 7-1 am; Sun 9 am-11 pm. Res accepted. Bar. A la carte entrees: breakfast $2.95-$7.50, lunch $3.95-$8.95, dinner $7.95-$18.95. Specializes in seafood, pasta, salads. Piano. European bistro-style cafe; art deco decor. Cr cds: A, C, D, DS, MC, V.

D ⌐

★ ★ **FIGLIO.** *209 W 46th Terrace, in Country Club Plaza. 816/561-0505.* Hrs: 11:30 am-2:30 pm, 5-10 pm; Fri, Sat to 11 pm; Sun 10:30 am-2:30 pm. Closed Dec 25. Res accepted. Italian, Amer menu. Bar. Semi-a la carte: lunch $5.95-$8.95, dinner $7.95-$16.95. Child's meals. Specializes in pasta, gourmet pizza, fresh fish. Accordionist Wed-Sun. Valet parking wkends. Outdoor porch dining. Cr cds: A, C, D, DS, MC, V.

D SC ⌐

★ ★ **GOLDEN OX.** *1600 Genessee (64102), south of downtown. 816/842-2866.* Hrs: 11:20 am-10 pm; Sat 4-10:30 pm; Sun 4-9 pm. Closed Dec 25. Bar. Semi-a la carte: lunch $4.50-$7.95, dinner $7.50-$19.95. Child's meals. Specializes in steak, prime rib. Parking. Western decor with stockyard influence. Family-owned. Cr cds: A, C, D, DS, MC, V.

D ⌐

★ ★ **GRAND STREET CAFE.** *4740 Grand Ave (64112), south of downtown. 816/561-8000.* Hrs: 11 am-10 pm; Fri & Sat to midnight; Sun from 10:30 am; Sun brunch to 3 pm. Closed Dec 25. Res accepted. Bar. Semi-a la carte: lunch $3.95-$10.95, dinner $5.95-$18.95. Sun brunch $4.95-$9.95. Child's meals. Specializes in lamb chops, pork chops, grilled tenderloin. Parking. Outdoor dining. Eclectic, contemporary decor. Cr cds: A, C, D, DS, MC, V.

D ⌐

★ ★ ★ **HARRY STARKER'S.** *200 Nichols Rd (64112), in Country Club Plaza. 816/753-3565.* Hrs: 11 am-3 pm, 5-10 pm; Sat to 11 pm; Sun from 5 pm. Closed major hols. Res accepted. Bar. Extensive wine list. A la carte entrees: lunch $4.95-$8.75, dinner $13-$23. Specializes in steak, fresh seafood. Entertainment, dancing. Valet parking. Country French decor; featuring 9,000 bottles of wine. Cr cds: A, C, D, DS, MC, V.

⌐

★ ★ **HEREFORD HOUSE.** *2 E 20th St, at Main St, south of downtown. 816/842-1080.* Hrs: 11 am-10 pm; Fri to 10:30 pm; Sat 4-10:30 pm; Sun 4-9 pm. Closed major hols. Res accepted. Bar. Semi-a la carte: lunch $5-$15, dinner $12-$30. Child's meals. Specializes in steak, Maine lobster tails. Parking. Casual atmosphere. Cr cds: A, C, D, DS, MC, V.

D ⌐

✔ ★ ★ **ITALIAN GARDENS.** *1110 Baltimore, downtown. 816/221-9311.* Hrs: 11 am-10 pm; Fri to 11 pm; Sat noon-11 pm. Closed Sun; major hols. Res accepted. Italian, Amer menu. Bar. Semi-a la carte: lunch $4.10-$6, dinner $7-$15. Child's meals. Specializes in pasta, veal, seafood, chicken, steak. Valet parking. Cr cds: A, C, D, DS, MC, V.

D ⌐

★ ★ **JASPER'S.** *405 W 75th St, south of downtown. 816/363-3003.* Hrs: 6-10 pm. Closed Sun exc Mother's Day; major hols; also 1st wk July. Res accepted. Northern Italian menu. Bar. Wine cellar. A la carte entrees: dinner $16.95-$25.95. Child's meals. Specialties: Cappeli Angelina, Gambere a la Livornese, Vitello alla Valdostana. Own pastries, pasta. Parking. Large grappa bar. Chef-owned. Jacket (dinner). Cr cds: A, C, D, DS, MC, V.

⌐

✔ ★ **JENNIE'S.** *511 Cherry St, downtown. 816/421-3366.* Hrs: 11 am-9 pm; Fri, Sat to 10 pm; Sun noon-8 pm. Closed most major hols. Res accepted. Italian, Amer menu. Bar. Semi-a la carte: lunch

$4.95-$7.95, dinner $5.25-$12.50. Child's meals. Specializes in lasagna, pizza. Parking. Family-owned. Cr cds: A, C, D, MC, V.

D ⌐

★ ★ **JESS & JIM'S STEAK HOUSE.** *517 E 135th St (64145), south of downtown. 816/941-9499.* Hrs: 11 am-11 pm; Sun noon-9 pm. Closed July 4, Thanksgiving, Dec 25. Bar. Semi-a la carte: lunch $4.25-$5.95, dinner $9.95-$37.50. Child's meals. Specializes in steak, seafood. Parking. Casual atmosphere, Western decor. Family-owned since 1938. Cr cds: A, C, D, DS, MC, V.

D ⌐

✔ ★ ★ **K.C. MASTERPIECE.** *4747 Wyandotte St (64112), in Country Club Plaza. 816/531-3332.* Hrs: 11 am-10 pm; Fri & Sat to 11 pm; Sun to 9:30 pm. Closed Thanksgiving, Dec 25. Bar. Semi-a la carte: lunch $6.95-$14.25, dinner $5.95-$15.50. Child's meals. Specializes in barbecued meats, filet of pork, turkey brisket. Parking. Kansas City memorabilia. Casual atmosphere. Cr cds: A, C, D, DS, MC, V.

D ⌐

★ ★ **METROPOLIS AMERICAN GRILL.** *303 Westport Rd (64111), in Westport. 816/753-1550.* Hrs: 11:30 am-2:30 pm, 5:30 pm-10 pm; wkends to 11 pm. Closed Sun; major hols. Res accepted. Bar. A la carte entrees: lunch $4.95-$11.95, dinner $8.50-$20.95. Specialties: stuffed Norwegian salmon, seared scallops, parmesan lamb chops. Parking. Contemporary decor. Cr cds: A, C, D, DS, MC, V.

★ ★ **MILANO.** *2450 Grand Ave (64108), in Crown Center. 816/426-1130.* Hrs: 11:30 am-9 pm; Fri & Sat to 10 pm; Sun noon-9 pm. Closed major hols. Res accepted. Italian menu. Bar. Semi-a la carte: lunch $4.25-$10.50, dinner $8.95-$16.95. Child's meals. Specializes in pasta. Own ice cream. Parking. Patio dining. Casual Italian decor. Cr cds: A, D, DS, MC, V.

D SC ⌐

✔ ★ **PARADISE GRILL.** *5225 NW 64th St, north of downtown. 816/587-9888.* Hrs; 11 am-10 pm; Fri & Sat to 11 pm; Sun from 10:30 am. Closed Thanksgiving, Dec 25. Res accepted. Bar. Semi-a la carte: lunch, dinner $4.95-$14.95. Child's meals. Specializes in chicken, fish. Bright, modern decor. Cr cds: A, D, DS, MC, V.

D ⌐

★ ★ **PARKWAY 600.** *600 Ward Pkwy (64112), in Country Club Plaza. 816/931-6600.* Hrs: 7 am-11 pm; early-bird dinner Sun-Thurs 4:30-6:30 pm. Closed Jan 1, July 4, Dec 25. Res accepted. Bar to 1 am. Semi-a la carte: bkfst $3.95-$7.95, lunch $5.95-$17.95, dinner $6.95-$38.95. Child's meals. Specializes in seafood, beef, chicken. Valet parking. Outdoor dining. Brass chandelier in lobby. Casual atmosphere. Cr cds: A, DS, MC, V.

D SC ⌐

★ ★ ★ **PLAZA III THE STEAKHOUSE.** *4749 Pennsylvania (64112), in Country Club Plaza. 816/753-0000.* Hrs: 11:30 am-2:30 pm, 5:30-10 pm; Fri, Sat to 11 pm; Sun 5-10 pm. Res accepted. Bar 11-1 am; Sun to midnight. Extensive wine list. A la carte entrees: lunch $5.95-$8.95, dinner $14.95-$26.95. Child's meals. Specializes in veal chops, prime-aged beef, seafood. Entertainment. Valet parking. Cr cds: A, C, D, DS, MC, V.

D ⌐

★ ★ ★ **RAPHAEL DINING ROOM.** *(See Raphael) 816/756-3800.* Hrs: 11 am-3 pm, 5-11 pm. Closed Sun; some major hols. Res accepted. Continental menu. Bar. Semi-a la carte: lunch $5.50-$9.50, dinner $12-$21. Specializes in fresh fish, veal, New Zealand rack of lamb. Jazz Fri & Sat. Valet parking. Romantic elegance in European-style setting. Cr cds: A, C, D, DS, MC, V.

D

★ ★ ★ **THE ROOFTOP.** *(See The Ritz-Carlton, Kansas City Hotel) 816/756-1500.* Hrs: 5:30-10 pm; Sun brunch 10:30 am-2 pm. Res accepted. Bar 5 pm-midnight. Wine cellar. Semi-a la carte: dinner $29-$43. Sun brunch $24.50. Child's meals. Specializes in steak, chicken, seafood. Own pastries. Pianist. Parking. Rooftop dining rm; panoramic view of city. Cr cds: A, C, D, DS, ER, JCB, MC, V.

D ⊡

★ ★ ★ **SAVOY GRILL.** (See Savoy Hotel) 816/842-3890. Hrs: 11 am-11 pm; Fri, Sat to midnight; Sun 4-10 pm. Closed Dec 25. Res accepted. Bar. Semi-a la carte: lunch $4.50-$12, dinner $14-$27. Specializes in fresh seafood, Maine lobster, prime dry-aged beef. Parking. 19th-century hotel dining rm; oak paneling, stained-glass windows, murals of Santa Fe Trail. Ornate back bar. Cr cds: A, C, D, DS, MC, V.

D ⊡

★ ★ **SMOKE STACK BAR-B-Q OF MARTIN CITY.** 13441 Holmes St (64145), south of downtown. 816/942-9141. Hrs: 11 am-10 pm. Closed Thanksgiving, Dec 25. Semi-a la carte: lunch $4.75-$10, dinner $6.75-$20. Specializes in barbecue, fresh seafood, steak. Parking. Many interesting antiques give this restaurant a museum-like atmosphere. Cr cds: A, D, MC, V.

D ⊡

★ ★ **SMUGGLER'S.** 1650 Universal Plaza Dr, east of downtown. 816/483-0400. Hrs: 11 am-10 pm; Fri to 11 pm; Sat 5-11 pm; Sun 4-9 pm. Closed Jan 1, Thanksgiving, Dec 25. Res accepted. Bar to 1 am. Complete meals: lunch $4.95-$9.95, dinner $9.95-$21.95. Specializes in prime rib, fresh fish. Salad bar. Entertainment Tues-Sat. Parking. Casual atmosphere; wood-burning fireplaces. Cr cds: A, C, D, DS, MC, V.

D ⊡

★ ★ ★ **STEPHENSON'S APPLE FARM.** 16401 E US 40, south of downtown. 816/373-5400. Hrs: 11:30 am-10 pm; Sun 10 am-9 pm; Sun brunch 10 am-2 pm exc hols. Closed Dec 24 & 25. Res accepted. Bar. Semi-a la carte: lunch $6-$11.50, dinner $12.95-$17.95. Sun brunch $10.95. Child's meals. Specializes in hickory-smoked meats, apple fritters and dumplings. Own baking. Parking. Outdoor dining. Started as a fruit stand (1900). Early Amer decor; farm implements, cider keg in lobby. Country store. Family-owned. Cr cds: A, C, D, DS, MC, V.

D ⊡

★ ★ **STROUD'S.** 1015 E 85th St (64131), south of downtown. 816/333-2132. Hrs: 4-10 pm; Fri 11 am-11 pm; Sat 2 -11 pm; Sun 11 am-10 pm. Closed Thanksgiving, Dec 25. Bar. Semi-a la carte: lunch $5.25-$10.95, dinner $7.95-$16.95. Child's meals. Specializes in pan-fried chicken. Child's meals. Pianist. Parking. Although there is nothing fancy about this restaurant it remains one of the more popular establishments in KC, guests have been known to wait 2 hrs for a table. Cr cds: A, C, D, DS, MC.

D ⊡

★ ★ **STROUD'S.** 5410 NE Oak Ridge Dr (64119), north of downtown. 816/454-9600. Hrs: 5-9:30 pm; Fri 11 am-10:30 pm; Sat 2-10:30 pm; Sun 11 am-9:30 pm. Closed Dec 25. Bar. Semi-a la carte: lunch $5.50, dinner $7.95-$18.95. Child's meals. Specializes in pan-fried chicken, chicken fried steak, pork chops. Pianist exc Mon. Parking. Outdoor dining. Converted log house (1829) in scenic setting. Country, rustic decor. Cr cds: A, D, DS, MC, V.

D ⊡

✔ ★ **TRATTORIA MARCO POLO.** 7514 Wornall Rd, south of downtown. 816/361-0900. Hrs: 11:30 am-2 pm, 5:30-10 pm; Fri & Sat to 11 pm. Closed Sun; major hols. Res accepted. Italian menu. Bar. Semi-a la carte: lunch $4.95-$8.95, dinner $6.95-$15.95. Child's meals. Specialties: polenta con funghi ala Milanese, pollo alla saltimboco, linguine Fra Diavolo, salciccia Marco Polo. Parking. Decorated to suggest outdoor trattoria. Cr cds: A, C, D, DS, MC, V.

D ⊡

Unrated Dining Spots

ANDRÉ'S CONFISERIE SUISSE. 5018 Main St, south of downtown. 816/561-3440. Hrs: 11 am-2:30 pm. Closed Sun, Mon; major hols. Swiss menu. Complete meal: lunch $7.50. Specializes in quiche, chocolate candy, pastries. Parking. Swiss chalet atmosphere. Family-owned. Founded in 1955 by Andre Bollier and continues to be operated by the Bollier family. Totally nonsmoking. Cr cds: A, MC, V.

D

CLASSIC CUP. 4130 Pennsylvania, in Westport. 816/756-0771. Hrs: 11 am-3 pm, 5-10 pm, Sat to 11 pm; Sun brunch 11 am-2 pm. Closed most major hols. Continental menu. Wine, beer. Semi-a la carte: lunch $4.25-$8.75, dinner $7.95-$15. Sun brunch $8.95. Specializes in homemade soups, pastries, creative American cuisine. Parking. European bistro atmosphere. Cr cds: A, MC, V.

D SC ⊡

LE PICNIQUE. 301 E 55th St, in Sebree Galleries, south of downtown. 816/333-3387. Hrs: 11 am-2 pm. Closed Sun; most major hols. Res accepted. Country French menu. Wine, beer. Semi-a la carte: lunch $4.50-$8.50. Specialties: French herb garden sandwich, freshly grilled fish & chicken, gateau au chocolat, tarte citron. Parking. Located in European antique and gift shop; brick floor, fountain; unique courtyard atmosphere. Cr cds: A, MC, V.

D

Kirksville (A-4)

(See Macon)

Founded 1841 **Pop** 17,152 **Elev** 981 ft **Area code** 816 **Zip** 63501
Information Chamber of Commerce, 304 S Franklin, Box 251; 816/665-3766.

Kirksville is a trade center for surrounding communities and the home of Kirksville College of Osteopathic Medicine (1892), the world's first such college. An early pioneer, Jesse Kirk, traded a turkey dinner for the right to name the town after himself.

What to See and Do

Northeast Missouri State University (1867). (6,000 students) E.M. Violette Museum on campus has gun collection, Native American artifacts, historical items (by appt only). Pickler Memorial Library has Schwengel-Lincoln Collection of memorabilia on Abraham Lincoln (Mon-Fri); also historical textiles and related arts (by appt). Campus tours. Phone 816/785-4016.

Thousand Hills State Park. More than 3,000 acres. Swimming, bathhouse; fishing; boating (ramp, marina, rentals), canoeing. Hiking trails. Picnicking, dining lodge, store. Improved camping (dump station), cabins. (Daily) Standard fees. 4 mi W on MO 6, then 2 mi S on MO 157. Phone 816/665-6995. **Free.**

Motels

✔ ★ ★ **BEST WESTERN SHAMROCK INN.** Box 1005, 2 mi S on US 63 Business. 816/665-8352. 45 rms. S $36-$44; D $46-$53; each addl $5; under 12 free. Crib free. Pet accepted, some restrictions. TV; cable (premium). Pool. Playground. Restaurant 6 am-10 pm. Ck-out 11 am. Meeting rms. Sundries. Cr cds: A, C, D, DS, MC, V.

🐾 ⊠ ⊠ 🔥 SC

✔ ★ **BUDGET HOST VILLAGE INN.** PO Box 673, 1304 S Baltimore. 816/665-3722; FAX 816/665-6334. 30 rms, 1-2 story. S $34-$36; D $38-$40; each addl $4; under 10 free. Crib free. Pet accepted. TV; cable (premium). Complimentary coffee in office. Restaurant nearby. Ck-out noon. Business servs avail. In-rm modem link. In-rm steam baths. Cr cds: A, C, D, DS, ER, MC, V.

[icons] SC

★ **SUPER 8.** *1101 Country Club Dr. 816/665-8826; FAX 816/665-8826, ext. 403.* 64 rms, 2-3 story. No elvtr. S $38.88; D $47.88; under 12 free. Crib $2. TV; cable. Complimentary coffee. Restaurants nearby. Ck-out 11 am. Cr cds: A, C, D, DS, MC, V.

[icons] SC

Hotel

✔★ **TRAVELER'S.** *301 W Washington. 816/665-5191; FAX 816/665-0825.* 66 rms, 4 story. S $23-$32.95; D $39.95; each addl $5; suites $60; wkly, monthly rates. Crib free. TV; cable (premium), VCR avail. Bar 3 pm-1:30 am, Sun noon-midnight. Ck-out noon. Meeting rms. Business center. In-rm modem link. Barber, beauty shop. Built in 1923. Cr cds: A, D, DS, MC, V.

[icons]

Restaurant

★ **MINN'S.** *216 N Franklin. 816/665-2842.* Hrs: 5-10 pm. Closed Sun; Memorial Day, July 4, Dec 25. Res accepted. International menu. Bar. Semi-a la carte: dinner $9-$26. Specializes in seafood, medallions of beef in peppercorn sauce, lamb, duck. Parking. Elegant decor. Cr cds: A, MC, V.

Lake of the Ozarks (D-4)

(See Camdenton, Lake Ozark, Osage Beach)

Area code 314
Information Lake of the Ozarks Convention & Visitors Bureau, US 54 Business, PO Box 98, Lake Ozark 65049; 314/365-3371 or 800/386-5253.

(Approx 42 mi SW of Jefferson City on US 54)

Bagnell Dam, 2,543 feet long, completed in 1931, impounds the Osage River to form this recreational lake, which has a very irregular 1,150-mile shoreline. Fishing, boating and swimming are excellent. Boats may be rented.

What to See and Do

Lake cruises.

Casino Pier. One-hour and two-hour cruises aboard the *Commander* depart hourly (Apr-Oct, daily); also breakfast, brunch and dinner & dance cruises. 1/2 blk S of Bagnell Dam, on US 54 Business. Phone 314/365-2020. ¢¢¢¢¢

Paddle-wheeler *Tom Sawyer* Excursion Boat. One- and two-hour narrated sightseeing excursions on sternwheeler (Apr-Oct, daily); charters avail. Scenic helicopter rides (fee). W end of Bagnell Dam. Phone 314/365-3300. ¢¢¢

Lake of the Ozarks State Park. This more than 17,000-acre park, the largest in the state, has 89 miles of shoreline with 2 public swimming and boat launching areas. Public Beach #1 is at end of MO 134, and Grand Glaize Beach is 1/2 mile from US 54, 2 miles south of Grand Glaize Bridge. On the grounds is a large cave with streams of water that continuously pour from stalactites. Fishing; canoeing. Hiking; horseback riding. Picnicking. Improved camping (dump station). Naturalist. (Daily) Standard fees. SE of Osage Beach on MO 42. Phone 314/348-2694. **Free.**

Osage Power Plant (Bagnell Dam). Tours (daily). 1/2 mi off US 54. Phone 314/365-9202. **Free.**

Cottage Colony

★ **BASS POINT RESORT.** *(Rte 1, Box 127, Sunrise Beach 65079) 314/374-5205.* 35 kit. cottages. No rm phones. June-Aug: S, D $67-$116; each addl $8; wkly rates; lower rates Apr-May & Sept-Oct. Closed rest of yr. TV; cable. 2 pools, 1 indoor; whirlpool. Playground. Ck-out 11 am, ck-in 4 pm. Grocery 3 mi. Coin lndry. Pkg store 3 mi. Lighted tennis. Boats. Water skiing. Game rm. Picnic tables. Cr cds: DS, MC, V.

[icons]

Lake Ozark (D-4)

(See Camdenton, Lake of the Ozarks, Osage Beach)

Pop 681 **Elev** 703 ft **Area code** 314 **Zip** 65049

Motor Hotel

★★ **HOLIDAY INN.** *Box 1930, 2 mi S of Bagnell Dam on US 54 Business. 314/365-2334; FAX 314/365-6887.* 213 rms, 2 story. Late May-early Sept: S $85-$147; D $89-$149; each addl $5; suites $220; under 20 free; lower rates rest of yr. Crib free. TV; cable (premium), VCR avail. 3 pools, 1 indoor; whirlpool, steam rm, sauna. Playground. Restaurant 6:30 am-10 pm. Rm serv. Bar noon-midnight. Ck-out noon. Coin lndry. Meeting rms. Business servs avail. Bellhops. Gift shop. Miniature golf. Game rm. Rec rm. Lawn games. On lake. Cr cds: A, C, D, DS, JCB, MC, V.

[icons] SC

Resort

★★★ **LODGE OF FOUR SEASONS.** *Box 215, 1 mi S of Bagnell Dam, 3 mi W of US 54 Business on State Rd HH. 314/365-3000; res: 800/THE-LAKE; FAX 314/365-8525.* 294 lodge rms, 17 rms over marina, 1-4 story. May-Sept: S, D $99-$179; suites $175-$450; 2-3 bedroom condos $180-$320; under 18 free; package plans; varied lower rates rest of yr. Crib free. TV; cable (premium), VCR avail. 5 pools, 1 indoor/outdoor; wading pool, poolside serv. Playground. Supervised child's activities (Memorial Day-Labor Day); ages 2-16. Restaurants 7 am-midnight (also see TOLEDO'S). Rm serv 6 am-10 pm. Box lunches, snacks; barbecues, outdoor buffets. Bars 11-1 am, Sun noon-midnight. Ck-out noon, ck-in 4 pm. Meeting rms. Business servs avail. Valet serv. Airport transportation. Package store 2 mi. Lighted & indoor tennis, pro. Two 18-hole golf courses, greens fee $49-$68, pro, putting greens, driving range, executive 9-hole. Private beach; waterskiing; boats, motors, fishing guides; marina. X-country ski on site. Trap shooting. Skeet shooting. Lawn games. Soc dir; movies, entertainment, dancing. Rec rm. Game rm. Bowling alley. Exercise rm; instructor, weights, bicycles, whirlpool, steam rm, sauna. Private patios, balconies. Sidewalk cafe by waterfall. More than 200 acres of natural wooded Ozark countryside. Japanese garden & tropical fish. Panoramic views of lake. Cr cds: A, D, DS, MC, V.

[icons] SC

Restaurants

★★ **BENTLEY'S RESTAURANT AND PUB.** *2 mi S of Bagnell Dam on US 54 Business. 314/365-5301.* Hrs: 5-10 pm; Fri, Sat to 11 pm. Closed Sun off-season; also Jan-Feb. Res accepted. Bar. Semi-a la carte: dinner $11.95-$19.95. Child's meals. Specializes in prime rib, seafood. Parking. English decor. Cr cds: A, C, D, DS, MC, V.

[icons]

★ ★ ★ **TOLEDO'S.** *(See Lodge Of Four Seasons Resort)* *314/365-8507.* Hrs: 5:30-10 pm; Sun brunch 10 am-2 pm. Res accepted. Bar. A la carte entrees: dinner $15.95-$27.50. Child's meals. Own baking. Entertainment. Valet parking. Mediterranean decor; scenic view of Japanese garden & lake. Cr cds: A, D, DS, MC, V.

🅓

Lamar (D-3)

(See Carthage, Nevada)

Pop 4,168 **Elev** 985 ft **Area code** 417 **Zip** 64759
Information Chamber of Commerce, 900 Gulf; 417/682-3595.

What to See and Do

⭐ **Harry S Truman Birthplace State Historic Site.** Restored 1½-story house where Truman was born May 8, 1884, and lived until he was 11 months old; 6 rooms with period furnishings, outdoor smokehouse and hand-dug well. Guided tours. (Mon-Sat, also Sun afternoons; closed some major hols) 1009 Truman Ave. Phone 417/682-2279. **Free.**

Prairie State Park. This nearly 3,000-acre park preserves an example of Missouri's original prairie; on site are a flock of prairie chickens and small herd of buffalo. Hiking. Picnicking. Visitor center; wildlife observation. Standard fees. (Daily) 16 mi W on US 160. Phone 417/843-6711. **Free.**

Annual Events

Truman Days. Arts & crafts, special events. 1st wkend June.

Lamar Free Fair, Farm & Industrial Exposition. Livestock exhibits; contests, displays; parade, carnival. Lamar Square. Phone 417/682-3911. Last wkend Aug.

Motel

★ **BEST WESTERN BLUE TOP INN.** *65 SE 1st Lane, 1 blk S of jct US 71 & 160. 417/682-3333.* 25 rms. S $28-$35; D $35-$45; each addl $3. Crib $3. TV; cable (premium). Pool. Restaurant adj 6 am-9 pm; winter hrs vary. Ck-out 11 am. Cr cds: A, C, D, DS, MC, V.

Lebanon (D-4)

(See Camdenton, Waynesville)

Founded 1849 **Pop** 9,983 **Elev** 1,266 ft **Area code** 417 **Zip** 65536
Information Lebanon Area Chamber of Commerce, 321 S Jefferson; 417/588-3256.

Lebanon was founded in the mid-1800s beside an Indian trail that today is Interstate 44. As the seat of the newly created Laclede County, the town was originally called Wyota; however, the name was changed when a respected minister asked that it be renamed after his hometown, Lebanon, Tennessee.

What to See and Do

Bennett Spring State Park. Nearly 1,500 acres. Swimming pool; trout fishing (Mar-Oct). Picnicking, store, dining lodge. Improved camping (dump station), cabins. Nature center, naturalist. Standard fees. (Daily) 12 mi W on MO 64. Phone 417/532-4338 or -4307 (cabins). (See ANNUAL EVENTS) **Free.**

Laclede County Museum (ca 1872). County jail until 1955; exhibits. (May-Sept, Mon-Fri; closed Memorial Day, July 4, Labor Day) 262 Adams St. Phone 417/588-2441. ¢

Annual Events

Bennett Spring Hillbilly Days. Bennett Spring State Park. Arts & crafts, contests, country music, antique cars. Father's Day wkend.

Laclede County Fair. Fairgrounds. 1 wk mid-July.

Motels

✔★ **BEST WESTERN WYOTA INN.** *Box 9, E I-44 Business Loop & I-44 exit 130. 417/532-6171.* 52 rms, 1-2 story. May-Oct: S $36-$40; D $42-$52; each addl $5; under 12 free; lower rates rest of yr. Crib $5. Pet accepted, some restrictions. TV; cable (premium). Pool. Restaurant 6 am-9 pm. Ck-out 11 am. Coin lndry. Cr cds: A, C, D, DS, MC, V.

★ **HOLIDAY INN.** *Box 972, I-44 Business Loop W exit 127. 417/532-7111; FAX 417/532-7005.* 82 rms, 2 story. S, D $40-$56; each addl $5; under 19 free. Crib free. Pet accepted. TV; cable, VCR avail. Pool; poolside serv. Restaurant 6:30 am-2 pm, 5-10 pm. Rm serv. Bar 3 pm-midnight. Ck-out noon. Coin lndry. Meeting rm. Business servs avail. Cr cds: A, C, D, DS, JCB, MC, V.

🅓 🐾 ☄ ⊠ 🅰 SC

Restaurant

✔★ **STONEGATE STATION.** *1475 S Jefferson. 417/588-1387.* Hrs: 11 am-9 pm; Fri, Sat to 10 pm; Sun buffet 11 am-2:30 pm. Closed some major hols. Serv bar exc Sun. Semi-a la carte: lunch $2.95-$7.65, dinner $4.95-$15.95. Child's meals. Specializes in steak, seafood, Mexican dishes. Salad bar. Parking. Rustic atmosphere; antique farm implements. Totally non smoking. Cr cds: MC, V.

Lexington (B-3)

(See Independence, Kansas City)

Settled 1822 **Pop** 4,860 **Elev** 849 ft **Area code** 816 **Zip** 64067
Information Tourism Bureau, Main & Broadway, PO Box 132; phone 816/259-4711.

This historic city with more than 110 antebellum houses was founded by settlers from Lexington, Kentucky. The site of a three-day battle during the Civil War, many of the Union Army's entrenchments are still visible today. Situated on bluffs overlooking the Missouri River, Lexington was an important river port during the 19th century. Today the area is one of the state's largest producers of apples.

What to See and Do

Battle of Lexington State Historic Site. Site of one of the Civil War's largest western campaign battles (Sept 18-20, 1861). Anderson House, which stood in the center of the battle, has been restored. Guided tours. (Daily; closed some major hols) MO 13 N. Phone 816/259-4654. ¢

Lafayette County Courthouse (1847). Oldest courthouse in constant use west of Mississippi. Has Civil War cannonball embedded in east column. (Mon-Fri; closed hols) 10th & Main Sts. Phone 816/259-4315.

Lexington Historical Museum. Built as a Presbyterian church in 1846; contains Pony Express and Battle of Lexington relics, photographs and other historical Lexington items. (Mid-Apr-mid-Oct, daily) MO 13 & US 224. Phone 816/259-6313. ¢

Log House Museum. Exhibits include candle making, quilting, hearth cooking. Also houses Tourism Bureau. (Wed-Sat & Sun afternoons; also by appt) Main St at Broadway. Phone 816/259-4711. ¢

Motel

✔★ **LEXINGTON INN.** *Jct US 24 & MO 13.* 816/259-4641; res: 800/289-4641. 60 rms, 2 story. S $35; D $42; each addl $5; under 5 free. Crib $3. Pet accepted, deposit required. TV; cable. Pool. Restaurant 6 am-9 pm; Fri, Sat to 10 pm; Sun 7 am-2 pm. Bar 4 pm-1:30 am; entertainment, dancing Fri, Sat. Ck-out 11 am. Coin lndry. Meeting rms. Cr cds: A, C, D, DS, MC, V.

[D] [✔] [👥] [≈] [✕] [🔥] [🐾] [SC]

Macon (B-4)

(See Kirksville)

Pop 5,571 **Elev** 859 ft **Area code** 816 **Zip** 63552
Information Macon Area Chamber of Commerce, 116 Bourke St; 816/385-2811.

What to See and Do

Long Branch State Park. Approximately 1,800-acre park on western shore of Long Branch Lake offers swimming, beach; fishing; boating (ramps, marina). Picnicking (shelters). Camping (hookups, dump station). Standard fees. (Daily) 2 mi W on US 36. Phone 816/773-5229. **Free.**

Motel

✔★ **BEST WESTERN INN.** *28933 Sunset Dr, 1¹/₂ mi W of US 63, Long Branch Lake exit.* 816/385-2125. 46 rms, 2 story. S $39-$43; D $47; each addl $4. Crib $4. Pet accepted, some restrictions. TV; cable. Pool. Coffee in rms. Restaurant adj 6 am-9 pm; Sun 7 am-8 pm. Ck-out 11 am. Meeting rm. Cr cds: A, C, D, DS, MC, V.

[✔] [≈] [✕] [🔥] [SC]

Restaurants

★★ **GASLIGHT ROOM.** *205 N Rollins.* 816/385-4013. Hrs: 10 am-9:30 pm; Sun 11 am-2 pm. Closed Jan 1, Thanksgiving, Dec 25. Res accepted. Bar. Semi-a la carte: lunch $2.50-$6, dinner $6.50-$15. Sun brunch $6.49. Specializes in seafood, steak, pork chops. Salad bar. Entertainment Fri & Sat. In historic hotel. Cr cds: A, D, DS, MC, V.

[D]

✔★ **LONG BRANCH.** *On US 36W, 1¹/₂ mi W of US 63, Long Branch Lake exit.* 816/385-4600. Hrs: 6 am-9 pm; Sun 7 am-8 pm; Sun brunch to 3 pm. Closed Jan 1, Dec 25. Res accepted. Bar 3:30 pm-1 am. Semi-a la carte: bkfst $1.49-$6.50, lunch $1.59-$5.25, dinner $4.39-$12.99. Sun brunch $5.99. Child's meals. Salad bar. Parking. Western decor. Cr cds: A, C, D, DS, MC, V.

[D] [SC]

Mexico (B-5)

(See Columbia)

Founded 1836 **Pop** 11,290 **Elev** 802 ft **Area code** 314 **Zip** 65265
Information Mexico Area Chamber of Commerce, 111A N Washington, PO Box 56; phone 314/581-2765 or 800/581-2765.

According to local lore, Mexico got its name from a sign on a local tavern reading "Mexico that-a-way." Known as an agricultural trade center, its heritage includes world-famous saddlehorse breeding and training stables. The Missouri Military Academy, founded in 1889, is located on a beautiful 70-acre campus at the eastern end of Jackson Street.

What to See and Do

Graceland: Audrain County Historical Society Museum. Restored 1857 mansion; Victorian parlor, dining room, library, period bedroom, children's room with doll collection; Audrain Country School, original rural schoolhouse and furnishings. Also here is American Saddle Horse Museum. (Mar-Dec, Tues-Sun afternoons; closed hols) 501 S Muldrow St. Phone 314/581-3910. ¢

Motel

✔★ **BEST WESTERN STEPHENSON.** *1010 E Liberty.* 314/581-1440; FAX 314/581-1487. 63 rms, 2 story. S $36-$40; D $41-$46; each addl $4; under 12 free. Crib $4. Pet accepted; deposit. TV; cable (premium). Pool. Complimentary continental bkfst. Complimentary coffee in rms. Restaurant 11 am-2 pm, 5-9 pm; closed Sun. Rm serv. Bar 11-1:30 am; closed Sun. Ck-out noon. Coin lndry. Meeting rm. Sundries. Refrigerators. Cr cds: A, C, D, DS, ER, MC, V.

[✔] [≈] [✕] [🔥] [SC]

Unrated Dining Spot

G & D STEAK HOUSE. *US 54 S.* 314/581-0171. Hrs: 11 am-9 pm. Closed Dec 25. Avg ck: lunch, dinner $5. Specializes in steak, Greek dishes, spaghetti. Salad bar. Cafeteria-style line service. Cr cds: DS, MC, V.

[D] [SC]

Monroe City (B-5)

(See Hannibal)

Founded 1857 **Pop** 2,701 **Elev** 749 ft **Area code** 314 **Zip** 63456
Information Chamber of Commerce, 314 S Main St, in Nutrition Center, Box 22; 314/735-4391.

What to See and Do

[★] **Mark Twain Birthplace and State Park.** Almost 2,000 acres of wooded park; museum has frame house where Samuel Clemens (Mark Twain) was born Nov 30, 1835, exhibits on Clemens' life and some personal artifacts; slide show (daily); movies (summer wkends). Swimming; fishing; boating. Picnicking. Camping (dump station; standard fees). (Daily; museum closed some major hols) 9 mi SW on US 24 to MO 107, then 7 mi S. Phone 314/565-3449. Museum ¢

Motels

★ **ECONO LODGE.** *#3 Gateway Square, US 36 Business & US 24.* 314/735-4200; FAX 314/735-3493. 47 rms, 2 story. Mar-Oct: S $40-$50; D $45-$50; under 12 free; lower rates rest of yr. Crib free. Pet accepted; some restrictions; $5. TV; cable. Indoor pool; whirlpool. Ck-out 11 am. Meeting rm. Cr cds: A, D, DS, MC, V.

[D] [✔] [≈] [✕] [🐾] [SC]

✔★ **RAINBOW.** *308 5th St, off US 24/Business 36.* 314/735-4526. 20 rms. S $32-$34; D $36-$38; each addl $5; under 6 free. Crib

$4. TV; cable (premium). Pool. Complimentary coffee. Ck-out 11 am. Cr cds: A, DS, MC, V.

Mound City (A-2)

(For accommodations see St Joseph)

Pop 1,273 **Elev** 900 ft **Area code** 816 **Zip** 64470

What to See and Do

Big Lake State Park. Located at 625-acre natural oxbow lake. Swimming pool; fishing; boating, canoeing. Picnicking, dining lodge. Improved camping (dump station); cabins. Standard fees. (Daily) 7 mi SW on US 118, then S on MO 111. Phone 816/442-3770. **Free.**

Squaw Creek National Wildlife Refuge. View bald eagles, geese, ducks, pelicans (during migrations), deer and pheasant along 10-mi auto tour route; hiking trail; display in office (Mon-Fri). Refuge (daily). 5 mi S via I-29, exit 79, then 2 mi W on US 159. For information contact Refuge Manager, PO Box 101. Phone 816/442-3187. **Free.**

Mount Vernon (E-3)

(See Joplin, Springfield)

Pop 3,726 **Elev** 1,176 ft **Area code** 417 **Zip** 65712

Motels

★ **BEST WESTERN BEL-AIRE.** *Box 366, at jct I-44, MO 39.* 417/466-2111. 43 rms. S $36-$42; D $45-$51; each addl $3; under 12 free. Crib free. TV; cable. Pool. Restaurant adj open 24 hrs. Ck-out 11 am. Meeting rm. Picnic tables. Cr cds: A, C, D, DS, MC, V.

✔ ★ **BUDGET HOST RANCH.** *Rte 1, Box 6B, on MO 39 at jct I-44, exit 46.* 417/466-2125; FAX 417/466-4440. 21 rms. S $38-$40; D $38-$46; each addl $3; wkly rates winter, extended stay rates. Crib $3. Pet accepted, some restrictions. TV; cable (premium), VCR avail. Pool. Restaurant nearby. Ck-out 11 am. Picnic tables. Cr cds: A, DS, MC, V.

Nevada (D-3)

(See Lamar; also see Fort Scott, KS)

Founded 1855 **Pop** 8,597 **Elev** 880 ft **Area code** 417 **Zip** 64772
Information Chamber of Commerce, 110 S Adams; 417/667-5300.

Settled by families from Kentucky and Tennessee, Nevada became known as the "bushwhackers capital" due to the Confederate guerrillas headquartered here during the Civil War. The town was burned to the ground in 1863 by Union troops and was not rebuilt until after the war. Today Nevada is a shopping and trading center for the surrounding area.

What to See and Do

Bushwhacker Museum. Museum, operated by Vernon County Historical Society, was a jail from 1860 to 1960; exhibits include original cell room; Civil War relics; period clothing, tools, medical items; Osage artifacts. (May-Sept, daily; Oct, Sat & Sun) 231 N Main St at Hunter St, 3 blks N of US 54. Phone 417/922-3227. ¢

Schell Osage Wildlife Area. Winter home to bald eagles and thousands of wild ducks and geese. (Daily; some areas closed during duck hunting season) 12 mi E on US 54 then 12 mi N on County AA, near Schell City. Phone 417/432-3414. **Free.**

Annual Event

Bushwhacker Days. Parade; arts & crafts, antique machine & car shows; street square dance, midway. Mid-June.

Motels

✔ ★ **BEST WESTERN RAMBLER.** *1401 E Austin.* 417/667-3351. 54 rms. S $34-$36; D $44-$46; each addl $4. Crib $4. TV; cable (premium). Pool. Ck-out 11 am. Business servs avail. Cr cds: A, C, D, DS, MC, V.

★ ★ **COMFORT INN.** *2345 Marvel Dr, US 71 exit Camp Clark W.* 417/667-6777; FAX 417/667-6135. 46 rms, 2 story. S $41.95; D $45.95; each addl $2; suites $59.95; under 12 free; higher rates special events. Pet accepted, some restrictions; $25. TV; cable (premium). Indoor pool; whirlpool. Complimentary continental bkfst. Restaurant nearby. Ck-out 11 am. Coin lndry. Meeting rms. Some minibars. Cr cds: A, C, D, DS, MC, V.

✔ ★ ★ **RAMSEY'S NEVADA.** *1514 E Austin.* 417/667-5273. 26 rms. S $30; D $42; each addl $2. Crib $5. TV; cable (premium). Pool. Coffee avail 6-10 am. Ck-out 11 am. Meeting rm. Airport transportation. Cr cds: A, C, D, DS, MC, V.

★ **SUPER 8.** *2301 E Austin.* 417/667-8888. 60 rms, 2 story. S $36.88-$46.88; D $41.88-$46.88; each addl $2. Crib avail. Pet accepted. TV; cable (premium), VCR avail. Continental bkfst. Restaurant nearby. Ck-out 11 am. Business center. In-rm modem link. Coin lndry. Cr cds: A, C, D, DS, MC, V.

Restaurants

✔ ★ **EL SAMBRE.** *1402 W Austin.* 417/667-8242. Hrs: 11 am-9 pm; Fri, Sat to 10 pm; Sun to 9 pm. Closed Easter, Thanksgiving, Dec 25. Mexican menu. Semi-a la carte: lunch, dinner $1.20-$13.35. Child's meals. Parking. Mexican decor. Cr cds: A, DS, MC, V.

★ **J.T. MALONEY'S.** *2117 E Austin.* 417/667-7719. Hrs: 11 am-2 pm, 4-10 pm; Sat from 4 pm; Sun brunch 11 am-3 pm. Closed major hols. Mexican, Amer menu. Bar to midnight. Semi-a la carte: lunch $3-$5.25, dinner $4-$19. Sun brunch $2.75-$5. Child's meals. Specializes in prime rib, chicken, seafood. Parking. Cr cds: A, DS, MC, V.

Osage Beach (D-4)

(See Camdenton, Lake Ozark)

Pop 2,599 **Elev** 895 ft **Area code** 314 **Zip** 65065
Information Lake Area Chamber of Commerce, US 54, PO Box 193; 314/348-2730.

A major resort community on the Lake of the Ozarks (see), the town came into existence with the completion, in 1931, of the lake. Today, Osage Beach features some of the lake area's most popular attractions.

What to See and Do

Big Surf Water Park. This 22-acre park features river and tube rides, wave pool, body flumes; volleyball; changing facilities; concession. (Memorial Day-Labor Day, daily) 3 mi SW on US 54 to County Y. Phone 314/346-6111. ¢¢¢¢ Adj is

Big Shot Family Action Park. Miniature golf, bumper boats, go-carts and other rides. Gift shop; concession. (Mar-Nov; daily, weather permitting) Admission to park is free; fees charged at each attraction. Phone 314/346-6111.

Seasonal Events

Country music and variety shows.

Main Street Opry. On US 54. Nightly exc Sun. Phone 314/348-4848. Mid-Apr-Oct.

Lee Mace's Ozark Opry. On US 54. Nightly exc Sun. Phone 314/348-2270. Late Apr-Nov.

Motels

✔ ★ ★ **BEST WESTERN DOGWOOD HILLS RESORT INN.** *Rte 4, Box 1300, off US 54, 1 mi on MO KK.* 314/348-1735; FAX 314/348-0014. 47 rms, 4 fairway villas, 2 story. S, D $44-$89; each addl $8; villas $90-$333; under 19 free; wkend rates. Crib $5. Pet accepted, some restrictions. TV; cable. Heated pool; whirlpool. Dining rm 7 am-2 pm; closed Nov-Feb. Bar. Ck-out 11 am, ck-in 4 pm. Grocery 1 mi. Coin lndry ½ mi. Package store 1 mi. Meeting rm. Business servs avail. 18-hole golf, pro, putting green, driving range. Some refrigerators. Some private patios, balconies. Extensive grounds. Cr cds: A, C, D, DS, MC, V.

D ⊬ ⚼ ≋ ⚶ SC

★ ★ **BEST WESTERN LAKE CHATEAU.** *Rte 2, Box 3985, ¼ mi W of Grand Glaize Bridge on US 54.* 314/348-2791; FAX 314/348-1340. 49 rms, 2 story. Mid-May-mid-Sept, D $74-$84; each addl $5; under 18 free; lower rates rest of yr. Crib free. TV; cable (premium). 2 pools; whirlpool. Playground. Restaurant 7 am-10 pm. Bar. Ck-out noon. Coin lndry. Meeting rm. Private patios, balconies. On lake; private sand beach, dock. Cr cds: A, C, D, DS, MC, V.

⊬ ≋ ⚶ ⚶

✔ ★ **POINT BREEZE RESORT.** *Rte 4, Box 2130, 2 blks W of Grand Glaize Bridge on US 54, then ¼ mi NW on Lake Rd 54-37.* 314/348-2929. 35 rms, 1-2 story, 34 kits. No rm phones. Memorial Day-Labor Day: S $58; D $72; each addl $5; suites $85; lower rates Apr-before Memorial Day, after Labor Day-Oct. Closed rest of yr. Crib $5. TV; cable. Pool; wading pool. Playground. Restaurant nearby. Ck-out 11 am. Tennis. Rec rm. Lawn games. Private patio, balconies. Boats, motors. Picnic tables, grills. No cr cds accepted.

⊬ ⚼ ≋ ⚶

★ ★ **SUMMERSET INN RESORT & VILLAS.** *Rte 4, Box 2220, US 54 and Lake Rd 37.* 314/348-5073; FAX 314/348-4676. 35 units, 33 kits, 1-3 story. No rm phones. June-Aug: S, D $53-$250; wkly rates; golf plans; lower rates Mar-May & Sept-Oct. Closed rest of yr. Crib free. TV; cable (premium). Pool; wading pool, whirlpool. Playgrounds. Restaurant nearby. Ck-out 10:30 am, ck-in 4 pm. Grocery store 1½ mi. Coin lndry. Package store ½ mi. Dockage. Lawn games. Game rm. Fishing guide. Picnic tables, grills. No cr cds accepted.

≋ ⚶

Motor Hotel

★ ★ **INN AT GRAND GLAIZE.** *PO Box 969, US 54 & Lake Rd 40.* 314/348-4731; FAX 314/348-4694. 151 rms, 5 story. May-Oct: S, D $100-$147; each addl $10; suites $250; under 18 free; lower rates rest of yr. Crib free. TV; cable. Heated pool; wading pool, whirlpool, sauna, poolside serv. Supervised child's activities (ages 3-14). Restaurant 6:30 am-10 pm. Rm serv. Bar 5 pm-1 am; entertainment wkends. Ck-out noon. Meeting rms. Business servs avail. In-rm modem link. Bellhops. Tennis. Game rm. Fishing guides. Some bathrm phones, refrigerators. Private patios, balconies. Cr cds: A, C, D, DS, MC, V.

D ⊬ ⚼ ≋ ⚶ ⚶ SC

Resorts

★ **KALFRAN LODGE.** *Box 221, ¼ mi W of Grand Glaize Bridge, off US 54; Lake Rd 54-39.* 314/348-2266; res: 800/417-2266. 56 rms, 1-2 story, 44 kits. June-Aug: S, D $65-$75; each addl $5; kit. units $68-$98; cottages with kit. $52-$92; lower rates Apr-May, Sep-Oct. Closed rest of yr. Crib $5. TV; cable. 2 heated pools; wading pool. Playground. Restaurant nearby. Ck-out 10 am, ck-in 3 pm. Grocery ¼ mi. Coin lndry. Package store ¼ mi. Meeting rms. Tennis. Boats. Lawn games. Rec rm. Refrigerators. Some private patios, balconies. Picnic tables, grills. Cr cds: MC, V.

⊬ ⚼ ≋ ⚶

★ ★ **THE KNOLLS.** *Rte 1, Box 435, 3 mi W off US 54 on MO KK and Baydy Peak Rd.* 314/348-2236; res: 800/648-0339; FAX 314/348-7198. 60 kit. condo units. Mid-May-mid-Sept: 1-bedrm $134-$194; 2-bedrm $159-$224; 3-bedrm $184-$284; 4-bedrm $304-$369; lower rates rest of yr. Crib $5. TV; cable. 2 pools, 1 indoor; poolside serv. Playground. Coffee in rms. Box lunches. Snack bar in season. Picnic area. Bar in season. Ck-out noon, ck-in 4 pm. Grocery 1 mi. Meeting rms. Business servs avail. Lighted & indoor tennis. Lawn games. Dock; waterskiing; boats, pontoons. Fishing guides. Game rm. Fireplaces; some in-rm whirlpools. Balconies, grills. Cr cds: A, DS, MC, V.

⊬ ⚼ ≋ ⚶

★ ★ ★ **MARRIOTT'S TAN-TAR-A RESORT, GOLF CLUB & SPA.** *PO Box 188, 2 mi SW of Grand Glaize Bridge on US 54, then 2 mi W on MO KK.* 314/348-3131; res: 800/826-8272; FAX 314/348-3206. 365 lodge rms, 1-8 story; 195 kit. units, 1-3 story. Apr-Oct: S, D $89-$165; suites, kit. units $170-$335; family rates; wkend, package plans; lower rates rest of yr. Crib free. TV; cable (premium), VCR avail. 5 pools, 1 indoor, 2 heated; 2 wading pools, poolside serv, lifeguard. Playground. Supervised child's activities (Memorial Day-Labor Day, daily; rest of yr, Fri-Sun; also major hols). Coffee in rms. Restaurant (public by res) 6-2 am. Box lunches. Snack bar. Picnics. Rm serv 7 am-11 pm. Bars to 1 am, Sun to midnight. Ck-out noon, ck-in 4 pm. Grocery nearby. Coin lndry. Meeting rms. Business center. Valet serv. Shopping arcade. Airport transportation. Rec dir. Indoor, outdoor tennis, pro. 27-hole golf, greens fee $49-$60, putting green, driving range. Waterskiing, instruction; para sailing; marina, excursion boat. Lawn games. Mountain bikes, minibikes. Soc dir; entertainment, dancing, movies. Indoor ice rink (Oct-Apr). Racquetball courts. Bowling. Rec rm. Exercise rm; instructor, weights, bicycles, whirlpool, sauna. Fishing guides. Refrigerators, fireplaces. Many private patios; balconies overlook lake. On 550-acre peninsula. Cr cds: A, C, D, DS, ER, JCB, MC, V.

D ⊬ ⚼ ⚼ ⚼ ≋ ⚷ ⚶ ⚶ ⚶ SC ⚶

Restaurants

★ ★ **BRASS DOOR.** *¼ mi W of Grand Glaize Bridge on US 54.* 314/348-9229. Hrs: 5-11 pm. Res accepted. Semi-a la carte: dinner $10.95-$25.95. Child's meals. Specializes in seafood, prime rib, steak. Parking. Cr cds: A, DS, MC, V.

✔★ ★ **DOMENICO'S AT THE LAKE.** *1/2 mi E of Grand Glaize Bridge on US 54.* 314/348-5335. Hrs: 5-11 pm; to 10 pm off season. Closed some major hols; also Super Bowl Sun. Italian, Amer menu. Bar. Semi-a la carte: dinner $4.75-$17.95. Child's meals. Specializes in char-broiled prime rib, pasta, chicken. Parking. Cr cds: A, D, DS, MC, V.

D

★ **HAPPY FISHERMAN.** *1/4 mi E of Grand Glaize Bridge on US 54.* 314/348-3311. Hrs: 11:30 am-10 pm. Closed mid-Dec-mid-Jan. Bar. Semi-a la carte: lunch, dinner $3.95-$24.50. Child's meals. Specializes in seafood. Salad bar. Parking. Nautical decor. Cr cds: A, MC, V.

D

✔★ **JUST LIKE HOME.** *US 54 & Lake Rd.* 314/348-1135. Hrs: 5-9:30 pm; Sun brunch 8:30 am-1:30 pm. Closed wk of Dec 25. Semi-a la carte: dinner $7.95-$16.95. Sun brunch $7.95. Specializes in chicken, barbecued ribs, catfish. Parking. Cr cds: A, DS, MC, V.

D

✔★ **VISTA GRANDE.** *US 54, opp Factory Outlet Village.* 314/348-1231. Hrs: 11:30 am-10 pm. Closed Thanksgiving, Dec 24-25. Mexican, Amer menu. Bar. Semi-a la carte: lunch $3.95-$6.50, dinner $6.25-$13.95. Child's meals. Mexican decor. Cr cds: A, DS, MC, V.

D

Pilot Knob (D-6)

(See Bonne Terre)

Pop 783 **Elev** 1,000 ft **Area code** 314 **Zip** 63663

What to See and Do

Johnson's Shut-Ins State Park. This nearly 2,800-acre area, left in its wilderness state, has a spectacular canyon-like defile along river. The park is at the southern end of 20-mile-long Taum Sauk backpacking trail, which traverses Missouri's highest mountain, Taum Sauk. Swimming; fishing. Hiking. Picnicking, playground. Improved camping (dump station). Standard fees. (Daily) 4 mi N on MO 21 to Graniteville, then 14 mi SW on County N. Phone 314/546-2450. **Free.**

Sam A. Baker State Park. The St François and Big Creek rivers flow through this more than 5,000-acre park. Hiking trails. Picnicking, playground, cabins, store. Improved camping (dump station). Nature center. Standard fees. (Daily) 30 mi S on MO 21 & MO 49 to Des Arc, then 12 mi SE on MO 143. Phone 314/856-4411 or -4223 (cabins). **Free.**

Resort

★ ★ **WILDERNESS LODGE.** *(Box 90, Lesterville 63654)* 1 mi E on MO 21, 72, Peola Rd exit to Gravel Rd, 2 1/4 mi. 314/296-2011. 27 cottages (1-3 bedrm). MAP, Apr-Oct: S $60; D $120; each addl $60; suites $75/person; under 5 free; family rates; lower rates rest of yr. Crib free. TV; cable (premium), VCR avail. Pool. Playground. Complimentary coffee in rms. Dining rm (public by res) 8-9 am, 11:30 am-1 pm, 7-8 pm. Box lunches. Bar 6-9 pm. Ck-out 1 pm, ck-in 4:30 pm. Meeting rms. Business center. Tennis. Private beach, canoes, inner tube rentals. Lawn games. Hiking trails with maps. Hay rides (fee). Refrigerators; some screened porches, fireplaces. Some private patios, balconies. On Black River. Cr cds: A, D, DS, MC, V.

D ✔ ⚹ ⚹ ⚹ ⚹ ⚹

Poplar Bluff (E-7)

(See Sikeston, Van Buren)

Settled 1819 **Pop** 16,996 **Elev** 344 ft **Area code** 314 **Zip** 63901

Information Chamber of Commerce, 1111 W Pine, PO Box 3986; phone 314/785-7761.

Solomon Kittrell, the first settler here, immediately set up two vital industries—a tannery and a distillery. Poplar Bluff is now an industrial and farm marketing center.

What to See and Do

Lake Wappapello State Park. Approx 1,800 acres. Swimming; fishing; boating (rentals, marina), canoeing. Hiking. Playground. Improved camping (dump station), cabins. Standard fees. (Daily) 15 mi N on US 67, then 9 mi E on MO 172. Phone 314/297-3232. **Free.**

Mark Twain National Forest (Poplar Bluff Ranger District). More than 150,000 acres on rolling hills of Ozark Plateau, with 49 acres of lakes, 33 miles of horseback riding trails. Fishing; hunting; float trips (Black River). Hiking. Camping (standard fees). 7 mi N on US 67. Contact Ranger District office phone 314/785-1475.

Motels

✔★ ★ **DRURY INN.** *2220 Westwood Blvd N.* 314/686-2451. 78 rms, 3 story. S $48-$53; D $54-$58; each addl $5; under 18 free. Crib free. TV; cable. Pool. Complimentary bkfst. Restaurant adj 6 am-11 pm. Ck-out noon. Valet serv. Cr cds: A, C, D, DS, MC, V.

D ✔ ⚹ ⚹ ⚹ SC

★ ★ **HOLIDAY INN.** *2115 N Westwood Blvd (US 67N).* 314/785-7711; FAX 314/785-7711, ext. 379. 143 rms, 1-2 story. S $55; D $63; each addl $8; suites $150; under 18 free. Crib free. TV; cable (premium). Pool. Restaurant 6 am-10 pm. Rm serv. Bar 11-1:30 am, Sun 1-10 pm; entertainment, dancing exc Sun. Ck-out noon. Meeting rms. Business servs avail. Free airport transportation. Cr cds: A, C, D, DS, JCB, MC, V.

D ✔ ⚹ ⚹ ⚹ SC

✔★ **SUPER 8.** *2831 N Westwood Blvd (US 67N).* 314/785-0176. 63 rms, 2 story. S $39.88; D $45.88-$53.88; each addl $4; under 12 free. Crib free. TV; cable. Restaurant adj 6 am-10 pm. Ck-out 11 am. Cr cds: A, C, D, DS, MC, V.

D ⚹ ⚹ SC

Rockaway Beach (E-4)

(See Branson/Table Rock Lake Area)

Pop 275 **Elev** 800 ft **Area code** 417 **Zip** 65740

Information Bureau of Tourism; PO Box 1004; phone 561-4280 or 800/798-0178.

This popular resort area is on the shores of Lake Taneycomo, which was created by the impounding of the White River by a 1,700-foot dam near Ozark Beach. Attractions include fishing, boating (rentals), tennis, golf, flea markets and arcades.

Motel

✔★ **TANEYCOMO MOTOR LODGE.** *PO Box 336, 1101 Beach Blvd.* 417/561-4141. 27 rms. S $35; D $39-$43. Crib free. TV; cable (premium). Pool. Playground. Complimentary morning coffee.

Restaurant nearby. Ck-out 11 am. On lake; marina. Cr cds: A, DS, MC, V.

Restaurant

✔★ **HILLSIDE INN.** *On Main St.* 417/561-8252. Hrs: 7 am-10 pm. Closed Dec 24-25. Res accepted. Mexican, Amer menu. Semi-a la carte: bkfst $2.50-$5.25, lunch $2.75-$7, dinner $4-$11.95. Child's meals. Specializes in chicken, Mexican dishes. No cr cds accepted.

D

Rolla (D-5)

(See Sullivan, Waynesville)

Settled 1855 **Pop** 14,090 **Elev** 1,119 ft **Area code** 314 **Zip** 65401
Information Rolla Area Chamber of Commerce, 1301 Kingshighway; phone 314/364-3577.

According to legend, the town was named by a homesick settler from Raleigh, North Carolina, who spelled the name as he pronounced it. Called "the child of the railroad," because it began with the building of the St Louis-San Francisco RR, the town is located in a scenic area with several fishing streams nearby. Mark Twain National Forest maintains its headquarters in Rolla.

What to See and Do

Ed Clark Museum of Missouri Geology. Displays of mineral resources, geological history and land surveying. (Mon-Fri; closed hols) In Buehler Park, on City I-44, 111 Fairgrounds Rd. Phone 314/368-2100. **Free.**

Maramec Spring Park and Remains of Old Ironworks. The spring discharges an average of 96.3 million gallons per day. The ironworks was first established in 1826; the present furnace was built in 1857. Trout fishing (Mar-Oct). Trails, scenic road. Picnicking, playground. Campground (fee). Nature center; observation tower; two museums. (Daily) 8 mi E on I-44 to St James, then 7 mi SE on MO 8. Phone 314/265-7387 or 314/265-7124. Vehicle (Mar-Oct) ¢

Mark Twain National Forest (Rolla-Houston Ranger Districts). More than 192,000 acres; cradles headwaters of Gasconade, Little Piney and Big Piney rivers. Swimming; fishing; hunting; boating. Picnicking. Camping (standard fees). Paddy Creek Wilderness Area covers about 6,800 acres with 30 miles of hiking, riding trails. SW via I-44, US 63. Contact Ranger District office 314/364-4501 (Rolla) or 417/967-4194 (Houston).

Memoryville, USA. More than 30 antique cars; art gallery, restoration shop; antique, gift shop; lounge, restaurant. (Daily; closed Jan 1, Thanksgiving, Dec 25) Sr citizen rate. On US 63N at jct I-44. Phone 314/364-1810. ¢¢

Montauk State Park. Approx 1,300 acres. Trout fishing. Hiking trail. Picnicking, store, motel, dining lodge. Improved camping (dump station), cabins. Standard fees. (Daily) 35 mi S on US 63 to Licking, then 2 mi S on MO 137, then 10 mi E on County VV. Phone 314/548-2201 or -2434 (cabins). **Free.**

St James Winery. Dry and semi-dry wines, champagne, sparkling wines, Concord, Catawba and berry wines all produced here. Hourly tours; tasting room; gift shop. (Daily; closed Dec 25) 10 mi E via I-44, St James exit, then 3 blks E on County B (north access road). Phone 314/265-7912. **Free.**

University of Missouri-Rolla (1870). (5,000 students) N Pine St. Phone 314/341-4328. On campus are

Minerals Museum. Begun in 1904 as part of the Missouri mining exhibit for the St Louis World's Fair, today the exhibit contains 4,000 specimens from around the world. (Mon-Fri; closed hols) First floor, McNutt Hall. Geology Department, Phone 314/341-4616. **Free.**

UMR Nuclear Reactor. Swimming pool-type reactor, contains 32,000 gallons of water. Tours. (Mon-Fri; closed hols & Aug; phone for appt) Phone 314/341-4236. **Free.**

UM-Rolla Stonehenge. Partial reproduction of Stonehenge, the ancient circle of megaliths on Salisbury Plain in England. Features five trilithons standing 13 feet high. Interpretive guides avail. Phone 314/341-4328. **Free.**

Annual Events

St Pat's Celebration. University of Missouri students' 87th celebration of St Patrick, patron saint of engineers; parade, painting Main St green, beard judging contests, shillelagh judging, entertainment. St Patrick's Day wkend.

Central Missouri Regional Fair. Fairgrounds, 1/2 mi S on US 63. Early Aug.

Motels

✔★ **BEST WESTERN COACHLIGHT.** *Box 826, I-44 at exit 184, on Martin Spring Dr.* 314/341-2511. 88 rms, 2 story. May-Oct: S $44; D $55; each addl $4; under 12 free; higher rates special events; lower rates rest of yr. Crib $8. Pet accepted. TV; cable (premium). Pool. Playground. Continental bkfst. Restaurant adj 11 am-10 pm. Ck-out noon. Meeting rms. Business servs avail. In-rm modem link. Some refrigerators. Cr cds: A, C, D, DS, ER, MC, V.

★★ **DRURY INN.** *PO Box 130, 2006 N Bishop Ave, I-44 exit 186.* 314/364-4000; FAX 314/364-4000, ext. 475. 86 rms, 2 story. S, D $49-$59; each addl $7; under 18 free. Crib free. Pet accepted. TV; cable. Complimentary continental bkfst. Pool. Ck-out noon. Meeting rms. Valet serv. Cr cds: A, C, D, DS, MC, V.

✔★★ **ZENO'S.** *1621 Martin Spring Dr.* 314/364-1301. 54 rms. S $35-$40; D $45; each addl $3; higher rates special events. Crib $3. TV; cable. 2 pools, 1 indoor; whirlpool, sauna. Restaurant 7 am-10 pm. Bar 4 pm-midnight. Ck-out noon. Meeting rms. Valet serv. Tennis. Cr cds: A, C, D, DS, MC, V.

Restaurant

✔★ **JOHNNY'S SMOKE STAK.** *201 US 72 at Rolla St.* 314/364-4838. Hrs: 11 am-9 pm; Fri & Sat to 10 pm. Closed Jan 1, Thanksgiving, Dec 25. Semi-a la carte: lunch $3.95-$4.95, dinner $4.65-$15.95. Sun buffet $7.95. Child's meals. Specializes in hickory-smoked beef, ribs, sausage, turkey. Salad bar. Parking. Cr cds: A, D, MC, V.

D

St Charles (C-6)

(See St Louis, Wentzville)

Settled 1769 **Pop** 54,555 **Elev** 536 ft **Area code** 314
Information Convention and Visitors Bureau, 230 S Main, PO Box 745, 63302; 314/946-7776 or 800/366-2427.

St Charles, one of the early settlements on the Missouri River, was the first capital of the state (1821-26). Between 1832 and 1870 a wave of German immigrants settled here and developed the town, but St Louis, by virtue of its location on the Mississippi, became the state's most important city. St Charles is the home of Sacred Heart Convent (1818) and the Lindenwood Colleges (1827). Frenchtown, a northern ward of old St Charles, is home to many antique shops.

What to See and Do

Goldenrod **Showboat.** Restored 1909 showboat dinner theater. Show only or dinner/show seating combination. (Thurs-Sat evenings; matinees Wed & Sun) 1000 blk Riverside Dr. Phone 314/946-2020. ¢¢¢¢

✖ **St Charles Historic District.** Nine-block area along S Main Street with restored houses, antique and gift shops, restaurants, the 1836 Newbill-McElhiney House and the restored Missouri, Kansas and Texas Railroad Depot, which now serves as a visitor information center. Also here are

First Missouri State Capitol State Historic Site. Eleven rooms of capitol have been restored to original state; nine rooms have 1820 period furnishings; also restoration of Peck Brothers General Store and house. Interpretive center. (Daily; closed some major hols) 200-216 S Main St. Phone 314/946-9282. ¢

Lewis and Clark Center. Museum depicts the 1804-06 expedition from St Charles to the Pacific Ocean. Hands-on exhibits, lifesize models of Sacagawea and the men of the expedition; Mandan & Sioux villages, display of Missouri River; gift shop. (Daily exc Jan 1, Easter, Thanksgiving, Dec 25) 701 Riverside Dr. Phone 314/947-3199. ¢

Annual Events

Lewis & Clark Rendezvous. Frontier Park, on Riverside Dr. Re-enactment of the explorers' encampment in 1804 prior to embarking on their exploration of the Louisiana Purchase; parade, fife and drum corps, frontier dinner and ball. 3rd wkend May.

Festival of the Little Hills. Main St. Bluegrass and country music; 19th-century crafts, antiques; muzzle loading rifle shoot. 3rd wkend Aug.

Motels

★ ★ **HAMPTON INN.** 3720 W Clay (63301), approx 4 mi W on I-70 at Cave Springs exit 225. 314/947-6800; FAX 314/947-0020. 122 rms, 4 story. S $52-$62; D $58-$69; under 19 free. Crib free. TV; cable. Pool. Complimentary continental bkfst, coffee. Restaurant nearby. Ck-out 11 am. Meeting rms. Bellhops. Valet serv. Airport transportation. Exercise equipt; weight machines, bicycles. Cr cds: A, C, D, DS, MC, V.

D ⊠ 🏋 ⊠ 🐾 SC

✔★ **KNIGHTS INN.** 3800 Harry S Truman Blvd (63301). 314/925-2020; res: 800/843-5644. 110 rms. S $35; D $39; each addl $5; kits. $41-$53; under 18 free. Crib free. TV; cable. Pool. Complimentary coffee in lobby. Restaurant opp 6 am-10:30 pm. Ck-out noon. Some refrigerators. Cr cds: A, C, D, DS, MC, V.

D 🐾 ⊠ ⊠ 🐾 SC

Motor Hotels

★ ★ ★ **BEST WESTERN NOAH'S ARK.** 1500 S 5th St (63303), I-70 exit 229. 314/946-1000; FAX 314/946-7767. 122 rms, 6 story. S $45-$65; D $50-$70; each addl $5; suites $125-$165; under 12 free; wkend, hol rates; higher rates special events. Crib free. TV; cable. Indoor pool. Complimentary continental bkfst. Restaurant 5-9 pm. Ck-out 11 am. Coin lndry. Meeting rms. Bellhops. Free Lambert Airport transportation. Exercise equipt; weight machine, treadmill, whirlpool, sauna. Game rm. Lawn games. Minibar. Picnic tables. Luxury level. Cr cds: A, C, D, DS, MC, V.

D ⊠ 🏋 ⊠ 🐾 SC

★ ★ **HOLIDAY INN-ST PETERS.** (4221 S Outer Rd, St Peters 63376) I-70 E to Cave Springs exit. 314/928-1500; FAX 314/928-1500, ext. 449. 199 rms, 6 story. S, D $59-$89; suites $89; under 18 free; wkly rates. Crib free. TV; cable. Indoor/outdoor pool; whirlpool, sauna, poolside serv. Restaurant 6 am-2 pm, 5-10 pm. Rm serv. Bar 11-1 am; entertainment, dancing Tues-Sat. Ck-out noon. Coin lndry. Meeting rms. Bellhops. Valet serv. Free airport, RR station, bus depot transportation. Game rm. Rec rm. Some bathrm phones. Refrigerators avail. Luxury level. Cr cds: A, C, D, DS, JCB, MC, V.

D ⊠ ⊠ 🐾 SC

Restaurants

★ ★ ★ **BOCCACIO'S.** 820 S Main. 314/947-7737. Hrs: 11 am-2 pm, 5-10 pm; Sat from 5 pm; early-bird dinner Tues-Fri 5-6:30 pm. Closed Sun; major hols. Res accepted; required wkends. Continental menu. Bar. A la carte entrees: lunch $4.95-$6.95, dinner $13.95-$22. Specialties: châteaubriand, rack of lamb. Own baking. Pianist Fri, Sat. Parking. Cr cds: A, C, D, DS, MC, V.

D

✔★ ★ **CIAO.** 1050 Park Place. 314/949-5410. Hrs: 11 am-2:30 pm, 4-10 pm; Sat & Sun 4-9 pm. Closed Mon; some major hols. Res accepted. Italian menu. Bar. Semi-a la carte: lunch $4.95-$6.75, dinner $7.95-$13.95. Child's meals. Specialties: pollo Ciao, beefsteak Ciao. Parking. Outdoor dining. Italian cafe atmosphere. Fireplace, hanging plants. Cr cds: A, C, D, DS, MC, V.

D SC

✔★ **RIVERSTAR CAFE.** 117 S Main St. 314/949-2525. Hrs: 11 am-9 pm; Fri & Sat to midnight; Sun noon-8 pm; Mon to 3 pm. Closed some major hols. Res accepted. Bar. Semi-a la carte: lunch $4.25-$11.95, dinner $5.95-$13.95. Child's meals. Specialties: crab phyllo, prime rib, chicken Marsala. Entertainment Fri-Sun (seasonal). Outdoor dining. Built in 1875. Cr cds: A, C, D, DS, MC, V.

★ ★ **ST CHARLES VINTAGE HOUSE & WINE GARDEN.** 1219 S Main St. 314/946-7155. Hrs: 11 am-10 pm; Fri, Sat to midnight; Sun 10 am-8 pm; early-bird dinner Tues-Sat 5-7 pm; Sun brunch to 1 pm. Closed Mon; Dec 25. Res accepted. German, Amer menu. Bar. Semi-a la carte: lunch $3.95-$6.50, dinner $7.95-$15.95. Sun brunch $5.50. Child's meals. Specializes in barbecued ribs, fresh seafood, German dishes. Parking. Outdoor dining. Former winery (1860). Cr cds: A, C, D, DS, MC, V.

SC

Sainte Genevieve (D-7)

(See St Louis)

Founded 1735 **Pop** 4,411 **Elev** 401 ft **Area code** 314 **Zip** 63670
Information Great River Road Interpretive Center, 66 S Main; 314/883-7097.

Sainte Genevieve, the first permanent settlement in Missouri, developed on the banks of the Mississippi River early in the 18th century when Frenchmen began mining lead in the region. After a great flood in 1785, the village was moved to higher ground. Once St Louis' chief rival, Sainte Genevieve preserves its French heritage in its festivals, old houses and massive red brick church. Today, the town is an important lime-producing center.

What to See and Do

Bolduc House Museum (ca 1770). Restored French house with walls of upright heavy oak logs; period furnishings, orchard and herb garden. (Apr-Nov, daily) 125 S Main St. Phone 314/883-3105. ¢

Felix Valle Home State Historic Site (1818). Restored and furnished Federal-style stone house of early fur trader. Guided tours. (Daily; closed some major hols) 198 Merchant St. Phone 314/883-7102. ¢

Guibourd-Valle House Late 18th-century restored vertical log house on stone foundation; French heirlooms. Attic with Norman truss and hand-hewn oak beams secured by wooden pegs. Courtyard; rose garden; stone well; costumed guides. (Apr-Oct, daily; Mar & Nov wkends only; closed rest of yr) 1 N 4th St. Phone 314/883-7544. ¢

Sainte Genevieve Museum. Display of salt manufacturing, state's first industry. Scale model of rail car transfer boat *Ste Genevieve*, which carried trains across the Mississippi. Native American artifacts; local mementos. (Daily; closed some major hols) Merchant St & DuBourg Place. Phone 314/883-3461. ¢

Annual Event

Jour de Fête à Ste Geneviève. 4 mi E via I-55, MO 32. Tours of historic French houses; art show, French market, antiques. Phone 314/883-7097. 2nd wkend Aug.

Inns

★ ★ **SOUTHERN HOTEL.** *146 S 3rd St. 314/883-3493; res: 800/275-1412.* 8 rms, 2 story. No rm phones. S $65-$80; D $80-$110. Children over 12 yrs only. Complimentary full bkfst, refreshments. Restaurant nearby. Ck-out 11 am, ck-in 4-6 pm. Built 1791. Totally nonsmoking. Cr cds: MC, V.

✔ ★ **ST GEMME BEAUVAIS.** *78 N Main St. 314/883-5744; res: 800/818-5744.* 7 rms, 3 story. No elvtr. No rm phones. S, D $69-$125; each addl $15. TV; cable, VCR avail. Bkfst avail. Afternoon refreshments. Ck-out 11 am, ck-in 2 pm. Business servs avail. Columned, red-brick Greek-revival inn (1848); antiques. Cr cds: MC, V.

Restaurants

✔ ★ **ANVIL SALOON.** *46 S 3rd St. 314/883-7323.* Hrs: 11 am-11 pm. Closed major hols. German, Amer menu. Bar. Semi-a la carte: lunch, dinner $2.75-$12.95. Specializes in steak, catfish, fried chicken, homemade pies. Oldest commercially operated building in city (ca 1850); early Western saloon decor. Cr cds: A, MC, V.

★ ★ **LUCRETIA'S.** *242 Merchant St. 314/883-5647.* Hrs: 11 am-4 pm; Fri-Sun to 9 pm. Closed Mon & Tues; major hols. Res accepted. French, Amer menu. Wine, beer. A la carte entrees: lunch $4-$10, dinner $8-$20. Child's meals. Specializes in quiche, shrimp scampi, beef tenderloin. 3 dining rms in Victorian house. Cr cds: MC, V.

★ **OLD BRICK HOUSE.** *Market & 3rd Sts. 314/883-2724.* Hrs: 8 am-9 pm; Sat to 10 pm; Sun 11 am-7 pm. Closed Thanksgiving, Dec 25. Bar to 1 am. Semi-a la carte: bkfst $2.50-$4.50, lunch $2-$4, dinner $4.95-$18.95. Child's meals. Specializes in fried chicken. Salad bar. Parking. Said to be first brick building (1785) west of Mississippi. Cr cds: MC, V.

St Joseph (B-2)

(See Cameron, Kansas City, Mound City; also see Atchison, KS)

Settled 1826 **Pop** 71,852 **Elev** 833 ft **Area code** 816

Information Convention & Visitors Bureau, 109 S 4th St, 64502; 816/233-6688 or 800/785-0360.

A historic city with beautiful parks and large industries, St Joseph retains traces of the frontier settlement of the 1840s in the "original town" near the Missouri River. It was founded and named by Joseph Robidoux III, a French fur trader from St Louis, who established his post in 1826. St Joseph, the western terminus of the first railroad to cross the state, became the eastern terminus of the Pony Express, whose riders carried mail to and from Sacramento, California, from 1860-61, using relays of fast ponies. The record trip, which carried copies of President Lincoln's inaugural address, was made in 7 days and 17 hours. The telegraph ended the need for the Pony Express. The Civil War disrupted the region, largely Southern in sympathy, but postwar railroad building and cattle trade restored the city.

What to See and Do

Albrecht-Kemper Museum of Art. Exhibits of 18th-, 19th-, & 20th-century American paintings, sculpture, graphic art. Formal gardens. (Daily exc Mon; closed major hols) 2818 Frederick Blvd. Phone 816/233-7003. ¢¢

Doll Museum. More than 500 antique dolls; miniature rooms and houses, old toys, antique clothing. (Daily exc Mon; tour by appt) 1115 S 12th St. Phone 816/233-1420. ¢

Glore Psychiatric Museum. Housed in a ward of the original 1874 administration building, the museum displays the evolution of treatment philosophy and techniques over a 400-year period. (Mon-Fri; also Sat, Sun & holiday afternoons) St Joseph State Hospital, 3400 Frederick Ave. Phone 816/387-2300. **Free.**

Jesse James Home. One-story frame cottage where the outlaw had been living quietly as "Mr. Howard," until he was killed here April 3, 1882, by an associate, Bob Ford. Some original furnishings. (Daily) 12th & Penn Sts. Phone 816/232-8206. ¢

Patee House Museum. Built in 1858 as a hotel; in 1860 it served as headquarters of the Pony Express. Contains pioneer exhibits related to transportation and communication; includes restored 1860 Buffalo Saloon; woodburning engine and the original last mail car from the Hannibal and St Joseph railroad. Also 1917 Japanese tea house; ice cream parlor. (Apr-Oct, daily; Feb-Mar & Nov, wkends) 12th & Penn Sts. Phone 816/232-8206. ¢

Pony Express National Memorial. Museum in old Pike's Peak (Pony Express) Stables, the starting point of the first westward ride. Original stables; displays illustrate the creation, operation, management and termination of the famed mail service. (Daily; closed Jan 1, Thanksgiving, Dec 24, 25 & 31) 914 Penn St. Phone 816/279-5059 or 800/530-5930. ¢¢

Pony Express Region Tourist Information Centers. Housed in historic railroad cabooses, centers provide brochures and information on St Joseph, northwest Missouri and northeast Kansas; free maps. (Apr-Oct, daily) W of I-29 exit 47; also at I-35 and US 36 at Cameron. Phone 816/232-1839 or 816/632-5466 (Cameron).

Robidoux Row Museum (ca 1850). Built by city's founder, French fur trader Joseph Robidoux, as temporary housing for the newly arrived settlers who had purchased land from him. Authentically restored; some original furnishings. Tours. (Tues-Fri, also Sat & Sun afternoons; closeds major hols) 3rd & Poulin Sts. Phone 816/232-5861. ¢

St Joseph Museum. Native American collections; natural history; local and western history exhibits, including Civil War, Pony Express and Jesse James era. (Daily; closed Jan 1, Thanksgiving, Dec 24, 25, 31) **Free** on Sun, hols. 11th & Charles Sts. Phone 816/232-8471. ¢

St Joseph Park System. Approximately 26 miles of parkway system stretching over 1,500 acres of land. Of the more than 40 parks and facilities, most are along a 9½-mile drive from **Krug Park** (W of St Joseph Ave in the N end of the city) to **Hyde Park** (4th & Hyde Pk Ave in the S end of the city). The park system provides a variety of recreational facilities, including 18-hole golf, tennis courts, ballfields and an indoor ice arena. (Daily) Phone 816/271-5500.

Annual Events

Apple Blossom Parade & Festival. Originally celebration of area apple growers. Parade with more than 200 entries; food, music, crafts. 1st wkend May.

Annual Homes Tour. Historic mansions open for tours. Styles range from pre-Civil War to Victorian. Wkend mid-Aug.

Motels

✔ ★ **DAYS INN.** *4312 Frederick Ave (64506).* 816/279-1671; FAX 816/279-6729. 100 rms, 2 story. S $38-$43; D $43-$52; each addl $6; under 12 free. Crib free. TV; cable (premium), VCR avail (movies avail $3). Pool. Restaurant 6:30-9:30 am, 5:30-9 pm. Rm serv. Bar 5 pm-9 pm. Ck-out 11 am. Meeting rms. Business center. Cr cds: A, C, D, DS, ER, JCB, MC, V.

★ ★ **DRURY INN.** *4213 Frederick Blvd (64506).* 816/364-4700; FAX 816/364-4700, ext. 491. 139 rms, 4 story. S $47-$57; D $57-$67; each addl $7; under 18 free. Crib free. TV; cable (premium). Pool. Complimentary bkfst, coffee. Restaurant adj 6 am-11 pm. Ck-out noon. Meeting rms. Business servs avail. In-rm modem link. Valet serv. Sundries. Cr cds: A, C, D, DS, MC, V.

★ ★ **RAMADA INN.** *4016 Frederick Blvd (64506).* 816/233-6192; FAX 816/233-6001. 161 rms, 2 story. S, D $48-$69; suites $85-$125; under 18 free. Crib free. Pet accepted. TV; cable (premium). Indoor pool; whirlpool. Restaurants 6 am-2 pm, 5-10 pm. Rm serv. Bar 4 pm-midnight. Ck-out noon. Coin lndry. Meeting rms. Valet serv. Rec rm. Picnic tables. Cr cds: A, C, D, DS, ER, JCB, MC, V.

Motor Hotel

★ ★ **HOLIDAY INN-DOWNTOWN.** *102 S 3rd St (64501).* 816/279-8000; FAX 816/279-8000, ext. 698. 170 rms, 6 story. S $63-$93; D $63-$93; suites $85-$125; under 18 free; wkend rates. Crib free. Pet accepted. TV; cable. Indoor pool; whirlpool, sauna. Restaurant 6:30 am-2 pm, 5:30-10:30 pm. Rm serv. Bar 4:30-1 am, Sun to midnight. Ck-out noon. Meeting rms. Bellhops. Sundries. Gift shop. Game rm. Refrigerator, wet bar in suites. Opp river. Cr cds: A, C, D, DS, JCB, MC, V.

Restaurants

★ ★ **36TH STREET FOOD & DRINK COMPANY.** *501 N Belt Hwy.* 816/364-1564. Hrs: 11 am-11 pm. Closed Sun; most major hols. Res accepted. Bar 11-1:30 am. Semi-a la carte: lunch $5.95-$19.25, dinner $5.95-$27.95. Specializes in barbecued ribs, steak, fresh seafood. Parking. Country French decor. Cr cds: A, D, DS, MC, V.

✔ ★ **BARBOSA'S CASTILLO.** *906 Sylvanie St (64501).* 816/233-4970. Hrs: 11 am-9 pm; Fri & Sat to 10 pm. Closed Sun; major hols. Mexican menu. Bar. Semi-a la carte: lunch $2-$8.95, dinner $5.75-$8.95. Child's meals. Specializes in enchiladas, tamales, tacos. Parking. Dining on 2 levels in restored Victorian mansion (1891). Enclosed rooftop beer garden. Cr cds: A, C, D, DS, MC, V.

Unrated Dining Spots

THE DELI. *2316 North Belt (64506).* 816/279-3354. Hrs: 9 am-6 pm. Closed Sun; major hols. Bar. A la carte entrees: bkfst $3.50-$8.50; lunch, dinner $3.50-$9.50. Child's meals. Specializes in mesquite-smoked meats, salads, St Brendan's Irish cream cheese cake. Own desserts. Parking. Old World deli atmosphere. Extensive wine selection. No cr cds accepted.

JERRE ANNE CAFETERIA & BAKERY. *2640 Mitchell Ave.* 816/232-6585. Hrs: 11 am-7 pm. Closed Sun, Mon; major hols. Avg ck: lunch $5, dinner $6. Specialties: scalloped eggplant, fruit salad pie, pork tenderloin. Own baking. Family-owned. No cr cds accepted.

St Louis (C-7)

Settled 1764 **Pop** 396,685 **Elev** 470 ft **Area code** 314

One of the oldest settlements in the Mississippi Valley, St Louis was founded by Pierre Laclede as a fur-trading post. It was named for Louis IX of France. Early French settlers, a large German immigration in the mid-1800s and a happy mix of other national strains contribute to the city's cosmopolitan flavor. A flourishing French community by the time of the Revolutionary War, St Louis was attacked by a band of British-led Indians but was successfully defended by its citizens and a French garrison. In 1804, it was the scene of the transfer of Louisiana to the United States, which opened the way to the westward expansion that overran the peaceful town with immigrants and adventurers. The first Mississippi steamboat docked at St Louis in 1817. Missouri's first constitutional convention was held here in 1820. During the Civil War, though divided in sympathy, the city was a base of Union operations. In 1904, the Louisiana Purchase Exposition, known as the St Louis World's Fair, brought international fame to the city and added to its cultural resources; its first art museum was established in connection with the fair.

For more than 200 years St Louis has been the dominant city in the state. It is the home of St Louis University (1818), the University of Missouri-St Louis (1963) and Washington University (1853), which lies at the border of St Louis and Clayton (see). Distinguished by wealth, grace and culture, St Louis is also a city of solid and diversified industry. It is one of the world's largest markets for wool, lumber and pharmaceuticals and a principal grain and hog center. It is also the center for the only industrial area in the country producing six basic metals: iron, lead, zinc, copper, aluminum and magnesium. St Louis is an important producer of beer, chemicals and transportation equipment. Strategically located near the confluence of the Missouri and Mississippi rivers, the city is one of the country's major railroad terminals and trucking centers. Seven bridges span the Mississippi here.

After the steamboat era, St Louis grew westward, away from the riverfront, which deteriorated into slums. This original center of the city has now been developed as the Jefferson National Expansion Memorial. Municipal and private redevelopment of downtown and riverfront St Louis also has been outstanding: Cervantes Convention Center is the hub of the 16-square-block Convention Plaza; Busch Stadium brings St. Louis Cardinals fans into the downtown area; and the rehabilitated Union Station offers visitors a unique shopping experience within a restored turn-of-the-century railroad station.

Transportation

Airport: See ST LOUIS LAMBERT AIRPORT AREA.

Car Rental Agencies: See toll-free numbers under Introduction.

Public Transportation: Tri-State Transit System, phone 314/231-2345.

Rail Passenger Service: Amtrak phone 800/872-7245.

What to See and Do

Aloe Plaza. Across from Union Station. Contains extensive fountain group, by Carl Milles, symbolizing the meeting of the Mississippi and Missouri rivers. Market St between 18th & 20th Sts.

Anheuser-Busch, Inc. Guided brewery tours. (Daily exc Sun; closed hols) 13th & Lynch St. Phone 314/577-2626. **Free.**

Campbell House Museum. Mansion with original 1840-80 furnishings. (Mar-Dec, daily exc Mon; closed hols) 1508 Locust St. Phone 314/421-0325. ¢¢

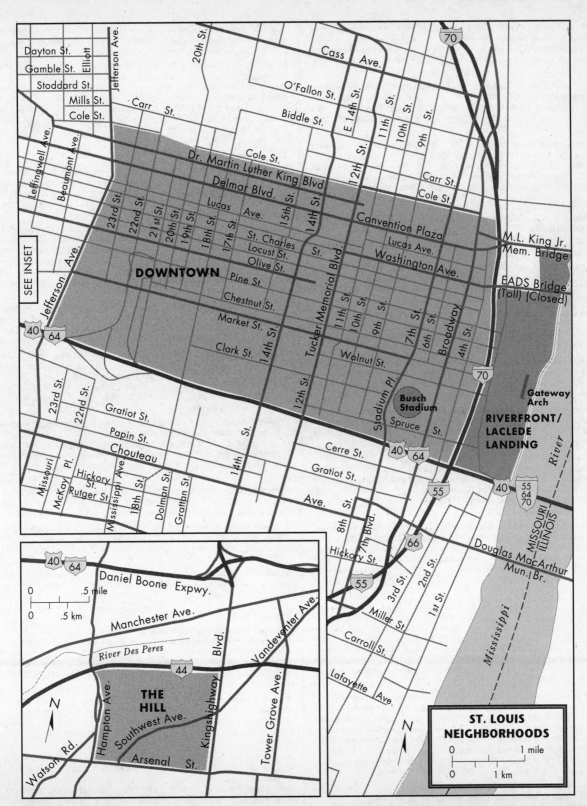

Dayton St.
Gamble St. Elliott
Stoddard St.
Mills St.
Cole St.

Jefferson Ave.
20th St.

Cass Ave.
70

O'Fallon St.

Carr St.
Biddle St.
E 14th St.
11th St.
10th St.
9th St.

Leffingwell Ave.
Beaumont Ave.

Cole St.
Dr. Martin Luther King Blvd
Delmar Blvd.
Lucas Ave.
12th St.
Carr St.
Cole St.

23rd St.
22nd St.
21st St.
20th St.
19th St.
18th St.
17th St.
15th St.
14th St.

Convention Plaza

M.L. King Jr.
Mem. Bridge

St. Charles St.
Locust St.
Olive St.
Lucas Ave.
Washington Ave.

EADS Bridge
(Toll) (Closed)

DOWNTOWN
Pine St.
Chestnut St.

Jefferson Ave.
40 64

Market St.
14th St.
Clark St.
Tucker Memorial Blvd.
11th St.
10th St.
9th St.
7th St.
6th St.
Broadway
4th St.

70

12th St.
Walnut St.
Stadium Pl.
Busch Stadium
Spruce St.

Gateway Arch

RIVERFRONT/
LACLEDE
LANDING

River

23rd St.
22nd St.
Gratiot St.
Papin St.
Chouteau

14th St.

Cerre St.
Gratiot St.
40 64

Missouri
McKay Pl.
Hickory St.
Rutger St.
Mississippi Ave.
18th St.
Dolman St.
Grattan St.

Ave.
St.
8th St.
7th Blvd.

55

40
55
64
70

SEE INSET

66

Hickory St.

Douglas MacArthur
Mun. Br.

MISSOURI
ILLINOIS

55

3rd St.
2nd St.

Miller St.

1st St.

Mississippi

Carroll St.

Lafayette Ave.

Inset map (THE HILL)

40 64
Daniel Boone Expwy.
Manchester Ave.
River Des Peres
44
THE HILL
Hampton Ave.
Kingshighway Blvd.
Vandeventer Ave.
Southwest Ave.
Tower Grove Ave.
Watson Rd.
Arsenal St.

0 .5 mile
0 .5 km
N

ST. LOUIS NEIGHBORHOODS legend

ST. LOUIS
NEIGHBORHOODS
0 1 mile
0 1 km
N

Cathedral of St Louis (1907). The city's cathedral is a fine example of Romanesque architecture with Byzantine details; the interior mosaic work is among the most extensive in the world. Mosaic museum (fee). Tours (by appt, fee). 4431 Lindell Blvd, at Newstead Ave. Phone 314/533-2824. **Free.**

Chatillon-De Menil Mansion. Antebellum, Greek-revival house with period furnishings; restaurant (lunch) in carriage house. Mansion on old Arsenal Hill in the colorful brewery district. Gift shop. (Wed-Sat; closed early-mid-Jan) 3352 De Menil Place. Phone 314/771-5828. Mansion ¢¢

Christ Church Cathedral (1859-1867). The first Episcopal parish west of the Mississippi River, founded 1819. English-Gothic, sandstone building; altar carved in England from stone taken from a quarry in Caen, France; Tiffany windows on north wall. Occasional concerts. (Daily exc Sat) Tours (Sun). 1210 Locust St. Phone 314/231-3454.

County parks.

Edgar M. Queeny Park. A 569-acre park. Swimming pool; hiking trail; tennis; ice rink (fee); picnicking, playground. (Daily) 19 mi W via I-64 (US 40) or Clayton Rd, S on Mason Rd. Phone 314/889-2863. **Free.**

Lone Elk Park. Approximately 400-acre preserve for bison, elk, deer and Barbados sheep. Picnicking. (Daily) MO 141 & N Outer Rd, 23 mi SW on I-44, adj Castlewood State Park. Phone 314/889-2863. **Free.**

Laumeier Sculpture Park. Sculpture of contemporary artists on grounds of the Laumeier mansion; art gallery (Wed-Sun). Nature trails. Picnic area. (Daily) Geyer & Rott Rds. Phone 314/821-1209. **Free.**

Eugene Field House and Toy Museum. (1845). Birthplace of famous children's poet; mementos, manuscripts and many original furnishings; antique toys and dolls. (Wed-Sat, also Sun afternoons; closed hols) 634 S Broadway. Phone 314/421-4689. ¢¢

✪ **Forest Park.** This 1,200-acre park was the site of most of the 1904 Louisiana Purchase Exposition. Many of the city's major attractions are here. (See SEASONAL EVENTS) W via I-64 (US 40), bounded by Skinker & Kingshighway Blvds and Oakland Ave. Phone 314/535-0100.

St Louis Science Center. Features eleven galleries with more than 600 exhibits. Also Omnimax theater, planetarium, Alien Research Project, childrens discovery room (various fees). Outdoor science park. Gift shops. Restaurant. (Daily; closed Jan 1, Thanksgiving, Dec 25) 5050 Oakland Ave. Phone 314/289-4400 or 800/456-SLSC. Exhibit areas **Free.**

History Museum-Missouri Historical Society. Exhibits on St Louis and the American West; artwork, costumes and decorative arts; toys, firearms; 19th-century fire-fighting equipment; St Louis history slide show; ragtime-rock 'n' roll music exhibit; 1904 World's Fair and Charles A. Lindbergh collections. (Daily exc Mon; closed some major hols) Jefferson Memorial Bldg, Lindell Blvd & DeBaliviere. Phone 314/746-4599. **Free.**

The St Louis Art Museum. Built for 1904 World's Fair as Palace of Fine Arts. Collections of American and European paintings, prints, drawings and decorative arts. Also African, Oriental and pre-Columbian art; 47-foot statue in front depicts St Louis the Crusader astride his horse. Lectures, films, workshops. Restaurant, museum shop. (Wed-Sun, also Tues afternoons; closed Jan 1, Thanksgiving, Dec 25) 1 Fine Arts Dr. Phone 314/721-0072. Admission **free.** Special exhibits ¢¢

St Louis Zoological Park. More than 3,400 animals in natural settings on 83 acres; apes and monkeys; walk-through aviary; big cat exhibit, cheetah survival exhibit; herpetarium; aquatic house. Living World education and visitor center features interactive computers, video displays, animatronic robot of Charles Darwin and live animals. Animal shows (summer; fee); children's zoo with contact area (fee); miniature railroad (mid-Mar-Nov, daily; fee). Zoo (daily; closed Jan 1, Dec 25). S side of park. Phone 314/781-0900. **Free.**

Steinberg Memorial Skating Rink. Roller-skating (May-Sept), ice-skating (Nov-Mar); rentals. Phone 314/361-5103. ¢¢

Jewel Box Floral Conservatory. 17½-acre site with formal lily pools; floral displays; special holiday shows. Free admission Mon & Tues mornings. (Daily) Wells & McKinley Drs. ¢

Grant's Farm. This 281-acre wooded tract contains a log cabin (1856) and land once owned by Ulysses S. Grant. Anheuser-Busch Clydesdale barn; carriage house with horse-drawn vehicles, trophy room; deer park where deer, buffalo, longhorn steer and other animals roam freely in their natural habitat; bird and elephant show, small animal feeding area. Tours by miniature train. (May-Sept, daily exc Mon; mid-Apr-May, Sept-mid-Oct, Thurs-Sun) 10501 Gravois Rd, SW via I-55. Phone 314/843-1700. **Free.**

Gray Line bus tours. Phone 314/241-1224.

Hidden Valley Ski Area. 2 triple chairlifts, 4 rope tows; patrol, school, rentals, snowmaking; cafeteria, restaurant, concession, bar. Longest run 1,760 ft; vertical drop 282 ft. (Dec-Mar, daily; closed Dec 24, 25) 28 mi W on I-44, then 3 mi S on MO F to Hidden Valley Dr in Eureka. Phone 314/938-5373 or -6999 (snow conditions). ¢¢¢¢¢

Jefferson Barracks Historical Park. Army post established in 1826, used through 1946. St Louis County now maintains 424 acres of the original tract. Restored buildings include stable (1851), laborer's house (1851), two powder magazines (1851 & 1857), ordnance room and visitor center. Picnicking. Buildings (Wed-Sun; closed Jan; also closed major hols). S Broadway at Kingston, 10 mi S on I-55, S Broadway exit. Phone 314/544-5714. **Free.**

Mercantile Money Museum. Counterfeiting, topical and informative money exhibits. Talking Benjamin Franklin mannequin tells money-related witticisms; "make-your-own" souvenir. (Daily) Mercantile Tower, 7th & Washington. Phone 314/421-1819. **Free.**

Missouri Botanical Garden. This 79-acre park includes rose, woodland and herb gardens; scented garden for the blind; electric tram rides (fee). Restaurant, floral display hall. Sections of the botanical garden are well over a century old. (Daily; closed Dec 25) Sr citizen rate. 4344 Shaw Blvd. Phone 314/577-9400 or 800/642-8842. Garden ¢¢ Included in admission are

Climatron. Seventy-foot high, prize-winning geodesic dome—first of its kind to be used as a conservatory—houses a two-level, half-acre tropical rain forest with canopies, rocky outcrops, waterfalls and mature tree collection; exhibits explain the many facets of a rain forest. Entrance to Climatron through series of sacred lotus and lily pools.

Japanese Garden. Largest traditional Japanese Garden in North America, with lake landscaped with many varieties of water iris, waterfalls, bridges and teahouse. Also here is

Tower Grove House (ca 1859). Restored country residence of garden founder, Henry Shaw; Victorian furnishings. In grove of trees before house is Shaw's Gothic-revival tomb. (Feb-Dec, daily; closed Dec 25) Phone 314/577-5150. ¢-¢¢

Museum of Transportation. Collection of locomotives, railway cars; city transit conveyances from horse-pulled carts to buses; highway vehicles. (Daily; closed Jan 1, Thanksgiving, Dec 25) Sr citizen rate. 16 mi SW via I-44, N on I-270 to Big Bend & Dougherty Ferry Rd exits, at 3015 Barrett Station Rd in Kirkwood. Phone 314/965-7998. ¢¢

National Bowling Hall of Fame & Museum. Exhibits and displays trace history of bowling from Egyptian child's game to present. Computerized and old-time alleys where visitors may bowl. Gift and snack shop. (Daily; closed Jan 1, Thanksgiving, Dec 24, 25, 31) Sr citizen rate. 111 Stadium Plaza, across from Busch Stadium. Phone 314/231-6340. ¢¢

Powell Symphony Hall (1925). Decorated in ivory and 24-karat gold leaf, the hall, built as a movie and vaudeville house, is now home of the **Saint Louis Symphony Orchestra** (mid-Sept-mid-May). 718 N Grand Blvd. Phone 314/533-2500 or 314/534-1700 (box office). After concert tours avail by appt.

Purina Farms. Domestic animals, educational graphic displays, videos, hands-on activities. Grain-bin theater. Petting areas, animal demonstrations, play area with maze, ponds. Snack bar, gift shop. Self-guided tours. (June-Aug, daily exc Mon; mid-Mar-May & Sept-Nov, Wed-Sun) Reservations required. 35 mi W via I-44, Gray Summit exit, then 2 blks N on MO 100 & 1 mi W on County MM, in Gray Summit. Phone 314/982-3232. **Free.**

⭐ **Riverfront area.**

Jefferson National Expansion Memorial. Eero Saarinen's **Gateway Arch** is a 630-foot, stainless steel arch that symbolizes the starting point of the westward expansion of the US. Visitor center (fee) includes capsule transporter to observation deck (fee). **Museum of Westward Expansion** offers exhibits on people and events of 19th-century western America, special exhibits and films (fee) on St Louis, construction of the arch and the westward movement (daily; closed Jan 1, Thanksgiving, Dec 25). Videotapes for the hearing impaired; tours for the visually impaired. Observation deck inaccessable to wheelchairs. **Note:** There is often a wait for observation-deck capsules, which are small and confining. 11 N 4th St. Phone 314/425-4465. Capsule to observation deck ¢¢; Museum ¢

Eads Bridge (1874). Designed by engineer James B. Eads, the Eads was the first bridge to span the wide, southern section of the Mississippi and the first bridge in which steel and the cantilever were used extensively; approach ramps are carried on enormous, Romanesque stone arches.

Laclede's Landing. Early St Louis commercial district (mid-1800s) includes nine-block area of renovated pre-Civil War and Victorian buildings that house specialty shops, restaurants and nightclubs. N edge of riverfront, between Eads and King bridges.

Delta Queen and *Mississippi Queen.* Paddlewheelers offer 3-12 night cruises on the Ohio, Cumberland, Mississippi and Tennessee rivers. Contact Delta Queen Steamboat Co, 30 Robin St Wharf, New Orleans, LA 70130-1890; phone 800/543-1949.

Gateway Riverboat Cruises. One-hour narrated cruise of the Mississippi River aboard the *Huck Finn*, *Tom Sawyer* and *Becky Thatcher* riverboats, replicas of 19th-century stern-wheelers. (Memorial Day-Labor Day, daily) Dock below Gateway Arch. Phone 314/621-4040 or 800/878-7411. ¢¢¢

Admiral Riverboat Casino. (Daily) Dock below Gateway Arch. Phone 314/621-4040. Admission ¢¢¢

Old Courthouse. Begun in 1837 and completed in 1862, this building houses five museum galleries on St Louis history, including various displays, dioramas and films; two restored courtrooms. First two trials of the Dred Scott case were held in this building. Guided tour. (Daily; closed Jan 1, Thanksgiving, Dec 25) 11 N 4th St, at Market St. Phone 314/425-4465. **Free.**

Old Cathedral (1831). Basilica of St Louis, King of France, on the site of the first church built in St Louis in 1770; museum on the west side contains the original church bell and other religious artifacts. (Daily) 209 Walnut St, at Memorial Dr, under Gateway Arch. Phone 314/231-3250. **Free.** Museum ¢

Shopping.

St Louis Union Station. This block-long, stone, chateauesque railroad station (1894) was the world's busiest passenger terminal from 1905 to the late 1940s. After the last train pulled out—on Oct 31, 1978—the station and train shed were restored and redeveloped as a marketplace with more than 100 specialty shops and restaurants, nightclubs and hotel (see HOTELS), as well as entertainment areas, plazas and a 1½-acre lake. The station was designed by a local architect to be modeled after a walled medieval city in Southern France; its interior features high Romanesque and Sullivanesque design. "Memories," a collection of photographs, letters, memorabilia and films, brings the history of the station to life. Special historical tours and festivities will be held during the 1994 centennial. Market St, between 18th & 20th Sts. For more information phone 314/421-6655 or -4314.

St Louis Centre. One of the largest urban shopping malls in the country, features 130 shops and Taste of St Louis food court with 28 restaurants. (Daily) Locust & 6th Sts, downtown.

West Port Plaza. Alpine-like setting with approximately 30 European-style shops and 20 restaurants. (Daily). Approx 15 mi W via I-64 (US 40), N on I-270, E on Page Blvd to West Port Plaza Dr, in Maryland Heights.

Six Flags Over Mid-America. A 200-acre entertainment park with more than 100 rides, shows and attractions, including wooden and looping steel roller coasters and whitewater raft rides. (Late May-late Aug, daily; Mar-late May & late Aug-late Oct, wkends) Sr citizen rate. 30 mi SW via I-44, exit 261, in Eureka. Phone 314/938-4800. ¢¢¢¢

Soldiers' Memorial Military Museum. Honoring St Louis' war dead; memorabilia from pre-Civil War, World War I, World War II, Korea and Vietnam. (Daily; closed Jan 1, Thanksgiving, Dec 25) 1315 Chestnut St. Phone 314/622-4550. **Free.**

St Louis Cardinals Hall of Fame Museum. St Louis baseball from 1860 to present; Stan Musial memorabilia. Gift shop. Also stadium tours (Apr-Dec, daily; rest of yr, limited hrs). Building (daily). Busch Stadium, 100 Stadium Plaza; between gates 5 & 6. Phone 314/421-3263. ¢¢

St Louis University (1818). (10,000 students) Oldest university west of the Mississippi River; includes Pius XII Memorial Library with Vatican Microfilm Library—the only depository for copies of Vatican documents in the Western Hemisphere (academic yr, daily; closed hols). 221 N Grand. Phone 314/977-3087 or -2222. Also here is

Cupples House and Art Gallery. Historic Romanesque building (1889) with 42 rooms, 22 fireplaces, original furnishings, period pieces; houses 20th-century graphics collection. (Tues-Fri & Sun, limited hrs) Sr citizen rate. 3673 W Pine Blvd. Phone 314/977-3025. ¢

State parks.

Mastodon. Excavation of mastodon remains and Native American artifacts; museum (fee). Fishing. Hiking. Picnicking. Standard fees. (Daily) 20 mi S off US 55, near US 67 Imperial exit. Phone 314/464-2976. **Free.**

Dr. Edmund A. Babler Memorial. Approx 2,500 acres. Swimming pool. Hiking trail. Picnicking, playground. Improved camping (dump station). Interpretive center, naturalist. Standard fees. (Daily) 25 mi W on MO 100, then N on MO 109. Phone 314/458-3813. **Free.**

The Dog Museum. Museum with exhibits of dog-related art; reference library, videotapes. (Tues-Sat, also Sun afternoons; closed major hols) Sr citizen rate. W via I-64 (US 40) to 1721 Mason Road, in Edgar M. Queeny Park. Phone 314/821-3647. ¢¢

The Magic House, St Louis Children's Museum. Hands-on exhibits include electrostatic generator and a three-story circular slide. (Memorial Day-Labor Day , daily exc Mon; rest of yr limited hrs; closed some major hols) 8 mi W via I-44, Lindbergh exit at 516 S Kirkwood Rd in Kirkwood. Phone 314/822-8900. ¢¢

Annual Events

Gypsy Caravan. One of the largest flea markets in the midwest, with more than 600 vendors; arts & crafts, entertainment, concessions. Memorial Day.

VP Fair. On riverfront. Three-day festival with parade, food, air & water shows, entertainment. July 4 wkend.

Great Forest Park Balloon Race. Forest Park. Food, entertainment, parachute jumps and other contests. Sept.

Seasonal Events

Muny Opera. Forest Park. 12,000-seat outdoor theater. Light opera and musical comedy. Phone 314/361-1900. Mid-June-Aug.

Saint Louis Symphony Orchestra. Edgar M. Queeny Park. Outdoor pops concerts. July-early Aug.

Repertory Theatre of St Louis. 130 Edgar Rd, off I-44 Elm St exit in Webster Groves. Nine-play season includes classics and new works. Phone 314/968-4925. Sept-Apr.

Muny Student Theater. 560 Trinity Ave. Childrens and family performances. Phone 314/862-1255. Sept-May.

Professional sports. Busch Stadium, Broadway & Walnut Sts, Cardinals (baseball), phone 314/421-3060. St Louis Arena, 5700 Oakland Ave: Blues (hockey), phone 314/622-2500.

Additional Visitor Information

The St Louis Convention & Visitors Commission, 10 S Broadway, Suite 1000, 63102, has brochures on things to see in St Louis; phone 314/421-1023 or 800/325-7962. Also obtain brochures at the St Louis Visitors Center, 308 Washington Ave, 63102; phone 314/241-1764. *St Louis Magazine*, at newsstands, has up-to-date information on cultural events and articles of interest to visitors. For 24-hour tourist information phone 314/421-2100.

St Louis Area Suburbs

The following suburbs in the St Louis area are included in the *Mobil Travel Guide*. For information on any one of them, see the individual alphabetical listing. Clayton, St Charles, Wentzville.

St Louis Lambert Airport Area

For additional accommodations, see ST LOUIS LAMBERT AIRPORT AREA, which follows ST LOUIS.

City Neighborhoods

Many of the restaurants, unrated dining establishments and some lodgings listed under St Louis include neighborhoods as well as exact street addresses. A map showing these neighborhoods can be found immediately following the city map. Geographic descriptions of these areas are given, followed by a table of restaurants arranged by neighborhood.

Downtown: South of Martin Luther King Blvd, west of I-70, north of I-64 (US 40) and east of Jefferson Ave. **North of Downtown:** North of Martin Luther King Blvd. **South of Downtown:** South of I-64. **West of Downtown:** West of Jefferson Ave.

The Hill: South of I-44, west of Kingshighway Blvd, north of Arsenal St and east of Hampton Ave.

Riverfront/Laclede Landing: On Mississippi River south of Eads Bridge, east of I-70 and north of I-40; Laclede Landing on riverfront directly north of Eads Bridge and south of M.L. King Jr Memorial Bridge.

ST LOUIS RESTAURANTS BY NEIGHBORHOOD AREAS

(For full description, see alphabetical listings under Restaurants)

DOWNTOWN

Cafe De France. 410 Olive St

Charlie Gitto's. 207 N 6th St

Faust's (Adam's Mark Hotel). 4th & Chestnut

Hannegan's. 719 N Second St

J.F. Sanfilippo's. 705 N Broadway

Just Jazz (Hotel Majestic). 1019 Pine St

Kemoll's. 1 Metropolitan Square

Mike Shannon's. 100 N 7th St

Premio. 7th & Market Sts

Tony's. 410 Market St

NORTH OF DOWNTOWN

Crown Candy Kitchen. 1401 St Louis Ave

Mandarin House. 9150 Overland Plaza

SOUTH OF DOWNTOWN

Bevo Mill. 4749 Gravois Ave

Patty Long's 9th Street Abbey. 1808 S 9th St

Sidney Street Cafe. 2000 Sidney St

WEST OF DOWNTOWN

Blueberry Hill. 6504 Delmar Blvd

Chuy Arzola's. 6405 Clayton Ave

Dierdorf & Hart's. 323 West Port Plaza

Harry's. 2144 Market St

House Of India. 8501 Delmar Blvd

Lombardo's (Drury Inn Union Station). 201 S 20th St

Mandarin House. 194 Union Station

Marciano's. 333 West Port Plaza

Robata Of Japan. 111 West Port Plaza

Saleem's. 6501 Delmar Blvd

Sunshine Inn. 8 1/2 S Euclid Ave

THE HILL

Bruno's Little Italy. 5901 Southwest Ave

Cunetto House Of Pasta. 5453 Magnolia Ave

Dominic's. 5101 Wilson Ave

Gian Peppe's. 2126 Marconi Ave

Gino's. 4502 Hampton Ave

Giovanni's. 5201 Shaw Ave

Lorusso's Cucina. 3121 Watson Rd

Mama Campisi's. 2132 Edwards St

O'Connells Pub. 4652 Shaw Ave

Zia's. 5256 Wilson Ave

Note: When a listing is located in a town that does not have its own city heading, it will appear under the city nearest to its location. In these cases, the address and town appear in parenthesis immediately following the name of the establishment.

Motels

✔ ★ **COMFORT INN SOUTHWEST.** *(3730 S Lindbergh Blvd, Sunset Hills 63127) SW via I-44 to S Lindbergh Blvd, south of downtown.* 314/842-1200; FAX 314/849-7220. 100 rms, 2 story. S $49-$61; D $57-$78; each addl $4; under 18 free. Crib $3. Pet accepted, some restrictions; $25 deposit. TV; cable (premium). Pool. Complimentary continental bkfst. Restaurant 11 am-10 pm; Sat to 11 pm. Bar. Ck-out noon. Business servs avail. In-rm link. Exercise equipt: weight machine, bicycle, whirlpool. Cr cds: A, C, D, DS, ER, MC, V.

🐾 🖾 🏋 🐾 🐾 SC

★ ★ **COURTYARD BY MARRIOTT.** *2340 Market St (63103), near Union Station, west of downtown.* 314/241-9111; FAX 314/241-8113. 151 rms, 4 story, 12 suites. S, D $72-$115; suites $98-$135; under 18 free; wkly rates. Crib free. TV; cable (premium). Indoor pool. Complimentary coffee in rms. Bkfst avail. Ck-out noon. Business servs avail. In-rm modem link. Valet serv. Exercise equipt: weight benches, bicycles, whirlpool. Some balconies. Cr cds: A, C, D, DS, MC, V.

D 🖾 🏋 🐾 🐾 SC

★ ★ **RESIDENCE INN BY MARRIOTT.** *1881 Craigshire Rd (63146), north of downtown.* 314/469-0060; FAX 314/469-3751. 128 kit. suites, 2 story. Suites $109-$159; wkly, wkend plans. Crib free. Pet accepted; $25. TV; cable (premium), VCR (movies avail $4). Heated pool; whirlpool. Complimentary continental bkfst. Restaurant adj 6 am-10:30 pm. Ck-out noon. Coin lndry. Meeting rm.

Business servs avail. In-rm modem link. Airport transportation. Health club privileges. Lawn games. Refrigerators; many fireplaces. Private patios, balconies. Picnic tables, grills. Library. Cr cds: A, C, D, DS; MC, V.

D ✋ ≈ ⊠ ⋒ SC

★ ★ SUMMERFIELD SUITES. *1855 Craigshire Rd (63146), I-270, Page Ave exit E to Craigshire Rd, north of downtown.* 314/878-1555; res: 800/833-4353; FAX 314/878-9203. 106 kit. suites, 2 story. 1-bedrm $139; 2-bedrm $159; wkend rates. Crib free. Pet accepted, some restrictions; $75. TV; cable (premium), VCR (movies avail $2). Heated pool. Complimentary continental bkfst. Complimentary coffee in rms. Restaurant nearby. Ck-out noon. Coin lndry. Meeting rms. Business servs avail. In-rm modem link. Valet serv. Sundries. Free airport transportation. Exercise equipt; weight machine, bicycles, whirlpool. Picnic tables, grills. Cr cds: A, C, D, DS, MC, V.

D ✋ ≈ 🕴 ⊠ ⋒ SC

Motor Hotels

★ ★ ★ HILTON FRONTENAC. *(1335 S Lindbergh Blvd 63131 W via I-64 (US 40), at S Lindbergh Blvd.* 314/993-1100; FAX 314/993-8546. 266 rms, 3 story. S, D $89-$180; each addl $10; suites $120-$500; under 14 free; wkend, wkly rates. Crib free. TV; cable (premium), VCR avail. Pool; poolside serv, lifeguard. Restaurant 6:30 am-10 pm. Rm serv. Bar 11-1 am; entertainment, dancing Thurs-Sat. Ck-out noon. Convention facilities. Business center. In-rm modem link. Bellhops. Valet serv. Sundries. Gift shop. Free airport transportation. Exercise equipt; weights, bicycles, sauna. Luxury level. Cr cds: A, C, D, DS, ER, MC, V.

D ≈ 🕴 🕴 ⊠ ⋒ SC 🕴

✔ ★ ★ HOLIDAY INN-SOUTHWEST. *10709 Watson Rd (63127), SW via I-44 exit 277B, Lindbergh Blvd to Watson Rd, south of downtown.* 314/821-6600; FAX 314/822-7614. 144 rms, 4 story. May-Sept: S $84-$109; D $87-$109; each addl $10; suites $100-$130; under 18 free; lower rates rest of yr. Crib free. TV; cable (premium). Pool. Complimentary coffee in rms. Restaurant 6:30 am-2 pm, 5-10 pm. Rm serv. Bar 11-1 am; entertainment, dancing. Ck-out noon. Meeting rms. Business servs avail. In-rm modem link. Bellhops. Valet serv. Airport transportation. Health club privileges. Game rm. Some bathrm phones; refrigerators. Cr cds: A, C, D, DS, ER, JCB, MC, V.

D ≈ ⊠ ⋒ SC

Hotels

★ ★ ★ ADAM'S MARK. *4th & Chestnut (63102), opp Gateway Arch, downtown.* 314/241-7400; res: 800/444-2326; FAX 314/241-9839. 910 rms, 18 story. S $149-$179; D $169-$199; each addl $15; suites $185-$1,200; under 18 free; wkend packages. Crib free. Garage parking $1/hr, in/out $10 unlimited; valet $3. TV; cable, VCR avail. 2 heated pools, 1 indoor; poolside serv. Afternoon tea. Restaurant 6 am-midnight (also see FAUST'S). Rm serv 24 hrs. Bar 11-2 am; entertainment, dancing exc Sun. Ck-out noon. Convention facilities. Business center. In-rm modem link. Concierge. Shopping arcade. Barber, beauty shop. Exercise rm; instructor, weight machines, bicycles, whirlpool, sauna. Bathrm phones; some refrigerators. Three-story atrium lobby decorated with bronze equestrian sculpture by De Luigi. View of Gateway Arch & riverfront from many rms; near Laclede's Landing & riverfront showboats. Luxury level. Cr cds: A, C, D, DS, MC, V.

D ≈ 🕴 🕴 ⊠ ⋒ SC 🕴

★ ★ DOUBLETREE DOWNTOWN. *806 St Charles St (63101), downtown.* 314/421-2500; FAX 314/421-6254. 184 units, 18 story. S $125-$145; D $135-$155; each addl $10; under 18 free. Crib free. Parking $9-$11. TV; cable. Restaurants 6:30 am-10:30 pm. Bar 11:30 am-midnight. Ck-out noon. Meeting rms. Business servs avail. In-rm modem link. Exercise equipt; weight machine, bicycles. Bathrm phones, refrigerators, minibars; some wet bars, fireplaces. Renovated

1925 landmark hotel with preserved millwork. Cr cds: A, C, D, DS, ER, JCB, MC, V.

D 🕴 ⊠ ⋒ SC

★ ★ ★ DOUBLETREE HOTEL & CONFERENCE CENTER. *(16625 Swingley Ridge Rd, Chesterfield 63017) Approx 20 mi W on I-64 (US 40), exit 19A, N to Swingley Ridge Rd.* 314/532-5000; FAX 314/532-9984. 223 rms, 12 story. S $150; D $165; under 18 free; wkend rates. Crib free. TV; cable (premium), VCR avail. 2 pools, 1 indoor; wading pool, poolside serv, lifeguard. Supervised child's activities; ages 1-13. Restaurant 6:30-10 pm. Bar 11-1 am. Ck-out noon. Meeting rms. Business center. In-rm modem link. Gift shop. Free airport, local transportation. Lighted tennis. Exercise rm; instructor, weights, bicycles, whirlpool, steam rm, sauna. Rec rm. Refrigerators avail. Luxury level. Cr cds: A, C, D, DS, ER, JCB, MC, V.

D 🕴 ≈ 🕴 🕴 ⊠ ⋒ SC 🕴

★ ★ DRURY INN UNION STATION. *201 S 20th St (63103), west of downtown.* 314/231-3900. 176 rms, 7 story. Apr-Oct: S $94-$119; D $104-$129; each addl $10; suites $135; under 18 free; hol rates; lower rates rest of yr. Crib avail. Pet accepted, some restrictions. TV; cable (premium), VCR avail. Indoor pool; whirlpool, lifeguard. Complimentary continental bkfst. Restaurant (see LOMBARDO'S). Bar. Ck-out noon. Coin lndry. Meeting rms. Business servs avail. In-rm modem link. No bellhops. Exercise equipt; weight machine, treadmill. Some refrigerators. Restored 1907 railroad hotel. Cr cds: A, C, D, DS, MC, V.

D ✋ ≈ 🕴 ⊠ ⋒ SC

★ ★ DRURY INN-GATEWAY ARCH. *711 N Broadway (63102), in Union Market Building, downtown.* 314/231-8100. 178 rms, 2 flrs in 6 story bldg. May-Sept: S $89-$104; D $99-$104; each addl $10; under 18 free; wkend rates; higher rates July 4th; lower rates rest of yr. Crib free. Pet accepted, some restrictions. TV; cable (premium). Indoor pool; whirlpool, poolside serv, lifeguard. Complimentary continental bkfst. Restaurant adj 11 am-2 pm, 4:30-11 pm; wkend hrs vary. Ck-out noon. Meeting rms. Business servs avail. In-rm modem link. No bellhops. Health club privileges. Some refrigerators. Cr cds: A, C, D, DS, MC, V.

D ✋ ≈ ⊠ SC

★ ★ EMBASSY SUITES. *901 N 1st St (63102), downtown.* 314/241-4200; FAX 314/241-6513. 297 suites, 8 story. S, D $140-$180; each addl $15; under 18 free; wkend rates. Crib free. Pet accepted, some restrictions; $200 deposit. TV; cable (premium), VCR avail (movies avail). Indoor pool; wading pool, lifeguard. Complimentary bkfst served in atrium. Restaurant 11 am-11 pm. Bar to 3 am. Ck-out noon. Lndry facilities. Meeting rms. Business servs avail. In-rm modem link. Exercise equipt; treadmill, bicycles, whirlpool. Game rm. Refrigerators, wet bars. Balconies. 8-story atrium courtyard. Cr cds: A, C, D, DS, JCB, MC, V.

D ✋ ≈ 🕴 ⊠ ⋒ SC

★ ★ HAMPTON INN. *2211 Market St (63103), opp Union Station, west of downtown.* 314/241-3200. 239 rms, 11 story, 9 suites. S $79-$89; D $85-$94; suites $110-$125; under 18 free; wkend rates. Crib free. Pet accepted, some restrictions. TV; cable (premium), VCR avail. Indoor pool. Complimentary continental bkfst. Restaurant 11-3 am. Bar. Ck-out noon. Coin lndry. Business servs avail. In-rm modem link. No bellhops. Free garage parking. Exercise equipt; weights, bicycles, whirlpool. Cr cds: A, C, D, DS, MC, V.

D ✋ ≈ 🕴 ⊠ ⋒ SC

✔ ★ ★ HOLIDAY INN-DOWNTOWN RIVERFRONT. *200 N 4th St (63102), downtown.* 314/621-8200; FAX 314/621-8073. 456 rms, 29 story, 167 kits. S $49-$89; D $59-$99; each addl $10; suites $69-$175; under 17 free; wkend rates; higher rates: July 4th. Crib free. Pet accepted, some restrictions. TV; VCR avail. Pool; lifeguard. Restaurant 6:30 am-2 pm, 4:30-10 pm; 24-hr deli. Bar 11-3 am; Sun 1 pm-midnight. Ck-out noon. Meeting rms. Business servs avail. Gift shop. Garage. Game rm. Some balconies. Cr cds: A, C, D, DS, ER, MC, V.

D ✋ ≈ ⊠ ⋒ SC

★ ★ ★ **HOTEL MAJESTIC.** *1019 Pine St (63101), downtown.* 314/436-2355; res: 800/451-2355; FAX 314/436-0223. 91 units, 9 story. S, D $155; each addl $15; suites $290-$850; studio rms $290; under 12 free; wkend rates. Crib free. Valet, in/out parking $8. TV; cable (premium), VCR avail. Coffee in rms. Complimentary continental bkfst. Restaurant (see JUST JAZZ). Rm serv 24 hrs. Bar 11-1 am; in season to 3 am; entertainment 8 pm-midnight. Ck-out noon. Meeting rms. Business servs avail. In-rm modem link. Concierge. Airport transportation. Bathrm phones, minibars. European elegance in 1914 building; marble floors, Oriental rugs. Individually decorated rms. Cr cds: A, C, D, DS, ER, MC, V.

[D] [≈] [⩩] [🔥] [SC]

★ ★ ★ **HYATT REGENCY AT UNION STATION.** *One St. Louis Union Station (63103), west of downtown.* 314/231-1234; FAX 314/923-3971. 538 rms, 6 story. S, D $114-$160; each addl $25; under 18 free; wkend rates. Crib free. Valet parking $12. TV; cable (premium), VCR avail. Outdoor pool; lifeguard. Restaurant 6:30 am-10:30 pm. Bar 11-1:30 am. Ck-out noon. Convention facilities. Business center. In-rm modem link. Shopping arcade. Exercise equipt; weight machine, stair machine, bicycles. Refrigerators avail. Bathrm phones. In renovated Union Station railroad terminal (1894); main lobby and lounge occupy Grand Hall, which features rare marble, barrel-vaulted frescoed ceilings, elaborate gold-leafed plasterwork and stained-glass window depicting St Louis as "Crossroads of America." Luxury level. Cr cds: A, C, D, DS, ER, JCB, MC, V.

[D] [≈] [🕴] [⩩] [🔥] [SC] [👤]

★ ★ ★ **MARRIOTT PAVILION.** *1 Broadway (63102), downtown.* 314/421-1776; FAX 314/331-9269. 672 rms, 22-25 story. S $125; D $145; each addl $15; under 18 free; wkend rates. Garage, in/out $11, valet $14. Pet accepted, some restrictions. TV; cable (premium), VCR avail. Pool; poolside serv, lifeguard. Restaurant 6:30 am-11 pm. Bar 11-1 am. Ck-out noon. Coin lndry. Convention facilities. Business center. In-rm modem link. Concierge. Gift shop. Exercise equipt; weights, bicycles, whirlpool, sauna. Some bathrm phones, refrigerators. Luxury level. Cr cds: A, C, D, DS, MC, V.

[D] [🐾] [≈] [🕴] [⩩] [🔥] [SC] [👤]

★ ★ ★ **REGAL RIVERFRONT.** *200 S 4th St (63102), downtown.* 314/241-9500; res: 800/222-8888; FAX 314/241-9977. 780 rms, 28 story. S $117-$137; D $132-$152; each addl $15; suites $350-$1,000; under 18 free; weekly, wkend rates; higher rates: baseball games, some hols. Crib free. Garage parking $9.50. TV; cable (premium), VCR avail. 2 pools, 1 indoor; wading pool, poolside serv, lifeguard. Restaurant 6:30 am-10 pm. Bar. Ck-out noon. Coin lndry. Convention facilities. Business center. Gift shop. Barber, beauty shop. Exercise equipt; weight machine, bicycles. Game rm. Renovated hotel near river. Luxury level. Cr cds: A, C, D, DS, ER, JCB, MC, V.

[D] [≈] [🕴] [⩩] [🔥] [SC] [👤]

★ ★ ★ ★ **THE RITZ-CARLTON, ST LOUIS.** *100 Carondelet Plaza (63105), 7 mi W on I-64, Hanley exit, in downtown Clayton.* 314/863-6300; res: 800/241-3333; FAX 314/863-4325. Fine oil paintings and 18th- and 19th-century antiques decorate public areas throughout the hotel. Some guest rooms on the top floors offer views of the skyline. 301 rms, 18 story, 34 suites. S, D $155-$215; suites $295-$1,500; under 12 free; wkend, package plans. Crib free. Garage, valet parking in/out $10/day. TV; cable (premium), VCR avail. Indoor pool; poolside serv. Restaurant (see THE GRILL). Rm serv 24 hrs. Bar 11-1 am; entertainment. Ck-out noon. Convention facilities. Business center. In-rm modem link. Concierge. Gift shop. Airport transportation. Exercise rm; instructor (by appt), weight machine, bicycles, whirlpool, sauna, steam rm. Massage. Bathrm phones, refrigerators, minibars. Complimentary newspaper. Luxury level. Cr cds: A, C, D, DS, JCB, MC, V.

[D] [≈] [🕴] [⩩] [🔥] [👤]

★ ★ ★ **SHERATON PLAZA.** *900 West Port Plaza (63146), W via I-64 (US 40), N on I-270 to Page Ave exit, west of downtown.* 314/434-5010; FAX 314/434-0140. 209 rms, 12 story. S $115; D $125-$129; each addl $10; suites $179-$338; under 18 free; wkend rates. Crib free. TV; cable (premium), VCR avail. Indoor pool; whirlpool, sauna. Complimentary coffee in rms. Restaurant 6:30 am-10:30 pm. Bar 11-1 am.

Ck-out 1 pm. Meeting rms. Business servs avail. In-rm modem link. Concierge. Free covered parking. Free airport transportation. Tennis & health club privileges. Some refrigerators. Fully landscaped pool area. Cr cds: A, C, D, DS, JCB, MC, V.

[D] [≈] [🕴] [⩩] [🔥] [SC]

★ ★ ★ **SHERATON-WEST PORT INN.** *191 West Port Plaza (63146), W via I-64 (US 40), N on I-270 to Page Ave exit, west of downtown.* 314/878-1500; FAX 314/878-2837. 300 rms, 4-6 story. S, D $125-$135; suites $160-$265; under 18 free; wkend rates. Pet accepted, some restrictions. TV; cable (premium), VCR avail. Pool; poolside serv, lifeguard. Complimentary coffee in rms. Restaurant 6:30 am-10:30 pm. Bar 11-1 am; pianist Tues-Sat. Ck-out 1 pm. Convention facilities. Business servs avail. In-rm modem link. Concierge. Free covered parking. Free airport transportation. Health club privileges. Some refrigerators. Some balconies. In shopping plaza. Cr cds: A, C, D, DS, JCB, MC, V.

[D] [🐾] [≈] [🕴] [⩩] [🔥] [SC]

Restaurants

★ ★ ★ **AGOSTINO'S COLOSSEUM.** *(12949 Olive Blvd, Creve Coeur 63141) 14 mi W on I-64 (US 40) to I-270, N on I-270 to Olive Blvd, 2 mi W.* 314/434-2959. Hrs: 5 pm-midnight. Closed Sun; major hols. Res accepted. Italian menu. Bar. Wine cellar. A la carte entrees: dinner $12.95-$15.95. Child's meals. Specialties: salmone al Siciliana, costoletta di vitello alla Sicilia, maccheroni del Vesuvio. Own baking. Jacket. Cr cds: A, C, D, DS, ER, MC, V.

[D] [⩩]

★ ★ **BEVO MILL.** *4749 Gravois Ave (63116), south of downtown.* 314/481-2626. Hrs: 11 am-9 pm; Sat to 10 pm; early-bird dinner Mon-Fri 3-5 pm; Sun brunch 10 am-2 pm. Closed Dec 25. Res accepted. German menu. Bar. Semi-a la carte: lunch $4.95-$7.95, dinner $10.95-$17.95. Sun brunch $8.95. Child's meals. Specializes in sauerbraten, Wienerschnitzel, fresh seafood. Own baking. Parking. Large stone fireplace. Bavarian exterior; operable windmill. Cr cds: A, C, D, MC, V.

[D] [⩩]

✔ ★ ★ **BIG SKY CAFE.** *(47 S Old Orchard, Webster Groves 63119) 8 mi W on I-44, Shrewsbury West exit, S on Big Bend.* 314/962-5757. Hrs: 5:30-10 pm; Fri & Sat 5-11 pm; Sun 4:30-9:30 pm. Closed some major hols. Res accepted. Bar. A la carte entrees: dinner $7.50-$12.95. Specialties: pecan encrusted catfish, barbecued salmon, roasted garlic mashed potatoes. Parking. Outdoor dining. Eclectic decor. Cr cds: MC, V.

[D]

★ ★ **BRISTOL BAR & GRILL.** *(11801 Olive Blvd, Creve Coeur 63141) 14 mi W on I-64 to I-270, N to Olive Blvd, turn E.* 314/567-0272. Hrs: 11:30 am-2:30 pm, 5:30-10 pm; Fri & Sat 5-10:30 pm; Sun 10 am-2 pm, 5-9 pm. Closed Memorial Day, July 4, Dec 25. Res accepted. Bar to 11:30 am. Semi-a la carte: lunch $5.95-$10.95, dinner $7.95-$19.95. Sun brunch $13.95. Child's meals. Specializes in mesquite-grilled seafood, steak, fresh fish. Own pastries. Stained-glass windows. Cr cds: A, C, D, DS, MC, V.

[D] [⩩]

★ ★ ★ **BRUNO'S LITTLE ITALY.** *5901 Southwest Ave (63139), on The Hill.* 314/781-5988. Hrs: 5-11 pm. Closed Mon; major hols. Res accepted Fri-Sun. Italian menu. Bar. Wine cellar. Semi-a la carte: dinner $12-$18. Specialties: papardelle alla Genovese, veal Vesuvio, fresh salmon. Own pastries. Located in old Italian neighborhood. Antiques, stained glass, original art. Cr cds: A, C, D, DS, MC, V.

[D]

★ ★ ★ **CAFE DE FRANCE.** *410 Olive St, downtown.* 314/231-2204. Hrs: 11:30 am-2 pm, 5:30-10:30 pm; Fri to 11:30 pm; Sat 5:30-11:30 pm. Closed Sun; most major hols. Res accepted. French menu. Bar. Wine cellar. A la carte entrees: lunch $5-$12, dinner $15-$22.

Complete meals: dinner (3, 4 & 5 courses) $18.50, $25.50 & $28.50. Specializes in fresh seafood, breast of duck, game. Own baking. Valet parking. European ambience. Jacket. Cr cds: A, C, D, DS, ER, MC, V.

★ **CHANEY'S.** *(8224 Olive St Rd, University City 63132) W on I-64 to US 170, N to Olive St (exit 3A), then E for 6 blks.* 314/993-1716. Hrs: 10:30 am-10 pm; Fri & Sat 11 pm; Sun 2-9 pm. Closed Easter, Thanksgiving, Dec 25; also Sun Nov-Feb. Res accepted Sat & Sun. Bar. Semi-a la carte: lunch, dinner $3.50-$13.85. Specializes in barbecue. Parking. Outdoor dining. Family-owned since 1945. Cr cds: A, D, DS, MC, V.

✔ ★ **CHARLIE GITTO'S.** *207 N 6th St (63101), downtown.* 314/436-2828. Hrs: 11 am-10:30 pm, to 11:30 Fri & Sat. Closed Sun; some major hols. Italian, Amer menu. Bar. A la carte entrees: lunch $5-$8, dinner $7.95-$14.95. Child's meals. Specializes in veal, seafood, pasta. Sports bar atmosphere. Cr cds: A, D, DS, MC, V.

★ **CHUY ARZOLA'S.** *6405 Clayton Ave (63139), west of downtown.* 314/644-4430. Hrs: 11 am-10 pm; Fri & Sat to 11 pm; Sun 4-9 pm. Closed most major hols. Mexican menu. Bar. Semi-a la carte: lunch, dinner $3.95-$7.95. Specializes in fajitas. Parking. Casual neighborhood establishment. Cr cds: DS, MC, V.

✔ ★ ★ **CUNETTO HOUSE OF PASTA.** *5453 Magnolia Ave (63139), on The Hill.* 314/781-1135. Hrs: 11 am-2 pm, 5-10:30 pm; Fri to 11:30 pm; Sat 5-11:30 pm. Closed Sun; major hols. Italian menu. Bar 11 am-11:30 pm. Semi-a la carte: lunch $4-$9, dinner $6.75-$12. Child's meals. Specialties: linguine tutto mare, veal with crabmeat, Sicilian steak. Parking. In old Italian neighborhood. Cr cds: A, C, D, MC, V.

★ ★ **DIERDORF & HART'S.** *323 West Port Plaza (63146), W via I-64 (US 40) to I-270, N on I-270 to Page Ave exit, west of downtown.* 314/878-1801. Hrs: 11 am-10 pm; Fri to 11 pm; Sat 4:30-11 pm; Sun 4:30-10 pm. Closed July 4, Thanksgiving. Res accepted. Bar to 12:30 am; Fri & Sat to 1:30 am. Semi-a la carte: lunch $5.95-$11.95, dinner $13.50-$39.50. Specializes in steak, broiled seafood. Pianist Tues-Sat. 1940s steakhouse atmosphere. Jacket. Cr cds: A, C, D, DS, MC, V.

★ ★ **DOMINIC'S.** *5101 Wilson Ave (63110), on The Hill.* 314/771-1632. Hrs: 5 pm-midnight. Closed Sun; major hols. Res accepted. Italian menu. Bar. Wine cellar. Semi-a la carte: dinner $14.50-$23. Specialties: osso buco, shrimp elegante, artichoke stuffed with shrimp, fresh seafood, pasta dishes. Own pastries, pasta. Tableside service. Valet parking. Family-owned. Jacket. Cr cds: A, C, D, DS, ER, MC, V.

★ ★ **FAUST'S.** *(See Adam's Mark Hotel)* 314/342-4690. Hrs: 11:30 am-2 pm, 5:30-10 pm; Fri to 10:30 pm; Sat 5:30-10:30 pm; Sun 10:30 am-2:30 pm. Res accepted. French, Amer menu. Bar. Extensive wine list. Semi-a la carte: lunch $6.25-$13.95, dinner $18-$27.25. Child's meals. Specializes in rack of lamb, halibut Chardonnay, crispy duck. Own bread, pastries. Valet parking. Two-tiered dining rm with beamed ceilings; upper tier with view of Gateway Arch. Jacket (dinner). Cr cds: A, C, D, DS, MC, V.

★ ★ ★ **G P AGOSTINO'S.** *(15846 Manchester Rd, Ellisville 63011) 22 mi W on I-64 (US 40) to Clarkson Rd, 4 mi S to Manchester Rd.* 314/391-5480. Hrs: 11 am-2:30 pm, 5 pm-midnight. Closed Jan 1, Thanksgiving, Dec 25. Res accepted. Italian menu. Bar. Wine cellar. Semi-a la carte: lunch $3.95-$9.95, dinner $8.95-$19.95. Sun brunch $11.95 Specialties: veal salto in bocca Romano, ossobuco Milanese, salmon con pappardelle. Parking. Chef-owned. Jacket (dinner). Cr cds: A, C, D, DS, MC, V.

★ ★ ★ **GIAN PEPPE'S.** *2126 Marconi Ave (63110), on The Hill.* 314/772-3303. Hrs: 11 am-2 pm, 5-11 pm; Sat from 5 pm. Closed Sun; major hols; also Mon Oct-Jan. Res accepted. Italian menu. Bar. Wine list. Semi-a la carte: lunch $6.25-$13.95, dinner $12.50-$24.50. Specializes in veal, fresh seafood. Own pastries. Valet parking. Jacket. Cr cds: A, C, D, MC, V.

✔ ★ **GINO'S.** *4502 Hampton Ave (63109), on The Hill.* 314/351-4187. Hrs: 11 am-2 pm, 5-10 pm; Fri to 11 pm; Sat 5-11 pm; Sun 5-9 pm. Closed Mon; major hols. Italian menu. Bar. Semi-a la carte: lunch $3.95-$9, dinner $6.95-$15.95. Child's meals. Specialties: veal Spedine, linguine Pescatore, veal chops. Cafe atmosphere. Cr cds: A, MC, V.

★ ★ **GIOVANNI'S.** *5201 Shaw Ave (63110), on The Hill.* 314/772-5958. Hrs: 5-11 pm; Fri & Sat to midnight. Closed Sun; major hols. Res accepted. Italian menu. Bar. A la carte entrees: dinner $14.50-$24. Specialties: tuna San Martino, maltagliati al funchetto, vitello con porcini, "presidential bow tie" al salmone. Own pastries. Most pasta homemade. Valet parking. Cr cds: A, C, D, DS, ER, MC, V.

★ ★ **GIOVANNI'S LITTLE PLACE.** *(14560 Manchester Rd, Ballwin 63011) 14 mi W on I-64 (US 40) to I-270, S on I-270 to Manchester Rd, in Winchester Plaza Center.* 314/227-7230. Hrs: 5-10 pm. Closed hols. Res accepted. Italian menu. Bar. Wine cellar. Semi-a la carte: dinner $10.95-$24. Specialties: fusilli ai quattro formaggi, involtini di vitello alla villa Igea, vitello alla Maria. Own pastries. Cr cds: A, C, D, DS, ER, MC, V.

★ ★ ★ **THE GRILL.** *(See The Ritz-Carlton, St Louis Hotel)* 314/863-6300. Hrs: 5-11 pm. Res accepted. Continental menu. Bar. Wine cellar. A la carte entrees: dinner $16-$28. Child's meals. Specialties: Dover sole, double-cut lamb chops, Norwegian salmon. Own baking. Valet parking. Marble fireplace in main rm; English pub atmosphere. Cr cds: A, C, D, DS, ER, JCB, MC, V.

✔ ★ ★ **HACIENDA.** *(9748 Manchester Rd, Rock Hill 63119) W of downtown via Manchester Rd (MO 100).* 314/962-7100. Hrs: 11 am-10 pm; Fri, Sat to midnight; Sun noon-9 pm. Closed some major hols. Res accepted. Mexican menu. Bar. Semi-a la carte: lunch, dinner $4.95-$10.95. Specialties: chicken mole, fajitas. Parking. Built as residence for steamboat captain (1861). Cr cds: A, C, DS, MC, V.

★ ★ **HANNEGAN'S.** *719 N Second St (63102), downtown.* 314/241-8877. Hrs: 11 am-10 pm; Fri & Sat to midnight. Closed Thanksgiving, Dec 25. Bar. Semi-a la carte: lunch $4-$8, dinner $10-$17. Child's meals. Specializes in fresh seafood, steak. Oyster bar in season. Jazz Fri & Sat. Parking. Outdoor dining. Replica of US Senate dining rm; political memorabilia. Cr cds: A, C, D, MC, V.

★ ★ **HARRY'S.** *2144 Market St (63103), west of downtown.* 314/421-6969. Hrs: 11 am-3 pm, 5-11 pm; Sun 5-10 pm. Closed some major hols. Res accepted. Bar. Semi-a la carte: lunch $5-$12, dinner $8-$20. Specializes in smoked meats & fish. Entertainment Wed, Fri & Sat. Valet parking. Patio dining with spectacular view of Union Station and skyline. Cr cds: A, D, DS, MC, V.

★ **HOUSE OF INDIA.** *8501 Delmar Blvd (63124), west of downtown.* 314/567-6850. Hrs: 11:30 am-2:30 pm, 5-10 pm. Res accepted. Indian menu. Serv bar. Buffet lunch $5.95. Semi-a la carte: dinner $6.95-$12.95. Child's meals. Specialty: yogi thali. Parking. Small dining rm features Indian art. Cr cds: A, D, DS, MC, V.

★ ★ **J.F. SANFILIPPO'S.** *705 N Broadway (63102), downtown.* 314/621-7213. Hrs: 11 am-2 pm, 4:30-11 pm; Sat from 4:30 pm. Closed Sun; some major hols. Res accepted. Italian menu. Bar. Semi-a la carte: lunch $4.50-$10.25, dinner $4.75-$18.50. Child's meals. Specializes in pasta, fresh seafood, veal. Garage parking. Low slatted ceiling of metal and wood. Casual, trattoria atmosphere. Cr cds: A, C, D, DS, MC, V.

D ◩

★ ★ ★ **JOHN MINEO'S.** *(13490 Clayton Rd, Town & Country 63131) 15 mi W of downtown via I-64 (US 40), exit Mason Rd, 1 mi S to Clayton Rd.* 314/434-5244. Hrs: 5 pm-midnight. Closed Sun. Res accepted. Italian menu. Bar. Wine list. A la carte entrees: dinner $9.95-$18.95. Specialties: veal alla panna, Dover sole, fresh fish. Parking. Chef-owned. Jacket. Cr cds: A, C, D, DS, ER, MC, V.

◩

★ ★ **JUST JAZZ.** *(See Hotel Majestic)* 314/436-2355. Hrs: 6:30-1 am. Continental menu. Bar 11-1 am. Semi-a la carte: bkfst $2.50-$8.25, lunch $5.95-$12.95, dinner $15.95-$21.95. Jazz Wed-Sun evenings. Casual dining in elegant atmosphere. Cr cds: A, C, D, DS, MC, V.

D ◩

★ ★ ★ **KEMOLL'S.** *1 Metropolitan Square, downtown.* 314/421-0555. Hrs: 11 am-2 pm, 5-9 pm; Fri & Sat to 10 pm; early-bird dinner 5-6:30 pm. Closed major hols. Res accepted. Italian menu. Bar. Semi-a la carte: lunch $11-$15.75, dinner $15-$32. Specializes in fresh seafood, veal Francesco, carciofi fritti. 3 dining rms. Family-owned. Cr cds: A, C, D, DS, MC, V.

D

★ ★ **LOMBARDO'S.** *(See Drury Inn Union Station)* 314/621-0666. Hrs: 11 am-10 pm; Fri to 11 pm; Sat 3-11 pm. Closed Sun; most major hols. Res accepted. Italian menu. Bar. Wine list. Semi-a la carte: lunch $4.75-$8.95, dinner $7.50-$22. Child's meals. Specialties: ravioli, calzoni. Valet parking (dinner). Several dining areas on lower level of historic hotel. Cr cds: A, C, D, MC, V.

D ◩

★ ★ **LORUSSO'S CUCINA.** *3121 Watson Rd (63139), on The Hill.* 314/647-6222. Hrs: 11:30 am-2 pm, 5-10 pm; Fri & Sat 5-11 pm; early-bird dinner Mon-Sat 5-6 pm. Closed Sun; major hols. Italian menu. Bar. Semi-a la carte: lunch $5.50-$9.50, dinner $8.50-$18.95. Child's meals. Specialties: risotto, vitello, tenderloin Mudega. Cr cds: A, C, D, DS, MC, V.

D ◩

★ ★ **MAMA CAMPISI'S.** *2132 Edwards St (63110), on The Hill.* 314/771-1797. Hrs: 11 am-3 pm, 5-10 pm; Fri & Sat to 11 pm; Sun 11:30 am-8:30 pm. Closed Mon; most major hols. Res accepted. Italian menu. Bar. Semi-a la carte: lunch $6.50-$8.95, dinner $7.25-$15.95. Specialties: petto de polo picante, vitello alla parmigiano, lasagna al forno. Parking. Casual, family atmosphere. Cr cds: A, C, D, DS, MC, V.

D ◩

★ ★ **MANDARIN HOUSE.** *194 Union Station (63103), in Union Station, west of downtown.* 314/621-6888. Hrs: 10 am-10 pm. Res accepted. Chinese menu. Bar. Semi-a la carte: lunch, dinner $4.50-$12. Sun brunch $6.95. Specialzies in Szechuan, Peking dishes. Chinese decor. Inside shopping mall at Union Station. Cr cds: A, C, D, DS, ER, JCB, MC, V.

D ◩

★ ★ **MANDARIN HOUSE.** *9150 Overland Plaza (63114), north of downtown.* 314/427-8070. Hrs: 11:30 am-2 pm, 5-9:30 pm; Fri to 10:30 pm; Sat 5-10:30 pm. Closed Labor Day, Thanksgiving. Res accepted. Chinese menu. Bar. Semi-a la carte: lunch $5.25-$6.55, dinner $5.55-$15.95. Sun brunch $8.95. Parking. Chinese decor featuring tapestry of Great Wall; fish pond. Cr cds: A, C, D, DS, MC, V.

D ◩

★ **MARCIANO'S.** *333 West Port Plaza (63146), west of downtown.* 314/878-8180. Hrs: 11 am-11 pm; Fri & Sat to midnight; Sun from 3 pm. Closed Easter, Thanksgiving, Dec 25. Res accepted. Italian menu. Bar. Semi-a la carte: lunch $4.95-$6.95. A la carte entrees: dinner $6.95-$15.95. Child's meals. Specializes in pasta. Parking. Outdoor dining. Multi-level dining; Italian posters. Cr cds: A, DS, MC, V.

D ◩

★ ★ **MIKE SHANNON'S.** *100 N 7th St (63101), at Chestnut, downtown.* 314/421-1540. Hrs: 11 am-11 pm; Sat & Sun 5-10 pm. Closed Easter, Thanksgiving, Dec 25. Res accepted. Bar. Semi-a la carte: lunch $5.25-$10.95, dinner $11.95-$35.95. Specializes in prime rib, steak, seafood. Sports memorabilia. Cr cds: A, DS, MC, V.

D

✔ ★ **PASTA HOUSE COMPANY.** *(295 Plaza Frontenac, Frontenac 63131) 10 mi NW on I-40, exit Lindbergh S.* 314/569-3040. Hrs: 11 am-10:30 pm; Sun noon-8 pm. Closed Thanksgiving, Easter, Dec 25. Italian menu. Bar. Semi-a la carte: lunch $4.50-$9.50, dinner $6-$15.99. Specializes in pasta. Contemporary decor, casual atmosphere. Cr cds: A, DS, MC, V.

D SC

★ ★ **PATTY LONG'S 9TH STREET ABBEY.** *1808 S 9th St (63104), south of downtown.* 314/621-9598. Hrs: 11 am-2 pm; Sun from 10 am. Closed Sat, Mon; some major hols. Res accepted. Bar. Semi-a la carte: lunch $7.95-$9.95. Specialties: almond chicken salad, grilled beef tenderloin, fish of the day. Valet parking. In former church (ca 1895); stained-glass windows and paneling. Cr cds: A, D, MC, V.

D ◩

★ ★ **PREMIO.** *7th & Market Sts (63101), downtown.* 314/231-0911. Hrs: 11 am-10 pm; Fri to 11 pm; Sat 5-11 pm. Closed Sun; major hols. Res accepted. Italian menu. Bar. Semi-a la carte: lunch $6.25-$12.95, dinner $7.95-$21. Specializes in fresh seafood, veal, creative pasta. Garage parking. Outdoor dining. Modern decor. Cr cds: A, C, D, DS, MC, V.

D ◩

★ ★ **ROBATA OF JAPAN.** *111 West Port Plaza (63146), on 12th fl of office bldg, west of downtown.* 314/434-1007. Hrs: 11:30 am-1:30 pm, 5:30-9 pm; wkend hrs vary. Closed Thanksgiving. Res accepted. Japanese menu. Bar. Semi-a la carte: lunch $5-$11, dinner $11-$22. Child's meals. Specializes in steak, seafood, chicken. Parking. Japanese decor; teppanyaki cooking. Cr cds: A, D, DS, MC, V.

★ **SALEEM'S.** *6501 Delmar Blvd (63130), west of downtown.* 314/721-7947. Hrs: 5-10 pm; Fri & Sat to 11:30 pm. Closed Sun; Thanksgiving, Dec 25. Middle Eastern menu. Serv bar. Semi-a la carte: dinner $9.95-$13.95. Specializes in vegetarian, chicken, lamb. Salad bar. Middle Eastern decor. Cr cds: D, MC, V.

D ◩

★ ★ **SCHNEITHORST'S HOFAMBERG INN.** *(1600 S Lindbergh Blvd, Ladue 63131) W of downtown, via I-64 (US 40), exit Lindbergh Blvd, S to Clayton Rd.* 314/993-5600. Hrs: 11 am-10 pm; Fri, Sat to 11 pm; Sun 10 am-8 pm; early-bird dinner Mon-Fri 4-6:30 pm (exc hols); Sun brunch to 1:30 pm. Closed Dec 25. Res accepted. German, Amer menu. Bar. Semi-a la carte: lunch $5.95-$16.95, dinner $8.95-$24.50. Sun brunch $10.95. Child's meals. Specializes in steak, prime rib, fresh seafood. Parking. Outdoor dining. Antique clocks, stein display. Cr cds: A, C, D, DS, MC, V.

D ◩

★ ★ **SIDNEY STREET CAFE.** *2000 Sidney St (63104), south of downtown.* 314/771-5777. Hrs: 5-9:45 pm; Fri & Sat 5-10:45 pm. Closed Sun & Mon. Res accepted. Bar. Semi-a la carte: dinner $16-$22. Specializes in grilled seafood, lamb, steak au poivre. In restored building (ca 1885); antiques. Dinner menu recited. Cr cds: A, C, D, DS, MC, V.

D

★ **SUNSHINE INN.** *8¹/₂ S Euclid Ave (63108), west of downtown.* 314/367-1413. Hrs: 11:30 am-10 pm; Sun 10 am-9 pm. Closed Mon. Res accepted. Bar. Semi-a la carte: lunch $6-$9, dinner $9-$12. Specializes in vegetarian, all natural dishes. Outdoor dining. Storefront cafe. Cr cds: A, D, DS, MC, V.

★ ★ ★ **TONY'S.** *410 Market St, downtown.* 314/231-7007. A St Louis favorite, ornamented by classical statues, this restaurant has been operated by the Bommarito family for three generations. Hrs: 5-11 pm; Fri & Sat to 11:30 pm. Closed Sun; major hols; also 1st wk Jan, 1st wk July. Res accepted. Italian menu. Bar. Extensive wine cellar. Semi-a la carte: dinner $18.75-$28.75. Child's meals. Specializes in prime veal and beef, fresh seafood, homemade pasta. Own baking. Valet parking. Family-owned. Jacket. Cr cds: A, C, D, DS, ER, MC, V.

★ ★ **ZIA'S.** *5256 Wilson Ave (63110), on The Hill.* 314/776-0020. Hrs: 11 am-10:30 pm. Closed Sun; Memorial Day, July 4. Italian menu. Bar. Semi-a la carte: lunch $5-$8, dinner $7.50-$16.25. Specializes in veal, pasta, chicken. Informal, modern corner restaurant. Cr cds: A, D, MC, V.

Unrated Dining Spots

BARN DELI. *(180 Dunn Rd, Florissant)* N on I-70 to I-270. 314/838-3670. Hrs: 11 am-4 pm. Closed Sun; major hols. Wine, beer. Semi-a la carte: lunch $3.50-$4.95. Specializes in deli sandwiches, salads. Own soups, desserts. Parking. In late 1800s barn. Cr cds: MC, V.

BLUEBERRY HILL. *6504 Delmar Blvd, west of downtown.* 314/727-0880. Hrs: 11 am-midnight; Sun to 11 pm. Closed Jan 1. Res accepted Sun-Thurs. Bar to 1:30 am; Sun to midnight. Semi-a la carte: lunch, dinner $3.25-$7. Specializes in hamburgers, vegetarian platters, soups. Own beer. Entertainment Fri & Sat evenings. Large display of pop culture memorabilia including Chuck Berry and Elvis. Vintage jukeboxes. Sidewalk has "Walk of Fame" stars for celebrities from St Louis. Cr cds: A, C, D, DS, MC, V.

CROWN CANDY KITCHEN. *1401 St Louis Ave, north of downtown.* 314/621-9650. Hrs: 10:30 am-10 pm; Sun from noon. Closed some major hols. Specialty: ice cream. Also sandwiches, chili $2-$4. Homemade candy. Old neighborhood building (1889) with old-fashioned soda fountain (1930s), antique juke box and Coca-Cola memorabilia. No cr cds accepted.

O'CONNELLS PUB. *4652 Shaw Ave, on The Hill.* 314/773-6600. Hrs: 11 am-midnight, Sun noon-10 pm. Closed major hols. Bar. Semi-a la carte: lunch, dinner $3.50-$6.50. Specializes in hamburgers, roast beef sandwiches, soup. Parking. Pub atmosphere; antique bar, blackboard menu. Cr cds: A, D, DS, MC, V.

St Louis Lambert Airport Area (C-6)

(See St Charles, St Louis)

Services and Information

Information: 314/426-8000.
Lost and Found: 314/426-8100.

Weather: 314/321-2222.

Cash Machines: Main Terminal, concourse level.

Club Lounges: Admirals Club (American), Main Terminal, lower level; TWA Ambassador Clubs, Main Terminal, lower level & Concourse C.

Motels

✔ ★ ★ **BEST WESTERN AIRPORT INN.** *(10232 Natural Bridge Rd, Woodson Terrace 63134)* I-70 exit 236. 314/427-5955; FAX 314/427-3079. 138 rms, 2 story. May-Sept: S $56-$76; D $54-$70; under 12 free; lower rates rest of yr. Crib free. TV; cable (premium). Pool. Restaurant adj. Ck-out noon. Coin lndry. Meeting rms. Business servs avail. In-rm modem link. Free airport transportation. Cr cds: A, C, D, DS, ER, JCB, MC, V.

★ ★ **DRURY INN.** *(10490 Natural Bridge Rd, St Louis 63134)* W via I-70, 1 blk N of exit 236. 314/423-7700; FAX 314/423-7700. 172 rms, 6 story. S $75-$95; D $85-$105; under 18 free; some wknd rates. Crib free. TV; cable (premium), VCR avail. Heated pool. Complimentary continental bkfst. Restaurant adj noon-10 pm. Ck-out noon. Meeting rms. Business servs avail. Free airport transportation 24 hrs. Cr cds: A, C, D, DS, MC, V.

✔ ★ **FAIRFIELD INN BY MARRIOTT.** *(9079 Dunn Rd, Hazelwood 63042)* 6 mi NW on I-270, exit 25. 314/731-7700. 135 rms, 3 story. May-Sept: S, D $35.95-$62.95; each addl $7; under 12 free; wknd rates; higher rates VP Fair. Crib free. TV; cable (premium). Pool. Complimentary continental bkfst, coffee in lobby. Restaurant adj 7 am-10pm. Ck-out noon. Business servs avail. In-rm modem link. Cr cds: A, D, DS, MC, V.

Motor Hotels

★ ★ ★ **HOLIDAY INN AIRPORT OAKLAND PARK.** *(4505 Woodson Rd, St. Louis 63134)* E on Natural Bridge Rd to Woodson Rd, S on Woodson. 314/427-4700; FAX 314/427-6086. 155 rms, 5 story. S $84.50; D $89.50; each addl $5; suites $100-$230; under 19 free; wknd rates. Crib free. TV; cable (premium), VCR avail (movies avail). Pool. Restaurant 6:30 am-2 pm, 5-10 pm. Rm serv. Bar 4:30 pm-midnight. Ck-out 1 pm. Coin lndry. Meeting rms. Business servs avail. In-rm modem link. Bellhops. Valet serv. Free airport transportation. Exercise equipt; bicycles, weight machine, whirlpool, sauna. Cr cds: A, C, D, DS, JCB, MC, V.

✔ ★ ★ **RAMADA-HENRY VIII.** *(4690 N Lindbergh, St Louis 63044)* W via I-70 N Lindbergh exit. 314/731-3040; FAX 314/731-4210. 386 units, 2-5 story. 190 suites, 35 kit. units. S $69-$89; D $79-$99; suites $89-$115; under 18 free; wkly, monthly rates. Crib free. TV; cable (premium). 2 pools, 1 indoor. Restaurant 6:30 am-midnight; Sun to 11 pm. Rm serv. Bar from 11 am. Ck-out 11 am. Coin lndry. Convention facilities. Business servs avail. Bellhops. Gift Shop. Free airport transportation. Lighted tennis. Exercise equipt; weights, weight machine, whirlpool, sauna. Game rm. Refrigerators, wet bars. Some bathrm phones. Some balconies. English Tudor architecture. Cr cds: A, C, D, DS, MC, V.

Hotels

★ ★ ★ **EMBASSY SUITES.** *(11237 Lone Eagle Dr, Bridgeton 63044)* I-70 exit Lindbergh S. 314/739-8929; FAX 314/739-6355. 159 suites, 6 story. S, D $129; wknd rates; higher rates special events. Crib avail. TV; cable (premium). Indoor pool; whirlpool, poolside serv. Complimentary coffee in rms; full bkfst. Restaurant 11 am-11 pm. Bar 4 pm-midnight. Ck-out 1 pm. Coin lndry. Meeting rms. Business center. In-rm modem link. Gift shop. Free airport transportation. Exercise equipt; weights, treadmill, sauna. Game rm. Refrigerators. Cr cds: A, C, D, DS, MC, V.

★ ★ ★ **HILTON.** *(10330 Natural Bridge Rd, Woodson Terrace 63134) E on Natural Bridge Rd.* 314/426-5500; FAX 314/426-3429. 220 rms, 9 story. S, D $99-$150; each addl $15; suites $200-$350; under 18 free; wknd package plan. Crib free. TV; cable, VCR avail. Indoor pool; poolside serv. Complimentary coffee in rms. Restaurant 6 am-10 pm; wkends to 11 pm. Bars 11-1:30 am, Sun to midnight; entertainment. Coin lndry. Ck-out 1 pm. Meeting rms. Business servs avail. In-rm modem link. Gift shop. Free airport transportation. Exercise equipt; weights, bicycles, whirlpool, sauna. Game rm. Some refrigerators. Luxury level. Cr cds: A, C, D, DS, ER, MC, V.

★ ★ ★ **MARRIOTT.** *(I-70 at Lambert St Louis Intl Airport, St Louis 63134) S on Airflight Dr to Pear Tree Ln.* 314/423-9700; FAX 314/423-0213. 601 rms, 9 story. S, D $99-$124; suites $200-$375; studio rms $99. Crib free. Pet accepted. TV; cable (premium), VCR avail. 2 pools, 1 indoor/outdoor; poolside serv. Restaurant 6 am-midnight. Bars 11:30-1 am; dancing. Ck-out 1 pm. Coin lndry. Convention facilities. Business center. In-rm modem link. Gift shop. Free airport transportation. 2 lighted tennis courts. Exercise rm; weights, bicycles, whirlpool, sauna. Luxury level. Cr cds: A, C, D, DS, ER, JCB, MC, V.

✔ ★ ★ **QUALITY HOTEL.** *(9600 Natural Bridge Rd, Berkeley 63134) 2 mi E on Natural Bridge Rd.* 314/427-7600; res: 800/221-2222; FAX 314/427-4972. 197 rms, 7 story. S, D $62-$74; each addl $7; under 18 free; wknd, extended stay rates. Crib free. Pet accepted, some restrictions. TV; cable. Pool. Complimentary continental bkfst. Bar 4 pm-1:30 am. Ck-out noon. Meeting rms. Business servs avail. In-rm modem link. Free airport transportation. Exercise equipt; weight machine, stair machine, whirlpool, sauna. Some bathrm phones, refrigerators, minibars. Balconies. Cr cds: A, C, D, DS, MC, V.

★ ★ **RADISSON ST LOUIS AIRPORT.** *(11228 Lone Eagle Dr, Bridgeton 63044) I-70 exit 235, S on Lindberg Dr.* 314/291-6700; FAX 314/770-1205. 353 rms, 8 story. S $109-$119; D $119-$129; each addl $10; suites $379; under 17 free; wknd rates. Crib $10. TV. Indoor pool. Restaurant 6:30 am-midnight. Bar from 11 am. Ck-out noon. Convention facilities. Business servs avail. In-rm modem link. Gift shop. Free airport transportation. Exercise equipt; weight machine, bicycles, whirlpool. Game rm. Some balconies. Wet bar in suites. Atrium with waterfall. Cr cds: A, C, D, DS, ER, JCB, MC, V.

★ ★ **STOUFFER RENAISSANCE.** *(9801 Natural Bridge Rd, St Louis 63134) 1 mi E on Natural Bridge Rd, adj to airport.* 314/429-1100; FAX 314/429-3466. 393 rms, 12 story. S $122-$152; D $137-$167; each addl $10; suites $175-$700; under 18 free; wknd rates. Crib free. TV; cable (premium), VCR avail. 2 pools, 1 indoor; poolside serv. Coffee in rms. Restaurant 6:30 am-11 pm. Rm serv until 1 am. Bar 3 pm-1 am. Ck-out 1 pm. Convention facilities. Business center. In-rm modem link. Gift shop. Concierge. Free airport transportation. Exercise equipt; weights, bicycles, whirlpool, sauna. Bathrm phones, minibars. Luxury level. Cr cds: A, C, D, DS, ER, JCB, MC, V.

Restaurants

★ **CHINA ROYAL.** *(5911 N Lindbergh, St Louis 63042) I-70 exit Lindbergh Blvd N.* 314/731-1313. Hrs: 11 am-9:30 pm; wkends to 10:30 pm. Chinese menu. Bar. Semi-a la carte: lunch $4.25-$4.95, dinner $6.75-$24.95. Specializes in dim sum, seafood. Parking. Chinese decor. Cr cds: A, C, D, MC, V.

★ ★ ★ **KREIS'S.** *(535 S Lindbergh, St Louis 63131)* 314/993-0735. Hrs: 5-10:30 pm; Sat to 11 pm; Sun 4:30-9:30 pm. Closed some major hols. Res accepted. Bar. Semi-a la carte: dinner $10.95-$37.50. Child's meals. Specializes in prime rib, steak, fresh fish. Valet parking. In renovated 1930s brick house with beamed ceilings. Cr cds: A, D, MC, V.

★ ★ **LOMBARDO'S.** *(10488 Natural Bridge Rd, St Louis 63134) adj to Drury Inn.* 314/429-5151. Hrs: 11 am-10 pm; Sat from 5 pm. Closed Sun; most major hols. Res accepted. Italian menu. Bar. Semi-a la carte: lunch $4.95-$12.75, dinner $9-$24. Specializes in fresh seafood, steak. Parking. Original art; sculptures. Family-owned since 1934. Cr cds: A, C, D, MC, V.

★ ★ ★ **TORNATORE'S.** *(12315 Natural Bridge Rd, Bridgeton 63044) 3 mi W on Natural Bridge Rd.* 314/739-6644. Hrs: 11 am-3 pm, 5-10 pm; Sat from 5 pm; early-bird dinner Mon-Fri 5-6:30 pm. Closed Sun; major hols. Res accepted. Continental Italian menu. Bar. Extensive wine list. Semi-a la carte: lunch $7.95-$15.95, dinner $14.95-$30.95. Specializes in fresh seafood, Sicilian veal chops. Own pastries. Parking. Modern art; etched glass-paneled room divider. Cr cds: A, C, D, DS, MC, V.

Unrated Dining Spot

PICCADILLY CAFETERIA. *(10906 St Charles Rock Rd, St Ann 63074) S on Lindbergh Dr, then E on St Charles Rock Rd.* 314/770-1131. Hrs: 11 am-8:30 pm. Closed Dec 25. Avg ck: lunch $5.50, dinner $6.20. Child's meals. Parking. Cr cds: A, C, D, DS, MC, V.

Sedalia (C-4)

(See Jefferson City)

Pop 19,800 **Elev** 919 ft **Area code** 816 **Zip** 65301
Information Chamber of Commerce, 113 E 4th St; 816/826-2222 or 800/827-5295.

Known as the "queen city of the prairies," Sedalia was a prosperous railhead town in the 1800s with great cattle herds arriving for shipment to eastern markets. During the Civil War the settlement functioned as a military post. A monument at Lamine and Main streets marks the site of the Maple Leaf Club, one of the city's many saloons that catered to railroad men. The monument is dedicated to Scott Joplin, who composed and performed the "Maple Leaf Rag" here, triggering the ragtime craze at the turn of the century. Whiteman Air Force Base is 21 miles to the west of Sedalia.

What to See and Do

Bothwell Lodge State Historic Site. Approx 180 acres, includes hiking trails; picnicking. Tours of stone lodge (Mon-Sat & Sun afternoons). 6 mi N on US 65. Phone 816/827-0510. ¢

Knob Noster State Park. Lakes and streams on more than 3,500 acres. Fishing; boating, canoeing. Hiking. Picnicking. Improved camping (dump stations), laundry facilities. Visitor center, naturalist program. Standard fees. (Daily) 20 mi W on US 50, then S on MO 132. Phone 816/563-2463. **Free.**

Pettis County Courthouse. Historic courthouse contains local artifacts and exhibits. (Mon-Fri; closed major hols) 415 S Ohio, downtown. Phone 816/826-4892. **Free.**

Sedalia Ragtime Archives. Includes original sheet music, piano rolls, tapes of interviews with Eubie Blake. (Mon-Fri; closed school hols) State Fair Community College Library, Maple Leaf Rm, 3201 W 16th St. Phone 816/530-5800. **Free.**

Annual Events

Scott Joplin Ragtime Festival. Entertainment by ragtime greats. Phone 816/826-2271. Early June.

Missouri State Fair. Fairgrounds, 16th St & Limit Ave. One of the country's leading state fairs; held here since 1901. Stage shows, rodeo, competitive exhibits, livestock, auto races. Phone 816/530-5600. August 16-25.

Seasonal Event

Band concerts. Liberty Park band shell. Thurs evenings. Mid-June-early Aug.

Motels

(Rates usually higher State Fair)

✔★ **BEST WESTERN STATE FAIR MOTOR INN.** *3120 S Limit (US 65).* 816/826-6100; FAX 816/827-3850. 119 rms, 2 story. S $37-$48; D $42-$53; each addl $5; under 18 free. Crib free. Pet accepted. TV; cable. Indoor pool; wading pool; poolside serv. Restaurant 5:45 am-2 pm, 5-9:30 pm. Rm serv. Bar. Ck-out noon. Coin lndry. Meeting rms. Free airport transportation. Exercise equipt; weights, bicycles, whirlpool, sauna. Miniature golf. Game rm. Cr cds: A, C, D, DS, MC, V.

★ **RAMADA INN.** *3501 W Broadway.* 816/826-8400; FAX 816/826-1230. 124 rms, 2-3 story. No elvtr. S $39-$45; D $45-$53; each addl $6; under 12 free. Crib free. TV; cable. Pool. Restaurant 6:30 am-2 pm, 5-9 pm. Rm serv. Bar 4 pm-1:30 am. Ck-out noon. Meeting rms. Sundries. Health club priveleges. Cr cds: A, C, D, DS, ER, MC, V.

Restaurant

★ **AROUND THE FIRESIDE.** *1975 W Broadway.* 816/826-9743. Hrs: 11 am-10 pm; Sat from 4 pm; early-bird dinner 4-6 pm. Closed Sun; major hols. Res accepted. Bar to 11:30 pm. Semi-a la carte: lunch $4.95-$7.95, dinner $6-$25. Child's meals. Specializes in steak, seafood. Salad bar. Parking. Cr cds: A, C, D, DS, MC, V.

Sikeston (E-7)

(See Cape Girardeau)

Founded 1860 **Pop** 17,641 **Elev** 325 ft **Area code** 314 **Zip** 63801

Information Sikeston Area Chamber of Commerce, 1 Industrial Dr; 314/471-2498.

Although settlers were in this region before the Louisiana Purchase, John Sikes established the town of Sikeston in 1860 on El Camino Real, the overland route from St Louis to New Orleans, at the terminus of the Cairo and Fulton Railway, now the Union Pacific.

Annual Events

Bootheel Rodeo. Country music and rodeo events; parade. 4 days mid-Aug.

Cotton Carnival. Parades, contests. Last full wk Sept.

Motel

✔★ **SUPER 8.** *Box 1653, 2609 E Malone.* 314/471-7944. 63 rms, 2 story. Apr-Sept: S $38; D $48; suites $67; under 12 free; higher rates rodeo; lower rates rest of yr. Crib free. TV; cable. Restaurant adj 10:30 am-10:30 pm. Ck-out 11 am. Cr cds: A, C, D, DS, MC, V.

Restaurants

★ **FISHERMAN'S NET.** *915 Kingsway Plaza, in Kingsway Plaza Shopping Center.* 314/471-8102. Hrs: 11 am-9 pm; Fri, Sat to 9 pm. Res accepted. Closed Sun; major hols. Semi-a la carte: lunch, dinner $3.95-$17.95. Buffet: lunch $5.49, dinner (Fri, Sat) $6.95. Child's meals. Specializes in catfish. Parking. Nautical decor. Cr cds: A, DS, MC, V.

✔★ **LAMBERT'S.** *2515 E Malone.* 314/471-4261. Hrs: 10:30 am-9 pm. Closed most major hols. Semi-a la carte: lunch, dinner $7.99-$12.50. Child's meals. Specialties: throwed rolls & sorghum molasses, chicken & dumplings, chicken-fried steak. Entertainment Thurs-Sun. Parking. Country decor. Family-owned. No cr cds accepted.

Silver Dollar City (E-4)

(see Branson/Table Rock Lake Area)

Springfield (E-4)

(See Branson/Table Rock Lake Area)

Pop 140,494 **Elev** 1,316 ft **Area code** 417

Information Convention & Visitors Bureau, 3315 E Battlefield, 65804-4048; phone 417/881-5300 or 800/678-8766.

In the southwest corner of the state, at the northern edge of the Ozark highlands, Springfield, known as the Gateway to Ozark Mountain Country, is near some of Missouri's most picturesque scenery and recreational areas. A few settlers came here as early as 1821, but settlement was temporarily discouraged when the government made southwestern Missouri an Indian reservation. Later the tribes were moved west, and the town began to develop. Its strategic location made it a military objective in the Civil War. The Confederates took the town in the Battle of Wilson's Creek, August 10, 1861; Union forces recaptured it in 1862. Confederate attempts to regain it were numerous but unsuccessful. "Wild Bill" Hickok, later one of the famous frontier marshals, was a scout and spy for Union forces headquartered in Springfield.

Springfield's growth has been largely due to a healthy economy based on diversified industry; manufacturing and the service industry provide the majority of jobs. Springfield is the home of six major colleges and universities, including Southwest Missouri State University.

What to See and Do

Crystal Cave. Once a Native American habitat; contains a variety of colorful formations; temperature 59°F; guided tours. Gift shop, picnic area. (Daily) 5 mi N of I-44 on MO H, exit 80B. For hrs phone 417/833-9599. ¢¢¢

Dickerson Park Zoo. Animals in naturalistic setting; features elephant herd; animal rides. Playground; concession, picnic area. Gift shop. (Daily; closed Jan 1, Thanksgiving, Dec 25) 3043 N Fort. Phone 417/833-1570. ¢¢

Exotic Animal Paradise. Approximately 3,000 wild animals and rare birds may be seen along 9-mile drive. (Daily; closed Thanksgiving, Dec 25; winter hours vary according to weather) 12 mi E on I-44 exit 88, Strafford, then E on outer road to entrance. Phone 417/859-2159. ¢¢¢

Fantastic Caverns. Cave tours (45-min) in jeep-drawn tram. (Daily; closed Jan 1, Thanksgiving, Dec 25) Restaurant (May-Oct). 4 mi NW via I-44, then N 1½ mi at MO 13. Phone 417/833-2010. ¢¢¢¢

★ **Laura Ingalls Wilder-Rose Wilder Lane Museum and Home.** House where Laura Ingalls Wilder wrote the *Little House* books; artifacts and memorabilia of Laura, husband Almanzo and daughter Rose Wilder Lane; four handwritten manuscripts; many items mentioned in Wilder's books, including Pa's fiddle. (Mid-Mar-mid-Nov, Mon-Sat; also Sun afternoons) 50 mi E on US 60, at MO 5 in Mansfield. Phone 417/924-3626. ¢¢

Snow Bluff Ski Area. Chairlift, 3 rope tows; school, rentals; snowmaking; restaurant; night skiing. (Dec & Jan, daily; Feb & Mar, wkends only) 12 mi N on US 13 in Brighton. Phone 417/376-2201. ¢¢¢¢

Springfield Art Museum. American and European paintings, sculpture and graphics. (Tues-Sat, also Wed evenings & Sun afternoons; closed hols) (See SEASONAL EVENTS) 1111 E Brookside Dr. Phone 417/866-2716. **Free.**

Springfield National Cemetery. One of the few national cemeteries where Union and Confederate soldiers from the same state are buried side by side. (Daily)

The History Museum. Permanent and rotating exhibits on Springfield, Greene County and the Ozarks. Donation. (Daily exc Sun, Mon; limited hrs) 830 Boonville, in City Hall. Phone 417/864-1976.

Wilson's Creek National Battlefield. Scene of battle, Aug 10, 1861, between Confederate and Union forces for control of Missouri during the Civil War. At entrance is the visitor center, which has film, battle map light display and a museum area. Also here are maps of self-guided 5-mile road tour featuring waysides, exhibits and walking trails. Highlights are the Bloody Hill trail, the Ray House and the headquarters of General Price. Living History program (Memorial Day-Labor Day, Sun & hols). Battlefield (daily; closed Jan 1, Dec 25). Sr citizen rate. 10 mi SW via I-44, County M & County ZZ, near Republic. Contact Superintendent, Rte 2, Box 75, Republic 65738; 417/732-2662. ¢¢

Annual Event

Ozark Empire Fair (regional). Phone 417/833-2660. Late July-early Aug.

Seasonal Events

Watercolor USA. Springfield Art Museum. National competitive exhibition of aquamedia painting. Phone 417/866-2716. Early June-late July.

Tent Theater. Southwest Missouri State University campus. Dramas, comedies and musicals in repertory in circus-like tent. Phone 417/836-5979. Late June-early Aug.

Motels

★★ **BEST WESTERN DEERFIELD INN.** 3343 E Battlefield (65804). 417/887-2323. 104 rms, 3 story. S $58-$63; D $63-$69; each addl $6; suites $110; under 12 free. TV; cable (premium). Indoor pool. Complimentary continental bkfst, coffee. Restaurant adj open 24 hrs. Ck-out noon. Meeting rm. Business servs avail. Cr cds: A, C, D, DS, ER, JCB, MC, V.

D ≈ ⊁ 🐾 SC

★★ **BEST WESTERN SYCAMORE.** 203 S Glenstone (65802), one block S of I-44 exit 80A. 417/866-1963. 93 rms. May-Oct: S, D $48-$53; each addl $5; suites $60-$65; under 18 free; lower rates rest of yr. Crib free. Pet accepted, some restrictions. TV; cable (premium), VCR avail. Pool; whirlpool. Complimentary continental bkfst. Restaurant adj open 24 hrs. Ck-out noon. Valet serv. Refrigerator in suites. Cr cds: A, C, D, DS, MC, V.

🐾 ⊁ 🐾 SC

✔★ **ECONO LODGE.** 2611 N Glenstone (65803), I-44 exit 80A. 417/864-3565; FAX 417/865-0567. 122 rms, 2 story. S $40-$47; D $45-$52; each addl $5; under 18 free. Crib free. TV; cable (premium), VCR avail. Pool. Complimentary continental bkfst. Complimentary coffee in lobby. Restaurant nearby. Ck-out 11 am. Valet serv. Cr cds: A, C, D, DS, MC, V.

D ≈ ⊁ 🐾 SC

★ **ECONO LODGE.** I-44 at MO 13 (65803). 417/869-5600; FAX 417/869-3421. 83 rms, 2-3 story. S $38.95-$43.95; D $45.95; suites $85.95; under 18 free. Crib free. Complimentary coffee in lobby. Restaurant adj 6 am-9:30 pm. Ck-out 11 am. Business servs avail. Cr cds: A, C, D, DS, ER, MC, V.

D ⊁ 🐾 SC

★★ **HAMPTON INN.** 222 N Ingram Mill Rd (65802), US 65 exit Chestnut Expwy. 417/863-1440; FAX 417/863-2215. 99 rms, 2 story. S $50-$60; D $55-$65; suites $65-$75; under 18 free. Crib free. TV; cable (premium), VCR avail. Pool. Complimentary continental bkfst, coffee. Restaurant adj 6 am-midnight. Bar 5-10 pm. Ck-out noon. Meeting rm. Business servs avail. In-rm modem link. Sundries. Free airport transportation. Exercise equipt; bicycle, stair machine, whirlpool. Cr cds: A, C, D, DS, MC, V.

D ≈ 🏃 ⊁ 🐾 SC

★★ **RADISSON INN.** 3333 S Glenstone (65804). 417/883-6550; FAX 417/887-1823. 199 rms (11 with shower only), 2 story. S, D $69-$75; each addl $5; suites $150; under 18 free. Crib free. Pet accepted, some restrictions; $10. TV; cable (premium). Restaurant 6 am-2 pm, 5-10 pm. Rm serv to 2 pm. Bar 11-1 am. Ck-out noon. Meeting rms. Business servs avail. Bellhops. Valet serv. Sundries. Free airport transportation. Health club privileges. Some refrigerators. Picnic tables. Cr cds: A, D, DS, MC, V.

D 🐾 ≈ ⊁ 🐾 SC

★★ **RAMADA INN.** 2820 N Glenstone (65803); I-44 exit 88. 417/869-3900. 130 rms, 2-3 story. May-Oct: S, D $55-$65; each addl $5; suites $89; under 18 free; higher rates special events; lower rates rest of yr. Crib avail. Pet accepted. TV; cable (premium), VCR avail. Pool. Complimentary coffee in rms; continental bkfst. Restaurant 6 am-10 pm. Bar. Ck-out noon. Meeting rms. Business servs avail. In-rm modem link. Bellhops. Valet serv. Free airport transportation. Game rm. Some refrigerators. Balconies. Cr cds: A, C, D, DS, MC, V.

D 🐾 ≈ ⊁ 🐾 SC

★★ **RESIDENCE INN BY MARRIOTT.** 1550 E Raynell Pl (65804). 417/883-7300; FAX 417/883-5779. 80 kit. suites, 2 story. S, D $99-$139. Crib $5. Pet accepted, some restrictions; $100 deposit ($75 refundable). TV; cable (premium). Pool; whirlpool. Complimentary continental bkfst. Restaurant nearby. Ck-out noon. Coin lndry. Meeting rms. Business servs avail. Valet serv. Health club privileges. Picnic tables, grills. Gazebo. Cr cds: A, C, D, DS, MC, V.

D 🐾 ≈ ⊁ 🐾 SC

Motor Hotel

★★ **HOLIDAY INN NORTH.** 2720 N Glenstone (65803), I-44 exit 80A. 417/865-8600; FAX 417/862-9415. 188 rms, 6 story, 36 suites. S, D $88.50-$100; suites $200; under 18 free. Crib free. TV; cable (premium), VCR avail. 2 pools, 1 indoor; whirlpool, poolside serv. Restaurant 6 am-2 pm, 5-10:30 pm. Rm serv. Bar 4 pm-1 am. Ck-out noon. Meeting rms. Business servs avail. In-rm modem link. Bellhops. Valet serv. Free airport, bus depot transportation. Exercise equipt; weights, bicycle, sauna. Some refrigerators. Cr cds: A, C, D, DS, MC, V.

D ≈ 🏃 ⊁ 🐾 SC

Hotels

★ ★ ★ **HOLIDAY INN UNIVERSITY PLAZA & CONVENTION CENTER.** *333 John Q. Hammons Pkwy (65806). 417/864-7333; FAX 417/831-5893.* 271 rms. S, D $79.50-$98.50; each addl $10; suites $111.50; under 19 free. Crib free. Pet accepted, some restrictions. TV; cable (premium), VCR avail. 2 pools, 1 indoor; poolside serv. Restaurant 6 am-10 pm. Bar noon-1 am; entertainment. Ck-out noon. Coin lndry. Convention facilities. Business center. In-rm modem link. Concierge. Gift shop. Barber, beauty shop. Free airport, bus depot transportation. Lighted tennis. Exercise equipt; weights, bicycles, whirlpool, sauna. Game rm. Refrigerators. Some private patios. 9-story atrium tower with multi-tiered waterfall. Cr cds: A, C, D, DS, JCB, MC, V.

D 🐾 🏃 ≋ 🏋 🐬 🔥 SC 🚶

★ ★ ★ **SHERATON HAWTHORNE PARK.** *2431 N Glenstone (65803), I-44 exit 80A. 417/831-3131; FAX 417/831-9786.* 203 rms, 10 story. S $89-$99; D $89-$109; under 18 free. Crib free. Pet accepted, some restrictions; $25 deposit. TV; cable, (premium). Indoor/outdoor pool; whirlpool, sauna. Complimentary coffee in rms. Restaurant 6:30 am-1:30 pm, 5:30-10:30 pm. Bar 1 pm-1 am; Sun to midnight. Ck-out 11 am. Coin lndry. Meeting rms. Business servs avail. In-rm modem link. Concierge. Free airport, bus transportation. Game rm. Luxury level. Cr cds: A, C, D, DS, MC, V.

D 🐾 ≋ ⊠ 🔥 SC

Inns

★ ★ **MANSION AT ELFINDALE.** *1701 S Fort St (65807). 417/831-5400; res: 800/443-0237; FAX 417/831-2965.* 13 suites, 3 story. S, D $70-$125; each addl $10. Children over 11 yrs only. TV in sitting rm, VCR avail. Complimentary full bkfst. Dinner avail. Ck-out 11 am, ck-in 3 pm. Business servs avail. Ornate 35-rm Victorian mansion (1892) built by stone masons brought from Germany; fireplaces, stained-glass windows. Variety of specimen trees on grounds. Totally nonsmoking. Cr cds: A, D, DS, MC, V.

D ⊠ 🔥

★ ★ **WALNUT STREET INN.** *900 E Walnut St (65806). 417/864-6346; res: 800/593-6346; FAX 417/864-6184.* 14 rms, 3 story. S, D $80-$135; each addl $20. TV; cable. Complimentary full bkfst, coffee. Restaurant nearby. Ck-out 11 am, ck-in 5 pm. Concierge. Queen Anne-style Victorian inn built 1894. Antiques; sitting rm on 2nd floor. Some in-rm whirlpools, fireplaces. Totally nonsmoking. Cr cds: A, C, D, DS, MC, V.

D ⊠ 🔥

Restaurants

✔ ★ **DIAMOND HEAD.** *2734 S Campbell Ave (US 160), in Village Shopping Center. 417/883-9581.* Hrs: 11 am-9:30 pm; Fri, Sat to 10:30 pm. Closed Thanksgiving, Dec 25. Res accepted. Chinese, Polynesian menu. Bar. Semi-a la carte: lunch $2.95-$4.95, dinner $4.95-$10.95. Buffet: lunch $5.45, dinner $6.45. Child's meals. Specialties: Mongolian barbecue, steak teriyaki. Oriental decor. Cr cds: A, DS, MC, V.

D

★ ★ **GEE'S EAST WIND.** *2951 E Sunshine. 417/883-4567.* Hrs: 11 am-9:30 pm. Closed Sun; Thanksgiving, Dec 25; also last wk June, 1st wk July. Res accepted. Chinese, Amer menu. Bar 11 am-9:30 pm. Semi-a la carte: lunch $4.50-$10, dinner $6.65-$22.75. Child's meals $4.50. Specialties: cashew chicken, moo goo gai pan. Parking. Chinese screens, wood carvings. Cr cds: A, MC, V.

D

★ **J PARRINO'S.** *1550 E Battlefield (65806), in Galleria Center shopping center. 417/882-1808.* Hrs: 10:30 am-11 pm; Fri & Sat to midnight; Sun 4-7 pm. Closed Dec 25. Italian menu. Bar. Semi-a la

carte: lunch $5-$10, dinner $5-$15. Child's meals. Specializes in pasta. Tableside magician Sat eves. Cr cds: A, C, D, DS, MC, V.

★ ★ ★ **LE MIRABELLE.** *2620 S Glenstone Ave (65804), in Brentwood Shopping Ctr. 417/883-2550.* Hrs: 5-9:30 pm. Closed Sun; major hols. Res accepted. French menu. Bar. Wine list. Semi-a la carte: dinner $12-$20. Specialties: beef Wellington, duck à l'orange, seafood. Own pastries. 3 dining rms, one with fireplace. Cr cds: A, C, D, DS, MC, V.

D

★ ★ **SHADY INN.** *524 W Sunshine St (65804). 417/862-0369.* Hrs: 11 am-10 pm. Closed Sun; Thanksgiving, Dec 25. Res accepted. Bar 10-1 am. Semi-a la carte: lunch $3.95-$7.95, dinner $6.95-$38. Child's meals. Specializes in prime rib, steak, seafood, lobster. Pianist, entertainment. Parking. Old English decor; fireplace. Family-owned. Cr cds: A, MC, V.

D SC

Unrated Dining Spot

HERITAGE CAFETERIA. *1310 S Glenstone Ave. 417/881-7770.* Hrs: 11 am-2 pm, 4:30-7:30 pm; Fri, Sat to 8 pm; Sun 11 am-7 pm. Closed Dec 25. Avg ck: lunch $4.50, dinner $5. Specializes in salads, fried chicken, homemade desserts. Parking. New Orleans decor. Cr cds: A, DS, MC, V.

D

Stockton (D-3)

Pop 1,579 **Elev** 965 ft **Area code** 417 **Zip** 65785

Stockton is the seat of Cedar County. The Stockton Dam, located two miles from the town square, offers many recreational activities.

What to See and Do

Stockton State Park. On shore of 25,000-acre Stockton Lake, impounded by Stockton Dam. Swimming; fishing in stocked lake for bass, crappie, walleye, catfish, pike and bluegill; boating, canoeing. Playground; lodging, restaurant. Improved camping, laundry facilities. Standard fees. (Daily) On MO 215. Phone 417/276-4259. **Free.**

Sullivan (D-6)

Pop 5,661 **Elev** 987 ft **Area code** 314 **Zip** 63080

What to See and Do

Jesse James Wax Museum. Life-size wax figures of the James gang; $100,000 gun collection; personal belongings of notorious raiders of the Old West; antiques; doll collection. Guided tours. (Mar-mid-Dec, daily; closed Thanksgiving, Dec 25) Sr citizen rate. 5 mi E on I-44 exit 230, on S Service Rd in Stanton. Phone 314/927-5233. ¢¢

Meramec Caverns. Cave used for gunpowder manufacture during Civil War and by Jesse James as a hideout in the 1870s; five levels; lighted; concrete walks; 60°F; guided tours (1 hr, 20 min). Picnicking. Camping; motel, restaurant, gift shop. Canoe rentals; boat rides. (Daily; closed Thanksgiving, Dec 25) 5 mi E on I-44 exit 230, then 3 mi S through La Jolla Park, follow signs. Phone 314/468-3166. ¢¢¢

Meramec State Park. This is one of the largest and most scenic of the state's parks. In its more than 6,700 acres are 30 caves and many springs. Swimming on the Meramec River; fishing; boating (ramp, rentals), canoeing. Hiking trails. Picnicking, playground, dining lodge.

Camping (trailer hookups, dump station), cabins, motel, laundry facilities. Nature center, naturalist. Cave tours. Standard fees. (Daily) 4 mi SE on MO 185; off I-44 exit 226. Phone 314/468-6072. **Free.**

Onondaga Cave State Park. Contains historical cave site in 1,300-acre park. Canoe rentals. Camping. Visitor center; dining lodge (Memorial Day-Labor Day, daily). Cave tour (Mar-Oct, daily). Park (daily). 10 mi SW on I-44, then 6 mi SE on County H, past Leasburg. Phone 314/245-6600 or -6576. **Free.** Cave tour ¢¢¢

Motels

★ **BEST WESTERN PENBERTHY INN.** *307 N Service Rd.* 314/468-3136. 48 rms. S $42; D $55; each addl $5; cottage $150. Crib $5. TV. Pool. Complimentary continental bkfst. Restaurant adj 6 am-10 pm. Ck-out 11 am. Cr cds: A, C, D, DS, MC, V.

⊠ ⊠ 🐾 SC

✔ ★ **FAMILY MOTOR INN.** *209 N Service Rd.* 314/468-4119; FAX 314/468-3891. 63 rms, 14 kits. Late May-early Sept: S $33.95; D $39.95; each addl $4; suites $45-$55; under 12 free (max 2); lower rates rest of yr. Crib $4. TV; VCR avail (movies $4.99). Pool; whirlpool, sauna. Complimentary coffee. Restaurant nearby. Ck-out 11 am. Meeting rm. Business servs avail. Coin lndry. Game rm. Antique shop adj. Cr cds: A, C, D, DS, MC, V.

D ⊠ ⊠ 🐾 SC

★ **SUPER 8.** *PO Box 69, 601 N Service Rd.* 314/468-8076. 60 rms, 3 story. No elvtr. S $37.88; D $44.88-$53.88; each addl $3; suites $61.88; under 12 free. Crib $3. TV; cable. Complimentary coffee. Ck-out 11 am. Coin lndry. Whirlpool in suites. Cr cds: A, C, D, DS, MC, V.

D ⊠ 🐾 SC

Table Rock Lake Area (F-3 - E-4)

(see Branson/Table Rock Lake Area)

Theodosia (F-4)

(see Bull Shoals Lake Area, AR)

Van Buren (E-6)

(For accommodations see Poplar Bluff)

Pop 893 **Elev** 475 ft **Area code** 314 **Zip** 63965
Information Van Buren-Big Spring Area Chamber of Commerce, US 60 E, PO Box 356; 314/323-4782.

A Ranger District office of the Mark Twain National Forest is located here.

What to See and Do

Clearwater Lake. Formed by dam on Black River. Five different parks surround lake. Swimming, waterskiing; fishing, hunting; boating (ramps, dock, rentals). Nature, exercise trails. Picnicking. Camping (spring-fall, fee; electric hookups, dump stations). Nature trail paved for wheelchair access. Visitor center. (Daily) 12 mi E on US 60, then 6 mi N on MO 34, then NE on County HH, near Piedmont. Phone 314/223-7777. **Free.**

✪ **Ozark National Scenic Riverways.** More than 80,000 acres with 134 miles of riverfront along the Current and Jacks Fork rivers, both clear, free-flowing streams that are fed by numerous springs. Big Spring, south of town, is one of the largest single-outlet springs in the US with a flow of 276 million gallons daily. Swimming; fishing; floating; boat trips (Memorial Day-Labor Day; some fees). Picnicking. Seven campgrounds (daily; fee). Cave tours (Memorial Day-Labor Day, daily; fee) Cultural demonstrations, including corn milling, at Alley Spring Mill; tours; quilting and wooden jon-boat making at Big Spring. Off US 60, reached from MO 17, 19, 21 or 106.

There is a visitor center at Alley Spring Mill, 6 miles west of Eminence on MO 106 (Memorial Day-Labor Day, daily). Contact the Superintendent, Ozark National Scenic Riverways, PO Box 490; 314/323-4236.

Waynesville (D-5)

(See Lebanon, Rolla)

Pop 3,207 **Elev** 805 ft **Area code** 314 **Zip** 65583
Information Waynesville/St Robert Chamber of Commerce, PO Box 6; phone 314/336-5121.

Motels

✔ ★ **BEST WESTERN MONTIS INN.** *14086 Hwy Z, I-44 at jct MO 28 exit 163.* 314/336-4299; FAX 314/336-2872. 45 rms, 2 story, 4 kit. units. May-Oct: S, D $47-$57; each addl $5; lower rates rest of yr. Crib $5. Pet accepted. TV; cable. Pool. Complimentary continental bkfst. Restaurant adj 6 am-9 pm. Ck-out noon. Coin lndry. Some refrigerators. Cr cds: A, C, D, DS, ER, JCB, MC, V.

✔ ⊠ ⊠ 🐾 SC

★ ★ **RAMADA INN.** *PO Box L, at I-44, Ft Leonard Wood exit 161.* 314/336-3121; FAX 314/336-4752. 82 rms, 2 story. S $49-$59; D $57-$68; each addl $9; suites $69-$98; under 18 free. Crib free. TV; cable (premium); VCR avail. 2 pools, 1 indoor. Restaurant 6 am-2 pm, 5-10 pm. Bar 3 pm-1:30 am, Sun to midnight; entertainment Wed-Sun, dancing. Ck-out noon. Meeting rms. Business center. In-rm modem link. Gift shop. Barber, beauty shop. Exercise rm; instructor, weights, bicycles, whirlpool, sauna. Game rm. Near Ft Leonard Wood. Cr cds: A, C, D, DS, JCB, MC, V.

D ⊠ 🏃 ⚹ ⊠ 🐾 SC 🚶

Wentzville (C-6)

(See St Charles, St Louis)

Pop 5,088 **Elev** 603 ft **Area code** 314 **Zip** 63385
Information Chamber of Commerce, 9 West Allen, PO Box 11; phone 314/327-6914.

Daniel Boone and his family were the first to settle in the area around Wentzville, which was named after Erasmus L. Wentz, principal engineer of the North Missouri Railroad. Between 1850 and 1880, the area was devoted to growing tobacco; the original Liggett and Myers Tobacco Company factory still stands in Wentzville.

What to See and Do

Cuivre River State Park. One of the state's largest and most natural parks, this 6,251-acre area contains rugged, wooded terrain, native prairie and an 88-acre lake. Swimming, beach; fishing; boating (ramp). 30 miles of hiking & horseback riding trails. Picnicking. Camping (hookups, dump station). Standard fees. (Daily) 13 mi N on US 61, then 3 mi E on MO 47 to MO 147. Phone 314/528-7247. **Free.**

Daniel Boone Home (ca 1803). Built by Boone and his son Nathan, this stone house is where Boone died in 1820; restored and authentically furnished; museum. Guided tours. Picnicking, snack bar. (Mid-Mar-mid-Dec, daily; rest of yr, Sat & Sun; closed Thanksgiving, Dec 25) 5 mi SE via County Z, F, near Defiance. Phone 314/987-2221. ¢¢

Motor Hotel

★★ **HOLIDAY INN.** *900 Corporate Pkwy, I-70 exit 212.* 314/327-7001; FAX 314/327-7019. 133 rms, 4 story. S, D $55-$65; each addl $5; suites $115; under 18 free. Crib free. Pet accepted, some restrictions. TV; cable (premium). Pool; poolside serv. Restaurant 6 am-10 pm. Rm serv. Bar 4-11 pm. Ck-out 1 pm. Meeting rms. In-rm modem link. Bellhops. Valet serv. Sundries. Free airport transportation. Some refrigerators. Cr cds: A, C, D, DS, ER, JCB, MC, V.

Weston (B-2)

(See Kansas City, St Joseph)

Settled 1837 **Pop** 1,528 **Elev** 800 ft **Area code** 816 **Zip** 64098
Information Weston Information Center, 502 Main St, PO Box 53; phone 816/386-2909.

Before the Civil War, Weston was at its peak. Founded on whiskey, hemp and tobacco, it rivaled St Louis as a commercial trade center and promised to become a major US city. But disasters—fire, floods and the Civil War—felled Weston's urban future. Today Weston, the first "district" west of the Mississippi entered into the National Register of Historic Sites, is a quiet town with more than 100 antebellum homes and other buildings.

What to See and Do

Historical Museum. On the site of the International Hotel, built by stagecoach king and distillery founder Benjamin Holladay. (Mid-Mar-mid-Dec, daily exc Mon; closed some major hols) 601 Main St. Phone 816/640-2977 or -2650. **Free.**

Lewis & Clark State Park. Approx 120 acres on southeast shore of Sugar Lake. Swimming; fishing; boating, canoeing. Picnicking, playground. Improved camping (dump station). Standard fees. (Daily) 17 mi NW on MO 45 & MO 138. Phone 816/579-5564. **Free.**

McCormick Distilling Co. Oldest continuously active distillery in the country, founded by Ben Holladay in 1856. Tour (Mar-Nov, daily; no tour hols). Country store (daily). 1¼ mi S via County JJ. Phone 816/640-2276. **Free.**

Mission Creek Winery. Tours and wine tasting. Picnicking. (Daily; closed some major hols) 1099 Welt St. Phone 816/386-5770. **Free.**

Pirtle's Weston Winery. Winery in old brick church (1867); tasting room furnished with antiques; stained-glass windows. (Daily; closed some major hols) 502 Spring St. Phone 816/386-5588 or -5728. **Free.**

Seasonal Event

Tobacco Auctions. Three warehouses handle six million pounds of tobacco annually in this "tobacco capital of the west." Thanksgiving-Jan.

Inns

★ **APPLE CREEK.** *908 Washington St.* 816/640-5724. 4 rms, 2 with bath, 2 story. No rm phones. S, D $65-$75; each addl $20.

Ck-out 11 am, ck-in 5 pm. Downhill ski 5 mi. 1897 house; country decor, sitting rm with fireplace. No cr cds accepted.

★★ **INN AT WESTON LANDING.** *500 Welt St, 500 Welt St,* on grounds of Old Royal Brewery. 816/386-5788. 4 rms, 2 story. No rm phones. S, D $75-$90. TV in sitting rm; cable. Complimentary full bkfst. Restaurant adj 11:30 am-3 pm, dinner seating 6:30 pm. Ck-out 11 pm, ck-in 4-6 pm. Downhill ski 5 mi. Built atop the cellars of former brewery (1842). British atmosphere; each rm individually decorated. Cr cds: MC, V.

Restaurant

★ **AMERICA BOWMAN.** *500 Welt St, on grounds of Old Royal Brewery.* 816/640-5235. Hrs: 11:30 am-3 pm, dinner seating 6:30 pm. Closed Mon; most major hols. Res accepted. Bar. Complete meals: lunch $5.65-$6.95, dinner $12.95-$16.95. Specializes in desserts. Entertainment; Irish balladeer, wkends. Parking. Mid-19th-century Irish pub atmosphere. Cr cds: DS, MC, V.

D

Unrated Dining Spot

PLUM PUDDING TEAROOM. *519 Main St.* 816/386-5510. Hrs: 11:30 am-3 pm. Closed Sun & Mon; Thanksgiving, Dec 25. Semi-a la carte: lunch $5.25. Specializes in croissant sandwiches with soup or salad. Own desserts. In Victorian bldg. Gift shop. Cr cds: MC, V.

West Plains (E-5)

Settled 1840 **Pop** 8,913 **Elev** 991 ft **Area code** 417 **Zip** 65775
Information Greater West Plains Area Chamber of Commerce, 401 Jefferson Ave; phone 417/256-4433.

Motel

✔★ **DAYS INN.** *PO Box 278, MO 63, at N end of town.* 417/256-4135; FAX 417/256-1106. 109 rms, 2 story. S $30-$40; D $36-$46; each addl $5; suite $95; under 12 free; wkly rates. TV; cable (premium). VCR avail (movies avail). Pool. Complimentary coffee in rms. Restaurant 6 am-1 pm, 5-9 pm. Rm serv. Bar 4 pm-1 am; closed Sun. Ck-out noon. Coin lndry. Meeting rms. Business servs avail. Free local airport transportation. Cr cds: A, C, D, DS, MC, V.

Motor Hotel

★★ **RAMADA INN.** *1301 Preacher Roe.* 417/256-8191. 80 rms, 2 story. S $38-$60; D $48-$60; each addl $7; suites $50-$60; under 18 free. Crib free. Pet accepted. TV; cable (premium), VCR avail. Pool. Restaurant 6 am-10 pm. Rm serv. Bar 4 pm-midnight. Ck-out noon. Meeting rms. Business servs avail. Coin lndry. Sundries. Cr cds: A, C, D, DS, MC, V.

New Mexico

Population: 1,515,069

Land area: 121,336 square miles

Elevation: 2,817-13,161 feet

Highest point: Wheeler Peak (Taos County)

Entered Union: January 6, 1912 (47th state)

Capital: Santa Fe

Motto: It grows as it goes

Nickname: Land of Enchantment

State flower: Yucca

State bird: Chaparral (roadrunner)

State tree: Piñon

State fair: September 6-22, 1996, in Albuquerque

Time zone: Mountain

Fray Marcos de Niza first saw what is now New Mexico in May, 1539. From a nearby mesa he viewed the Zuni pueblo of Hawikúh, not far from the present Gallup. He returned to Mexico with tales of cities of gold, which so impressed the Viceroy that in 1540 he dispatched Francisco Vásquez Coronado with an army and Fray Marcos as his guide. They found no gold and very little of anything else. Coronado returned home two years later a broken man.

While others came to New Mexico before him for a variety of purposes, Don Juan de Oñate established the first settlement in 1598. Don Pedro de Peralta founded Santa Fe as the capital in 1609. Spanish villages were settled all along the Rio Grande until 1680, when the Pueblo Indians, with Apache help, drove every Spaniard out of New Mexico in the famous Pueblo Revolt.

Twelve years later, Don Diego de Vargas reconquered the province with little resistance. The territory grew and prospered, though not entirely without conflict, since the Spanish were determined to maintain control at any cost. They forbade trade with the French of Louisiana, their nearest neighbors and rivals.

In 1810, Napoleon overran Spain; in 1821, Mexico won its independence and formed a republic. The following year, William Becknell of Missouri brought the first wagons across the trackless plains and blazed what was later called the Santa Fe Trail. After the Mexican War of 1846, New Mexico became a US territory, joining the Union in 1912.

New Mexico is a land of contrasts. Traces of prehistoric Folsom Man and Sandia Man, whose ancestors may have trekked across the Bering Strait land bridge from Asia, have been found here. Working in the midst of antiquity, scientists at Los Alamos opened up the new atomic world.

Southern New Mexico has fascinating desert country and cool, green, high forests popular with campers, anglers and vacationers. In the north it also has desert lands, but most of this area is high mountain country with clear streams and snow, which sometimes stays all year.

Spanish-speaking farmers mix with Indians and urban Americans in the plazas of Santa Fe and Albuquerque.

Where sheep and cattle were once the only industry, extractive industries—of which oil and uranium are a part—now yield nearly five billion dollars a year.

Native Americans in New Mexico

Native Americans occupied New Mexico for centuries before the arrival of Europeans. The exploring Spaniards called them Pueblo Indians because their tightly clustered communities were not unlike Spanish *pueblos*, or villages. The Apache and Navajo Indians, who arrived in New Mexico after the Pueblo people, were semi-nomadic wanderers. The Navajo eventually adopted many of the Pueblo ways, although their society is less structured and more individualistic than the Pueblo. The main Navajo reservation straddles New Mexico and Arizona (see SHIPROCK). The Apache, living closer to the Plains Indians, remained more nomadic.

The 19 pueblo groups have close-knit communal societies and cultures, even though they speak six different languages. Their pueblos are unique places to visit. In centuries-old dwellings craftsmen make and sell a variety of wares. The religious ceremonies, which include many dances and songs, are quite striking and not to be missed. While some pueblos are adamantly uninterested in tourists, others are trying to find a way to preserve those aspects of their ancient culture they most value, while taking advantage of what is most beneficial to them in non-Indian culture and ways.

Tourists are welcome at all Indian reservations in New Mexico on most days, though there are various restrictions. Since the religious ceremonies are sacred, photography is generally prohibited. This may also be true of certain sacred areas of the pueblo (in a few cases, the entire pueblo). Sometimes permission to photograph or draw is needed, and fees may be required. The ancient culture and traditions of these people hold great meaning; visitors should be as respectful of them as they would be of their own. Questions should be directed to the pueblo governor or his representative at the tribal office.

More can be learned about New Mexico's Native Americans and their origins at the many museums and sites in Santa Fe (see), the visitor center at Bandelier National Monument (see) and the Indian Pueblo Cultural Center (see ALBUQUERQUE). For further information contact the Office of Indian Affairs, 228 E Palace Ave, Santa Fe 87501; 505/827-6440.

National Park Service Areas

New Mexico has Carlsbad Caverns National Park (see); Chaco Culture (see) and Pecos (see SANTA FE) National Historical Parks; Bandelier, El Morro, Salinas Pueblo Missions and White Sands national monuments (see all), as well as Aztec Ruins (see AZTEC), Capulin Volcano (see RATON), Fort Union (see LAS VEGAS), Petroglyph (see ALBUQUERQUE) and Gila Cliff Dwellings (see SILVER CITY) national monuments, and El Malpais National Monument & National Conservation Area (see GRANTS). Forty-five percent of all land in the state is federally owned or controlled. Nineteen Indian pueblos and five non-pueblo reservations are located in New Mexico. They are colorful places to visit and some offer recreational facilities.

National Forests

The following is an alphabetical listing of National Forests and towns they are listed under.

Carson National Forest (see TAOS): Forest Supervisor in Taos; Ranger offices in Blanco*, Canijilon*, El Rito*, Penasco*, Questa*, Taos, Tres Piedras*.

Cibola National Forest (see ALBUQUERQUE): Forest Supervisor in Albuquerque; Ranger offices in Cheyenne, OK*, Clayton*, Grants, Magdalena*, Mountainair*, Texline, TX*, Tijeras*.

Gila National Forest (see SILVER CITY): Forest Supervisor in Silver City; Ranger offices in Glenwood*, Luna*, Mimbres*, Quemado*, Reserve*, Silver City, Truth or Consequences.

Lincoln National Forest (see ALAMOGORDO): Forest Supervisor in Alamogordo; Ranger offices in Carlsbad, Cloudcroft, Mayhill*, Ruidoso.

Santa Fe National Forest (see SANTA FE): Forest Supervisor in Santa Fe; Ranger offices in Coyote*, Cuba*, Española, Jemez Springs*, Las Vegas, Los Alamos, Pecos*.

*Not described in text

State Recreation Areas

The following towns list state recreation areas in their vicinity under What to See and Do; refer to the individual town for directions and park information.

Listed under **Alamogordo:** see Oliver Lee State Park.

Listed under **Aztec:** see Navajo Lake State Park.

Listed under **Carlsbad:** see Brantley Lake and Living Desert Zoo and Gardens state parks.

Listed under **Chama:** see El Vado Lake and Heron Lake state parks.

Listed under **Deming:** see City of Rocks, Rockhound and Pancho Villa state parks.

Listed under **Eagle Nest:** see Cimarron Canyon State Park.

Listed under **Gallup:** see Red Rock State Park.

Listed under **Grants:** see Bluewater Lake State Park.

Listed under **Las Vegas:** see Storrie Lake and Morphy Lake state parks.

Listed under **Portales:** see Oasis State Park.

Listed under **Raton:** see Sugarite Canyon State Park.

Listed under **Roswell:** see Bottomless Lakes State Park.

Listed under **Santa Fe:** see Hyde Memorial State Park.

Listed under **Santa Rosa:** see Sumner Lake State Park.

Listed under **Truth or Consequences:** see Caballo Lake and Elephant Butte Lake state parks.

Listed under **Tucumcari:** see Conchas Lake and Ute Lake state parks.

Water-related activities, hiking, riding, various other sports, picnicking, camping and visitor centers are available in many of these areas. Most parks are open all year. Day-use fee per vehicle is $3 at most parks. Camping: $6-$7/day; electrical hookups $4 (where available); sewage hookups $2. Limit 14 consecutive days during any 20-day period; pets on leash only. Annual entrance passes and camping permits available. For further information contact the New Mexico State Park and Recreation Division, PO Box 1147, Santa Fe 87504-1147; 505/827-7465.

Fishing & Hunting

Nonresident fishing license (includes trout stamp): annual $41; 5-day $15; 1-day $8.50. Nonresident hunting license: deer $181; bear $151; cougar $201; elk $356; antelope $192; turkey $76.

New Mexico, with six of the seven life zones found on the North American continent, has a large number of wildlife species, among them four varieties of deer, as well as mountain lion, bear, elk, bighorn sheep, oryx, antelope, javelina, Barbary sheep, ibex, wild turkey, goose, duck, quail, pheasant and squirrel. There is good fishing for trout in mountain streams and lakes; bass, bluegill, crappie, walleye and catfish can also be found in many of the warmer waters.

Hunting and fishing regulations are complex and vary from year to year. For detailed information contact the New Mexico Game and Fish Department, Villagra Building, State Capitol, Santa Fe 87503; 505/827-7911.

Skiing

The following towns list ski areas in their vicinity under What to See and Do; refer to the individual town for directions and information.

Listed under **Albuquerque:** see Sandia Peak Ski Area.

Listed under **Cloudcroft:** see Snow Canyon.

Listed under **Eagle Nest:** see Angel Fire Ski Resort.

Listed under **Red River:** see Red River Ski Area.

Listed under **Ruidoso:** see Ski Apache Resort.

Listed under **Santa Fe:** see Santa Fe Ski Area.

Listed under **Taos:** see Sipapu and Taos Ski Valley ski areas.

For ski reports call Snowphone from Nov-Apr for a two-minute tape on snow conditions, 505/984-0606.

Safety Belt Information

Safety belts are mandatory for all persons in front seat of vehicle. Children under 11 years must be in an approved passenger restraint anywhere in vehicle: ages 5-10 may use a regulation seat belt; ages 1-4 may use a regulation seat belt in back seat, however, in front seat children must use an approved safety seat; under age 1 must be in an approved safety seat. For further information phone 505/827-0427.

Interstate Highway System

The following alphabetical listing of New Mexico towns in *Mobil Travel Guide* shows that these cities are within 10 miles of the indicated Interstate highways. A highway map should, however, be checked for the nearest exit.

INTERSTATE 10: Deming, Las Cruces.

INTERSTATE 25: Albuquerque, Las Cruces, Las Vegas, Raton, Santa Fe, Socorro, Truth or Consequences.

INTERSTATE 40: Albuquerque, Gallup, Grants, Santa Rosa, Tucumcari.

Additional Visitor Information

For free information, contact the New Mexico Department of Tourism, Lamy Building, Rm 751, 491 Old Santa Fe Trail, Santa Fe 87503; 505/827-7400 or 800/545-2040. *New Mexico*, a colorful, illustrated magazine, is published monthly; to order, contact *New Mexico Magazine* at the Lew Wallace Bldg, 495 Old Santa Fe Trail, Santa Fe 87501; 505/827-7447 or 800/435-0715.

There are several welcome centers in New Mexico; visitors who stop by will find information and brochures helpful when planning stops at points of interest. They are located in Anthony (24 mi S of Las Cruces on I-10); Chama (just off US 64/84); Gallup (I-40 exit 22); Glenrio (31 mi E of Tucumcari on I-40); La Bajada (11 mi S of Santa Fe on I-25); Lordsburg (on I-10); Raton (off I-25); Santa Fe (downtown); and Texico (7 mi E of Clovis on US 70/84).

Acoma Pueblo (E-2)

(For accommodations see Albuquerque, Grants)

Pop Reservation, 4,000 (est) **Elev** 7,000 ft
Information Tourist Visitation Center, PO Box 309, Acoma 87034; 505/740-7966 or 800/747-0181.

On a mesa rising 367 feet from the surrounding plain is perhaps the oldest continuously inhabited town in the United States. The exact date of establishment is not known, but archaeologists have dated occupation of the "Sky City" to at least 1150. Legend says it has been inhabited since the time of Christ.

Acoma is a beautiful pueblo with the mission church, San Esteban del Rey. This mission probably includes part of the original built by Fray Ramirez in 1629. Beams 40 feet long and 14 inches square were carried from the mountains 30 miles away; even the dirt for the graveyard was carried up by Indians. They farmed on the plain below and caught water in rock basins on top. Acoma Indians are skilled potters and excellent stockmen.

The pueblo is about 12 miles south of I-40 and is accessible from exit 102. Tours leave from the base of the pueblo at the Visitors Center, where a shuttle bus takes visitors to the pueblo on top of the mesa (fee). Visitors may walk down the steep, narrow "padre's trail" to the Visitors Center after the tour.

There is a museum with Indian pottery and history exhibits (ca 1400 to the present). (Daily) **Free.**

Acoma-made crafts, native foods, tours and a cultural and historical exhibit can be seen at the Visitor Center below Sky City.

Once or twice a year, special religious ceremonials are held at which no outsiders are permitted, but there are several festivals (see ANNUAL EVENTS) to which the public is welcome. (Daily; closed pueblo hols, July 10-13 and 1st or 2nd wkend Oct) Your guide will explain the rules and courtesies of taking pictures (picture-taking fee; no movie cameras).

Approximately 1 mile north on NM 23 is the **Enchanted Mesa,** 400 feet high. According to an Acoma legend, the tribe lived on top of this mesa until a sudden, violent storm washed out the only way up. Visitors are not permitted to climb to the mesa.

Annual Events

Governor's Feast. Old Acoma; dances. Early Feb.

Santa Maria Feast. McCartys Village Mission. 1st Sun May.

Fiesta (St Lorenzo's) Day. In Acomita. Mid-Aug.

Feast of St Estevan. Old Acoma; harvest dance. Early Sept.

Christmas Festivals. San Estevan del Rey Mission, Old Acoma; dances, luminarias. Late Dec.

Alamogordo (G-4)

(See Cloudcroft, Mescalero, Ruidoso)

Founded 1898 **Pop** 27,596 **Elev** 4,350 ft **Area code** 505 **Zip** 88310
Information Chamber of Commerce, 1301 N White Sands Blvd, PO Box 518; 505/437-6120.

Alamogordo is a popular tourist destination because of its proximity to Mescalero Apache Indian Reservation, Lincoln National Forest and White Sands National Monument. A branch of New Mexico State University is located here. Surrounded by desert and mountains, Alamogordo is the home of Holloman AFB and the 49th Fighter Wing, home of the Stealth fighter. The first atomicbomb was set off nearby.

What to See and Do

Alameda Park Zoo. A 7-acre zoo with more than 275 native and exotic animals. (Daily; closed Jan 1, Dec 25) 10th & White Sands Blvd (US 54/70). Phone 505/439-4290 or 505/437-1292. ¢¢

Lincoln National Forest. Fishing, hunting,picnicking, camping, wild cave tours and winter sports in the Sacramento, Capitan and Guadalupe mountains. Backpack trips in the White Mt Capitan Wildernesses. Some campsites in developed areas free, some require fee. E of town. Contact the Supervisor's Office, Federal Bldg, 1101 New York Ave; 505/437-6030.

Oliver Lee State Park (Dog Canyon). Mecca for mountain climbers, photographers and history buffs. Early Apache stronghold, site of at least five major battles, box canyon protected by 2,000-foot bluff; mossy bluffs, cottonwood trees; Frenchy's Place, a substantial rock house with miles of stone fence. Hiking. Camping (hookups, dump station). Visitor center (daily), museum, tours of restored ranchhouse (Sat & Sun, mid-afternoon). 12 mi S via US 54, E on County A16. Phone 505/437-8284. Day use per vehicle ¢¢; Camping ¢¢¢-¢¢¢¢

★ **Space Center-International Space Hall of Fame.** Museum features space-related artifacts and exhibits;one-hour tour (daily; closed Dec 25). Sr citizen rate. 2 mi E via US 54, Indian Wells & Scenic Drive. Phone 505/437-2840 or 800/545-4021. ¢¢¢ Combination ticket includes Hall of Fame and

Tombaugh Space Theater. Planetarium with Omnimax movies (daily). Features laser light shows (winter, Fri-Sun evenings; summer, every evening; fee). Combination ticket including Space Hall of Fame ¢¢¢

Three Rivers Petroglyph Site. Twenty thousand rock carvings made between A.D. 900 and 1400 by the Jornada Branch of the Mogollon Indian Culture; semi-desert terrain; interpretive signs; reconstructed prehistoric village; six picnic sites; tent and trailer sites (no hookups). 29 mi N on US 54 to Three Rivers, then 5 mi E on county road. Phone 505/525-4300. Day use per vehicle ¢¢

White Sands National Monument (see). 15 mi SW on US 70.

Annual Events

Trinity Site Tour. Visit to the site of the first A-bomb explosion; only time the site is open to the public. Contact the Chamber of Commerce. 1st Sat Apr & Oct.

Space Hall of Fame Induction Ceremonies. Phone 505/437-2840. 1st Sat Oct.

Motels

★★**BEST WESTERN DESERT AIRE.** *1021 S White Sands Blvd (US 54, 70, 82).* 505/437-2110; FAX 505/437-1898. 100 rms, 2 story. S $47-$57; D $58; each addl $5; under 12 free. Crib free. TV; cable, VCR avail. Heated pool, sauna. Complimentary continental bkfst. Ck-out noon. Coin lndry. Business servs avail. In-rm modem link. Valet serv. Sundries. Game rm. Cr cds: A, C, D, DS, MC, V.

D ≈ ⊠ ⋒ SC

★★**DAYS INN.** *907 S White Sands Blvd (US 54, 70, 82).* 505/437-5090; FAX 505/434-5667. 40 rms, 2 story. S $38-$46; D $46-$52; each addl $8. TV; cable. Pool. Continental bkfst. Restaurant adj open 24 hrs. Ck-out 11 am. Coin lndry. Some refrigerators. Cr cds: A, C, D, DS, MC, V.

≈ ⊠ ⋒ SC

✔★**SATELLITE INN.** *2224 N White Sands Blvd (US 54, 70, 82), at 23rd St.* 505/437-8454; res: 800/221-7690. 40 rms, 1-2 story. S $32-$34; D $34-$38; each addl $2; kit. unit $38-$46; family unit $32-$42. Crib free. Pet accepted. TV; cable (premium). Pool. Continental bkfst. Restaurant adj 6 am-9 pm. Ck-out noon. Refrigerators. Cr cds: A, C, D, DS, MC, V.

✔ ≈ ⊠ ⋒ SC

★★**WHITE SANDS INN.** *1020 S White Sands Blvd (US 54, 70, 82).* 505/434-4200; res: 800/255-5061; FAX 505/437-8872. 92 units, 2 story, 16 suites. S $38-$45; D $45-$49; each addl $5; suites $55; under 12 free. Crib free. TV; cable. Heated pool; whirlpool. Complimentary continental bkfst, coffee. Restaurant adj open 24 hrs. Ck-out noon. Coin lndry. Meeting rms. Business servs avail. In-rm modem link. Valet serv. Refrigerators, microwaves avail. Cr cds: A, C, D, DS, MC, V.

D ≈ ⊠ ⋒ SC

Restaurant

★**EAGLE'S NEST.** *905 S White Sands Blvd.* 505/437-8644. Hrs: 11 am-9:30 pm. Closed Sun; Thanksgiving, Dec 25. Res accepted. Bar. A la carte entrees: lunch $3.75-$5.75, dinner $4.95-$22.95. Specializes in prime rib. Salad bar. Western decor. Cr cds: DS, MC, V.

D

Albuquerque (D-3)

Founded 1706 **Pop** 384,736 **Elev** 5,311 ft **Area code** 505

In 1706, Don Francisco Cuervo y Valdés, then governor of New Mexico, moved 30 families from Bernalillo to a spot some 15 miles south on the Rio Grande, where there was better pasturage. He named this community after the Duke of Alburquerque, then Viceroy of New Spain. With a nice sense of diplomatic delicacy, the Viceroy renamed it San Felipe de Alburquerque (the first "r" was dropped later), in limited deference to King Philip V of Spain. He also named one of the first structures, a church (still standing), San Felipe de Neri.

The pasturage proved good, and by 1790, the population grew to almost 6,000 (a very large city for New Mexico at the time). Today, Albuquerque is the largest city in New Mexico.

Albuquerque was an important US military outpost from 1846 to 1870. In 1880, when a landowner near the Old Town refused to sell, the Santa Fe Railroad chose a route two miles east, forming a new town called New Albuquerque. It was not long before the new town had enveloped what is still called "Old Town," now a popular tourist shopping area.

Surrounded by mountains, Albuquerque continues to grow. The largest industry is Sandia Laboratories, a national laboratory engaged in solar and nuclear research and the testing and development of nuclear weapons. More than 100 firms are engaged in electronics manufacturing and research and development. The city is also the center for the livestock business.

Dry air and plentiful sunshine (76% of the time) have earned it a reputation as a health center. Adding to that reputation is the Lovelace Medical Center (similar to the Mayo Clinic in Rochester, MN), which gave the first US astronauts their qualifying examinations. The University of New Mexico is also located in Albuquerque.

What to See and Do

Albuquerque Museum. Regional museum of art and history; traveling exhibits; solar heated building. (Daily exc Mon; closed hols) 2000 Mountain Rd NW. Phone 505/242-4600. **Free.**

Cibola National Forest. More than 1.5 million acres located throughout central New Mexico. Includes Mt Taylor (11,301 ft), several mountain ranges and four wilderness areas: Sandia Mt, Manzano Mt, Apache Kid and Withington. Scenic drives; bighorn sheep in Sandia Mts. Fishing, hunting. Picnicking. Camping (some fees). La Cienega Nature Trail is for the disabled and visually impaired. Contact the Supervisor, 2113 Osuna Rd NE, Ste A, 87113-1001; 505/761-4650. Also phone 800/280-2267 for camping reservations.

Coronado State Monument. Coronado is said to have camped near this excavated pueblo in 1540 on his famous, but unsuccessful quest for the seven golden cities of Cibola. Reconstructed, painted kiva; visitor center devoted to Southwestern Indian culture and the Spanish influence on the area. Picnicking. (Daily; closed state hols in winter) 15 mi N on I-25, then 1 mi W on NM 44. Phone 505/867-5351. ¢

Indian Pueblo Cultural Center. Owned and operated by the 19 Indian pueblos of New Mexico. Exhibits in museum feature the story of Pueblo Indian culture; Pueblo Gallery with handcrafted art; Indian dance and craft demonstrations (wkends). Restaurant. (Daily; closed Jan 1 & 6, Thanksgiving, Dec 25) 2401 12th St NW. Phone 505/843-7270. ¢¢

Isleta Pueblo (population: 1,703; altitude: 4,885 ft). A prosperous pueblo with church originally built by Fray Juan de Salas. The church was burned during the Pueblo Rebellion of 1680 and later rebuilt; beautiful sanctuary and altar. Recreation area 4 mi NE across river includes stocked fishing lakes (fee). Picnicking. Camping (electricity, water avail; 2-wk limit); concession. Pueblo (daily). 13 mi S, just off US 85. Contact General Manager, PO Box 383, Isleta 87022; 505/877-0370. Camping ¢¢¢-¢¢¢¢

National Atomic Museum. History and nuclear energy science center; films; tours; exhibits depicting history of atomic age. (Daily; closed major hols) Necessary identification for admission to the base includes: valid driver's license (driver only); vehicle registration; proof of insurance; car rental paperwork. Kirtland Air Force Base (East), Bldg 20358; 2¹/₂ mi S of I-40 on Wyoming Blvd. Phone 505/845-6670. **Free.**

New Mexico Museum of Natural History. Exhibits on botany, geology, paleontology and zoology; naturalist center; Dynamax theater; cafe; shop. (Daily; closed some major hols) Sr citizen rate. 1801 Mountain Rd NW. Phone 505/841-8837. ¢¢

⚹ **Old Town.** The original settlement is one block N of Central Ave, the city's main street, at Rio Grande Blvd. Old Town Plaza retains a lovely Spanish flavor, with many interesting shops and restaurants. (See ANNUAL EVENTS)

Petroglyph National Monument. In the West Mesa area; contains concentrated groups of rock drawings believed to have been carved on lava formations by ancestors of the Pueblo Indians. Three walking trails along the 17-mile escarpment. Picnicking. (Daily) 9 mi W on Unser Blvd. Phone 505/897-8814 or 505/873-6620. Per car ¢

Rio Grande Nature Center State Park. Visitor center, glass-enclosed observation room overlooking 4¹/₂-acre pond; interpretive displays on wildlife of the *bosque* (cottonwood groves) along the river; two miles of nature trails. (Daily; closed Jan 1, Thanksgiving, Dec 25) E bank of Rio Grande, at 2901 Candelaria Rd NW. Phone 505/344-7240. ¢

Rio Grande Zoological Park. More than 1,200 exoticanimals in exhibits among a grove of cottonwoods. Rain forest; reptile house; Ape Country; Cat Walk; white tigers. (Daily; closed Jan 1, Thanksgiving, Dec 25) Sr citizen rate. 903 10th St SW. Phone 505/843-7413. **¢¢**

Sandia Peak Ski Area. Areahas 4 double chairlifts, 1 surface lift; patrol, school, rentals; snack bar, restaurant, bar. Aerial tramway on W side of mountain meets lifts at top. Longest run over 2¹/₂ miles; vertical drop 1,700 feet. (Mid-Dec-Mar, daily) Chairlift also operates July-Labor Day (Thurs-Sun; fee). 16 mi E on I-40, then 7 mi N on NM 14, then 6 mi NW on NM 536, in Cibola National Forest, Sandia Mts. Phone 505/242-9133 or -9052 (snow report). **¢¢¢¢**

Sandia Peak Aerial Tramway. From tram base at 6,559-feet, travels almost three miles up west slope of Sandia Mts to 10,378-feet. Hiking trail, restaurant at summit. Cactus garden, restaurant at base terminal. (Daily; closed 1 wk late Apr & 1 wk late Oct) Parking fee. Sr citizen rate. 5 mi NE of city limits via I-25 and Tramway Rd. Phone 505/298-8518. **¢¢¢¢**

Sightseeing. Gray Line bus tours. For information, reservations contact 800 Rio Grande Blvd NW, Ste 22, 87104; 505/242-3880.

Telephone Pioneer Museum. Displays tracethe development of the telephone from 1876 to the present. More than 100 types of telephones; switchboards; early equipment; pioneer telephone directories. 201 3rd NW, Ste 710. Phone 505/245-5883 for days open. **Free.**

University of New Mexico (1889). (25,009 students) This campus, seated at the foot of the SandiaMountains, shows both Spanish and Pueblo Indian architectural influences. It is one of the largest universities in the Southwest. Special outdoor sports course for the disabled, north of Johnson Gym (phone 505/277-4347). E of I-25, CentralAve exit. Contact Visitors Center at the corner of Las Lomas and Redondo Sts or phone 505/277-1989. On campus are

Maxwell Museum of Anthropology. Permanent and changing exhibits of early man andNative American cultures with an emphasis on the Southwest. (Mon-Sat, also Sun afternoons; closed major hols) Redondo Dr at Ash St NE, in Anthropology Building. Phone 505/277-4405. **Free.**

Museum of Geology and Institute of Meteoritics Meteorite Museum. Museum of Geology contains numerous samples of ancient plants, minerals, rocks and animals. Meteorite Museum has major collection of over 200 meteorites. Both museums (Mon-Fri). 200 Yale Blvd NE, both part of Geology Department. **Free.**

Jonson Gallery. Houses archives andwork of modernist painter Raymond Jonson (1891-1982) and a few works by his contemporaries. Also exhibitions on the arts in New Mexico. (Tues-Fri, also Tues evenings; closed hols) 1909 Las Lomas NE. Phone 505/277-4967. **Free.**

Fine Arts Center. Houses University Art Museum, featuring more than 23,000 pieces in collection of fine arts (Mon-Fri, also Tues evenings & Sun afternoons; phone 505/277-4001; free). Fine Arts Library, which contains the Southwest Music Archives; Rodey Theatre; 2,094-seat Popejoy Hall, home of New Mexico Symphony Orchestra & host to Best of Broadway International Theatre seasons of plays, dance and music (phone 505/277-3121). Just NW of university's Stanford Dr & Central Ave main entrance. Phone 505/277-4402.

Annual Events

New Year's Celebration. Taos Pueblo. Turtle dance. Jan 1.

Kings' Day. Dances at most pueblos. Early Jan.

Founders Day. In Old Town. Late Apr.

Fiesta Artistica de Colores. At Civic Plaza. Celebrating more than400 years of Hispanic heritage. Arts & crafts, entertainment. May.

San Antonio Feast Day. Sandia and Taos Pueblos. Corn dance. Mid-June.

San Pedro Feast Day. Santa Ana Pueblo. Corn dance. Late June.

New Mexico Arts & Crafts Fair. At Fairgrounds. Exhibits and demonstrations by craftsworkers representing Spanish, Indian and other North American cultures. Last wkend June.

Santa Ana Feast Day. Santa Ana & Taos Pueblos. Corndance. Late July.

St Augustin's Feast Day. Dances at Isleta Pueblo. Late Aug.

New Mexico State Fair. Fairgrounds, San Pedro Dr between Lomas and Central Blvds. Horseracing, rodeo, midway; entertainment. Phone 505/265-1791. Sept 6-22.

International Balloon Fiesta. First 2 wkends Oct beginning with 1st Sat.

San Diego Feast Day. Jemez & Tesuque Pueblos. Buffalo, Comanche, Deer and Flag dances. Mid-Nov.

Seasonal Events

Albuquerque Civic Light Opera. Popejoy Hall on University of New Mexico campus. Five musicals each season. Phone 505/345-6577. Apr-Dec.

New Mexico Symphony Orchestra. Concerts in Popejoy Hall on the University ofNew Mexico campus. Phone 505/881-9590 or 800/251-NMSO. Sept-May.

Albuquerque Ballet Co. Full-length productions of contemporary and classical works, often featuring internationally known guest stars. For schedule phone 505/265-8150.

Albuquerque Little Theatre. Historic community theater; Broadway productions. Phone 505/242-4750. Sept-May.

Additional Visitor Information

For further information and a list of sightseeing tours contact the Convention & Visitors Bureau, 121 Tijeras NE, PO Box 26866, 87102; 505/842-9918 or 800/733-9918. For information on public transportation phone 505/843-9200.

Motels

(Rates may be higher during the Balloon Fiesta, the State Fair and other special events)

★ ★ ★ **BEST WESTERN INN AT RIO RANCHO.** *(1465 Rio Rancho Dr, Rio Rancho 87124) 3 mi W on I-40 exit 155, then 8 mi N on NM 45.* 505/892-1700; FAX 505/892-4628. 106 rms, 10 kits. S $55-$73; D $61-$73; each addl $6; suites $115; kit. units $61-$67; under 12 free. Crib $6. Pet accepted, some restrictions; $3 per day. TV; cable (premium), VCR avail. Pool; whirlpool, poolside serv. Coffee in rms. Restaurant 6:30 am-10 pm. Rm serv. Bar 11-2 am; entertainment, dancing Fri & Sat. Ck-out 11 am. Coin lndry. Meeting rms. Business servs avail. In-rm modem link. Valet serv. Sundries. Gift shop. Free airport, RR station, bus depot transportation. Golf privileges, greens fee, pro, putting green, driving range. Downhill/x-country ski 20 mi. Lawn games. Picnic tables, grills. Cr cds: A, C, D, DS, JCB, MC, V.

D 🐾 ⚓ 🏃 🏊 ⌦ 🐾 **SC**

★ **CLUBHOUSE INN.** *1315 Menaul Blvd NE (87107), at I-25.* 505/345-0010; FAX 505/344-3911. 137 units, 2 story, 17 kit. suites. S $65; D $75; each addl $5; kit. suites $89-$93; under 10 free; wkly, wkend rates. Crib free. TV; cable. Heated pool; whirlpool. Complimentary full bkfst buffet. Ck-out noon. Meeting rms. Private patios, balconies. Picnic tables, grills. Cr cds: A, C, D, DS, MC, V.

D ⌦ ⌦ 🐾 **SC**

✔ ★ ★ **COMFORT INN EAST.** *13031 Central NE (87123), I-40 at Tramway exit 167.* 505/294-1800; FAX 505/293-1088. 122 rms, 2 story. June-mid-Oct: S $46-$52; D $49-$55; each addl $5; under 17 free; lower rates rest of yr. Crib free. Pet accepted; $3 non-refundable per day. TV; cable (premium). Pool; whirlpools. Complimentary full bkfst. Coffee in rms. Restaurant 6-10 am, 5-8 pm. Ck-out 11 am. Coin lndry. Meeting rms. Business servs avail. Downhill ski 9 mi. Cr cds: A, C, D, DS, MC, V.

★ ★ ★ **COURTYARD BY MARRIOTT.** *1920 Yale SE (87106), near Intl Airport.* 505/843-6600; FAX 505/843-8740. 150 rms, 4 story. S $84; D $94; suites $99-$109; under 12 free; wkend rates. Crib free. TV; cable (premium), VCR avail. Indoor pool. Complimentary coffee in rms. Restaurant 6 am-10 am, 5-10 pm; Sat & Sun 7 am-11 am. Rm serv. Bar 4-11 pm. Ck-out 1 pm. Meeting rms. Business center. In-rm modem link. Valet serv. Free airport transportation. Downhill/x-country ski 15 mi. Exercise equipt; weights, bicycles, whirlpool. Refrigerator in suites. Balconies. Picnic tables. Cr cds: A, C, D, DS, MC, V.

☐ ☒ ☒ ☒ ✕ ✕ ☒ ☒ SC ☒

✔ ★ **DAYS INN.** *6031 Iliff Rd NW (87121), I-40 exit 155.* 505/836-3297; FAX 505/836-1214. 81 rms, 2 story. June-Oct: S $45-$70; D $50-$75; each addl $5; under 12 free; lower rates rest of yr. Crib free. Pet accepted; $5 per day. TV; cable (premium). Indoor pool; whirlpool, sauna. Complimentary continental bkfst, coffee. Restaurant nearby. Ck-out 11 am. Guest lndry. Downhill/x-country ski 10 mi. Cr cds: A, C, D, DS, MC, V.

☐ ☒ ☒ ☒ ☒ ☒ ☒ SC

✔ ★ **DAYS INN.** *13317 Central Ave NE (87123).* 505/294-3297; FAX 505/293-3973. 72 rms, 2 story. S $52-$60; D $55-$65; each addl $5; under 12 free. Crib free. TV; cable (premium). Indoor pool; whirlpool, sauna. Complimentary coffee in lobby. Restaurant adj open 24 hrs. Ck-out 11 am. Cr cds: A, C, D, DS, MC, V.

☒ ☒ ☒ SC

★ **HAMPTON INN.** *5101 Ellison NE (87109), I-25 exit 231.* 505/344-1555; FAX 505/345-2216. 125 rms, 3 story. May-Aug: S $52-$66; D $59-$64; under 18 free. Crib free. Pet accepted, some restrictions. TV; cable (premium), VCR avail. Heated pool. Complimentary continental bkfst, coffee. Restaurant nearby. Ck-out noon. Business servs avail. In-rm modem link. Valet serv. Cr cds: A, C, D, DS, MC, V.

☐ ☒ ☒ ☒ ☒ ☒ SC

★ ★ **HOLIDAY INN EXPRESS.** *10330 Hotel Ave (87123).* 505/275-8900; FAX 505/275-6000. 104 rms, 2 story. S $60-$75; D $65-$80; each addl $5; suites $85-$90; under 19 free. Crib free. Pet accepted; $5. TV; cable (premium), VCR avail. Indoor pool; whirlpool. Complimentary coffee in rms. Complimentary continental bkfst. Restaurant nearby. Ck-out noon. Coin lndry. Meeting rms. Business servs avail. In-rm modem link. Valet serv. Free airport transportation. Downhill ski 15 mi. Exercise equipt; weight machine, bicycle, sauna. Refrigerator in suites. Cr cds: A, C, D, DS, JCB, MC, V.

☐ ☒ ☒ ☒ ☒ ✕ ☒ ☒ SC

★ **HOWARD JOHNSON.** *15 Hotel Circle (87123), 6 mi E on I-40, exit 165.* 505/296-4852; FAX 505/293-9072. 150 rms, 2 story. S, D $48-$80; each $5; under 18 free. Crib free. TV; cable (premium). Heated pool. Restaurant 6 am-10 pm. Rm serv. Ck-out noon. Coin lndry. Business servs avail. Bellhops. Valet serv. Free airport, RR station, bus depot transportation. Exercise equipt; weight machine, rowers, whirlpool. Some refrigerators. Cr cds: A, C, D, DS, ER, JCB, MC, V.

☐ ☒ ✕ ☒ ☒ SC

★ ★ **LA QUINTA-AIRPORT.** *2116 Yale Blvd SE (87106), 1 mi E of I-25 Gibson Airport exit, near Intl Airport.* 505/243-5500; FAX 505/247-8288. 105 rms, 3 story. S $56; D $64; each addl $8; suites $79; under 18 free. Crib free. Pet accepted; some restrictions. TV; cable (premium), VCR avail. Pool. Continental bkfst 6-10 am. Restaurant adj open 24 hrs. Ck-out noon. Business servs avail. In-rm modem link. Valet serv. Free airport transportation 7 am-10:30 pm. Downhill ski 20 mi. Cr cds: A, C, D, DS, MC, V.

☐ ☒ ☒ ☒ ✕ ☒ ☒ SC

★ ★ **LE BARON INN.** *2120 Menaul Blvd NE (87107), at jct I-25 Menaul exit, I-40.* 505/884-0250; res: 800/444-7378; FAX 505/883-0594. 200 units, 2 story, 33 suites. S, D $52-$62; suites $72-$125; under 12 free. Crib free. TV; cable (premium), VCR avail. Pool. Complimentary continental bkfst. Restaurant adj open 24 hrs. Ck-out noon. Coin lndry. Meeting rms. Business servs avail. Valet serv. Free airport transportation. Downhill ski 15 mi. Bathrm phones; some refrigerators. Cr cds: A, C, D, DS, MC, V.

☐ ☒ ☒ ☒ ☒ SC

★ **TRAVELERS INN.** *411 McKnight Ave NW (87102), I-40 at 4th St.* 505/242-5228; res: 800/633-8300; FAX 505/766-9218. 99 rms, 4 story. S $40.95; D $47.95; each addl $4; under 12 free. Crib free. TV; cable (premium). Heated pool; whirlpool. Complimentary coffee in lobby. Complimentary continental bkfst. Restaurant adj open 24 hrs; Sun to midnight. Ck-out 11 am. Business servs avail. Some minibars. Cr cds: A, C, D, DS, MC, V.

☐ ☒ ☒ ☒ SC

✔ ★ **TRAVELODGE.** *13139 Central Ave NE (87123).* 505/292-4878; FAX 505/299-1822. 40 rms, 2 story. May-Oct: S, D $40-$100; each addl $5; under 17 free; higher rates for special events; lower rates rest of yr. Crib free. Pet accepted, some restrictions; $5. TV; cable (premium). Complimentary coffee in lobby. Complimentary bkfst. Restaurant adj open 24 hrs. Ck-out 11 am. Downhill ski 8 mi; x-country ski 8 mi. Cr cds: A, C, D, DS, MC, V.

☐ ☒ ☒ ☒ ☒ SC

Motor Hotels

★ **AMBERLY SUITE HOTEL.** *7620 Pan American Frwy NE (87109), I-25 & San Antonio Rd N.* 505/823-1300; res: 800/333-9806; FAX 505/823-2896. 170 suites, 3 story. S, D $94-$114; each addl $10; under 16 free; wkly rates. Crib free. Pet accepted; $2 per stay. TV; cable (premium), VCR avail. Heated pool. Complimentary full bkfst, afternoon refreshments. Restaurant 6 am-10 pm. Bar 4 pm-midnight. Ck-out noon. Coin lndry. Meeting rms. Business servs avail. In-rm modem link. Shopping arcade. Free airport, RR station, bus depot transportation. Downhill ski 5 mi. Exercise equipt; weights, bicycles, whirlpool, sauna. Refrigerators. Courtyard; fountain. Cr cds: A, C, D, DS, MC, V.

☐ ☒ ☒ ☒ ✕ ☒ ☒ SC

★ **BEST WESTERN WINROCK INN.** *18 Winrock Center NE (87110), in Winrock Shopping Center.* 505/883-5252; FAX 505/889-3206. 173 rms, 2 story. S, D $67-$82; each addl $7; suites $110; under 12 free. Crib free. TV; cable. Heated pool. Complimentary bkfst buffet. Restaurant adj open 24 hrs. Ck-out noon. Coin lndry. Meeting rms. Business servs avail. Bellhops. Free airport transportation. Health club privileges. Game rm. Some refrigerators. Cr cds: A, C, D, DS, MC, V.

☒ ☒ ☒ SC

★ ★ **HOLIDAY INN-MIDTOWN.** *2020 Menaul Blvd NE (87107), 1 blk E of I-25, I-40, Menaul Blvd exit.* 505/884-2511; FAX 505/884-5720. 363 rms, 4-5 story. S, D $99-$109; each addl $10; under 18 free. Crib free. TV; cable (premium). Heated pool; wading pool, poolside serv. Restaurant 6:30 am-2 pm, 5-10 pm. Rm serv. Bar 11-1 am, Sun noon-midnight; entertainment, dancing. Ck-out noon. Coin lndry. Meeting rms. Business servs avail. Bellhops. Valet serv. Sundries. Free airport, RR station, bus depot transportation. Downhill ski 15 mi. Exercise equipt; bicycles, whirlpool, sauna. Game rm. Some private patios, balconies. Cr cds: A, C, D, DS, JCB, MC, V.

☐ ☒ ☒ ✕ ☒ ☒ SC

✔ ★ ★ **PLAZA INN.** *900 Medical Arts Ave NE (87102), I-25 Lomas Blvd exit.* 505/243-5693; res: 800/237-1307; FAX 505/843-6229. 120 rms, 5 story. S, D $65-$85; each addl $5; under 17 free. Crib $5. Pet accepted. TV. Heated pool. Complimentary coffee 24 hrs. Restaurant 6 am-midnight. Bar 11-2 am, Sun noon-midnight. Ck-out noon. Coin lndry. Meeting rms. Business servs avail. Valet serv. Free airport, RR station, bus depot transportation. Downhill ski 14 mi. Exercise equipt; weight machine, bicycle, whirlpool. Some refrigerators. Private patios, balconies. Cr cds: A, C, D, DS, ER, MC, V.

☐ ☒ ☒ ☒ ✕ ☒ ☒ SC

★ ★ ★ **RADISSON INN AIRPORT.** *1901 University SE (87106), I-25 exit 222, near Intl Airport.* 505/247-0512; FAX 505/843-7148. 150 rms, 2-3 story. S $75-$95; D $85-$105; each addl $10; suite $95-$110; under 18 free; wkly, wkend rates. Crib free. TV; cable (premium), VCR avail. Heated pool; poolside serv. Restaurant 6 am-10 pm. Rm serv. Bar 2 pm-midnight. Ck-out noon. Meeting rms. Business center. In-rm modem link. Bellhops. Free airport, RR station, bus depot transportation. Downhill ski 20 mi. Health club privileges. Cr cds: A, C, D, DS, ER, MC, V.

[icons]

★ ★ **RAMADA INN.** *25 Hotel Circle NE (87123), I-40 Eubank Blvd exit E 165.* 505/271-1000; FAX 505/291-9028. 205 rms, 2 story. S $63-$83; D $73-$93; each addl $10; suites $99-$150; under 18 free; wkend rates. Crib free. TV; cable (premium). Heated pool. Restaurant 6 am-2 pm, 5-10 pm. Rm serv. Bar 2 pm-2 am, Sun 1 pm-midnight; video entertainment. Ck-out noon. Coin lndry. Meeting rms. Business servs avail. Valet serv. Free airport transportation. Downhill ski 10 mi. Cr cds: A, C, D, DS, MC, V.

[icons]

Hotels

★ ★ ★ **BEST WESTERN FRED HARVEY.** *2910 Yale Blvd SE (87106), 2 blks E of I-25 Gibson Blvd exit, at Intl Airport.* 505/843-7000; FAX 505/843-6307. 266 rms, 14 story. S $82-$87; D $92-$97; each addl $10; suites $150-$300; under 12 free; wkend rates. Crib free. TV; cable (premium). Heated pool; poolside serv. Restaurant 6 am-11 pm. Bar 11-1:30 am, Sun to midnight. Ck-out 1 pm. Coin lndry. Meeting rms. Business center. In-rm modem link. Gift shop. Free airport transportation. Tennis. Downhill ski 15 mi. Exercise equipt; bicycles, stair machine, sauna. Some refrigerators. Balconies. Cr cds: A, C, D, DS, MC, V.

[icons]

★ ★ ★ **DOUBLETREE.** *201 Marquette Ave NW (87102).* 505/247-3344; FAX 505/247-7025. 294 rms, 15 story. S, D $125-$145; each addl $20; suites $140-$475; under 18 free. Crib free. TV; cable (premium), VCR avail. Pool. Restaurant 6 am-10 pm. Bar 11:30-2 am, Sun from noon. Ck-out noon. Convention facilities. Business servs avail. In-rm modem link. Gift shop. Downhill ski 15 mi. Exercise equipt; weights, bicycles. Health club privileges. Cr cds: A, C, D, DS, ER, JCB, MC, V.

[icons]

★ ★ ★ **HILTON INN.** *1901 University Blvd (87125), 1 blk E of I-25 Menaul Blvd exit.* 505/884-2500; FAX 505/889-9118. 262 rms, 12 story. S $79-$119; D $89-$125; each addl $10; suites $395-$495; under 18 free. Crib free. TV; cable (premium), VCR avail. 2 pools, 1 indoor; whirlpool, sauna, poolside serv. Restaurants 6 am-11 pm. Bar 11-1 am, Sun from noon; entertainment. Ck-out noon. Convention facilities. Business center. In-rm modem link. Free airport, RR station, bus depot transportation. Tennis. Downhill ski 15 mi. Exercise rm; stair machine, weights, bicycles. Some bathrm phones, refrigerators. Balconies. Luxury level. Cr cds: A, C, D, DS, ER, JCB, MC, V.

[icons]

★ ★ ★ **HOLIDAY INN PYRAMID.** *5151 San Francisco Rd NE (87109), I-25 at Paso Del Norte exit 232.* 505/821-3333; FAX 505/828-0230. 311 units, 10 story. S, D $104-$124; each addl $12; suites $118-$275; under 19 free. Crib free. TV; cable (premium), VCR avail. Indoor/outdoor pool; poolside serv. Restaurant 6 am-10 pm. Bar 11-2 am; dancing Tues-Sat evenings. Ck-out noon. Convention facilities. Business center. In-rm modem link. Concierge. Shopping arcade. Free airport, RR station, bus depot transportation. Downhill ski 8 mi. Exercise equipt; weights, bicycles, whirlpool, sauna. Some refrigerators. Private patios. Atrium lobby; waterfall. Luxury level. Cr cds: A, C, D, DS, JCB, MC, V.

[icons]

★ ★ ★ **HYATT REGENCY.** *330 Tijeras NW (87102).* 505/842-1234; FAX 505/766-6710. 395 rms, 20 story. S $105-$135; D $130-$160; each addl $25; suites $310-$725; under 18 free. Crib free. Garage parking $7; valet $11. TV; cable (premium), VCR avail. Heated pool; poolside serv. Restaurant 6 am-10:30 pm. Bar 11-2 am; entertainment. Ck-out noon. Convention facilities. Business center. In-rm modem link. Shopping arcade. Beauty shop. Downhill/x-country ski 18 mi. Exercise equipt; weights, bicycles, sauna. Refrigerator, wet bar in suites. Convention center adj. Cr cds: A, C, D, DS, JCB, MC, V.

[icons]

★ ★ **LA POSADA DE ALBUQUERQUE.** *125 2nd St NW (87102), at Copper.* 505/242-9090; res: 800/777-5732; FAX 505/242-8664. 114 rms (2 with shower only), 10 story. No A/C. S $72-$92; D $82-$102; each addl $10; under 17 free; wkend rates. Crib free. TV; cable (premium), VCR avail. Restaurant (see CONRAD'S DOWNTOWN). Bar 11 am-midnight. Ck-out noon. Meeting rms. Business servs avail. Shopping arcade. Downhill ski 15 mi. Refrigerator in suites. Cr cds: A, C, D, DS, MC, V.

[icons]

★ ★ ★ **MARRIOTT.** *2101 Louisiana Blvd NE (87110).* 505/881-6800; FAX 505/888-2982. 411 rms, 17 story. S $130; D $145; each addl $10; suites $250-$500; under 18 free; wkend rates. Crib free. TV; cable (premium), VCR avail. Indoor/outdoor pool; poolside serv. Restaurant 6:30 am-11 pm. Bar noon-midnight, Sat & Sun from 2 pm. Ck-out noon. Coin lndry. Convention facilities. Business center. In-rm modem link. Gift shop. Downhill ski 10 mi. Exercise rm; weights, bicycles, whirlpool, sauna. Rec rm. Luxury level. Cr cds: A, C, D, DS, ER, JCB, MC, V.

[icons]

★ ★ **RAMADA HOTEL CLASSIC.** *6815 Menaul Blvd NE (87110), I-40 Louisiana Blvd exit N.* 505/881-0000; FAX 505/881-3736. 296 rms, 8 story. S $99-$125; D $109-$135; each addl $10; suites $150-$300; under 18 free; wkend rates. Crib free. Pet accepted. TV; cable, VCR avail (movies avail). Indoor pool. Restaurant 6 am-11 pm. Bar 11-2 am; entertainment Thur-Sat. Ck-out noon. Coin lndry. Convention facilities. Business center. Gift shop. Airport, bus depot transportation. Downhill ski 7 mi. Exercise equipt; weight machines, bicycles, whirlpool, sauna. Refrigerators. Tennis, golf nearby. Cr cds: A, C, D, DS, MC, V.

[icons]

★ ★ ★ **SHERATON-OLD TOWN.** *800 Rio Grande Blvd NW (87104), 2 blks S of I-40 Rio Grande exit.* 505/843-6300; FAX 505/842-9863. 190 rms, 11 story. S $105-$115; D $115-$125; each addl $10; suites $150; under 18 free; wkend rates. Crib free. TV; cable (premium). Heated pool; poolside serv. Restaurant 6 am-2 pm; dining rm 11:30 am-10:30 pm. Bar 11:30-1:30 am. Ck-out noon. Meeting rms. Business servs avail. In-rm modem link. Shopping arcade. Barber, beauty shop. Downhill ski 20 mi. Exercise equipt; weight machine, bicycles, whirlpool, steam rm. Some refrigerators. Some balconies. In historic Old Town. Cr cds: A, C, D, MC, V.

[icons]

Inns

★ ★ **CASA LA RESOLANA.** *(7887 Corralles Rd, Corrales 87048) 7 mi N on I-25, exit Alameda.* 505/898-0203; res: 800/884-0203. 3 rms. No A/C. Rm phone avail. S $75-$85; D $85-$110; each addl $15. Children over 10 yrs only. Complimentary coffee in rms. Complimentary full bkfst. Ck-out 11 am, ck-in 4 pm. Luggage handling. In-rm modem link. Country adobe; kiva fireplaces, beamed ceilings. View of the Sandia Mountains. Totally nonsmoking. Cr cds: A, DS, MC, V.

[icons]

★ ★ ★ **CASAS DE SUEÑOS.** *310 Rio Grande SW (87104).* 505/247-4560; res: 800/242-8987; FAX 505/842-8493. 17 units, 4 suites, 8 with kit. S, D $85-$225; each addl $15; suites, kit. units $110-$225; 2-day min Balloon Fiesta. Children over 12 yrs only. TV;

cable (premium), VCR avail. Complimentary full bkfst, tea/sherry. Restaurant nearby. Ck-out 11 am, ck-in 2 pm. Business servs avail. In-rm modem link. Separate adobe units surround courtyard; European antiques. Totally nonsmoking. Cr cds: A, D, DS, MC, V.

⊠ 🌫

★ ★ **HACIENDA ANTIQUA.** 6708 Tierra Dr NW (87107). 505/345-5399; FAX 505/345-3855. 5 rms. No A/C. No rm phones. S $75-$90; D $85-$110; each addl $15; 3-day min Balloon Festival. Children over 6 yrs only. TV in common rm. Pool; whirlpool. Complimentary full bkfst; afternoon tea/sherry. Ck-out 11 am, ck-in 4-6 pm. Downhill/x-country ski 12 mi. Refrigerators. Picnic tables. Spanish colonial house built 1790 that once served as stagecoach stop. Many antiques. Cr cds: MC, V.

D ⊁ 🌊 ⊠ 🌫

↩ ★ **W.E. MAUGER ESTATE.** 701 Roma Ave NW (87102). 505/242-8755; FAX 505/842-8835. 8 air-cooled rms, shower only, 3 story. No rm phones. S $65-$95; D $75-$115; each addl $15; monthly, wkly rates. Crib free. Pet accepted. TV; in-rm movies in sitting rm. Complimentary gourmet bkfst, refreshments. Complimentary coffee in rms. Restaurant nearby. Ck-out noon, ck-in 4-6 pm. Business servs avail. Downhill/x-country ski 12 mi. Sun porch. Restored Queen Anne house (1897); library; antiques. Cr cds: A, C, D, MC, V.

↩ ⊁ ⊠ 🌫 .

Restaurants

↩ ★ **505.** 6601 Uptown Blvd NE. 505/884-8383. Hrs: 11 am-9 pm; Fri, Sat to 10 pm; Sun 11 am-8 pm. Closed Dec 25. New Mexican menu. Bar. Semi-a la carte: lunch $5.95-$8.95, dinner $5.95-$11.95. Child's meals $3.25. Specializes in pasta, fajitas. Parking. Outdoor dining. Festive decor. Cr cds: A, D, DS, MC, V.

D

★ ★ **ANTIQUITY.** 112 Romero St NW (87104). 505/247-3545. Hrs: 5-9 pm; Fri & Sat to 9:30 pm. Closed Jan 1, Easter, Dec 25. Res accepted. Continental menu. Wine, beer. Semi-a la carte: dinner $12.95-$28.95. Specialties: seafood, steaks, salmon papillote. Romantic atmosphere. Antiques. Cr cds: C, D, MC, V.

★ ★ **THE ARTICHOKE.** 424 Central St (87102). 505/243-0200. Hrs: 11 am-2:30 pm, 5:30-10 pm; Sat from 5:30 pm. Closed Sun; Jan 1, Thanksgiving, Dec 25. Res accepted. Continental menu. Wine, beer. Semi-a la carte: lunch $4.95-$10.95, dinner $8.95-$19.95. Child's meals. Specializes in pasta, fresh seafood, lamb. Own bread. Parking. Outdoor dining. Contemporary decor. Cr cds: A, C, D, MC, V.

★ ★ **CAFE OCEANA.** 1414 Central SE. 505/247-2233. Hrs: 11 am-11 pm; Fri to 11:30 pm; Sat 5-11:30 pm. Closed Sun; most major hols. Bar. Semi-a la carte: lunch $5-$11, dinner $6.95-$21. Child's meals. Specializes in fresh seafood. Patio dining. Cr cds: A, D, DS, MC, V.

D

↩ ★ **CHRISTY MAE'S.** 1400 San Pedro NE. 505/255-4740. Hrs: 11 am-8 pm. Closed Sun; hols. Semi-a la carte: lunch $4.50-$6, dinner $5.50-$9.50. Child's meals. Specializes in croissant sandwiches, barbecued ribs, homemade soup. Parking. Cr cds: A, D, DS, MC, V.

D SC

★ ★ **CONRAD'S DOWNTOWN.** (See La Posada De Albuquerque Hotel) 505/242-9090. Hrs: 6:30 am-10 pm; Sun brunch 11:30 am-2 pm. Res accepted dinner. No A/C. Spanish, Amer menu. Bar. Semi-a la carte: bkfst $3.95-$7.50, lunch $3.95-$8, dinner $14.50-$22. Sun brunch $14.95. Specializes in veal, paella, salmon. Guitarist Thurs-Sat eves & Sun brunch. Valet parking. Tapas bar. Cr cds: A, C, D, DS, MC, V.

D

★ **THE COOPERAGE.** 7220 Lomas Blvd NE, 1 mi S of I-40 Louisiana Blvd exit. 505/255-1657. Hrs: 11 am-2:30 pm, 5-10 pm; Fri to 11 pm; Sat noon-2:30 pm, 5-11 pm; Sun noon-9 pm; early-bird dinner 5-7 pm. Closed Dec 25. Res accepted. Bar to 2 am, Sun to 10 pm. Semi-a la carte: lunch $4.50-$7.50, dinner $12.95-$27.95. Child's meals. Specializes in prime rib, lobster. Salad bar. Entertainment Fri & Sat 9:30 pm-1:30 am. Parking. Built like an enormous barrel; circular rms with many intimate corners & booths; atrium dining rm. Cr cds: A, C, D, DS, MC, V.

D

★ **COUNTY LINE BBQ.** 9600 Tramway Blvd NE. 505/856-7477. Hrs: 5-9 pm; Fri, Sat to 10 pm; Sun 4-9 pm. Closed some major hols. Bar. Semi-a la carte: dinner $7.95-$16.95. Child's meals. Specializes in barbecue ribs, steak. Parking. View of mountains, valley, city. Cr cds: A, C, D, DS, MC, V.

D

↩ ★ ★ **EL PINTO.** 10500 4th St NW, off I-25, Tramway Rd exit 234W, in valley. 505/898-1771. Hrs: 11 am-9 pm; Fri & Sat to 10 pm; Sun 11 am-9 pm. Closed Jan 1, Thanksgiving, Dec 25. New Mexican, Amer menu. Bar. Semi-a la carte: lunch $4.15-$10.95, dinner $5.95-$13.55. Child's meals. Specialties: chile rellenos, chile con carne. Patio dining with waterfall. Hacienda decor. Cr cds: A, DS, MC, V.

D

↩ ★ **GARDUÑO'S.** 10551 Montgomery NE. 505/298-5000. Hrs: 11 am-10 pm; Fri to 10:30 pm; Sun 10:30 am-9:30 pm; Sun brunch to 2:30 pm. Closed Thanksgiving, Dec 25. New Mexican menu. Bar. Semi-a la carte: lunch $4.95-$7.75, dinner $5.95-$13.95. Sun brunch $7.95. Child's meals. Specializes in enchiladas, fajitas. Entertainment exc Mon. Parking. Outdoor dining. Festive atmosphere; Mexican decor. Family-owned. Cr cds: A, C, D, DS, MC, V.

★ **HIGH NOON.** 425 San Felipe St NW, in Old Town Plaza. 505/765-1455. Hrs: 11 am-9 pm; Fri, Sat to 10:30 pm; Sun noon-9 pm. Closed Jan 1, Dec 25. Res accepted. Southwestern menu. Bar. Semi-a la carte: lunch $4.95-$8.95, dinner $8.75-19.95. Specializes in pepper steak, seafood, game. Guitarist Thurs-Sat. Parking. Original 2 rooms built in 1785. Mexican decor; kiva fireplaces. Cr cds: A, C, D, DS, MC, V.

D

★ **LA HACIENDA DINING ROOM.** 302 San Felipe NW, Old Town Plaza, 3 blks S of I-40 Rio Grande exit S. 505/243-3131. Hrs: 11 am-9 pm; summer to 10 pm. Closed Dec 25. Res accepted. Mexican, Amer menu. Serv bar. Semi-a la carte: lunch $4.25-$7.95, dinner $6.95-$13.95. Child's meals. Specialties: enchiladas New Mexican, sopaipillas, seafood. Entertainment Wed-Sun. Patio dining. Mexican decor in old hacienda; antiques, Native American art. Cr cds: A, C, D, MC, V.

D

↩ ★ ★ **LE CAFE MICHE.** 1431 Wyoming NE, in shopping center. 505/299-6088. Hrs: 11 am-1:30 pm, 5:30-8:30 pm; Sat from 5:30 pm. Closed Sun, Mon; major hols. Res accepted. Continental menu. A la carte entrees: lunch $4.25-$6.25, dinner $9.50-$13. Specialties: veal piccata, chow-chow, seafood, veal. European cafe atmosphere. Totally nonsmoking. Cr cds: D, DS, MC, V.

D

★ ★ **LE MARMITON.** 5415B Academy Blvd NE. 505/821-6279. Hrs: 5-9 pm; Fri, Sat to 9:30 pm. Closed Thanksgiving. Res accepted. French menu. Wine, beer. Semi-a la carte: dinner $12.95-$19.95. Specialties: fantaisie aux fruits de mer, canard aux framboises. Parking. French art; hand-painted plate display. Cr cds: A, D, DS, MC, V.

D

↩ ★ **M & J.** 403 2nd St SW. 505/242-4890. Hrs: 9 am-4 pm. Closed Sun; major hols. Mexican menu. Semi-a la carte: lunch, dinner

$4.20-$8. Child's meals. Specialties: tamales, carne adovada, blue corn enchilada plate. No cr cds accepted.

D SC

★ ★ **MAINE-LY LOBSTER & STEAKHOUSE.** *6220 San Mateo NE. 505/822-1200.* Hrs: 5:30-9:30 pm; Fri, Sat 5:30-10 pm; Sun 5-8:30 pm. Res accepted. Wine, beer. Semi-a la carte: dinner $9.99-$28.95. Child's meals. Specializes in fresh seafood, steak. Parking. Nautical decor. Patrons may choose own lobster. Cr cds: A, C, D, MC, V.

D

★ ★ **MARIA TERESA.** *618 Rio Grande Blvd NW, 1/4 mi S of I-40, Rio Grande Blvd exit in Old Town Albuquerque. 505/242-3900.* Hrs: 11 am-9 pm; Sun brunch 10 am-2 pm. Res accepted. Mexican, Amer menu. Bar 11 am-9 pm. Semi-a la carte: lunch $4.75-$9.95, dinner $8.95-$28. Sun brunch $5.95-$9.95. Child's meals. Specializes in steak, seafood. Parking. Fountain Courtyard for lunch & cocktails. Restored adobe hacienda (1840); antique decor; art, fireplaces, walled gardens. Cr cds: A, C, D, MC, V.

D

★ ★ **MONTE VISTA FIRE STATION.** *3201 Central NE. 505/255-2424.* Hrs: 11 am-2:30 pm, 5-10:30 pm; Fri to 11 pm; Sat 5-11 pm; Sun 5-10:30 pm. Closed Thanksgiving, Dec 25. Res accepted. Bar 11-2 am; Sat from noon; Sun to midnight. Wine cellar. Semi-a la carte: lunch $4.95-$9.95, dinner $8.95-$19.95. Child's meals. Specializes in seafood, game, pasta. Own pastries, breads. Outdoor dining. In old fire station (1936); brass fire pole; bar upstairs in former sleeping quarters. Cr cds: A, D, MC, V.

D

✔ ★ **NEW CHINATOWN.** *5001 Central Ave NE (US 66). 505/265-8859.* Hrs: 11 am-10 pm; Fri, Sat to 11 pm. Closed Thanksgiving. Res accepted. Chinese menu. Bar to midnight. Semi-a la carte: lunch $3.25-$5.75, dinner $6.50-$14.95. Buffet: lunch $4.95. Child's meals. Specializes in Cantonese, Szechwan dishes. Piano bar. Parking. Unusual modern Chinese decor; artwork; Chinese garden. Family-owned. Cr cds: A, C, D, DS, MC, V.

D

★ **OASIS.** *5400 San Mateo NE, Sun West Center. 505/884-2324.* Hrs: 11:30 am-9:30 pm; Fri to 10 pm; Sat noon-10 pm; Sun 5-9 pm. Closed Thanksgiving, Dec 25. Res accepted. Continental menu. Bar. Semi-a la carte: lunch $3.75-$6, dinner $7.50-$19.95. Child's meals. Specialties: lamb, seafood. Belly dancer Wed-Sat. Parking. Enclosed garden dining. Cr cds: A, C, D, DS, MC, V.

D

★ ★ **PRAIRIE STAR.** *(255 Prairie Star Rd, Bernalillo) 17 mi N on I-25 exit 242, W on NM 44 to Jemez Dam Rd. 505/867-3327.* Hrs: 5-10 pm; Fri & Sat to 11 pm. Closed Dec 25-Jan 1. New American menu. Bar. Wine cellar. Semi-a la carte: dinner $15-$26. Specialties: châteaubriand, venison, crisp duck. Own baking. Menu changes seasonally. Adobe building; art. View of river valley, mountains. Cr cds: A, C, D, DS, MC, V.

D

★ ★ **RATTLESTEAKS.** *1100 San Mateo, at Lomas. 505/268-5354.* Hrs: 11:30 am-2:30 pm, 5-10 pm; Fri-Sun 5-11 pm. Closed some major hols. Res accepted. Bar. Semi-a la carte: lunch $5-$10, dinner $9-$22. Child's meals. Specializes in fresh seafood, Omaha steaks. Own baking. Parking. Outdoor dining. Contemporary Southwestern decor. Cr cds: A, C, D, DS, MC, V.

D

★ ★ **RIO BRAVO.** *515 Central Ave (87102). 505/242-6800.* Hrs: 11:30 am-10 pm. Closed Sun; some major hols. Res accepted. Southwestern menu. Bar. Semi-a la carte: lunch $5.95-$10.95, dinner $7.95-$18.95. Child's meals. Specialties: wild mushroom enchiladas,

New Mexico fettucine Alfredo, handcrafted beer. Microbrewery on site. Cr cds: A, DS, MC, V.

D

★ ★ **RIO GRANDE YACHT CLUB.** *2500 Yale Blvd SE (87106). 713/243-6111.* Hrs: 11-2 am; Sat from 4:30 pm; Sun 4:30 pm-midnight. Closed most hols. Res accepted. Bar. Semi-a la carte: lunch $5.95-$8.95, dinner $9.95-$37.50. Child's meals. Parking. Outdoor dining. Nautical decor. Cr cds: A, C, D, DS, MC, V.

D

★ ★ ★ **SCALO.** *3500 Central Ave SE, near Carlisle. 505/255-8782.* Hrs: 11:30 am-2:30 pm, 5-11 pm; Sun 5-9 pm. Closed most major hols. Res accepted. Italian menu. Bar. Semi-a la carte: lunch $4.95-$10.95, dinner $7.95-$16.75. Specialties: salmon padellata, bianchire herring, grilled fish. Own pasta. Parking. Patio dining. Dining areas on several levels. Cr cds: A, MC, V.

D

★ ★ ★ **STEPHENS.** *1311 Tijeras Ave, at 14th & Central NW. 505/842-1773.* Hrs: 11 am-2 pm, 5-9:30 pm; Fri to 10:30; Sat 5-10:30 pm; Sun 5-9:30 pm. Closed Jan 1, Dec 25. Res accepted. Bar. Wine cellar. A la carte entrees: lunch $6.50-$12, dinner $16-$25. Specializes in pasta, grilled salmon, prime beef. Parking. Elegant dining. Cr cds: A, D, MC, V.

D

★ ★ **TRATTORIA TROMBINO.** *5415 Academy Blvd NE. 505/821-5974.* Hrs: 11 am-9:30 pm; Fri & Sat to 11 pm; Sun to 10 pm. Closed Thanksgiving, Dec 25. Italian menu. Bar. Semi-a la carte: lunch $4.95-$7.95, dinner $6.75-$16.95. Child's meals. Specializes in pasta, seafood, steak. Parking. Cr cds: A, C, D, DS, MC, V.

D

✔ ★ **YESTER-DAVE'S GRILL, BAR & BAKERY.** *10601 Montgomery NE. 505/293-0033.* Hrs: 11 am-10 pm; Fri & Sat to 11 pm; Sun 10 am-9:30 pm; Sun brunch to 3 pm. Closed Thanksgiving, Dec 25. Bar. Semi-a la carte: lunch $4.50-$8.50, dinner $5.75-$11. Complete meals: dinner $9.50-$12.50. Sun brunch $7.50. Specializes in hamburgers & shakes, chicken-fried steak, barbecued ribs & chicken, blue-plate specials, soup & salad bar. Entertainment. Parking. Outdoor dining. Vintage car on display; soda fountain and soda jerk; decor and atmosphere reminiscent of rock 'n roll era. DJ takes requests. Cr cds: A, C, D, DS, MC, V.

D SC

Unrated Dining Spots

66 DINER. *1405 Central Ave NE. 505/247-1421.* Hrs: 9 am-11 pm; Fri to midnight; Sat 8 am-midnight; Sun 8 am-10 pm. Closed major hols. Wine, beer. Semi-a la carte: bkfst $1.95-$4.25, lunch, dinner $3-$6.95. Child's meals. Specialty: green chile cheeseburger. Parking. Outdoor dining. Roadside diner; photographs, music of the 40s, 50s and 60s. Cr cds: A, DS, MC, V.

D

CAFE ZURICH. *3513 Central NE. 505/265-2556.* Hrs: 10 am-midnight. Continental menu. Serv bar. Semi-a la carte: lunch, dinner $2.50-$6.95. Specializes in gourmet pizzas, pastas, salads, sandwiches. Outdoor dining. Unique decor. Cr cds: A, MC, V.

D

FURRS CAFETERIA. *2272 Wyoming Blvd NE, 1 mi N of I-40 Wyoming Blvd exit, in Wyoming Mall. 505/298-6886.* Hrs: 11 am-8 pm; Fri & Sat to 8:30 pm. Closed Dec 25. Avg ck: lunch, dinner $5.99. Specializes in roast beef, baked fish. Pianist Mon, Wed, Fri, Sun nights. Fireplace. Cr cds: A, MC, V.

D

SOUPER SALAD. *4411 San Mateo NE, on grounds of Montgomery Plaza Ctr. 505/883-9534.* Hrs: 11 am-9 pm; Sun noon-8 pm. Closed Jan 1, Thanksgiving, Dec 25. Semi-a la carte: lunch, dinner $2.65-$5.95. Specializes in homemade soup, baked potatoes. Salad bar. No cr cds accepted.

◨ D

Artesia (G-5)

(See Carlsbad)

Founded 1903 **Pop** 10,610 **Elev** 3,380 ft **Area code** 505 **Zip** 88210
Information Chamber of Commerce, 408 W Texas, PO Box 99; 505/746-2744.

Artesia was named for the vast underground water supplies, which once rushed up through drilled wells, now used to irrigate the area's farmland. The first underground school in the US, Abo Elementary School at 18th St & Centre Ave, was built here for safety from radiation effects of fallout. Potash, natural gas, oil and petroleum products are processed near here. Artesia is the home of the Federal Law Enforcement Training Center. The area offers wild turkey, deer, bear and upland game for hunting enthusiasts.

What to See and Do

Historical Museum and Art Center. Pioneer and Native American artifacts; changing art exhibits. (Tues-Sat; closed major hols) 503 & 505 W Richardson Ave. Phone 505/748-2390. **Free.**

Annual Event

Eddy County Fair. 1st wk Aug.

Motel

★★**BEST WESTERN PECOS INN.** *2209 W Main St. 505/748-3324; FAX 505/748-2868.* 81 rms, 2 story. S $56; D $63; each addl $7; suites $90-$110. Crib free. TV; cable. Indoor pool; whirlpool, sauna. Restaurant 6-10 am, 11 am-2 pm, 5-9 pm; Rm serv. Bar 4 am-midnight, closed Sun. Ck-out 11 am. Coin lndry. Meeting rms. Local airport, bus depot transportation. Refrigerators. Some balconies. Cr cds: A, C, D, DS, MC, V.

◨ D 🏊 🖨 🔥 SC

Restaurant

✔★★**LA FONDA.** *206 W Main. 505/746-9377.* Hrs: 11 am-2 pm, 5-9 pm; Sat, Sun 11 am-9 pm. Closed Thanksgiving, Dec 25. Mexican, Amer menu. Semi-a la dinner carte: dinner $4.50-$8.75. Buffet: lunch $5.99. Child's meals. Specialties: fajitas, burritos, enchiladas. Parking. Waterfall in lobby; arched doorways. Cr cds: A, DS, MC, V.

◨ D SC

Aztec (B-2)

(See Farmington)

Founded 1890 **Pop** 5,479 **Elev** 5,686 ft **Area code** 505 **Zip** 87410
Information Chamber of Commerce, 203 N Main St; 505/334-9551.

Aztec is the seat of San Juan County, a fruit-growing and cattle-grazing area. This town is filled with history; architectural and historic commentary for walking tours may be obtained at the Aztec Museum.

What to See and Do

Aztec Museum and Pioneer Village. Main museum houses authentic pioneer artifacts, including mineral and fossil display, household items, farm and ranch tools; Native American artifacts. Atwood Annex has authentically furnished pioneer rooms, farm equipment, sleighs, buggies and wagons. Oil Field Museum has 1920s cable tool oil rig, oil well pumping unit, "doghouse" and tools. Pioneer Village has reconstructed buildings, including doctor's and sheriff's offices, blacksmith shop and foundry, pioneer cabin (1880), general store and post office, church. (Daily exc Sun) 125 N Main. Phone 505/334-9829. ¢

✴ **Aztec Ruins National Monument.** One of the largest prehistoric Indian towns, it was occupied between 1100 and 1300. These are ancient Pueblo ruins, misnamed Aztec by early settlers in the 1800s. The partially excavated pueblo contains nearly 450 rooms, with its plaza dominated by the Great Kiva (48 feet in diameter). Instructive museum; interpretive programs in summer. Self-guided tours, trail guide available at visitor center for the one-quarter-mile trail. Some portions accessible by wheelchair. (Daily; closed Jan 1, Dec 25) 1/2 mi N of US 550. Contact Superintendent, PO Box 640; 505/334-6174 (voice or TDD). Golden Eagle & Golden Age Passports (see INTRODUCTION). ¢

Navajo Lake State Park. Surrounded by sandstone mesas and stands of piñon and juniper. Part of Colorado River Storage Project; reservoir extends 35 miles upstream into Colorado, totaling 15,000 surface acres of water. Standard fees. (Daily) 18 mi E via NM 173, 511. Phone 505/632-2278. Per vehicle ¢¢ Also in the area are

Pine River Site. Swimming, waterskiing; fishing (panfish, catfish, bass, salmon and trout); boating (ramps, rentals, marina). Picnicking (fireplaces), concession. Camping (hookups). Visitor center with interpretive displays. West side.

Sims Mesa Site. Boat ramp. Camping (dumpstation). East side.

San Juan River Recreation Area. Below the dam. Fishing (trout). Camping.

Motel

★ **ENCHANTMENT LODGE.** *1800 W Aztec Blvd (US 550). 505/334-6143; res: 800/847-2194.* 20 rms. Apr-Sept: S $29-$34; D $36-$46; each addl $7; lower rates Nov-Mar. Crib $5. TV; cable. Heated pool. Playground. Complimentary coffee in lobby. Restaurant nearby. Ck-out 11 am. Coin lndry. Gift shop. Picnic tables, grills. Cr cds: DS, MC, V.

🏊 🖨 🔥 SC

Restaurants

✔★ **AZTEC.** *107 E Aztec Blvd. 505/334-9586.* Hrs: 5 am-9 pm. Closed Thanksgiving, Dec 25. Mexican, Amer menu. Semi-a la carte: bkfst $2.25-$6.25, lunch $1.50-$6.25, dinner $3.95-$9.95. Child's meals. Specialties: chicken-fried steak, tiger burger, Mexican chili. Salad bar. Own pies. Entertainment Fri, Sat. Parking. No cr cds accepted.

★★ **THE TROUGH.** *(Aztec Blvd, Flora Vista) 5 mi W on US 550. 505/334-6176.* Hrs: 5:30-10:30 pm; Fri, Sat to 11 pm. Closed Sun; Jan 1, Thanksgiving, Dec 25. Bar. Complete meals: dinner $12-$35. Specializes in prime rib, seafood, duck. Parking. Rustic decor. Cr cds: A, DS, MC, V.

Bandelier National Monument (D-3)

(For accommodations see Los Alamos, Santa Fe)

(From Los Alamos, 6 mi SW on NM 502, then 6 mi SE on NM 4 to turnoff sign)

A major portion of this 34,000-acre area is designated wilderness. The most accessible part is in Frijoles Canyon, which features cave dwellings carved out of the soft volcanic tuff and houses built out from the cliffs. There is also a great circular pueblo ruin (Tyuonyi) on the floor of the canyon. These houses and caves were occupied from about 1150-1550. The reason for their abandonment is not known, although climatic changes and depletion of resources may have forced the residents to leave. Some of the modern pueblos along the Rio Grande are related to the prehistoric Anasazi people of the canyon and the surrounding mesa country. There is a paved 1-mile self-guided trail to walk and view these sites. The monument is named after Adolph Bandelier, ethnologist and author of the novel, *The Delight Makers,* which used Frijoles Canyon as its locale. There are 70 miles of trails (free permits required for overnight trips; no pets allowed on the trails); visitor center with exhibits devoted to the dwellings and ruins of this particular area, as well as the entire pueblo region (daily); ranger-guided tours (summer); campfire programs (Memorial Day-Labor Day). Campground (Mar-Nov, daily) with tent & trailer sites (fee; no hookups or reservations); grills, tables & water. Golden Access, Golden Age, Golden Eagle Passport (see INTRODUCTION). Contact the Superintendent, Los Alamos 87544; 505/672-3861. Per car ¢¢

Capulin Volcano National Monument (B-5)

(see Raton)

Carlsbad (G-5)

(See Artesia)

Founded 1893 **Pop** 24,952 **Elev** 3,110 ft **Area code** 505 **Zip** 88220
Information Convention & Visitors Bureau, 302 S Canal, PO Box 910; 505/887-6516 or 800/221-1224 outside NM.

Like many towns in New Mexico, explorers such as Antonio de Espejo and Alvar Nuñez Cabeza de Vaca probably traveled through this area as they made their way down the Pecos River during the 1500s. Carlsbad is also on the famous Goodnight-Loving cattle-drive trail.

Irrigation of the rich alluvial bottomland began with the earliest Spanish settlements in the early 1600s. In 1911, the US Bureau of Reclamation began its Carlsbad Project, building three dams and an intricate network of canals that now irrigate more than 25,000 acres. Cotton, alfalfa and vegetables are the principal crops.

In 1925, potash was discovered by a company drilling for oil; six years later active mining began.

A Ranger District office of the Lincoln National Forest (see ALAMO-GORDO) is located here.

What to See and Do

Brantley Lake State Park. This 3,000-acre park is adj to Brantley Lake on the Pecos River. Fishing; boating (ramps). Picnicking (shelters). Camping (hookups, dump station, showers). Visitor center. Standard fees. (Daily) 12 mi N on US 285, then 5 mi E on County Rd 30. Phone 505/457-2384. ¢¢

Carlsbad Caverns National Park (see). 27 mi SW on US 62/180.

Carlsbad Museum & Art Center. Bones of prehistoric animals that once roamed the state. Pueblo pottery, art, meteorite remains. Potash & mineral exhibits. Pioneer & Apache relics. McAdoo collection of paintings; bird carvings by Jack Drake; changing temporary exhibits. (Daily exc Sun; closed major hols) Donation. 418 W Fox St, 1 blk W of Canal St. Phone 505/887-0276.

Guadalupe Mountains National Park (see TEXAS). 55 mi SW via US 62/180 in Texas.

Lake Carlsbad Water Recreation Area. Swimming, water sports; fishing; boating. Tennis, golf (fee). Picnic area. E end of Church St, on the Pecos River.

Living Desert Zoo and Gardens State Park. This 1,100-acre park is an indoor/outdoor living museum of the Chihuahuan Desert's plants and animals. The Desert Arboretum has an extensive cactus collection. Living Desert Zoo has over 60 animal species native to the region including mountain lions, bear, wolf, elk, bison and an extensive aviary. Hiking trails. (Daily; closed Dec 25) 1½ mi NW, off US 285. Phone 505/887-5516. ¢¢

Million Dollar Museum. Early Americana collection; 31 antique European doll houses; $25,000 doll collection; first car west of the Pecos; Whittlin' Cowboys Ranch. (Daily; closed Dec 25) Sr citizen rate. 20 mi SW on US 62/180 to White's City, then W on NM 7. Phone 505/785-2291. ¢¢

Sitting Bull Falls. Day-use area near spectacular desert waterfall. Hiking trail to piñon and juniper forest, diverse vegetation along trail with scenic overlooks of canyons and plains. Picnicking. (Daily) 11 mi NW on US 285 to NM 137, then 30 mi SW, in Lincoln National Forest (see ALAMOGORDO). Phone 505/885-4181. **Free.**

Motels

★ ★ **BEST WESTERN STEVENS INN.** *(Box 580) 1829 S Canal St.* 505/887-2851; FAX 505/887-6338. 202 rms, 1-2 story. S $45; D, suites $55-$65; each addl $5. Crib $4. TV; cable (premium), VCR (movies avail $4). Pool. Playground. Restaurant 5:30 am-10 pm, Sun 6 am-9 pm. Rm serv 7 am-9 pm. Bar 11-2 am; entertainment, dancing exc Sun. Ck-out noon. Meeting rms. Business servs avail. Sundries. Some refrigerators. Some patios. Cr cds: A, C, D, DS, MC, V.

D ✦ ⌧ ⌧ 🐾 SC

★ ★ **CONTINENTAL INN.** *3820 National Parks Hwy.* 505/887-0341. 58 units, 2 story. S $34.95; D $39.95-$44.95; each addl $5; suites $49.95-$79.95. Crib free. TV; cable (premium). Heated pool. Restaurant nearby. Ck-out 11 am. In-rm modem link. Free airport, bus depot transportation. Some refrigerators. Cr cds: A, C, D, DS, MC, V.

D ⌧ ⌧ 🐾 SC

✔ ★ **TRAVELODGE CARLSBAD SOUTH.** *3817 National Parks Hwy, near Cavern City Air Terminal.* 505/887-8888; FAX 505/885-0126. 60 units, 3 story. S $29-$39; D $33-$44; each addl $4; under 16 free. Crib free. TV; cable (premium). Heated pool; whirlpool. Complimentary buffet bkfst for adults. Ck-out noon. Coin lndry. Free airport, bus depot transportation. Cr cds: A, C, D, DS, MC, V.

D ✦ ⌧ ✈ ⌧ 🐾 SC

Carlsbad Caverns National Park (H-5)

(For accommodations see Carlsbad)

(27 mi SW of Carlsbad on US 62/180)

One of the largest and most remarkable in the world, this cavern extends approximately 30 miles and is as deep as 1,037 feet below the surface.

It was once known as Bat Cave because of the spectacular bat flights, still a daily occurrence at sunset during the warmer months. Cowboy and guano miner Jim White first explored and guided people through the caverns in the early 1900s, later working for the National Park Service as the Chief Park Ranger. Carlsbad Cave National Monument was established in 1923 and in 1930 the area was enlarged and designated a national park. The park contains 46,755 acres and more than 80 caves. Carlsbad Cavern was formed by the dissolving action of acidic water in the Tansill and Capitan limestones of the Permian age. When an uplift drained the cavern, mineral-laden water dripping from the ceiling formed the stalactites and stalagmites.

The main cavern has two self-guided routes, a Ranger-led guided tour and several "off-trail" trips. Also available are tours in two backcountry caves: Slaughter Canyon Cave and Spider Cave. All guided tours require reservations.

Since the temperature in the cavern is always 56°F, be sure to carry a sweater even if it is hot outside; comfortable rubber-soled shoes are also recommended for safety. No pets; kennel available. Photography, including flash and time exposures, is permitted on self-guided trips and some guided tours. (Closed Dec 25). Wheelchairs can be accommodated in the elevator for a partial tour. Rangers patrol the cave. Holders of Golden Access and Golden Age Passports (see INTRODUCTION) receive a 50% discount. Box lunches available in underground lunchroom. Picnic area at Rattlesnake Springs. Scenic 9½-mile loop drive; hiking trails; observation tower; exhibits on surface; restaurant. No camping in park, but available nearby. Bat flight programs are held each evening during the summer at the cavern entrance amphitheater.

Visitor center and museum with educational exhibits and displays. For tour reservations and fees contact the Superintendent, 3225 National Parks Hwy, Carlsbad 88220; 505/785-2232.

Cerrillos (D-3)

(see Santa Fe)

Chaco Culture National Historical Park (C-2)

(For accommodations see Farmington, Gallup, Grants)

(From NM 44, 29 mi S on NM 57 from Blanco Trading Post; from I-40, 60 mi N of Thoreau on NM 57. Check road conditions locally; may be extremely difficult when wet)

From A.D. 900 to 1150, Chaco Canyon was a major center of Anasazi culture. A prehistoric roadway system, which included masonry walls and stairways carved into sandstone cliffs, extends for hundreds of miles in all directions. Within the park, the roads connect twelve large pueblo ruins and many smaller ruins. Ancient roads up to thirty feet wide represent the most developed and extensive road network of this period north of Central America. Researchers speculate that Chaco Canyon was the center of a vast, complex and interdependent civilization in the American Southwest.

There are five self-guided trails with tours conducted (times vary), as well as evening campfire programs in summer. Visitor center has museum (daily; closed Jan 1, Dec 25). Camping. Contact Superintendent, Star Rte 4, Box 6500, Bloomfield 87413; 505/786-7014. Per vehicle ¢¢

Chama (B-3)

(See Dulce)

Pop 1,048 **Elev** 7,800 ft **Area code** 505 **Zip** 87520

What to See and Do

Cumbres & Toltec Scenic Railroad, New Mexico Express. Round-trip excursion to Osier, Colorado on 1880s narrow-gauge steam railroad. Route passes through backwoods country and spectacular mountain scenery; includes the four percent-grade climb to Cumbres Pass. Warm clothing advised due to sudden weather changes. (Memorial Day-mid-Oct, daily) Also through trips to Antonito, Colorado with van return. Reservations advised; contact PO Box 789; 505/756-2151. The Colorado Limited runs to Osier from Antonito, CO (see ALAMOSA, CO). ¢¢¢¢

El Vado Lake State Park. This park features an irrigation lake withwater sports; fishing, ice fishing; boating (dock, ramps). Hiking trail connects to Lake Heron. Picnicking, playground. Camping (hookups, dump station). Standard fees. (Daily) 15 mi S on US 84 to Tierra Amarilla, then 13 mi SW on NM 112. Phone 505/588-7247. Per vehicle ¢¢

Lake Heron State Park. Region of tall ponderosa pines. Swimming; fishing (trout, salmon), ice fishing; boating (ramp, dock). Hiking. Winter sports. Picnicking. Camping (hookups; fee). Visitor center. (Daily) 10 mi S on US 84, then 6 mi SW on NM 95. Phone 505/588-7470. Per vehicle ¢¢

Motel

(Because of the altitude, air-conditioning is rarely necessary)

★ **ELK HORN LODGE.** *Rte 1, Box 45, On US 84.* 505/756-2105; res: 800/532-8874; FAX 505/756-2638. 22 motel rms, 1-2 story, 11 kit. cottages. June-Dec: S $42-$48; D $59-$62; each addl $6; kit cottages $64-$101; wkly & lower rates rest of yr. Crib $6. Pet accepted. TV; cable. Restaurant 6 am-10 pm. Ck-out 11 am. X-country ski 5 mi. Balconies. Porches on cottages. Picnic tables, grills. On Chama River. Cr cds: DS, MC, V.

Restaurants

✔ ★ **BRANDING IRON.** *1551 W Main.* 505/756-2808. Hrs: 7 am-8:30 pm. Closed Dec 25. Southwestern menu. Bar. Semi-a la carte: bkfst, lunch $3-$7, dinner $5-$10. Child's meals. Specializes in combination plates, steak. Salad bar. Parking. Outdoor dining. Casual atmosphere. Cr cds: A, C, D, DS, MC, V.

★ **HIGH COUNTRY.** *At jct NM 17 & US 64/84.* 505/756-2384. Hrs: (summer) 7 am-11 pm; Sun to 10 pm; (winter) to 10:30 pm. Closed Easter, Thanksgiving, Dec 25. Mexican menu. Bar. Semi-a la carte: bkfst $3-$6.25, lunch $2.50-$11.95, dinner $6-$21.95. Child's meals. Specializes in steak, seafood. Parking. Outdoor dining. Bar located in 19th-century portion of building. Cr cds: A, DS, MC, V.

Cimarron (C-4)

(See Eagle Nest, Raton, Red River)

Pop 774 **Elev** 6,427 ft **Area code** 505 **Zip** 87714
Information Chamber of Commerce, PO Box 604; 505/376-2417 or 800/700-4298.

This historic Southwestern town was part of Lucien B. Maxwell's land holdings on the Santa Fe Trail. The St James Hotel (1872), where

Buffalo Bill Cody held his Wild West Shows, the gristmill, the old jail (1872) and several other historic buildings still stand.

What to See and Do

Old Aztec Mill Museum (1864). Built as gristmill. Chuckwagon, mill wheels and local historical items. (Memorial Day-Labor Day, daily; early-late May & rest of Sept, wkends) On NM 21, S of US 64 in Old Town. Phone 505/376-2913.   ¢

Philmont Scout Ranch. A138,000-acre camp for some 15,000 Boy Scouts. Kit Carson Museum (7 mi S of headquarters); Ernest Thompson Seton Memorial Library and Philmont Museum includes several thousand drawings, paintings and Native American artifacts (Mon-Fri; closed hols). Camp also has buffalo, deer, elk, bear and antelope. Headquarters is 4 mi S on NM 21. Phone 505/376-2281. **Free.**

Annual Events

Maverick Club Rodeo. Rodeo for working cowboys. Parade, fireworks. July 4.

Cimarron Days. Crafts, entertainment. Labor Day wkend.

Cloudcroft (G-4)

(See Alamogordo, Mescalero, Ruidoso)

Pop 636 **Elev** 8,700 ft **Area code** 505 **Zip** 88317
Information Chamber of Commerce, US 82, PO Box 1290; 505/682-2733.

One of the highest golf courses in North America is Cloudcroft's most publicized claim to distinction, but this is also a recreation area for non-golfers. It is at the crest of the Sacramento Mountains in the Lincoln National Forest (see ALAMOGORDO), among fir, spruce, pine and aspen. A Ranger District office of the forest is located here. The area is popular with writers, photographers and artists. Several art schools conduct summer workshops here. There are many miles of horseback trails through the mountains, and skiing, snowmobiling and skating in winter. Deer, elk, turkey and bear hunting is good in season. Several campgrounds are located in the surrounding forest. During the day temperatures seldom reach 80°F; nights are always crisp and cool.

What to See and Do

Sacramento Mountains Historical Museum. Exhibits depict 1880-1910 life in the Sacramento Mountains area. (Tues-Sat) US 82, in town. Phone 505/682-2932.   ¢

Snow Canyon. Double chairlift, beginner tows; snowmaking; patrol, school, rentals; lodge, snack bar, cafeteria, restaurant. (Mid-Dec-mid-Mar, daily) Snow boarding. Elev 8,350-8,950 feet. 2¹/₂ mi E on US 82. Phone 800/333-SKI-2 (winter) or 505/682-2566 (off season).   ¢¢¢¢

Annual Event

Western Roundup. Contests, parade, street dance. Mid-June.

Inn

(Because of the altitude, air-conditioning is rarely necessary)

★ ★ ★ **THE LODGE.** Box 497, On US 82. *505/682-2566; res: 800/395-6343; FAX 505/682-2715.* 60 air-cooled rms, 3 story, 9 suites. No elvtr. S $59-$90; D $69-$105; each addl $10; suites $115-$185; ski, golf package plans. Crib free. TV; cable (premium), VCR avail. Heated pool; sauna, hot tub. Restaurant (see REBECCA'S). Box lunches, picnics. Bar 11-2 am; entertainment. Ck-out noon, ck-in after 4 pm. Meeting rms. Business center. Bellhops. Gift shop. Airport transporta-

tion. 9-hole golf, greens fee, pro, putting green. Downhill ski 3 mi; x-country ski on site. Historic building (1899). Cr cds: A, D, DS, MC, V.

★ ♣ ≋ ≍ ≋ SC ≋

Restaurant

★ ★ ★ **REBECCA'S.** *(See The Lodge Inn)* 505/682-2566. Hrs: 7-10:30 am, 11:30 am-2 pm, 5:30-10 pm; Sun to 10 am; Sun brunch 11 am-2 pm. Res accepted. Continental menu. Bar 11 am-midnight. Wine list. Semi-a la carte: bkfst $3.25-$9.95, lunch $5.95-$9.95, dinner $12.95-$25. Sun brunch $16.95. Child's meals. Own pastries. Pianist. Parking. Mountain view; early 1900s atmosphere. Cr cds: A, D, DS, MC, V.

Clovis (E-6)

(See Portales)

Founded 1907 **Pop** 30,954 **Elev** 4,280 ft **Area code** 505 **Zip** 88101
Information Chamber of Commerce, 215 N Main; 505/763-3435.

Established as a town for Santa Fe railroad stops, Clovis is named for the first Christian king of France, who ruled from A.D. 481-511. It is surrounded by cattle ranches and dairies, alfalfa, wheat, milo and corn farms. Cannon AFB is located 8 miles west on US 60. Clovis is also home of the Norman Petty Recording Studio, where Buddy Holly, Roy Orbison and others recorded some of their first hits.

What to See and Do

Hillcrest Park and Zoo. Second largest zoo in New Mexico; over 500 animals, most of which are exhibited in natural environments. Informational programs. Park has kiddieland with amusement rides, outdoor and indoor swimming pool. Golf course, picnic areas, sunken garden. 10th St and Sycamore. Phone 505/769-7870. Zoo ¢; Pool ¢¢

Annual Events

Pioneer Days & PRCA Rodeo. Parade, chili cook-off, Little Buckaroo Rodeo. 1st wkend June.

Clovis Music Festival. Nightly concerts; daily tours of original Norman Petty Studio; classic car show. Phone 505/763-3435. 2nd wkend July.

Curry County Fair. Mid-Aug.

Motels

★ ★ **BEST WESTERN LA VISTA INN.** *1516 Mabry Dr (US 60, 70, 84).* 505/762-3808; FAX 505/762-1422. 47 rms. S $30-$40; D $34-$44; each addl $5; under 12 free. Crib $4. TV; cable. Heated pool. Ck-out 11 am. Sundries. Airport, bus depot transportation. Game rm. Some refrigerators. Cr cds: A, C, D, DS, MC, V.

≋ ♣ SC

✔ ★ **BISHOPS INN.** *2920 Mabry Dr (US 60).* 505/769-1953; res: 800/643-9239. 59 rms, 2 story. S $27-$30; D $31.50-$35; each addl $5; under 12 free. Crib free. Pet accepted. TV; cable. Heated pool; whirlpool. Complimentary continental bkfst. Ck-out 11 am. Coin lndry. Cr cds: A, C, D, DS, MC, V.

D ♣ ≋ ≍ ≋ SC

★ **CLOVIS INN.** *2912 Mabry Dr.* 505/762-5600; res: 800/535-3440; FAX 505/762-6803. 97 rms, 2 story. Mar-Nov: S $38-$52; D $40-$65; each addl $4; under 12 free; lower rates rest of yr. Crib free. TV; cable. Heated pool; whirlpool. Complimentary continental bkfst. Restaurant nearby. Ck-out noon. Coin lndry. Meeting rms. Some refrigerators. Picnic tables. Cr cds: A, C, D, DS, MC, V.

⊡ ≋ ⬚ ⬚ SC

★ ★ **COMFORT INN.** *1616 E Mabry Dr (US 60, 70, 84). 505/762-4591; FAX 505/763-6747.* 50 rms, 2 story. S $33-$38; D $33-$43; each addl $5; under 18 free. Crib free. TV; cable, in-rm movies. Heated pool. Restaurant adj open 24 hrs. Ck-out 11 am. Meeting rm. Cr cds: A, C, D, DS, ER, JCB, MC, V.

≋ SC

✔ ★ **DAYS INN.** *1720 E Mabry Dr (US 60, 70, 84). 505/762-2971; FAX 505/762-2735.* 92 rms, 1-2 story. S $27-$32; D $33-$38; each addl $6. Crib free. TV; cable (premium). Pool; wading pool. Complimentary coffee. Restaurant adj open 24 hrs. Ck-out noon. Cr cds: A, C, D, DS, MC, V.

≋

★ ★ **HOLIDAY INN.** *Box 973, 2700 Mabry Dr (US 60, 70, 84). 505/762-4491; FAX 505/769-0564.* 120 rms, 2 story. S $48; D $55; each addl $5; under 18 free. Crib free. TV; cable. 2 pools, 1 indoor; whirlpool, sauna. Restaurant 6 am-2 pm, 5-10 pm. Rm serv. Bar noon-11 pm; exc Sun. Ck-out noon. Meeting rms. Holidome. Game area. Cr cds: A, C, D, DS, JCB, MC, V.

≋ ⬚ ⬚ SC

Restaurants

✔ ★ **GUADALAJARA.** *916 L Casillas St. 505/769-9965.* Hrs: 11 am-2 pm, 5-9 pm; Sat from 5 pm. Closed Sun. Mexican menu. Semi-a la carte: lunch, dinner $2.50-$6.05. Specialties: chile relleno con carne, enchiladas. Parking. No cr cds accepted.

★ **LEAL'S MEXICAN FOOD.** *3100 E Mabry Dr (US 60/70/84). 505/763-4075.* Hrs: 11 am-9 pm; Sun to 8 pm. Closed Thanksgiving, Dec 25. Res accepted. Mexican, Amer menu. Semi-a la carte: lunch, dinner $3.25-$9.99. Child's meals. Specializes in enchiladas, tacos, tamales. Parking. Cr cds: A, DS, MC, V.

★ ★ **POOR BOY'S STEAKHOUSE.** *2115 N Prince. 505/763-5222.* Hrs: 11 am-9 pm; Fri, Sat to 10 pm. Res accepted. Closed Thanksgiving, Dec 25. Semi-a la carte: lunch $3.99-$9.99, dinner $3.99-$12.99. Child's meals. Specializes in steak, seafood. Salad bar. Parking. Antiques. Cr cds: A, DS, MC, V.

Unrated Dining Spots

EL CHARRO STEAKHOUSE. *805 E 1st St. 505/769-1345.* Hrs: 11 am-9 pm. Closed Sun; major hols. Mexican menu. Avg ck: lunch, dinner $8.50. Parking. Cr cds: DS, MC, V.

FURRS CAFETERIA. *200 W 22nd St, in Hilltop Plaza. 505/762-3741.* Hrs: 11 am-2 pm, 4:30-8 pm; Sat, Sun 11 am-8 pm. Closed Dec 24, 25. Avg ck: lunch, dinner $4.65. Specialties: chicken-fried steak, jalapeño cornbread. No cr cds accepted.

⊡ SC

Deming (H-2)

(See Las Cruces)

Founded 1881 **Pop** 10,970 **Elev** 4,335 ft **Area code** 505 **Zip** 88031
Information Chamber of Commerce, 800 E Pine St, PO Box 8; 505/546-2674.

This is a livestock, cotton, and feed grain town in the Mimbres Valley. The old Butterfield Trail, route of an early stagecoach line to California, passed about 12 miles north of here; there is a marker on US 180.

Hunting enthusiasts will find deer, antelope, ibex, bear and blue quail plentiful in the surrounding mountains.

What to See and Do

City of Rocks State Park. This 680-acre park features fantastic rock formations formed by a thick blanket of volcanic ash that hardened into tuff, and subsequently was sculpted by wind and water; extensive cactus garden. Hiking. Picnicking, playground. Camping. Standard fees. (Daily) 28 mi NW on US 180, then E on NM 61. Phone 505/536-2800. Per vehicle ¢¢

Columbus Historical Museum. Housed in restored Southern Pacific Depot (1902). Memorabilia of 1916 Pancho Villa raid and Camp Furlong (Pershing expedition into Mexico); headquarters of Columbus Historical Society. (Daily; closed major hols) 32 mi S via NM 11 in Columbus. Phone 505/531-2620. **Free.**

Deming-Luna-Mimbres Museum. Mining, military, ranching, railroad, Indian and Hispanic artifacts of the Southwest. Mimbres pottery; Indian baskets; chuckwagon with equipment; photographic display; antique china, crystal; quilt room; antique dolls; bell and bottle collections; gems and minerals. Musical center; art gallery. (Daily; closed Thanksgiving, Dec 25) 301 S Silver St. Phone 505/546-2382. **Free.**

Pancho Villa State Park. Commemorates Pancho Villa's famous raid (March 9, 1916) into American territory. On site of Camp Furlong, from which Brigadier General John "Black Jack" Pershing pursued Villa into Mexico; the first US military action to employ motorized vehicles and airplanes. Some original buildings still stand. Garden of desert vegetation, hundreds of different cacti. Picnicking, playground. Camping (hookups, dump station). Standard fees. Three miles south is Las Palomas, Mexico. (Daily) (For Border Crossing Regulations, see INTRODUCTION) 32 mi S on NM 11 near Columbus. Phone 505/531-2711. Per vehicle ¢¢

Rock hunting. "Deming Agate," jasper, onyx, nodules and many other types of semiprecious stones abound in area. Local gem and mineral society sponsors field trips (see ANNUAL EVENTS).

Rockhound State Park. This 1,000-acre park is on the rugged western slope of the Little Florida Mts. An abundance of agate, geodes and other semiprecious stones for collectors (free; limit 15 lbs). Display of polished stones. Hiking. Picnicking, playground. Camping (hookups). Standard fees. (Daily) 5 mi S on NM 11, then 9 mi E on access road 549. Phone 505/546-6182. Per vehicle ¢¢

Annual Events

Rockhound Roundup. Fairgrounds. More than 6,000 participants. Guided field trips for agate, geodes, candy-rock, marble, honey onyx. Auctions; exhibitions; demonstrations. Contact Deming Gem & Mineral Society, PO Box 1459. 2nd wkend Mar.

Great American Duck Race. Live duck racing; duck queen, darling duckling, best-dressed duck contests; hot air balloon race; tortilla toss; parade. 4th wkend Aug.

Southwestern New Mexico State Fair. Fairgrounds. Livestock shows, midway, parade. Last wkend Sept.

Motels

✔ ★ **DAYS INN.** *PO Box 790, 1709 Spruce St. 505/546-8813; FAX 505/546-7095.* 57 rms, 2 story. S $39; D $45; each addl $5; suites $48-$54; under 18 free; wkly rates. Crib free. Pet accepted, some restrictions. TV; cable. Pool. Restaurant 5:30 am-9:30 pm. Ck-out noon. Meeting rms. Business servs avail. Beauty shop. Picnic tables. Cr cds: A, C, D, DS, MC, V.

⊡ ⬚ ≋ ⬚ ⬚ SC

★ ★ **GRAND MOTOR INN.** *1721 E Spruce St. 505/546-2632; FAX 505/546-4446.* 62 rms, 2 story. S $42; D $45-$50; each addl $6; suites $65; under 12 free. Crib free. Pet accepted. TV; cable (premium). Heated pool; wading pool, poolside serv. Restaurant 6 am-10 pm. Rm serv. Bar noon-12:30 am. Ck-out noon. Meeting rms. Business servs avail. Valet serv. Free local airport, RR station, bus depot transportation. Golf privileges. French Provincial decor. Cr cds: A, C, D, DS, MC, V.

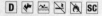

★ ★ **HOLIDAY INN.** *Box 1138, I-10 E, exit 85.* 505/546-2661; *FAX 505/546-6308.* 85 rms, 2 story. S $50-$60; D $58-$68; each addl $6; suites $75-$125; under 19 free; higher rates last wknd Aug. Crib free. Pet accepted. TV; cable. Pool. Restaurant 6 am-10 pm. Ck-out 11 am. Coin lndry. Meeting rms. Business servs avail. Sundries. Free airport, RR station, bus depot transportation. Cr cds: A, C, D, DS, MC, V.

Dulce (B-3)

(See Chama)

Pop 2,438 **Elev** 6,769 ft **Area code** 505 **Zip** 87528

A section of Carson National Forest (see TAOS) is located southwest on US 64.

What to See and Do

Jicarilla Apache Indian Reservation. The Jicarilla Apaches came from a group that migrated from southwestern Canada several centuries ago. The reservation is at an elevation of 6,500-8,500 feet and has excellent fishing and hunting (guides available; tribal permit required; phone 505/759-3255 for information); boating. On US 64. Phone 505/759-3442. Primitive camping ¢¢

Annual Events

Little Beaver Roundup. Jicarilla Apache Reservation (see). Parade, rodeo, dances, arts and crafts, carnival, 62-mile pony express race. Phone 505/759-3242. Mid-July.

Go-Gee-Yah. Stone Lake. Rodeo, powwow, foot races. Phone 505/759-3242. Mid-Sept.

Motel

★ ★ **BEST WESTERN JICARILLA INN.** *US 64 & Hawks Dr, US 64 & Hawks Dr.* 505/759-3663; *FAX 505/759-3170.* 42 units, 2 story. June-Dec: S $60; D $75; each addl $5; suites $85-$90; under 10 free; lower rates rest of yr. TV; cable. Restaurant 6:30 am-9 pm. Bar 4 pm-1:30 am. Ck-out 11 am. Meeting rms. Gift shop. Local airport transportation. Some refrigerators. Cr cds: A, C, D, DS, ER, JCB, MC, V.

Eagle Nest (C-4)

(For accommodations see Red River, Taos, also see Cimarron)

Pop 189 **Elev** 8,300 ft **Area code** 505 **Zip** 87718
Information Angel Fire Chamber of Commerce, PO Box 547, Angel Fire 87710; 800/446-8117.

On Eagle Nest Lake, this area is a summer and winter ski resort high in the Sangre de Cristo Mountains. The lake features trout fishing.

What to See and Do

Angel Fire Ski Resort. Resort has 2 triple, 4 double chairlifts; patrol, school, rentals; snowmaking; cafeteria, restaurants, bars. 67 runs, longest run over 3 miles; vertical drop 2,180 feet. (Early Dec-Mar, daily) Also cross-country trails, snowmobiling. **Summer resort** includes 18-hole golf, tennis, fishing, boating, Jeep tours, riding stables, lake. Conference center (all yr). 12 mi S on US 64, NM 434. Phone 505/377-6401 or 800/633-7463. ¢¢¢¢¢

Cimarron Canyon State Park. Region of high mountains and deep canyons has scenic 200-foot palisades; winding mountain stream has excellent trout fishing; state wildlife area. Hiking, rock climbing; wildlife viewing. Winter sports. Camping (fishing license required). Standard fees. (Daily) 12 mi E on US 64. Phone 505/377-6271.   **Free.**

DAV Vietnam Veterans National Memorial. This beautiful, gracefully designed building stands on a hillside overlooking Moreno Valley and the Sangre de Cristo Mountains. Maintained by the Disabled American Veterans, the Memorial is dedicated to all who fought in Vietnam. Chapel (daily). Visitors Center (May-Sept, daily exc Mon; rest of yr, Wed-Sun). 10 mi S on US 64.   **Free.**

El Morro National Monument (Inscription Rock) (D-1)

(For accommodations see Gallup, Grants)

(From I-40, 43 mi SW of Grants off NM 53)

Here, on the ancient trail taken by the Conquistadores from Santa Fe to Zuni, is the towering cliff that served as the guest book of New Mexico. Don Juan de Oñate carved his name here in 1605; others followed him in 1629 and 1632. Don Diego de Vargas, reconqueror of New Mexico after the Pueblo Rebellion of 1680, registered his passing in 1692, and scores of other Spaniards and Americans added their names to the cliff at later dates.

The rock is pale buff Zuni sandstone. The cliff, 200 feet high, has pueblo ruins on its top; pre-Columbian petroglyphs. Visitor center and museum (daily; closed Jan 1, Dec 25).   **Free.**

Trail (fee). Picnic facilities. Ranger on duty. Golden Eagle and Golden Age Passports (see INTRODUCTION). Primitive camping (fee). Contact the Superintendent, El Morro National Monument, Rte 2, Box 43, Ramah 87321; 505/783-4226.

Española (C-3)

(See Los Alamos, Santa Fe)

Pop 8,389 **Elev** 5,585 ft **Area code** 505 **Zip** 87532
Information Española Valley Chamber of Commerce, 417 Big Rock Center; 505/753-2831.

First settled 700 years ago by the Pueblo Indians, then by Don Juan de Oñate in 1598, Española was claimed by the United States in 1846. Prosperity came with the railroad in the 1870s. A Ranger District office of the Santa Fe National Forest (see SANTA FE) is located here.

What to See and Do

Ghost Ranch Living Museum. Operated by the US Forest Service. Animals native to the area: bears, mountain lions, snakes and reptiles. Beaver National Forest and displays by the Soil Conservation Service. (May-Sept, daily; rest of yr, daily exc Mon) Donation. Approx 34 mi NW on US 84. Phone 505/685-4312. Also here is

Florence Hawley Ellis Museum of Anthropology. Exhibits of Indian/Spanish history. (Daily exc Mon; closed Dec) Phone 505/685-4333. **Free.**

Ruth Hall Museum of Paleontology. Exhibits on Traisic animals, Coelophysis, New Mexico state fossil. (Daily exc Mon; closed Dec) Phone 505/685-4333. **Free.**

Ortega's Weaving Shop. Near the *Plaza del Cerro* (plaza of the hill), an example of an old-style protected Spanish colonial village. Generations of noted weavers make blankets, coats, vests, purses, rugs. (Daily exc Sun) 10 mi NE via NM 76, jct NM 520 in Chimayo. Phone 505/351-4362. **Free.** Directly north of the shop is

Galeria Ortega. Contains works by artists of northern New Mexico depicting the region's unique tri-cultural heritage. (May-Oct, daily; rest of yr, daily exc Sun) Phone 505/351-2288.

Puye Cliff Dwellings. Owned by the Puebloof Santa Clara, Puye means "where the rabbits assemble." Occupied from 1250 to 1577. Road and walking trails lead to top of mesa. Visitor Center (at Tribal Administrative Office). (Daily) Sr citizen rate. May close due to weather in winter. 2 mi S on NM 30. Contact PO Box 580, 87532; 505/753-7326. **¢¢**

Whitewater rafting. Guided river excursions; half-day, full-day and multi-day tours arranged. (May-Sept) Contact Rio Grande Rapid Transit, PO Box A, Pilar 87531; 505/758-9700 or 800/222-RAFT. **¢¢¢¢¢**

Annual Events

Rio Grande White Water Race. Canoe, kayak, raft experts challenge 14 miles of white water below Pilar; canoe marathon; canoe/kayak slalom. Phone 505/758-9700 or 800/222-RAFT. Mother's Day.

San Juan Feast Day. San Juan Pueblo, 5 mi N via US 84, NM 68. Dancing; food; carnival. Late June.

Fiesta de Oñate. Celebrates establishment of New Mexico's first Spanish settlement in 1598. Torch relay; vespers, candlelight procession; street dancing; arts & crafts; food; entertainment; fireworks (Sat); parade (Sun). Phone Chamber of Commerce. 2nd wkend July.

Santa Clara Feast Day. Santa Clara Pueblo, 2 mi S via NM 30. Dancing; food; market. Mid-Aug.

Tri-cultural Arts Festival. Northern New Mexico Community College. Features local artisans and their works; includes potters, weavers, woodworkers, photographers, painters, singers and dancers. Phone Chamber of Commerce. Usually 1st wkend Oct.

Motels

★ **PARK INN.** *PO Box 3617 (87533), 920 N Riverside Dr (NM 68).* 505/753-7291; res: 800/766-7943; FAX 505/753-1218. 51 rms. S $48; D $53.95; each addl $5. Pet accepted; $10. TV; cable (premium). Heated pool. Continental bkfst 7-9:30 am. Bar 2 pm-2 am; Sun to 10 pm. Ck-out 11 am. Cr cds: A, C, D, DS, ER, JCB, MC, V.

✔ ★ **WESTERN HOLIDAY.** *Rte 3, Box 249, On US 68 E.* 505/753-2491. 24 rms. May-Sept: S $34-$38; D $46-$52; each addl $8; lower rates rest of yr. Crib $5. TV; cable. Heated pool. Complimentary coffee in rms. Ck-out 11 am. Cr cds: A, C, D, MC, V.

Inn

★ ★ ★ **INN AT THE DELTA.** *(304 Paseo de Onate, Española)* 505/753-9466; res: 800/995-8599. 10 rms, 2 story. Late May-Sept, mid-Dec-Jan 1: S $75-$125; D $85-$150; each addl $10; under 12 free; hol plans; lower rates rest of yr. Crib avail. TV; cable (premium), VCR avail. Complimentary coffee, tea. Complimentary full bkfst. Restaurant adj 7 am-10 pm. Ck-out noon, ck-in 3 pm. Concierge. Whirlpools. Adobe structure with Southwestern-style furnishings, many hand-

carved by local craftsmen. Totally nonsmoking. Cr cds: A, D, DS, MC, V.

Restaurants

★ ★ **ANTHONY'S AT THE DELTA.** *228 Onate NW (Chama Hwy), on west side.* 505/753-4511. Hrs: 5-9 pm; summer to 10 pm. Closed Jan 1, Thanksgiving, Dec 25. Res accepted. Bar. Semi-a la carte: dinner $10.95-$32. Specializes in prime rib, grilled salmon. Salad bar. Parking. 4 dining areas; 2 fireplaces; hand-carved wooden furniture; art collection displayed. Many plants and fragrant fresh flowers; courtyard with 200 rose bushes. Cr cds: A, D, DS, MC, V.

★ ★ **EL PARAGUA.** *603 Santa Cruz Rd, at NM 76.* 505/753-3211. Hrs: 11 am-9 pm; wkends to 9:30 pm. Closed Dec 25. Res accepted. Mexican menu. Bar. A la carte entrees: lunch $5.75-$8.50, dinner $7.50-$28. Child's meals. Specialties: tacos, carne adovada. Mariachi bands on wkends. Parking. Outdoor dining. Stone bldg (1877); many antiques, Mexican tiles, stone fireplace. Family-owned. Cr cds: MC, V.

✔ ★ ★ **RANCHO DE CHIMAYO.** *(PO Box 11, Chimayo 87522) 16 mi N on US 285, then 8 mi NE on NM 503, then 3 mi N on NM 520, in Chimayo.* 505/351-4444. Hrs: 11:30 am-9 pm. Closed Dec 25; Mon from Nov-May; also 1st full wk Jan. Res accepted. Mexican, Amer menu. Bar. Semi-a la carte: lunch $4.25-$12.95, dinner $5.50-$12.95. Child's meals. Specialties: carne adovada, sopaipillas. Entertainment June-Aug. Parking. Terrace dining. In old hacienda (1885); antiques, fireplace, original artwork. Family-owned. Cr cds: A, D, MC, V.

Farmington (B-2)

(See Aztec, Shiprock)

Founded 1876 **Pop** 33,997 **Elev** 5,395 ft **Area code** 505

Information Convention & Visitors Bureau, 203 W Main St, 87401; 505/326-7602 or 800/448-1240.

The Navajos call it Totah, the meeting place at the convergence of three rivers in the colorful land of the Navajo, Ute, Apache and Pueblo Indians. Once the home of of the ancient Anasazi, Farmington is now the largest city in the Four Corners area and supplies much of the energy to the Southwest. From Farmington, visitors may explore Mesa Verde, Chaco Canyon and the Salmon and Aztec ruins.

Visitors to the area can also enjoy some of the best year-round fishing in the state at Navajo Lake State Park (see AZTEC) and in the San Juan River. Farmington is also the home of the Navajo Indian Irrigation Project, which encompasses more than 100,000 acres.

There are many shops offering traditional Indian crafts in the immediate area—baskets, jewelry, pottery, rugs and sand paintings. Obtain a list of local art galleries and trading posts at the Convention and Visitors Bureau.

What to See and Do

Bisti Badlands. A federallyprotected wilderness area of strange geologic features; large petrified logs and other fossils are scattered among numerous scenic landforms. No vehicles permitted beyond boundary. 37 mi S via NM 371. **Free.**

Chaco Culture National Historic Park (see). 75 mi S.

❑ **Four Corners Monument.** Only point in the country common to four states: Arizona, Colorado, New Mexico and Utah. 64 mi NW via US 64, NM 504, US 160.

San Juan County Archaeological Research Center & Library at Salmon Ruin. Archaeological remains of a 250-room structure built by the Pueblo Indians (ca 1100). Museum and research center exhibit artifacts from excavation; historic structures; picnicking. (Daily; closed Jan 1, Easter, Thanksgiving, Dec 25) Sr citizen rate. 12 mi E on US 64 near Bloomfield. Phone 505/632-2013. ¢

Annual Events

Pro-Rodeo Roundup. McGee Park, US 64. Top professional rodeo cowboys from several states. Early Apr.

Farmington Invitational Balloon Rally. Hare & hound races; competitions. Memorial Day wkend.

Connie Mack World Series Baseball Tournament. Ricketts Park. Seventeen-game serieshosting teams from all over US & Puerto Rico. Aug.

San Juan County Fair. Parade; rodeo; fiddlers' contest; chili cook-off; exhibits. Mid-late Aug.

Seasonal Event

Anasazi, the Ancient Ones. Lions Wilderness Park Amphitheater. Musical pageant about the Southwest's multi-cultural heritage, presented in outdoor amphitheater. Contact Convention & Visitors Bureau for schedule. Mid-June-mid-Aug.

Motels

★ **BASIN LODGE.** 701 Airport Dr (87401). 505/325-5061. 21 rms. S $25-$27; D $29-$31; each addl $4; under 8 free. Crib $4. TV; cable. Complimentary coffee in lobby. Restaurant nearby. Ck-out 11 am. Cr cds: A, C, D, DS, MC, V.

★ ★ **BEST WESTERN INN & SUITES.** 700 Scott Ave (87401), at Bloomfield Hwy. 505/327-5221. 194 rms, 3 story. S $59-$62; D $67-$69; each addl $10; under 12 free; wkend rates. Crib free. TV; cable (premium). Indoor pool; poolside serv. Restaurant 6-10 am, 5-10 pm. Rm serv. Bar 4 pm-midnight. Ck-out noon. Coin lndry. Meeting rms. Business servs avail. In-rm modem link. Bellhops. Valet serv. Gift shop. Free airport, bus depot transportation. Exercise equipt; weights, bicycles, whirlpool, sauna. Rec rm. Some refrigerators. Cr cds: A, C, D, DS, MC, V.

★ **COMFORT INN.** 555 Scott Ave (87401). 505/325-2626; FAX 505/325-7675. 60 rms, 2 story, 18 suites. May-Oct: S $52-$54; D $60-$64; each addl $8; suites $60-$70; under 18 free; lower rates rest of yr. Crib free. Pet accepted. TV; cable (premium). Pool. Complimentary continental bkfst. Complimentary coffee in rms. Ck-out 11 am. Business servs avail. In-rm modem link. Valet serv. Refrigerator in suites. Cr cds: A, C, D, DS, ER, JCB, MC, V.

★ ★ **HOLIDAY INN.** 600 E Broadway (87499), US 64 at Scott Ave. 505/327-9811; FAX 505/325-2288. 149 rms, 2 story. S $64; D $70; each addl $6; under 19 free. Crib free. Pet accepted. TV; cable (premium). Pool. Restaurant 6 am-10 pm. Rm serv. Bar. Ck-out noon. Business servs avail. Bellhops. Free airport, bus depot transportation. Exercise equipt; weights, bicycles, whirlpool, sauna. Cr cds: A, C, D, DS, JCB, MC, V.

★ ★ **LA QUINTA.** 675 Scott Ave (87401). 505/327-4706. 106 rms, 2 story. S, D $62; each addl $8; under 18 free. Crib free. Pet accepted. TV; cable. Heated pool. Complimentary continental bkfst. Complimentary coffee in lobby. Restaurant adj open 24 hrs. Ck-out

noon. Meeting rm. Valet serv. Refrigerators avail. Picnic tables, grills. Cr cds: A, C, D, DS, MC, V.

✔ ★ **MOTEL 6.** 510 Scott Ave (87401). 505/327-0242. 98 rms, 3 story. S, D $26.95; each addl $6; under 18 free. Crib free. Pet accepted. TV; cable. Heated pool. Restaurant adj 5:30 am-midnight. Ck-out noon. Cr cds: A, D, DS, MC, V.

Restaurants

✔ ★ **CLANCY'S PUB.** 2701 E 20th, at Hutton. 505/325-8176. Hrs: 11-2 am; Sun noon-midnight. Closed Easter, Thanksgiving, Dec 25. Res accepted. Mexican, Amer menu. Bar. Semi-a la carte: lunch, dinner $2.50-$7.50. Child's meals. Specializes in prime rib, hamburgers. Parking. Outdoor dining. Casual dining. Cr cds: A, D, DS, MC, V.

✔ ★ **LA FIESTA GRANDE.** 1916 E Main St. 505/326-6476. Hrs: 11 am-9:30 pm; Fri, Sat to 10 pm; Sun to 3 pm. Closed Jan 1, Thanksgiving, Dec 25. Mexican, Amer menu. Semi-a la carte: lunch $3-$4.95, dinner $3-$8.50. Lunch buffet $4.95, Sun $5.95. Child's meals. Specializes in fajitas, sopaipillas, green chili cheeseburgers. Salad bar. Parking. Cr cds: DS, MC, V.

Gallup (D-1)

Founded 1881 **Pop** 19,154 **Elev** 6,600 ft **Area code** 505 **Zip** 87301
Information Gallup Convention & Visitors Bureau, 701 E Montoya Blvd, PO Box 600, 87305; 505/863-3841 or 800/242-4282.

Gallup, originally a railroad town, was established to take advantage of the coal reserves nearby and has grown into a retail center serving a large area. The Navajo reservation is north and west of town. Navajo, Zuni, Hopi and Acoma Indians trade here.

What to See and Do

McGaffey Recreation Area. 1/2 mi to lake. Fishing. Picnicking (fireplaces, tables). Tent & trailer sites. Ranger District headquarters at Grants. Fees for some activities. (Daily) 12 mi E on I-40, then 10 mi S on NM 400 in Cibola National Forest (see ALBUQUERQUE). Phone 505/287-8833. **Free.**

Red Rock State Park. Desertsetting with massive red sandstone buttes. Nature trail, boarding stable. Picnicking, concession. Camping (hookups). Interpretive displays; auditorium/convention center, 7,000-seat arena; site of Inter-Tribal Indian Ceremonial (see ANNUAL EVENTS) and rodeos. 5 mi E via I-40 & NM 566. Phone 505/722-3839. Camping **Free.** In the park is

Red Rock Museum. Hopi, Navajo and Zuni artifacts; gift shop. (Summer, daily; winter, Mon-Fri; closed winter hols) Phone 505/722-3839. ¢

Window Rock. This is the capital of the Navajo Reservation. The Navajo Nation Council Chambers, Navajo Tribal Museum and Navajo Nation Zoological and Botanical Park are here. 8 mi N on US 666, then 18 mi W on NM 264, in Arizona.

Zuni Pueblo (see). 31 mi S on NM 602, then 8 mi W on NM 53.

Annual Events

Inter-Tribal Indian Ceremonial. Red Rock State Park. A major Indian festival; more than 50 tribes from the US, Canada and Mexico participate in parades, rodeos, games, contests, dances; arts and crafts sales. Contact Exec Dir, PO Box 1, Church Rock 87311; 505/863-3896 or 800/233-4528. 2nd wk Aug.

Navajo Nation Fair. Fairgrounds in Window Rock, AZ. Dances, ceremonials, rodeo, arts and crafts, educational and commercial exhibits, food, traditional events. Contact PO Box Drawer U, Window Rock, AZ 86515; 602/871-6478. Five days beginning Wed after Labor Day.

Red Rock Balloon Rally. Red Rock State Park. Contact Convention & Visitors Bureau for more information. 1st wkend Dec.

Motels

(Rates may be higher during Intertribal Indian Ceremonial week. All properties listed on US 66 are parallel to the main line of the Santa Fe Railroad.)

★ ★ **BEST WESTERN ROYAL HOLIDAY.** *1903 W US 66 (Historic Rte 66).* 505/722-4900. 50 rms, 2 story. May-Oct: S $50-$65; D $55-$65; each addl $5; suites $58-$95; lower rates rest of yr. TV; cable (premium). Indoor pool; whirlpool. Complimentary coffee in rms. Restaurant nearby. Ck-out 11 am. Exercise equipt; bicycle, treadmill, sauna. Cr cds: A, C, D, DS, MC, V.

✔ ★ **DAYS INN CENTRAL.** *1603 W US 66.* 505/863-3891; FAX 505/863-3891, ext. 300. 78 rms, 2 story. Apr-Oct: S $30-$40; D $35-$50; each addl $3; under 12 free; lower rates rest of yr. Crib free. TV; cable (premium). Heated pool. Playground. Complimentary continental bkfst. Restaurant nearby. Ck-out 11 am. Business servs avail. Cr cds: A, C, D, DS, MC, V.

★ **ECONO LODGE.** *3101 W US 66.* 505/722-3800. 51 rms, 2 story. May-Oct: S, D $38.95-$51.95; each addl $5; under 12 free; higher rates mid-Aug; lower rates rest of yr. Crib $5. TV; cable (premium). Coffee in rms. Restaurant nearby. Ck-out 11 am. Airport, RR station, bus depot transportation. Cr cds: A, C, D, DS, JCB, MC, V.

★ ★ **EL RANCHO.** *1000 E US 66.* 505/863-9311. 75 rms, 6 kit. units. S $34-$51; D $44-$55; each addl $5; suites $75. Crib free. Pet accepted. TV. Pool. Restaurant 6:30 am-10 pm. Bar 5 pm-1 am. Ck-out noon. Coin lndry. Meeting rms. Gift shop. Free RR station, bus depot transportation. Cr cds: A, C, D, DS, MC, V.

✔ ★ **ROSEWAY INN.** *2003 W US 66.* 505/863-9385; res: 800/454-5444; FAX 505/863-6532. 92 rms, 2 story. S, D $33.40-$44; each addl $4; under 18 free; wkly rates. Crib free. TV; cable (premium). Heated pool; whirlpool, sauna. Restaurant adj 6 am-10 pm. Ck-out noon. Meeting rm. Business servs avail. Near municipal airport. Cr cds: A, C, D, DS, ER, JCB, MC, V.

✔ ★ **TRAVELERS INN.** *3304 W US 66.* 505/722-7765; res: 800/633-8300; FAX 505/722-4752. 105 rms, 2 story. June-Sept: S $35.95; D $42.95; each addl $4; suites $56.95-$61.95; under 12 free; lower rates rest of yr. Crib free. TV; cable (premium). Heated pool. Complimentary coffee in lobby. Restaurant nearby. Ck-out 11 am. Business servs avail. Refrigerator in suites. Cr cds: A, C, D, DS, MC, V.

Motor Hotel

★ ★ **HOLIDAY INN HOLIDOME.** *2915 W US 66, near Municipal Airport.* 505/722-2201; FAX 505/722-9616. 212 rms, 2 story. June-Aug: S $62-$67; D $67-$73; each addl $5; under 19 free; lower rates rest of yr. Crib free. TV; cable (premium). Indoor pool. Restaurant 6 am-10 pm. Rm serv. Bar 4 pm-12:30 am, closed Sun; entertainment, dancing. Ck-out noon. Coin lndry. Meeting rms. Business servs avail.

Bellhops. Valet serv. Sundries. Free airport, RR station, bus depot transportation. Exercise equipt; weights, bicycles, whirlpool, sauna. Game rm. Cr cds: A, C, D, DS, JCB, MC, V.

Restaurants

★ **EARL'S.** *1400 E US 66.* 505/863-4201. Hrs: 6 am-9:30 pm; Fri, Sat to 10 pm. Closed most major hols. Res accepted. Mexican, Amer menu. Semi-a la carte: bkfst $3.50-$5.50, lunch, dinner $4.50-$9.29. Child's meals. Salad bar. Parking. Casual family dining. Family-owned. Cr cds: A, C, D, MC, V.

✔ ★ **RANCH KITCHEN.** *3001 W US 66.* 505/722-2537. Hrs: 6 am-10 pm. Closed Dec 25. Res accepted. Mexican, Amer menu. Wine, beer. Semi-a la carte: bkfst $2.95-$5.50, lunch $3.50-$7.95, dinner $4.95-$12.95. Child's meals. Specialties: beef chimichanga, Navajo taco, mesquite smoked barbecue. Salad bar. Parking. Cr cds: A, C, D, DS, MC, V.

Grants (D-2)

Founded 1882 **Pop** 8,626 **Elev** 6,460 ft **Area code** 505 **Zip** 87020

Information Chamber of Commerce, 100 N Iron St, PO Box 297; 505/287-4802.

A Navajo named Paddy Martinez revolutionized the life of this town in 1950, when he discovered uranium ore. More than half the known domestic reserves of uranium ore are in this area.

About 12 miles east, I-40 (US 66) crosses one of the most recent lava flows in the continental United States. Indian pottery has been found under the lava, which first flowed about four million years ago from Mt Taylor, to the north. Lava also flowed less than 1,100 years ago from fissures that, today, are near the highway. The lava is sharp and hard; heavy shoes are advisable for walking on it. A Ranger District office of the Cibola National Forest (see ALBUQUERQUE) is located here.

What to See and Do

Acoma Pueblo, Sky City (see). Oldest continuously inhabited Indian Pueblo in North America. Provides a glimpse into well-preserved Native American culture. 32 mi SE via I-40, NM 23. For information phone 800/747-0181.

Bluewater Lake State Park. Rolling hills studded with piñon and juniper trees encircle the Bluewater Reservoir. Swimming, waterskiing; fishing (trout, catfish); boating (ramps). Winter sports. Picnicking. Camping (hookups, dump station). Standard fees. (Daily) 19 mi W on I-40, then 7 mi S on NM 412. Phone 505/876-2391. Per vehicle ¢¢

El Malpais National Monument & National Conservation Area. These two areas total 376,000 acres of volcanic formations and sandstone canyons. Monument features splatter cones, 17-mile-long system of lava tubes and ice caves. Conservation area, which surrounds the monument, includes: La Ventana Natural Arch, one of the state's largest free standing natural arches; Cebolla and West Malpais wildernesses; and numerous Anasazi ruins. The Sandstone Bluffs Overlook off NM 117 offers an excellent view of lava-filled valley and surrounding area. Facilities include hiking, bicycling, horseback riding; scenic drives. Primitive camping (acquire Back-country Permit at Information Center or Ranger Station). Lava is rough; caution is advised. Most lava tubes accessible only by hiking trails; check with Information Center in Grants before attempting any hikes. Monument, Conservation area (daily). Information Center and visitor facility on NM 117 (daily; closed Jan 1, Thanksgiving, Dec 25). S on NM 53; or 6 mi SE on I-40, then S on NM 117. Contact Interpretive Specialist, El Malpais Information Center, PO Box 939; 505/287-3407. **Free.**

El Morro National Monument (see). Approx 43 mi SW off NM 53.

Laguna Pueblo (population approx 7,000). This is one of the 19 pueblos located in the state of New Mexico. The people here speak the Keresan language. The pueblo consists of 6 villages: Encinal, Laguna, Mesita, Paguate, Paraje and Seama. These villages are located along the western boundary of the pueblo. The Pueblo people sell their arts & crafts on the reservation; items such as Indian belts, pottery, jewelry, baskets, paintings, Indian kilts and moccasins can be purchased. Visitors are welcomed to the pueblo throughout the year and may encounter various religious observances, some of which are open to the public. However, questions concerning social and religious ceremonies should be directed to the Governor of the Pueblo. As a general rule, photographs, sketches and tape recordings of Pueblo ceremonials are strictly forbidden. Therefore, it is most important that visitors observe these restrictions and first obtain permission from the Governor of the Pueblo before engaging in such activities. Fiestas and dances are held throughout the year. 33 mi E off I-40. Phone 505/552-6654.

New Mexico Mining Museum. Only uranium mining museum in the world. Also has Indian artifacts and relics; native mineral display. (May-Sept, daily; rest of yr, daily exc Sun) 100 N Iron St. Phone 505/287-4802. ¢

Motels

★ ★ **BEST WESTERN.** *1501 E Santa Fe Ave, at I-40, exit 85.* 505/287-7901; FAX 505/285-5751. 126 rms, 2 story. S $54-$64; D $64-$69; each addl $10; under 12 free. Crib free. Pet accepted, some restrictions. TV; cable (premium). Indoor pool; whirlpool, sauna. Restaurant 6-10 am; dining rm 5-9 pm. Rm serv. Bar 4 pm-midnight; Fri, Sat to 1:30 am: Sun to 11:30 pm; entertainment, dancing Thur-Sat. Ck-out noon. Coin lndry. Meeting rms. Business servs avail. Valet serv. Sundries. Game rm. Refrigerators avail. Cr cds: A, C, D, DS, MC, V.

✔ ★ **LEISURE LODGE.** *1204 E Santa Fe Ave, 1204 E Santa Fe Ave (Old US 66), I-40 exit 85.* 505/287-2991. 32 rms, 2 story. S $24.95-$26.95; D $30-$34; each addl $3; under 12 free. Crib $3. Pet accepted. TV; cable. Heated pool. Complimentary coffee in lobby. Restaurant adj 9 am-9 pm. Ck-out 11 am. Cr cds: A, C, D, DS, MC, V.

Hobbs (G-6)

Founded 1927 **Pop** 29,115 **Elev** 3,650 ft **Area code** 505 **Zip** 88240
Information Chamber of Commerce, 400 N Marland; 800/658-6291.

A chance meeting between two covered wagons on a trail across the *Llano Estacado* (Staked Plain) led to the founding of Hobbs. James Hobbs and his family were headed for Alpine, Texas, when they met an eastbound wagon of pioneers returning from Alpine because they couldn't make a living there. Hearing this, James turned his wagon north and eventually settled in what is now Hobbs. This was primarily an agrarian community until the discovery of "black gold" turned it into a booming oil town.

Oil, natural gas and potash are the big products here; however, Lea County has long been (and still is) an important cattle ranch and dairy territory. Because there is a plentiful supply of shallow water in the ground, cotton, alfalfa, grain and vegetables have been grown successfully.

What to See and Do

Lea County Cowboy Hall of Fame & Western Heritage Center. Local memorabilia and artifacts with emphasis on the cowboy, Indian and oil

eras. Permanent displays of Lea County history. (Mon-Fri, Sat afternoons; closed hols) New Mexico Junior College. Phone 505/392-1275 or -5518. **Free.**

Annual Events

Cinco de Mayo Celebration. City Park. Includes parade; Mexican food booths; arts and crafts booths. Early May.

Lea County Fair. In Lovington, 20 mi NW on NM 18. Phone 505/396-5344. Aug.

Motels

✔ ★ ★ **BEST WESTERN LEAWOOD.** *1301 E Broadway.* 505/393-4101. 70 rms. S $37-$41; D $41-$45; each addl $4. Crib $3. TV; cable. Pool. Complimentary full bkfst. Restaurant opp 11 am-10 pm. Ck-out noon. Airport transportation. Cr cds: A, C, D, DS, MC, V.

★ ★ **RAMADA INN.** *501 N Marland Blvd.* 505/397-3251; res: 800/635-6639. 75 rms, 2 story. S $35-$38; D $42-$45; each addl $3; suites $82; under 12 free. Crib free. TV; cable. Heated pool. Restaurant 5 am-8 pm; dining rm 5:30-10 pm. Rm serv 6 am-10 pm. Bar 11-2 am; entertainment, dancing exc Sun. Ck-out 1 pm. Meeting rms. Sundries. Cr cds: A, C, D, DS, MC, V.

Restaurant

★ ★ **CATTLE BARON STEAK & SEAFOOD.** *1930 N Grimes.* 505/393-2800. Hrs: 11 am-9:30 pm; Fri, Sat to 10 pm; Sun to 9 pm. Closed Dec 25. Bar. Semi-a la carte: lunch $4.95-$7, dinner $7.25-$22. Child's meals. Specializes in steak, seafood. Salad bar. Parking. Cr cds: A, C, D, DS, MC, V.

Unrated Dining Spot

FURRS CAFETERIA. *N Turner & Sanger, in Broadmoor Mall.* 505/397-3211. Hrs: 6-9:30 am, 10:30 am-2 pm, 4-8 pm. Closed Dec 25. Avg ck: bkfst $3; lunch, dinner $6.70. Specializes in roast beef, baked cod. Old English decor. No cr cds accepted.

Las Cruces (H-3)

(See El Paso, TX)

Founded 1848 **Pop** 62,126 **Elev** 3,896 ft **Area code** 505
Information Convention & Visitors Bureau, 311 N Downtown Mall, 88001; 505/524-8521.

In 1830, a group of people from Taos were traveling on the Spanish highway El Camino Real; they camped here and were massacred by Apache Indians. They were buried under a field of crosses; hence the name Las Cruces ("the crosses"). Situated in the vast farming area of the fertile lower Rio Grande Valley, this region is especially noted for its homegrown green chile as well as pecans, cotton, lettuce and corn.

What to See and Do

Aguirre Spring Recreation Site. Organ Mountain area formed by monzonite intrusions—molten rock beneath the surface. Wearing away of the crust left organ pipe rock spires. Baylor Pass and Pine Tree hiking trails. Picnicking. Camping (centrally located rest rms; no drinking water). Managed by the Department of the Interior, Bureau of Land Management, Mimbres Resource Area. (Daily) 17 mi E via US 70, 5 mi S on unnumbered road. Phone 505/525-4300. Per car ¢¢

Exploring by car. There are ghost mining towns, extinct volcanoes, frontier forts, mountains and pecan orchards in the area.

Fort Selden State Monument. Frontier cavalry fort established in 1865; partial ruins now stabilized. General Douglas MacArthur lived here as a boy (1884-1886) when his father was post commander. Famed Buffalo Soldiers were stationed here. Self-guided, bilingual trail. Visitor center has history exhibits. Picnicking. (Daily; closed state hols) 12 mi N on I-25. Phone 505/526-8911. ¢

Gadsden Museum. Native American and Civil War artifacts; paintings; hand-painted china; Santo collection; history of the Gadsden Purchase. (Daily; closed some major hols) 2 mi SW on W Barker Rd in Mesilla. Phone 505/526-6293. ¢

Mesilla. Historic village that briefly served as the Confederate capital of the Territory of Arizona. Billy the Kid stood trial for murder here and escaped; the Gadsden Purchase was signed here. La Mesilla State Monument consists of the original plaza and surrounding adobe buildings. There are numerous specialty shops, restaurants, art galleries and museums. 2 mi SW.

New Mexico State University (1888). (15,500 students) On the 950-acre campus are a history museum (daily exc Mon; free), an art gallery and an 18-hole public golf course. University Ave. Phone 505/646-3221.

White Sands Missile Range. Missiles and related equipment tested here. Actual range closed to the public; visitors welcome at the outdoor missile park and the Visitors Center at the Public Affairs Office, Building 122. (Mon-Fri; closed hols) 25 mi E on US 70. Phone 505/678-1134. **Free.**

Annual Events

Southern New Mexico State Fair & Rodeo. Phone 505/526-1106. Late Sept.

Whole Enchilada Fiesta. Downtown Mall. Street dancing, entertainment, crafts, food including world's largest enchilada. Phone 505/527-3939. Early Oct.

Renaissance Arts & Craftfaire. Young Park. Juried fair with participants in Renaissance costume. Food, entertainment. Phone 505/523-6403. Early Nov.

Our Lady of Guadalupe Fiesta. Tortugas Village, adj to town. Evening Indian dances, vespers; daytime ascent of Mount Tortugas; Mass, bonfire and torchlight descent; fiesta. Phone 505/526-8171. Dec.

Motels

★ ★ **BEST WESTERN MESILLA VALLEY INN.** 901 Avenida de Mesilla (88005), at jct I-10 exit 140. 505/524-8603; FAX 505/526-8437. 167 units, 2 story. S, D $48-$64; each addl $8; under 12 free. Crib free. Pet accepted, some restrictions. TV; cable. Heated pool; whirlpool. Restaurant 6 am-10 pm. Rm serv. Bar 11-1:30 am, Sun noon-11 pm; entertainment. Ck-out 11 am. Coin lndry. Meeting rms. Some refrigerators. Cr cds: A, C, D, DS, MC, V.

D ⚡ ≈ ⊠ 🐾 SC

✔ ★ **DAY'S END LODGE.** 755 N Valley Dr (88005), at jct US 70, 85. 505/524-7753; FAX 505/523-2127. 32 rms, 2 story. S $31; D $37-$41; each addl $3; family unit $43-$50. Crib free. TV; cable (premium). Pool. Complimentary continental bkfst. Ck-out 11 am. Business servs avail. In-rm modem link. Cr cds: A, DS, MC, V.

≈ ⊠ 🐾 SC

★ ★ **DAYS INN.** 2600 S Valley Dr (88005), at I-10 exit 142. 505/526-4441; FAX 505/526-3713. 132 rms, 2 story. S $45-$60; D $50-$65; each addl $10; under 18 free. TV; cable. Indoor pool; sauna, poolside serv. Restaurant 6-10 am, 5:30-9 pm. Bar 4-11 pm; Sat, Sun 4-10 pm. Ck-out noon. Coin lndry. Meeting rms. Valet serv. Game rm. Some balconies. Cr cds: A, C, D, DS, MC, V.

≈ ⊠ 🐾 SC

✔ ★ **ECONOMY INN.** 2160 W Picacho (88005). 505/524-8627. 90 rms, 2 story, 6 suites, 15 kit. units (no equipt). S $25-$35; D $30-$50; each addl $4; suites $30-$50; kit. units $26-$40; under 12 free; wkly rates. TV; cable. Pool. Complimentary coffee in lobby. Restaurant adj 11 am-9 pm. Ck-out 11 am. Coin lndry. Meeting rms. Picnic tables, grills. Cr cds: A, DS, MC, V.

≈ ⊠ 🐾 SC

★ ★ **HAMPTON INN.** 755 Avenida de Mesilla (88004). 505/526-8311; FAX 505/527-2015. 119 rms, 2 story. S $54-$58; D $59-$63; under 18 free. Crib free. Pet accepted. TV; cable (premium). Pool. Complimentary continental bkfst. Restaurant opp 6 am-10 pm. Ck-out noon. Meeting rm. In-rm modem link. Health club privileges. Cr cds: A, C, D, DS, MC, V.

D ⚡ ≈ ⊠ 🐾 SC

★ ★ **HOLIDAY INN DE LAS CRUCES.** 201 E University Ave (88001), 201 E University Ave. 505/526-4411; FAX 505/524-0530. 110 rms, 2 story. S, D $69-$79; suites $150; under 19 free. Crib free. Pet accepted, some restrictions. TV; cable (premium). Indoor pool; wading pool. Restaurant 6 am-10 pm. Rm serv. Bar 11-1 am. Ck-out noon. Coin lndry. Meeting rms. Bellhops. Valet serv. Free airport, bus depot transportation. Game rm. Enclosed courtyard re-creates Mexican plaza; original 1870s saloon; many antiques. Tennis, golf nearby. Cr cds: A, C, D, DS, MC, V.

D ⚡ ≈ ⊠ 🐾 SC

Hotel

★ ★ ★ **HILTON.** 705 S Telshor Blvd (88011). 505/522-4300; FAX 505/522-7657. 203 units, 7 story. S $67-$107; D $77-$117; each addl $10; suites $104-$300. Crib free. TV; cable. Pool; whirlpool, poolside serv. Coffee in rms. Restaurant 6 am-2 pm, 5-10 pm. Rm serv. Bar 11-2 am; entertainment. Ck-out 1 pm. Meeting rms. Gift shop. Free local airport, bus depot transportation. Golf privileges. Some refrigerators. Overlooks valley. Cr cds: A, C, D, DS, ER, JCB, MC, V.

D 🏋 ≈ ⊠ 🐾 SC

Inns

★ ★ **INN OF THE ARTS.** 618 S Alameda (88005). 505/526-3327; FAX 505/526-3355. 21 units, 2 story, 5 suites, 6 kits. Some rm phones. S $55; D $61-$95; each addl $15; suites, kit. units $95; wkly rates. Crib $15. TV in some rms, also sitting rm; cable (premium), VCR avail. Complimentary full bkfst, coffee & tea. Restaurant nearby. Ck-out 11 am, ck-in 4 pm. Business center. Bellhops. Health club privileges. Lawn games. Some balconies. Picnic tables, grills. Built 1890; antique furnishings. Library, sitting rm. Art gallery; each rm named for an artist. Cr cds: A, D, DS, MC, V.

D ⊠ 🐾 SC ⛷

★ ★ **MESÓN DE MESILLA.** (Box 1212, 1803 Avenida de Mesilla, Mesilla 88046) Just S of I-10 exit NM 28 (Avenida de Mesilla). 505/525-9212; res: 800/732-6025. 15 rms, 2 story. Phones avail. S $50-$60; D $60-$85; each addl $10; AP, MAP avail; wkly rates. TV; cable (premium). Pool; poolside serv. Complimentary full bkfst. Restaurant (see MESÓN DE MESILLA). Bar 11:30 am-9:15 pm. Ck-out 11 am, ck-in 1:30 am. Balconies. Picnic tables. Scenic views. Antique furnishings, brass beds; fireplace. Cr cds: C, D, DS, MC, V.

≈ 🐾

Restaurants

★ ★ **CATTLE BARON.** 790 S Telshor. 505/522-7533. Hrs: 11 am-9:30 pm; Fri, Sat to 10 pm. Closed Dec 25. Bar. Lunch $4.25-$6.50, dinner $6.95-$20.95. Child's meals. Specialties: blackened catfish, prime rib, shrimp teriyaki. Salad bar. Parking. Cr cds: A, C, D, DS, MC, V.

[D]

★ ★ ★ **DOUBLE EAGLE.** *3 mi SW on the Mesilla Plaza.* *505/523-6700.* Hrs: 11 am-10 pm; Sun brunch 11 am-3 pm. Res accepted. Bar. Wine list. Semi-a la carte: lunch $4.95-$7.45, dinner $10.95-$24.95. Sun champagne brunch $15.95. Specializes in steak, seafood. Outdoor dining. Fountain in patio. Restored adobe house (1848); Victorian decor, antiques. Cr cds: A, C, D, DS, ER, MC, V.

[D]

✔ ★ **MAMA MARIE'S.** *(2190 Avenida de Mesilla, Mesilla 88046)* *2 mi W on NM 28.* 505/524-0701. Hrs: 11 am-1:15 pm; Fri, Sat to 9:15 pm; Sun 4:30-8:15 pm. Closed Tues; most major hols. Res accepted. Italian menu. Wine, beer. Semi-a la carte: lunch $4.15-$10.85, dinner $4.15-$14.25. Specialties: Marie's fettucine, egg plant parmigiana, lasagne. Parking. Cr cds: MC, V.

[D]

★ ★ **MESÓN DE MESILLA.** *(See Mesón De Mesilla Inn)* *505/525-2380.* Hrs: 11:30 am-2 pm, 5:30-9 pm; Sun brunch 11 am-1:45 pm. Closed Mon; Jan 1, Dec 25. Res accepted. Continental menu. Bar. Semi-a la carte: lunch $4.95-$7.95. Buffet: lunch $7.50. Complete meals: dinner $15-$25. Sun brunch $14.95. Specializes in beef, seafood. Guitarist wkends. Parking. Adobe building. Cr cds: C, D, DS, MC, V.

[D]

Las Vegas (D-4)

(See Santa Fe)

Founded 1835 **Pop** 14,753 **Elev** 6,470 ft **Area code** 505 **Zip** 87701
Information Las Vegas-San Miguel Chamber of Commerce, 727 Grand Ave, PO Box 148; 505/425-8631.

Las Vegas once was a stopover on the old Santa Fe Trail. The town prospered as a shipping point, and after the arrival of the railroad in 1879, it began an active period of building and rebuilding. Consequently, there are 900 historic buildings (1851-1898). A Ranger District office of the Santa Fe National Forest (see SANTA FE) is located here, as are the New Mexico Highlands University and the Armand Hammer United World College of the American West.

What to See and Do

Fort Union National Monument. Established at this key defensive point on the Santa Fe Trail in 1851, the third and last fort built here was the largest post in the Southwest and the supply center for nearly 50 other forts in the area. It was abandoned by the military in 1891; 100 acres of adobe ruins remain. Self-guided trail with audio stations, living history programs featuring costumed demonstrations (summer). Visitor center depicts the fort's history; artifacts. (Daily; closed Jan 1, Dec 25) 20 mi NE on I-25 to Watrous/Ft Union exit 366, then 8 mi NW on NM 161. Contact Superintendent, PO Box 127, Watrous 87753; 505/425-8025. ¢

Las Vegas National Wildlife Refuge. Nature trail, observation of wildlife, including migratory water fowl. Hunting for dove (permit required), Canada goose (permit required; limited drawing); user's fee for hunts. (Daily; some areas Mon-Fri) 2 mi E via NM 104, then 4 mi S via NM 281. Phone 505/425-3581. **Free.**

Morphy Lake State Park. Towering ponderosa pines surround 15-acre mountainlake in Carson National Forest. Primitive-use area. Fishing (trout); restricted boating (oars or electric motors only; ramp). Winter sports. Primitive camping. Accessible to backpackers, horses or trucks; four-wheel drive vehicle advisable. No drinking water available. Standard fees. (Daily) 11 mi N on NM 518 to Sapello, then 16 mi NW off NM 94. Phone 505/387-2328. Per vehicle ¢¢

Storrie Lake State Park. Swimming, waterskiing; fishing; boating (ramp); windsurfing (special regattas in July). Winter sports. Picnicking, playground. Camping (hookups). (Daily) Standard fees. 4 mi N on NM 518. Phone 505/425-7278. Per vehicle ¢¢

Theodore Roosevelt Rough Riders' Memorial and City Museum. Mementos and relics. (Mon-Fri; closed hols) Donation. Municipal Bldg, 727 Grand Ave. Phone 505/425-8726.

Motels

★ ★ **COMFORT INN.** *2500 N Grand Ave.* 505/425-1100; FAX 505/454-8404. 101 rms, 2 story. Mar-Oct: S $49-$53; D $54-$59; each addl $5; under 18 free; lower rates rest of yr. Crib $5. TV; cable (premium), VCR avail. Indoor pool; whirlpool. Complimentary continental bkfst, coffee. Ck-out 11 am. Meeting rms. Business servs avail. In-rm modem link. Patio. Picnic tables, grill. Cr cds: A, C, D, DS, ER, JCB, MC, V.

[D] [symbols] SC

★ ★ **INN OF SANTA FE TRAIL.** *1133 Grand Ave.* 505/425-6791; res: 800/425-6791; FAX 505/425-0417. 42 rms, 12 suites. Mid-May-mid-Oct: S $46-$52; D $51-$65; each addl $5; suites $54-$65; under 12 free; wkly rates; lower rates rest of yr. Pet accepted; deposit & $5 per day. TV; cable (premium), VCR avail. Heated pool; whirlpool. Complimentary continental bkfst. Restaurant opp 6:30 am-9 pm. Ck-out 11 am. Business servs avail. In-rm modem link. Lawn games. Refrigerator in suites. Picnic tables. Cr cds: A, C, D, DS, MC, V.

[D] [symbols] SC

★ **REGAL.** *1809 N Grand.* 505/454-1456. 50 rms. Mid-May-mid-Sept: S $30-$39; D $35-$49; under 17 free; higher rates special events; lower rates rest of yr. Crib $5. Pet accepted. TV; cable (premium). Complimentary coffee in lobby. Restaurant adj 6 am-9 pm. Ck-out 11 am. Cr cds: A, C, D, DS, MC, V.

[D] [symbols] SC

✔ ★ **SCOTTISH INN.** *1216 N Grand Ave.* 505/425-9357; FAX 505/425-9357, ext. 18. 45 rms, 2 story. May-Aug: S $28-$36; D $38-$60; each addl $3; under 3 free; lower rates rest of yr. Crib $3. TV; cable (premium). Complimentary coffee in lobby. Restaurant nearby. Ck-out 11 am. Meeting rms. Free airport, RR station, bus depot transportation. Cr cds: A, C, D, DS, MC, V.

[symbols] SC

★ **TOWN HOUSE.** *1215 N Grand Ave.* 505/425-6717; res: 800/679-6717. 42 rms. May-Oct: S $27-$36; D $36-$44; each addl $3; under 8 free; wkly rates; higher rates graduation, family reunions; lower rates rest of yr. Pet accepted, some restrictions; $2. TV; cable (premium). Restaurant nearby. Ck-out 11 am. Picnic tables. Cr cds: A, C, D, DS, MC, V.

[D] [symbols]

Hotel

★ ★ **PLAZA.** *230 Old Town Plaza.* 505/425-3591; res: 800/328-1882; FAX 505/425-9659. 38 rms, 3 story. S $55-$110; D $65-$110; each addl $6; suites from $85; under 17 free; ski rates; some wkend rates. Crib free. Pet accepted. TV; cable (premium), VCR avail. Coffe in rms. Restaurant 7 am-2 pm, 5-9 pm. Bar noon-midnight. Ck-out 11 am. Meeting rms. Business servs avail. In-rm modem link. Airport, RR station, bus depot transportation. X-country ski 5 mi. Historic hotel built 1882 in the Victorian Italianate-bracketed style; interior renovated; period furnishings, antiques. Cr cds: A, D, DS, MC, V.

[D] [symbols] SC

Restaurants

★ **EL RIALTO.** *141 Bridge St, ¹/₂ blk from Plaza in Old Town.* 505/454-0037. Hrs: 10:30 am-9 pm. Closed Sun; major hols. Res accepted. Mexican, Amer menu. Bar 11 am-midnight. Complete meals: lunch, dinner $1.59-$19.99. Child's meals. Specializes in Mexican dishes, seafood. Salad bar. Parking. Quaint, historic building (1890s); antiques. Cr cds: A, DS, MC, V.

D **SC**

★ **PINO'S.** *1901 N Grand Ave.* 505/454-1944. Hrs: 6 am-9 pm. Closed Dec 25. Mexican, Amer menu. Wine, beer. Semi-a la carte: bkfst $1.95-$7.95, lunch $3.25-$9.95, dinner $6.95-$23.95. Child's meals. Specialties: enchilada plate, super burger. Salad bar. Parking. Casual dining. Cr cds: MC, V.

D **SC**

Los Alamos (C-3)

(See Española, Santa Fe)

Pop 11,455 **Elev** 7,410 ft **Area code** 505 **Zip** 87544
Information Los Alamos County Chamber of Commerce, PO Box 460; 505/662-8105.

On high mesas between the Rio Grande Valley floor and the Jemez Mountain peaks, Los Alamos offers spetacular views and outdoor activities. The city was originally the site of a boys' school; it was acquired by the government in 1942 for nuclear research. In 1967, the city property was turned over to Los Alamos County. The scientific laboratories, where research continues, remain a classified installation.

What to See and Do

Bandelier National Monument (see). 6 mi SW on NM 502, then 6 mi SE on NM 4 to turnoff sign.

Bradbury Science Museum of the Los Alamos National Laboratory. Displays artifacts relating to the history of the laboratory and the atomic bomb; exhibits on modern nuclear weapons, life sciences, materials sciences, computers, particle accelerators; geothermal, fusion and fission energy sources. (Daily; closed major hols) 15th & Central. Phone 505/667-4444. **Free.**

County Historical Museum. Fuller Lodge Cultural Center. Artifacts, photos, other material tracing local history from prehistoric to present times; exhibit on the Manhattan Project; traveling exhibits from Smithsonian and other institutions. (Daily;closed some major hols) 1921 Juniper. Phone 505/662-4493 or -6272. **Free.** Also here is

Fuller Lodge Art Center. 2nd floor of Fuller Lodge's west wing. Historic log building provides setting for changing exhibits. Features arts & crafts of northern New Mexico. (Daily; closed major hols) Phone 505/662-9331. **Free.**

Jemez State Monument. Stabilized Spanish mission (1621) built by Franciscan missionaries next to a prehistoric Indian pueblo. Self-guided bilingual trail. Visitor center has anthropology and archaeology exhibits. Picnicking. (Daily; closed state hols) 31 mi W on US 4, then 9 mi S in Jemez Springs. Phone 505/829-3530. ¢

Motels

★ ★ **HILLTOP HOUSE & LOS ALAMOS SUITES.** *400 Trinity Dr (NM 502), at Central, near airport.* 505/662-2441; res: 800/462-0936; FAX 505/662-5913. 100 rms, 3 story, 33 kits. S $65-$78; D $73-$83; each addl $10; kit. units $77-$87; suites $98-$225; under 12 free; long term rates. Crib $10. Pet accepted; $25 deposit. TV; cable (premium). Indoor pool. Complimentary bkfst. Restaurant 6:30-9:30 am, 11:30 am-2 pm, 5-9 pm. Rm serv. Ck-out 11 am. Coin lndry. Meeting rms.

Business servs avail. In-rm modem link. Sundries. Airport transportation. Downhill/x-country ski 10 mi. Cr cds: A, C, D, MC, V.

D **⟲** **≥** **≈** **⊠**

★ **LOS ALAMOS INN.** *2201 Trinity Dr.* 505/662-7211; res: 800/279-9279. 116 rms, 2-3 story. S $66-$70; D $71-$75; each addl $5; under 12 free. Crib free. TV; cable (premium). Pool; whirlpool. Restaurant 6:30 am-2 pm, 5-9 pm; Sun from 7 am. Bar 11 am-midnight; Sun noon-9 pm. Ck-out 12:30 pm. Meeting rms. Business servs avail. Airport transportation. Cr cds: A, C, D, DS, ER, JCB, MC, V.

D **≈** **⊠** **🔥** **▨**

Inn

✔ ★ **ORANGE STREET INN.** *3496 Orange St.* 505/662-2651. 8 air-cooled rms, 4 with bath, 2 story. S, D $55-$75; ski, golf plans. Children over 5 yrs only. TV in sitting rm; cable. Complimentary full bkfst, coffee & tea/sherry. Restaurant nearby. Rm serv. Ck-out 11 am, ck-in 4-8 pm. Concierge. Street parking. Airport transportation. Downhill/x-country ski 8 mi. Lawn games. Picnic tables, grills. Southwest and country decor; antiques, library. Totally nonsmoking. Cr cds: A, D, MC, V.

D **≥** **⊠** **🔥** **▨**

Restaurant

✔ ★ **BLUE WINDOW.** *800 Trinity, Suite H, in Mari Mack Village.* 505/662-6305. Hrs: 11 am-2 pm, 5-8:30 pm; Sat from 5 pm. Closed Sun; Dec 25. Res accepted. Wine, beer. Semi-a la carte: lunch $2.75-$6.50, dinner $6.25-$14.95. Child's meals. Specializes in home-made pastas, desserts. Dining rm upstairs; excellent view of mountains. Totally nonsmoking. Cr cds: MC, V.

D

Mescalero (G-4)

(For accommodations see Alamogordo, Cloudcroft, Ruidoso)

Pop 1,159 **Elev** 6,605 ft **Area code** 505 **Zip** 88340

What to See and Do

Mescalero Apache Reservation. Approximately 2,700 Native Americans live on this reservation. Timber, cattle and recreation are sources of income. There is also a store, museum and national fish hatchery. Ceremonials may sometimes be observed (fee); inquire at the community center or at the Mescalero store. Most famous dances are on or around July 4 (see ANNUAL EVENT). For information contact Main Tribal Office, 505/671-4494. Also on reservation are

Silver Lake, Mescalero Lake, Inn of the Mountain Gods and Ruidoso Recreation Areas. Fishing, hunting for elk, deer, antelope and bear (fall). Picnicking. Camping (exc at Mescalero Lake and Inn of the Mountain Gods; hookups at Silver and Eagle lakes only). Some fees. Phone 505/671-4427 for information and schedule. Per vehicle ¢¢

Mescalero National Fish Hatchery. Produces 500,000 trout annually; brood stockfor rare and endangered trout species are also developed. (Daily) ¹/₂ mi E of US 70 exit 246, on the reservation. Phone 505/671-4401. **Free.**

Annual Event

Mescalero Apache Maidens' Ceremonial. Colorful & interesting series of dances; Mountain Spirits dance at dusk. All-Indian rodeo. 4 days including pre-dawn ceremony July 4.

Pecos (D-4)

(see Santa Fe)

Portales (E-6)

(See Clovis)

Founded 1890 **Pop** 10,690 **Elev** 4,000 ft **Area code** 505 **Zip** 88130
Information Roosevelt County Chamber of Commerce, 7th & Abilene Sts; 505/356-8541 or 800/635-8036.

The land near Portales, irrigated with water from several hundred wells, produces a wide variety of crops. The county is the Valencia peanut capital of the US.

What to See and Do

Blackwater Draw Museum. Operated by Eastern New Mexico University. Includes 12,000-yr-old artifacts and fossils from nearby archaeological site (Mar-Oct); displays, murals tell story of early inhabitants. Films; tours (by appt). Museum (Memorial Day-Labor Day, Mon-Sat, also Sun afternoons; rest of yr, Tues-Sat, also Sun afternoons). Sr citizen rate. 7 mi N on US 70. Phone museum 505/562-2202. Museum & site ¢

Eastern New Mexico University (1934). (4,000 students) On campus is the Roosevelt County Museum; exhibits depict daily lives of early Western pioneers (daily; closed hols; museum phone 505/562-2592); university phone 505/562-2131 or -1011 for general information. SW corner of town.

Oasis State Park. Shifting sand dunes and towering cottonwood trees, planted in 1902 by a homesteader, form an oasis. Small fishing lake. Picnicking. Camping (hookups, dump station). Standard fees. (Daily) 7 1/2 mi NE, off NM 467. Phone 505/356-5331. Per vehicle ¢¢

Annual Events

Roosevelt County Heritage Days. Rodeo, dance, barbecue, parade, contests, entertainment. Late Apr.

Roosevelt County Fair. Mid-Aug.

Peanut Valley Festival. 3rd wkend Oct.

Motel

✔ ★ **CLASSIC AMERICAN ECONOMY INN.** *1613 W 2nd St, NM 70 W.* 505/356-6668; res: 800/344-9466; FAX 505/356-6668, ext. 13. 40 units. S $28-$38; D $32-$45; each addl $5; suite $35-$45; under 12 free; wkly rates. Crib free. Pet accepted. TV; cable (premium), VCR avail (movies avail). Heated pool. Playground. Complimentary coffee in rms. Restaurant adj. Ck-out 11 am. In-rm modem link. Coin lndry. Sundries. Airport, bus depot transportation. Some refrigerators. Picnic tables, grills. Adj to Eastern New Mexico University. Cr cds: A, C, D, DS, MC, V.

🆔 ✔ 🏊 ⊠ 🔥 SC

Hotel

★ ★ **PORTALES INN.** *218 W 3rd.* 505/359-1208. 39 rms, 4 story. S $30-$35; D $36-$40; each addl $4; under 12 free; wkly rates. TV; cable. Restaurant 6 am-8 pm. Ck-out noon. Meeting rms. Cr cds: A, C, D, DS, MC, V.

✔ ⊠ 🔥 SC

Questa (B-4)

(see Taos)

Raton (B-5)

(See Cimarron; also see Trinidad, CO)

Founded 1880 **Pop** 7,372 **Elev** 6,666 ft **Area code** 505 **Zip** 87740
Information Chamber & Economic Development Council, 100 Clayton Rd, PO Box 1211; 505/445-3689 or 800/638-6161.

Raton is at the southern foot of famous Raton Pass, on the original Santa Fe Trail (the main road to Denver). The road over the pass is a masterpiece of engineering; the view from several points is magnificent.

What to See and Do

Capulin Volcano National Monument. This is a dormant volcano, which last erupted approximately 10,000 years ago. The strikingly symmetrical cinder cone rises more than 1,500 feet from the plains. It has a crater 1 mile in circumference and 415 feet deep. Visitors can spiral completely around the mountain on a paved road to the rim (daily); four states can be seen on clear days. Picnic area. Visitor Center with exhibits of geology, flora and fauna of the area (daily; closed Jan 1, Dec 25). Uniformed personnel occasionally on duty at the crater rim (summer only). 29 mi E on US 64/87 to Capulin, then 3 1/2 mi N. Contact the Superintendent, Box 40, Capulin 88414; 505/278-2201. Per car ¢¢

Folsom Museum. Artifacts and fossils of Folsom Man (ca 12,000 B.C.). (Memorial Day-Labor Day, daily; May & Sept, wkends) 29 mi E on US 64/87, then 10 mi N on NM 325, on Main St in Folsom. Phone 505/278-2122 or -3616. ¢

Raton Museum. Collections relating to the Indian, Hispanic, ranch, railroad and mining cultures in New Mexico. (May-Sept, Tues-Sat; rest of yr, Wed-Sat or by appt; closed hols) 216 S 1st St. Phone 505/445-8979. **Free.**

Sugarite Canyon State Park. This park contains 3,500 acres on the New Mexico side and offers fishing, ice fishing, seasonal bow hunting for deer & turkey. Boating (oars or electric motors only); tubing. Cross-country skiing, ice skating. Picnicking. Camping. Visitor center. (Daily) 10 mi NE on NM 72 & NM 526. Phone 505/445-5607. Camping ¢¢¢; Per vehicle ¢¢

Motels

(Rates may be higher during racing wkends)

★ ★ **BEST WESTERN SANDS MANOR.** *350 Clayton Rd, 2 blocks W of I-25 on US 87/64.* 505/445-2737; FAX 505/445-4053. 50 rms. June-Aug: S $68; D $73; each addl $3; some lower rates rest of yr. Crib $2. TV; cable (premium), VCR avail (movies avail $3.73). Heated pool. Playground. Coffee in rms. Restaurant 6:30 am-8 pm. Ck-out 11 am. Business servs avail. In-rm modem link. Free RR station transportation. Cr cds: A, C, D, DS, MC, V.

🆔 ⊠ ⊠ 🔥 SC

✔ ★ **MELODY LANE.** *136 Canyon Dr, I-25 N Business Loop exit 454.* 505/445-3655; FAX 505/445-3461. 26 rms. May-early Oct: S $32-$49; D $39-$55; each addl $5; lower rates rest of yr. Crib $5. Pet accepted. TV; cable (premium). Continental bkfst. Ck-out 11 am. RR station transportation. Some in-rm steam baths. Cr cds: A, C, D, DS, MC, V.

✔ ⊠ 🔥 SC

Restaurant

★ ★ **PAPPAS' SWEET SHOP.** *1201 S 2nd St.* 505/445-9811. Hrs: 9 am-2 pm, 5-9 pm. Closed Jan 1, Dec 25; also Sun Sept-May. Res accepted. Bar. Semi-a la carte: bkfst $3.25-$7.95, lunch $4.25-$8.95, dinner $8.95-$27.95. Child's meals. Specializes in prime rib, pasta, seafood. Pianist Sat. Parking. Decorated with many collectibles & antiques. Cr cds: A, C, D, DS, MC, V.

D

Red River (B-4)

(See Cimarron, Eagle Nest, Taos)

Pop 387 **Elev** 8,676 ft **Area code** 505 **Zip** 87558
Information Chamber of Commerce, Main St, PO Box 870; 505/754-2366 or 800/348-6444.

This was a gold-mining boomtown with a population of 3,000 in the early days of this century. Today, it is a summer vacation and winter ski center. Trout fishing, hunting for deer, elk and small game, snowmobiling, horseback riding and backpacking are popular sports here.

What to See and Do

Red River Ski Area. 2 triple, 3 double chairlifts, surface tow; patrol, school, rentals; snowmaking; snack bar, cafeteria. 51 runs, longest run over 2 1/2 miles; vertical drop, 1,600 feet. (Thanksgiving-late Mar, daily) Chairlift also operates Memorial Day-Labor Day (daily; fee). SE via NM 38 to Pioneer Rd. Phone 505/754-2382 or 800/348-6444 (reservations). ¢¢¢¢¢

Annual Events

Winter Carnival. Snowmobile, cross-country & downhill ski races; dinner shows; snow and ice sculpture contests. Late Jan.

Mardi Gras in the Mountains. Ski slope parades, cajun food. Late Feb.

Enchanted Circle Century Bike Tour. Nearly 1,000 cyclists participate in a 100-mile tour around the Enchanted Circle (Red River, Angel Fire, Taos, Questa). 2nd wkend Sept.

Motels

(Because of the altitude, air-conditioning is rarely necessary)

✔ ★ ★ **ALPINE LODGE.** *Box 67 Main St (NM 38), at Mallette.* 505/754-2952; res: 800/252-2333. 45 rms, 1-3 story, 15 kits. No A/C. No elvtr. S $29-$40; D $33-$70; kit. units for 2-12, $38-$136; ski packages. Crib $5. TV; cable (premium). Playground. Restaurant 7 am-2 pm. Bar 3-9 pm. Ck-out 10 am. Business servs avail. Downhill ski opp; x-country ski 2 mi. Some balconies. On river; at ski lift. Cr cds: A, DS, MC, V.

D ⊠ 🔥 SC

★ **ARROWHEAD SKI LODGE.** *Box 261, Pioneer Rd, 2 blks S off NM 38.* 505/754-2255. 19 rms, 10 kits. No A/C. S, D $40-$60; each addl $10; kit. units $46-$175. TV; cable. Complimentary coffee in lobby. Restaurant nearby. Ck-out 10 am. Airpot transportation. Downhill ski on site; x-country ski 4 mi. Picnic tables, grill. Sun deck. On river. Cr cds: DS, MC, V.

⊠ SC

★ ★ **LIFTS WEST CONDOMINIUM RESORT HOTEL.** *Box 330 Main St, NM 38.* 505/754-2778; res: 800/221-1859 (exc NM); FAX 505/754-6617. 75 kit. units, 3 story. Dec-Mar: S, D $35-$389; each addl $15; suites $71-$389; studio rms $54-$198; under 12 free; ski rates; higher rates Christmas hols; lower rates rest of yr. Crib free. TV; cable

(premium), VCR (movies avail $3.49). Heated pool; whirlpools. Restaurant 7 am-9 pm. Ck-out 10 am. Lndry facilities. Meeting rms. Business servs avail. Shopping arcade. Downhill ski adj; x-country ski 4 mi. Private patios, balconies. Picnic tables. Large atrium lobby with fireplace. Cr cds: A, C, D, DS, MC, V.

D ⊠ ≈ SC

★ **LODGE AT RED RIVER.** *400 E Main (NM 38).* 505/754-6280. 26 rms, 2 story. No A/C. No rm phones. July-Sept, late Nov-Mar: S $64; D $78; each addl $11; MAP avail; ski plans; higher rates hols; lower rates May-June, Oct. Restaurant 7 am-9 pm. Bar 5-10 pm. Ck-out 11 am. Meeting rms. Business servs avail. Downhill ski on site; x-country ski 3 mi. Rustic lodge. Cr cds: A, MC, V.

🖝 ⊠ SC

★ ★ **PONDEROSA LODGE.** *Box 528 Main St, NM 38.* 505/754-2988; res: 800/336-7787. 17 rms, 2 story, 17 kit. apts. No A/C. Dec-Mar: S, D $61-$74; each addl $10; suites $116-$232; under 12 free; lower rates rest of yr. Crib free. TV; cable. Coffee in rms. Restaurant opp 8 am-9 pm. Ck-out 10 am. Downhill ski adj; x-country ski 4 mi. Whirlpool, sauna. Cr cds: A, DS, MC, V.

⊠ ⊠ 🔥 SC

★ **RED RIVER INN.** *Main St (NM 68).* 505/754-2930; res: 800/365-2930. 16 rms, 3 kit. units. No A/C. June-Sept: S $32-$77; D $38-$97; kit. units $32-$97; family, wkly, wkend, hol rates; ski plans; higher rates hols; lower rates rest of yr. Crib free. TV; cable (premium). Complimentary coffee in lobby. Restaurant nearby. Ck-out 10 am. Gift shop. Downhill ski 1 blk, x-country ski 1 mi. Picnic tables, grills. Totally nonsmoking. Cr cds: A, DS, MC, V.

⊠ ⊠ 🔥

★ ★ **RIVERSIDE.** *201 E Main St, NM 38.* 505/754-2252; res: 800/432-9999; FAX 505/754-2495. 8 rms in 2-story lodge, 30 winterized kit. cabins. No A/C. Dec-Mar: S, D $49.50-$89.50; each addl $10; kit. units to 6, $89.50-$150; higher rates Christmas hols; lower rates rest of yr. Crib $5. TV; cable. Playground. Restaurant opp 7 am-10 pm. Ck-out 10 am. Meeting rm. Business servs avail. Downhill ski adj; x-country ski 2 mi. Lawn games. Some fireplaces. Patio area with picnic tables, grills. Sun deck. Cr cds: A, DS, MC, V.

D ⊠ ⊠ 🔥 🔥

★ ★ **TALL PINE RESORT.** *PO Box 567, 1 1/2 mi S on NM 578.* 505/754-2241; res: 800/573-2241. 19 kit. cabins (1-2-bedrm). No A/C. No rm phones. May-Sept: S $60-$70; D $80-$95. Closed rest of yr. Crib free. Pet accepted. Playground. Ck-out 10 am, ck-in 1 pm. Maid serv wkly. Grocery, coin lndry, package store 1 1/2 mi. Picnic tables, grills. 27 acres in forest; cabins along Red River. Cr cds: MC, V.

D 🖝 🖝 🔥

✔ ★ **TERRACE TOWERS LODGE.** *712 W Main St.* 505/754-2962; res: 800/69-LODGE. 26 kit. suites, 2 story. S, D $49.50-$115; under 12 free; higher rates Spring Break, Christmas hols. Pet accepted. TV; cable VCR avail (movies avail $3). Whirlpool. Playground. Restaurant nearby. Ck-out 10 am. Lndry facilities. Downhill/x-country ski 1/2 mi. View of valley and mountains. Cr cds: A, D, MC, V.

🖝 ⊠ 🔥

Restaurants

★ ★ **BRETT'S HOMESTEAD STEAKHOUSE.** *W Main St (NM 38) & High Cost Trail.* 505/754-6136. Hrs: 5-9 pm. Closed Easter-mid-May & Nov. Res accepted. Wine, beer. Semi-a la carte: dinner $87.95-$30. Child's meals. Specialties: fresh trout, choice steaks, prime rib, Southwest cuisine. Parking. Outdoor dining. Fireplace; many antiques. Cr cds: A, DS, MC, V.

D

✔ ★ **SUNDANCE.** *401 High St, 1 blk off Main St.* 505/754-2971. Hrs: 11 am-2 pm, 5-9 pm. Closed Apr-mid-May. Mexican menu.

Wine, beer. Semi-a la carte: lunch, dinner $6.50-$13.95. Child's meals. Specialties: stuffed sopaipilla, fajitas, super burrito. Parking. Southwestern decor; fireplace. Gift shop. Cr cds: A, DS, MC, V.

★★ **TEXAS REDS STEAK HOUSE.** *Main St (NM 38). 505/754-2964.* Hrs: 5-9:30 pm. Semi-a la carte: dinner $6-$28.50. Child's meals. Specialties: NY strip steak, smoked pork chops, charbroiled beef steak. Parking. Western decor. Family-owned. Cr cds: A, C, D, DS, MC, V.

D

Roswell (F-5)

(See Artesia)

Founded 1871 **Pop** 44,654 **Elev** 3,981 ft **Area code** 505 **Zip** 88201
Information Chamber of Commerce, 131 W 2nd St, PO Drawer 70; 505/623-5695.

Roswell was a cattle town in its early days, with Goodnight-Loving cattle trail passing through and the Chisholm Trail starting here.

Farming, ranching, livestock-feeding, oil and gas exploration and development as well as other industrial areas surround the town. The Roswell campus of Eastern New Mexico University is located here.

What to See and Do

Bitter Lake National Wildlife Refuge. Wildlife observation, auto tour, picnicking. Hunting in season with state license. (Daily) 13 mi NE, via US 70, 285 and US 380 exits. Phone 505/622-6755. **Free.**

Bottomless Lakes State Park. Bordered by high red bluffs, seven small lakes were formed when circulating underground water formed caverns that collapsed into sinkholes. Headquarters at Cottonwood Lake has displays and a network of trails. Beach and swimming at Lea Lake only, bathhouse, skin diving; some lakes have fishing (trout); paddleboat rentals. Picnicking, concession (summer). Camping. (Daily) 10 mi E on US 380, then 6 mi S on NM 409. Phone 505/624-6058. Per vehicle ¢¢

Dexter National Fish Hatchery and Technology Center. This facility is the US Fish and Wildlife Service's primary center for the study and culture of endangered fish species of the American Southwest. (Daily) Also visitor's center (Apr-Oct, daily). 20 mi SE via US 285 or NM 2. Phone 505/734-5910. **Free.**

Historical Center for Southeast New Mexico. Antiques, period rooms (early 1900s); turn-of-the-century furnishings, clothes; communications exhibits; research library and archives. (Fri-Sun, afternoons) Tours by appt. 200 N Lea. Phone 505/622-8333. ¢

New Mexico Military Institute (1891). (900 cadets) State-supported high school and junior college. Alumni Memorial Chapel, near the entrance, has beautiful windows. Also here is the General Douglas L. McBride Military Museum with an interpretation of 20th-century American military history (Tues-Fri; free). Occasional marching formations & parades. Tours. N Main St & College Blvd. Phone 505/622-6250 or 800/421-5376.

Roswell Museum and Art Center. Southwest arts collection including Georgia O'Keeffe, Peter Hurd, Henriette Wyeth; Native American, Mexican American and western arts; Dr Robert H. Goddard's early liquid-fueled rocketry experiments. (Mon-Sat, also Sun & hol afternoons; closed Jan 1, Thanksgiving, Dec 25) 100 W 11th St. Phone 505/624-6744. **Free.**

Spring River Park & Zoo. Zoo and children's zoo area; small lake with fishing for children 11 & under only; miniature train; antique wooden-horse carousel. Picnicking, playground. (Daily; closed Dec 25) 1306 E College Blvd. Phone 505/624-6760 or -6700. **Free.**

★ **The International UFO Museum & Research Center.** Museum includes exhibits on various aspects of UFO phenomena and a video viewing room. Various video tapes can be viewed upon request. (Daily, afternoons) 400-402 N Main St. Phone 505/625-9495. **Free.**

Annual Events

Eastern New Mexico State Fair and Rodeo. 2 mi S on US 285, at Fair Park. Phone 505/623-9411. Oct.

Motels

★★ **BEST WESTERN SALLY PORT INN.** *2000 N Main St, US 70, 285.* 505/622-6430; FAX 505/623-7631. 124 rms, 2 story. S, studio rms $49-$69; D $59-$79; each addl $10; suites $53-$83; under 18 free. Crib free. TV; cable (premium). Indoor pool. Restaurant 6-10 am, 5-10 pm. Rm serv. Bar 3-9 pm; Fri, Sat to 11 pm; closed Sun. Ck-out noon. Coin lndry. Meeting rms. Business servs avail. In-rm modem link. Sundries. Beauty shop. Free airport, bus depot transportation. 18-hole golf privileges adj, putting green, driving range. Exercise equipt; weights, rower, whirlpool, sauna. Refrigerators. Cr cds: A, C, D, DS, MC, V.

D ✦ 🏋 🏌 ≈ 🍴 🔥 SC

✔★ **BUDGET INN.** *2200 W 2nd St.* 505/623-3811; res: 800/752-INNS. 29 rms, 2 story. S $26-$29; D $31-$35; each addl $4; kit. units $175/wk; under 17 free. Crib free. TV; cable. Pool. Complimentary coffee in rms. Ck-out noon. Some refrigerators. Cr cds: A, C, D, DS, MC, V.

≈ 🔧 SC

★★ **COMFORT INN.** *2803 W 2nd St.* 505/623-9440; FAX 505/622-9708. 61 rms, 2 story. S $34-$38; D $38-$42; each addl $4; under 18 free. Crib free. TV; cable. Heated pool. Complimentary continental bkfst. Ck-out noon. Meeting rms. Refrigerators. Cr cds: A, C, D, DS, ER, JCB, MC, V.

D ≈ 🔧 🔥 SC

✔★ **FRONTIER.** *3010 N Main St (US 70, US 70, 285.)* 505/622-1400; res: 800/678-1401; FAX 505/622-1405. 38 rms. S $28-$36; D $32-$40; each addl $3; higher rates NMMI events. Pet accepted. TV; cable (premium). Pool. Free continental bkfst. Restaurant adj 5:30 am-9 pm. Ck-out 11 am. Some refrigerators. Cr cds: A, C, D, DS, MC, V.

D ✦ ≈ 🔧 🔥 SC

★★★ **ROSWELL INN.** *Box 2065 1815 N Main St, US 70, 285.* 505/623-4920; res: 800/323-0913 (exc NM), 800/426-3052 (NM); FAX 505/622-3831. 121 rms, 2 story. S $62; D $65; each addl $7; suites $95-$145; under 18 free. Crib free. TV; cable (premium), VCR avail. Heated pool; poolside serv. Restaurant 6 am-10 pm, Sun to 9 pm. Rm serv. Bar 11-1 am; closed Sun. Ck-out noon. Meeting rms. Business center. In-rm modem link. Free airport transportation. 18-hole golf privileges opp. Balconies. Cr cds: A, C, D, DS, MC, V.

D 🏋 ≈ 🔥 SC 🏌

Restaurant

✔★ **EL TORO BRAVO.** *102 S Main.* 505/622-9280. Hrs: 11 am-2:30 pm, 5-9 pm; Sat 11 am-9 pm. Res accepted. Closed Sun; most major hols. Mexican menu. Wine, beer. Semi-a la carte: lunch, dinner $1.95-$10.95. Lunch buffet (Mon-Fri) $4.95. Child's meals. Specialties: chimichangas, chile Colorado, fajitas. Bull fighting and Mexican pictures. Cr cds: A, MC, V.

Ruidoso (F-4)

(See Alamogordo, Carrizozo, Cloudcroft, Mescalero)

Pop 4,600 **Elev** 6,911 ft **Area code** 505 **Zip** 88345
Information Ruidoso Valley Chamber of Commerce, PO Box 698; 505/257-7395 or 800/253-2255.

This resort town in the Sierra Blanca Mountains, surrounded by the trees of the Lincoln National Forest, has had spectacular growth. It is a thriving town and an all-year resort with skiing in winter and fishing and horseback riding in summer. If planning to visit during June, July or August, secure confirmed reservations before leaving home. Few mountain resorts have such a variety of attractions. The forested mountain slopes and streams are idyllic, the air is clear and cool, especially at night, and there are many interesting ways to spend time. A Ranger District Office of the Lincoln National Forest (see ALAMOGORDO) is located here.

What to See and Do

Lincoln State Monument. Lincoln was the site of the infamous Lincoln County War and hangout of Billy the Kid. Several properties have been restored, including the Old Lincoln County Courthouse and the mercantile store of John Tunstall. Guided tours (summer). (Daily; closed state hols) 30 mi E on US 70, then 10 mi NW on US 380. Phone 505/653-4372. ¢¢

Museum of the Horse. Dedicated to the heritage of the horse; collection of more than 10,000 horse-related items. (Daily; winter, daily exc Mon; closed Thanksgiving, Dec 25) Sr citizen rate. US 70E, Ruidoso Downs. Phone 505/378-4142. ¢¢

Old Dowlin Mill. A 20-foot waterwheel still drives a mill more than 100 years old. In town.

Ski Apache Resort. Resort has 4-passenger gondola, quad, 5 triple, 2 double chairlifts, surface lift; patrol, school, rentals; snack bars, cafeteria, bar. 52 runs, longest run over 2 miles; vertical drop 1,900 feet. (Thanksgiving-Easter, daily) 16 mi NW on NM 48, 352 in Lincoln National Forest. Phone 505/336-4356; for snow report phone 505/257-9001. ¢¢¢¢

Smokey Bear Historical State Park. Commemorates the history and development of the national symbol of forest fire prevention. The original Smokey, who was orphaned by a fire raging in the Lincoln National Forest, is buried here, within sight of the mountain where he was found. Fire prevention exhibit; film. (Daily; closed Jan 1, Thanksgiving, Dec 25) 22 mi N via NM 37/48 on US 380 in Capitan. Phone 505/354-2748. ¢ Nearby is

Smokey Bear Museum. Features 1950s memorabilia of famed firefighting bear found in the nearby Capitan Mountains. (Daily; closed major hols) Phone 505/354-2298. **Free.**

Annual Events

Smokey Bear Stampede. 22 mi N via NM 48 in Capitan. Rodeo, parade, dances, barbecue. Early July.

Arts Festival. Last full wkend July.

Aspenfest. Includes motorcycle convention, official state chili cook-off, arts and crafts. Early Oct.

Seasonal Event

Horse racing. Ruidoso Downs. Thoroughbred and quarter horse racing, parimutuel betting. Home of All-American Futurity, world's richest quarter horse race (Labor Day); All-American Derby and All-American Gold Cup. Estimated purses: All-American Futurity, $2 million; All-American Derby, $500,000; All-American Gold Cup, $50,000. Phone 505/378-4431. Thurs-Sun & hols. Early May-Labor Day.

Motels

(Because of the altitude, air-conditioning is rarely necessary)

★ ★ ★ **BEST WESTERN SWISS CHALET INN.** *Box 759, 3 mi N on NM 48.* 505/258-3333; *FAX* 505/258-5325. 81 rms, 2 story. June-Sept: S $58-$85; D $66-$92; each addl $6; suites $76-$150; under 12 free; lower rates rest of yr. Pet accepted, some restrictions; $20. TV; cable (premium), VCR avail. Indoor pool; whirlpool. Restaurant 7-11 am, 5:30-9 pm; closed Mon. Rm serv. Bar 5-10 pm. Ck-out noon. Coin lndry. Meeting rms. Business servs avail. In-rm modem link. Sundries. Balconies. On hilltop. Cr cds: A, C, D, DS, JCB, MC, V.

⊞ ⊠ ⊠ ⊠ SC

★ **ENCHANTMENT INN.** *PO Box 4210, 307 US 70W.* 505/378-4051; *res:* 800/435-0280; *FAX* 505/378-5427. 80 rms, 2 story 40 suites. S, D $65-$80; suites, kit. units $65-$185; under 18 free. Crib free. TV; cable (premium). Indoor pool; whirlpool. Restaurant 7-11 am, 5-9 pm. Rm serv. Bar. Ck-out 11 am. Coin lndry. Meeting rms. Business servs avail. Downhill ski 20 mi. Game rm. Picnic tables, grills. Cr cds: A, C, DS, MC, V.

D ⊠ ⊠ ⊠ ⊠ SC

★ **HIGH COUNTRY LODGE.** *(Box 137, Alto 88312) 5 mi N on NM 48.* 505/336-4321. 32 kit. apts (2-bedrm). No A/C. S, D $99; each addl $10; under 13 free; higher rates hol wknds. Pet accepted. TV; cable (premium). Indoor pool; whirlpool, sauna. Playground. Ck-out 11 am. Business servs avail. Tennis. Game rm. Lawn games. Fireplaces. Picnic table, grills. Scenic location, lake opp. Cr cds: A, DS, MC, V.

⊞ ⊠ ⊠ ⊠ SC

★ **INNSBRUCK LODGE.** *601 Sudderth Dr.* 505/257-4071; *FAX* 505/257-7536. 48 rms (18 with shower only), 2 story. No A/C. Mid-June-Sept: S, D $26-$52; under 10 free; wkly rates; higher rates hols; lower rates rest of yr. Crib $4-$6. Pet accepted. TV; cable. Restaurant nearby. Ck-out 11 am. Business servs avail. Gift shop. Downhill ski 16 mi. Cr cds: A, DS, MC, V.

⊞ ⊠ ⊠

★ ★ **SHADOW MOUNTAIN LODGE.** *PO Box 211, 107 Main Rd, Upper Canyon.* 505/257-4886; *res:* 800/441-4331; *FAX* 505/257-2000. 19 kit. units. No A/C. Memorial Day-Labor Day: S, D $84; each addl $10; ski plans; lower rates rest of yr. Children over 15 yrs only. TV; cable (premium). Complimentary coffee in rms. Restaurant nearby. Ck-out 11 am. Business servs avail. Downhill ski 18 mi. Wet bars. Grills. Opp river. Cr cds: A, C, D, DS, MC, V.

D ⊠ ⊠ ⊠ SC

✔ ★ **SUPER 8.** *Box 2600, US 70 at NM 48.* 505/378-8180; *FAX* 505/378-8180. 63 rms, 2½ story. May-Sept: S $43.88; D $51.88; each addl $4; suites $74.88; lower rates rest of yr. Crib $3. TV; cable (premium), VCR avail (movies avail). Whirlpool, sauna. Ck-out 11 am. Coin lndry. Business servs avail. In-rm modem link. Sundries. Picnic table. Cr cds: A, C, D, DS, MC, V.

D ⊠ ⊠ SC

★ ★ **VILLAGE LODGE AT INNSBROOK.** *1000 Meachum Dr.* 505/258-5442; *res:* 800/722-8779. 26 kit. suites, 2 story. Mid-May-mid-Sept, Nov-Easter: S, D $79-$109; each addl $10; under 13 free; higher rates hols; lower rates rest of yr. TV; cable (premium). Ck-out 11 am. Business servs avail. Downhill ski 14 mi. Cr cds: A, C, D, DS, MC, V.

⊞ ⊠ ⊠ SC

✔ ★ **WEST WINDS LODGE & CONDOMINIUMS.** *PO Box 1458 208 Eagle Dr, N of NM 48.* 505/257-4031; *res:* 800/421-0691. 21 rms, 15 condos. No A/C. No rm phones. Dec-Jan, July-Sept: S, D $42-$75; each addl $5-$10; kit. units $54-$75; condominiums $75-$169; lower rates rest of yr. TV; cable. Indoor pool; whirlpool. Restaurant nearby. Ck-out 11 am. Free bus depot transportation. Downhill/x-country ski 16 mi. Grills. Cr cds: DS, MC, V.

Inns

★ ★ ★ **CASA DE PATRON.** *(US 380, Lincoln 88338) 20 mi N on US 70, then 10 mi W on US 380. 505/653-4676; FAX 505/653-4671.* 3 rms (shower only), 2 suites. No A/C. No rm phones. S $69-$83; D $79-$97; each addl $6-$13; suites $97-$109; 2-day min some hols & special events. Complimentary coffee in rms; full bkfst. Restaurant nearby. Ck-out noon, ck-in 3-8 pm. Luggage handling. Business servs avail. Whirlpool, sauna. Refrigerator in suites. Picnic tables. Built in 1860 and filled with antiques, this inn was the home of Juan Patron, the youngest Speaker of the House in the Territorial Legislature. Legendary figures, such as Billy the Kid & Pat Garrett, are said to have spent the night here. Totally nonsmoking. Cr cds: MC, V.

★ ★ **SIERRA MESA LODGE.** *(Box 463, Alto 88312) 6 mi N via NM 48, then 2 mi E on Sierra Blanca Airport Rd. 505/336-4515.* 5 rms. No A/C. No rm phones. S $80; D $90. Children over 14 yrs only. Complimentary full gourmet bkfst, coffee & tea, homemade pastries. Ck-out noon, ck-in 3 pm. Concierge serv. Bellhops. Tennis privileges. Whirlpool. Downhill ski 14 mi. Located along hillside; view of mountains. Antiques. Game rm/sitting rm with fireplace. Totally nonsmoking. Cr cds: A, DS, MC, V.

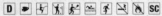

Resort

★ ★ ★ **INN OF THE MOUNTAIN GODS.** *(PO Box 269, Mescalero 88340) 3½ mi SW of town, on Carrizo Canyon Rd. 505/257-5141; res: 800/545-9011; FAX 505/257-6173.* 253 rms, 2-5 story. June-Sept: S, D, suites $120-$150; each addl $12; under 12 free; tennis, golf, ski, hunting, honeymoon plans; lower rates rest of yr. Crib $12. TV; cable (premium), VCR avail. Heated pool; wading pool, whirlpool, sauna, poolside serv. Dining rm 7 am-10 pm. Box lunches. Rm serv. Bars 10-1 am; entertainment, dancing. Ck-out noon, ck-in 4 pm. Convention facilities. Business servs avail. Valet serv. Gift shop. Airport transportation. Lighted tennis, pro. 18-hole golf, greens fee $35, pro, putting green. Dock; rowboats, pedal-boats, canoes. Bicycles. Trap & skeet shooting. Game rm. Lawn games. Some refrigerators. Private patios, balconies. Casino. Cr cds: A, C, D, DS, MC, V.

Restaurants

✔ ★ **CAFE CARRIZO.** *On Carrizo Canyon Rd, historic Corrizo Lodge. 505/257-3607.* Hrs: 11 am-2 pm, 5-10 pm; wkends to 11 pm. Closed Dec 24. Southwestern menu. Bar. Semi-a la carte: lunch $4.25-$7.25, dinner $7.25-$13.95. Child's meals. Specializes in beef, poultry, seafood. Parking. Outdoor dining. Southwestern decor; fireplaces. Cr cds: DS, MC, V.

★ ★ **VICTORIA'S HIDEWAY.** *2103 Sudderth Dr. 505/257-5440.* Hrs: 7 pm (each reservation is for 3 hrs min). Closed Dec 25. Res required. No A/C. Sicilian menu. Wine, beer. Prix fixe: dinner $50. Specialties: traditional Sicilian entrees. Romantic, intimate dining that caters to couples only. Cr cds: C, D, DS, MC, V.

Salinas Pueblo Missions National Monument (E-3)

(For accommodations see Socorro)

(Approx 75 mi SE of Albuquerque via I-40, NM 337, 55)

This monument was established to explore European-Indian contact and the resultant cultural changes. The stabilized ruins of the massive 17th-century missions are basically unaltered, preserving the original design and construction. All three units are open (daily; closed Jan 1, Dec 25). The Monument Headquarters, 1 blk W of NM 55 on US 60 in Mountainair, has an audiovisual presentation and an exhibit of paintings and drawings depicting the Salinas story. (Daily; closed Jan 1, Dec 25) Contact the Superintendent, PO Box 496, Mountainair 87036; 505/847-2585. The three units of this monument are

Gran Quivira. Here are the massive walls of the 17th-century San Buenaventura Mission (begun in 1659 but never completed), "San Isidro" Church (ca 1630) and 21 pueblo mounds, 2 of which have been excavated. A self-guided trail and museum-visitor center (exhibits, 7-min video, 40-min video) combine to vividly portray Indian life and the cultural change that has occurred over the past thousand years. Various factors led to the desertion of the pueblo and the mission around 1671. Tompiro Indians occupied this and the Abó site. Picnicking. 25 mi SE of Mountainair on NM 55. Phone 505/847-2770.

Abó. Ruins of the mission church of San Gregorio de Abó (ca 1630), built by Native Americans under the direction of the Spanish. This is the only early church in New Mexico with 40-foot buttressed curtain walls—a style typical of medieval European architecture. The pueblo adjacent to the church was abandoned about 1673 because of drought, disease and Apache raids. These Indians and others from the Salinas jurisdiction eventually moved south with the Spanish to El Paso del Norte, where they established the pueblo of Isleta del Sur and other towns still in existence today. There are self-guided trails throughout the mission compound and Indian pueblo mounds. Picnicking (no water). 9 mi W of Mountainair on US 60, then ¾ mi N on NM 513. Phone 505/847-2400.

Quarai. Ruins of the Mission de la Purísima Concepción de Cuarac, other Spanish structures and unexcavated Indian mounds, all built of red sandstone. Built about 1630, it was abandoned along with the pueblo about 1677, most likely for the same reasons. Unlike the other two, this site was occupied by Tiwa-speaking Indians. Much of the history is related to the conflict between Spanish civil and church authorities. The church ruins have been excavated and it is the most complete church in the monument. The visitor center has a museum and interpretive displays. Wayside exhibits, trail guides. Picnicking. 8 mi N of Mountainair on NM 55, then 1 mi W on a countyroad from Punta. Phone 505/847-2290.

Santa Fe (D-4)

(See Española, Las Vegas, Los Alamos)

Founded 1610 **Pop** 55,859 **Elev** 7,000 ft **Area code** 505

Information Convention & Visitors Bureau, PO Box 909, 87504; 505/984-6760 or 800/777-2489.

This picturesque city, the oldest capital in the United States, is set at the base of the Sangre de Cristo (Blood of Christ) Mountains. A few miles south, these mountains taper down from a height of 13,000 feet to a rolling plain, marking the end of the North American Rocky Mountains. Because of the altitude, the climate is cool and bracing. Tourists and vacationers will find much to do and see here all year.

Santa Fe was founded by Don Pedro de Peralta, who laid out the plaza and built the Palace of the Governors in 1610. In 1680, the Pueblo Indians revolted and drove the Spanish out. In 1692, led by General Don Diego de Vargas, the Spanish made a peaceful re-entry. Mexico gained its independence from Spain in 1821. This was followed by the opening of the Santa Fe Trail. In 1846, General Stephen Watts Kearny led US troops into the town without resistance and hoisted the American flag. During the Civil War, Confederate forces occupied the town for two weeks before they were driven out.

In addition to its own attractions, Santa Fe is also the center of a colorful area, which can be reached by car. It is in the midst of the Pueblo Indian country. The Pueblo, farmers for centuries, are also extremely gifted craftsworkers and painters. Their pottery, basketry and jewelry are especially beautiful. At various times during the year, especially on the saint's day of their particular pueblo, they present dramatic ceremonial dances. Visitors are usually welcome. Since these are sacred rites, however, visitors should be respectful. As a rule, photographs are forbidden. A list of many of these ceremonies is given under ANNUAL EVENTS.

The high altitude may cause visitors accustomed to lower altitudes to have a little shortness of breath for a day or two. A short walking tour taken slowly will be helpful; the tour covers many centrally located sights.

What to See and Do

✪ **Canyon Road tour.** This is considerably longer than the walking tour, totaling about two or three miles, but there is no better way to savor the unique character of Santa Fe than to travel along its narrow, picturesque old streets. Go E on San Francisco St to the cathedral and bear right to the end of Cathedral Pl. Turn left on Alameda. On the left is

St Francis School. Turn right across first bridge and immediately bear left onto

Canyon Road. Many artists now live on this old thoroughfare. Continue along Canyon Rd several miles to

Cristo Rey Church. This is the largest adobe structure in the US. It contains beautiful ancient stone *reredos* (altar screens). (Mon-Fri; closed hols) Return on Canyon Road to

Camino del Monte Sol. Famous street on which many artists live and work. Turn left up the hill. Off this road are a number of interesting streets worth exploring. If traveling by car, continue down the hill on Camino del Monte Sol about 1 mi to

St John's College in Santa Fe (1964). (400 students) A second campus of St John's College is in Annapolis, MD (1696). Liberal arts. On Camino Cruz Blanca, just E of Camino del Monte Sol. Phone 505/982-3691. From its intersection with Camino Cruz Blanca, walk S approx 2 blks on Camino del Monte Sol to Old Santa Fe Trail, then turn E. On the right is the

National Park Service, Southwest Regional Office (1939). Adobe-building with central patio. (Mon-Fri; closed hols) 1100 Old Santa Fe Trail. Phone 505/988-6012. **Free.** From here, go W a short distance on Old Santa Fe Trail, then S on Camino Lejo to the

Museum of Indian Arts and Culture. Displays outstanding collection of the Laboratory of Anthropology; Southwestern Indian basketry, pottery, weaving, jewelry and other cultural artifacts. (Mar-Dec, daily; rest of yr, daily exc Mon; closed Jan 1, Easter, Thanksgiving, Dec 25) 710 Camino Lejo. Phone 505/827-6344. ¢¢ Across the yard is the

Museum of International Folk Art. Folk art collections with more than 125,000 objects from around the world: textiles; woodcarvings; toys; jewelry; paintings; religious articles. (Same days as Museum of Indian Arts and Culture) 706 Camino Lejo. Phone 505/827-6350. ¢¢ On the same road, less than one long block beyond the museum, is the

Wheelwright Museum. Exhibits of the arts and culture of Native Americans. Collections of Navajo textiles, silver, baskets and Southwest pottery; contemporary Indian artists' exhibitions; turn-of-the-century replica of Navajo Trading Post. (Mon-Sat, also Sun

afternoons; closed Jan 1, Thanksgiving, Dec 25) Donation. 704 Camino Lejo. Phone 505/982-4636. Shortest way back to town is via the Old Santa Fe Trail.

College of Santa Fe (1947). (1,400 students) On campus are the Greer Garson Theatre Center and Communications Center and Fogelson Library. 3 mi SW at Cerrillos Rd & St Michael's Dr. Phone 505/473-6011.

El Rancho de las Golondrinas. Village and agricultural museum depicting Spanish Colonial life in New Mexico from 1700-1900. (June-Sept, Wed-Sun) Tours by appt (Apr-Oct). (See SEASONAL EVENTS) Sr citizen rate. 15 mi S, off I-25. Phone 505/471-2261. ¢¢

Hyde Memorial State Park. Perched 8,500 feet up in the Sangre de Cristo Mountains near the Santa Fe Ski Basin; used as base camp for backpackers and skiers in the Santa Fe National Forest. Cross-country skiing, rentals, sledding hill. Picnicking (shelters), playground, concession, restaurant. Camping (electric hookups, dump station). Standard fees. (Daily) 8 mi NE via NM 475. Phone 505/983-7175. Per vehicle ¢¢

Institute of American Indian Arts Museum. The National Collection of Contemporary Indian Art contains more than 8,000 pieces of contemporary Native American art and some historial material. Collection includes paintings, prints, drawings, sculpture, weavings, costumes, jewelry and other artwork. (Mar-Dec, daily; rest of yr, Tues-Sat, also Sun afternoons) 108 Cathedral Place. Phone 505/988-6211 or -6281. ¢¢

Pecos National Historical Park. Ruins of two large Spanish mission churches and unexcavated multi-story communal pueblo dwelling, which once housed 2,000 Indians; it was occupied for 500 years. The final 17 occupants left the pueblo in 1838, and relocated to Jemez Pueblo. Once a landmark on the Santa Fe Trail. Self-guided walk through pueblo and mission. Restored kivas. Visitor center with introductory film, exhibits. (Daily; closed Dec 25) 25 mi SE via US 25. Contact Superintendent, PO Box 418, Pecos 87552-0418; 505/757-6414 or -2616. ¢

San Ildefonso Pueblo (pop: 447). This pueblo is famous for its beautiful surrounding sand its black, red and polychrome pottery, made famous by Maria Poveka Martinez. (Daily; closed winter wknds; visitors must register at the Visitor Center) Photography permit may be purchased at the Visitor Center (fee). Various festivals take place here throughout the year (see ANNUAL EVENTS). The circular structure with the staircase leading up to its rim is a *kiva*, or ceremonial chamber. In the pueblo plaza are two Indian shops, and a tribal museum adjoins the governor's office. One-half mile W is a fishing lake. 16 mi N on US 84, 285, then 6 mi W on NM 502. Phone 505/455-2273. Per car ¢¢

Santa Fe Children's Museum. Participatory children's exhibits of science and arts in play-like environment. Giant soap bubbles; greenhouse with pond and working microscopes; simulated rock climbing activity involving 18-foot-high climbing wall (days vary); toddler waterplay area. Also art & science programs. (June-Aug, Wed-Sun; rest of yr, Thurs-Sun; closed major hols) 1050 Old Pecos Trail. Phone 505/989-8359. ¢¢

Santa Fe National Forest. This forest consists of over 1½ million acres. Fishing is excellent in the Pecos and Jemez rivers and tributary streams. Hiking trails are close to unusual geologic formations. Hot springs in the Jemez Mts. Four wilderness areas within the forest total more than 300,000 acres. Campgrounds are provided by the Forest Service at more than 40 locations; for reservations call 800/280-2267. There are user fees for many areas. Forest headquarters are located here. Contact the Forest Supervisor, 1220 St Francis Dr, PO Box 1689, 87504; 505/988-6940.

Santa Fe Ski Area. Area has 4 chairlifts, 3 surface lifts; patrol, school, rentals; snowmaking; concession, cafeteria, restaurant, bar. 38 runs, longest run 3 miles; vertical drop 1,650 feet. (Thanksgiving-mid-Apr, daily) 16 mi NE via NM 475. Phone 505/982-4429, 505/983-9155 (snow conditions). ¢¢¢¢

Santuario de Guadalupe (ca 1785). Adobe church museum featuring Spanish Colonial art; changing exhibits; the only existing complete *lienzo* in New Mexico, the Jose de Alzibar oil on canvas of *Our Lady of Guadalupe;* garden; authentic 18th-century sacristy. (Daily; winter, Mon-Fri; closed major hols) Donation. 100 Guadalupe St. Phone 505/988-2027.

Sightseeing tours.

Gray Line. Tours of Santa Fe and surrounding area. For information, reservations contact 1330 Hickox St, 87501; 505/983-9491.

Discover Sante Fe, Inc. Tour & other packages. Contact PO Box 2847, 87504; 505/982-4979. ¢¢¢¢-¢¢¢¢¢

✪ **Walking tour.** Start on Palace Ave at

The Plaza. Laid out in 1610, this famous square is where the old Santa Fe Trail ended. It includes the Soldier's Monument at the center, the "End of the Santa Fe Trail" marker at the SE corner, and the Kearny Proclamation marker on the N side. The colorful plaza is the center of informal civic social life and the scene of fiestas and markets. Cross Palace Ave toward the roofed portal under which Indians sell jewelry, pottery and blankets and enter

Palace of the Governors. Built in 1610, this is the oldest public building in continuous use in the United States. It was the seat of government in New Mexico for more than 300 years. Lew Wallace, governor of the territory (1878-81), wrote part of *Ben Hur* here in 1880. It is now a major museum of Southwestern history. The Palace, Museum of Fine Arts, Museum of Indian Arts and Culture, Museum of International Folk Art and state monuments all make up the Museum of New Mexico. (Mar-Dec, daily; rest of yr, daily exc Mon; closed Jan 1, Thanksgiving, Dec 25) Phone 505/827-6483. ¢¢ Turn right (W) onto the Plaza and walk across Lincoln Ave to the

Museum of Fine Arts (1917). Classic Southwestern pueblo-revival architecture. More than 10,000 art objects; focus on Santa Fe and Taos artists of the early 20th century. Changing exhibits of American art and photography. Research library. (Same days as Palace of the Governors) 107 W Palace Ave. Phone 505/827-4455. ¢¢ Turn left (N) two blocks to Federal Place. Turn right, passing the

Federal Court House. There is a monument to Kit Carson in front. NE of this is the monumental

Scottish Rite Temple. Modeled after part of the Alhambra. Return to the plaza along Washington Ave, turn left (E) on Palace Ave, and explore

Sena Plaza and Prince Plaza. Small shops, formerly old houses, built behind portals and around central patios. Next street E is Cathedral Pl. Turn right. On the left is the

Cathedral of St Francis (1869). French Romanesque Cathedral built under the direction of Sante Fe's first archbishop, Archbishop Lamy (prototype for Bishop Latour in Willa Cather's *Death Comes for the Archbishop*). La Conquistadora Chapel, said to be the country's oldest Marian shrine, is here. (Daily) Tours (summer). Phone 505/982-5619. This is the E end of San Francisco St, Santa Fe's main street. Turn right and drop in at

La Fonda Hotel. A long-time center of Santa Fe social life. Former meeting place of trappers, pioneers, merchants, soldiers and politicians; known as the "Inn at the End of the Trail." Just beyond, walk left (S) one block on Old Santa Fe Trail. Here is

Loretto Chapel (Chapel of Our Lady of Light). Gothic chapel built by the Sisters of Loretto, the first religious women to come to New Mexico. (Daily) Old Santa Fe Trail. Phone 505/984-7971. The problem of constructing a staircase to the choir loft here baffled workmen until an unknown carpenter appeared and built

The Famous Staircase. A circular stairway 22 feet high, built without central support and, according to legend, put together with wooden pegs. It makes two complete 360° turns and has 33 steps. (Daily; closed Dec 25) Phone 505/984-7971. ¢ Continue S Along Santa Fe Trail crossing the bridge over the Santa Fe River. One block beyond is

San Miguel Mission. Oldest church still in use in the United States, originally built in the early 1600s. Santa Fe's oldest wooden *reredos* (altar screen), dated 1798. Much of the interior has been restored; audio tours. (Mon-Sat, also Sun afternoons; closed Jan 1, Easter, Thanksgiving, Dec 25) Donation. 401 Old Santa Fe Trail. Phone 505/983-3974. A few yards E, on narrow De Vargas St, is the

Oldest House. Believed to be pre-Spanish; built by Indians more than 800 years ago. Walk W along De Vargas St. S is the new

State Capitol (1966). This unique building, in modified Territorial style, is round and intended to resemble a Zia sun symbol; inspired by an Indian kiva (underground ceremonial chamber). (Mon-Fri; closed most hols) Tours. Phone 505/986-4589. **Free.** Return to the Plaza via Old Santa Fe Trail, just E of the capitol.

Annual Events

Buffalo and Comanche dances. Fiesta at San Ildefonso Pueblo. Late Jan.

Fiesta and Green Corn Dance. San Felipe Pueblo. Early May.

Spring Corn Dances. Cochiti, San Felipe, Santo Domingo and other pueblos. Races, contests. Late May-early June.

St Anthony's Feast-Comanche Dance. San Juan pueblo. Late June.

Santa Fe Rodeo. 4 days mid-July.

Northern Pueblo Artist & Craftsman Show. Santa Clara pueblo. Mid-July.

Spanish Market. Palace of the Governors' porch. Artisans display Spanish crafts. Phone 505/983-4038. Last full wkend July.

Fiesta at Santo Domingo Pueblo. Corn dance. This fiesta is probably the largest and most famous of the Rio Grande pueblo fiestas. Early Aug.

Indian Market. Plaza. One of largest in the world with tribes from all over US. Dances, Indian art. Make reservations at lodgings well in advance. Phone 505/983-5220. 2 days mid-Aug.

Invitational Antique Indian Art Show. Sweeney Center. Largest show of its kind in the country. Pre-1935 items; attracts dealers, collectors, museums. 2 days mid-Aug.

Santa Fe Fiesta. This ancient folk festival, dating back to 1712, features historical pageantry, religious observances, arts and crafts shows, street dancing. Celebrates the reconquest of Santa Fe by Don Diego de Vargas in 1692. Make reservations well in advance. 2nd wkend Sept.

Christmas Eve Celebrations. In Santa Fe and nearby villages with street fires and *farolitos* (paper bag lanterns) "to guide the Christ Child," candlelit Nacimientos (nativity scenes) and other events. Santo Domingo, Tesuque, Santa Clara and other pueblos have Christmas dances the following three days.

Seasonal Events

Horse racing. The Downs. 5 mi S on I-25. Thoroughbred and quarter horse racing. For reservations phone 505/471-3311. June-Labor Day.

Santa Fe Opera. 7 mi N on US 84/285. Presents combination of operatic classics with neglected masterpieces and an American premiere in an outdoor setting. Backstage tours (during season, daily exc Sun). Reservations suggested. For schedule and prices contact PO Box 2408, 87504; 505/986-5955 or -5900 (box office). Early July-late Aug.

Santa Fe Chamber Music Festival. For information contact PO Box 853, 87504; 505/983-2075. July-Aug.

Orchestra of Santa Fe. Chamber orchestra performs classical and contemporary music; also performance of *Messiah* during Christmas season, Mozart Festival in Feb. For schedule contact PO Box 2091, 87504; 505/988-4640. Sept-May.

Motels

(Because of the altitude, air-conditioning is rarely necessary)

★ ★ **BEST WESTERN HIGH MESA INN.** *3347 Cerrillos Rd* (87505). 505/473-2800; FAX 505/473-5128. 211 rms, 3 story. May-Oct: S $89-$105; D $99-$115; each addl $12; under 12 free; ski rates; higher rates: Dec 25, Indian Market; lower rates rest of yr. Crib free. TV; cable (premium). Indoor pool. Restaurant 7 am-1 pm, 5-10 pm. Bar 11 am-midnight; entertainment Wed & Sat evening. Ck-out 11 am. Coin lndry. Meeting rms. Business servs avail. Gift shop. Free airport transportation. Downhill/x-country ski 17 mi. Exercise equipt; weights, bicycles, whirlpools. Refrigerators. Some private patios, balconies. Cr cds: A, C, D, DS, ER, JCB, MC, V.

[D] [≋] [≈] [✗] [⊠] [⊠] [SC]

★ **DAYS INN.** *3650 Cerrillos Rd (87505).* 505/438-3822; FAX 505/438-3795. 97 rms, 2 story. Memorial Day-Labor Day: S $65-$105; D $66-$120; each addl $10; suites $95-$195; under 12 free; higher rates hols; lower rates rest of yr. Crib free. Pet accepted, some restrictions. TV; cable (premium), VCR avail. Indoor pool; whirlpool. Complimentary continental bkfst. Restaurant adj open 24 hrs. Ck-out 11 am. Coin lndry. Business servs avail. Downhill, x-country ski 20 mi. Some refrigerators. Balconies. Cr cds: A, C, D, DS, MC, V.

[D] [✦] [≋] [≈] [⊠] [⊠] [SC]

✔ ★ ★ **EL REY INN.** *Box 4759, 1862 Cerrillos Rd (87502), I-25 Business Loop.* 505/982-1931; FAX 505/989-9249. 86 rms, 1-2 story, 7 kits. May-Oct: S, D $56-$110; each addl $12; kit. suites $98-$155. Crib free. TV; cable (premium). Pool; whirlpool. Playground. Complimentary continental bkfst. Restaurant nearby. Ck-out noon. Coin lndry. Business servs avail. Downhill/x-country ski 17 mi. Some fireplaces. Picnic tables. Cr cds: A, C, D, MC, V.

[D] [≋] [≈] [🔥]

★ ★ **HOMEWOOD SUITES.** *400 Griffin St (87501).* 505/988-3000; FAX 505/988-4700. 105 kit. suites, 2 story. Mid-June-Oct: 1-bedrm $150-$190; 2-bedrm $255-$310; wkly & monthly rates; higher rates Indian Market & hols; lower rates rest of yr. Crib free. Pet accepted; $150 deposit and $10 per day. TV; cable, VCR (movies avail $5). Heated pool. Complimentary coffee in rms. Complimentary continental bkfst buffet. Restaurant nearby. Ck-out noon. Coin lndry. Meeting rms. Business center. In-rm modem link. Bellhops. Concierge. Gift shop. Airport transportation. Grocery store. Exercise equipt; weights, bicycles, whirlpools. Many balconies. Picnic tables. Cr cds: A, C, D, DS, JCB, MC, V.

[D] [✦] [≋] [✗] [⊠] [🔥] [SC] [🚶]

★ **HOWARD JOHNSON.** *4044 Cerrillos Rd (87505), 1 mi N of I-25 exit 278.* 505/438-8950. 47 rms, 2 story. Mid-May-Aug: S $54-$98; D $65-$120; each addl $6; under 18 free; lower rates rest of yr. Crib avail. TV; cable (premium). Complimentary continental bkfst. Restaurant adj 6:30 am-10 pm. Ck-out noon. Downhill/x-country ski 20 mi. Near airport. Cr cds: A, D, DS, MC, V.

[D] [≋] [⊠] [🔥] [SC]

★ ★ **INN ON THE ALAMEDA.** *303 E Alameda (87501), 2 blks from Plaza.* 505/984-2121; res: 800/289-2122; FAX 505/986-8325. 66 rms, 2-3 story. July-Oct: S $155-$335, D $170-$350; each addl $15; suites $260-$375; lower rates rest of yr. Pet accepted; $50 refundable. TV; cable (premium), VCR avail. Complimentary continental bkfst buffet. Restaurant nearby. Bar 4-11 pm. Ck-out noon. Meeting rm. Business servs avail. In-rm modem link. Valet serv. Downhill/x-country ski 15 mi. Exercise equipt; stair machine, bicycles, treadmill. Library. Kiva fireplaces. Private patios, balconies. Cr cds: A, C, D, DS, MC, V.

[D] [✦] [≋] [✗] [⊠] [🔥]

★ ★ **LA QUINTA.** *4298 Cerrillos Rd (Business Loop I-25) (87505).* 505/471-1142; FAX 505/438-7219. 130 rms, 3 story. Mid-May-Late Oct: S $81-$90; D $89-$96; each addl $8; suites $125; under 18 free; lower rates rest of yr. Crib free. Pet accepted. TV; cable (premium). Pool. Complimentary continental bkfst in lobby. Restaurant adj open 24 hrs. Ck-out noon. Coin lndry. Downhill/x-country ski 14 mi. Cr cds: A, C, D, DS, MC, V.

[D] [✦] [≋] [≈] [⊠] [🔥] [SC]

★ **LAMPLIGHTER.** *2405 Cerrillos Rd (87505).* 505/471-8000; res: 800/767-5267; FAX 505/471-1397. 80 rms, 2 story, 16 kits. May-Oct: S $49-$56; D $52-$87; each addl $5; suites $78-$100; kit. units $72-$95; under 18 free; lower rates rest of yr. Crib free. TV; cable (premium). Indoor pool; sauna. Complimentary coffee in rms. Restau-

rant 7 am-10 pm. Bar. Ck-out 11 am. Business servs avail. Airport transportation. Cr cds: A, C, D, DS, ER, JCB, MC, V.

[≈] [⊠] [🔥] [SC]

★ **LUXURY INN.** *3752 Cerrillos Rd (87505), 3 mi N of I-25 exit 278.* 505/473-0567; FAX 505/471-9139. 51 rms, 2 story. No A/C. May-Oct: S $35-$55; D $70-$90; under 10 free; wkly rates; higher rates special events; lower rates rest of yr. Crib free. TV; cable (premium). Pool; whirlpool. Complimentary continental bkfst. Restaurant adj 11 am-9 pm. Ck-out 11 am. Cr cds: A, C, D, DS, JCB, MC, V.

[D] [≈] [⊠] [🔥] [SC]

✔ ★ **QUALITY INN.** *3011 Cerrillos Rd (I-25 Business Loop) (87501).* 505/471-1211; FAX 505/438-9535. 99 rms, 2 story. May-Oct: S $63-$90; D $70-$90; each addl $10; under 18 free; lower rates rest of yr. Crib free. Pet accepted; some restrictions. TV; cable (premium). Pool. Restaurant 7 am-9 pm. Rm serv. Ck-out noon. Meeting rm. Business servs avail. Airport transportation. Downhill/x-country ski 17 mi. Some refrigerators. Balconies. Cr cds: A, C, D, DS, ER, JCB, MC, V.

[D] [✦] [≋] [≈] [⊠] [🔥] [SC]

★ **RAMADA INN.** *2907 Cerrillos Rd (87505), 3 mi N of I-25 exit 278.* 505/471-3000. 103 rms, 2 story. June-Oct: S $35-$70; D $40-$75; each addl $5; under 18 free; wkly & wkend rates; ski plan; higher rates special events; lower rates rest of yr. Crib free. Pet accepted; $10. TV; cable, VCR avail. Pool. Complimentary continental bkfst. Restaurant 11 am-10 pm. Bar. Meeting rms. Business servs avail. Downhill/x-country ski 20 mi. Game rm. Cr cds: A, C, D, DS, ER, JCB, MC, V.

[D] [✦] [≋] [≈] [⊠] [🔥] [SC]

★ ★ **RESIDENCE INN BY MARRIOTT.** *1698 Galisteo St (87501).* 505/988-7300; FAX 505/988-3243. 120 kit. suites, 2 story. June-late Oct: kit. suites $169; under 12 free; wkly, ski rates; lower rates rest of yr. Crib free. Pet accepted, some restrictions; $150 deposit and $8 per day. TV; cable (premium). Heated pool; whirlpools. Complimentary continental bkfst, coffee. Ck-out noon. Coin lndry. Meeting rms. Business servs avail. Valet serv. Airport transportation. Downhill ski 16 mi. Health club privileges. Some private patios, balconies. Picnic tables, grills. Cr cds: A, C, D, DS, JCB, MC, V.

[D] [✦] [≋] [≈] [⊠] [🔥] [SC]

✔ ★ **STAGE COACH.** *3360 Cerrillos Rd (I-25 Business Loop) (87505).* 505/471-0707. 14 rms, 1-2 story. Mid May-mid-Oct: S, D $49-$80; each addl $5; lower rates rest of yr. TV. Restaurant nearby. Ck-out 11 am. Downhill/x-country ski 20 mi. Picnic tables, grills. Cr cds: DS, MC, V.

[≋] [⊠] [🔥]

Motor Hotels

★ ★ ★ **BEST WESTERN INN AT LORETTO.** *Box 1417 (87504), 211 Old Santa Fe Trail, just off the plaza.* 505/988-5531; FAX 505/984-7988. 136 rms, 4 story. July-Aug: S $170-$210; D $185-$225; each addl $15; under 12 free; lower rates rest of yr. Crib free. TV; cable (premium), VCR avail. Heated pool; poolside serv. Restaurant 6:30 am-9 pm; dining rm from 5:30 pm. Rm serv. Bar 11-1 am, Sun noon-midnight; entertainment; dancing Thurs-Sat. Ck-out noon. Free lndry facilities. Meeting rms. Business center. In-rm modem link. Bellhops. Shopping arcade. Barber, beauty shop. Downhill/x-country ski 15 mi. Refrigerators. Private patios, balconies. Indian-style adobe building. Cr cds: A, C, D, DS, MC, V.

[D] [≋] [≈] [⊠] [🔥] [SC] [🚶]

★ **GARRETT'S DESERT INN.** *311 Old Santa Fe Trail (87501).* 505/982-1851; res: 800/888-2145; FAX 505/989-1657. 82 rms, 2 story. July & Aug: S, D $89-$99; suites $109; lower rates rest of yr.

TV; cable. Heated pool. Restaurant 7 am-9 pm. Bar. Ck-out noon. Meeting rms. Business servs avail. Cr cds: A, C, D, DS, MC, V.

★ ★ ★ **HILTON OF SANTA FE.** *100 Sandoval St (87501), just off Plaza, downtown.* 505/988-2811; FAX 505/986-6439. 158 rms, 3 story. Mid-June-Oct: S $139-$229; D $159-$249; each addl $20; suites $275-$675; family rates; ski packages; lower rates rest of yr. Crib free. TV; cable (premium), VCR avail. Heated pool; whirlpool. Restaurants 6:30 am-11 pm (also see PIÑON GRILL). Rm serv. Bar 7 pm-midnight. Ck-out noon. Meeting rms. Business servs avail. In-rm modem link. Bellhops. Concierge. Gift shop. Airport transportation. Downhill skiing 15 mi. Minibars. Cr cds: A, C, D, DS, JCB, MC, V.

★ ★ **HOLIDAY INN.** *4048 Cerrillos Rd (I-25 Business Loop) (87501).* 505/473-4646; FAX 505/473-2186. 130 rms, 4 story. Mid-June-Sept: S $85-$149; D $95-$159; each addl $10; under 20 free; ski plans; lower rates rest of yr. Crib free. Pet accepted. TV; cable (premium). Indoor/outdoor pool; whirlpool, sauna, poolside serv. Complimentary coffee in rms. Restaurant 6:30 am-10 pm. Rm serv. Bar from noon. Ck-out noon. Meeting rms. Business servs avail. In-rm modem link. Bellhops. Sundries. Airport, bus depot transportation. Downhill/x-country ski 20 mi. Exercise rm; treadmill, weight station. Game rm. Refrigerator. Private patios, balconies. Cr cds: A, C, D, DS, JCB, MC, V.

★ ★ **HOTEL PLAZA REAL.** *125 Washington Ave (87501), 1 blk north of plaza.* 505/988-4900; res: 800/279-REAL; FAX 505/988-4900, ext. 490. 56 rms, 3 story, 44 suites. June-Oct: S, D $159-$249; each addl $15; suites $249-$475; under 12 free; ski plans; lower rates rest of yr. Underground garage parking $5. TV; cable, VCR avail. Complimentary continental bkfst 7-10 am, coffee. Restaurant adj 9 am-6 pm. Bar 3-11 pm. Ck-out noon, ck-in 3 pm. Meeting rms. Business servs avail. Bellhops. Concierge. Health club privileges. Downhill/x-country ski 15 mi. Wet bar in suites. Refrigerators. Some balconies. Territorial-style architecture; fireplaces, handcrafted Southwestern furniture. Cr cds: A, D, MC, V.

★ ★ **HOTEL SANTA FE.** *1501 Paseo de Peralta (87501), at Cerrillos Rd.* 505/982-1200; res: 800/825-9876; FAX 505/984-2211. 131 rms, 3 story, 91 suites. Late June-Aug: S, D $114-$144; suites $144-$224; under 17 free; ski plans; lower rates rest of yr. Crib free. TV; cable (premium), VCR avail (movies avail). Pool; whirlpool. Restaurant 7 am-10 pm. Bar 4 pm-midnight; entertainment Fri, Sat. Ck-out noon. Coin lndry. Meeting rms. Business servs avail. Bellhops. Valet serv. Concierge. Gift shop. Airport transportation. Downhill & x-country ski 10 mi. Health club privileges. Minibars. Balconies. Pueblo-revival architecture; original art by Native Americans. A Native American enterprise. Cr cds: A, C, D, DS, MC, V.

★ ★ **INN OF THE GOVERNORS.** *234 Don Gaspar Ave (87501).* 505/982-4333; res: 800/234-4534; FAX 505/989-9149. 100 rms, 2-3 story. S, D $90-$249; each addl $10; under 12 free. Crib free. TV; cable, VCR avail. Pool. Restaurant (see MAÑANA). Rm serv. Bar 11:30 am-midnight, Sun from noon; entertainment. Ck-out noon. Meeting rm. Business servs avail. In-rm modem link. Bellhops. Concierge. Downhill/x-country ski 14 mi. Some minibars, fireplaces. Balconies. Cr cds: A, C, D, MC, V.

★ ★ **LA POSADA DE SANTA FE.** *330 E Palace Ave (87501), 2 blks from Plaza.* 505/986-0000; res: 800/727-5276; FAX 505/982-6850. 119 rms, 1-2 story. May-Oct & hols: S, D $115-$330; suites $195-$395; under 12 free; package plans; lower rates rest of yr. Crib $3. TV; cable (premium). Pool; poolside serv. Restaurant (see STAAB HOUSE). Rm serv. Bar 11 am-midnight, Sun noon-11 pm. Ck-out noon, ck-in 3 pm. Meeting rms. Business servs avail. Concierge. Bellhops. Beauty shop. Downhill/x-country ski 15 mi. Health club privileges.

Many fireplaces. Adobe casitas, or cottages constructed in the ancient manor, surround Victorian/Second Empire Staab Mansion (1882); guest rms either pueblo revival or Victorian in style. On 6 acres; gardens. Cr cds: A, C, D, DS, MC, V.

★ ★ **RADISSON PICACHO PLAZA.** *750 N St Francis Dr (87501), US 84, 285.* 505/982-5591; FAX 505/988-2821. 129 rms, 2 story. May-Dec: S, D, studio rms $128-$158; each addl $20; suites $148-$454; ski packages; lower rates rest of yr. Crib $15. TV; cable (premium), VCR avail. Heated pool; poolside serv. Restaurant 6:30 am-10 pm. Rm serv. Bar 11 am-midnight; entertainment. Ck-out 11 am. Meeting rms. Business servs avail. In-rm modem link. Bellhops. Free airport, RR station, bus depot transportation. Downhill/x-country ski 18 mi. Health club privileges. Cr cds: A, C, D, DS, MC, V.

★ ★ ★ **ST FRANCIS.** *210 Don Gaspar Ave (87501).* 505/983-5700; res: 800/529-5700; FAX 505/989-7690. 83 rms, 3 story. May-Oct: S, D $85-$185; each addl $15; suites $225-$350; under 12 free; lower rates rest of yr. Crib free. TV; cable (premium), VCR avail. Tea 3-5:30 pm. Restaurant 7-10 am, 11:30 am-2 pm, 5:30-9:30 pm; Sun brunch 7 am-2 pm. Rm serv. Bar noon-midnight. Ck-out 11 am. Meeting rms. Business servs avail. Concierge. Skiing 15 mi. Health club privileges. Refrigerators. European ambience; antiques, original artwork. Cr cds: A, D, DS, MC, V.

Hotels

★ ★ ★ **ELDORADO.** *309 W San Francisco (87501), 2 blks from the Plaza.* 505/988-4455; res: 800/955-4455; FAX 505/988-5376. In this Pueblo revival-style hotel in the town's historic district, all the chic Southwestern guest rooms have views of the Santa Fe mountains. 219 rms, 5 story. S, D $169-$309; suites $280-$750; under 18 free. Crib free. Garage parking $5.75. Pet accepted. TV; cable (premium), VCR avail (movies avail $5.95). Rooftop heated pool; poolside serv. Restaurant 7 am-10 pm (also see THE OLD HOUSE). Bar 11:30-2 am; entertainment. Ck-out 11:30 am. Convention facilities. Business center. In-rm modem link. Concierge. Butler service avail in 41 upscale rms. Shopping arcade. Barber, beauty shop. Downhill ski 12 mi; x-country ski 7 mi. Exercise equipt; weight machine, treadmill, whirlpool, sauna. Refrigerators, minibars. Balconies. Cr cds: A, C, D, DS, MC, V.

★ ★ ★ **INN OF THE ANASAZI.** *113 Washington Ave (87501), just off the Plaza, in the historic Plaza District.* 505/988-3030; res: 800/688-8100; FAX 505/988-3277. This sophisticated adobe hotel one block from the Plaza embodies Santa Fe style. Contained within are native and Southwestern art and artifacts, four-poster beds, and kiva fireplaces in the guest rooms. 59 units, 3 story, 8 suites. Apr-Oct: S, D $235-$395; each addl $20; under 12 free; lower rates rest of yr. Crib free. Valet parking $10/night. Pet accepted, some restrictions; $30 non-refundable. TV; cable (premium), VCR (movies avail $5). Complimentary coffee in rms. Restaurant (see THE ANASAZI). Ck-out noon, ck-in 3 pm. Business servs avail. Concierge. Tennis privileges. 18-hole golf privileges, putting green, driving range. Downhill ski 13 mi; x-country ski 7 mi. Health club privileges. Cr cds: A, C, D, DS, MC, V.

Inns

★ ★ **ALEXANDER'S INN.** *529 E Palace Ave (87501).* 505/986-1431. 7 rms (2 share bath, 2 with shower only), 2 story. Mid-Mar-mid-Nov: S, D $85-$150; each addl $15; higher rates Indian Market, Dec 25; lower rates rest of yr. Pet accepted, some restrictions. TV; cable, VCR avail. Complimentary continental bkfst; afternoon tea & lemonade. Ck-out 11 am, ck-in by arrangement. Concierge serv. Luggage handling. Downhill ski 17 mi; x-country ski 10 mi. Health club privileges. Five rms in renovated house built 1903; one cottage & one casita. Totally nonsmoking. Cr cds: MC, V.

★ **DANCING GROUND OF THE SUN.** 711 Paseo de Peralta (87501). 505/986-9797; res: 800/645-5673; FAX 505/986-8082. 7 kit. units, 2 story. May-Oct: S, D $115-$160; each addl $20; lower rates rest of yr. TV; cable. Complimentary coffee in rms. Complimentary continental bkfst. Restaurant nearby. Ck-out 11 am, ck-in 3-6 pm. Concierge serv. Balconies. Most rms with Native American theme. Totally nonsmoking. Cr cds: MC, V.

★ ★ **DOS CASAS VIEJAS.** 610 Agua Fria St (87501), 2 blks SW off Guadalupe. 505/983-1636. 2 rms, 3 suites. No A/C. D $145-$195; suites $195. TV; cable, VCR avail. Heated pool. Complimentary continental bkfst. Coffee in rms. Restaurant nearby. Ck-out noon, ck-in 3-6 pm. Some refrigerators. Two historical buildings in a 1/2-acre walled compound; renovated to restore 1860s architecture. Mexican tiled floors and wood-burning kiva fireplaces. Authentic southwestern antiques, original art. Some rms with canopy beds. Lobby/library and dining area in main building. Brick patio enclosed by 6-ft high adobe walls. Totally nonsmoking. Cr cds: MC, V.

✔ ★ ★ **EL PARADERO.** 220 W Manhattan (87501), near Capitol. 505/988-1177. 14 rms, 2 kit. suites. A/C in suites. Apr-Oct: S $50-$115; D $60-$130; each addl $15; kit. suites $130; lower rates rest of yr. Children over 4 yrs only. Pet accepted. TV in sitting rm; cable in suites. Complimentary full bkfst, tea. Restaurant nearby. Ck-out 11 am, ck-in 2 pm. Downhill ski 18 mi; x-country ski 9 mi. Balconies. Renovated Spanish adobe house (ca 1820) with details from 1880 & 1912 remodelings. Library/sitting rm; skylights, fireplaces, antiques. No cr cds accepted.

★ ★ **GRANT CORNER.** 122 Grant Ave (87501). 505/983-6678; FAX 505/984-9003. 12 rms, 10 with bath, 2 share bath, 3 story. June-Oct: S, D $85-$140; each addl $20; lower rates rest of yr. Children over 8 yrs only. TV; cable. Complimentary full bkfst, tea & wine. Restaurant nearby. Rm serv. Ck-out noon, ck-in 2-6 pm. Downhill/x-country ski 15 mi. Colonial manor house built 1905; antiques. Totally nonsmoking. Cr cds: MC, V.

★ ★ ★ **GUADALUPE.** 604 Agua Fria (87501), near La Tertuliana. 505/989-7422. 12 rms, 2 story. Mid-Apr-mid-Jan: S, D $125-$175; each addl $15; 2-day min Indian Market; lower rates rest of yr. Crib $25. TV; cable (premium). Complimentary full bkfst. Restaurant adj. Ck-out 11 am, ck-in 3-6 pm. Concierge serv. Business servs avail. Downhill ski 15 mi, x-country ski 10 mi. Balconies. Picnic tables. Some in-rm whirlpools. Individually decorated rms; many antiques. Totally nonsmoking. Cr cds: A, DS, MC, V.

★ **INN OF THE ANIMAL TRACKS.** 707 Paseo de Peralta (87501), east of the plaza. 505/988-1546. 5 rms. S, D $90-$130; each addl $20. TV; cable (premium). Complimentary full bkfst, coffee. Restaurant nearby. Ck-out noon, ck-in 4 pm. Downhill/x-country ski 15 mi. Picnic tables. In 1890 adobe house; fireplaces. Guest rms overlook tree-shaded lawn, garden. Small animals roam inn freely. Totally nonsmoking. Cr cds: A, MC, V.

★ ★ **INN ON THE PASEO.** 630 Paseo de Peralto (87501). 505/984-8200; res: 800/457-9045; FAX 505/989-3979. 18 rms, 2-3 story. No A/C. Mid-May-Oct: S, D $99-$175; suite $175; min stay required: summer wkends, Indian market. TV; cable (premium). Complimentary bkfst buffet, afternoon refreshments. Restaurant nearby. Ck-

out 11 am, ck-in 3 pm. Balconies. Totally nonsmoking. Cr cds: A, D, MC, V.

★ ★ **PRESTON HOUSE.** 106 Faithway St (87501), 4 blks E of the plaza. 505/982-3465; FAX 505/982-3465. 15 rms, 13 with bath, 3 story, 2 suites. Some A/C. Mar-Nov & hols: S, D $75-$160; each addl $20; suites $150-$160; lower rates rest of yr. Pet accepted, some restrictions. TV. Complimentary continental bkfst, coffee 8-10 am & high tea 3-5 pm. Restaurant nearby. Ck-out 11 am, ck-in 3 pm. Downhill/x-country ski 17 mi. Fireplace in some rms. Queen Anne house (1886) with antique furnishings and sitting rm. Totally nonsmoking. Cr cds: A, MC, V.

✔ ★ ★ **PUEBLO BONITO.** 138 W Manhattan (87501), near Capitol. 505/984-8001; FAX 505/984-3155. 18 rms, 1-2 story, 7 suites, 6 kits. No A/C. May-Oct: S $90; D $90-$140; each addl $10; suites, kit. units $140; lower rates rest of yr. TV; cable. Complimentary continental bkfst, coffee & afternoon tea. Restaurant nearby. Ck-out noon, ck-in 2 pm. Downhill/x-country ski 18 mi. Fireplaces. Some balconies. Renovated adobe casitas on 1880s estate; private courtyards, gardens, mature trees. Antique furnishings; baskets, sand paintings. Cr cds: MC, V.

★ **A STARRY NIGHT.** 324 McKenzie St (87501). 505/820-7117. 2 rms (1 with shower only). No A/C. S, D $116; 2-day min wkends. Adults only. TV; cable. Complimentary coffee in rms. Complimentary continental bkfst. Restaurant nearby. Ck-out 11 am, ck-in by arrangement. Lndry facilities. Concierge serv. Downhill ski 15 mi; x-country 10 mi. Adobe building (c.1900); many antiques. Totally nonsmoking. Cr cds: MC, V.

★ **TERRITORIAL INN.** 215 Washington Ave (87501), 1 blk from plaza. 505/989-7737; FAX 505/986-1411. 11 rms, 8 with bath, 2 story. S, D $80-$150; each addl $15; higher rates: Thanksgiving wkend, Christmas hols, Indian Market. Children over 10 yrs only. TV; cable (premium). Complimentary continental bkfst & coffee, also evening refreshments. Restaurant nearby. Ck-out 11 am, ck-in 3 pm. Business servs avail. Downhill/x-country ski 15 mi. Whirlpool. Some fireplaces. House (ca 1895) blends New Mexico's stone & adobe architecture with pitched roof, Victorian-style interior; sitting rm, antiques; garden and tree-shaded lawns more typical of buildings in the East. Cr cds: MC, V.

★ ★ **WATER STREET INN.** 427 W Water St (87501). 505/984-1193; FAX 505/984-1193. 8 rms. S, D $90-$155; each addl $15. Crib free. TV; cable. Complimentary continental bkfst in rms. Complimentary coffee, wine. Restaurant nearby. Ck-out 11 am, ck-in 2-6 pm. Business servs avail. Downhill/x-country ski 17 mi. Restored adobe building; fireplaces, antique stoves. Totally nonsmoking. Cr cds: MC, V.

Guest Ranches

★ ★ ★ **BISHOP'S LODGE.** Box 2367 (87504), Bishop's Lodge Rd, 3 mi N of the Plaza. 505/983-6377; res: 800/732-2240; FAX 505/989-8739. 88 rms in 1-3 story lodges. No elvtr. June 1-Sept 7: S, D $160-$431; each addl up to 3 from $53; lower rates rest of yr. Crib $10. TV; cable (premium), VCR avail. Heated pool; poolside serv, lifeguard. Playground. Supervised child's activities (June-Sept); ages 4-12. Dining rm 7:30 am-9 pm. Child's dining rm. Rm serv. Box lunches; picnics. Bar 11:30 am-midnight; Sun from noon. Ck-out noon, ck-in mid-late afternoon. Business servs avail. Concierge. Sports dir. Tennis, pro. 18-hole golf privileges. Stocked pond. Fishing pond for children. Downhill/x-country ski 18 mi. Skeet, trap shooting; pro. Riding instruction; bkfst & lunch rides as scheduled; children's rides. Lawn games. Exercise equipt; stair machine, bicycles, whirlpool, sauna. Soc dir;

entertainment, movies in season. Rec rm. Many refrigerators. Fireplace in some rms. Some private patios. Nestled in foothills of the Sangre de Cristo Mts; Old West charm in 1,000-acre resort. Cr cds: A, MC, V.

⬛ 🚶 🎣 ⛷ 🏊 🎿 🏊 🏃 ⛵

★ ★ ★ **RANCHO ENCANTADO.** *Rte 4, Box 57C, N on US 285 to North Tesuque exit, SE on NM 592 to ranch.* 505/982-3537; res: 800/722-9339; FAX 505/983-8269. 88 units, 15 cottages. June-Oct: S, D $110-$415; each addl $10; kits. $175-$415; cottages $125-$260; min stay 3-days; ski plan; higher rates Indian Market; lower rates rest of yr. Crib avail. TV; VCR avail. Pool; whirlpool. Complimentary coffee in rms. Dining rm 7-10:30 am, 6-9 pm. Box lunches. Picnics. Bar 5-11 pm. Ck-out 11 am, ck-in 3 pm. Gift shop. Grocery 3 mi. Coin lndry 8 mi. Bellhops. Concierge. Valet serv. Meeting rms. Business servs avail. In-rm modem link. Tennis; pro. X-country skiing 12 mi. Hiking trails. Minibars. Picnic tables. Cr cds: A, C, D, DS, MC, V.

⬛ 🎣 🏊 🎿 🏊 🎣 🏊 ⛷ SC

Restaurants

★ ★ ★ ★ **THE ANASAZI.** *(See Inn Of The Anasazi Hotel)* 505/988-3236. Stone walls, a beamed ceiling, artwork, and antiques set the scene for innovative takes on local and regional cuisine. Hrs: 7-10:30 am, 11:30 am-2:30 pm, 5:30-10 pm; Sun brunch 7 am-2:30 pm. Res accepted. Southwestern menu. Bar 11 am-midnight; wkends to midnight. Wine cellar. A la carte entrees: bkfst $5.25-$9.50, lunch $4-$12.75, dinner $6.50-$29. Sun brunch $6-$12.75. Child's meals. Specialties: tortilla soup, white cheddar mashed potatoes, fresh fish, organically grown foods. Menu changes seasonally. Classical guitarist (brunch). Cr cds: A, C, D, DS, MC, V.

⬛

★ ★ **BABBO GANZO.** *130 Lincoln Ave, in Lincoln Place shopping mall.* 505/986-3835. Hrs: 11:30 am-2:30 pm, 5:30-10 pm; Sun from 5:30 pm. Closed most major hols. Res accepted. Northern Italian menu. Bar. A la carte entrees: lunch $5.25-$9.75, dinner $9.25-$24. Complete meals: lunch, dinner $12-$35. Specializes in classic Tuscan dishes, fresh fish, free range veal. Own pasta. Tuscan trattoria decor; murals. Located on upper level of building. Cr cds: MC, V.

⬛

✔ ★ **BLUE CORN CAFE.** *133 Water St, on 2nd floor.* 505/984-1800. Hrs: 11 am-11 pm. Closed Jan 1, Thanksgiving, Dec 25. Mexican menu. Bar to 1:30 am. Semi-a la carte: lunch, dinner $5.95-$8.25. Child's meals. Specialties: chile rellenos, achiote grilled half-chicken. Entertainment Fri, Sat. Southwestern decor, fireplace. Cr cds: A, C, D, DS, MC, V.

⬛

★ ★ **CAFE ESCALERA.** *130 Lincoln Ave (87501).* 505/989-8188. Hrs: 11:30 am-2:30 pm, 5:30-9:30 pm. Closed Dec 25. Mediterranean menu. Bar. A la carte entrees: Semi-a la carte: lunch, dinner $5-$24.50. Specialties: artichoke bruschetta, fried oyster sandwich with green chili, grilled sea bass with fennel. Contemporary decor. Cr cds: A, MC, V.

★ ★ **CAFE PASQUAL'S.** *121 Don Gaspar, just off the plaza.* 505/983-9340. Hrs: 7 am-3 pm, 6-10 pm; wkends to 10:30 pm; Sun brunch 8 am-2 pm. Closed Thanksgiving, Dec 25. Res accepted. New Mexican, Amer menu. Wine, beer. Semi-a la carte: bkfst $4.25-$9.95, lunch $5.95-$9.95, dinner $14.75-$23.75. Sun brunch $4.25-$9.95. Child's meals. Specialties: chorizo burrito, char-grilled chicken quesadillas, char-grilled rack of lamb. Hand-painted murals; festive Old Santa Fe decor. Totally nonsmoking. Cr cds: A, MC, V.

✔ ★ **CELEBRATIONS.** *618 Canyon Rd.* 505/989-8904. Hrs: 7:30 am-2:30 pm, 5:30-9:30 pm; Wed & Thurs to 9 pm; Sun brunch 11 am-2:30 pm. Closed Jan 1, Thanksgiving, Dec 25. Res accepted. No A/C. Continental menu. Wine, beer. Semi-a la carte: bkfst $3.95-$5.95, lunch $4.75-$7.95, dinner $7.95-$14.95. Sun brunch $5.95-$9.95. Spe-

cializes in Northern New Mexican dishes, New Orleans dishes, rack of lamb. Outdoor dining. 3 dining areas; fireplaces. Cr cds: MC, V.

⬛

★ ★ ★ **COMPOUND.** *653 Canyon Rd.* 505/982-4353. Hrs: from 6 pm. Closed Sun, Mon; major hols; also Jan. Res required. Continental menu. Serv bar. Wine cellar. Dinner $18-$28. Specialties: fresh foie gras, roast loin of lamb, baked filet of salmon, breast of chicken in champagne. Fresh fish from Europe, caviar from Russia. Own baking. Parking. Family-owned. With its heavy crystal and fine artwork, this restaurant shimmers with Old World elegance. The main dining room overlooks a formal Italian garden; a smaller one has a view of a Spanish patio. Totally nonsmoking. Cr cds: A, MC.

⬛

★ ★ ★ **CORN DANCE CAFE.** *409 W Water (87501).* 505/986-1662. Hrs: 11:30 am-2:30 pm, 5-10 pm. Closed Tues during winter months. Res required. Native American menu. Wine, beer. Semi-a la carte: lunch $9.95-$12.95, dinner $12.95-$25.95. Specialties: buffalo rib-eye steak, wild turkey with corn bread dressing, Little Big pies. Native American musicians Thurs-Sun during summer months. Patio dining. Native American decor. Cr cds: A, C, D, DS, MC, V.

⬛

★ ★ ★ **COYOTE CAFE.** *132 W Water St, off the plaza.* 505/983-1615. Hrs: 5:30-9:45 pm; Sat-Sun 11 am-1:45 pm, 5:30-9:45 pm. Southwestern menu. Bar/cantina (May-Oct) 11 am-10 pm. Semi-a la carte: lunch $7-$13, dinner $39.50. Specialties: cowboy rib chop, chile relleno platter, griddled corn cakes with shrimp. Outdoor dining on rooftop cantina. Adobe structure; Southwestern decor; fireplace. Cr cds: A, C, D, DS, MC, V.

★ ★ **EL NIDO.** *(Box 488, Tesuque 87574) 6 mi N on NM 591 (Bishops Lodge Rd).* 505/988-4340. Hrs: 5:30-9:30 pm; Fri & Sat to 10 pm; Sun from 6 pm. Closed Mon; Jan 1, Super Bowl Sun, Thanksgiving, Dec 25. Res accepted. Bar. Semi-a la cart: dinner $8.95-$29.95. Specializes in fresh seafood, beef, lamb. Parking. 1920 adobe building; fireplaces. Folk art of Tesuque Valley. Cr cds: MC, V.

★ ★ **ENCORE PROVENCE.** *548 Agua Fria (87501).* 505/983-7470. Hrs: 6-9 pm; Fri & Sat to 10 pm. Closed Jan. Res accepted. French menu. Wine, beer. Semi-a la carte: dinner $15-$18.50. Specializes in dishes of Provence, Chilean black bass, leg of lamb. Parking. Outdoor dining. Three intimate dining rms in house of former congressman. Cr cds: A, MC, V.

⬛

★ ★ **THE EVERGREEN.** *7¹/₂ mi NE of the plaza, on Hyde Park Rd, in Hyde Memorial State Park.* 505/984-8190. Hrs: 5-9 pm; Fri, Sat 11 am-4 pm (summer); Sun brunch 11 am-4 pm. Closed Mon. Res accepted. Bar. Wine cellar. Semi-a la carte: lunch $7.95-$10, dinner $12.95-$21.95. Sun brunch $17.95. Specializes in smoked salmon, grilled smoked lamb chops, smoked trout. Parking. Outdoor dining (seasonal). Historic mountainside Alpine-style log and stone building, built in 1935 by the CCC. Fireplace at each end and middle of restaurant; tall windows offer scenic view of evergreens. Cr cds: A, C, D, DS, MC, V.

⬛

✔ ★ **GARDUÑO'S.** *130 Lincoln Ave, 2nd fl.* 505/983-9797. Hrs: 11 am-10 pm; Fri, Sat to 10:30 pm; Sun 10:30 am-10 pm; Sun brunch to 3 pm. Closed Thanksgiving, Dec 25. Mexican menu. Bar. Semi-a la carte: lunch $4.95-$12.95, dinner $4.75-$13.95. Sun brunch $9.95. Child's meals. Specializes in chimichangas, fajitas, seafood. Entertainment. Southwest decor. Family-owned. Cr cds: A, C, D, DS, MC, V.

⬛ SC

★ ★ **GERONIMO.** *724 Canyon Rd.* 505/982-1500. Hrs: 11:30 am-2:30 pm, 6-10:30 pm; Mon from 6 pm. Res accepted. Bar to midnight. Semi-a la carte: lunch $8-$12, dinner $15-$20. Specializes in southwestern fare. Parking. Outdoor dining. Historic adobe house (1753). Cr cds: A, MC, V.

D

★ ★ **IMPERIAL WOK.** *731 Canyon Rd (87501).* 505/988-7100. Hrs: 11:30 am-9:30 pm; Fri & Sat to 10:30 pm. Closed Thanksgiving. Res accepted. Chinese menu. Bar. Semi-a la carte: lunch $6.75-$8.25, dinner $7.50-$17.75. Specializes in Szechuan and Hunan dishes. Entertainment exc Mon. Parking. Atrium dining, fountain in center. Cr cds: A, C, D, DS, MC, V.

★ ★ ★ **JULIAN'S.** *221 Shelby St, just off the plaza.* 505/988-2355. Hrs: 11:30 am-2 pm, 6-10 pm; Sun from 6 pm. Closed Thanksgiving. Res accepted. Italian menu. Bar. Semi-a la carte: lunch $7-$21, dinner $12-$24. Specialties: pollo al agro dolci, gamberi alla marinara, piccata di vitello. Outdoor dining. Fine art; etched-glass windows; 2 fireplaces. Cr cds: A, D, DS, MC, V.

★ ★ ★ **LA CASA SENA.** *20 Sena Plaza, 125 E Palace, on grounds of Sena Plaza Center.* 505/988-9232. Hrs: 11:30 am-3 pm, 5:30-10 pm; Sun from 11 am; Sun brunch 11 am-3 pm. Res accepted. Santa Fe, continental menu. Bar 11:30 am-midnight; Sun from noon. Wine cellar. Semi-a la carte: lunch $7-$10, dinner $18-$24. Sun brunch $7-$10. Specialties: trucha en adobe, grilled venison, seasonal fish, rack of lamb. Own baking. Entertainment 6-11 pm. Outdoor dining. Adobe house (late 1860s); art work; old Santa Fe decor. Singing waiters in cantina. Cr cds: A, C, D, DS, MC, V.

D

★ ★ ★ **LA TERTULIA DE SANTA FE.** *416 Agua Fria St.* 505/988-2769. Hrs: 11:30 am-2 pm, 5-9:30 pm; Sept-May to 9 pm. Closed Mon; major hols; also 1st wk Dec. Res accepted. Mexican, Amer menu. Serv bar. Semi-a la carte: lunch $5.50-$8.50, dinner $6.50-$18. Child's meals. Specialties: chiles rellenos, carne adovada, pollo adovo. Parking. Elegant Spanish decor; Spanish-colonial art collection. Garden rm & outdoor garden area. Located in restored area of 18th-century convent. Cr cds: A, D, MC, V.

D

★ ★ **LA TRAVIATA.** *95 W Marcy (87501).* 505/984-1091. Hrs: 8:30 am-2:30 pm, 6-10 pm; Sun to 2:30 pm. Closed Jan 1, Thanksgiving, Dec 25; also Super Bowl Sun. Res accepted. Italian menu. Semi-a la carte: bkfst $1.25-$3.50, lunch $7-$15, dinner $14.50-$21. Specializes in lasagne. Opera theme. Cr cds: MC, V.

D

★ ★ **MAÑANA.** *(See Inn Of The Governors Motor Hotel)* 505/982-4333. Hrs: 6:30 am-midnight. Res accepted. Southwestern menu. Bar. A la carte entrees: bkfst $4.95-$6.75, lunch $4.95-$7.50, dinner $5.95-$15.25. Child's meals. Specializes in woodfired pizza, woodroasted salmon, blue corn pancakes. Pianist, vocalist. Parking. Patio dining. Two dining rms. Cr cds: A, MC, V.

D

★ ★ **MARIA'S KITCHEN.** *555 W Cordova Rd (87501).* 505/983-7929. Hrs: 11 am-10 pm; Sat & Sun from noon. Closed Thanksgiving, Dec 25. Res accepted. Bar. Semi-a la carte: lunch $4.95-$8.95, dinner $7.25-$15.75. Child's meals. Specialty: tortillas. Famous for magaritas, this restaurant also has an extensive Mexican beer selection. Parking. Patio dining. Original art. Cr cds: A, C, D, DS, MC, V.

★ **MONROE'S.** *727 Cerrillos Rd (87501).* 505/989-7575. Hrs: 7 am-9 pm; Fri & Sat to 10 pm. Closed July 4, Thanksgiving, Dec 25. Wine, beer. Semi-a la carte: bkfst $2.10-$7.75, lunch $4.75-$9.50, dinner $7.15-$9.50. Child's meals. Specializes in blue corn enchiladas. Parking. Patio dining. Family-owned. Cr cds: A, D, DS, MC, V.

★ **NATURAL CAFE.** *1494 Cerrillos Rd (87505).* 505/983-1411. Hrs: 11:30 am-2:30 pm, 5-9:30 pm; Sat & Sun from 5 pm. Closed Mon; Dec 25. Res accepted. Eclectic menu. Semi-a la carte: lunch $4.75-$8.50, dinner $8.50-$16. Child's meals. Specialties: New Mexi-

can polenta, Szechuan chicken, grilled salmon. Entertainment. Parking. Patio dining. Totally nonsmoking. Cr cds: DS, MC, V.

D

★ ★ ★ **THE OLD HOUSE.** *(See Eldorado Hotel)* 505/988-4455. Hrs: 5:30-10 pm; Sun brunch 11 am-2 pm. Closed Mon. Res required. Southwestern menu. Bar. Wine list. Semi-a la carte: dinner $16.95-$29.95. Sun brunch $18. Specialties: roasted achiote rubbed halibut, smoked antelope and wild mushrooms, roast rack of lamb in pepita-garlic crust. Valet parking. Intimate dining in elegant surroundings. Contemporary Southwestern decor. Cr cds: A, C, D, DS, MC, V.

D

★ **OLD MEXICO GRILL.** *2434 Cerrillos Rd.* 505/473-0338. Hrs: 9:30 am-10 pm. Winter hrs vary. Closed Jan 1, Dec 25. Mexican menu. Bar. A la carte entrees: lunch $5.95-$9.95, dinner $8.50-$17.50. Specializes in fajitas, old Mexico sauces, steak. Parking. Cr cds: DS, MC, V.

D

★ ★ **ORE HOUSE.** *50 Lincoln Ave, on the plaza.* 505/983-8687. Hrs: 11:30 am-2:30 pm, 5:30-10 pm; Sun from noon. Closed Thanksgiving, Dec 25. Res accepted. Bar to 1 am; entertainment. Semi-a la carte: lunch $3.75-$8.95, dinner $36. Child's meals. Specializes in steak, seafood, rack of lamb. Outdoor dining (lunch). Cr cds: A, MC, V.

D

★ ★ ★ **PALACE.** *142 W Palace Ave, just off the plaza.* 505/982-9891. Hrs: 11:30 am-4 pm, 5:45-10 pm; Sun from 5:45 pm. Closed Dec 25. Res accepted. Continental menu. Bar 11:30 am-10 pm. Semi-a la carte: lunch $4.50-$12, dinner $9.50-$20. Specializes in New Mexican lamb, seafood, pasta, steak. Pianist. Patio dining. Turn-of-the-century Victorian decor. Cr cds: A, D, MC, V.

D

★ ★ **PIÑON GRILL.** *(See Hilton Of Santa Fe Motor Hotel)* 505/986-6400. Hrs: 11 am-2 pm, 5-10 pm. Res accepted. Bar. A la carte entrees: lunch $4.95-$11.95, dinner $13-$23. Child's meals. Specializes in wild game, fish, free range poultry. Parking. High-beamed, mission style ceilings; Native American artifacts. Cr cds: A, C, D, DS, MC, V.

D

★ ★ **PINK ADOBE.** *406 Old Santa Fe Trail (US 84, 85, 285), just off the plaza.* 505/983-7712. Hrs: 11:30 am-2:30 pm, 5:30-10 pm; Sat & Sun from 5:30 pm. Closed major hols. Res accepted. Some A/C. Bar. New Mexican, continental menu. Semi-a la carte: lunch $6.50-$8.50, dinner $10.25-$22.25. Specialties: porc Napoleone, poulet Marengo, steak Dunigan. Entertainment in Dragon Room Tues-Thurs, Sat 7-10 pm. Fireplace in dining rms. Historic building ca 1700. Family-owned. Cr cds: A, C, D, DS, MC, V.

D

★ ★ ★ **SANTACAFE.** *231 Washington Ave, just off the plaza.* 505/984-1788. Hrs: 11:30 am-2 pm, 5:30-10:30 pm; Sun from 5:30 pm. Res accepted. Bar. A la carte entrees: lunch $8-$12, dinner $18-$28. Specializes in Southwestern cuisine with Asian flare. Own baking. Patio dining. Historic adobe house (1850); landscaped courtyard. Cr cds: MC, V.

D

✔ ★ **THE SHED.** *Prince Patio, 113½ E Palace Ave, ½ blk E of plaza.* 505/982-9030. Hrs: 11 am-2:30 pm, 5:30-9 pm Closed Sun; major hols. New Mexican, Amer menu. Wine, beer. Semi-a la carte: lunch $3.75-$7. Specializes in blue corn enchiladas, mocha cake. Patio dining. Unusual restaurant in oldest part of town. Artwork, wall hangings. Family-owned. No cr cds accepted.

D

★ **SHOHKO-CAFE.** *321 Johnson St, downtown, off the Plaza.* 505/983-7288. Hrs: 11:30 am-2 pm, 5:30-9 pm; Fri, Sat to 9:30

pm. July & Aug: Sun from 5:30 pm. Closed hols. Res accepted. Chinese, Japanese menu. Wine, beer. Semi-a la carte: lunch $6-$12, dinner $9-$18. Specialties: tempura, sushi, seafood. Parking. Cr cds: A, MC, V.

D

★ ★ ★ STAAB HOUSE. *(See La Posada De Santa Fe Motor Hotel)* 505/986-0000. Hrs: 7 am-10 pm. Res accepted. Continental menu. Bar 11-2 am; Sun from noon. Semi-a la carte: bkfst $4.25-$9.95, lunch $5.95-$9.95, dinner $9.95-$19.95. Child's meals. Specializes in creative Southwest cuisine. Entertainment (seasonal). Parking. Outdoor dining. In historic Staab mansion (1882); hand-crafted furniture; fireplace. On 6 acres. Cr cds: A, C, D, MC, V.

D

★ ★ STEAKSMITH AT EL GANCHO. *Old Las Vegas Hwy, approx 5 mi S of plaza, at El Gancho Tennis Club.* 505/988-3333. Hrs: 5:30-10 pm; Sun 5-9 pm. Closed most major hols. Res accepted. Continental menu. Bar from 4 pm. Complete meals: dinner $8.95-$26.95. Specializes in prime rib, fresh seafood, aged beef. Parking. Southwestern decor. Cr cds: A, MC, V.

D

✔ ★ TECOLOTE CAFE. *1203 Cerrillos Rd (87501).* 505/988-1362. Hrs: 7 am-2 pm. Closed Mon; Dec 24 & 25; also wk of Thanksgiving. Southwestern, Mexican menu. Semi-a la carte: bkfst, lunch $3.25-$10. Child's meals. Specializes in breakfast dishes. Original Southwestern art. Cr cds: A, C, D, DS, MC, V.

D

✔ ★ TOMASITA'S. *500 S Guadalupe.* 505/983-5721. Hrs: 11 am-10 pm. Closed Sun; Jan 1, Thanksgiving, Dec 25. Northern New Mexican, Amer menu. Bar. Semi-a la carte: lunch $4.50-$9.50, dinner $4.95-$9.95. Child's meals $1.95. Specializes in quesidillas, burritos, enchiladas. Parking. Outdoor dining. Old train station (1894). Cr cds: MC, V.

D

★ ★ VANESSIE OF SANTA FE. *434 W San Francisco St.* 505/982-9966. Hrs: 5:30-10 pm. Closed Easter, Thanksgiving, Dec 25. Bar to 2 am. A la carte entrees: dinner $10.95-$37.95. Specializes in rack of lamb, lobster, steak, chicken. Pianist evenings. Parking. Outdoor dining. Cr cds: A, C, D, DS, MC, V.

D

Unrated Dining Spots

THE BURRITO COMPANY. *111 Washington Ave (87501).* 505/982-4453. Hrs: 7:30 am-7 pm; Sun 10 am-5 pm. Closed Dec 25. Mexican menu. A la carte entrees: bkfst $2-$3.50, lunch & dinner $1.65-$4.75. Child's meals. Specializes in burritos, enchiladas. Fast-food style restaurant famous for bkfst burritos. No cr cds accepted.

FURRS CAFETERIA. *522 Cordova Rd.* 505/982-3816. Hrs: 11 am-9 pm. Closed Sun; Dec 24 (eve), Dec 25. Avg ck: lunch, dinner $4.85. Specializes in chicken-fried steak, baked fish. Extra coffee, tea serv. Cr cds: MC, V.

D SC

GRANT CORNER INN. *122 Grant Ave (87501).* 505/983-6678. Hrs: 8-9:30 am; Sat to 11 am; Sun to 1 pm. Res accepted. Brunch menu: $8.50-$10.50; Sun $10.50. Child's meals. Specialties: hearts of palm eggs Benedict, chile rellenos souffle, pumpkin raisin pancakes. Guitarist Sun. Outdoor dining. Colonial-style house built 1905. Cr cds: MC, V.

PLAZA. *54 Lincoln Ave, on the plaza.* 505/982-1664. Hrs: 7 am-9 pm; wkends 8 am-10 pm. Closed Thanksgiving, Dec 25. Continental menu. Wine, beer. Semi-a la carte: bkfst $2.50-$6.50, lunch $4.50-$8, dinner $6-$15. Child's meals. Specialties: blue corn

enchiladas, chicken chimichanga, Greek baked pasta, Greek lemon garlic chicken. Century-old building with many original fixtures; stamped-tin ceiling; photos of early Santa Fe. Art deco lunch-counter design. Family-owned since 1947. Cr cds: DS, MC, V.

Santa Rosa (E-5)

Settled 1865 **Pop** 2,263 **Elev** 4,620 ft **Area code** 505 **Zip** 88435
Information Chamber of Commerce, 486 Parker Ave; 505/472-3763.

In grama-grass country on the Pecos River, Santa Rosa has several natural and man-made lakes.

What to See and Do

Billy the Kid Museum. Contains 60,000 items, including relics of the Old West, Billy the Kid and Old Fort Sumner. On display is rifle once owned by Billy the Kid. (Mid-May-mid-Sept, daily; Mar-early May & late Sept-Dec, daily exc Sun; closed Thanksgiving, Dec 25) 1601 E Sumner Ave, 44 mi SE via US 84, in Fort Sumner. Phone 505/355-2380. ¢¢

City parks. Fishing in stocked lakes. Picnicking. (Daily) Phone 505/472-3404. Free.

Park Lake. Also swimming, lifeguard (June-Aug); children's fishing only. Tennis courts. Playground. Park Lake Dr.

Janes-Wallace Memorial Park. Also camping, small trailers allowed. 1 mi S on 3rd St.

Blue Hole. Clear blue lake in rock setting fed by natural artesian spring, 81 feet deep; scuba diving (permit fee). Nature trails. 1 mi E on La Pradira Lane.

Tres Lagunas. Fishing. Hiking. Nine-hole golf (fee). Wilderness camping. 1/4 mi N of US 66, E end of town.

Santa Rosa Dam & Lake. Army Corps of Engineers project for flood control and irrigation. No permanent pool; irrigation pool is often available for recreation. Fishing, small-game hunting; boating (ramp, launch). Nature trails, also trail for the disabled. Picnicking. Camping (fee; electricity addl). Information center. Excellent area for photography. (Daily) 7 mi N via access road. Contact ACE, PO Box 345; 505/472-3115. Per vehicle ¢¢

Puerta de Luna. Founded about 1862, this Spanish-American town of 250 persons holds to old customs in living and working. 10 mi S on NM 91. Phone 505/472-3763. Also here is

Grzelachowski Territorial House. Store and mercantile built in 1800; this house was visited frequently by Billy the Kid. Grzelachowski had a major role in the Civil War battle at Glorieta Pass. (Daily, mid-morning-early evening; closed hols) Donation. Phone 505/472-5320.

Fort Sumner State Monument. Original site of the Bosque Redondo, where thousands of Navajo and Mescalero Apache people were held captive by the US Army from 1863-1868. The military established the adobe fort of Fort Sumner to oversee the containment. (See ANNUAL EVENTS) Visitor center has exhibits relating to the period. (Daily; closed winter hols) 3 mi E on US 54/66, then 44 mi SE on US 84, near Fort Sumner. Phone 505/355-2573. ¢

Rock Lake Rearing Station. State fish hatchery, rearing rainbow trout and walleyed pike. (Daily) 2 mi S off I-40. Phone 505/472-3690. Free.

Sumner Lake State Park. 4,500-surface-acre reservoir created by irrigation dam. Swimming, waterskiing; fishing (bass, crappie, channel catfish); boating (ramps). Picnicking. Camping (hookups, dump station). (Daily) Standard fees. 3 mi E on US 54/66, then 32 mi S on US 84, near Fort Sumner. Phone 505/355-2541. Per vehicle ¢¢

Annual Events

Santa Rosa Day Celebration. Sports events, contests, exhibits, car show, dances. Memorial Day wkend.

Old Fort Days. Ft Sumner, downtown & County Fairgrounds. Parade, rodeo, bank robbery, barbecue, contests, exhibits. June.

Motels

★★ **BEST WESTERN ADOBE INN.** *Drawer 410, Will Rogers Dr (US 54, 66, 84).* 505/472-3446. 58 rms, 2 story. S $38-$52; D $48-$58; each addl $2. Crib $4. TV; cable. Heated pool. Ck-out 11 am. Sundries. Gift shop. Airport, bus depot transportation. Cr cds: A, C, D, DS, MC, V.

✔★ **HOLIDAY INN EXPRESS.** *Box E, Will Rogers Dr (US 54, 66, 84) at jct I-40, exit 277.* 505/472-5411; FAX 505/472-3537. 100 rms, 2 story. S $29.95-$49.95; D $39.95-$69.95; each addl $10. TV; cable. Pool. Ck-out 10 am. Coin lndry. Meeting rm. Cr cds: A, C, D, DS, MC, V.

Shiprock (B-1)

(For accommodations see Farmington)

Founded 1904 **Pop** 7,687 **Elev** 4,903 ft **Area code** 505 **Zip** 87420

Named for a 1,865-foot butte rising out of the desert, Shiprock is on the Navajo Reservation. The tribe, largest in the US, numbers about 200,000. Once almost exclusively shepherds and hunters, the Navajos have acquired some wealth by discoveries of oil, coal and uranium on their lands—oil wells are found in the Four-Corners area nearby and throughout San Juan County. The Navajo people are applying this income to urgent needs in educational and economic development. The Navajo Tribal Council has its headquarters at Window Rock, AZ. For information contact Navajoland Tourism Dept, PO Box 663, Window Rock, AZ 86515; 602/871-6659; or the Superintendent, Shiprock Agency, PO Box 966; 505/368-4427.

Annual Event

Shiprock Navajo Fair. Powwow, carnival, parade. 1st wkend Oct.

Silver City (G-1)

(See Deming)

Founded 1870 **Pop** 10,683 **Elev** 5,895 ft **Area code** 505 **Zip** 88061
Information Chamber of Commerce, 1103 N Hudson; 505/538-3785.

The rich gold and silver ores in the foothills of the Mogollon (pronounced MUG-ee-yone) Mountains are running low, but copper mining has now become important to the economy. Cattle ranching thrives on the plains. The forested mountain slopes to the north are the habitat of turkey, deer, elk and bear, and the streams and lakes provide excellent trout fishing.

What to See and Do

✪ **Gila** (HEE-la) **National Forest.** Administers more than three million-acres, including the New Mexico part of Apache National Forest. Also includes Gila, Blue Range and Aldo Leopold wildernesses. Hunting. Backpacking, horseback riding. Lakes Quemado, Roberts and Snow also have fishing, boating, picnicking and camping. Fees for some activities. Surrounds town on all borders except on SE. Contact the Information Desk, 3005 E Camino del Bosque; 505/388-8201. In forest are

Gila Cliff Dwellings National Monument. There are 42 rooms in 6 caves (accessible by a 1-mi hiking trail) which were occupied by Mogollon Indians circa 1300. Well-preserved masonry dwellings in natural alcoves in the face of an overhanging cliff. Self-guided tour. Camping. Forest naturalists conduct programs (Memorial Day-Labor Day). Ruins and visitor center (daily; closed Jan 1, Dec 25). 44 mi N of Silver City on NM 15. Contact District Ranger, Rte 11, Box 100; 505/536-9461. **Free.**

Catwalk of Whitewater Canyon. National recreation trail. Steel Causeway follows the course of two former pipelines that supplied water and water power in the 1890s to the historic gold and silver mining town of Graham. Causeway clings to sides of the sheer box canyon of Whitewater Creek. Access is by foot trail from Whitewater picnic ground (no water avail); access also to Gila Wilderness. (Daily) 63 mi NW of Silver City via US 180, then 5 miNE on NM 174. Phone 505/539-2481. **Free.**

Mogollon Ghost Town (1878-1930s). Former gold-mining town. Weathered buildings, beautiful surroundings; nearby Whitewater Canyon was once the haunt of Butch Cassidy and his gang, as well as Vitorio and Geronimo. 75 mi NW of Silver City via US 180 & NM 159. Phone 505/539-2481. **Free.**

Phelps Dodge Copper Mine. Open-pit mine and leach plant process more than 65,000 tons of material each day; solvent-extraction/electrowinning plant. Tours (Mon-Fri; closed hols). 12 mi SW on NM 90. Phone 505/538-5331, 24 hrs in advance. **Free.**

Silver City Museum. In restored 1881 house of H. B. Ailman, owner of a rich silver mine; Victorian antiques and furnishings; Casas Grandes Indian artifacts; memorabilia from mining town of Tyrone. (Daily exc Mon, also open Memorial Day, July 4 & Labor Day; closed Jan 1, Thanksgiving, Dec 24-25) 312 W Broadway. Phone 505/538-5921. **Free.**

Western New Mexico University (1893). (1,800 students) W part of town. Phone 505/538-6011. On campus is

Fleming Hall Museum. Depicts contribution of American Indian, Hispanic, black and European cultures to history of region; Mimbres Indian artifacts; photography, archive and mineral collections. (Daily; closed hols) 1000 College Ave. Phone 505/538-6386. **Free.**

Annual Event

Frontier Days. Parade, dances, exhibits, food. Western dress desired. July 4.

Motels

✔★ **COPPER MANOR.** *Box 1405, 710 Silver Heights Blvd (US 180).* 505/538-5392; res: 800/853-2996. 68 rms, 2 story. S $35-$40; D $42-$49; each addl $3. Crib free. TV; cable. Indoor pool. Restaurant 11 am-10 pm. Rm serv. Ck-out 11 am. Meeting rm. Business servs avail. Valet serv. Cr cds: A, C, D, DS, MC, V.

★ **DRIFTER.** *Silver Heights Blvd (88062), on US 180.* 505/538-2916; res: 800/853-2916. 69 rms, 2 story. No A/C. S $36-$53; D $40-$53; each addl $3; under 10 free. Crib free. TV; cable. Indoor/outdoor pool; sauna. Complimentary coffee in lobby. Restaurant adj 11 am-10 pm. Bar 4 pm-2 am. Meeting rms. Business servs avail. Rec rm. Cr cds: A, C, D, DS, MC, V.

★★ **HOLIDAY MOTOR HOTEL.** *Box 3420 (88062), 2¹/₂ mi E on US 180.* 505/538-3711; res: 800/828-8291; FAX 505/538-3711, ext. 300. 79 rms, 2 story. S $40; D $46; each addl $4; under 12 free. Pet accepted. TV; cable (premium). Pool. Restaurant 6 am-2 pm, 5-8:30 pm; Sun 7 am-3 pm, 5-8:30 pm. Ck-out noon. Guest lndry. Meeting rms. Business servs avail. Free airport transportation. Cr cds: A, C, D, DS, MC, V.

Restaurant

★ ★ **BUCKHORN SALOON.** *(32 Main St, Pinos Altos 88053) 6 mi N on NM 15.* 505/538-9911. Hrs: 6-10 pm. Closed Sun; Jan 1, Thanksgiving, Dec 25. Res accepted. No A/C. Bar to midnight. Semi-a la carte: dinner $5.50-$35. Specializes in steak, seafood. Entertainment Thurs-Sat. Parking. Four dining rms in house designed to look like Western opera house; melodrama performed some wkends. Cr cds: MC, V.

Socorro (F-3)

Pop 8,159 **Elev** 4,620 ft **Area code** 505 **Zip** 87801
Information Socorro County Chamber of Commerce, 103 Francisco de Avondo, PO Box 743; 505/835-0424.

Originally a Piro Indian town, Socorro had a Franciscan mission as early as 1598. In 1817, a Spanish land grant brought the ancestors of the present families here.

In an area once rich in silver, zinc and other materials, Socorro was, in 1880, the largest city in New Mexico, with 44 saloons along its main street. Farming, stock raising and research are the main income sources in this part of the Rio Grande Valley.

What to See and Do

Bosque del Apache National Wildlife Refuge. A 15-mile, self-guided auto tour loop allows visitors to view a variety of wildlife, including the endangered whooping crane. Nov-mid-Feb are best viewing months. Visitor center has brochures and exhibits (daily). Tour loop (daily; phone for hrs and fee). 18 mi S via I-25 and NM 1. Phone 505/835-1828.

Mineral Museum. More than 12,000 mineral specimens from around the world. Free rockhounding and prospecting information. (Mon-Fri) 1 mi W of I-25 on campus of New Mexico Institute of Mining and Technology (College Ave & Leroy) at Workman Center. Phone 505/835-5616 or -5246. **Free.**

National Radio Astronomy Observatory. The VLA (Very Large Array) radio telescope consists of 27 separate antennas situated along three arms of railroad track. Self-guided walking tour of grounds and visitor center. (Daily) 52 mi W on US 60, then S on NM 52. Phone 505/835-7000. **Free.**

Old San Miguel Mission (1615-26). Restored; south wall was part of the original 1598 mission. Carved ceiling beams and corbels; walls are five feet thick. (Daily) Artifacts on display in church office (building S of church) (Mon-Fri). 403 El Camino Real NW, 2 blks N of the plaza. Phone 505/835-1620 or -2750. **Free.**

Annual Events

Conrad Hilton Open Golf Tournament. Early June
Socorro County Fair & Rodeo. Labor Day wkend.

Motels

★ **BEST WESTERN GOLDEN MANOR.** *507 N California St (US 60, 85, I-25 Business).* 505/835-0230; FAX 505/835-1993. 41 rms, 2 story. S $43; D $50; each addl $3. Crib $4. Pet accepted, some restrictions; $50 refundable. TV; cable (premium). Heated pool. Restaurant 6-10 am, 5-9 pm. Rm serv. Ck-out noon. Cr cds: A, C, D, DS, MC, V.

✔ ★ **SAN MIGUEL.** *916 California St NE, US 60, 85, I-25 Business.* 505/835-0211. 40 rms. S $37; D $44; each addl $3. TV; cable. Heated pool. Restaurant opp open 24 hrs. Ck-out noon. Coin lndry. Refrigerator in rm. Cr cds: A, C, D, DS, MC, V.

★ **SUPER 8.** *1121 Frontage Rd NW, I-25 exit 150.* 505/835-4626; FAX 505/835-3988. 88 rms, 2 story. S $42.88-$46.88; D $49.88-$52.88; each addl $4; under 12 free. Crib $5. TV; cable (premium). Heated pool; whirlpool. Complimentary coffee in lobby. Restaurant nearby. Ck-out 11 am. Coin lndry. Business servs avail. 18-hole golf privileges, greens fee. Refrigerator in rm. Cr cds: A, C, D, DS, MC, V.

★ **WESTERN.** *(US 60, Magdalena 87825) 20 mi W on US 60.* 505/854-2415. 6 rms (shower only). No A/C. S $26-$39; D $34-$49; each addl $4; under 12 free; wkly rates. Pet accepted. TV; cable (premium). Complimentary coffee in rms. Restaurant opp 8 am-8 pm; closed Sat. Ck-out noon. Cr cds: A, C, D, DS, MC, V.

Taos (C-4)

(See Eagle Nest, Red River)

Founded 1615 **Pop** 4,065 **Elev** 6,950 ft **Area code** 505 **Zip** 87571
Information Taos County Chamber of Commerce, 1139 Paseo Del Pueblo Sur, PO Drawer I; 505/758-3873

On a high plateau flanked by mountains, low, flat-roofed houses hug the ground. D.H. Lawrence said, "I think the skyline of Taos the most beautiful of all I have ever seen in my travels around the world."

Other artists and writers agree with him, for many now live and work amid this stimulating mixture of three peoples and three cultures: American Indian, Spanish-American, Anglo-American. They like it for its clear air, magnificent surroundings and exciting and congenial atmosphere.

Taos is actually three towns: the Spanish-American settlement into which Anglos have infiltrated, which is Taos proper; Taos Pueblo, two and one-half miles north; and Ranchos de Taos, four miles south. Each is distinct, yet all are closely allied. In the surrounding mountains are many other towns, Spanish-American farming communities and fishing resorts.

As early as 1615, a handful of Spanish colonists settled in this area; in 1617, a church was built. After the Pueblo Rebellion of 1680, and the reconquest by De Vargas in 1692, the town was a farming center plagued by Apache raids and disagreements with the Taos Indians and the government of Santa Fe. The first artists came in 1880; since then, it has flourished as an art colony.

What to See and Do

Carson National Forest. 1½ million acres, includes Wheeler Peak, New Mexico's highest mountain, 13,161 feet, and the Valle Vidal, home to 2,000 Rocky Mountain elk. Fishing (good in the 425 mi of streams and numerous small mountain lakes). Hunting. Hiking. Winter sports. Picnicking. Camping (some fees). Ghost Ranch Living Museum has injured and orphaned native animals. (Daily) Contact Forest Supervisor, Cruz Alta Rd, PO Box 558; 505/758-6200.

D. H. Lawrence Ranch & Memorial. A 160-acre education, conference and recreational facility maintained by University of New Mexico. Memorial open to public (daily). 15 mi N on NM 522, then 5 mi E on dirt road (bad in inclement weather). Phone 505/776-2245. **Free.**

Ernest L. Blumenschein Home. Restored adobe house includes furnishings and exhibits of paintings by the Blumenschein family and other early Taos artists. Co-founder of Taos Society of Artists. (Daily) Combination tickets to other museums avail. 222 Ledoux St. Phone 505/758-0505. ¢¢

Fort Burgwin Research Center. Restored fort was occupied by 1st Dragoons of the US Calvary (1852-1860). Summer lecture series; music and theater performances. Operated by Southern Methodist University. (Schedule varies) 8 mi S on NM 518. Phone 505/758-8322. **Free.**

Governor Bent House Museum and Gallery. Home of New Mexico's first American territorial governor; scene of his death in 1847. Bent family possessions; Native American artifacts; western Americana art. (Daily; closed Jan 1, Thanksgiving, Dec 25) 117A Bent St, 1 blk N of plaza. Phone 505/758-2376. Gallery **free.** Museum **¢**

Harwood Foundation. Founded in 1923; features paintings, drawings, prints, sculptures and photographs by artists of Taos from 1800 to the present. (Mon-Fri afternoons, also Sat; closed hols) 238 Ledoux St. Phone 505/758-9826. **Free.**

Kit Carson Home and Museum (1825). Restored house with mementos of the famous scout; mountain man and trappers rooms; Indian artifacts, gun exhibit. (Daily) Combination tickets to other museums avail. Kit Carson Rd, on US 64, ½ blk E of plaza. Phone 505/758-0505. **¢¢** Nearby is

Kit Carson Park. A 20-acre plot with bicycle/walking path. Ice-skating. Picnic tables (grills), playground. No camping. Graves of Kit Carson and his family. (Daily) Phone 505/758-4160. **Free.**

The Martinez Hacienda. 708 Ranchitos Rd. Contains early Spanish-colonial hacienda with period furnishings; 21 rooms, two large patios. Early Taos, Spanish culture exhibits. Used as fortress during Indian raids. Living museum demonstrations. (Daily) Combination tickets to other museums avail. 2 mi W of plaza on NM 240. Phone 505/758-1000. **¢¢**

Millicent Rogers Museum. Native American and Hispanic arts and crafts. (Daily; closed major hols) Sr citizen rate. 4 mi N on NM 522. Phone 505/758-2462. **¢¢**

Skiing.

Taos Ski Valley. Area has 10 chairlifts, surface lift; patrol, school, rentals; cafeteria, restaurants, bar; nursery, lodges. Longest run more than 4 mi; vertical drop 2,612 ft. (Nov-Apr, daily) 18 mi NE via NM 522, 150. Phone 505/776-2233 or 800/776-1111 (exc NM) for reservations; 505/776-2916 (24-hr snow reports). **¢¢¢¢¢**

Sipapu Ski Area. Area has triple chairlift, 2 Pomalifts; patrol, school, rentals; accommodations, restaurant, lounge. Longest run more than 1 mi; vertical drop 865 ft. (Mid-Dec-Mar, daily) Cross-country skiing on forest roads and trails. 25 mi SE on NM 518, 3 mi W of Tres Ritos. Phone 505/587-2240. **¢¢¢¢**

Orilla Verde Recreation Area. Offers spectacular views. Park runs along banks of the Rio Grande, offering some of the finest trout fishing in the state; whitewater rafting through deep chasm N of park. Hiking. Picnicking. Standard fees. (Daily) 16 mi SW via NM 68. Phone 505/758-8851. Per vehicle **¢¢**

Ranchos de Taos (ca 1800). This adobe-housed farming and ranching center has one of the most beautiful churches in the Southwest, the San Francisco de Asis Church. Its huge buttresses and twin bell towers only suggest the beauty of its interior. (Mon-Sat, morning-mid-afternoon; inquire for schedule) Donation. 4 mi S on NM 68. Phone 505/758-2754.

Rio Grande Gorge Bridge. Bridge is 650 feet above the Rio Grande; observation platforms, picnic and parking areas. 11 mi NW on US 64.

Taos Pueblo (pop: 1,187). This is one of the most famous pueblos and is believed to be more than 1,000 years old. Within the pueblo is a double apartment house; the north and south buildings, separated by a river, are five stories tall and form a unique communal dwelling. Small buildings and corrals are scattered around these impressive Indian architectural masterpieces. The residents here live without modern utilities such as electricity and plumbing and get their drinking water from the river. The people are independent, conservative and devout in their own religious observances. Fees are charged for parking, photography permits. Photographs of individual Indians may be taken only with their consent. Do not enter any buildings that do not indicate a shop. Pueblo (daily; closed for special occasions in spring). 2½ mi N. For further information contact the Tourism Office, PO Box 1846; 505/758-9593. (See ANNUAL EVENTS) Per vehicle **¢¢**

Annual Events

Spring Arts Celebration. Three-week festival featuring visual, performing and literary arts. May.

Taos Rodeo. County Fairgrounds. Late June or earlyJuly.

Annual Pow-Wow. Taos Pueblo. Intertribal dancers from throughout US, Canada and Mexico participate; competition. Phone 505/758-7762. 2nd wkend in July.

Fiestas de Santiago y Santa Ana. Traditional festival honoring the patron saints of Taos. Candlelight procession, parade, crafts, food, entertainment. Late July.

San Geronimo Eve Sundown Dance. Taos Pueblo. Traditional men's dance followed next day by **San Geronimo Feast Day,** with intertribal dancing, trade fair, pole climb, footraces. Late Sept.

Taos Arts Festival. Arts and crafts exhibitions, music, plays, poetry readings. Late Sept-early Oct.

Yuletide in Taos. Ski area festivities, *farolito* (paper bag lantern) tours, food and craft fairs, art events, dance performances. Early-mid-Dec.

Taos Pueblo Deer or *Matachines* **Dance.** Symbolic animal dance or ancient Montezuma dance. Dec 25.

Taos Pueblo Dances. For a complete list of annual dances, contact the pueblo.

Seasonal Event

Chamber Music Festival. Taos Community Auditorium & Hotel St Bernard in Taos Ski Valley. Phone 505/776-2388. Mid-June-early Aug.

Motels

✔ ★ **EL PUEBLO LODGE & CONDOMINIUMS.** PO Box 92, 412 Paseo del Pueblo Norte. 505/758-8700; res: 800/433-9612; FAX 505/758-7321. 60 rms, 1-2 story, 16 kits. Mid-June-Oct, mid-Dec-early Apr: S $48; D $63; each addl $7; suites $105-$215; kit. units $73; wkly rates; ski plans; lower rates rest of yr. Crib free. TV; cable (premium). Heated pool; whirlpool. Complimentary continental bkfst. Ck-out 11:30 am. Downhill ski 17 mi; x-country ski 5 mi. Refrigerators. Some balconies. Cr cds: A, MC, V.

⊠ ≋ 🐾 SC

★ **HACIENDA INN.** Box 5758, 1321 Paseo del Pueblo Sur (NM 68). 505/758-8610; res: 800/858-8543; FAX 505/751-0807. 51 rms, 2 story. S $60; D $65; under 12 free; higher rates Christmas hols. TV; cable (premium), VCR avail (movies 99¢). Indoor pool; whirlpool. Complimentary coffee in lobby. Bar 5 pm-midnight. Ck-out 11 am. Business servs avail. Downhill ski 18 mi; x-country ski 5 mi. Balconies. Picnic tables. Cr cds: A, C, D, DS, MC, V.

D ⊠ ≋ 🐾

★ **QUALITY INN.** Box 2319, 1043 Camino del Pueblo Sur, NM 68. 505/758-2200; FAX 505/758-9009. 99 rms, 2 story. Mid-June-Oct: S, D $55-$109; each addl $7; suites $150; under 18 free; ski plans; higher rates Christmas hols; lower rates rest of yr. Crib free. TV; cable (premium), VCR avail. Heated pool; poolside serv. Restaurant 6:30 am-2 pm, 5-9 pm. Rm serv. Bar 11 am-11 pm. Ck-out 11 am. Meeting rms. Business servs avail. In-rm modem link. Valet serv. Downhill ski 20 mi; x-country ski 5 mi. Refrigerator, wet bar in suites. Picnic tables. Cr cds: A, C, D, DS, ER, JCB, MC, V.

D ✔ ⊠ ≋ ⊠ 🐾 SC

✔ ★ ★ **RANCHO RAMADA DE TAOS.** 615 Paseo del Pueblo Sur (NM 68), at Frontier Rd. 505/758-2900; res: 800/659-8267; FAX 505/758-1662. 124 rms, 2 story. Mid-June-Sept, mid-Dec-mid-Apr: S, D $69-$84; each addl $15; suites $189; under 18 free; rafting, ski plans. Crib free. TV; cable (premium). Indoor pool; whirlpool. Restaurant 6 am-1 pm, 5-9 pm. Rm serv. Bar 5-9 pm. Ck-out noon. Meeting rms.

Business servs avail. Valet serv. Downhill ski 17 mi. X-country ski 5 mi. Some fireplaces. Cr cds: A, C, D, DS, MC, V.

⊡ 🚶 ≋ ⊠ 🔥 SC

★ ★ **SAGEBRUSH INN.** *Box 557, 3 mi S of Plaza on Paseo del Pueblo Sur (NM 68).* 505/758-2254; res: 800/428-3626. 100 rms, 2 story. S $70-$95; D $70-$100; each addl $10; suites $100-$140; under 12 free. Crib $7. Pet accepted. TV; cable (premium). Pool; whirlpools. Complimentary full bkfst. Restaurant 6:30-11 am, 5:30-10 pm. Bar 3 pm-midnight; entertainment. Ck-out 11 am. Meeting rms. Business servs avail. Tennis. X-country ski 10 mi. Many fireplaces. Some refrigerators. Built in 1929 of adobe in pueblo-mission style; extensive art collection, antiques, Navajo rugs, Indian pottery. Cr cds: A, C, D, MC, V.

⊡ 🚶 ≋ 🎿 🏊 ≋ ⊠ 🔥 SC

★ ★ **SIERRA DEL SOL.** *(Box 84, Taos Ski Valley 87525) 5 mi N on US 64, then 15 mi E on Taos Ski Valley Rd (NM 150) to Taos Ski Valley.* 505/776-2981; res: 800/523-3954. 32 kit. units, 2 story. No A/C. Nov-Apr: D, studio rm $165; suites $220-$330; wkly rates; ski packages; higher rates Christmas hols; lower rates rest of yr. TV; cable (premium), VCR. Ck-out 11 am. Business servs avail. Downhill ski on site. Whirlpool, sauna. Fireplaces, dishwashers. Balconies. Cr cds: A, DS, MC, V.

🚶 ≋ ⊠ 🔥

Motor Hotel

★ ★ ★ **HOLIDAY INN DON FERNANDO DE TAOS.** *PO Drawer V, 1005 Paseo del Pueblo Sur (NM 68).* 505/758-4444; FAX 505/758-0055. 124 rms, 2 story. S, D $79-$135; under 19 free; wkly rates; ski plans; higher rates Christmas hols. Crib free. Pet accepted; $75 deposit. TV; cable, VCR avail. Pool; whirlpool, poolside serv. Restaurant 6:30 am-2 pm, 5-10 pm. Rm serv. Bar 3-11 pm; Fri, Sat to 1 am; Sun noon-11 pm. Ck-out 11 am. Meeting rm. Business servs avail. Free airport, RR station, bus depot transportation. Tennis. 18-hole golf privileges, greens fee $25, pro, putting green, driving range. Downhill ski 20 mi; x-country ski 5 mi. Health club privileges. Fireplace in suites. Pueblo-style building; central courtyard. Cr cds: A, C, D, DS, MC, V.

⊡ 🚶 ≋ 🎿 🏊 ≋ ⊠ 🔥 SC

Inns

★ ★ **AUSTING HAUS.** *(Box 8, Taos Ski Valley 87525) 5 mi N on US 64, then east 13 1/2 mi on Taos Ski Valley Rd (NM 150).* 505/776-2649; res: 800/748-2932; FAX 505/776-8751. 34 rms, 2 story. No A/C. Mid-Nov-mid-Apr: S $98; D $100; each addl $15; under 5 free; ski plans; wkday rates; lower rates mid-May-mid-Nov. Closed mid-Apr-mid-May. Pet accepted. TV; cable (premium). Complimentary continental bkfst. Dining rm 6-9 am, 6-9 pm. Ck-out 10 am, ck-in 2 pm. Lndry facilities. Business servs avail. In-rm modem link. Downhill ski 2 mi. 3 whirlpools. Game rm. Constructed of oak-pegged heavy timbers with beams exposed inside and out; built by hand, entirely without nails or metal plates. Cr cds: C, D, MC, V.

🚶 🚶 ≋ 🔥

★ ★ **BROOKS STREET.** *Box 4954 119 Brooks St.* 505/758-1489. 6 rms. No A/C. No rm phones. S $70-$95; D $75-$100; each addl $15; 3-night min stay Christmas hols. Adults perferred. Complimentary full bkfst, coffee. Ck-out 11 am, ck-in 4-6 pm. Free airport, bus depot transportation. Downhill ski 18 mi; x-country ski 5 mi. Rambling adobe house; stone fireplace in sitting rm; artwork. Patio. Totally nonsmoking. Cr cds: A, MC, V.

⊡ ≋ ⊠ 🔥

★ ★ ★ **CASA DE LAS CHIMENEAS.** *Box 5303, 405 Cordoba Ln.* 505/758-4777; FAX 505/758-3976. 3 rms, 1 suite. No A/C. S, D $108-$143; each addl $15; suite $143-$163. Crib $10. TV; cable (premium). Complimentary full bkfst. Coffee in rms. Restaurant nearby.

Ck-out 11 am, ck-in 3-6 pm. Downhill ski 18 mi; x-country ski 15 mi. Refrigerators. Rambling adobe house within walled garden with fountains. Library. Kiva fireplaces; hand-carved & antique furniture; regional art. Totally nonsmoking. Cr cds: MC, V.

≋ ⊠ 🔥

★ ★ ★ **CASA EUROPA.** *157 Upper Ranchitos Rd.* 505/758-9798. 7 rms, 2 story. No A/C. Some rm phones. S $65-$100; D $70-$135; each addl $20. Crib $5. TV in sitting rm; cable (premium). Complimentary full bkfst, coffee. Complimentary refreshments (seasonal). Ck-out 11 am, ck-in 3 pm. Free airport, bus depot transportation. Downhill/x-county ski 16 mi. Whirlpools, sauna. Picnic tables. Old adobe structure with courtyard. European antiques, artwork. Cr cds: MC, V.

≋ ⊠ 🔥

✔ ★ ★ **EL RINCON.** *114 E Kit Carson.* 505/758-4874. 16 rms, 3 story. No rm phones. S, D $59-$125; each addl $10. Crib $10. TV; VCR (movies avail). Complimentary continental bkfst. Complimentary coffee in rms. Restaurant nearby. Ck-out 11 am, ck-in 2-6 pm. Downhill ski 18 mi; x-country ski 5 mi. Many fireplaces. Picnic tables. Adobe building (1800); antiques, contemporary & Indian art; Indian-made fireplaces. Cr cds: A, DS, MC, V.

⊡ 🚶 ≋ 🔥

✔ ★ **MOUNTAIN LIGHT.** *PO Box 241, 10 mi N on NM 522; on Altalaya Rd in Arroyo Hondo.* 505/776-8474. 2 rms. No A/C. No rm phones. S $35-$48; D $52-$62; each addl $15; under 6 free; monthly rates; higher rates hols. TV in sitting rm. Complimentary full bkfst, coffee. Ck-out 11 am, ck-in 3 pm. Downhill ski 20 mi; x-country ski 10 mi. Rustic adobe; view of Sangre de Cristo Mountain Range. Fireplaces. Cr cds: MC, V.

≋ ⊠ 🔥 SC

★ ★ **THE RUBY SLIPPER.** *Box 2069, 416 La Lomita.* 505/758-0613. 7 rms. No A/C. No rm phones. S $64-$90; D $79-$104; wkly rates; ski plans; higher rates Christmas hols. Crib $5. Coffee, tea in rms. Complimentary full bkfst. Ck-out 11 am, ck-in 4-6 pm. Downhill ski 18 mi; x-country ski 5 mi. Whirlpool. Library; works by local artists; kiva fireplaces. Cr cds: A, DS, MC, V.

⊡ ≋ ⊠ 🔥

★ ★ **SALSA DEL SALTO BED & BREAKFAST.** *(PO Box 1468, El Prado 87529) 10 mi NE via NM 64; 1 mi N of Arroyo Seco on Taos Ski Valley Rd (NM 150).* 505/776-2422; res: 800/530-3097. 8 rms, 2 story. No A/C. No rm phones. S, D $85-$160. Children over 6 yrs only. TV in sitting rm. Heated pool; whirlpool. Complimentary full bkfst, coffee & tea. Restaurant nearby. Ck-out 11 am, ck-in 3-7 pm. Concierge. Tennis. Downhill/x-country ski 8 mi. Lawn games. Balconies. Picnic tables. Fireplace. Each rm with spectacular view of mountains or mesas. Totally nonsmoking. Cr cds: MC, V.

≋ 🎿 ≋ 🔥

★ ★ ★ **TAOS INN.** *125 Paseo del Pueblo Norte, in heart of historic district.* 505/758-2233; res: 800/826-7466; FAX 505/758-5776. 39 rms. Some A/C. S, D $75-$160. Crib free. TV; cable (premium), VCR avail (movies avail). Pool; whirlpool. Restaurant (see DOC MARTIN'S). Bar noon-11 pm; entertainment. Ck-out 11 am, ck-in 4 pm. Business servs avail. Downhill ski 17 mi; x-country ski 5 mi. Balconies. Inn consists of number of structures, some dating from 17th century, that were joined, in mid-1930s, to enclose patio, forming present lobby. Unique guest rms overlook old patio or open to tree-shaded courtyard. Pueblo fireplaces; antique Taos-style furniture; colorful hand-loomed Indian textiles; Mexican tile-work. "Meet-the-Artist" series, in spring & fall. Cr cds: D, MC, V.

⊡ ≋ ≋ ⊠ 🔥

★ ★ **TOUCHSTONE.** *110 Mabel Dodge Lane.* 505/758-0192; FAX 505/758-3498. 6 rms, 2 story. No A/C. S, D $75-$150; each addl $30. TV; cable, VCR (movies avail). Complimentary full bkfst; afternoon tea/sherry. Ck-out 11 am, ck-in 4 pm. Downhill ski 15 mi; x-country ski

10 mi. Adobe hacienda filled with original art; bkfst rm has splendid view of Taos Mt. Totally nonsmoking. Cr cds: MC, V.

Resort

★ ★ **QUAIL RIDGE INN.** *Box 707, 5 mi N on US 64, then 6 mi E on Taos Ski Valley Rd (NM 150).* 505/776-2211; res: 800/624-4448; FAX 505/776-2949. 110 condos, 65 kits. No A/C. S, D $60-$130; each addl $10; suites $170-$300; studio rms $110-$140; under 18 free; tennis plans; higher rates ski season. TV; cable (premium), VCR. Pool. Supervised child's activities (June-Labor Day); ages 5-15. Dining rm 7-10 am, 6-9 pm. Bar from 4 pm. Ck-out 11 am. Meeting rms. Business center. Lighted indoor tennis, pro. Soc dir. Exercise equipt; weights, bicycles, whirlpools, saunas. Fireplaces. Balconies. Cr cds: C, D, DS, JCB, MC, V.

Restaurants

★ ★ **APPLE TREE.** *123 Bent St.* 505/758-1900. Hrs: 11:30 am-3 pm, 5:30-9 pm; Sat, Sun brunch 11:30 am-3 pm. Res accepted. Wine, beer. Semi-a la carte: lunch $5.95-$7.95, dinner $7.95-$19.95. Sat, Sun brunch $5.95-$9.95. Specializes in fresh seafood, New Mexican dishes. Outdoor dining. Cr cds: A, MC, V.

D

★ ★ **BRETT HOUSE.** *US 64 at NM 150/522.* 505/776-8545. Hrs: 6-9 pm. Res accepted. Continental menu. Wine, beer. Semi-a la carte: dinner $11.50-$21.50. Child's meals. Specializes in fresh fish, rack of lamb. Parking. Adobe house built for artist Dorothy Brett on land given to her by Mrs D.H. Lawrence. Relaxing atmosphere, view of mountains. Totally nonsmoking. Cr cds: MC, V.

★ ★ ★ **CASA CORDOVA.** *(Ski Valley Rd, Arroyo Seco) 5 mi N on US 64, then 3 mi E on Taos Ski Valley Rd (NM 150).* 505/776-2500. Hrs: from 4:30 pm. Closed Sun; Jan 1, Dec 25. Res accepted. Continental menu. Bar from 4:30 pm. Wine list. Semi-a la carte: dinner $10.95-$20.25. Child's meals. Specialties: veal piccata, lamb, prawns à la maison, châteaubriand. Own baking. Pianist & guitarist wkends. Parking. Outdoor dining. Paintings by leading Taos artists. Fireplaces. Family-owned. Cr cds: A, MC, V.

D

★ ★ **CASA DE VALDEZ.** *1401 Paseo del Pueblo Sur (NM 68), at Estes Rd.* 505/758-8777. Hrs: 11:30 am-9:30 pm; Sun from 4 pm. Closed Wed; Thanksgiving, Dec 25; also 3 wks after Thanksgiving. Res accepted. Regional Southwestern menu. Serv bar. Semi-a la carte: lunch $5.95-$9.95, dinner $8.95-$18.95. Specializes in barbecue, steak. Patio. Parking. Cr cds: A, MC, V.

D

★ ★ ★ **DOC MARTIN'S.** *(See Taos Inn)* 505/758-1977. Hrs: 8 am-2:30 pm, 5:30-9:30 pm. Res accepted. No A/C. Southwestern menu. Extensive wine list. Semi-a la carte: bkfst $3-$7, lunch $5.50-$9, dinner $14-$19. Specializes in fresh seafood, pasta, green chili. Own baking. Parking. In colorful, historic structure; fireplaces. Cr cds: A, D, MC, V.

D

★ ★ **EL PATIO DE TAOS.** *121 Teresino Lane, near Plaza.* 505/758-2121. Hrs: 11:30 am-10 pm. Res accepted. Regional, Mexican menu. Bar. Semi-a la carte: lunch $3-$10, dinner $8-$16.95. Child's meals. Specialties: pork loin with mole, achiote salmon. Outdoor dining. Atrium with fountain; fireplace. Cr cds: DS, MC, V.

★ ★ **HOUSE OF TAOS.** *(1587 US 64, El Prado) N on US 64.* 505/758-3456. Hrs: 6-9:30 pm. Closed Sun & Mon; Jan 1, Easter, Dec 25; also 1 month/yr (varies). Res required. French menu. Wine, beer. Complete meals: dinner $20-$30. Own desserts. Parking. Outdoor

dining. Menu changes daily. Intimate dining in small adobe; fireplaces, view of mountains. Original artwork. Semi-formal dress. Cr cds: A, C, D, MC, V.

D

✔ ★ **MICHAEL'S KITCHEN & BAKERY.** *3 blks N of Plaza on N Pueblo Rd.* 505/758-4178. Hrs: 7 am-8:30 pm. Closed hols. Mexican, Amer menu. Semi-a la carte: bkfst $2.55-$7.45, lunch $2.85-$7.55, dinner $6.05-$9.75. Child's meals. Specialties: stuffed sopapillas, Indian tacos. Parking. Cr cds: DS, MC, V.

D

★ ★ **OGELVIE'S.** *103 Suite I, East Plaza.* 505/758-8866. Hrs: 11 am-10 pm. Bar. Semi-a la carte: lunch $4.95-$9.50, dinner $4.95-$18.50. Child's meals. Specializes in Angus beef, fresh seafood, New Mexican dishes. Outdoor dining. Eclectic Southwestern decor. Cr cds: A, MC, V.

D

★ ★ **STAKEOUT AT OUTLAW HILL.** *8 1/2 mi S on NM 68.* 505/758-2042. Hrs: 5-10 pm. Res accepted. No A/C. Bar from 4 pm. Semi-a la carte: dinner $9.95-$27.50. Child's meals. Specializes in steak, seafood, lamb. Entertainment. Parking. Outdoor dining. Adobe pueblo-style building. Cr cds: A, C, D, DS, MC, V.

D

★ ★ ★ **VILLA FONTANA.** *5 mi N on NM 522.* 505/758-5800. Hrs: 11:30 am-2 pm (June-Oct, Tues-Fri); 5:30 pm-closing. Closed Sun; also Sun-Wed mid-Apr-mid-May & mid-Nov-mid-Dec. Res accepted. Bar. Northern Italian menu. A la carte entrees: lunch $6.50-$10.50, dinner $19.50-$25. Specializes in wild mushrooms (seasonal), veal, fresh fish. Outdoor dining. Cr cds: A, C, D, MC, V.

Truth or Consequences (G-2)

Pop 6,221 **Elev** 4,240 ft **Area code** 505 **Zip** 87901

Information Truth or Consequences/Sierra County Chamber of Commerce, 201 S Foch St, PO Drawer 31; 505/894-3536.

Formerly called Hot Springs, for the warm mineral springs, the town changed its name in 1950 to celebrate the tenth anniversary of Ralph Edwards' radio program, "Truth or Consequences."

In the early 1500s, the Spanish Conquistadores came through this area, and legends of lost Spanish gold mines and treasures in the Caballo Mountains persist today. There are numerous ghost towns and old mining camps in the area. A Ranger District office of the Gila National Forest (see SILVER CITY) is located here.

What to See and Do

Caballo Lake State Park. Caballo Mts form a backdrop for this lake. Swimming, windsurfing, waterskiing; fishing (bass, crappie, pike, trout, catfish); boating (ramp, marina). Hiking, Picnicking, playground, concession. Camping (hookups). Standard fees. (Daily) 18 mi S on I-25. Phone 505/743-3942. Per vehicle ¢¢

Canoeing, boating and tubing on the Rio Grande, which flows through the city.

Elephant Butte Lake State Park. This 40-mile long lake was created in 1916 for flood control; later adapted to hydroelectric power and irrigation. Swimming, windsurfing, waterskiing; fishing (bass, crappie, pike, catfish); boating (ramp, rentals, slips, mooring, 3 marinas). Hiking. Picnicking, playground, concession, restaurant, lodge. Camping (hookups), cabins. (Daily) Standard fees. 5 mi N via I-25. Phone 505/744-5421. Per vehicle ¢¢

Geronimo Springs Museum. Exhibits of Mimbres Indian Pottery, fossils and photographs and articles on local history. Ralph Edwards Room, Apache Room, Hispanic Room and log cabin. Gift shop. (Daily exc Sun; closed some major hols) 211 Main St. Phone 505/894-6600. ¢

Motels

✔★ **ACE LODGE.** *1302 N Date St (I-25 Business).* *505/894-2151.* 38 rms. S $29-$32; D $34-$40; each addl $2; suites $50-$60; wkly rates. Crib $2. Pet accepted, some restrictions. TV; cable. Heated pool. Playground. Restaurant 6 am-9 pm. Bar 5 pm-2 am. Ck-out 11 am. Free airport transportation. Golf privileges. Picnic tables. Cr cds: A, C, D, MC, V.

[icons] SC

★★ **BEST WESTERN HOT SPRINGS INN.** *PO Box 2080, 2270 N Date St (I-25 Business), exit 79.* *505/894-6665; FAX 505/894-6665.* 40 rms. S $45; D $50; each addl $7; under 12 free (2 max). Crib free. TV; cable (premium). Heated pool. Complimentary coffee in lobby. Restaurant adj 7 am-8 pm. Ck-out noon. Business servs avail. Cr cds: A, C, D, DS, MC, V.

[D] [icons] SC

Restaurant

★★ **LOS ARCOS STEAK HOUSE.** *1400 N Date St (I-25 Business).* *505/894-6200.* Hrs: 5-10:30 pm; Fri, Sat to 11 pm. Closed Thanksgiving, Dec 25. Res accepted. Bar to 2 am. Semi-a la carte: dinner $5.95-$38.95. Specializes in steak, lobster tail. Salad bar. Open grill. Parking. Mexican decor. Cr cds: A, C, D, DS, MC, V.

[D]

Tucumcari (D-6)

Settled 1901 **Pop** 6,831 **Elev** 4,096 ft **Area code** 505 **Zip** 88401

Information Tucumcari/Quay County Chamber of Commerce, PO Drawer E; 505/461-1694.

A convenient stopping point between Amarillo, Texas and Albuquerque, this is a trading center for a 45,000-acre irrigated and industrial water area. New energy is focused on carbon-dioxide, petroleum and natural gas. There is also a thriving cattle business. Tucumcari has become a transportation center with many trucking companies and much railroad traffic. Tucumcari Mt (4,957 ft) is to the south. Born when the railroad reached its site, Tucumcari was once known as "six-shooter siding."

What to See and Do

Conchas Lake State Park. Lake is 25 miles long. Swimming, waterskiing; fishing; boating. Picnicking. Camping (hookups, dump station), cabins. Standard fees. (Daily) 33 mi NW via NM 104, 433. Phone 505/868-2270. Per vehicle ¢¢

Tucumcari Historical Museum. Western Americana; Indian artifacts; gems, minerals, rocks, fossils; restored fire truck and caboose. (Early June-early Sept, daily; rest of yr, daily exc Mon; closed hols) 416 S Adams St. Phone 505/461-4201. ¢¢

Ute Lake State Park. Created by a dam on the Canadian River. Swimming, waterskiing; fishing (bass, crappie, channel catfish); boating (marina, ramp, slips, mooring). Hiking trails. Picnicking, playground. Camping (hookups, dump station). Standard fees. (Daily) 22 mi NE on US 54, NM 540. Phone 505/487-2284. Per vehicle ¢¢

Annual Event

Piñata Festival. Parade, dances, pageant, other events; food booths. Last full wk June.

Motels

★★★ **BEST WESTERN DISCOVERY INN.** *200 E Estrella.* *505/461-4884; FAX 505/461-2463.* 107 units, 2 story. May-mid Sept: S $42-$48; D $54-$58; each addl $4; suites $60; under 12 free; lower rates rest of yr. Crib free. TV; VCR avail (movies avail $3.49). Pool; whirlpool. Restaurant 6 am-10 pm. Ck-out 11 am. Coin lndry. Meeting rms. Business servs avail. In-rm modem link. Sundries. Airport transportation. Exercise equpt: stair machine, bicycle, weights. Some refrigerators. Some balconies. Cr cds: A, C, D, DS, MC, V.

[D] [icons] SC

✔★ **BUDGET HOST ROYAL PALACIO.** *1620 E Tucumcari Blvd (I-40 Business).* *505/461-1212.* 23 rms. S $27; D $35; each addl $3. Pet accepted. TV; cable. Restaurant nearby. Ck-out 11 am. Coin lndry. Sundries. Picnic tables. Cr cds: A, C, D, DS, MC, V.

[icons] SC

✔★ **ECONO LODGE.** *3400 E Tucumcari Blvd, I-40 exit 335.* *505/461-4194; FAX 505/461-4911.* 41 rms, 2 story. S $22.95; D $29.95-$43.95; each addl $7; under 17 free. Crib free. TV; cable. Complimentary coffee in lobby. Restaurant nearby. Ck-out 11 am. Cr cds: A, C, D, DS, MC, V.

[D] [icons] SC

★★ **HOLIDAY INN.** *Box 808, E I-40 at exit 335.* *505/461-3780; FAX 505/461-3931.* 100 rms, 2 story. S $55-$65; D $63-$73; each addl $8; under 18 free. Crib free. Pet accepted. TV; cable. Heated pool. Playground. Restaurant 6 am-10 pm. Rm serv. Bar 5 pm-2 am. Ck-out noon. Coin lndry. Meeting rms. Sundries. Cr cds: A, C, D, DS, ER, JCB, MC, V.

[D] [icons] SC

★ **SUPER 8.** *PO Box 1223, 4001 E Tucumcari Blvd, I-40 exit 335.* *505/461-4444; FAX 505/461-4320.* 63 rms, 2 story, 13 suites. S $32.88-$42.88; D $38.88-$46.88; each addl $2; suites $39.88-$49.88; under 12 free. TV; cable. Continental bkfst. Indoor pool. Restaurant nearby. Ck-out 11 am. Coin lndry. Cr cds: A, C, D, DS, MC, V.

[D] [icons] SC

White Sands National Monument (G-3)

(For accommodations see Alamogordo)

(15 mi SW of Alamogordo on US 70/82)

These shifting, dazzling white dunes are a challenge to plants and animals. Here, lizards and mice are white like the sand, helping them to blend in with the background. (Similarly, mice are reddish in the red sand country nearby, and black in the black lava area only a few miles north.)

Plants elongate their stems up to 30 feet so that they can keep their leaves and flowers above the sand. When the sands recede, the plants are sometimes left on elevated pillars of hardened gypsum bound together by their roots. Even an ancient two-wheeled Spanish cart, now on display in the visitor center, was laid bare when the sands shifted.

Beach sand is usually silica, but White Sands National Monument sand is gypsum, from which plaster of Paris is made. Dunes often rise to 60 feet; it is the largest gypsum dune field in the world.

White Sands National Monument encloses 143,732 acres of this remarkable area. The visitor center has a sound and light program, exhibits concerning the dunes and how they were formed and other related material (daily exc Dec 25). Evening programs and guided nature walks in the dunes area are conducted (Memorial Day-Labor Day). There is a 16-mile round-trip drive from the center; free printed guide leaflet. Picnic area with shaded tables and grills. Primitive back country campsite (by permit only). Dunes Drive (daily exc Dec 25). Per car ¢¢

For further information contact the Superintendent, PO Box 1086, Holloman AFB, NM 88330-1086; 505/479-6124.

Zuni Pueblo (D-1)

(For accommodations see Gallup)

Pop 5,857 **Elev** 6,283 ft **Area code** 505 **Zip** 87327

Thirty-nine miles south of Gallup, via NM 602 and W on NM 53, is one of Coronado's "Seven Cities of Cibola." Fray Marcos de Niza reported that these cities were built of gold. When looking down on the Zuni pueblo from a distant hilltop at sunset, it does seem to have a golden glow. Marcos' story was partly responsible for Coronado's expedition of the area in 1540, which found no riches for Spain.

Zuni is linguistically unique and distinct from the other Rio Grande pueblos. The people here make beautiful jewelry and fine pottery. They also have a furniture and woodworks center with colorful and uniquely painted and carved items. The pueblo, built mainly of stone, is one-story high for the most part. The old Zuni mission church has been restored and its interior painted with murals of Zuni traditional figures. A tribal permit is required for photography; certain rules must be observed.

The famous Shalako Dance, usually in late November or early December, is one of the best known and most spectacular Native American ceremonies. Attendance is frequently restricted at Shalako.

Picnicking and camping at Eustace, Ojo Caliente, Pescado, Nutria #2 and Nutria #4 lakes. Lakes stocked by Tribal Fish & Wildlife Service; a tribal permit as well as a state fishing license is required. For further information contact the Pueblo of Zuni, PO Box 339; 505/782-4481.

Oklahoma

Population: 3,145,585

Land area: 68,656 square miles

Elevation: 287-4,973 feet

Highest point: Black Mesa (Cimarron County)

Entered Union: November 16, 1907 (46th state)

Capital: Oklahoma City

Motto: Labor conquers all

Nickname: Sooner State

State flower: Mistletoe

State bird: Scissortailed flycatcher

State tree: Redbud

State fair: 17 days late September, 1996, in Oklahoma City

Time zone: Central

Populated by Native Americans, the area that was to become the state of Oklahoma was practically unknown to Americans at the time of the Louisiana Purchase of 1803. Believing these unsettled lands to be of little value, the government set them aside as "Indian Territory" in 1830, assigning a portion to each of the Five Civilized Tribes. Between 1830 and 1846, 20,000 Creeks of Georgia and Alabama, 5,000 Choctaws of Mississippi and Louisiana, 4,000 Chickasaws of Mississippi and 3,000 Seminoles of Florida were forced to move to Oklahoma. In 1838 some 16,000 Cherokees were marched west from their lands in North Carolina, Tennessee and Georgia by troops under the command of General Winfield Scott. Many hid out in the hills and swamps of their homeland, where their descendants still remain. About one-fourth of those forced west over this "Trail of Tears" died en route of hunger, disease, cold and exhaustion. But those who reached Indian Territory were soon running their own affairs with skill and determination. By 1890, 67 different tribal groups resided in Oklahoma. Today, Oklahoma has the largest Native American population of the United States.

As the nation moved west, settlers squatted in Indian Territory, wanting the land for their own. On April 22, 1889, portions of the land were opened for settlement. In the next few years, all unassigned Oklahoma land was opened by a series of six "runs." People who jumped the gun were called "Sooners," hence Oklahoma's nickname, the "Sooner State." Close to 17 million acres of land in the state were settled in this way; the last "lottery," a form of run, took place on August 16, 1901. Previously unsettled tracts became cities in eight hours.

Oklahoma produces many millions of barrels of oil a year and great quantities of natural gas. It is a leader in coal production and produces gypsum limestone, tripoli, granite and other minerals. The state's three largest industries are agriculture, tourism and petroleum. The McClellan-Kerr Arkansas River Navigation System has given Oklahoma a direct water route to the Mississippi River and to the Gulf of Mexico. The ports of Muskogee on the Arkansas River and Catoosa on the Verdigris River connect Oklahoma to the inland waterway system and to major US markets.

Oklahoma is developing its recreational resources at a rapid rate. Every year millions of tourists and vacationers visit the growing number of lakes, built mostly for electric power, and the state park system, one of the best in the country.

National Park Service Areas & Lakes

Oklahoma has Chickasaw National Recreation Area (see SULPHUR), as well as Fort Smith National Historic Site (see FORT SMITH, AR). Of the state's more than 10 million acres of forest lands, almost 6 million acres are protected by the State Division of Forestry.

The state has more than 200 lakes, of which 40 are large enough to provide first-class lake fishing, and 60 cover more than 1,000 acres each; more are under construction. These, with Oklahoma's 55 state parks, have made tourism Oklahoma's second largest industry, preceded only by its oil industry. The state's year-round vacation and recreation facilities are excellent.

National Forest

Ouachita National Forest (see HOT SPRINGS & HOT SPRINGS NATIONAL PARK, AR): Forest Supervisor in Hot Springs, AR; Ranger offices in Booneville, AR*, Danville, AR*, Glenwood, AR*, Heavener*, Hot Springs, AR, Idabel, Mena, AR, Mount Ida, AR*, Oden, AR*, Perryville, AR*, Talihina*, Waldron, AR*.

*Not described in text

State Recreation Areas

The following towns list state recreation areas in their vicinity under What to See and Do; refer to the individual town for directions and park information.

Listed under **Alva:** see Alabaster Caverns, Great Salt Plains and Little Sahara state parks.

Listed under **Anadarko:** see Fort Cobb State Park.

Listed under **Atoka:** see Boggy Depot State Park.

Listed under **Boise City:** see Black Mesa State Park.

Listed under **Broken Bow:** see Beavers Bend Resort and Hochatown state parks.

Listed under **Clinton:** see Foss State Park.

Listed under **Eufaula:** see Arrowhead and Fountainhead state parks.

Listed under **Hugo:** see Raymond Gary State Park.

Listed under **Lake Murray State Park:** see Lake Murray State Park.

Listed under **Lake Texoma:** see Lake Texoma State Park.

Listed under **McAlester:** see Robber's Cave State Park.

Listed under **Muskogee:** see Greenleaf Lake State Park.

Listed under **Norman:** see Little River State Park.

Listed under **Okmulgee:** see Okmulgee State Park.

Listed under **Pawhuska:** see Osage Hills State Park.

Listed under **Poteau:** see Lake Wister State Park.

Listed under **Quartz Mountain State Park:** see Quartz Mountain State Park.

Listed under **Roman Nose State Park:** see Roman Nose State Park.

Listed under **Sallisaw:** see Sallisaw State Recreation Area.

Listed under **Sequoyah State Park:** see Sequoyah State Park.

Listed under **Tenkiller Ferry Lake:** see Tenkiller State Park.

Listed under **Tulsa:** see Feyodi Creek, Keystone and Walnut Creek state parks.

Listed under **Weatherford:** see Red Rock Canyon State Park.

Listed under **Woodward:** see Boiling Springs State Park.

Water-related activities, hiking, riding, various other sports, picnicking and visitor centers, as well as camping, are available in many of these areas. Many of the state parks have lodges and cabins as well as campsites and trailer parks. Camping fee ($12-$15) required for assigned campgrounds and trailer hookups; tent camping ($6); camping fee ($10-$13) in unassigned areas. For state park reservations, phone the park directly. Pets on leash only. For further information contact the Division of State Parks, 2401 N Lincoln, Suite 500, Oklahoma City 73105-4492; 405/521-3411.

For further information write Oklahoma Tourism & Recreation Dept, Literature Distribution Center, PO Box 60789, Oklahoma City 73146.

Fishing & Hunting

Nonresident fishing license: 5-day, $10; 14-day, $20; annual, $28.50; nonresident hunting license: small game, 5-day, $35 (except pheasant, turkey or deer), annual, $85; deer, $201; elk, $251 (by drawing only). Trout fishing license: $7.75.

Many species of fish are found statewide: largemouth bass, white bass, catfish, crappie and bluegill. Rainbow trout can be found throughout the year in the Illinois River, Mountain Fork River and Broken Bow Lake; during the winter at Lake Watonga, Blue River, Lake Carl Etling and below Altus-Lugert dam; striped bass in Lake Keystone, Lake Texoma and the Arkansas River Navigation System; and small-mouth bass in several eastern streams as well as in Broken Bow, Murray and Texoma lakes.

For information about fishing and hunting regulations and changes in fees, write Oklahoma Department of Wildlife Conservation, 1801 N Lincoln Blvd, Oklahoma City 73105. For boating regulations contact Lake Patrol Division, Dept of Public Safety, 3600 N Martin Luther King Ave, Oklahoma City 73136; 405/425-2143.

Safety Belt Information

Safety belts are mandatory for all persons in front seat of vehicle. Children under 6 years must be in an approved passenger restraint anywhere in vehicle: ages 4 and 5 may use a regulation safety belt; age 3 and under may use a regulation safety belt in back seat, however, in front seat children must use an approved safety seat. For further information phone 405/521-3314.

Interstate Highway System

The following alphabetical listing of Oklahoma towns in *Mobil Travel Guide* shows that these cities are within 10 miles of the indicated Interstate highways. A highway map should, however, be checked for the nearest exit.

INTERSTATE 35: Ardmore, Guthrie, Marietta, Norman, Oklahoma City, Pauls Valley, Perry

INTERSTATE 40: Clinton, Elk City, El Reno, Henryetta, Oklahoma City, Sallisaw, Shawnee, Weatherford

INTERSTATE 44: Chickasaw, Lawton, Miami, Oklahoma City, Tulsa

Additional Visitor Information

Free information on the state may be obtained from the Oklahoma Tourism & Recreation Department, Literature Distribution Center, PO Box 60789, Oklahoma City 73146; 405/521-3831 or 800/652-6552. Also available from the Tourism Dept, *Oklahoma Today* magazine, published bi-monthly. The Department of Wildlife Conservation produces a monthly publication, *Outdoor Oklahoma*.

There are 10 traveler information centers in Oklahoma; visitors who stop will find information and brochures most helpful in planning stops at points of interest. Their locations are as follows: from the north, 10 mi S of OK-KS border on I-35; from the east, 14 mi W of OK-AR border on I-40; from the south, 2 mi N of OK-TX border on US 69/75, or 4 mi N of OK-TX border on I-35; from the southwest, on I-44 at the Walters exit; from the west, 9 mi E of OK-TX border on I-40. (Daily, summer, 7 am-7 pm; winter, 8:30 am-5 pm) Also: from the northeast, on Will Rogers Tpke E of Miami, Catoosa-Intersection of Will Rogers Tpke & US 66; at intersection of I-35 and NE 50th in Oklahoma City; and, at the State Capitol Building, NE 23rd & Lincoln Blvd; all centers are closed Dec 25.

Ada (D-8)

(See Pauls Valley, Sulphur)

Founded 1890 **Pop** 15,820 **Elev** 1,010 ft **Area code** 405 **Zip** 74820

Information Chamber of Commerce, 300 W Main, PO Box 248, 74821; 405/332-2506.

Ada is one of the principal cities of southeastern Oklahoma. Important manufactured products here are automotive parts, farm implements, furniture, feed, denim clothing and biomedical supplies. South of the city are fine silica sand and limestone quarries that provide the raw material for cement. Cattle operations are still important, and oil is produced throughout the county.

What to See and Do

East Central University (1909). (4,000 students) At the entrance to the campus is the fossilized stump of a rare giant Callixylon tree of the Devonian Age. Main St & Francis Ave. For campus tours phone 405/332-8000.

Wintersmith Park. Park covering approx 140 acres has arboretum, restored 1-room schoolhouse (1907), small zoo, carousel, 1/2-mi miniature train ride, concerts. Swimming pool; stocked fishing lake. Miniature golf. Picnic area. Fee for some activities. (Daily) 18th St at Scenic Dr. Phone 405/436-6300. **Free.**

Annual Event

Western Heritage Week. 5 days of celebration. 1st full wk Aug.

Motor Hotel

★ **BEST WESTERN-RAINTREE.** *1100 N Mississippi.* 405/332-6262; FAX 405/436-4929. 40 rms, 2 story. S $44-$48; D $48-$50; each addl $4; suites $50; under 12 free. Crib $4. TV; cable. Indoor pool. Restaurant 6 am-9 pm; closed Mon; Sun to 2:30 pm. Rm serv. Ck-out noon. Meeting rms. Bathrm phones. Cr cds: A, C, D, DS, MC, V.

Altus (D-5)

Founded 1891 **Pop** 21,910 **Elev** 1,398 ft **Area code** 405 **Zip** 73521
Information Chamber of Commerce, 100 N Main, PO Box 518; 405/482-0210.

In the spring of 1891 a flood on Bitter Creek forced a group of settlers to flee to higher ground, taking with them what possessions they could. Gathered together to escape destruction, they founded a town and called it Altus because one of them said the word meant "high ground."

On the border between the high plains and the southland, Altus lies between winter wheat on the north and cotton on the south. The Lugert-Altus irrigation district, using water from Lake Altus on the North Fork of the Red River, feeds 70,000 acres of prosperous farmland growing cotton, wheat, alfalfa seed and cattle. Nearby Altus Air Force Base is the home of the Air Mobility Command, 97th Air Mobility Wing, the training unit for the C-5.

What to See and Do

Museum of the Western Prairie. Changing exhibits depict all aspects of pioneer living in southwestern Oklahoma. Also, building featuring displays of early farm implements, coaches, wagons; original reconstructed half-dugout house. Reference library. (Daily exc Mon; closed some major hols) 1100 N Hightower St. Phone 405/482-1044. **Free.**

Quartz Mountain State Park (see). 18 mi N via US 283, OK 44, 44A.

Annual Events

Jackson County Fair. Livestock, carnival, games, food. Late Aug.

Great Plains Stampede Rodeo. PRCA-sanctioned rodeo; special events. Mid-Sept.

Motels

★ ★ **BEST WESTERN.** *2804 N Main.* 405/482-9300; FAX 405/482-2245. 100 rms, 2 story. S, D $44-$58; each addl $6; under 12 free. Crib free. TV; cable (premium). Indoor/outdoor pool; sauna. Complimentary continental bkfst. Ck-out noon. Coin lndry. Meeting rms.

Business servs avail. In-rm modem link. Some bathrm phones, refrigerators. Cr cds: A, C, D, DS, JCB, MC, V.

✔ ★ **DAYS INN.** *3202 N Main.* 405/477-2300. 36 rms, 2 story. S $27-$33; D $35-$40; each addl $5; under 18 free. Crib free. TV; cable (premium). Complimentary continental bkfst. Ck-out 11 am. Cr cds: A, C, D, DS, ER, MC, V.

★ **RAMADA INN.** *2515 E Broadway.* 405/477-3000; FAX 405/477-0078. 121 units, 12 suites, 2 story. S $47-$53; D $53-$59; each addl $6; suites $86-$102. Crib free. Pet accepted. TV; cable. Indoor pool. Restaurant 6:30 am-10 pm. Rm serv. Bar 5 pm-2 am; dancing. Ck-out noon. Meeting rms. Valet serv. Balconies. Cr cds: A, C, D, DS, MC, V.

Unrated Dining Spot

FURRS CAFETERIA. *1400 N Main (US 283), in Bunker Hill Shopping Ctr.* 405/482-5823. Hrs: 11 am-2 pm, 4:30-8 pm; Sat, Sun 11 am-8 pm. Closed Dec 24 from 4 pm, Dec 25. Avg ck: lunch, dinner $5.25. Specialties: chicken-fried steak, roast beef, baked fish. Cr cds: A, DS, MC, V.

Alva (A-6)

Pop 5,495 **Elev** 1,350 ft **Area code** 405 **Zip** 73717
Information Chamber of Commerce, 410 College; 405/327-1647.

What to See and Do

Cherokee Strip Museum. Historical display of Cherokee Strip; Lincoln pictures; collection of flags, soldiers' uniforms; antiques, dolls, toys, furniture; general store, kitchen; miniature trains; authentic covered wagon; adj annex houses small farm machinery. Old schoolhouse. (Summer hrs vary; rest of yr, Sat-Sun afternoons; closed major hols) 901 14th St. Phone 405/327-2030. **Free.**

State Parks.

Alabaster Caverns. On approximately 200 acres, Alabaster is said to be largest known natural gypsum cavern in world; tours (daily); Cedar Canyon. Swimming, bathhouse. Picnicking, playground. Camping area, trailer sites. (Daily) 25 mi W on US 64, then 7 mi S via OK 50, 50A. Phone 405/621-3381. Cavern tours ¢¢

Great Salt Plains. Approx 840 acres with 9,300-acre lake. Swimming, waterskiing; fishing; boating (ramps). Nature trails. Picnic area, playground. Camping areas, trailer hookups (fee), cabins. (Daily) 16 mi E on US 64, then 11 mi E on OK 11, then S on OK 38. Phone 405/626-4731.

Little Sahara. Approx 1600 acres. Sand dunes. Picnicking, playground. Trailer hookups (fee). (Daily) 28 mi S & W on US 281. Phone 405/824-1471.

Motels

✔ ★ **HOLIDAY.** *701 E Oklahoma Blvd (US 64), at jct US 281.* 405/327-3333. 32 rms. S $25-$28; D $30-$39; each addl $3. Crib free. TV; cable (premium). Pool. Complimentary coffee in lobby. Restaurant nearby. Ck-out 11 am. Business servs avail. Refrigerators avail. Cr cds: A, DS, MC, V.

★ **RANGER INN.** *420 E Oklahoma Blvd (US 64). 405/327-1981; FAX 405/327-1981, ext. -142.* 41 rms. S $30-$32; D $36; up to 2 addl free; under 16 free. Pet accepted, some restrictions. TV; cable (premium), VCR avail (movies avail $1). Complimentary coffee. Restaurant adj 6 am-10 pm. Ck-out 11 am. Cr cds: A, C, D, DS, MC, V.

[D] [icons]

✔ ★ **WESTERN MOTEL.** *608 E Oklahoma Blvd (US 64), at jct US 281. 405/327-1363; FAX 405/327-1364.* 21 rms. S $28-$30; D $34; each addl $3; under 12 free. Crib $4. TV; cable (premium). Pool. Complimentary coffee in rms. Restaurant nearby. Ck-out 11 am. Business servs avail. In-rm modem link. Free airport transportation. Refrigerators avail. Picnic tables. Cr cds: A, C, D, DS, MC, V.

[icons] [SC]

Anadarko (C-6)

(For accommodations see Chickasha)

Founded 1901 **Pop** 6,586 **Elev** 1,183 ft **Area code** 405 **Zip** 73005
Information Chamber of Commerce, 516 W Kentucky, PO Box 366; 405/247-6651.

Anadarko first came into being in 1859 as the Wichita Indian Agency after eastern tribes were relocated here. The Bureau of Indian Affairs area office is located here.

What to See and Do

Anadarko Philomathic Museum. Railroad memorabilia displayed in old ticket office; American Indian doll collection; paintings, costumes and artifacts; military equipment and uniforms; excellent photographic collection; early physician's office; country store. (Daily exc Mon; closed hols) 311 E Main St, in Rock Island Depot. Phone 405/247-3240. **Free.**

Fort Cobb State Park. A 2,850-acre park; 4,100-acre lake. Swimming, waterskiing; fishing, hunting; boating (ramps, marina). 18-hole golf. Picnic facilities. Camping, trailer hookups (fee). (Daily) 8 mi W on US 62, then 12 mi NW off OK 9. Phone 405/643-2249. **Free.**

Indian City—USA. Authentic reconstruction of seven Plains tribes' villages (Pawnee, Wichita, Caddo, Kiowa, Navajo, Pueblo and Apache) with Native American guides (45-min tours) and actual dance ceremonies (summer, daily; winter, wkends). Petting zoo. Arts and crafts shop. Swimming. Concession. Camping. (Daily; closed Jan 1, Thanksgiving, Dec 25) (See ANNUAL EVENTS) 2½ mi SE on OK 8. Phone 405/247-5661. **¢¢¢**

National Hall of Fame for Famous American Indians. Outdoor museum with sculptured bronze busts of famous Native Americans (daily). Visitor center (daily; closed Thanksgiving, Dec 25). E on US 62E. Phone 405/247-5555. **Free.**

Southern Plains Indian Museum and Crafts Center. Exhibits of historic and contemporary Native American arts from the southern plains region. (June-Sept, daily; rest of yr, daily exc Mon; closed Jan 1, Thanksgiving, Dec 25) E on US 62 E. Phone 405/247-6221. **Free.**

Annual Events

Kiowa Veterans Blackleggins Ceremonial. Indian City. Mid-May & Mid-Oct.

American Indian Exposition. Held at Caddo County Fairground. Parade, dances, horse races, arts & crafts. Mid-Aug.

Wichita-Caddo-Delaware Ceremonial. Wichita Park. Late Aug.

Caddo County Free Fair. Early Sept.

Ardmore (D-7)

(See Marietta, Sulphur)

Founded 1887 **Pop** 23,079 **Elev** 881 ft **Area code** 405 **Zip** 73401
Information Chamber of Commerce, 410 W Main, PO Box 1585; 405/223-7765.

This is an oil and cattle town and a good center for recreation. The Arbuckle Mountains are a few miles north of town.

What to See and Do

Charles B. Goddard Center. Contemporary Western graphics, painting and sculpture. National touring exhibits. Community theater, dance, concerts. (Mon-Fri, also wkend afternoons; closed major hols) First Ave & D Street SW. Phone 405/226-0909.

Eliza Cruce Hall Doll Museum. Collection of more than 300 antique dolls, some dating to 1728; display includes porcelain, bisque, leather, wood, wax dolls. (Daily exc Sun; closed hols) 320 E Street NW, in public library. Phone 405/223-8290. **Free.**

Greater Southwest Historical Museum. "Living" history exhibits; oil and agricultural machinery; military memorabilia; re-creation of a pioneer community. (Wed-Sat, Sun afternoon) Donation. 35 Sunset Dr. Phone 405/226-3857.

Lake Murray State Park. 7 mi SE, off I-35 exit 24 or 29.

Annual Events

Shrine Rodeo. Hardy Murphy Coliseum. PRCA sanctioned. Phone 405/226-1422. Early Apr.

Carter County Free Fair. Hardy Murphy Coliseum. Various festivities. Phone 405/223-5934. Early Sept.

CRRA Cowboy Regional Rodeo Finals. Hardy Murphy Coliseum. Phone 405/223-7765. 3rd wk Oct.

Motels

✔ ★ **GUEST INN.** *2519 W OK 142. 405/223-1234; res: 800/460-4064.* 126 rms, 2 story. S $28.80-$33; D $33-$38; suites $42-$65; each addl $5; under 12 free; wkly rates. Crib $2. Pet accepted, some restrictions. TV; cable, VCR avail (movies avail $5.99). Pool. Complimentary coffee in lobby. Restaurant adj 6 am-9 pm. Ck-out 1 pm. Coin lndry. Business servs avail. Valet serv. Airport transportation. Cr cds: A, C, D, DS, MC, V.

[D] [icons] [SC]

★ ★ **HOLIDAY INN.** *2705 Holiday Dr, at jct I-35 & US 70. 405/223-7130; FAX 405/223-7130, ext. 390.* 171 rms, 2 story. S $48-$60; D $54-$60; each addl $6; suites $95. Crib free. Pet accepted. TV; cable. Pool; wading pool. Playground. Complimentary continental bkfst. Ck-out noon. Coin lndry. Valet serv. Sundries. Cr cds: A, C, D, DS, JCB, MC, V.

[D] [icons] [SC]

Restaurants

✔ ★ **BILL AND BARB'S.** *1225 N Washington. 405/223-1976.* Hrs: 6 am-9 pm; Sun to 3 pm. Closed Mon; July 4, Thanksgiving, Dec 25-Jan 1. Res accepted Sun. Semi-a la carte: bkfst $3.50-$6.50, lunch, dinner $4.50-$9.45. Specialties: fresh vegetables, corn bread. Salad bar. Parking. Family-owned. Cr cds: C, D, DS, MC, V.

[D] [SC]

★ **GOURMET.** *1606 McLish Ave SW. 405/223-0369.* Hrs: 11 am-2 pm; Sun brunch to 2:30 pm. Closed Sat; some major hols. Res accepted. Semi-a la carte: lunch $6.95-$11. Sun brunch $11. Specializes in turkey, prime rib, seafood. Salad bar. Parking. Family-owned. Cr cds: A, MC, V.

Atoka (D-8)

Founded 1867 **Pop** 3,298 **Elev** 583 ft **Area code** 405 **Zip** 74525
Information Chamber of Commerce, US 69 N, PO Box 778; 405/889-2410.

What to See and Do

Boggy Depot State Park. Approx 420 acres. Picnicking, playgrounds. Camping areas, trailer hookups (fee). Historical area. (Daily) 11 mi W on OK 7, then 4 mi S on Park Lane. Phone 405/889-5625. **Free.**

Motels

★ ★ **BEST WESTERN ATOKA INN.** *2101 S Mississippi Ave.* 405/889-7381; FAX 405/889-6695. 54 rms, 2 story. S $40-$44; D $48-$52; each addl $4; under 12 free. TV; cable. Pool. Restaurant open 24 hrs. Ck-out noon. Meeting rms. Cr cds: A, C, D, DS, MC, V.

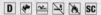

✔ ★ **THUNDERBIRD LODGE.** *402 N Mississippi Ave.* 405/889-3315. 24 rms. S $23; D $32-$35; each addl $3; under 12 free. TV; cable. Pool. Ck-out noon. Sundries. Cr cds: A, D, DS, MC, V.

Bartlesville (A-8)

(See Pawhuska)

Founded 1875 **Pop** 34,256 **Elev** 715 ft **Area code** 918
Information Bartlesville Area Chamber of Commerce, 201 SW Keeler, PO Box 2366, 74005; 918/336-8708.

The Bartlesville area is proud of its Western and Native American heritage, which involves three tribes—the Cherokee, Delaware and Osage. Oklahoma's first electricity was produced here in 1876 when Jacob Bartles, an early settler, hitched a dynamo to the Caney River. Oil, first tapped in the area in 1897, is the economic base of the city, which is the headquarters of the Phillips Petroleum Company.

Bartlesville has become internationally known for its distinguished, modern architecture, a building trend initiated by the H.C. Price family. The town boasts a number of both public and private buildings by Frank Lloyd Wright and Bruce Goff.

What to See and Do

Dewey Hotel Museum. Victorian structure built by Jacob Bartles. Period furnishings. (Apr-Nov, Tues-Sat & Sun afternoon; closed hols) 801 N Delaware. Phone 918/534-0215. **¢**

Frank Phillips Mansion. Built in 1908 by the founder of the Phillips Petroleum Co. This Greek-revival house has been restored to 1930s period; interior includes imported woods, marble, Oriental rugs and original furnishings. (Daily exc Mon; closed most major hols) Donation. 1107 S Cherokee Ave. Phone 918/336-2491.

Nellie Johnstone Oil Well. Replica of the original rig, first commercial oil well in state. An 83-acre park with a low water dam on the Caney River. Fishing. Picnicking, playgrounds, children's rides (late May-La-

bor Day, daily; closed July 4). Park (daily). In Johnstone Park, 300 blk of N Cherokee. **Free.**

Price Tower. Designed by Frank Lloyd Wright, this 221-foot office building was built by pipeline construction pioneer H.C. Price as headquarters for his company. The building design is based on a diamond modular of 30-60 degree triangles. Although Wright designed many skyscrapers, Price Tower was his only tall building to be completed. Guided tours (45 min). (Thurs or by appt) On Sixth & Dewey Sts. Phone 918/333-8558.

Shin 'en Kan (House of the Far Away Heart). Largest and most elaborate house designed by Bruce Goff, whose work, like Frank Lloyd Wright's, is considered organic, or an architectural interpretation of nature. The house, constructed of such building materials as cullets, or waste glass, and anthracite coal, was completed in 1956 and added to in 1966 and again in 1974. Built by Joe Price, son of H.C. Price, Shin 'en Kan includes part of Price's Edo collection (17th-19th-century Japanese art) and functions, in part, as a conference center for creative thinking. Tours (Thurs & some Sat mornings). Tourists must remove shoes and are supplied with sanitized footwear. 2919 Price Rd. Approx 1/4 mi W of OK 75. Phone 918/333-3275. **¢¢**

Tom Mix Museum. Exhibits and memorabilia of silent movie star Tom Mix, the first "King of the Cowboys"; displays of his cowboy gear; stills from his films. (Daily exc Mon; closed major hols) 6 mi N on OK 123 at jct Delaware & Don Tyler Aves, in Dewey. Phone 918/534-1555. **Free.**

★ **Woolaroc.** Complex covering 3,500 acres with wildlife preserve for herds of American bison, longhorn cattle, Scottish Highland cattle, elk, deer and other native wildlife. These are wild animals and may be dangerous; it is mandatory to stay in car. At museum are paintings by Russell, Remington and other great Western artists; exhibits on the development of America; artifacts of several Native American tribes, pioneers and cowboys; also one of the finest collections of Colt firearms in the country. The Woolaroc Lodge (1927), once a private dwelling, has paintings, bark-covered furnishings and Indian blankets. The National Y-Indian Guide Center has multimedia shows, authentic Native American crafts, art displays and a nature trail (1 1/2-mi). Picnic area. (Late May-early Sept, daily; rest of yr, daily exc Mon; closed Thanksgiving, Dec 25) Sr citizen rate. 13 mi SW on OK 123, Woolaroc exit. Phone 918/336-0307. **¢¢**

Motels

★ ★ **BEST WESTERN WESTON INN.** *222 SE Washington Blvd (74006).* 918/335-7755; FAX 918/335-7763. 111 rms, 2 story, 5 suites. S $42-$49; D $45-$53; each addl $6; suites $49-$60; under 12 free. Crib free. TV; cable (premium). Pool. Complimentary continental bkfst. Complimentary coffee in rms. Restaurant 6 am-9 pm. Rm serv. Ck-out noon. Coin lndry. Meeting rms. Business servs avail. Some refrigerators, in-rm whirlpools. Cr cds: A, C, D, DS, ER, JCB, MC, V.

★ ★ **HOLIDAY INN.** *1410 SE Washington Blvd (US 75) (74006).* 918/333-8320; FAX 918/333-8979. 107 rms, 3 story, 8 kits. S $44-$52; D $52-$54; each addl $6; suites $65; under 18 free. Crib free. Pet accepted; $15 deposit. TV; cable (premium). Indoor pool. Complimentary coffee in rms. Restaurant 6 am-1:30 pm, 5-10 pm; Sun to 1:30 pm. Rm serv. Bar. Ck-out noon. Coin lndry. Meeting rm. Business servs avail. In-rm modem link. Valet serv. Free local airport transportation. Exercise equipt; weight machine, bicycle, sauna. Game rm. Cr cds: A, C, D, DS, MC, V.

✔ ★ **TRAVELERS.** *3105 E Frank Phillips Blvd (74006).* 918/333-1900. 24 rms. S $28-$30; D $30-$36; Crib $6. TV; cable (premium). Complimentary continental bkfst. Restaurant nearby. Ck-out 11 am. Cr cds: A, C, D, DS, MC, V.

Hotel

★ ★ ★ **HOTEL PHILLIPS.** *821 Johnstone (74003). 918/336-5600; res: 800/331-0706; FAX 918/336-0350.* 165 rms, 7 story, 28 suites. S, D $65; each addl $10; suites $75-$150; under 16 free. Crib free. TV; cable (premium). Restaurant 6:30 am-10 pm; Sun to 2 pm. Rm serv. Bar 11 am-midnight. Ck-out noon. Meeting rms. Business servs avail. In-rm modem link. Concierge. Airport transportation. Gift shop. Free parking. Exercise equipt; weight machines, bicycles. Health club privileges. Rms individually decorated. Rooftop terrace. Luxury level. Cr cds: A, C, D, DS, MC, V.

Restaurant

★ **MURPHY'S STEAK HOUSE.** *1625 W Frank Phillips Blvd. 918/336-4789.* Hrs: 11 am-11:30 pm. Closed Mon; Thanksgiving, Dec 25. Semi-a la carte: lunch, dinner $4-$16.95. Specializes in steak, hamburgers. Open kitchen. Parking. Family-owned. No cr cds accepted.

D

Boise City (A-2)

(See Dalhart, TX)

Pop 1,509 **Elev** 4,165 ft **Area code** 405 **Zip** 73933
Information Chamber of Commerce, 6 NE Square, in red caboose, PO Box 1027; 405/544-3344.

What to See and Do

Black Mesa State Park. Lake Carl Etling (260 acres) offers fishing facilities; boating (ramps). Picnic area, playground. Camping, trailer hookups (fee). (Daily) 19 mi NW on OK 325, then 9 mi W on unnumbered roads. Phone 405/426-2222. **Free.**

Annual Event

Santa Fe Trail Daze Celebration. Guided tour of Santa Fe Trail crossing, autograph rock, dinosaur tracks and excavation site. Phone 405/544-3344. 1st wkend June.

Broken Bow (E-10)

(See Idabel)

Pop 3,961 **Elev** 467 ft **Area code** 405 **Zip** 74728
Information Chamber of Commerce, 214 Craig Rd; 405/584-3393.

What to See and Do

Beavers Bend Resort State Park. This 3,522-acre mountainous area is crossed by the Mountain Fork River and includes the Broken Bow Reservoir. Swimming, bathhouse; fishing; boating (no motors). Nature trail. Picnic areas, playground, grocery, restaurant. Camping, trailer hookups (fee), cabins. Nature center. (Daily) 6 mi N on US 259, then 3 mi E on OK 259A. Phone 405/494-6300. **Free.**
Hochatown State Park. Covers 1,713 acres on 14,220-acre Broken Bow Lake. Swimming, waterskiing; fishing, bait and tackle shop; boating (ramps, marina, rentals, gas dock, boathouses). Hiking trails; 18-hole golf course. Picnicking, playground, snack bar. Trailer hookups

(fee), dump station, rest rms. (Daily) 10 mi N on US 259. Phone 405/494-6452. **Free.**

Annual Event

Kiamichi Owa Chito Festival. Beavers Bend Resort State Park. Contests, entertainment, food. 3rd wkend June.

Motel

✔ ★ **CHARLES WESLEY MOTOR LODGE.** *302 N Park Dr. 405/584-3303; FAX 405/584-3433.* 50 rms, 1-2 story, 6 kits. S $32; D $39; each addl $4. Crib $4. TV; cable. Pool. Restaurant 6 am-10 pm; Sun to 9 pm. Ck-out 11 am. Cr cds: A, C, D, DS, MC, V.

Chickasaw National Recreation Area (D-7)

(see Sulphur)

Chickasha (C-6)

(See Anadarko)

Founded 1892 **Pop** 14,988 **Elev** 1,095 ft **Area code** 405
Information Chamber of Commerce, 221 W Chickasha Ave, PO Box 1717, 73018; 405/224-0787.

Established to serve as a passenger and freight division point for the Rock Island and Pacific Railroad in 1892, this townsite was on land originally given to the Choctaws in 1820. It became part of the Chickasaw Nation in 1834. In 1907, when the Oklahoma and Indian territories were joined to form the forty-sixth state, Chickasha became the county seat of Grady County. Today, agriculture, livestock, dairy production, manufacturing and energy-related industries play an important part in the economy of the city and surrounding area.

What to See and Do

Recreation areas. Lake Burtschi, Fishing. Picnic areas. Camping. 11 mi SW on OK 92. **Lake Chickasha,** Swimmimg, waterskiing; fishing, hunting. Picnic areas. Camping. 15 mi NW off US 62.

Annual Events

Grady County Rodeo. 3 days mid-June.

Grady County Fair. Last wk Aug.

Antique Car Swap Meet. 1st wkend Nov & late May.

Motel

✔ ★ ★ **BEST WESTERN INN.** *2101 S 4th (73018), on US 81, 7 blks N of H.E. Bailey Tpke. 405/224-4890; FAX 405/224-3411.* 154 rms, 2 story. S $37-$47; D $42-$53; each addl $5; under 18 free. Crib free. TV; cable. Heated pool; whirlpool, sauna, poolside serv. Restaurant 6 am-9 pm. Rm serv. Ck-out noon. Meeting rms. Valet serv. Refrigerator in suites. Cr cds: A, C, D, DS, MC, V.

Restaurant

★ **JAKES RIB.** 100 Ponderosa. 405/222-2825. Hrs: 10:30 am-9 pm; Fri, Sat to 10 pm; Sun to 4 pm. Closed Dec 25. Beer. Semi-a la carte: lunch, dinner $2.75-$14.95. Specializes in barbecued ribs, steak. Salad bar. Parking. Cr cds: MC, V.

D SC

Claremore (B-9)

(See Pryor, Tulsa)

Pop 13,280 **Elev** 602 ft **Area code** 918 **Zip** 74017
Information Claremore Area Chamber of Commerce, 419 W Will Rogers Blvd, 918/341-2818.

Claremore is most famous as the birthplace of Will Rogers. He was actually born about halfway between this city and Oologah but used to talk more of Claremore because, he said, "nobody but an Indian could pronounce Oologah."

There is a national Indian Hospital in Claremore. Rogers County, of which this is the seat, was named not for Will Rogers but for his father, Clem.

What to See and Do

J.M. Davis Firearms & Historical Museum. Houses 20,000 firearms, steins, arrowheads, saddles, posters, other historical and Native American artifacts, collection of "John Rogers Groups" statuaries. (Mon-Sat, also Sun afternoons; closed Thanksgiving, Dec 25) Donation. 333 N Lynn Riggs Blvd (OK 66). Phone 918/341-5707.

Lynn Riggs Memorial. Houses author's personal belongings, sculpture of Riggs, original manuscripts and the original "surrey with the fringe on top" from *Oklahoma!* (Mon-Fri; closed some hols) Rogers State College, Meyer Hall. Phone 918/341-7510, ext 241 or 218. **Free.**

Will Rogers Birthplace and Dog Iron Ranch. Home where "Oklahoma's favorite son" was born Nov 4, 1879. (Daily; closed Thanksgiving, Dec 25) Donation. 12 mi NW on OK 88, then 2 mi N. Phone 918/341-0719.

⭐ **Will Rogers Memorial.** Rogers' mementos; murals; saddle collection; dioramas of 13 episodes of his life; theater, films, tapes, research library. Jo Davidson's statue of Rogers stands in the foyer. The memorial is on 20 acres once owned by the humorist. Garden with Rogers' tomb. (Daily) Donation. 1720 W Will Rogers Blvd (OK 88). Phone 918/341-0719.

Annual Events

Rogers County Free Fair. Mid-Sept.

Will Rogers Birthday Celebration. Early Nov.

Motel

✔★★ **BEST WESTERN WILL ROGERS MOTOR INN.** 940 S Lynn Riggs Blvd (OK 66). 918/341-4410; FAX 918/341-6045. 52 rms. S $41; D $47; each addl $4. Crib $5. Pet accepted. TV; cable (premium). Pool. Playground. Restaurant adj 6 am-9:30 pm; closed Sun. Bar noon-1:30 am, closed Sun, hols. Ck-out noon. Meeting rm. Business servs avail. In-rm modem link avail. Many refrigerators. Cr cds: A, C, D, DS, ER, JCB, MC, V.

Unrated Dining Spot

PINK HOUSE. 210 W 4th St. 918/342-2544. Hrs: 11 am-3 pm. Closed wk of July 4, Thanksgiving wkend, wk of Dec 25. A la carte entrees: lunch $3-$7. Child's meals. Specializes in soups, desserts. Parking. House (1902) with Victorian decor; antiques. Cr cds: A, DS, MC, V.

Clinton (C-5)

(For accommodations see Elk City, Weatherford)

Founded 1903 **Pop** 9,298 **Elev** 1,592 ft **Area code** 405 **Zip** 73601
Information Chamber of Commerce, 400 Gary Blvd, PO Box 1595; 405/323-2222.

This is a cattle, farming, manufacturing and shipping center founded when Congress approved the purchase of acreage owned by Native Americans at the junction of two railroads. Oil and gas drilling and production take place here.

What to See and Do

Foss State Park. An 8,800-acre lake created by dam on Washita River. Waterskiing; fishing, enclosed dock; boating (ramps, docks, marina). Picnic facilities, playgrounds. Camping, trailer hookups (fee). (Daily) 14 mi W on I-40, then 6 mi N on OK 44. Phone 405/592-4433. **Free.**

Annual Event

Art in the Park Festival. McLain-Rogers Park. Features art from Oklahoma and surrounding states. 2nd Sat May.

Duncan (D-6)

(See Lawton, Waurika)

Founded 1893 **Pop** 21,732 **Elev** 1,126 ft **Area code** 405 **Zip** 73533
Information Chamber of Commerce, 911 Walnut; 405/255-3644.

Once a cattle town on the old Chisholm Trail, Duncan has become an oil-services and agricultural center. It was here that Erle P. Halliburton developed his oil-well cementing business, which now operates all over the world.

What to See and Do

Stephens County Historical Museum. Houses pioneer and Native American artifacts, antique toys, gem and lapidary display; Plains Indian exhibit. Also log cabin, old schoolhouse, pioneer kitchen (1892), blacksmith shop, dentist's office, law office. (Thurs, Sat & Sun; closed hols) On E side of US 81 & Beech Ave, in Fuqua Park. Phone 405/252-0717. **Free.**

Motels

✔★ **DUNCAN INN.** 3402 N US 81. 405/252-5210. 92 rms, 2 story. S $25-$30; D $30-$36; each addl $4; wkly, monthly rates. Pet accepted. TV; cable (premium). Pool. Complimentary coffee in lobby. Restaurant. Ck-out 11 am. Coin lndry. Meeting rm. Cr cds: A, C, D, DS, MC, V.

★**HERITAGE INN.** *1515 S US 81. 405/252-5612; FAX 405/252-5620.* 37 rms, 2 story. S $24.95; D $28.95; under 12 free. Crib free. TV; cable. Restaurant adj. Ck-out 11 am. Cr cds: A, D, MC, V.

🔥

Durant (E-8)

(See Lake Texoma)

Settled 1832 **Pop** 12,823 **Elev** 647 ft **Area code** 405 **Zip** 74701
Information Chamber of Commerce, 215 N 4th St, PO Box 517; 405/924-0848.

Long a farm and livestock-producing town in Oklahoma's Red River Valley, Durant has become a recreation center since the completion of Lake Texoma. Oil and industry have also stimulated the city's economy. Durant, home of Southeastern Oklahoma State University (1909), has many mansions, magnolia trees and gardens.

What to See and Do

Fort Washita. Originally built in 1842 to protect the Five Civilized Tribes from the Plains Indians; used during the Civil War as Confederate supply depot; remains of 48 buildings are visible. Picnicking. (Daily; closed major hols) 16 mi NW via OK 78, 199, on N shore of Lake Texoma. Phone 405/924-6502. **Free.**

Lake Texoma (see). 14 mi W on US 70.

Three Valley Museum. Museum housed in the Choctaw Nation Head-quarters building; contains turn-of-the-century artifacts, antique dolls, art & beadwork. (Mon-Fri; also by appt; closed Thanksgiving, Dec 25) 16th & Locust. Phone 405/920-1907. **Free.**

Annual Events

Durant Western Heritage Days. Rodeo. Mid-June.

The Oklahoma Shakespearean Festival. On the campus of Southeastern Oklahoma State University. Musical; children's show, teen cabaret; dinner theatre. Phone 405/924-0121, ext 2442. Late June-July.

Motels

✔★★**BEST WESTERN MARKITA INN.** *2401 W Main (US 70). 405/924-7676; FAX 405/924-3060.* 60 rms, 2 story. S $35; D $42; each addl $3; suites $50-$90; under 12 free. Crib $5. TV; cable. Pool. Restaurant open 24 hrs. Rm serv 7-11 am. Ck-out noon. Meeting rm. Picnic tables, grills. Near Eaker Field Airport. Cr cds: A, C, D, DS, MC, V.

🏊 ✕ 🔥 SC

★★**HOLIDAY INN.** *2121 W Main St, US 69, 70, 75 Bypass. 405/924-5432; FAX 405/924-9721.* 81 rms, 2 story. May-mid-Sept: S $49-$59; D $54-$64; each addl $5; under 18 free. Crib free. TV; cable (premium), VCR avail (movies avail $6.99-$9.99). Pool. Restaurant open 24 hrs. Rm serv. Ck-out noon, ck-in 2 pm. Meeting rm. In-rm modem link. Cr cds: A, C, D, DS, JCB, MC, V.

D 🏊 ✕ 🔥 SC

Elk City (C-5)

(See Clinton)

Pop 10,428 **Elev** 1,928 ft **Area code** 405 **Zip** 73644
Information Chamber of Commerce, 1016 Airport Blvd, PO Box 972; 405/225-0207 or 800/280-0207.

This was once a stopping point for cattlemen driving herds from Texas to railheads in Kansas. Just northwest of town is the Sandstone Creek Project, a flood-control and soil-conservation project with upstream dams on an area of 65,000 acres. Elk City lies near the center of the Anadarko Basin, where extensive natural gas exploration takes place.

What to See and Do

Old Town Museum. Turn-of-the-century house has Victorian furnishings, Native American artifacts, Beutler Brothers Rodeo memorabilia; Memorial Chapel; early one-room school; wagon yard; gristmill; depot and caboose. (Daily exc Mon; closed hols) Pioneer Rd & US 66. Phone 405/225-2207. ¢¢

Annual Events

Rodeo of Champions. Rodeo grounds, A Ave at W edge of town. PRCA sanctioned. Labor Day wkend.

Fall Festival of the Arts. Exhibits, children's show, performing arts & music. 3rd wkend Sept.

Motels

★**DAYS INN.** *1100 OK 34, I-40 exit 41. 405/225-9210.* 135 rms, 63 kits. S $27-$35; D $34-$40; kit. units $27-$40. Crib free. TV; cable. Pool. Complimentary continental bkfst, coffee. Restaurant opp open 24 hrs. Ck-out noon. Gift shop. Some refrigerators. Cr cds: A, C, D, DS, MC, V.

D 🐾 🏊 ✕ 🔥 SC

✔★**FLAMINGO INN & RESTAURANT.** *2000 W 3rd St, on Old 66 Business. 405/225-1811; res: 800/466-1811; FAX 405/225-6525.* 42 rms, 1-2 story. S $24-$35; D $26-$37; each addl $3; family rms up to 6, $45. Pet accepted. TV; cable. Pool. Restaurant 6 am-10 pm. Ck-out 11 am. Meeting rms. Cr cds: A, C, D, DS, MC, V.

🐾 🏊 ✕ 🔥 SC

★★**HOLIDAY INN.** *Box 782 (73648), I-40 at OK 6, exit 38. 405/225-6637; FAX 405/225-6637, ext. 290.* 151 rms, 2 story. S $57-$65; D $63-$71; each addl $6; suites $85-$105; studio rms from $82; under 19 free. Crib free. Pet accepted. TV; cable (premium), VCR avail (movies avail $8.55). Indoor pool. Complimentary coffee in rms. Restaurant 6 am-10 pm. Rm serv. Bar 5 pm-2 am; dancing. Ck-out noon. Meeting rms. Business servs avail. Valet serv. Exercise equipt; stair machine, treadmill, whirlpool, sauna. Holidome. Lawn games. Wet bar in suites. Cr cds: A, C, D, DS, JCB, MC, V.

D 🐾 🏊 🏋 ✕ 🔥 SC

★**QUALITY INN.** *102 Hughes Access Rd. 405/225-8140.* 50 rms, 2 story, 6 kits. S $30.95; D $40.95; kits. $38.95; family, wkly rates. Pet accepted. TV; cable (premium). Indoor pool; whirlpool. Complimentary continental bkfst. Restaurant opp 6-9:30 am. Ck-out 11 am. Business servs avail. Game rm. Cr cds: A, C, D, DS, ER, JCB, MC, V.

🐾 🏊 ✕ 🔥 SC

Restaurant

✔★**LUPE'S.** *905 N Main. 405/225-7109.* Hrs: 11 am-2 pm, 4-11 pm; Sat from 4 pm. Closed Sun; most major hols. Mexican, Amer menu. Serv bar. Semi-a la carte: lunch $3.95-$5.95, dinner $4.25-$14.95. Child's meals. Specializes in rib-eye steak, fajitas. Parking. Mexican decor. Cr cds: MC, V.

El Reno (C-6)

Founded 1889 **Pop** 15,414 **Elev** 1,365 ft **Area code** 405 **Zip** 73036

Information Chamber of Commerce, 206 N Bickford, PO Box 67; 405/262-1188.

Established in 1889, El Reno was named for Civil War General Jesse L. Reno, who was killed during the Battle of Antietam in 1862. The city lies in the heart of the Canadian River valley. Farming, livestock and cotton are its principal agricultural pursuits.

What to See and Do

Canadian County Historical Museum. Former Rock Island Depot (1907) houses Native American and pioneer artifacts; Agriculture Exhibit Barn; railroad exhibit and caboose; historical hotel, log cabin, jail and rural schoolhouse on grounds. (Wed-Sun; closed some hols) Wade & Grand Sts. Phone 405/262-5121. **Free.**

Darlington Game Bird Hatchery. A state game farm. (Daily; closed hols) 3 mi N on US 81, then 3 mi W on Darlington Rd. Phone 405/262-2372. **Free.**

Motel

★ **BEST WESTERN HENSLEY'S.** Country Club Rd, I-40 exit 123. 405/262-6490; FAX 405/262-7642. 60 rms, 2 story. $40-$45; D $45-$48; each $4; under 12 free. Crib $2. Pet accepted, some restrictions. TV; cable (premium). Heated pool. Complimentary bkfst. Restaurant (see HENSLEY'S). Ck-out 11 am. Meeting rms. Business servs avail. Cr cds: A, C, D, DS, MC, V.

⊡ ➹ ⚞ ⌦ 🔥 SC

Restaurant

✔★ **HENSLEY'S.** Country Club Rd, I-40 exit 123. 405/262-3535. Hrs: 6 am-10 pm. Closed Dec 25. Buffet: lunch $4.99, dinner $5.99. Sunday buffet $6.45. Semi-a la carte: dinner $5.60-$10.95. Child's meals. Specializes in chicken-fried steak. Salad bar. Parking. Gift shop. Cr cds: A, DS, MC, V.

⊡ SC

Enid (B-6)

Founded 1893 **Pop** 45,309 **Elev** 1,246 ft **Area code** 405

Information Chamber of Commerce, 210 Kenwood Blvd, PO Box 907, 73702; 405/237-2494.

Like many Oklahoma cities, Enid was born of a land rush. When the Cherokee Outlet (more popularly known as the Cherokee Strip) was opened to settlement on September 16, 1893, a tent city sprang up. It is now a prosperous community, a center for farm marketing and oil processing. Just south of town is Vance Air Force Base, a training base for jet aircraft pilots.

What to See and Do

Homesteader's Sod House (1894). A 2-room sod house built by Marshall McCully in 1894; said to be the only original example of this type of structure still standing in Oklahoma. Period furnishings; farm machinery. (Tues-Fri, also Sat & Sun afternoons; closed hols) 30 mi W on US 60, then 5½ mi N of Cleo Springs on OK 8. Phone 405/463-2441. **Free.**

Museum of the Cherokee Strip. Artifacts covering Oklahoma history of the Plains Indians, the Land Run of 1893 and events from 1900 to present. (Tues-Fri, also Sat & Sun afternoons; closed major hols) 507 S 4th St. Phone 405/237-1907. **Free.**

Annual Events

Tri-State Music Festival. 1 wk early May.

Cherokee Strip Celebration. City-wide festival commemorates opening of the Cherokee Strip to settlers. Includes turtle races, beard-growing contest, bike races, pageants. 4 days mid-Sept.

Grand National Quail Hunt. Early Dec.

Motels

★ **BEST WESTERN.** 2818 S Van Buren (US 81) (73703). 405/242-7110; FAX 405/242-6202. 100 rms, 2 story. S $43; D $48; each addl $5. Crib free. TV; cable (premium). Indoor pool. Restaurant 6 am-2 pm, 5-10 pm. Bar 5 pm-2 am, closed Sun. Ck-out noon. Meeting rms. Business servs avail. In-rm modem link. Valet serv. Game rm. Cr cds: A, C, D, DS, MC, V.

⊡ ⚞ ⌦ 🔥 SC

✔★★ **HOLIDAY INN.** 2901 S Van Buren (US 81) (73703). 405/237-6000; FAX 405/237-6000, ext. 177. 100 rms, 2 story. S $46-$50; D $52-$56; each addl $6. Crib free. TV; cable (premium). Pool. Restaurant 6 am-10 pm; Sun to 2 pm. Rm serv. Bar 5 pm-2 am, closed Sun. Ck-out noon. Meeting rms. Business servs avail. Sundries. Cr cds: A, C, D, DS, JCB, MC, V.

⊡ ⚞ ⌦ 🔥 SC

★★ **RAMADA INN.** 3005 W Owen K. Garriott Rd (73703). 405/234-0440; FAX 405/233-1402. 125 rms, 2 story. S $51; D $59; each addl $6; under 18 free. Crib free. TV; cable (premium). Pool. Restaurant 6 am-2 pm, 5-9 pm; Sun to 2 pm. Rm serv. Ck-out noon. Coin lndry. Meeting rms. Cr cds: A, C, D, DS, JCB, MC, V.

⊡ ⚞ ⌦ 🔥 SC

Restaurants

★★ **SAGE ROOM.** 1927 S Van Buren (US 81). 405/233-1212. Hrs: 5:30-9:30 pm; Fri, Sat to 10 pm. Closed Sun; major hols. Serv bar. Semi-a la carte: dinner $4.95-$35.95. Child's meals. Specializes in choice beef, seafood and chicken. Pianist exc Mon. Parking. Antique clock collection. No cr cds accepted.

⊡ SC

✔★ **SNEAKERS.** 1710 W Willow. 405/237-6325. Hrs: 11 am-11 pm. Closed some major hols. Res accepted. Bar. Semi-a la carte: lunch $2.95-$4.95, dinner $4.95-$11.95. Specializes in gourmet hamburgers, prime rib. Parking. Antique chandeliers and art objects. Cr cds: A, D, DS, MC, V.

Unrated Dining Spot

WYATT'S CAFETERIA. 4125 W Garriott, in Oakwood Mall. 405/233-3180. Hrs: 11 am-2:30 pm, 4:30-8 pm; Sat 11 am-8 pm; Sun 11 am-7 pm. Closed Dec 25. Avg ck: lunch, dinner $4.25-$6.75. Cr cds: A, DS, MC, V.

Eufaula (C-9)

(See McAlester)

Settled 1836 **Pop** 2,652 **Elev** 617 ft **Area code** 918 **Zip** 74432

Information Greater Eufaula Area Chamber of Commerce, 64 Memorial Dr; 918/689-2791.

Eufaula was first a Native American settlement and, later, a trading post. The town is still the home of the Eufaula Boarding School for Indian Girls (1849), which was renamed the Eufaula Dormitory after becoming co-educational. The town is also the home of the state's oldest continually published newspaper, *The Indian Journal,* and the location of the Eufaula Dam, which impounds the Canadian River to form one of the largest man-made lakes in the world.

What to See and Do

Arrowhead State Park. Approximately 2,450 acres located on south shore of 102,500-acre Lake Eufaula. Beach, bathhouse, waterskiing; fishing; boating (ramps, marina). Golf. Nature walk, hiking. Picnicking, playground, restaurant, lodges, full resort facilities. Camping, trailer hookups (fee), cabins. Airstrip. (Daily) 11 mi S on US 69, then E. Phone 918/339-2204. **Free.**

Eufaula Dam. Tours of powerhouse, 45-min (Mon-Fri). Camping at Damsite S (early Apr-Oct, fee; rest of yr, free). Swimming beach. Nature trail. 18 mi NE via OK 9, 71. Phone 918/484-5135. Powerhouse tour **Free.**

Fountainhead State Park. Approximately 3,400 acres on shore of Lake Eufaula. Beach, bathhouse, waterskiing; fishing; boating (ramps, marina). Golf, tennis. Nature walk, hiking, bridle paths. Picnicking, playground, restaurant, lodges, full resort facilities (see RESORT). Camping, trailer hookups (fee). Airstrip. (Daily) 6 mi N on US 69, then 2 mi NW on OK 150. Phone 918/689-5311. **Free.**

Annual Event

McIntosh County Fair. 3 days late Aug.

Motel

✔ ★ **BEST WESTERN LA DONNA INN.** *(Box 427, Checotah 74426)* 7 mi W of Checotah, just S of I-40, Fountainhead exit 259. 918/473-2376; FAX 918/473-5774. 48 rms. S $34; D $38-$48; each addl $5. Crib $3. TV. Pool. Continental bkfst 6-9 am. Ck-out noon. Coin lndry. Cr cds: A, C, D, DS, MC, V.

D ⊠ ⊠ ⊠ SC

Resort

★ ★ **FOUNTAINHEAD.** *(Box 1355, HC 60 Checotah 74426)* N on OK 150, adj to Lake Eufaula in Fountainhead State Park. 918/689-9173; res: 800/345-6343; FAX 918/689-9493. 205 units, 5 story, 14 cottages. Apr-Oct: S, D $75-$95; each addl $10; suites $200-$250; cottages $85; treehouses $100; under 16 free; lower rates rest of yr. Crib free. TV. 2 pools, 1 indoor; wading pool, poolside serv. Playground. Supervised child's activities (Memorial Day-Labor Day). Dining rm 7 am-10 pm. Box lunches, picnics. Rm serv. Bar 4 pm-1 am, Sat to 2 am; entertainment Thurs-Sat. Ck-out 1 pm, ck-in 3 pm. Coin lndry. Grocery, package store 7 mi. Meeting rms. Bellhops. Gift shop. Sports dir. Lighted tennis. 18-hole golf, greens fee $8.50, putting green, driving range. Miniature golf. Swimming beach. Hiking. Lawn games. Soc dir. Rec rm. Game rm. Sauna. Fishing/hunting guides. Some refrigerators. Fountainhead State Park facilities avail to guests. Cr cds: A, C, D, DS, MC, V.

D ⊠ 🏊 🎿 ⊠ 🚣 SC

Grand Lake (A-10)

(See Miami, Pryor, Vinita)

Information Grand Lake Assn, 6807 US 59 N, Grove 74344; 918/786-2289.

Also called "Grand Lake O' the Cherokees," this 66-mile, 59,200-acre lake above Pensacola Dam is primarily a source of electric power. It also offers swimming, water sports, fishing, boating and camping along 1,300 miles of shoreline. It is a popular resort area that has drawn millions of visitors. There are more than 100 resorts and fishing camps. Twenty-nine enclosed fishing docks; some are heated for year-round use. Grove is a major center of activity, but Ketchum, Langley and Disney are also important. The lake is convenient to Miami, Pryor and Vinita (see all).

What to See and Do

Boat cruises. *Cherokee Queen I & II.* Narrated cruise (1½ hrs) on Grand Lake O' the Cherokees; entertainment, refreshments. Honey Creek Bridge on US 59, S end of Grove. Phone 918/786-4272 for schedule. ¢¢¢¢

Har-Ber Village. Reconstructed old-time village with 90 buildings and shops typical of a pioneer town; also a variety of memorabilia collections. Picnicking. (Mar-Nov, daily) 3½ mi W of Grove, Har-ber Rd 1. Phone 918/786-6446. **Free.**

Annual Event

Pelican Festival. Grand Lake O' The Cherokees, in Grove. Viewing of white pelicans on their southward migration; tours and cruises to view pelicans; events; parade. Phone 918/786-2289. Last wkend Sept.

Seasonal Event

Picture in Scripture Amphitheater. 6 mi S via OK 85 & OK 82, 3 mi E via OK 28, in Disney. Biblical drama of Jonah and the Whale. Phone 918/435-8207. June-Aug.

Resort

★ ★ ★ **SHANGRI-LA.** *(Rte 3, Afton 74331)* At end of OK 125, 18 mi S of I-44, Afton exit. 918/257-4204; res: 800/331-4060; FAX 918/257-5619. 391 units, 101 suites. Memorial Day-Labor Day: S, D $79-$119; each addl (after 2nd person) $15; suites $99-$387; under 18 free; tennis, golf packages; lower rates rest of yr. Crib free. TV; cable (premium), VCR avail (movies avail $7.95). 2 pools, 1 indoor; lifeguard (wkends). Playground. Supervised child's activities (Memorial Day-Labor Day); ages 5-12. Dining rms 6:30 am-10 pm; Thurs-Sat to 11 pm. Box lunches, snack bar. Bar 1 pm-1 am. Ck-out noon, ck-in 4 pm. Convention facilities. Business servs avail. Valet serv. Gift shop. Beauty shop. Sports dir. Lighted & indoor tennis. 36-hole golf, pro, putting green, driving range. Private beach; marina, boats, waterskiing, swimming. Bicycles. Lawn games. Soc dir. Game rm. Bowling. Exercise equipt; weight machines, bicycles, whirlpool, sauna, steam rm. Fireplace in houses. Some balconies. Picnic tables. 660-acre resort on shores of Grand Lake O' the Cherokees. Cr cds: A, C, D, DS, MC, V.

D 🚣 🎿 🎿 ⊠ 🚶 ⊠ ⊠ SC

Guthrie (B-7)

(See Oklahoma City)

Founded 1889 **Pop** 10,518 **Elev** 946 ft **Area code** 405 **Zip** 73044
Information Chamber of Commerce, 212 W Oklahoma, PO Box 995; 405/282-1947.

Guthrie was founded in just a few hours during the great land rush. Prior to the "run" only a small frame railroad station and a partially completed land registration office stood on the site. A few hours later perhaps 20,000 inhabited the tent city on the prairie.

Oklahoma's territorial and first state capital, Guthrie now has the most complete collection of restored Victorian architecture in the United States, with 1,600 acres of the city listed on the National Historical Register. Included are 160 buildings in the central business district and the center of town and numerous Victorian mansions. The town is being restored to the 1907-1910 era, including the expansive Guthrie Railroad Hotel and the former opera house, the Pollard Theatre. Some who have called Guthrie home at one time or another are Tom Mix, Lon Chaney, Will Rogers, Carry Nation and O. Henry.

What to See and Do

Oklahoma Territorial Museum. Exhibits and displays of life in territorial Oklahoma during the turn of the century. Adj is the Carnegie Library (1902-1903), the site of the inaugurations of the last territorial and the first state governor. (Daily exc Mon; closed hols) 402 E Oklahoma Ave. Phone 405/282-1889. **Free.**

Scottish Rite Masonic Temple. A multi-million dollar classical-revival building, said to be the largest structure used for Masonic purposes. Building contains the original state capitol; 13 artistic rooms; 200 stained glass windows. Surrounding it is a 10-acre park. Visitors welcome; children must be accompanied by adult. (Mon-Fri; closed most hols) 900 E Oklahoma Ave. Phone 405/282-1281. ¢

State Capital Publishing Museum. Located in the 4-story State Capital Publishing Company building (1902). Houses a collection of original furnishings, vintage letterpress equipment; exhibits featuring the history of the first newspaper in Oklahoma Territory and period printing technology. (Daily exc Mon; closed hols) 301 W Harrison. Phone 405/282-4123. **Free.**

Annual Events

Eighty-niner Celebration. PRCA rodeo, parade, carnival, races. Mid- or late Apr.

Road Show. Street display of antique automobiles. Mid-Sept.

Seasonal Event

Territorial Christmas. Seven miles of lights outline architecture in Historic District; streets are filled with persons clad in turn-of-the-century style clothes; horse drawn vehicles; window displays echo 1890-1920 era. Fri after Thanksgiving-late Dec.

Motel

★ ★ **BEST WESTERN TERRITORIAL INN.** 2323 Territorial Dr, 2323 Territorial Trail (OK 33) at jct I-35, exit 157. 405/282-8831. 84 units, 2 story. S $43-$49; D $53-$59; each addl $6; under 12 free. Crib free. Pet accepted, some restrictions. TV; cable. Pool. Restaurant 6 am-2 pm, 5-9 pm; Fri, Sat to 10 pm. Rm serv. Bar 5 pm-2 am. Ck-out 11 am. Meeting rms. Cr cds: A, C, D, DS, MC, V.

D ☯ ⌘ ⊠ 🔥 SC

Inn

★ ★ **HARRISON HOUSE.** 124 W Harrison. 405/282-1000; res: 800/375-1001; FAX 405/282-4304. 30 rms, 3 story. S $50-$55; D $57-$102; each addl $10; under 12 free. Crib $10. TV in parlor; VCR avail. Complimentary continental bkfst. Restaurant (see SAND PLUM). Ck-out 11 am, ck-in after 3 pm. Pollard Theatre adj. Cr cds: A, C, D, DS, MC, V.

D ⊠ 🔥 SC

Restaurants

★ ★ ★ **SAND PLUM.** (See Harrison House Inn) 405/282-7771. Hrs: 11 am-2 pm, 5:30-9 pm; Sat to 10 pm; Mon to 2 pm. Closed July 4. Res accepted. Continental menu. Serv bar. Wine list. A la carte entrees: lunch $3.75-$7, dinner $11.95-$16.95. Buffet: lunch $5.95. Specializes in steak, veal. Own baking. Pianist. Restored Victorian building. Cr cds: A, D, MC, V.

D

✔ ★ **STABLES CAFE.** 223 N Division. 405/282-0893. Hrs: 11 am-9 pm; Fri & Sat to 10 pm. Closed Thanksgiving, Dec 25. Res accepted. Semi-a la carte: lunch, dinner $3.65-$14. Child's meals. Specializes in barbecue, steak, hamburgers. Salad bar. Parking. Western atmosphere; pictures, memorabilia. Cr cds: A, C, D, DS, MC, V.

D SC

Guymon (A-3)

Founded 1890 **Pop** 7,803 **Elev** 3,121 ft **Area code** 405 **Zip** 73942
Information Chamber of Commerce, Rte 3, Box 120; 405/338-3376.

Located approximately at the center of Oklahoma's panhandle, Guymon owes its growth to oil, natural gas, irrigation, manufacturing and commercial feed lots.

What to See and Do

Oklahoma Panhandle State University (1909). (1,200 students) Agricultural research station; golf course (fee). 10 mi SW on US 54, in Goodwell. Campus tours; phone 405/349-2611, ext 275. On campus is

No Man's Land Museum (1932). Exhibit divisions relating to panhandle region include archives, anthropology, biology, geology, pioneer history and art gallery; changing exhibits; notable archaeological collection and alabaster carvings. (Daily exc Sun, Mon; closed hols) 207 W Sewell St. Phone 405/349-2670. **Free.**

Sunset Lake. Fishing. Picnicking, playground. Miniature train rides, paddle boats. Fee for activities. Adjacent game preserve has buffalo, llamas, aoudad sheep, longhorn cattle and elk. (Daily) W end of 5th St in Thompson Park. Phone 405/338-5838. **Free.**

Annual Events

Pioneer Days. Chuck wagon breakfast, parade, PRCA rodeo, dancing, entertainment. 1st wkend May.

Panhandle Exposition. Texas County Fairgrounds, 5th and Sunset. Livestock, field and garden crop displays; grandstand attractions; midway. Phone 405/338-5446. Mid-Sept.

Motels

(Rates vary during pheasant season, Pioneer Days)

★ ★ **AMBASSADOR INN.** PO Box 5, US 64 at 21st St. 405/338-5555; FAX 405/338-1784. 70 rms, 2 story. S $40-$50; D

$46-$58; each addl $4; under 12 free. Crib free. TV; cable (premium). Pool. Restaurant 6 am-9 pm. Private club; dancing. Ck-out 11 am. Meeting rms. Business servs avail. Valet serv. Cr cds: A, C, D, DS, MC, V.

D ≈ ⊠ 🔥 SC

✔★ ECONO LODGE. *923 US 54E. 405/338-5431; FAX 405/338-0554.* 40 rms. S $37-$42; D $46-$58; each addl $4; under 12 free. Crib $4. TV; cable (premium). Complimentary coffee in lobby. Restaurant adj open 24 hrs. Ck-out 11 am. Business servs avail. Cr cds: A, C, D, DS, JCB, MC, V.

D ⊠ 🔥 SC

Henryetta (C-8)

(See Okmulgee)

Founded 1900 **Pop** 5,872 **Elev** 691 ft **Area code** 918 **Zip** 74437
Information Chamber of Commerce, 115 S 4th St; 918/652-3331.

Motels

★ HOLIDAY INN. *Box 789, E Trudgeon & US 75, 1/2 mi N of jct I-40. 918/652-2581; FAX 918/652-2581, ext. 149.* 84 rms, 2 story. S $65-$73; D $72-$79; each addl $7; under 19 free. Crib free. TV; cable. Indoor pool. Restaurant 6 am-10 pm. Rm serv. Bar 5 pm-2 am; closed Sun. Ck-out 1 pm. Meeting rms. Sundries. Exercise rm; treadmill, weight machine, sauna. Holidome. Rec rm. Cr cds: A, C, D, DS, JCB, MC, V.

D ✔ ≈ 🏋 ⊠ 🔥 SC

✔★ LE BARON. *Rte 2, Box 170, E Main & US 75. 918/652-2531; res: 800/868-3562.* 24 rms, 2 story. S $29.95; D $36.85-$39.95. Crib free. Pet accepted. TV; cable (premium). Cafe nearby. Ck-out noon. Sundries. Some in-rm whirlpools. Cr cds: A, C, D, DS, MC, V.

✔ ⊠ 🔥 SC

Hugo (E-9)

Pop 5,978 **Elev** 541 ft **Area code** 405 **Zip** 74743
Information Hugo Chamber of Commerce, 200 S Broadway; 405/326-7511.

What to See and Do

Hugo Lake. Nine recreation areas. Swimming; beaches; boat ramps. Picnicking. Tent & trailer sites (fee). Electrical, water hookups in some areas. (Daily) 8 mi E on US 70. Phone 405/326-3345. **Free.**

Raymond Gary State Park. Approx 46 acres with 295-acre lake. Swimming beach; fishing; boating. Picnicking, playgrounds. Camping (showers, dump station). Standard fees. (Daily) 16 mi E on US 70; 2 mi S of Fort Towson on OK 209. Phone 405/873-2307. **Free.**

Annual Event

Grant's Bluegrass & Old-Time Music Festival. Salt Creek Park. Bluegrass performances. Phone 405/326-5598. Mid-Aug.

Motel

✔★ VILLAGE INN. *610 W Jackson St (US 70/271). 405/326-3333.* 50 rms. S $29-$36; D $39; each addl $4; higher rates music festival. Crib $6.25. TV; cable. Pool. Restaurant 6 am-9 pm; Fri, Sat to 9:30 pm; Sun 7 am-8 pm. Ck-out 11 am. Meeting rm. Cr cds: A, C, D, MC, V.

≈ ⊠ 🔥 🐾

Idabel (E-10)

(See Broken Bow)

Pop 6,957 **Elev** 489 ft **Area code** 405 **Zip** 74745
Information Chamber of Commerce, 13 N Central; 405/286-3305.

The western portion of the Ouachita National Forest (see HOT SPRINGS & HOT SPRINGS NATIONAL PARK, ARKANSAS) is located to the east of Idabel. Although predominantly evergreen, the deciduous growth, a mixture of oak, gum, maple, sycamore, dogwood and persimmon, makes the forest notable for its magnificent fall color. For information contact Supervisor, PO Box 1270, Federal Building, Hot Springs National Park, AR 71902; 501/321-5202. A Ranger District office of the forest is also located in Idabel; phone 405/286-6564.

What to See and Do

Museum of the Red River. Interpretive exhibits of historic and prehistoric Native Americans; local archeology; changing exhibits. (Daily exc Mon; closed Jan 1, Thanksgiving, Dec 25) Just S of city on US 70/259 Bypass. Phone 405/286-3616. **Free.**

Annual Event

Kiamichi Owa Chito Festival of the Forest. 3rd wkend June.

Motel

★★ HOLIDAY INN. *Box 1498, 2 mi NW on US 70W. 405/286-6501; FAX 405/286-7482.* 99 rms, 2 story. S $53; D $59; each addl $6; under 18 free. Crib free. TV; cable (premium), VCR avail. Pool. Restaurant 6 am-10 pm. Rm serv. Private club 5 pm-1 am, closed Sun; dancing. Ck-out noon. Meeting rm. Business servs avail. In-rm modem link. Cr cds: A, C, D, DS, JCB, MC, V.

D ≈ ⊠ 🔥 SC

Lake Murray State Park (E-7)

(See Ardmore)

(7 mi SE of Ardmore, off I-35 exit 24 or 29)

This 12,496-acre state park, which includes a 5,728-acre, man-made lake, can be reached from either Marietta or Ardmore. The museum in Tucker Tower (Feb-Nov, Wed-Sun; free) has historical and mineral exhibits, including a large, rare meteorite. The park is hilly and wooded, with beach, bathhouse, swimming pool, waterskiing; two fishing piers, heated fishing dock; boating (rentals, ramps, marina). Horseback riding; 18-hole golf, tennis. Picnic facilities, playground, ping pong, shuffleboard, grocery, lodge (see RESORT), club. Camping areas, trailer hookups (fee). Airstrip. (Daily) Phone 405/223-4044. **Free.**

Resort

✔★ LAKE MURRAY. *(3310 S Lake Murray Dr, #12A, Ardmore 73401) 7 mi S of Ardmore on Scenic US 77, 2 mi E of I-35, Lake Murray exit 24. 405/223-6600; res: 800/654-8240; FAX 405/223-6154.* 55 rms in lodge, 88 cottages. Mid-May-mid-Sept: S, D $49-$54; each addl $10; suites $75-$150; lower rates rest of yr; kit. cottages (no equipt) $35-$65; cottages for 6-12, $100-$150; 1-2 bedrm cottages $75-$95; under 18 free in lodge rms; golf plans. Crib free. Pet accepted. TV in lodge rms, 44 cottages, lobby; VCR avail. Pool; lifeguard. Playgrounds. Free supervised child's activities; ages 6-18. Dining rm 7 am-10 pm. Take outs, snacks. Rm serv. Bar 1 pm-midnight. Ck-out noon, ck-in 3 pm. Meeting rms. Business servs avail. Airport transportation. Gift shop. Grocery. Tennis. 18-hole golf privileges. Miniature golf. Paddleboats. Sport facilities of Lake Murray State Park. Lawn games. Soc dir. Rec rm. Movies. Chapel; services Sun. Some refrigerators, fireplaces. Cottages widely spaced. 2,500-ft lighted, paved airstrip. On Lake Murray. State operated. Cr cds: A, C, D, DS, MC, V.

Restaurant

★★ **FIRESIDE DINING.** *Lake Murray Village, 2 mi E of I-35, Lake Murray exit 24.* 405/226-4070. Hrs: 5-10 pm. Closed Sun, Mon; major hols. Continental menu. Semi-a la carte: dinner $11.95-$16.95. Child's meals. Specialties: prime cut aged beef, fresh seafood. Parking. Western decor; pioneer artifacts, fireplace, gardens. Cr cds: A, DS, MC, V.

D

Lake Texoma (E-8)

(See Durant, Marietta; also see Denison and Sherman, TX)

Area code 405
Information Project Office, Lake Texoma, Rte 4, Box 493, Denison TX 75020; 903/465-4990.

(On US 70, 12 mi E of Madill, 14 mi W of Durant)

This lake is so named because it is impounded behind Denison Dam on the Red River, the boundary between Oklahoma and Texas. With shores in both states, this is one of the finest and most popular of the lakes in either.

Approximately two-thirds of the lake's 89,000 acres are in Oklahoma. The total shoreline is 580 miles. Approximately 105,000 acres surrounding the lake are federally owned, but the state of Oklahoma has leased 1,600 acres between Madill and Durant for Lake Texoma State Park. The remainder of the lake is under control of the US Army Corps of Engineers, which built the dam. Project office (Mon-Fri; closed major hols).

Fishing boats and outboard motors may be rented at several locations on the lake. Guides are available. Duck and goose hunting is good. Swimming beaches have been developed at many points on the lake. Picnicking, camping and trailer hookups (fee charged), cabins and supplies at many points, some privately operated and some state owned. Also here are beach, swimming pool, bathhouse, waterskiing; fishing dock; boat dock, storage and marina; horseback riding; 18-hole golf course, driving range, putting range, tennis courts, shuffleboard; three playgrounds, restaurant, grocery, lodging (see RESORT); cabins and a 2,500-foot airstrip at Lake Texoma State Park.

At the northern end of the lake, on the courthouse grounds in Tishomingo is the Chickasaw Council House, the log cabin used as the first seat of government of the Chickasaw Nation in Indian territory. Enclosed in a larger building, it has displays on Native American history (daily exc Mon; closed major hols; free).

Fees may be charged at federal recreation sites.

Resort

★★ **LAKE TEXOMA.** *(Box 248, Kingston 73439) 5 mi E of Kingston on US 70 in Lake Texoma State Park.* 405/564-2311; res: 800/654-8240. 100 rms in main lodge; 20 rms in annex (dorm-type baths, phone in lobby); 67 cottages with kits. (no equipt). Mid-Apr-mid-Sept: S, D $55-$66; suites $88-$91; kit. cottages for 1-8, $63-$99; MAP, golf, fishing, honeymoon plans; some lower rates rest of yr. Crib free. TV in main lodge, cottages; cable. Pool; wading pool, lifeguard in summer. Playground. Free supervised child's activities. Dining rm 6:30 am-9:30 pm. Rm serv in lodge. Box lunches, snacks in summer. Ck-out noon, ck-in varies. Coin lndry. Convention facilities. Bellhops. Gift shop. Lighted tennis. 18-hole golf, greens fee $8-$10, pro. Miniature golf. Volleyball, horseshoe pit. Go-carts; bumper boats. Full-service marina. Exercise equipt; weights, bicycles, sauna. Sports dir; all facilities of state park. Fishing guides. Rec rm. Indoor, outdoor games. Refrigerator, wet bar in suites. Fireplace in cottages. Airstrip in park. State-owned, operated. Cr cds: A, C, D, DS, MC, V.

Restaurants

✔★ **NAIFEH'S STEAK HOUSE.** *(Rte 1, Box 17, Mead 73449) 9 mi W of Durant on US 70, 3 mi E of Roosevelt Bridge.* 405/924-7211. Hrs: 4-10 pm; Sat & Sun from 11 am. Closed Mon; Thanksgiving; also Dec 25-Jan 2. Res accepted. Bar. Semi-a la carte: lunch, dinner $3.50-$13.95. Child's meals. Specialties: tabuli salad, farm-raised catfish. Salad bar. Parking. Open grill. Cr cds: MC, V.

D

★ **SANFORD'S.** *(Box 1040, Kingston 73439) 4 mi E on US 70.* 405/564-3764. Hrs: 4-10 pm. Closed Sun, Mon; Thanksgiving, Dec 25. Semi-a la carte: dinner $7.45-$21.95. Specializes in catfish, steak. Salad bar. Cr cds: A, DS, MC, V.

D SC

Lawton (D-6)

(See Duncan)

Founded 1901 **Pop** 80,561 **Elev** 1,109 ft **Area code** 405
Information Chamber of Commerce, 607 C Ave, PO Box 1376, 73502; 405/355-3541.

Last of the many Oklahoma cities that sprang up overnight, Lawton had its land rush on August 6, 1901. The local tales—of the bank that was a shack on wheels, so that it could be moved to the lot its owner had chosen; the man who earned the name "Hog" by selecting a lot so shaped that it blocked off a woman's land from the town; the saloon that put out a sign "All nations welcome except CARRY"—are typical of Oklahoma's historical land rush. Lawton is the trading center of a large farm territory, but perhaps it owes most of its prosperity to Fort Sill, established in 1869 just north of town. Lawton is the state's third largest city.

What to See and Do

Fort Sill Military Reservation. A 94,268-acre army installation, US Army Field Artillery Center and School. Geronimo, war leader of the Apaches, spent his final years here and is buried in the post's Apache cemetery. There are many historic sites here. (Daily) 4 mi N on US 277. Phone 405/442-8111. **Free.**

Fort Sill National Historic Landmark. 43 buildings built of native stone during the 1870s, many of which are still being used for their original purpose. Includes

Sherman House, commandant's home. In 1871 General William Tecumseh Sherman was almost killed by Kiowa Indians on the front porch. Not open to the public.

Old Post Headquarters, from which Generals Grierson and Mackenzie conducted Indian campaigns.

Old Post Chapel, one of the oldest houses of worship still in use in state.

Old Guardhouse, Commissary Storehouse, Quartermaster warehouse, School of Fire, Quartermaster Corral, Visitor Center and Cannon Walk. Depicts history of field artillery and missiles. Cavalry, Native American relics. Film presentation of Fort Sill history, 25 min (daily). Self-guided tour map. (Daily; closed Jan 1, 2, Dec 25, 26) Phone 405/442-8111. **Free.**

Museum of the Great Plains. Displays on Native Americans, fur trade, exploration, cattle industry and settlement of the area; period rooms depict Main St of frontier town; outdoor exhibits of a 300-ton Baldwin steam locomotive, depot and wooden threshers; fortified trading post with a 100-sq-ft log stockade, 2-story blockhouses and furnished trader's cabin representing such a post in the 1830s-1840s. Trading post (Wed-Sun) has living history programs. (Daily; closed Jan 1, Thanksgiving, Dec 25) In Elmer Thomas Park, 601 Ferris Blvd. Phone 405/581-3460. ¢

Wichita Mountains Wildlife Refuge. This 59,060-acre refuge has 12 man-made lakes. Man-powered boating permitted on four lakes, trolling motors on three lakes. Picnicking. Camping only at Doris Campground; limited backcountry camping by reservation only (camping fee). Quanah Parker Visitor Center (Mar-Nov, Fri-Sun); self-guided trails. Longhorn cattle, herds of buffalo, elk, deer and other wildlife can be viewed from several wildlife/scenic viewing areas. (Daily) (See ANNUAL EVENTS) Headquarters are 13 mi W on US 62 to Cache, then 12 mi N on OK 115. Phone 405/429-3222. **Free.**

Annual Events

Easter Sunday Pageant. Holy City of the Wichitas, in Wichita Mountains National Wildlife Refuge. Phone 405/429-3361. Begins Sat evening before Easter.

Lawton Birthday and Rodeo Celebration. Street dancing, rodeo, races, parade. 3 days early Aug.

Motels

★ **EXECUTIVE INN.** 3110 NW Cache Rd (US 62) (73505). 405/353-3104; FAX 405/353-0992. 96 rms, 2 story. S, D $40-$54; each addl $6; under 16 free. Crib free. Pet accepted. TV; cable. Indoor/outdoor pool; sauna. Complimentary full bkfst. Ck-out noon. Valet serv. Free airport, bus depot transportation. Some bathrm phones, refrigerators. Cr cds: A, C, D, DS, MC, V.

★★ **HOLIDAY INN.** 3134 Cache Rd (US 62) (73505). 405/353-1682; FAX 405/353-1682, ext. 286. 171 rms, 2 story. S $48-$56; D $48-$61; each addl $5; under 17 free. Crib free. TV; cable. Pool. Restaurant 6 am-11 pm; Fri to midnight; Sat 7 am-midnight; Sun 7 am-10 pm. Rm serv. Bar 6 pm-2 am; dancing. Ck-out noon. Coin lndry. Meeting rms. Valet serv. Sundries. Some minibars. Cr cds: A, C, D, DS, JCB, MC, V.

✔★ **HOSPITALITY INN.** 202 E Lee Blvd (73501). 405/355-9765; FAX 405/355-2360. 106 rms, 2 story. S $33-$36; D $36-$40; each addl $4; under 16 free. Crib free. TV; cable. Pool. Continental bkfst. Complimentary coffee. Ck-out 12:30 pm. Coin lndry. Sundries. Cr cds: A, D, DS, MC, V.

★★ **HOWARD JOHNSON.** 1125 E Gore Blvd (73501), off I-44. 405/353-0200; FAX 405/353-6801. 142 rms, 2 story. S $44; D $49; suites $110-$140; each addl $5; under 16 free. Crib free. TV; cable (premium), VCR avail. 3 pools, 1 indoor; wading pool, sauna, poolside serv. Restaurant 6 am-9 pm. Rm serv. Bar 4 pm-2 am. Ck-out noon. Meeting rms. Business center. Free airport transportation. Lighted tennis. Some refrigerators. Private patios, balconies. Picnic tables. Cr cds: A, C, D, DS, JCB, MC, V.

★★ **RAMADA INN.** 601 N 2nd St (73507). 405/355-7155; FAX 405/353-6162. 98 rms, 2 story. S $44-$46; D $50-$52; each addl $6; under 18 free. Crib free. Pet accepted, some restrictions; $10. TV; cable (premium), VCR avail (movies avail $6.99). Pool. Complimentary coffee in rms. Restaurant 6 am-10 pm. Rm serv. Bar. Ck-out noon. Meeting rms. Cr cds: A, C, D, DS, JCB, MC, V.

Restaurants

★★ **FISHERMEN'S COVE.** OK 49, 10 mi N on I-44 (H.E. Bailey Tpke) Medicine Park exit, then 2 mi W on OK 49. 405/529-2672. Hrs: 4-10 pm; Sun 11 am-9 pm. Closed Mon, Tues; Thanksgiving, Dec 25. Res accepted. Semi-a la carte: dinner $4.95-$23.95. Child's meals. Specializes in seafood, hickory-smoked meat, Cajun dishes. Parking. Nautical decor. Family-owned. Cr cds: A, DS, MC, V.

★★★ **MARTIN'S.** 2107 NW Cache Rd (US 62). 405/353-5286. Hrs: 11 am-2 pm, 5:30-10:30 pm; Fri to 11pm, Sat 5-11 pm; Sun brunch on 1st Sun of each month 10:30 am-3 pm. Closed major hols; Dec 24-26. Res accepted. Bar. Wine list. Semi-a la carte: dinner $9.95-$39.95. Sun brunch $14.95. Child's meals. Specialties: veal Oscar, duck a l'orange, prime rib. Own baking. Piano. Family-owned. Cr cds: A, C, D, DS, MC, V.

✔★★ **SALAS.** 111 W Lee Blvd (OK 7). 405/357-1600. Hrs: 11 am-10 pm. Closed Mon, Tues; Jan 1, Thanksgiving, Dec 25. Res accepted. Mexican, Amer menu. Semi-a la carte: lunch, dinner $4.50-$8.50. View of kitchen. Parking. Family-owned. Cr cds: A, C, D, DS, MC, V.

Marietta (E-7)

(For accommodations see Ardmore, Lake Texoma)

Pop 2,306 **Elev** 841 ft **Area code** 405 **Zip** 73448
Information Love County Chamber of Commerce, 104 W Main, Box 422; 405/276-3102.

What to See and Do

Lake Murray State Park (see). 11 mi NE, off I-35 or OK 77.

Annual Event

Love County Frontier Days Celebration. Courthouse lawn. Parade, musical entertainment, games, races. 1st wkend June.

Restaurant

✔★ **McGEHEE CATFISH.** 407 W Broadway, 5 mi SW of I-35 Marietta exit (follow signs). 405/276-2751. Hrs: 5-9:30 pm; Sat, Sun from 1 pm. Closed Wed; Thanksgiving, 3 days Christmas. Semi-a la carte: dinner $9.49-$10.95. Child's meals. Specialities: catfish, hot cherry tarts. Limited menu. Parking. Old West decor; fireplace, antiques. Overlooks Red River. Cr cds: DS, MC, V.

McAlester (D-9)

(See Eufaula)

Founded 1870 **Pop** 16,370 **Elev** 723 ft **Area code** 918 **Zip** 74501

Information Chamber of Commerce, 17 E Carl Albert Pkwy, PO Box 759, 74502; 918/423-2550.

James J. McAlester came to Indian Territory in 1870 armed with a geologist's notebook describing some coal deposits and a fine sense of commercial strategy. He set up a tent store where the heavily traveled Texas Road crossed the California Trail and later married a Native American woman, which made him a member of the Choctaw Nation with full rights. When the railroad came through, he started mining coal. After a dispute with the Choctaw Nation over royalties, McAlester came to terms with the Indians, and in 1911 became lieutenant governor of the state.

Cattle raising, peanut farming, women's sportswear and lingerie, aircraft, electronics, boat and oil field equipment give the town's economy diversification.

What to See and Do

Lake McAlester. Fishing; boating. Stocked by the city. Supplies available on road to lake. (Daily) NW of town. Phone 918/423-1212.   **Free.**

McAlester Scottish Rite Temple. Unusual copper dome containing multicolored lenses makes this a landmark when lighted. One of its most illustrious members was Will Rogers, taking degrees in 1908. Tours (Mon-Fri by appt; closed most hols). Adams Ave & 2nd St. Phone 918/423-6360.   **Free.**

Robber's Cave State Park. Approximately 8,200 acres include lakes, alpine forests, "outlaw cave." Swimming, bathhouse; fishing; boating. Hiking, horseback riding trails. Picnicking, playground, restaurant, grocery. Camping, trailer hookups (fee), cabins. Amphitheater. (Daily) 35 mi E to Wilburton on US 270, then 5 mi N on OK 2. Phone 918/465-2565.   **Free.**

Annual Event

Sanders Family Bluegrass Festival. 5 mi W via US 270. Bluegrass performances, entertainment. Phone 918/423-4891. Early-mid-June.

Motels

✔★★ **COMFORT INN.** *1215 George Nigh Expy (74502), 4 mi S of jct US 270 & US 69 Bypass.* 918/426-0115; FAX 918/426-3634. 61 rms, 2 story. S $36-$40; D $44-$50; each addl $4; suite $75; under 18 free. Crib free. Pet accepted. TV; cable (premium). Pool. Restaurant 6 am-10 pm. Ck-out noon. Business servs avail. Some refrigerators. Cr cds: A, C, D, DS, ER, JCB, MC, V.

★★ **DAYS INN.** *1217 George Nigh Expy.* 918/426-5050; FAX 918/426-5055. 100 rms, 2 story. S $45; D $50; each addl $5; under 18 free. Crib free. Pet accepted. TV; cable (premium), VCR avail (movies avail). Indoor pool; hot tub. Restaurant 6-10 am, 5-10 pm. Rm serv. Bar 5 pm-midnight, closed Sun. Ck-out noon. Meeting rm. Some refrigerators. Near Municipal Airport. Cr cds: A, C, D, DS, JCB, MC, V.

★★ **HOLIDAY INN.** *Box 430 (74502), 2 mi SE on US 69 Bypass S.* 918/423-7766; FAX 918/426-0068. 161 rms, 2 story. S $45-$48; D $50-$55; each addl $5; suites $89-$178; under 19 free. Crib free. TV; cable. Heated pool. Restaurant 6 am-10 pm. Rm serv. Bar 4 pm-2 am; dancing; closed Sun. Ck-out noon. Coin lndry. Meeting rms. Bellhops. Valet serv. Sundries. Miniature golf. Exercise equipt; weight machine, bicycle, whirlpool, sauna. Holidome. Game rm. Near Municipal Airport. Cr cds: A, C, D, DS, JCB, MC, V.

Restaurants

★ **GIACOMO'S.** *19th & Comanche Sts, 1 mi SE on US 69 Bypass, 1 mi S of cloverleaf.* 918/423-2662. Hrs: 11:30 am-9:30 pm. Closed Sun, Mon; major hols; also wk after Memorial Day and Labor Day. Italian, Amer menu. Beer. Complete meals: lunch, dinner $8.50-$15.50. Child's meals. Specializes in steak, lamb fries, shrimp scampi. Parking. Family-owned. Cr cds: DS, MC, V.

★★ **ISLE OF CAPRI.** *(Box 1103, Krebs 74554) 1 blk N of US 270, 1 blk S of OK 31.* 918/423-3062. Hrs: 5-10:30 pm. Closed Sun; major hols; also wks of July 4 & Thanksgiving. Res accepted. Italian, Amer menu. Bar. Complete meals: dinner $8-$14. Child's meals. Specializes in steak, shrimp, lamb fries. Parking. Family-owned. Cr cds: A, MC, V.

★★ **PETE'S PLACE.** *(Box 66, Krebs 74554) Jct of US 270 & OK 31.* 918/423-2042. Hrs: 4-10 pm; Sun noon-9 pm. Closed major hols. Res accepted. Italian menu. Serv bar. Complete meals: dinner $7-$14.50. Child's meals. Specializes in lamb fries, steak. Parking. Family-owned. Cr cds: A, DS, MC, V.

✔★★ **TROLLEY'S.** *21 E Monroe St.* 918/423-2446. Hrs: 5-10 pm. Closed Thanksgiving, Dec 25. Res accepted. Serv bar. Semi-a la carte: dinner $5.75-$14.75. Child's meals. Specializes in seafood, steak, Cajun dishes. Own desserts. Parking. Located in restored house (1886) with former streetcar (1908) addition; decor from early movie theaters. Cr cds: A, C, D, DS, MC, V.

Miami (A-10)

(See Vinita)

Founded 1891 **Pop** 13,142 **Elev** 798 ft **Area code** 918 **Zip** 74354

Information Chamber of Commerce, 111 N Main, PO Box 760, phone 918/542-4481; or Traveler Information Center, E on Will Rogers Turnpike, phone 918/542-9303.

Situated on the headwaters of Grand Lake, Miami boasts many recreational facilities. Agriculture is diversified, and a number of outstanding foundation breeding herds are raised in the area. In recent years many industries have been attracted to Miami by the low-cost electricity generated by the Grand River Dam Authority.

What to See and Do

Grand Lake (see). S on US 59.

Riverview Park. Swimming; fishing; boating. Picnicking. Camping. On Neosho River, end of S Main St.

Motel

✔★★ **BEST WESTERN CONTINENTAL MOTOR INN.** *2225 E Steve Owens Blvd.* 918/542-6681; FAX 918/542-3777. 80 rms. S $44-$48; D $49-$52; each addl $4; under 12 free. Crib $3. Pet accepted. TV; cable (premium). Pool. Restaurant 6 am-10 pm. Rm serv. Bar 5 pm-midnight. Ck-out noon. Business servs avail. Airport transportation. Valet serv. Refrigerators. Cr cds: A, C, D, DS, MC, V.

Muskogee (B-9)

Founded 1872 **Pop** 37,708 **Elev** 602 ft **Area code** 918

Information Greater Muskogee Area Chamber of Commerce, 425 Boston, PO Box 797, 74402; 918/682-2401.

Located near the confluence of the Verdigris, Grand and Arkansas rivers, Muskogee was a logical site for a trading center, especially since it was in Indian country (Cherokee and Creek). On the old Texas Road, southward, over which families moved to Texas, and northward, over which cattle were driven to market, the town's location was commercially ideal. The railroad superseded the rivers in transportation importance, however, almost before the town was settled.

Today, Muskogee is a diversified agricultural and industrial center in which glass, paper products and paper containers, rare metals, structural steel and iron, optical machinery and many other products are manufactured. It is an attractive town, dotted with 32 small parks, and is the gateway to the eastern lakes area. The port of Muskogee is part of the McClellan-Kerr Arkansas River Navigation System, handling barges that go through the inland waterway system from Pittsburgh and Minneapolis to Houston and New Orleans.

Its Indian country surroundings made it a logical location for the US Union Agency for the Five Civilized Tribes (Cherokee, Chickasaw, Choctaw, Creek and Seminole). The agency is in the Old Union Building, Honor Heights Dr.

What to See and Do

Five Civilized Tribes Museum (1875). Art and artifacts of the Cherokees, Chickasaws, Choctaws, Creeks and Seminoles; displays relating to their history and culture. (Mar-Dec, daily; rest of yr Tues-Sat; closed Jan 1, Thanksgiving, Dec 25) Sr citizen rate. Agency Hill in Honor Heights Park. Phone 918/683-1701. ¢

Fort Gibson Military Park. Established as state's first military post in 1824, park includes 12 reconstructed or restored buildings on 55-acre site; period rooms depict army life in the 1830s and 1870s. Fort Gibson National Cemetery 1½ mi east. (Daily) 7 mi E on US 62 to Fort Gibson, then 1 mi N on OK 80. Phone 918/478-2669. **Free.**

Greenleaf Lake State Park. On a 930-acre lake stocked with crappie, channel catfish and black bass. Beach, swimming pool, bathhouse; enclosed fishing dock; boating (boat and equipment rentals, marina, boathouse). Hiking. Picnicking, playground. Camping trailer hookups (fee), cabins. (Daily) 20 mi SE on OK 10. Phone 918/487-5196. **Free.**

Honor Heights Park. A 112-acre park with azalea (mid-Apr), rose (May-Oct) and chrysanthemum gardens (Sept-Nov); nature walks, lakes, waterfall. Picnicking. (Daily) Honor Heights Dr, 3 mi NW. Phone 918/684-6302. **Free.**

Lake Tenkiller State Park (see TENKILLER FERRY LAKE). 30 mi SE on US 64, N on OK 10, 10A.

USS *Batfish.* World War II submarine. Also military museum; Teddy Roosevelt Historical Monument. (Mid-Mar-mid-Oct, daily) Sr citizen rate. 2 mi NE via Muskogee Tpke, Hyde Pk Rd at Port of Muskogee. Phone 918/682-6294. ¢¢

Annual Events

Azalea Festival. Parade, art shows, garden tours, entertainment. Mid-Apr.

Muskogee State Fair. 5 days early or mid-Sept.

Motels

★ ★ **BEST WESTERN TRADE WINDS.** *534 S 32nd St (US 64/69) (74401).* 918/683-2951. 109 rms, 2 story. S $43; D $47; each addl $4; suites $59; under 12 free. Crib $4. Pet accepted, some restrictions. TV; cable (premium). Pool; poolside serv. Complimentary coffee

in lobby. Restaurant 6 am-10 pm. Rm serv. Bar 4:30 pm-2 am, closed Sun; dancing. Ck-out noon. Meeting rms. Business servs avail. Valet serv. Cr cds: A, C, D, DS, MC, V.

★ **DAYS INN.** *900 S 32nd St (US 69) (74401).* 918/683-3911; FAX 918/683-5744. 43 rms, 2 story. S $38; D $45; each addl $5; under 12 free. Crib $5. TV; cable (premium). VCR avail. Pool. Complimentary coffee in rms. Restaurant nearby. Ck-out 11 am. Meeting rms. Business servs avail. Some refrigerators. Cr cds: A, C, D, DS, MC, V.

✔ ★ **QUALITY INN.** *2300 E Shawnee Ave (US 62/OK 16) (74403).* 918/683-6551; FAX 918/682-2877. 122 rms, 2 story. S $36-$41; D $41-$46; each addl $5; under 16 free. Crib free. TV; cable (premium). Pool. Restaurant 6 am-2 pm. Bar 4 pm-2 am, closed Sun; dancing. Ck-out noon. Meeting rms. Cr cds: A, C, D, DS, ER, MC, V.

★ ★ **RAMADA INN.** *800 S 32nd St (US 69) (74401).* 918/682-4341; FAX 918/682-7400. 135 rms, 2 story. S $48; D $53; each addl $5; suites $95-$125; under 18 free. Crib free. Pet accepted. TV; cable (premium). VCR avail. Indoor pool; whirlpool, sauna. Restaurant 6 am-2 pm, 5-9 pm; Sun to 2 pm; summer 5-10 pm. Rm serv. Bar 5 pm-2 am; Sun 6 am-2 pm; dancing. Ck-out noon. Meeting rms. Business servs avail. In-rm modem link avail. Game rm. Cr cds: A, C, D, DS, MC, V.

Restaurant

★ **OKIE'S.** *219 S 32nd St (US 69).* 918/683-1056. Hrs: 11 am-10 pm. Closed Sun; Jan 1, Thanksgiving, Dec 25. Res accepted. Bar. Semi-a la carte: lunch, dinner $4.75-$24.95. Child's meals. Specialties: marinated chicken breast, prime rib. Own ice cream. Parking. Antiques. Cr cds: A, C, D, DS, MC, V.

Norman (C-7)

Founded 1889 **Pop** 80,071 **Elev** 1,104 ft **Area code** 405

Information Chamber of Commerce, 115 E Gray, PO Box 982, 73070; 405/321-7260.

Norman was founded on April 22, 1889, in the famous land rush known as the "Oklahoma run." The run opened what was once Indian Territory to modern-day settlement. A year later the University of Oklahoma was founded. The city now offers numerous restaurants, museums, shopping areas, parks and lodgings as well as convention, conference and symposium sites. The city of Norman has a well-balanced economy with education, oil, industry, tourism, high technology, research and development and agriculture.

What to See and Do

Hunting preserves. Lexington, Lake Thunderbird, Little River Arm & Hog Creek Arm, NE of town. 9 mi S, off US 77.

Little River State Park. A 4,010-acre park on 6,070-acre Thunderbird Lake. Swimming, bathhouse; fishing; boating (ramp, rentals, marina). Hiking, riding; archery; minature golf (fee). Picnicking, playground, grocery. Camping, trailer hookups (fee). (Daily) 12 mi E on OK 9. Phone 405/360-3572. **Free.**

Sooner Theatre (1929). Seasonal concerts, ballets and theater productions.101 E Main at Norman's Performing Arts Center. Phone 405/321-9600. ¢¢¢

University of Oklahoma (1890). (20,000 students) An approx 3,100-acre campus with more than 225 buildings. Its University of Oklahoma

Press is a distinguished publishing house. On campus are the Fred Jones, Jr Museum of Art (daily exc Mon; phone 405/325-3272); Oklahoma Museum of Natural History (daily exc Mon; phone 405/325-4711); Rupel Jones Theater (phone 405/325-4101); University Research Park. (Museums closed major hols) 660 Parrington Oval. Phone 405/325-0311.

Annual Events

Chocolate Festival. 444 S Flood, in Firehouse Art Center. Artwork with chocolate theme; culinary delights. 1st wkend Feb.

Medieval Fair. Brandt Park duck pond at University of Oklahoma. Living history fair depicting life in the Middle Ages; strolling minstrels, jugglers, jesters; knights in armor joust; storytellers. Phone 405/321-7227. 2nd wkend Apr.

89er Celebration. Parade, contests, wagon train river crossing. 3rd wk Apr.

Motels

★ **DAYS INN.** 609 N Interstate Dr (73069). 405/360-4380; FAX 405/321-5767. 76 rms, 2 story. S $38; D $47; each addl $5; suites $55; under 12 free. TV; cable. Ck-out 11 am. Some refrigerators. Cr cds: A, C, D, DS, MC, V.

D ⊠ 🐾 **SC**

✔ ★ ★ **RAMADA INN.** 1200 SW 24th St (73072). 405/321-0110; FAX 405/360-5629. 150 rms, 2 story. S $46-$58; D $52-$64; each addl $6; suites $95; under 12 free; higher rates football wkends. Crib free. TV; cable. Pool. Restaurant 6 am-1:30 pm, 5:30-9 pm. Rm serv. Bar 2 pm-2 am; band wkends. Ck-out noon. Meeting rms. Valet serv. Game rm. Cr cds: A, D, DS, MC, V.

D ⊠ 🐾 **SC**

★ ★ **RESIDENCE INN BY MARRIOTT.** 2681 Jefferson St (73072). 405/366-0900; FAX 405/360-6552. 126 kit. suites, some rms with shower only, 2 story. Kit. suites from $89; family, wkly, monthly rates. Crib free. Pet accepted; $75. TV; cable. Pool; whirlpool. Complimentary coffee in rms. Restaurant nearby. Ck-out noon. Coin lndry. Meeting rms. Lighted tennis. Cr cds: A, C, D, DS, JCB, MC, V.

D 🐾 🎾 ⊠ 🔥 **SC**

✔ ★ **STRATFORD HOUSE INN.** 225 N Interstate Dr (73069). 405/329-7194. 40 rms, 2 story. S $34.92; D $42.95; each addl $3; under 18 free. Crib free. TV; cable. Complimentary continental bkfst. Restaurant nearby. Ck-out 11 am. In-rm whirlpools. Cr cds: A, C, D, DS, MC, V.

D ⊠ 🐾 **SC**

Hotel

★ ★ **HOLIDAY INN.** 1000 N Interstate Dr (73072). 405/364-2882; FAX 405/321-5264. 149 rms, 6 story. S $70-$100; D $80-$100; each addl $10; suites $90-$150; studio rms $60; under 18 free; higher rates football wkends. Crib free. TV; cable (premium). Indoor/outdoor pool. Restaurant 6 am-2 pm, 5-10 pm. Bar from 5 pm. Ck-out noon. Meeting rms. Business servs avail. In-rm modem link. Exercise equipt; weights, bicycles, whirlpool. Game rm. Some refrigerators. 3-story atrium. Cr cds: A, C, D, DS, JCB, MC, V.

D ⊠ 🍴 ⊠ 🐾 **SC**

Restaurants

★ **INTERURBAN.** 105 W Main. 405/364-7942. Hrs: 11 am-midnight; Fri, Sat to 2 am; Sun to 10 pm. Closed major hols. Bar. Semi-a la carte: lunch, dinner $2.45-$14.99. Child's meals. Specializes in gourmet hamburgers, own beer, baby back ribs. Outdoor dining.

Parking. Building (1917) was originally a trolley depot. Cr cds: A, C, D, DS, MC, V.

D

★ ★ ★ **LEGENDS'.** 1313 W Lindsey St. 405/329-8888. Hrs: 11 am-11 pm; Sun from 10 am; Sun brunch 10 am-4:30 pm. Closed Jan 1, Dec 25. Continental menu. Bar. Semi-a la carte: lunch $4.25-$6.95, dinner $4.95-$15.95. Sun brunch $4.25-$6.95. Specializes in fresh seafood, steak, pasta. Salad bar. Own desserts. Parking. Garden dining. Eclectic decor. Cr cds: A, C, D, DS, MC, V.

D

★ ★ **LUCIANO'S.** 1816 W Lindsey St. 405/366-1800. Hrs: 11:30 am-2 pm, 5-10 pm; Fri, Sat to 10:30 pm; Sun to 9 pm. Closed major hols. Res accepted. Italian menu. Bar. Wine list. Semi-a la carte: lunch $4.95-$7.95, dinner $8.95-$17.50. Sun brunch $3.95-$9.95. Specialties: chicken Marsala, fettucine Alfredo. Own breads. Parking. Outdoor dining. Cr cds: A, C, D, MC, V.

D

✔ ★ **VISTA SPORTS GRILL.** 111 N Peters, 6th floor. 405/447-0909. Hrs: 11 am-midnight; Fri & Sat to 2 am. Closed major hols. Bar. Semi-a la carte: lunch $2.95-$5.95, dinner $4.75-$9.95. Sun brunch $4.95-$5.95. Child's meals. Specializes in steaks, burgers, pasta. Sports memorabilia. Cr cds: A, C, D, DS, MC, V.

D

Oklahoma City (C-7)

Founded 1889 **Pop** 444,719 **Elev** 1,207 ft **Area code** 405

What is now the site of Oklahoma's capital was barren prairie on the morning of April 22, 1889. Unassigned land was opened to settlement that day, and by nightfall the population numbered 10,000. No city was ever settled faster or harder than during this famous run.

The city sits atop one of the nation's largest oilfields, with wells even on the lawn of the Capitol. First discovered in 1928, the field was rapidly developed throughout the city. It still produces large quantities of high-gravity oil. Oil-well equipment manufacture became one of the city's major industries.

Oklahoma City's stockyards and meatpacking plants are the largest in the state. The city is also a grain-milling and cotton-processing center. Iron and steel, furniture, tire manufacturing, electrical equipment, electronics, aircraft and automobile assembly are other industries. Tinker Air Force Base is southeast of the city.

Transportation

Car Rental Agencies: See toll-free numbers under Introduction.

Public Transportation: Buses (Central Oklahoma Transportation and Parking Authority), phone 405/235-7433.

Airport Information

Will Rogers World Airport: Information 405/681-5311; lost and found 405/681-3233; weather 405/478-3377; cash machines, located at upper level Main Terminal.

What to See and Do

45th Infantry Division Museum. Exhibits state military history from its beginnings in the early Oklahoma Territory through World War II, Korea to the present National Guard; uniforms, vehicles, aircraft, artillery and an extensive military firearms collection with pieces dating from the American Revolution; memorabilia and original cartoons by Bill Mauldin. (Daily exc Mon; closed some hols) 2145 NE 36th St. Phone 405/424-5313. **Free.**

Civic Center Music Hall. Home of the Oklahoma City Philharmonic, Canterbury Choral Society and Ballet Oklahoma. A variety of entertainment is provided, including Broadway shows and popular concerts. 201 Channing Sq. For schedule phone 405/297-2584.

Enterprise Square, USA. Exhibits celebrate the free enterprise system. Hands-on projects, computer games, electronic displays and other exhibits, including giant talking currency. (Daily; closed some major hols) Sr citizen rate. 2501 E Memorial Rd, between I-35 and Broadway Extension. Phone 405/425-5030. ¢¢

Frontier City. A 40-acre Western theme park; includes more than 60 rides, shows and attractions; entertainment; shops, restaurants. (Memorial Day-late Aug, daily; Easter-Memorial Day & late Aug-Oct, wkends only) 11501 NE Expy (I-35N). Phone 405/478-2412. ¢¢¢¢¢

Garden Exhibition Building and Horticulture Gardens. Azalea trails; butterfly garden; rose, peony and iris gardens; arboretum; conservatory has one of the country's largest cactus and succulent collections (daily). Exhibition Building (Mon-Fri; closed some hols; open Sat, Sun during flower shows). 3400 NW 36th St. Phone 405/943-0827. **Free.**

Harn Homestead and 1889er Museum. Historic homestead claimed in Land Run of 1889; 1904 farmhouse furnished with pre-statehood objects dating from period of the run. Three-story stone and cedar barn; one-room schoolhouse; working farm. Ten acres of picnic area, shade trees. (Tues-Sat; closed hols) 313 NE 16th St. Phone 405/235-4058. ¢¢

★ **Kirkpatrick Center.** Houses seven museums, including Oklahoma Air Space Museum and Red Earth Indian Center. (Daily; closed Thanksgiving, Dec 25) Sr citizen rate. 2100 NE 52nd St. Phone 405/427-5461. ¢¢¢   Also includes

International Photography Hall of Fame and Museum. Permanent and traveling exhibits; one of world's largest photographic murals. (Daily; closed Thanksgiving, Dec 25) Phone 405/424-4055.

Kirkpatrick Planetarium. Shows change quarterly. (Daily; closed Thanksgiving, Dec 25) Phone 405/424-5545.

OMNIPLEX Science Museum. Features more than 300 hands-on science exhibits, including enchanted tree, earthquake exhibit, Gravitram, Geovator, two-story dinosaur, weather station; changing exhibits. (Daily; closed Thanksgiving, Dec 25) Phone 405/424-5545.

Metro Concourse. A downtown "city beneath the city," the underground tunnel system connects nearly all the downtown buildings in a 20-square-block area. It is one of the most extensive all-enclosed pedestrian systems in the country. Offices, shops and restaurants line the concourse system. (Daily exc Sun)

Myriad Botanical Gardens. A 12-acre botanical garden in the heart of the city's redeveloping central business district. Features lake, amphitheater, botanical gardens and seven-story Crystal Bridge Tropical Conservatory Reno & Robinson Sts. Phone 405/297-3995. ¢¢. Myriad Botanical Gardens **Free.**

★ **National Cowboy Hall of Fame & Western Heritage Center.** Major art collections depict America's Western heritage; West of Yesterday Gallery features life-size re-creations of early pioneer life; Rodeo Hall of Fame; sculpture, including *End of the Trail, Buffalo Bill* and *Coming Through the Rye;* the John Wayne collection of guns, knives, kachina dolls and art; portrait gallery of Western film stars; landscaped gardens. (Daily; closed Jan 1, Thanksgiving, Dec 25) 1700 NE 63rd St, off I-44 near I-35, between Martin Luther King, Jr & Kelley Aves. Phone 405/478-2250. ¢¢¢

National Softball Hall of Fame and Museum. Displays of equipment and memorabilia trace the history of the sport; Hall of Fame; stadium complex. (Mar-Oct, daily; rest of yr, Mon-Fri) 2801 NE 50th St, just W of I-35. Phone 405/424-5266. ¢

OCAM at ArtsPlace. Features art by regional artists, crafts, handblown glass, jewelry; monthly changing exhibits. Offer walking tours of city (fee). (Mon-Fri; closed most major hols) 20 W Main, downtown. Phone 405/232-1787. **Free.**

Oklahoma City Art Museum. Permanent collection of 13th-20th-century European and American paintings, prints, drawings, photographs, sculpture and decorative arts; also temporary loan exhibits. Changing

exhibitions of regional, national and international artists. (Daily exc Mon; closed Jan 1, Easter, Thanksgiving, Dec 25) 3113 Pershing Blvd. Phone 405/946-4477. ¢¢

Oklahoma City Zoo. Covers 110 acres with more than 2,000 animals representing 500 species; expansive hoofstock collection; naturalistic island life exhibit; walk-through aviaries; herpetarium; pachyderm building; primate and gorilla exhibit; children's zoo with discovery area; Safari Tram, Sky Safari. (Daily; closed Jan 1, Dec 25) Exit 50th St off I-35, 1 mi W to zoo entrance. Phone 405/424-3344. ¢¢ On zoo grounds is

Aquaticus. A unique marine-life science facility contains comprehensive collection of aquatic life; dolphin/sea lion shows; shark tank; adaptations and habitat exhibits; underwater viewing. (Daily; closed Jan 1, Dec 25) Phone 405/424-3344. Shows ¢

Oklahoma Firefighters Museum. Antique fire equipment dating back to 1736; also first fire station (1869) in Oklahoma reassembled here. (Daily; closed hols) Sr citizen rate. 2716 NE 50th St. Phone 405/424-3440. ¢¢

Oklahoma Heritage Center. Restored Hefner family mansion (1917) maintained as a museum; antique furnishings; collection of bells, art; Oklahoma Hall of Fame galleries (3rd floor); memorial chapel and gardens. (Daily; closed Jan 1, Dec 25) 201 NW 14th St. Phone 405/235-4458. ¢¢

Oklahoma National Stockyards. One of world's largest cattle markets; auction of cattle, hogs, and sheep; Livestock Exchange Bldg. (Mon, Tues; closed hols) 2500 Exhange Ave. Phone 405/235-8675. **Free.**

Remington Park. Thoroughbred racing with 4-level grandstand and over 300 video monitors. Restaurants. (Feb-July, Sept-Dec; Wed-Sun) One Remington Place, at jct I-35 & I-44. For schedule phone 405/424-9000. General admission ¢¢

State Capitol. Greco-Roman, neoclassical building designed by S.A. Layton and Wemyss Smith. Oil well beneath Capitol building reaches 1.25 miles underground. After pumping oil from 1941-1986, it is now preserved as a monument. Legislature meets annually for 78 days beginning on the first Mon in Feb. Tours (daily; closed Dec 25) NE 23rd St & Lincoln Blvd. Phone 405/521-3356, **Free.**   Opp is

State Museum of History. Exhibits on the history of Oklahoma; extensive collection of Native American artifacts. (Daily exc Sun; closed major hols) Phone 405/521-2491. **Free.**

White Water Bay. Outdoor water park, with body surfing, water chutes, slides, rapids and swimming pool; special playland for tots. (June-Aug, daily; May & Sept, wkends) 3908 W Reno, via I-40, Meridian exit. Phone 405/943-9687. ¢¢¢¢

Annual Events

International Finals Rodeo. Myriad Convention Center. International Pro Rodeo Association's top 15 cowboys and cowgirls compete in 7 events to determine world championships. Phone 405/297-3000 or 405/236-5000. Late Jan.

Arts Festival. International foods, entertainment, children's learning & play area; craft market; artists from many states display their work. 6 days late Apr.

Red Earth. Native American heritage and culture featuring dancers and artists from most North American tribes. Dance competition, arts festival. Phone 405/427-5228. Mid-June.

Aerospace America. Will Rogers World Airport. Air show includes precision performers, aerobatics, parachute jumpers, warbird displays. June.

State Fair of Oklahoma. Fair Park. NW 10th St & N May Ave. Livestock, crafts, art exhibits; ice show, circus, rodeo; truck pull contests; auto races; concerts; international show, flower and garden show; Native American ceremonial dances; carriage collection; monorail, space tower, carnival, parades. Arena and grandstand attractions. Phone 405/948-6700. 17 days late Sept.

World Championship Quarter Horse Show. State fairgrounds. More than 1,800 horses compete. Mid-Nov.

Seasonal Events

Lyric Theatre. 2501 N Blackwelder Ave, in Kirkpatrick Fine Arts Auditorium of Oklahoma City University. Professional musical theatre. Phone 405/524-7111. Mid-June-mid-Aug.

Oklahoma City Philharmonic Orchestra. Civic Center Music Hall. Phone 405/843-0900. Sept-Apr.

Ballet Oklahoma. 201 Channing Sq. Phone 405/843-9898 or 405/848-TOES. Oct-Apr.

Additional Visitor Information

The following organizations can provide travelers with assistance and additional information: Oklahoma City Convention and Visitors Bureau, Four Santa Fe Plaza, 73102, phone 405/278-8912 or 800/225-5652; Oklahoma City Chamber of Commerce, 123 Park Ave, 73102, phone 405/278-8900; Oklahoma Tourism and Recreation Dept, 505 Will Rogers Building, 73105, phone 405/521-2406. *Oklahoma Today,* the state's official magazine, has up-to-date information and articles of interest to the tourist.

City Neighborhoods

Many of the restaurants, unrated dining establishments and some lodgings listed under Oklahoma City include neighborhoods as well as exact street addresses. Geographic descriptions of Downtown and Bricktown are given, followed by a table of restaurants arranged by neighborhood.

Bricktown: South of Sheridan Ave, west of Oklahoma Ave, east of the railroad tracks and along California St from Oklahoma Ave.

Downtown: South of 10th St, west of Walnut St, north of I-40/US 270 and east of Classen Blvd. **North of Downtown:** North of 10th St. **South of Downtown:** South of I-40/US 270. **West of Downtown:** West of Western Ave.

OKLAHOMA CITY
RESTAURANTS BY
NEIGHBORHOOD AREAS

(For full description, see alphabetical listings under Restaurants)

NORTH OF DOWNTOWN

Bellini's. 63rd & Pennsylvania

Classen Grill. 5124 N Classen Blvd

Coach House. 6437 Avondale Dr

The County Line. 1226 NE 63rd St

Don Serapio's. 11109 N May

Eagle's Nest. 5900 Mosteller Dr

Eddy's Of Oklahoma City. 4227 N Meridian Ave

Furrs Cafeteria. 2842 NW 63rd St

Jamil's. 4910 N Lincoln

La Baguette. 7408 N May Ave

Michael's Supper Club. 1601 Northwest Expy (OK 3)

Sleepy Hollow. 1101 NE 50th St

Waterford (The Waterford Hotel). 6300 Waterford Blvd

SOUTH OF DOWNTOWN

Aloha Garden. 2219 SW 74th St

Cattleman's Steakhouse. 1309 S Agnew St

WEST OF DOWNTOWN

Applewoods. 4301 SW 3rd St

Molly Murphy's House Of Fine Repute. 1100 S Meridian Ave

Shorty Small's. 4500 W Reno

Texanna Red's. 4600 W Reno

Note: When a listing is located in a town that does not have its own city heading, it will appear under the city nearest to its location. In these cases, the address and town appear in parenthesis immediately following the name of the establishment.

Motels

★ ★ ★ **BEST WESTERN-SADDLEBACK INN.** *4300 SW 3rd St (73108), 1/2 blk NE of I-40 Meridian Ave exit, west of downtown.* 405/947-7000; FAX 405/948-7636. 220 rms, 2-3 story. S $53-$60; D $60-$67; each addl $7; suites $68-$75; under 17 free; wkend rates. Crib free. TV; cable (premium), VCR avail. Heated pool; poolside serv. Coffee in rms. Restaurant 6 am-2 pm, 5-10 pm; Sat, Sun to 9 pm. Rm serv. Bar 4 pm-midnight. Ck-out noon. Coin lndry. Meeting rms. Business servs avail. In-rm modem link. Bellhops. Valet serv. Gift shop. Sundries. Free airport transportation. Exercise equipt; weights, bicycles, whirlpool, sauna. Southwestern decor. Cr cds: A, C, D, DS, MC, V.

[D] [≈] [🖈] [🚫] [🔥] [SC]

✔ ★ **COMFORT INN.** *4017 NW 39th Expy (US 66/270) (73112), north of downtown.* 405/947-0038; FAX 405/946-7450. 112 rms, 2 story, 15 kit. units. S, D $44-$54; each addl $6; kit. units $54-$66; under 18 free. Crib $6. Pet accepted, some restrictions. TV; cable (premium), VCR avail (movies avail $6.99). Pool. Complimentary continental bkfst, coffee in rms. Restaurant adj open 24 hrs. Ck-out noon. Coin lndry. Meeting rms. Business center. In-rm modem link avail. Valet serv. Some refrigerators. Cr cds: A, C, D, DS, ER, JCB, MC, V.

[D] [🐾] [≈] [🚫] [🔥] [SC] [🖈]

★ ★ ★ **COURTYARD BY MARRIOTT.** *4301 Highline Blvd (73108), near Will Rogers World Airport, west of downtown.* 405/946-6500; FAX 405/946-7638. 149 rms, 3 story. S $79; D $89; suites $99-$109; under 12 free; wkend rates. TV; cable (premium), VCR avail (movies avail $8). Heated pool. Complimentary coffee in rms. Restaurant 6:30-10:30 am; wkends 7-11 am. Bar 4-11 pm. Ck-out 1 pm. Coin lndry. Meeting rms. Business servs avail. In-rm modem link. Valet serv. Sundries. Free airport transportation. Exercise equipt; weight machine, bicycles, whirlpool. Refrigerator in suites. Balconies. Cr cds: A, C, D, DS, MC, V.

[D] [≈] [🖈] [🚫] [🔥] [SC]

✔ ★ ★ **DAYS INN-NORTHWEST.** *2801 NW 39th St (73112), north of downtown.* 405/946-0741; FAX 405/942-0181. 191 rms, 2 story. S $42-$48; D $46-$55; each addl $6; suites $75; under 16 free; wkend rates. Crib free. TV; cable (premium), VCR avail. Pool. Restaurant 6:30 am-1 pm, 5-10 pm. Rm serv. Bar 4 pm-midnight. Ck-out 11 am. Coin lndry. Meeting rms. Business center. In-rm modem link. Valet serv. Sundries. Free airport transportation. Some bathrm phones, refrigerators. Cr cds: A, C, D, DS, JCB, MC, V.

[D] [≈] [🚫] [🔥] [SC] [🖈]

★ **GOVERNORS SUITES.** *2308 S Meridian (73108), near Will Rogers World Airport, west of downtown.* 405/682-5299; FAX 405/682-3047. 50 units, 3 story. S, D $59-$95. Crib free. Pet accepted, some restrictions; $10. TV; cable. Pool; whirlpool, sauna. Complimentary coffee in rms; continental bkfst. Restaurant nearby. Ck-out noon. Meeting rm. Free airport transportation. Cr cds: A, C, D, DS, MC, V.

[D] [🐾] [≈] [🖈] [🚫] [🔥] [SC]

★ ★ **HAMPTON INN.** *1905 S Meridian Ave (73108), 1 mi S of I-40, near Will Rogers World Airport, west of downtown.* 405/682-2080; FAX 405/682-3662. 134 rms, 3 story. S $59-$65; D $66-$70; each addl

$7; suites $76; under 18 free; wkend rates. Crib free. Pet accepted, some restrictions. TV; cable (premium). Pool. Complimentary continental bkfst. Ck-out noon. Meeting rms. Business servs avail. In-rm modem link. Valet serv. Free airport transportation. Some refrigerators. Some private patios, balconies. Cr cds: A, C, D, DS, ER, JCB, MC, V.

⊡ 🏄 ≈ ⊠ 🔥 SC

★ **HOLIDAY INN NORTH.** 12001 NE Expressway (73131), I-35 exit 137. 405/478-0400; FAX 405/478-2774. 213 rms, 2 story. June-Aug: S $55-$60; D $60-$65; each addl $5; suites $75-$125; under 18 free; higher rates special events; lower rates rest of yr. Crib free. Pet accepted. TV; cable (premium), VCR avail. Pool; sauna. Playground. Restaurant 6 am-2 pm, 5-10 pm. Rm serv. Bar 5 pm-midnight. Ck-out noon. Coin lndry. Meeting rms. Business servs avail. Game rm. Lawn games. Cr cds: A, C, D, DS, JCB, MC, V.

⊡ 🏄 ≈ ⊠ 🐾 🔥 SC

★★ **LA QUINTA.** 8315 S I-35 (73149), 7 mi SE on I-35, exit 121A, south of downtown. 405/631-8661; FAX 405/631-1892. 121 rms, 2 story. S, D $53-$60; each addl $8; under 18 free. Crib free. TV; cable (premium). Pool. Complimentary bkfst in lobby. Restaurant opp open 24 hrs. Ck-out noon. Meeting rm. Business servs avail. In-rm modem link avail. Valet serv. Cr cds: A, C, D, DS, MC, V.

⊡ ≈ ⊠ 🔥 SC

★★ **RAMADA INN-AIRPORT WEST.** 800 S Meridian Ave (73108), west of downtown. 405/942-0040; FAX 405/942-0638. 171 rms, 2 story S $54-$58; D $54-$58; suites $75; each addl $8; under 18 free. Pet accepted, some restrictions. TV; cable, VCR avail (movies avail $9.47). Pool; wading pool, poolside serv. Restaurant 6:30 am-midnight. Rm serv. Bar from 10 am. Ck-out noon. Meeting rms. Business servs avail. Free airport, bus depot transportation. Refrigerators avail. Cr cds: A, C, D, DS, MC, V.

⊡ 🏄 ≈ ⊠ 🔥 SC

★★ **RESIDENCE INN BY MARRIOTT.** 4361 W Reno Ave (73107), 2 blks NE of I-40 Meridian exit, west of downtown. 405/942-4500; FAX 405/942-7777. 135 kit. suites, 1-2 story. 1-bedrm suites $95; 2-bedrm suites $115. Crib free. Pet accepted, some restrictions; $25 and $6 per day. TV; cable (premium), VCR avail. Heated pool; whirlpool. Complimentary continental bkfst. Complimentary coffee in rms. Ck-out noon. Coin lndry. Meeting rms. Business servs avail. In-rm modem link. Valet serv. Airport transportation. Health club privileges. Refrigerators, fireplaces. Private patios, balconies. Picnic tables, grills. Cr cds: A, C, D, DS, JCB, MC, V.

⊡ 🏄 ≈ ⊠ 🔥 SC

★★ **RICHMOND SUITES HOTEL.** 1600 Richmond Square (73118), north of downtown. 405/840-1440; res: 800/843-1440; FAX 405/843-4272. 50 suites, 2 story. S, D $80-$125; under 18 free; wknd, hol rates. Crib $5. Pet accepted, some restrictions; $50. TV; cable (premium). Pool. Complimentary continental bkfst. Complimentary coffee in rms. Restaurant 11:30 am-2 pm, 6:30-10 pm; Sat from 6 pm; closed Sun. Rm serv. Bar, closed Sun; pianist. Meeting rms. Business servs avail. In-rm modem link. Free airport transportation. Refrigerators, minibars. Cr cds: A, C, D, DS, MC, V.

⊡ 🏄 ≈ ⊠ 🔥 SC

✔★ **RODEWAY INN.** 4601 SW 3rd (73128), west of downtown. 405/947-2400; FAX 405/947-2931. 183 rms, 2 story. S $38; D $42; each addl $4; suites $65-$125; under 17 free. Crib free. TV; cable (premium), VCR avail. Pool. Complimentary continental bkfst. Restaurant adj open 24 hrs. Ck-out noon. Coin lndry. Business servs avail. Valet serv. Free airport transportation. Cr cds: A, C, D, DS, JCB, MC, V.

⊡ ≈ ⊠ 🔥 SC

★ **TRAVELERS INN.** 504 S Meridan (73108), jct I-40, west of downtown. 405/942-8294; FAX 405/947-3529. 136 rms, 2 story. S $30.95; D $37.95; each addl $4; suites $43.95-$50.95; under 11 free. Crib free. TV; cable (premium). Pool. Complimentary continental bkfst. Restaurant adj 11 am-11 pm. Ck-out 11 am. Coin lndry. Business servs

avail. In-rm modem link. Valet serv. Near airport. Cr cds: A, C, D, DS, MC, V.

⊡ ≈ ⊠ 🔥 SC

Motor Hotels

★★ **BEST WESTERN SANTA FE INN.** 6101 N Santa Fe (73118), I-44 exit 127. 405/848-1919; FAX 405/840-1581. 96 rms, 3 story. S $51-$56; D $63-$70; each addl $7; suites $65-$85; under 12 free. Crib free. TV; cable (premium). Pool; whirlpool. Complimentary coffee in rms. Complimentary full bkfst. Restaurant 6 am-1:30 pm, 5-9 pm. Rm serv. Bar 5 pm-midnight. Ck-out 11 am. Meeting rms. Business servs avail. In-rm modem link. Valet serv. Health club privileges. Refrigerator in suites. Cr cds: A, C, D, DS, JCB, MC, V.

⊡ ≈ ⊠ 🔥 SC

★★★ **CLARION.** 4345 N Lincoln Blvd (73105). 405/528-2741; FAX 405/525-8185. 68 rms, 3 story. S $92; D $102; under 18 free; wkend rates. Crib $10. TV; cable (premium). Pool; wading pool, poolside serv. Complimentary continental bkfst. Restaurant 6:30 am-9 pm. Rm serv to 10 pm. Bar 11-2 am. Ck-out noon. Meeting rms. Business center. In-rm modem link. Free airport transportation. Bellhops. Concierge. Gift shop. Valet serv. Lighted tennis. Exercise equipt; weight machine, stair machine, sauna. Minibars. Cr cds: A, C, D, DS, JCB, MC, V.

🏄 ≈ 🏃 ⊠ 🔥 SC 🏃

★★ **COMFORT INN.** 4445 N Lincoln Blvd (73105), off I-44. 405/528-6511; FAX 405/525-8185. 240 rms, 7 story. S $62; D $68; each addl $6; suites $125-$175; under 18 free; wkend rates. Crib free. TV; cable (premium). Pool; wading pool, poolside serv. Complimentary continental bkfst. Restaurant 6:30 am-9 pm. Rm serv. Bar 11-2 am. Ck-out noon. Meeting rms. Business servs avail. Bellhops. Gift shop. Valet serv. Free airport transportation. Lighted tennis. Exercise equipt; weight machine, stair machine, sauna. Cr cds: A, C, D, DS, MC, V.

⊡ 🏄 ≈ 🏃 ⊠ 🔥 SC

★★★ **RADISSON.** 401 S Meridian Ave (73108), at I-40, Meridian Ave exit, west of downtown. 405/947-7681; FAX 405/947-4253. 509 rms, 2 story. S $61-$81; D $71-$91; each addl $10; suites $89-$185; family, wkend rates. Crib free. Pet accepted, some restrictions. TV; cable (premium), VCR avail. 4 pools, 1 indoor; poolside serv. Restaurants 6 am-11 pm. Rm serv. Bars 11:30-2 am; entertainment, dancing. Ck-out noon. Meeting rms. Business servs avail. Bellhops. Sundries. Gift shop. Barber shop. Free airport transportation. Tennis. Paddle tennis. Exercise equipt; weights, bicycles, whirlpool, sauna. Bathrm phone, wet bar in townhouse suites; whirlpool in some suites. Cr cds: A, C, D, DS, ER, JCB, MC, V.

⊡ 🏄 🏃 ≈ 🏃 ⊠ 🔥 SC

Hotels

★★★ **EMBASSY SUITES.** 1815 S Meridian Ave (73108), west of downtown. 405/682-6000; FAX 405/682-9835. 236 suites, 6 story. S, D $115-$125; each addl $10; under 12 free; wkend rates. Crib free. Pet accepted. TV; cable (premium). Indoor pool. Complimentary bkfst. Complimentary coffee in rms. Restaurant 6 am-10 pm; Sat, Sun from 6:30 am. Bar 4 pm-2 am. Ck-out noon. Meeting rms. Business servs avail. In-rm modem link. Gift shop. Airport transportation. Exercise equipt; weights, bicycles, whirlpool, steam rm, sauna. Refrigerators, wet bars. Some balconies. Atrium. Cr cds: A, C, D, DS, MC, V.

⊡ 🏄 ≈ 🏃 ⊠ 🔥 SC

★★ **FIFTH SEASON.** 6200 N Robinson Ave (73118), north of downtown. 405/843-5558; res: 800/682-0049 (exc OK), 800/522-9458 (OK); FAX 405/840-3410. 202 rms, 3 story, 27 suites. S, D $65-$80; each addl $10; suites $85-$95; under 12 free; wknd rates; race track plans. Crib free. Pet accepted, some restrictions. TV; cable (premium). Indoor pool; poolside serv. Complimentary full bkfst. Restaurant 6:30

am-2 pm, 5-10 pm. Bar 4 pm-2 am. Ck-out noon. Coin lndry. Meeting rms. Business servs avail. Gift shop. Free airport transportation. Health club privileges. Refrigerator, minibar in suites. Cr cds: A, C, D, DS, JCB, MC, V.

D 🖐 ≈ 🏃 🔥 SC

★ ★ ★ **HILTON-NORTHWEST.** *2945 Northwest Expy (OK 3) (73112), west of downtown.* 405/848-4811; FAX 405/843-4829. 212 rms, 9 story. S $89-$129; D $99-$139; each addl $10; suites $175-$299; under 18 free; wkend rates. Crib free. TV; cable (premium), VCR avail. Heated pool; poolside serv. Complimentary coffee in rms. Restaurant 6 am-10 pm. Bar 4 pm-midnight; Fri, Sat to 1 am; Sun to 10 pm; pianist exc Sun. Ck-out noon. Meeting rms. Business servs avail. In-rm modem link. Free airport transportation. Exercise equipt; weights, bicycles. Refrigerator in suites. Cr cds: A, C, D, DS, ER, MC, V.

D ≈ 🏃 🔥 SC

★ ★ ★ **MARRIOTT.** *3233 Northwest Expy (OK 3) (73112), northwest of downtown.* 405/842-6633; FAX 405/842-3152. 354 rms, 15 story. S, D $129-$139; suites $175-$350; studio rms $89; under 18 free; wkend rates. Crib free. Pet accepted, some restrictions. TV; cable (premium). Indoor/outdoor pool. Restaurant 6:30 am-11 pm. Bar 4 pm-2 am, Sun to midnight; entertainment Sat; dancing. Ck-out noon. Coin lndry. Convention facilities. Business servs avail. In-rm modem link. Concierge. Gift shop. Exercise equipt; weights, bicycles. Health club privileges. Some balconies. Luxury level. Cr cds: A, C, D, DS, ER, JCB, MC, V.

D 🖐 ≈ 🏃 🔥 SC

★ ★ **MEDALLION.** *One N Broadway (73102), downtown.* 405/235-2780; res: 800/285-2780; FAX 405/272-0369. 399 rms, 15 story. S $99; D $109; suites $150-$350; wkend rates. Crib free. Garage $4. TV; cable (premium), VCR avail. Pool. Restaurant 6:30 am-10 pm. Rm serv 24 hrs. Bar 11-2 am. Ck-out noon. Convention facilities. Business servs avail. In-rm modem link. Valet parking. Health club privileges. Luxury level. Cr cds: A, C, D, DS, MC, V.

D ≈ 🏃 🔥 SC

★ ★ **RAMADA EDMOND.** *(930 E 2nd St, Edmond 73034) 10 mi N, 1 1/2 mi W of I-35 exit Edmond-2nd St, opp University of Central OK.* 405/341-3577; res: 800/322-4686; FAX 405/341-9279. 145 rms, 8 story. S $55-$65; D $60-$75; each addl $10; suites $85-$150; under 18 free; wkend rates. Crib free. TV; cable. Pool; whirlpool. Complimentary coffee in rms. Complimentary full bkfst. Restaurant 6 am-2 pm, 5-10 pm. Rm serv. Bar 4 pm-midnight, Sat to 1:30 am, Sun 4-10 pm; entertainment Fri & Sat, dancing. Ck-out 11 am. Meeting rms. Business servs avail. Exercise rm: treadmills, stair machine. Cr cds: A, C, D, DS, JCB, MC, V.

D ≈ 🏃 🔥 SC

★ ★ ★ **THE WATERFORD HOTEL.** *6300 Waterford Blvd (73118), north of downtown.* 405/848-4782; res: 800/992-2009; FAX 405/843-9161. 197 rms, 9 story. S $118-$145; D $128-$155; each addl $10; suites $165-$750; under 18 free; honeymoon, wkend packages. Crib free. TV; cable (premium), VCR avail. Heated pool; poolside serv. Restaurant (see WATERFORD). Bar 11-1 am; entertainment, dancing. Ck-out noon. Business center. In-rm modem link. Concierge. Airport transportation; free transportation to Remington Park race track. Exercise rm; instructor, weights, bicycles, whirlpool, sauna, steam rm. Massage. Squash. Bathrm phones; some refrigerators. Some balconies. Luxury level. Cr cds: A, C, D, DS, MC, V.

D ≈ 🏃 🌴 🔥 🏃

Restaurants

✔ ★ ★ **ALOHA GARDEN.** *2219 SW 74th St, in Walnut Square Shopping Center, I-240 exit Pennsylvania Ave S, south of downtown.* 405/686-0288. Hrs: 11 am-9:30 pm; Fri, Sat to 10:30 pm; Sun brunch 11 am-2:30 pm. Closed major hols. Res accepted. Chinese, Amer menu. Bar. Semi-a la carte: lunch $3.95-$5.50, dinner $4.25-$13.95.

Sun brunch $6.25. Buffet: lunch $4.95, dinner (Fri, Sat) $7.25. Child's meals. Specializes in seafood combinations, willow beef. Own sauces. Oriental decor. Cr cds: A, C, D, DS, MC, V.

D 🍽

★ ★ **APPLEWOODS.** *4301 SW 3rd St (73108), west of downtown.* 405/947-8484. Hrs: 11 am-2 pm, 5-10 pm; Fri to 11 pm; Sat 4-11 pm; Sun 11 am-3 pm, 4:30-10 pm. Closed major hols. Bar. Semi-a la carte: lunch $3.95-$8.95, dinner $8.95-$17. Buffet: lunch (Sun) $6.50. Child's meals. Specializes in pot roast, pork chops, hot apple dumplings. Magician on wkends. Cr cds: A, C, D, DS, MC, V.

D 🍽

★ ★ ★ **BELLINI'S.** *63rd & Pennsylvania (73188), in underground parking garage, north of downtown.* 405/848-1065. Hrs: 11 am-10:30 pm; Fri & Sat to 11:30 pm; Sun to 9 pm; Sun brunch to 2:30 pm. Closed some major hols. Italian, Amer menu. Bar. Semi-a la carte: lunch $5.95-$10.95, dinner $6.95-$17.95. Sun brunch $5.95-$7.95. Specializes in pasta, pizza. Parking. Patio dining, view of park and fountain. Open brick pizza oven. Cr cds: A, C, D, DS, MC, V.

D 🍽

★ ★ **CATTLEMAN'S STEAKHOUSE.** *1309 S Agnew St (73108), south of downtown.* 405/236-0416. Hrs: 6 am-2 pm; Fri & Sat to midnight. Closed Thanksgiving, Dec 25. Serv bar. Semi-a la carte: bkfst $1.40-$6, lunch $2.25-$17.95, dinner $5.95-$17.95. Sat & Sun bkfst buffet $4.50. Specializes in steak, lamb fries. Parking. In historic Stockyards City district, first opened in 1910. Cr cds: A, C, D, DS, MC, V.

D 🍽

★ ★ ★ **COACH HOUSE.** *6437 Avondale Dr, north of downtown.* 405/842-1000. Hrs: 11:30 am-2 pm, 6-10 pm; Sat from 6 pm. Closed Sun; major hols. Res accepted. French, Amer menu. Serv bar. A la carte entrees: lunch $6-$12, dinner $18-$26. Specializes in rack of lamb, Dover sole, Grand Marnier souffle. Parking. Formal dining. Cr cds: A, C, D, DS, MC, V.

D 🍽

★ **THE COUNTY LINE.** *1226 NE 63rd St (73111), north of downtown.* 405/478-4955. Hrs: 11 am-10 pm; Fri & Sat to 11 pm. Closed some major hols. Bar. Semi-a la carte: lunch $4.95-$10.95, dinner $6.95-$16.95. Child's meals. Specializes in barbecue, prime rib. Parking. Nostalgic decor and atmosphere. Cr cds: A, D, DS, MC, V.

D 🍽

★ **DON SERAPIO'S.** *11109 N May (73120), north of downtown.* 405/755-1664. Hrs: 11 am-10 pm; Fri & Sat to 11 pm; Sun to 9 pm. Closed Mon; major hols. Res accepted. Mexican menu. Bar. Semi-a la carte: lunch $5.29; dinner $4.95-$11.95. Child's meals. Specializes in fajitas, chile belleno, chile burrito. Own tamales. Parking. Mexican cantina-style dining. Cr cds: A, C, D, DS, MC, V.

D SC 🍽

★ ★ ★ **EAGLE'S NEST.** *5900 Mosteller Dr, top of United Founder's Tower, north of downtown.* 405/840-5655. Hrs: 11 am-2 pm, 6-10 pm; Fri to 10:30 pm; Sat 6-10:30 pm; Sun 6-9 pm. Closed major hols. Res accepted. Bar. Semi-a la carte: lunch $5.95-$8.25, dinner $14.95-$25.95. Buffet: lunch $7.95. Child's meals. Specializes in steak, fresh seafood. Entertainment Wed, Fri & Sat. Parking. Scenic view of city; revolving room. Family-owned. Cr cds: A, C, D, DS, MC, V.

D 🍽

★ ★ ★ **EDDY'S OF OKLAHOMA CITY.** *4227 N Meridian Ave, north of downtown.* 405/787-2944. Hrs: 5-10:30 pm; Fri, Sat to 11 pm; Easter, Mother's Day & Father's Day 11 am-8:30 pm. Closed Sun; Thanksgiving, Dec 25. Semi-a la carte: dinner $9.95-$18.95. Child's meals. Specialties: Lebanese hors d'oeuvres, steak, seafood. Own pastries. Parking. Display of Jack Riley bronze Western sculpture. Family-owned. Cr cds: A, C, D, DS, MC, V.

D 🍽

★★ **GREYSTONE.** *(1 N Sooner Rd, Edmond) 10 mi N on I-35 to exit 141, west to Sooner Rd, turn right. 405/340-4400.* Hrs: 11 am-2 pm, 5-9 pm; Fri, Sat to 10 pm; early-bird dinner Tues-Fri 5-6:30 pm; Sun brunch 10 am-2:30 pm. Closed Mon; July 4, Dec 25. Res accepted. Continental menu. Bar. Semi-a la carte: lunch $5.75-$9.95, dinner $10.75-$42.50. Sun brunch $11.95. Child's meals. Specializes in steak, lobster. Valet parking. Elegant dining in quiet atmosphere. Cr cds: A, C, D, DS, MC, V.

★★ **JAMIL'S.** *4910 N Lincoln, north of downtown. 405/525-8352.* Hrs: 11 am-2 pm, 5-10 pm; Fri, Sat to 11 pm; Sun 5-10 pm. Closed most major hols. Res accepted. Bar. Complete meals: lunch $3.95-$7.95, dinner $9.95-$26.95. Child's meals. Specializes in steak. Parking. Antiques from frontier period; Tiffany-style lamps, etched-glass doors. Family-owned. Cr cds: A, MC, V.

★ **LA BAGUETTE.** *7408 N May Ave, north of downtown. 405/840-3047.* Hrs: 8 am-10 pm; Mon to 5 pm; Sun 10 am-2 pm. Closed some major hols. Res accepted. French menu. Bar. Semi-a la carte: bkfst $2.75-$6.95, lunch $3.50-$10.50, dinner $6.95-$20.95. Sun brunch $4.95-$8.95. Parking. Bistro atmosphere. Cr cds: A, C, D, DS, MC, V.

★★ **MICHAEL'S SUPPER CLUB.** *1601 Northwest Expy (OK 3), in Bank IV Tower, north of downtown. 405/842-5464.* Hrs: 11 am-2 pm, 5:30-11 pm. Closed Sun; most major hols. Res accepted. Bar to 2 am. Wine list. Semi-a la carte: lunch $6-$8, dinner $11.95-$31.95. Specializes in steak, seafood, veal. Own baking. Pianist evenings. Parking. Skylight, Italian chandelier. Cr cds: A, C, D, MC, V.

★★ **MOLLY MURPHY'S HOUSE OF FINE REPUTE.** *1100 S Meridian Ave (73108), west of downtown. 405/942-8589.* Hrs: 5-10 pm; Fri, Sat to 11 pm. Closed Jan 1, Dec 25. Bar. A la carte entrees: dinner $12.95-$17.95. Child's meals. Specialties: prime rib, Bacchus Feast. Salad bar. Parking. Entertainment. The salad bar is set within a 1962 Jaguar XKE convertible. A unique dining experience featuring costumed servers portraying various characters and an eclectic atmosphere replete with antiques and varied design motifs. Cr cds: A, MC, V.

✔★ **SHORTY SMALL'S.** *4500 W Reno, west of downtown. 405/947-0779.* Hrs: 11 am-10 pm; Fri, Sat to 11 pm. Closed Thanksgiving, Dec 25. Bar. Semi-a la carte: lunch, dinner $2.99-$16.99. Child's meals. Specializes in St Louis-style ribs, barbecued brisket, steak. Parking. Rustic decor. Cr cds: A, C, D, DS, MC, V.

★★ **SLEEPY HOLLOW.** *1101 NE 50th St, north of downtown. 405/424-1614.* Hrs: 11 am-2 pm, 5-10 pm; Sat from 5 pm; Sun brunch 10:30 am-3 pm. Closed Dec 25. Res accepted. Semi-a la carte: lunch $3.50-$9. Complete meals: dinner $10.95-$24.95. Specializes in pan-fried chicken, steak, seafood. Own biscuits. Valet parking. Cr cds: A, DS, MC, V.

✔★ **TEXANNA RED'S.** *4600 W Reno, west of downtown. 405/947-8665.* Hrs: 11 am-10:30 pm; Fri, Sat to 11 pm; Sun to 10 pm. Closed major hols. Res accepted exc Fri & Sat. Mexican menu. Bar. Semi-a la carte: lunch, dinner $4.95-$15.95. Child's meals. Specializes in fajitas, mesquite-broiled dishes. Parking. Southwestern decor. Game rm in bar. Cr cds: A, C, D, DS, MC, V.

★★★ **WATERFORD.** *(See The Waterford Hotel) 405/848-4782.* Hrs: 6-10:30 pm; Fri & Sat to 11 pm. Closed Sun. Res accepted. Continental menu. Bar. Wine list. A la carte entrees: dinner $9.75-$32. Specializes in Black Angus beef. Own baking, sauces. Valet parking. English country decor. Cr cds: A, C, D, DS, MC, V.

Unrated Dining Spots

CLASSEN GRILL. *5124 N Classen Blvd, north of downtown. 405/842-0428.* Hrs: 7 am-10 pm; Sat from 8 am; Sun 8 am-2 pm. Closed Mon; some major hols. Bar from 10 am. Semi-a la carte: bkfst $2.50-$5.95, lunch $4-$6, dinner $5-$9. Child's meals. Specializes in chicken-fried steak, fresh seafood. Parking. Local artwork. Cr cds: C, D, DS, MC, V.

FURRS CAFETERIA. *2842 NW 63rd St, in French Market Mall, north of downtown. 405/848-5656.* Hrs: 10:45 am-2:30 pm, 4-8 pm; Sat, Sun 11 am-8 pm. Closed Dec 24 eve, 25. Avg ck: lunch, dinner $5. Specializes in chicken-fried steak, millionaire pie. Cr cds: MC, V.

Okmulgee (C-8)

(See Henryetta)

Founded ca 1900 **Pop** 13,441 **Elev** 670 ft **Area code** 918 **Zip** 74447
Information Chamber of Commerce, 112 N Morton, PO Box 609; 918/756-6172.

The capital of the Creek Nation was established in 1868 and operates out of a Creek Indian Complex. The Creeks gave the town its name, which means "bubbling water." Within Okmulgee County nearly five million pounds of wild pecans are harvested annually. The city is the home of Oklahoma State University/Okmulgee, one of the country's largest residential-vocational training schools and a branch of Oklahoma State University.

What to See and Do

Creek Council House Museum. Museum houses displays of Creek tribal history. Capital of the old Muscogee Nation. (Tues-Sat; closed hols) Council House, 6th St between Grand & Morton Aves. Phone 918/756-2324. **Free.**

Okmulgee State Park. Covers 575 acres; 678-acre lake. Fishing; boating (ramps). Picnicking, playground. Camping, trailer hookups (fee). (Daily) 5 mi W on OK 56. Phone 918/756-5971. **Free.**

Annual Events

Creek Nation Rodeo and Festival. 3rd wkend June.

Pecan Festival. Carnival, entertainment, arts & crafts. Phone 918/756-6172. 3rd wkend June.

Motel

★★ **BEST WESTERN.** *3499 N Wood Dr. 918/756-9200; FAX 918/756-9200, ext. 300.* 50 units, 2 story, 6 suites. S $40; D $45; suites $75; under 17 free. Crib avail. Pet accepted. TV; cable (premium), VCR avail. Pool. Restaurant 6 am-10 pm. Rm serv. Bar 4 pm-2 am; entertainment, dancing Mon, Fri & Sat. Ck-out 11 am. Meeting rms. Business servs avail. In-rm modem link. Refrigerators. Cr cds: A, C, D, DS, JCB, MC, V.

Pauls Valley (D-7)

Settled 1847 **Pop** 6,150 **Elev** 876 ft **Area code** 405 **Zip** 73075
Information Chamber of Commerce, 112 E Paul St, Box 638; 405/238-6491.

What to See and Do

Murray-Lindsay Mansion (1880). A three-story Classic-revival mansion built by Frank Murray, an Irish immigrant who married a woman of Choctaw descent. Starting small, Murray eventually controlled over 20,000 acres of land within the Chickasaw Nation. The mansion, a showplace within the Nation, contains original period furnishings. (Tues-Sun afternoons; closed hols) 21 mi W on OK 19, 2 mi S on OK 76, in Erin Springs. Phone 405/756-2121. **Free.**

Pauls Valley City Lake. Fishing; boating (ramps, dock). Hiking. Picnicking. Camping. (Daily) Fee for some activities. 2 mi E on OK 19, then 1 mi N. Phone 405/238-5134.

Washita Valley Museum. Artifact collection of the Washita River Culture People (A.D. 600-800) with paintings by a local artist; collection of antique medical and surgical instruments; Pioneer clothing, photos and other memorabilia from the early 1900s. (Sat, Sun; closed Thanksgiving, Dec 25) 1100 N Ash St. Phone 405/238-3048. **Free.**

Annual Events

International Rodeo Assn Competition. Last wkend June.

Garvin County Free Fair. Fairgrounds. Early Sept.

Motels

★ **BEST WESTERN 4 SANDS INN.** *Box 505, 2 mi W at jct OK 19, I-35, exit 72.* 405/238-6416; FAX 405/238-6416, ext. 171. 55 rms. S $34; D $45-$51; each addl $5. Crib $5. Pet accepted. TV; cable (premium). Pool. Complimentary continental bkfst, coffee. Restaurant 10 am-9 pm; Sun to 2 pm. Ck-out noon. Business center. In-rm modem link. Free airport transportation. Cr cds: A, C, D, DS, MC, V.

✔ ★ **DAYS INN.** *I-35 & US 19.* 405/238-7548. 54 rms, 2 story. May-Sept: S $34-$39; D $44; each addl $5; under 16 free. Crib free. Pet accepted, some restrictions. TV; cable. Complimentary continental bkfst. Restaurant nearby. Ck-out noon. Meeting rooms. Cr cds: A, C, D, DS, MC, V.

Pawhuska (A-8)

(For accommodations see Bartlesville)

Pop 3,825 **Elev** 818 ft **Area code** 918 **Zip** 74056
Information Chamber of Commerce, 114 W Main St; 918/287-1208.

This is a county seat and Osage Indian capital (county boundaries are same as those of the Osage Nation). This is a good fishing and hunting area with approximately 5,000 private lakes and five major lakes nearby.

The first Boy Scout troop in America was organized here in May 1909, by the Reverend John Mitchell.

What to See and Do

Drummond Home (1905). Restored three-story Victorian house of merchant/cattleman Fred Drummond. Native sandstone, central square tower, second floor balcony and false dormers; original furnishings. (Fri, Sat & Sun afternoons; closed major hols) 21 mi S on OK 99, in Hominy. Phone 918/885-2374. **Free.**

Osage County Historical Society Museum. Old Santa Fe depot; chuck wagon display; saddles, Western, Native American, pioneer and oil exhibits. Monument to the first Boy Scout troop in America (1909); correspondence and pictures about the beginning of the Boy Scouts. (Mon-Fri, also Sat & Sun afternoons; closed Thanksgiving, Dec 25) 700 N Lynn Ave. Phone 918/287-9924. **Free.**

Osage Hills State Park. A 1,005-acre park with 18-acre lake. Swimming pool; fishing. Picnic facilities, playgrounds. Camping areas, trailer hookups (fee). (Daily) 11 mi NE on US 60. Phone 918/336-4141. **Free.**

Osage Tribal Museum. Treaties; costumes, beadwork; arts and crafts center. (Mon-Fri; closed hols) 814 Grandview Ave. Phone 918/287-4622. **Free.**

Annual Events

Ben Johnson Memorial Steer-Roping Contest. Father's Day wkend.

International Roundup Cavalcade. State's largest amateur Western show. 3rd wkend July.

Osage County Fair. Late Aug-early Sept.

Pawnee (B-8)

(For accommodations see Perry)

Pop 2,197 **Elev** 900 ft **Area code** 918 **Zip** 74058
Information Chamber of Commerce, 608 Harrison St; 918/762-2108.

What to See and Do

Pawnee Bill Ranch Site. House of Pawnee Bill, completed in 1910; 14 rooms with original furnishings; Wild West show mementos. Buffalo, longhorn cattle pasture. (Daily; closed Jan 1, Dec 25) On US 64. Phone 918/762-2513. **Free.**

Annual Events

Steam Show and Threshing Bee. Fairgrounds. Steam engine races; exhibits. 1st full wkend May.

Indian Powwow. Tribal dances, contests. 1st wkend July.

Perry (B-7)

(See Pawnee, Stillwater)

Pop 4,978 **Elev** 1,002 ft **Area code** 405 **Zip** 73077
Information Chamber of Commerce, PO Box 426; 405/336-4684.

What to See and Do

Cherokee Strip Museum. Schoolhouse (1895), implement building, pioneer artifacts and documents depict era of the 1893 land run; picnic area. (Daily exc Mon; closed major hols) 2617 W Fir. Phone 405/336-2405. **Free.**

Annual Event

Cherokee Strip Celebration. Commemorates opening of Cherokee Strip to settlers. Parade, entertainment, rodeo, contests, Noble County Fair. Mid-Sept.

Motel

★ ★ **BEST WESTERN CHEROKEE STRIP.** *Box 529, 2 mi W at I-35, US 77. 405/336-2218; FAX 405/336-9753.* 90 rms. S $45-$51; D $51-$57; each addl $5. Crib free. Pet accepted, some restrictions. TV; cable (premium), VCR avail. Indoor pool. Restaurant 6 am-10 pm. Bar 5-11 pm; closed Sun. Ck-out noon. Driving range. Cr cds: A, C, D, DS, MC, V.

D ✔ ⌧ ⋈ ⋒ SC

Ponca City (A-7)

Founded 1893 **Pop** 26,359 **Elev** 1,019 ft **Area code** 405

Information Convention & Visitors Bureau, PO Box 1109, 74602; 405/765-4400 or 800/475-4400.

Ponca was founded in a single day, in the traditional Oklahoma land rush manner. Although in the Cherokee Strip, the town was named for the Ponca tribe. Ponca is a modern industrial town surrounded by cattle and wheat country.

What to See and Do

Cultural Center & Museums. Indian Museum; 101 Ranch Room; Bryant Baker studio and D.A.R. Memorial Museum. (Daily exc Tues; closed Jan 1, Thanksgiving, Dec 24, 25, 31) 1000 E Grand Ave, in Marland-Paris Historic House. Phone 405/767-0427. ¢

Kaw Lake. On the Arkansas River; shoreline covers 168 miles. Water sports; fishing, hunting; boating. Recreation and camping areas (fee) located 1 mile off US 60. (Daily) 8 mi E on Lake Rd. Phone 405/762-5611. **Free.**

Lake Ponca. Waterskiing (licenses required); fishing; boating. Camp and trailer park (fee). 4 mi NE.

Marland Mansion. A 55-room mansion built in 1927 by E.W. Marland, oil baron, governor and philanthropist. Modeled after the Davanzati Palace in Florence, Italy; features elaborate artwork and hand-painted ceilings. Tours. (Daily; closed Jan 1, Thanksgiving, Dec 25) Sr citizen rate. 901 Monument Rd. Phone 405/767-0420. ¢¢

Pioneer Woman Museum. Imposing bronze statue by Bryant Baker memorializing the courage of the women who pioneered America; pioneer home and ranch exhibits; costumes and memorabilia of family life in the pioneer era; rose garden. (Tues-Sat, also Sun afternoons; closed most hols) 701 Monument Rd. Phone 405/765-6108. **Free.**

Motels

✔ ★ **DAYS INN.** *1415 E Bradley (74604). 405/767-1406; FAX 405/762-9589.* 59 rms, 3 story. No elvtr. S $34; D $36; each addl $3; suites $46; under 12 free. Crib free. TV; cable (premium). Complimentary continental bkfst. Restaurant nearby. Ck-out 11 am. In-rm modem link. Cr cds: A, C, D, DS, MC, V.

D ✔ ⋈ ⋒ SC

★ ★ **HOLIDAY INN.** *2215 N 14 St (US 77) (74601). 405/762-8311; FAX 405/765-0014.* 139 rms, 2 story. S $48-$53; D $53-$58; each addl $5; under 18 free. Crib free. TV; cable (premium). Pool. Restaurant 6 am-2 pm, 5-10 pm; Sat & Sun 7 am-2 pm, 5-9 pm. Rm serv. Bar 5 pm-midnight. Ck-out noon. In-rm modem link. Valet serv. Cr cds: A, C, D, DS, JCB, MC, V.

D ⌧ ⋈ ⋒ SC

Poteau (C-10)

(For accommodations see Fort Smith, AR)

Founded 1898 **Pop** 7,210 **Elev** 480 ft **Area code** 918 **Zip** 74953

Information Chamber of Commerce, 201 S Broadway St; 918/647-9178.

Rich in ancient history and pioneer heritage, Poteau is located in an area of timber and high hills. Just off US 271, a 4½-mile paved road winds to the peak of Cavanal Hill for a spectacular view of the entire Poteau River Valley. Poteau lies approximately 15 miles north of Ouachita National Forest (see HOT SPRINGS, AR).

What to See and Do

Heavener Runestone. Scandinavian cryptograph in 8 runes that scholars believe were inscribed by Vikings in A.D. 1012. Other runes, from the Scandinavian alphabet of the 3rd-10th centuries, have been found engraved on several stones in the area. NE of Heavener off US 59.

Kerr Museum. Home of former Senator Robert S. Kerr contains material detailing the history and development of eastern Oklahoma; includes natural history, pioneer, Choctaw and special exhibits. (Daily afternoons exc Mon; also by appt; closed Jan 1, Thanksgiving, Dec 25) 6 mi SW. Phone 918/647-8221. ¢

Lake Wister State Park. On 4,000-acre lake, facilities include swimming pool, waterskiing; fishing; boating (ramps). Also picnic facilities, playground, restaurant, grocery. Camping, trailer hookups (fee), cabins. (Daily) 9 mi SW on US 271, then 2 mi SE on US 270. Phone 918/655-7756 or -7212 (reservations). **Free.**

Spiro Mound Archeological State Park. A 138-acre site with 12 earthen mounds dated from A.D. 600 to A.D. 1450. Reconstructed Native American house; excavated items on display in the Interpretive Center (summer, daily exc Mon; winter, Wed-Sun). Hiking trails. Picnicking. 17 mi N on US 59, 6 mi E on OK 9, then 4 mi N on Spiro Mounds Rd. Phone 918/962-2062. **Free.**

Annual Event

Poteau Frontier Days Rodeo. Memorial Day wkend.

Pryor (B-9)

(See Claremore, Grand Lake, Miami, Vinita)

Pop 8,327 **Elev** 626 ft **Area code** 918 **Zip** 74361

Information Chamber of Commerce, PO Box 367, 74362; 918/825-0157

Pryor was named in honor of Nathaniel Pryor, a scout with Lewis and Clark, who built a trading post near the town to do business with the Osage. For years a simple farming community, Pryor has become industrialized, with plants producing cement, fertilizers and chemicals, castings and wallboard.

What to See and Do

Coo-Y-Yah Country Museum. Artifacts from Mayes County representing several cultures including clothing, artwork, Native American and pioneer items; also temporary exhibits. The museum is housed in an old railroad depot. (Apr-Dec, Wed-Fri & Sun afternoons; rest of yr by appt) 8th St at US 69S. Phone 918/825-2222. **Free.**

Lake Hudson. Robert S. Kerr Dam impounds waters of Grand River. Swimming, waterskiing; fishing; boating. Camping. 10 mi E on OK 20. **Free.**

Motel

★ **PRYOR HOUSE MOTOR INN.** *123 S Mill St (US 69).* *918/825-6677.* 35 rms, 2 story. S $33; D $33-$38; each addl $5; suites $40-$42; under 12 free. Pet accepted. TV; cable. Pool. Complimentary continental bkfst. Restaurant opp open 24 hrs. Ck-out 11 am. Cr cds: A, C, D, MC, V.

Quartz Mountain
State Park (D-5)

(18 mi N of Altus via US 283, OK 44, 44A)

This 4,284-acre scenic preserve is on Lake Altus-Lugert, a 6,260-acre lake, with excellent fishing for bass, catfish and crappie. The wild rock-strewn park has 29 varieties of trees and 140 species of wildflowers.

Recreational facilities include beach, swimming pool, bathhouse, waterskiing; fishing; boating (ramps). Hiking. Golf, tennis. Picnic facilities, playground, cafe, grocery, lodge (see LODGE). Camping, trailer hookups (fee), cabins. Amphitheater. For camping reservations and additional information, phone 800/654-8240 or contact Oklahoma Tourism and Recreation Department, 505 Will Rogers Building, Oklahoma City 73105; 405/521-2406.

Lodge

★ **QUARTZ MOUNTAIN.** *(Rte 1, Lone Wolf 73655) 22 mi N of Altus on OK 44A.* *405/563-2424; FAX 405/563-9125.* 42 lodge rms, 3 suites, 14 cottages with kit. Early Apr-late Nov: lodge: S $50-$58; cottages for 1-6, $68-$88; under 18 free; MAP avail; lower rates rest of yr. Crib free. TV in lodge rms, lobby; cable. 2 pools, 1 indoor; lifeguard in summer. Playground. Dining rm 7 am-2 pm, 5-10 pm. Ck-out noon, ck-in 3 pm. Grocery 1½ mi. Lighted tennis. 18-hole golf, pro, putting green. Lawn games. Recreation program. Game rm. Rustic lodge. Water slide nearby. All facilities of state park avail. On Lake Altus. Cr cds: A, C, D, DS, MC, V.

Roman Nose
State Park (B-6)

(7 mi N of Watonga via OK 8, 8A)

Named after Chief Henry Roman Nose of the Cheyenne, this is a 750-acre area with a 55-acre artificial lake stocked with bass, crappie, bluegill, rainbow trout and catfish. It has many recreational facilities including swimming pool, bathhouse; fishing; boating, paddleboats on Lake Boecher. Golf, tennis. Picnicking (grills), playgrounds, concession, lodge (see RESORT). Campsites, trailer hookups (fee). Contact Park Manager, Rte 1, Box 2-2, Watonga 73772; 405/623-4215.

Resort

★★ **ROMAN NOSE LODGE.** *(Rte 1, Watonga 73772) 7 mi N of Watonga on OK 8A, just off OK 8.* *405/623-7281; res: 800/654-8240; FAX 405/623-2538.* 57 units, 1-3 story; 47 lodge rms, 10 cottages with kits. Mid-May-mid-Sept: S, D $65-$68; each addl $10; kit. cottages $70-$73; under 18 free; lower rates rest of yr. TV; VCR avail (movies avail $10.95). Pool. Supervised child's activities (Memorial Day-Labor

Day); ages 3 and up. Playground. Restaurant 7 am-9 pm; summer to 10 pm. Box lunches. Ck-out noon, ck-in 3 pm. Meeting rm. Business servs avail. Free local airport transportation. Lighted tennis. 9-hole golf, pro, greens fee $8-$10, putting green. Recreation program. Paddle boats, canoes. Social dir. State-owned, operated; all facilities of state park avail. On bluff overlooking Lake Boecher. Cr cds: A, C, D, DS, MC, V.

Sallisaw (C-10)

(See Fort Smith, AR)

Pop 7,122 **Elev** 533 ft **Area code** 918 **Zip** 74955
Information Chamber of Commerce, 111 N Elm, PO Box 251; 918/775-2558.

What to See and Do

Blue Ribbon Downs. Parimutuel horse racing. Thoroughbred, quarter horse, appaloosa and paint horse racing. (All-yr, schedule varies) Phone 918/775-7771. Admission ¢

Robert S. Kerr Lake. Approximately 42,000 acres with 250 miles of shoreline, Kerr Lake was formed with the creation of the inland waterway along the Arkansas River. Swimming; fishing; hunting (in season); boating (ramps). Picnicking. Camping (fee). (Daily) 8 mi S on OK 59. Phone 918/775-4474. **Free.**

Sallisaw State Recreation Area. Fishing; boating (ramp). Picnicking. Camping (fee). (Daily) 8 mi N on Marble City Rd, then 1 mi W on county road. Phone 918/775-6507. **Free.**

 **Sequoyah's Home** (ca 1830). Historic 1-room log cabin built by Sequoyah, the famous Cherokee who created an 86-character alphabet for the Cherokee language. Historic landmark includes visitor center, mini-museum, artifacts; picnicking. (Daily exc Mon; closed major hols) 11 mi NE on OK 101. Phone 918/775-2413. **Free.**

Motels

★★ **BEST WESTERN-BLUE RIBBON.** *PO Box 828 706 S Kerr Blvd, at jct I-40 & US 59.* *918/775-6294.* 81 rms, 2 story. June-Aug: S $39; D $45; each addl $5; suites $60-$75; under 12 free; lower rates rest of yr. Crib $5. Pet accepted; $5. TV; cable (premium). 2 pools, 1 indoor. Restaurant adj 6 am-10 pm. Ck-out 11 am. Lndry facilities. Meeting rms. Gift shop. Exercise equipt; weights, bicycles, whirlpool. Some refrigerator. Cr cds: A, C, D, DS, MC, V.

✔★ **DAYS INN.** *Rte 2, Box 13, On US 64W at jct US 59.* *918/775-4406; FAX 918/775-4406.* 33 rms, 2 story, 3 kits. S, kits. $34; each addl $5; suites $44-$46; under 12 free. Crib $5. Pet accepted, some restrictions. TV; cable (premium). Complimentary coffee in lobby. Restaurant adj 6 am-8:30 pm. Ck-out 11 am. Some refrigerators. Cr cds: A, C, D, DS, JCB, MC, V.

✔★ **GOLDEN SPUR INN.** *Box 828, I-40 & US 59.* *918/775-4443.* 29 rms, 2 story. S $30; D $32-$34; each addl $5; under 12 free. Crib $3. Pet accepted, some restrictions. TV; cable (premium). Pool. Complimentary coffee in lobby. Ck-out 11 am. Cr cds: A, C, D, DS, MC, V.

★ **McKNIGHT.** *1611 W Ruth St, I-40 exit 308.* *918/775-9126; res: 800/842-9442.* 39 units, 2 story. S $26-$33; D $33-$50; wkly rates. Crib free. TV; cable (premium), VCR (movies avail $2-$3). Pool. Restaurant nearby. Ck-out 11 am. Coin lndry. Cr cds: A, DS, MC, V.

★**RAMADA INN LIMITED.** *1300 E Cherokee (US 64). 918/775-7791; FAX 918/775-7795.* 50 rms. S $40; D $44 each addl $4; under 18 free. Crib free. Pet accepted. TV; cable (premium). Continental bkfst. Restaurant nearby. Ck-out noon. Meeting rm. Business servs avail. In-rm modem link. Cr cds: A, C, D, DS, JCB, MC, V.

D ⚑ ⚒ 🐾 SC

Sequoyah State Park (B-9)

(See Tahlequah)

(8 mi E of Wagoner on OK 51)

These approx 2,800 acres in Oklahoma's Cookson Hills, once a bandits' hideout, offer many attractions to vacationers. The park is on Fort Gibson Reservoir, which was created by the dam of the same name. This 19,100-acre reservoir shifts its level less than most hydroelectric-power lakes in Oklahoma. It is stocked with bass, catfish and crappie. Fees may be charged at federal recreation sites at the reservoir.

The park has many features of a resort: beach, swimming pool, bathhouse, water sports; fishing; boating (ramps, docks, marina, rentals). Hiking trail, mountain bike trail, horseback riding; 18-hole golf, tennis. Picnic facilities, playgrounds, games, grocery, lodge (see RESORT). Camping area, trailer hookups (fee), cabins. Contact Park Manager, Rte 1, Box 198-3, Hulbert 74441; 918/772-2046.

Motel

✔★**INDIAN LODGE.** *(Rte 2, Box 393, Wagoner 74467) 5 mi E on OK 51. 918/485-3184.* 25 rms, 9 kits. Apr-Oct: D $37.50-$50; each addl $7.50; kit. units $50-$55; suites $80-$95. Closed rest of yr. Crib $5. TV; cable. Pool. Playground. Restaurant nearby. Ck-out noon. Some carports. Lawn games. Picnic tables, grill. Shaded grounds, near Fort Gibson Reservoir. No cr cds accepted.

Resort

★★★**WESTERN HILLS GUEST RANCH.** *(Box 509, Wagoner 74477) 8 mi E on OK 51, then 3 mi S into park. 918/772-2545; res: 800/654-8240; FAX 918/772-2030.* 98 rms in lodge; 44 cottages (1-2 bedrm) avail, 18 kits. (no equipt). Mid-Apr-mid-Sept: lodge: S, D $63-$68; each addl $10; studio rms from $58; cabana $99; suites $100-$175; under 18 free; golf package plans; lower rates rest of yr. Crib free. TV; VCR avail (movies avail $9.95). Pool; wading pool, lifeguard in summer. Supervised child's activities (Memorial Day-Labor Day). Playground. Dining rm 7 am-9 pm. Box lunches, snack bar. Rm serv, lodge only. Bar 6 pm-1 am. Ck-out noon, ck-in 3 pm. Meeting rms. Business servs avail. Local airport transportation. Grocery 3 mi. Gift shop. Sundries. Lighted tennis. Golf, greens fee Fri, Sat $10.50; pro. Miniature golf. Boats, paddleboats. Bicycles, lawn games, hayrides. Soc dir. Rec rm. Poolside, lakeside rms. State owned, operated; all facilities of park avail. On Fort Gibson Reservoir. Cr cds: A, D, DS, MC, V.

D ⚑ ⚒ 🏇 ♿ ⚒ 🏊 ⚒ 🐾 SC

Restaurant

★★**SKIDMORE' LAKESIDE.** *(Rte 2, Box 480, Wagoner 74467) Approx 7 mi E on OK 51. 918/485-3350.* Hrs: 5-9 pm; Fri & Sat to 10 pm; Sun 11 am-7 pm. Closed Mon & Tues; Dec 25; also Jan. Res accepted. Bar. Semi-a la carte: lunch $3.99-$5.99, dinner $6.95-$14.95. Child's meals. Specializes in steak, shrimp, catfish, chicken & hot rolls. Parking. Overlooks Lake Fort Gibson. Cr cds: A, DS, MC, V.

D

Shawnee (C-7)

Founded 1895 **Pop** 26,017 **Elev** 1,055 ft **Area code** 405 **Zip** 74801
Information Chamber of Commerce, 131 N Bell, PO Box 1613; 405/273-6092.

The history of Shawnee is that of Oklahoma in miniature. In the center of the state, it stands on what was originally Sac and Fox Indian land, which was also claimed at various times by Spain, France and England. It was opened by a land rush on Sept 22, 1891. Oil was struck in 1926. Now it has diversified industries in addition to fruits, vegetables, poultry and dairy products that are processed here.

Shawnee is the home of Oklahoma Baptist University (1910). Jim Thorpe, the great Indian athlete, and Dr. Brewster Higley, the physician who wrote "Home on the Range," lived here. Astronaut Gordon Cooper was born and raised in Shawnee.

What to See and Do

Mabee-Gerrer Museum of Art. Art gallery features works by 19th- and 20th-century European and American artists as well as works from the Middle Ages and the Renaissance. Museum features artifacts of Egyptian, Babylonian, Grecian, Roman, Persian, Chinese, African and Polynesian civilizations as well as North, Central and South American native civilizations. (Daily exc Mon; closed major hols) Donation. St Gregory's College, 1900 W MacArthur Dr. Phone 405/878-5300.

Seminole Nation Museum. Traces the tribe's history from its removal in Florida over "Trail of Tears" to establishing the capital. Displays include collection of Native American peace medals; replicas of a Chické (Florida Seminole house), dioramas of the stickball game, the Whipping tree, the Old Wewoka Trading Post; artifacts from pioneer through oil boom days of 1920s. Art gallery with Native American paintings and sculpture. (Daily exc Mon; closed Jan, Thanksgiving, Dec 24, 25) 524 S Wewoka Ave, 30 mi SE via US 177, OK 9, US 270, in Wewoka. Phone 405/257-5580. **Free.**

Shawnee Twin Lakes. Fishing, hunting; boating, swimming. Fee. 8 mi W.

Annual Events

Potawatomie Powwow. Late June.

Pott County Fair. Late Aug.

Heritage Fest. Late Sept.

Motels

★★**BEST WESTERN CINDERELLA.** *623 Kickapoo Spur, 2¹/₂ mi S of I-40. 405/273-7010.* 92 rms, 2 story. S $46-$56; D $60-$67; each addl $5; under 18 free. Crib free. Pet accepted. TV; cable (premium). Indoor pool; poolside serv, whirlpool. Restaurant 6 am-10 pm. Rm serv. Bar 4 pm-midnight, closed Sun; dancing. Ck-out noon. Coin lndry. Meeting rms. Business servs avail. In-rm modem link. Sundries. Cr cds: A, C, D, DS, MC, V.

⚑ ⚒ 🏊 ⚒ 🐾 SC

★**FLEETWOOD.** *1301 N Harrison St. 405/273-7561.* 17 rms. S $20-$22; D $25-$29; each addl $2. Crib $2. TV; cable. Restaurant nearby. Ck-out 11 am. Cr cds: MC, V.

🐾

Stillwater (B-7)

(See Perry)

Founded 1889 **Pop** 36,676 **Elev** 900 ft **Area code** 405

Information Visitors and Special Events Bureau, 409 S Main, PO Box 1687, 74076; 405/372-5573.

Stillwater was born overnight in the great land run of 1889. The settlement was less than a year old when, on Christmas Day 1890, the territorial legislature established Oklahoma State University (formerly Oklahoma A & M). At the time, the settlement had a mayor, but no real town government. Yet less than four months later, the new settlers voted to incorporate as a city and to issue $10,000 in bonds to help build the college.

What to See and Do

Lake Carl Blackwell. A 19,364-acre recreation area operated by Oklahoma State University. Swimming, waterskiing; fishing, hunting; boating, sailing. Picnic areas. Campgrounds, cabins. Fees for various activities. 9 mi W on OK 51. Phone 405/372-5157. ¢

National Wrestling Hall of Fame. Houses Museum of Wrestling History and Honors Court. (Mon-Fri; also open Sat during university sports events; closed hols) 405 W Hall of Fame Ave. Phone 405/377-5243. **Free.**

Oklahoma State University (1890). (18,567 students) On a campus of 840 acres with an additional 4,774 acres of experimental university farms statewide. On campus is the Noble Research Center for Agriculture and Renewable Natural Resources, education/research complex with emphasis on the biological sciences. Buildings vary in style from "Old Central," the oldest collegiate building in the state, built in 1894 of pink brick, to attractive modified Georgian buildings of red brick with slate roofs. Of special interest are Museum of Higher Education in Oklahoma (daily exc Mon; phone 405/624-3220); Bartlett Center for Studio Arts (Mon-Fri; phone 405/744-6016); and Gardiner Art Gallery (daily; phone 405/744-9086). Relief maps for the visually impaired. Washington St & University Ave, jct US 177 & OK 51. For tours of campus phone 405/744-9341.

Sheerar Museum. Historical building houses local history museum, including a 4,000-specimen button collection; also changing exhibits. (Daily exc Mon; closed major hols) 7th & Duncan. Phone 405/377-0359. **Free.**

Annual Events

Run for the Arts. Fine arts & jazz festival. Fiddle, banjo and guitar contests; antique auto show. Apr.

Taylorsville Country Fair. Early Oct.

Stillwater Cheese & Sausage Festival. Many exhibits, some samples. Wkend late Oct.

Motor Hotels

✔★★ **BEST WESTERN.** *600 E McElroy (74075). 405/377-7010; FAX 405/743-1686.* 122 rms, 4 story. S $41-$50; D $46-$55; each addl $5; suites $85-$110; under 12 free. Crib free. Pet accepted, some restrictions. TV; cable (premium), VCR avail. Indoor pool. Restaurant 6 am-9 pm, Sun to 11 am. Rm serv. Bar 11-2 am, closed Sun. Ck-out noon. Coin lndry. Meeting rms. Business center. In-rm modem link. Valet serv. Free airport transportation. Exercise equipt; treadmill, bicycles, whirlpool, sauna. Game rm. Some refrigerators. Balconies. Glass elevators. Cr cds: A, C, D, DS, MC, V.

D ✔ ⇆ ✗ ⋈ ⋈ SC ⋔

★★ **HOLIDAY INN.** *2515 W 6th (OK 51) (74074). 405/372-0800; FAX 405/377-8212.* 141 rms, 2 story. S $46-$65; D $53-$70; each addl $7; suites from $65; town house $125; under 19 free. Crib

free. TV; cable (premium), VCR avail. Indoor pool; whirlpool, steam rm. Restaurant 6 am-8 pm. Rm serv. Bar 4 pm-midnight. Ck-out noon. Coin lndry. Meeting rms. Business servs avail. Valet serv. Free airport transportation. Holidome. Miniature golf. Game rm. Cr cds: A, C, D, DS, JCB, MC, V.

D ⇆ ⋈ ⋈ SC

Restaurants

★★ **THE ANCESTOR.** *1324 S Main, at 14th St. 405/372-2915.* Hrs: 11:30 am-2 pm, 5-9 pm; Sat from 5 pm; Sun 8 am-2 pm. Closed major hols. Res accepted. Bar; live jazz, blues Fri & Sat. Semi-a la carte: lunch $3.25-$5.95, dinner $7.95-$13.95. Child's meals. Specializes in steak, pan-fried chicken, seafood. Salad bar. Parking. Antiques. Cr cds: A, D, DS, MC, V.

D

✔★★ **BOBO'S MEXICAN RESTAURANTE.** *5020 W 6th St (OK 51). 405/372-9353.* Hrs: 10:30 am-10 pm; Thurs to 11 pm; Fri, Sat to midnight. Closed Thanksgiving, Dec 25. Res accepted wkends. Mexican, Southwestern menu. Bar. Semi-a la carte: lunch $4.45-$5.95, dinner $5.50-$12.50. Child's meals. Specializes in authentic Mexican and Southwestern dishes. Parking. Mexican hacienda motif. Cr cds: A, C, D, DS, MC, V.

D

★★ **STILLWATER BAY.** *623½ S Husband, opp courthouse. 405/743-2780.* Hrs: 11 am-10 pm; Fri, Sat to 11 pm; Sun to 9 pm; Sun brunch to 2 pm. Closed some major hols. Bar. Semi-a la carte: lunch $2.95-$8.95, dinner $4.95-$19.95. Sun brunch $2.95-$8.95. Child's meals. Specializes in fresh seafood, prime rib, chicken. Cr cds: A, D, DS, MC, V.

Sulphur (D-7)

(See Ada, Ardmore)

Pop 4,824 **Elev** 976 ft **Area code** 405 **Zip** 73086

Information Chamber of Commerce, 113 Muskogee; 405/622-2824.

What to See and Do

Arbuckle Wilderness. An 8-mile scenic drive-through animal park; 2,000 free-roaming animals; aviaries, zoo, hayrides, camel rides; petting park, catfish feeding; paddle and bumper boats; go carts; playground; snack bar; gifts. (Daily, weather permitting; closed Dec 25) Approx 9 mi W via OK 7, 3 mi S of Davis near jct I-35, US 77; exit 51. Phone 405/369-3383. ¢¢¢¢

Chickasaw National Recreation Area. Travertine District (912 acres), near Sulphur, has mineral and freshwater springs, which contain sulphur, iron, bromide and other minerals. There are streams for wading and swimming and trails for hiking. Travertine Nature Center (daily; closed hols) has exhibits of natural history of area. Guided tours (summer and wkends; rest of yr by appt). Veterans Lake has a fishing dock with access for the disabled. Lake of the Arbuckles offers fishing for catfish, largemouth bass, sunfish, crappie and walleyed pike. There is also swimming, waterskiing; boating (launching at three designated ramps only). Picnicking. Camping (fee); first-come, first-served basis; (Daily) S off OK 7. Phone 405/622-6677. **Free.** Contact Superintendent, PO Box 201; 405/622-3165. Camping per night ¢¢¢

Motel

★ **CHICKASAW MOTOR INN.** *W First & Muskogee. 405/622-2156; FAX 405/622-3094.* 71 rms, 1-2 story. S $30-$34; D $36-$37; each addl $5. Crib $5. TV; cable. Pool; wading pool. Restaurant 6 am-8 pm. Ck-out noon. Meeting rms. Sundries. Cr cds: A, C, D, MC, V.

Restaurant

✔ ★ **THE BRICKS.** *2112 W Broadway (OK 7). 405/622-3125.* Hrs: 11 am-9 pm. Closed Jan 1, Thanksgiving, Dec 25. Semi-a la carte: lunch, dinner $2.95-$10.95. Child's meals. Specializes in barbecue, catfish. Parking. Cr cds: A, MC, V.

Tahlequah (B-10)

Founded 1845 **Pop** 10,398 **Elev** 800 ft **Area code** 918 **Zip** 74464
Information Tahlequah Area Chamber of Commerce, 123 E Delaware St; 918/456-3742.

Tribal branches of the Cherokee met here in 1839 to sign a new constitution forming the Cherokee Nation. They had been driven by the US Army from North Carolina, Alabama, Tennessee and Georgia over the "Trail of Tears." Many died during the long forced march; a new life then began for the survivors, whose influence has since permeated the history and life of Tahlequah.

Sequoyah had created a written alphabet. The Cherokee were the only tribe with a constitution and a body of law written in their own language. These talented people published the first newspaper in Indian Territory (Oklahoma) and, in 1885, established the first commercial telephone line in Oklahoma. The Southwestern Bell Telephone Company, to which it was later sold, established a monument to this remarkable enterprise on the Old Courthouse Square.

The scene of these historic events is now rapidly growing as a vacation area with lakes and a river offering fishing and water sports of all types.

What to See and Do

⭐ **Cherokee Heritage Center.** National Museum of Cherokee artifacts; also reconstructed 1890 rural village (weather permitting). Guided tours of 1650 ancient village (May-late Aug, daily). *Trail of Tears* drama (see SEASONAL EVENTS) is presented in Tsa-La-Gi outdoor amphitheater. Museum (daily; closed Jan 1, Thanksgiving, Dec 25). Combination ticket available. 3½ mi S on US 62, then 1 mi E on Willis Rd. For schedule, information phone 918/456-6007. Museum ¢¢; Ancient village ¢¢

Float trips on the Illinois River. Contact the Chamber of Commerce.

Murrell Home. Pre-Civil War mansion; many original furnishings. (Spring-fall, daily exc Mon; rest of yr, Wed-Sun; closed Jan 1, Thanksgiving, Dec 25) 3 mi S on OK 82, then 1 mi E on Murrell Rd. Phone 918/456-2751. **Free.** Also park and

Murrell Home Nature Trail. ¾ mile trail with special features for those in wheelchairs. Railroad ties along edges as guides; bird sanctuary, flower beds. **Free.**

Northeastern State University (1909). (9,500 students) Founded on site of National Cherokee Female Seminary (1889), now Seminary Hall; John Vaughan Library; arboretum; theater productions. Tours of campus and Tahlequah historic places. On OK 82. Phone 918/458-2088.

Sequoyah State Park (see). 17 mi W on OK 51.

Tenkiller Ferry Lake (see). S on US 62, OK 82.

Annual Events

Cherokee National Holiday. Celebration of Constitutional Convention. Championship Cornstalk bow & arrow shoot, powwow. Labor Day wkend.

Cherokee County Fair. Mid-Sept.

Seasonal Event

Trail of Tears. Tsa-La-Gi Amphitheater. Professional cast presents musical drama depicting history of Cherokee Tribe. Nightly Tues-Sat. Phone 918/456-6007. Late May-early June.

Motel

✔ ★ **TAHLEQUAH MOTOR LODGE.** *Box 495 2501 S Muskogee. 918/456-2350; FAX 918/456-4580.* 53 rms, 2 story. S $32-$44; D $38-$52. TV; cable. Pool. Restaurant 6:30 am-8 pm. Ck-out 11 am. Meeting rm. Cr cds: A, C, D, DS, MC, V.

Restaurant

✔ ★ **JASPER'S.** *2600 S Muskogee, on US 62. 918/456-0100.* Hrs: 11 am-10 pm. Closed Sun; Thanksgiving, Dec 25. Bar. Semi-a la carte: lunch $3.79-$5.95, dinner $8.95-$19.95. Child's meals. Specializes in steak, seafood. Parking. Cr cds: A, D, DS, MC, V.

Tenkiller Ferry Lake (C-10)

(See Muskogee, Tahlequah)

Area code 918

(40 mi SE of Muskogee, off US 64)

This is one of Oklahoma's most beautiful lakes. Its shores consist of recreation areas, cliffs, rock bluffs and wooded slopes. The Tenkiller Ferry Dam on the Illinois River is 197 feet high and backs up the stream for 34 miles, creating more than 130 miles of shoreline. There are 12,900 acres of water surface.

Tenkiller State Park is on OK 100, 9 miles north of Gore. There are 4 recreation areas on its 1,180 acres, with beach, pool, bathhouse, waterskiing; fishing; boating (rentals, ramps, marina); picnic facilities, playground, restaurant, grocery; camping areas, trailer hookups (fee), plus cabins.

Like other Oklahoma lakes, Tenkiller is lined with marinas, lodges and boat docks; and the lower Illinois River is famous for its striped bass fishing. It is stocked with 96,000 trout annually. Black bass and channel catfish are also plentiful, but the fish causing the most excitement among fishermen are white bass and crappie.

There are 12 federal recreational areas that provide camping for the public. Six of these have electrical hookups, showers and other facilities.

Resort

★ ★ **FIN AND FEATHER.** *(Rte 1, Box 194, Gore 74435) 8 mi N of Gore on OK 10A; I-40 Webbers Falls exit. 918/487-5148; FAX 918/487-5025.* 82 units (1-5 bedrm), 35 kits. Easter-Sept (wkends, 2-day min; kit. units, 3-day min): 1-bedrm $52-$58; 2-bedrm kit. units $88-$132; 3-5-bedrm $265. Closed rest of yr. Crib $5. TV; cable (premium), VCR avail. Indoor/outdoor pool; wading pool, whirlpool. Playground. Dining rms 8 am-2 pm, 6-8:30 pm. Box lunch, snacks. Ck-out noon, ck-in 2 pm. Grocery. Coin lndry. Convention facilities. Business servs avail. Gift shop. Tennis. Private pond. Basketball. Volleyball. Roller-skating. Lawn games. Entertainment. Theater. Rec rm. Game rm. Fishing guides. Refrigerators. Picnic tables, grills. Cr cds: A, D, DS, MC, V.

Tulsa (B-8)

Founded 1879 **Pop** 367,302 **Elev** 750 ft **Area code** 918

Not an oil derrick is visible to the casual tourist, yet Tulsa is an important energy city. Oil and gas fields surround it; offices of energy companies are prevalent; more than 600 energy and energy-oriented firms employ 30,000 people. It is the second largest city in Oklahoma; its atmosphere is cosmopolitan.

The first well came in across the river in 1901; Tulsa invited oilmen to "come and make your homes in a beautiful little city that is high and dry, peaceful and orderly, where there are good churches, stores, schools and banks, and where our ordinances prevent the desolation of our homes and property by oil wells."

More oil discoveries came in 1905 and 1912, but Tulsa maintained her aloof attitude. Although most of the town owned oil, worked in oil or supplied the oil fields, culture remained important. Concerts, theater, museums and activities at three universities, including the University of Tulsa (1894) and Oral Roberts University (1963), give the city a sophisticated quality.

Tulsa has a well-balanced economy. Aviation and aerospace is the city's second largest industry; it includes the McDonnell-Douglas plant, Rockwell International and the American Airlines maintenance base, engineering center, reservations center and revenue and finance division.

With the completion of the Arkansas River Navigation System, Tulsa gained a water route to the Great Lakes and the Gulf of Mexico. The Port of Catoosa, three miles from the city and located on the Verdigris River, is at the headwaters of the waterway and is now America's westernmost inland water port.

Transportation

Car Rental Agencies: See toll-free numbers under Introduction.

Public Transportation: Buses (Tulsa Transit), phone 918/585-1195.

Airport Information

Tulsa Intl Airport: Information 918/838-5000; lost and found 918/838-5012; weather 918/743-3311; cash machines, Main Terminal, upper level.

What to See and Do

Allen Ranch. A working horse ranch offering horseback riding, hayrides, children's barnyard and animal park, camping and chuck-wagon dinners with entertainment. (Daily; closed Thanksgiving, Dec 25) Reservations requested. 19600 S Memorial Dr. Phone 918/366-3010. Per activity **¢¢-¢¢¢¢¢**

Arkansas River Historical Society Museum. Located in the Port Authority Building; pictorial displays and operating models trace the history of the 1,450-mile Arkansas River and McClellan-Kerr Navigation System. (Mon-Fri; closed major hols) Tulsa Port of Catoosa, 5350 Cimarron Rd, 17 mi E on I-44 in Catoosa. Phone 918/266-2291. **Free.**

Bell's Amusement Park. Rides include large wooden roller coaster, log ride, skyride; two miniature golf courses. (June-Aug, evenings, also Sat & Sun afternoons; Apr-May, Fri-Sun; Sept, Sat & Sun) Free parking. 21st & S New Haven Sts. Phone 918/744-1991. Admission (includes rides & golf) **¢¢¢¢-¢¢¢¢¢**

Big Splash Water Park. Park with 2 speed slides (75 ft), 3 flume rides, wave pool, tube ride; children's pool. (May-Labor Day) 21st St and Yale. Phone 918/749-7385. **¢¢¢¢**

Boston Avenue United Methodist Church (1929). Designed by Adah Robinson, the church facade was executed in art deco, the first large-scale use of the style in sacred architecture, and features a main 225-foot tower and many lesser towers decorated with bas-relief pioneer figures. The sanctuary is ornamented with Italian mosaic on the reredos. (Daily exc Sat; closed hols) 1301 S Boston Ave, at 13th St. Phone 918/583-5181.

Creek Council Oak Tree. Landscaped plot housing the "Council Oak," which stands as a memorial to the Lochapokas Creek tribe. In 1834 this tribe brought law and order to a near wilderness. 18th & Cheyenne.

Frankoma Pottery. Guided tour, 20 min (Mon-Fri). Shop (Sun afternoons). 2400 Frankoma Rd, 4 mi SW off I-44, in Sapulpa. Phone 918/224-5511. **Free.**

Gershon and Rebecca Fenster Museum of Jewish Art. Southwest's largest collection of Judaica contains objects representative of Jewish history, art, ceremonial events and daily life from around the world. (Mon-Thurs, also Sun afternoons; closed Jewish hols) 1223 E 17th Pl, in the B'nai Emunah Synagogue. Phone 918/582-3732. **Free.**

★ **Gilcrease Museum.** Founded by Thomas Gilcrease, oil man of Creek descent. Collection of art concerning westward movement, North American development and the Native American. Works by Frederic Remington, Thomas Moran, Charles Russell, George Catlin and others, including colonial artists such as Thomas Sully; Native American artifacts from 12,000 years ago to the present. Library houses some 90,000 items, including the earliest known letter sent to Europe from the New World. Beautiful grounds with historic theme gardens. (Daily; closed Dec 25) Donation. 1400 Gilcrease Museum Rd. Phone 918/596-2700.

Mohawk Park. Fishing. Golf course (fee). Picnicking, restaurant. Nature center by appt. Park entrance fee. E 36th St N. Phone 918/836-4489. Within the park at 5701 E 36th St is

Tulsa Zoological Park. More than 200 varieties of animals set within 68 acres of landscaped grounds. North American Living Museum features Native American artifacts, geological specimens, dinosaur replica, live plants and animals; train ride **¢**. (Daily; closed Dec 25) Sr citizen rate. Phone 918/669-6200. **¢¢**

Philbrook Museum of Art. Exhibits include Italian Renaissance, 19th-century English, American and Native American paintings; Native American baskets and pottery; Chinese jades and decorative material; Southeast Asian tradeware; African sculpture. Housed in Italian Renaissance-revival villa on 23 acres; formal and sculpture gardens. Many national touring exhibitions. A 75,000-square-foot addition houses an auditorium, museum school and restaurant. (Daily exc Mon; closed hols) Sr citizen rate. 2727 S Rockford Rd. Phone 918/749-7941 or 800/324-7941. **¢¢**

State Parks.

Feyodi Creek. Covers 140 acres on the W shore of Keystone Lake. Fishing; boat ramp. Picnicking, playground. Camping (hookups; rest rms). Standard fees. (Daily) 32 mi W on US 64. Phone 918/358-2844. **Free.**

Keystone. Covers 715 acres on S shore of 26,300-acre Keystone Lake. Swimming, waterskiing; fishing; boating (marina, boathouse). Hiking trails. Picnicking, playground; grocery, snack bar (seasonal). Camping, 14-day limit (fee), trailer hookups, cabins. Standard fees. (Daily) (Fees may be charged at federal recreation sites on Keystone Lake.) 16 mi W on US 64, then S on OK 151. Phone 918/865-4991. **Free.**

Walnut Creek. Covers 1,429 acres on N side of Keystone Lake. Beach swimming, bathhouse, waterskiing; fishing; boating (ramps). Picnicking, playground. Camping, trailer hookups. Standard fees. (Daily) 19 mi W on US 64, then NW on North Loop Hwy. Phone 918/242-3362. **Free.**

Tulsa Garden Center. Library, arboretum; extensive dogwood and azalea plantings. Directly north are rose and iris display gardens (late Apr-early May). East of the Center is the Tulsa Park Dept Conservatory, with five seasonal displays each year. Garden Center (Mon-Fri; also wkends during some events; closed most major hols & Dec 25-Jan 1). 2435 S Peoria Ave. Phone 918/746-5125. **Free.**

Tulsa Historical Society Museum. Located in the Gilcrease residence. Features photographs, rare books and furniture. (Tues-Thurs & Sat-Sun; closed major hols) Phone 918/585-5520. **Free.**

Annual Events

Gilcrease Rendezvous. Patterned after fur traders' engagements of days gone by. Early May.

Tulsa Indian Powwow. Expo Square. June.

Arkansas River Sand Castle Contest. 61st St and Riverside Dr. Sand castle/sculpture judged on originality, composition and design; musical entertainment; dog show, children's activities. Phone 918/596-2001. July.

Chili Cookoff & Bluegrass Festival. Sept.

Tulsa State Fair. Expo Square. Phone 918/744-1113. Late Sept-early Oct.

Seasonal Events

Professional Sports. Tulsa Drillers (AA baseball), Tulsa Drillers Stadium. Phone 918/744-5901. Apr-Aug. Tulsa Oilers (minor league hockey), Tulsa Convention Center. Phone 918/663-5888. Nov-Mar.

Discoveryland! Outdoor Theater. 10 mi W via W 41st St. Presents Rodgers and Hammerstein's *Oklahoma!* in a 2,000-seat outdoor theater complex with western theme. Authentic Native American dancing, Western musical revue and barbecue dinner prior to performance. Daily exc Sun. Phone 918/245-6552. June-Aug.

Additional Visitor Information

The Metro Tulsa Chamber of Commerce, 616 S Boston Ave, 74119, 918/585-1201, can provide travelers with assistance and additional information.

Motels

★ ★ **BEST WESTERN GLENPOOL.** (14831 S Casper, Glenpool 74033) 15 mi S, just off US 75. 918/322-5201; FAX 918/322-9604. 63 rms, 2 story. S $40-$50; D $45-$55; each addl $5; under 18 free; higher rates special events. Crib free. Pet accepted. TV; cable (premium). Pool. Complimentary coffee in rms; continental bkfst. Restaurant adj 11 am-11 pm. Ck-out 11 am. Coin lndry. Business servs avail. In-rm modem link. Many refrigerators. Cr cds: A, C, D, DS, JCB, MC, V.

[D] [⚟] [≈] [⊠] [🔥] [SC]

★ ★ **BEST WESTERN TRADE WINDS CENTRAL INN.** 3141 E Skelly Dr (74105), I-44 Harvard exit. 918/749-5561; FAX 918/749-6312. 167 rms, 2 story. S $56; D $63-$66; each addl $4; studio rms $66-$74; under 18 free; wkend rates. Crib free. Pet accepted, some restrictions. TV; cable (premium), VCR avail (movies avail $7.95). Heated pool; poolside serv. Restaurant 6 am-10 pm. Rm serv. Bar 11-2 am, closed Sun; entertainment, dancing. Ck-out noon. Meeting rms. Business servs avail. In-rm modem link. Valet serv. Sundries. Airport transportation. Wet bar, whirlpool in suites. Some balconies. Cr cds: A, C, D, DS, MC, V.

[D] [⚟] [≈] [⊠] [🔥] [SC]

✔ ★ **COMFORT INN.** 4717 S Yale Ave (74135), I-44 exit 229. 918/622-6776; FAX 918/622-1809. 109 rms, 3 story. S $38-$43; D $45-$48; suites $55-$110; under 18 free. Crib free. TV; cable. Pool. Complimentary continental bkfst. Restaurant adj. Ck-out 1 pm. Cr cds: A, C, D, DS, ER, MC, V.

[D] [≈] [⊠] [🔥] [SC]

★ ★ **COMFORT SUITES.** 8338 E 61st St S (74133). 918/254-0088; FAX 918/254-6820. 49 suites, 3 story. S $65; D $70; each addl $8; under 18 free; wkend rates. Crib free. TV; cable (premium), VCR avail. Pool. Complimentary full bkfst. Complimentary coffee in rms. Restaurant 6:30-10 am, 6-10 pm. Bar. Ck-out 11 am. Meeting rm. Business servs avail. In-rm modem link. Sundries. Health club privileges. Bathrm phones; some refrigerators, wet bars. Cr cds: A, C, D, DS, ER, JCB, MC, V.

[D] [≈] [⊠] [🔥] [SC]

★ **DAYS INN.** 8201 E Skelly Dr (74129), I-44E, exit 231. 918/665-6800; FAX 918/665-7653. 195 rms, 2 story, 21 kit. suites. S $38-$42; D $42-$50; each addl $4; kit. suites $44-$56; under 18 free. Crib free. Pet accepted, some restrictions; $25 refundable. TV; cable (premium). Pool. Complimentary continental bkfst. Complimentary coffee. Restaurant nearby. Ck-out noon. Coin lndry. Meeting rms. Business servs avail. Valet serv. Cr cds: A, C, D, DS, MC, V.

[D] [⚟] [≈] [⊠] [🔥] [SC]

★ ★ **HAMPTON INN.** 3209 S 79th E Ave (74145). 918/663-1000; FAX 918/663-0587. 148 rms, 4 story. S $58-$60; D $65-$67; suites $71-$78; under 18 free; wkend rates. Crib free. TV; cable. Heated pool. Complimentary continental bkfst, coffee. Restaurant adj open 24 hrs. Ck-out noon. Meeting rms. In-rm modem link. Health club privileges. Refrigerator in suites. Cr cds: A, C, D, DS, ER, JCB, MC, V.

[D] [≈] [⊠] [🔥] [SC]

★ ★ **HAWTHORN SUITES.** 3509 S 79th East Ave (74145), at jct I-44 & Broken Arrow Expy. 918/663-3900; FAX 918/664-0548. 131 units, 3 story. S, D $59-$69; 1-bedrm suites $89-$109; 2-bedrm suites $139-$169; wkend rates. Crib free. TV; cable (premium). Heated pool; whirlpool. Complimentary full bkfst, evening refreshments Mon-Thurs. Coin lndry. Meeting rms. Business servs avail. Free airport transportation 8 am-10 pm. Bellhops. Valet serv. Game court. Health club privileges. Refrigerator in suites. Fireplaces. Private patios, balconies. Cr cds: A, C, D, DS, MC, V.

[D] [≈] [⊠] [🔥] [SC]

★ ★ **HOLIDAY INN-EAST/AIRPORT.** 1010 N Garnett Rd (74116), near Intl Airport. 918/437-7660; FAX 918/438-7538. 158 rms, 2 story. S $59-$85; D $59-$90; each addl $5; under 19 free. Pet accepted, TV; cable (premium). Indoor pool. Restaurant 6 am-2 pm, 5-10 pm; Sat, Sun from 7 am. Rm serv. Bar noon-2 am; Sat, Sun from 4 pm. Ck-out noon. Meeting rms. Business servs avail. In-rm modem link. Bellhops. Valet serv. Free airport transportation. Health club privileges. Game rm. Cr cds: A, C, D, DS, ER, JCB, MC, V.

[D] [⚟] [≈] [✈] [⊠] [🔥] [SC]

★ **LA QUINTA INN.** 35 N Sheridan Rd (74115), jct I-244. 918/836-3931; FAX 918/836-5428. 101 rms, 2 story. S $47; D $55; each addl (after 2nd person) $5; units for 6, $75; suites $63-$76; under 18 free. Crib free. Pet accepted, some restrictions. TV; cable (premium). Heated pool. Continental bkfst in lobby. Restaurant adj open 24 hrs. Ck-out noon. Meeting rm. Business servs avail. Valet serv. Free airport transportation. Cr cds: A, C, D, DS, JCB, MC, V.

[D] [⚟] [≈] [⊠] [🔥] [SC]

✔ ★ ★ **QUALITY INN.** 6030 E Skelly Dr (74135), I-44 exit 230. 918/665-2630; FAX 918/665-2630, ext. 476. 131 rms, 4 story. S $42; D $47; each addl $5; suites $89; under 18 free. Crib free. TV; cable (premium), VCR avail. Pool. Complimentary continental bkfst. Ck-out noon. Meeting rms. Business servs avail. In-rm modem link. Cr cds: A, C, D, DS, ER, JCB, MC, V.

[D] [≈] [⊠] [🔥] [SC]

✔ ★ ★ **QUALITY INN AIRPORT.** 222 N Garnett St (74116). 918/438-0780. 118 rms, 2 story. S $40-$52; D $48-$56; each addl $4; suites $75; under 18 free. Crib $4. Pet accepted, some restrictions; $4. TV; cable. Pool. Restaurant 6 am-2 pm, 5-10 pm. Rm serv. Bar. Ck-out

11 am. Meeting rms. Business servs avail. In-rm modem link. Airport transportation. Cr cds: A, C, D, DS, ER, JCB, MC, V.

[D] [⌂] [≈] [⊠] [♨] [SC]

★ ★ **RESIDENCE INN BY MARRIOTT.** *8181 E 41st St (74145).* 918/664-7241; FAX 918/622-0314. 135 kit. units, 2 story. S, D $95-$115; under 12 free. Crib free. Pet accepted, some restrictions; $50. TV; cable (premium), VCR avail. Pool; whirlpool. Complimentary continental bkfst. Complimentary coffee in rms. Ck-out noon. Coin Indry. Meeting rms. Business center. In-rm modem link. Sundries. Valet serv. Free airport transportation. Health club privileges. Balconies. Picnic tables. Cr cds: A, C, D, DS, ER, JCB, MC, V.

[D] [⌂] [≈] [⊠] [⊠] [♨] [SC] [🏃]

Motor Hotels

★ **HOLIDAY INN-TULSA CENTRAL HOLIDOME.** *8181 E Skelly Dr (74129), at I-44, 31st St & Memorial Dr exit.* 918/663-4541; FAX 918/665-7109. 211 rms, 3 story. S, D $55-$64; suites $72-$130; under 18 free; wkend rates. Crib free. TV; cable (premium). Indoor pool; wading pool. Complimentary coffee in lobby. Restaurant 6:30 am-2 pm, 5:30-10 pm. Rm serv. Bar 4:30 pm-midnight, Fri & Sat to 2 am, closed Sun, hols. Ck-out noon. Coin Indry. Meeting rms. Business servs avail. In-rm modem link. Bellhops. Valet serv. Free airport transportation. Putting green. Exercise equipt; weight machine, bicycle, whirlpool, sauna. Holidome. Game rm. Cr cds: A, C, D, DS, JCB, MC, V.

[D] [≈] [🏃] [⊠] [♨] [SC]

✔ ★ ★ **LEXINGTON HOTEL SUITES.** *8525 E 41st (74145).* 918/627-0030; FAX 918/627-0587. 162 kit. suites, 3 story. S $59-$117; D $62-$124; each addl $7; under 16 free; wkly, monthly rates. Crib free. TV; cable (premium). Heated pool. Complimentary continental bkfst 6:30-9 am. Complimentary coffee in rms. Ck-out noon. Coin Indry. Meeting rms. Business servs avail. In-rm modem link. Valet serv. Free airport transportation. Cr cds: A, C, D, DS, JCB, MC, V.

[D] [≈] [⊠] [♨] [SC]

★ ★ **RADISSON INN-TULSA AIRPORT.** *2201 N 77 East Ave (74115), at Intl Airport.* 918/835-9911; FAX 918/838-2452. 171 rms, 2 story. S $76-$85; D $86-$95; each addl $10; suites from $110; under 17 free; wkend rates. Crib free. TV; cable (premium). Pool. Restaurants 6 am-10:30 pm; Sat & Sun 6:30 am-10 pm. Rm serv. Bar 11-midnight. Ck-out 1 pm. Meeting rms. Business servs avail. In-rm modem link. Bellhops. Valet serv. Free airport transportation. Exercise equipt; weights, bicycles, sauna. Grill. Cr cds: A, C, D, DS, MC, V.

[D] [≈] [🏃] [✈] [⊠] [♨] [SC]

★ ★ **RAMADA.** *5000 E Skelly Dr (74135).* 918/622-7000; FAX 918/664-9353. 318 rms, 4 story. S, D $55-$70; each addl $6; suites $95-$225; under 12 free. Crib free. Pet accepted. TV; cable (premium), VCR avail. Pool. Restaurant 6:30 am-2 pm, 5-10 pm. Rm serv. Bar 5 pm-2 am; entertainment Tues-Sat, dancing. Ck-out noon. Convention facilities. Business servs avail. Bellhops. Valet serv. Gift shop. Barber, beauty shop. Free airport transportation. Exercise equipt; weight machine, treadmill. Game rm. Private patios; balcony on suites. Cr cds: A, C, D, DS, MC, V.

[D] [⌂] [≈] [🏃] [⊠] [♨] [SC]

Hotels

★ ★ ★ **ADAMS MARK TULSA, AT WILLIAMS CENTER.** *100 E 2nd (74103), in town center.* 918/582-9000; FAX 918/560-2232. 462 rms, 15 story. S $120-$152; D $132-$152; suites $275-$975; under 18 free; wkend & honeymoon rates. Crib free. TV; cable, VCR avail. Heated pool. Restaurants 6:30 am-10 pm; Fri & Sat to 11 pm; Sun to 10 pm. Rm serv 24 hrs. Bar 11-1 am. Ck-out noon. Meeting rms. Business center. In-rm modem link. Gift shop. Free airport transportation. Exer-

cise equipt; bicycles, rowing machine. Minibars. Balconies. Luxury level. Cr cds: A, C, D, DS, ER, JCB, MC, V.

[D] [⌂] [≈] [🏃] [⊠] [♨] [SC]

★ ★ ★ **DOUBLETREE DOWNTOWN.** *616 W 7th St (74127).* 918/587-8000; FAX 918/587-1642. 418 rms, 18 story. S $76-$129; D $91-$144; each addl $15; suites $400-$700; under 18 free; wkend rates. Crib free. Pet accepted; $50 deposit ($25 refundable). Valet parking, garage. TV; cable (premium), VCR avail. Indoor pool; poolside serv. Restaurant 6:30 am-9:30 pm. Bar; entertainment. Ck-out noon. Convention facilities. Business servs avail. In-rm modem link. Gift shop. Free airport transportation. Exercise equipt; weight machine, treadmill, whirlpool, sauna. Picnic tables. Cr cds: A, C, D, DS, JCB, MC, V.

[D] [⌂] [≈] [🏃] [⊠] [⊠] [♨] [SC]

★ ★ ★ **DOUBLETREE HOTEL AT WARREN PLACE.** *6110 S Yale (74136).* 918/495-1000; FAX 918/495-1944. 371 rms, 10 story. S $123-$153; D $133-$173; each addl $15; suites $175-$400; under 18 free; wkend, honeymoon rates. Crib free. Valet parking $5. TV; cable (premium), VCR avail. Indoor pool; whirlpool, sauna. Restaurants 6:30 am-11 pm (also see WARREN DUCK CLUB). Bar 3 pm-1 am; dancing. Ck-out noon. Convention facilities. Business center. In-rm modem link. Concierge. Gift shop. Free covered parking. Free airport transportation. Health club privileges. Refrigerator, wet bar in suites. Some balconies. Elaborate landscaping. Common rms decorated with Chippendale, Hepplewhite furniture. Lighted 18-hole par 3 golf opp. Luxury level. Cr cds: A, C, D, DS, ER, JCB, MC, V.

[D] [⌂] [≈] [⛱] [⊠] [♨] [SC] [🏃]

★ ★ ★ **EMBASSY SUITES.** *3332 S 79th E Ave (74145), I-44 Memorial exit to 33rd.* 918/622-4000; FAX 918/665-2347. 240 kit. suites, 9 story. S, D $95-$115; each addl $10; exec suites $129-$149; under 12 free; wkend rates. Crib free. TV; cable (premium), VCR avail. Indoor pool. Complimentary full bkfst cooked to order 6-9:30 am; Sat 6:30-10 am. Coffee in rms. Restaurant 11 am-2 pm, 5-10 pm; Fri & Sat to 11 pm. Bar 11-2 am; entertainment exc Sun. Ck-out 1 pm. Coin Indry. Meeting rms. In-rm modem link. Gift shop. Free airport transportation. Exercise equipt; weights, bicycles, whirlpool, steam rm, sauna. Refrigerators, wet bars. Balconies. Skylight over atrium. Cr cds: A, C, D, DS, ER, JCB, MC, V.

[D] [≈] [🏃] [⊠] [♨] [SC]

★ ★ **MARRIOTT.** *10918 E 41st St (74146), at Garnett Rd, at jct Broken Arrow Expy & Mingo Valley Expy.* 918/627-5000; FAX 918/627-4003. 336 rms, 11 story. S, D $110; suites $200-$350; under 18 free; wkend plans. Crib free. Pet accepted. TV; cable (premium), VCR avail (movies avail $7.50). Indoor/outdoor pool; poolside serv. Restaurant 6 am-10 pm. Bar. Ck-out noon. Coin Indry. Convention facilities. Business center. In-rm modem link. Concierge. Gift shop. Free parking. Free airport transportation. Exercise equipt; weights, bicycles, whirlpool, sauna. Health club privileges. Lawn games. Traditional decor with brass accents. Many floral arrangements. Luxury level. Cr cds: A, C, D, DS, JCB, MC, V.

[D] [⌂] [≈] [🏃] [⊠] [♨] [SC] [🏃]

★ ★ **MARRIOTT SOUTHERN HILLS.** *1902 E 71st St S (74136).* 918/493-7000; FAX 918/481-7147. 383 rms, 11 story. S $98-$119; D $108-$134; each addl $10; suites $185-$600; under 18 free; wkend rates. Crib free. Valet parking $3. TV; cable (premium), VCR avail. Indoor pool; poolside serv. Restaurant 6:30 am-11 pm. Bar 4 pm-2 am; dancing. Ck-out noon. Convention facilities. Business servs avail. In-rm modem link. Concierge. Shopping arcade. Airport transportation. Lighted tennis privileges opp. Exercise equipt; weight machine, bicycle, sauna. Some bathrm phones. Fountain in lobby. Cr cds: A, C, D, DS, ER, JCB, MC, V.

[D] [≈] [🏃] [⊠] [♨] [SC]

Restaurants

★ ★ ★ **ATLANTIC SEA GRILL.** 8321-A E 61st St (74133). 918/252-7966. Hrs: 11:30 am-2:30 pm, 5:30-10 pm; Fri to 11 pm; Sat 5:30-11 pm; Sun 5:30-10 pm. Closed Jan 1, July 4, Thanksgiving, Dec 25. Res accepted. Continental menu. Bar. Wine list. Semi-a la carte: lunch $4.95-$9.95, dinner $7.95-$19.95. Specializes in fresh seafood, steak, veal. Own pastries. Parking. Outdoor dining. 350-gallon saltwater aquarium. Cr cds: A, C, D, DS, MC, V.
D

★ ★ **BODEAN SEAFOOD.** 3323 E 51st. 918/743-3861. Hrs: 11 am-2:30 pm, 5-10:30 pm; Sat from 5 pm; Sun 5-9 pm. Closed most hols. Res accepted. Bar 11 am-10:30 pm. Semi-a la carte: lunch $4.95-$15.95, dinner $11.95-$25.95. All seafood fresh daily. Parking. Cr cds: A, C, D, DS, MC, V.
D

✔ ★ ★ **CAMARELLI'S.** 1536 E 15th St (74120). 918/582-8900. Hrs: 11 am-2 pm, 5-10 pm; Fri, Sat 5-11 pm; Sun 5-9 pm. Closed Thanksgiving, Dec 25. Res accepted. Italian menu. Bar to 2 am. A la carte entrees: lunch $4.95-$8.95. Semi-a la carte: dinner $8.95-$12.95. Specializes in pasta, chicken, veal. Live entertainment Wed 9 pm-midnight. Parking. Cr cds: A, C, D, DS, MC, V.
D

★ **CAPISTRANO CAFE.** 1748 Utica Sq (74119). 918/747-2819. Hrs: 11 am-2:30 pm, 5-10:30 pm; Fri to 11 pm; Sat, Sun 11 am-3 pm, 5-9:30 pm. Closed some major hols. Res accepted. Italian, Southwestern menu. Bar. Semi-a la carte: lunch $2.95-$9.95, dinner $3.25-$17.95. Specialties: Santa Fe blue corn plato, chicken rotisserie, pasta. Outdoor dining. Art deco wall murals. Cr cds: A, C, D, DS, MC, V.
D

✔ ★ ★ **CHARLIE MITCHELL'S MIDTOWN.** 2705 E 21st St (74114). 918/747-8858. Hrs: 11 am-11 pm; Fri & Sat to midnight; Sun 10 am-10 pm. Closed Dec 25. Bar; entertainment Thurs-Sat. Semi-a la carte: lunch, dinner $4.95-$11.95. Child's meals. Specializes in fish & chips, prime rib, steak. Parking. Outdoor dining. Cr cds: A, C, D, DS, MC, V.
D

★ ★ **FOUNTAINS.** 6540 S Lewis Ave (74136). 918/749-9916. Hrs: 11:30 am-2 pm, 5:30-10 pm; Fri to 11 pm; Sat 5:30-11 pm; Sun to 9 pm; early-bird dinner 5:30-6:30 pm; Sun brunch 11 am-2 pm. Closed major hols. Res accepted. Bar. Wine list. Semi-a la carte: lunch $4.95-$7.95, dinner $9.95-$15.95. Buffet: lunch $6.95. Sun brunch $9.95. Child's meals. Specialties: veal Oscar, roast duck, seafood. Salad bar at lunch. Dessert bar. Entertainment Tues, Sat; pianist Sun. Parking. Multi-level dining overlooks pool and fountains. Cr cds: A, C, D, DS, MC, V.
D SC

★ ★ **FRENCH HEN.** 7143 S Yale, in the Lighthouse shopping center. 918/492-2596. Hrs: 11:30 am-2 pm, 5:30-10 pm; Sat from 5:30 pm; early-bird dinner Mon-Sat 5:30-6:30 pm. Closed Sun; most major hols. Res accepted. Continental menu. Bar. Semi-a la carte: lunch $5.50-$12.95. A la carte entrees: dinner $9-$26.95. Specializes in fresh game & seafood. French street cafe decor. Cr cds: A, C, D, DS, MC, V.
D

✔ ★ ★ **GRADY'S AMERICAN GRILL.** 7007 S Memorial Dr (74133). 918/254-7733. Hrs: 11 am-10:30 pm; Fri, Sat to midnight. Closed Thanksgiving, Dec 25. Res accepted. Bar. Semi-a la carte: lunch, dinner $4.95-$13.95. Specializes in prime rib, fresh seafood, pizza Florentine. Parking. Open kitchen. Rustic decor. Cr cds: A, C, D, DS, MC, V.
D

★ ★ **GREEN ONION.** 4532 E 51st. 918/481-3338. Hrs: 11:30 am-2 pm, 5:30-10 pm; Fri, Sat to 11 pm; Sun 5:30-9 pm; Sun brunch 11 am-2 pm. Closed major hols. Res accepted. Bar. Semi-a la carte: lunch $4.50-$7, dinner $11-$17. Sun brunch $9.95. Child's meals. Specializes in fresh seafood, steak, New Zealand lamb. Musical combo Tues-Sat, pianist Sun evenings. Parking. Local artwork in dining rm. Cr cds: A, C, D, DS, MC, V.
D

★ **JAMIL'S.** 2833 E 51st. 918/742-9097. Hrs: 5-11:30 pm; wkends to 12:15 am. Res accepted. Lebanese menu. Semi-a la carte: dinner $9-$27.50. Child's meals. Specializes in steak, smoked chicken, seafood. Parking. Family-owned. Cr cds: A, C, D, DS, MC, V.
D

★ ★ **JOSEPH'S STEAK HOUSE & SEAFOOD.** 4848 S Yale. 918/493-5888. Hrs: 11 am-1:30 pm, 5-10 pm; wkends to 11 pm. Closed Sun; Thanksgiving, Dec 25. Res accepted. Serv bar. Semi-a la carte: lunch $3.50-$6.95, dinner $8.95-$28.95. Child's meals. Specializes in prime rib, seafood, Lebanese hors d'oeuvrés. Parking. Extensive art and art objects from around the world; some antiques. Cr cds: A, C, D, DS, MC, V.
D

★ ★ **POLO GRILL.** 2038 Utica Square (74120). 918/744-4280. Hrs: 11 am-10 pm; Fri, Sat to 11 pm. Closed Sun; major hols. Res accepted. Bar. Semi-a la carte: lunch $4.95-$10.95, dinner $7.50-$21.95. Specializes in fresh seafood. Pianist evenings. Outdoor dining. English hunting decor, collectibles. Cr cds: A, C, D, MC, V.
D

✔ ★ **RICARDOS.** 5629 E 41st (74135). 918/622-2668. Hrs: 11 am-2 pm, 5-9:30 pm; Fri to 10 pm; Sat 11 am-10 pm. Closed Sun; July 4, Thanksgiving, Dec 24 (evening), Dec 25. Mexican menu. Serv bar. Semi-a la carte: lunch $3.50-$7.50, dinner $4-$8.95. Child's meals. Specializes in chili rellenos, chili con queso. Parking. Cr cds: A, DS, MC, V.
D

★ ★ **ROMANO'S MACARONI GRILL.** 8112 E 66th St (74133). 918/254-7800. Hrs: 11 am-10 pm; Fri & Sat to 11 pm. Closed Thanksgiving, Dec 25. Italian menu. Bar. Semi-a la carte: lunch $4.95-$8.95, dinner $6.95-$18.95. Child's meals. Specializes in Northern Italian cuisine. Entertainment; opera singers. Parking. Stone walls, archways. Fireplaces. Cr cds: A, C, D, DS, MC, V.
D

★ ★ **ROSIE'S RIB JOINT.** 8125 E 49th St (74145). 918/663-2610. Hrs: 11 am-2 pm, 5-10 pm; Sat from 5 pm; Sun 5-9 pm. Closed some major hols. Res accepted. Bar. Semi-a la carte: lunch $4.95-$9.95, dinner $9.95-$27.95. Specializes in smoked ribs, prime rib, seafood. Salad bar. Parking. Cr cds: A, C, D, DS, MC, V.
D SC

★ ★ **URSULA'S BAVARIAN INN.** 4932 E 91st St, in Hunters Glen Shopping Center. 918/496-8282. Hrs: 5-9 pm; Fri, Sat to 10 pm. Closed Sun, Mon; some major hols. Res accepted. German menu. Bar. Semi-a la carte: dinner $7.50-$17. Specialties: Wienerschnitzel, beef rouladen, Schweizer schnitzel. Accordianist Thurs evenings. Outdoor dining in beer garden. Extensive beer selection. German decor; tapestries, murals. Cr cds: A, C, D, MC, V.
D

★ ★ ★ **WARREN DUCK CLUB.** (See Doubletree Hotel At Warren Place) 918/495-1000. Hrs: 11:30 am-2 pm, 6-10 pm; Fri, Sat 6-11 pm. Closed Sun; some major hols. Res accepted. Continental menu. Bar. Semi-a la carte: lunch $8.95-$13.95, dinner $17.95-$25.95. Child's meals. Specialties: blackened tenderloin, rotisserie duck, seafood. Pianist Fri & Sat. Valet parking. Cr cds: A, C, D, DS, ER, JCB, MC, V.
D SC

Unrated Dining Spots

CASA BONITA. *2120 S Sheridan Rd, in Alameda Shopping Ctr. 918/836-6464.* Hrs: 11 am-9:30 pm; Fri, Sat to 10 pm. Closed Thanksgiving, Dec 24-25. Mexican, Amer menu. Semi-a la carte: lunch $4.99-$7.99, dinner $5.49-$7.99. Child's meals. Specializes in all-you-can-eat Mexican dinner. Strolling Mexican musicians; entertainment, puppet shows. Mexican village decor; waterfalls, caves. Gift shop. Game rm. Cr cds: A, C, D, DS, MC, V.

D **SC**

INTERURBAN. *717 S Houston. 918/585-3134.* Hrs: 11 am-10:30 pm; Fri, Sat to midnight; Sun 5-10:30 pm. Closed some major hols. Bar to midnight. Semi-a la carte: lunch, dinner $4.95-$12.95. Child's meals. Specializes in gourmet hamburgers, salads, Mexican dishes. Parking. Trolley theme. Cr cds: A, C, D, MC, V.

D

METRO DINER. *3001 E 11th St. 918/592-2616.* Hrs: 6:30 am-10 pm; Fri to midnight; Sat 7 am-midnight; Sun 7 am-10 pm. Closed Easter, Thanksgiving, Dec 25. Bar. Semi-a la carte: bkfst $2.95-$6.50, lunch, dinner $3.99-$10. Child's meals. Specializes in chicken-fried steak, homemade pies. Parking. 1950s diner atmosphere. Cr cds: A, DS, MC, V.

D **SC**

Vinita (A-9)

(For accommodations see Grand Lake, Miami, Pryor)

Pop 5,804 **Elev** 700 ft **Area code** 918 **Zip** 74301
Information Chamber of Commerce, 104 E Illinois, PO Box 882; 918/256-7133.

Among the oldest towns in the state, Vinita was established in 1871 within the Cherokee Nation. Many stately homes attest to the town's cultural significance during the late 1800s. Vinita is also home to one of the world's largest McDonald's restaurants.

What to See and Do

Eastern Trails Museum. Historic displays, articles belonging to Vinnie Ream, Native American artifacts. (Mon-Sat afternoons; closed most major hols) 215 W Illinois. Phone 918/256-2115. **Free.**

Annual Event

Will Rogers Memorial Rodeo and Parade. Late Aug.

Waurika (D-6)

(For accommodations see Duncan)

Pop 2,088 **Elev** 881 ft **Area code** 405 **Zip** 73573

Waurika is the site of Monument Rocks, a high point of the Chisholm Trail in southern Oklahoma. Early drovers made two piles of sandstone boulders, each about 12 feet high on a flat-topped mesa, enabling the viewer to see 10 to 15 miles in either direction.

What to See and Do

Chisholm Trail Historical Museum. Chisholm Trail Gallery depicts history and artifacts from 1867-1889; Pioneer Gallery shows development of local history; slide presentation. (Daily exc Mon; closed major hols) 1 mi E via US 70. Phone 405/228-2166. **Free.**

Waurika Lake. Dam on Beaver Creek, a tributary of the Red River. Swimming, waterskiing; fishing, hunting; boating. Picnicking. Camping (fee; many sites have electrical hookups). Information center (Mon-Fri). (Daily) 6 mi NW via OK 5. Phone 405/963-2111. **Free.**

Weatherford (C-6)

(See Clinton)

Settled 1898 **Pop** 10,124 **Elev** 1,647 ft **Area code** 405 **Zip** 73096
Information Chamber of Commerce, 522 W Rainey, PO Box 729; 405/772-7744 or 800/725-7744.

Weatherford is a progressive, growing city with a diversified economy and is the home of Southwestern Oklahoma State University (1901) as well as Gemini and Apollo astronaut Thomas P. Stafford.

What to See and Do

Crowder Lake. Swimming; fishing; boating. 9 mi S on OK 54, then 3/4 mi E.

Red Rock Canyon State Park. Covers 310 acres. Swimming pool, bathhouse. Hiking. Picnicking, playground. Camping, trailer hookups (fee). (Daily) 20 mi E on I-40, then 4 1/2 mi S on US 281, near Hinton. Phone 405/542-6344. **Free.**

Annual Event

Southwest Festival of the Arts. Crafts, performing arts, concerts. 2nd Sat Sept.

Motel

BEST WESTERN-THE MARK. *525 E Main St. 405/772-3325; FAX 405/772-8950.* 59 rms, 1-2 story. S $37-$45; D $41-$45; each addl $3. Crib $4. Pet accepted. TV; cable (premium), VCR avail. Pool. Complimentary coffee in rms. Restaurant opp 6 am-10 pm. Ck-out noon. Meeting rms. Business servs avail. In-rm modem link. Refrigerators. Cr cds: A, C, D, DS, MC, V.

Restaurant

T-BONE STEAK HOUSE. *1805 E Main St. 405/772-6329.* Hrs: 5-10 pm; Sun to 9 pm; Sun brunch 11 am-2 pm. Bar. Semi-a la carte: dinner $5.99-$16.99. Sun brunch $7.49, $8.99. Child's meals. Specialties: hickory-smoked prime rib, mushrooms tempura, mud pie. Parking. Outdoor dining. Fireplace. Cr cds: DS, MC, V.

Woodward (B-5)

Pop 12,340 **Elev** 1,905 ft **Area code** 405 **Zip** 73801
Information Chamber of Commerce, 1006 Oklahoma Ave, PO Box 1026; 405/256-7411.

What to See and Do

Boiling Springs State Park. Covers 790 acres with 7-acre lake. Swimming pool, bathhouse; fishing. Hiking. Picnicking, playground, concession. Camping, trailer hookups (fee), cabins. (Daily) 1 mi N on OK 34, then 5 mi E on OK 34C. Phone 405/256-7664. **Free.**

Fort Supply Lake. Swimming; fishing, hunting. Camping (hookups; fees). (Daily) 15 mi NW via US 270; 1 mi S of Fort Supply. Phone 405/766-2701. **Free.**

Glass Mountains. Name derived from the mountains' surface, which is made up of sparkling selenite crystals. Roadside rest area. E on OK 15, just E of jct US 281, OK 15, W of Orienta.

Plains Indians & Pioneers Museum. Changing and permanent displays depict Native American culture and early life on the plains. Pioneer, cowboy and Native American artifacts and clothing; collection of personal belongings of Temple Houston, son of Sam Houston; exhibits from early-day banks; original building from historic Fort Supply; agriculture building; art center with changing exhibits. (Daily exc Mon; closed hols) 2009 Williams St (US 270). Phone 405/256-6136. **Free.**

Motels

✔★ **HOSPITALITY INN.** *4120 Williams Ave, off US 270S.* 405/254-2964; res: 800/454-2964; FAX 405/254-2897. 60 rms, 2 story. S $26.50; D $34.50; each addl $4; kit. units $29.50-$37.50; under 12 free; wkly rates. Crib avail. TV; cable (premium). Pool. Complimentary continental bkfst. Restaurant nearby. Ck-out 11 am. Business servs avail. Lawn games. Picnic table. Cr cds: A, DS, MC, V.

[D] [⚓] [≈] [✕] [🐾]

★★ **NORTHWEST INN.** *Box 1006 (73802), US 270 & 1st St.* 405/256-7600; res: 800/727-7606; FAX 405/254-2274. 124 rms, 2 story. S, D $47.50-$57.50; each addl $6; under 18 free. Crib free. Pet accepted. TV; cable (premium). Indoor pool; poolside serv. Restaurant 6 am-2 pm, 5-10 pm. Rm serv. Bar 5 pm-2 am, closed Sun; entertainment, dancing. Ck-out noon. Coin lndry. Meeting rms. Business servs avail. Exercise equipt; bicycles. Game rm. Some refrigerators. Cr cds: A, C, D, DS, MC, V.

[D] [⚓] [≈] [🏋] [✕] [🐾] [SC]

Restaurant

✔★★ **RIB RANCH.** *2424 Williams Ave.* 405/256-6081. Hrs: 11 am-2 pm, 5-9 pm; Sat 11 am-9 pm. Closed Mon; Jan 1, Thanksgiving, Dec 25. Res accepted. Semi-a la carte: lunch, dinner $3.45-$12. Child's meals. Specializes in barbecued beef, ribs. Parking. Log building; antiques, player piano. Cr cds: DS, MC, V.

[D] [SC]

Unrated Dining Spot

BUFFY'S BUFFET. *US 270S.* 405/256-5873. Hrs: 11 am-2 pm, 5-8:30 pm; Wed to 2 pm; Sun 11 am-7 pm. Closed Dec 25. Buffet: lunch $4.92, dinner $5.99; Sun $5.99. Specialties: seafood (Fri), barbecued ribs (Tues, Sat). Parking. Cr cds: MC, V.

[D]

Texas

Population: 16,986,510

Land area: 262,017 square miles

Elevation: 0-8,749 feet

Highest point: Guadalupe Peak (Culberson County)

Entered Union: December 29, 1845 (28th state)

Capital: Austin

Motto: Friendship

Nickname: Lone Star State

State flower: Bluebonnet

State bird: Mockingbird

State tree: Pecan

State fair: September 27-October 20, 1996, in Dallas

Time zone: Central and Mountain

The long, turbulent history of Texas as we know it goes back to 27 years after Columbus invaded America. In 1519 Alonzo Alvarez de Piñeda explored and charted the Texas coast. Alvar Núñez Cabeza de Vaca, shipwrecked near Galveston, wandered across Texas in 1528 and the following years. Inspired by the tales of de Vaca, Coronado entered the state from New Mexico, bringing with him Fray Juan de Padilla, the first missionary, who was later murdered by the Indians he tried to convert.

In 1821 Mexico won its independence from Spain, and Texas became a part of the new Mexican republic. At about this time, Moses Austin and his son, Stephen F. Austin, received permission to settle 300 American families on the Brazos. This was the beginning of Anglo-American Texas. Dissatisfaction with Mexican rule led to the Texas Revolution and the taking of San Antonio, later temporarily lost when the Alamo fell. The Revolution came to an end on the plain of San Jacinto when General Sam Houston's outnumbered troops successfully charged the Mexican Army on April 21, 1836, and Texas became an independent republic. It remained so until December 29, 1845, when Texas became the 28th state of the Union.

The character of Texas changes markedly from region to region. While the face of western Texas is largely that of the open range, eastern Texas is home to plantations where rice, sugar cane and cotton are grown. Northern Texas is the land of the *Llanos Estacado* (staked plains), but to the southwest stand mountain ranges with 59 peaks at an altitude of more than 6,000 feet. South Texas is dotted with citrus groves that thrive in its semi-tropical climate, as do the beach lovers that populate hundreds of miles of sand along the Gulf Coast and on the barrier islands. Central areas have an abundance of man-made lakes, making fishing and boating popular pastimes.

Industry exceeds agriculture in the Houston-Beaumont area, including a space industry that contributes millions of dollars to the state's economy. Much of the nation's oil is produced in Texas, and it also ranks at the top of the cotton and livestock industries.

National Park Service Areas

Texas has two national parks, Big Bend and Guadalupe Mountains (see both); one national seashore, Padre Island (see); two national historical parks, Lyndon B. Johnson (see JOHNSON CITY) and San Antonio Missions (see SAN ANTONIO); two national historic sites, Fort Davis (see ALPINE) and Palo Alto Battlefield (see BROWNSVILLE); and two national recreation areas, Amistad (see DEL RIO) and Lake Meredith (see FRITCH). There is also Alibates Flint Quarries National Monument (see FRITCH) and Chamizal National Memorial (see EL PASO). Big Thicket National Preserve, headquartered at Beaumont, is not one contiguous area but consists of several tracts of land north and west of there—a total of 84,550 acres.

The US Forest Service manages two national grasslands and four national forests in Texas. They are visited by thousands of people each year. Recreation facilities include picnicking, hiking, swimming, boating, hunting, bird-watching and sightseeing. For information on national forests contact Public Affairs Officer, US Forest Service, 701 N First St, Lufkin 75901-3088; 409/639-8501. For state forests contact Texas Forest Service, College Station 77843; 409/845-2641.

National Forests

The following is an alphabetical listing of National Forests and the towns they are listed under.

Angelina National Forest (see LUFKIN): Forest Supervisor in Lufkin; Ranger office in Lufkin.

Davy Crockett National Forest (see LUFKIN): Forest Supervisor in Lufkin; Ranger offices in Apple Springs*, Crockett.

Sabine National Forest (see JASPER): Forest Supervisor in Lufkin; Ranger offices in Hemphill*, San Augustine*.

Sam Houston National Forest (see HUNTSVILLE): Forest Supervisor in Lufkin; Ranger offices in Cleveland*, New Waverly*.

*Not described in text

State Recreation Areas

The following towns list state recreation areas in their vicinity under What to See and Do; refer to the individual town for directions and park information.

Listed under **Abilene**: see Abilene State Park.

Listed under **Alice**: see Lake Corpus Christi State Park.

Listed under **Alpine**: see Davis Mountains State Park.

Listed under **Austin**: see McKinney Falls State Park.

Listed under **Bastrop**: see Bastrop and Buescher state parks.

Listed under **Big Spring**: see Lake Colorado City State Park.

Listed under **Bonham**: see Bonham State Park.

Listed under **Brenham**: see Lake Somerville and Stephen F. Austin state parks.

Listed under **Brownwood**: see Lake Brownwood State Park.

Listed under **Burnet**: see Inks Lake State Park.

Listed under **Canyon**: see Palo Duro Canyon State Park.

Listed under **Cleburne**: see Cleburne and Dinosaur Valley state parks.

Listed under **Crockett**: see Mission Tejas State Historical Park.

Listed under **Del Rio**: see Seminole Canyon State Historical Park.

Listed under **Denison**: see Eisenhower State Park.

Listed under **El Paso**: see Hueco Tanks State Historical Park.

Listed under **Fairfield**: see Fairfield Lake State Park.

Listed under **Galveston**: see Galveston Island State Park.

Listed under **Goliad**: see Goliad State Historical Park.

Listed under **Gonzales**: see Palmetto State Park.

Listed under **Graham**: see Fort Richardson State Historical Park.

Listed under **Groesbeck**: see Fort Parker State Park.

Listed under **Huntsville**: see Huntsville State Park.

Listed under **Jasper**: see Martin Dies, Jr State Park.

Listed under **Johnson City**: see Lyndon B. Johnson State Historical Park and Pedernales Falls State Park.

Listed under **Kerrville**: see Kerrville-Schreiner State Park.

Listed under **Lake Whitney**: see Lake Whitney State Park.

Listed under **Laredo**: see Lake Casa Blanca State Park.

Listed under **Marshall**: see Caddo Lake State Park.

Listed under **Mission**: see Bentsen-Rio Grande Valley State Park.

Listed under **Monahans**: see Monahans Sandhills State Park.

Listed under **Pecos**: see Balmorhea State Park.

Listed under **Port Aransas**: see Mustang Island State Park.

Listed under **Port Arthur**: see Sea Rim State Park.

Listed under **Possum Kingdom State Park**: see Possum Kingdom State Park.

Listed under **Quanah**: see Copper Breaks State Park.

Listed under **Rockport**: see Copano Bay Causeway and Goose Island state parks.

Listed under **Rusk**: see Rusk-Palestine State Park.

Listed under **San Marcos**: see Lockhart State Park.

Listed under **Tyler**: see Tyler State Park.

Listed under **Uvalde**: see Garner State Park.

Listed under **Wichita Falls**: see Lake Arrowhead State Park.

Water-related activities, hiking, riding, various other sports, picnicking and camping, as well as visitor centers, are available in many of these areas. The daily per vehicle entrance fee at most parks ranges from $3-$5; annual Texas Conservation Passport, $25. Camping: primitive $4-$7/night; water only $6-$9/night; water & electricity $9-$12/night; water, electricity & sewer $10-$14/night; screened shelter $15-$18/night. Cabins $35-$55/night, depending on size. Pets on leash only; pets not allowed in buildings, cabins or screened shelters. Most parks accept reservations up to 90 days in advance; continuous occupancy limited to 14 days. Reservations made more than 10 days in advance require a reservation fee for each facility reserved in an amount equal to one day's user fee. Contact Parks & Wildlife, Park Operations Branch, 4200 Smith School Rd, Austin 78744; 512/389-4890 or 800/792-1112.

There are also approximately 1,000 roadside parks maintained by the Texas Dept of Transportation. Tables, benches, grills and rubbish incinerators are provided. Some have water.

Fishing & Hunting

Nonresident fishing license: 14-day $10; annual $30. Freshwater trout or saltwater finfish stamp, $7. Annual nonresident hunting license: $75 for small game; $200 for big game. Nonresident 5-day small game license, $25. Nonresident spring turkey license, $75. Banded bird area license $10. Stamps required for white-winged dove, $7; turkey, $5; and migratory waterfowl, $7 (state) & $15 (federal). All annual licenses expire Aug 31. Fees subject to change. For complete information, send for "Texas Hunting Guide," "Texas Saltwater Fishing Guide" and "Texas Freshwater Fishing Guide" from the Parks & Wildlife Dept, 4200 Smith School Rd, Austin 78744. Phone 512/389-4800 or 800/792-1112 in TX. To report hunting and fishing violations call Operation Game Thief 800/792-GAME.

Safety Belt Information

Safety belts are mandatory for all persons in front seat of vehicle. Children under 5 years must be in an approved passenger restraint anywhere in vehicle: ages 2-4 may use a regulation safety belt; age 2 and under must use an approved safety seat. For further information phone 512/465-2110.

Interstate Highway System

The following alphabetical listing of Texas towns in *Mobil Travel Guide* shows that these cities are within 10 miles of the indicated Interstate highways. A highway map should, however, be checked for the nearest exit.

INTERSTATE 10: Baytown, Beaumont, El Paso, Fort Stockton, Gonzales, Houston, Kerrville, Orange, Ozona, San Antonio, Seguin, Sonora, Van Horn.

INTERSTATE 20: Abilene, Arlington-Grand Prairie, Big Spring, Dallas, Dallas/Fort Worth Airport Area, Eastland, Fort Worth, Kilgore, Longview, Marshall, Midland, Monahans, Odessa, Pecos, Sweetwater, Tyler, Weatherford.

INTERSTATE 27: Amarillo, Canyon, Lubbock, Plainview.

INTERSTATE 30: Arlington-Grand Prairie, Dallas, Dallas/Fort Worth Airport Area, Greenville, Mount Pleasant, Sulphur Springs, Texarkana.

INTERSTATE 35: Arlington-Grand Prairie, Austin, Cleburne, Dallas, Dallas/Fort Worth Airport Area, Denton, Fort Worth, Gainesville, Georgetown, Hillsboro, Laredo, New Braunfels, Salado, San Antonio, San Marcos, Temple, Waco.

INTERSTATE 37: Corpus Christi, San Antonio.

INTERSTATE 40: Amarillo, Shamrock.

INTERSTATE 45: Corsicana, Dallas, Ennis, Fairfield, Galveston, Houston, Huntsville, Texas City.

Additional Visitor Information

The *Texas Almanac,* an excellent compendium published every two years by the Dallas *Morning News,* may be obtained from the Gulf Publishing Company, PO Box 2608, Houston 77252-2608.

The Texas Department of Transportation operates 12 travel information centers on main highways entering the state, and also the Judge Roy Bean Visitor Center in Langtry and an information center in the state capitol. They also distribute free maps and travel literature by mail, including the *Texas State Travel Guide.* Write to *Texas,* Dept of Transportation, PO Box 5064, Austin 78763-5064; phone 800/452-9292 (daily; 8 am-9 pm) or 800/888-8TEX (24-hr travel kit hotline).

Abilene (B-5)

(See Sweetwater)

Founded 1881 **Pop** 106,654 **Elev** 1,738 ft **Area code** 915
Information Convention & Visitors Bureau, 1101 N 1st St, PO Box 2281, 79604; phone 915/676-2556 or 800/727-7704.

Abilene is a major retail, educational, medical and employment center for a 22-county area. Its economy is based primarily on the petroleum industry, agribusiness and a major military installation.

What to See and Do

Abilene State Park. Approx 600 acres with Texas Longhorn herd. Swimming pool (Memorial Day-Labor Day; ¢), bathhouse. Picnicking. Improved campsites (dump station). Standard fees. Nearby **Lake Abilene** has fishing. (Daily) 16 mi SW on FM 89 to Park Rd 32. Phone 915/572-3204. Per vehicle **¢¢**

Abilene Zoological Gardens. Approx 13 acres; includes indoor plant and animal habitat facility with live specimens in museum setting. (Daily; closed Jan 1, Thanksgiving, Dec 25) Sr citizen rate. In Nelson Park, near jct Loop 322, TX 36. Phone 915/676-6085. ¢

Buffalo Gap Historic Village. More than 15 restored original buildings, including the first Taylor County Courthouse and jail; Museum of the Old West. Tour includes a film on history of Texas. (Mid-Mar-mid-Oct, daily; rest of yr, Fri-Sun; closed Thanksgiving, Dec 25) Sr citizen rate. William & Elm Sts, Buffalo Gap, 8 mi S on US 89. Phone 915/572-3365. **¢¢**

Dyess AFB. An Air Combat Command base, first home of the B-1B bomber. Also has KC-135s, C-130s, T-38s. Linear Air Park includes two dozen vintage display aircraft (daily). W on US 80, then S on Spur 312. Flight line tours by two-week advance arrangement. Phone 915/696-5609. **Free.**

Fort Phantom Hill & Lake. Ruins of 1850s frontier fort, built to protect gold miners traveling to California. Lake has water sports (some fees). (Daily) 14 mi N on FM 600. Phone 915/677-1309. **Free.**

Oscar Rose Park. Picnicking, playground; pool, gym, tennis center; community and children's theater, amphitheater; senior citizen center. There are 25 other city parks. 7th & Mockingbird Sts. Phone 915/676-6217. **Free.**

Annual Events

Buffalo Gap Art Festival. Arts & crafts, entertainment, food, dancing, children's activity area. Last wkend Apr.

West Texas Fair & Rodeo. Phone 915/670-1311. 2nd & 3rd wkend Sept.

Motels

✔★★ **BEST WESTERN COLONIAL INN.** *3210 Pine St (79601).* 915/677-2683; FAX 915/677-8211. 102 rms. S $37-$43; D

$42-$54; each addl $6; under 12 free. Crib free. Pet accepted, some restrictions. TV; cable (premium), VCR avail. Pool; wading pool. Restaurant 6 am-10 pm. Rm serv. Ck-out noon. Meeting rms. Business servs avail. Cr cds: A, C, D, DS, ER, MC, V.

Ⓓ 🐾 ≈ 🛏 🔥 SC

✔★★ **BEST WESTERN MALL SOUTH.** *3950 Ridgemont Dr (79606).* 915/695-1262; res: 800/346-1574; FAX 915/695-2593. 61 rms, 2 story. S $47-$55; D $56.50-$63; under 12 free. Crib free. Pet accepted, some restrictions. TV; cable (premium). Pool. Complimentary continental bkfst. Restaurant adj open 24 hrs. Ck-out noon. Meeting rm. In-rm modem link. Airport, bus depot transportation. Refrigerators. Cr cds: A, C, D, DS, MC, V.

Ⓓ 🐾 ≈ 🛏 🔥

★★ **HOLIDAY INN EXPRESS.** *1625 TX 351 (79601), 1 blk N of I-20.* 915/673-5271; FAX 915/673-8240. 161 rms, 2 story. S $56; D $62. Crib free. Pet accepted, some restrictions. TV; cable (premium). Pool. Continental bkfst 6:30-9:30 am. Ck-out noon. Free lndry facilities. Business servs avail. Free airport transportation. Cr cds: A, C, D, DS, JCB, MC, V.

Ⓓ 🐾 ≈

★★★ **KIVA.** *5403 S 1st St (79605).* 915/695-2150; res: 800/592-4466 (TX); FAX 915/698-6742. 185 rms, 3 story. S, D $49-$65; each addl $5; suites $95-$125; under 16 free. Crib free. Pet accepted; some restrictions. TV; cable (premium), VCR avail. 2 pools, 1 indoor; wading pool, whirlpool, sauna. Restaurant 6 am-10 pm. Rm serv. Bar 4:30 pm-midnight; Sat to 1 am. Ck-out 11 am. Meeting rms. Business servs avail. In-rm modem link. Sundries. Free airport transportation. Putting green. Some refrigerators. Cr cds: A, C, D, DS, MC, V.

Ⓓ 🐾 ≈ 🛏 🔥 SC

★★ **LA QUINTA.** *3501 W Lake Rd (79601).* 915/676-1676; FAX 915/672-8323. 106 rms, 2 story. S $55-$62; D $62-$69; each addl $7; suites $65-$72; under 18 free. Crib avail. Pet accepted; some restrictions. TV; cable (premium). Pool. Complimentary continental bkfst. Ck-out noon. Cr cds: A, C, D, DS, MC, V.

Ⓓ 🐾 ≈ 🛏 🔥 SC

★★ **QUALITY INN.** *505 Pine St (79601).* 915/676-0222; FAX 915/676-0513. 118 rms, 2 story. S $48-$53; D $53-$60; each addl $5; suites $65-$180; under 18 free. Crib free. Pet accepted, some restrictions; $10. TV; cable (premium), VCR avail. Pool. Complimentary full bkfst. Restaurant 6 am-9 pm. Rm serv. Bar 4-11 pm. Ck-out noon. Meeting rms. Business servs avail. Sundries. Free airport transportation. Some refrigerators. Cr cds: A, C, D, DS, ER, JCB, MC, V.

Ⓓ 🐾 ≈ 🛏 🔥 SC

★★ **RAMADA INN.** *3450 S Clack (79606).* 915/695-7700; FAX 915/698-0546. 148 rms, 2 story. S $44-$53; D $49-$58; each addl $5; under 18 free. Crib avail. TV; cable (premium), VCR avail. Pool. Restaurant 6-10 am, 6-9 pm. Rm serv. Bar 5 pm-midnight; entertainment, dancing. Ck-out noon. Meeting rms. Business servs avail. In-rm modem link. Cr cds: A, C, D, DS, MC, V.

Ⓓ ≈ 🛏 🔥 SC

✔★ **ROYAL INN.** *5695 S 1st St (79605).* 915/692-3022; res: 800/588-4386; FAX 915/692-3137. 150 rms. S $27-$35; D $34-$40; each addl $3-$5; suites $44. Crib $5. Pet accepted, some restrictions. TV; cable (premium). Pool. Restaurant 6 am-2 pm, 5-9 pm; wkend hrs vary. Rm serv. Bar 4 pm-midnight. Ck-out noon. Meeting rms. Business servs avail. Sundries. Cr cds: A, C, D, DS, MC, V.

Ⓓ 🐾 ≈ 🛏 🔥 SC

Motor Hotel

★★★ **EMBASSY SUITES.** *4250 Ridgemont Dr (79606).* 915/698-1234; FAX 915/698-2771. 176 kit. suites, 3 story. S, D $92; each addl $10; under 12 free. Crib free. Pet accepted, some restrictions. TV; cable (premium). Indoor pool; whirlpool, sauna, steam rm. Complimentary full bkfst. Coffee in rms. Restaurant 11 am-2 pm, 5-9 pm. Bar to midnight; entertainment. Ck-out noon. Coin lndry. Meeting rms. Business servs avail. Bellhops. Sundries. Airport, RR station, bus depot transportation. Game rm. Refrigerators, wet bars. Garden atrium. Cr cds: A, C, D, DS, MC, V.

Restaurant

✔ ★ ★ **OUTPOST.** 3126 S Clack. 915/692-3595. Hrs: 5:30-10 pm; Fri & Sat to 10:30 pm. Closed Thanksgiving, Dec 24-25. Bar; Fri & Sat to midnight. A la carte entrees: dinner $8.95-$13.95. Child's meals. Specializes in steak, seafood. Parking. Cr cds: A, D, DS, MC, V.

D

Alice (E-6)

(For accommodations see Corpus Christi, Kingsville)

Pop 19,788 **Elev** 205 ft **Area code** 512 **Zip** 78332
Information Chamber of Commerce, 612 E Main, PO Box 1609; 512/664-3454.

This is a farming, livestock, natural gas and oil town. It is situated on the gently sloping subtropical Gulf Plain, where mesquite, hackberry and live oak flourish. Alice is also a center of uranium production in southern Texas.

What to See and Do

Lake Corpus Christi State Park. Approx 21,000 acres. Swimming, waterskiing; fishing; boating (ramp). Picnicking (shelters), playground. Tent & trailer sites (dump station). Standard fees. (Daily) 25 mi NE on TX 359, then 2 mi NW on Park Rd 25. Phone 512/547-2635. Per vehicle ¢¢

Annual Events

Fiesta Bandana. Plaza park. Nightly entertainment; carnival, queen's court, talent show, folkloric dancers, softball, tournaments. 10 days early May.

Jim Wells County Fair. JWC Fairgrounds. Mid-Oct.

Alpine (C-3)

(See Fort Stockton, Marfa)

Founded 1882 **Pop** 5,637 **Elev** 4,481 ft **Area code** 915 **Zip** 79830
Information Chamber of Commerce, 106 N Third St; 915/837-2326.

Alpine lies in a high valley, with the Glass Mountains to the east, the Davis Mountains to the north and the Del Norte Mountains to the south. It is the home of Sul Ross State University, and it serves as a business center for ranching in the Big Bend area of west Texas.

Local mountain and desert plants include piñon pine, juniper, sotol and a great variety of cacti. Pronghorn antelope, mountain lions, white-tailed deer and javelina can be seen in the area.

What to See and Do

Big Bend National Park (see). 103 mi S on TX 118.

Driving tour. Davis Mountains and McDonald Observatory. (Approx 100 mi). Drive 26 mi NW on TX 118, a mountain road through scenic country, to

Fort Davis (population: 900; altitude: 5,050 ft), the highest town in Texas. Just outside town are the restored ruins of

Fort Davis National Historic Site. A famous frontier outpost garrisoned from 1854 until 1891. Museum, visitor center; restored and refurnished officers' quarters, barracks, commissary and kitchen; sound reproduction of 1875 Retreat Parade; slide show; living history programs in summer. Self-guided trail; transportation for handicapped (free). (Daily; closed Dec 25) Golden Age Passport accepted (see INTRODUCTION). Contact Superintendent, PO Box 1456, Fort Davis 79734; 915/426-3224. ¢

Continue NW approx 4 mi on TX 118 to

Davis Mountains State Park. A 2,250-acre park. Picnicking, playground. Hiking trails. Restaurant, lodge. Tent & trailer sites (dump station). Standard fees. (Daily) Phone 915/426-3337. Per vehicle ¢¢

Continue on TX 118 approx 11 mi to turnoff for

McDonald Observatory. Atop Mt Locke. Has a 107-inch reflecting telescope; solar viewing, video presentations. Guided tours; evening star parties at Visitors Center (Tues, Fri & Sat evenings). (Daily; closed Jan 1, Thanksgiving, Dec 25) Phone 915/426-3640. ¢

To drive further into the mountains, use TX 166, which makes a loop between Fort Davis and a point on TX 118 some 8 miles northwest of the observatory. Return to Alpine from Fort Davis either via less mountainous TX 17 to Marfa (see), then over US 90, or via TX 118, which is shorter.

Museum of the Big Bend. Local Spanish, Native American, Mexican and pioneer artifacts and historical displays. (Daily exc Mon) Donation. Sul Ross State University, E of town via US 90. Phone 915/837-8143.

Annual Event

Big Bend Bash. Pro Rally car races sanctioned by SCCA. Late Feb.

Motel

✔ ★ **SUNDAY HOUSE INN.** Box 578, 1 mi E on US 90. 915/837-3363. 80 rms, 2 story. S $34-$36; D $38-$42; under 12 free. Crib $4. Pet accepted. TV; cable (premium), VCR avail. Pool; wading pool. Restaurant 24 hrs. Private club 5 pm-midnight. Ck-out 1 pm. Meeting rm. Free airport, bus depot transportation. Cr cds: A, C, D, DS, MC, V.

Lodge

★ ★ **INDIAN LODGE.** (Box 1458, Fort Davis 79734) 24 mi NW in Davis Mountains State Park, 4 mi NW of TX 118. 915/426-3254; FAX 915/426-2022. 39 rms, 2-3 levels. S, D $55-$85; each addl $10; suites $75-$85; under 12 free. Closed 2 wks beginning 2nd Mon in Jan. TV; cable (premium). Heated pool. Restaurant 7:30 am-9 pm. Ck-out noon. Meeting rm. Picnic tables, grills. Pueblo-style lodge on hillside. Rustic decor. State-owned, operated. All park facilities avail. Cr cds: MC, V.

Inn

★ ★ **HOTEL LIMPIA.** (Fort Davis 79734) Approx 20 mi N on TX 118, on Town Square. 915/426-3237; res: 800/662-5517; FAX 915/426-2113. 33 rms, 2 story, 8 with kit., 12 suites, 1 cottage. No rm phones. Mar-Oct: S $49-$65; D $65; each addl $7; suites $79-$90; kit. units $79; cottage $95; under 12 free; lower rates rest of yr. Pet accepted; $7. TV; cable (premium). Complimentary tea and sherry in afternoons, coffee in library. Restaurant adj 5:30-9:30 pm; closed Mon.

Ck-out noon. Some refrigerators. Balconies. Picnic tables. Built in 1912 of locally mined pink limestone. Cr cds: A, DS, MC, V.

D ✔ ⚒ SC

Amarillo (F-2)

(See Canyon, Pampa)

Settled 1887 **Pop** 157,615 **Elev** 3,676 ft **Area code** 806
Information Convention and Visitor Council, 1000 Polk St, PO Box 9480, 79105; 806/374-1497 or 800/692-1338.

This is the Panhandle, once known as the *Llano Estacado* (staked plain). It is open-range, cattle country covered by tall, robust buffalo grass. It was, and in many ways still is, the raw, weather-beaten, hearty, old West. But the hide huts of the buffalo hunters on the prairie have given way to a modern, attractive city where the economy is based on cattle, irrigated farming, tourism, diversified industry, oil, natural gas and helium production.

The flatlands of the Panhandle were once generally regarded as worthless and uninhabitable. But buffalo hides at $3.75 and the use of buffalo bones for fertilizer made buffalo hunting a source of wealth for those who dared to cross into this area heavily populated with Native Americans. Later, ranchers moved in to graze their cattle and in 1877 the railroad arrived. "Ragtown," as it was first called, became Amarillo, which is Spanish for "yellow." An early promoter was so delighted with the name, which was derived from the color of a nearby creek bank, that he painted all his buildings a bright yellow. The yellow rose remains a symbol of Amarillo's colorful past.

Oil and copper refining, packing plants, farm machinery and tourism have added wealth to modern Amarillo. Most of the world's helium is produced within a 150-mile radius, and there is abundant natural gas here. The town's livestock auction attracts buyers from all over the country.

What to See and Do

American Quarter Horse Heritage Center & Museum. Many hands-on and interactive exhibits, video presentations, artifacts and live demonstrations on the history and significance of "America's breed." Heritage Gallery traces chronology of development; Performance Gallery includes rodeo, ranching and racing aspects and features the American Quarter Horse Hall of Fame. Research library; 70-seat orientation theater. (May-Aug, daily; rest of yr, daily exc Sun, Mon; closed Jan 1, Thanksgiving, Dec 25) Sr citizen rate. 2601 I-40E, at Quarter Horse Dr. Phone 806/376-5181. ¢¢

Carson County Square House Museum. Museum depicts the history and development of the Texas Panhandle region from the era of Native American hunters through ranching and railroads to the discovery of oil and the industrialization of the region. Complex includes historic house, furnished dugout dwelling, Santa Fe caboose, barn, branding diorama, pioneer bank, general store, windmill, blacksmith shop, natural history hall and two art galleries. (Mon-Sat, also Sunday afternoons; closed Jan 1, Thanksgiving, Dec 24, 25) 26 mi NE via US 60 at 5th & Elsie Sts (TX 207) in Panhandle. Phone 806/537-3524. **Free.**

Cattle auction. One of world's largest. More than 600,000 cattle sold each year for more than $100 million. (All yr, Tues) E 3rd & Manhattan Sts. Phone 806/373-7464. **Free.**

Don Harrington Discovery Center. Exhibits focus on science, health and technology; more than 75 hands-on exhibits. Planetarium shows; 360° films (summer, fee). Helium Monument is a steel memorial to the gas found in abundance in the area. Monument is also a time capsule. Fee for some special exhibits. (Tues-Sat, also Sun afternoons; closed major hols) 1200 Streit Dr, 5 mi W on I-40, 1 mi N of Coulter exit. Phone 806/355-9547 or -9548. **Free.**

Palo Duro Canyon State Park. (See CANYON) 18 mi S on I-27, then 10 mi E on TX 217.

Thompson Park. Pool (June-Aug, daily; ¢); amusement park (mid-Mar-Sept, daily; fee). Amarillo Zoo has animals indigenous to the plains (Tues-Sun). NE 24th St & US 87. Phone 806/378-3036. **Free.**

Wonderland Amusement Park. More than 20 rides and 30 attractions, including a double-loop roller coaster and water rides. (Apr-Sept, wkends after noon; June-Aug, nightly, exc Mon & Wed in May) N on US 87/287N, River Rd exit. Phone 806/383-4712. ¢¢¢¢

Annual Events

Inter-Tribal Powwow. 2nd wkend Aug.

Boys Ranch Rodeo. Phone 805/372-2341. Labor Day wkend.

Tri-State Fair. 2nd largest after State Fair. Mid-Sept.

Seasonal Event

Cowboy Morning Breakfast. Horse-drawn wagons run to breakfast site, rim of Palo Duro Canyon; breakfast cooked on open fire. Exhibition roping & branding. May-Sept.

Motels

✔ ★ **BUDGET HOST LA PALOMA.** 2915 I-40 E (79104), exit 72 A. 806/372-8101. 96 rms, 2 story. S $29.95-$49.95; D $39.95-$59.95; each addl $10. Crib free. TV; cable (premium). Indoor pool; whirlpool. Complimentary coffee in lobby. Restaurant nearby. Ck-out noon. Meeting rms. Free airport transporatation. Cr cds: A, C, D, DS, MC, V.

≈ ⊠

★ ★ **DAYS INN.** 1701 I-40E (79102). 806/379-6255; FAX 806/379-8204. 119 rms, 5 story. S $55-$80; D $65-$80; each addl $5; under 12 free. Crib free. TV; cable. Heated pool. Complimentary continental bkfst. Restaurant opp 6 am-9 pm. Ck-out noon. Meeting rm. Airport transportation. Cr cds: A, C, D, DS, MC, V.

D ≈ ⊠ ⚒ SC

★ ★ **HAMPTON INN.** 1700 I-40 E (79103). 806/372-1425; FAX 806/379-8807. 116 rms, 2 story. June-Sept: S $58-$60; D $60-$68; under 18 free; lower rates rest of yr. Crib free. TV; cable (premium). Pool. Complimentary continental bkfst, coffee. Restaurant adj open 24 hrs. Ck-out noon. In-rm modem link. Cr cds: A, C, D, DS, MC, V.

D ✔ ≈ ⊠ ⚒ SC

★ **TRAVELODGE-WEST.** 2035 Paramount (79109). 806/353-3541; FAX 806/353-0201. 100 rms, 2 story. S $38-$43; D $43-$58; each addl $5; under 17 free. Crib free. TV; cable. Heated pool. Restaurant nearby. Ck-out noon. Meeting rm. Health club privileges. Cr cds: A, C, D, DS, ER, JCB, MC, V.

≈ ⚒

★ ★ **WESTAR SUITES.** 6800 I-40 W (79106), 6 mi W on I-40, Bell St exit. 806/358-7943; FAX 806/358-8475. 126 kit. suites, 2 story. S $62; D $70; each addl $8; under 18 free. Crib free. TV; cable. Heated pool; whirlpool, hot tub. Complimentary continental bkfst. Meeting rms. Business servs avail. In-rm modem link. Valet serv. Health club privileges. Refrigerators. Picnic tables, grills. Cr cds: A, C, D, DS, ER, JCB, MC, V.

D ≈ ⊠ ⚒ SC

Motor Hotels

★ ★ **HOLIDAY INN.** 1911 I-40 (79102), at Ross & Osage. 806/372-8741; FAX 806/372-2913. 247 rms, 4 story. S $74-$75; D $84-$85; each addl $10; under 19 free. Crib free. TV; cable (premium). Indoor pool; wading pool. Restaurants 6 am-1 pm, 5:30-10 pm. Rm serv. Bar 4 pm-2 am. Ck-out noon. Coin lndry. Meeting rms. Business servs avail. In-rm modem link. Bellhops. Sundries. Free airport transportation. Exercise equipt; weight machine, bicycle. Holidome. Game rm. Balconies. Cr cds: A, C, D, DS, JCB, MC, V.

⊡ 🏊 🏋 ✈ ⊠ 🔥 SC

★ ★ ★ **RADISSON INN AIRPORT.** *7909 I-40 E (79104), near Intl Airport. 806/373-3303; FAX 806/373-3353.* 208 rms, 2 story. June-Aug: S, D $59.95-$89.95; each addl $10; suites $149.95-$199.95; under 12 free; lower rates rest of yr. Crib free. Pet accepted. TV; cable. Indoor pool; poolside serv. Complimentary continental bkfst. Restaurant 6 am-11 pm. Rm serv. Bar; entertainment Thurs-Sat. Ck-out noon. Meeting rms. Bellhops. Gift shop. Valet serv. Free airport transportation. Exercise equipt; weight machine, bicycles, whirlpool. Game rm. Mini bars. Cr cds: A, C, D, DS, ER, JCB, MC, V.

⊡ 🐾 🏊 🏋 ✈ ⊠ 🔥 SC

Restaurants

★ ★ **BIG TEXAN STEAK RANCH.** *7701 I-40E. 806/372-5000.* Hrs: 10:30 am-10:30 pm. Res accepted. Bar. Semi-a la carte: lunch, dinner $4.50-$29.95. Child's meals. Specializes in Texas prime beef steak, rattlesnake, buffalo. Strolling musicians. Frontier Western decor. Family-owned. Cr cds: A, C, D, DS, MC, V.

⊡ SC

★ ★ **COUNTRY BARN.** *1805 Lakeside Dr. 806/335-2325.* Hrs: 11 am-10:30 pm; Sun 5-10 pm. Closed Thanksgiving, Dec 25. Mexican, Amer menu. Bar. Semi-a la carte: lunch $3.99-$18, dinner $3.99-$18. Child's meals. Specializes in Texas steak, barbecue, calf fries. Parking. Rustic Western decor; antiques. Family-owned. Cr cds: A, C, D, DS, MC, V.

⊡

★ **PEKING.** *2511 Paramount Blvd, .in shopping center. 806/353-9179.* Hrs: 11 am-9:30 pm; Fri & Sat 11:30 am-10 pm. Closed Sun; Thanksgiving. Chinese menu. Bar. Semi-a la carte: lunch $3.95-$4.95, dinner $3.95-$19.95. Specializes in shrimp, scallops. Cr cds: A, D, DS, MC, V.

★ ★ **STEAK & ALE.** *2915 I-40W. 806/359-1631.* Hrs: 11:15 am-10 pm; Fri, Sat 4-11 pm; Sun to 10 pm. Bar. Semi-a la carte: lunch $3.85-$13.95, dinner $9-$20.25. Child's meals. Specializes in prime rib, marinated steak, chicken, seafood. Salad bar. Parking. Old English atmosphere. Cr cds: A, C, D, DS, MC, V.

⊡

Unrated Dining Spot

FURRS CAFETERIA. *2640 Wolfin Sq. 806/355-5661.* Hrs: 11 am-8:30 pm. Avg ck: lunch, dinner $4-$6.50. Specializes in Mexican dishes, liver & onions. Parking. Fireplace. Cr cds: A, DS, MC, V.

Angleton (D-8)

(For accommodations see Brazosport, Galveston, Houston)

Pop 17,140 **Elev** 31 ft **Area code** 409 **Zip** 77515
Information Chamber of Commerce, 445 E Mulberry, PO Box 1356, 77516; 409/849-6443.

What to See and Do

Varner-Hogg Plantation State Historical Park. Stately house (ca 1835) in 66-acre park. Period furnishings; family memorabilia. Tours (Wed-Sun, fee). Picnicking. 15 mi W via TX 35, FM 2852 in West Columbia. Phone 409/345-4656.

Annual Event

Brazoria County Fair. Rodeo, livestock exhibition, exhibits. 1 wk early Oct.

Aransas Pass (E-7)

(For accommodations see Corpus Christi, Port Aransas, also see Rockport)

Founded ca 1830 **Pop** 7,180 **Elev** 5 ft **Area code** 512 **Zip** 78336
Information Chamber of Commerce, 452 W Cleveland Blvd; 512/758-2750 or 800/633-3028.

Shipping from Corpus Christi passes through the waterway called Aransas Pass to the Gulf. The town is a shrimp boat and resort headquarters, with some industrial plants. Boats for deep-sea and bay fishing can be rented; duck hunting in December and January is popular. Aransas Pass is the northern gateway to Port Aransas (see) and Mustang Island.

Annual Event

Shrimporee. Parade, arts & crafts. Late Sept.

Arlington-Grand Prairie (B-7)

(See Dallas, Dallas/Fort Worth Airport Area, Fort Worth)

Pop Arlington, 261,721; Grand Prairie, 99,616 **Elev** 616 ft **Area code** Arlington, 817; Grand Prairie, 214
Information Arlington Convention & Visitors Bureau, 1250 E Copeland Rd, Ste 650, 76011, phone 817/265-7721; or the Grand Prairie Convention & Visitors Bureau, 900 Conover Dr, PO Box 531227, Grand Prairie 75053, phone 214/263-9588 or 800/288-8386.

What to See and Do

Six Flags Over Texas. This 205-acre entertainment center has more than 100 rides, shows and other attractions. Texas history under flags of Spain, France, the Republic of Texas, the Confederacy, Mexico and the US is presented, with a separate section of the park devoted to each flag. Skylines of Dallas and Fort Worth are visible from 300-foot-high observation deck atop oil derrick. Park is circled by narrow-gauge railway; other rides include wooden roller coaster, Runaway Mine Train, parachute ride, double loop roller coaster, biplane ride, Roaring Rapids river rafting; Looney Tunes Land, with special rides and play activities for small children; Southern Palace ice revue and other attractions. Restaurants. (Late May-early Sept, daily; mid-Mar-late May & early Sept-mid-Nov, Sat & Sun only) Admission includes all rides. Just W of jct TX 360, I-30, Arlington. Contact PO Box 191, Arlington 76010. 817/640-8900. ¢¢¢¢

The Palace of Wax. Onion-domed structure houses a collection of wax figures in exhibits with themes including Hollywood, history, religion, fairy tales, horrors and the Old West. Visitors can view figure-making studio to see actual pieces under construction. Gift shop, concession, arcade. (Daily; closed Jan 1, Thanksgiving, Dec 25) 601 E Safari Pkwy, I-30 at Belt Line Rd exit N, Grand Prairie. Phone 214/263-2391. ¢¢¢ Also here is

Ripley's Believe It or Not! Features galleries filled with antiques, oddities, curiosities and illusions from the collection of Robert L. Ripley. ¢¢¢ Combination ticket ¢¢¢¢

Seasonal Event

Professional baseball. Texas Rangers. Arlington Stadium, just W of jct TX 360, Dallas-Ft Worth Tpke. Apr-early Oct.

Motels

(Most accommodations near Six Flags Over Texas have higher rates when the park is open daily.)

★ ★ **COUNTRY SUITES BY CARLSON.** *(1075 Wet & Wild Way, Arlington 76011)* I-30 exit Collins St. 817/261-8900; FAX 817/274-0343. 132 kit. suites, 3 story. May-Sept: suites $79-$121; each addl $6; under 18 free; lower rates rest of yr. TV; cable (premium), VCR avail. Heated pool; wading pool, whirlpool. Playground. Complimentary continental bkfst 6-9:30 am; Sat, Sun 7-10:30 am. Restaurant nearby open 24 hrs. Ck-out noon. Coin lndry. Meeting rms. Business servs avail. Sundries. Valet serv. Free airport transportation. Health club privileges. Cr cds: A, C, D, DS, ER, MC, V.

[D] [≈] [⊁] [⊁] [🔥] [SC]

★ ★ **COURTYARD BY MARRIOTT.** *(1500 Nolan Ryan Expy, Arlington 76011)* 817/277-2774; FAX 817/277-3103. 147 rms, 2-3 story, 14 suites. S, D $84-$94; suites $100-$110. Crib free. TV; cable (premium). Indoor/outdoor pool. Complimentary coffee in rms. Restaurant 6:30-10:30 am; Sat, Sun 7 am-1 pm. Bar 4-11 pm. Ck-out noon. Coin lndry. Meeting rms. Business center. In-rm modem link. Valet serv. Sundries. Exercise equipt; weight machine, bicycles, whirlpool. Refrigerator in suites. Opp Arlington Stadium, Six Flags. Cr cds: A, D, DS, MC, V.

[D] [≈] [⊁] [⊁] [🔥] [SC] [⊁]

★ **DAYS INN DOWNTOWN.** *(910 N Collins, Arlington 76011)* just S of I-30. 817/261-8444; FAX 817/860-8326. 87 rms, 4 story. Mid-May-mid-Sept: S $45-$75; D $55-$75; each addl $5; under 13 free; higher rates hols; lower rates rest of yr. Crib free. Pet accepted; $5. TV; cable (premium); VCR avail. Pool. Complimentary continental bkfst. Restaurant adj open 24 hrs. Ck-out noon. Business servs avail. Valet serv. Some refrigerators. Cr cds: A, D, DS, MC, V.

[D] [⊁] [≈] [⊁] [🔥] [SC]

✔ ★ **FAIRFIELD INN BY MARRIOTT.** *(2500 E Lamar Blvd, Arlington 76006)* 817/649-5800. 109 rms, 3 story. May-Sept: S $69; D $79; under 18 free; lower rates rest of yr. Crib free. TV; cable (premium). Heated pool. Complimentary continental bkfst. Restaurant nearby. Ck-out noon. Business servs avail. In-rm modem link. Sundries. Cr cds: A, D, DS, MC, V.

[D] [≈] [⊁] [🔥] [SC]

✔ ★ ★ **HAMPTON INN.** *(2050 TX 360 N, Grand Prairie 75050)* Jct TX 360 & Carrier Pkwy. 214/988-8989; FAX 214/988-8989. 140 rms, 4 story. S $60; D $69; under 18 free. TV; cable (premium). Pool. Continental bkfst. Complimentary coffee. Restaurant nearby. Ck-out noon. Coin lndry. Business servs avail. In-rm modem link. Valet serv. Free airport transportation. Exercise equipt; weights, bicycles. Cr cds: A, C, D, DS, MC, V.

[D] [≈] [⊁] [⊁] [🔥] [SC]

Motor Hotels

★ **HAWTHORN SUITES.** *(2401 Brookhollow Plaza Dr, Arlington 76006)* I-30 at Lamar Blvd exit. 817/640-1188; res: 800/527-1133; FAX 817/640-1188. 130 suites, 3 story, 104 kit. suites. Suites $110-$180; wkend rates. Crib free. Pet accepted, some restrictions; $5. TV; cable (premium), VCR avail (movies avail $2). Pool. Complimentary full bkfst. Restaurant nearby. Ck-out noon. Coin lndry. Meeting rms. Business servs avail. In-rm modem link. Valet serv. Private patios, balconies. Cr cds: A, D, DS, MC, V.

 [⊁] [≈] [⊁] [🔥]

★ ★ **HOLIDAY INN.** *(1507 N Watson Rd, Arlington 76006)* Jct TX 360 & Brown Blvd. 817/640-7712; FAX 817/640-3174. 237 rms, 5 story. S $84-$104; D $89-$109; each addl $5; under 19 free; wkend rates Sept-Apr. Crib free. TV; cable (premium), VCR avail. Indoor/outdoor pool; wading pool. Restaurant 6:30 am-2 pm, 5-10 pm. Rm serv. Bar 11:30 am-midnight, Sun from 5 pm. Ck-out noon. Coin lndry. Meeting rms. Business center. In-rm modem link. Bellhops. Valet serv. Free airport transportation. Exercise equipt; weights, bicycles, whirlpool. Some refrigerators. Some private patios, balconies. Cr cds: A, C, D, DS, ER, JCB, MC, V.

[D] [≈] [⊁] [⊁] [⊁] [SC] [⊁]

Hotels

★ ★ ★ **HILTON.** *(2401 E Lamar Blvd, Arlington 76006)* I-30 exit at TX 360. 817/640-3322; FAX 817/633-1430. 310 rms, 16 story. S $115-$140; D $125-$150; each addl $10; under 18 free; wkend rates. Crib free. TV; cable (premium), VCR avail. Indoor/outdoor pool; poolside serv. Restaurant 6 am-11 pm. Bar 11-2 am; dancing. Ck-out 11 am. Coin lndry. Convention facilities. Business center. In-rm modem link. Gift shop. Airport transportation. Golf, tennis privileges. Exercise equipt; weight machine, bicycles, whirlpool, sauna. Health club privileges. Cr cds: A, C, D, DS, JCB, MC, V.

[D] [⊁] [⊁] [≈] [⊁] [⊁] [🔥] [SC] [⊁]

★ ★ ★ **MARRIOTT.** *(1500 Convention Center Drive, Arlington 76011)* I-30, Six Flags exit. 817/261-8200; FAX 817/469-8815. 310 rms, 18 story. S $124-$140; D $134-$150; each addl $10; suites $145-$350; under 16 free; wkend rates. Crib free. TV; cable (premium). Pool; poolside serv. Bkfst buffet. Restaurant 6:30 am-10 pm. Bar 2 pm-2 am. Ck-out noon. Meeting rms. Business center. In-rm modem link. Concierge. Sundries. Gift shop. Exercise equipt; bicycles, rower. Some refrigerators. Luxury level. Cr cds: A, C, D, DS, ER, JCB, MC, V.

[D] [≈] [⊁] [⊁] [⊁] [🔥] [⊁]

★ ★ **RADISSON SUITE.** *(700 Avenue H East, Arlington 76011)* At I-30 & TX 360 exit Six Flags Dr. 817/640-0440; FAX 817/649-2480. 202 rms, 7 story, 184 suites. S, D $114-$134; each addl $10; under 18 free. Crib free. TV; cable. Indoor pool; whirlpool, sauna, steam rm. Complimentary full bkfst 6:30-9:30 am. Restaurant 11 am-2 pm, 5:30-10 pm. Bar 11 am-midnight. Ck-out noon. Meeting rms. Business servs avail. In-rm modem link. Gift shop. Health club privileges. Game rm. Refrigerators, wet bars. Luxury level. Cr cds: A, C, D, DS, ER, JCB, MC, V.

[D] [≈] [⊁] [⊁] [🔥] [SC]

Restaurants

★ ★ ★ **CACHAREL.** *(2221 E Lamar Blvd, Arlington 76006)* In the Brookhollow II Bldg. 817/640-9981. Hrs: 11:30 am-2 pm, 6-11 pm; Sat from 6 pm. Closed Sun; major hols. Res accepted. French, Amer menu. Serv bar. Complete meals: lunch $12-$15, dinner $30. Child's meals. Specializes in seafood, chicken, lamb. Own pastries. Parking. Country French decor. Menu changes daily. View of city. Jacket. Cr cds: A, C, D, DS, MC, V.

[D]

✔ ★ ★ **KEY WEST GRILL.** *(919 Six Flags Dr, Arlington 76011)* 817/640-3157. Hrs: 11 am-10 pm; Fri, Sat to 11 pm. Closed Thanksgiving, Dec 25. Caribbean, Amer menu. Bar to 11 pm; Sun 11 am-10 pm. Semi-a la carte: lunch, dinner $5.95-$16.95. Specializes in steak, fresh seafood, homemade soups. Parking. Outdoor dining. Tropical decor. Cr cds: A, D, DS, MC, V.

[D]

★ ★ **PICCOLO MONDO.** *(829 Lamar Blvd E, Arlington 76011)* 817/265-9174. Hrs: 11:30 am-2:30 pm, 5:30-10:30 pm; Fri, Sat to 11 pm; Sun 5-10 pm. Closed Jan 1, Thanksgiving, Dec 25. Res accepted. Italian menu. Bar. Semi-a la carte: lunch $6-$11.75, dinner $9-$19.75.

Child's meals. Specialties: chicken alla forestiera, gnocchi Piemontese, capelli d'Angelo alla pescatora. Pianist Tues-Sat. Parking. Cozy Italian atmosphere. Cr cds: A, C, D, DS, MC, V.

D

★★ ROYAL CATHAY CHINESE CUISINE. *(740 Lincoln Sq, Arlington 76011) In Lincoln Sq Shopping Ctr.* 817/860-2662. Hrs: 11:30 am-10 pm; Fri to 11 pm; Sat noon-11 pm. Closed Thanksgiving, Dec 25. Res accepted. Chinese menu. Serv bar. Semi-a la carte: lunch $4.50-$5.95, dinner $6.95-$22.95. Buffet: lunch $4.75-$5.25. Sun brunch $5.95. Specialties: royal chicken, sesame beef, beef with hot orange sauce, garlic shrimp. Ornate Chinese decor. Cr cds: A, D, DS, MC, V.

D

Athens (B-7)

(See Corsicana, Palestine, Tyler)

Pop 10,967 **Elev** 492 ft **Area code** 903 **Zip** 75751
Information Chamber of Commerce, 1206 S Palestine, PO Box 2600; 903/675-5181.

Annual Events

Texas Fiddlers' Contest and Reunion. Last Fri May.

Black-Eyed Pea Jamboree. Arts & crafts, bike races, food, pea popping & shelling contests, terrapin races, cook-off. 3rd wkend July.

Motels

✔★★ BEST WESTERN INN & SUITES. *2050 TX 31, 2¹/₂ mi E on TX 31.* 903/675-9214; FAX 903/675-5963. 110 rms, 2 story. S $39-$50; D $45-$56; each addl $6; suites $70-$80. Crib free. TV; cable (premium). Pool. Restaurant 6 am-1 pm, 6-9 pm; Sun to 2 pm. Rm serv. Bar; dancing. Ck-out noon. Meeting rms. Business servs avail. Cr cds: A, C, D, DS, MC, V.

D ⊠ ⊠ ⊠ SC

★★ SPANISH TRACE INN. *716 E Tyler St.* 903/675-5173; res: 800/488-5173; FAX 903/677-1529. 80 rms, 2 story. S $41-$45; D $46-$50; each addl $6; suites $76; under 12 free. Crib free. Pet accepted. TV; cable (premium). Pool. Restaurant (see TRACER'S). Rm serv. Private club 5 pm-midnight, closed Sun. Ck-out noon. Meeting rms. Business servs avail. Health club privileges. Private patios, balconies. Cr cds: A, C, D, DS, MC, V.

D ✔ ⊠ ⊠ ⊠ SC

Restaurant

✔★ TRACER'S. *(See Spanish Trace Inn Motel)* 903/675-5173. Hrs: 6 am-2 pm, 5-10 pm; Sun brunch 11:30 am-2 pm. Res required hols. Bar 5 pm-midnight. Semi-a la carte: bkfst $2.95-$7.25, lunch $4.25-$5.95, dinner $7.95-$14.95. Sun brunch $8.95. Child's meals. Specializes in chicken, steak, seafood. Salad bar (lunch). Parking. Old Spanish decor. Cr cds: A, C, D, DS, MC, V.

D SC

Austin (C-6)

(See Georgetown, San Antonio, San Marcos)

Founded 1839 **Pop** 465,622 **Elev** 550 ft **Area code** 512
Information Convention & Visitors Bureau, 201 E 2nd St, PO Box 1088, 78767; 512/478-0098 or 800/888-8-AUS.

In 1838 a party of buffalo hunters that included Mirabeau B. Lamar, vice president of the Republic of Texas, camped at a pleasant spot on the Colorado River. In 1839, Lamar, then president of the republic, suggested this same spot as the site of a permanent capital. Situated on high ground and far away from the fever dangers of the coast country, the site was selected even though it was on the frontier. Named for Stephen F. Austin, son of Moses Austin, leader of the first American colony in Texas, the new capital was planned and planned well. Situated at the foot of the Highland Lakes chain, the site was blessed with lakes—Austin and Town—which today wind their way through the heart of the city. The Capitol building, at the head of Congress Avenue, was later built on one of the hills that rises from the Colorado River Valley.

A city of handsome buildings, modern Austin boasts a unique version of New Orleans' Bourbon Street—Old Pecan Street. This seven block strip of renovated Victorian and native limestone buildings on East 6th Street between Congress Ave and I-35 is a National Registered Historic District with more than 60 restaurants, clubs and shops. On weekends, thousands gather to enjoy the street performers and nightlife.

As a state center of science, research, education and government, Austin's economy is diversified between the state bureaucracy, the University of Texas and the research and manufacturing of high-technology electronics.

What to See and Do

⊠ **Elisabet Ney Museum.** Former studio of Elisabet Ney, 19th-century German-Texan portrait sculptor. Houses collection of her works, some of which stand in the Texas and US capitols. (Wed-Sat, also Sun afternoons; closed hols) 304 E 44th St, at Avenue H. Phone 512/458-2255. **Free.**

French Legation Museum (1841). Housed the *chargé d'affaires* to the Republic of Texas. Creole architecture and furnishings. Restored house and gardens; reconstructed barn, French Creole kitchen. (Daily exc Mon; closed major hols) 802 San Marcos St. Phone 512/472-8180. ¢¢

Governor's Mansion (1856). Greek-revival architecture, American Federal & Empire furnishings. Contains former governors' memorabilia. Tours (Mon-Fri mornings; closed some state hols, special occasions) 1010 Colorado between 10th & 11th Sts, in Capitol Complex. Phone 512/463-5516 (tape) or -5518 (for required group reservations). **Free.**

Gray Line bus tours. Depart from downtown hotels. Narrated bus tours (2¹/₂ hrs) of scenic and historic sites with visits to various points of interest. Contact Gray Line Tours, PO Box 9802-557, 78766; 512/345-6789 or 800/950-8285.

Highland Lakes. Seven hydroelectric dams cross the Colorado River, creating a continuous series of lakes for nearly 150 miles upstream. Lake Buchanan and Lake Travis are the largest; Town Lake and Lake Austin are located within the Austin city limits. Fishing, boating; camping (exc on Town Lake). Many varied accommodations on the shores of each.

Inner Space Cavern (See GEORGETOWN). 27 mi N off I-35.

Laguna Gloria Art Museum. Changing exhibits of American art since 1900; performances, films, lectures, art classes. (Daily exc Mon; closed some major hols) (See ANNUAL EVENTS) 3809 W 35th St, on Lake Austin. Phone 512/458-8191. ¢

McKinney Falls State Park. A 641-acre park containing two waterfalls. Fishing. Nature trail, hiking. Picnicking. Camping (dump station). Standard fees. (Daily) 7 mi SE on US 183. Phone 512/243-1643. Per vehicle ¢¢

Neill-Cochran House (ca 1855). Greek-revival house built of native Austin limestone and Bastrop pine; furnishings from 18th-20th centuries. (Wed-Sun; closed hols) 2310 San Gabriel. Phone 512/478-2335. ¢

O. Henry Home and Museum. Victorian cottage was the residence of writer William Sydney Porter (O. Henry); original furnishings. Special events. (Wed-Sun afternoons; closed Jan 1, Thanksgiving, Dec 25) Donation. 409 E 5th St. Phone 512/472-1903.

State Capitol. A conventionally domed state capitol, larger than that of other states; built in 1888 of pink granite taken from Marble Falls near Burnet. A special narrow-gauge railroad was built to bring the stone to Austin. Fine statuary surrounds the building, which also has murals by W.H. Huddle. In the west wing is a tourist information center (daily; closed Jan 1, Dec 25). Guided tours (daily; schedule may vary). 11th & Congress Ave. Phone 512/463-0063. **Free.** On grounds is

Texas State Library. Houses historical documents inoluding Texas Declaration of Independence; 45-foot mural offers view of Texas history. (Mon-Fri; genealogy library Tues-Sat; closed hols) Lorenzo de Zavala State Archives & Library Building, 1201 Brazos St. Phone 512/463-5480. **Free.**

University of Texas at Austin (1883). (48,000 students) Its 16 colleges and schools and 75 departments offer some 6,500 courses, providing 268 different degree programs. The visitor center in Sid Richardson Hall (adj Lyndon Baines Johnson Presidential Library & Museum) offers schedules of campus events. Red River, Guadalupe, 26th Sts & Martin Luther King Jr Blvd. Phone 512/471-1420. Attractions include

Texas Memorial Museum. Natural history exhibits dedicated to geology, paleontology, zoology, anthropology and history. Special events. (Daily; closed major hols) 2400 Trinity St. Phone 512/471-1604. **Free.**

Archer M. Huntington Art Gallery. Permanent exhibits housed in the Ransom Center, 21st & Guadalupe, and temporary exhibitions housed in the Art Bldg, 23rd & San Jacinto. With a permanent collection of more than 9,000 objects, the gallery is the only encyclopedic fine arts museum in the area. (Mon-Sat, also Sun afternoons; closed hols) Phone 512/471-7324. **Free.**

Lyndon Baines Johnson Library & Museum. Exhibits on "Great Society," international affairs, oval office, head-of-state gifts; presidential history presented through memorabilia of political campaigns from Washington to Reagan. Changing exhibits on US history. Archives collection of documents available for research. (Daily; closed Dec 25) 2313 Red River. On campus, 1 blk W of I-35. Phone 512/482-5137. **Free.**

Harry Ransom Humanities Research Center. Collections of rare books and manuscripts. Gutenberg Bible on display. (Mon-Fri; closed some major hols) Guadalupe & 21st Sts. Phone 512/471-8944. **Free.**

Zilker Park. Austin's largest and most beautiful city park. 2100 Barton Springs Rd.

Austin Area Garden Center. Rose garden, Oriental garden, cactus garden, xeriscape garden, fragrance garden for the visually impaired; butterfly trail; historical area including Swedish pioneer cabin (ca 1840) with period artifacts, log school, replica of blacksmith shop. (Daily) Phone 512/477-8672. **Free** exc during Flora Rama (1st wkend May).

Barton Springs Pool. Spring-fed natural swimming pool nearly as long as a football field. (Apr-Oct) Phone 512/476-9044. ¢¢

Zilker Hillside Theater. (See SEASONAL EVENT)

Annual Events

Livestock Show. Features rodeo performances. Late Mar.

Highland Lakes Bluebonnet Trail. Highland Lakes communities feature arts and crafts and activities during wildflower season. 2 wkends early Apr.

Old Pecan Street Arts Festival. 1st wkend May & last wkend Sept.

Laguna Gloria Fiesta. Fine arts & crafts, children's events, music, food. 3rd wkend May.

Austin Aqua Festival. Water parade & sports, dances, music, entertainment. First 2 wkends Aug.

Seasonal Events

Congress Avenue Bridge Bat Colony. 7 blks S of State Capitol. The largest urban bat colony in North America, this 81-foot span across Town Lake provides roosting for more than a million Mexican free-tailed bats. The bats emerge from beneath the bridge each night at dusk to forage for insects. The spectacle of the colony taking flight has become one of the most popular tourist attractions in Texas, and draws thousands of people each summer. An educational kiosk is located on the north bank of the river, just east of the bridge. Best viewing is in Aug. For further information and locations for viewing, phone 512/327-9721. Late Mar-early Nov.

Zilker Park Hillside Theater. Zilker Park. Free drama, ballet, classic films, musicals & symphony concerts under the stars. Major Broadway musical featured each summer. Phone 512/499-6700. Early Apr-Oct.

Motels

✔ ★ **HAMPTON INN.** 7619 I-35N (78752), exit 240A. 512/452-3300; FAX 512/452-3124. 122 rms, 4 story. S $61; D $69; under 18 free. Crib free. TV; cable (premium). Pool. Complimentary continental bkfst. Restaurant adj 11 am-midnight. Ck-out noon. Meeting rm. In-rm moden link. Exercise equipt; weights, bicycles. Cr cds: A, C, D, DS, ER, JCB, MC, V.

D ⊠ 🏋 ⊠ 🔥 **SC**

★ ★ **HAWTHORN SUITES SOUTH.** 4020 I-35 S (78704). 512/440-7722; FAX 512/440-4815. 127 suites, 2 story. S $99-$129; D $109-$139; each addl $10; under 18 free; wkend rates. Crib free. Pet accepted; $50 non-refundable deposit, $5 per day. TV; cable (premium). Heated pool; whirlpool. Complimentary coffee in rms. Complimentary continental bkfst. Restaurant nearby open 24 hrs. Bar. Ck-out noon. Coin lndry. Meeting rms. Valet serv. Refrigerators. Picnic tables, grills. Cr cds: A, C, D, DS, JCB, MC, V.

D 🐾 ⊠ ⊠ 🔥 **SC**

★ ★ **HAWTHORN SUITES-NORTHWEST.** 8888 Tallwood Dr (78759). 512/343-0008; res: 800/527-1133; FAX 512/343-6532. 103 rms, 3 story, 89 kit. units. S $129-$159, D $169-$199; wkly, wkend rates. Crib free. TV; cable (premium). VCR avail. Pool; whirlpool. Complimentary buffet bkfst. Coffee in rms. Ck-out noon. Coin lndry. Meeting rms. Business servs avail. In-rm modem link. Valet serv. Health club privileges. Refrigerators. Private patios, balconies. Picnic tables. Cr cds: A, C, D, DS, MC, V.

D ⊠ ⊠ 🔥 **SC**

★ ★ **HOLIDAY INN EXPRESS.** 7622 N I-35 (78752), exit 240 A. 512/467-1701. 125 rms, 4 story. S $57-$75; D $63-$96; each addl $6; under 19 free. Crib free. TV; cable, VCR avail. Pool; spa. Complimentary continental bkfst. Restaurant adj open 24 hrs. Ck-out noon. Meeting rms. In-rm modem link. Free airport transportation. Some refrigerators. Cr cds: A, C, D, DS, JCB, MC, V.

D ⊠ ⊠ 🔥 **SC**

★ ★ **LA QUINTA NORTH.** 7100 I-35N (78752). 512/452-9401; FAX 512/452-0856. 115 rms, 2 story. S $59-$66; D $69-$76; each addl $10; suites $67-$81; under 18 free. Crib free. Pet accepted, some restrictions. TV; cable. Pool. Continental bkfst. Restaurant adj open 24 hrs. Ck-out noon. In-rm modem link. Free airport transportation. Cr cds: A, C, D, DS, MC, V.

D 🐾 ⊠ ⊠ 🔥 **SC**

✔ ★ **QUALITY INN AIRPORT.** *909 E Koenig Lane (78751), near jct I-35 & US 290.* 512/452-4200; FAX 512/452-4200, ext. 303. 91 rms, 2 story. S $50-$60; D $55-65; each addl $5; under 17 free. Crib free. Pet accepted; $25. TV; cable (premium). Pool. Complimentary bkfst buffet. Ck-out noon. Meeting rm. Free airport transportation. Exercise equipt; bicycles, stair machine. Cr cds: A, C, D, DS, MC, V.

D ⚬ ≈ ✈ 🔥 🐾 SC

Motor Hotels

★ ★ **COURTYARD BY MARRIOTT.** *5660 N I-35 (78751), near Robert Mueller Airport.* 512/458-2340; FAX 512/458-8525. 198 rms, 9 story. S $99; D $109; each addl $10; under 12 free; wkend rates. Crib free. TV; cable (premium). Pool; whirlpool. Complimentary coffee in rms. Restaurant 6 am-10 pm; wkends 7 am-midnight. Bar 5-9 pm. Ck-out noon. Meeting rms. Business servs avail. Free airport transportation. Exercise equipt; weights, bicycle. Cr cds: A, C, D, DS, MC, V.

D ≈ ✈ 🔥 🐾 SC

★ **DRURY INN-AUSTIN NORTH.** *6511 I-35N (78752).* 512/467-9500; FAX 512/467-9500, ext. -489. 156 rms, 4 story. S $65-$72; D $75-$82; each addl $10; under 18 free; some wkend rates. Pet accepted, some restrictions. TV; cable (premium) Pool. Complimentary bkfst. Restaurant adj 6 am-midnight. Ck-out noon. Meeting rms. Business servs avail. In-rm modem link. Valet serv. Sundries. Free airport transportation. Some refrigerators. 4-story atrium lobby. Cr cds: A, C, D, DS, MC, V.

D ≈ 🔥 🐾 SC

✔ ★ **EXEL INN.** *2711 I-35 S (78741).* 512/462-9201; FAX 512/462-9371. 90 rms, 3 story. S $34.99-$49.99; D $41.99-$59.99; each addl $5; under 18 free. Pet accepted, some restrictions. TV; cable (premium), VCR avail. Pool. Complimentary continental bkfst. Restaurant adj open 24 hrs. Ck-out noon. Coin lndry. Game rm. Cr cds: A, C, D, DS, MC, V.

D ≈ 🔥 🐾 SC

★ ★ **HOLIDAY INN SOUTH.** *3401 I-35S (78741).* 512/448-2444; FAX 512/448-4999. 210 rms, 5 story. S $89-$129; D $99-$139; each addl $10; suites $119-$139; under 18 free; wkend rates. TV; cable. Pool; whirlpool, poolside serv. Restaurant 6:30 am-10 pm; Sat, Sun from 7 am. Rm serv. Bar 4 pm-midnight, Sat from 4:30 pm. Ck-out noon. Coin lndry. Meeting rms. In-rm modem link. Bellhops. Gift shop. Free airport transportation. Refrigerators; many bathrm phones. Private patios. Cr cds: A, C, D, DS, MC, V.

D ≈ 🔥 🐾 SC

★ ★ **HOLIDAY INN-TOWNLAKE.** *20 N Interregional (78701), I-35N at Town Lake exit.* 512/472-8211; FAX 512/472-4636. 320 rms, 11 story. S $94-$114; D $104-$134; each addl $10; under 18 free; wkend rates. Crib avail. TV; cable (premium). Pool. Restaurant 6:30 am-2 pm, 5:30-10 pm. Rm serv. Bar noon-midnight; Fri, Sat to 1 am. Ck-out noon. In-rm modem link. Bellhops. Valet serv. Sundries. Gift shop. Free covered parking. Free airport, RR station transportation. Exercise equipt; bicycle, stair machine, whirlpool, sauna. Two towers. On lake. Cr cds: A, C, D, DS, JCB, MC, V.

D ≈ ✈ 👟 🐾 🔥 🐾 SC

✔ ★ **NORTHPARK SUITES.** *7685 Northcross Dr (78757), 4 mi N via TX L-1, E at Anderson Lane exit.* 512/452-9391; res: 800/851-9111; FAX 512/459-4433. 180 units. S, D $60-$70; each addl $10; kit. suites $139-$169. TV; cable, VCR (movies free). Heated pool; whirlpool. Complimentary full bkfst. Ck-out noon. Coin lndry. Meeting rms. Business center. In-rm modem link. Bellhops. Valet serv. Airport transportation. Health club privileges. Picnic tables, grills. Cr cds: A, C, D, DS, MC, V.

D ≈ 🐾 🔥 SC 🛼

★ ★ **RED LION.** *6121 I-35N (78752), at US 290.* 512/323-5466; FAX 512/453-1945. 300 rms, 7 story. S $109-$129; D $119-$139;

each addl $10; suites $225; under 18 free; wkend rates. Crib free. Pet accepted. TV; cable. Heated pool; poolside serv. Coffee in rms. Restaurant 6 am-10 pm. Rm serv. Bar 3 pm-midnight; Fri, Sat to 2 am; dancing. Ck-out noon. Coin lndry. Meeting rms. Business servs avail. In-rm modem link. Bellhops. Valet serv. Gift shop. Sundries. Free airport transportation. Exercise equipt; weights, bicycles, whirlpool, sauna. Some refrigerators. Private patios. Cr cds: A, C, D, DS, ER, MC, V.

D ⚬ ≈ ✈ 🐾 🔥 🐾 SC

Hotels

★ ★ **DOUBLETREE.** *6505 I-35N (78752).* 512/454-3737; FAX 512/454-6915. 350 rms, 6 story. S $109-$140; D $129-$160; each addl $20; suites $135-$375; under 18 free; wkend rates. Crib free. TV; cable. Pool; poolside serv, hot tub. Restaurant 6:30 am-10 pm; wkends to 11 pm. Bar 3 pm-2 am; wkends noon-2 am. Ck-out noon. Convention facilities. Business center. In-rm modem link. Concierge. Gift shop. Valet parking. Airport transportation. Exercise equipt; weights, bicycles, whirlpool, sauna. Bathrm phones; some refrigerators. Balconies. Luxury level. Cr cds: A, C, D, DS, ER, JCB, MC, V.

D ⚬ ≈ ✈ 🐾 🔥 SC 🛼

★ ★ ★ **DOUBLETREE GUEST SUITES.** *303 W 15th St (78701).* 512/478-7000; FAX 512/478-5103. 189 suites, 15 story. S $155-$165; D $175-$185; each addl $10; 2-bedrm suites $205-$275; under 18 free; wkly, wkend rates. Crib free. Pet accepted, some restrictions; $5 per day. Garage parking, valet $6. TV; cable (premium), VCR avail. Heated pool; poolside serv. Complimentary coffee in rms. Restaurant 6:30 am-10 pm. Rm serv 24 hrs. Bar 11 am-midnight. Ck-out noon. Coin lndry. Meeting rms. Business servs avail. In-rm modem link. Exercise equipt; stair machines, bicycles, whirlpool, sauna. Refrigerators. Balconies. Lending library. Cr cds: A, C, D, DS, MC, V.

D ⚬ ≈ ✈ 🐾 🔥 🐾 SC

★ ★ **DRISKILL.** *604 Brazos (78701).* 512/474-5911; FAX 512/474-2188. 177 rms, 5-12 story. S $112-$122; D $122-$132; each addl $10; suites $200-$500; under 12 free; wkend rates. Crib free. Garage $4; valet $6. TV; cable, VCR avail. Restaurant 6:30 am-2 pm, 6-10 pm. Rm serv 6:30 am-10:30 pm. Bar 11-2 am; entertainment. Ck-out noon. Meeting rms. Business servs avail. Health club privileges adj. Restored 1886 hotel. Cr cds: A, C, D, DS, MC, V.

D 🐾 🔥 SC

★ ★ ★ **EMBASSY SUITES.** *300 S Congress (78704).* 512/469-9000; FAX 512/480-9164. 262 kit. suites, 9 story. S, D $102-$169; each addl $10; under 12 free; wkend rates. Crib free. Pet accepted; $25 per 2 days (max 6 days). TV; cable (premium). Indoor pool; poolside serv. Complimentary full bkfst. Restaurant 11 am-10 pm. Bar to 2 am. Ck-out noon. Coin lndry. Meeting rms. Business servs avail. In-rm modem link. Free airport transportation. Exercise equipt; weights, bicycles, whirlpool, sauna. Refrigerators. Cr cds: A, C, D, DS, JCB, MC, V.

D ⚬ ≈ ✈ 🐾 🔥 🐾 SC

★ ★ ★ ★ **FOUR SEASONS.** *98 San Jacinto Blvd (78701), downtown.* 512/478-4500; FAX 512/478-3117. Queen Elizabeth II has stayed at this property. Facilities combine European tone with Texas Hill Country comfort; many rooms have lovely Town Lake views. 292 units, 9 story, 27 suites. S $155-$195; D $175-$220; each addl $20; suites $210-$1,200; under 18 free; wkend rates. Crib free. Covered parking $7; valet parking $12. Pet accepted, some restrictions. TV; cable (premium), VCR avail. Heated pool; poolside serv. Restaurant 6:30 am-11 pm (also see THE CAFE AT THE FOUR SEASONS). Rm serv 24 hrs. Bar 11-2 am. Ck-out 1 pm. Convention facilities. Business center. In-rm modem link. Concierge. Gift shop. Exercise rm; instructor, weights, bicycles, whirlpool, sauna. Massage. Bathrm phones; some refrigerators. Balconies. Complimentary newspaper. Cr cds: A, C, D, ER, JCB, MC, V.

D ⚬ ≈ ✈ 👟 🐾 🔥 🛼

★ ★ ★ **HILTON-NORTH.** 6000 Middle Fiskville Rd (78752). 512/451-5757; FAX 512/467-7644. 237 rms, 9 story. S $109-$129, D $119-$139; each addl $10; suites $195-$310; family, wkend rates. Crib avail. Pet accepted, some restrictions. TV; cable (premium). Pool. Restaurant 6:30 am-10 pm; Sat, Sun from 7 am. Bar 2 pm-midnight. Ck-out noon. Meeting rms. Business servs avail. In-rm modem link. Gift shop. Free airport transportation. Exercise equipt; bicycles, treadmill. Balconies. Luxury level. Cr cds: A, C, D, DS, MC, V.

D ✍ ≈ ✕ 🐾 🏊 SC

★ ★ ★ **HYATT REGENCY.** 208 Barton Springs Rd (78704). 512/477-1234; FAX 512/480-2069. 448 rms, 17 story. S, D $145-$170; each addl $25; suites $250-$650; under 18 free; wkend rates. Crib free. TV; cable (premium), VCR avail. Pool; whirlpool, poolside serv. Playground. Restaurant 6:30 am-11 pm; wkends to midnight. Bar 2 pm-2 am; dancing. Ck-out noon. Meeting rms. Business center. In-rm modem link. Concierge. Gift shop. Airport transportation. Exercise equipt; treadmill, stair machine. Balconies. Open atrium lobby. On lake. Cr cds: A, C, D, DS, JCB, MC, V.

D ≈ ✕ 🐾 🏊 SC

★ ★ **MARRIOTT AT THE CAPITOL.** 701 E 11th St (78701), jct I-35. 512/478-1111; FAX 512/478-3700. 365 rms, 15 story. S, D $90-$140; suites $250-$450; wkend rates. Crib free. TV; cable (premium). Indoor/outdoor pool; poolside serv. Restaurant 6:30 am-10 pm. Rm serv to midnight. Bar 2 pm-2 am. Ck-out noon. Convention facilities. Business center. In-rm modem link. Gift shop. Free airport transportation. Exercise equipt; weight machines, bicycles, whirlpool, saunas. Game rm. Some bathrm phones, refrigerators. Scenic view of city. Luxury level. Cr cds: A, C, D, DS, ER, JCB, MC, V.

D ≈ ✕ 🐾 🏊 SC 🏊

★ ★ **OMNI AUSTIN.** 700 San Jacinto (78701), at Austin Centre. 512/476-3700; FAX 512/320-5882. 304 units, 14 story. S $140-$160; D $160-$180; each addl $20; suites $250-$800; under 18 free; wkend rates. Crib free. Parking $5, valet $9. TV; cable (premium), VCR avail. Pool; poolside serv, hot tub. Restaurant 6:30 am-10 pm. Rm serv. Bar 11-1 am, Fri & Sat to 2 am; entertainment. Ck-out noon. Convention facilities. Business center. In-rm modem link. Shopping arcade. Free airport transportation. Exercise equipt; weights, bicycles, whirlpool, sauna. Some refrigerators. Luxury level. Cr cds: A, C, D, DS, ER, JCB, MC, V.

D ≈ ✕ 🐾 🏊 SC 🏊

★ ★ **STOUFFER RENAISSANCE.** 9721 Arboretum Blvd (78759), jct US 183, TX 360, north of downtown. 512/343-2626; FAX 512/346-7953. 478 units, 9 story, 16 suites. S, D $152-$212; each addl $20; suites $275-$1,500; under 18 free; package plans. Crib free. Pet accepted, some restrictions; $50 refundable. TV; cable (premium), VCR avail. 2 heated pools, 1 indoor; poolside serv. Restaurant open 24 hrs (also see TRATTORIA GRANDE). Bar noon-2 am; entertainment, dancing exc Sun. Ck-out 1 pm. Convention facilities. Business servs avail. In-rm modem link. Concierge. Shopping arcade. Airport transportation. Exercise rm; instructor, weight machines, bicycles, whirlpool, sauna. Some refrigerators. Balconies. Elegant skylit atrium lobby. Luxury level. Cr cds: A, C, D, DS, ER, JCB, MC, V.

D ✍ ≈ ✕ 🐾 🏊 🏊 SC 🏊

★ ★ **WYNDHAM AUSTIN AT SOUTHPARK.** 4140 Governor's Row (78744). 512/448-2222; FAX 512/442-8028. 313 rms, 12 story. S $119; D $129; each addl $10; suites $250-$350; under 18 free; wkend rates. Crib free. Pet accepted, some restrictions; $35 refundable. TV; cable (premium), VCR avail. Indoor/outdoor pool; poolside serv. Restaurant 6:30 am-2:30 pm, 5-10 pm. Rm serv 6 am-11 pm; wkends to midnight. Bar 11 am-midnight, Fri, Sat to 2 am. Ck-out noon. Business center. In-rm modem link. Gift shop. Free airport, RR station, bus depot transportation. Exercise equipt; weights, bicycles, whirlpool, sauna. Basketball court. Some refrigerators. Balconies. Cr cds: A, C, D, DS, JCB, MC, V.

D ✍ ≈ ✕ 🐾 🏊 🏊 SC 🏊

Inn

★ ★ **FAIRVIEW.** 1304 Newning Ave (78704). 512/444-4746; res: 800/310-4746. 6 rms (1 with shower only), 2 story, 2 kit. S, D $89-$129; each addl $15; wkly rates. TV; cable. Complimentary full bkfst; tea/sherry. Restaurant nearby. Ck-out noon, ck-in 3 pm. Luggage handling. Some refrigerators. Restored 1910 Colonial-style house; antiques. Smoking on porches only. Cr cds: A, C, D, MC, V.

🐾 🏊

Resorts

★ ★ ★ ★ **BARTON CREEK RESORT.** 8212 Barton Club Dr (78735), 13 mi W of downtown on FM 2244 (Bee Cave Rd). 512/329-4000; res: 800/336-6158; FAX 512/329-4597. Recreational facilities are top-notch at this deluxe conference resort, with its gently rolling grounds and appealing restaurants and watering holes. 147 rms, 5 story, 4 suites. Mar-Nov: S $175; D $190; suites $275-$725; under 17 free; golf & spa plans; AP avail; lower rates rest of yr. Crib free. TV; cable (premium), VCR avail. 2 pools, 1 indoor; poolside serv, lifeguard (summer). Supervised child's activities; ages 6 months-8 yrs. Dining rm 7 am-10 pm. Snack bar. Grill rm. Rm serv to midnight. Bar 11-1 am. Ck-out noon, ck-in 4 pm. Valet serv. Barber, beauty shop. Gift shop. Convention facilities. Business servs avail. In-rm modem link. Airport transportation. Limo service avail. Sports dir. Lighted tennis, pro. 54-hole golf, greens fee $80-$135, pro, putting green, driving range. Golf school. Exercise rm; instructor, weight machines, bicycles, whirlpool, sauna, steam rm. Massage. Lawn games. Soc dir. Game rm. Refrigerators, minibars; fireplace in suites. Some balconies. Cr cds: A, C, D, MC, V.

D 🏊 🏊 🐾 ≈ ✕ 🏊 🐾 🏊

★ ★ ★ **LAKEWAY RESORT AND CONFERENCE CENTER.** 101 Lakeway Dr (78734), 18 mi W on FM 620, off TX 71, on Lake Travis. 512/261-6600; res: 800/525-3929; FAX 512/261-7311. 137 rms, 10 kit. town houses. EP: S, D $160; under 18 free; suites $320-$360; kit. town houses $240-$480; golf package. Crib free. TV; cable (premium), VCR avail. 2 pools; whirlpool, poolside serv. Playground. Supervised child's activities (Mar-Nov); ages 5-15. Dining rm 7 am-10 pm. Rm serv 6:45 am-10 pm. Bar 11-2 am; Sun from noon. Ck-out noon, ck-in 4 pm. Gift shop. Meeting rms. Business center. In-rm modem link. Airport transportation. Lighted tennis, pro. 36-hole golf, greens fee $49-$57; driving ranges, putting greens. Marina; charter boats, motor boats; water sports. Lawn games. Exercise equipt; stair machine, bicycles, sauna. Some refrigerators, fireplaces (wood in winter); wet bar. Private patios, balconies. Cr cds: A, C, D, DS, MC, V.

D ✍ 🏊 🏊 🐾 ≈ ✕ 🐾 🏊 🏊 SC 🏊

Restaurants

✔ ★ ★ **BASIL'S.** 900 W 10th St. 512/477-5576. Hrs: 6-10 pm; Fri, Sat to 10:30 pm. Closed Dec 25. Res accepted. Italian menu. Wine, beer. Semi-a la carte: dinner $8.25-$16.95. Specializes in veal chops, fresh seafood. Own pasta. Parking. Dining in several rooms. Cr cds: A, C, D, DS, MC, V.

D

★ ★ **THE BELGIAN, L'ESTRO ARMONICO.** 3520 Bee Caves Rd (78746). 512/328-0580. Hrs: 11:30 am-2 pm, 6-10 pm; Fri, Sat 6-11 pm; Sun 6-10 pm. Closed Jan 1, July 4, Dec 25. Res accepted. Continental menu. Wine, beer. Semi-a la carte: lunch $5.45-$6.95, dinner $8.75-$19.50. Child's meals. Specialties: Dover sole meunière, beef tenderloin béarnaise. Guitarist, harpist Wed-Sat. Parking. Totally nonsmoking. Cr cds: A, C, D, DS, MC, V.

D

★ ★ **CAFE AT THE FOUR SEASONS.** (See Four Seasons Hotel) 512/478-4500. Hrs: 6:30 am-11 pm; Sat, Sun from 7 am; Sun brunch 10:30 am-2 pm. Res accepted. Bar. Wine cellar. Complete meals: bkfst $7-$15. Semi-a la carte: lunch $7-$12.50, dinner $16-$26. Sun brunch $26. Child's meals. Specialties in game, seafood, pasta. Own baking. Valet parking. Outdoor dining. Overlooks Town Lake. Southwestern decor. Cr cds: A, C, D, ER, JCB, MC, V.

D

★ **CHEZ NOUS.** *510 Neches St (78701). 512/473-2413.* Hrs: 11:45 am-2 pm, 6-10:30 pm; Sat, Sun from 6 pm. Closed Mon; Thanksgiving, Dec 25. French menu. Wine, beer. Semi-a la carte: lunch $4-$7.50, dinner $12.50-$18.50. Complete meal: dinner $15.50. Specializes in duck, lamb. Valet parking (eves). Bistro-style cafe. Cr cds: A, MC, V.

✔ ★ **COUNTY LINE ON THE HILL.** *6500 W Bee Cave Rd.* *512/327-1742.* Hrs: 5:30-9:30 pm; Sat 5-10 pm; Sun 5-9 pm. Closed Dec 24-Jan 1. Bar. Semi-a la carte: dinner $8.95-$16.95. Child's meals. Specializes in barbecued meats. Own desserts. Parking. Outdoor dining. 1940s roadhouse atmosphere. Cr cds: A, C, D, DS, MC, V.

D

★ ★ **FONDA SAN MIGUEL.** *2330 W North Loop (53rd St)* *(78756). 512/459-4121.* Hrs: 5:30-9:30 pm; Fri & Sat to 10:30 pm. Sun brunch 11:30 am-2 pm. Mexican menu. Bar. Semi-a la carte: dinner $9.95-$18.95. Sun brunch $19.95. Child's meals. Specialities: chiles rellenos, shrimp Veracruz, costillas estilo Yucatan. Parking. Classic Mexican decor. Cr cds: A, C, D, DS, MC, V.

D

★ ★ **GREEN PASTURES.** *811 W Live Oak. 512/444-4747.* Hrs: 11 am-2 pm, 6-10 pm; Sun brunch 11 am-2 pm. Closed Jan 1, Dec 25. Res accepted. Continental menu. Bar. Semi-a la carte: lunch $6.50-$12.25, dinner $10.75-$23.95. Sun brunch $19.50. Child's meals. Specialties: blackened tenderloin, asparagus struedel, snapper Florentine. Pianist Sun. Parking. Southern mansion built 1894. Family-owned. Cr cds: A, C, D, DS, MC, V.

D

★ ★ **HUDSON'S ON THE BEND.** *3509 Ranch Rd 620 N, near* *Mansfield Dam. 512/266-1369.* Hrs: 6-10 pm; Fri & Sat from 5:30 pm; Sun to 9 pm. Closed Dec 25. Res accepted. Continental menu. Bar. Wine list. Semi-a la carte: dinner $18.95-$26. Specializes in smoked quail, smoked shrimp quesadilla, pecan wood-smoked meats. Parking. Outdoor dining. Native stone house surrounded by flower and herb gardens; patio. Cr cds: A, C, D, MC, V.

★ ★ **JEAN-PIERRE'S UPSTAIRS.** *3500 Jefferson, #201.* *512/454-4811.* Hrs: 11:30 am-2 pm, 6-10 pm; Fri, Sat to 11 pm. Closed Sun; some major hols. Res accepted. Continental, Southwestern menu. Bar. Semi-a la carte: lunch $5-$10, dinner $12-$17. Specialties: spinach duck salad, marinated lamb chops, Texas bobwhite quail. Covered parking. Outdoor dining. Dining on 2nd-floor terrace of office building. Cr cds: A, D, MC, V.

D

★ ★ **JEFFREY'S.** *1204 W Lynn. 512/477-5584.* Hrs: 6-10 pm; Fri, Sat to 10:30 pm. Closed Sun; major hols. Res accepted. Continental menu. Bar. Semi-a la carte: dinner $12.75-$27.75. Specializes in fish, rabbit, lamb. Original paintings. Menu changes daily. Cr cds: A, D, DS, MC, V.

D

★ ★ **LOUIE'S 106.** *106 E 6th (78701). 512/476-1997.* Hrs: 11:15 am-10:30 pm; Fri to 11 pm; Sat 5-11 pm; Sun 5-10:30 pm. Mediterranean menu. Bar. Semi-a la carte: lunch $6-$10, dinner $10-$16. Child's meals. Specialties: Blue Island mussels, veal chop with carmelized onion, bouillabaisse. Guitarist Fri, Sat. Valet parking. Cr cds: A, C, D, DS, MC, V.

D

★ ★ **MAMA MIA'S.** *8015 Shoal Creek Blvd (78757). 512/451-0177.* Hrs: 11 am-10 pm; Fri, Sat to 11 pm. Closed some major hols. Italian menu. Bar. Semi-a la carte: lunch $5-$10, dinner $7-$18. Child's meals. Specializes in Northern Italian cuisine. Pianist wkends. Parking. Cr cds: A, C, D, DS, JCB, MC, V.

✔ ★ ★ **MATT'S EL RANCHO.** *2613 S Lamar Blvd. 512/462-9333.* Hrs: 11 am-10 pm; Fri, Sat to 11 pm. Closed Tues; some major hols. Mexican menu. Bar. Semi-a la carte: lunch, dinner $5.50-$12.25. Child's meals. Specialties: chile rellenos, Mexican seafood entrees. Parking. Patio dining. Mexican hacienda. Family-owned. Cr cds: A, C, D, DS, MC, V.

D

✔ ★ **THE OASIS-LAKE TRAVIS.** *6550 Comanche Trail, on* *Lake Travis. 512/266-2441.* Hrs: 11 am-10 pm; Fri, Sat to 11 pm. Closed Thanksgiving, Dec 25. Mexican menu. Bar. Complete meals: lunch, dinner $6-$18. Specializes in beef, chicken, fajitas. Parking. Outdoor dining. Outstanding view of Lake Travis. One of largest restaurants in Texas; 26 levels of outdoor dining. Cr cds: A, DS, MC, V.

D

★ **OLD SAN FRANCISCO STEAK HOUSE.** *8709 I-35N.* *512/835-9200.* Hrs: 4:30-11 pm; Fri to midnight; Sat 4 pm-midnight; Sun 4-10 pm. Res accepted. Bar. Semi-a la carte: dinner $10.95-$29.95. Child's meals. Specializes in steak, fresh seafood. Pianist; girl on swing. Valet parking. Gay 90s atmosphere. Cr cds: A, C, D, DS, MC, V.

D **SC**

★ **PAPPADEAUX.** *6319 I-35N. 512/452-9363.* Hrs: 11 am-10 pm; Fri, Sat to 11 pm. Closed Thanksgiving, Dec 25. Cajun menu. Bar. A la carte entrees: lunch, dinner $8.20-$17.95. Child's meals. Specializes in Gulf coast seafood. Parking. Cr cds: A, MC, V.

D

★ ★ **SHORELINE GRILL.** *98 San Jacinto Blvd. 512/477-3300.* Hrs: 11 am-2 pm, 5-10 pm; Fri to 10:30 pm; Sat 5-10:30 pm; Sun 5-10 pm. Closed some major hols. Res accepted. Bar. Semi-a la carte: lunch $5.95-$11.95, dinner $9.95-$17.95. Child's meals. Specializes in prime rib, seafood. Outdoor dining. Parking. Overlooks Town Lake. Cr cds: A, C, D, DS, MC, V.

D

★ ★ **TRATTORIA GRANDE.** *(See Stouffer Renaissance Hotel) 512/343-2626.* Hrs: 11:30 am-2 pm, 6-10 pm; Fri to 11 pm; Sat 6-11 pm; Sun 6-10 pm. Res accepted. Italian menu. Bar. A la carte entrees: lunch $8.50-$9.75, dinner $10.95-$19.50. Child's meals. Specialties: sauteed gulf snapper, filet algorgonzola, pasta flutes, sautéed salmon. Entertainment Fri, Sat. Free valet parking. Arched windows overlooking arboretum. Cr cds: A, C, D, DS, ER, JCB, MC, V.

D **SC**

★ **U.R. COOKS.** *9012 Research Blvd (78758). 512/453-8350.* Hrs: 5-11 pm; Sat, Sun from noon. Closed Jan 1, Dec 25. Bar. Semi-a la carte: lunch, dinner $9.95-$13.95. Child's meals. Specializes in steak, seafood. Salad bar. Parking. Cooking area for guests to select and grill their own food. Cr cds: A, C, D, DS, MC, V.

D

★ ★ **ZOOT.** *509 Hearn St (78703), off Lake Austin Blvd.* *512/477-6535.* Hrs: 5:30-10:30 pm. Closed some major hols. Res accepted. Wine, beer. Semi-a la carte: dinner $9.95-$18.95. Specializes in pork loin, roast chicken, tenderloin of beef. 4 small dining rms in older house. Totally nonsmoking. Cr cds: A, C, D, DS, MC, V.

D

Bandera (D-5)

(See Kerrville, San Antonio)

Founded 1850 **Pop** 877 **Elev** 1,257 ft **Area code** 210 **Zip** 78003
Information Convention & Visitors Bureau, PO Box 171; 800/364-3833.

This authentic Western town, known as the "cowboy capital of the world," offers fishing all year and hunting for wild turkey and white-tailed deer in season. Rodeos and country & western dances are popular pastimes here.

What to See and Do

Frontier Times Museum. Early Texas and frontier items; Western art gallery; bell collection; South American items; genuine shrunken head. (Daily; closed major hols) 506 13th St. Phone 210/796-3864. ¢

Annual Event

Cowboy Capital PRCA Rodeo. Mansfield Park Rodeo Arena. Parade, dances. Labor Day wkend.

Motel

✔ ★ **BANDERA LODGE.** *PO Box 1959, 1900 TX 16. 210/796-3093; FAX 210/796-3191.* 44 rms. Feb-Nov: S $41-$44; D $49-$58; each addl $5; under 18 free; lower rates rest of yr. Crib $5. TV; cable. Pool. Restaurant 6 am-2 pm, 5-10 pm. Bar 11 am-midnight. Ck-out 11 am. Meeting rms. Trail rides avail. Cr cds: A, D, DS, MC, V.

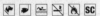

Resort

★ **FLYING L.** *PO Box 1959, 1 1/2 mi S on TX 173. 210/460-3001; res: 800/292-5134; FAX 210/796-8455.* 41 cottages (1- & 2-bedrm). Late May-early Sept: S, D $105-$157; under 2 free; golf plans; lower rates rest of yr. Crib free. TV; cable (premium) . Pool. Playground. Free supervised child's activities (May-Sept & hols, ages 3-12). Complimentary coffee in rms. Dining rm 8-9:30 am, 5:30-7 pm. Snacks. Cookouts. Bar 4 pm-midnight; entertainment. Ck-out 11 am, ck-in 4 pm. Grocery 1 1/2 mi. Coin lndry. Meeting rms. Business servs avail. Gift shop. Lighted tennis. 18-hole golf, greens fee $11-$16, pro, putting green, driving range. Some in-rm whirlpools. Cr cds: A, DS, MC, V.

Guest Ranches

★ ★ **DIXIE DUDE RANCH.** *Box 548, 9 mi SW, off TX 173, FM 1077. 210/796-4481; res: 800/375-9255; FAX 210/796-3217.* 3 rms in ranch house, 15 cottages, 1-4 bedrm. AP: S $90-$95; D $160-$170; family rates. Crib avail. TV. Pool; wading pool. Playground. Dining rm, 3 sittings: 8:30 am, 12:30 pm, 6:30 pm. Family-style meals; buffets, cookouts. Setups. Ck-out 11 am, ck-in 4 pm. Coin lndry 9 mi. Golf privileges 10 mi; greens fee $18. Rec rm. Lawn games. Soc dir; dancing, Western entertainment. Fireplaces. Private patios, porches. Horseback rides twice daily. On 725-acre working ranch. Cr cds: A, DS, MC, V.

★ ★ ★ **MAYAN DUDE RANCH.** *Box 577, follow signs from center of town. 210/796-3312; FAX 210/796-8205.* 67 cottages, 1-4 bedrm, 1-2 story. AP: S, D $98-$125/person; under 13, $40; 13-17, $70; wkly rates. TV. Pool. Playground. Free supervised child's activities (June-Sept). Dining rm (public by res) 7:30-10 am, 12:30-1:30 pm, 7-8 pm. Box lunches, snack bar, picnics. Bar noon-midnight. Ck-out 1 pm, ck-in 4 pm. Coin lndry. Meeting rms. Airport transportation. Tennis. Tubing on Medina River. Lawn games. Soc dir (June-Sept). Entertain-

ment, dancing. Movies. Game rm. Rec rm. Fireplace in some rms. Private patios. Picnic tables. Authenticated dinosaur tracks on property. Family-owned over 40 years. Cr cds: A, C, D, DS, MC, V.

★ **SILVER SPUR.** *TX 1077, 10 mi S of downtown Bandera. 210/796-3037.* 9 rms, 6 cottages. AP: S $85; D $150; each addl $75; cottages $150; family rates; 2-day min stay. Crib free. TV. Pool. Restaurant. Picnics. Gift shop. Grocery, coin lndry 10 mi. Meeting rms. Horse stables. Hiking. Rec rm. Lawn games. Cr cds: DS, MC, V.

Bastrop (D-6)

(For accommodations see Austin, San Marcos, also see La Grange)

Pop 4,044 **Elev** 374 ft **Area code** 512 **Zip** 78602
Information Chamber of Commerce, PO Box 681; 512/321-2419.

Bastrop, named for Felipe Enrique Neri, Baron de Bastrop, is the seat of Bastrop County, one of the 23 original counties of the Republic of Texas. First settled in 1829 to protect commerce on the Old San Antonio Road, the town was subjected to many Indian raids and was virtually abandoned in 1836. In 1839 it was resettled and has since flourished. The timber from the "Lost Pines of Texas", so named because the nearest similar vegetation is 100 miles away, was used in the building of the capitol at Austin.

What to See and Do

Lake Bastrop Park (Lower Colorado River Authority). Includes a 906-acre lake. Daily entrance permit includes swimming, waterskiing; fishing; boating (launch fee). Picnicking. Camping (hookups, dump station); unfurnished cabins. (Daily) North Shore Recreation Area, 3 mi N on TX 95, then E on FM 1441. Contact Lake Bastrop Park, PO Box 546; 512/321-3307. Per vehicle ¢¢

State parks.

Bastrop. These 3,500 acres include forest of "Lost Pines of Texas." Swimming pool (Memorial Day-Labor Day, daily; fee); fishing. Hiking trail; 9-hole golf. Picnicking. Improved campsites, RV facilities, cabins. Standard fees. (Daily) 1 mi E via TX 71, Park Rd 1. Phone 512/321-2101. Per vehicle ¢¢

Buescher. Approx 1,000 acres. Swimming (no supervision): fishing; boating (no gasoline motors permitted). Hiking trail. Picnicking; playground. Improved campsites (dump station); shelters. Standard fees. (Daily) 12 mi SE via TX 71, then NE on FM 153, Park Rd 1. Phone 512/237-2241. Per vehicle ¢¢

Baytown (D-8)

(For accommodations see Galveston, Houston)

Settled 1824 **Pop** 63,850 **Elev** 33 ft **Area code** 713
Information Chamber of Commerce, #2 W Texas Ave, PO Box 330, 77522; 713/422-8359.

Progressing from a small sawmill and store settlement to a Confederate shipyard to an oil boomtown in 1916, Baytown today has industries related to oil refineries, petrochemicals and synthetic rubber. Water sports, fishing and hunting are popular pastimes.

What to See and Do

Anahuac National Wildlife Refuge. This 28,564-acre refuge, bounded by East Galveston Bay and the Intracoastal waterway, is primarily for migrating and wintering waterfowl; more than 250 bird species include

30 varieties of geese and duck as well as pelicans, roseate spoonbills, ibis and egrets. Natural marshlands provide food and shelter. Animals include American alligator, nutria and river otter. Saltwater fishing for crab and flounder; freshwater fishing only in designated areas; seasonal waterfowl hunting east of Oyster Bayou. Rest rms but no drinking water avail. 20 mi S of I-10 on TX 61, 562 to FM 1985, connecting with gravel road for 3 mi. Phone 409/267-3337. **Free.**

Lynchburg Ferry. Oldest operating ferry in Texas, shuttling travelers across the mouth of the San Jacinto River since 1824. Trip provides access to San Jacinto Battleground and Battleship USS *Texas* (see HOUSTON).

Beaumont (D-8)

(See Orange, Port Arthur)

Founded 1835 **Pop** 114,323 **Elev** 24 ft **Area code** 409
Information Convention & Visitors Bureau, 801 Main, PO Box 3827, 77704; 409/880-3749 or 800/392-4401.

On January 10, 1901, a group of men working under Anthony Lucas were glumly but determinedly drilling for oil. Suddenly the pipe catapulted into the air, and oil spouted 200 feet high. This was the Lucas well in the Spindletop field. Promoters, toughs, petty thieves and soldiers of fortune rushed to Beaumont, but the town soon brought things under control. Later another oil pool deeper than the original was discovered.

Located on the Neches River deep ship channel, which connects with the Intracoastal Waterway and the Gulf of Mexico, Beaumont is an important inland port and industrial city. Chemicals, synthetic rubber, oil equipment, forest products and ships are produced here. Rice is grown in the surrounding area and milled in Beaumont.

What to See and Do

Art Museum of Southeast Texas. A permanent collection of 19th- and 20th-century American paintings, sculpture, prints, drawings, photography; folk art of Felix "Fox" Harris, decorative arts. Hosts national and international traveling exhibitions. Gift shop. (Daily; closed major hols) 500 Main St. Phone 409/832-3432. **Free.**

Babe Didrikson Zaharias Memorial Museum. Trophies, artifacts and memorabilia of "the world's greatest woman athlete." (Daily; closed Dec 25) 1750 East I-10, exit 854. Phone 409/833-4622. **Free.**

Edison Plaza Museum. Largest collection of Thomas A. Edison artifacts west of the Mississippi and the only electric industry museum in the South. Exhibits focus on Edison's inventions concerning electric light and power, the rising costs of electricity today, the future of electricity and alternative energy sources. Includes Edison phonographs, mimeograph, dictating machine and personal items from Edison's estate. (Mon-Fri or by appt; closed hols) 350 Pine St. Phone 409/839-3089. **Free.**

Jefferson Theater. Host to vaudeville in 1927 and various live performances today, this theater is the subject of a long-term, gradual restoration program. Located in the orchestra pit is the original Robert Morton Wonder Organ with 778 pipes. Guided tours (by appt). 345 Fannin St. Phone 409/832-6649. **Free.**

John Jay French Museum (Historic House) (1845). Restored Greek-revival country house, re-created tannery and blacksmith shop. (Daily exc Mon; closed hols) 2995 French Rd. Phone 409/898-3267. **¢**

McFaddin-Ward House (1906). Historic house museum, Beaux-Arts Colonial style with original family furnishings. Silver collection, Oriental rugs, porcelain and glass; carriage house. (Daily exc Mon; closed major hols) Res requested. Children over 8 yrs only. 1906 McFaddin Ave. Phone 409/832-2134. **¢¢**

Police Museum. Former jail building houses police memorabilia dating from the turn of the century; displays of confiscated weapons, contraband, jail cells. (Mon-Fri and by appt; closed hols) 255 College St. Phone 409/880-3825. **Free.**

Spindletop/Gladys City Boomtown Museum. Re-creation of turn-of-the-century oil town; 15 buildings including pharmacy, surveyor's office, saloon, photography studio; all contain period furnishings, artifacts. Self-guided tour. (Tues-Sun afternoons; closed major hols) 3 mi S of I-10, on US 69/96/287; Lamar Univ campus, at US 69 & University Dr. Phone 409/835-0823. **¢¢** On grounds is

Lucas Gusher Monument. A Texas granite shaft, 58 feet high, erected to commemorate the discovery of the first major oil field on the Gulf Coastal Plain.

Texas Energy Museum. Extensive modern facility encompassing history, science and technology of energy. Permanent educational exhibits include a 120-foot long "History Wall," which traces energy from the 18th into the 21st century; a 135-gallon saltwater aquarium; and an exhibit on the 1901 "Spindletop" oil boom, featuring two lifelike animated robots. (Tues-Sat, also Sun afternoons; closed hols) 600 Main St. Phone 409/833-5100. **¢**

Tyrrell Historical Library (1903). Served as the First Baptist Church until 1926. It now houses historical documents, art collections and serves as a center for genealogical research. (Tues-Sat) 695 Pearl St. Phone 409/833-2759. **Free.**

Annual Events

Neches River Festival. Mid-Apr.

Kaleidoscope. Creative arts festival. Early May.

South Texas State Fair. 10 days mid-Oct.

Motels

✔ ★ ★ **BEST WESTERN-JEFFERSON INN.** *1610 I-10S (77707). 409/842-0037; FAX 409/842-0057.* 120 rms, 12 kits. S $45; D $57; each addl $6; kit. units $57-$63; under 18 free. Crib free. Pet accepted, some restrictions. TV; cable (premium). Pool. Complimentary continental bkfst in lobby. Ck-out noon. Coin lndry avail. Meeting rms. In-rm modem link. Some refrigerators. Cr cds: A, C, D, DS, MC, V.

D ✎ ≋ ⊠ ⊠ **SC**

★ ★ **LA QUINTA.** *220 I-10N (77702). 409/838-9991; FAX 405/832-1266.* 122 rms, 2 story. S $51-$59; D $59-$65; under 18 free. Crib free. Pet accepted, some restrictions. TV; cable (premium), VCR avail. Pool. Complimentary continental bkfst. Ck-out 1 pm. Meeting rms. Business servs avail. In-rm modem link. Valet serv. Sundries. Cr cds: A, C, D, DS, JCB, MC, V.

D ✎ ≋ ⊠ ⊠ **SC**

Motor Hotel

★ **HOLIDAY INN MIDTOWN.** *2095 N 11th St (77703). 409/892-2222; FAX 409/892-2231.* 190 rms, 6 story. S $79; D $86; each addl $7; under 18 free; wkend rates. Crib free. Pet accepted; some restrictions. TV; cable (premium). Pool; poolside serv. Restaurant 6 am-10 am, 5:30-10 pm. Rm serv. Bar. Ck-out noon. Coin lndry. Meeting rms. Business servs avail. Bellhops. Free airport transportation. Health club privileges. Cr cds: A, C, D, DS, JCB, MC, V.

D ✎ ≋ ⊠ ⊠ **SC**

Hotels

★ ★ ★ **HILTON.** *2355 I-10S (77705). 409/842-3600; FAX 409/842-1355.* 284 rms, 9 story. S $79-$125; D $69-$135; each addl $10; suites $129-$299; under 18 free; wkend rates. Crib free. Pet accepted. TV; cable (premium). Pool. Complimentary coffee. Restaurant 6 am-10:30 pm. Bar 5 pm-2 am; DJ, dancing. Ck-out noon. Business center. Gift shop. Free airport transportation. Golf privileges.

Exercise equipt; weights, stair machine. Game rm. Balconies. Cr cds: A, C, D, DS, ER, MC, V.

D ✦ ⅓ ≈ ⅓ ⅓ ≈ SC ⚓

★ ★ ★ HOLIDAY INN-BEAUMONT PLAZA. *3950 I-10S (77705), Walden exit. 409/842-5995; FAX 409/842-0315.* 253 rms, 80 suites, 8 story. S $89-$99; D $94-$104; each addl $10; suites $96-$225; under 20 free; wkend rates. Crib free. Pet accepted; $15 refundable. TV; cable (premium), VCR avail. Indoor pool; poolside serv. Restaurant 6 am-10 pm. Bar; pianist, dancing. Ck-out noon. Business center. In-rm modem link. Gift shop. Free airport transportation. Golf privileges. Exercise equipt; weights, bicycles, whirlpool, sauna. Game rm. Some refrigerators. 3-story waterfall in lobby. Convention center adj. Cr cds: A, C, D, DS, MC, V.

D ✦ ⅓ ≈ ⅓ ⅓ ≈ SC ⚓

Restaurants

★ CHULA VISTA. *1135 N 11th St (77702). 409/898-8855.* Hrs: 11 am-10 pm; Fri, Sat to 11 pm. Closed Thanksgiving, Dec 25; also half-day Jan 1. Res accepted. Mexican menu. Bar. Semi-a la carte: lunch $3.95-$4.95, dinner $4.75-$14.95. Child's meals. Specializes in fajitas, beef enchiladas. Parking. Outdoor dining. Cr cds: A, D, DS, MC, V.

D SC

✔ ★ HOFFBRAU STEAKS. *2310 N 11th St (77703). 409/892-6911.* Hrs: 11 am-10 pm; Fri to 11 pm; Sat 4-11 pm. Closed Sun; Jan 1, Dec 25. Res accepted. Bar. Semi-a la carte: lunch, dinner $4.25-$13.50. Child's meals. Specializes in char-grilled steak with lemon butter sauce. Entertainment exc Sun. Parking. Outdoor dining. Cr cds: A, C, D, DS, MC, V.

D

★ ★ PATRIZI'S. *2050 I-10S (77707), Washington Blvd exit. 409/842-5151.* Hrs: 11 am-10 pm; Fri to 11 pm; Sat 5-11 pm. Closed Dec 25. Res accepted. Italian, Amer menu. Bar. Buffet: lunch $7.50. Semi-a la carte: dinner $4-$16. Child's meals. Specializes in fresh seafood, steak, pasta. Entertainment. Parking. Multi-level dining. Family-owned. Cr cds: A, C, D, DS, MC, V.

D

Unrated Dining Spot

PICCADILLY CAFETERIA. *6155 Eastex Frwy, in Parkdale Mall. 409/892-9498.* Hrs: 11 am-8:30 pm. Closed Dec 25. Avg ck: lunch, dinner $4.62. Specializes in seafood gumbo, vegetable plate, crawfish in season. No cr cds accepted.

SC

Belton (C-6)

(see Temple)

Big Bend National Park (D-3)

(See Alpine, Fort Stockton)

(103 mi S of Alpine on TX 118 or 68 mi S of Marathon on US 385 to Park Headquarters.)

In this park the Rio Grande, southern boundary of the US, flows through awe-inspiring canyons with sheer rock walls rising 1,500 feet above the water; south of Marathon, the river makes the extraordinary 90 degree bend for which the park is named. This rocky wilderness, once home to dinosaurs, boasts hundreds of species of plants, particularly cacti in the lowest areas and juniper, piñon, oak and scattered stands of Arizona pine, Douglas fir, Arizona cypress and aspen in the uplands. Deer, coyote, peccaries (javelina) and more than 400 bird species may be found amid scenery as stark and magnificent as anywhere in the US. The Sierra del Carmen and other mountain ranges visible from the park are across the border in Mexico.

The park administration building at Panther Junction contains orientation exhibits for visitors (daily); at Persimmon Gap, the entrance from Marathon, there is also a visitor contact station. At Chisos Basin, about seven miles off the connecting road within the park (watch for sign), there is a visitor contact station, a store, restaurant and motel; tent and trailer campgrounds (no hookups; limit 24 feet). Rio Grande Village, 20 mi SE of Panther Junction, offers a visitor center; tent and trailer campground and RV park (vehicle must accept full hookups); a store; shower facilities; gas; laundromat. Castolon, 35 miles southwest of Panther Junction, has a tent and trailer campground (no hookups; 24-ft limit) and small store. Some fees.

Floating the Rio Grande and overnight backpacking is free by permit only; inquire at visitor centers. Several self-guided trails. Park Service naturalists frequently conduct nature walks and talks. Further information, including activity schedules, can be obtained at all visitor centers in park or by contacting the Superintendent, Big Bend National Park 79834; phone 915/477-2251.

It is possible to drive within this 800,000-acre park to Santa Elena Canyon and to Boquillas Canyon. Both drives offer much scenery. The trip between Alpine, the park and Marathon totals about 190 miles. To get the most out of Big Bend, plan to spend at least one night.

Fill gas tank, check oil before entering the park and carry water. Most people go into the park by one route and out by the other.

Big Spring (B-4)

(See Midland)

Founded 1881 **Pop** 23,093 **Elev** 2,397 ft **Area code** 915 **Zip** 79720
Information Chamber of Commerce, 215 W 3rd St, PO Box 1391, 79721; 915/263-7641.

Big Spring was once a feeding ground for buffalo. Comanches and pioneers fought bitterly for hunting and water rights in the early years. Big Spring is now a farm and ranch center with varied industries. Nearby lakes offer fishing, boating, picnicking and camping.

What to See and Do

Big Spring State Park. A 370-acre park, with picnic grounds & playground. View from top of mountain; prairie dog colony. Hiking; interpretive trail. (Day use only) Standard fees. (Daily) 1 mi W on FM 700 to Park Rd 8. Phone 915/263-4931. Per vehicle ¢¢

Heritage Museum. Themed exhibits, including Indian artifacts, ranching and oil production; large longhorn collection; Western art; changing exhibits, demonstrations. (Tues-Sat; closed major hols) 510 Scurry St. Phone 915/267-8255. ¢

Lake Colorado City State Park. A 500-acre area. Swimming, waterskiing; fishing; boating (ramp). Picnicking, playground. Improved camping, tent & trailer sites. Standard fees. (Daily) 36 mi E via I-20, then 6 mi S via FM 2836. Phone 915/728-3931. Per vehicle ¢¢

Potton House (1901). Restored turn-of-the-century Victorian-style house; furnishings brought from England by original owners. (Tues-Sat; closed hols) 200 Gregg St. Phone 915/263-0511. ¢

Annual Events

Gem & Mineral Show. Dora Roberts Bldg, Fairgrounds. 1st wkend Mar.

Rattlesnake Roundup. Late Mar.

Square Dance Festival. Mid-May.

Howard County Fair. Early Sept.

Motels

✔★★ **BEST WESTERN MID-CONTINENT INN.** Box 1333, at jct I-20 & US 87. 915/267-1601; FAX 915/263-0418. 153 rms, 2 story. S $40-$46; D $48-$54; each addl $6; suites $70; under 12 free. Crib free. Pet accepted, some restrictions. TV; cable, VCR avail. Heated pool. Restaurant open 24 hrs. Rm serv. Bar 5 pm-midnight. Ck-out noon. Coin lndry. Business servs avail. Cr cds: A, C, D, DS, JCB, MC, V.

★ **DAYS INN.** 300 Tulane Ave. 915/263-7621; FAX 915/263-2790. 103 rms. S $42; D $48; under 18 free. Crib free. TV; cable (premium). Pool. Bar 5 pm-midnight. Coin lndry. Meeting rms. Business servs avail. In-rm modem link. Cr cds: A, C, D, DS, MC, V.

Bonham (A-7)

(For accommodations see Greenville, Paris, Sherman)

Founded 1837 **Pop** 6,686 **Elev** 605 ft **Area code** 903 **Zip** 75418

Information Chamber of Commerce, 110 E First St; 903/583-4811.

Bonham was named for James Butler Bonham, a defender of the Alamo. It is located in the blackland prairie south of the Red River, near the boundary between Texas and Oklahoma.

What to See and Do

Bonham State Park. Entrance on Park Rd 24. On 261 acres. Swimming; fishing. Picnicking. Improved campsites (dump station). (Daily) 3¹/2 mi SE via TX 78, FM 271. Phone 903/583-5022. Per vehicle ¢¢

Fort Inglish Village. Blockhouse is replica of first building in Bonham (1837), built to protect settlers from Indians. Log structures, including blacksmith shop, residential cabin and general store have been moved from surrounding county to form a settlement. (Apr-Aug, Tues-Fri, also Sat & Sun afternoons) (See ANNUAL EVENTS) 1/2 mi W on US 82. Phone 903/583-3441. **Free.**

Lake Bonham Recreation Area. Swimming, waterskiing; fishing; boating (launch). Nine-hole, miniature golf; playground. Tent & trailer sites (dump station, no hookups). Some fees. 6 mi N. Phone 903/583-8001.

Sam Rayburn House (1916). Guided tour of house and grounds. (Tues-Fri, hrs vary; closed hols) 1 mi W on US 82. Phone 903/583-5558. **Free.**

Sam Rayburn Library. Affiliated with the University of Texas at Austin. Honors the man who was Speaker of the US House of Representatives for 17¹/2 years. In the library is an exact copy of the Speaker's Capitol office, which contains a fireplace that was in the US House of Representatives for 92 years and a crystal chandelier, more than a century old, that has hung in both the White House and the Capitol. The library also contains Rayburn's papers; published proceedings of Congress from the first Continental Congress; books by and about leading political figures and American history. (Daily; closed major hols) 800 W Sam Rayburn Dr, 1/2 mi W on US 82. Phone 903/583-2455. **Free.**

Annual Events

Bois d'Arc Festival. Fort Inglish Park. Historical re-enactments; arts & crafts; demonstrations of 19th-century skills and pioneering life. 3rd wkend May.

Fannin County Free Fair. National Guard Armory Grounds. 4th wkend Oct.

Brackettville (D-4)

(For accommodations see Eagle Pass, Uvalde, also see Del Rio)

Pop 1,740 **Elev** 1,110 ft **Area code** 210 **Zip** 78832

Information Kinney County Chamber of Commerce, PO Box 386; 210/563-2466.

What to See and Do

⊠ **Alamo Village.** Built for the John Wayne movie *The Alamo* (1959). Buildings include stage depot, bank, jail and a replica of the Alamo. Entertainment (Memorial Day-Labor Day); walk-in museums, trading post, Indian store; cantina. (Daily; closed Dec 21-26) 7 mi N on Ranch Rd 674. Phone 210/563-2580. ¢¢¢

Brazosport (D-8)

(See Angleton, Houston)

Pop 49,541 (area) **Elev** 0-20 ft **Area code** 409

Information Visitor & Conv Bureau, 420 TX 332, Clute 77531; 409/265-2508 or 800/WET-GULF.

Brazosport, with the deepwater Brazos Harbor on the Gulf, is a composite of cities including Brazoria, Clute, Freeport, Jones Creek, Lake Jackson, Oyster Creek, Quintana, Richwood and Surfside. One of the state's largest chemical plants extracts chemicals from seawater here. Fishing, both sport and commercial (shrimp), is important to the area.

What to See and Do

Brazosport Museum of Natural Science. Emphasizing local flora, fauna; archaeological finds. Shell exhibits with collections for public study; Children's Hall; paleontology, mineralogy and ivory displays; marine life exhibits; aquarium, simulated underwater diorama. (Tues-Sat, also Sun afternoons; closed some major hols) 400 College Dr. Phone 409/265-7831. **Free.**

City Docks. Tour of the Public Port Authority. (Mon-Fri; closed hols) Reservations advised. 1001 Pine Street, in Freeport. Phone 409/233-2667. **Free.**

Annual Events

Blessing of the Fishing Fleet. Last wkend Apr.

Great Mosquito Festival. Last wkend July.

Shrimp Boil and Auction. Late Aug.

Festival of Lights. Sat before Thanksgiving.

Motels

✔★★ **LA QUINTA.** (1126 TX 332W, Clute 77531) 409/265-7461; FAX 409/265-3804. 136 rms, 2 story. S $49-$63; D $56-$66.50; each addl $7; suites $66-$73; under 18 free. Pet accepted. TV; cable (premium). Pool. Complimentary continental bkfst in lobby. Restaurant adj open 24 hrs. Ck-out noon. Meeting rm. In-rm modem link. Cr cds: A, C, D, DS, JCB, MC, V.

★ **RAMADA INN.** *(925 TX 332W, Lake Jackson 77566) 409/297-1161; FAX 409/297-1249.* 147 rms, 2 story. S, D $77-$92; each addl $10; family, wkend, wkly rates. Crib free. Pet accepted, some restrictions. TV; cable. Indoor pool. Restaurant 6 am-2 pm, 5-10 pm. Rm serv. Bar 4 pm-midnight. Ck-out 1 pm. Meeting rms. 8 mi from Gulf. Cr cds: A, C, D, DS, JCB, MC, V.

Brenham (D-7)

(For accommodations see Bryan/College Station)

Founded 1844 **Pop** 11,952 **Elev** 350 ft **Area code** 409 **Zip** 77833
Information Washington County Convention & Visitors Bureau, 314 S Austin; 409/836-3695.

Brenham is a commercial center for the surrounding farming community. It is located in the east central area of Washington County, part of an original Spanish land grant. Bluebonnets and wild flowers bloom in profusion along country roads in April.

What to See and Do

Blue Bell Creamery. Tours of ice cream manufacturing plant. Free samples. (Mon-Fri, phone for tour info) Loop 577. Phone 409/830-2197 or 800/327-8135. ¢

Lake Somerville. Fishing; boating (ramps). Hiking. Picnicking, concession. Camping, cabins, tent & trailer facilities. The state of Texas operates **Birch Creek** (phone 409/535-7763) and **Nails Creek** (phone 409/289-2392) state parks on the lake. 15 mi NW on TX 36. The US Army Corps of Engineers operates four additional recreation areas; contact PO Box 549, 77879; phone 409/596-1622.

St. Clare Monastery Miniature Horse Ranch. Pastures, barn, trophy shop. Miniature carousel and carriage displays, ceramic art barn. Tours, horse shows. (Limited hrs; closed religious hols) Contact the Convention & Visitors Bureau for schedule. 9 mi NE via TX 105. ¢¢

Stephen F. Austin State Historical Park. Site of San Felipe, seat of Anglo-American colonies in Texas. Monuments; replica of Austin's house. Swimming pool (fee); bathhouse; fishing. Picnicking, playground, concession. Camping (tent & trailer sites, shelters). Some fees. (Daily) Approx 30 mi S via TX 36, off I-10. Phone 409/885-3613. Per vehicle ¢¢

Texas Baptist Historical Center. Museum with exhibits on Sam Houston, including wardrobe; history of Texas Baptists; history of city of Independence. Baptist Church (organized in 1839, present building 1872) was site of baptism of Sam Houston. Contains historic century-old church bell, relics. (Wed-Sat; closed Jan 1, Dec 25) Across the highway are the graves of Houston's wife and mother-in-law, who requested burial within sound of the church bell. Ruins of old Baylor College, 1/2 mi W on FM 390. 12 mi N at intersection of FM 50 & 390 in Independence. Phone 409/836-5117. **Free.**

Washington-on-the-Brazos State Historical Park. A 200-acre park, site of signing of Texas Declaration of Independence (1836). Picnic area. (Daily) 14 mi NE on TX 105, then 5 mi NE on FM 912. Phone 409/878-2214. (See ANNUAL EVENTS) **Free.** On grounds are

Independence Hall. Replica of hall in which Texan Declaration of Independence was signed. (Daily) **Free.**

Anson Jones Home. Residence of last president of the Republic of Texas; period furnishings. Guided tours (Mar-Aug, daily; rest of yr, wkends). ¢

Star of the Republic Museum. Exhibits on history and culture of the Republic of Texas; audiovisual programs; research library. (Daily; closed Thanksgiving, Dec 24-Jan 1) Phone 409/878-2461. **Free.**

Annual Events

Texas Independence Day Celebration. Washington-on-the-Brazos State Historical Park. Wkend nearest Mar 2.

Bluebonnet Trails. Drive through countryside combining wildflowers with early Texas history; free maps. Phone 409/836-3695. Late Mar-Apr.

Washington County Fair. Held annually since 1868. Phone 409/836-4112. 4 days mid-Sept.

Brownsville (F-6)

(See Harlingen, Port Isabel, South Padre Island)

Founded 1848 **Pop** 98,962 **Elev** 33 ft **Area code** 210
Information Convention & Visitors Bureau, 650 FM 802, PO Box 4697, 78523; 210/546-8455 or 800/626-2639.

While breezes off the Gulf make Texas' southernmost city cooler than many other cities farther north, its tropical climate remains clear. Palms, royal poinciana, citrus trees, bougainvillea, papaya and banana trees line the streets. Brownsville and nearby South Padre Island are year-round resort areas.

Brownsville is an air, rail and highway port of entry between the US and Mexico and an international seaport with a 17-mile ship channel to the Gulf. Red grapefruit, oranges, lemons, limes, sorghum and winter vegetables are grown and shipped from here. Brownsville is also an important shrimp boat port and deep-sea fishing center. The Mexican city of Matamoros is just across the Rio Grande.

Fort Taylor (later Fort Brown) was established in 1846, after Texas entered the Union. Construction of the fort precipitated the Mexican War, which began at Palo Alto Battlefield. The final land battle of the Civil War was also fought nearby. Raids of the area by Mexican bandits continued well into the early 20th century.

What to See and Do

Fishing.

Freshwater fishing in the many lakes and canals. Bass, crappie and catfish.

Saltwater fishing on Laguna Madre Bay, in the ship channels or in the Gulf by charter boats from Port Isabel or South Padre Island.

Gladys Porter Zoo. Outstanding 31-acre zoo with more than 1,900 animals in their natural setting; reptile collection; free-flight aviary; children's zoo; aquarium; Australian exhibit. (Daily) 500 Ringgold St. Phone 210/546-7187. ¢¢

Gray Line bus tours. Contact 508 E Jefferson and Garcia, PO Box 2422, South Padre Island 78597; 210/542-8962 or 800/321-8720.

Matamoros, Tamaulipas, Mexico (population: 500,000), across the Rio Grande. This is a colorful and interesting Mexican city, with diversified industry making it one of Mexico's wealthiest towns. Life centers around the Plaza de Hidalgo and the streets that reach out from it. The market, four blocks from the plaza on Calle (street) 9 & Calle 10, is an open mall of small stands. (No fruit may be brought back to the US. For Border Crossing Regulations, see INTRODUCTION.)

Palmitto Ranch Battlefield. Site of the final land engagement of the Civil War (May 12-13, 1865). Confederate troops prevailed, but were ordered to surrender upon learning of Lee's capitulation at Appomattox more than a month before. Marker is 12 mi E on TX 4.

Palo Alto Battlefield National Historic Site. Historical marker gives details of the artillery battle that began the Mexican War here on May 8, 1846. 6 mi N of town on FM 1847, near jct FM 511.

Port Brownsville. Harbor for shrimp boats and ships transporting various commodities. 6 mi NE on International Blvd.

Resaca de la Palma. Site of the second Mexican War battle, May 9, 1846. Gen. Zachary Taylor defeated Mexican Gen. Mariano Arista.

Historical markers give details. N end of town, vicinity Paredes Line Rd and Coffee Port Rd.

Annual Event

Charro Days. Parades, fireworks, concerts, special events. 4th Thurs Feb.

Motels

★ ★ **HOWARD JOHNSON.** *1945 N Expy (78520). 210/546-4591; FAX 210/544-1246.* 162 rms, 2 story. S $50-$68; D $66-$68; each addl $9; family rates. Crib free. Pet accepted; $50. TV; cable. Pool; wading pool. Playground. Restaurant 6 am-2 pm, 5-10 pm. Rm serv. Bar 4 pm-2 am; entertainment, dancing. Ck-out noon. Coin lndry. Meeting rms. Bellhops. Valet serv. Health club privileges. Lawn games. Some refrigerators. Picnic table. Cr cds: A, C, D, DS, JCB, MC, V.

✔ ★ **LA QUINTA.** *55 Sam Perl Blvd (78520), 4 blks SW of Gateway Bridge. 210/546-0381; FAX 210/541-5313.* 143 rms, 2 story. S $44-$51; D $52-$59; each addl $8; suites $75; under 18 free. Crib free. TV; cable. Pool. Continental bkfst. Complimentary coffee. Restaurant adj open 24 hrs. Ck-out noon. Meeting rms. Valet serv. Picnic table, grill. Cr cds: A, C, D, DS, ER, MC, V.

Motor Hotels

★ ★ **HOLIDAY INN FORT BROWN.** *Box 2255 (78520), 1900 E Elizabeth St, 2 blks E of Gateway Bridge. 210/546-2201; FAX 210/546-0756.* 174 rms, 2-3 story. S $70; D $78; each addl $8; suites $85-$200; under 12 free. Crib free. TV; cable (premium). Heated pool; wading pool, poolside serv. Restaurant 6 am-10 pm. Rm serv. Bar noon-2 am; entertainment, dancing. Ck-out noon. Convention facilities. Business center. In-rm modem link. Bellhops. Valet serv. Gift shop. Lighted tennis. Picnic tables. Private patios, balconies. Intl Gateway Bridge nearby. Cr cds: A, C, D, DS, MC, V.

★ ★ **SHERATON INN.** *3777 N Expy (78520). 210/350-9191; FAX 210/350-4153.* 142 rms. S $80-$91; D $90-$101; each addl $10; suites $225; under 17 free; some wkend rates. TV; cable. Indoor/outdoor pool; whirlpool. Coffee in rms. Restaurant 6 am-11 pm. Rm serv. Bar 4 pm-2 am; entertainment, dancing. Ck-out noon. Meeting rms. Bellhops. Refrigerator, whirlpool in suites. Cr cds: A, C, D, DS, MC, V.

Resort

★ ★ ★ **RANCHO VIEJO.** *(1 Rancho Viejo Dr, Rancho Viejo 78520) 11 mi NW on US 77. 210/350-4000; res: 800/531-7400; FAX 210/350-9681.* 80 units, 1-2 story, 30 kits. S $95-$118; D $95-$118; each addl $10; villas (1-3 bedrm) with kit. $118-$314; under 14 free; golf plans. Crib $15. TV; cable. Pool; wading pool, poolside serv. Dining rm 7 am-10 pm. Bar noon-10 pm; entertainment, dancing Thurs-Sat. Ck-out noon, ck-in 4 pm. Free lndry facilities in some villas. Convention facilities. Bellhops. Barber, beauty shop. Tennis. 36-hole golf, greens fee $35, putting green, driving range. Rec rm. Some refrigerators. Private patios, balconies. Cr cds: A, C, D, DS, MC, V.

Unrated Dining Spot

LUBY'S CAFETERIA. *2124 Boca Chica Blvd. 210/546-1062.* Hrs: 10:45 am-8 pm; summer to 8 pm. Closed Dec 25. Avg ck:

lunch, dinner $4.95. Specializes in baked fish, homemade pies. Cr cds: DS, MC, V.

Brownwood (C-5)

(See Comanche)

Pop 18,387 **Elev** 1,342 ft **Area code** 915 **Zip** 76801
Information Chamber of Commerce, 521 E Baker, PO Box 880; 915/646-9535.

Almost in the exact center of Texas, Brown County is rich farm and ranch land, producing cattle, sheep, goats, poultry, pecans and grain crops.

What to See and Do

Douglas MacArthur Academy of Freedom. Includes Hall of Christian Civilization, with one of Texas' largest murals; Mediterranean Hall, with reproduction of the Rosetta Stone; and MacArthur Exhibit Gallery, containing memorabilia of the famous general. Tours (daily exc univ hols). Howard Payne Univ campus, Austin & Coggin Sts. Phone 915/643-7830. **Free.**

Lake Brownwood State Park. Approx 540 acres on a 7,300-acre lake. Swimming; fishing; boating (ramps). Hiking trails. Picnicking; concessions (seasonal). Multi-use campsites, RV facilities, cabins, shelters. (Daily) Standard fees. 16 mi NW on TX 279, then 6 mi E on Park Rd 15. Phone 915/784-5223. Per vehicle ¢¢

Annual Event

Lone Star Fair & Rattlesnake Roundup. 3 days mid-Mar.

Motel

★ ★ **GOLD KEY INN.** *515 E Commerce. 915/646-2551; res: 800/646-0912; FAX 915/643-6064.* 137 rms, 2 story. S, D $29.95-$44; each addl $4; under 18 free. Crib free. Pet accepted. TV; cable (premium). Pool; whirlpool, sauna. Restaurant 6-9 am. Private club 5-10 pm, Sat to 10 pm; closed Sun. Ck-out noon. Coin lndry. Meeting rms. Business servs avail. Cr cds: A, D, DS, MC, V.

Unrated Dining Spot

UNDERWOOD'S CAFETERIA. *404 W Commerce. 915/646-6110.* Hrs: 10 am-9 pm. Closed Wed; Thanksgiving, Dec 25. Avg ck: lunch, dinner $6.39. Specializes in barbecue, fried chicken, chicken-fried steak. Parking. Western decor. Family-owned. No cr cds accepted.

Bryan/College Station (C-7)

(See Huntsville)

Pop Bryan, 55,002; College Station, 52,456 **Elev** Bryan, 367 ft; College Station, 308 ft **Area code** 409
Information Bryan/College Station Convention & Visitors Bureau, 715 University Dr E, College Station 77840; 409/260-9898 or 800/777-8292.

This rich farming area is home to a number of nationalities, blended together into a thriving community. Bryan and College Station have become a space research, industrial and wholesale-retail trade center. Hunting, fishing and camping are popular year-round.

What to See and Do

Messina Hof Wine Cellars. Winery and vineyard tours, lakeside picnic area. Tasting room, gift shop. Tours (res required). (Daily; closed some major hols) 5 mi NE of Bryan on TX 21, Wallis Rd exit, then follow signs. Phone 409/778-9463 or 800/736-9463 (TX). **Free.**

Texas A&M University (1876). (43,000 students) This school is the oldest public institution of higher education in the state. It ranks among the top 10 institutions in research and development. Enrollments in engineering, agriculture, business, veterinary medicine and architecture are among the largest in the country. On its attractive 5,200-acre campus, limited tours are available of the creamery, the oceanography-meteorology building with observation deck, the Memorial Student Center art exhibits, rare gun collection, nuclear science center, cyclotron and branding iron exhibit. Aggieland Visitor Center has audiovisual programs (Mon-Fri; 2-wk advance notice requested). Phone 409/845-5851.

The Brazos Valley Museum of Natural History. Exhibits focus on archeology and natural history of the Brazos Valley; includes hands-on Discovery Room featuring live animals. (Tues-Sat; closed major hols) 3232 Briarcrest Dr, Bryan. Phone 409/776-2195.

Annual Event

Jazzfest. Apr.

Motels

★ **BEST WESTERN CHIMNEY INN.** (901 E University, College Station 77840) 409/260-9150; FAX 409/846-0467. 98 rms, 2 story. S $47-$59; D $52-$64; suites $125-$150; under 16 free. Crib avail. TV; cable. Pool. Complimentary continental bkfst, coffee in lobby. Restaurant adj 6 am-10 pm. Bar 4 pm-midnight. Ck-out noon. Coin lndry. Cr cds: A, C, D, DS, MC, V.

☑ ✆ ≋ ✗ 🔥 SC

✔ ★ **COMFORT INN.** (104 Texas Ave S, College Station 77840) 409/846-7333; FAX 409/846-5479. 114 rms, 3 story. S $45-$70; D $50-$75; each addl $5; under 18 free; higher rates special events. TV; cable (premium) Pool; whirlpool. Complimentary continental bkfst. Ck-out noon. Coin lndry. Meeting rm. Valet serv. Free airport, bus depot transportation. Picnic tables, grills. Cr cds: A, C, D, DS, MC, V.

☑ ≋ ✗ 🔥 SC

★ ★ **HAMPTON INN.** (320 Texas Ave S, College Station 77840) 409/846-0184; FAX 409/846-0184, ext. 104. 134 rms, 4 story. S, D $54-$59; under 17 free; higher rates special events. Crib free. TV; cable. Pool. Complimentary continental bkfst. Restaurant nearby. Ck-out noon. Meeting rm. In-rm modem link. Valet serv. Airport, bus depot transportation. Cr cds: A, C, D, DS, MC, V.

☑ ≋ ✗ 🔥 SC

★ **HOLIDAY INN.** (1503 Texas Ave S, College Station 77840) 409/693-1736; FAX 409/693-1736. 126 rms, 6 story. S, D $53-$55; each addl $6; under 19 free. Crib free. Pet accepted, some restrictions. TV; cable. Pool; poolside serv. Restaurant 6 am-2 pm, 5-10 pm; wkends 7 am-2 pm. Rm serv. Bar. Ck-out noon. Coin lndry. Meeting rms. Free airport transportation. Some refrigerators. Cr cds: A, C, D, DS, JCB, MC, V.

☑ ✆ ≋ ✗ 🔥 SC

★ ★ **LA QUINTA.** (607 Texas Ave S, College Station 77840) 409/696-7777; FAX 409/696-0531. 176 rms. S, D $56-$63; each addl $7; under 18 free. Crib free. Pet accepted. TV; cable (premium). Pool. Complimentary continental bkfst. Restaurant adj 11 am-11 pm; Fri, Sat to midnight. Ck-out noon. Meeting rms. In-rm modem link. Free airport transportation. Texas A & M Univ opp. Picnic tables. Cr cds: A, C, D, DS, MC, V.

☑ ✆ ≋ ✗ 🔥 SC

★ ★ **MANOR HOUSE.** (2504 Texas Ave S, College Station 77840) 409/764-9540; res: 800/231-4100; FAX 409/693-2430. 117 rms, 2 story. S, D $39-$75; under 12 free; higher rates: hols, special events. Crib $7. Pet accepted; $7 per day. TV; cable (premium). Pool. Complimentary continental bkfst. Restaurant adj open 24 hrs. Ck-out noon. Meeting rms. In-rm modem link. Valet serv. Free airport transportation. Health club privileges. All refrigerators. Cr cds: A, C, D, DS, MC, V.

☑ ✆ ≋ ✗ 🔥 SC

Motor Hotel

★ **FAIRFIELD INN BY MARRIOTT.** (4613 S Texas Ave, Bryan 77802) 409/268-1552; FAX 409/268-1552. 62 rms, 4 story. S $45.95-$59.95; D $47.95-$59.95; under 18 free; higher rates special events. Pet accepted; some restrictions. TV; cable (premium). Indoor pool; whirlpool. Complimentary continental bkfst. Restaurant opp 10 am-11 pm. Ck-out 11 am. Game rm. Some refrigerators. Cr cds: A, C, D, DS, MC, V.

☑ ✆ ≋ ✗ 🔥 SC

Hotel

★ ★ ★ **HILTON COLLEGE STATION.** (801 University Dr E, College Station 77840) 409/693-7500; FAX 409/846-7361. 303 rms, 11 story. S $61-$100; D $71-$120; each addl $14; suites $110-$250; family rates. Crib free. Pet accepted, some restrictions; $50 refundable. TV; cable. Pool; poolside serv. Restaurant 6 am-10 pm; Fri, Sat to 11 pm. Bar 11 am-midnight, Fri, Sat to 1 am, Sun noon-midnight; entertainment Thurs-Sat, dancing. Meeting rms. Gift shop. Free airport transportation. Exercise equipt; weights, bicycle, stair machine. Some refrigerators, in-rm whirlpools. Private patios, balconies. Cr cds: A, C, D, DS, ER, JCB, MC, V.

☑ ✆ ≋ ✗ ✗ 🔥 SC

Restaurants

✔ ★ ★ **CENARE.** (404 University Dr, College Station 77840) 409/696-7311. Hrs: 11 am-11 pm; Sun 11 am-10 pm. Closed Dec 25. Res accepted. Italian menu. Bar. Semi-a la carte: lunch $4.50-$6.75, dinner $6.50-$12. Specialties: veal Marsala, orange roughy Roosa, fettucine, cannelloni. Own pasta. Parking. Contemporary Italian decor. Cr cds: A, C, D, DS, MC, V.

★ **JOSE'S.** (3824 Texas Ave S, Bryan) 409/268-0036. Hrs: 11 am-9:45 pm. Closed Mon; most major hols. Mexican menu. Bar. Semi-a la carte: lunch $4.50-$16.95, dinner $4.50-$16.99. Child's meals. Specialties: tacos al carbon, chimichangas, filet de Huachinango. Parking. Cr cds: A, C, DS, MC, V.

☑

Unrated Dining Spot

LUBY'S CAFETERIA. (4401 Texas Ave S, Bryan) 409/846-3729. Hrs: 10:45 am-8 pm. Closed Dec 25. Mexican, Amer menu. Avg ck: lunch $5, dinner $6. Specializes in roast beef, chicken, fresh strawberry pie. Parking. Cr cds: DS, MC, V.

☑

Burnet (C-6)

(See Austin, Georgetown, Johnson City)

Founded 1849 **Pop** 3,423 **Elev** 1,300 ft **Area code** 512 **Zip** 78611

Information Chamber of Commerce, 705 Buchanan Dr, PO Drawer M; 512/756-4297.

This resort town is in the Highland Lakes region, an area of geologic interest that attracts many rockhounds.

What to See and Do

Fort Croghan Museum. One of 8 frontier forts established 1848-49 to protect settlements. Original stone building, blacksmith shop, relocated buildings; visitor center; museum displays early pioneer artifacts; displays relating to Civilian Conservation Corps. (Apr-mid-Oct, Thurs-Sun) 1 mi W on TX 29. Phone 512/756-8281. **Free.**

Inks Lake State Park. A 1,200-acre recreation area. Swimming, fishing; boating (ramps). Hiking. Golf. Concessions. Campsites (dump station). Standard fees. (Daily) 9 mi W on TX 29, then S on Park Rd 4. Phone 512/793-2223. Per vehicle **¢¢**

Lake Buchanan. Larger than Inks Lake; water sports. 3 mi W on TX 29.

Longhorn Cavern State Park. In the Highland Lakes country on the Colorado River, this 639-acre tract provides picnicking facilities in addition to a museum of the Civilian Conservation Corps (CCC) and the extremely large cavern. Robert E. Lee is said to have driven a band of Indians into the big entrance to capture them, not realizing there were at least six other exits. Guided tours. (Daily) 5 mi S on US 281, then 5 1/2 mi W on Park Rd 4. Phone 512/756-6976. **¢¢¢**

Annual Event

Bluebonnet Festival. On the square. Mid-Apr.

Motel

✔★ **HoJo INN.** *908 Buchanan Dr (TX 29W). 512/756-4747; FAX 512/756-7839.* 46 rms. S $35.95-$49.95; D $49.95-$59.95; each addl $5; under 12 free. TV; cable (premium). Pool. Restaurant 6 am-2 pm, 5-9 pm. Rm serv. Ck-out noon. Cr cds: A, C, D, DS, MC, V.

⊠ ⊁ 🐾 **SC**

Canyon (F-2)

(For accommodations see Amarillo, Hereford)

Pop 11,365 **Elev** 3,551 ft **Area code** 806 **Zip** 79015

Information Chamber of Commerce, 1600 4th Ave, PO Box 8; 806/655-1183.

This former cattle town, now the seat of Randall County, originated as the headquarters of the once huge T-Anchor Ranch.

What to See and Do

Palo Duro Canyon State Park. Approx 16,400 acres of colorful scenery. Hiking trail, saddle horses (fee); miniature train trips (fee). Picnicking, concession; improved campsites (dump station). (See SEASONAL EVENT) Standard fees. (Daily) 12 mi E on TX 217 to Park Rd 5. Phone 806/488-2227. Per vehicle **¢¢**

Panhandle-Plains Historical Museum. Texas' largest state museum; exhibits include Western heritage, petroleum, paleontology, transportation and fine art. (Daily; closed Jan 1, Thanksgiving, Dec 24-25) Dona-

tion. 2401 4th Ave, on campus of West Texas A&M University. Phone 806/656-2244.

Seasonal Event

Texas. Amphitheater, Palo Duro Canyon State Park. Musical drama by Paul Green depicting Texas life in the 1880s. Outdoors. Pre-performance barbecue. Nightly exc Sun. Contact PO Box 268, Canyon; 806/655-2181. Mid-June-late Aug.

Childress (A-5)

(See Quanah, Vernon)

Pop 5,055 **Elev** 1,877 ft **Area code** 817 **Zip** 79201

Information Chamber of Commerce, PO Box 35; 817/937-2567.

What to See and Do

Childress County Heritage Museum. Housed in historic US Post Office building; prehistoric and Native American artifacts; cattle, cotton and railroad industry exhibits; farming, ranching and pioneer displays; period rooms, antique carriage room. (Mon-Fri or by appt) 210 3rd St NW. Phone 817/937-2261. **Free.**

Annual Event

Childress County Old Settlers' Reunion. Rodeo Old Settlers Arena. Celebrated for more than 100 yrs. Memorial, parade, barbecue, rodeo, dance. 3 days 3rd wkend July.

Motel

✔★★ **ECONO LODGE.** *1612 Avenue F NW, 3 blks E of jct US 62 & 83. 817/937-3695; res: 800/542-4229; FAX 817/937-6956.* 28 rms, 2 story. June-Aug: S $38; D $42-$48; each addl $3; lower rates rest of yr. Crib free. TV; cable (premium). Pool; whirlpool. Restaurant 6 am-10 pm; summer hrs vary. Ck-out noon. Cr cds: A, D, DS, JCB, MC, V.

⊠ ⊁ 🐾 **SC**

Ciudad Juárez, Chihuahua, Mexico (B-1)

(For accommodations see El Paso)

Pop 700,000 (est) **Elev** 4,693 ft

Juárez changed its name from El Paso del Norte to Juárez in 1888 in honor of Benito Juárez, a Zapotec who became president of Mexico. The city later built a monument to its hero in Benito Juárez Park.

Nightlife in Juárez is definitely mixed. There are many pleasant restaurants and nightclubs; others, however, are honky-tonk. It is advisable to exercise discretion in listening to hawkers. (For Border Crossing Regulations, see INTRODUCTION.)

For further information contact the Mexico Tourism Office; 312/606-9252.

What to See and Do

Greyhound racing. Glass-enclosed A/C grandstand. Greyhound racing (Wed-Sun). Parimutuels (US currency). Admission charged. Juárez Racetrack. 6 mi S, off Ave 16 de Septiembre at E edge of town. Contact

Juárez Racetrack Public Relations Center, 5959 Gateway West, Suite 112, El Paso, TX 79925; 915/775-0555.

Mision de Nuestra Senora de Guadalupe (1659). Still in use. On the Plaza de Armas near Ave 16 de Septiembre.

PRONAF Center. National Border Complex just across the Cordova Bridge from El Paso. Shops, the Museum of Art & History (daily exc Mon; closed national hols) and the

    Centro Artesanal. National Arts & Crafts Center; handmade products from all parts of Mexico; folk art. (Daily; closed Mexican natl hols) **Free.**

Seasonal Events

Rodeo. Lienzo Charro Adolfo Lopez Mateos. Sun, Apr-Oct.

Ballet Folklorico. PRONAF Center. Sun in summer.

Clarendon (F-2)

(See Amarillo)

Founded 1878 **Pop** 2,067 **Elev** 2,727 ft **Area code** 806 **Zip** 79226
Information Chamber of Commerce, 120 W 3rd St, PO Box 730; 806/874-2421.

What to See and Do

Greenbelt Lake. Swimming, waterskiing; fishing; boating (ramps, marina). 18-hole golf (fee). Picnicking. Camping, tent & trailer sites (hookups, dump station). (All yr) Some fees. (Daily) 4 mi N on TX 70. Phone 806/874-3650. ¢

Motel

    ✔ ★ **WESTERN SKIES.** *Box 769, 6 blks NW on US 287, TX 70.* 806/874-3501. 23 rms. S $35-$38; D $36-$42; each addl $3. Crib $4. TV; cable. Heated pool. Playground. Complimentary morning coffee. Restaurant nearby. Ck-out 11 am. Cr cds: A, C, D, DS, MC, V.

D ≊ 🔥

Cleburne (B-6)

(For accommodations see Arlington-Grand Prairie, Dallas, Fort Worth)

Pop 22,205 **Elev** 764 ft **Area code** 817 **Zip** 76031
Information Chamber of Commerce, 1511 W Henderson St, PO Box 701, 76033; 817/645-2455.

Cleburne is an industrial, trading and shipping town with surrounding dairy, small grain and livestock farms and several manufacturing plants.

What to See and Do

Layland Museum. Southwest Native American collection, early pottery; fossils; Civil War exhibit, local history, Santa Fe RR caboose and artifacts; research library. (Daily exc Sun; closed hols) 201 N Caddo St. Phone 817/645-0940. **Free.**

State Parks.

    Cleburne. Approx 500 acres. Swimming; fishing; boating (ramp, rentals). Hiking. Picnicking (shelters), playground; concession. Improved camping, tent & trailer sites (dump station). Standard fees. (Daily) 6 mi SW on US 67, then 6 mi SW on Park Rd 21. Phone 817/645-4215. Per vehicle ¢¢

    Dinosaur Valley. Approx 1,500 acres. Swimming; fishing. Hiking. Picnicking. Playground. Camping, tent & trailer sites (hookups, dump station). Standard fees. (Daily) 24 mi SW on US 67 to Park Rd 59, near Glen Rose. Phone 817/897-4588. Per vehicle ¢¢

Annual Events

Sheriff's Posse PRCA Rodeo. Wkend mid-June.

Christmas Candle Walk. Tour of houses. Early Dec.

College Station (C-7)

(see Bryan/College Station)

Comanche (B-6)

(For accommodations see Brownwood, Stephenville)

Pop 4,087 **Elev** 1,358 ft **Area code** 915 **Zip** 76442
Information Chamber of Commerce, 100 Indian Creek Dr, PO Box 65; 915/356-3233.

In its early days, Comanche was a supply point for ranchers who dared to push their herds into Indian country. Gangs of outlaws, including John Wesley Hardin, raided the town periodically. Comanche's commerce is based on agriculture, cattle, dairy products and light manufacturing.

What to See and Do

Bicentennial Park. Features Fleming Oak (more than 200 yrs old), historical markers and stone columns from 1890 courthouse. On town square.

Comanche County Museum. Area history; 13 rooms of memorabilia. (Sat & Sun, limited hrs; also by appt) 1 mi W via TX 36 on Moorman Rd. Phone 915/356-3187. **Free.**

Old Cora (1856). Oldest original existing courthouse in state. SW corner of town square.

Proctor Lake. Swimming, waterskiing; fishing; boating (ramps). Picnicking (fee). Camping, tent & trailer sites (most with electricity; fee). Off-road vehicle area. (Daily) 10 mi NE on US 67/377. Phone 817/879-2424. **Free.**

Corpus Christi (E-6)

(See Alice, Aransas Pass, Kingsville, Port Aransas, Rockport)

Founded 1839 **Pop** 257,453 **Elev** 35 ft **Area code** 512
Information Convention & Visitors Bureau, 1201 N Shoreline Dr, PO Box 2664, 78403; 512/882-5603 or 800/678-6232.

Corpus Christi was established as a trading post by Colonel Henry L. Kinney in 1839. When the US Army moved in for the Mexican War in 1846, it was described as a "small village of smugglers and lawless men with but few women and no ladies." In its early days Corpus Christi grew and prospered as ranching prospered. Natural gas and oil were discovered in the early 1900s, but the city has remained a livestock and industrial center.

    Corpus Christi Bay provides a landlocked harbor with a ship channel to the Gulf through Aransas Pass and Port Aransas. The bay also makes this a resort area, with fishing, swimming and water sports.

What to See and Do

Art Museum of South Texas. Building designed by Philip Johnson; permanent and changing exhibits. (Daily exc Mon; closed major hols) 1902 N Shoreline Blvd. Phone 512/884-3844. **Free.**

Corpus Christi Museum of Science & History. Permanent exhibits focus on reptiles, minerals, prehistoric and marine life, history of native cultures of Central and North America, ranching, local history. Features 1554 shipwreck artifacts, including full-scale ship replica, and the Children's Exhibit for young children. (Daily exc Mon; closed some hols) 1900 N Chaparral St. Phone 512/883-2862. ¢

Fishing. Fishing boats leave downtown Corpus Christi marina for bay fishing trips and at other piers including Deep Sea Headquarters and Fisherman's Wharf in Port Aransas for Gulf trips. Skiffs for redfish trout fishing in Laguna Madre may be rented at John F. Kennedy Causeway.

Las Carabelas—The Columbus Fleet. Authentic replicas of the Nina, the Pinta and the Santa Maria. (Daily) Sr citizen rate. 1900 N Chaparral St, near Museum of Science & History. Phone 512/886-4492. ¢¢

Museum of Oriental Cultures. Exhibits on the cultures of Japan, India, China, Korea and the Philippines. (Mon-Fri; closed hols) 418 Peoples St, Suite 200. Phone 512/883-1303. ¢

Padre Island (see) and **Mustang Island.** These can be reached via the John F. Kennedy Causeway or from Port Aransas.

Sidbury House. One of eight turn-of-the-century houses in this district and the only remaining sample of high Victorian architecture in Corpus Christi. (Tues, Wed, Sat; closed hols) 1609 N Chaparral, Heritage Park. Phone 512/883-9352. **Free.**

Sightseeing tours.

Gray Line bus tours. Contact 5875 Agnes, 78406; 512/289-7113.

Flagship Cruises. Peoples St T-Head dock, Corpus Christi Marina. Phone 512/643-7128.

Tours Unlimited. Guide service. 109 Lakeshore Dr. Phone 512/991-3302.

Texas State Aquarium. Ten major indoor and outdoor exhibit areas focus on marine plant and animal life indigenous to the Gulf of Mexico; changing exhibits; approx 350,000 gallons of saltwater and more than 250 species of sea life. (Daily; closed Dec 25) Sr citizen rate. On Corpus Christi Beach. Phone 512/881-1200 or 800/477-GULF. ¢¢¢

US Naval Air Station Corpus Christi. Home of basic and advanced prop pilot training. Tour leaves North Gate, Ocean Dr entrance (Wed afternoons exc hols). No cameras. 17 mi S of downtown on Ocean Dr. Phone 512/939-2811 or -2674. **Free.**

USS *Lexington.* Recently decommissioned World War II aircraft carrier nicknamed the "Blue Ghost" by Tokyo Rose. Now serves as a floating naval museum. (Daily; closed Dec 25) Sr citizen rate. Phone 512/888-4873 or 800/678-OCEAN. ¢¢¢

Annual Events

Buccaneer Days. Beauty pageant, parades, sports events, carnival, music festival, art jamboree and drama. 10 days late Apr-early May.

Texas Jazz Festival. Concerts, jazz boat cruises. Late July.

Bayfest. Six blocks downtown closed to private vehicles; shuttle buses & trains. International foods, arts & crafts, entertainment. Late Sept-Early Oct.

Harbor Lights Celebration. Lighting of boats in marina. Christmas trees at Art Museum of South Texas. 1st wkend Dec.

Seasonal Event

Summer Bayfront Concerts. Cole Park Amphitheater under the Stars. Sun evenings in summer.

Motels

★ **DAYS INN.** 4302 Surfside Blvd (78402). 512/882-3297; FAX 512/882-6865. 56 rms, 3 story. Mid-May-Labor Day: S, D $59-$89; each addl $5; under 12 free; lower rates rest of yr. Crib free. TV; cable, VCR (movies avail $3.76). Complimentary continental bkfst. Ck-out 11 am. On beach. Cr cds: A, C, D, DS, MC, V.

D ⤵ ≈ ⊠ 🐾 SC

★ ★ **DRURY INN.** 2021 N Padre Island Dr (78408). 512/289-8200. 105 units, 4 story, 10 suites. S $59-$67; D $67-$75; suites $67-$75; under 18 free. Crib free. Pet accepted. TV; cable (premium), VCR avail. Pool. Complimentary continental bkfst. Ck-out noon. Meeting rms. Business servs avail. In-rm modem link. Valet serv. Free airport transportation. Refrigerator in suites. Cr cds: A, C, D, DS, MC, V.

D ⤵ ≈ ⊠ 🐾 SC

★ **GULFSTREAM.** 14810 Windward Dr (78418), on Padre Island. 512/949-8061; res: 800/542-7368. 96 kit. apts (2-bedrm), 6 story. Mar-Aug: S, D $105-$160 under 12 free; lower rates rest of yr. Crib free. TV; cable. Heated pool. Complimentary coffee. Restaurant nearby. Ck-out noon. Coin lndry. Game rm. Lawn games. Balconies. Cr cds: A, DS, MC, V.

⤵ ≈ 🔥 SC

★ **ISLAND HOUSE.** 15340 Leeward Dr (78418), on Padre Island. 512/949-8166; res: 800/333-8806; FAX 512/949-8904. 62 kit. apts, 1-3-bedrm, 3 story. May-Sept: S, D $90-$230; lower rates rest of yr. Crib free. TV; cable. Heated pool; wading pool. Restaurant nearby. Ck-out noon. Coin lndry. Business servs avail. Balconies. Picnic tables, grills. On beach. Cr cds: A, DS, MC, V.

⤵ ≈ 🐾

✔ ★ ★ **LA QUINTA NORTH.** 5155 I-37N (78408), at Navigation Blvd. 512/888-5721. 122 rms, 2 story. S $46-$53; D $54-$61; each addl $7; suites $60-$75; under 18 free. Crib free. TV; cable. Pool. Complimentary coffee in lobby. Restaurant open 24 hrs. Ck-out noon. Meeting rms. Valet serv. Cr cds: A, C, D, DS, ER, JCB, MC, V.

D ⤵ ≈ ⊠ 🐾 SC

★ **SEA SHELL INN.** 202 Kleberg Place (78402), at foot of Harbor Bridge on Corpus Christi Beach. 512/888-5391. 24 rms, 2 story, 16 kits. Mid-May-mid-Sept: S $69; D $75; each addl $6; kits. $79; under 12 free; lower rates rest of yr. Crib free. TV; cable (premium). Heated pool. Complimentary coffee in lobby. Restaurant nearby. Ck-out 11 am. Coin lndry. Lawn games. On beach. Cr cds: A, C, D, DS, MC, V.

⤵ ≈ ⊠ 🐾 SC

Motor Hotels

★ ★ **BEST WESTERN SANDY SHORES BEACH HOTEL.** Box 839 (78403), 3200 Surfside, on Corpus Christi Beach. 512/883-7456; FAX 512/883-1437. 251 rms, 7 story. Mid-May-mid-Sept: S $49-$119; D $69-$119; each addl $10; under 12 free; lower rates rest of yr. Crib $5. TV; cable (premium). Heated pool; wading pool, whirlpool, sauna, poolside serv. Restaurant 6:30 am-10 pm. Rm serv. Bar 5 pm-midnight. Ck-out noon. Coin lndry. Meeting rms. Business servs avail. Valet serv. Sundries. Lawn games. Balconies. On beach. Kite museum on grounds. Near Texas State Aquarium. Cr cds: A, C, D, DS, MC, V.

D ⤵ ≈ ⊠ 🐾 SC

✔ ★ **HARBOR INN BAYFRONT.** 411 N Shoreline Blvd (78401). 512/884-4815; res: 800/538-4238; FAX 512/884-3111. 99 rms, 4 story. S, D $39.95-$79.95; each addl $5; under 18 free; wkly, wkend & hol rates. Crib free. Pet accepted, some restrictions; $5. TV; cable (premium). Outdoor pool. Supervised child's activities March-Oct. Restaurant 7-2 am. Rm serv. Ck-out noon. Meeting rms. Business center.

In-rm modem link. Bellhops. Valet serv. On ocean. Cr cds: A, C, D, DS, MC, V.

⊡ ⌕ ⇆ ≋ ⤩ ♨ SC ✈

★ ★ ★ **HOLIDAY INN-EMERALD BEACH.** *1102 S Shoreline Blvd (78401).* 512/883-5731; FAX 512/883-9079. 368 rms, 2-7 story. S, D $89-$129; each addl $5; under 19 free; some wkend rates. TV; cable. Heated pool; wading pool, poolside serv summer. Playground. Restaurant 6 am-2 pm, 5-10 pm. Rm serv. Bar 11 am-midnight. Ck-out noon. Meeting rms. Bellhops. Exercise equipt; weights, bicycles, whirlpool, sauna. Holidome. Game rm. Some private patios, balconies. On beach. Cr cds: A, C, D, DS, ER, JCB, MC, V.

⊡ ⌕ ≋ ⅄ ⤩ ♨ SC

★ **HOLIDAY INN-GULF BEACH RESORT.** *15202 Windward Dr (78418), on Padre Island.* 512/949-8041; FAX 512/949-9139. 148 rms, 6 story. Mar-early Sept: S, D $99-$149.95; each addl $10; under 19 free; wkly rates; lower rates rest of yr. Crib free. Pet accepted; $10. TV; cable (premium), VCR avail (movies avail). Pool; poolside serv. Restaurant 6:30 am-2 pm, 5-10 pm. Rm serv. Bar 5 pm-2 am. Ck-out 11 am. Meeting rms. Business center. Tennis privileges; pro. 18-hole golf privileges; greens fee $30, pro. Health club privileges. Game rm. Refrigerators avail. Some balconies. Picnic tables. Swimming beach. Cr cds: A, C, D, DS, JCB, MC, V.

⊡ ⌕ ⇆ ⅄ ⅄ ≋ ≋ ♨ SC ✈

✔ ★ **RAMADA HOTEL BAYFRONT.** *601 N Water St (78401).* 512/882-8100; FAX 512/888-6540. 200 rms, 10 story. Mid-June-early Sept: S $49-$79; D $49-$89; each addl $10; suites $79-$89; under 18 free; some wkend rates; lower rates rest of yr. Crib free. TV; cable. Pool. Restaurant 6 am-10 pm. Rm serv. Bar 11-2 am; entertainment. Ck-out noon. Meeting rms. Business servs avail. Bellhops. Valet serv. Sundries. Gift shop. Free garage parking. Free airport transportation. Exercise equipt; bicycles, rower. Balconies. Lobby with 10-story atrium ceiling. Cr cds: A, C, D, DS, MC, V.

⊡ ≋ ⅄ ⅄ ≋ SC

Hotels

★ ★ ★ **EMBASSY SUITES.** *4337 S Padre Island Dr (78411).* 512/853-7899; FAX 512/851-1310. 150 kit. suites, 3 story. S $115; D $125; each addl $10; under 17 free; wkend rates. Crib free. Pet accepted. TV; cable (premium). Indoor pool. Complimentary bkfst. Meeting rms. Business servs avail. Free airport transportation. Exercise equipt; bicycles, stair machine, whirlpool, sauna. Game rm. Refrigerators. Atrium lobby with fountain, plants. Cr cds: A, C, D, DS, MC, V.

⊡ ⌕ ≋ ⅄ ⤩ ♨ SC

★ ★ ★ **MARRIOTT BAYFRONT.** *900 N Shoreline Blvd (78401).* 512/887-1600; FAX 512/883-8084. 474 units, 20 story. S, D $89-$145; each addl $10; suites $160-$500; under 18 free; wkend rates. Crib free. TV; cable (premium), VCR avail.. Indoor/outdoor pool. Restaurant 6:30 am-11 pm. Bar 11 am-midnight. Ck-out noon. Meeting rms. Business center. Gift shop. Barber, beauty shop. Free garage parking. Free airport transportation. Exercise equipt; weights, bicycles, whirlpool, sauna. Some refrigerators. Balconies. Rms have view of bay. Cr cds: A, D, DS, JCB, MC, V.

⊡ ≋ ⅄ ⅄ ≋ SC ✈

★ ★ ★ **SHERATON BAYFRONT.** *707 N Shoreline Blvd (78401).* 512/882-1700; FAX 512/882-3113. 346 units, 17 story, 19 suites. S, D $69-$99; each addl $10; suites $145-$275; under 18 free; wkend rates. Crib free. TV; cable (premium), VCR avail. Indoor/outdoor pool. Restaurant 6:30 am-10 pm. Bar noon-midnight. Ck-out noon. Meeting rms. Business center. Gift shop. Free garage parking. Free airport transportation. Exercise equipt; weights, bicycles, whirlpool, sauna. Some refrigerators. Private balconies. Rms have view of bay. Cr cds: A, D, DS, MC, V.

⊡ ⇆ ≋ ⅄ ⅄ ≋ SC ✈

Restaurants

✔ ★ **ELMO'S CITY DINER.** *622 N Water St.* 512/883-1643. Hrs: 11 am-9 pm; Fri, Sat to 10 pm; Sun 11:30 am-9 pm. June-Sept, hrs vary. Closed Jan 1, Thanksgiving, Dec 24. Bar. Semi-a la carte: lunch $4.50-$9.95, dinner $6.50-$14.95. Child's meals. Specializes in seafood, chicken. 1950s diner decor. Cr cds: A, C, D, DS, MC, V.

⊡

★ ★ **LANDRY'S SEAFOOD HOUSE.** *600 N Shoreline Blvd.* 512/882-6666. Hrs: 11 am-10 pm; Fri, Sat to 11 pm. Bar. Semi-a la carte: lunch $5.95-$7.95, dinner $7.95-$31.95. Child's meals. Specializes in seafood, steak. Own desserts. Parking. Former army housing barge. Views of bay and yacht mooring area. Cr cds: A, C, D, DS, MC, V.

⊡

★ ★ **LIGHTHOUSE.** *444 N Shoreline Blvd.* 512/883-3982. Hrs: 11 am-10 pm. Bar. Lunch $5.95-$22.95, dinner $8.95-$22.95. Child's meals. Specializes in fresh seafood. Parking. Outdoor dining. Located on bayfront. Cr cds: A, C, D, DS, MC, V.

⊡ SC

✔ ★ **WATER STREET OYSTER BAR AND SEAFOOD COMPANY.** *309 N Water St.* 512/881-9448. Hrs: 11 am-11 pm; Fri, Sat to midnight. Closed Dec 25. Bar. Semi-a la carte: lunch, dinner $4.95-$15. Child's meals. Specializes in Gulf seafood. Parking. Patio. High ceilings, oak furniture. Cr cds: A, C, D, MC, V.

⊡

Unrated Dining Spot

LUBY'S CAFETERIA. *3217 S Alameda St, in Alameda Shopping Ctr.* 512/854-4373. Hrs: 10:45 am-8:30 pm. Closed Dec 25. Avg ck: lunch $4.50, dinner $5. Specializes in fish, liver, chicken. Wide variety of dishes. Cr cds: DS, MC, V.

⊡ SC

Corsicana (B-7)

(For accommodations see Dallas, also see Ennis)

Pop 22,911 **Elev** 411 ft **Area code** 903 **Zip** 75110
Information Chamber of Commerce, 120 N 12th St; 903/874-4731.

While drilling for fresh water in 1894, citizens of Corsicana were surprised to strike oil instead. With that discovery one of the first commercial wells west of the Mississippi was dug. This site has now been preserved as Petroleum Park, located on 12th Street in town. Mobil Oil had its beginnings in Corsicana as Magnolia Oil with the construction of the first oil refinery in Texas built in 1897. This refinery was also the first of its kind in the west. The rotary drill bit now in universal use was developed by a Corsicanan.

Industries include oil field machinery, textiles, clothing and food products. Cotton and small grains are grown in the rich blackland of the area, and beef cattle are another important industry.

What to See and Do

Navarro Mills Lake. Swimming, waterskiing; fishing; boating (ramps). Nature trail. Picnicking, playgrounds. Tent & trailer sites (hookups, dump station; fee), shower facilities. (Daily) 20 mi SW on TX 31, then 1 mi N on FM 667. Phone 817/578-1431; camping reservations accepted nine days in advance, phone 800/284-2267. **Free.**

Pioneer Village. Seven restored log buildings, including house, store, blacksmith shop, tack shed, children's play house; gristmill; carriage house with antique vehicles; museums; pre-Civil War documents.

(Daily; closed most major hols) 912 W Park Ave. Phone 903/654-4846.
¢

Robert S. Reading Indian Artifact Collection. One of the largest collections of arrow points (47,000) and artifacts in the Southwest. Tours. (Mon-Fri; closed hols) Navarro College. 3 mi W on US 31. Phone 903/874-6501. **Free.**

Crockett (C-8)

(For accommodations see Huntsville, Lufkin, Palestine)

Pop 7,024 **Elev** 366 ft **Area code** 409 **Zip** 75835

Information Houston County Chamber of Commerce, 1100 Edmiston Dr, PO Box 307; 409/544-2359.

Incorporated as the seat of Houston County on December 29, 1837, Crockett is one of the oldest towns in Texas. The town site was donated by A.E. Gossett, a veteran of the Battle of San Jacinto; he named the town in honor of Davy Crockett and the county in honor of Sam Houston. There are historic structures in town and a spring where Davy Crockett is said to have camped on the way to the Alamo.

The 161,478-acre Davy Crockett National Forest (see LUFKIN) lies six miles to the east. The ranger station for the Neches Ranger District is in Crockett.

What to See and Do

Mission Tejas State Historical Park. Named for Mission San Francisco de los Tejas, the first Spanish mission in Texas. Mission commemorative building; log house (1828-38). Swimming; lake fishing. Hiking, nature trails. Picnicking, playground. Tent & trailer sites (hookups). (Daily) Standard fees. (Daily) 22 mi NE via TX 21 near Weches, enter on Park Rd 44. Located adj to the Davy Crockett National Forest. Phone 409/687-2394. Per vehicle ¢¢

Monroe Crook House. Greek-revival house built by the great-nephew of James Monroe. (Wed, Sat, Sun) 707 E Houston. Phone 409/544-5820. ¢

Annual Events

World's Champion Fiddlers' Festival. 1st wkend June.

Fall Pilgrimage to St Francis de los Tejas Mission. 1st Sun Oct.

Dalhart (E-1)

(See Amarillo)

Pop 6,246 **Elev** 3,985 ft **Area code** 806 **Zip** 79022

Information Chamber of Commerce, 102 E 7th St, PO Box 967; 806/249-5646.

Annual Event

XIT Rodeo & Reunion. One of the world's largest amateur rodeos. Junior rodeo, 5K "Empty Saddle" run, parade, one of world's largest free barbecues, pony express races, dances, antique car show. 3 days 1st full wkend Aug.

Motels

★ ★ **BEST WESTERN NURSANICKEL.** *US 87S, at jct US 54. 806/249-5637; FAX 806/249-5803.* 55 rms, 2 story. Late May-mid-Sept: S $36-$45; D $42-$49; each addl $4; higher rates rodeos; lower rates rest of yr. Crib $5. Pet accepted. TV; cable. Heated pool. Restau-

rant 6 am-10 pm. Ck-out 11 am. Meeting rm. Some refrigerators. Cr cds: A, C, D, DS, MC, V.

☞ ⚡ ≋ 🐾 SC

✔ ★ ★ **COMFORT INN.** *HCR #2, Box 22, US 54E.* 806/249-8585. 36 rms. S $36-$51; D $45-$65. Crib $5. Pet accepted. TV; cable (premium). Heated pool. Continental bkfst avail. Coffee in rms. Restaurant adj 11 am-9 pm. Ck-out 11 am. Airport, bus depot transportation. Some refrigerators. Cr cds: A, C, D, DS, ER, MC, V.

D ⚡ ☞ ≋ 🐾 SC

Dallas (B-7)

Founded 1841 **Pop** 1,006,877 **Elev** 468 ft **Area code** 214

The city of Dallas, the Southwest's largest business center, is also one of the nation's leading fashion centers. A variety of businesses and industries make their homes in Dallas, primarily those involved in oil, aerospace and insurance. Far from the typical image of a Texas city, Dallas is a well-dressed, sophisticated city that tends toward formality. A major convention city, Dallas is accustomed to showing visitors a good time and is well-equipped to do so.

The city originated with the establishment of John Neely Bryan's trading post on the Upper Trinity River in 1841. Two years later the town was named Dallas, after one of several men by that name—no one is quite sure who. By the mid-1870s, Dallas had become a thriving business town, with a cosmopolitan air unique to the region.

The cultivation of Dallas' urbane, cultural persona began in 1855, with the arrival of French, Swiss and Belgian settlers looking to build a Utopian colony. Among them were scientists, artists, writers, naturalists and musicians. The colony was a failure, but the nucleus of culture remained in the heart of this young community on the frontier. Today ballet, the symphony, opera and theater are still enjoyed in Dallas, as are numerous museums and exhibitions.

Transportation

Airports: Love Field, phone 214/670-6080; also see DALLAS/FORT WORTH AIRPORT AREA.

Car Rental Agencies: See toll-free numbers under Introduction.

Public Transportation: Buses (Dallas Area Rapid Transit), phone 214/979-1111.

Rail Passenger Service: Amtrak 800/872-7245.

What to See and Do

Biblical Arts Center. Building features early Christian-era architecture; museum/gallery areas display Biblical art. Life-size replica of Garden Tomb of Christ located in Atrium Courtyard. Light and sound presentation of 124-by-20-foot oil painting featuring more than 200 Biblical characters (fee). (Tues-Sat, also Sun afternoons; closed Jan 1, Thanksgiving, Dec 24-25) Sr citizen rate. 7500 Park Lane at Boedeker; 1 blk W of Central Expy (US 75). Phone 214/691-4661. ¢¢

Dallas Arboretum and Botanical Garden. Four permanent, themed gardens situated on 66 acres; featured areas include Mimi's Garden, with 2 acres of perennials, Jonsson Color and Palmer Fern Dell gardens. Self-guided tours. (Daily) Sr citizen rate. 8525 Garland Rd, on White Rock Lake. Phone 214/327-8263. ¢¢¢

Dallas Market Center Complex. One of the World's largest wholesale merchandise marts, consists of the World Trade Center, Dallas Trade Mart, Market Hall, Apparel Mart, Menswear Mart and Home Furnishings Mart; also Design District and Infomart (information processing market center). Infomart and first floor of Trade Center are open to the public. Tours by appt. 2100 Stemmons Frwy. Phone 214/655-6100. **Free.**

Dallas Museum of Art. Pre-Columbian, 18th- and 19th-century and contemporary American art; African and Asian art; European painting

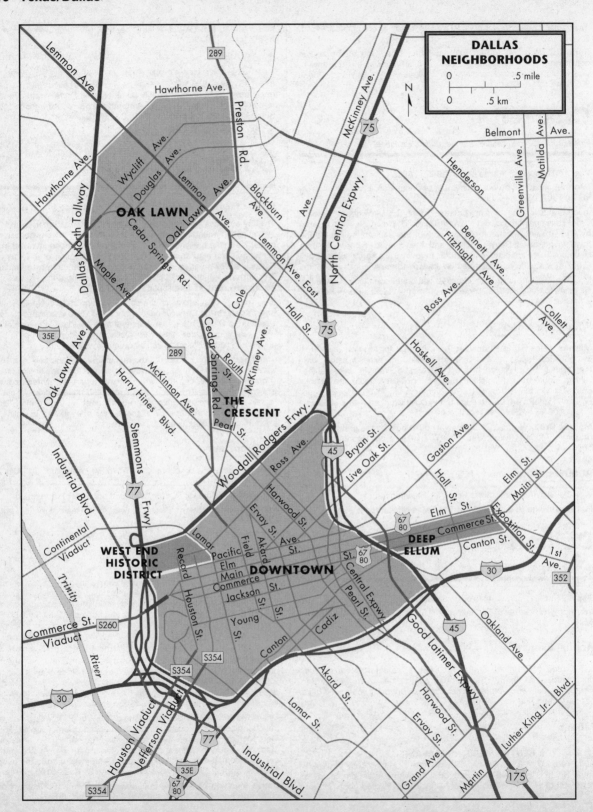

DALLAS NEIGHBORHOODS

0   .5 mile

0   .5 km

N

OAK LAWN

THE CRESCENT

WEST END HISTORIC DISTRICT

DOWNTOWN

DEEP ELLUM

and sculpture; decorative arts including Bybee Collection of American Furniture and Emery Reves Collection. Special exhibitions. (Daily exc Mon; closed Jan 1, Thanksgiving, Dec 25) 1717 N Harwood St. Phone 214/922-1200 **Free.** Fees for special exhibits.

Dallas Symphony Orchestra. Classical and pops programs; also pop, jazz and country artists. (Late Sept-late May) Morton H. Meyerson Symphony Center, Pearl and Flora Sts. Phone 214/692-0203.

Dallas Theater Center (1959). Professional theater, occupies two performing spaces. The building at 3636 Turtle Creek Blvd, designed by Frank Lloyd Wright, houses the Kalita Humphreys Theater (approx 500 seats); at 2401 Flora St is the Arts District Theater, with flexible seating and staging arrangements. (Sept-May, daily exc Mon) Phone 214/526-8210.

Dallas Zoo. More than 1,400 mammals, reptiles and birds on 70 landscaped acres. The 25-acre "Wilds of Africa" exhibit features a one-mile monorail ride, nature trail, African Plaza and gorilla conservation research center; animals roam freely through six naturalistic habitats. (Daily; closed Dec 25) Parking fee. 621 E Clarendon Dr, S on I-35, Ewing exit. Phone 214/946-5154. **¢¢**

Fair Park Dallas. Comprised of 277 landscaped acres with art deco buildings and numerous entertainment and cultural facilities. Site of the annual state fair (see ANNUAL EVENTS), one of the world's largest expositions. (Daily) 2 mi E via I-30. Phone 214/670-8400. Here are

Age of Steam Railroad Museum. Collection of steam locomotives and passenger cars, including a locomotive weighing more than 600 tons; electric locomotive that pulled Robert F. Kennedy's funeral train. (Thurs-Sun, weather permitting; during State Fair, daily) 1105 Washington Ave. Phone 214/428-0101. **¢**

The Cotton Bowl. Scene of the college football classic each Jan 1 (see ANNUAL EVENTS) and other special events throughout the year.

Hall of State. Historic landmark; fine example of American art deco architecture. Murals, statuary and changing exhibits depict the history of Texas. (Daily exc Mon; closed Jan 1, Dec 25) Research Center located in West Texas Room; lower floor houses Dallas Historical Society offices. Phone 214/421-4500. **Free.**

Dallas Museum of Natural History. Fifty habitat groups exhibit diverse plant and animal life of Texas. Fossil hall exhibits animals of prehistoric Texas, including a reconstructed tenontosaurus. Changing exhibits (some fees). (Daily; closed Thanksgiving, Dec 25) Cullum Blvd & Grand Ave entrance to Fair Park. Phone 214/421-3466. **¢¢**

Dallas Aquarium. More than 375 species of marine, freshwater and tropical fish; amphibians and reptiles. (Daily; closed Thanksgiving, Dec 25) 1st Ave & M.L. King Jr Blvd. Phone 214/670-8443. **¢**

The Science Place. Hands-on exhibits on energy, chemistry, physics, medical sciences, growth and development; "Kids Place" exhibit. (Daily; closed Dec 25) Planetarium shows (daily). Sr citizen rate. 1318 2nd Ave. Phone 214/428-5555. **¢¢¢**

Music Hall. Performances by the Dallas Opera; Dallas Summer Musicals and concerts. (See SEASONAL EVENTS) 909 1st Ave, at Parry St. Phone 214/565-1116.

Dallas Civic Garden Center. Gardens; tropical conservatory; Xeriscape Garden; display with Braille markers. (Daily exc Mon; closed major hols) 2nd Ave & M.L. King Jr Blvd. Phone 214/428-7476. **Free.**

Grapevine Lake. Swimming, waterskiing; fishing; boating (ramps, rentals). Hiking, bicycle, bridle trails. Picnicking. Camping (tent & trailer sites; hookups, dump station). Fee for camping, some recreation areas. (Daily) 9½ mi NW on US 77/I-35, then 12 mi NW on TX 114, ½ mi N on TX 114 Business, then N on TX 26. Phone 817/481-4541.

Gray Line bus tours. Contact PO Box 1769, 75221; 214/824-2424.

John F. Kennedy Memorial Plaza. A 30-foot monument, designed by Philip Johnson, is situated 200 yards from the spot where the president was assassinated. Main, Commerce & Market Sts.

McKinney Ave Trolley Line. Four restored, vintage electric trolley cars operate over a 2.8-mile route, mainly along McKinney Ave, which connects central Dallas (beginning at Ross Ave & St Paul St) with McKinney Avenue's popular restaurants, nightclubs and shops. Some

track dates back 100 years to Dallas' original trolley system. (Daily) Phone 214/855-0006. **¢**

Meadows School of the Arts. Houses Greer Garson Theatre, with classic thrust stage design, Bob Hope and Margo Jones theaters, with university productions; Caruth Auditorium, a 490-seat concert hall with Fisk pipe organ. (Aug-May; some fees). Also Meadows Museum, with the most encyclopedic collection of 15th-20th century Spanish art in the US; sculpture garden (daily exc Wed; hrs vary). (Daily) Southern Methodist Univ campus, Bishop & Binkley Blvd. For information phone 214/768-ARTS. **¢¢¢**

Old City Park Museum. Museum of architectural and cultural history, operated by the Dallas County Heritage Society. A 13-acre park with 37 restored north-central Texas structures (1840-1910). Guided tours (1 & 2 hrs) of buildings (daily exc Mon). Sights include Millermore house, gazebo, Lively log cabin, McCall's store, Brent Place restaurant. Jct I-30, Gano & Harwood Sts. Phone 214/421-5141. Tours **¢¢**

Six Flags Over Texas. 16 mi W, at jct TX 360, I-30. (See ARLINGTON-GRAND PRAIRIE)

Telephone Pioneer Museum of Texas. Story of the telephone, from birth to development into widely diversified telecommunications, is told through the use of interactive audiovisual displays. Antique phones, related equipment. (Tues-Fri; closed hols) One Bell Plaza, Akard & Commerce Sts, 2nd floor. Phone 214/464-4359. **Free.**

⭐ **"The Sixth Floor."** On sixth floor of former Texas School Book Depository Building; films, photographs and original documents examining the life, death and legacy of President Kennedy within the context of American history. Audio tour avail (fee). (Daily; closed Dec 25) 411 Elm St. Phone 214/653-6666 (recording). **¢¢**

White Rock Lake Park. Fishing; boating (marina), sailboat races (summer, most Sundays). Jogging & hiking trails; nature areas. Picnicking, cultural center. (Daily) 5 mi NE on Garland Rd. Phone 214/670-8281. **Free.**

Annual Events

Cotton Bowl Classic. Jan 1.

Boat Show. Market Hall. Late Jan-early Feb & late July.

Scarborough Faire Renaissance Village. 30 mi S on I-35E, exit 399A, near Waxahachie. Re-creation of a 16th-century English village at market time; entertainment, jousting, crafts, games, food & drink. Phone 214/938-1888. 8 wkends, late Apr-mid-June.

Byron Nelson Golf Classic. Four Seasons Club Resort. Phone 214/717-1200. May.

State Fair of Texas. State Fair Park. Phone 214/565-9931. Sept 27-Oct 20.

Seasonal Events

Mesquite Championship Rodeo. I-635 at Military Pkwy in Mesquite. Barbecue pavilion, pony rides, children's barnyard. Phone 214/285-8777. Fri & Sat, Apr-Sept.

Summer musicals. Music Hall, Fair Park. Featuring Broadway musicals; daily exc Mon. Phone 214/691-7200. Early June-late Aug.

Dallas Opera. Music Hall, Fair Park. Internationally famed opera seasons. For schedule & tickets contact 3102 Oak Lawn Ave, Suite 450, 75219; 214/443-1000. Nov-Feb.

Professional sports. Cowboys (football), Texas Stadium, TX 183 at Loop 12. Texas Rangers (baseball), Arlington Stadium, just W of jct TX 360, Dallas-Ft Worth Tpke (I-30). Mavericks (basketball), Stars (hockey) & Sidekicks (soccer), Reunion Arena, 777 Sports St.

Additional Visitor Information

For further information contact the Dallas Convention & Visitors Bureau, 1303 Commerce, 75270; phone 214/746-6679; the Visitors Information Center, Union Station, 400 S Houston St, 75202; or the Visitors Information Center at West End Marketplace, 603 Menger.

Dallas Area Suburbs and Towns

The following suburbs and towns in the Dallas area are included in the *Mobil Travel Guide*. For information on any one of them, see the individual alphabetical listing. Arlington-Grand Prairie, Denton, Ennis, Fort Worth, Greenville, McKinney.

Dallas/Fort Worth Airport Area

For additional accommodations, see DALLAS/FORT WORTH AIRPORT AREA, which follows DALLAS.

City Neighborhoods

Many of the restaurants, unrated dining establishments and some lodgings listed under Dallas include neighborhoods as well as exact street addresses. A map showing these neighborhoods can be found immediately following the city map. Geographic descriptions of these areas are given, followed by a table of restaurants arranged by neighborhood.

The Crescent: North of Downtown; bounded by Cedar Springs Rd, Maple Ave, McKinney Ave and Pearl St; also Routh St between Cedar Springs Rd and McKinney Ave.

Deep Ellum: East of Downtown; south of Elm St, west of Exposition St, north of Canton St and east of I-45.

Downtown: South of Woodall Rodgers Frwy, west of I-45, north of I-30 and east of I-35E/US 77. **North of Downtown:** North of Woodall Rodgers Frwy.

Oak Lawn: North of Downtown; along Oak Lawn Ave between Hawthorne and Maple Aves; also along Lemon Ave between Oak Lawn Ave and Dallas North Tollway.

West End Historic District: Woodall Rogers Frwy, west of Lamar St, north of Pacific Ave and east of Record St and railroad tracks.

DALLAS RESTAURANTS BY NEIGHBORHOOD AREAS

(For full description, see alphabetical listings under Restaurants)

DEEP ELLUM

Deep Ellum Cafe. 2706 Elm St
Momo's Pasta. 2704 Elm St

DOWNTOWN

Dakota's. 600 N Akard St
French Room (The Adolphus Hotel). 1321 Commerce St
Lombardi's. 311 N Market
Pyramid Room (Fairmont Hotel). 1717 N Akard St

NORTH OF DOWNTOWN

Adelmo's. 4537 Cole Ave
Alessio's. 4117 Lomo Alto
Arthur's. 1000 Campbell Center
Athenee Cafe. 5365 Spring Valley #150
Cafe Pacific. 24 Highland Park Village
Calluad's. 5405 W Lovers Lane
Capriccio. 3005 Routh at Cedar Springs
Celebration. 4503 W Lovers Lane
Chaplin's. 1928 Greenville Ave
Chez Gerard. 4444 McKinney Ave
Del Frisco's. 5251 Spring Valley Rd

The Enclave. 8325 Walnut Hill
Highland Park Cafeteria. 4611 Cole St
J Pepe's. 2800 Routh St
Javier's. 4912 Cole Ave
Jennivine. 3605 McKinney Ave
Juniper. 2917 Fairmount St
L'Ancestral. 4514 Travis #124
La Trattoria Lombardi. 2916 N Hall St
Le Chardonnay. 500 Crescent Court, suite 165
Luby's Cafeteria. 10425 N Central Expy
Mario's Chiquita. 4514 Travis #105
Patrizio. 25 Highland Park Village
Restaurant At The Mansion On Turtle Creek (Mansion On Turtle Creek Hotel). 2821 Turtle Creek Blvd
Riviera. 7709 Inwood Rd
Royal Tokyo. 7525 Greenville Ave
Star Canyon. 3102 Oak Lawn Ave, suite 144
Uncle Tai's. 13350 Dallas Pkwy

OAK LAWN

The Landmark (Melrose). 3015 Oak Lawn Ave
Old Warsaw. 2610 Maple Ave

WEST END HISTORIC DISTRICT

Morton's Of Chicago. 501 Elm St
Newport's Seafood. 703 McKinney Ave

Note: When a listing is located in a town that does not have its own city heading, it will appear under the city nearest to its location. In these cases, the address and town appear in parenthesis immediately following the name of the establishment.

Motels

(Rates may be higher State Fair, Cotton Bowl, Texas/OU wkend and city-wide conventions. Most accommodations near Six Flags Over Texas have higher rates when the park is open daily.)

✔ ★ ★ **BEST WESTERN.** *13333 N Stemmons Frwy (75234), north of downtown.* 214/241-8521; FAX 214/243-4103. 186 rms, 2 story. S $59, D $69; each addl $6; under 12 free; pet accepted; $10. TV; cable (premium). Pool; sauna. Restaurant 6:30 am-10 pm; hrs vary Sat, Sun. Rm serv. Bar 4 pm-midnight. Ck-out noon. Coin lndry. Meeting rms. Business servs avail. In-rm modem link. Valet serv. Airport transportation. Health club privileges. Cr cds: A, C, D, DS, ER, MC, V.

⏺ 🏊 ➖ 🎿 SC

★ ★ **BEST WESTERN WINDSOR SUITES.** *2363 Stemmons Tr (75220), north of downtown.* 214/350-2300; FAX 214/350-5144. 96 suites, 3 story. S $85-$110; D $85-$125; each addl $5; under 18 free; wkend rates. Crib free. TV; cable (premium). Pool; whirlpool. Complimentary continental bkfst. Restaurant adj 6 am-midnight. Ck-out noon. Coin lndry. Meeting rms. Business servs avail. In-rm modem link. Valet serv. Gift shop. Free Love Field airport transportation. Exercise equipt; weight machine, bicycle. Refrigerators. Cr cds: A, C, D, DS, ER, JCB, MC, V.

D 🏊 🏋 ➖ SC

✔ ★ ★ **CLASSIC MOTOR INN.** *9229 Carpenter Frwy (75247), north of downtown.* 214/631-6633; res: 800/662-7437; FAX 214/631-6616. 135 rms, 2 story. S $41-$46; D $51-$55; each addl $5; suites $68. Crib free. TV; cable, VCR avail. Pool. Complimentary continental bkfst. Restaurant adj. Ck-out noon. Coin lndry. Meeting rms. Business servs avail. In-rm modem link. Valet serv. Free airport transportation. Exercise equipt; weights, bicycles, sauna. Bathrm phones; some refrigerators. Cr cds: A, C, D, DS, MC, V.

[D] [≈] [✕] [⋈] [🔥] [SC]

★ ★ **COURTYARD BY MARRIOTT.** 2383 Stemmons Trail (75220), 8 mi N on I-35 E, Northwest Hwy exit 436, north of downtown. 214/352-7676; FAX 214/352-4914. 146 rms, 3 story. S $79; D $89; suites $89-$109; under 12 free; wkly, wkend rates. Crib free. TV; cable, VCR avail. Pool. Complimentary coffee in rms. Bkfst avail 6:30-9:30 am; Sat, Sun 7-11 am. Bar 4-11 pm. Ck-out 1 pm. Coin Indry. Meeting rms. Business servs avail. In-rm modem link. Valet serv. Sundries. Exercise equipt; weight machine, bicycles, whirlpool. Refrigerators avail. Cr cds: A, D, DS, MC, V.

[D] [≈] [✕] [⋈] [⋈] [SC]

★ ★ **DRURY INN-NORTH.** 2421 Walnut Hill (75229), north of downtown. 214/484-3330; FAX 214/484-3330. 130 rms, 4 story. S $60-$65; D $70-$75; each addl $10; under 18 free. TV; cable (premium). Pool. Complimentary bkfst, coffee. Restaurant adj open 24 hrs. Ck-out noon. Meeting rms. Business servs avail. In-rm modem link. Sundries. Cr cds: A, C, D, DS, MC, V.

[D] [↩] [≈] [⋈] [🔥] [SC]

★ **HAMPTON INN.** 4154 Preferred Place (75237), south of downtown. 214/298-4747; FAX 214/283-1305. 119 rms, 2 story. June-Sept: S $57-$63; D $60-$65; family, wkly, wkend & hol rates; higher rates auto races (Oct); lower rates rest of yr. Crib free. TV; cable (premium). Complimentary continental bkfst, coffee. Restaurant nearby. Ck-out noon. Coin Indry. Meeting rms. Business servs avail. In-rm modem link. Valet serv. Sundries. Cr cds: A, C, D, DS, ER, JCB, MC, V.

[D] [≈] [⋈] [🔥] [SC]

✔ ★ ★ **HAMPTON INN-GARLAND.** 12670 E Northwest Hwy (75228), I-635 exit 11B, north of downtown. 214/613-5000; FAX 214/613-4535. 126 rms, 3 story. S $56; D $63; under 18 free. Crib free. Pet accepted, some restrictions. TV; cable (premium). Pool. Complimentary continental bkfst, coffee. Restaurant opp 11-2 am. Ck-out noon. Meeting rm. Business servs avail. Valet serv. Health club privileges. Cr cds: A, C, D, DS, ER, MC, V.

[D] [↩] [≈] [⋈] [🔥] [SC]

★ ★ **HAWTHORN SUITES.** 7900 Brookriver Dr (75247), north of downtown. 214/688-1010; res: 800/527-1133; FAX 214/688-1010. 97 kit. suites, 3 story. S $117; D $147; wkend, wkly, hol rates. Crib free. Pet accepted; some restrictions; $50 plus $6/day. TV; cable (premium). Pool. Complimentary full bkfst. Complimentary coffee in rms. Ck-out noon. Coin Indry. Meeting rms. Business servs avail. In-rm modem link. Valet serv. Sundries. Free airport transportation. Health club privileges. Lawn games. Balconies. Cr cds: A, C, D, DS, MC, V.

[D] [↩] [≈] [✕] [⋈] [⋈]

★ **LA QUINTA INN.** 8303 E RL Thornton Frwy (I-30) (75228), I-30 exit Jim Miller, east of downtown. 214/324-3731; FAX 214/324-1652. 102 rms, 2 story. Mar-Oct: S $50-$65; D $60-$75; suites $125; each addl $10; under 18 free; higher rates wkends; lower rates rest of yr. Crib free. Pet accepted, some restrictions. TV; cable (premium). Pool. Complimentary continental bkfst. Restaurant adj 6 am-midnight. Ck-out noon. Business servs avail. Sundries. Valet serv Mon-Fri. Cr cds: A, C, D, DS, MC, V.

[D] [↩] [≈] [⋈] [⋈] [SC]

✔ ★ ★ **LA QUINTA NORTHWEST-FARMERS BRANCH.** 13235 Stemmons Frwy (75234), north of downtown. 214/620-7333; FAX 214/484-6533. 122 rms, 2 story. S $53; D $61; each addl $8; under 18 free. Crib free. Pet accepted, some restrictions. TV; cable (premium). Pool. Complimentary continental bkfst in lobby, 6-10 am. Complimentary coffee. Restaurant adj 6 am-midnight. Ck-out noon. Meeting rms. Business servs avail. Cr cds: A, C, D, DS, MC, V.

[D] [↩] [≈] [⋈] [SC]

✔ ★ **RED ROOF INN.** 10335 Gardner Rd (75220), I-35 E at TX L-12, north of downtown. 214/506-8100; FAX 214/556-0072. 112 rms, 2 story. S $32.99-$42.99; D $38.99-$53.99; each addl $7; under 18 free. Crib free. Pet accepted, some restrictions. TV; cable (premium). Complimentary coffee. Restaurant nearby. Ck-out noon. Business servs avail. Near Texas Stadium. Cr cds: A, C, D, DS, MC, V.

[D] [↩] [⋈] [🔥]

★ ★ **RESIDENCE INN BY MARRIOTT.** 13636 Goldmark Dr (75240), north of downtown. 214/669-0478; FAX 214/644-2632. 70 kit. suites, 1-2 story. Suites $110-$160; wkend rates. Crib free. Pet accepted, some restrictions; $60 non-refundable and $6 per day. TV; cable (premium), VCR avail. Pool; whirlpool. Complimentary continental bkfst. Ck-out noon. Coin Indry. Business servs avail. In-rm modem link. Valet serv. Health club privileges. Refrigerators. Fireplaces. Private patios, balconies. Grill. Cr cds: A, C, D, DS, MC, V.

[D] [↩] [≈] [⋈] [⋈] [SC]

★ ★ **RESIDENCE INN BY MARRIOTT.** 6950 N Stemmons (75247), north of downtown. 214/631-2472; FAX 214/634-9645. 142 kit. suites, 3 story. S $75; D $145; wkend rates. Crib free. Pet accepted; $50. TV; cable (premium). Pool; whirlpool. Complimentary continental bkfst. Complimentary coffee in rms. Ck-out noon. Coin Indry. Meeting rms. Business servs avail. Valet serv. Exercise equipt; weight machine, bicycle. Picnic tables. Cr cds: A, D, DS, JCB, MC, V.

[D] [↩] [≈] [✕] [⋈] [🔥]

★ **SLEEP INN.** (4801 W Plano Pkwy, Plano 75093) 20 mi N on North Tollway, Plano Parkway exit. 214/867-1111; FAX 214/612-6753. 104 rms, 2 story. S $49-$69; D $54-$74; each addl $6; under 19 free; wkend rates. Crib free. TV; cable (premium), VCR avail. Heated pool. Complimentary continental bkfst. Restaurant nearby. Ck-out noon. Meeting rms. Business servs avail. In-rm modem link. Valet serv. Cr cds: A, C, D, DS, ER, JCB, MC, V.

[D] [≈] [⋈] [⋈] [🔥] [SC]

Motor Hotels

★ ★ **BEST WESTERN PRESTON SUITES HOTEL.** 6104 LBJ Frwy (75240), Preston Rd exit, north of downtown. 214/458-2626; FAX 214/385-8331. 98 units, 2 story, 86 kit. S, D $55; kit units $115-$135; under 12 free; wkly rates. Crib free. TV; cable (premium). Pool; whirlpool. Complimentary full bkfst. Restaurant nearby. Ck-out noon. Coin Indry. Meeting rm. Business servs avail. In-rm modem link. Valet serv. Cr cds: A, C, D, DS, MC, V.

[≈] [⋈] [🔥] [SC]

★ ★ **COURTYARD BY MARRIOTT.** 2150 Market Center Blvd (75207), north of downtown. 214/653-1166; FAX 214/653-1892. 184 rms, 5 story. S $94-$104; D $104-$114; each addl $10; under 12 free. Crib free. TV; cable (premium), VCR avail. Pool. Complimentary coffee in rms. Restaurant 6:30 am-2 pm, 4:30-10:30 pm. Bar. Ck-out 1 pm. Coin Indry. Meeting rms. Business servs avail. In-rm modem link. Sundries. Valet serv. Airport transportation. Exercise equipt; weight machine, bicycles, whirlpool. Some refrigerators, balconies. Cr cds: A, C, D, DS, MC, V.

[D] [≈] [✕] [⋈] [⋈] [SC]

★ ★ **HARVEY HOTEL ADDISON.** 14315 Midway Rd (75244), I-635 exit Midway Rd, north of downtown. 214/980-8877; FAX 214/788-2758. 429 rms, 3 story. Feb-May: S $99-$120; D $109-$135; each addl $10; under 12 free; wkly, wkend & hol rates. Crib free. Free garage parking. TV; cable (premium), VCR avail. Pet accepted, some restrictions; $25. Restaurant 7 am-10 pm. Coin Indry. Business center. In-rm modem link. Airport transportation. Exercise equipt; weight machine, treadmill, whirlpool. Health club privileges. Some refrigerators. Cr cds: A, C, D, DS, ER, MC, V.

[D] [↩] [≈] [✕] [⋈] [⋈] [SC] [🚶]

★ ★ **HARVEY HOTEL-DALLAS.** *7815 LBJ Frwy (75240), north of downtown. 214/960-7000; res: 800/922-9222; FAX 214/788-4227.* 313 rms, 3 story. S $75-$89; D $85-$95; each addl $10; suites $125-$250; under 17 free. Crib free. Pet accepted; $125 ($100 refundable). TV; cable (premium), VCR avail. Pool. Restaurant 6:30 am-11 pm. Rm serv. Bar 11 am-midnight. Ck-out 1 pm. Meeting rms. Business servs avail. In-rm modem link. Valet serv. Gift shop. Refrigerators, wet bars; bathrm phone in suites. Cr cds: A, C, D, DS, MC, V.

★ ★ **HARVEY HOTEL-PLANO.** *(1600 N Central Expy, Plano 75074) 12 mi N on Central Expy, 15th St exit. 214/578-8555; FAX 214/578-9720.* 279 rms, 3 story. S $89-$109; D $94-$114; each addl $10; suites $120-$165; under 16 free. Crib $10. Pet accepted; $100 ($25 non-refundable). TV; cable, VCR avail. Pool; poolside serv. Restaurants 6:30 am-10 pm. Rm serv. Private club 11 am-midnight. Ck-out 1 pm. Coin lndry. Meeting rms. Business servs avail. In-rm modem link. Bellhops. Valet serv. Sundries. Gift shop. Beauty shop. Exercise equipt; weight machine, treadmill, whirlpool. Some bathrm phones; refrigerator, wet bar in suites. Cr cds: A, C, D, DS, MC, V.

★ ★ **HOLIDAY INN-LBJ NORTHEAST.** *11350 LBJ Frwy (75238), at Jupiter Rd exit, downtown. 214/341-5400; FAX 214/553-9349.* 244 rms, 3-5 story. S, D $62-$80; suites $80-$150; under 18 free. Crib free. TV; cable (premium), VCR avail. Pool. Restaurant 6:30 am-2 pm, 5-10 pm. Rm serv. Bar 2 pm-1 am; entertainment, dancing. Ck-out noon. Coin lndry. Meeting rms. Business servs avail. Bellhops. Valet serv. Gift shop. Exercise equipt; weight machine, treadmill, sauna. Luxury level. Cr cds: A, C, D, DS, JCB, MC, V.

Hotels

★ ★ ★ ★ **THE ADOLPHUS.** *1321 Commerce St (75202), downtown. 214/742-8200; res: 800/221-9083; FAX 214/651-3588.* 17th-century Flemish tapestries grace the lobby of the Beaux Arts hotel created by beer baron Adolphus Busch in 1912. Guest rooms, unusually soundproof, are furnished in Queen Anne and Chippendale styles. 425 rms, 22 story. S $180-$295; D $200-$320; each addl $20; suites $375-$2,000; under 12 free; wkend rates. Crib free. Valet parking $10. TV; cable (premium), VCR avail. Restaurant 6:30 am-10:30 pm (also see FRENCH ROOM). Rm serv 24 hrs. Bar 11-2 am. Ck-out 1 pm. Convention facilities. Business center. In-rm modem link. Concierge. Shopping arcade. Barber, beauty shop. Complimentary downtown transportation. Tennis & golf privileges. Exercise equipt; weight machine, bicycles. Health club privileges. Bathrm phones, refrigerators, minibars. Some private patios. Grand Lobby is the setting for afternoon tea; pianist signals evening cocktails. Cr cds: A, C, D, DS, ER, JCB, MC, V.

★ ★ **BRISTOL SUITES.** *7800 Alpha Rd (75240), north of downtown. 214/233-7600; res: 800/922-9222; FAX 214/701-8618.* 295 suites, 10 story. Suites $129-$239; each addl $15; under 17 free; wkly rates; some lower rates summer. Crib free. Pet accepted; $125 ($100 refundable). TV; cable, VCR avail. Indoor/outdoor pool; poolside serv. Complimentary full bkfst, coffee. Restaurant 6:30 am-10 pm. Bar 11-2 am. Ck-out 1 pm. Convention facilities. Business servs avail. In-rm modem link. Gift shop. Exercise equipt; weights, bicycles, whirlpool. Refrigerators; some bathrm phones. Cr cds: A, C, D, DS, MC, V.

★ ★ **CLARION.** *1241 W Mockingbird Lane (75247), near Love Field Airport, north of downtown. 214/630-7000; FAX 214/638-6943.* 350 rms, 13 story. S $109; D $119; each addl $10; suites $225-$450; under 18 free; wkly, wkend, hol rates. Crib $10. Pet accepted; $20. TV; cable (premium), VCR avail. Pool; wading pool, poolside serv. Restaurant 6:30 am-2 pm, 4-10 pm. Bar. Ck-out 1 pm. Coin lndry. Convention facilities. Business servs avail. Gift shop. Free Love

Field transportation. Exercise equipt; bicycle, weight machine, stair machine. Health club privileges. Cr cds: A, C, D, DS, ER, JCB, MC, V.

★ ★ ★ ★ **CRESCENT COURT.** *400 Crescent Court (75201), at Maple & McKinney Ave, in the Crescent area, just north of downtown. 214/871-3200; res: 800/654-6541; FAX 214/871-3272.* Modeled after the Royal Crescent spa in Bath, England, this hotel is part of a castle-like complex that includes a posh retail gallery. Furnishings are reminiscent of those in an English manor house; all the suites have hardwood floors and some have lofts. 216 rms, 7 story. S $255-$320; D $285-$350; each addl $30; suites $450-$1,200; under 12 free; wkend rates. Crib free. Pet accepted, some restrictions; $25. Garage $10; valet $5. TV; cable (premium), VCR avail. Pool; poolside serv. Restaurant 6:30 am-midnight. Afternoon tea served 3-5 pm. Rm serv 24 hrs. Bar 11:30-2 am. Ck-out 1 pm. Meeting rms. Business servs avail. In-rm modem link. Concierge. Shopping arcade. Free Love Field airport transportation. Exercise rm; instructor, weights, bicycles, whirlpool, sauna, steam rm. Massage. Fully equipped spa. Bathrm phones; some refrigerators. Cr cds: A, C, D, DS, ER, JCB, MC, V.

★ ★ **DALLAS GRAND.** *1914 Commerce St (75201), downtown. 214/747-7000; res: 800/421-0011; FAX 214/749-0231.* 709 rms, 20 story. S $115-$125; D $125-$135; each addl $10; suites $175-$550; under 17 free; wkend, honeymoon packages; Dallas Cowboy wkend rates. Crib free. TV; cable (premium), VCR avail. Restaurant 6:30 am-11 pm. Bar 11:30-2 am. Ck-out noon. Coin lndry. Convention facilities. Business servs avail. Gift shop. Valet parking. Exercise equipt; weights, rower, rooftop whirlpools. Some refrigerators. Sun deck. Cr cds: A, C, D, DS, ER, JCB, MC, V.

★ ★ ★ **DOUBLETREE AT PARK WEST.** *1590 LBJ Frwy (75234), off I-635 Luna Rd exit, north of downtown. 214/869-4300; FAX 214/869-3295.* 339 rms, 12 story. S $139-$149; D $149-$159; each addl $10; suites $160-$895; under 17 free; wkend rates. Crib free. TV; cable. Heated pool; poolside serv. Restaurant 6 am-10 pm. Bar 11-1 am. Ck-out noon. Convention facilities. Business center. In-rm modem link. Concierge. Gift shop. Free airport transportation. Exercise equipt; weight machine, bicycles, whirlpool, sauna. Luxury level. Cr cds: A, C, D, DS, ER, JCB, MC, V.

★ ★ ★ **EMBASSY SUITES LOVE FIELD.** *3880 W Northwest Hwy (75220), near Love Field Airport, north of downtown. 214/357-4500; FAX 214/357-0683.* 248 suites, 9 story. S $149-$169; D $159-$179; each addl $10; wkly, wkend rates. TV; cable (premium). Indoor pool; wading pool, poolside serv. Complimentary full bkfst. Restaurant 11 am-2 pm; wkends also 5-10 pm. Bar 4 pm-midnight. Ck-out noon. Guest lndry. Meeting rms. Business servs avail. In-rm modem link. Covered parking. Free Love Field airport transportation. Exercise equipt; weight machines, treadmill, sauna. Refrigerators; some bathrm phones. Cr cds: A, C, D, DS, MC, V.

★ ★ ★ **FAIRMONT.** *1717 N Akard St (75201), at Ross, in Dallas arts district, downtown. 214/720-2020; FAX 214/720-5269.* 550 rms, 25 story. S, D $135-$215; salon suites $325; under 17 free; wkend rates. Crib free. Garage parking $12. TV; cable (premium), VCR avail. Pool; wading pool, poolside serv. Restaurant 5:50 am-midnight (also see PYRAMID ROOM). Rm serv 24 hrs. Bar 11-2 am; entertainment. Ck-out 1 pm. Convention facilities. Business center. In-rm modem link. Shopping arcade. Tennis & golf privileges. Health club privileges adj. Bathrm phones. Cr cds: A, C, D, DS, ER, JCB, MC, V.

★ ★ ★ ★ **FOUR SEASONS RESORT & CLUB.** *(4150 N MacArthur Blvd, Irving 75038) NW via TX 114, exit MacArthur Blvd, S 2 mi. 214/717-0700; FAX 214/717-2550.* This property combines top-notch resort amenities—including a superb health center and spa—and state-of-the-art conference facilities with the comforts of an elegant hotel. 357 rms, 9 story. S, D $230-$270; suites $375-$950; under 18 free; golf, spa, wknd plans. Valet parking $5. TV; cable (premium), VCR avail. 4 heated pools, 1 indoor & 1 child's; poolside serv, lifeguard (wknds in season). Supervised child's activities; ages 6 months-8 yrs. Restaurant (see CAFE ON THE GREEN). Rm serv 24 hrs. Bar 11-2 am. Ck-out 1 pm. Convention facilities. Business center. In-rm modem link. Concierge. Gift shop. Barber, beauty shop. 12 tennis courts, 4 indoor, pro. 18-hole TPC golf, greens fee $100, pro, 2 putting greens, driving range. Exercise rm; instructor, weight machines, bicycles, whirlpool, sauna, steam rm. Massage. Lawn games. Minibars. Private patios, balconies. Cr cds: A, C, D, ER, JCB, MC, V.

★★★ **THE GRAND KEMPINSKI.** *15201 Dallas Pkwy (75248), north of downtown.* 214/386-6000; res: 800/426-3135; FAX 214/991-6937. 529 rms, 15 story. S $165; D $185; each addl $20; suites $325-$1,250; under 17 free. Crib free. Valet parking $9 overnight. TV; cable, VCR avail (movies avail). Indoor/outdoor pool; poolside serv. 2 restaurants 6 am-11 pm. Rm serv 24 hrs. Bars 11-2 am; dancing. Ck-out noon. Convention facilities. Business center. In-rm modem link. Concierge. Shopping arcade. Barber, beauty shop. Lighted tennis. Golf privileges. Exercise rm; instructor, weight machine, bicycles, whirlpool, steam rm, sauna. Bathrm phones; some refrigerators. Private patios. Luxury level. Cr cds: A, C, D, DS, MC, V.

★★ **HARVEY.** *400 N Olive (75201), in Skyway Tower, downtown.* 214/922-8000; FAX 214/969-7650. 502 rms, 29 story. S $79-$165; D $94-$180; each addl $15; suites $240-$600; under 18 free; honeymoon, wknd rates. Valet parking $10 Mon-Thurs. Pet accepted; $125 fee, $100 refundable. TV; cable, VCR avail. Restaurant 6:30 am-11 pm. Bar 11-2 am. Ck-out 1 pm. Convention facilities. Business center. Concierge. Shopping arcade. Exercise equipt; weights, bicycles. Health club privileges. Some bathrm phones. Luxury level. Cr cds: A, C, D, DS, ER, MC, V.

★★ **HARVEY HOTEL-BROOKHOLLOW.** *7050 N Stemmons Frwy (75247), near Market Center, north of downtown.* 214/630-8500; FAX 214/630-9486. 356 rms, 21 story. S $99-$119; D $109-$129; each addl $10; under 18 free; wknd rates. Crib free. TV; cable (premium), VCR avail. Indoor pool. Restaurant 6 am-2 pm, 5-11 pm. Bar 2 pm-midnight, Sat & Sun to 2 am. Ck-out 1 pm. Coin lndry. Convention facilities. Business servs avail. In-rm modem link. Gift shop. Love Field airport transportation. Exercise equipt; weight machines, bicycles, whirlpool, sauna. Luxury level. Cr cds: A, C, D, DS, MC, V.

★★ **HILTON DALLAS PARKWAY.** *4801 LBJ Frwy (75244), jct Dallas N Tollway, north of downtown.* 214/661-3600; FAX 214/385-3156. 310 rms, 15 story. S $99-$150; D $109-$160; each addl $10; suites $250-$375; under 18 free; wknd, special rates. Crib free. TV; cable (premium). Indoor/outdoor pool, whirlpool, sauna. Restaurant 6:30 am-10 pm. Bar 11 am-midnight. Ck-out 1 pm. Convention facilities. Business center. In-rm modem link. Gift shop. Exercise equipt: treadmill, weight machine. Cr cds: A, C, D, DS, ER, MC, V.

★★★ **HOLIDAY INN SELECT.** *2645 LBJ Frwy (75234), north of downtown.* 214/243-3363; FAX 214/243-6682. 375 rms, 6 story. S, D $129; each addl $10; suites $149-$600; under 18 free; wknd, honeymoon rates. Crib free. TV; cable (premium), VCR avail. Indoor/outdoor pool; poolside serv. Coffee in rms. Restaurants 6:30 am-midnight. Rm serv 7 am-midnight. Bar 11-1 am; Fri, Sat to 2 am; entertainment, dancing. Ck-out 1 pm. Convention facilities. Business servs avail. In-rm modem link. Gift shop. Exercise equipt; weight machine, bicycle, whirlpool. Some refrigerators. Some balconies. Cr cds: A, C, D, DS, ER, JCB, MC, V.

★★★ **HOLIDAY INN-ARISTOCRAT.** *1933 Main St (75201), at Harwood, downtown.* 214/741-7700; res: 800/231-4235; FAX 214/939-

3639. 172 rms, 15 story. S $109-$160; D $119-$160; under 12 free; wknd rates. Crib $10. TV; cable (premium), VCR avail. Complimentary coffee in lobby. Restaurant 6:30 am-10:30 pm. Bar 11-1 am. Ck-out noon. Meeting rms. Business servs avail. In-rm modem link. Concierge. Free business district transportation. Exercise equipt; weights, bicycles. Health club privileges. Bathrm phones, refrigerators, minibars. Historic landmark, built in 1925 by Conrad Hilton and the first to bear his name; restored to its original Sullivanesque style. Cr cds: A, C, D, DS, ER, JCB, MC, V.

★★★ **HYATT REGENCY.** *300 Reunion Blvd (75207), downtown.* 214/651-1234; FAX 214/742-8126. 943 rms, 28 story. S $175; D $200; each addl $25; suites $300-$1,200; under 18 free; wkend rates. Valet parking $12. TV; cable (premium), VCR avail. Pool; poolside serv. Restaurant 6 am-midnight. Bar noon-1:30 am; dancing. Ck-out noon. Convention facilities. Business center. In-rm modem link. Gift shop. Free airport transportation. Lighted tennis. Golf privileges 12 mi, greens fee $50. Exercise equipt; weights, bicycles, whirlpool, sauna. Minibars; some refrigerators. Luxury level. Cr cds: A, C, D, DS, ER, JCB, MC, V.

★★★★ **MANSION ON TURTLE CREEK.** *2821 Turtle Creek Blvd (75219), north of downtown.* 214/559-2100; res: 800/527-5432 (exc TX), 800/442-3408 (TX); FAX 214/528-4187. This well-known hotel was converted from the 1926 home of a cotton baron. It retains an atmosphere of privilege and calm, thanks to a turret-shaped white-marble lobby with European antiques and a glass-domed roof, and deep-carpeted guest rooms with French windows. 140 rms, 9 story, 5 kits. S $280-$360; D $310-$380; each addl $40; suites, kit. units $495-$1,350; wkend packages. Crib free. Valet parking $10. TV; cable (premium), VCR avail. Heated pool; poolside serv. Restaurant 7 am-10:30 pm (also see RESTAURANT AT THE MANSION ON TURTLE CREEK). Rm serv 24 hrs. Bar 11-2 am; entertainment. Ck-out 2 pm. Meeting rms. Business center. In-rm modem link. Concierge. Beauty salon. Airport, downtown transportation. Lighted tennis privileges. Golf privileges. Health club. Bathrm phones; wet bar in suites. Private patios, balconies. Cr cds: A, C, D, DS, ER, JCB, MC, V.

★★★ **MARRIOTT HOTEL QUORUM.** *14901 Dallas Pkwy (75240), north of downtown.* 214/661-2800; FAX 214/934-1731. 548 rms, 12 story. S, D $129-$149; suites $250-$450; under 12 free; honeymoon, wkend rates. Crib free. Pet accepted. Free covered parking. TV; cable (premium), VCR avail. Heated indoor/outdoor pool; poolside serv. Restaurants 6:30 am-midnight. Bar 11-2 am; dancing exc Sun. Ck-out 1 pm. Lndry serv. Convention facilities. Business center. In-rm modem link. Concierge. Gift shop. Tennis. Golf privileges. Exercise equipt; weights, bicycles, whirlpool, sauna. Health club privileges. Luxury level. Cr cds: A, C, D, DS, ER, JCB, MC, V.

★★★ **MEDALLION.** *4099 Valley View Lane (75244), I-635 Midway Rd exit, north of downtown.* 214/385-9000; FAX 214/788-1174. 289 rms, 10 story. S $119-$149; D $129-$159; each addl $10; suites $350-$850; under 18 free; wknd, hol rates. Crib free. TV; cable (premium); VCR avail. Heated pool. Restaurant 6:30 am-10 pm. Bar 4 pm-1 am. Ck-out noon. Meeting rms. Business servs avail. In-rm modem link. Concierge. Tennis privileges. 18-hole golf privileges. Exercise equipt; weight machine, stair machine, bicycle. Health club privileges. Cr cds: A, C, D, DS, MC, V.

★★★ **MELROSE.** *3015 Oak Lawn Ave (75219), in Oak Lawn.* 214/521-5151; res: 800/MEL-ROSE; FAX 214/521-2470. 184 rms, 8 story. S $135-$155; D $140-$160; each addl $10; suites $250-$400; wkend rates; honeymoon packages. Crib free. TV; cable (premium), VCR avail. Pool privileges. Restaurant (see THE LANDMARK). Rm serv 6 am-midnight. Bar 11-2 am; entertainment. Ck-out noon. Meeting rms. Business servs avail. In-rm modem link. Concierge. Gift shop. Valet parking. Free Love Field airport transportation. Health club privileges.

Some refrigerators. Beautifully restored 1924 hotel; library. Luxury level. Cr cds: A, C, D, DS, JCB, MC, V.

⬚ ⬚ ⬚ SC

★ ★ ★ **OMNI MANDALAY AT LAS COLINAS.** *(221 E Las Colinas Blvd, Irving 75039) W on I-35E to TX 114, O'Connor exit, right to Las Colinas Blvd.* 214/556-0800; FAX 214/556-0729. Located on five elaborately landscaped acres, this luxury property is conveniently located on the Mandalay Canal as well as Lake Carolyn. An extensive art collection gives the public areas a special touch. 410 rms, 28 story. S, D $160-$170; each addl $10; suites $180-$1,300; under 18 free; wkend, honeymoon rates. Crib free. Valet parking $5 overnight. TV; cable, VCR avail. Heated pool; whirlpool, poolside serv (seasonal). Supervised child's activities (Memorial Day-Labor Day). Restaurant (see ENJOLIE). Rm serv 24 hrs. Bar 11:30-1:30 am. Ck-out noon. Convention facilities. Business center. In-rm modem link. Concierge. Gift shop. Free airport transportation. Golf privileges. Exercise rm; instructor, weights, bicycles, sauna. Masseur. Bathrm phones. Some private patios, balconies. On lake; lakeside restaurant. Cr cds: A, C, D, DS, ER, JCB, MC, V.

⬚ ⬚ ⬚ ⬚ ⬚ ⬚ SC ⬚

✔ ★ **QUALITY HOTEL-MARKET CENTER.** *2015 N Market Center Blvd (75207), north of downtown.* 214/741-7481; FAX 214/747-6191. 250 rms, 11 story. S $60-$95; D $70-$105; each addl $10; suites, kit. unit $135-$200; under 18 free. Crib free. TV; cable (premium). Pool. Restaurant 6:30-10 am, 5-10 pm. Ck-out noon. Coin lndry. Meeting rms. Business center. In-rm modem link. Exercise equipt; weights, bicycles. Private patios, balconies. Cr cds: A, C, D, DS, ER, JCB, MC, V.

⬚ ⬚ ⬚ ⬚ ⬚ SC ⬚

★ ★ **RADISSON CENTRAL.** *6060 N Central Expy (75206), US 75 at Mockingbird Blvd exit, north of downtown.* 214/750-6060; FAX 214/750-5959. 288 rms, 9 story. S, D $89-$119; each addl $10; suites $140-$400; under 18 free; wkend rates. Crib free. TV; cable (premium), VCR avail. Indoor/outdoor pool; whirlpool, sauna, poolside serv. Restaurant 6:30 am-2 pm, 5-10 pm. Bar noon-1 am. Ck-out noon. Meeting rms. Business servs avail. Gift shop. Free Love Field airport transportation avail. Some refrigerators. Cr cds: A, C, D, DS, ER, MC, V.

⬚ ⬚ ⬚ ⬚ ⬚ SC

★ ★ **RADISSON STEMMONS.** *2330 W Northwest Hwy (75220), north of downtown.* 214/351-4477; FAX 214/351-4499. 198 rms, 8 story. S $109-$139; D $119-$149; each addl $10; suites $129-$139; under 18 free; wkly, wkend, hol rates. Crib free. Pet accepted, some restrictions; $50 refundable. TV; cable (premium), VCR avail. Pool; poolside serv. Restaurant 6:30 am-10 pm. Bar. Ck-out noon. Coin lndry. Meeting rms. Business servs avail. In-rm modem link. Concierge. Gift shop. Free Love Field transportation. Exercise equipt; weight machine, treadmill, whirlpool. Balconies. Cr cds: A, C, D, DS, ER, JCB, MC, V.

⬚ ⬚ ⬚ ⬚ ⬚ ⬚ SC

✔ ★ **RAMADA.** *1011 S Akard (75215), downtown.* 214/421-1083; FAX 214/428-6827. 238 rms, 12 story. S $55-$125; D $65-$135; each addl $10; suites $350-$450; under 18 free; wkend rates. Crib free. Pet accepted. TV; cable (premium); VCR avail. Indoor pool. Restaurant 6 am-2 pm, 5-10 pm. Bar 3 pm-1 am. Ck-out noon. Meeting rms. Business center. In-rm modem link. Free garage parking. Love Field airport, downtown transportation. Exercise equipt; weights, bicycles, whirlpool. Balconies. Cr cds: A, C, D, DS, ER, JCB, MC, V.

⬚ ⬚ ⬚ ⬚ ⬚ ⬚ SC ⬚

✔ ★ **RAMADA-MARKET CENTER.** *1055 Regal Row (75247), north of downtown.* 214/634-8550; FAX 214/634-8418. 360 units, 12 story. S $79-$99; D $79-$99; each addl $10; suites $125-$350; under 19 free. Pet accepted, some restrictions; $25 refundable. TV; cable, VCR avail (movies avail $4.95). Pool; poolside serv. Restaurant 6:30 am-2 pm, 5-10 pm. Bar 4 pm-11 pm. Ck-out noon. Convention facilities. Business servs avail. Gift shop. Free covered parking. Free airport

transportation. Game rm. Tennis. Some refrigerators. Cr cds: A, C, D, DS, JCB, MC, V.

⬚ ⬚ ⬚ ⬚ ⬚ ⬚ SC

★ ★ **SHERATON PARK CENTRAL.** *12720 Merit Dr (75251), I-635 N at Coit Rd, north of downtown.* 214/385-3000; FAX 214/991-4557. 545 rms, 20 story. S $165; D $185; each addl $10; under 18 free; wkend rates. Crib free. Pet accepted, some restrictions. Valet parking $5. TV; cable (premium), VCR avail. Pool; poolside serv. Restaurant 6 am-11 pm. Rm serv 24 hrs. Private club. Ck-out 1 pm. Convention facilities. Business center. In-rm modem link. Gift shop. Concierge. Exercise equipt; weight machine, bicycles. Bathrm phones. Luxury level. Cr cds: A, C, D, DS, ER, JCB, MC, V.

⬚ ⬚ ⬚ ⬚ ⬚ ⬚ SC ⬚

★ ★ **SHERATON SUITES-MARKET CENTER.** *2101 Stemmons Frwy (75207), northwest of downtown.* 214/747-3000; FAX 214/742-5713. 253 suites, 11 story. S $175; D $190; each addl $10; under 18 free; wkend rates. TV; cable (premium). Indoor/outdoor pool; poolside serv. Complimentary coffee in rms. Complimentary bkfst buffet. Restaurant 6 am-11 pm. Bar 11-1 am. Ck-out noon. Guest lndry. Business servs avail. In-rm modem link. Sundries. Exercise equipt; weight machine, treadmill, whirlpool. Refrigerators, wet bars. Some balconies. Cr cds: A, C, D, DS, ER, JCB, MC, V.

⬚ ⬚ ⬚ ⬚ ⬚ SC

★ ★ **STONELEIGH.** *2927 Maple Ave (75201), north of downtown.* 214/871-7111; res: 800/255-9299; FAX 214/871-9379. 153 units, 11 story, 12 kits. S $140-$175; D $150-$185; each addl $15; suites $200-$450; kit. units from $160; family, wkend rates. Crib free. TV; cable (premium), VCR avail. Pool. Playground. Restaurant 6:30 am-10 pm. Bar 11-1 am. Ck-out noon. Business servs avail. In-rm modem link. Concierge. Valet parking. Free Love Field airport transportation. Health club privileges. Refrigerator in some suites. Restored 1924 hotel. Cr cds: A, C, D, DS, MC, V.

⬚ ⬚ ⬚ ⬚ SC

★ ★ **STOUFFER RENAISSANCE.** *2222 Stemmons Frwy (I-35E) (75207), near Market Center, north of downtown.* 214/631-2222; FAX 214/905-3814. 540 rms, 30 story. S $159-$179; D $179-$199; each addl $20; suites $199-$1,000; under 18 free; wkend rates. Crib free. Pet accepted, some restrictions. TV; cable (premium), VCR avail. Heated pool. Complimentary coffee. Restaurant 6:30 am-10 pm. Bar 3 pm-2 am; entertainment. Ck-out 1 pm. Convention facilities. Business center. In-rm modem link. Gift shop. Love Field airport transportation. Exercise equipt; weights, bicycles, whirlpool, steam rm, sauna. Some refrigerators. Three-story chandelier; art objects. Luxury level. Cr cds: A, C, D, DS, ER, JCB, MC, V.

⬚ ⬚ ⬚ ⬚ ⬚ ⬚ SC ⬚

★ ★ ★ **THE WESTIN.** *13340 Dallas Pkwy (75240), north of downtown.* 214/934-9494; FAX 214/851-2869. 431 rms, 21 story. S $119-$177; D $182-$192; each addl $20; suites $350-$1,250; under 18 free; wkend rates. Crib free. TV; cable (premium), VCR avail. Heated pool; poolside serv. Supervised child's activities. Restaurants 6:30 am-10 pm. Rm serv 24 hrs. Bar 11-2 am. Ck-out 1 pm. Convention facilities. Business center. Concierge. Shopping arcade. Barber, beauty shop. Garage parking, valet $10. Free airport transportation. Health club privileges. Refrigerators. Balconies. Adj Galleria Mall complex. Luxury level. Cr cds: A, C, D, DS, ER, JCB, MC, V.

⬚ ⬚ ⬚ ⬚ ⬚ ⬚ SC ⬚

★ ★ ★ **WYNDHAM ANATOLE HOTEL.** *2201 Stemmons Frwy (75207), opp Dallas Market Center, north of downtown.* 214/748-1200; FAX 214/761-7520. 1,620 rms, 27 story. S $149-$215; D $175-$240; each addl $15; suites $275-$1,000; under 18 free; wkend, honeymoon packages. TV; cable (premium), VCR avail. 3 pools, 2 indoor; poolside serv. Restaurants open 24 hrs. Bar 11-2 am; entertainment, dancing. Ck-out noon. Convention facilities. Business center. Concierge. Shopping arcade. Barber, beauty shop. Garage parking; valet. Lighted tennis. Exercise rm; instructor, weights, bicycles, whirlpool, steam rm, sauna. Bathrm phones, refrigerators, minibars. Luxury level. Cr cds: A, C, D, DS, JCB, MC, V.

D 🏃 🏊 🏋 🏃 🏄 🏂 🔥 SC 🏃

Inn

★ ★ ★ **HOTEL ST GERMAIN.** *2516 Maple Ave (75201), Oak Lawn.* 214/871-2516; res: 800/638-2516; FAX 214/871-0740. Combining Old World character with modern amenities, this restored 1906 Victorian house features elegant French antiques and wood-burning fireplaces. The dining room opens onto a New Orleans-style walled courtyard. 7 suites, 3 story. EP: S, D $200-$600; wkly rates. TV; cable (premium), VCR (movies avail). Complimentary refreshments. Dining rm: bkfst hrs flexible for inn guests; dinner res required; public by res (wkends only, dinner). Rm serv 24 hrs. Ck-out noon, ck-in 4 pm. Business servs avail. Bellhops. Valet serv. Concierge. Wraparound balcony; library/sitting rm. Cr cds: A, C, MC, V.

D 🏂 🔥

Restaurants

★ ★ **ADELMO'S.** *4537 Cole Ave (75205), north of downtown.* 214/559-0325. Hrs: 11:30 am-2 pm, 6-10:30 pm; Sat from 6 pm. Closed Sun; major hols. Res accepted. Mediterranean menu. Bar. Semi-a la carte: lunch $8.50-$14.50, dinner $12-$29. Specializes in Mediterranean dishes. Parking. Cr cds: A, C, D, DS, MC, V.

🏂

★ ★ **ALESSIO'S.** *4117 Lomo Alto (75219), north of downtown.* 214/521-3585. Hrs: 11:30 am-2 pm, 6-10 pm. Closed some major hols. Res accepted. Italian menu. Bar. Semi-a la carte: lunch $9-$15, dinner $16-$28. Specialties: jumbo scallops Madagascar, fettuccine Genovese, scaloppine al Marsala. Pianist Fri & Sat. Valet parking. Wood paneling. Original paintings. Jacket. Cr cds: A, D, MC, V.

D 🏂

★ ★ **ARTHUR'S.** *1000 Campbell Center (75206), 8350 Central Expy, north of downtown.* 214/361-8833. Hrs: 11:30 am-2:30 pm, 6-10:30 pm; Fri, Sat 6-11 pm. Closed Sun; major hols. Res accepted. Bar to 2 am; Sat from 6 pm. Semi-a la carte: lunch $7.25-$12, dinner $10-$20. Specializes in veal, steak, seafood. Entertainment. Valet parking. Cr cds: A, C, D, DS, MC, V.

D 🏂

✔ ★ ★ **ATHENEE CAFE.** *5365 Spring Valley #150 (75240), north of downtown.* 214/239-8060. Hrs: 11 am-2 pm, 5:30-11 pm; Sat from 5:30 pm. Closed Sun; Thanksgiving, Dec 25. Res accepted; required Fri, Sat. European menu. Bar. A la carte entrees: lunch $5.95-$8.95, dinner $11.95-$14.95. Specialties: stuffed cabbage, eggplant moussaka, gypsy sausage, chicken dolma. Library paneling. Fountain. Cr cds: A, D, DS, MC, V.

D 🏂

✔ ★ ★ ★ **CAFE ON THE GREEN.** *(See Four Seasons Resort & Club Hotel)* 214/717-0700. Hrs: 6:30 am-11 pm; Sat & Sun from 7 am; Sun brunch 11 am-2 pm. Res accepted. Bar. Wine cellar. A la carte entrees: bkfst $5.75-$12, lunch $8-$12.75, dinner $15-$24. Buffet: bkfst $12.50, lunch $18.50, dinner $24. Sun brunch $24.50. Serv charge 16%. Specialties: rack of lamb with rosemary vegetable risotto, sirloin of Black Angus with tobacco onions, mushroom crusted Pacific sea bass. Own baking. Valet parking. Garden-like setting; overlooks villas & pool. Cr cds: A, C, D, ER, JCB, MC, V.

D 🏂

★ ★ ★ **CAFE PACIFIC.** *24 Highland Park Village (75205), at Mockingbird & Preston Rd, north of downtown.* 214/526-1170. Hrs: 11:30 am-2 pm, 6-10 pm; Fri to 11 pm; Sat 11:30 am-2:30 pm, 5:30-11 pm. Closed Sun; some major hols. Res accepted. Bar 11 am-midnight. Wine cellar. A la carte entrees: lunch $6.90-$11.90, dinner $10.90-

$23.50. Specializes in seafood. Own baking. Valet parking. Outdoor terrace dining. View of kitchen behind glass. Cr cds: A, C, D, DS, MC, V.

🏂

★ ★ ★ **CALLUAD'S.** *5405 W Lovers Lane (75209), north of downtown.* 214/352-1997. Hrs: 11 am-2 pm, 6-11 pm; Sat from 6 pm. Closed Sun; some major hols. Res accepted Fri & Sat. French menu. Bar. Wine list. A la carte entrees: lunch $8-$14, dinner $16-$28. Specializes in sweetbreads, rack of lamb, Dover sole. Valet parking. Antique furnishings, original art and several tapestries add a touch of elegance to this local favorite. Family-owned. Totally nonsmoking. Cr cds: A, C, D, DS, MC, V.

D

★ ★ **CAPRICCIO.** *3005 Routh at Cedar Springs (75201), north of downtown.* 214/871-2004. Hrs: 11 am-3 pm, 5-10 pm; Sat 5 pm-midnight; Sun 5-11 pm. Closed Jan 1, Dec 25. Res accepted. Northern Italian menu. Bar. A la carte: lunch $8.75-$14, dinner $10.75-$24. Specialties: salmon Basil, duck à l'orange, veal chop Milanese, fettucine pescatore. Valet parking. Outdoor dining. Cr cds: A, C, D, DS, ER, JCB, MC, V.

D 🏂

✔ ★ **CELEBRATION.** *4503 W Lovers Lane (75209), north of downtown.* 214/351-5681. Hrs: 11 am-2:30 pm, 5-10 pm; Fri, Sat to 10:30 pm; Sun 11 am-10 pm. Closed Thanksgiving, Dec 24-25. Bar. Semi-a la carte: lunch $4-$9, dinner $5.95-$13. Child's meals. Specializes in fresh vegetables, fish, pot roast. Own breads and desserts. Parking. Rustic decor; copper tables. Cr cds: A, C, D, DS, MC, V.

D SC 🏂

★ ★ **CHAPLIN'S.** *1928 Greenville Ave, north of downtown.* 214/823-3300. Hrs: 6-11 pm. Closed Jan 1, Thanksgiving, Dec 25. Res required wkends. American menu with Northern Italian influence. Bar. A la carte entrees: dinner $12-$20. Child's meals. Specializes in seafood, steak, pasta. Valet parking. Cr cds: A, C, D, DS, MC, V.

D 🏂

★ ★ **CHEZ GERARD.** *4444 McKinney Ave (75205), north of downtown.* 214/522-6865. Hrs: 11:30 am-2:30 pm, 6-10:30 pm; Sat from 6 pm. Closed Sun; major hols. Res accepted. French menu. Bar. A la carte entrees: lunch $6.50-$9.50, dinner $13.50-$16.50. Specializes in fish, rack of lamb. Parking. Outdoor dining. Cr cds: A, C, D, DS, MC, V.

🏂

★ ★ ★ **DAKOTA'S.** *600 N Akard St (75201), downtown.* 214/740-4001. Hrs: 11 am-2:30 pm, 5-10 pm; Fri, Sat to 10:30 pm; Sun 5:30-9 pm. Closed some major hols. Res accepted. A la carte entrees: lunch $6.50-$12, dinner $9.95-$19.95. Specializes in fresh seafood, steaks. Own breads, pasta. Pianist Fri, Sat. Valet parking. Patio dining. Ceiling fans; unusual 5-tiered waterfall outside. Cr cds: A, C, D, DS, MC, V.

D 🏂

★ **DEEP ELLUM CAFE.** *2706 Elm St (75226), in Deep Ellum.* 214/741-9012. Hrs: 11 am-10 pm; Thurs to 11 pm; Fri, Sat to midnight; Sun brunch to 2:30 pm. Closed Thanksgiving, Dec 25. Res accepted. Bar. Semi-a la carte: lunch, dinner $6.25-$14.95. Sun brunch $5.95-$10.95. Specialties: Vietnamese grilled chicken salad, southern fried steak, vegetarian entrees. Outdoor dining. Renovated bldg from the 30s; eclectic decor. Cr cds: A, C, D, DS, MC, V.

D 🏂

★ ★ ★ **DEL FRISCO'S.** *5251 Spring Valley Rd (75240), north of downtown.* 214/490-9000. Hrs: 5-10 pm; Fri & Sat to 11 pm. Closed Sun; Thanksgiving, Dec 25. Res accepted. Bar. Wine list. A la carte entrees: dinner $15.50-$29. Specializes in steak & lobster. Valet parking. 2-story steakhouse. Native American, Western artwork. Cr cds: A, C, D, DS, MC, V.

[D] [⌐]

★ ★ ★ **THE ENCLAVE.** *8325 Walnut Hill (75231), north of downtown.* 214/363-7487. Hrs: 11 am-2:30 pm, 5:30-11 pm; Sat from 5:30 pm. Closed Sun; major hols. Res accepted. Continental menu. Bar to 2 am. Semi-a la carte: lunch $7.25-$14, dinner $14-$26. Specializes in French cuisine, veal, seafood. Pianist. Valet parking. Elegant dinner club atmosphere. Family-owned. Cr cds: A, C, D, MC, V.

[D] [⌐]

★ ★ ★ **ENJOLIE.** *(See Omni Mandalay At Las Colinas Hotel)* 214/556-0800. Hrs: 6:30-10 pm. Closed Sun, Mon. Res accepted. Bar. Wine list. Semi-a la carte: dinner $19-$28. Prix fixe: dinner $45. Child's meals. Specializes in grilled fish, roast game. Own baking, smoked meats and seafood. Valet parking. Outstanding view of grounds. Cr cds: A, C, D, DS, ER, JCB, MC, V.

[D] [SC] [⌐]

★ ★ ★ **FRENCH ROOM.** *(See The Adolphus Hotel)* 214/742-8200. Exceptionally detailed presentations—such as veal that arrives looking like a declicately wrought hummingbird—match the ornate Louis XIV style and service of this gorgeous restaurant. Hrs: 6-10:30 pm. Closed Sun. Res accepted. Neo-classic cuisine. Bar 4 pm-1:30 am. Wine list. A la carte entrees: dinner $22-$52. Specialties: Dover sole, foie gras, roast rack of lamb, sautéed Norwegian salmon. Menu changes with season. Valet parking. Jacket. Cr cds: A, C, D, DS, ER, MC, V.

[D] [⌐]

✔ ★ **J PEPE'S.** *2800 Routh St (75201), north of downtown.* 214/871-0366. Hrs: 11 am-10 pm; Thur-Sat to 11 pm. Closed Thanksgiving, Dec 25. Res accepted. Mexican menu. Bar. Semi-a la carte: lunch $5.25-$10.95, dinner $6.25-$10.95. Child's meals. Specializes in fajitas, Margarita shrimp, chicken Mazatlan. Valet parking. Outdoor dining. Cantina decor. Cr cds: A, C, D, DS, MC, V.

[⌐]

★ ★ **JAVIER'S.** *4912 Còle Ave, north of downtown.* 214/521-4211. Hrs: 5:30-10:30 pm; Fri, Sat to 11 pm; Sun to 10 pm. Closed major hols. Res accepted. Continental, Mexican menu. Bar. Semi-a la carte: dinner $12.85-$18.95. Specialties: filete Cantinflas, red snapper mojo de ajo. Complimentary valet parking. Eclectic decor; antiques from Mexico. Cr cds: A, C, D, DS, MC, V.

[D] [⌐]

★ ★ **JENNIVINE.** *3605 McKinney Ave (75204), north of downtown.* 214/528-6010. Hrs: 11:30 am-10 pm. Closed Sun; most major hols. Res accepted. Bar. A la carte entrees: lunch $7-$8, dinner $12-$19. Specializes in rack of lamb, beef tenderloin, duck, fresh fish. Parking. Outdoor dining. British pub atmosphere. Cr cds: A, C, D, DS, MC, V.

[D]

★ ★ ★ **JUNIPER.** *2917 Fairmount St (75201), north of downtown.* 214/855-0700. Hrs: 6-10:30 pm; Thurs-Sat to 11 pm. Closed Sun & Mon; some major hols. Res accepted. French Provençale menu. Bar. A la carte entrees: dinner $14-$24. Specialties: fish soup, crab cakes, rack of lamb. Own desserts. Valet parking. Outdoor dining. French Provincial decor in converted house. Cr cds: A, C, D, DS, MC, V.

[D] [⌐]

★ ★ **L'ANCESTRAL.** *4514 Travis #124 (75205), north of downtown.* 214/528-1081. Hrs: 11:30 am-2 pm, 6-10 pm; Fri, Sat to 11 pm. Closed Sun; some major hols. Res accepted. Country French menu. Bar. A la carte entrees: lunch $6.50-$13.50, dinner $12.50-$19.50. Complete meals: dinner $22.50. Specializes in pepper steak, lamb tenderloin, grilled salmon. Outdoor dining. Cr cds: A, C, D, DS, MC, V.

[D] [⌐]

★ ★ ★ **LA TRATTORIA LOMBARDI.** *2916 N Hall St (75204), north of downtown.* 214/954-0803. Hrs: 11 am-2 pm, 5:30-10:30 pm; Fri & Sat to 11 pm. Closed some major hols. Res accepted. Italian menu. Bar. Wine cellar. A la carte entrees: lunch $6-$12.50, dinner $10-$21. Child's meals. Specializes in pasta, seafood, veal. Valet parking. Outdoor dining. Mediterranean decor. Cr cds: A, C, D, MC, V.

[D] [SC] [⌐]

★ ★ ★ **THE LANDMARK.** *(See Melrose Hotel)* 214/521-5151. Hrs: 6 am-2 pm, 5:30-10 pm; Sat 6 am-noon, 6-11 pm; Sun 6 am-2 pm, brunch from 11 am. Res accepted; required Fri, Sat eve. Bar. Wine cellar. Semi-a la carte: bkfst $8-$12, lunch $9-15, dinner $17-$35. Sun brunch $24.95. Valet parking. Specialties: bkfst entrees, pasta-crusted salmon, grilled veal medallions. Attractive decor in same 20s style as hotel. Cr cds: A, C, D, DS, JCB, MC, V.

[D]

★ ★ ★ **LE CHARDONNAY.** *500 Crescent Court, suite 165 (75201), north of downtown.* 214/922-4555. Hrs: 11 am-10 pm; Fri & Sat to 11 pm. Closed Sun; Jan 1, July 4, Dec 25. Res accepted. French menu. Bar. Wine cellar. Semi-a la carte: lunch $6-$11, dinner $11-$20. Specialties: la tarte a l'oignons aux pommes, les cotes d'agneau Montrachet. Valet parking. Parisian atmosphere, objets d'art. Cr cds: A, C, D, DS, MC, V.

[D]

✔ ★ **LOMBARDI'S.** *311 N Market (75202), downtown.* 214/747-0322. Hrs: 11 am-11 pm; Fri to midnight; Sat 5 pm-midnight; Sun 5-10 pm. Italian menu. Bar. A la carte entrees: lunch, dinner $4.95-$21. Specializes in pasta, pizza. Outdoor dining. Valet parking. Cr cds: A, C, D, MC, V.

[D] [⌐]

✔ ★ ★ **MARIO'S CHIQUITA.** *4514 Travis #105 (75205), north of downtown.* 214/521-0721. Hrs: 11:30 am-9 pm; Fri, Sat to 10 pm. Closed Jan 1, Thanksgiving, Dec 25. Mexican menu. Bar. Semi-a la carte: lunch, dinner $3.95-$9.95. Child's meals. Specialties: carne asada, chile rellenos, chicken a la parrilla. Colorful Mexican decor. Cr cds: A, D, DS, MC, V.

[D] [⌐]

★ **MOMO'S PASTA.** *2704 Elm St (75226), in Deep Ellum.* 214/748-4222. Hrs: 11 am-2 pm, 5-10:30 pm; Fri to 11:30 pm; Sat 5-11:30 pm; Sun 5-10 pm. Closed some major hols. Res accepted; required Fri, Sat. Italian menu. Bar. A la carte entrees: lunch $5.95-$7.50, dinner $8.95-$15.95. Specialties: capelli d'angelo alla Momo, conchiglie a modo mio. Totally nonsmoking. Cr cds: A, C, D, DS, MC, V.

[D]

★ ★ ★ **MORTON'S OF CHICAGO.** *501 Elm St (75202), in West End Historic District.* 214/741-2277. Hrs: 5:30-11 pm; Sun 5-10 pm. Closed major hols. Res accepted. Bar. A la carte entrees: dinner $18.50-$29.95. Specializes in steak, seafood, lamb. Valet parking. Open grill; meat displayed at table for patrons to select. Cr cds: A, D, DS, JCB, MC, V.

[D] [⌐]

★ ★ **NEWPORT'S SEAFOOD.** *703 McKinney Ave (75202), in the Brewery, in West End Historic District.* 214/954-0220. Hrs: 11:30 am-2:30 pm, 5:30-10:30 pm; Fri to 11 pm; Sat 5:30-11 pm; Sun 5:30-10 pm. Closed major hols. Bar. A la carte entrees: lunch $7.95-$10.50, dinner $12.95-$16.95. Specializes in mesquite-grilled seafood, steak, chicken. Extensive seafood selection. Parking. Tri-level dining in turn-of-the-century brewery; 50-ft-deep freshwater well in dining area. Cr cds: A, C, D, DS, MC, V.

[D] [⌐]

★ ★ ★ **OLD WARSAW.** *2610 Maple Ave (75201), in Oak Lawn.* 214/528-0032. Hrs: 5:30-10:30 pm. Res required. French, continental menu. Bar. Wine cellar. A la carte entrees: dinner $21-$28. Specializes in lobster Thermidor, salmon tartare, steak au poivre. Own baking. Violinist, pianist. Valet parking. Lobster tank. Family-owned. Jacket. Cr cds: A, C, D, DS, MC, V.

✔ ★ ★ **PATRIZIO.** *25 Highland Park Village (75205), north of downtown.* 214/522-7878. Hrs: 11:30 am-11 pm; Sun & Mon to 10 pm; Fri & Sat to midnight. Closed Jan 1, Thanksgiving, Dec 25. Italian menu. Bar 11 am-midnight. A la carte entrees: lunch $4.90-$8.10, dinner $5.75-$13.95. Specialties: angel hair pasta with basil & tomato, sautéed crab claws, chicken Parmesan salad. Valet parking. Outdoor dining. Oriental rugs, many large oil paintings. Cr cds: A, D, DS, MC, V.

★ ★ ★ **PYRAMID ROOM.** *(See Fairmont Hotel)* 214/720-5249. Hrs: 11:30 am-2 pm, 6-10:30 pm; Fri, Sat 6-10:30 pm; Sun 10:30 am-2:30 pm. Res accepted. Continental menu. Bar 11:30-1:30 am. Wine list. A la carte entrees: lunch $7.50-$14, dinner $18.50-$35. Specializes in beef, veal, seafood. Own baking. Entertainment. Valet parking. Jacket. Cr cds: A, C, D, DS, MC, V.

★ ★ ★ ★ **RESTAURANT AT THE MANSION ON TURTLE CREEK.** *(See Mansion On Turtle Creek Hotel)* 214/559-2100. Dean Fearing's exuberant cuisine is a perfect match for this famous hotel's gorgeous dining rooms, entered through a fantastical circular black-and-white marble-floored lobby. A capacious living room with an intricately carved ceiling, an oak-paneled library, and the sweeping veranda of a former cotton baron's mansion have been transformed into this nationally known restaurant. Hrs: noon-2:30 pm, 6-10:30 pm; Fri & Sat to 11 pm. Brunch: Sat noon-2:30 pm; Sun 11 am-2:30 pm. Res accepted; required Fri & Sat. Amer Southwest menu. Bar 11-2 am. Wine cellar. A la carte entrees: lunch from $15, dinner from $30. Brunch $26.50. Specialties: tortilla soup, lobster taco, crème brulée, rack of lamb. Own baking. Valet parking. Private dining areas. Jacket, tie. Cr cds: A, C, D, DS, ER, JCB, MC, V.

★ ★ ★ **RIVIERA.** *7709 Inwood Rd, north of downtown.* 214/351-0094. Hrs: 6:30-10:30 pm; Fri, Sat to 11 pm. Closed most major hols. Res accepted. Continental menu. Bar. Wine list. A la carte entrees: dinner $25-$34. Complete meals: dinner $45-$65. Specialties: escargots and tortilloni, glazed salmon, gulf shrimp pancake with scallops. Valet parking. Country French decor. Jacket. Cr cds: A, C, D, MC, V.

★ ★ **ROYAL TOKYO.** *7525 Greenville Ave (75231), 2 mi S of LBJ Frwy; 3/4 mi E of US 75, Walnut Hill exit, north of downtown.* 214/368-3304. Hrs: 11:30 am-2 pm, 5:30-11 pm; Fri to 11:30 pm; Sat noon-2:30 pm, 5:30-11:30 pm; Sun 5:30-10:30 pm; Sun brunch 11:30 am-2:30 pm. Closed Jan 1, Thanksgiving, Dec 25. Res accepted. Japanese menu. Bar. Semi-a la carte: lunch $4-$15, dinner $12.95-$25. Sun brunch $16.95. Child's meals. Hibachi chefs. Specialties: tempura, shabu-shabu, hibachi steak. Sushi bar. Piano. Parking. Traditional seating avail. Japanese motif; outdoor water gardens. Cr cds: A, C, D, DS, JCB, MC, V.

★ ★ **STAR CANYON.** *3102 Oak Lawn Ave, suite 144 (75219), in Centrum Bldg, north of downtown.* 214/520-7827. Hrs: 11 am-2 pm, 6-10:30 pm; Fri to 11 pm; Sat 6-11 pm; Sun 6-10 pm. Closed some major hols. Res accepted. Bar. Wine list. Semi-a la carte: lunch $6.50-$10.75, dinner $13.50-$21. Specialties: tamale tart with roast garlic custard and Gulf crabmeat, bone-in cowboy ribeye with red chile onion rings. Valet parking. Outdoor dining. Stylish yet unpretentious dining experience among award winning Texan decor. Cr cds: A, D, DS, MC, V.

★ ★ **UNCLE TAI'S.** *13350 Dallas Pkwy (75240), in the Galleria Shopping Plaza, north of downtown.* 214/934-9998. Hrs: 11 am-10 pm;

Fri, Sat to 10:30 pm; Sun noon-9:30 pm. Closed some major hols. Res accepted. Chinese menu. Serv bar. A la carte entrees: lunch $7-$10.50, dinner $11-$17. Specializes in beef, chicken, seafood. Valet parking. Cr cds: A, C, D, MC, V.

Unrated Dining Spots

HIGHLAND PARK CAFETERIA. *4611 Cole St, north of downtown.* 214/526-3801. Hrs: 11 am-8 pm. Closed July 4, Dec 25. Buffet: lunch, dinner $10.49. Avg ck: lunch, dinner $6. Specializes in no-sugar-added desserts. Parking. Display of Meissen china. Cr cds: A, DS, MC, V.

LUBY'S CAFETERIA. *10425 N Central Expy (10425), 8 1/2 mi N, at Meadow Rd, north of downtown.* 214/361-9024. Hrs: 10:45 am-8 pm; late spring-early fall to 8:30 pm. Closed Dec 24 eve-Dec 25. Avg ck: lunch, dinner $5.50. Specializes in prime rib, baked fish, home-made carrot cake. Parking. Cr cds: DS, MC, V.

Dallas/Fort Worth Airport Area (B-7)

(See Dallas, Fort Worth)

Services and Information

Information: 214/574-8888.

Lost and Found: 214/574-4454.

Cash Machines: Terminals 2E, 3E, 4E.

Club Lounges: Admirals Clubs (American), Terminals 2E & 3E; Crown Room (Delta), Terminal 4E; Ambassadors Club (TWA), Terminal 2W.

Terminals

Terminal 2E: American, American Eagle

Terminal 2W: America West, Continental, Lone Star, Lufthansa, Mesa, Midwest Express, Northwest, TWA, United, USAir

Terminal 3E: American

Terminal 4E: British Airways, Delta

(Airlines and their terminal locations may change. Before leaving for the airport, you should phone the airline to confirm terminal location for your flight.)

Motels

✔ ★ ★ **COUNTRY SUITES BY CARLSON.** *(4100 W John Carpenter Frwy, Irving 75063) TX 114 exit Esters Rd.* 214/929-4008; FAX 214/929-4224. 72 kit. suites, 18 kit. units, 3 story. S $59-$119; D $69-$129; each addl $6; under 16 free. Crib free. TV; cable (premium), VCR avail. Heated pool; wading pool, whirlpool. Complimentary continental bkfst. Ck-out noon. Meeting rms. Business servs avail. Coin lndry. Free airport transportation. Health club privileges. Refrigerators. Cr cds: A, C, D, DS, JCB, MC, V.

★ ★ **DRURY INN.** *(4210 W Airport Frwy, Irving 75062) TX 183 & Esters Rd.* 214/986-1200. 129 rms, 4 story. S $64; D $74; each addl $10; under 18 free. Crib free. Pet accepted; some restrictions. TV; cable (premium), VCR avail. Pool. Complimentary continental bkfst. Restaurant adj 11-2 am. Ck-out noon. Meeting rms. Business servs avail.

DALLAS/FORT WORTH INTERNATIONAL AIRPORT

TERMINAL 1W
Long Term Parking

TERMINAL 2W
TWA AMBASSADOR CLUB,
United,
US Air,
Midwest Express,
Am. West,
Northwest,
Continental,
Exec Express II,
Lone Star,
Lufthansa,
Mesa

TERMINAL 3W
General Aviation

TERMINAL 4W
Long Term Parking

Terminals
Parking Lot

TERMINAL 2E
AMERICAN ADMIRALS CLUB,
American Eagle

TERMINAL 3E
AMERICAN ADMIRALS CLUB

TERMINAL 4E
DELTA CROWN ROOM,
British Airways,
Atlantic Southeast

TERMINAL 5E
Long Term Parking

N
W E
S

In-rm modem link. Sundries. Free airport transportation. Cr cds: A, C, D, DS, MC, V.

[icons] D ⤢ ≋ ✈ ⤳ 🔥 SC

✔★★ LA QUINTA DFW-IRVING. *(4105 W Airport Frwy, Irving 75062)* TX 183 & Esters Rd. 214/252-6546; FAX 214/570-4225. 166 rms, 2 story. S $56-$66; D $69-$76; each addl $10; under 18 free. Crib free. Pet accepted. TV; cable (premium). Pool. Complimentary continental bkfst. Restaurant adj open 24 hrs. Ck-out noon. Meeting rm. Free airport transportation. Health club privileges. Cr cds: A, C, D, DS, MC, V.

[icons] D ⤢ ≋ ✈ ⤳ 🔥 SC

★★ WESTAR SUITES. *(3950 W Airport Frwy, Irving 75062)* W on TX 183 at Esters. 214/790-1950; res: 800/255-1755; FAX 214/790-4750. 126 one-rm suites, 2 story. S $68; D $72; each addl $8; under 18 free; wkly, wkend rates. Crib free. TV; cable. Pool; whirlpool. Complimentary continental bkfst 6-9 am; Sat, Sun 7-10 am. Ck-out noon. Coin lndry. Meeting rms. Business servs avail. In-rm modem link. Valet serv. Free airport transportation. Health club privileges. Refrigerators. Grills. Cr cds: A, C, D, DS, ER, MC, V.

[icons] D ≋ ✈ ⤳ 🔥 SC

Motor Hotels

★★★ HARVEY SUITES. *(4550 W John Carpenter Frwy, Irving 75063)* TX 114 off Esters Blvd exit. 214/929-4499; res: 800/922-9222; FAX 214/929-0774. 164 suites, 3 story. S $119-$134; D $124-$144; each addl $15; under 12 free; wkend rates. Crib free. Pet accepted; $25 deposit. TV; cable, VCR avail (movies avail). Pool; poolside serv. Complimentary continental bkfst. Complimentary coffee in rms. Restaurant 6:30 am-1:30 pm; Sat & Sun 7-11 am. Bar 4 pm-midnight. Ck-out 1 pm. Coin lndry. Meeting rms. Business center. In-rm modem link. Valet serv. Sundries. Gift shop. Free airport transportation. Exercise equipt; weights, bicycles, whirlpool. Refrigerators, wet bars. Picnic tables, grills. Cr cds: A, C, D, DS, MC, V.

[icons] D ⤢ ≋ ✈ ✈ ⤳ 🔥 SC 🚶

★★ HOLIDAY INN-AIRPORT NORTH. *(4441 US 114, Irving 75063)* 214/929-8181; FAX 214/929-8233. 275 rms, 8 story. S $85-$89; D$95-$99; each addl $10; suites $125-$250; under 18 free; wkend & hol rates. Crib free. TV; cable (premium). Pool; poolside serv. Restaurant 6:30 am-11 pm. Rm serv. Bar 11 am-1 am. Ck-out noon. Coin lndry. Meeting rms. Business servs avail. In-rm modem link. Gift shop. Valet serv. Free airport transportation. Exercise equipt; weight machine, bicycles. Some refrigerators. Cr cds: A, C, D, DS, ER, JCB, MC, V.

[icons] D ≋ ✈ ✈ ⤳ 🔥 SC

★★ HOLIDAY INN-DFW AIRPORT SOUTH. *(4440 W Airport Frwy, Irving 75062)* 214/399-1010; FAX 214/790-8545. 409 rms, 4 story. S $89-$119; D $99-$129; each addl $10; suites $150-$300; under 18 free; wkend rates. TV; cable (premium), VCR avail. Indoor/outdoor pool; wading pool, whirlpool, sauna. Exercise equipt: stair machine, treadmill, bicycle. Restaurant 5:30 am-midnight. Rm serv. Bar 3 pm-2 am; dancing. Ck-out noon. Coin lndry. Meeting rms. Business servs avail. In-rm modem link. Bellhops. Valet serv. Sundries. Gift shop. Free airport transportation. Exercise equipt; stair machine, treadmill, bicycle. Health club privileges. Holidome. Game rm. Rec rm. Cr cds: A, C, D, DS, ER, JCB, MC, V.

[icons] D ≋ ✈ ✈ ⤳ 🔥 SC

★ WILSON WORLD. *(4600 W Airport Frwy, Irving 75062)* 214/513-0800; FAX 214/513-0106. 200 rms, 5 story, 100 suites. S, D $79.95-$99.95; each addl $6; suites $89.95-$99.95; under 18 free; wkend rates. Crib free. Pet accepted, some restrictions. TV; cable (premium), VCR avail. Indoor pool. Coffee in rms. Restaurant 6 am-2 pm, 5:30-10 pm. Bar 4:30 pm-midnight. Ck-out noon. Meeting rms. Business servs avail. In-rm modem link. Gift shop. Free airport trans-

portation. Exercise equipt; weight machine, stair machine, whirlpool. Refrigerators. Cr cds: A, C, D, DS, MC, V.

[icons] D ⤢ ≋ ✈ ✈ ⤳ 🔥 SC

Hotels

★★★ DFW HILTON EXECUTIVE CONFERENCE CENTER. *(1800 TX 26E, Grapevine 76051)* TX 121N, Bethel Rd exit. 817/481-8444; FAX 817/481-3160. 395 rms, 9 story. S $99-$149; D $114-$164; each addl $15; suites $225-$950; family, wkend rates. Crib free. TV; cable (premium), VCR avail. 2 pools, 1 indoor; poolside serv. Restaurant 6:30 am-midnight (also see COPPERFIELD'S). Bars 11-2 am; entertainment, dancing. Ck-out noon. Convention facilities. Business center. In-rm modem link. Concierge. Gift shop. Free parking, valet avail. Free airport transportation. 6 outdoor tennis courts, 2 indoor. Golf privileges, driving range. Exercise rm; instructor, weights, bicycles, whirlpool, steam rm. Minibars; some bathrm phones, refrigerators. Wooded grounds with lake. Luxury level. Cr cds: A, C, D, DS, ER, JCB, MC, V.

[icons] D 🧖 🏋 ≋ ✈ 🚶 ✈ ⤳ 🔥 SC

★★★ DOUBLETREE GUEST SUITES. *(4650 W Airport Frwy, Irving 75062)* TX 183 & Valley View Ln. 214/790-0093; FAX 214/790-4768. 308 suites, 10 story. S, D $149; each addl $10; under 12 free; wkend rates. Crib free. TV; cable (premium), VCR avail. Indoor pool; whirlpool, sauna. Restaurant 11 am-10 pm. Bar 11-midnight, Fri & Sat to 2 am; dancing. Ck-out noon. Coin lndry. Meeting rms. Business servs avail. In-rm modem link. Gift shop. Free airport transportation. Health club privileges. Balconies. Atrium lobby with tropical plants. Cr cds: A, C, D, DS, ER, MC, V.

[icons] D ≋ ✈ ⤳ 🔥 SC

★★ HYATT REGENCY-DFW. *(PO Box 619014, DFW Airport 75261)* At airport. 214/453-1234; FAX 214/456-8668. 1,367 rms, 12 story. S $145; D $170; each addl $25; suites $275-$1,200; under 18 free; wkend, honeymoon rates. TV; cable (premium, VCR avail. Heated pool; poolside serv. Supervised child's activities; ages 2-15. Restaurant open 24 hrs. Rm serv. Bar 11-2 am; entertainment, dancing. Ck-out noon. Convention facilities. Business center. In-rm modem link. Concierge. Shopping arcade. Free Airport transportation. Indoor & outdoor tennis, pro. 36-hole golf, greens fee $50-$60, pro, putting green, driving range. Exercise rm; weights, bicycles, steam rm, sauna. Game rm. Many refrigerators; some bathrm phones. Balconies. Luxury level. Cr cds: A, C, D, DS, ER, JCB, MC, V.

[icons] D 🧖 🏋 🚶 ≋ ✈ 🚶 ✈ ⤳ 🔥 SC 🚶

★★ MARRIOTT-DFW AIRPORT. *(8440 Freeport Pkwy, Irving 75063)* TX 114 at N entrance to airport. 214/929-8800; FAX 214/929-6501. 491 rms, 20 story. S, D $135-$155; suites $175-$400; under 12 free; wkend plans. Crib free. Pet accepted, some restrictions. TV; cable (premium). Indoor/outdoor pool; poolside serv. Restaurants 6 am-11 pm. Bar 11-2 am. Ck-out 1 pm. Coin lndry. Convention facilities. Business center. In-rm modem link. Sundries. Gift shop. Free airport transportation. Tennis, golf privileges. Exercise rm; instructor, weights, bicycles, whirlpool, sauna. Some bathrm phones, refrigerators. Luxury level. Cr cds: A, C, D, DS, ER, JCB, MC, V.

[icons] D ⤢ 🧖 🏋 ≋ 🚶 ✈ ⤳ 🔥 D

Restaurants

★★★ COPPERFIELD'S. *(See DFW Hilton Executive Conference Center Hotel)* 817/481-8444. Hrs: 5:30-10 pm; Fri & Sat to 11 pm. Closed Sun; major hols. Res accepted. Southwestern menu. Bar. Wine list. A la carte entrees: dinner $15.75-$24.75. Specializes in fresh seafood, beef. Valet parking. Dark wood paneling gives this hotel dining rm an Old World club atmosphere; view of gardens. Cr cds: A, C, D, DS, MC, V.

[icons] D

★ ★ **DORRIS HOUSE CAFE.** *(224 E College St, Grapevine 76051)* 817/421-1181. Hrs: 11:30 am-2 pm, 5:30-10 pm; Sat from 5:30 pm. Closed Sun & Mon; major hols. Res accepted. New American menu. Bar. Wine list. A la carte entrees: lunch $5.95-$13.95, dinner $13.95-$24.95. Child's meals. Specialties: potato wrapped shrimp, mushroom crusted medallions of beef, pan-seared salmon. Parking. Fine dining in Victorian house filled with antiques. Cr cds: A, C, D, DS, MC, V.

 D

★ ★ **MONET'S.** *(5005 Colleyville Blvd, Colleyville 76034)* 817/498-5525. Hrs: 5:30-10 pm; Sun brunch 11 am-3 pm. Closed most major hols. Res accepted. Continental menu. Bar to midnight. Wine list. Semi-a la carte: dinner $14-$24. Sun brunch $13.95. Child's meals. Specialties: feta-crusted lamb chops, venison tenderloin with blackberry port, crayfish cakes. Pianist Fri & Sat. Parking. Outdoor dining. Elegant dining among Claude Monet prints; some menu items selected from his journals. Totally nonsmoking. Cr cds: A, D, DS, MC, V.

D

★ ★ **VIA REÁL.** *(4020 N MacArthur, Ste 100, Irving 75038)* in Las Colinas Plaza. 214/255-0064. Hrs: 11 am-10 pm; Fri, Sat to 11 pm; Sun brunch to 3 pm. Closed Jan 1, Thanksgiving, Dec 25. Res accepted. Mexican menu. Bar. Semi-a la carte: lunch $5.50-$18, dinner $8-$18. Sun brunch $8. Child's meals. Specialties: grilled chicken cilantro, skewered sea scallops, beef tenderloin. Stone fireplaces; Southwestern decor. Cr cds: A, C, D, DS, MC, V.

 D SC

Del Rio (D-4)

(See Brackettville, Eagle Pass, Uvalde)

Founded 1868 **Pop** 30,705 **Elev** 948 ft **Area code** 210 **Zip** 78840
Information Chamber of Commerce, 1915 Avenue F; 210/775-3551.

The San Felipe Springs supply water to thousands of acres, making Del Rio a green spot in the desert. This is Texas' top-ranking sheep, lamb and wool producing county. Laughlin Air Force Base, of the Air Training Command, is six miles east. Private ranches in the area offer hunting for a variety of game including whitetail deer, javelina and turkey.

What to See and Do

Amistad (Friendship) National Recreation Area. An international project. Six-mile-long, S-shaped dam, forms a lake of more than 67,000 acres extending up the Rio Grande, Devil's and Pecos rivers. Stone statue of Tlaloc, Aztec rain god, towers over Mexican end of dam; 4,000-year-old Indian pictographs in rock shelters in the area. Two marinas with boat ramps, gas, stores and full facilities. Water sports, seven other shallow launch ramps; primitive camping. (Daily) 12 mi NW on US 90. Contact Amistad National Recreation Area, PO Box 420367, 78842-0367. Phone 210/775-7491. **Free.**

Ciudad Acuña, Mexico. Across the border. Visitors often make the short trip over the river to this quaint Mexican town. Shopping, restaurants and nightlife all serve as attractions to the tourist. (For Border Crossing Regulations see INTRODUCTION)

Firehouse Gallery. The Council for the Arts maintains an art gallery; classes & workshops in arts and special interest areas. (Mon-Fri; closed most major hols) 120 E Garfield. Phone 210/775-0888. **Free.**

Judge Roy Bean Visitor Center. For years, Bean was "the law west of the Pecos." Preserved by the state of Texas, his saloon-courtroom, the "Jersey Lily," is a historic landmark. Dioramas with sound; cactus garden. Dept of Transportation visitor center. (Daily; closed Jan 1, Thanksgiving, Dec 24, 25) 60 mi NW on US 90 in Langtry. Phone 915/291-3340. **Free.**

Seminole Canyon State Historical Park. On 2,172 acres. Hiking. Picnicking. Camping. Prehistoric Native American pictograph sites.

Guided tours into canyon (Wed-Sun). 41 mi NW via US 90, W of Comstock. Phone 915/292-4464. Per vehicle ¢¢

Val Verde Winery. Texas' oldest licensed winery, founded in 1883, is operated by the third generation of the Qualia family. Tours, tasting. (Daily exc Sun; closed major hols) 100 Qualia Dr. Phone 210/775-9714. **Free.**

Whitehead Memorial Museum. Memorabilia of early Southwest; Cadena folk art; grave of Judge Roy Bean; replica of Bean's Jersey Lily Saloon, hacienda and chapel, doctor's office; cabins, store, barn. (Tues-Sat; closed hols) 1308 S Main St. Phone 210/774-7568. ¢

Annual Events

George Paul Memorial Bull-Riding. Top riders in the world compete. Late Apr-early May.

Diez y Seis de Septiembre. Brown Plaza. Concerts, food booths, music. Sept. Cinco de Mayo Celebration. May 5.

Fiesta de Amistad. Mid-late Oct.

Motels

★ ★ **BEST WESTERN.** 810 Ave F. 210/775-7511; FAX 210/774-2194. 62 rms, 2 story. S $49; D $57; each addl $8; under 4 free. Pet accepted; $4. TV; cable (premium). Pool; whirlpool. Complimentary full bkfst. Complimentary coffee in rms. Ck-out noon. Coin lndry. Business servs avail. Cr cds: A, C, D, DS, MC, V.

D ☒ ☒ ☒ SC

★ **LA QUINTA.** 2005 Ave F. 210/775-7591; FAX 210/774-0809. 101 rms, 2 story. S $54-$70; D $62-$77; under 18 free. Crib free. Pet accepted. TV; cable. Pool. Complimentary continental bkfst, coffee in lobby. Ck-out noon. Coin lndry. Cr cds: A, C, D, DS, MC, V.

D ☒ ☒ ☒ ☒ SC

★ **RAMADA INN.** 2101 Ave F. 210/775-1511. 127 rms. S $55-$63; D $60-$68; each addl $8; suites $123; under 18 free; higher rates special events. Crib free. Pet accepted; some restrictions. TV; cable (premium), VCR (movies avail). Pool; poolside serv, whirlpool. Complimentary coffee in rms. Restaurant 6 am-1 pm, 3-10 pm; Sun 6 am-3 pm. Rm serv. Bar 4 pm-2 am. Ck-out noon. Coin lndry. Valet serv. Exercise equipt; weight machine, bicycle. Some refrigerators. Cr cds: A, C, D, MC, V.

D ☒ ☒ 🖾 ☒ ☒ SC

Unrated Dining Spot

WYATT'S CAFETERIA. Plaza Del Sol, 2 mi W of US 90W, in Plaza Del Sol Shopping Plaza. 210/775-3438. Hrs: 11 am-8:30 pm. Closed Dec 25. Avg ck: lunch, dinner $6.50. Specializes in roast beef, strawberry shortcake, fried okra. Cr cds: A, DS, MC, V.

Denison (A-7)

(For accommodations see Gainesville, Sherman, also see Bonham)

Founded 1872 **Pop** 21,505 **Elev** 767 ft **Area code** 903 **Zip** 75020
Information Chamber of Commerce, 313 W Woodard St, PO Box 325; 903/465-1551.

President Dwight D. Eisenhower was born in Denison. It is an industrial and transportation center manufacturing clothing, fabricated metal, food products and drilling equipment.

What to See and Do

Denison Dam. Large earth-filled dam impounds Lake Texoma. Water sports; resorts. Camping (fees in some areas). Visitor center, power-house tours (Mon-Fri or by appt). (See LAKE TEXOMA, OK) 5 mi NW on TX 75A. Phone 903/465-4990. Tours **Free.**

Eisenhower Birthplace State Historical Park. Restored house; fur-nishings; some of Eisenhower's personal items. Interpretive center; picnicking. (Daily; closed Jan 1, Dec 25) 208 E Day St at Lamar Ave, 4 blks E of US 69/75. Phone 903/465-8908. ¢

Eisenhower State Park. Approx 450 acres. Swimming; fishing (lighted pier); boating (ramps, marina). Hiking trails. Picnicking, playground. Improved campsites, RV facilities (dump stations). Standard fees. (Daily) 5 mi NW on TX 75A, then 2 mi W on FM 1310 to Park Rd 20. Phone 903/465-1956. Per vehicle ¢¢

Grayson County Frontier Village. Town replica from 1800s; 15 origi-nal structures, museum. (May-Oct, Wed-Sun) 2 mi SW via TX 75, Loy Lake Rd exit. Phone 903/463-2487. **Free.**

Annual Events

Texoma Lakefest Regatta. Regatta, dance, lake activities. Mid-Apr.

Western Week. Rodeo, parade, square dance. Mid-July.

Denton (A-7)

(See Arlington-Grand Prairie, Dallas, Fort Worth, Gainesville)

Pop 66,270 **Elev** 662 ft **Area code** 817
Information Convention & Visitors Bureau, 414 Parkway St, PO Drawer P, 76202; 817/382-7895.

This pleasant town and county seat has diversified industry; it also serves as a farm supply and shipping point. Much scientific research is carried on at the University of North Texas and Texas Woman's Univer-sity.

What to See and Do

Denton County Historical Museum. Memorabilia & artifacts depicting Denton County history; large collections of rare antique dolls & guns; rare blue glass; Native American artifacts. (Mon-Sat afternoons; closed major hols) 1st Floor, Courthouse on the Square, 110 W Hickory. Phone 817/565-8693, -8697 or 800/346-3189. **Free.**

Lewisville Lake. This 23,000-acre lake is surrounded by 11 developed park areas. Three marinas and a fishing barge provide service to boaters and fishermen; swimming; hunting. Some fees. (Daily) 15 mi SE via I-35E. Contact Reservoir Manager, 1801 N Mill St, Lewisville 75057; 214/434-1666.

Ray Roberts Lake. Formed by the damming of the Trinity River; recreation areas around the new lake are still being developed. Isle duBois and Johnson Branch areas each offer swimming; fishing piers (cleaning stations); boating (launch, docks). Nature, hiking, bridle trails. Picnicking, playgrounds. Primitive & improved camping, tent & trailer sites. Other areas offer limited facilities. Some fees. (Daily) Approx 12 NE via US 380 & US 377. Phone 817/686-2148 or 817/334-2150. Per vehicle ¢¢

Texas Woman's University (1901). (9,400 students) Graduate school and Institute of Health Sciences are coeducational. This 270-acre cam-pus includes University Gardens; art galleries in Fine Arts Building; DAR Museum with "Gowns of First Ladies of Texas" collection in Human Development Building, 1117 Bell Ave (by appt); and the Blagg-Huey Library with "Texas Women—A Celebration of History," a self-guided tour with photos and artifacts (daily; closed hols). University Dr & Bell Ave, NE part of town. Phone 817/898-3456. **Free.** Also on campus is

Little-Chapel-in-the-Woods. Designed by O'Neil Ford. Stained glass windows, carved wood, mosaics made by students. A National Youth Administration (NYA) project dedicated by Eleanor Roosevelt in 1939. (Daily) **Free.**

Annual Event

North Texas State Fair and Rodeo. 9 days 4th full wk Aug.

Motels

★ ★ **HOLIDAY INN.** *1500 Dallas Dr (76205). 817/387-3511; FAX 817/387-7917.* 144 rms, 2 story. S, D $52-$68; each addl $5; suites $95-$150; under 18 free. Crib free. TV; cable (premium). Pool. Restaurant 6:30 am-2 pm, 5-10 pm. Rm serv. Private club 5 pm-mid-night; closed Sun; dancing. Ck-out noon. Coin lndry. Meeting rms. Business servs avail. Sundries. Cr cds: A, C, D, DS, MC, V.

🄳 ⊠ ⊠ 🛇 🄢🄲

✔ ★ ★ **LA QUINTA.** *700 Ft Worth Dr (76201), I-35E, Ft Worth Dr exit. 817/387-5840; FAX 817/387-2493.* 100 rms, 2 story. S $45-$55; D $50-$60; each addl $8; under 18 free. Crib free. TV; cable (premium). Pool. Continental bkfst. Restaurant adj open 24 hrs. Ck-out noon. Meeting rms. Cr cds: A, C, D, DS, MC, V.

🄳 ✔ ⊠ ⊠ 🛇 🄢🄲

Hotel

★ ★ **RADISSON.** *2211 I-35 E North (76205), at University of North Texas. 817/565-8499; FAX 817/387-4729.* 150 rms, 8 story. S, D $69-$95; each addl $10; suites $150-$295; under 18 free; golf plans. TV; cable (premium), VCR avail. Pool. Complimentary coffee in rms. Restaurant 7 am-10 pm. Rm serv. Bar noon-midnight. Meeting rms. Business center. In-rm modem link. Tennis privileges. 18-hole golf, pro, putting green, driving range. Exercise equipt; weights, treadmill. Cr cds: A, C, D, DS, ER, MC, V.

🄳 ✔ 🏋 ⊠ 🚶 🛇 🛇 🄢🄲 ⛷

Restaurant

★ **TRAIL DUST.** *(Rte 1, Box 106, Aubrey 76227) 10 mi E on US 380. 817/383-4731.* Hrs: 5-11 pm; Fri, Sat to midnight; Sun noon-10 pm. Closed Thanksgiving, Dec 25. Western Amer menu. Bar. A la carte entrees: lunch, dinner $8.99-$19.99. Child's meals. Specialties: 14-oz or 24-oz T-bone steak, barbecued ribs, mesquite-broiled chicken. Parking. Traditional Texas atmosphere; "No ties allowed." Cr cds: A, DS, MC, V.

🄳

Dumas (F-2)

(See Amarillo)

Pop 12,871 **Elev** 3,668 ft **Area code** 806 **Zip** 79029
Information Chamber of Commerce, PO Box 735; 806/935-2123.

Oil was discovered in Dumas in 1926. Today Dumas is noted for its large natural gas fields and for the production of between 60 and 70 percent of the nation's helium.

Annual Event

Dogie Days Celebration. McDade Park. Food booths, carnival rides, dances; barbecue, parade. 1st wkend June.

Motels

★ ★ **BEST WESTERN DUMAS INN.** *1712 S Dumas Ave. 806/935-6441; FAX 806/935-9331.* 100 rms, 2 story. S $49-$89; D $53-$97; each addl $8; suites $125. Crib $8. Pet accepted. TV; cable (premium). Indoor pool; whirlpool. Restaurant 6 am-10 pm. Rm serv. Private club 5 pm-2 am. Ck-out noon. Meeting rms. Business servs avail. In-rm modem link. Game rm. Cr cds: A, C, D, DS, MC, V.

✔ ★ **ECONO LODGE OLD TOWN INN.** *1719 S Dumas Ave. 806/935-9098; FAX 806/935-7483.* 40 rms, 2 story. May-July: S $38.95-$50; D $47.95-$70; each addl $3; under 18 free; wkly, wkend rates; lower rates rest of yr. Crib $3. Pet accepted. TV; cable. Heated pool; whirlpool. Complimentary continental bkfst. Restaurant nearby. Ck-out 11 am. Coin lndry. Some refrigerators. Cr cds: A, C, D, DS, ER, JCB, MC, V.

★ **SUPER 8.** *119 W 17th St. 806/935-6222.* 30 rms, 2 story. Apr-Sept: S $39-$49; D $46-$56; each addl $5; under 10 free; lower rates rest of yr. Pet accepted; $5. TV; cable. Complimentary continental bkfst. Restaurant nearby. Ck-out 11 am. Cr cds: A, C, D, DS, MC, V.

Eagle Lake (D-7)

(For accommodations see Houston)

Pop 3,551 **Elev** 170 ft **Area code** 409 **Zip** 77434
Information Chamber of Commerce, 408 E Main St; 409/234-2780.

A popular area for duck and goose hunting, this region produces large rice harvests, oil, natural gas, sand and gravel. A sanctuary for the coastal prairie chicken is nearby.

What to See and Do

Attwater Prairie Chicken National Wildlife Refuge. Approx 8,000 acres along banks of San Bernard River. Protected area for the endangered Attwater prairie chicken; large numbers of migratory and resident species. In spring refuge is filled with wildflowers. (Daily; office Mon-Fri) 7 mi NE off FM 3013. Phone 409/234-3021. **Free.**

Prairie Edge Museum. Exhibits depicting area history, life on the prairie, flora & fauna, early rice farming equipment. (Daily in Apr; rest of yr Sat, Sun and by appt) 408 E Main. Phone 409/234-2780. **Free.**

Annual Event

Magnolia Homes Tour. 18 mi NW, in Columbus. Ten early Texas and Victorian houses are opened for tours; antique show; parade; food. Phone 409/732-5881. 10 days mid-May.

Eagle Pass (E-4)

(See Brackettville, Del Rio, Uvalde)

Founded 1849 **Pop** 20,651 **Elev** 726 ft **Area code** 210 **Zip** 78852
Information Chamber of Commerce, 400 Garrison St, PO Box 1188, 78853; 210/773-3224.

Eagle Pass is across the Rio Grande from Piedras Negras, Coahuila, Mexico (for Border Crossing Regulations see INTRODUCTION). A toll bridge connects the two cities. Eagle Pass is the port of entry to Mexican Highway 57, the Constitution Highway to Mexico City via Saltillo and San Luis Potosi.

What to See and Do

Fort Duncan Park. Ten restored buildings of the fort (1849) that once housed 10,000 troops; museum (Mon-Fri). In park are ballfields, picnic area, playground, tennis court and golf course. (Daily) Enter at Adams or Monroe Sts. Phone 210/773-4343. **Free.**

Piedras Negras, Mexico (population: 230,000). Many pleasant restaurants and nightclubs. Contact the Chamber of Commerce.

Motel

★ ★ **LA QUINTA.** *2525 Main St. 210/773-7000.* 130 rms, 2 story. S $60-$67; D $68-$75; each addl $8; under 18 free. Crib free. TV; cable (premium). Pool. Complimentary coffee in lobby. Complimentary continental bkfst. Restaurant adj open 24 hrs. Ck-out noon. Valet serv. Meeting rms. In-rm modem link. Cr cds: A, C, D, DS, MC, V.

Eastland (B-5)

(See Abilene, Fort Worth, Weatherford)

Pop 3,690 **Elev** 1,421 ft **Area code** 817 **Zip** 76448
Information Chamber of Commerce, 102 S Seaman; 817/629-2332.

Eastland is the home of the legend of "Old Rip," a Texas horned toad alleged to have survived for 31 years (1897-1928) sealed in the cornerstone of the county courthouse. A minor publicity sensation resulted for the town when the cornerstone was opened and the reptile discovered. Today, the remains of Old Rip are on view in the new county courthouse.

Motel

✔ ★ **BUDGET HOST INN.** *I-20 Exit 343, 3 mi SE at I-20 exit 343 (FM 570). 817/629-2655; FAX 817/629-1914.* 69 rms, 2 story. S $33-$37; D $35-$47; each addl $4; under 12 free. Crib $3. Pet accepted; $3-$5. TV; cable (premium). Pool. Restaurant 6 am-10 pm; Sun to 9 pm. Rm serv. Private club 5:30 pm-midnight; Sat 6 pm-1 am. Ck-out noon. Meeting rms. Business servs avail. Cr cds: A, C, D, DS, MC, V.

Edinburg (F-6)

(For accommodations see Harlingen, McAllen, also see Mission)

Founded 1907 **Pop** 29,885 **Elev** 91 ft **Area code** 210 **Zip** 78539
Information Chamber of Commerce, 109-B W Mahl, PO Box 85; 210/383-4974.

Edinburg is an educational center as well as a leading agricultural, citrus market (with year-round growing conditions) and shipping point for oranges, grapefruit and vegetables.

What to See and Do

Hidalgo County Historical Museum. Exhibits depict regional history of Rio Grande Valley, south Texas and northern Mexico; includes Native American items, Spanish exploration, Mexican War, ranch life, steamboats, bandit era. Special exhibits; education gallery. Housed partly in 1910 County Jail Bldg with hanging room (used once in 1913) and original gallows trapdoor. (Tues-Sat, also Sun afternoons; closed major hols) 121 E McIntyre (on Courthouse Square). Phone 210/383-6911. ¢

Annual Event

Fiesta Hidalgo. 12 days, late Feb-early Mar.

El Paso (B-1)

(See Ciudad Juárez, Chihuahua, Mexico; also see Las Cruces, NM)

Founded 1827 **Pop** 515,342 **Elev** 3,762-6,700 ft **Area code** 915

Information El Paso Tourist Bureau, 1 Civic Center Plaza, 79901; 915/534-0653 or 800/351-6024.

The first authenticated expedition here was by Rodriguez Chamuscado in 1581. Juan de Oñate named the place El Paso del Norte in 1598. Several missions were founded in the area from 1659 on. They are now considered to be among the oldest continuously active parishes in the US. Over the years several ranches were established. The first actual settlement in what is now downtown El Paso was in 1827, adjacent to the ranch of Juan Maria Ponce de Leon.

The town remained wholly Mexican throughout the Texas Revolution. In 1846 it surrendered to US forces engaged in fighting the Mexican War. In 1848 it was divided between present-day Ciudad Juárez and what was to become El Paso proper. The border was placed in the middle of the Rio Grande, according to the terms of the treaty of Guadalupe Hidalgo. By provision of the Chamizal Treaty of 1963, the boundary has been changed, giving back to Mexico about 700 acres cut off by the shifting of the river. The disputed area was made into parkland on both sides of the border.

A military post was established in 1846 and a trading post in 1852. In 1854 the military post was named Fort Bliss. By this time the Butterfield Stage Line from St Louis to San Francisco was carrying gold seekers to California through El Paso.

Fort Bliss was captured by Texas troops of the Confederate Army in 1861 as part of a campaign to win New Mexico. The campaign failed, and the troops gradually withdrew. El Paso returned to Union hands by the end of the Civil War.

Spanish and English are mutually spoken in both El Paso and Ciudad Juárez. International spirit runs heavy between these two cities as, does the traffic. This spirit is reflected in the Civic Center complex and in Chamizal National Memorial.

Along with more than 400 manufacturing plants ranging from oil refineries to food processing facilities, El Paso is also home to a military training center and one of the largest air defense centers in the world.

What to See and Do

Bus tours of El Paso, Ciudad Juárez. Golden Tours, for information, reservations phone 915/779-0555.

Chamizal National Memorial. The 55-acre area commemorates peaceful settlement of a boundary dispute between Mexico and the US. Exhibits and bilingual movie tell story of the settlement; bilingual guide service. Special events include theater performances (see ANNUAL EVENTS). Visitor center (daily). Enter from Paisano Dr; near Cordova Bridge. Contact Superintendent, 800 S San Marcial, 79905. 915/532-7273. **Free.**

Ciudad Juárez (see) offers a different and fascinating experience. The markets in Ciudad Juárez have a wide variety of goods, and the stores offer better shopping than most Mexican border cities. Bullfights, dog racing, fairs and festivals abound. The best way to cross the border is to park in a lot on El Paso St, at the bridge, and walk. Take advantage of the El Paso/Juárez trolley. (For Border Crossing Regulations, see INTRODUCTION)

El Paso Mission Trail. (Approx 20 mi) Drive E 12 mi on I-10 to Zaragosa Rd, then S 2½ mi to Alameda St; turn left and then immediate right onto Old South Pueblo Rd, which leads to

Ysleta (1682), the oldest mission in Texas. When founded, Ysleta was on the Mexican side of the Rio Grande, but the river shifted, leaving it in Texas. The Mission Nuestra Señora del Carmen is on US 80 and S Old Pueblo Rd. Preservation and upkeep is continuous. Some of the surrounding lands have been in cultivation every year since its founding. This is one of the few places in the US where Egyptian long-staple cotton has been grown successfully. Also here is the

Tigua Indian Reservation. The Tigua people, whose origins can be traced to 1500 B.C., maintain a cultural center, two restaurants and a gift shop. Presentations of Tigua dances (summer, Fri-Sun; fee). (See ANNUAL EVENTS) (Daily exc Mon; closed Jan 1, Easter, Thanksgiving, Dec 25) Phone 915/859-7913. Performances ¢¢

Take Socorro Rd E 2 mi from Ysleta Mission to

Socorro. The Mission here (ca 1680) is the oldest parish church in continual use in the US. Continue E approx 9 mi to

San Elizario. The Presidio Chapel (1843) was built to replace the one first established in 1780. San Elizario was the site of the Salt War, a bitter struggle over rights to salt found in flats to the east.

Scenic drive to S end of Mt Franklin gives a magnificent view of El Paso and Ciudad Juárez, particularly at night. Go N on Mesa St to Rim Rd and turn E, which will lead you to Scenic Dr.

El Paso Museum of Art. Exhibits spanning six centuries of paintings and sculpture include American, Mexican-colonial and pre-Columbian art, Kress Collection of Italian Renaissance works; changing exhibits. (Daily exc Mon; closed major hols) 1211 Montana Ave. Phone 915/541-4040. **Free.**

El Paso Museum of History. Hispanic, Native American, US artifacts and El Paso history dioramas; changing exhibits. (Daily exc Mon; closed hols) Donation. 12901 Gateway West, I-10 & Americas Ave. Phone 915/858-1928.

Fort Bliss. Enter at Robert E. Lee Gate, 1 mi E of airport. Once the largest cavalry post in the US, Fort Bliss is now the home of the US Army Air Defense Center, one of the largest air defense centers in the world, where troops from all allied nations train. On base are

Fort Bliss Museum. Five adobe buildings replicate the original Fort Bliss army post. Period rooms contain items pertaining to the history of the fort, military & civilian artifacts from 1850s to present. (Daily; closed some major hols) Pershing & Pleasanton Rds. Phone 915/568-4518. **Free.**

3rd Cavalry Museum. Depicts the history of the 3rd Cavalry from its beginnings as the Regiment of Mounted Riflemen in 1846. (Mon-Fri; closed hols) S of Forest & Chafee Rds. Phone 915/568-1922. **Free.**

US Army Air Defense Artillery Museum. Audiovisual exhibits on history of US antiaircraft gunnery and other military subjects. Changing exhibits; weapons park. (Daily; closed some major hols) Pershing & Pleasanton Rd. Phone 915/568-5412. **Free.**

Guadalupe Mountains National Park (see). 110 mi E on US 62/180.

Hueco Tanks State Historical Park. More than 850 acres of cave and rock formations, rock art, vegetation and wildlife. This is a semi-oasis in the desert where rainfall is trapped in natural basins or "huecos." Park facilities include picnicking, improved campsites (hookups, dump station). Standard fees. (Daily) 32 mi NE off US 62, Ranch Rd 2775. Phone 915/857-1135. ¢

Magoffin Home State Historic Site. Example of early Texas architecture (1875). Sun-dried adobe combined with Greek-revival detail created the Southwestern living style. Regional antiques. (Wed-Sun) 1120 Magoffin Ave. Phone 915/533-5147. ¢

University of Texas at El Paso (1914). (17,000 students) The Sun Bowl, seating 53,000, is on campus along with the Centennial Museum. Fine Arts Center with art exhibits, drama and musical productions (fee). Off I-10, Schuster exit. Phone 915/747-5526.

Wilderness Park Museum. Archaeological and ethnological exhibits of the Southwest, and man's adaptation to a desert environment; nature trail. Guided tours (by appt). (Daily exc Mon; closed hols) Transmountain Rd at Gateway South. Phone 915/755-4332. **Free.**

Annual Events

Southwestern Intl Livestock Show & PRCA Rodeo. 1st wk Feb.

Siglo de Oro. Chamizal National Memorial. Festival of Classical Spanish drama. 2 wks Mar.

Tiqua St. Anthony's Day. Tigua Indian Reservation. Religious patron saint of the Tiquas; special food and ceremonies. June 13.

Fiesta de las Flores. Carnival festivities with a Latin flavor. Labor Day wkend.

Border Folk Festival. Chamizal National Memorial. 1st full wkend Oct.

Seasonal Events

Viva El Paso. McKelligon Canyon Amphitheater. Musical history of the Southwest. Phone 915/565-6900 for schedule information.

El Paso Symphony Orchestra. Civic Center. Sixteen concerts with solo artists Sept-Apr. Also summer concerts and special events. Phone 915/532-3776.

Horse racing. Sunland Park Race Course. 6 mi W, just off I-10 in New Mexico. Thoroughbred and quarter horse racing. Parimutuel betting. Major race: $175,000 (est) Riley Allison Thoroughbred Futurity. Waterski shows on infield lake (Sat & Sun, weather permitting). Contact PO Box 1, Sunland Park, NM 88063; 505/589-1131. Mid-Oct-early May.

Sun Carnival. Festivities and sporting events; ending with the John Hancock Bowl. Thanksgiving wkend-Dec.

Motels

✔ ★ **BUDGET LODGE.** 1301 N Mesa St (79902). 915/533-6821; FAX 915/534-9130. 48 rms, 2-3 story. S, D $29.57-$34.13; each addl $4.50; under 12 free; wkly rates. Pet accepted, some restrictions; $25. TV; cable. Pool. Restaurant 7:30 am-3:30 pm; Sun 7 am-3 pm. Ck-out 11 am. Refrigerator avail. Balconies. Cr cds: A, C, D, DS, MC, V.

✔ ★ ★ **COMFORT INN.** 900 N Yarbrough (79915). 915/594-9111; FAX 915/590-4364. 185 units, 3 story, 7 kit. suites. S $50 D $56; each addl $6; suites $75; under 18 free. Crib free. Pet accepted; $25. TV; cable (premium), VCR avail. Heated pool; whirlpool. Complimentary continental bkfst. Restaurant adj 10 am-8 pm. Ck-out noon. Coin Indry. Meeting rms. Business servs avail. In-rm modem link. Airport transportation. Balconies. Cr cds: A, C, D, DS, ER, JCB, MC, V.

★ ★ **HOWARD JOHNSON.** 8887 Gateway W (79925). 915/591-9471; FAX 915/591-5602. 140 rms, 1-2 story. S $52-$61; D $56-$64; each addl $3. Crib free. TV; cable (premium). Pool; wading pool. Restaurant adj open 24 hrs. Bar 4 pm-midnight. Ck-out 2 pm. Coin Indry. Meeting rms. Business servs avail. In-rm modem link. Bellhops. Valet serv. Free airport transportation. Some refrigerators. Private patios, balconies. Cr cds: A, C, D, DS, JCB, MC, V.

★ ★ **LA QUINTA.** 6140 Gateway E (79905). 915/778-9321. 121 rms, 2 story. S $54; D $62; each addl $8; suites $70-$83; under 18 free. Crib free. Pet accepted. TV; cable (premium), VCR avail. Heated pool. Restaurant adj open 24 hrs. Ck-out noon. Meeting rm. Business servs avail. In-rm modem link. Free airport transportation. Cr cds: A, C, D, DS, ER, JCB, MC, V.

★ ★ **QUALITY INN.** 6201 Gateway W (79925), near Intl Airport. 915/778-6611; FAX 915/779-2270. 308 rms, 2-3 story. No elvtr. S $46; D $51; suites $74-$95. Crib $5. Pet accepted. TV; cable, VCR avail. Pool; wading pool. Restaurant 6 am-10 pm. Rm serv. Bar 4 pm-1:30 am; entertainment, dancing. Ck-out 2 pm. Convention facili-

ties. Business servs avail. Bellhops. Gift shop. Free airport transportation. Cr cds: A, C, D, DS, JCB, MC, V.

★ ★ **RESIDENCE INN BY MARRIOTT.** 6791 Montana Ave (79925), near Intl Airport. 915/772-8000; FAX 915/772-8000, ext. 407. 200 rms, 2 story. S, D $99-$130; family, wkly, wkend rates. Crib free. TV; cable (premium), VCR avail. 2 heated pools; whirlpools. Complimentary buffet bkfst. Restaurant adj 11 am-midnight. Ck-out noon. Meeting rms. Business servs avail. Bellhops. Valet serv. Airport transportation. Refrigerators. Private patios, balconies. Grills. Attractive grounds. Cr cds: A, C, D, DS, MC, V.

Motor Hotels

★ ★ ★ **HILTON-AIRPORT.** 2027 Airway Blvd (79925), near Intl Airport. 915/778-4241; FAX 915/772-6871. 272 rms, 4 story. S $97-$111; D $107-$121; each addl $10; suites $101-$185; family, wkend rates. Pet accepted. TV; cable (premium). Heated pool; whirlpool, sauna, poolside serv. Bkfst buffet 6-9:30 am. Restaurant 6 am-11 pm. Rm serv. Bar noon-2 am. Ck-out noon. Convention facilities. Business center. In-rm modem link. Bellhops. Valet serv. Sundries. Barber, beauty shop. Free airport transportation. Airport opp. Cr cds: A, C, D, DS, ER, JCB, MC, V.

★ ★ **HOLIDAY INN-SUNLAND PARK.** 900 Sunland Park Dr & I-10W (79922). 915/833-2900; FAX 915/833-2900, ext. 646. 178 rms, 2 story. S $67, D $75; each addl $8; suites $100-$125; under 18 free. Crib free. TV; cable (premium). Pool; wading pool, whirlpool, poolside serv. Restaurant 6 am-2 pm, 5-10 pm; wkends 7 am-10 pm. Rm serv. Bar. Ck-out noon. Meeting rms. Business servs avail. Bellhops. Valet serv. Sundries. Airport, bus depot transportation. On hill overlooking Sunland Park. Cr cds: A, C, D, DS, MC, V.

Hotels

★ ★ ★ **CAMINO REAL.** 101 S El Paso St (79901). 915/534-3000; FAX 915/534-3024. 360 units, 17 story. S, D $125-$275; each addl $15; suites $275-$900; under 18 free. Crib free. Pet accepted, some restrictions; $50. TV; cable. Pool; sauna. Restaurants 6 am-10 pm. Rm serv 24 hrs. Bar 11-1 am; entertainment. Ck-out 1 pm. Convention facilities. Business center. In-rm modem link. Free airport transportation. Renovated historic hotel (1912). Luxury level. Cr cds: A, C, D, DS, ER, JCB, MC, V.

★ ★ **EMBASSY SUITES.** 6100 Gateway E (79905). 915/779-6222; FAX 915/779-8846. 185 kit. suites, 8 story. S, D $169; under 12 free; wkend rates. Pet accepted, some restrictions; $50. TV (2 per unit); cable (premium), VCR avail. Indoor pool; whirlpool, sauna. Complimentary bkfst 6-9:30 am; wkends 7-10:30 am. Ck-out 1 pm. Coin Indry. Meeting rms. Business servs avail. Free airport transportation. Refrigerators. Large atrium with fountain, pools, plants. Cr cds: A, C, D, DS, MC, V.

✔ ★ **INTERNATIONAL.** 113 W Missouri (79901). 915/544-3300; FAX 915/533-2136. 200 rms, 17 story. S, D $55; each addl $5; suites $100-$130; under 18 free. Crib free. Pet accepted; $10. TV; cable. Pool. Restaurant 6:30 am-10 pm. Bar 4 pm-2 am, closed Sun & Mon; dancing. Ck-out noon. Meeting rms. Business servs avail. Free airport, RR station, bus depot transportation. Balconies. Cr cds: A, C, D, DS, JCB, MC, V.

★ ★ ★ **MARRIOTT.** *1600 Airway Blvd (79925), near Intl Airport. 915/779-3300; FAX 915/772-0915.* 296 rms, 6 story. S $99; D $114; each addl $15; suites $225-$300; wkend rates. Crib free. Pet accepted, some restrictions. TV; cable (premium). Indoor/outdoor pool; poolside serv. Restaurant 6:30 am-11 pm. Bar noon-2 am; entertainment, dancing. Ck-out 1 pm. Coin lndry. Convention facilities. Business servs avail. In-rm modem link. Valet serv. Shopping arcade. Free airport transportation. 18-hole golf, greens fee $35, putting green. Exercise equipt; weight machines, bicycles, whirlpool, sauna. Private patios. Southwest decor and art. Luxury level. Cr cds: A, C, D, DS, ER, JCB, MC, V.

D ⚓ 🏌 ≋ 🏋 ✈ ⊠ ⊠ SC

Inn

★ ★ ★ **SUNSET HEIGHTS.** *717 W Yandell Ave (79902). 915/544-1743; res: 800/767-8513; FAX 915/544-5119.* 5 rms, 3 story. S, D $70-$165; higher rates Sun Bowl, hols. Adults preferred. TV; cable, VCR avail. Pool. Spa. Complimentary full bkfst, tea/sherry & champagne. Complimentary coffee in rms. Ck-out, ck-in noon. Business servs avail. Airport, RR station, bus depot transportation. Picnic tables, grills. Victorian-style building (1905); leaded glass, Tiffany chandeliers. Totally nonsmoking. Cr cds: A, DS, MC, V.

≋ ⊠ 🔥 ▨

Restaurants

★ ★ **BELLA NAPOLI.** *6331 N Mesa St. 915/584-3321.* Hrs: 5-10 pm; Sun from 11:30 am. Closed Mon; Thanksgiving, Dec 25. Res accepted. Italian, Amer menu. Wine, beer. Semi-a la carte: dinner $6.50-$18.95. Specializes in osso bucco, veal parmigiana, chicken Jerusalem. Entertainment Wed & wkends. Outdoor dining. Italian decor; twin fireplaces; gardens. Cr cds: A, DS, MC, V.

D

✔ ★ **BILL PARK'S BAR-B-Q.** *3130 Gateway E. 915/542-0960.* Hrs: 11 am-8 pm. Closed Sun & Mon. Wine, beer. A la carte entrees: lunch, dinner $2-$8.90. Child's meals. Specializes in barbecued meats. Parking. Family-owned. Cr cds: A, D, DS, MC, V.

✔ ★ **CASA JURADO.** *4772 Doniphan Dr. 915/833-1151.* Hrs: 11 am-9 pm; Fri, Sat to 10 pm; Sun noon-8 pm. Closed Mon; major hols. Mexican menu. A la carte entrees: lunch, dinner $3.85-$11.95. Specializes in chicken mole, tacos, enchiladas. Parking. Mexican decorations. Cr cds: A, C, D, DS, MC, V.

D

★ ★ **CATTLEMAN'S STEAK HOUSE.** *(Box 1056, Fabens 79838) 28 mi E via I-10, exit 49; on grounds of Indian Cliffs Ranch. 915/544-3200.* Hrs: 5-10 pm; Sat from 4 pm; Sun 12:30-9 pm. Bar. Semi-a la carte: lunch, dinner $6.95-$22.95. Child's meals. Specialties: 2-lb T-bone steak, mesquite-smoked brisket, seafood. Parking. Replica 1890s frontier fort; rustic decor. Family-owned. Cr cds: A, C, D, MC, V.

D

★ ★ **JAXON'S.** *4799 N Mesa St. 915/544-1188.* Hrs: 11 am-10 pm; Fri, Sat to 11 pm; Sun 11 am-9 pm. Closed some major hols. Mexican, Amer menu. Bar 11 am-midnight. Semi-a la carte: lunch, dinner $3.89-$14.99. Specializes in a variety of salads, steak, Southwestern dishes. Fireplace. Cr cds: A, C, D, DS, MC, V.

D SC

★ ★ **SAN FRANCISCO GRILL.** *127A Pioneer Plaza (79901). 915/545-1386.* Hrs: 11 am-11 pm; Fri, Sat to midnight; Sun to 10 pm; Sun brunch to 4 pm. Closed Thanksgiving, Dec 25. Res accepted. Semi-a la carte: lunch $4.95-$7.95, dinner $8.95-$18.95. Sun brunch $8. Specializes in salmon, prime rib, pasta. Cr cds: A, D, DS, MC, V.

D

✔ ★ ★ **SEÑOR JUAN'S GRIGGS.** *9007 Montana Ave. 915/598-3451.* Hrs: 11 am-9 pm. Closed Thanksgiving, Dec 25. Res accepted. Mexican, Amer menu. Bar. A la carte entrees: lunch, dinner $3.95-$9.75. Entertainment Thur-Sun. Specializes in beef and chicken enchiladas, chili. Atrium; antiques. Family recipes. Cr cds: MC, V.

Unrated Dining Spots

FURRS CAFETERIA. *119 N Balboa. 915/833-1197.* Hrs: 11 am-2 pm, 4-8 pm; Sat, Sun 11 am-8 pm. Closed Dec 24 evening-Dec 25. Avg ck: lunch, dinner $4.75. Specializes in chicken-fried steak, corned beef & cabbage. Parking. Southwest decor. No cr cds accepted.

D SC

LUBY'S CAFETERIA. *3601 N Mesa St. 915/533-0502.* Hrs: 10:45 am-8 pm. Closed Dec 25. Avg ck: lunch, dinner $5. Specializes in salad, fresh vegetables. Parking. Cr cds: DS, MC, V.

D

Ennis (B-7)

(For accommodations see Arlington-Grand Prairie, Dallas, also see Corsicana)

Pop 13,883 **Elev** 548 ft **Area code** 214 **Zip** 75119
Information Chamber of Commerce, 108 Wagon Wheel Dr, PO Box 1177; 214/878-2625.

Ennis has preserved many historical buildings in the downtown area. The town is also noted for the Bluebonnet Trails, which are at their best in April (see ANNUAL EVENTS).

What to See and Do

Bardwell Lake. Beaches, waterskiing; fishing; boating (ramps, marina). Nature trail. Picnic facilities. Tent & trailer sites (electric & water hookups, dump station). (All yr) Some fees. (Daily) 4½ mi SW on TX 34. Phone 214/878-5711.

Annual Events

Bluebonnet Trails. Garden Club-sponsored 40-miles of fields in profusion of blooming wildflowers. Contact the Chamber of Commerce. Mid-late Apr.

National Polka Festival. Parade, Czech costumes, arts & crafts fair. Late Apr-early May.

Fairfield (B-7)

(For accommodations see Palestine)

Pop 3,234 **Elev** 461 ft **Area code** 903 **Zip** 75840
Information Chamber of Commerce, 820 E Commerce, PO Box 956; 903/389-5792.

What to See and Do

Burlington-Rock Island Railroad Museum. Housed in the 1906 depot of the old Trinity & Brazos Valley RR, railroad artifacts, items of local history, genealogical records; also two-room log house. (Sat & Sun afternoons; closed Jan 1, Easter, Dec 25) 208 S 3rd Ave, 10 mi SW via US 84 in Teague. Phone 817/739-2408. ¢

Fairfield Lake State Park. More than 1,400 acres. Swimming, water-skiing; fishing; boating (ramps). Hiking trails. Picnicking, playground. Improved campsites (dump station). Guided boat tours of bald eagle habitats (fee). Standard fees. (Daily) NE on US 84 to FM 2570, then E on Park Rd 64. Phone 903/389-4514. Per vehicle ¢¢

Freestone County Historical Museum. Old county jail (1857), two log cabins, W.L. Moody House; old church, antiques exhibit, county history items, old telephone exhibit, artifacts of seven wars, Civil War letters; quilts. Guided tours. (Wed-Sat, also Sun afternoons; closed major hols) 302 E Main St. Phone 903/389-3738. ¢

Fort Davis National Historic Site (C-2)

(see Alpine)

Fort Stockton (C-3)

(See Alpine)

Founded 1859 **Pop** 8,524 **Elev** 2,954 ft **Area code** 915 **Zip** 79735
Information Chamber of Commerce Tourist Center, 222 W Dickinson Blvd, PO Box C; 915/336-2264.

Fort Stockton grew around a military post established in 1859 at Comanche Springs; the springs had previously been a watering place on the California Trail, the San Antonio-San Diego Stage Line and on the Comanche War Trail, which extended from Chihuahua to Arkansas. Today, the area surrounding Fort Stockton has more than 100,000 acres of irrigated land producing pecans, vegetables, alfalfa, grain, wine grapes and cotton; the area is also known for cattle, sheep and goat ranches and for its many oil and gas wells. Fort Stockton is rich in preserved landmarks.

What to See and Do

Annie Riggs Hotel Museum (1899). Turn-of-the-century hotel, later run as a boarding house; 14 of the original 15 rooms feature displays on local history and the town's development. Self-guided tours. (Daily; closed major hols) 301 S Main St. Phone 915/336-2167. ¢

Auto tours. Five self-guided, one-day trips from 40-310 miles in length. Markers indicate route to 14 state historic sites. Contact Chamber of Commerce Tourist Center.

Big Bend National Park (see). Approx 120 mi S via US 385.

Old Fort Stockton. Some of the original 24-inch adobe-walled officers' quarters, the old guardhouse and the fort cemetery remain; rebuilt barracks kitchen. Self-guided tours (maps avail at Chamber of Commerce Tourist Center). 4 blks off US 290 at Rooney St, between 2nd & 5th Sts and at Water & 8th Sts.

Annual Events

Pecos County Livestock Show. Wkend mid-Jan.

Fiesta de San Juan. 3 days mid-June.

Motels

✔ ★ ★ **BEST WESTERN SWISS CLOCK INN.** *3201 W Dickinson.* 915/336-8521; FAX 915/336-6513. 112 rms, 2 story. S $44-$48; D $45-$54; each addl $6; studio rms $60; under 12 free. Crib free. Pet accepted. TV; cable (premium), VCR avail. Pool. Restaurant 6 am-2 pm, 5-10 pm. Rm serv. Private club 5-10 pm. Ck-out noon. Meeting

rms. Business servs avail. Valet serv. Some private patios. Cr cds: A, C, D, DS, JCB, MC, V.

D ✔ ≈ ⊁ ⚓ SC

★ ★ **LA QUINTA.** *Box 596, Near jct I-10 & US 285.* 915/336-9781; res: 800/531-5900 (TX); FAX 915/336-3634. 97 rms, 2 story. S $49; D $56; each addl $7; suite $66; under 18 free. Crib free. Pet accepted, some restrictions. TV; cable (premium), VCR avail. Pool. Restaurant opp 6 am-10 pm. Ck-out noon. Guest lndry. Business servs avail. Cr cds: A, C, D, DS, JCB, MC, V.

D ✔ ≈ ⊁ ⚓ SC

✔ ★ **SANDS.** *1801 W Dickinson Blvd.* 915/336-2274; FAX 915/336-2738. 78 rms. S $28.95; D $32.95. Crib $5. Pet accepted. TV; cable. Heated pool; whirlpool. Ck-out noon. Business servs avail. In-rm modem link. Cr cds: A, C, D, DS, MC, V.

✔ ≈ ⚓ SC

Fort Worth (B-6)

Founded 1849 **Pop** 447,619 **Elev** 670 ft **Area code** 817

Somewhere between Dallas and Fort Worth is the dividing line between the East and the West. Dallas is sophisticated and fashionable; Fort Worth is proudly simple and open. The city's predominant industry, cattle (for a long time symbolized by the historic Fort Worth Stockyards), has been joined by the oil, grain, aircraft and computer industries, creating a modern metropolis full of shops, restaurants and nightspots that somehow continue to reflect a distinctly Western character.

In the mid-nineteenth century, Fort Worth was a camp (never a fort) with a garrison to protect settlers. It was later named Fort Worth in honor of General William J. Worth, a Mexican War hero. After the Civil War, great herds of longhorn cattle were driven through the area en route to the Kansas railheads. Cowboys camped with their herds outside of town and "whooped it up" at night.

By 1873 the Texas & Pacific Railroad had reached a point 26 miles east when its backers, Jay Cooke & Co, failed. The population fell from 4,000 to 1,000, and a Dallas newspaper commented that Fort Worth was a place so dead that a panther was seen sleeping on the main street. In response to this insult, Fort Worth called itself "Panther City," and the long-term feud between Fort Worth and Dallas had begun.

A group of citizens headed by K.M. Van Zandt formed the Tarrant County Construction Co and continued the building of the railroad. In 1876 the T & P had a state land grant that would expire unless the road reached Fort Worth before the legislature adjourned. While efforts were made to keep the legislature in session, practically everybody in Fort Worth went to work on the grading and laying of track.

The legislature finally decided to adjourn in two days. It seemed impossible that the line could be finished. The desperate Fort Worthians improvised cribs of ties to bridge Sycamore Creek and for two miles laid the rails on ungraded ground. The city council is said to have moved the city limits east to meet it. The first train, its whistle tied down, wheezed into town on July 19, 1876. Fort Worth had become a shipping point.

In 1882 the free school system was begun, and the first flour mill started operations. In 1883 the Greenwall Opera House was host to many famous stars. In 1870 a local banking institution, now known as NationsBank, opened. Oil did not come in until 1917, but in the years before and since, Fort Worth has continued to grow. The headquarters for several well-known American companies are located in Fort Worth.

Transportation

Airport: See DALLAS/FORT WORTH AIRPORT AREA.

Car Rental Agencies: See toll-free numbers under Introduction.

Public Transportation: Buses (Transportation Authority of Ft Worth), phone 817/871-6200.

Rail Passenger Service: Amtrak 800/872-7245.

What to See and Do

Benbrook Lake. Swimming, waterskiing; fishing; boating (ramps, marinas). Horseback riding; golf. Picnicking, concession. Camping (tent & trailer sites). Fees may be charged at some recreation areas. (Daily) 12 mi SW on US 377. Phone 817/292-2400. Per vehicle ¢¢

Botanic Garden. More than 150,000 plants of 2,000 species including native plants and tropical plant. Conservatory (fee); fragrance garden; rose gardens; perennial garden; trial garden. Extensive Japanese garden with bridges, waterfalls, teahouses (daily exc Mon). (Daily) 3220 Botanic Garden Blvd. Phone 817/871-7686 or -7689 (recording). **Free.**

★ **Cultural District.**

Will Rogers Memorial Center. Will Rogers statue, Memorial Coliseum, Tower, Auditorium, Amon Carter, Jr Exhibit Hall, Equestrian Center. Many community events are held here—horse shows, boxing, circuses, rodeos. 3401 W Lancaster St. Phone 817/871-8150.

Casa Mañana Theater. Large geodesic dome houses professional performances ranging from Broadway shows to children's theater. (Nightly exc Mon; Sat & Sun matinees) 3101 W Lancaster, at University Dr. Phone 817/332-CASA.

Kimbell Art Museum. Permanent collection dating from ancient times to early 20th century includes masterworks by El Greco, Rembrandt, Picasso, Velázquez and many others. Asian, Mesoamerican, African and ancient Mediterranean collections. Special exhibits. Building designed by Louis I. Kahn. (Daily exc Mon; closed hols) 3333 Camp Bowie Blvd. Phone 817/332-8451. **Free.**

Amon Carter Museum. Major collection of American paintings, photography and sculpture includes works by Winslow Homer, Georgia O'Keeffe, Grant Wood, Thomas Cole, Frederic Remington and Charles Russell; changing exhibits. Building designed by Philip Johnson. (Daily exc Mon; closed most hols) 3501 Camp Bowie Blvd. Phone 817/738-1933. **Free.**

Modern Art Museum of Fort Worth. Permanent and traveling exhibits of 20th-century paintings, sculpture, drawings and prints, including works by Picasso, Kelly, Pollock and Warhol. (Daily exc Mon; closed most hols) 1309 Montgomery St. Phone 817/738-9215. **Free.** Adj is

Fort Worth Theater. Plays, operas. (All yr) 3505 W Lancaster. Phone 817/738-6509.

Fort Worth Museum of Science & History. Exhibits on fossils, anthropology, geology, natural sciences and history, medical science; calculators & computers. Participatory exhibits. (Daily; closed Thanksgiving, Dec 24-25) 1501 Montgomery St. Phone 817/732-1631. ¢¢ Also here are

Omni Theater. 70mm Omnimax films are screened on an 80-foot projection dome. Films change periodically. (Daily; closed Thanksgiving, Dec 24-25) Sr citizen rate. ¢¢¢ Adj is

Noble Planetarium. Shows change periodically. Public shows (June-Aug, daily; rest of yr, Sat, Sun only). Sr citizen rate. ¢¢

Downtown.

Sundance Square. Shopping, dining and entertainment district of brick streets and renovated turn-of-the-century buildings. Markers along a self-guided walking tour commemorate historic locations and events; the 300 block of Main St is especially associated with the city's colorful history and with such characters of the Old West as Butch Cassidy, the Sundance Kid and Luke Short, an infamous western gambler who gunned down the town's marshall in front of the notorious White Elephant Saloon. Houston & Main Sts between 2nd & 4th Sts.

Sid Richardson Collection of Western Art. Permanent exhibit of 52 original paintings by renowned western artists Frederic Remington and Charles M. Russell from the private collection of oil man Sid W.

Richardson. (Daily exc Mon; closed hols) 309 Main St. Phone 817/332-6554. **Free.**

150 Years of Fort Worth Museum. Museum recounts the history of the city in a series of photographs and artifacts on view in Fire Station No. 1, the city's first fire station, built in 1907. (Daily) 203 Commerce St, at 2nd St. **Free.**

Fort Worth Water Garden. Enormous concrete, terraced water gardens containing a wide variety of foliage, trees and spectacular water cascades and fountains. (Daily) Just S of Fort Worth/Tarrant County Convention Center. **Free.**

Fort Worth Nature Center & Refuge. A 3,400-acre wildlife habitat. Nature trails. Picnicking. Visitor center. (Tues-Sat, also Sun afternoons; closed some hols) 9 mi NW via TX 199 to Buffalo Rd, on Lake Worth. Phone 817/237-1111. **Free.**

★ **Fort Worth Stockyards National Historic District.** Renovated buildings now house Western-style retail shops, nightclubs and restaurants. 130 E Exchange Ave. A visitor center is located on E Exchange St, opp the Livestock Exchange Bldg, (daily; closed Jan 1, Dec 25); phone 817/625-9715. Tours ¢¢¢. Site of the annual Chisholm Trail Roundup (see ANNUAL EVENTS) as well as other livestock shows and rodeos. A restored steam train travels to the stockyards from the city's south side; phone 817/625-7245. Also here is

Stockyards Museum. Featuring the 1986 Texas Sesquicentennial Wagon Train Collection, the museum also contains memorabilia and hands-on artifacts of the stockyards era, the meatpacking industry and the railroad. (Daily exc Sun; closed major hols) 131 E Exchange Ave, Suite 111-114. Phone 817/625-5082. **Free.**

Old Trail Driver's Park, east of the stockyards at 28th and Decatur Sts; adjacent to the stockyards to the west is Rodeo Park.

Fort Worth Zoo. More than 4,400 exotic and native specimens in a tree-shaded setting. Exhibits include Raptor Canyon, Asian Rhino Ridge, featuring greater one-horned Asian rhinos; also World of Primates, Asian Falls, African Savannah, TEXAS; herpetarium and large aquarium. (Daily) 1989 Colonial Pkwy, in Forest Park; I-30 to University Dr, then 1 mi S (follow signs). Phone 817/871-7050. ¢¢ Also in Forest Park is

Log Cabin Village. Pioneer houses used by early settlers. (Daily; closed Jan 1, Thanksgiving, Dec 25) 2100 Log Cabin Village Lane at South University Dr. Phone 817/926-5881. ¢

Lake Worth. Boating, fishing, picnicking. 9 mi NW on TX 199.

Scenic drive. Through Trinity and Forest Parks on the Clear Fork of the Trinity River. These beautiful parks have a swimming pool, duck pond, zoo and miniature train.

Six Flags Over Texas. (See ARLINGTON-GRAND PRAIRIE) 16 mi E on I-30, just W of jct TX 360.

Thistle Hill (1903). Restored mansion built by one of the cattle barons who made Fort Worth a major city. Guided tours (daily exc Sat). 1509 Pennsylvania Ave, at Summit Ave. Phone 817/336-1212. ¢¢

Annual Events

Southwestern Exposition & Livestock Show. Will Rogers Memorial Coliseum. Mid-Jan-early Feb.

Chisholm Trail Roundup. Fort Worth Stockyards. Trail ride, parade, historical tours, chili cookoff, square dancing & street dances. Early June.

Shakespeare in the Park. Trinity Park. Shakespeare's plays are presented under the stars. Phone 817/924-3701. June & July.

Pioneer Days. Fort Worth Stockyards. Commemorates pioneer settlement along the Trinity River and early days of the cattle industry. Wkend late Sept.

Additional Visitor Information

For further information contact the Fort Worth Convention & Visitors Bureau, located in the Sundance Square area at 415 Throckmorton, 76102; phone 817/336-8791 or 800/433-5747.

Fort Worth Area Suburbs and Towns

The following suburbs and towns in the Fort Worth area are included in the *Mobil Travel Guide.* For information on any one of them, see the individual alphabetical listing. Arlington-Grand Prairie, Cleburne, Denton, Granbury, Weatherford.

Dallas/Fort Worth Airport Area

For additional accommodations, see DALLAS/FORT WORTH AIRPORT AREA, which follows DALLAS.

City Neighborhoods

Many of the restaurants, unrated dining establishments and some lodgings listed under Fort Worth include neighborhoods as well as exact street addresses. Geographic descriptions of the Downtown and Museum/Cultural District are given, followed by a table of restaurants arranged by neighborhood.

Downtown: South of Heritage Park, west of I-35W and the railroad yards, north of Lancaster Ave and east of Henderson Ave (TX 199). **North of Downtown:** North of TX 199 & US 377. **South of Downtown:** South of I-30. **West of Downtown:** West of Trinity River.

Museum/Cultural District: South of Camp Bowie Blvd, west of University Dr, north of Crestline St and east of Montgomery St; also along Lancaster Ave.

FORT WORTH RESTAURANTS
BY NEIGHBORHOOD AREAS

(For full description, see alphabetical listings under Restaurants)

DOWNTOWN

Juanita's. 115 W Second St

Reflections (Worthington Hotel). 200 Main St

NORTH OF DOWNTOWN

Joe T. Garcia's. 2201 N Commerce

SOUTH OF DOWNTOWN

Le Chardonnay. 2443 Forest Park Blvd

WEST OF DOWNTOWN

Balcony. 6100 Camp Bowie Blvd

Celebration. 4600 Dexter

Edelweiss. 3801-A Southwest Blvd

Lucile's. 4700 Camp Bowie

MUSEUM/CULTURAL DISTRICT

7th Street Cafe. 3500 W 7th St

Saint-Emilion. 3617 W 7th St

Note: When a listing is located in a town that does not have its own city heading, it will appear under the city nearest to its location. In these cases, the address and town appear in parenthesis immediately following the name of the establishment.

Motels

✔ ★ **BEST WESTERN-WEST BRANCH INN.** 7301 W Freeway (76116), I-30 at TX 183, west of downtown. 817/244-7444; FAX 817/244-7902. 120 rms, 2 story. S $39-$45; D $50; each addl $5; suites $60-$80; under 12 free. Crib free. Pet accepted, some restrictions. TV; cable (premium), VCR avail. Pool. Complimentary continental bkfst. Restaurant adj 5 pm-1 am; closed Sun-Tues. Ck-out noon. Coin lndry. Meeting rms. Business servs avail. Some refrigerators. Cr cds: A, C, D, DS, JCB, MC, V.

⊠ ➦ ⊠ ⊠ SC

★ **COMFORT INN.** 4850 N Freeway (76137), north of downtown. 817/834-8001; FAX 817/834-3159. 60 rms, 2 story. Apr-Oct: S $55; D $65; under 18 free; lower rates rest of yr. Crib $4. TV; cable (premium). Pool. Complimentary continental bkfst. Complimentary coffee in lobby. Ck-out noon. Coin lndry. Business servs avail. Sundries. Cr cds: A, D, DS, JCB, MC, V.

D ⊠ ⊠ ⊠ SC

★ ★ **COURTYARD BY MARRIOTT.** (2201 Airport Frwy, Bedford 76021) 13 mi E on TX 121, Central Dr N exit, north of downtown. 817/545-2202; FAX 817/545-2319. 145 rms, 3 story, 14 suites. S $82-$85; D $92-$95; suites $97-$107; under 12 free; wkly, wkend rates. Crib free. TV; cable (premium), VCR avail. Pool. Complimentary coffee in rms. Restaurant 6:30-10:30 am; wkends 7 am-noon. Bar 4-11 pm. Ck-out 1 pm. Coin lndry. Meeting rms. Business servs avail. In-rm modem link. Valet serv. Sundries. Exercise equipt; weight machine, bicycles, whirlpool. Refrigerator in suites. Patios, balconies. Cr cds: A, C, D, DS, MC, V.

D ⊠ ✈ ⊠ ⊠

✔ ★ **LA QUINTA NORTHEAST.** (7920 Bedford-Euless Rd, North Richland Hills 76180) 817/485-2750; FAX 817/656-8977. 100 rms, 2 story. S $49-$61; D $54-$66; each addl $5; under 18 free. Crib free. Pet accepted; some restrictions. TV; cable (premium). Pool. Complimentary continental bkfst. Restaurant adj. Ck-out noon. Meeting rms. In-rm modem link. Valet serv. Cr cds: A, C, D, DS, MC, V.

⊠ ⊠ ⊠ SC

✔ ★ ★ **LA QUINTA-WEST.** 7888 I-30W (76108), west of downtown. 817/246-5511; FAX 817/246-8870. 106 rms, 3 story. S $52; D $60; each addl $8; under 18 free. Crib free. Pet accepted. TV; cable (premium), VCR avail. Pool. Complimentary continental bkfst. Restaurant adj open 24 hrs. Meeting rms. Cr cds: A, C, D, DS, MC, V.

D ➦ ⊠ ⊠ SC

★ ★ **RESIDENCE INN BY MARRIOTT.** 1701 S University Dr (76107), west of downtown. 817/870-1011; FAX 817/877-5500. 120 kit. suites, 2 story. Suites: 1-bedrm $110-$120; 2-bedrm $130-$150; studio rms $95-$110; wkly, some wkend rates. Crib free. Pet accepted; $5 per day. TV; cable (premium). Heated pool; whirlpool. Complimentary continental bkfst. Restaurant nearby. Ck-out noon. Coin lndry. Meeting rm. Business servs avail. Valet serv. Private patios, balconies. Picnic tables, grills. Cr cds: A, C, D, DS, ER, JCB, MC, V.

D ➦ ⊠ ⊠ ⊠

Motor Hotels

★ ★ **GREEN OAKS INN AND CONFERENCE CENTER.** 6901 W Frwy (76116), I-30 at TX 183, west of downtown. 817/738-7311; res: 800/433-2174 (exc TX), 800-772-7341 (TX); FAX 817/377-1308. 284 rms, 2-3 story. S $79; D $89; suites $109-$112; each addl $10; under 18 free; wkend, honeymoon packages. Crib free. Pet accepted. TV; cable (premium). 2 pools; poolside serv. Coffe in rms. Restaurant 6 am-2 pm, 5-10 pm. Rm serv. Bars 4 pm-2 am; entertainment, dancing exc Sun. Ck-out noon. Convention facilities. Business center. In-rm modem link. Sundries. Lighted tennis. Exercise equipt;

weights, bicycles, sauna. Adj Carswell AFB, 18-hole golf course. Cr cds: A, C, D, DS, MC, V.

★ ★ ★ **HOLIDAY INN CENTRAL.** *2000 Beach St (76103), off I-30, east of downtown.* 817/534-4801; FAX 817/534-3761. 194 rms, 2-3 story. S, D $69-$89; each addl $10; suites $89-$225; under 18 free; some wkend rates. Crib free. TV; cable (premium). Pool. Restaurant 6 am-2 pm, 5-10:30 pm. Rm serv. Bar 2 pm-midnight. Ck-out noon. Meeting rms. Business servs avail. In-rm modem link. Tennis. Exercise equipt; weight machine, bicycles, whirlpool. Cr cds: A, C, D, DS, ER, MC, V.

★ ★ **HOLIDAY INN-NORTH.** *2540 Meacham Blvd (76106), I-35W at Meacham Blvd exit, north of downtown.* 817/625-9911; FAX 817/625-5132. 247 rms, 6 story. S, D $89; suites $185; under 18 free; some wkend rates. Crib free. TV; cable (premium), VCR avail. Indoor pool. Restaurant 6 am-2 pm, 5-11 pm; Sat, Sun from 7 am. Rm serv. Bar noon-2 am, Sun to midnight; entertainment, dancing. Ck-out noon. Coin lndry. Meeting rms. Business servs avail. Airport transportation. Bellhops. Sundries. Gift shop. Exercise equipt; bicycles, whirlpool, sauna. Bathrm phone, wet bar, whirlpool in suites. Cr cds: A, C, D, DS, ER, JCB, MC, V.

Hotels

★ ★ ★ **STOCKYARDS.** *109 E Exchange St (76106), north of downtown.* 817/625-6427; res: 800/423-8471 (exc TX); FAX 817/624-2571. 52 rms, 3 story. S, D $120; each addl $15; suites $160-$350; higher rates: Chisholm Trail Round-up, Pioneer Days, Dec 31. Valet parking $5. TV. Restaurant 6:30 am-10 pm; Fri, Sat to 11 pm. Bar 11 am-midnight, Fri, Sat to 2 am. Ck-out noon. Business servs avail. Valet serv. Restored turn of the century hotel. Western decor. Cr cds: A, C, D, DS, MC, V.

★ ★ ★ ★ **WORTHINGTON.** *200 Main St (76102), downtown.* 817/870-1000; res: 800/433-5677; FAX 817/882-1755. This ultra-modern high-rise stretches along two city blocks, forming a dramatic glassed-in bridge over Houston Street. Fresh flowers in every room are among the many luxurious touches. 504 rms, 12 story. S, D $149-$189; each addl $10; suites $375-$950; under 18 free; wkend, honeymoon rates. Crib free. Covered parking $5.50, valet parking $8.50. TV; cable (premium), VCR avail. Indoor pool; poolside serv. Restaurant 6 am-11 pm (also see REFLECTIONS). Rm serv 24 hrs. Bar 11-1:30 am; Sun from noon. Ck-out 11 am. Convention facilities. Business center. In-rm modem link. Concierge. Shopping arcade. Tennis. Golf privileges. Exercise rm; instructor, weights, bicycles, whirlpool, sauna. Some refrigerators. Private patios, balconies. Cr cds: A, C, D, DS, MC, V.

Restaurants

✔ ★ ★ **7TH STREET CAFE.** *3500 W 7th St (76107), in Museum/Cultural District.* 817/870-1672. Hrs: 11:30 am-9:30 pm; Fri, Sat to 11 pm. Closed Sun; most major hols. Res accepted. Regional menu. Bar to 11 pm. Semi-a la carte: lunch, dinner $5.95-$14.95. Specialties: pan-fried tilapia with mustard sauce, boule de Niege. Parking. Outdoor dining on patio with view of downtown. Cr cds: A, C, D, MC, V.

★ ★ **BALCONY.** *6100 Camp Bowie Blvd (76116), in Ridglea Village, west of downtown.* 817/731-3719. Hrs: 11:30 am-2 pm, 6-10 pm; Fri to 10:30 pm; Sat 6-10:30 pm. Closed Sun; major hols. Res accepted. Continental menu. Bar. Semi-a la carte: lunch $5.25-$12.95, dinner $12-$25. Child's meals. Specializes in châteaubriand, rack of lamb. Pianist wkends. Parking. Glassed-in balcony. Cr cds: A, C, D, DS, MC, V.

★ ★ **CAFE MATTHEW.** *(8251 Bedford-Euless Rd, North Richland Hills 76180) Northeast of downtown via S-121.* 817/577-3463. Hrs: 11:30 am-2 pm, 5:30-10 pm; Sat from 5:30 pm. Closed Sun; most major hols. Res accepted. Continental menu. Bar. A la carte entrees: lunch $9.50-$14.95, dinner $10.50-$26. Specialties: poached Norwegian salmon, angel hair pasta & chicken breast, roasted rack of lamb, grilled beef tenderloin. Parking. Contemporary decor. Cr cds: A, MC, V.

✔ ★ **CELEBRATION.** *4600 Dexter (76107), west of downtown.* 817/731-6272. Hrs: 11 am-2:30 pm, 5-9 pm; Fri, Sat 11 am-10 pm; Sun 11 am-9 pm. Res accepted. Bar. Semi-a la carte: lunch $4.50-$8.50, dinner $6.50-$13. Child's meals. Specializes in fresh vegetables, fish, pot roast. Own desserts. Parking. Outdoor dining. Converted ice house. Cr cds: A, C, D, DS, MC, V.

★ **EDELWEISS.** *3801-A Southwest Blvd (76116), west of downtown.* 817/738-5934. Hrs: 5-10:30 pm; Fri, Sat to 11 pm. Closed Sun, Mon; some major hols. German menu. Bar. Semi-a la carte: dinner $9.95-$17.95. Specializes in Wienerschnitzel, sauerbraten, red cabbage. Entertainment. Parking. Beer garden atmosphere. Family-owned. Cr cds: A, C, D, DS, MC, V.

★ **JOE T. GARCIA'S.** *2201 N Commerce (76106), north of downtown.* 817/626-8571. Hrs: 11 am-2:30 pm, 5-10 pm; Fri, Sat to 11 pm. Closed Easter, Thanksgiving, Dec 25. Mexican menu. Bar. Semi-a la carte: lunch $5.25-$9, dinner $9-$11. Child's meals. Specialties: chicken and beef fajitas, family-style dinners. Mariachi band Fri-Sun. Parking. Outdoor dining; courtyard with fountain, garden. Family-owned more than 50 years. No cr cds accepted.

✔ ★ ★ **JUANITA'S.** *115 W Second St, downtown.* 817/335-1777; FAX 817/335-1779. Hrs: 11 am-midnight; Fri to 1 am; Sat noon-1 am; Sun noon-midnight. Closed some major hols. Res accepted. Mexican menu. Bar. Semi-a la carte: lunch, dinner $2.50-$12. Specialties: quail braised in tequila, chile butter chicken, fajitas. Valet parking (dinner, exc Sun). Outdoor dining. Victorian decor. Cr cds: A, D, DS, MC, V.

★ ★ **LE CHARDONNAY.** *2443 Forest Park Blvd (76110), south of downtown.* 817/926-5622. Hrs: 11 am-10 pm; Fri & Sat to 11 pm. Closed July 4, Dec 25. Res accepted. French menu. Bar. A la carte entrees: lunch $4.95-$11.95, dinner $9.95-$19.95. Specialties: steak Parisienne, chocolate soufflé, fresh seafood. Parking. Outdoor dining. Toy train runs on overhead track. Cr cds: A, C, D, DS, MC, V.

★ ★ **LUCILE'S.** *4700 Camp Bowie (76107), west of downtown.* 817/738-4761. Hrs: 11:30 am-10 pm; Fri to 11 pm; Sat 9 am-11 pm; Sun 9 am-10 pm. Closed Dec 25. Res accepted. Bar. Semi-a la carte: bkfst $3.95-$9.95, lunch, dinner $5.25-$25.95. Specialties: angel hair pasta, woodroasted entrees. Pianist Fri, Sat. Parking. Outdoor dining. Bldg used as a restaurant since 30s; original pressed tin ceiling. Cr cds: A, D, DS, MC, V.

★ ★ **REFLECTIONS.** *(See Worthington Hotel)* 817/870-1000. Hrs: 6-10 pm; Sun brunch 10 am-2:30 pm. Res accepted. Continental menu. Bar 11:30-2 am; Sun noon-1 am. Wine cellar. A la carte entrees: dinner $17.95-$40. Sun brunch $22.95. Specializes in beef, seafood, veal. Own baking. Pianist. Valet parking. Multi-level dining. Cr cds: A, C, D, DS, JCB, MC, V.

★ ★ **SAINT-EMILION.** *3617 W 7th St (76107), near Museum/Cultural District. 817/737-2781.* Hrs: 6-10 pm; Sun 5:30-9 pm. Closed some major hols. Res accepted. French menu. Fixed price: dinner $19.75-$28.75. Specializes in roast duck, imported fresh fish, Myers black rum Creme Brulee. Parking. Cr cds: A, C, D, DS, MC, V.

Fredericksburg (C-5)

(See Johnson City, Kerrville, Mason)

Founded 1846 **Pop** 6,934 **Elev** 1,742 ft **Area code** 210 **Zip** 78624
Information Chamber of Commerce, 106 N Adams; 210/997-6523.

Nearly 600 Germans came here to settle under the auspices of the Society for the Protection of German Immigrants in Texas. Surrounded by Comanches, isolated, plagued with epidemics, unfamiliar with the country, they fought a bitter battle for survival. Upright and industrious, they prospered until the Civil War when, disapproving of slavery, men hid out in the hills and fled to Mexico to avoid joining the Confederate Army. Their troubles continued during Reconstruction, but these folk persevered by being self-reliant. In 1912 they built their own railroad to connect with the nearest line; this was discontinued in 1941. In 1937, US 87 was built through the town; now US 290 and TX 16 also run through here. Today, Fredericksburg, the center of diversified farming and ranching activity, is a picturesque community with many stone houses. Fleet Admiral Chester W. Nimitz was born here.

What to See and Do

Admiral Nimitz Museum State Historical Park. Dedicated to the more than two million men and women of all services who served under Fleet Admiral Chester W. Nimitz. The restored steamboat-shaped Nimitz Hotel (1852) contains three floors of exhibits in the Museum of the Pacific War. History Walk is lined with rare guns, planes and tanks from Pacific theater. Captured Japanese minisub. The Garden of Peace was built by the Japanese. (Daily; closed Dec 25) 340 E Main St. Phone 210/997-4379. ¢¢

Enchanted Rock State Natural Area. A 1,643-acre park with massive, 500-foot high dome of solid granite famed in Indian legend. Indians believed ghost fires flickered upon crest on moonlit nights. Geologists say creaking, groaning sounds emitted at night are result of cooling and contraction after day's heat. Nature & hiking trails. Picnicking. Primitive camping (no vehicular camping permitted). Standard hrs & fees. (Daily) 18 mi N off RR 965. Phone 915/247-3903. Per vehicle ¢¢

Pioneer Museum. Complex of several buildings, including Sunday house, log cabin. Relics of German colonists. (Apr-mid-Dec, Wed-Mon; rest of yr, wkends; closed Jan 1, Dec 25) 309 W Main St. Phone 210/997-2835. ¢¢

Vereins Kirche (Pioneer Memorial Building). Reproduction of the original (1847), octagonal community building; archives and local history collection. (Mon-Sat) Market Square, opp courthouse. Phone 210/997-7832. ¢

Annual Events

Easter Fires Pageant. Dates back more than 100 years. Sat eve before Easter.

Night in Old Fredericksburg. German food, entertainment. 3rd wkend July.

Gillespie County Fair. Oldest county fair in Texas. 4th wkend Aug.

Kristkindl Market. Market Square. Christmas fair & candlelight tour of homes. 2nd wkend Dec.

Motels

★ **BEST WESTERN SUNDAY HOUSE.** *501 E Main St. 210/997-4484; FAX 210/997-5607.* 97 rms, 2 story. S $62.95; D $67.95; each addl $6; suites $86.95; under 12 free. Crib $6. TV; cable. Pool. Restaurant 7 am-9 pm; Sat, Sun to 10 pm. Ck-out noon. In-rm modem link. Cr cds: A, C, D, DS, MC, V.

★ **COMFORT INN.** *908 S Adams. 210/997-9811; FAX 210/997-2068.* 46 rms, 2 story. S $54; D $59; each addl $5. Crib free. TV; cable. Pool. Complimentary continental bkfst. Ck-out noon. Bus depot transportation. Tennis. Picnic tables, grills. Cr cds: A, C, D, DS, ER, JCB, MC, V.

✔ ★ **DIETZEL.** *PO Box 266, 905 W Main St. 210/997-3330.* 20 rms. S $32-$44; D $34-$48; each addl $5. Crib free. Pet accepted, some restrictions; $2. TV; cable. Pool. Complimentary coffee in lobby. Restaurant adj 11 am-10 pm. Ck-out 11 am. Picnic tables. Cr cds: A, DS, MC, V.

★ **PEACH TREE INN.** *401 S Washington (US 87 S). 210/997-2117; res: 800/843-4666; FAX 210/997-0827.* 24 rms (shower only). S $28.33-$66.50; D $32.75-$66.50; under 16 free. Crib free. Pet accepted; some restrictions. TV; cable. Pool. Playground. Complimentary coffee in lobby, continental bkfst. Restaurant nearby. Ck-out 11 am. Lawn games. Some refrigerators. Cr cds: A, DS, MC, V.

★ **SAVE INN.** *514 E Main St. 210/997-6568.* 61 rms, 2 story. S $37-$50; D $50-$53; each addl $5; wkend rates (summer). Crib $5. TV; cable (premium). Pool. Complimentary coffee in lobby. Restaurant adj 6 am-10 pm. Ck-out noon. Cr cds: A, C, D, DS, MC, V.

Restaurants

★ **FRIEDHELM'S BAVARIAN INN.** *905 W Main St. 210/997-6300.* Hrs: 11 am-10 pm; Sun 11:30 am-8:30 pm. Closed Mon; Thanksgiving, Dec 25. Res accepted. German menu. Bar 3-10 pm. Semi-a la carte: lunch $4.95-$14.95, dinner $6.95-$16.95. Child's meals. Specialties: jägerschnitzel, schweinerippchen. Parking. Bavarian tavern decor. Cr cds: A, DS, MC, V.

★ ★ **THE GALLERY.** *230 E Main St. 210/997-8777.* Hrs: 7 am-10 pm; Blue Room from 6 pm Wed-Sun only. Closed Dec 25. Res accepted. Italian, German, Amer menu. Bar. Semi-a la carte: bkfst $2.95-$7.50, lunch, dinner $4.50-$16.95. A la carte entrees (Blue Room): dinner $8.50-$21. Specialties: rigatoni a pollo, Blue Room Decadence. Combo Wed-Sun (Blue Room). Four dining areas: Grille, Garden and Garden Room, main level; Blue Room, upstairs. Cr cds: A, MC, V.

★ **MAMACITA'S.** *506 Main St E. 210/997-9546.* Hrs: 11 am-9:30 pm; Fri, Sat to 10 pm. Closed Thanksgiving, Dec 25. Res accepted. Mexican menu. Bar. Semi-a la carte: lunch $4.25-$5.25, dinner $4.95-$9.95. Child's meals. Specialties: chalupas, quesadillas, enchiladas. Parking. Mexican decor; stone fountain. Cr cds: A, DS, MC, V.

Freeport (D-8)

(see Brazosport)

Fritch (F-2)

(For accommodations see Amarillo, Pampa)

Pop 2,335 **Area code** 806 **Zip** 79036
Information Chamber of Commerce, 104 N Robey, PO Box 396; 806/857-2458.

What to See and Do

Hutchinson County Historical Museum. Professionally designed museum emphasizes oil boom of the 1920s and the story of Hutchinson County. Photos of Boomtown Borger; models of early houses and Fort Adobe Walls. Painting of Chief Quanah Parker, the Battle of Adobe Walls and early Indian fighter Billy Dixon. Tools and oil field equipment, Panhandle Pueblo artifacts; dancehall, pioneer house, changing exhibits. (Memorial Day-Labor Day, daily; rest of yr, daily exc Sun; closed major hols) 12 mi E, at 618 N Main St in Borger. Phone 806/273-0130. **Free.**

Lake Meredith Aquatic & Wildlife Museum. Life-size dioramas of small game found around lake area. Five aquariums holding 11,000 gallons of water display the variety of fish found in Lake Meredith. (Daily; closed Jan 1, Thanksgiving, Dec 25) 104 N Robey. Phone 806/857-2458. **Free.**

Lake Meredith National Recreation Area. Created by Sanford Dam on the Canadian River and stocked with walleye, bass, channel and blue catfish, crappie and perch. Swimming, waterskiing; fishing; boating (ramps). Primitive camping. (Daily) Phone 806/857-3151 **Free.** On S edge of lake is

Alibates Flint Quarries National Monument. Includes area of flint quarries used by Indians of several periods from 10,000 B.C. to A.D. 1700. Bates Canyon Information Station (summer, daily) is departure point for ranger-guided tours (Memorial Day-Labor Day, daily; rest of yr, by res). Contact Lake Meredith Recreation Area, PO Box 1460; 806/857-3151. **Free.**

Annual Event

World's Largest Fish Fry. Borger. 1st Sat June.

Gainesville (A-7)

(See Denton, Sherman)

Founded 1849 **Pop** 14,256 **Elev** 738 ft **Area code** 817 **Zip** 76240
Information Chamber of Commerce, PO Box 518, phone 817/665-2831; the Tourist Information Center is located at 101 Culberson, I-35 California St exit.

Once a stop on the Butterfield Stage Line, Gainesville today is an industrial center producing airplane interiors, cutting tools and foodstuffs.

What to See and Do

Lake Texoma. (See DENISON, TX; LAKE TEXOMA, OK) E on US 82 then N via US 377 or US 69/75.

Leonard Park. Swimming pool, bathhouse (mid-May-Labor Day; fee); picnicking; playground, ballfields. 1000 W California. Phone 817/668-6291. Frank Buck Zoo is also here. Park (daily).

Morton Museum of Cooke County. Former city fire station (1884) now houses items of county history back to 1850. Tours of historic downtown area (by appt). (Tues-Sat afternoons; closed major hols) 210 S Dixon St. Phone 817/668-8900. **Free.**

Moss Lake. A 1,125-acre lake with 15 miles of shoreline. Fishing; boating (launch). Picnicking. 12 mi NW. Phone 817/668-8420.

Motels

✔ ★ ★ **BEST WESTERN SOUTHWINDS.** *2103 N I-35. 817/665-7737; FAX 817/668-2651.* 35 rms. S $34-$37; D $38-$44; each addl $5; under 12 free. Crib free. TV; cable (premium). Pool. Continental bkfst. Complimentary coffee in rms. Restaurant nearby. Ck-out 11 am. Cr cds: A, C, D, DS, MC, V.

⊞ ≈ ⊠ ⊠ SC

★ **COMFORT INN.** *Box 76, 1936 N I-35, exit 499. 817/665-5599; FAX 817/665-4266.* 30 rms, 2 story. S $38; D $42; each addl $5; under 18 free. Crib $3. TV; cable. Pool. Complimentary continental bkfst, coffee. Restaurant adj open 24 hrs. Ck-out noon. Meeting rms. Cr cds: A, C, D, DS, ER, JCB, MC, V.

D ≈ ⊠ ⊠ SC

★ ★ **HOLIDAY INN.** *600 Fair Pk Blvd, I-35 California St exit. 817/665-8800; FAX 817/665-8709.* 118 rms, 2 story. S, D $45-$50; each addl $5; under 18 free. Crib $3. TV; cable. Pool. Restaurant 6:30 am-9:30 pm. Rm serv. Bar 5 pm-midnight, Sat to 1 am, closed Sun. Ck-out noon. Coin lndry. Meeting rms. Game rm. Cr cds: A, C, D, DS, ER, JCB, MC, V.

D ≈ ⊠ ⊠ SC

Galveston (D-8)

(See Houston)

Founded 1816 **Pop** 59,070 **Elev** 20 ft **Area code** 409
Information Galveston Island Convention & Visitors Bureau, 2106 Seawall Blvd, 77550; 409/763-4311.

Few American cities have histories as romantic and adventurous as Galveston's. It is generally agreed that the Spanish explorer Cabeza de Vaca, first European to see Texas, was shipwrecked on Galveston Island in 1528. From here he began his wanderings through Texas, New Mexico and finally to Mexico, where his tales inspired later expeditions.

The pirate Jean Lafitte was lord of Galveston from 1817 until 1821. He built a house and fortress called Maison Rouge (Red House). Under Lafitte, the town was a nest of slave traders, saloon keepers, gamblers, smugglers and pirates. One hundred Spanish ships were seized and looted during Lafitte's time, but Spain was powerless against him. Many slaves were on the pirated vessels; Lafitte's standard price for slaves was a dollar a pound.

Lafitte's occupation ended in May 1821, after the US Navy ordered him to leave. He set fire to the town, fleeing southward and into oblivion with his remaining followers.

During the Texas Revolution the four ships of the Texas Navy were based in Galveston and managed to prevent a blockade of the Texas coast. When David Burnet, interim President of the Republic of Texas, and his cabinet came here in 1836, fleeing from Santa Anna, the town became the capital of Texas.

After the Civil War, Congress appropriated money to make Galveston a deep-water port. The town had a population of 38,000 in 1900. On September 8 of that year a hurricane with 110-mph winds struck, flooding the city, killing 6,000 and leaving 8,000 homeless. The storm drove a 4,000-ton vessel to a point 22 miles from deep water. Galveston rebuilt itself with inspired fortitude. The level of land was raised from 5 to 17 feet and a 17-foot high, 16-foot wide reinforced concrete seawall was built. The wall has withstood subsequent hurricane tides.

Galveston's wharves can berth 38 oceangoing vessels. It is the state's leading cotton port and is a sulphur and grain shipping center. It is an island city colored with blooming tropical flora. Forty blocks of the East End Historical District, protected from future development, may be seen on walking or driving tours.

With 32 miles of sandy beaches, fishing piers, deep-sea fishing, cool breezes off the Gulf and plenty of places to stay, eat and enjoy oneself, Galveston is an ideal spot for a seaside vacation. Such vacations are its specialty, although the city is also an important medical center and international seaport.

What to See and Do

1839 Williams Home. Home of Texas pioneer, patriot and entrepreneur Samuel May Williams, the house was saved from the wrecker's ball and meticulously restored. Combines historical restoration with advanced audiovisual techniques. (Daily; closed Jan 1, Thanksgiving & Dec 24-25) Sr citizen rate. 3601 Ave P. Phone 409/765-1839. ¢¢

Ashton Villa (1859). This 3-story brick Italianate mansion has been restored to reflect life in Galveston during the late 1800s; period furniture; many interesting details including ornate cast-iron verandas in Gothic-revival style. Tours begin in carriage house, located on grounds, and include the ornate Gold Room and second-floor family quarters. A permanent archaeology exhibit, "Ashton Villa through the Back Door," shows domestic 19th-century life. (Daily; closed Thanksgiving & Dec 24-25) Sr citizen rate. 2328 Broadway at 23rd St. Phone 409/762-3933. ¢¢

Factory Stores of America. Over 30 outlet stores can be found in this outdoor shopping area. (Mon-Sat, Sun afternoons) Approx 5 min on I-45, exit 13, in La Marque. Phone 409/938-3333.

Galveston Island State Park. A 2,000-acre recreational area. Swimming, fishing, boating in bay and gulf. Nature trails. Picnicking (shelters). Improved campsites (hookups, showers, dump station). Standard fees. (Daily) 11 mi SW on FM 3005. Phone 409/737-1222. Per vehicle ¢¢

Galveston-Port Bolivar Ferry. Operated by Texas Dept of Transportation. (Daily) Ferry Rd (Hwy 87). Phone 409/763-2386. **Free.**

Moody Gardens. A 142-acre recreation and educational facility featuring Rain Forest Pyramid, 3-D IMAX theater, Palm Beach (Memorial Day-Labor Day, daily) and Seaside Safari. (Daily) 1 Hope Blvd. Phone 409/744-1745. ¢¢¢

Railroad Museum at the Center for Transportation and Commerce. At the foot of the historic Strand in the restored Santa Fe Union Station, the five-acre museum contains the largest collection of restored railroad equipment in the Southwest. Sound and light shows portray the history and development of Galveston Island; the miniature layout of the Port of Galveston features an HO-scale railroad. Building includes a 1930s waiting room. (Daily; closed Thanksgiving, Dec 25) Sr citizen rate. 123 Rosenberg. Phone 409/765-5700. ¢¢

Recreational facilities. The 32-mile beach, with fishing piers, boats for rent and amusements, is Galveston's prime attraction. Stewart Beach, a municipal development, is at the east end of the island. Fishing is allowed from five free county piers, by boat rental or by charter boat for deep-sea sport. There are riding stables at Jamaica Beach on Stewart Rd and two golf courses and several tennis courts in the area. Anchorage for 300 pleasure boats and yachts at the Galveston Yacht Club, 715 Holiday Dr; also for 556 (400 covered) at the marina, 11th St at Pier 7. Phone 409/763-5668.

Seawolf Park. World War II submarine USS *Cavalla* and destroyer escort USS *Stewart* are located here; also Army tank, Navy fighter plane. Playground, picnicking, fishing pier (fee), pavilion. Parking (fee). Park (daily; closed Dec 25). Pelican Island. Phone 409/744-5738. ¢

Texas Seaport Museum. Features the "tall ship" *Elissa*, built in Scotland in 1877. The ship, crafted by Alexander Hall & Co, shipbuilders famous for their beautiful iron sailing ships, traded under five different flags and visited ports throughout the world. Rescued from the scrapyard in 1974 and restored by Galveston Historical Foundation. Audiovisual presentation on *Elissa*; galleries with maritime exhibits. (Daily; closed Thanksgiving, Dec 25) Sr citizen rate. Pier 21. Phone 409/763-1877. ¢¢

The Bishop's Palace (1886). Four-story stone, Victorian mansion, former residence of Bishop Byrne (1923-50), is outstanding example of this style and period; marble, mosaics, stained- and jeweled-glass windows, hand-carved stairwell and woodwork, art objects from many lands. Tours (Memorial Day wkend-Labor Day wkend, Mon-Sat, also Sun afternoons; rest of yr, Wed-Mon afternoons; closed some major hols) Sr citizen rate. 1402 Broadway. Phone 409/762-2475. ¢¢

⭐ **The Strand National Historic Landmark District.** Extends between 20th and 25th Sts. This historic area is restored to late 1800s appearance. The Strand, once known as the "Wall Street of the Southwest," contains one of the finest concentrations of 19th-century commercial structures in the United States. Many are now restored and used as apartments, restaurants, shops and galleries. A Visitors Center is located at 2016 Strand. Various events take place here throughout the year (see ANNUAL EVENTS). For additional information contact the Galveston Historical Foundation, 2016 Strand, 77550; 409/765-7834.

Treasure Isle Tour Train. One and one-half hour, 17-mile trip around Galveston. (Daily, weather permitting) Moody Center, 2106 Seawall Blvd. Phone 409/765-9564. ¢¢

Annual Events

Mardi Gras. On the Strand. Late Feb.

Historic Homes Tour. Tour of 19th-century private houses not normally open to the public. Contact Galveston Historical Foundation. 1st 2 wkends May.

Dickens on the Strand. Located in the Strand National Historic Landmark District. Yuletide celebration recreates 19th-century London street scene including live representations of Charles Dickens' characters, carolers, dancers, puppeteers and outdoor handbell festival. Contact Galveston Historical Foundation. 1st wkend Dec.

Seasonal Event

Galveston Island Outdoor Musicals. Amphitheater, N of Seawall Blvd (FM 3005) on 13-mile Rd in Galveston Island State Park. Broadway, other productions. Phone 800/54-SHOWS. Memorial Day-Labor Day.

Motel

⭐⭐ **LA QUINTA.** *1402 Seawall Blvd (77550). 409/763-1224; FAX 409/765-8663.* 117 rms. May-mid-Sept: S $73-$106; D $80-$109; each addl $10; under 18 free; higher rates wkends; lower rates rest of yr. Crib free. Pet accepted, some restrictions. TV; cable (premium). Pool. Complimentary continental bkfst. Restaurant adj open 24 hrs. Ck-out 11 am. Meeting rms. Valet serv. On Gulf. Cr cds: A, C, D, DS, MC, V.

Motor Hotels

⭐⭐ **HARBOR HOUSE.** *No. 28 (77550), Pier 21. 409/763-3321; res: 800/874-3721; FAX 409/765-6421.* 42 rms, 3 story. S $115; D $130; each addl $10; suites $175; under 18 free; package plans; higher rates Mardi Gras. Crib free. TV; cable (premium). Restaurant 7 am-10 pm. Rm serv. Bar. Ck-out noon. Meeting rms. Business servs avail. In-rm modem link. Bellhops. Shopping arcade. On harbor. Marina for guest's boats. Cr cds: A, C, D, MC, V.

🅳 🈁 🔥 🆂🅲

✔⭐⭐ **INN AT SAN LUIS.** *5400 Seawall Blvd (77551). 409/744-5000; res: 800/392-5937; FAX 409/740-2209.* 150 rms, 6 story. S, D $59-$119; each addl $10; under 12 free; lower rates winter. Crib free. TV; cable (premium). Pool; poolside serv. Restaurant 7-11 am. Bar 11 am-11:30 pm. Ck-out noon. Meeting rms. Gift shop. Lighted tennis.

Exercise equipt; weight machines, bicycles, whirlpool. Balconies. Opp beach. Cr cds: A, C, D, DS, MC, V.

D 🚭 🏊 🏃 ⛷ 🎿 🔥 SC

Hotels

★ **HOLIDAY INN ON THE BEACH.** 5002 Seawall Blvd (77551). 409/740-3581; FAX 409/744-6677. 178 rms, 8 story. Mar-Aug: S, D $89-$124; each addl $5; under 18 free; suites $395; higher rates special events; lower rates rest of yr. Crib free. TV; cable (premium). Pool; wading pool, poolside serv. Restaurant 6 am-10 pm. Bar 11:30-2 am; entertainment. Ck-out noon. Gift shop. Exercise equipt; weights, bicycles, sauna. Balconies. Gulf view. Cr cds: A, C, D, DS, JCB, MC, V.

D 🚭 🏊 🏃 🎿 🔥 SC

★ ★ **HOTEL GALVEZ.** 2024 Seawall Blvd (77550). 409/765-7721; res: 800/392-4285. 228 rms, 7 story. S, D $105-$135; suites $175-$350; under 18 free. Crib free. Free garage parking; valet $5. TV; cable (premium). Pool; wading pool, whirlpool. Restaurant 7 am-2 pm, 5:30-10 pm. Bar noon-1 am; entertainment Fri, Sat. Ck-out noon. Meeting rms. Business servs avail. In-rm modem link. Gift shop. Refrigerator in suites. On beach. Cr cds: A, C, D, MC, V.

D 🏊 🎿 🔥

★ ★ ★ **SAN LUIS.** 5222 Seawall Blvd (77551). 409/744-1500; res: 800/327-2029; FAX 409/744-8452. 244 rms, 96 condominiums, 16 story. Memorial Day-Labor Day: S, D $99-$169; each addl $10; suites $135-$320; under 12 free; package plans; lower rates rest of yr. TV; cable. Heated pool. Restaurant 6:30 am-10 pm. Bar 11 am-11:30 pm, Sun from noon; dancing Thurs-Sat. Business center. In-rm modem link. Lighted tennis. Golf privileges. Exercise equipt; weight machine, treadmill, whirlpool. Balconies overlook Gulf. Cr cds: A, C, D, DS, MC, V.

D 🚭 🏋 ⛷ 🏊 🏃 🎿 🔥 SC ✈

★ ★ ★ **TREMONT HOUSE.** 2300 Ship's Mechanic Row (77550). 409/763-0300; res: 800/874-2300; FAX 409/763-1539. A hand-carved mahogany bar is but one of the magnificent details of the public spaces in this grand 1879 building. Guest rooms feature Italian tile, soaring ceilings, and 11-foot windows. 117 rms, 4 story. S, D $130-$175; each addl $15; suites $250-$350; under 18 free. Crib free. TV; cable (premium), VCR avail (movies avail). Restaurant 6:30 am-10:30 pm. Rm serv 24 hrs. Bar 11-2 am; pianist. Ck-out noon. Meeting rms. Business servs avail. Concierge. Shopping arcade. Free downtown transportation. Cr cds: A, C, D, MC, V.

D 🎿 🔥 SC

Restaurants

★ ★ **CLARY'S.** 8509 Teichman Rd. 409/740-0771. Hrs: 11:30 am-2:30 pm, 5:30-10 pm; Sat 5-10 pm. Closed Mon. Bar. Wine list. Semi-a la carte: lunch $7.50-$11, dinner $12.25-$18.75. Specializes in fresh seafood, steak. Own baking. Glass garden rm overlooks bayou. Cr cds: A, C, D, DS, MC, V.

D

★ ★ **GAIDO'S.** 3828 Seawall Blvd (77550). 409/762-9625. Hrs: 11:45 am-9 pm; Fri, Sat to 10 pm. Closed Thanksgiving, Dec 25. Bar. Semi-a la carte: lunch & dinner $12-$18. Complete meals: dinner $16.15-$23.70. Child's meals. Specializes in Gulf seafood. Parking. Nautical decor. Gulf opp. Established 1911. Family-owned. Cr cds: A, DS, MC, V.

D SC

★ ★ **LANDRY'S.** 5310 Seawall Blvd (77551). 409/744-1010. Hrs: 11 am-11 pm; Fri, Sat to midnight; winter hrs vary. Closed Dec 25. Bar. Semi-a la carte: lunch, dinner $4.95-$18.95. Child's meals. Specialties: seafood gumbo, whole gulf flounder, Angus steak. Parking. Outdoor dining. Casual dining. Cr cds: A, D, DS, MC, V.

D

✔ ★ **NASH D'AMICO'S.** 2328 Strand. 409/763-6500. Hrs: 11:30 am-10 pm; Fri, Sat to 11 pm. Closed Jan 1, Thanksgiving, Dec 25. Res accepted. Italian menu. Bar. Semi-a la carte: lunch, dinner $6.25-$14.95. Child's meals. Specializes in seafood, veal. Own desserts. Art deco and neon decor in historic Victorian building (1895). Cr cds: A, C, D, DS, MC, V.

★ ★ ★ **WENTLETRAP.** 2301 Strand, at Tremont. 409/765-5545. Hrs: 11:30 am-2:30 pm, 6-10 pm; Fri, Sat to 10:30 pm; Sun 11:30 am-2:30 pm. Res accepted. Continental menu. Bar. Semi-a la carte: lunch $8.95-$12.95, dinner $14.95-$24.95. Sun brunch $16.95. Specializes in seafood, beef. Pianist Fri-Sun. Valet parking. Restored 1871 building, 3-story atrium. Cr cds: A, C, D, MC, V.

D

Georgetown (C-6)

(See Austin, Burnet, Salado)

Founded 1848 **Pop** 14,842 **Elev** 758 ft **Area code** 512
Information Chamber of Commerce, 100 Stadium Dr, PO Box 346, 78627; 512/930-3535.

Established as a trade center for this agricultural region, Georgetown is the seat of Williamson County, one of Texas' most productive farming areas and home of Southwestern University. The town's Main Street has some of the best Victorian architecture in the state.

What to See and Do

Inner Space Cavern. Large stalactites, stalagmites; lighting, acoustical effects; cable car-type elevator. Cave temp constant 70°F. Guided tours (1¼ hr); 30-min max wait for tours to depart. (Daily; closed 2 wks before Dec 25) 1 mi S off I-35 exit 259. Phone 512/863-5545. ¢¢¢

Lake Georgetown. This 1,300-acre lake is surrounded by 3 developed park areas. Hiking trail (16½ mi). Camping (fee). (Daily) 4 mi W via FM 2338. Contact the Project Manager, Rte 5, Box 500; 512/863-3016. **Free.**

San Gabriel Park. Eighty acres with fishing, swimming; picnicking (shelters, barbecue facilities); ballfield, hiking; livestock show barns, rodeo arena. N edge of town, on the San Gabriel River. Phone 512/869-3595. **Free.**

Southwestern University (1840). (1,200 students) Oldest university in Texas. Several historic buildings; chapel, museum. Self-guided tours. (Mon-Fri) 1001 E University Ave. Phone 512/863-6511.

Annual Event

Williamson County Gem & Mineral Show. Mid-Feb.

Motels

✔ ★ **COMFORT INN.** 1005 Leander Rd (78628). 512/863-7504. 55 rms. S $54-$69; D $59-$74; each addl $5; under 12 free. Crib free. Pet accepted; some restrictions. TV; cable, VCR avail (movies avail). Pool. Complimentary continental bkfst, coffee. Restaurant nearby. Ck-out noon. In-rm modem link. Cr cds: A, C, D, DS, JCB, MC, V.

D 🐾 🏊 🎿 🔥

★ ★ **LA QUINTA INN.** 333 I-35N (78628), off exit 262. 512/869-2541; FAX 512/863-7073. 98 rms, 3 story. May-Aug: S $59-$66; D $69-$79; each addl $10; suites $85-$150; under 18 free. Crib free. TV; cable (premium). Pool. Complimentary continental bkfst. Restaurant 6:30 am-9:30 pm. Rm serv. Ck-out noon. Meeting rms. In-rm modem link. Valet serv. Cr cds: A, C, D, DS, MC, V.

D 🏊 🎿 🔥 SC

Restaurant

✔ ★ ★ **CAFE ON THE SQUARE.** *119 W 7th St. 512/863-0596.* Hrs: 11 am-9 pm; Fri, Sat to 10 pm; Sun 10 am-9 pm. Closed Thanksgiving, Dec 25. Private club. Semi-a la carte: lunch $3.95-$7.95; dinner $6.95-$15.95. Child's meals. Specializes in chicken-fried steak, seafood. In 1870 native stone building that was a frontier general store. Cr cds: A, DS, MC, V.

D

Goliad (E-6)

(For accommodations see Victoria)

Founded 1749 **Pop** 1,946 **Elev** 171 ft **Area code** 512 **Zip** 77963
Information Chamber of Commerce, Market & Franklin Sts, PO Box 606; 512/645-3563.

A Mexican garrison stationed in Goliad was conquered in 1835 by Americans settlers in Texas; in December of that year the first Declaration of Texas Independence was issued from the city of Goliad. Three weeks after the fall of the Alamo, in March 1836, Colonel James W. Fannin and 350 men holding the town were overwhelmed by Mexican forces and surrendered. They were promised they would be treated as prisoners of war; instead, they were massacred. Spurred on by the resultant wrath and the battle cry "Remember the Alamo, remember Goliad," Texas Republic forces devastated Santa Anna at San Jacinto.

Now a farm and ranching market town, Goliad remains a monument to the Texas Revolution.

What to See and Do

Goliad State Historical Park. A 186-acre recreational area. Swimming; fishing. Nature, hiking trails. Picnicking (shelters), playground. Improved camping, tent & trailer sites (dump station). Standard fees. (Daily) 1 mi S on US 183 to Park Rd 6. Phone 512/645-3405. Includes

Mission Espiritu Santo de Zuñiga. Reconstruction of the original established in 1749. Interpretive center in the mission contains artifacts and displays illustrating Spanish colonial era. ¢

Market House Museum. The Market House, restored in 1967 as a museum, was built in 1870 with stalls that were rented to sellers of meat and produce. In 1886 the building became a firehouse, home to the volunteer fire department. Chamber of Commerce offices are here as well. (Daily exc Sun; closed major hols) Corner Franklin & Market Sts. Phone 512/645-3563. **Free.**

Presidio La Bahia (1721). The only completely restored Spanish Colonial Presidio in the western hemisphere and the only one in North America to have participated in six wars for independence. Spanish, Mexican and Texan soldiers once garrisoned its fortified walls. The first Declaration of Texas Independence was signed here; the first flag of Texas independence flew here. Site of the longest seige in American military history (1812-13) and the Goliad Massacre (1836), the largest loss of life for Texas independence. Living history programs, battle reenactments, seasonal fiestas throughout the year. (Daily; closed major hols) 1 mi S on US 183. Phone 512/645-3752. ¢

Annual Events

Goliad County Fair & Rodeo. Fairgrounds. 3rd wkend Mar.

Cinco de Mayo Fiesta. Honoring victory of Mexican troops under General Ignacio Zaragosa against invading French troops at Battle of Puebla (1862). Wkend nearest May 5.

Seasonal Event

Stock car racing. Shady Oaks Speedway. 6 mi N off US 77A on FM 622. Phone 512/645-2840. Mar-Oct.

Gonzales (D-6)

(For accommodations see San Marcos, also see Seguin)

Settled 1825 **Pop** 6,527 **Elev** 292 ft **Area code** 210 **Zip** 78629
Information Chamber of Commerce, 414 St Lawrence St, PO Box 134; 210/672-6532.

In 1835 the city of Gonzales had a small brass cannon that the Mexican government had left for defense in case of Indian attack. When the American settlers grew dissatisfied with Mexican rule, they refused to return the cannon. Mexico then sent a detachment to take it by force. The first Texas battle flag, with a single star and the words "Come and Take It," was unfurled. When the Mexicans came, the first shots of the Texas Revolution were fired (October 2, 1835), and the Mexicans withdrew. Later Gonzales' men went to the Alamo to aid Col. William Travis although they knew the cause was hopeless.

What to See and Do

Gonzales County Jail. Restored cells, gallows, dungeon, jailer's room. (Mon-Sat, also Sun afternoons; closed hols) 414 St Lawrence. Phone 210/672-6532. **Free.**

Gonzales Memorial Museum. Collection of toys, guns, clothing, pictures & letters that depict Gonzales and its history. Includes the legendary cannon. (Daily exc Mon) 414 Smith St. Phone 210/672-6350. **Free.**

Gonzales Pioneer Village. Village consists of ten reconstructed buildings from before 1900. Includes log house, blacksmith shop, working broom factory, 1890s house and 1870s church. Special tours, programs. Adj is Ft Waul, an earthen-walled Confederate fort (1864). 1 mi N on US 183. For tour information phone 210/672-2157. ¢¢

Palmetto State Park. Approx 250 acres. Swimming; fishing (pier). Picnicking (shelter; fee), playground. Nature, hiking trails. Improved camping (hookups, dump station). Standard fees. (Daily) 12 mi NW on US 183, 2 mi W on Park Rd 11. Phone 210/672-3266.

Annual Event

Come and Take It Celebration. Honors first shot fired for Texas independence. Parade, street dance, vintage house tours; battle re-enactments. 1st wkend Oct.

Graham (B-6)

(See Mineral Wells)

Founded 1872 **Pop** 8,986 **Elev** 1,045 ft **Area code** 817 **Zip** 76450
Information Chamber of Commerce, 608 Elm St, PO Box 299; 817/549-3355 or 800/256-4844.

The Cattle Raisers Association of Texas was organized here in 1877. Today Graham is a farming, ranching and oil commercial center.

What to See and Do

Fort Richardson State Historical Park. Approx 400 acres. Most northerly of frontier army posts in Texas, active 1867-78. Seven restored buildings and two replicas. Interpretive center and period displays. Fishing. Hiking; nature study. Picnicking. Improved campsites (hookups, dump station). Standard fees. (Daily) 30 mi NE via US 380 in Jacksboro. Phone 817/567-3506. Per vehicle ¢¢

Possum Kingdom State Park (see). Approx 30 mi SW via TX 67, then S on FM 717.

Motel

✔★★ **GATEWAY INN.** *1401 TX 16S.* 817/549-0222; FAX 817/549-4301. 77 rms, 2 story. S $32; D $36-$39; each addl $4. Pet accepted; $5. TV; cable. Pool; whirlpool. Complimentary coffee in rms. Restaurant 6 am-10 pm. Rm serv. Private club 11 am-midnight, Sat to 1 am. Ck-out noon. Coin lndry. Free airport transportation. Cr cds: A, C, D, DS, MC, V.

D ✦ ≈ ⊠ 🔥 SC

Granbury (B-6)

(See Arlington-Grand Prairie, Cleburne, Fort Worth)

Pop 4,045 **Elev** 722 ft **Area code** 817 **Zip** 76048
Information Granbury Convention and Visitors Bureau, 100 N Crockett; 817/573-5548 or 800/950-2212.

What to See and Do

Fossil Rim Wildlife Center. A 3,000-acre wildlife conservation center with more than 1,000 endangered, threatened and exotic animals. Breeding programs for endangered species including white rhinoceros, Mexican wolf, red wolf, Grevy's zebra, Arabian oryx, scimitar-horned oryx, addax and cheetah. Ten-mile drive-through with Nature trail; fossil area; petting pasture. Restaurant; gift shop. Some fees. (Daily; closed Thanksgiving, Dec 25) Sr citizen rate. S on TX 144, then 3 mi SW of Glen Rose off US 67. Phone 817/897-2960. ¢¢¢¢

Granbury Opera House (1886). Restored opera house on historic town square. Musicals, plays, special events. (Summer, Thurs-Sun; rest of yr, Fri-Sun) 116 E Pearl St. Phone 817/573-9191.

Granbury Queen **Riverboat.** Authentic 2-story paddlewheeler offers 1½-hour excursions on river. (Daily; 1 wk advance notice advised; closed Jan-Feb) Also 2½-hour dinner excursion (Fri, Sat evenings; res required). Sr citizen rate. Accessible to wheelchairs. 1 mi S via TX 144, adj McElvey Marina. Phone 817/573-6822. Daily cruise ¢¢¢

Annual Event

Civil War Reeanactment. Sept 28, 29.

Motels

★ **BEST WESTERN CLASSIC INN.** *1209 N Plaza Drive.* 817/573-8874. 42 rms. S $59; D $64; each addl $5; under 12 free. Crib $4. Pet accepted, some restrictions. TV; cable (premium). Pool. Complimentary continental bkfst, coffee. Restaurant adj open 24 hrs. Ck-out 11 am. Business servs avail. In-rm modem link. Health club privileges. Refrigerators. Lake ¼ mi; swimming beach. Cr cds: A, C, D, DS, JCB, MC, V.

D ✦ ✱ ≈ ⊠ 🔥 SC

★ **COMFORT INN.** *1201 N Plaza Dr, off US 377.* 817/573-2611; FAX 817/573-2695. 48 rms, 2 story. Apr-Aug: S $50-$60; D $60-$70; each addl $5; under 18 free; lower rates rest of yr. Crib $10. TV; cable (premium). Pool; whirlpool. Complimentary coffee in lobby, continental bkfst. Restaurant adj open 24 hrs. Ck-out noon. Meeting rms. Business servs avail. Some refrigerators. Cr cds: A, C, D, DS, MC, V.

D ≈ ⊠ 🔥 SC

★ **LODGE OF GRANBURY.** *400 E Pearl St.* 817/573-2606; res: 800/551-6388; FAX 817/573-2077. 58 suites, 3 story. May-Oct: suites $89-$165; lower rates rest of yr. TV; cable (premium). Pool; whirlpool. Complimentary coffee in rms. Private club 4 pm-midnight. Ck-out noon. Business servs avail. Lighted tennis. 18-hole golf privi-

leges. Refrigerators. Private patios, balconies. Picnic tables. On lake. Cr cds: A, C, D, DS, MC, V.

D ✦ 🎿 ≈ ⊠ 🔥 SC

★★ **PLANTATION INN.** *1451 E Pearl St.* 817/573-8846; res: 800/422-2402; FAX 817/579-0917. 53 rms, 2 story. S $60-$65, D $65-$70; each addl $5; suites $70-$75; under 6 free. TV; cable. Pool; wading pool. Complimentary continental bkfst. Ck-out 11 am. Meeting rms. Business servs avail. Free airport transportation. Refrigerators. Some private patios, balconies. Cr cds: A, D, DS, MC, V.

≈ ⊠ 🔥 SC

Restaurants

✔★ **CUCKOO'S NEST.** *On the Square, downtown.* 817/573-9722. Hrs: 11:30 am-9 pm. Closed Mon; also Dec 24-Jan 1. Res accepted. Private club to midnight; Sat to 1 am. Semi-a la carte: lunch $4.95-$14.95. Child's meals. Specializes in country-fried steak, marinated rib-eye steak, dessert crêpes. Entertainment Sat. Parking. Historic building; antique furnishings. Cr cds: A, C, D, DS, MC, V.

★ **KEY LARGO.** *1333 N Plaza Dr.* 817/573-7031. Hrs: 5-9:30 pm. Closed Sun; Dec 25. Res accepted. Private club 11 am-midnight; Sat to 1 am. Semi-a la carte: dinner $4.95-$14.95. Child's meals. Specializes in steak, seafood, prime rib. Salad bar. Parking. Nautical motif. Cr cds: A, DS, MC, V.

D

Grand Prairie (B-7)

(see Arlington-Grand Prairie)

Greenville (B-7)

(See Bonham, Dallas, McKinney)

Pop 23,071 **Elev** 550 ft **Area code** 903
Information Chamber of Commerce, 2713 Stonewall St, PO Box 1055, 75403; 903/455-1510.

A manufacturing and processing center of aerospace, electronics, food and other products, Greenville is in a rich livestock area near Lake Tawakoni. Fishing is available in five city reserviors and a number of nearby streams.

What to See and Do

Lake Tawakoni. Fishing; boating (ramps, marinas), waterskiing. Picnicking. Tent & trailer sites. Some fees. (Daily) 16 mi S off US 69. For information phone Wind Point Park, 903/662-5134. Per vehicle ¢¢

Annual Events

Hunt County Fair. Fairgrounds. Sept.

Cotton Jubilee. Downtown. Multicultural & environmental fair; dancing, carnival, gospel sing; arts & crafts show. 4 days mid-Oct.

Motels

✔★★ **BEST WESTERN INN.** *1216 I-30W (75401).* 903/454-1792. 99 rms, 2 story. S $36-$40; D $42-$50; each addl $4; suites $55-$65; under 12 free. Crib free. TV; cable. Pool. Complimentary coffee. Restaurant adj open 24 hrs. Bar 4 pm-midnight, Sat from 6 pm, closed Sun; dancing. Ck-out noon. Coin Indry. Meeting rm. Valet serv. Health club privileges. Cr cds: A, C, D, DS, MC, V.

★ ★ **HOLIDAY INN.** 1215 I-30 (75401), at US 69 Business. 903/454-7000; FAX 903/454-7000, ext. 284. 138 rms, 2 story. S $39-$51; D $43-$55; each addl $4; under 18 free. Crib free. TV; cable. Pool; whirlpool, sauna. Complimentary coffee. Restaurant 6 am-10 pm. Rm serv. Private club 4 pm-midnight, Sat 5 pm-1 am; dancing. Ck-out noon. Coin Indry. Meeting rm. Valet serv. Sundries. Cr cds: A, C, D, DS, JCB, MC, V.

Unrated Dining Spot

PUDDIN HILL STORE. 201 E I-30 (75401), at exit 95. 903/455-6931. Hrs: 10 am-5 pm; Sun from 1 pm. Closed hols. A la carte entrees: lunch $3-$7.50. Child's meals. Specializes in homemade soups, gourmet sandwiches, carrot cake. Western country atmosphere; chocolate doll house and carousel on display. Tours of confectionery (Oct-Dec); special events. Cr cds: A, MC, V.

D

Groesbeck (C-7)

(For accommodations see Waco)

Founded 1869 **Pop** 3,185 **Elev** 478 ft **Area code** 817 **Zip** 76642
Information Chamber of Commerce, 112 1/2 N Ellis, PO Box 326; 817/729-3894.

Groesbeck is a trade center for area farms and ranches. Site of several small manufacturing industries and large deposits of lignite coal, it has some oil and gas production.

What to See and Do

Confederate Reunion Grounds State Historical Park. Approx 80 acres. Encampment formed in 1889 to perpetuate memories of fallen Confederate soldiers and to aid disabled survivors and indigent widows and orphans of the deceased. Canoeing to Fort Parker State Park on Navasota River. Swimming; fishing. Hiking, birdwatching. Picnicking, playground. Standard fees. (Daily) 7 mi N via TX 14, then 2 1/2 mi W on FM 2705. Contact Park Superintendent, c/o Fort Parker State Park, Rte 3, Box 95, Mexia 76667; 817/562-5751. Per vehicle ¢¢

Fort Parker State Park. On Lake Fort Parker, approx 1,500 acres. Swimming; fishing; boating (ramp), canoeing. Hiking. Picnicking; concession. Improved campsites (hookups, shelters, dump station). Standard fees. (Daily) 6 mi N via TX 14, to entrance on Park Rd 28. Phone 817/562-5751. Per vehicle ¢¢

Lake Limestone. This 14,200-acre dammed lake offers two marinas with public access areas at various locations. (Daily) 18 mi SE via FM 937.

Limestone County Historical Museum. Artifacts and information relating to Limestone County; Old Fort Parker memorabilia. (Mon-Fri; closed major hols) 210 W Navasota St. Phone 817/729-5064. ¢

Old Fort Parker State Historical Park (1834). Built by the Parker family to protect a small settlement of families. In 1836 Comanches overran the fort, killing 5 persons and capturing 5 more, including Cynthia Ann Parker, 9 years old. She grew up, married a Comanche chief and lived with the Indians until captured 24 years later. She was the mother of the last great Comanche chief, Quanah Parker. Log blockhouse and stockade. (Daily) Standard fees. (Daily) 4 mi N via TX 14 & Park Rd 35. Phone 817/729-5253. ¢

Annual Event

Red Stocking Follies. Last wkend Apr.

Guadalupe Mountains National Park (B-2)

(For accommodations see El Paso, Van Horn; also Carlsbad, NM)

(Approx 50 mi N of Van Horn via TX 54)

Standing like an island in the desert, this spectacular expanse of the Capitan Reef is part of the world's most extensive fossil reef complex (Permian reef complex). The 86,416-acre park encompasses the most scenic and rugged portion of these mountains. Elevations range from 3,650 feet to 8,749 feet at Guadalupe Peak, the highest point in Texas. Beside the lofty peaks and coniferous forests there are deep canyons, a tremendous earth fault, desert lowlands, historic sites, unusual flora and fauna, outstanding scenery and more than 80 miles of hiking trails, with possible trips ranging from 5 minutes to 5 days. Several precautions are necessary. Check with a ranger before leaving the main road; do not climb the cliffs; many desert plants have sharp spines; watch for and respect rattlesnakes; be prepared in the backcountry (stout shoes, sun protection, appropriate clothing and water). Pets must be leashed or restrained and are not permitted on the trails or in the back country; firearms are not permitted in the park; wood or charcoal fires are not permitted in the park. Plan to cook on a stove using containerized fuel. Sightseeing by car is limited to the highway, but scenic. Camping, backpacking, hiking and horseback trails (no rentals). Two drive-in campgrounds: one on the southeast side at Pine Springs, and one on the north at Dog Canyon. All individual campsites are on a first-come first-served basis. Permits (free) required for backpacking; check with the Visitors Center first. For information contact the Superintendent, HC 60, Box 400, Salt Flat, TX 79847-9400 or phone 915/828-3251.

Harlingen (F-6)

(See Brownsville, McAllen, Port Isabel)

Pop 48,735 **Elev** 36 ft **Area code** 210
Information Chamber of Commerce, 311 E Tyler St, 78550; 210/423-5440 or 800/531-7346.

Formerly known as Six-shooter Junction because in the 1800s there were more six-shooters than city residents, Harlingen has become the transportation and medical center of a rich farming territory. It is also a central area of distribution, processing and marketing. The Harlingen Channel (Arroyo Colorado Canal) links the Port of Harlingen with the Intracoastal Waterway and 30,000 miles of inland waterways.

What to See and Do

Laguna Atascosa National Wildlife Refuge. Approx 45,000 acres with walking trails. Fishing along the Harlingen Ship Channel only. Visitor center (Oct-Apr, daily) Administrative office (all yr, Mon-Fri; closed some major hols). 18 mi E on FM 106, then follow signs. Phone 210/748-3607. Per vehicle ¢

Annual Event

RioFest. Valley Fair Park. Phone 210/425-2705. Early Apr.

Motels

✔★ **DAYS INN.** *1901 W Tyler (48550). 210/425-1810; FAX 210/425-7227.* 148 rms, 2 story. S $49-$64; D $61-$71; each addl $7; under 18 free. Pets accepted. TV; cable. Heated pool. Complimentary coffee in lobby. Restaurant 7 am-2 pm, 5-9 pm. Rm serv. Bar 5 pm-2 am. Ck-out noon. Coin lndry. Meeting rms. Free airport transportation. Refrigerators avail. Picnic tables. Cr cds: A, C, D, DS, MC, V.

★★ **LA QUINTA.** *1002 S US 83 (78550). 210/428-6888.* 130 rms, 2 story. S $49-$56; D $59-$66; each addl $8; under 18 free. Crib free. Pet accepted. TV; cable. Pool. Complimentary continental bkfst. Complimentary coffee in lobby. Restaurant adj open 24 hrs. Ck-out noon. Coin lndry. Meeting rms. Valet serv. Free airport transportation. Health club privileges. Cr cds: A, C, D, DS, MC, V.

Unrated Dining Spot

LUBY'S CAFETERIA. *709 N 77 Sunshine Strip (US 77). 210/423-4812.* Hrs: 11 am-8 pm; summer to 8:30 pm. Closed Dec 24 eve-Dec 25. Avg ck: lunch, dinner $5.40. Specializes in fresh vegetables, fish, strawberry pie. Parking. Cr cds: DS, MC, V.

SC

Henderson (B-8)

(For accommodations see Longview, Tyler)

Founded 1844 **Pop** 11,139 **Elev** 506 ft **Area code** 903 **Zip** 75652
Information Tourist Development Dept, Chamber of Commerce, 201 N Main St; 903/657-5528.

What to See and Do

Depot Museum and Children's Discovery Center. Covers Rusk County history; many activities for children ages 3-11 in renovated cotton warehouse. Several other buildings include T.J. Walling Cabin (1841) and Arnold Outhouse (1908), the first such structure to receive a state historical marker. (Daily exc Sun; closed major hols) 514 N High St. Phone 903/657-4303. ¢

Howard-Dickinson House (1855). First brick house in county. Frame wing added in 1905. Period furnishings; books, paintings, photographs, original documents. (Mon-Fri afternoons; also by appt; closed hols) 501 S Main St. Phone 903/657-6925. ¢

Annual Events

Syrup Festival. Syrup making, arts & crafts, entertainment. Mid-Nov.

Hereford (F-1)

(See Amarillo, Canyon)

Pop 14,745 **Elev** 3,806 ft **Area code** 806 **Zip** 79045
Information Chamber of Commerce, 701 N Main, PO Box 192; 806/364-3333.

Seat of Deaf Smith County and named for the many herds of Hereford cattle, this area's economy is mostly related to agriculture. Huge quantities of wheat, grain sorghum, corn and sugar beets are produced; more than 3 million cattle are raised in feed-lots.

What to See and Do

Deaf Smith County Historical Museum. Furniture, clothes, farming tools, artifacts used by pioneers of the area; also E.B. Black Home (1909). (Daily exc Sun; closed some major hols) 400 Sampson St. Phone 806/364-4338. **Free.**

National Cowgirl Hall of Fame & Western Heritage Center. Celebrates notable women in rodeo history and those who helped develop the American West. Western art collection, library. (Mon-Fri; wkends by appt) 515 Avenue B. Phone 806/364-5252. ¢¢

Motel

✔★★ **BEST WESTERN RED CARPET INN.** *830 W First. 806/364-0540; FAX 806/364-0540.* 90 rms, 2 story. S $36-$38; D $40-$44; each addl $4; under 12 free. Crib free. Pet accepted. TV; cable. Pool. Restaurant adj 11 am-9 pm. Ck-out noon. Some refrigerators. Cr cds: A, C, D, DS, ER, JCB, MC, V.

Hillsboro (B-6)

(See Arlington-Grand Prairie, Cleburne, Corsicana, Dallas, Waco)

Founded 1853 **Pop** 7,072 **Elev** 634 ft **Area code** 817 **Zip** 76645
Information Chamber of Commerce, PO Box 358; 817/582-2481.

Center of a rich agricultural region and gateway to lakes Aquilla and Whitney, Hillsboro is also noted for its many antique and crafts shops. The imposing Hill County Courthouse (1890) at the center of town square is surrounded by many restored turn-of-the-century buildings.

What to See and Do

Confederate Research Center. Archives and displays with emphasis on Confederate military history. Also here is the Audie L. Murphy Gun Museum. (Mon-Fri; closed college hols) Hill College, 112 Lamar Dr, in Library Bldg. Phone 817/582-2555, ext 242. **Free.**

Southwest Outlet Center. Farm Rd 286 & TX 22. Over 25 outlet stores can be found here. Cafe. (Mon-Sat, Sun afternoons) Phone 817/582-9205.

Annual Events

Hill County Fair. Livestock, food, arts & crafts exhibits. 2nd wk Mar.

Bond's Alley Holiday Bazaar. Homemade gifts, food items. Wkend before Thanksgiving.

Motel

★ **RAMADA INN.** *Box 1205, Jct I-35 & TX 22. 817/582-3493; FAX 817/582-2755.* 94 rms, 2 story. S $50-$60; D $55-$65; each addl $8; under 18 free; wkend rates. Crib free. Pet accepted (some restrictions). TV; cable (premium). Pool. Restaurant 6:30 am-1 pm, 5-8:30 pm. Ck-out noon. Cr cds: A, C, D, DS, MC, V.

Houston (D-8)

(See Galveston)

Founded 1836 **Pop** 1,630,553 **Elev** 55 ft **Area code** 713

Houston and Texas, it has been said, grew up together. The city was founded in the same year as the Republic of Texas by brothers Augustus and John Allen, speculators from New York. The town became the new nation's first capital, named after Sam Houston, hero of the Battle of San Jacinto and the first elected president of the Republic. When the first steamboat chugged up the Buffalo Bayou, its captain found stakes marking the streets of what is today the largest city in both Texas and the South.

Buffalo Bayou is now part of the Houston Ship Channel, a 400-foot-wide, 40-foot-deep, 52-mile-long man-made waterway flowing into the Gulf of Mexico. More than 200 industries, including petrochemical and steel plants, line its shore. Houston is a leader in both total tonnage and foreign tonnage handled by a US port.

The space industry has thrived here for years, following the establishment in 1962 of NASA's Mission Control Center (now known as the NASA Lyndon B. Johnson Space Center), 16 miles southeast, near Clear Lake City. A number of research and development and other space-related concerns are located in the greater Houston area.

In recent years, several construction and redevelopment projects have been undertaken in Houston. The city already boasts the tallest building in the US west of the Mississippi in the Texas Commerce Tower. Newer projects include a new convention center, theater center and Space Center Houston. The face of Houston promises to change continuously into the 21st century.

Conventions and tourism play an important role in the local economy. Relying on its cosmopolitan image, temperate climate, Gulf Coast location and a myriad of shops, accomodations and recreational and cultural activities, Houston attracts millions of visitors each year.

Transportation

Car Rental Agencies: See toll-free numbers under Introduction.

Public Transportation: Buses (Metro Transit), phone 713/635-4000.

Rail Passenger Service: Amtrak 800/872-7245.

Airport Information

Hobby: Information 713/643-4597; lost and found 713/643-4597; weather 713/529-4444; cash machines, near Southwest Airlines. **Intercontinental:** Information 713/230-3000; lost and found 713/230-3032; weather 713/529-4444; cash machines, Terminals A, B, C.

Terminals (Intercontinental): Terminal A: Southwest, United, USAir; Terminal B: America West, American, Delta, UltrAir; Terminal C: Continental, Continental Express; International Terminal: AeroMexico, Air France, Aviateca, British Airways, Cayman, Continental Airlines, KLM, Lufthansa, TACA, SAHSA, VIASA

(Airlines and their terminal locations may change. Before leaving for the airport, you should phone the airline to confirm terminal location for your flight.)

What to See and Do

Armand Bayou Nature Center. A 1,900-acre wilderness preserve and environmental education center. Interpretive building. Hiking, nature trails; birdwatching. Public demonstrations and tours (wkends). (Wed-Sun; closed major hols) Sr citizen rate. 8500 Bay Area Blvd, SE of town near University of Houston-Clear Lake. Phone 713/474-2551. ¢¢

Astrodomain. Complex of entertainment and meeting/display facilities includes Astrohall, Astroarena and

Astrodome. This enclosed stadium is the home of baseball's Houston Astros and the Houston Oilers football team. Site of sporting events, conventions, exhibitions and concerts. Tours (daily). Parking (fee). South Loop 610 & Kirby Dr. Phone 713/799-9544. ¢¢

Six Flags AstroWorld. A 75-acre theme park with more than 100 rides, shows and attractions. Includes Texas Cyclone roller coaster; suspended coaster; white-water river rapids ride; children's section. Concerts at the Southern Star Amphitheatre (adj). (Summer, daily; spring & fall, wkends) Phone 713/799-1234. ¢¢¢¢¢

Six Flags WaterWorld. A 15-acre family water recreation park, featuring water slides, river rapids ride, wave pool, speed slides, diving platforms; children's play area. (May, wkends; June-Aug, daily) Phone 713/799-1234. ¢¢¢¢

Bayou Bend Collection. American decorative arts from the late 17th, 18th and early 19th centuries; displayed in 24-room former residence of philanthropist Miss Ima Hogg; 14-acre gardens. 1 Westcott St. For hours, tour schedule & fee information contact PO Box 6826, 77265; 713/520-2600.

Children's Museum of Houston. Nine galleries cover topics ranging from science and health to history and the arts. Changing exhibits. (Daily exc Mon; closed most hols) 1500 Binz, at La Branch. Phone 713/522-1138. ¢¢

Contemporary Arts Museum. Changing exhibits by international and regional artists of contemporary painting, sculpture, photography, video. (Daily exc Mon; closed most hols) 5216 Montrose Blvd. Phone 713/526-3129. ¢¢

Gray Line bus tours. Contact 602 Sampson St, 77003; 713/223-8800 or 800/334-4441.

Heritage Society Tours. Museum complex of 7 historic structures dating from 1820-1905; structures include frontier cabin, Texas plantation house, Greek-revival and Victorian houses, church (ca 1890) and museum gallery. Period furnishings. One-hour tours through four structures. (Daily; no tours major hols) 1100 Bagby St, in Sam Houston Park. Phone 713/655-1912. ¢¢

★ **Hermann Park.** Approx 400 acres donated by businessman and philanthropist George Hermann. A bronze statue and fountain honoring him are located at the intersection of Fannin and N MacGregor Dr. Bounded by Fannin & Main Sts on the west, Hermann Dr on the north, Alameda Rd on the east and N MacGregor Dr on the south. Also in the park are the Garden Center, an ancient Korean pavilion, a Japanese garden, the Miller Outdoor Theatre, which stages free summer music, ballet, and theater productions and

Mecom Rockwell Fountain. Considered one of the most beautiful structures in the city. Colonnade around the fountain resembles a Roman temple; the water jet in the pool rises 12 feet. Between Fannin & San Jacinto Sts.

Houston Zoological Gardens. Small mammals, including vampire bat colony; reptile and primate houses, hippopotamus building, alligator display, gorilla habitat, birdhouse with tropical rain forest; aquarium with marine life; large cat facility; education center. Three-acre discovery zoo with separate contact areas. (Daily) Free admission city hols. 6300 S Main or 1513 North MacGregor Way, near Texas Medical Center. Phone 713/525-3300. ¢¢

Museum of Natural Science. Archaeological, geological, petroleum, space, wildlife and prehistoric animal exhibits. World-class gem & mineral collection. (Daily; closed Jan 1, Dec 25) Free admission on Thurs after 2 pm. One Hermann Circle Dr. Phone 713/639-4600. ¢¢

Wortham IMAX Theatre. Multimedia auditoruim (seats 400) featuring films on natural science topics shown on 80-foot by 6-story-high screen. (Daily; closed Jan 1, Dec 25) Phone 713/639-4629. ¢¢ Museum/IMAX ticket ¢¢¢

Burke Baker Planetarium. Shows (daily; closed Jan 1, Dec 25; hrs & fees vary). Phone 713/639-4600.

Historical parks.

Allen's Landing Park. Site where Houston was founded (1836) by the Allen brothers. Served as first port for steamers and sailing

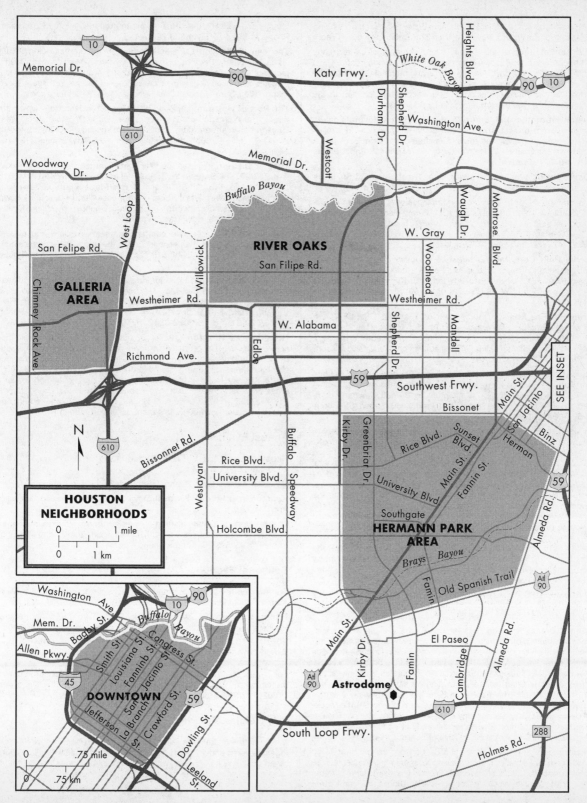

vessels from 1837. A project to renovate the old boat landing is being considered. (Daily) Downtown. At Main St & Buffalo Bayou. **Free.**

Old Market Square. Site of city's first commercial center (early 1800s). An extensive redevelopment project features a central plaza and sidewalks paved with collages of paving material taken from old Houston buildings. Photos commemorating city history are reproduced on porcelain-enameled panels decorating benches in the square. (Daily) One block park on Congress. **Free.**

Houston Arboretum and Nature Center. A 155-acre nonprofit nature sanctuary for the protection of native trees, shrubs & wildlife. Five miles of nature trails (daily). Guided tours (Sun afternoons). Special events & educational programs. 4501 Woodway, in Memorial Park. Phone 713/681-8433. **Free.**

Houston Ballet. Wortham Theater Center, Texas Ave and Smith St. Aug-June. Phone 713/227-2787 or 800/828-2787 (ticket office).

Houston Grand Opera. Multiple performances of eight major productions featuring international stars (Oct-June); also special events. Wheelchair seating, infra-red & live narration headphones. Wortham Theater Center, 501 Texas Ave. Phone 713/546-0200 (information), 713/227-ARTS or 800/828-ARTS (tickets).

Imperial Holly Corporation. Oldest continuously operated business on original site in Texas. Guided tours of all processes of sugar cane refining (Mon-Fri). Reservations advised. 198 Kempner St, in Sugar Land, approx 20 mi SW via US 90A, or US 59. Phone 713/491-9181. **Free.**

Museum of Fine Arts. Sculpture, paintings, graphics, Oriental & Oceanic art, photographs, decorative arts; African, Native American, pre-Columbian artifacts and changing exhibits. Gallery lectures & tours. (Daily exc Mon; closed major hols) Free admission Thurs. 1001 Bissonnet. Phone 713/639-7300. **¢¢**

Rothko Chapel. Octagonal chapel houses final canvases of the late Mark Rothko, Russian-born painter. On the grounds are a reflecting pool and the *Broken Obelisk*, a sculpture by Barnett Newman, dedicated to Dr. Martin Luther King, Jr. (Daily) 3900 Yupon St. Phone 713/524-9839. **Free.**

San Jacinto Battleground. A 570-foot reinforced concrete shaft, faced with Texas fossilized buff limestone and a lone star on top, marks the site of the Battle of San Jacinto. On April 21, 1836, General Sam Houston suddenly attacked the superior forces of Dictator-General Santa Anna of Mexico, routed them and took Santa Anna himself prisoner. This victory ended Texas' War of Independence with Mexico, avenged the massacre at the Alamo six weeks earlier and led to the founding of the Republic of Texas. Elevator in monument (fee). Free museum with exhibits on the cultural development of Texas from Indian civilization to statehood. Multimedia presentation (fee). Monument and museum (daily; closed 24-25). Battleground (daily). 6 mi SE on Gulf Frwy (I-45) to I-610 (South Loop), then 1½ mi E to TX 225 (La Porte Frwy), then 10½ mi E to TX 134 and 3 mi W to Battleground; highway signs identify the battlefield exits beginning on the Gulf Frwy. Phone 713/479-2421. **Free.** Moored nearby is the

Battleship USS *Texas*. Presented to the state by the US Navy. The ship, a dreadnought built in 1914, saw action in World Wars I and II. Restoration in progress. (Wed-Sun) Phone 713/479-2411. **¢¢**

★ **Space Center Houston.** This hands-on facility explores the past, present and future of America's space program. **Mission Status Center** has monitors showing live pictures from Mission Control, Kennedy Space Center and space shuttle missions; briefings on current NASA projects. **NASA Tour** is a guided tram excursion through actual Johnson Space Center facilities, including Mission Control and astronaut training areas. **The Feel of Space** lets visitors wear a space helmet or pilot a manned maneuvering unit. Also Space Shuttle Mock-Up, Starship Gallery, 5-story movie screen in Space Center Theater and Space Center Plaza. (Daily; closed Dec 25) Sr citizen rate. 25 mi S on I-45, exit 2351 (Clear Lake City Blvd). Phone 713/244-2100. **¢¢¢¢**

The Houston Symphony. Classical & Exxon Pops series (Sept-May). Sounds Like Fun children's festival (various locations; June, free). Free summer concerts at Miller Outdoor Theatre in Hermann Park. Summer concerts at Cynthia Woods Mitchell Pavilion, Jones Hall and other

locations. Jesse H. Jones Hall for the Performing Arts, 615 Louisiana. Phone 713/227-ARTS or 800/828-ARTS.

The Menil Collection. Considered one of the most outstanding private art collections in the world, endowed by Mr. & Mrs. John de Menil. Includes contemporary, surrealistic and prehistoric art and antiquities. Housed in museum designed by renowned Italian architect Renzo Piano. (Wed-Sun) 1515 Sul Ross. Phone 713/525-9400. **Free.**

The Port of Houston maintains an observation deck from which the turning basin and port can be seen. Take Clinton Dr E to the port area. Observation platform (daily; closed Thanksgiving, Dec 25) on top of Wharf 9. Drive-through of facilities permitted Sun. Phone 713/670-2400. **Free.**

Theater District. Includes the **Wortham Theater Center,** 500 Texas Ave, 713/237-1439; **Jesse H. Jones Hall for the Performing Arts,** 615 Louisiana Ave, 713/227-3974; also **Jones Plaza,** 600 Louisiana Ave, which occasionally hosts outdoor performances; and **Tranquility Park,** 400 Rusk St, a small park opp Federal Bldg. Bounded by Milam, Smith, Preston & Rusk Sts, downtown. Also here are

Alley Theatre. Resident company presents modern and classic plays and musical theater works. (Nightly exc Mon; matinees Sat, Sun; also summer events) 615 Texas Ave, at Louisiana Ave. Phone 713/228-8421.

Music Hall. Presents six major indoor musical productions by Theatre under the Stars (Oct-May, fee) and other shows. TUTS also gives free summer performances at Miller Outdoor Amphitheater, Hermann Park. 810 Bagby St, adj Sam Houston Coliseum. Phone 713/520-0111 or 713/622-8887 (TUTS).

University of Houston (1927). (33,000 students) Located on 392 acres. University Center has an arboretum; the Hofheinz Pavilion is site of many sports events & concerts. The Lyndall Finley Wortham Theater complex offers mime and drama productions; phone 713/743-2929. Blaffer Gallery features classical and modern art; changing exhibits (Tues-Fri, also Sat & Sun afternoons; closed most hols; phone 713/743-9530). Hilton College of Hotel & Restaurant Management operates a hotel on campus. Main campus: 4800 Calhoun Rd.

Annual Events

Houston Livestock Show & Rodeo. Astrodome. Phone 713/791-9000. Late Feb-early Mar.

Houston Azalea Trail. Phone 713/523-2483. First 2 wkends Mar.

Houston International Festival. Downtown area. Dance, food, music. Apr.

Greek Festival. Annunciation Greek Orthodox Cathedral, 3511 Yoakum St. Cultural festival with Greek food, music and dancing. Phone 713/526-5377. 1st full wkend Oct.

Seasonal Events

Summer concerts. Various parks & plazas throughout the city. May-Aug.

Professional sports. Astros (baseball), Oilers (football), Astrodome. Rockets (basketball), the Summit, 10 Greenway Plaza; 713/627-3865.

Additional Visitor Information

For details on industrial tours, special events and pamphlets, contact the Greater Houston Convention and Visitors Bureau, 801 Congress, 77002; 713/227-3100 or 800/231-7799.

City Neighborhoods

Many of the restaurants, unrated dining establishments and some lodgings listed under Houston include neighborhoods as well as exact street addresses. A map showing these neighborhoods can be found immediately following the city map. Geographic descriptions of these areas are given, followed by a table of restaurants arranged by neighborhood.

Downtown: South of Buffalo Bayou, west of US 59, north of I-45 and east of Bagby St. **North of Downtown:** North of Buffalo Bayou. **South of Downtown:** South of I-45 & US 59. **West of Downtown:** West of I-45.

Galleria Area: South of San Felipe, west of Loop 610, north of Richmond Ave and east of Chimney Rock Ave.

Hermann Park Area: South of Bissonnet and Binz Sts, west of Almeda Rd, north of Old Spanish Trail and east of Kirby Dr; included in this area are the Museum District, Medical Center, Rice University, Astrodome and Montrose areas.

River Oaks: South of Buffalo Bayou, west of S Shepherd Dr, north of Westheimer Rd and east of Willowick Rd.

HOUSTON RESTAURANTS BY NEIGHBORHOOD AREAS

(For full description, see alphabetical listings under Restaurants)

DOWNTOWN

Birraporetti's. 500 Louisiana St

Bistro Lancaster (Lancaster Hotel). 701 Texas Ave

Charley's 517. 517 Louisiana St

Damian's. 3011 Smith St

Dong Ting. 611 Stuart St

Deville (Four Seasons Hotel-Houston Center). 1300 Lamar St

Kim Son. 2001 Jefferson St

Nino's. 2817 W Dallas St

NORTH OF DOWNTOWN

Glass Menagerie (Woodlands). 2301 N Millbend St

La Tour d'Argent. 2011 Ella Blvd

SOUTH OF DOWNTOWN

Brennan's. 3300 Smith St

Goode Co. Texas Bar-B-Q. 5109 Kirby Dr

Luby's Cafeteria. 5215 Buffalo Speedway

Maxim's. 3755 Richmond Ave

WEST OF DOWNTOWN

Anthony's. 4007 Westheimer

Bistro Vino. 819 W Alabama St

Butera's On Montrose. 4621 Montrose Blvd

Captain Benny's Half Shell. 8018 Katy Frwy

Chez Georges. 11920-J Westheimer

Churrasco's. 2055 Westheimer Rd

Confederate House. 2925 Weslayan St

The Dining Room (The Ritz-Carlton, Houston Hotel). 1919 Briar Oaks Lane

Doneraki. 7705 Westheimer Rd

Great Caruso. 10001 Westheimer Rd

Guadalajara. 210 Town & Country Dr

Jags. 5120 Woodway Dr

La Colombe d'Or (La Colombe d'Or Inn). 3410 Montrose Blvd

La Reserve (Omni Houston Hotel). 4 Riverway

Montesano Ristorante Italiano. 6009 Beverly Hill Lane

Otto's Barbecue. 5502 Memorial Dr

Pappadeaux. 6015 Westheimer Rd

Pappasito's Cantina. 6445 Richmond Ave

Rainbow Lodge. 1 Birdsall St

Rivoli. 5636 Richmond Ave

Rotisserie For Beef And Bird. 2200 Wilcrest Dr

Ruggles Grill. 903 Westheimer Rd

Ruth's Chris Steak House. 6213 Richmond Ave

Sierra. 4704 Montrose Blvd

Vargo's. 2401 Fondren Rd

GALLERIA AREA

Americas. 1800 S Post Oak Blvd

The Bar And Grill. 1919 Briar Oaks Lane

Cafe Annie. 1728 Post Oak Blvd

Chianti Cucina Rustica. 1515 S Post Oak Lane

Gugenheim's Delicatessen. 1708 Post Oak Blvd

Hunan. 1800 Post Oak Blvd

Post Oak Grill. 1415 S Post Oak Lane

HERMANN PARK AREA

Kaphan's. 7900 S Main St

Prego. 2520 Amherst St

RIVER OAKS

Armando's. 2300 Westheimer

Brownstone. 2736 Virgina St

Carrabba's. 3115 Kirby Dr

Grotto. 3920 Westheimer Rd

La Griglia. 2002 W Gray St

River Oaks Grill. 2630 Westheimer Rd

Shanghai River. 2407 Westheimer Rd

Tony Mandola's Gulf Coast Kitchen. 1962 W Gray St

Note: When a listing is located in a town that does not have its own city heading, it will appear under the city nearest to its location. In these cases, the address and town appear in parenthesis immediately following the name of the establishment.

Motels

(Rates may be higher for sports & special events in Astrodome.)

★ ★ **DRURY INN.** *1000 N TX 6 (77079), just off I-10, west of downtown.* 713/558-7007. 120 rms, 5 story. S $59-$74; D $69-$84; each addl $10; under 18 free; wkend rates. Crib free. Pet accepted. TV; cable (premium). Indoor pool; whirlpool. Complimentary continental bkfst. Restaurant adj 11 am-10 pm. Ck-out noon. Meeting rm. Some refrigerators. Cr cds: A, C, D, DS, MC, V.

D 🐾 ⊠ ⊠ 🐾 SC

★ ★ **DRURY INN.** *1615 W Loop 610 S (77027), in Galleria Area.* 713/963-0700. 134 rms, 5 story. S $68-$83; D $78-$83; under 12 free; wkend rates. Crib avail. Pet accepted. TV; cable (premium). Indoor/outdoor pool; whirlpool. Complimentary continental bkfst. Ck-out noon. Meeting rm. In-rm modem link. Some refrigerators. Cr cds: A, C, D, DS, MC, V.

D 🐾 ⊠ ⊠ 🐾 SC

✔ ★ **HAMPTON INN.** *828 Mercury Dr (77013), east of downtown.* 713/673-4200; FAX 713/674-6913. 89 rms, 6 story. S $60-$65; D $60-$70; under 18 free. Crib free. Pet accepted. TV; cable. Pool.

Complimentary continental bkfst. Complimentary coffee in lobby. Restaurant adj 6 am-2 pm, 5-10 pm. Ck-out noon. Coin lndry. Valet serv. Some refrigerators. Cr cds: A, C, D, DS, MC, V.

D ⚓ ≋ ⊠ 🔥 SC

★ ★ **LA QUINTA GREENWAY PLAZA.** 4015 Southwest Frwy (77027), Weslayan Rd exit, south of downtown. 713/623-4750; FAX 713/963-0599. 131 rms, 2-3 story. S, D $59-$66; each addl $8; suites $75-$83; under 18 free; family units. Crib free. Pet accepted, some restrictions. TV; cable. Pool. Complimentary continental bkfst. Ck-out noon. Coin lndry. Meeting rms. Cr cds: A, C, D, DS, MC, V.

D ⚓ ≋ ⊠ 🔥 SC

★ ★ **LA QUINTA WEST.** 11113 Katy Freeway (77079), west of downtown. 713/932-0808; FAX 713/973-2352. 176 rms, 2 story. S $55-$65; D $61-$71; each addl $6; under 18 free. Crib free. Pet accepted. TV. Pool. Complimentary continental bkfst. Restaurant adj open 24 hrs. Ck-out noon. Meeting rms. In-rm modem link. Cr cds: A, C, D, DS, MC, V.

D ⚓ ≋ ⊠ 🔥 SC

✔ ★ **LEXINGTON HOTEL SUITES.** 16410 I-45N (77090), 25 mi N, north of downtown. 713/821-1000; FAX 713/821-1420. 248 kit. suites, 3 story. Suites $55-$99; each addl $5; under 18 free; wkly rates. Crib free. TV; cable (premium). Heated pool. Complimentary continental bkfst. Complimentary coffee in rms. Restaurant adj 6:30 am-10 pm. Ck-out noon. Coin lndry. Meeting rms. In-rm modem link. Valet serv. Free airport transportation. Health club privileges. Cr cds: A, C, D, DS, MC, V.

D ≋ ⊠ 🔥 SC

★ **QUALITY INN INTERCONTINENTAL AIRPORT.** PO Box 60135 (77205), 6115 Will Clayton Pkwy, near Intercontinental Airport, north of downtown. 713/446-9131; FAX 713/446-2251. 135 rms, 2 story. S $56-$66; D $66-$75; each addl $7; suites $75; studio rms $60-$69; under 18 free; wkend rates. Crib free. Pet accepted; $15. TV; cable (premium). Pool; poolside serv. Restaurant 6 am-10 pm. Rm serv. Bar 4 pm-midnight; entertainment, dancing Fri. Ck-out 11 am. Meeting rms. Business servs avail. In-rm modem link. Bellhops. Sundries. Free 24-hour airport transportation. Tennis. Balconies. Cr cds: A, C, D, DS, ER, JCB, MC, V.

D ⚓ ⛽ ≋ ✈ ⊠ 🔥 SC

★ **RAMADA LIMITED.** 15350 JFK Blvd (77032), near Intercontinental Airport, north of downtown. 214/258-0900; FAX 214/252-1335. 125 rms, 3 story. S $45-$85; D $51-$85; each addl $6; under 15 free; wkend, hol rates. Crib free. TV; cable (premium). Pool; whirlpool. Complimentary continental bkfst. Restaurant adj open 24 hrs. Ck-out noon. Free airport transportation. Exercise equipt; weights, rowers. Cr cds: A, C, D, DS, MC, V.

D ≋ ✗ ✈ ⊠ 🔥 SC

★ **RESIDENCE INN BY MARRIOTT.** 525 Bay Area Blvd (77058), off I-45. 713/486-2424; FAX 713/488-8179. 110 kit. units, 2 story. S, D $140-$170; under 16 free; wkend rates. Crib free. Pet accepted; $50 and $6 per day. TV; cable (premium), VCR avail. Heated pool. Complimentary coffee in rms. Complimentary continental bkfst, evening refreshments. Restaurant adj 11 am-11 pm. Ck-out noon. Coin lndry. Meeting rm. Business center. In-rm modem link. Airport transportation. Lawn games. Exercise equipt; weight machine, stair machine. Cr cds: A, C, D, DS, JCB, MC, V.

D ⚓ ≋ ✗ ⊠ 🔥 SC 🏃

★ ★ **RESIDENCE INN BY MARRIOTT-ASTRODOME.** 7710 S Main St (77030), S edge of Medical center, in Hermann Park Area. 713/660-7993; FAX 713/660-8019. 285 kit. suites. Kit. suites $95-$125; family, medical rates. Crib free. Pet accepted; $25 and $5 per day. TV; cable (premium). Heated pool; whirlpool. Complimentary continental bkfst. Bar. Ck-out noon. Meeting rms. In-rm modem link. Valet serv. Lawn games. Private patios, balconies. Picnic tables, grills. Cr cds: A, C, D, DS, MC, V.

D ⚓ ≋ ⊠ 🔥 SC

Motor Hotels

★ ★ ★ **ALLEN PARK INN.** 2121 Allen Parkway (77019), downtown. 713/521-9321; res: 800/231-6310; FAX 713/521-9321. 249 rms, 3 story. S, D $78-$98; each addl $8; suites $275; under 10 free; wkly, wkend rates. Crib free. TV; cable (premium), VCR avail. Pool; poolside serv. Restaurant open 24 hrs. Rm serv 24 hrs. Bar 10-2 am, Sun from noon. Ck-out noon. Coin lndry. Meeting rms. In-rm modem link. Gift shop. Barber, beauty shop. Exercise equipt; weights, bicycles, whirlpool, sauna. Bathrm phones. Some refrigerators. Private patios, balconies. Cr cds: A, C, D, DS, MC, V.

D ≋ ✗ ⊠ 🔥 SC

★ ★ **COURTYARD BY MARRIOTT.** 2504 N Loop West (77092), north of downtown. 713/688-7711; FAX 713/688-3561. 202 rms, 3 story. S $79-$89; D $89-$99; each addl $10; suite $175; wkend rates. Crib free. TV; cable (premium). Heated pool. Restaurant 6:30 am-10 pm. Bar 11:30 am-10 pm. Ck-out 1 pm. Coin lndry. Meeting rms. In-rm modem link. Valet serv. Exercise equipt; weights, bicycles, whirlpool. Some refrigerators, wet bars. Cr cds: A, C, D, DS, ER, MC, V.

D ≋ ✗ ⊠ 🔥 SC

★ ★ **HOLIDAY INN-ASTRODOME.** 8111 Kirby Dr (77054), south of downtown. 713/790-1900; FAX 713/799-8574. 235 rms, 11 story. S $79; D $89; each addl $10; suites $220-$275; under 19 free; wkend rates; higher rates Livestock Show & Rodeo. Crib free. TV; cable (premium), VCR. Pool. Restaurant 6 am-10 pm. Rm serv. Bar 11-2 am. Ck-out noon. Meeting rms. In-rm modem link. Bellhops. Valet serv. Sundries. Gift shop. Astrodomain, Medical Center, Galleria transportation. Exercise equipt; weights, bicycles, whirlpool. Some bathrm phones, refrigerators, wet bars. Cr cds: A, C, D, DS, JCB, MC, V.

D ≋ ✗ ⊠ 🔥 SC

★ **RAMADA HOTEL.** 12801 Northwest Frwy (77040), north of downtown. 713/462-9977; FAX 713/460-8725. 296 rms, 10 story. S $79-$82, D $89-$92; each addl $10; suites $105-$210; under 12 free; wkend rates. Pet accepted, some restrictions. TV; cable (premium). Pool; poolside serv. Restaurant 6 am-10 pm. Rm serv. Bar 11-2 am; dancing. Ck-out 1 pm. Meeting rms. In-rm modem link. Bellhops. Valet serv. Sundries. Gift shop. Free bus depot transportation. Exercise equipt; weights, stair machine, sauna. Health club privileges. Some bathrm phones; refrigerator, wet bar, in suites. Cr cds: A, C, D, DS, MC, V.

D ⚓ ≋ ✗ ⊠ 🔥 SC

★ **RAMADA HOTEL.** 2100 S Braeswood Blvd (77030), at Greenbriar, in Hermann Park Area. 713/797-9000; FAX 713/799-8362. 331 rms, 2-3 story. S $49-$79; D $59-$89; suites $150-$275; family, medical rates. Crib free. Pet accepted; some restrictions. TV; cable (premium). Pool; wading pool, poolside serv. Restaurants 6:30 am-2 pm, 5-10 pm. Bar. Ck-out noon. Coin lndry. Meeting rms. Valet serv. Gift shop. Barber. Free bus terminal (airport link), Medical Center transportation. Exercise equipt; weight machines, bicycles. Game rm. Private patios. Cr cds: A, C, D, DS, ER, JCB, MC, V.

D ⚓ ≋ ✗ ⊠ 🔥 SC

Hotels

★ ★ **ADAM'S MARK.** 2900 Briar Park (77042), west of downtown. 713/978-7400; res: 800/444-ADAM; FAX 713/735-2726. 604 rms, 10 story. S, D $89-$149; each addl $15; suites $190-$730; under 18 free; wkend rates. Crib free. TV; cable (premium). Heated indoor/outdoor pool; wading pool, hot tub, poolside serv. Restaurant 6 am-midnight. Rm serv 24 hrs. Bars 11-2 am; entertainment, dancing. Ck-out noon. Meeting rms. Business center. Concierge. Gift shop. Galleria transportation. Exercise equipt; weights, bicycles, whirlpool, sauna. Game rm. Some refrigerators. Some balconies. Artwork in lobby. Cr cds: A, C, D, DS, MC, V.

D ≋ ✗ ⊠ 🔥 SC 🏃

★ ★ **CROWNE PLAZA-GALLERIA.** *2222 West Loop S (77027), in Galleria Area.* 713/961-7272; FAX 713/961-3327. 477 rms, 23 story. S $89-$135; D $99-$145; each addl $10; suites $150-$250; under 19 free; wkend rates. Valet parking $8. Crib free. TV; cable (premium). Indoor pool; poolside serv, hot tub. Complimentary coffee in rms. Restaurants 6 am-10 pm. Bar 11-2 am; entertainment. Ck-out noon. Coin lndry. Convention facilities. In-rm modem link. Concierge. Gift shop. Free garage parking. Galleria area transportation. Exercise equipt; weights, bicycles, whirlpool, sauna. Some refrigerators. Luxury level. Cr cds: A, C, D, DS, JCB, MC, V.

D ⇌ ✗ ⊠ 🔥 SC

★ ★ ★ **DOUBLETREE.** *15747 John F. Kennedy Blvd (77032), north of downtown.* 713/442-8000; FAX 713/590-8461. 309 rms, 7 story. S $103-$133; D $113-$150; each addl $10; each addl. Crib free. Pet accepted; $25. TV; cable. Pool; poolside serv. Restaurant 6 am-2 pm, 5-11 pm. Bar 11 am-midnight. Ck-out noon. Meeting rms. Gift shop. Free Intl Airport transportation. Exercise equipt; weight machine, treadmill, whirlpool. Cr cds: A, C, D, DS, ER, JCB, MC, V.

D ⇌ ≋ ✗ ⊠ 🐾 SC

★ ★ ★ **DOUBLETREE AT ALLEN CENTER.** *400 Dallas St (77002), downtown.* 713/759-0202; FAX 713/752-2734. 341 rms, 20 story. S $125-$150; D $140-$170; each addl $20; suites $225-$675; under 17 free; wkend rates. Crib free. Pet accepted, some restrictions; $75 refundable. TV; cable (premium). Restaurants 6 am-10 pm. Bar 11-2 am; entertainment Mon-Fri. Ck-out noon. Meeting rms. In-rm modem link. Concierge. Gift shop. Free downtown area transportation. Exercise rm; bicycle, stair machine. Elegant hanging tapestries. Cr cds: A, C, D, DS, ER, JCB, MC, V.

D ⇌ ✗ ⊠ 🐾 SC

★ ★ ★ **DOUBLETREE GUEST SUITES.** *5353 Westheimer Rd (77056), in Galleria Area.* 713/961-9000; FAX 713/877-8835. 335 kit. suites, 26 story. S, D $189; each addl $20; 2-bedrm suites $289; under 18 free; wkend rates. Crib free. Pet accepted; $10 per night. TV; cable (premium), VCR avail. Pool; poolside serv. Restaurant 6:30 am-10 pm; Sat, Sun 8 am-1 pm, 5-10 pm. Rm serv 24 hrs. Bar 5 pm-midnight. Ck-out noon. In-rm modem link. Coin lndry. Valet serv. Local area, Medical Center transportation. Tennis privileges. Exercise equipt; weights, bicycles, whirlpool. Health club privileges. Game rm. Refrigerators. Some balconies. Cr cds: A, C, D, DS, MC, V.

D ⇌ 🏊 ≋ ✗ ⊠ 🐾 SC

★ ★ ★ **DOUBLETREE POST OAK.** *2001 Post Oak Blvd (77056), in Galleria Area.* 713/961-9300; FAX 713/623-6685. 449 rms, 14 story. S $125-$190; D $145-$210; each addl $20; suites $190-$1,200; under 18 free; wkend rates. Crib free. Valet parking $11; garage $2. TV; cable (premium). Pool; poolside serv. Restaurant 6:30 am-11 pm. Rm serv 24 hrs. Bar 11-1 am; wkends to 2 am; Sun from noon. Ck-out noon. Convention facilities. Business center. In-rm modem link. Concierge. Shopping arcade. Barber, beauty shop. Free transportation to Galleria area. Exercise equipt; weights, stair machine, sauna. Health club privileges adj. Many bathrm phones; some refrigerators. Balconies. Cr cds: A, C, D, DS, JCB, MC, V.

D ≋ ✗ ⊠ 🐾 SC ⚑

★ ★ **EMBASSY SUITES.** *9090 Southwest Frwy (77074), south of downtown.* 713/995-0123; FAX 713/779-0703. 243 suites, 9 story. Suites $104-$139; each addl $10; under 12 free; wkend rates. Crib free. TV; cable (premium). Indoor pool. Complimentary full bkfst 6-9 am; Sat, Sun 7-10:30 am. Complimentary coffee in rms. Restaurant adj 11:30 am-11 pm. Ck-out noon. Meeting rms. In-rm modem link. Gift shop. Exercise equipt; weights, stair machine, whirlpool, sauna. Game rm. Refrigerators, wet bars; some bathrm phones. Balconies. Cr cds: A, C, D, DS, JCB, MC, V.

D ≋ ✗ ⊠ 🐾 SC

★ ★ ★ ★ **FOUR SEASONS HOTEL-HOUSTON CENTER.** *1300 Lamar St (77010), downtown.* 713/650-1300; FAX 713/650-1203. This toney high-rise with etched-glass doors and thick carpeting is all marble, fresh flowers, and antiques. 10 floors of the 30 stories are occupied by apartments that are home to well-to-do Houstonians. 399 rms, 30 story. S $180-$250; D $205-$275; each addl $25; suites $495-$1,175; under 18 free; wkend rates. Crib free. Pet accepted. Valet & covered parking $13/day. TV; cable (premium), VCR avail (movies avail). Heated pool; poolside serv. Restaurant (see DeVILLE). Rm serv 24 hrs. Bar 11-1 am; entertainment. Ck-out 1 pm. Meeting rms. Business servs avail. In-rm modem link. Concierge. Shopping arcade. Free transportation to downtown area. Exercise rm; instructor, bicycles, rowing machine, whirlpool, sauna. Massage. Health club privileges. Bathrm phones, minibars; some refrigerators. Cr cds: A, C, D, ER, JCB, MC, V.

D ⇌ ≋ ✗ ⊠

★ ★ **HARVEY SUITES-MEDICAL CENTER.** *6800 Main St (77030), in Hermann Park Area.* 713/528-7744; res: 800/922-9222; FAX 713/528-6983. 287 rms, 12 story, 212 kit. suites. S $84; D $94; kit. suites $90-$159; under 18 free. Crib free. TV; cable, VCR avail. Pool. Complimentary coffee in rms. Restaurant 6:30 am-11 pm. Rm serv. Bar from 11 am. Ck-out 1 pm. Coin lndry. Meeting rms. In-rm modem link. Bellhops. Concierge. Valet serv. Gift shop. Free medical center transportation. Health club privileges. Cr cds: A, C, D, DS, MC, V.

D ≋ ⊠ 🐾 SC

✔ ★ ★ **HILTON NASSAU BAY.** *3000 NASA Rd 1 (77058), south of downtown.* 713/333-9300; FAX 713/333-3750. 244 rms, 13 story. S $89-$134; D $99-$134; each addl $10; suites $250-$400; family rates; wkend packages. Crib avail. TV; cable (premium). Pool; poolside serv. Restaurant 6 am-11 pm. Bar 5 pm-2 am; entertainment, dancing Thurs-Sat. Ck-out 1 pm. Meeting rms. Exercise equipt; weights, bicycles, whirlpool. Sailboating, windsurfing, waterskiing. Many bathrm phones. Marina shops. Balconies with view of lake, marina. Luxury level. Cr cds: A, C, D, DS, ER, MC, V.

D ⇌ 🐾 ≋ ✗ ⊠ 🐾 SC

★ ★ ★ **HILTON PLAZA.** *6633 Travis St (77030), adj Medical Center, in Hermann Park Area.* 713/313-4000; FAX 713/313-4660. 185 units, 19 story. S $110-$145; D $120-$155; each addl $10; medical, wkend rates. Crib free. Garage $7 (wkends $4). TV; cable (premium). Heated rooftop pool; poolside serv. Restaurant 6:30 am-10 pm. Bar 4 pm-midnight; pianist. Ck-out 1 pm. Meeting rms. Free Medical Center, Galleria transportation. Exercise rm; instructor, weights, bicycles, whirlpool, sauna. Bathrm phones, refrigerators, wet bars. Adj to museums, parks, Rice Univ. Luxury level. Cr cds: A, C, D, DS, MC, V.

D ≋ ✗ ⊠ 🐾 SC

★ ★ ★ **HILTON WESTCHASE.** *9999 Westheimer Rd (77042), west of downtown.* 713/974-1000; FAX 713/974-2108. 300 rms, 13 story. S, D $99; $109; each addl $10; suites $114-$124; under 18 free; wkend rates. Crib free. TV; cable. Heated pool; poolside serv. Complimentary coffee in rms. Restaurant 6:30 am-10 pm. Rm serv 24 hrs. Bar 11:30 am-midnight. Ck-out 1 pm. Convention facilities. Business center. In-rm modem link. Concierge. Gift shop. Barber, beauty shop. Exercise equipt; weight machine, stair machine, whirlpool, sauna. Minibars. Luxury level. Cr cds: A, C, D, DS, ER, JCB, MC, V.

D ≋ ✗ ⊠ 🐾 SC ⚑

★ ★ **HOLIDAY INN HOBBY AIRPORT.** *9100 Gulf Freeway (I-45) (77017), near Hobby Airport, south of downtown.* 713/943-7979; FAX 713/943-2160. 288 rms, 10 story. S $99-$105; D $109-$119; each addl $10; under 12 free; wkend rates. Crib avail. Pet accepted. TV; cable (premium). Indoor pool; poolside serv. Restaurant 5:30 am-10 pm. Bar; piano. Ck-out noon. Meeting rms. Business servs avail. In-rm modem link. Concierge. Gift shop. Free Hobby Airport transportation. Exercise equipt; weight machine, stair machine, whirlpool, sauna. Game rm. Luxury level. Cr cds: A, C, D, DS, ER, JCB, MC, V.

D ⇌ ≋ ✗ ✗ ⊠ 🐾 SC

★ ★ **HOLIDAY INN-WEST.** *14703 Park Row (77079), west of downtown.* 713/558-5580; FAX 713/496-4150. 349 rms, 19 story. S $119; D $129; suites $250; under 18 free; wkend rates. TV; cable. Indoor pool; poolside serv. Restaurant 6 am-10 pm. Rm serv 6 am-10 pm. Bar 4 pm-midnight; Fri, Sat to 2 am. Ck-out noon. Convention facilities. Business center. Gift shop. Exercise equipt; weights, bicycles, whirlpool. Holidome. Luxury level. Cr cds: A, C, D, DS, MC, V.

[D] [≈] [✗] [⊠] [△] [SC] [⚇]

★★ **HOTEL SOFITEL.** *425 Sam Houston Pkwy E (77060), north of downtown.* 713/445-9000; FAX 713/445-9826. 337 rms, 8 story. S $115-$125; D $125-$135; each addl $20; suites $145-$300; under 18 free; wkend rates. Crib free. TV; cable. Pool; hot tubs. Restaurant 6 am-midnight. Rm serv 5:30-2 am. Bar 11-2 am; entertainment. Ck-out noon. Convention facilities. In-rm modem link. Concierge. Shopping arcade. Airport transportation. Exercise equipt; weight machine, bicycles, whirlpool, sauna. French bakery in lobby. Cr cds: A, C, D, JCB, MC, V.

[D] [≈] [✗] [☆] [⊠] [△] [SC]

★★ **HOUSTON MEDALLION.** *3000 North Loop W (77092), north of downtown.* 713/688-0100; res: 800/688-3000; FAX 713/688-9224. 382 rms, 10 story. S $145; D $155; each addl $10; family, wkend rates. Crib free. Pet accepted, some restrictions. TV; cable (premium), VCR avail. Pool; poolside serv. Restaurant 6 am-2 pm, 5-10 pm. Rm serv to 1 am. Bar 11-1 am. Ck-out 1 pm. Meeting rms. In-rm modem link. Gift shop. Free garage parking. Exercise equipt; weight machine, bicycles, whirlpool, sauna. Refrigerators avail. Luxury level. Cr cds: A, C, D, DS, ER, JCB, MC, V.

[D] [⚇] [≈] [✗] [⊠] [△] [SC]

★★★ **HOUSTONIAN.** *111 N Post Oak Lane (77024), west of downtown.* 713/680-2626; res: 800/231-2759; FAX 713/680-2992. 291 rms, 4 story. S, D $134-$184; suites $225-$925; under 18 free; wkend, hol rates, packages. Crib free. TV; cable (premium). 3 heated pools. Supervised child's activities (to age 11). Restaurant 6:30 am-10 pm. Bar 11-2 am; Sun from noon. Ck-out noon. Convention facilities. Business center. In-rm modem link. Concierge. Gift shop. Free garage parking; valet. Lighted tennis, pro. Exercise rm; instructor, weights, bicycles, whirlpool, sauna. Game rm. Lawn games. Minibars. Luxury level. Cr cds: A, C, D, DS, MC, V.

[D] [⚇] [≈] [✗] [☆] [⊠] [△] [SC] [⚇]

★★★ **HYATT REGENCY.** *1200 Louisiana St (77002), at Polk St, downtown.* 713/654-1234; FAX 713/951-0934. 959 rms, 30 story. S $130-$145; D $155-$200; each addl $25; suites $300-$850; under 18 free; wkend rates. Crib free. Valet parking $11. TV; cable (premium). Heated pool; poolside serv. Restaurant 6 am-11 pm. Bar 11-2 am; entertainment. Ck-out 1 pm. Convention facilities. Business center. In-rm modem link. Concierge. Airport transportation. Exercise equipt; weights, bicycles. Bathrm phones, refrigerators. Built around spectacular 30-story atrium; glass-enclosed elvtrs. Covered passage to downtown buildings. Cr cds: A, C, D, DS, ER, JCB, MC, V.

[D] [≈] [✗] [⊠] [△] [SC] [⚇]

★★★ **J.W. MARRIOTT-HOUSTON.** *5150 Westheimer Rd (77056), in Galleria Area.* 713/961-1500; FAX 713/961-5045. 502 rms, 23 story. S $139-$159; D $149-$169; suites $175-$600; under 18 free; wkend rates. Valet parking $13.25, self-park $6. TV; cable (premium), VCR avail. Indoor/outdoor pool; poolside serv. Restaurant 6:30 am-2 pm, 5:30-11 pm. Bar 11-1 am. Ck-out noon. Convention facilities. In-rm modem link. Concierge. Gift shop. Barber, beauty shop. Exercise rm; instructor, weights, bicycles, whirlpool, sauna, steam rm. Game rm. Bathrm phones. Refrigerator in suites. Lobby furnished with marble, rich paneling and artwork. Luxury level. Cr cds: A, C, D, DS, MC, V.

[D] [≈] [✗] [⊠] [△] [SC]

★★★★ **LANCASTER.** *701 Texas Ave (77002), downtown.* 713/228-9500; FAX 713/223-4528. In this beautifully refurbished theater district hotel dating from the 1920s, rich hunter green and Chinese red draperies provide a backdrop for gleaming antiques. 93 rms, 12 story. S $180-$220; D $190-$230; each addl $25; suites $325-$825; under 16 free; wkend rates. Crib free. Valet parking $12. TV; cable, VCR. Restaurant (see BISTRO LANCASTER). Rm serv 24 hrs. Bars 11 am-midnight. Ck-out 1 pm. Meeting rms. Business servs avail. In-rm modem link. Concierge. Downtown transportation 7 am-11 pm. Health

club privileges. Bathrm phones, refrigerators, minibars. Complimentary newspaper, shoe shine. Cr cds: A, C, D, DS, JCB, MC, V.

[D] [⊠] [△]

★★★ **MARRIOTT AIRPORT.** *18700 Kennedy Blvd (77032), at Intercontinental Airport, north of downtown.* 713/443-2310; FAX 713/443-5294. 566 rms, 3 & 7 story. S, D $110-$130; suites $250-$350; studio rms $150-$250; under 18 free; wkend rates. Crib free. Pet accepted. TV; cable (premium). Pool; poolside serv. Restaurant 5:30 am-10:30 pm. Bar 11-2 am, Sat from 4 pm, Sun noon-midnight; dancing. Ck-out 1 pm. Free lndry facilities. Convention facilities. Business center. In-rm modem link. Shopping arcade. Barber, beauty shop. Free subway to airport terminals. Exercise equipt; stair machine, treadmill. Some bathrm phones, refrigerators. Some private patios. Luxury level. Cr cds: A, C, D, DS, ER, JCB, MC, V.

[D] [⚇] [≈] [✗] [✈] [⊠] [△] [SC] [⚇]

★★★ **MARRIOTT MEDICAL CENTER.** *6580 Fannin St (77030), at Texas Medical Center, in Hermann Park Area.* 713/796-0080; FAX 713/770-8100. 386 rms, 26 story. S, D $124; suites $165-$600; under 18 free; wkend, medical rates. Crib free. Garage $7; valet parking $13. TV; cable (premium), VCR avail. Indoor pool; whirlpool, sauna, poolside serv. Restaurant 6:30 am-11 pm. Ck-out noon. Coin lndry. Convention facilities. In-rm modem link. Concierge. Shopping arcade. Bus depot, medical center transportation. Exercise rm; bicycles, weights. Refrigerators. Connected to Medical Center; covered walks. Luxury level. Cr cds: A, C, D, DS, JCB, MC, V.

[D] [≈] [✗] [⊠] [△] [SC]

★★ **MARRIOTT NORTH AT GREENSPOINT.** *255 N Sam Houston Pkwy E (77060), adj Greenspoint Mall, north of downtown.* 713/875-4000; FAX 713/875-6208. 391 rms, 12 story. S, D $119-$146; suites $250-$350; under 17 free; wkend rates. Crib free. Pet accepted. TV; cable (premium). Indoor/outdoor pool; poolside serv. Restaurant 6:30 am-11 pm. Bar 2 pm-2 am. Ck-out 1 pm. Coin lndry. Convention facilities. Business center. In-rm modem link. Concierge. Gift shop. Free garage parking. Free airport, mall transportation. Exercise equipt; weights, bicycles, whirlpool, sauna. Luxury level. Cr cds: A, C, D, DS, ER, JCB, MC, V.

[D] [⚇] [≈] [✗] [⊠] [△] [SC] [⚇]

★★★ **MARRIOTT WESTSIDE.** *13210 Katy Frwy (77079), west of downtown.* 713/558-8338; FAX 713/558-4028. 400 rms, 5 story. S, D $119-$130; under 10 free; wkend rates. Crib free. Valet parking $7. Pet accepted, some restrictions. TV; cable (premium). Heated pool; poolside serv. Restaurant 6 am-3 pm, 5-11 pm. Bar; pianist Mon-Fri. Ck-out noon. Convention facilities. In-rm modem link. Gift shop. Lighted tennis. Exercise equipt; weight machine, rowers, whirlpool. Cr cds: A, C, D, DS, MC, V.

[D] [⚇] [☆] [≈] [✗] [⊠] [△] [SC]

★★★★ **OMNI HOUSTON HOTEL.** *4 Riverway (77056), west of downtown.* 713/871-8181; res: 800/843-6664; FAX 713/871-0719. This striking-curvilinear resort-style high-rise has an especially large pool, a dramatic modern lobby and bar with fountains and sculpture. Guest rooms have sitting areas, marble and dark-wood furniture, and floor-to-ceiling windows. 381 rms, 11 story. S $145-$195; D $170-$220; each addl $25; suites $225-$650; under 17 free; wkend rates. Crib free. Garage: valet parking $11, self-park free. TV; cable (premium), VCR avail. 2 pools, 1 heated; poolside serv. Restaurant (see LA RESERVE). Rm serv 24 hrs. Bar 11:30-2 am; entertainment, dancing. Ck-out 1 pm. Meeting rms. Business center. In-rm modem link. Concierge. Transportation to Galleria area, airport. Tennis. Exercise rm; instructor, weights, bicycles, whirlpool, sauna. Minibars. Cr cds: A, C, D, DS, ER, JCB, MC, V.

[D] [☆] [≈] [✗] [⊠] [△] [SC] [⚇]

★★★★ **THE RITZ-CARLTON, HOUSTON.** *1919 Briar Oaks Lane (77027), near Galleria Center, west of downtown.* 713/840-7600; res: 800/241-3333; FAX 713/840-8036. Margaret Thatcher and Adnan Khashoggi patronize this elegant property, convenient to the Galleria shops and to many museums. Exotic flowers perfume the hallways; some rooms afford views of the Houston skyline. 232 rms, 12 story. 3

kits. S, D $175-$280; each addl $30; suites $395-$2,000; kit. units $1,500-$2,000; under 18 free; wkend rates. Valet parking $14. Crib free. TV; cable (premium). Heated pool; poolside serv. Restaurant (see THE DINING ROOM and THE BAR AND GRILL). Bar; entertainment. Harpist at afternoon tea (3-5 pm). Ck-out noon. Meeting rms. Business center. Concierge. Gift shop. Free transportation within 3 mi radius. Exercise equipt; treadmill, bicycle. Health club privileges. Bathrm phones; whirlpool in suites. Luxury level. Cr cds: A, C, D, DS, ER, JCB, MC, V.

[D] [icons]

★★ **SHERATON CROWN HOTEL & CONFERENCE CEN-TER.** 15700 John F Kennedy Blvd (77032), north of downtown. 713/442-5100; FAX 713/987-9130. 418 rms, 10 story. S $105-$120; D $115-$130; each addl $10; suites $150-$600; under 18 free; wkend rates. Crib free. TV; cable (premium). 2 pools, 1 indoor. Coffee in rms. Restaurants 6 am-11 pm. Bars 11 am-1 am. Ck-out noon. Convention facilities; amphitheater. Business servs avail. Gift shop. Free Intercontinental Airport transportation. Putting greens. Exercise equipt; treadmill, stair machine, whirlpool. Some refrigerators. Luxury level. Cr cds: A, C, D, DS, ER, JCB, MC, V.

[D] [icons]

★★ **SHERATON GRAND.** 2525 West Loop South (77027), in Galleria area. 713/961-3000; FAX 713/961-1490. 321 rms, 14 story. S $136-$159; D $146-$169; each addl $10; suites $325-$500; under 18 free; wkend rates. Crib free. Pet accepted; $50 deposit. Valet parking $9. TV; cable (premium), VCR avail. Pool; poolside serv. Restaurant 6 am-10 pm. Bar 4 pm-midnight. Ck-out noon. Convention facilities. Gift shop. Exercise equipt; weight machine, treadmill, whirlpool, sauna. Cr cds: A, D, DS, JCB, MC, V.

[D] [icons]

★★ **STOUFFER RENAISSANCE.** 6 Greenway Plaza E (77046), west of downtown. 713/629-1200; FAX 713/629-4702. 389 rms, 20 story. S $119-$159; D $129-$169; each addl $10; suites $300-$750; under 18 free; wkend rates. Crib free. Pet accepted, some restrictions. Garage parking; valet $10, self-park free. TV; cable (premium). Pool; poolside serv, hot tub. Complimentary coffee in rms. Restaurant 6:30 am-10 pm. Rm serv 24 hrs. Bar 11:30-2 am; entertainment Mon-Sat. Ck-out 1 pm. Convention facilities. In-rm modem link. Tennis privileges. Exercise equipt; weights, bicycles, sauna. Bathrm phones; some refrigerators. Cr cds: A, C, D, DS, ER, JCB, MC, V.

[D] [icons]

★★ **WYNDHAM GREENSPOINT.** 12400 Greenspoint Dr (77060), adj Greenspoint Mall, north of downtown. 713/875-2222; res: 800/822-4200; FAX 713/875-1652. 472 rms, 16 story. S $139-$179; D $159-$199; each addl $10; suites $185-$500; studio rms $129; under 18 free; wkend rates. TV; cable. Pool. Restaurant 6 am-11 pm. Bar 4 pm-2 am; entertainment. Ck-out noon. Coin lndry. Convention facilities. Shopping arcade. Free airport transportation. Exercise equipt; weights, bicycles, whirlpool, sauna. Some refrigerators; bathrm phone in suites. Distinctive architectural design & decor. Cr cds: A, C, D, DS, JCB, MC, V.

[D] [icons]

★★ **WYNDHAM WARWICK.** 5701 Main St (77005), near Rice University, in Hermann Park Area. 713/526-1991; FAX 713/639-4545. 308 rms, 12 story, 46 suites, 5 kits. S, D $135-$195; each addl $20; suites $175-$450; kits. $175-$195; under 18 free; wkend plans. Self-parking $6.50, valet parking $10. TV; cable (premium). Pool; poolside serv. Complimentary coffee in rms. Restaurant 6:30 am-11 pm. Bar 3 pm-1 am. Ck-out noon. Convention facilities. Concierge. Gift shop. Beauty shop. Free medical center, downtown transportation. Exercise equipt; weight machine, bicycles, whirlpool, sauna. Bathrm phones; some refrigerators, wet bars. Balconies. Hotel offers luxury, elegance, and personal service in the grand European manner; many antiques and objets d'art displayed. Cr cds: A, C, D, DS, ER, JCB, MC, V.

[D] [icons]

Inns

★★★ **LA COLOMBE D'OR.** 3410 Montrose Blvd (77006), west of downtown. 713/524-7999; FAX 713/524-8923. Walter Fondren, founder of Humble Oil (now Exxon), built this huge 21-room Prairie-style mansion in 1923. Guest quarters are stunning, with private dining rooms, marble baths, and artwork from local and well-known artists. 6 suites, 3 story. Suites $195-$295. TV; cable (premium), VCR avail. Restaurant (see LA COLOMBE D'OR). Rm serv. Bar 11 am-midnight. Concierge. Ck-out noon, ck-in 3 pm. Whirlpool. Fruit furnished daily. Cr cds: A, C, D, DS, MC, V.

[icons]

✔★★★ **SARA'S BED & BREAKFAST.** 941 Heights Blvd (77008), north of downtown. 713/868-1130; res: 800/593-1130; FAX 713/868-1160. 14 rms (2 share bath), 2 story. S, D $55-$95; each addl $10; suites $150; wkly rates. TV; VCR. Complimentary bkfst, coffee. Restaurant nearby. Ck-out noon, ck-in 3 pm. Victorian house (1900); antiques, collectibles. Totally nonsmoking. Cr cds: A, C, D, DS, JCB, MC, V.

[icons]

Resort

★★★ **WOODLANDS.** 2301 N Millbend St (77380), north of downtown. 713/367-1100; res: 800/433-2624 (exc TX), 800/533-3052 (TX); FAX 713/298-1621. 268 rms, 2 story. S $125-$160; D $140-$180; each addl $15; suites $145-$350; kit. units $145-$225; under 12 free; AP avail; wkend rates (seasonal), golf, tennis, package plans. TV; cable, VCR avail. 2 pools; wading pool, poolside serv. Restaurants 6 am-11 pm (also see GLASS MENAGERIE). Rm serv. 3 bars 11-2 am, Sun from noon. Ck-out noon, ck-in after 3 pm. Meeting rms. Business center. In-rm modem link. Valet serv. Airport transportation. Indoor & outdoor lighted tennis, pro. 36-hole golf, greens fee $50-$95, 3 putting greens, 3 driving ranges, pro shop. Hiking, bicycle trails. Bicycle rentals. Game rm. Exercise rm; instructor, weights, bicycles, whirlpool, steam rm, sauna. Health spa. Lawn games. Refrigerators. Private patios, balconies. Some lake views. Cr cds: A, C, D, DS, MC, V.

[icons]

Restaurants

✔★★ **AMERICAS.** 1800 S Post Oak Blvd (77056), in Galleria Area. 713/961-1492. Hrs: 11 am-10 pm; Fri to 11 pm; Sat 5-11 pm. Closed Sun; most major hols. Res accepted. South American menu. Bar. Semi-a la carte: lunch $6-$12, dinner $10-$18. Child's meals. Specialties: roasted quail breast, filet of red snapper with fresh corn, plantain chips. Rain forest, Inca decor. Suspension bridge to second level. Cr cds: A, C, D, DS, MC, V.

[D] [icon]

★★★ **ANTHONY'S.** 4007 Westheimer, west of downtown. 713/961-0552. Hrs: 11:30 am-2 pm, 5:30-11 pm; Fri to 11:30 pm; Sat 5:30-11:30 pm. Closed Sun; major hols. Res accepted. Italian, Amer menu. Bar. Wine list. Semi-a la carte: lunch $8.95-$13, dinner $11.95-$25. Specializes in seafood, veal, beef. Own baking. Valet parking. Open hearth cooking. Cr cds: A, D, MC, V.

[D] [icon]

★★ **ARMANDO'S.** 2300 Westheimer, in River Oaks. 713/521-9757. Hrs: 11 am-2 pm, 5:30-11 pm; Sun from 5:30 pm, Mon to 10 pm. Closed Thanksgiving, Dec 25. Res accepted. Mexican, Amer menu. Bar. Semi-a la carte: lunch $6.95-$16.95, dinner $8.95-$18.95. Specializes in chicken enchiladas, fajitas. Own tortillas. Valet parking. Outdoor dining. Local modern art displays. Cr cds: A, D, MC, V.

[D] [icon]

★★★★ **THE BAR AND GRILL.** (See The Ritz-Carlton, Houston Hotel) 713/840-7600. There's a masculine, clubby atmosphere to this restaurant in the Ritz-Carlton hotel. Dinners feature fresh seafood, grilled meats, and farm-raised poultry. Hrs: dinner 6-10:30 pm; lite menu 3-6 pm & 10:30 pm-1:30 am. Res accepted. Bar. Wine cellar. Semi-a la carte: dinner $21-$29; lite menu $5.95-$14. Child's meals. Specialties: chili-roasted filet, grilled salmon, Felix's mixed grill. Pianist Tues-Sat. Valet parking. Jacket. Cr cds: A, C, D, DS, ER, JCB, MC, V.

[D] [symbol]

✔ ★ **BIRRAPORETTI'S.** 500 Louisiana St, adj to Alley Theatre, downtown. 713/224-9494. Hrs: 11 am-11 pm; Fri-Sat to midnight. Italian menu. Bar. Semi-a la carte: lunch, dinner $6.95-$12.95. Child's meals. Specializes in lasagne, pollo poretti, chicken alfredo. In Theater District. Cr cds: A, C, D, DS, MC, V.

[D] [symbol]

★ ★ **BISTRO LANCASTER.** (See Lancaster Hotel) 713/228-9502. Hrs: 6:30 am-11 pm; Fri, Sat to midnight; Sun 7:30 am-11 pm. Res accepted. Bar. A la carte entrees: bkfst $6-$9.95, lunch $6.50-$17.95, dinner $17.95-$23.95. Specializes in wild mushroom quesadillas, pecan & black pepper crusted venison, crawfish. Valet parking. Beautifully restored hotel built 1926. Cr cds: A, C, D, JCB, MC, V.

[D] [symbol]

★ ★ **BISTRO VINO.** 819 W Alabama St, west of downtown. 713/526-5500. Hrs: 11:30 am-11 pm; Fri & Sat to midnight. Closed Sun. Closed most major hols. Res accepted. French, Italian menu. Bar. Semi-a la carte: lunch $6.95-$15, dinner $7.95-$18. Complete meals: dinner $18.95-$26.95. Specialties: veal Milanese, osso buco, filet au poivre. Entertainment. Valet parking. Outdoor dining. Romantic atmosphere. Cr cds: A, C, D, MC, V.

[D] [symbol]

★ ★ ★ **BRENNAN'S.** 3300 Smith St, south of downtown. 713/522-9711. Hrs: 11:30 am-2 pm, 5:45-10 pm; Sat from 5:45 pm; Sun 5:45-9:30 pm; Sat brunch 11 am-1:30 pm, Sun brunch 10 am-2 pm. Closed Dec 24, 25. Res accepted. Creole, Southwestern menu. Bar. A la carte entrees: lunch $14-$24, dinner $21-$28. Complete meals: lunch $15.50-$16.50. Sat & Sun brunch $18-$24. Specialties: turtle soup, grilled veal chop with tchoupitoulas sauce, bananas Foster. Own baking. Jazz Sat, Sun brunch. Valet parking. Outdoor dining. Elegant decor in unique building designed by John Staub as headquarters of Junior League. Family-owned. Jacket. Cr cds: A, C, D, DS, MC, V.

[D] [symbol]

★ ★ **BROWNSTONE.** 2736 Virgina St, at Westheimer Rd, in River Oaks. 713/520-5666. Hrs: 11:30 am-2:30 pm, 6-10:30 pm; Fri, Sat to 11 pm; Sun 11 am-2:30 pm. Closed Dec 25. Res accepted. Continental menu. Bar. Semi-a la carte: lunch $6.95-$13.95, dinner $14.95-$24.95. Sun brunch $18.95. Specializes in herb encrusted salmon, beef Wellington. Harpist Thurs-Sat. Valet parking. Outdoor poolside dining. Elegant, numerous antiques. Cr cds: A, D, DS, MC, V.

[D] [symbol]

★ ★ **CAFE ANNIE.** 1728 Post Oak Blvd, in Galleria Area. 713/840-1111. Hrs: 11:30 am-2 pm, 6-10 pm; Fri to 10:30 pm; Sat 6-10:30 pm. Closed Sun; most major hols. Res accepted. Bar. A la carte entrees: lunch $9-$14, dinner $18-$32. Complete meals: lunch $16-$20. Specialties: poached shrimp with Dallas mozzarella, muscovy duckling, grilled Texas ostrich. Own pastries. Valet parking. Seasonal floral arrangements; harvest mural by local artist. Cr cds: A, D, DS, MC, V.

[D]

★ ★ **CARRABBA'S.** 3115 Kirby Dr, in River Oaks. 713/522-3131. Hrs: 11 am-11 pm; Fri to midnight; Sat 11:30 am-midnight; Sun noon-10 pm. Closed Thanksgiving, Dec 25. Italian menu. Bar. Semi-a la carte: lunch, dinner $7.95-$20.95. Specialties: pasta Carrabba, pollo Rosa Maria, veal chop. Own desserts. Valet parking. Outdoor dining. Modern decor; wood-burning pizza oven. Cr cds: A, C, D, MC, V.

[D] [symbol]

★ ★ ★ **CHARLEY'S 517.** 517 Louisiana St, downtown. 713/224-4438. Hrs: 11:30 am-2 pm, 5:30-11 pm. Closed Sun; major hols. Res accepted. Bar. Wine cellar. A la carte entrees: lunch $8.50-$16, dinner $19-$32. Specializes in domestic and imported game, seafood. Own pastries. Valet parking. In Theater District. Jacket (dinner). Cr cds: A, C, D, MC, V.

[D] [symbol]

★ ★ **CHEZ GEORGES.** 11920-J Westheimer, at Kirkwood, west of downtown. 713/497-1122. Hrs: 11 am-2 pm, 6-10 pm; Sat 6-10:30 pm. Closed Sun; Dec 25. Res accepted. French menu. Wine, beer. Semi-a la carte: lunch $7.95-$12.95. A la carte entrees: dinner $14-$23. Complete meals: lunch $12.95, dinner $21.95. Specialties: filet of red snapper with fennel & lime, french p&vates. Own pastries. Parking. Country French decor. Jacket. Cr cds: A, C, D, MC, V.

[D] [symbol]

★ ★ **CHEZ NOUS.** (217 S Ave G, Humble) Approx 22 mi NE on US 59, exit FM 1960. 713/446-6717. Hrs: 5:30-11 pm. Closed Sun. Res accepted. French menu. Bar. A la carte entrees: dinner $15.50-$27. Specializes in filet of king salmon, mesquite-grilled rib-eye steak, rack of lamb. Own desserts. Parking. French decor. Former Pentecostal church (1928). Cr cds: A, C, D, MC, V.

[symbol]

✔ ★ **CHIANTI CUCINA RUSTICA.** 1515 S Post Oak Lane, in Galleria Area. 713/840-0303. Hrs: 11:30 am-2:30 pm, 5:30-10:30 pm; Fri to 11 pm; Sat 5:30-11 pm. Closed Sun; some major hols. Res accepted. Italian menu. Bar. Semi-a la carte: lunch, dinner $4.50-$13. Child's meals. Specialties: antipasti misto, grilled pork chops, tortellini. Valet parking. Open hearth cooking. View of garden from dining rm. Cr cds: A, D, MC, V.

[D] [symbol]

★ ★ **CHURRASCO'S.** 2055 Westheimer Rd, in Shepherd Square Shopping Center, west of downtown. 713/527-8300. Hrs: 11:30 am-10 pm; Fri to 11 pm; Sat 5-11 pm; Sun brunch 11:30 am-3 pm. Closed Jan 1, July 4, Dec 25. Res accepted; required wkends. South American menu. Bar. A la carte entrees: lunch $7-$18, dinner $10.95-$22. Sun brunch $7-$18. Specialties: churrasco, empanadas, plantain chips. South American estancia atmosphere. Cr cds: A, C, D, DS, MC, V.

[D] [symbol]

★ ★ ★ **CONFEDERATE HOUSE.** 2925 Weslayan St, west of downtown. 713/622-1936. Hrs: 11:30 am-2:30 pm, 6-10:30 pm; Sat from 6 pm. Closed Sun; major hols. Res accepted. Bar. Wine list. Semi-a la carte: lunch $7.50-$13.75, dinner $13.75-$21. Specialties: grilled red snapper, rib-eye steak, shrimp salad, soft shell crab. Own desserts. Valet parking. Southern colonial decor. Family-owned. Jacket (dinner). Cr cds: A, C, D, DS, MC, V.

[symbol]

★ ★ ★ **DAMIAN'S.** 3011 Smith St, downtown. 713/522-0439. Hrs: 11 am-2 pm, 5:30-10 pm; Fri to 11:30 pm; Sat 5-11:30 pm. Closed Sun; some major hols. Res accepted. Italian menu. Bar. A la carte entrees: lunch, dinner $9.95-$24.95. Specialties: shrimp Damian, involtini di pollo, veal chop milanese. Valet parking. Terra cotta walls with hand-painted frescoes. Cr cds: A, C, D, MC, V.

[D]

★ ★ ★ **DeVILLE.** (See Four Seasons Hotel-Houston Center) 713/652-6250. Hrs: 6:30 am-1:30 pm, 6-10 pm; wkend hrs vary. Bar. Wine cellar. Complete meals: bkfst $5-$12. A la carte entrees: lunch $9-$17, dinner $16-$26. Sun brunch $27.50. Child's meals. Specializes in fresh regional cuisine. Own baking. Entertainment; pianist at Sun brunch. Valet parking. Art deco furnishings. Cr cds: A, C, D, ER, MC, V.

[D] [symbol]

★ ★ ★ **THE DINING ROOM.** (See The Ritz-Carlton, Houston Hotel) 713/840-7600, ext. 6110. Hrs: 6:30 am-2:30 pm; Sun brunch

10:30 am-2:30 pm. Res accepted. Continental menu. Bar. Wine cellar. A la carte entrees: bkfst $5.50-$15, lunch $8.50-$18. Sun brunch $32. Child's meals. Specialties: tortilla soup, grilled swordfish, crème brulée, she-crab soup, pecanwood smoked salmon. Own baking. Entertainment (Sun brunch). Valet parking. Jacket. Cr cds: A, C, D, DS, ER, JCB, MC, V.

✔ ★ **DONERAKI.** 7705 Westheimer Rd, west of downtown. 713/975-9815. Hrs: 11 am-midnight; Fri to 4 am; Sat 8-4 am; Sun 8 am-midnight. Res accepted. Mexican menu. Bar. Semi-a la carte: bkfst $3.95-$6.95, lunch, dinner $4.95-$11.95. Child's meals. Specialties: fajitas, shrimp a la Diabla, chicken enchiladas. Mariachis (dinner). Parking. Colorful Mexican decor. Cr cds: A, DS, MC, V.

✔ ★ ★ **DONG TING.** 611 Stuart St, downtown. 713/527-0005. Hrs: 11 am-2 pm, 5-10 pm; wkend hrs vary. Res accepted. Chinese menu. Semi-a la carte: lunch, dinner $7.50-$12. Specialties: lamb dumplings, clay pot pork, jalapeno steak. Valet parking. Heavy wood paneling; hand-painted murals, antiques. Cr cds: A, C, D, DS, MC, V.

★ ★ **THE FLYING DUTCHMAN.** (505 2nd Ave, Kemah 77565) 25 mi SE on US 45, exit 23, then E to Kemah. 713/334-7575. Hrs: 11 am-10:30 pm; wkends to 11 pm. Closed Thanksgiving, Dec 25. Res accepted. Bar. Semi-a la carte: dinner $13.95-$18.95. Child's meals. Specializes in broiled Gulf seafood, steak. Parking. Outdoor dining with view of boat channel. Cr cds: A, C, D, DS, MC, V.

★ ★ **GLASS MENAGERIE.** (See Woodlands Resort) 713/367-1000. Hrs: 11:30 am-2 pm, 6-10 pm; Sun brunch 11 am-3 pm. Res accepted. Continental menu. Bar. Buffet lunch $11.95. Semi-a la carte: dinner $16-$28. Sun brunch $20.95. Specializes in potato baskets, steak Diane, flambé desserts. Pianist exc Mon. Parking. Dining rm of resort with views of lake. Cr cds: A, C, D, DS, MC, V.

★ ★ **GROTTO.** 3920 Westheimer Rd, in River Oaks. 713/622-3663. Hrs: 11:30 am-11 pm; Fri, Sat to midnight; Sun to 10 pm. Closed major hols. Southern Italian menu. Bar. Semi-a la carte: lunch $6.95-$9.95, dinner $6.95-$15.95. Specialties: pasta al Bosco, linguine alle vongole. Own pizza. Parking. Outdoor dining. Neapolitan cafe setting; large mural on wall. Cr cds: A, C, D, MC, V.

★ **GUADALAJARA.** 210 Town & Country Dr (77024), at Kimberly Lane, in shopping center, west of downtown. 713/461-5300. Hrs: 11 am-10 pm; Fri & Sat to 11 pm. Closed Thanksgiving, Dec 25. Mexican menu. Bar. Semi-a la carte: lunch $5.50-$6.95, dinner $5.95-$13.95. Child's meals. Specializes in enchiladas, tortillas, seafood. Casual, family-friendly restaurant; Mexican decor. Cr cds: DS, MC, V.

✔ ★ **HUNAN.** 1800 Post Oak Blvd (77056), in Galleria Area. 713/965-0808. Hrs: 11:30 am-10:30 pm; Fri 11:30 am-11:30 pm; Sat noon-11:30 pm; Sun noon-10:30 pm. Closed Thanksgiving. Res accepted. Hunan menu. Bar. Semi-a la carte: lunch $6.50-$8.75, dinner $9.85-$14.95. Specializes in Hunan-style chicken & prawn, Peking duck. Parking. Chinese decor, large oriental mural. Cr cds: A, C, D, MC, V.

★ **KAPHAN'S.** 7900 S Main St, at Kirby Dr, in Hermann Park Area. 713/668-0491. Hrs: 11:30 am-9 pm; Fri, Sat to 10 pm. Closed Wed; Jan 1, Labor Day, Dec 25. Res accepted. Bar. Semi-a la carte: lunch $9.95, dinner $10.95-$15.95. Child's meals. Specializes in fresh Gulf Coast seafood, beef. Parking. Garden room. Family-owned. Cr cds: A, C, D, DS, MC, V.

★ ★ **KIM SON.** 2001 Jefferson St, downtown. 713/222-2461. Hrs: 10:30 am-midnight; Fri & Sat to 1 am. Vietnamese, Chinese menu. Bar. A la carte entrees: lunch, dinner $6.50-$13.95. Specialties: spring rolls, black pepper crab, Vietnamese fajitas. Parking. Cr cds: A, C, D, DS, MC, V.

★ ★ ★ **LA COLOMBE D'OR.** (See La Colombe d'Or Inn) 713/524-7999. Hrs: 11:30 am-2 pm, 6-10 pm; Fri to 11 pm; Sat, Sun 6-11 pm. Closed Dec 25. Res accepted. French menu. A la carte entrees: lunch $9.50-$15, dinner $19.50-$29. Specializes in rack of lamb, veal, fish. Own desserts. Valet parking. 21-rm residence decorated with artwork. Cr cds: A, C, D, MC, V.

★ ★ ★ **LA GRIGLIA.** 2002 W Gray St, in River Oaks Shopping Center, in River Oaks. 713/526-4700. Hrs: 11:30 am-2 pm, 5:30-11 pm; Fri to midnight; Sat 5:30 pm-midnight; Sun 5:30-10 pm. Closed Dec 25. Res accepted. Italian menu. Bar. A la carte entrees: lunch $6.95-$13.95, dinner $9.95-$24.95. Specialties: shrimp & crab cheesecake, red snapper La Griglia, linguine pescatore. Valet parking. Outdoor dining. Colorful tilework and murals; lively atmosphere. Cr cds: A, C, D, DS, MC, V.

★ ★ ★ **LA RESERVE.** (See Omni Houston Hotel) 713/871-8181. In this dusty-rose dining room, the many beveled mirrors seem to multiply the eye-catching central flower arrangement. Candlelight and antique accent pieces add intimacy to large contemporary space. Hrs: 11:30 am-2 pm, 6:30-10:30 pm; Sat from 6:30 pm. Closed Sun. Res accepted. Continental menu. Bar 5 pm-midnight. A la carte entrees: lunch $12-$18, dinner $19-$30. Table d'hôte: dinner $45-$65 (with wine). Specialties: morel-stuffed veal chops, charred citrus-pepper tuna, grilled double lamb chops, tian of freshwater prawns and Louisiana crab. Also dietary menu. Own baking. Menu changes daily; fresh food only. Valet parking. Jacket, tie (dinner). Cr cds: A, C, D, DS, ER, JCB, MC, V.

★ ★ ★ **LA TOUR D'ARGENT.** 2011 Ella Blvd, north of downtown. 713/864-9864. Hrs: 11:30 am-2 pm, 6-11 pm. Closed Sun; major hols. Res accepted; required wkends. French menu. Bar. A la carte entrees: lunch $8.50-$15, dinner $16-$26. Specializes in seafood, pheasant, duck. Pastry chef. Valet parking. Antiques. Dining in 1920s hunting lodge, Houston's oldest log cabin. Overlooks bayou. Jacket. Cr cds: A, C, D, DS, MC, V.

★ ★ ★ **MAXIM'S.** 3755 Richmond Ave, south of downtown. 713/877-8899. Hrs: 11:15 am-10:30 pm; Sat 5:30-11 pm. Closed Sun; major hols. Res accepted. French menu. Bar. Extensive wine cellar. Semi-a la carte: lunch $9.75-$11.75, dinner $15.75-$23.75. Table d'hôte: lunch $7-$11.75. Specialties: cream of lobster soup, Gulf seafood, fresh lump crabmeat, veal, lamb, flaming desserts. Own baking. Valet parking. Family-owned. Jacket. Cr cds: A, C, D, DS, MC, V.

★ ★ **MONTESANO RISTORANTE ITALIANO.** 6009 Beverly Hill Lane, west of downtown. 713/977-4565. Hrs: 11 am-2:30 pm, 5:30-11 pm; Fri to midnight; Sat 5:30 pm-midnight. Closed Sun; Thanksgiving, Dec 25. Res accepted. Italian menu. Bar. A la carte entrees: lunch $7.95-$13.95, dinner $8-$18.95. Specializes in chicken, veal, seafood. Valet parking. Cr cds: A, D, DS, MC, V.

★ ★ **NINO'S.** 2817 W Dallas St, downtown. 713/522-5120. Hrs: 11 am-2:30 pm, 5:30-10 pm; Fri to 11 pm; Sat 5:30-11 pm. Closed Sun; major hols. Res accepted. Italian menu. Bar. Semi-a la carte: lunch $8.95-$17.95, dinner $8.95-$21.95. Specializes in veal, seafood. Own pasta. Parking. Cr cds: A, C, D, MC, V.

★ ★ **PAPPADEAUX.** *6015 Westheimer Rd, west of downtown.* 713/782-6310. Hrs: 11 am-11 pm; Fri & Sat to midnight. Closed Thanksgiving, Dec 25. Cajun menu. Bar. Semi-a la carte: lunch $5-$9, dinner $7.95-$17.95. Specialties: fried alligator, crawfish etouffée, Angus steak. Parking. Patio dining. Lively atmosphere. Cr cds: A, MC, V.

D ⬛

✔ ★ **PAPPASITO'S CANTINA.** *6445 Richmond Ave, west of downtown.* 713/784-5253. Hrs: 11 am-10:30 pm; Fri, Sat to midnight. Mexican menu. Bar. A la carte entrees: lunch $5.95-$8.95, dinner $5.95-$15.95. Specializes in seafood, enchiladas, fajitas. Own tortillas, desserts. Mexican decor. Cr cds: A, MC, V.

D ⬛

★ ★ ★ **POST OAK GRILL.** *1415 S Post Oak Lane, in Galleria Area.* 713/993-9966. Hrs: 11 am-midnight; Sun 5-10 pm; Mon, Tues 11 am-11 pm; Sun brunch 11 am-3 pm. Closed some major hols. Res accepted. Bar to 2 am. Semi-a la carte: lunch $6.95-$14.95, dinner $8.25-$21.95. Sun brunch $11.95-$14.95. Specialties: tomatoes Manfred, fresh gulf snapper, lemon pepper chicken. Entertainment. Valet parking. Outdoor dining. Festive ambience, colorful Toulouse-Lautrec murals. Cr cds: A, C, D, DS, MC, V.

D ⬛

★ ★ **PREGO.** *2520 Amherst St, in Hermann Park Area.* 713/529-2420. Hrs: 11 am-10 pm; Fri to 11 pm; Sat noon-11 pm; Sun noon-10 pm. Closed some major hols. Res accepted. Italian menu. Bar. A la carte entrees: lunch, dinner $5-$20. Child's meals. Specialties: veal alla pego, wild mushroom ravioli, Gulf coast crab cakes. Parking. Bistro-style dining. Cr cds: A, C, D, MC, V.

D ⬛

★ ★ **RAINBOW LODGE.** *1 Birdsall St, west of downtown.* 713/861-8666. Hrs: 11:30 am-10:30 pm; Sat 6-10:30 pm; Sun 10:30 am-10:30 pm; Sun brunch 10:30 am-4 pm. Closed Mon; major hols. Res accepted. Bar. Semi-a la carte: lunch $7.25-$28, dinner $16.95-$32. Sun brunch $7.25-$15.95. Specializes in seafood, veal, wild game. Valet parking. Outdoor dining. On Buffalo Bayou; garden, gazebo. Cr cds: A, C, D, DS, MC, V.

D ⬛

★ ★ **RIVER OAKS GRILL.** *2630 Westheimer Rd, in River Oaks.* 713/520-1738. Hrs: 11 am-2:30 pm, 6-10:30 pm; Fri, Sat to 11:30 pm. Closed Sun; some major hols. Res accepted; required wkends. Bar 11 am-midnight, Sat from 5 pm. Semi-a la carte: lunch $6.95-$14.50, dinner $9.95-$24.95. Specializes in steak, fresh seafood, chops. Pianist Tues-Sat. Valet parking. Club atmosphere; dark paneled walls. Cr cds: A, C, D, MC, V.

D ⬛

★ ★ ★ **RIVOLI.** *5636 Richmond Ave, west of downtown.* 713/789-1900. Hrs: 11:30 am-2 pm, 6-11 pm; Sat from 6 pm. Closed major hols. Res accepted. Continental menu. Bar. Wine list. A la carte entrees: lunch $7.95-$14.95, dinner $16.95-$27. Specialties: Dover sole stuffed with crabmeat and shrimp, rack of lamb Diable, blackened shrimp with mustard sauce. Own pastries. Entertainment Tues-Sat. Valet parking. Jacket. Cr cds: A, D, DS, MC, V.

⬛

★ ★ ★ **ROTISSERIE FOR BEEF AND BIRD.** *2200 Wilcrest Dr, west of downtown.* 713/977-9524. Hrs: 11:30 am-2 pm, 6-10 pm; Sat from 6 pm. Closed Sun; Jan 1, Dec 25. Res accepted. Continental menu. Bar. Wine cellar. Semi-a la carte: lunch $6.95-$17.50, dinner $17.95-$27.50. Specializes in roast duckling, venison, lobster. Valet parking. New England-colonial atmosphere. Jacket (dinner). Cr cds: A, C, D, DS, MC, V.

D ⬛

★ ★ **RUGGLES GRILL.** *903 Westheimer Rd (77006), west of downtown.* 713/524-3839. Hrs: 11:30 am-2 pm, 5:30-11 pm; Fri to midnight; Sat 5:30 pm-midnight; Sun 11 am-2:30 pm, 5:30-10 pm.

Closed Mon; July 4, Thanksgiving, Dec 25. Res accepted. Bar. Semi-a la carte: lunch $5.95-$13.95, dinner $9.95-$16.95. Specialties: black pepper pasta, grilled beef filet, Texas goat cheese salad. Valet parking. Contemporary decor. Cr cds: A, D, MC, V.

⬛

★ ★ ★ **RUTH'S CHRIS STEAK HOUSE.** *6213 Richmond Ave, west of downtown.* 713/789-2333. Hrs: 5-11 pm. Closed most major hols. Res accepted. Bar. A la carte entrees: dinner $17-$29. Specializes in steak, lamb chops, lobster. Valet parking. Cr cds: A, C, D, DS, JCB, MC, V.

D ⬛

✔ ★ ★ **SHANGHAI RIVER.** *2407 Westheimer Rd, in River Oaks.* 713/528-5528. Hrs: 11 am-10 pm; Fri, Sat to 11 pm. Closed Thanksgiving. Res accepted. Chinese menu. Bar. Semi-a la carte: lunch $5.50-$6.95, dinner $5.50-$14.95. Specialties: crispy shrimp, General Tso's chicken, Peking duck. Parking. Chinese porcelains on display. Cr cds: A, C, D, MC, V.

D ⬛

★ ★ **SIERRA.** *4704 Montrose Blvd, west of downtown.* 713/942-7757. Hrs: 11 am-2:30 pm, 5-10:30 pm; Fri to 11:30 pm; Sat 5-11:30 pm. Closed Sun; most major hols. Res accepted. Southwestern menu. Bar. Semi-a la carte: lunch $5.95-$19.95, dinner $7.50-$19.95. Specialties: filet of salmon "campfire style," filet of beef tenderloin. Valet parking. Outdoor patio dining. Southwestern decor. Cr cds: A, C, D, DS, MC, V.

D ⬛

★ ★ **TONY MANDOLA'S GULF COAST KITCHEN.** *1962 W Gray St, in River Oaks.* 713/528-3474. Hrs: 11 am-10 pm; Fri & Sat to 11 pm; Sun to 9 pm. Closed some major hols. Res accepted. Italian, Amer menu. Bar. A la carte entrees: lunch, dinner $8.95-$18.95. Child's meals. Specialties: Mama's gumbo, crawfish ravioli, blackened soft shell crab. Parking. Outdoor dining. New Orleans bistro atmosphere. Cr cds: A, D, MC, V.

D ⬛

★ ★ **VARGO'S.** *2401 Fondren Rd (77063), west of downtown.* 713/782-3888. Hrs: 11 am-2 pm, 6-10:30 pm; Fri to 11:30 pm; Sat 5-11:30 pm; Sun 11 am-2:30 pm. Closed Jan 1, Dec 25. Res accepted. Continental menu. Bar 4 pm-midnight. Semi-a la carte: lunch $10.95-$19.50, dinner $18.95-$28. Specialties: Gulf shrimp Henry, Long Island duck, grilled snapper. Pianist (Thurs-Sun). Valet parking. View of lake and gardens. Tree in center of dining rm. Family-owned. Cr cds: A, C, D, DS, MC, V.

D ⬛

Unrated Dining Spots

BUTERA'S ON MONTROSE. *4621 Montrose Blvd, on grounds of Chelsea Market, west of downtown.* 713/523-0722. Hrs: 10:30 am-10 pm; Sat from 10:30 am; Sun 10:30 am-8 pm. Closed some major hols. Wine, beer. A la carte: lunch, dinner $6-$8. Specializes in chicken salad, sandwiches, pasta salad. Outdoor dining. Cafeteria-style serv. Cr cds: A, D, DS, MC, V.

D ⬛

CAPTAIN BENNY'S HALF SHELL. *8018 Katy Frwy, I-10, Wirt exit, west of downtown.* 713/683-1042. Hrs: 11 am-11:45 pm. Closed Sun; most major hols. Beer. Semi-a la carte: lunch, dinner $2.95-$7.95. Specializes in fried oysters, shrimp. Parking. Boat-shaped building; glass walls overlook freeway. No cr cds accepted.

⬛

GOODE CO. TEXAS BAR-B-Q. *5109 Kirby Dr, south of downtown.* 713/522-2530. Hrs: 11 am-10 pm. Closed Jan 1, Thanksgiving, Dec 25. Wine, beer. A la carte entrees: lunch, dinner $4-$9.75. Specializes in barbecued dishes, cheese bread, pecan pie. Entertainment first Fri of month. Parking. Outdoor dining. Laid-back Western atmosphere. Family owned. Cr cds: A, C, D, DS, MC, V.

GREAT CARUSO. *10001 Westheimer Rd, west of downtown.* 713/780-4900. Hrs: 6-10:30 pm; Fri, Sat to 11:30 pm. Closed Mon; Jan 1, Dec 25. Res accepted. Continental menu. Bar to 1 am. A la carte entrees: dinner $15.95-$34.95. Entertainment charge $3.50-$3.95. Specializes in veal, steak, fish. Valet parking. Unique antique decor. Broadway and light operetta performances nightly; singing waiters and dancers. Cr cds: A, C, D, DS, MC, V.

GUGENHEIM'S DELICATESSEN. *1708 Post Oak Blvd, in Galleria Area.* 713/622-2773. Hrs: 10 am-9 pm; Fri to 10 pm; Sat 9 am-9 pm; Sun 9 am-9 pm. Closed Jan 1, Thanksgiving, Dec 25. Wine, beer. Semi-a la carte: bkfst $1-$9.95, lunch, dinner $4.95-$9.95. Specializes in deli sandwiches, cheesecake. Own desserts. Parking. Outdoor dining. NY-style deli. Cr cds: A, C, D, DS, MC, V.

JAGS. *5120 Woodway Dr, in Decorative Ctr, west of downtown.* 713/621-4766. Hrs: 11:30 am-2:30 pm. Closed Sat, Sun; Memorial Day, Thanksgiving, Dec 25. Res accepted. Bar. A la carte entrees: lunch $8-$15. Specialties: blini Santa Fe, seared salmon with cucumber salsa. Multi-level dining area surrounded by running stream. Cr cds: A, MC, V.

LUBY'S CAFETERIA. *5215 Buffalo Speedway, south of downtown.* 713/664-4852. Hrs: 10:45 am-8:30 pm. Closed Dec 25. Continental menu. Avg ck: lunch $4.75, dinner $5. Specializes in fried & baked fish, roast beef, fried chicken. Parking. Cr cds: DS, MC, V.

OTTO'S BARBECUE. *5502 Memorial Dr, west of downtown.* 713/864-2573. Hrs: 11 am-9 pm. Closed Sun; some major hols. Beer. Semi-a la carte: lunch, dinner $4.75-$8.75. Child's meals. Specializes in barbecued meats. Parking. Outdoor dining. Rustic. Western decor; slogan-covered walls. No cr cds accepted.

Huntsville (C-8)

(See Bryan/College Station)

Pop 27,925 **Elev** 400 ft **Area code** 409 **Zip** 77340
Information Chamber of Commerce, 1327 11th St; 409/295-8113 or 800/289-0389.

Huntsville was the home of Sam Houston, winner of Texas independence at San Jacinto, first elected president of the Texas Republic and twice governor of Texas. It is the headquarters of the Texas Department of Criminal Justice. Lumber and woodworking are important part of its economy. Huntsville is the home of Sam Houston State University; the school's Criminal Justice Center is one of the largest criminal justice education and research facilities in the nation.

What to See and Do

Huntsville State Park. On Lake Raven, 2,083 acres. Swimming, fishing, boating (ramp, rentals). Nature & hiking trails. Picnicking, concession. Improved campsites (hookups, dump station). Standard fees. (Daily) 6 mi S on I-45, exit 109 at Park Rd 40. Phone 409/295-5644. Per vehicle ¢¢

Sam Houston Memorial Museum Complex. Eight-structure complex surrounding a 15-acre park. Exhibits with artifacts pertaining to the Republic of Texas and relating to Houston and his family. Tours. (Daily exc Mon; closed some hols). 1836 Sam Houston Ave. Phone 409/294-1832. **Free.** Includes

Woodland Home, Sam Houston's Residence (1848). Residence with original law office and detached replica log kitchen. Tours.

Steamboat House (1858), where Houston died. Built by Dr. Rufus W. Bailey, this is modeled after a Mississippi steamboat, with decklike galleries running its full length.

Sam Houston National Forest. Offers 161,500 acres with swimming (fee) & fishing in Double Lake and Lake Conroe for catfish, bass; hunting for deer, squirrel. Lone Star Hiking Trail (140 mi). Picnicking & camping at Double Lake (fee). Primitive camping (free). Recreation fees vary. S and E, via US 75, 190, 59, I-45. Contact San Jacinto (East) District Ranger Office, 713/592-6461, or Raven (West) District Ranger Office, 409/344-6205. **Free.**

Sam Houston's Grave. About 3 blks N of courthouse on side road, follow signs. Inscription is the tribute of Andrew Jackson, once his military commander: "The world will take care of Houston's fame."

Texas Prison Museum. Items on display include an electric chair ("Old Sparky"), rifles, contraband items and examples of inmate art. (Tues-Sun afternoons; closed major hols) 1113 12th St, opp courthouse. Phone 409/295-2155. ¢

Motels

★ **PARK INN INTERNATIONAL.** *1407 I-45, exit 116.* 409/295-6454; FAX 409/295-9245. 124 rms, 2 story. S $49; D $54-$58; each addl $5; under 18 free. Crib free. TV; cable (premium). Pool; wading pool. Complimentary coffee in rms. Restaurant 6 am-9 pm. Rm serv. Bar 3 pm-midnight, Sat 6 pm-1 am; dancing. Ck-out noon. Meeting rms. Some refrigerators. Picnic tables. Cr cds: A, C, D, DS, MC, V.

✔ ★ ★ **SAM HOUSTON INN.** *3296 I-45S, exit 114.* 409/295-9151; res: 800/395-9151. 76 rms, 2 story. S $42-$46; D $48-$76; each addl $8; under 16 free. Crib free. TV; cable. Pool. Complimentary continental bkfst, coffee. Ck-out noon. Coin lndry. Meeting rms. In-rm modem link. Cr cds: A, C, D, DS, MC, V.

Motor Hotel

✔ ★ **UNIVERSITY HOTEL.** *PO Box 2388 (77341), 1600 Avenue H.* 409/291-2151; FAX 409/294-1683. 95 rms, 4 story. S $35; D $40; each addl $3; under 18 free; monthly rates. Crib free. Pet accepted. TV; cable. Pool privileges. Bkfst avail. Ck-out noon. Meeting rms. In-rm modem link. Health club privileges. Refrigerators. On Sam Houston State University campus. Cr cds: A, C, D, MC, V.

Restaurant

★ **THE JUNCTION.** *2641 11th St.* 409/291-2183. Hrs: 11 am-10 pm; Fri, Sat to 11 pm. Closed Thanksgiving, Dec 24-25. Res accepted. Bar. Semi-a la carte: lunch $3.75-$6.45, dinner $5.95-$13.95. Child's meals. Specializes in prime rib, lobster, catfish, shrimp. Salad bar. Parking. Restored 1840s plantation house; many antiques. Cr cds: A, C, D, DS, MC, V.

Irving (B-7)

(see Dallas and Dallas/Fort Worth Airport Area)

Jacksonville (B-8)

(For accommodations see Palestine, Tyler, also see Rusk)

Pop 12,765 **Elev** 531 ft **Area code** 903 **Zip** 75766
Information Chamber of Commerce, 526 E Commerce, PO Box 1231; 903/586-2217.

What to See and Do

Lake Jacksonville. A 1,760-acre recreation area with swimming, waterskiing; bass fishing; boating. Camping and cabins (fee). (Daily) 3 mi SW via US 79, College Ave exit. Phone 903/586-4160. Per vehicle ¢¢

Love's Lookout Park. Large roadside park with beautiful overlook of countryside. Woodlands, play areas, picnicking, rest rms. (All yr) 3¹/₂ mi N via US 69, Lookout exit. **Free.**

Annual Events

Western Week. Different events each day. Tops-n-Texas Rodeo lasts four days. 2nd wk July.

Tomato Fest. Jacksonville Show & Expo Center. Barbecue cook-off, children's activities. Battle of San Tomato, diaper derby. Mid-Sept.

Jasper (C-8)

Founded 1837 **Pop** 6,959 **Elev** 228 ft **Area code** 409 **Zip** 75951
Information Chamber of Commerce, 246 E Milam; 409/384-2762.

Jasper is the seat of Jasper County, where much of the land is covered with timber. The economy is based on lumbering, wood products and by-products, but there are also many small industries.

The reservoirs resulting from the construction of dams on the Angelina, Sabine and Neches Rivers provide recreational facilities.

What to See and Do

Angelina National Forest. NW on TX 63 (see LUFKIN).

Beaty-Orton House. Restored Victorian gingerbread house. Museum; tours. (By appt) 200 S Main. Phone 409/383-6138. ¢¢

Martin Dies, Jr State Park. Approx 700 acres. Swimming, waterskiing; fishing piers; boating (ramps). Picnicking. Camping (tent & trailer sites, hookups, dump station). Standard fees. (Daily) 13 mi SW on US 190 to Park Rd 48, on E shore of B.A. Steinhagen Lake. Phone 409/384-5231. Per vehicle ¢¢

Reservoirs.

B.A. Steinhagen Lake. Waterskiing; fishing; boating (ramps). Picnicking; concession. Camping (tent & trailer sites, fee). (Daily) Headquarters located 15 mi SW on US 190, then 5 mi S on FM 92. Phone 409/429-3491. **Free.**

Sam Rayburn. Swimming, waterskiing; fishing; boating (ramps). Picnicking. Camping (tent & trailer sites, fee). Headquarters located 9 mi N on US 96, then 8 mi W on TX 255. Phone 409/384-5716. **Free.**

Toledo Bend Dam and Reservoir. Maintained by the Sabine River Authorities of Texas & Louisiana. Swimming, waterskiing; fishing; boating. Picnicking. Camping. Approx 1,200 mi of shoreline. Some fees. (Daily) Project HQ, 9 mi N on US 96, then 26 mi E on TX 255. Phone 409/565-2273. Per vehicle ¢¢

Sabine National Forest. Approx 160,600 acres of rolling clay, sand hills covered with pine, hardwood forests. Toledo Bend Reservoir is on the east boundary of forest. Five recreation areas. Swimming; boating (launch). Hiking. Camping (fee). (Daily) Fees vary. N & E via US 96. Contact District Ranger Office, 409/275-2632 or 409/787-3870.

Annual Event

PRCA Lion's Club Championship Rodeo. Usually 2nd wk May.

Motel

✔★★ **RAMADA INN.** *239 E Gibson. 409/384-9021; FAX 409/384-9021, ext. 309.* 100 rms. S, D $43-$58; under 18 free. Pet accepted. TV; cable (premium), VCR avail. Pool. Restaurant 6 am-9 pm, Sun to 2 pm. Rm serv. Bar 4 pm-midnight. Ck-out noon. Coin lndry. Meeting rms. Business servs avail. Valet serv. Some refrigerators. Picnic tables. Cr cds: A, C, D, DS, JCB, MC, V.

Resort

✔★★ **RAYBURN COUNTRY RESORT.** *(10 mi N of Jasper, Sam Rayburn)* 409/698-2444; res: 800/882-1442; FAX 409/6982372. 176 units, 50 rms in main bldg, 126 kit. condos. 2-day min: S $38.95-$43.95; D $43.95-$48.95; wkly, monthly rates; MAP avail. Crib free. TV; cable. Pool. Playground. Restaurant nearby. Bar noon-midnight. Gift shop. Grocery 2 mi. Coin lndry 5 mi. Meeting rms. Lighted tennis. 27-hole golf, greens fee $27-$35, putting green, driving range. Boats. Fishing guide, clean and store. Some balconies. On Lake Sam Rayburn. Cr cds: A, C, D, DS, MC, V.

Jefferson (B-8)

(See Marshall)

Founded 1836 **Pop** 2,199 **Elev** 200 ft **Area code** 903 **Zip** 75657
Information Marion County Chamber of Commerce, 116 W Austin St; 903/665-2672.

On Big Cypress Bayou, this was once Texas' largest inland river steamboat port. The town had gaslights in 1867, which used gas made from pine knots. Trees were harvested for lumber until the area was nearly stripped of its natural resource. Iron ore was found nearby, and Jefferson was the home of an early foundry. In 1872 this community had a population of more than 35,000.

What to See and Do

Atalanta. Personal rail car of railroad magnate and financier Jay Gould. Inquire at Excelsior House. (Daily; closed Dec 25) ¢

Caddo Lake State Park. E on TX 134 (see MARSHALL).

Excelsior House (see INNS). Built in the 1850s. President Ulysses S. Grant, President Rutherford B. Hayes, Jay Gould and Oscar Wilde stayed here. Period furnishings. Tours (daily; closed Dec 25). 211 W Austin St. Phone 903/665-2513. ¢

Freeman Plantation. Antebellum home built in 1850; restored and furnished with Victorian antiques. Tours (daily exc Wed; closed Easter, Thanksgiving, Dec 25) 1 mi W on TX 49. Phone 903/665-2320. ¢¢

Historical Museum. Former post office and federal court building (1888) houses Native American exhibits, gun collection, early American items, art display. (Daily; closed Dec 24-25) 223 W Austin St. Phone 903/665-2775. ¢

House of the Seasons (1872). Example of the transition period between the Greek-revival and Victorian styles of architecture. The unique feature of the house is the cupola, from which the house gets its name. Each wall contains a different color stained-glass window that creates the illusion of a season of the year. Many original furnishings and art pieces. Tours (daily; closed Thanksgiving, Dec 25). 409 S Alley. Phone 903/665-1218. ¢¢

Lake o' the Pines Swimming; fishing; boating. Picnicking. Camping (tent & trailer sites, dump station; fee). (Daily) 4 mi W on TX 49, then 4 mi W on FM 729, then 2 mi W on FM 726. Phone 903/665-2336 or for reservations 800/284-2267. Per vehicle ¢¢

Turning basin riverboat tours. Flat-bottom boat ride down Big Cypress Bayou. Historical sites are detailed. (Mar-Nov, daily) At Polk St Bridge. Phone 903/665-2222. ¢¢

Annual Events

Historical Pilgrimage. Tours of six old houses. Surrey rides, saloon show. *Diamond Bessie Murder Trial*, Jefferson Playhouse; Henderson & Market Sts. Contact 211 W Austin. Late Apr-early May.

Christmas Candlelight Tour. Tour of four Victorian houses decorated for the season. 1st 2 wkends Dec.

Motel

✔ ★ ★ **BEST WESTERN INN OF JEFFERSON.** *400 S Walcott (US 59).* 903/665-3983. 65 rms, 2 story. S $46-$56; D $50-$60; each addl $6; suites $79-$100; under 16 free; higher rates: Mardi Gras, hol wkends, Pilgrimage, Candlelight Tour. Pet accepted, some restrictions; $20 refundable. TV; cable (premium). Pool; whirlpool, sauna. Restaurant adj 6 am-9 pm; Fri, Sat to 10 pm. Ck-out noon. Business servs avail. Some in-rm whirlpools. Cr cds: A, C, D, DS, MC, V.

D ✔ 🏊 🏊 🐾 SC

Inns

★ ★ **EXCELSIOR HOUSE.** *211 W Austin St.* 903/665-2513. 13 rms, 2 story. No rm phones. S, D $45-$70; each addl $5; suites $80-$90. Closed Dec 24. TV. Bkfst avail. Ck-out noon, ck-in 2:30 pm. Restored hotel (1858); elegant antique Victorian furnishings. Jefferson museum adj. No cr cds accepted.

🏊 🐾

★ ★ **McKAY HOUSE.** *306 E Delta St.* 903/665-7322. 7 rms, 4 with bath, 3 shower only, 2 story, 3 suites. S, D $85-$95; each addl $25; suites $125-$145; wkly, wkday rates; 2-night min hols. TV; cable (premium). Complimentary full bkfst. Restaurant nearby. Ck-out 11 am. Meeting rms. Balconies. Romantic Victorian house restored with authentic antiques. Totally nonsmoking. Cr cds: MC, V.

🏊 🐾 SC

★ ★ **PRIDE HOUSE.** *409 Broadway.* 903/665-2675; res: 800/894-3526. 6 rms in house, 2 story, 4 rms in cottage. No rm phones. S, D $65-$100; each addl $15; suite $100; mid-wk rates. TV avail. Complimentary full bkfst. Restaurant nearby. Ck-out 11:30 am, ck-in noon-3 pm. Free airport transportation. Victorian residence (1889) restored with original materials. Ornate woodwork, period furnishings. Totally nonsmoking. Cr cds: MC, V.

🏊 🐾

Restaurants

✔ ★ **THE BAKERY.** *201 W Austin St.* 903/665-2253. Hrs: 7 am-4 pm; Sat, Sun to 5 pm. Closed Thanksgiving, Dec 25. Res accepted. Semi-a la carte: bkfst $2.50-$4.75, lunch, dinner $1.95-$5.50. Specializes in hot roast beef, pastries. Own baking. Parking. In historic district. Cr cds: A, MC, V.

D

★ ★ **STILLWATER INN.** *203 E Broadway, 1 blk E of jct TX 49, US 59.* 903/665-8415. Hrs: 6-10 pm. Closed Mon; Dec 25. Res ac-

cepted; required Sat. French, Amer menu. Private club. Wine list. Semi-a la carte: dinner $12.95-$24.50. Specializes in seafood, grilled meats. Own baking, ice cream. Parking. Intimate dining in restored Eastlake Victorian house (1893); antiques; herb garden. Guest rms avail. Cr cds: A, MC, V.

Johnson City (C-6)

(See Austin, Burnet, Fredericksburg)

Pop 932 **Elev** 1,193 ft **Area code** 210 **Zip** 78636
Information Tourism & Visitors Bureau, PO Box 485; 210/868-7684

President Lyndon B. Johnson's Hereford ranch is 13 miles west at Stonewall, just off US 290. During his term of office, it was referred to as the Texas White House. It is now a National Historical Park.

What to See and Do

⭐ **Lyndon B. Johnson National Historical Park.** Composed of two units: the Johnson City Unit consists of the boyhood home with visitor center and the 1860s Johnson Settlement; the LBJ Ranch Unit consists of the LBJ birthplace, family cemetery, Texas White House and the ranch. Access to Ranch Unit by bus tour only (1½ hrs; free). (Daily) Contact Superintendent, PO Box 329; 210/868-7128. **Free.**

Boyhood Home (1901). Victorian-style frame house, period furnishings, family heirlooms; Johnson lived here from 1913-34. (Daily; closed Jan 1, Dec 25) **Free.** 1 blk off Main St. From here walk to the

Johnson Settlement. Restoration of cabin and surrounding pastures owned by the President's grandfather, a longhorn cattle driver in the mid-1800s. (Daily; closed Jan 1, Dec 25) **Free.**

Birthplace. Reconstructed two-bedroom farmhouse, typical of late 1800s structures of this region, with "dog-trot," an open hallway for ventilation. Johnson family occupied the house from 1907-13 and 1920-22. Adj to Birthplace is family cemetery where Johnson is buried. LBJ State Park is nearby. 13 mi W via US 290, Park Rd 49. **Free.**

LBJ Ranch House ("Texas White House"). Built of limestone and wood; ranch has registered Hereford cattle. Bus tour drives by only (not open to public).

Lyndon B. Johnson State Historical Park. On Pedernales River, 733 acres. Swimming and wading pools (fee). Fishing. Nature & hiking trails. Picnicking, playground Tennis courts. Visitor center (daily; closed Dec 25) has Johnson family memorabilia and relics of previous settlers of the area. Adj is Behrens Cabin (1840), a "dog-trot" building with period furnishings. Sauer-Beckmann homestead of early 1900s is site of living history program; tours. (Daily) 14 mi W on US 290, enter on Park Rd 52. Phone 210/644-2252. **Free.**

Pedernales Falls State Park. Approx 4,800 acres. Swimming; fishing. Nature, hiking, bicycle trails. Picnicking. Primitive and improved camping (hookups, dump station). Standard fees. (Daily) 14 mi E on Ranch Rd 2766. Phone 210/868-7304. Per vehicle ¢¢

Motel

★ **SAVE INN MOTEL.** *PO Box 610, 107 US 281, jct US 281 & US 290.* 210/868-4044. 53 rms, 2 story. S $36; D $41-$46; under 6 free. Crib $5. TV; cable (premium). Pool. Restaurant 7 am-3 pm. Ck-out 11 am. Cr cds: A, C, D, DS, MC, V.

D 🏊 🏊 🐾 SC

Juárez, Chihuahua, Mexico (B-1)

(see Ciudad Juárez, Mexico)

Kerrville (D-5)

(See Bandera, Fredericksburg, San Antonio)

Pop 17,384 **Elev** 1,645 ft **Area code** 210 **Zip** 78028
Information Convention and Visitors Bureau, 1700 Sidney Baker, Suite 200; 210/792-3535.

A resort area in the hill country, this community is also a popular conference center and winter destination for Texans. Among the many activities available are fishing, swimming, boating, hunting, horseback riding, tennis and golf. River and ranch cabins are open year round.

What to See and Do

Cowboy Artists of America Museum. Rotating and permanent collections of works and memorabilia devoted to the art of the modern West; Western art library. (Memorial Day-Labor Day, daily; rest of yr, daily exc Mon) Sr citizen rate. 1550 Bandera Hwy (TX 173). Phone 210/896-2553. ¢¢

Hill Country Museum (Capt. Charles Schreiner Mansion). Residence restored to house the memorabilia of more than a century of area history. (Daily) 226 Earl Garrett. Phone 210/896-8633.   ¢¢

Kerrville-Schreiner State Park. Approx 500 acres. Swimming; fishing; boating (ramps). Hiking trail. Picnicking; playground. Camping (hookups, dump station). Standard fees. (Daily) 3 mi S via TX 16/173. Phone 210/257-5392. Per vehicle   ¢¢

Y.O. Ranch. Acquired in 1880 by Captain Charles Schreiner, this 60 square-mile ranch, one of the largest in Texas, has a herd of more than 1,500 longhorn cattle. The terrain resembles that of Africa. Approx 50 different species of exotic game animals, including antelopes, zebras, giraffes, ostriches, emus, roam free. Game animals are also abundant (limited hunting); photo safaris. Tours (by res). Ranch includes general store, cabins, pool, lodge. (Daily, by res only) (See ANNUAL EVENTS) Some fees. I-10W, 18 mi W to TX 41, then 16 mi SW. Phone 210/640-3222.

Annual Events

Longhorn Trail Drive. Y.O. Ranch. Heritage celebration, camping under the stars, covered wagons and "trailblazers." Wkend, spring.

Kerrville Folk Festival. Quiet Valley Ranch, 9 mi S on TX 16. Outdoor music festival. Children's concerts; crafts; camping. Phone 210/257-3600. Late May-early June.

Texas State Arts & Crafts Fair. Schreiner College campus. Concessions, entertainment, demonstrations. Phone 210/896-5711. Memorial Day wkend.

Kerr County Fair. Music, food, crafts, livestock. Oct.

Seasonal Event

Smith/Ritch Point Theatre. 6 mi W via TX 39, in Ingram. Four productions in outdoor amphitheater on the banks of the Guadalupe River. Wed-Sat, nightly. Phone 210/367-5122. May-Aug.

Motels

★ ★ **BEST WESTERN SUNDAY HOUSE INN.** *2124 Sidney Baker St. 210/896-1313; FAX 210/896-1336.* 97 rms, 2 story. S $60-

$70; D $62-$92; each addl $6; studio, family rms $72-$102; under 12 free. Crib $6. TV; cable (premium). Pool. Restaurant 6 am-9 pm. Bar 5-9 pm. Ck-out noon. Meeting rms. Cr cds: A, C, D, DS, MC, V.

★ ★ ★ **HOLIDAY INN-Y.O. RANCH HOTEL & CONFERENCE CENTER.** *2033 Sidney Baker, jct I-10, TX 16. 210/257-4440; FAX 210/896-8189.* 200 rms, 2 story. S $78-$105; D $85-$115; suites $150-$230; each addl $10; parlors $75; family rates; package plans. Crib free. Pet accepted. TV; cable (premium). Pool; wading pool, whirlpool. Restaurant 6 am-2 pm, 5-10 pm; Fri, Sat to 11 pm. Rm serv. Bar 4 pm-2 am. Ck-out noon. Meeting rms. Airport transportation. Tennis. 18-hole golf privileges, greens fee $35-$50. Some bathrm phones, refrigerators. Private patios, balconies. Western decor; Mexican tile floors. Cr cds: A, C, D, DS, ER, JCB, MC, V.

✔ ★ ★ **SHONEY'S INN.** *2145 Sidney Baker St. 210/896-1711.* 105 rms, 2 story. S $42-$64; D $44-$68; each addl $6; under 18 free. Crib free. TV; cable (premium), VCR avail. Pool; wading pool. Serv bar 4 pm-midnight, Sat to 1 am. Ck-out noon. Coin lndry. Meeting rms. Business servs avail. Valet serv. 18-hole golf privileges, greens fee $45. Cr cds: A, C, D, MC, V.

Inn

★ **RIVER BEND.** *(Rt 1, Box 114, Hunt 78024) 15 mi W on FM 1340. 210/238-4681; res: 800/472-3933; FAX 210/238-3180.* 16 rms (7 with shower only), 3 bldgs, 6 suites. No rm phones. S $70-$80; D $85-$95; each addl $15; suites $115; kit. unit $165; higher rates wknds & hols (2-3 day min), Crib free. TV in lobby. Complimentary full bkfst. Ck-out 11 am, ck-in 2 pm. Tennis privileges. Overlooks Guadalupe River; scenic views. Cr cds: A, DS, MC, V.

Resort

★ ★ **INN OF THE HILLS.** *1001 Junction Hwy. 210/895-5000; res: 800/292-5690; FAX 210/895-1277.* 218 units, 2-6 story, 37 kit. units. May-Oct: S $60-$80; D $65-$85; each addl $6; suites $100-$250; kits. $125-$130; under 12 free; wkly rates; lower rates rest of yr. Crib $3. TV; cable (premium). 4 pools, 2 indoor; wading pool; whirlpool, sauna, poolside serv (summer). Playground. Complimentary coffee in rms. Restaurant (see ALPINE LODGE). Rm serv. Bar 1 pm-1 am; entertainment, dancing exc Mon. Ck-out noon. Coin lndry. Meeting rms. In-rm modem link. Valet serv. Gift shop. Barber, beauty shop. Free bus depot transportation. Lighted tennis. 18-hole golf privileges, greens fee $50, pro, putting green. Canoes, paddleboats. Health club privileges. Lawn games. Game rm. Some balconies. Cr cds: A, C, D, DS, MC, V.

Guest Ranch

★ ★ **LAZY HILLS GUEST RANCH.** *(Box MG, Ingram 78025) 8 mi NW on TX 27. 210/367-5600; res: 800/880-0632; FAX 210/367-5667.* 25 units. S $95; D $70/person; each addl $62; under 1 yr $10; 1-8 yrs $20; 9-11 yrs $25; 12-16 yrs $35. TV in lobby. Pool; wading pool, whirlpool. Playground. Free supervised child's activities (June-Aug); ages 3-8. Dining rm sittings: 8-9 am, noon, 6 pm. Cookouts. Ck-out 2 pm, ck-in 4 pm. Business servs avail.Lighted tennis. Lawn games. Rec rm. Some fireplaces. Cr cds: DS, MC, V.

Restaurants

★ ★ **ALPINE LODGE.** *(See Inn Of The Hills Resort) 210/257-8282.* Hrs: 6 am-10 pm; Sun to 9 pm; Sun brunch from 11 am. Res accepted. Swiss, Amer menu. Bar. Semi-a la carte: bkfst $2.75-$8.50, lunch $4.75-$11.50, dinner $6.95-$14. Sun brunch $10.95. Child's meals. Specialties: Swiss Alpine platter, birchermuesli. Salad bar. Accordianist Wed & Thur. Swiss decor features Alpine horn and cow bells. Family-owned. Cr cds: A, C, D, DS, MC, V.

D SC

✔ ★ **MAMACITAS.** *215 Junction Hwy. 210/895-2441.* Hrs: 11 am-9:30 pm; Fri-Sun 11 am-10 pm. Closed Jan 1, Thanksgiving, Dec 25. Res accepted. Mexican menu. Bar. Semi-a la carte: lunch $4.25-$4.95, dinner $5.45-$9.95. Specializes in fajitas, enchiladas. Parking. Mexican courtyard decor; stained-glass windows, fountain. Cr cds: A, DS, MC, V.

D

★ **MENCIUS.** *208 Cully Dr (48028), behind River Hills Mall. 210/257-8868.* Hrs: 11 am-2:15 pm, 4:30-9:30 pm; early-bird dinner 4:30-6 pm; Sun brunch from 11:30 am. Closed Thanksgiving, Dec 25. Res accepted. Chinese menu. Bar. Semi-a la carte: lunch $4.25-$5.50, dinner $5.95-$14.95. Sun brunch $6.50-$7.50. Specializes in Hunan dishes. Parking. Asian decor. Cr cds: A, D, DS, MC, V.

D

★ **SUNDAY HOUSE.** *2124 Sidney Baker St. 210/257-7171.* Hrs: 6 am-9 pm; Fri & Sat to 9:30 pm; Sun brunch 11 am-4 pm. Res accepted. Continental menu. Bar. Semi-a la carte: bkfst $2.75-$6.50, lunch $3.95-$6.95, dinner $5.95-$13.95. Sun brunch $11.95. Specializes in German dishes, pasta, steak. Salad bar. Parking. Outdoor dining. German cafe atmosphere. Cr cds: A, C, D, DS, MC, V.

D SC

Kilgore (B-8)

(For accommodations see Longview, Marshall, Tyler)

Pop 11,066 **Elev** 370 ft **Area code** 903 **Zip** 75662
Information Chamber of Commerce, 1100 Stone Rd, Suite 104-A, PO Box 1582, 75663-1582; 903/984-5022.

The discovery of the largest oil field in the continental US transformed Kilgore into a thriving boomtown in the 1930s. More than 1,200 producing wells were drilled within the city limits during the boom, including 24 in a half-block area of downtown.

What to See and Do

East Texas Oil Museum at Kilgore College. Re-creation of oil discovery and production in 1930s in largest oil field in US. Full-scale town depicting oil boom days. (Daily exc Mon; special Dec holiday schedule; closed Easter, Thanksgiving) Kilgore College campus, jct US 259 & Ross St. Phone 903/983-8295. ¢¢ Also on campus is

Rangerette Showcase. Museum depicts history of the famous Kilgore Rangerettes, college football's first precision drill & dance team, with photographs, scrapbooks, memorabilia and film footage. (Daily exc Mon, hrs vary; closed some major hols) 1100 Broadway. Phone 903/983-8265. **Free.**

Killeen (C-6)

(See Burnet, Temple)

Pop 63,535 **Elev** 833 ft **Area code** 817
Information Convention & Visitors Bureau, PO Box 548, 76540; 817/526-9551 or 800/869-8265.

What to See and Do

Belton Lake. 8 mi E & N via US 190 then TX 317 (see TEMPLE).

Fort Hood. This 339-sq-mi army installation has the nation's largest concentration of armored power. Houses the US Army III Corps, the 1st Cavalry Division and the 2nd Armored Division. The 2nd Armored and 1st Cavalry museums feature military equipment and campaign exhibits (daily, limited hrs). W of town. Phone 817/287-8506. **Free.**

Stillhouse Hollow Lake. 6 mi SE via FM 2410 & US 190 (see SALADO).

Motel

★ ★ **LA QUINTA.** *1112 Ft Hood St (76541). 817/526-8331; FAX 817/526-0394.* 105 rms, 3 story. No elvtr. S $52-$59; D $59-$66; each addl $7; suites $59-$64; under 18 free. Crib free. Pet accepted. TV; cable (premium). Pool. Complimentary continental bkfst. Complimentary coffee in lobby. Restaurant adj open 24 hrs. Ck-out noon. Meeting rm. Valet serv. Free airport transportation. Cr cds: A, D, DS, MC, V.

D ✔ ≈ ⚓ 🔥 SC

Motor Hotel

★ ★ **PLAZA HOTEL.** *1721 Central Texas Expy (76541). 817/634-1555; FAX 817/519-2945.* 148 rms, 6 story. S $66; D $76; suites $83-$110; under 12 free; wkend rates. Crib free. TV; cable. Pool. Restaurant 6 am-10 pm; Fri, Sat to 11 pm. Rm serv. Private club noon-midnight, Fri, Sat to 2 am; dancing. Ck-out 1 pm. Meeting rms. Business servs avail. In-rm modem link. Bellhops. Valet serv. Free airport transportation. Exercise equipt; weights, bicycles. Whirlpool in some suites. Some refrigerators. Cr cds: A, C, D, DS, MC, V.

D ≈ 🏋 ⚓ 🔥 🐾 SC

Restaurant

★ ★ **DIVINO'S.** *2100 S W.S. Young (76543), in mall. 817/680-3383.* Hrs: 11 am-10 pm; Fri & Sat to 11 pm; Sun to 9 pm. Closed Thanksgiving, Dec 25. Res accepted. Italian menu. Bar. Semi-a la carte: lunch $4.95-$8.95, dinner $7.95-$15.95. Child's meals. Specialties: fettuccine Alfredo, veal Marsala. Italian country decor. Cr cds: A, C, D, DS, MC, V.

D

Kingsville (E-6)

(See Alice, Corpus Christi)

Founded 1904 **Pop** 25,276 **Elev** 66 ft **Area code** 512 **Zip** 78363
Information Visitors Center, 101 N 3rd St, PO Box 1562; 512/592-8516 or 800/333-5032.

This is the home of the King Ranch, an 825,000-acre property in four main sections stretching down the coastal bend between Corpus Christi and Harlingen. It is the world's largest privately owned ranch and one of the most scientifically run. Richard King, a steamboat captain, came into this unpromising area in 1853 and built an empire.

His son-in-law, Robert J. Kleberg, Jr, and Richard M. Kleberg, Sr, developed the first beef breed in the Western Hemisphere—the hardy, cherry-red Santa Gertrudis. Planning and genetic engineering went into the ranch's pursuit of the perfect cow horse, the Old Sorrel family of quarter horses. King's descendants still own and run the vast territory. Many varieties of wildlife live on the ranch. Driving south along US 77, traffic passes right through the ranch, though there are no signs to indicate this.

Also near Kingsville are a large petrochemical plant and the Kingsville Naval Air Station, a jet pilot training facility.

What to See and Do

King Ranch. Guided bus tours (90 min; fee) include cattle, horses, native wildlife, drive-by of historic buildings. Museum includes 20-minute film of King Ranch history, saddles, stagecoaches, automobiles. (Daily; closed major hols) 12-mile Loop Rd around headquarters area, just W of town via Santa Gertrudis Ave or TX 141. Phone 512/592-8055 or 800/333-5032. ¢¢¢

Texas A & M University-Kingsville (1925). (6,400 students) A 1,600-acre campus. Changing exhibits in Gallery of Art Bldg featuring famous southwestern artists. Observatory in Lon C. Hill Science Hall. Armstrong St between Santa Gertrudis & Corral Aves. Phone 512/595-2111. Also on campus is

John E. Conner Museum. Historical exhibits and collections of southern Texas; Kleberg Hall of Natural History; Peeler Hall of Horns. Regional and photo archives. Changing exhibits. (Daily exc Sun; closed hols) Donation. 821 W Santa Gertrudis Ave. Phone 512/595-2819.

Annual Events

Texas A & M National Intercollegiate Rodeo. Northway Exposition Center. Contestants from across Texas and Louisiana. Late Mar.

Fiesta de Colores. Northway Exposition Center. 1st wkend Oct.

Motel

✔★ **QUALITY INN.** 2502 E Kenedy St. 512/592-5251; FAX 512/592-6197. 117 rms, 2 story. S $40; D $45-$49; each addl $4; under 12 free. TV; cable. Pool; wading pool. Rm serv. Ck-out noon. Meeting rms. Cr cds: A, C, D, DS, JCB, MC, V.

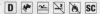

La Grange (D-7)

(See Austin, Bastrop)

Pop 3,951 **Elev** 277 ft **Area code** 409 **Zip** 78945
Information Chamber of Commerce, 129 N Main, "On the Square"; 409/968-5756.

What to See and Do

Fayette Heritage Museum. Historical museum; changing displays; archives. (Daily exc Mon; closed hols) 855 S Jefferson. Phone 409/968-6418. **Free.**

Fayette Power Project Lake & Parks. On 2,400-acre cooling pond for generating station. Swimming, waterskiing; fishing; boating (launch, ramps). Picnicking. Tent camping (showers). (Daily) 10 mi E via TX 159, jct TX 71. Phone 409/249-5208. Per car ¢¢¢

Monument Hill & Kreische Brewery State Historical Park. Memorial monument, tomb of Texans massacred during the Mexican uprisings (1842) and Black Bean Episode (1843). Ruins of a German brewery; guided tours (wkends). Picnic area, nature trails. (Daily) 2 mi S off US 77 on Spur 92, on bluff overlooking Colorado River. Phone 409/968-5658. ¢

Winedale Historical Center. Outdoor museum maintained by the University of Texas. Six restored farm buildings; antique furniture, tools; guided tours. (Sat, Sun; Mon-Fri by appt; closed hols) 17 mi NE on TX 237 to Round Top, then 4½ mi E via FM 1457, 2714. Phone 409/278-3530. ¢¢

Annual Events

Fayette County Country Fair. Labor Day wkend.

Czhilispiel. 20 mi SW on I-10 and TX 609, in Flatonia. Three-day festival is one of the largest chili cook-offs in Texas. 4th wkend Oct.

Inn

★ **MEERSCHEIDT HOUSE.** 485 N Monroe St. 409/968-9569; res: 800/725-3695. 4 rms (1 with shower only), 2 story. S, D $45-$85; adjoining rms $90-$110. Children over 12 yrs only. TV; cable (premium). Complimentary full bkfst. Ck-out 11 am, ck-in 3 pm. Victorian house built early 1880s, furnished with antiques. Totally nonsmoking. Cr cds: MC, V.

Lake Whitney (B-6)

(For accommodations see Hillsboro, Waco)

(17 mi SW of Hillsboro on TX 22)

This is one of the largest lakes in Texas: 49,710 acres on the Brazos River near Whitney. This area, offering many resorts and fishing camps, has been increasing in popularity among vacationers since 1953, when the Whitney Dam was completed.

What to See and Do

Whitney Lake. Swimming, waterskiing; fishing; boating (ramps). Picnicking, concession. Camping (tent & trailer sites, some fees). Headquarters is 7 mi SW of Whitney on TX 22. Phone 817/694-3189. An Army Corps of Engineers Project Office is located below the dam. On E shore of lake is

Lake Whitney State Park. More than 900 acres offering swimming, waterskiing; fishing; boating (ramp). Hiking. Picnicking, playground. Improved campsites (tent & trailer sites). Standard fees. (Daily) 4 mi SW of Whitney on FM 1244. Phone 817/694-3793. Per vehicle ¢¢

Laredo (E-5)

Founded 1755 **Pop** 122,899 **Elev** 420 ft **Area code** 210
Information Convention & Visitors Bureau, 2310 San Bernardo Ave, Box 790, 78042; 210/722-9895 or 800/292-2122.

Laredo is the most important US gateway to Mexico for rail, highway and tourist traffic, with a fine highway to Monterrey and Mexico City. Many white brick and stone buildings grace the streets of the business district; areas of the city date from the Spanish colonial period and reflect that heritage.

Thomas Sanchez founded the town in 1755 and established a ferry across the Rio Grande, for which he received 15 square leagues (about 110 square miles) of rangeland from the Spanish authorities. After the Texas Revolution, because of a dispute over the boundaries of Texas, Laredo was in a no man's land. For a time in the 1840s a government of "The Republic of the Rio Grande" was set up; the capitol building still stands opposite San Agustin Plaza, on Zaragoza Street.

Bermuda onions were a specialty crop introduced early on the 15,000 acres irrigated with Rio Grande water; since then other crops have been successfully grown. Large-scale cattle ranching is done in the mesquite, chaparral and cactus country north and east of town.

What to See and Do

Bus tours. Fiesta Time Tours. 1016 Grant; 210/727-3814. Ole Tours. PO Box 43; 210/726-4290.

LIFE Downs. Site of youth rodeos, livestock shows, other events. US 59E, near Casa Blanca Lake. Phone 210/722-9948. Fairgrounds **free;** Rodeo ¢¢¢

Lake Casa Blanca State Park. Swimming pool (Memorial Day-Labor Day), waterskiing; fishing (piers); boating (ramp). 18-hole golf adj. Picnicking, playground. Primitive camping. (Daily) 5 mi E off US 59 on Lake Casa Blanca Rd. Phone 210/725-3826. Per vehicle ¢¢

Laredo Children's Museum. Two fort buildings dating from the mid-1800s house the museum. Changing hands-on exhibits and demonstrations. (Thurs-Sun; closed hols) At Laredo Junior College, West End Washington St. Phone 210/725-2299. ¢

Nuevo Laredo, Tamaulipas, Mexico (population: 203,700) is across the bridge at the end of Convent Ave. For a limited visit, it is easier to park in Laredo and walk across. (For Border Crossing Regulations, see INTRODUCTION.) Nuevo Laredo is a typical border town, with stores and stands featuring Mexican goods lining the street south of the bridge. There are also many parks, fine restaurants and popular entertainment spots.

Villa de San Agustin. Downtown area. Laredo's historical district contains many of the city's older buildings. They include

Republic of the Rio Grande Museum (ca 1830). An example of "Laredo" architecture, this was the former capitol of the short-lived Republic; period rooms, furniture. (Daily exc Mon; closed some hols) 1003 Zaragoza St, opp San Agustin Plaza. Phone 210/727-3480. **Free.**

San Agustin Church (1872). The original church was built in 1767 on the site where the city was founded. Genealogical records date back to 1789. (Daily) 214 San Agustin Ave, E of Plaza. **Free.**

Annual Events

George Washington's Birthday Celebration. International fiesta with parades; jalapeño-eating festival, colonial pageant, dances, bullfights. 10 days mid-Feb.

Laredo International Fair & Exposition. LIFE Downs. Stock, arts and crafts shows; horse racing, barbecue, dance. Last wkend Mar.

Borderfest. Civic Center grounds. Arts & crafts, food & entertainment. 1st wkend July.

Expomex. Nuevo Laredo (Mexico), at Carranza Park. Fiesta, stock show, bullfight. 2nd wkend Sept.

"Fiestas Patrias." Laredo & Nuevo Laredo. Mexican National Independence Day celebration. Mid-Sept.

Motel

✓ ★ ★ **LA QUINTA.** 3610 Santa Ursula Ave (78041). 210/722-0511; FAX 210/723-6642. 152 rms, 2 story. S $56.70-$63; D $56.70-$73; each addl $10; suites $78; under 18 free. Crib free. TV; cable. Pool. Complimentary continental bkfst. Restaurant adj open 24 hrs. Ck-out noon. Cr cds: A, C, D, DS, MC, V.

🄳 🐾 ⌷ ⋈ ⊠ **SC**

Motor Hotel

★ ★ **LA POSADA.** 1000 Zaragoza St (78040), 1 blk E of Intl Bridge. 210/722-1701; res: 800/444-2099; FAX 210/722-4758. 208 rms, 4 story. S, D $79-$150; each addl $10; suites $129-$250; under 19

free. Crib $10. TV; cable (premium), VCR avail (movies avail). 2 heated pools; poolside serv. Restaurant 6 am-11 pm. Rm serv. Bars; entertainment, dancing Mon-Sat. Ck-out noon. Meeting rms. Business center. In-rm modem link. Bellhops. Valet serv. Gift shop. Free airport transportation. Tennis, golf privileges. Some refrigerators. Balconies. Spanish colonial architecture, decor. Rms vary. On Rio Grande. Luxury level. Cr cds: A, C, D, DS, MC, V.

🕴 🕴 ⌷ ⋈ ⊠ **SC** 🕴

Hotels

★ ★ **HOLIDAY INN.** 800 Garden St (78040). 210/727-5800; FAX 210/727-0278. 203 rms, 13 story. S $89-$95; D $95-$101; suites $130; under 17 free; package plans. Crib free. TV; cable. Pool; poolside serv. Restaurant 6:30 am-11 pm. Bar noon-2 am; entertainment, dancing. Ck-out noon. Coin lndry. Meeting rms. Free garage parking. Airport, bus depot, border transportation. Exercise equipt; weights, treadmill, whirlpool, sauna. Cr cds: A, C, D, DS, JCB, MC, V.

🄳 ⌷ 🕴 ⋈ ⊠ **SC**

★ ★ **HOLIDAY INN ON THE RIO GRANDE.** 1 S Main St (78040). 210/722-2411; FAX 210/722-4578. 207 rms, 15 story. S $82-$98; D $92-$108; each addl $10; under 19 free. Crib avail. Pet accepted. TV; cable (premium). Complimentary coffee in rms. Restaurant 6 am-10 pm. Bar 11 am-11 pm. Ck-out noon. Coin lndry. Meeting rms. Business servs avail. In-rm modem link. Free airport transportation. Refrigerators avail. On river, overlooking Mexico. Cr cds: A, C, D, DS, JCB, MC, V.

🄳 🐾 ⌷ ⋈ ⊠ **SC**

Restaurant

✓ ★ **UNICORN.** 3810 San Bernardo (78041). 210/727-4663. Hrs: 11 am-11 pm; Fri, Sat to midnight; Sun to 10 pm. Res accepted. Bar. Semi-a la carte: lunch, dinner $6.25-$14.95. Child's meals. Specializes in mesquite-broiled steak, Tex-Mex dishes. Parking. Cr cds: A, C, D, DS, MC, V.

🄳

Longview (B-8)

(See Marshall, Tyler)

Founded 1870 **Pop** 70,311 **Elev** 289 ft **Area code** 903

Longview, in the Sabine River Valley, is a center for beef cattle production. This is also a manufacturing center with petroleum and earthmoving equipment plants, a brewery and other diversified industry.

What to See and Do

Gregg County Historical Museum. Artifacts, photographs; displays on timber, cotton, corn, farming, railroads, printing, early business and commerce; extensive military collection. Period room settings include bank president's and dentist's offices, early 1900s parlor and bedroom, log cabin, general store. Audiovisual presentation. (Tues-Sat; closed major hols) 214 N Fredonia St, in Everett Bldg (1910), downtown. Phone 903/753-5840. ¢

LeTourneau University (1946). (1,700 students) Engineering, business, technology, education, aviation, arts and sciences. Displays on campus contain early scale models of earthmoving equipment invented by R.G. LeTourneau, founder of the university; also personal mementos. 2100 S Mobberly Ave, Memorial Student Center, 3rd floor. Phone 903/753-0231.

Longview Art Museum. Collection of Southwestern and contemporary artists; changing exhibits; lectures, workshops and classes. (Tues-Sat; closed hols) 102 W College St. Phone 903/753-8103. **Free.**

Stroh Brewery Co. Tours (Mon-Fri afternoons, 3 tours; closed hols). Beer not served to those under 21 years of age. 1400 W Cotton St. Phone 903/753-0371. **Free.**

Motels

✔★ **GUEST INN.** *419 North Spur 63 (75601), Towne Lake Square.* 903/757-0500. 142 rms, 2 story. S $49-$54; D $54-$59; each addl $5; under 12 free. Crib free. TV; cable (premium). Pool. Complimentary coffee in rms. Bkfst avail. Ck-out 1 pm. Meeting rms. Business servs avail. Sundries. Valet serv. Health club privileges. Many refrigerators. Cr cds: A, C, D, DS, MC; V.

D ⊠ ≋ ⋈ 🔥 SC

★★ **HOLIDAY INN.** *3119 Estes Pkwy (75602).* 903/758-0700; FAX 903/758-8705. 193 rms, 2-4 story. S, D $69-$75; each addl $7; suites $77-$175; under 18 free; wkend rates. Crib free. Pet accepted, some restrictions; $25 ($20 refundable). TV; cable (premium), VCR avail. Indoor/outdoor pool; whirlpool, poolside serv. Restaurant 6 am-2 pm, 5:30-10 pm. Rm serv. Private club 4 pm-2 am, closed Sun; dancing. Ck-out 1 pm. Coin lndry. Meeting rms. Business servs avail. In-rm modem link. Sundries. Free airport transportation. Game rm. Holidome. Cr cds: A, C, D, DS, ER, JCB, MC, V.

D ✋ ≋ ⋈ 🔥 SC

★★ **LA QUINTA INN.** *502 S Access Rd (75602), I-20 at Estes Pkwy.* 903/757-3663; FAX 903/753-3780. 106 rms, 2 story. S $49-$56; D $55-$66; each addl $6; under 18 free. Crib free. Pet accepted, some restrictions. TV; cable (premium). Pool. Complimentary continental bkfst. Complimentary coffee in lobby. Restaurant adj open 24 hrs. Ck-out noon. Meeting rms. Valet serv. Cr cds: A, C, D, DS, MC, V.

D ✋ ≋ ⋈ 🔥 SC

Restaurants

★★ **JOHNNY CACE'S SEAFOOD & STEAK HOUSE.** *1501 E Marshall (75601).* 903/753-7691. Hrs: 11 am-10 pm; Fri & Sat to 11 pm; Sun & Mon 3-10 pm. Closed some major hols. Creole, Cajun menu. Bar. Semi-a la carte: lunch $4.95-$6.25, dinner $7.45-$21. Child's meals. Specializes in fresh-shucked oysters, aged beef, broiled fresh fish. Family-owned. Cr cds: A, C, D, DS, MC, V.

D

✔★ **PAPACITA'S.** *305 Loop 281 (75601).* 903/663-1700. Hrs: 11 am-10 pm; Fri & Sat to 11 pm. Closed some major hols. Mexican menu. Bar. Semi-a la carte: lunch $2.95-$8.95, dinner $4.95-$11. Child's meals. Specialties: Papacita combination dinner, sizzling fajitas. Parking. Colorful Mexican decor. Cr cds: A, DS, MC, V.

D

Unrated Dining Spot

LUBY'S CAFETERIA. *118 Johnston, Chaparral Plaza Shopping Center, at Judson St.* 903/758-6496. Hrs: 10:45 am-2:30 pm, 4:15-8 pm; Sat, Sun 10:45 am-8 pm. Closed Dec 25. Avg ck: lunch $4.75, dinner $5. Cr cds: DS, MC, V.

Lubbock (A-4)

(See Plainview)

Founded 1891 **Pop** 186,206 **Elev** 3,241 ft **Area code** 806
Information Convention & Tourism Bureau, PO Box 561, 79408; 806/747-5232.

Named after Colonel Thomas S. Lubbock, Confederate officer and brother of Texas' Civil War governor, this was originally a headquarters for buffalo hunters, trail drivers and early ranchers. Lubbock is now an important commercial and shipping center for a large, rich ranching, oil and agricultural territory.

Lubbock is one of the largest inland cotton markets in the nation, the center of a farm area also producing grain sorghums, wheat and corn. Grain elevators dot the landscape. A number of manufacturing plants produce a wide variety of products. Reese AFB, a jet pilot training center, is just west of the city.

What to See and Do

Buddy Holly Statue and Walk of Fame. Bronze statue of the rock & roll pioneer and Lubbock native. Bronze plaques honor country & western musicians from the area. Sixth St & Avenue Q.

Buffalo Springs Lake Recreational Area. A 1,223-acre area with 225 acres of water. Waterskiing; fishing; boating. Picnicking, concession. Primitive & improved camping (tent & trailer sites; fee; 2-wk max). Store. (Daily) 5 mi SE on FM 835. Phone 806/747-3353. ¢

Mackenzie Park. Approx 500 acres. Includes 36-hole golf course (fee). Picnicking, grills. Amusement area (fee); prairie dog town. (Daily) Off I-27, 4 mi E on Broadway to Park Rd 18. Phone 806/767-2687. **Free.**

Texas Tech University (1923) and **Texas Tech University Health Sciences Center** (1969) (26,000 students). One of Texas' four major state universities; 1,800-acre campus. It offers major sports and arts attractions, including a noted Peter Hurd mural. University & Broadway Ave. Phone 806/742-2136. On campus are

Museum of Texas Tech University. Exhibits on art, natural sciences and history of semiarid & arid lands. (Daily exc Mon; closed major hols) Moody Planetarium ¢. 4th St & Indiana Ave. Phone 806/742-2456. **Free.** An outdoor addition to the museum is

Ranching Heritage Center. This 14-acre restoration of 33 structures represents the development of ranching in the West. (Daily; closed hols) **Free.**

Lubbock Lake Landmark State Historic Park. This major archaeological excavation is located two miles north of campus at Loop 289 and Indiana Ave. (Tues-Sat, also Sun afternoons) Phone 806/762-9773. Tours ¢

Annual Events

Lubbock Arts Festival. Lubbock Memorial Civic Center. 4 days Mar or Apr.

Panhandle South Plains Fair. Fairgrounds, 9th St. Late Sept.

Motels

★★★ **BARCELONA COURT.** *5215 Loop 289S (79424), Slide Rd exit.* 806/794-5353; res: 800/222-1122; FAX 806/798-3630. 161 rms, 3 story. S $75; D $85; each addl $10; under 16, $5, wkend rates. Crib free. TV; cable (premium). Heated pool. Complimentary full bkfst. Ck-out 1 pm. Coin lndry. Meeting rms. Business servs avail. In-rm modem link. Sundries. Gift shop. Free airport transportation. Balconies. Cr cds: A, C, D, DS, MC, V.

D ≋ 🔥 SC

✔★★ **LA QUINTA MOTOR INN.** *601 Avenue Q (79401).* 806/763-9441; FAX 806/747-9325. 137 rms, 2 story. S $53-$73; D $66-$73; each addl $5; under 18 free. Crib free. TV; cable. Pool. Complimentary continental bkfst, coffee. Restaurant adj open 24 hrs. Ck-out noon. Cr cds: A, C, D, DS, MC, V.

D ✋ ≋ ⋈ 🔥 SC

★★ **RESIDENCE INN BY MARRIOTT.** *2551 S Loop 289 (79423), 3 mi S on Loop 289, exit Indiana.* 806/745-1963; FAX 806/748-1183. 80 kit. suites, 2 story. S $82; D $82-$125; wkly rates. Pet accepted. TV; cable (premium). Heated pool; whirlpools. Complimentary continental bkfst. Ck-out noon. Coin lndry. Meeting rms. Business servs avail. In-rm modem link. Valet serv. Free airport transportation. Tennis. Refrigerators. Private patios, balconies. Picnic tables, grills. Cr cds: A, C, D, DS, JCB, MC, V.

⬜ ⛷ 🏌 ⊠ ⊠ ⊠ SC

Motor Hotels

✔ ★ ★ **LUBBOCK INN.** *Box 10404 (79408), 3901 19th St. 806/792-5181; res: 800/545-8226; FAX 806/792-1319.* 147 rms, 3 story, 28 kits. S $49.50-$56; D $57.50-$62; each addl $6; kit. units $48-$56; studio rms $90; under 12 free. Crib free. TV; cable (premium), VCR avail. Heated pool; wading pool. Restaurant 6 am-11 pm. Rm serv. Bar 10-2 am, Sun 1 pm-midnight. Ck-out noon. Meeting rms. Business servs avail. In-rm modem link. Bellhops. Sundries. Free airport, bus depot transportation. Bathrm phones; some refrigerators. Cr cds: A, C, D, DS, MC, V.

⬜ ⊠ ⊠ 🔥 SC

★ ★ **LUBBOCK PLAZA.** *3201 Loop 289 S (79423), at Indiana Ave. 806/797-3241; FAX 806/793-1203.* 202 rms, 2 story. S, D $59-$89.50; each addl $10; suites $99-$225; under 18 free; seasonal rates. Crib free. Pet accepted. TV; cable (premium). Indoor pool; wading pool. Restaurant 6 am-10 pm. Rm serv. Bars 4 pm-2 am. Ck-out noon. Coin lndry. Meeting rms. Business servs avail. In-rm modem link. Bellhops. Free airport transportation. Exercise equipt; weights, bicycles, sauna. Cr cds: A, C, D, DS, ER, JCB, MC, V.

⬜ ⛷ ⊠ 🏃 ⊠ 🔥

Hotels

★ ★ **HOLIDAY INN-CIVIC CENTER.** *801 Avenue Q (79401). 806/763-1200; FAX 806/763-2656.* 293 rms, 6 story. S $72-$78; D $74-$80; each addl $10; suites $84-$90; under 19 free. Crib free. Pet accepted. TV; cable, in-rm movies. Indoor pool; poolside serv. Restaurant 6 am-10 pm. Bar 4 pm-2 am, Sun noon-midnight; dancing. Ck-out noon. Coin lndry. Convention facilities. Free airport transportation. Exercise equipt; weight machines, bicycles, whirlpool, sauna. Cr cds: A, C, D, DS, ER, JCB, MC, V.

⬜ ⛷ ⊠ 🏃 🔥 SC

★ ★ **SHERATON INN.** *505 Avenue Q (79401). 806/747-0171; FAX 806/747-9243.* 145 rms, 6 story. S $64-$82; D $73-$82; each addl $10; suites $175-$275; under 18 free; higher rates football wknds. Crib free. TV; cable (premium). Indoor pool. Restaurant 6 am-10 pm. Bar 4 pm-midnight, closed Sun. Ck-out noon. Meeting rms. Business servs avail. Free airport transportation. Refrigerator, minibar in suites. Atrium. Cr cds: A, C, D, DS, MC, V.

⬜ ⊠ ⊠ 🔥 SC

Restaurants

✔ ★ ★ **CHEZ SUZETTE.** *4423 50th St, in Quaker Square Shopping Ctr. 806/795-6796.* Hrs: 11:30 am-2 pm, 5:30-10 pm; Fri to 10:30 pm; Sat 5:30-10:30 pm. Closed Sun; Jan 1, Thanksgiving, Dec 25. Res accepted. French, Italian menu. Bar. Semi-a la carte: lunch $4.50-$7.95, dinner $5.95-$13.95. Child's meals. Specializes in châteaubriand, snapper in puff pastry. Cr cds: A, C, D, DS, MC, V.

⬜

★ ★ **DEPOT.** *19th St, at I-27. 806/747-1646.* Hrs: 11 am-2 pm, 5:30-10 pm; Sat 5:30-11 pm. Closed major hols. Bar. Semi-a la carte: lunch $2.95-$8.95, dinner $8.50-$25.95. Specializes in prime rib, stuffed potato. Salad bar. Parking. Beer garden. Old railroad depot; Victorian decor. Cr cds: A, C, D, DS, MC, V.

SC

✔ ★ **GARDSKI'S LOFT.** *2009 Broadway. 806/744-2391.* Hrs: 11 am-11 pm; Fri, Sat to midnight. Closed Thanksgiving, Dec 25. Semi-a la carte: lunch, dinner $3.95-$10.95. Specializes in gourmet hamburgers, fully aged steak, soft tacos. Parking. In 50-yr-old mansion, garden decor. Cr cds: A, C, D, DS, MC, V.

★ ★ **HARRIGAN'S.** *3801 50th St. 806/792-4648.* Hrs: 11 am-2 pm, 5-10 pm; Fri, Sat to 11 pm. Bar. Semi-a la carte: lunch, dinner $2.50-$14.95. Specializes in prime rib. Antiques, early 1920s atmosphere. Cr cds: A, C, D, MC, V.

★ **ORLANDO'S.** *2402 Avenue Q (79405). 806/747-5998.* Hrs: 11 am-10 pm; Fri, Sat to 11 pm. Closed some major hols. Italian menu. Bar. Semi-a la carte: lunch, dinner $3.99-$15.99. Specializes in lasagne, fettucine, tortellini. Parking. Cr cds: A, C, D, DS, MC, V.

SC

✔ ★ ★ **SANTA FE.** *401 Avenue Q. 806/763-6114.* Hrs: 11 am-10 pm; Fri, Sat to 10:30 pm. Closed Thanksgiving, Dec 25. Mexican, Amer menu. Bar 4:30 pm-midnight; closed Sun. Semi-a la carte: lunch, dinner $3.95-$13.95. Child's meals. Parking. Cr cds: A, D, DS, MC, V.

⬜

Lufkin (C-8)

(See Nacogdoches)

Settled 1881 **Pop** 30,206 **Elev** 326 ft **Area code** 409 **Zip** 75901

Information Visitor & Convention Bureau, PO Box 1606; 409/634-6305.

Lumber and a newsprint mill combine with iron foundries, farming and ranching to give Lufkin a well-diversified income base. The headquarters for the Sam Houston (see HUNTSVILLE), Sabine (see JASPER), Angelina and Davy Crockett National Forests are here.

What to See and Do

Ellen Trout Park Zoo. More than 500 species of birds, reptiles, mammals; miniature train rides (summer, daily; rest of yr, wkends; fee); lake, fishing; picnicking, playground. (Daily) Loop 287N at Martin Luther King Dr, 2 mi N. Phone 409/633-0399. ¢

Museum of East Texas. Restored church houses museum; explores visual arts and history through changing exhibits, lectures, performances, multi-disciplinary programs and films. (Tues-Fri, also Sat & Sun afternoons; closed hols) 2nd & Paul Sts. Phone 409/639-4434. **Free.**

National Forests.

Davy Crockett. Ratcliff Lake is in the forest. Approx 163,000 acres. Includes Big Slough Wilderness Area. Swimming; fishing (bass, bream, catfish), hunting (deer); boating. Hiking. Picnicking, concession. Camping (fee) in shortleaf-loblolly pinewoods. Fees charged at recreation sites. Free audio tape tour of Ratcliff Lake and surrounding forest area avail from camp concessionaire. 17 mi W on TX 94 or TX 103. District Ranger Office phone 409/544-2046 or -2047.

Angelina. Approx 153,000 acres of rolling, forested sandhills; Sam Rayburn Reservoir (see JASPER) bisects the forest. Swimming; fishing, hunting; boating (ramps). Hiking. Picnicking. Camping (fee). Audio tape tour (free) avail at ranger station. Fees are charged at recreation sites. 21 mi E on TX 103 or 16 mi SE on US 69. District Ranger Office phone 409/639-8620.

Forest Information and a visitor guide to the forests may be obtained from Forest Supervisor, 701 N First St, Lufkin; 409/639-8501.

Texas Forestry Museum. Artifacts from early days of Texas logging and timber industry include logging train, working sawmill steam engine, 100-foot fire tower, photographs and memorabilia. (Daily; closed major hols) 1905 Atkinson Dr. Phone 409/632-9535. **Free.**

Motels

✔ ★ **DAYS INN.** 2130 S 1st St. 409/639-3301; FAX 409/634-4266. 124 rms, 2 story. S $46; D $42-$47; each addl $5; suites $65-$75; under 18 free; wkend rates. Crib free. Pet accepted, some restrictions. TV; cable. Pool; wading pool. Restaurant open 24 hrs. Rm serv. Bar 5 pm-midnight, Sat to 1 am, closed Sun. Ck-out noon. Coin lndry. Meeting rms. Some refrigerators. Whirlpool in some suites. Cr cds: A, C, D, DS, MC, V.

★ ★ **HOLIDAY INN.** 4306 S 1st St. 409/639-3333; FAX 409/639-3382. 104 rms, 2 story. S $55; D $60; each addl $5; suites $65-$75; under 19 free; wkend rates (min stay required). Crib free. Pet accepted, some restrictions; $5. TV; cable. Pool; poolside serv. Restaurant 6 am-2 pm, 5-10 pm. Rm serv. Bar. Ck-out noon. Coin lndry. Meeting rms. Sundries. Valet serv. Free airport transportation. Health club privileges. Some refrigerators; minibar in suites. Cr cds: A, C, D, DS, ER, JCB, MC, V.

✔ ★ ★ **LA QUINTA.** 2119 S 1st St. 409/634-3351; FAX 409/634-9475. 106 rms, 2 story. S $43-$50; D $48-$55; each addl $5; suites $67; under 18 free. Crib free. Pet accepted, some restrictions. TV; cable. Pool. Complimentary continental bkfst, coffee. Restaurant adj. Ck-out noon. Meeting rms. Valet serv. Cr cds: A, C, D, DS, MC, V.

Restaurant

★ **LEMKE'S WURST HAUS.** 4105 Ted Trout Dr. 409/875-2205. Hrs: 11 am-10 pm. Closed Sun; Jan 1, Thanksgiving, Dec 25. Res accepted. German menu. Bar. Semi-a la carte: lunch, dinner $2.95-$15.95. Cover charge $2 (outdoor entertainment). Child's meals. Specialties: sausage dinners, sauerbraten, schnitzel, seafood platter. Salad bar. Entertainment Fri-Sat. Parking. Outdoor dining. German decor. Extensive beer selection. Cr cds: A, C, D, DS, MC, V.

SC

Marfa (C-2)

(For accommodations see Alpine)

Founded 1883 **Pop** 2,424 **Elev** 4,688 ft **Area code** 915 **Zip** 79843
Information Chamber of Commerce, PO Box 635; 915/729-4942.

Texas's highest incorporated city, Marfa is surrounded by unspoiled mountain country, rising to more than 8,000 feet in some areas. Marfa is the best starting point to travel the highway to Mexico and Chihuahua City; the Camino del Rio (River road) to Big Bend National Park (see); and the Scenic Loop through the Davis Mountains. It offers various outdoor recreation activities and the puzzling "Marfa ghost lights," which have remained a mystery for more than 100 years. The Presidio County Courthouse (1886) and El Paisano Hotel (1930) are notable landmarks.

With mild winters and cool summers, the area offers abundant opportunities for camping, hunting, hiking, picnicking and golfing.

Annual Event

Marfa Lights Festival. Labor Day wkend.

Marshall (B-8)

(See Longview; also see Shreveport, LA)

Founded 1841 **Pop** 23,682 **Elev** 412 ft **Area code** 903 **Zip** 75670
Information Chamber of Commerce, 213 W Austin, PO Box 520; 903/935-7868.

For a time this was the Confederate state capital of Missouri. Orders were issued, vouchers drawn and official business transacted in exile; Missouri itself was in Northern hands, but the governor held himself to be legitimately in office nonetheless. Marshall was also important in the administration of Confederate affairs. The Confederate Trans-Mississippi Agency of the Post Office Department, Quartermaster and Commissary Departments were all in Marshall. The basements of the First Methodist Church and Odd Fellows Hall were used for storage of military supplies. Marshall is now an educational and manufacturing center.

What to See and Do

Caddo Lake State Park. Approx 500 acres. Oil wells have been drilled in the lake. Swimming, waterskiing; fishing; boating (ramp, rentals). Nature & hiking trails. Picnicking, playground. Screened shelters; improved campsites, RV facilities, cabins (dump station). Standard fees. (Daily) 14 mi NE on TX 43, then 3 mi E on FM 2198. Phone 903/679-3351. Per vehicle ¢¢

Harrison County Historical Museum. Business, transportation and communication displays; medical items; Victorian needlecraft; pressed glass; toys; Caddo Indian artifacts; pioneer relics. Memorabilia collections of Lady Bird Johnson, journalist Bill Moyers, Olympic gold medalist George Foreman and others. Military Room, Ethnic Group Heritage Room; Caddo Lake Room. Art gallery. (Tues-Sat; closed some hols) Old Courthouse, Peter Whetstone Square. Phone 903/938-2680. ¢

Michelson Museum of Art. Features paintings of Russian-born, post-impressionist Leo Michelson; special exhibits. (Daily exc Mon; closed most hols) Southwestern Bell Bldg, 216 N Bolivar. Phone 903/935-9480. ¢

T.C. Lindsey & Co. General store, in continuous operation since 1847; antiques, rural relics on display. Setting for two Walt Disney productions. (Daily exc Sun; closed hols) 2 mi W of Louisiana state line via I-20, 2 mi N on FM 134 in Jonesville. Phone 903/687-3382. **Free.**

Annual Events

Stagecoach Days Celebration. Stagecoach rides, gunfighters, arts & crafts. 3rd wkend May.

Central East Texas Fair. 1st wk Sept.

Wonderland of Lights. Christmas festival. Courthouse, entire neighborhoods decorated by four and one-half million lights. Thanksgiving-Dec.

Motels

✔ ★ **BEST WESTERN.** 5555 East End Blvd S, jct I-20, US 59. 903/935-1941; FAX 903/938-0071. 100 units, 2 story. S $42-$52; D $46-$56; each addl $5; suites $50-$60; under 16 free. Crib free. Pet accepted, some restrictions. TV; cable (premium), VCR avail. Pool. Restaurant 24 hrs. Ck-out noon. Business servs avail. Cr cds: A, C, D, DS, JCB, MC, V.

★ ★ **HOLIDAY INN EXPRESS.** 100 I-20 W, at jct US 59. 903/935-7923; FAX 903/938-2675. 96 rms, 2 story. S, D $48-$60; each addl $6; suites $125; under 18 free. Crib free. TV; cable (premium), VCR avail. Pool; whirlpool. Complimentary continental bkfst. Ck-out noon. Coin lndry. Meeting rms. Business servs avail. In-rm modem link. Valet serv. Cr cds: A, C, D, DS, JCB, MC, V.

★ **RAMADA INN.** *5301 East End Blvd S, I-20 exit 59N. 903/938-9261; FAX 903/935-1868.* 102 rms, 2 story. S $46-$52; D $48-$55; under 12 free. Crib free. Pet accepted; some restrictions. TV; cable (premium). Pool. Restaurant 6 am-9 pm. Rm serv. Bar 3 pm-midnight. Ck-out noon. Coin lndry. Meeting rms. Business servs avail. In-rm modem link. Sundries. Valet serv. Cr cds: A, D, DS, MC, V.

Mason (C-5)

(For accommodations see Fredericksburg, Kerrville)

Pop 2,041 **Elev** 1,550 ft **Area code** 915 **Zip** 76856
Information Mason County Chamber of Commerce, PO Box 156; 915/347-5758.

This town grew under the protection of Fort Mason in the rolling, scenic hill country. Hunting for white-tailed deer and wild turkey and fishing in the Llano River are popular. Citizens and cattle rustlers once participated in a bloody feud known as the Mason County War.

What to See and Do

Eckert James River Preserve Bat Cave. One of America's largest known Mexican free-tailed bat colonies and the only bat maternity cave owned by a conservation agency. Visitors are instructed on how best to view the colony without disturbing the bats (summer, Thurs-Sun evenings). Preserve (all yr). Contact Chamber of Commerce. Approx 14 mi SW via US 87, Ranch Road 1723. **Free.**

Fort Mason. Reconstructed four-room officers' quarters on crest of Post Hill. Original foundations and stone used in reconstruction. Robert E. Lee's last command before the Civil War. Picnicking. (Daily) Spruce St. **Free.**

Mason County Museum. Historical items housed in old schoolhouse (1870) built with stone from Fort Mason. (Mon-Fri or by appt) 300 Moody St. Phone 915/347-5752 or -6242. **Free.**

Rocks & Minerals. Collectors from all over the nation come to this area of ancient geologic outcroppings for variety of rocks and minerals, especially topaz, the state gemstone.

McAllen (F-6)

(See Edinburg, Harlingen, Mission)

Pop 84,021 **Elev** 124 ft **Area code** 210
Information Chamber of Commerce, 10 N Broadway, PO Box 790, 78505; 210/682-2871.

This is a winter resort area surrounded by orange and grapefruit groves and irrigated vegetable and cotton fields. McAllen packs and markets this produce. Food manufacturing and processing machinery, petroleum products, dehydrated foods and carotene are also local industries. McAllen is a favorite crossing place for excursions into Mexico.

Hunting for quail, whitewing dove and deer is popular in season, as well as fishing in both fresh and salt water.

What to See and Do

McAllen Botanical Gardens and Nature Trail. Sunken and cactus gardens; nature trails; bird-watching. (Daily) 2¹⁄₂ mi W on TX 83 Business. Phone 210/682-1517. **Free.**

McAllen International Museum. Art and natural science exhibits and programs. (Daily exc Mon; closed hols) Free admission Sun. Bicentennial Blvd at 1900 Nolana Loop. Phone 210/682-1564. ¢

Reynosa, Mexico (population: 206,500). Parking area on US side of bridge. (For Border Crossing Regulations, see INTRODUCTION) 8 mi S on TX 336.

Reynosa is a picturesque border town, well worth a leisurely visit. The plaza has a beautiful renovated church with high belfries and a soaring arched facade. There are nightclubs; several restaurants serve game dinners—venison and wild turkey. Dancing to Mexican music outdoors or indoors; occasional bullfights. The *Mercado* (market) tests visitors' bargaining skills.

Santa Ana National Wildlife Refuge. More than 2,000 acres of forest and lakes include 450 plant species, 380 species of North American and Mexican birds, 12 miles of hiking trails and 7 miles of wildlife auto tour road (avail when tram tour is not in operation). Interpretive tram tour ¢¢;   photo blinds; visitor center. Nature trail accessible to wheelchairs and the visually impaired. (Daily; closed Jan 1, Thanksgiving, Dec 25) 8 mi E on US 83, then 7 mi S on FM 907 and ¹⁄₄ mi E on US 281. Contact Refuge Manager, Rte 2, Box 202-A, Alamo 78516; 210/787-3079. **Free.**

Virgin de San Juan del Valle Shrine. Original statue of the Virgin, rescued from flames, now stands in a new shrine. E on US 83, between McAllen and San Juan.

Annual Event

Candleight Posada. Archer Park. Citywide Christmas celebration. Blends traditions of Mexico with those of America. 1st wkend Dec.

Motels

(Rates may be higher dove-hunting season)

★ **DRURY INN.** *612 W US 83 (78501). 210/687-5100.* 89 units. S $65-$75; D $75-$80; each addl $10; under 18 free. Crib free. TV; cable (premium), VCR avail. Pool. Complimentary continental bkfst, coffee. Restaurant adj. Ck-out noon. Meeting rm. Business servs avail. In-rm modem link. Refrigerator in suites. Cr cds: A, C, D, DS, MC, V.

★ ★ **HAMPTON INN.** *300 W US 83 (78501). 210/682-4900.* 91 rms, 2 story. S $62-$72; D $67-$77; under 18 free. Crib free. Pet accepted. TV; cable. Pool. Complimentary continental breakfast. Restaurant adj. Ck-out noon. Near airport. Cr cds: A, C, D, DS, JCB, MC, V.

✔ ★ ★ **LA QUINTA MOTOR INN.** *1100 S 10th St (78501), near Miller Intl Airport. 210/687-1101; FAX 210/687-9265.* 120 rms, 3 story. S $59-$65; D $61-$66; each addl $5; under 18 free. Crib free. TV; cable. Pool. Complimentary continental bkfst in lobby. Restaurant adj open 24 hrs. Bar 11-2 am. Ck-out 1 pm. Meeting rm. Valet serv. Free airport, bus depot transportation. Convention Center adj. Cr cds: A, C, D, DS, MC, V.

Motor Hotels

★ ★ **DOUBLETREE CLUB.** *101 N Main St (78501). 210/631-1101; FAX 210/631-7934.* 158 rms, 3 story. S $63-$79; D $69-$89; each addl $10; suites $89-$160; under 12 free. Crib free. TV. Pool. Complimentary full bkfst. Restaurant (see LA TERRAZA). Rm serv. Bar 11 am-10 pm. Ck-out 1 pm. Meeting rms. Free covered parking. Free airport, mall transportation. Golf privileges. Exercise equipt; weights, bicycles. Balconies. Some refrigerators, wet bars. Cr cds: A, C, D, DS, ER, JCB, MC, V.

★ **HOLIDAY INN-CIVIC CENTER.** *200 W US 83 (78501), at 2nd St (78501), near Miller Intl Airport. 210/686-2471; FAX 210/686-2038.* 173 rms, 2 story. S $65-$75; D $75-$85; each addl $10; under 18 free. Crib free. TV; cable (premium), VCR avail. 2 pools, 1 indoor; whirlpool. Restaurant 6 am-10 pm. Rm serv. Bar noon-2 am; Sun noon-midnight. Ck-out noon. Coin lndry. Meeting rms. Business servs avail. In-rm modem link. Bellhops. Free airport transportation. Lighted tennis. Exercise equipt; bicycle, stair machine, sauna. Holidome. Game rm. Rec rm. Cr cds: A, C, D, DS, JCB, MC, V.

⊡ 🏊 ⛷ ⚿ ✕ ✈ 🏊 🔥 SC

Hotels

★ ★ ★ **EMBASSY SUITES.** 1800 S 2nd St (78503). 210/686-3000; FAX 210/631-8362. 224 suites, 8 story. S, D $102-$117; each addl $15; under 12 free. Crib free. TV; cable (premium). Indoor pool. Complimentary bkfst, evening refreshments. Coffee in rms. Restaurant 11 am-2 pm, 5-10 pm. Bar 11-1 am; entertainment. Ck-out noon. Meeting rms. Gift shop. Free airport transportation. Exercise equipt; weights, bicycles, whirlpool, sauna. Refrigerators. Balconies. Cr cds: A, C, D, DS, MC, V.

⊡ 🏊 ⚿ ✕ 🏊 🔥 SC

★ ★ **HILTON INN.** 2721 S 10th St (78503), near Miller Intl Airport. 210/687-1161; FAX 210/687-8651. 150 rms, 5 story. S $70; D $76; each addl $10; under 12 free; wkend rates. Crib free. TV; cable. Pool; poolside serv, whirlpool. Restaurant 6 am-11 pm. Bar 4 pm-1 am. Ck-out noon. Meeting rms. Lighted tennis. Free airport transportation. Health club privileges. Balconies. Cr cds: A, C, D, DS, MC, V.

⊡ ⛷ 🏊 ✕ 🏊 🔥 SC

Restaurants

★ **JOHNNY'S.** 1010 Houston St (78501). 210/686-9061. Hrs: 9 am-10:30 pm; Fri & Sat to midnight. Res accepted. Mexican menu. Bar. Semi-a la carte: bkfst $2.95-$3.95, lunch & dinner $4.95-$14.95. Child's meals. Specializes in char-broiled dishes. Mariachi band. Parking. Family-owned. Cr cds: A, MC, V.

★ **LA TERRAZA.** (See Doubletree Club Motor Hotel) 210/631-1101. Hrs: 8 am-10 pm. Res accepted. Mexican, Amer menu. Bar from 5 pm. Complete meals: bkfst $3.30-$6.75. Semi-a la carte: lunch $5.50-$8, dinner $6.50-$14.95. Specialties: fajitas, tampiqueña platter. Salad bar. Covered parking. Outdoor dining. Spanish colonial-style decor. Cr cds: A, C, D, DS, ER, JCB, MC, V.

⊡

Unrated Dining Spot

LUBY'S CAFETERIA. 1215 S 10th St. 210/682-3115. Hrs: 10:45 am-8 pm; summer to 8:30 pm. Closed half day Dec 24; Dec 25. Avg ck: lunch, dinner $5.25. Specializes in baked haddock, strawberry pie. Parking. Cr cds: DS, MC, V.

⊡

McKinney (A-7)

(For accommodations see Dallas, Denton, Greenville, Sherman)

Founded 1848 **Pop** 21,283 **Elev** 632 ft **Area code** 214
Information Chamber of Commerce, PO Box 621, 75070; 214/542-0163.

The north Texas artificial lake area has 8 lakes of more than 10,000 acres each within 60 miles of this town. Chestnut Square is a block of restored 1800s houses.

What to See and Do

Heard Natural Science Museum and Wildlife Sanctuary. Natural history exhibits of north central Texas; marine life, rock and mineral displays; historical exhibit of museum founder Bessie Heard (1886-

1988); live animals; changing art shows; bird of prey rehabilitation facility; a 274-acre sanctuary along Wilson Creek includes bottomland, upland, woodland and prairie; guided & self-guided tours of nature trails ¢. (Daily exc Mon; closed major hols) Exit 38 E off US 75 to TX 5S, follow signs (FM 1378). Phone 214/562-5566. **Free.**

Lavon Lake. Swimming, waterskiing; fishing; boating. Hiking, horseback trail. Picnicking. Camping (tent & trailer sites). Some fees. (Daily) 15 mi E on US 380, then 10 mi S on TX 78. Phone 214/442-5711 (recording) or -3141. **Free.**

Annual Events

Mayfair. Downtown Square. House tours; antique, craft shows; parade, entertainment. 1st Sat May.

Heritage Guild's Christmas Tour of Homes. 1st wkend Dec.

Mexico (C-1 - F-7)

(see Brownsville, Del Rio, Eagle Pass, Ciudad Juárez, Laredo, McAllen)

Midland (B-4)

(See Big Spring, Odessa)

Pop 89,443 **Elev** 2,779 ft **Area code** 915
Information Chamber of Commerce, 109 N Main, PO Box 1890, 79702; 915/683-3381 or 800/624-6435.

Midland (midway between Fort Worth and El Paso) is at the south edge of the high plains. The administrative center for the Permian oil basin, many oil companies have their offices in Midland, as do manufacturers and distributors.

What to See and Do

Confederate Air Force Flying Museum. Dedicated to the preservation of World War II combat aircraft. Planes on display change every three months. (Daily; closed Thanksgiving, Dec 25) (See ANNUAL EVENT). 9600 Wright Dr, at Midland Intl Airport. Phone 915/563-1000. ¢¢

Midland Community Theatre. Eight dramas, comedies or musicals annually, including special summer features. (Thurs-Sat) 2000 W Wadley Ave. Phone 915/682-4111.

Museum of the Southwest. Former residence (1934) of Texas oil man Fred Turner houses permanent collection of Southwestern art and anthropology; traveling exhibits on display; children's museum with hands-on exhibits. Marian Blakemore Planetarium sky programs (Sun afternoons & Tues evenings; fee). (Daily exc Mon; closed some hols) 1705 W Missouri Ave. Phone 915/683-2882. **Free.**

Nita Stewart Haley Memorial Library. Rare books, archives and Western art. Emphasis on range country and cattle industry history in Texas and the Southwest. Includes original mission bell from the Alamo, cast in 1722. Research room. (Mon-Fri; closed hols) 1805 W Indiana. Phone 915/682-5785. **Free.**

The Petroleum Museum. Animated exhibits explain the history and development of the oil industry and the Permian Basin; walk-through diorama of ocean floor as it was 230 million years ago; oil well blowout action display; collection of paintings of west Texas and southeastern New Mexico. World's largest collection of antique drilling and production equipment. (Daily; closed 2nd Mon Jan, Thanksgiving, Dec 24-25) Sr citizen rate. 1500 I-20W at TX 136 exit. Phone 915/683-4403. ¢¢

Annual Event

World War II Flying Air Show. Midland Intl Airport. 2nd wkend Oct.

Seasonal Event

Summer Mummers. Yucca Theatre (1927), 208 N Colorado St. Topical satire staged in the manner of 1890s melodrama. Thurs-Sat, late June-early Sept.

Motels

★ ★ **BEST WESTERN.** *3100 W Wall (79701). 915/699-4144; FAX 915/699-7639.* 200 rms, 3 story. S $48; D $56; each addl $6; under 12 free. Crib free. Pet accepted. TV; cable (premium). Indoor pool. Restaurant 6-10 am, 5-10 pm. Rm serv. Bar 4 pm-midnight. Ck-out noon. Meeting rms. Business servs avail. In-rm modem link. Valet serv. Free airport, bus depot transportation. Cr cds: A, C, D, DS, JCB, MC, V.

D ✦ ≈ ⊠ ⊠ SC

✔ ★ **DAYS INN.** *4714 W US 80 (79703). 915/699-7727; FAX 915/699-7813.* 90 rms, 2 story. S $37; D $42; each addl $5; under 12 free. Crib free. Pet accepted, some restrictions. TV; cable (premium). VCR avail. Pool. Complimentary continental bkfst. Ck-out noon. Business servs avail. Picnic tables. Cr cds: A, C, D, DS, MC, V.

D ✦ ≈ ⊠ SC

★ ★ **HOLIDAY INN.** *4300 W US 80 (79703). 915/697-3181; FAX 915/694-7754.* 274 rms, 2 story, 6 suites. S $54-$71; D $61-$79; each addl $7; suite $132-$159; under 18 free. Crib free. TV; cable (premium). VCR avail. Indoor pool; whirlpool, sauna. Restaurant 6 am-10 pm. Rm serv. Bar 4-11 pm. Ck-out noon. Coin lndry. Meeting rms. Business servs avail. In-rm modem link. Free airport transportation. Holidome. Cr cds: A, C, D, DS, JCB, MC, V.

D ≈ ⊠

★ ★ **LA QUINTA.** *4130 W Wall (79703). 915/697-9900; FAX 915/689-0617.* 146 rms, 2 story. S $39-$49; D $46-$56; under 18 free. Crib free. TV; cable (premium). Pool. Complimentary continental bkfst. Ck-out noon. Coin lndry. Meeting rms. Business servs avail. Valet serv. Cr cds: A, C, D, DS, MC, V.

D ≈ ⊠ ⊠ SC

★ ★ **LEXINGTON HOTEL SUITES.** *1003 S Midkiff (79701). 915/697-3155; FAX 915/699-2017.* 182 kit. units, 2 story. 1-bedrm $54-$65; 2-bedrm $80-$108. Crib free. TV; cable (premium). Heated pool; whirlpool. Complimentary continental bkfst 7-8:30 am; Sat, Sun 8-10 am. Restaurant nearby. Ck-out noon. Coin lndry. Business servs avail. Airport transportation. Cr cds: A, C, D, DS, MC, V.

D ✦ ≈ ⊠ SC

★ ★ **PLAZA INN.** *4108 N Big Spring (79705). 915/686-8733; res: 800/365-3222; FAX 915/685-0530.* 115 rms, 3 story. S, D $55; each addl $8.50; under 16 free. Crib free. TV; cable (premium). Pool; sauna. Complimentary continental bkfst. Ck-out 1 pm. Meeting rms. Business servs avail. In-rm modem link. Free airport, bus depot transportation. Health club privileges. Picnic tables. Cr cds: A, C, D, DS, MC, V.

D ✦ ≈ ⊠ ⊠ SC

★ ★ **RAMADA INN AIRPORT.** *100 Airport Plaza Dr (79711), near Midland Intl Airport. 915/561-8000; res: 800/272-6232; FAX 915/561-5243.* 95 rms, 3 story. S $51; D $58; each addl $7; under 18 free; wkend rates. Crib free. Pet accepted, some restrictions. TV; cable (premium). Pool. Complimentary coffee in rms. Restaurant 6:30 am-2 pm, 6-10 pm. Rm serv. Bar 4 pm-midnight. Ck-out 11 am. Meeting rm. Business center. Many rms with modem link. Bellhops. Sundries. Coin lndry. Free airport transportation. Exercise equipt; weights, treadmill. Refrigerators avail. Cr cds: A, C, D, DS, JCB, MC, V.

D ✦ 🎿 ✈ ⊠ ⊠ SC ⊼

Hotel

★ ★ ★ **HILTON.** *117 W Wall (79701), Wall & Loraine Sts. 915/683-6131; FAX 915/683-0958.* 249 rms, 2-11 story. S, D $119; each addl $10; suites $180-$255; wkend rates; AP avail. Crib $10. Pet accepted, some restrictions; $100 refundable. TV; cable (premium), VCR avail. Pool; whirlpool, poolside serv. Restaurant 6:30 am-10 pm. Bar 4 pm-midnight; Sun from 7 pm. Ck-out noon. Meeting rms. Business servs avail. Gift shop. Free airport transportation. Exercise equipt; bicycles, stair machine. Health club privileges. Luxury level. Cr cds: A, C, D, DS, MC, V.

D ✦ ≈ ✈ ⊠ ⊠

Restaurants

✔ ★ **BLUE STAR INN.** *2501 W Wall (79707), on US 80 Business. 915/682-4231.* Hrs: 11 am-2 pm, 5-10 pm; Sat & Sun 11 am-10 pm. Chinese, Amer menu. Bar. A la carte entrees: lunch, dinner $3.50-$9.95. Parking. Family-owned. Cr cds: A, DS, MC, V.

✔ ★ **LUIGI'S ITALIAN.** *111 N Big Spring St. 915/683-6363.* Hrs: 11 am-10 pm; Fri to 11 pm; Sat 5-11 pm. Closed Sun, major hols. Res accepted. Bar. Semi-a la carte: lunch, dinner $3.50-$13.25. Child's meals. Specializes in lasagne, fettucine, spaghetti. Family-owned. Cr cds: A, D, DS, MC, V.

D SC

★ ★ **VENEZIA.** *20 Plaza Center, Wadley & Garfield. 915/687-0900.* Hrs: 11 am-1:45 pm, 5-10 pm; Sat from 5 pm. Closed Sun; major hols. Res accepted. Northern Italian menu. Wine, beer. Semi-a la carte: lunch $5.25-$8, dinner $6-$16. Specializes in fresh seafood. Parking. Outdoor patio dining. 2 dining areas; European decor; large fireplace. Cr cds: A, C, D, DS, MC, V.

D

Mineral Wells (B-6)

(For accommodations see Fort Worth, also see Weatherford)

Pop 14,870 **Elev** 911 ft **Area code** 817 **Zip** 76067
Information Chamber of Commerce, Box 1408; 817/325-2557 or 800/252-MWTX.

What to See and Do

Swimming, water sports, fishing, boating. On several nearby lakes and the Brazos River. **Lake Mineral Wells State Park**, 4 mi E; **Lake Palo Pinto**, 20 mi S; **Possum Kingdom Lake**, 25 mi NW.

Annual Event

Palo Pinto County Livestock Assn Rodeo. 2nd wk May.

Mission (F-6)

(For accommodations see McAllen, also see Edinburg)

Pop 28,653 **Elev** 134 ft **Area code** 210 **Zip** 78572
Information Chamber of Commerce, 220 E 9th St; 210/585-2727.

This center of the Texas citrus industry started when the Oblate Fathers planted a citrus grove on the north bank of the Rio Grande near here. La Lomita Mission, located south of town, has been restored using many of the original bricks and foundations.

What to See and Do

Bentsen-Rio Grande Valley State Park. Approx 600 acres. Fishing; boat ramp. Nature & hiking trails. Picnicking, playground. Camping, tent & trailer sites (dump station). Standard fees. (Daily) 3 mi W on US 83, then 3 mi S on FM 2062 to Park Rd 43. Phone 210/585-1107. Per vehicle **¢¢**

La Lomita State Historic Site. Spanish-style structure once used as novitiate for oblate priests now houses exhibits. (Mon-Fri) 3³/₄ mi S on FM 1016. Phone 210/581-2725. **Free.** Nearby is

La Lomita Mission. One of several missions established. Tiny (12 by 25 ft) chapel, still used as place of worship by local rancheros. Built by oblate priests in 1849; town of Mission is named for chapel. 3 mi S on FM 1016.

Los Ebanos International Ferry. Only hand-drawn ferry across US border. (Daily, weather permitting) 17 mi W via US 83. **¢**

Annual Event

Texas Citrus Fiesta. Phone 210/585-9724. Last wk Jan.

Restaurant

✔ ★ **FERRELL'S PIT.** 2¹/₂ mi E on US 83 Business. 210/585-2381. Hrs: 11 am-8:30 pm. Closed Tues. Mexican, Amer menu. Semi-a la carte: lunch, dinner $3.75-$7.50. Specializes in barbecued dishes. Parking. Pit barbecue. No cr cds accepted.

Monahans (C-3)

(For accommodations see Fort Stockton, Odessa, Pecos)

Pop 8,101 **Elev** 2,613 ft **Area code** 915 **Zip** 79756
Information Chamber of Commerce, 401 S Dwight; 915/943-2187.

What to See and Do

Million Barrel Museum. Texas oil boom prompted construction of an oil tank 522 feet by 426 feet to hold more than one million gallons; it was filled only once. Includes the Holman House with period furnishings; antique farming and railroad memorabilia, caboose; eclipse windmill; first Ward County jail; amphitheater; gift shop. (Daily exc Mon; closed Thanksgiving, Dec 25) 2 mi E on Business Loop 20. Phone 915/943-8401. **Free.**

Monahans Sandhills State Park. Sand dunes, some 60 ft high, believed to be from the Trinity sandstone formation and collected by the Permian Sea. On 3,840 acres. Nature trail. Picnicking. Improved campsites (dump station). Standard fees. (Daily) 6 mi E on I-20, exit mile marker 86 to Park Rd 41. Phone 915/943-2092. Per vehicle **¢¢** Also here is the

Sandhills Interpretive Center. Natural history, historical, archaeological, botanical and geological displays on the area. (Daily) Included with entrance to park.

Mount Pleasant (A-8)

Pop 12,291 **Elev** 416 ft **Area code** 903 **Zip** 75455
Information Titus County Chamber of Commerce, 1604 N Jefferson, PO Box 1237; 903/572-8567.

This town is a commercial center for farming, livestock and oil. State records for largemouth bass have been set in two nearby lakes; many catches have weighed in at seven pounds or more.

Annual Events

Mount Pleasant Championship Rodeo. 1st wkend June.

Titus County Fair. Civic Center area. Carnival, cattle show, entertainment. Last full wk Sept.

Nacogdoches (C-8)

(See Lufkin, Rusk)

Founded 1691 **Pop** 30,872 **Elev** 277 ft **Area code** 409 **Zip** 75961
Information Nacogdoches County Chamber of Commerce, 513 North St, PO Drawer 631918; 409/564-7351.

Nacogdoches was founded as one of the five original Spanish missions in Texas. The initial mission was abandoned until 1779, when Captain Antonio Gil Y'Barbo returned with a group of settlers who had been evicted from their land by Spanish authorities. Here in 1826 Haden Edwards brashly declared Texas independent of Mexico and named it the Republic of Fredonia. He got no support from other colonists and soon fled to the United States.

Surrounded by 460,000 acres of pine timber, Nacogdoches is in the east Texas pine belt. Chicken, egg and milk production along with industry, business and education are the mainstays of the town's economy.

What to See and Do

Millard's Crossing. Historic village of restored 19th-century east Texas homes furnished with period antiques. Log cabin, corn crib, chapel, Victorian parsonage and farmhouse reflect life of east Texas pioneers. Guided tours (daily; closed Jan 1, Easter, Thanksgiving, Dec 25). 4 mi N via US 59. 6020 North St. Phone 409/564-6631. **¢¢**

Sterne-Hoya Home (1830). Pioneer home of Adolphus Sterne. (Daily exc Sun; closed hols) 211 S LaNana St. Phone 409/560-5426. **Free.**

Stone Fort Museum. Rebuilt by state in 1936 from original structure probably erected by Gil Y'Barbo in 1779. Focus on east Texas history and Spanish Nacogdoches. (Daily exc Mon; closed univ hols) Clark & Griffith Blvds, Stephen F. Austin State Univ campus. Phone 409/568-2408. **Free.**

Motels

★ ★ **HOLIDAY INN.** 3400 South St. 409/569-8100; FAX 409/569-0332. 126 rms, 2 story. S $55-$69; D $61-$74; each addl $6; suites $69-$150; under 19 free. Crib free. TV; cable. Indoor/outdoor pool. Restaurant 6-11 am, 5-10 pm. Rm serv. Private club 5-11 pm. Ck-out noon. Meeting rms. Valet serv. Exercise equipt; bicycles, treadmill, whirlpool. Health club privileges. Cr cds: A, C, D, DS, JCB, MC, V.

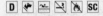

★ ★ **LA QUINTA.** 3215 South St. 409/560-5453; FAX 409/560-4372. 106 rms, 2 story. S $47-$55; D $53-$65; each addl $6; suites $62-$74; under 18 free. Crib free. Pet accepted, some restrictions. TV; cable (premium). Pool. Complimentary continental bkfst. Complimentary coffee in lobby. Restaurant adj open 24 hrs. Ck-out noon. Meeting rms. In-rm modem link. Valet serv. Cr cds: A, C, D, DS, MC, V.

D 🐾 ≈ ⊠ 🐾 **SC**

Hotel

★ ★ **FREDONIA.** 200 N Fredonia St. 409/564-1234; FAX 409/564-1234, ext. 240. 113 rms, 6 story. S $60-$79; D $70-$89; each addl $10; suites $135-$165; under 18 free; wkly. Crib free. TV; cable (premium). Pool; poolside serv. Complimentary full bkfst. Restaurant

6:30 am-2 pm, 5-9 pm. Private club 4 pm-midnight, closed Sun. Ck-out 1 pm. Meeting rms. Business center. In-rm modem link. Gift shop. Some private patios, balconies. Cr cds: A, C, D, DS, MC, V.

Restaurant

★ ★ **CALIFORNIAN.** *342 University Dr. 409/560-1985.* Hrs: 11 am-9:30 pm; Fri, Sat to 10:30 pm; Sun to 9:30 pm. Closed Dec 25. Bar to midnight; Sat to 1 am. A la carte entrees: lunch $4.95-$15.99, dinner $7.95-$29.95. Child's meals. Specializes in fresh seafood, prime rib. Entertainment Thur-Sat. Cr cds: A, D, DS, MC, V.

D

New Braunfels (D-6)

(See San Antonio, San Marcos)

Founded 1845 **Pop** 27,334 **Elev** 639 ft **Area code** 210

Information Chamber of Commerce, 390 S Seguin Ave, PO Box 311417, 78131; 210/625-2385 or 800/572-2626.

Prince Carl of Solms-Braunfels, Commissioner-General for the Society for the Protection of German Immigrants in Texas, founded New Braunfels in 1845. He built his headquarters on a hilltop, lived there for a short while and then returned to Germany to marry. Within a few months of his return to Texas, nearly 6,000 German immigrants followed him, landing at Indianola, 125 miles away from New Braunfels. There was little shelter; food and supplies were scarce; and no transportation to New Braunfels was available. In desperation, many began to walk. Disease, hunger and exposure wiped out as many as 2,000 of these pioneers. Unfamiliarity with the land and conditions in their new homeland caused much privation and suffering, but they persevered. Today New Braunfels still has a strong German influence.

What to See and Do

Canyon Lake. A 224-foot-high earthen dam. Swimming, waterskiing; fishing; boating (ramps), canoeing, tubing. Picnicking; concession. Camping (tent & trailer sites, some hookups; fee). Headquarters, 15 mi NW via FM 306. Phone 210/964-3341. **Free.**

Fishing. For bass, catfish, perch in Lake Dunlap and Canyon Lake; for rainbow trout in Guadalupe River.

Hummel Museum. World's largest collection of original paintings and drawings by Sister Maria Innocentia Hummel; the popular German porcelain figurines are modeled on her work. Rotating exhibits; guided tours; videos on Sr Hummel's life, the W. Goebel factory. Gift shop. (Mon-Sat, also Sun afternoons; closed some major hols) 199 Main Plaza. Phone 210/625-5636. ¢¢¢

Landa Park. A 190-acre park with spring-fed pool, swimming pool, tubing on river; glass-bottom boat rides. 18-hole golf, miniature golf. Miniature train. Picnicking; playground, concession. Historical markers, arboretum. Park (daily; schedule varies with season). Some fees. Landa St, 5 blks NW on TX 46. Phone 210/608-2160. **Free.**

Lindheimer Home (ca 1850). Restored house of Ferdinand Lindheimer (1801-79), educator, guide, botanist and editor. (May-Aug, daily exc Wed; rest of yr, Sat, Sun or by appt; closed Jan 1, Dec 25) 491 Comal Ave. Phone 210/625-8766 or 210/629-2943. ¢

Natural Bridge Caverns. 15 mi W via TX 46, FM 1863 (see SAN ANTONIO).

New Braunfels Factory Stores. Over 45 outlet stores can be found in this outdoor shopping mall. (Daily) 651 Hwy 81 E. Phone 210/620-6806.

Schlitterbahn Water Park. 305 W Austin. Waterslides, water rides, swimming pools. Gift shops, restaurants, hotels. (Late Apr-late Sept) Phone 210/625-2351. ¢¢¢¢¢

Sophienburg Museum & Archives. Memorabilia, archives of pioneer days. Changing exhibits. (Daily; closed major hols) 401 W Coll St. Phone 210/629-1900 or -1572. ¢

Annual Events

Comal County Fair. Carnival and rodeo. Late Sept.

Wurstfest. German music and food, displays, dancing. 10 days early Nov.

Motel

★ **HOLIDAY INN.** *1051 I-35 E (78130), exit 189. 210/625-8017; FAX 210/625-3130.* 140 rms, 2 story. Memorial Day-Labor Day: S, D $85; each addl $5; suites $125-$150; under 18 free; lower rates rest of yr. Crib free. Pet accepted. TV; cable (premium). Pool; wading pool. Complimentary coffee in rms. Restaurant 6 am-2 pm, 5:30-10 pm. Rm serv. Bar 4 pm-midnight. Ck-out noon. Meeting rms. Business servs avail. In-rm modem link. Coin lndry. Cr cds: A, C, D, DS, MC, V.

D

Inns

★ **HOTEL FAUST.** *240 S Seguin St (78130). 210/625-7791; FAX 210/620-1530.* 62 rms, 4 story. May-Sept: S $59; D $79; each addl $5; suite $125; under 5 free; lower rates rest of yr. TV; cable (premium). Complimentary continental bkfst. Restaurant adj 11 am-11 pm. Bar 4 pm-midnight. Ck-out noon. Built 1929; many period furnishings. Cr cds: A, C, D, DS, MC, V.

★ ★ **PRINCE SOLMS.** *295 E San Antonio (78130). 210/625-9169; res: 800/625-9169.* 10 rms, 2 story. S, D $60-$95; suites $110-$125. Adults only. Complimentary continental bkfst. Dining rm 6-10 pm; closed Mon. Bar 5-10 pm; entertainment Thurs-Sun. Ck-out 11:30 am, ck-in 2:30 pm. Antique furnishings. Cr cds: A, DS, MC, V.

Resort

★ ★ **JOHN NEWCOMBE'S TENNIS RANCH.** *Box 310469 (78131), 5 mi W on TX 46. 210/625-9105.* 46 rms in lodge, motel (1-2 story); 10 cottages. S, D $60-$140; 2-bedrm kit. condos $140; tennis plans; wkly rates. Crib free. Pool; whirlpool, lifeguard. Supervised child's activities (June-Aug); ages 8-18. Dining rm 7-9 am, 12:30-1:30 pm; 7-8 pm. Snack bar in summer, picnics. Bar 5 pm-midnight. Ck-out 2 pm, ck-in 4 pm. Coin lndry. Business servs avail. Airport transportation. Sports dir. 28 tennis courts (4 covered, 12 lighted), pro, tennis clinics. Soc dir; entertainment, dancing. Fireplace in condos. Some private patios, balconies. Cr cds: A, DS, MC, V.

Restaurants

★ **GRIST MILL.** *1287 Gruene Rd. 210/625-0684.* Hrs: 11 am-9 pm; Fri, Sat to 10 pm; summer 11 am-10 pm. No A/C. Bar. Semi-a la carte: lunch, dinner $3.99-$13.99. Child's meals. Specializes in chicken-fried steak, grilled chickadee. Entertainment Fri-Sat in summer. Parking. Outdoor dining. Overlooks Guadalupe River. Cr cds: A, C, D, DS, MC, V.

D

✔ ★ **NEW BRAUNFELS SMOKEHOUSE.** *146 TX 46E, at jct I-35. 210/625-2416.* Hrs: 7 am-9 pm. Closed Easter, Thanksgiving, Dec 25. German, Amer menu. Wine, beer. Semi-a la carte: bkfst $3-$6, lunch, dinner $4-$10. Child's meals. Specializes in smoked meat, German potato salad, strudel. Parking. Outdoor dining. Family-owned. Cr cds: A, DS, MC, V.

Odessa (B-3)

(See Midland, Monahans)

Founded 1881 **Pop** 89,699 **Elev** 2,890 ft **Area code** 915

Information Chamber of Commerce, 700 N Grant, Suite 100, 79761; 915/333-7871.

An oil field supply and equipment center for the Permian Basin, Odessa also has liquefied petroleum, synthetic rubber, cement and petrochemical plants.

Odessa is the home of the "Chuck Wagon Gang," a group of businessmen who travel world-wide each year preparing Texas-style barbecue "feeds" to promote good will for their city.

What to See and Do

Globe Theatre. Authentic re-creation of Shakespeare's original playhouse showcases drama ranging from Shakespeare to Broadway. Guided tours (Mon-Fri; wkends by appt). (See ANNUAL EVENTS) 2308 Shakespeare Rd. Phone 915/332-1586. Tours **free.** Also here is

Ann Hathaway Cottage Archival & Shakespearean Library. Contains many old books, documents pertaining to Shakespeare; costumes, furnishings and other items of the Elizabethan era.

Meteor Crater. Large crater formed more than 20,000 years ago. Paths through crater have interpretive signs. Picnic facilities. 8 mi W via I-20 or US 80 to Meteor Crater Rd exit. **Free.**

Presidential Museum. Changing exhibits & educational programs devoted to the people who have held or run for the office of President of the United States. Collections include images of the presidents, campaign memorabilia, signatures, political cartoons, miniature replicas of First Lady inaugural dresses. (Tues-Sat; closed most hols) Donation. 622 N Lee. Phone 915/332-7123.

Water Wonderland. The 18-acre park includes giant wave pools, swimming pools, water slides, inner-tube rides, bumper boats, go-karts, Kiddieland. (Late Apr-Memorial Day, wkends; Memorial Day-Labor Day, daily) 10113 US 80E, between Midland & Odessa; 2½ mi W of Midland Intl Air Terminal. Phone 915/563-2200. ¢¢¢¢¢

Annual Events

Sand Hills Hereford and Quarter Horse Show and Rodeo. 1st wk Jan.

Shakespeare Festival. Globe Theatre. Phone 915/332-1586. Feb or Mar.

Motels

★ ★ **BEST WESTERN GARDEN OASIS.** *110 W I-20 (79761), at Grant Ave.* 915/337-3006; FAX 915/332-1956. 118 rms, 2 story. S $39-$49; D $46-$56; each addl $5; suites $80-$90; under 12 free. Crib $8. Pet accepted, some restrictions. TV; cable (premium), VCR avail. Indoor pool; whirlpool, sauna, poolside serv. Restaurant 6 am-10 pm. Rm serv. Ck-out noon. Meeting rms. Business servs avail. In-rm modem link. Lndry facilities. Gift shop. Free airport, bus depot transportation. Cr cds: A, C, D, DS, ER, JCB, MC, V.

D 🐾 ⛖ 🏂 🐾 SC

★ ★ ★ **HOLIDAY INN CENTRE.** *Box 4891 (79760), 6201 E US 80, exit loop 338.* 915/362-2311; FAX 915/362-9810. 273 rms, 3 story. S $61-$71; D $67-$78; suites $125-$160. Crib free. Pet accepted, some restrictions. TV; cable (premium). Indoor/outdoor pool; poolside

serv. Restaurant 6 am-10 pm. Rm serv. Bar 4 pm-2 am; dancing. Coin Lndry. Business servs avil. In-rm modem link. Bellhops. Valet serv. Free airport, bus depot transportation. Putting green. Exercise equipt; weight machines, bicycles, whirlpool, sauna. Cr cds: A, C, D, DS, MC, V.

D 🐾 ⛖ 🏂 🏊 🐾 SC

★ ★ **LA QUINTA.** *5001 E US 80 (79761).* 915/333-2820; FAX 915/333-4208. 122 rms. S $51; D $58; each addl $7; under 18 free. Crib free. Pet accepted, some restrictions. TV; cable (premium). Pool. Restaurant adj open 24 hrs. Ck-out noon. Business servs avail. Picnic tables, grills. Cr cds: A, C, D, DS, MC, V.

D 🐾 ⛖ 🏊 🐾 SC

Restaurants

★ ★ **BARN DOOR.** *2140 N Andrew Hwy.* 915/337-4142. Hrs: 11 am-9:30 pm; Fri, Sat to 10:30 pm. Closed Sun; Labor Day, Dec 24 eve & Dec 25. Res accepted. Mexican, Amer menu. Semi-a la carte: lunch $3.95-$13.50, dinner $5.95-$19.50. Specializes in steak, seafood. Parking. Bar in old railroad depot. Victorian country decor. Cr cds: A, MC, V.

D SC

✔ ★ **LA BODEGA.** *1024 E 7th St.* 915/333-4469. Hrs: 11 am-10 pm; Fri, Sat to 10:30 pm. Closed major hols. Mexican, Amer menu. Bar to midnight. Semi-a la carte: lunch, dinner $4.75-$13.75. Child's meals. Specializes in Mexican seafood dishes. Parking. Mexican decor. Cr cds: A, D, MC, V.

D

★ **MANUEL'S.** *1404 E 2nd St (79761).* 915/333-2751. Hrs: 11 am-9 pm; Mon to 2 pm; Fri & Sat to 10 pm. Closed Jan 1, July 4, Dec 25. Res accepted. Mexican menu. Bar. Semi-a la carte: lunch, dinner $5.25-$14.50. Child's meals. Specializes in San Antonio-style cooking. Parking. Family-owned. Cr cds: A, C, D, DS, MC, V.

★ **SHOGUN.** *3952 E 42nd St, in Santa Fe Square Shopping Ctr.* 915/368-4711. Hrs: 5-10 pm. Japanese menu. Bar. A la carte entrees: dinner $9.95-$18.95. Child's meals. Specializes in chicken teriyaki, seafood, steak. Oriental decor. Cr cds: A, C, D, DS, ER, MC, V.

D

Orange (D-9)

(See Beaumont, Port Arthur; also Lake Charles, LA)

Founded 1836 **Pop** 19,381 **Elev** 14 ft **Area code** 409 **Zip** 77630

Information Convention & Visitors Bureau, 1012 Green Ave; 409/883-3536 or 800/528-4906.

Orange is on the Sabine River, at its junction with the Intracoastal Waterway. The deepwater port is connected with the Gulf by the Sabine-Neches Waterway. Bayous nearby are shaded with cypress and pine trees. Cattle, timber, shipbuilding, oil and chemical processing provide a diverse economy. There are several historic structures and a branch of Lamar University of Beaumont in town. The imposing First Presbyterian Church with art glass windows and a marble staircase was among the first public buildings in the country to be air-conditioned.

What to See and Do

Boating and fishing. On Sabine River and Lake and in surrounding bayous. Launching, dock facilities, marinas in area.

Heritage House Museum (1902). Historic house; changing exhibits. (Tues-Fri; closed major hols) 905 W Division St. Phone 409/886-5385. ¢

Lutcher Theater for the Performing Arts. Professional performances of top stars in concert, Broadway musicals and plays. Orange Civic Plaza. Box office 409/886-5535 or 800/828-5535. ¢¢¢¢

Stark Museum of Art. Built to house the collections of the Stark family. Fine collections of western art, including originals by Russell, Remington, Audubon and the Taos Society of Artists of New Mexico. The American Indian collection includes many art forms of the tribes of the Great Plains and the Southwest. Displays of Doughty & Boehm porcelain bird sculpture and Steuben crystal. (Wed-Sat, also Sun afternoons; closed major hols) 712 Green Ave. Phone 409/883-6661. **Free.**

W.H. Stark House (1894). Restored Victorian house typical of wealthy southeast Texas family; 15 rooms, 3 stories built of longleaf yellow pine with gables, galleries and windowed turret. Original furniture, silver, woodwork, lighting and decorative accessories; collection of cut glass in carriage house. Stairs major part of tour. Res advised. (Tues-Sat; closed major hols) Over 14 yrs only. Entrance through carriage house, 610 Main St. 6th & Green Sts. Phone 409/883-0871. ¢

Motels

✔★ ★ **BEST WESTERN.** *2630 I-10, exits 876 & 877.* 409/883-6616; FAX 409/883-3427. 60 rms, 2 story. S $40-$50; D $42-$50; each addl $5; under 18 free. Crib avail. Pet accepted, some restrictions. TV; cable (premium). Pool. Complimentary coffee in rms. Restaurant adj 6 am-10 pm; Sun 7 am-9 pm. Ck-out noon. Business servs avail. In-rm modem link. Some refrigerators. Some balconies. Near Orange County Airport. Cr cds: A, C, D, DS, MC, V.

★ ★ **RAMADA INN.** *Box 1839, 2610 I-10.* 409/883-0231; FAX 409/883-8839. 125 rms, 2 story. S, D $55; each addl $5; studio rms $58-$66; suites $55-$125; under 18 free. Crib free. TV; cable (premium). Pool; wading pool. Restaurant 6 am-10 pm. Rm serv. Bar 3 pm-2 am, Sat from 5 pm, closed Sun; entertainment Fri-Sat, dancing. Ck-out noon. Meeting rms. Business servs avail. In-rm modem link. Some refrigerators. Wet bar in some suites. Cr cds: A, C, D, DS, JCB, MC, V.

Ozona (C-4)

(See Sonora)

Pop 3,181 **Elev** 2,348 ft **Area code** 915 **Zip** 76943
Information Chamber of Commerce, 1110 Avenue E, PO Box 1135; 915/392-3737.

The only town in the 3,215-square-mile area of Crockett County, Ozona is a ranching community that calls itself the "biggest little town in the world."

What to See and Do

Crockett County Museum. Local historical exhibits, including objects from early Spanish explorers; minerals, mammoth bones. Murals depicting big-game animals hunted by Paleo-Indians; simulated rock overhang shelter, artifacts dating back to 10,000 B.C. (Mon-Fri; closed Jan 1, Thanksgiving, Dec 25) Donation. Courthouse Annex, 404 11th St. Phone 915/392-2837.

Davy Crockett Monument. Unveiled in 1939, this statue of the famous frontiersman bears the inscription "Be sure you are right, then go ahead." S end of town square.

Fort Lancaster State Historical Park. Ruins of Army outpost (1855-61); 82 acres. Museum containing exhibits relating to 18th century military life. (Thurs-Mon; closed Dec 25) 33 mi W on I-10, exit 343 then 11 mi W on US 290, near Sheffield. Phone 915/836-4391. ¢

Motels

★ **BEST WESTERN CIRCLE BAR.** *I-10 at Taylor Box Rd.* 915/392-2611; FAX 915/392-3651. 52 rms, 2 story. S, D $44-$70; each addl $10; under 12 free. TV; cable (premium). Indoor pool; wading pool, whirlpool, sauna. Complimentary coffee in lobby. Restaurant opp open 24 hrs. Ck-out noon. Coin lndry. Business servs avail. Some refrigerators, wet bars. Balconies. Cr cds: A, C, D, DS, MC, V.

✔ ★ **FLYING W LODGE.** *Box 985, Eight 11th St.* 915/392-2656. 40 rms, 1-2 story. S $22-$36; D $27-$46. Crib free. Pet accepted, some restrictions. TV; cable (premium). Pool. Complimentary coffee. Ck-out 11 am. Cr cds: A, C, D, DS, MC, V.

Padre Island (F-6 - F-7)

(North section: see ARANSAS PASS, CORPUS CHRISTI, *and* PORT ARANSAS. *South section: see* BROWNSVILLE, HARLINGEN, PORT ISABEL, SOUTH PADRE ISLAND)

In 1962 a stretch of this long, narrow island was made a national seashore. Stretching 113 miles from Corpus Christi to a point near Port Isabel (there is a causeway from each city), the island is rarely more than three miles wide. Drivers can navigate certain parts of the island, but the majority of the seashore is open only to four-wheel drive vehicles. The Port Mansfield Ship Channel, completed in 1964, essentially divides the island in two. There are no bridges or ferries across the channel, making it necessary to return to the mainland in order to reach the southern section.

Another way to explore the island is by hiking. The Grassland Trail (3/4 mi) makes a loop through a grassland-and-dunes area; a guide pamphlet is available at the trailhead. Birdwatching can be an interesting diversion; more than 350 species of birds inhabit the island or are seasonal visitors. Padre Island offers swimming, excellent surf fishing and picnicking. Camping is available at the Malaquite Beach Campground (fee) or free along the beach.

Nueces County Park, at the north end, offers picnicking, Gulf swimming and fishing; cabañas.

(For information contact Superintendent, 9405 S Padre Island Dr, Corpus Christi 78418; 512/937-2621 or 512/949-8068. The Corpus Christi Area Tourist Bureau also has details on the area; contact Box 604, Corpus Christi 78403; 800/678-OCEAN.)

Palestine (B-7)

(See Fairfield, Rusk)

Founded 1846 **Pop** 18,042 **Elev** 510 ft **Area code** 903
Information Convention and Visitors Bureau, PO Box 1177, 75802; 903/723-3014.

Surrounded by wooded areas and lakes, Palestine (pronounced PAL-es-teen) offers a wide array of outdoor recreation. It is the home of an atmospheric research station as well as petroleum, retail and agricultural operations.

What to See and Do

Community Forest. Fishing, piers; boat ramp. Nature trails. Picnicking. Fishing also on Lake Palestine, 20 mi N. 2 mi NW on US 287. **Free.**

National Scientific Balloon Facility. Research facility employs high-altitude balloons in various experiments. Interpretive video (30 min). Guided tour of facility (weather permitting; 1 wk advance notice requested) includes launch vehicle "Tiny Tim" and weather station. (Mon-Fri; closed major hols) 5 mi S via US 287 to FM 3224. Phone 903/729-0271. **Free.**

Rusk-Palestine State Railroad Park. 6 mi E on US 84. (See RUSK)

Annual Events

Texas Dogwood Trail Festival. Phone 903/729-7275. Last 2 wkends Mar and 1st wkend Apr.

Hot Pepper Festival. Last Sat Oct.

Motel

✔ ★ **BEST WESTERN PALESTINE INN.** *1601 W Palestine Ave (75801).* 903/723-4655; FAX 903/723-2519. 66 rms, 2 story. S $39; D $46; under 16 free. Crib $3. Pet accepted. TV; cable. Pool. Playground. Restaurant 6 am-9 pm. Ck-out 1 pm. Cr cds: A, C, D, DS, MC, V.

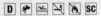

Palo Duro Canyon State Park (F-2)

(see Canyon)

Pampa (F-2)

(See Amarillo)

Pop 19,959 **Elev** 3,234 ft **Area code** 806 **Zip** 79065
Information Chamber of Commerce, 200 N Ballard, PO Box 1942; 806/669-3241.

From a little cattle town of perhaps 1,000 people, Pampa (so named because the country around it resembles the Argentine *pampas*) has grown, since the discovery of oil in 1926, into a thriving industrial city. Carbon black, petrochemical and manufacturing plants now stand alongside grain elevators and livestock businesses.

What to See and Do

White Deer Land Museum. Arrowhead and Native American photo collection, pioneer artifacts, historical records; room displays with antique furnishings, machines and utensils. (Daily exc Mon, limited hrs; closed hols) 116 S Cuyler St. Phone 806/669-8041. **Free.**

Annual Events

Top O'Texas Junior Livestock Show & Sale. Mid-Jan.

Top O'Texas Rodeo, PRCA. Wkend after July 4.

Motel

★ **CORONADO INN.** *1101 N Hobart St.* 806/669-2506; res: 800/388-5650; FAX 806/665-8502. 120 rms, 2 story. S $39-$46; D $46; each addl $7; suites $60-$90. Crib $5. TV; cable. Pool. Restaurant 5:30 am-11 pm. Private club 5 pm-midnight, Sat to 1 am; entertainment. Ck-out noon. Sundries. Game rm. Private patios, balconies. Cr cds: A, C, D, DS, MC, V.

Restaurant

✔ ★ **DANNY'S MARKET.** *2537 Perryton Parkway.* 806/669-1009. Hrs: 11 am-9 pm; Fri & Sat to 10 pm. Closed Sun; major hols. Res accepted. Semi-a la carte: lunch, dinner $2.95-$10.50. Child's meals. Specializes in steak. Parking. Kitchen visible behind glass partition. Cr cds: A, D, DS, MC, V.

D

Paris (A-7)

(See Bonham)

Settled 1836 **Pop** 24,699 **Elev** 602 ft **Area code** 903 **Zip** 75460
Information Visitors & Convention Office, 1651 Clarksville St; 903/784-2501.

Farm produce and cattle are raised outside the city limits; Paris proper relies on manufacturing. Rebuilt by plan after a great fire in 1916, the downtown area is a time capsule of the 1920s. Paris has nearly 1,400 acres of parks and flower beds.

What to See and Do

Fishing. Lake Crook, 3 mi N. Lake Pat Mayse, 12 mi N.

Sam Bell Maxey House State Historical Park. Two-story house (1867), in high Victorian Italianate style, was built by Sam Bell Maxey, Confederate major general and US Senator. Occupied by his family until 1966. Family heirlooms and furniture, some dating to 1795. (Wed-Sun; closed Jan 1, Dec 25) 812 S Church. Phone 903/785-5716. ¢

Senator A.M. and Welma Aikin, Jr Regional Archives. Includes a gallery of memorabilia from the noted senator's career as an educational reformer; replica of his office in Austin. Local and regional archives. (Mon-Fri; closed campus hols) On campus of Paris Junior College. Phone 903/784-9411. **Free.**

Annual Events

Municipal Band Concerts. Fri nights. 2nd wkend June-2nd wkend July.

CRCA Annual Rodeo. Fairgrounds. Aug.

Red River Valley Exposition. Fairgrounds. 8 days, 1st wk Sept.

Motels

✔ ★ **COMFORT INN.** *3505 NE Loop 286.* 903/784-7481. 64 rms, 2 story. S $32.95-$36.95; D $36.95-$44.95; each addl $4; under 18 free. Crib $4. TV; cable. Pool. Complimentary continental bkfst 6-9 am. Restaurant opp 6 am-10 pm. Ck-out noon. Free airport transportation. Cr cds: A, C, D, DS, ER, JCB, MC, V.

D

★ ★ **HOLIDAY INN.** *3560 NE Loop 286.* 903/785-5545; FAX 903/785-9510. 124 rms, 2 story. S $51-$63; D $56-$68; suites $64-$70; each addl $6; under 19 free; wkend rates. Crib free. Pet accepted.

TV; cable (premium). Pool; whirlpool. Restaurant 6 am-2 pm, 5-10 pm. Rm serv. Private club. Ck-out noon. Coin lndry. Meeting rms. Business center. In-rm modem link. Valet serv. Free airport transportation. Some bathrm phones. Cr cds: A, C, D, DS, ER, JCB, MC, V.

Restaurant

★ **FISH FRY.** *3500 NE Loop 286. 903/785-6144.* Hrs: 5-10 pm. Closed Sun & Mon; Jan 1, Thanksgiving, Dec 25. Res accepted. Dinner $10-$20. Child's meals. Specializes in catfish, steak, seafood. Parking. 5 dining areas. Wildlife motif. Totally nonsmoking. No cr cds accepted.

D

Pecos (C-3)

(See Fort Stockton, Monahans)

Pop 12,069 **Elev** 2,580 ft **Area code** 915 **Zip** 79772
Information Chamber of Commerce, 111 S Cedar, PO Box 27; 915/445-2406.

This one-time rough cattle town is now a modern producing and shipping point for cotton, cantaloupes and vegetables produced in the large area irrigated by water pumped from underground. It is also an oil, gas and sulphur center. The town has not forgotten its colorful past. The annual rodeo commemorates the fact that Pecos invented this sporting event in 1883, with a contest among cowpokes from local ranches.

What to See and Do

Balmorhea State Park. Swimming pool (late May-Labor Day, daily; fee). Picnicking, playground; lodging. Camping, tent & trailer sites (dump station). Standard fees. (Daily) 50 mi S on TX 17, near the Davis Mts. Phone 915/375-2370. Per vehicle ¢¢

West of the Pecos Museum. Renovated 1904 hotel; more than 30 rooms cover history of western Texas from the 1880s; includes restored old Pecos saloon (1896), where two gunslingers were killed. (Mon-Sat, also Sun afternoons; closed Thanksgiving; also 1 wk mid-Dec) Sr citizen rate. 1st St & US 285. Phone 915/445-5076. ¢¢

Annual Event

"West of the Pecos" Rodeo. Includes Golden Girl of the Old West contest, Old-Timer Reunion at museum, parade of floats, riding groups and old vehicles and barbecue. 4 days early July.

Motels

★★ **BEST WESTERN SWISS CLOCK INN.** *900 W Palmer, at I-20 exit 40. 915/447-2215; FAX 915/447-4463.* 104 rms. S $36-$44; D $42-$54; each addl $6. Crib free. TV; cable (premium). Pool. Restaurant 6 am-2 pm, 5-10 pm. Rm serv. Bar 5-10 pm. Ck-out noon. Meeting rm. Business servs avail. In-rm modem link. Valet serv. Cr cds: A, C, D, DS, MC, V.

✔★★ **HOLIDAY INN.** *Box 1777, 2 mi S at jct I-20, US 285. 915/445-5404; FAX 915/445-2484.* 96 rms, 2 story. S $56; D $61; each addl $5. Crib free. TV; cable. Pool; wading pool. Restaurant 6 am-9 pm. Rm serv. Private club. Ck-out 1 pm. Meeting rm. Business servs avail. In-rm modem link. Valet serv. Cr cds: A, C, D, DS, ER, JCB, MC, V.

Plainview (A-4)

(See Lubbock)

Founded ca 1880 **Pop** 21,700 **Elev** 3,300 ft **Area code** 806 **Zip** 79072
Information Chamber of Commerce, 710 W 5th; 806/296-7431.

This is one of the four chief commercial centers of the High Plains, where cotton, corn, castor beans and soybeans are nurtured by the vast, shallow, underground water belt.

What to See and Do

Llano Estacado Museum. Regional history and archaeology; art and science collections. Major events held yr-round. (Mar-Nov, daily; rest of yr, Mon-Fri; closed most major hols) 1900 W 7th St, on Wayland Baptist Univ campus. Phone 806/296-4735. **Free.**

Annual Events

High Plains Gem & Mineral Show. Late Feb.
Pioneer Roundup. 3rd wkend May.

Motels

★★ **BEST WESTERN-CONESTOGA.** *600 N I-27. 806/293-9454; FAX 806/293-9454, ext. 200.* 83 rms, 2 story. S $44; D $50; each addl $6; suites $90; under 12 free. Crib free. Pet accepted; some restrictions. TV; cable (premium), VCR avail. Pool. Complimentary continental bkfst. Restaurant adj open 24 hrs. Private club 5 pm-midnight; closed Sun. Ck-out noon. Meeting rm. In-rm modem link. Some bathrm phones. Some refrigerators. Cr cds: A, C, D, DS, MC, V.

D

✔★ **HOLIDAY INN.** *4005 Olton Rd (79073-1925). 806/293-4181.* 95 rms, 2 story. S $45-$48; D $46-$49; each addl $8; under 12 free; wkend rates; higher rates pheasant season. Crib free. Pet accepted. TV; cable. Private club. Ck-out noon. Meeting rms. Business servs avail. Some refrigerators. Picnic tables. Cr cds: A, C, D, DS, MC, V.

D

Restaurant

✔★ **GOLDEN CORRAL FAMILY STEAK HOUSE.** *2606 Olton Rd. 806/296-2235.* Hrs: 11 am-10 pm; Fri, Sat to 11 pm. Closed Dec 25. Res accepted. A la carte entrees: lunch, dinner $2.49-$12. Child's meals. Specializes in steak. Salad bar. Parking. Vaulted ceiling. Cr cds: DS, MC, V.

D SC

Plano (B-7)

(see Dallas)

Port Aransas (E-7)

(See Corpus Christi, Rockport)

Pop 2,233 **Elev** 7 ft **Area code** 512 **Zip** 78373
Information Chamber of Commerce, 421 W Cotter, PO Box 356; 512/749-5919 or 800/452-6278.

This resort town on Mustang Island is accessible from Aransas Pass by causeway and ferryboat or from Corpus Christi via causeway. Padre Island (see) is also nearby. Coastline of 20 miles provides good surf fishing as well as chartered-boat, deep-sea fishing for sailfish and kingfish. Swimming and surfing on the beach are popular activites. **Mustang Island State Park**, 14 miles south on TX 361, while relatively unspoiled, does have swimming with a bathhouse and showers; picnicking and camping. Beach driving is permitted. A hardtop road goes to Corpus Christi.

Annual Events

Deep-Sea Roundup. Fishing contest. Early July.

Port Aransas Days. Early Sept.

Motels

★ **DAYS INN SUITES.** *(US 361 Causeway, Aransas Pass 78336)* 6 mi N on US 361. 512/758-7375. 32 rms, 18 suites. S $40-$100; D $50-$100; each addl $8-$10; suites $70-$150. Crib free. TV; cable. Pool. Complimentary continental bkfst. Restaurant nearby. Ck-out noon. Meeting rms. Exercise equipt; bicycles, treadmill. Refrigerators. Cr cds: A, C, D, DS, MC, V.

[icons]

★ ★ **DUNES CONDOMINIUMS.** *Box 1238, 1000 Lantana Lane, on the beach.* 512/749-5155; res: 800/288-DUNE; FAX 512/749-5930. 48 kit. units, 9 story. Mid-Mar-Labor Day (2-night min wkends): 1-3 bedrm apts $127-$228; wkly rates; lower rates rest of yr. TV; cable (premium), VCR avail. Heated pool. Complimentary coffee in lobby. Restaurant nearby. Ck-out noon. Meeting rms. Tennis. Exercise equipt; bicycle, weights, whirlpool. Lawn games. Refrigerators. Private patios, balconies. Gulf view. Cr cds: A, C, D, MC, V.

[icons]

Restaurant

✔ ★ **SEAFOOD & SPAGHETTI WORKS.** *710 Alister St.* 512/749-5666. Hrs: 5:30-9:30 pm; Sun brunch 9 am-noon; Memorial Day-Labor Day 5-10 pm. Seafood menu. Bar. Semi-a la carte: dinner $6.95-$12.95. Child's meals. Specialties: grilled shrimp, spaghetti primavera. Salad bar. Parking. Geodesic dome building; balcony dining area encircles perimeter. Cr cds: A, C, D, DS, MC, V.

Port Arthur (D-9)

(See Beaumont, Orange)

Founded 1895 **Pop** 58,724 **Elev** 18 ft **Area code** 409
Information Convention & Visitors Bureau, 3401 Cultural Center Dr, 77642; 409/985-7822.

Hernando De Soto was shipwrecked nearby in 1543. Later a secret anchorage for the pirate Jean Lafitte, the area became known as the "Cajun Capital of Texas" when settled by thousands of French Acadians.

In 1895 Arthur Edward Stilwell, builder of the Kansas City, Pittsburg and Gulf Railroad (now the Kansas City Southern), chose Port Arthur as his Gulf terminus. He said the "brownies" had suggested the site, and that the plan of the city had been suggested to him in dreams inspired by the spirit world. He named the town after himself.

The Lucas well in the Spindletop field, 15 miles north, gushed forth in 1901, flooding 100 acres with oil before it was capped. John W. "bet-a-million" Gates came to town, lent Stilwell some needed money

and soon took over the industrial development of the booming new city.

This city on the shores of Lake Sabine is now called the "energy city" because it has the largest petroleum refining center in the country. It is also a thriving commercial, shipping and chemical center. Since the Sabine-Neches Ship Channel is built within the city, ships passing through appear to be moving through the city streets. An interesting mix of industry and tourism fuels the local economy.

What to See and Do

J.D. Murphree Wildlife Management Area. A 12,400-acre marsh. Fishing (spring, summer); waterfowl, alligator hunting (fall, winter). Some fees. W on TX 73. Phone 409/736-2551. ¢¢¢

Museum of the Gulf Coast. Exhibits cover history and culture of area; also history of oil refining; southeast Texas musical heritage exhibit includes Janis Joplin, Tex Ritter; sports legends exhibit features Jimmy Johnson, Babe Zaharias and others. (Daily exc Sat; closed hols) 700 Procter. Phone 409/982-7000. **Free.**

Nederland Windmill Museum. Located in Tex Ritter Park is replica of Dutch windmill built to honor 1898 immigrants from Holland; artifacts from Holland; memorabilia of country-western star Tex Ritter. (Mar-Labor Day, daily exc Mon; rest of yr, Thurs-Sun; closed major hols) 1500 Boston Ave, 5 mi N via TX 347 in Nederland. Phone 409/722-0279. **Free.** Adj is

La Maison Acadienne Museum. Replica of French Acadian home preserves heritage of French and Cajun immigrants who settled in Nederland in early 1900s; period furniture. (Days, phone same as Windmill Museum) **Free.**

Pleasure Island. Fishing (4 fishing piers, free; also charter boat fishing); crabbing (from 16¹/₂ mi of shoreline). Boating (launch, marina, supplies, repair; also regattas). Horseback riding (stables). Picnicking. Camping. Music park. Lake connects to the Intracoastal Waterway at its north end and the Port Arthur Ship Channel at its south end, 16 miles from the Gulf of Mexico. Sabine Lake, across the channel on TX 82. **Free.**

Pompeiian Villa. Built as a winter house for Isaac Ellwood of DeKalb, Illinois in 1900, the villa, with its three-sided courtyard and decorative trim, is a copy of a Pompeiian house of A.D. 79; furnishings include a Louis XVI parlor set; diamond-dust mirror; art nouveau Baccarat chandelier, French Savannerie rug. (Mon-Fri; closed hols) 1953 Lakeshore Dr. Phone 409/983-5977. ¢¢

Port of Port Arthur. Port where vessels are loaded and unloaded; 75-ton gantry crane, "Big Arthur." Tours (Mon-Fri; closed hols exc by appt). 900 4th St. Phone 409/983-2029. **Free.**

Rose Hill Manor. Palatial colonial residence of Rome H. Woodworth, early Port Arthur mayor. Greek-revival style; border the Interacoastal Waterway. Tours. (Tues-Sat, by appt; closed hols) 100 Woodworth Blvd. Phone 409/985-7292. ¢

Sabine Woods. The Audubon Society maintains two wooded bird sanctuaries near Pleasure Island. (Apr-Sept) 15 mi E on TX 87. **Free.**

Sea Rim State Park. Approx 15,000 acres with a 5¹/₂-mile long beach and some marsh areas. Swimming; fishing. Nature trail. Picnicking. Camping (hookups, dump station); primitive beach camping. Standard fees. (Daily) 24 mi SW on TX 87. Phone 409/971-2559. Per vehicle ¢¢

Annual Events

Mexican Independence Day Festival. Music, children's costume parade, folk dances, food. Sept.

Caymanfest. Entertainment, international soccer matches. 4th Sat Sept.

CavOILcade. Festival honoring the oil industry; coronation of queen; carnival, parades, fireworks. Early Oct.

Motor Hotels

★ ★ **HOLIDAY INN.** *2929 Jimmy Johnson Blvd. (77642). 409/724-5000; FAX 409/724-7644.* 163 rms, 4 story. S, D $61-$64; suites $125; under 18 free. TV; VCR avail. Pool. Restaurant 6 am-2 pm, 5-10 pm. Rm serv. Bar 4 pm-midnight; dancing. Ck-out noon. Meeting rms. Business servs avail. In-rm modem link. Bellhops. Free airport transportation. Some refrigerators. Cr cds: A, C, D, DS, JCB, MC, V.

D ⌨ ✕ 🔥 SC

★ ★ **RAMADA INN.** *Box 2826 (77643), 3801 TX 73. 409/962-9858; FAX 409/962-3685.* 125 rms, 2 story. S $53-$63; D $61-$71; each addl $8; suites $120-$135; studio rms $63-$71; under 18 free; wkend rates. Pet accepted, some restrictions. TV; cable (premium). Pool; wading pool. Restaurant 6 am-10 pm. Rm serv. Bar 4 pm-2 am; DJ, dancing. Ck-out noon. Meeting rms. Business servs avail. Bellhops. Sundries. Free airport transportation. Lighted tennis. Some refrigerators. Cr cds: A, C, D, DS, MC, V.

D ⌨ 🎿 ≋ ⚲ ✕ 🔥 SC

Unrated Dining Spot

LUBY'S CAFETERIA. *3533 Twin City Hwy, in Jefferson Shopping Ctr. 409/962-0261.* Hrs: 10:45 am-2:30 pm, 4:15-8 pm; Fri-Sun 10:45 am-8 pm. Closed Dec 24 evening-Dec 25. Avg ck: lunch, dinner $4.65. Specializes in roast beef, seafood, fresh vegetables. Cr cds: A, DS, MC, V.

D

Port Isabel (F-7)

(See Brownsville, Harlingen, South Padre Island)

Founded 1790 **Pop** 4,467 **Elev** 15 ft **Area code** 210 **Zip** 78578
Information Chamber of Commerce, 213 Yturria St; 210/943-2262 or 800/527-6102.

This is a fishing, shrimping and resort town near the southernmost tip of Texas. The Queen Isabella Causeway stretches to the town of South Padre Island (see) via the state's longest bridge (2.6 miles). Port Isabel has a yacht harbor, marinas and fishing charters for the Bay and Gulf.

What to See and Do

Port Isabel Lighthouse State Historic Park. Built in 1853 and abandoned 1905 after shipping traffic declined, this area was donated to the state in 1950 as a historic site. Nearby are Fort Brown, the camp and depot commanded by General Zachary Taylor during the Mexican War, and Palmito Hill, site of last land battle of Civil War. Self-guided tours (daily). W on TX 100. Phone 210/943-1172. ¢

Annual Event

Texas International Fishing Tournament. South Point Marina. Marlin, tarpon, sailfish and offshore categories; bay, tag and release and junior divisions. Phone 210/943-8438. 5 days early Aug.

Motel

★ ★ **YACHT CLUB RESORT.** *700 Yturria St (78758). 210/943-1301.* 24 rms, 2 story. S $35-$52; D $42-$59; each addl $10; under 12 free. Crib free. Pet accepted; $25. TV; cable. Heated pool. Complimentary coffee in rms. Complimentary continental bkfst. Res-

taurant (see YACHT CLUB). On bay. Historic yacht club built 1926. Cr cds: A, C, D, MC, V.

 ⌨ ≋ ⚲

Restaurants

★ **MARCELLO'S ITALIAN RESTAURANT.** *110 N Tarnava, in front of lighthouse. 210/943-7611.* Hrs: 11 am-10 pm; Fri to 11 pm; Sat, Sun 5-11 pm. Closed Thanksgiving, Dec 25. Res accepted; required Fri & Sat. Italian menu. Bar. Semi-a la carte: lunch $2.99-$5.99, dinner $7.25-$15.95. Child's meals. Specialties: fettucine, flounder primavera, pasta. Own desserts. Parking. Marble fountain at entrance. Cr cds: A, C, D, DS, MC, V.

D SC

★ ★ **YACHT CLUB.** *(See Yacht Club Resort Motel) 210/943-1301.* Hrs: 6-10 pm. Closed Wed. Res accepted. Bar. Semi-a la carte: dinner $12.95-$24.95. Child's meals. Specializes in seafood, prime rib, pasta. Parking. In former yacht club built 1926. Cr cds: A, C, D, MC, V.

D

Port Lavaca (E-7)

(See Victoria)

Founded 1815 **Pop** 10,886 **Elev** 22 ft **Area code** 512 **Zip** 77979
Information Port Lavaca-Calhoun Co Chamber of Commerce, 2300 TX 35 Bypass, PO Box 528; 512/552-2959.

Founded by the Spanish in 1815 and established as a community in 1840, Port Lavaca became an important shipping port. In 1856 camels were landed in nearby Indianola, bound for Camp Verde, Texas. They had been purchased for the US Army to transport supplies between forts along the western frontier. The camel experiment was abandoned following the Civil War, and the herd was sold to a San Antonio entrepreneur.

The great hurricane of 1886 destroyed Indianola, then the county seat. Port Lavaca became the county seat but did not regain its importance as a shipping point until much later. A deepwater port serves the city's major industries.

What to See and Do

Fishing. In Lavaca Bay (3,200-ft-long pier, lighted for night fishing) and the Gulf. Charter boats; also a number of fishing camps in area.

Annual Events

Summerfest. Centers on the town's man-made beach. Beauty pageant, music, evening dances, sports tournaments and recreational games. Mid-June.

Calhoun County Fair. Mid-Oct.

Motel

★ **DAYS INN.** *2100 N TX 35 Bypass. 512/552-4511.* 99 rms, 2 story. S $46-$52; D $52-$58; each addl $6; suites $71-$77; under 12 free. Crib free. Pet accepted. TV. Pool. Complimentary continental bkfst. Restaurant 6 am-2 pm, 5-10 pm; Bar 5 pm-midnight, Sat to 1 am. Ck-out noon. Coin lndry. Meeting rms. Cr cds: A, C, D, DS, MC, V.

D ⌨ ≋ ✕ 🔥 SC

Possum Kingdom State Park (B-6)

(For accommodations see Graham, also see Mineral Wells)

(15 mi E of Breckenridge on US 180 to Caddo, then 17 mi N on Park Road 33)

This park, on the shores of Possum Kingdom Reservoir, is located in the Brazos River Valley. The reservoir covers 19,800 acres behind the Morris Sheppard Dam and has a 310-mile shoreline. Water sports are popular; catfish, striped bass, white bass and crappie abound. Boats and supplies are available.

The park covers more than 1,500 acres and offers swimming, waterskiing; lighted fishing pier; boating (ramps). Picnicking, playground, concessions. Improved campsites, cabins. Standard fees. Phone 817/549-1803.

Quanah (A-5)

(For accommodations see Vernon)

Pop 3,413 **Elev** 1,568 ft **Area code** 817 **Zip** 79252
Information Chamber of Commerce, PO Box 158; 817/663-2222.

Named for Quanah Parker, last great war chief of the Comanche, who was the son of a Comanche chief and Cynthia Ann Parker, a captive girl raised by the Comanche, the town of Quanah is today a marketing and shipping point where cottonseed oil, dairy products and meat are processed.

What to See and Do

Copper Breaks State Park. Approx 1,900 acres. Swimming; fishing. Hiking. Picnicking, playground. Primitive & improved camping . Museum of local history with dioramas, artifacts; Texas Longhorn herd. Standard fees. (Daily) 12 mi S on TX 6. Phone 817/839-4331. Per vehicle ¢¢

Reynosa, Mexico (F-6)

(see McAllen)

Richardson (B-7)

(see Dallas)

Rockport (E-7)

(For accommodations see Corpus Christi)

Founded 1870 **Pop** 4,753 **Elev** 6 ft **Area code** 512 **Zip** 78382
Information Chamber of Commerce, 404 Broadway, 78382; 512/729-6445.

With its weathered buildings and wind-twisted trees, this resort town calls to mind a Maine fishing village. Year-round fishing in Aransas Bay and the Gulf, a mile-long sand beach and water sports add to its attractions. The town is also a haven for artists.

What to See and Do

Aransas National Wildlife Refuge. More than 110,000 acres, including Matagorda Island overlooking Gulf of Mexico. This is the principal wintering ground for the endangered whooping crane; it also houses deer, alligators and a variety of birds. Early mornings and late afternoons are best for viewing wildlife. Observation tower; interpretive center; 15-mile auto tour loop; nature trails. Wheelchair access to observation tower (ramps). (Daily; closed Thanksgiving, Dec 25) Nearest gas 14 miles. 22 mi N on TX 35, then 9 mi E on FM 774, then 7 mi SE on FM 2040. Contact Refuge Manager, PO Box 100, Austwell 77950; 512/286-3559. **Free.**

Beaches. Rockport. Sand beach; park; ski and yacht basins, boat launch. **Fulton.** 3 mi N on TX 35. Yacht basin, boat launch; 1,000-ft fishing pier; sand beach. N end of downtown on TX 35 Business.

Boat trips into Aransas National Wildlife Refuge. Bird watching, sightseeing & photography tours. *Lucky Day* leaves Rockport Harbor (Nov-Mar), phone 512/729-4855. *Pisces* leaves Rockport Harbor (Nov-Mar), phone 512/729-7525. *New Pelican* leaves Rockport Harbor (Nov-Mar), phone 512/729-8448. **Captain Ted's Whooping Crane Tours** leave from Sandollar Pavillion (Nov-Mar), also inquire about rookery tours (Apr-June), phone 512/729-9589. ¢¢¢¢

Fulton Mansion State Park. Second Empire/Victorian mansion, built in the mid-1870s. First and second floors authentically furnished. Spacious lawns slope toward the beach. (Wed-Sun; closed Dec 25) Between Fulton and Rockport via TX 35, turn E on Henderson St. Phone 512/729-0386. ¢¢

State parks.

Goose Island. Swimming permitted; lighted fishing pier; boating (ramp). Picnicking. Birdwatching. Improved campsites. Standard fees. (Daily) 10 mi NE on TX 35, then E on Park Rd 13, partly on mainland and partly on nearby islands. Phone 512/729-2858. Per vehicle ¢¢

Copano Bay Causeway. Fishing piers; boating (ramp). Picnicking. Some fees. 5 mi N on TX 35. Phone 512/729-8633.

Texas Maritime Museum. Explores Texas' seafaring history, from early Spanish discovery, through Texas independence, emergence of river trade, Civil War blockade-running and growth of fishing and offshore drilling industries. (Tues-Sat, also Sun afternoons; closed major hols) 1202 Navigation Blvd, at Rockport Harbor. Phone 512/729-1271. ¢¢

Annual Events

OysterFest. Food & music. 1st wkend Mar.

SeaFair Festival. Columbus Day wkend.

Rusk (B-8)

(For accommodations see Palestine, also see Jacksonville)

Pop 4,366 **Elev** 489 ft **Area code** 903 **Zip** 75785
Information Chamber of Commerce, 415 S Main St, PO Box 67; 903/683-4242.

Rusk was a supply center for salt, iron ore and lumber during the Civil War. Oil production began in 1914; fruit, vegetables and dairy products are handled here. Many old houses have been restored. A 546-foot wooden footbridge (1861) is thought to be the longest in the nation.

What to See and Do

Jim Hogg State Historical Park. Approx 170 acres. "Mountain Home" plantation; replica of the pioneer home of Governor Hogg and his family. Family cemetery, trails. Picnicking, playground. Flowering trees. (Thurs-Mon; closed Dec 25) 2 mi NE off US 84. Phone 903/683-4850. Per vehicle ¢¢ Museum **Free.**

Rusk-Palestine State Park. Includes a 15-acre lake, tennis courts, picnic area and campsites. Standard fees. (Daily) 3 mi W on US 84. Phone 903/683-5126. Per vehicle ¢¢ Also here is

Texas State Railroad Historical Park. Four-hour round-trip excursions aboard turn-of-the-century steam-powered train to Palestine (see). Tour through locomotive cab before departure; slide show. Also runs from Palestine. (Summer, Thurs-Mon; spring & fall, Sat & Sun only) Advance reservations recommended. Camping adj (full hookups). Phone 903/683-2561. Round trip ¢¢¢¢

Salado (C-6)

(See Georgetown, Temple)

Pop 1,216 **Elev** 520 ft **Area code** 817 **Zip** 76571

Information Chamber of Commerce, PO Box 81; 817/947-5040.

Established prior to 1860, this town has several interesting buildings including a stagecoach inn. The Scottish Clans of Texas meet here each year (see ANNUAL EVENT).

What to See and Do

Stillhouse Hollow Lake. Swimming; fishing; boating (ramps, storage). Picnicking; concession. Primitive & improved camping (fee). Fee for some recreation areas. (Daily) Approx 5 mi NW on FM 1670. Phone 817/939-2461. **Free.**

Annual Event

Gathering of the Clans. Village Green. Different events each year. 2nd wkend Nov.

Motel

✓★★ **STAGECOACH INN.** *Box 97, 1 Main St, just off I-34, exit 284. 817/947-5111; res: 800/732-8994; FAX 817/947-0671.* 82 rms, 2 story. S $42-$52; D $49-$59; each addl $3; suites $75; under 12 free. Crib free. TV; cable (premium), VCR avail. Pool; whirlpool. Playground. Restaurant (see STAGECOACH INN DINING ROOM). Rm serv 7 am-7 pm. Private club 10 am-10 pm; winter 5-9 pm. Ck-out 1 pm. Meeting rms. Business servs avail. Sundries. Lighted tennis. Golf privileges. Lawn games. Private patios; balconies. Landscaped grounds on Salado Creek. Cr cds: A, C, D, DS, MC, V.

Restaurants

★★ **LA MANSION DE SALADO.** *200 N Main St. 817/947-5157.* Hrs: 11 am-9 pm; Fri & Sat to 10 pm; Sun to 5 pm. Closed Mon; Jan 1, Thanksgiving, Dec 25. Southwestern, Mexican menu. Bar. Semi-a la carte: lunch $4.25-$6.95, dinner $6.95-$12.95. Specializes in mesquite-grilled trout, cayenne battered shrimp, woodgrilled vegetables. Parking. Patio dining with view of waterfall and pond. Built 1857 for a judge; antiques displayed. Cr cds: A, DS, MC, V.

★ **STAGECOACH INN DINING ROOM.** *(See Stagecoach Inn Motel) 817/947-9400.* Hrs: 11 am-9 pm. Res accepted; required wkends & hols. Complete meals: lunch $7.95-$10.95, dinner $12.95-$18.95. Child's meals. Specializes in prime rib, own pies. Parking. Former stagecoach stop; Early American decor. Family-owned since 1945. Cr cds: A, C, D, DS, MC, V.

San Angelo (C-5)

Founded 1867 **Pop** 84,474 **Elev** 1,847 ft **Area code** 915

Information Convention & Visitors Bureau, 500 Rio Concho Dr, 76903; 915/653-1206 or 800/375-1206.

The Goodnight-Loving cattle trail, the Chidester Stage Line and the California Trail once passed this way. San Angelo was once a wild Western town. Now a huge wool and mohair market, cattle and oil also support the area. San Angelo is where the North and South Concho rivers combine to form the Concho River. Goodfellow AFB is at the southeast corner of town.

What to See and Do

Fishing and boating. Lake Nasworthy, 6 mi SW on Knickerbocker Rd. Twin Buttes Lake, 5 mi W of city, off US 67. O.C. Fisher Reservoir, 4 mi N on Arden Rd, off Mercedes St. North, Middle & South Concho rivers.

Fort Concho National Historic Landmark. Indian Wars fort comprised of 20 restored stone buildings on 40 acres. Museum covers infantry, cavalry and civilian life during fort's active period (1867-89). San Angelo Museum of Fine Arts occupies 1868 Quartermaster Storehouse. Tours start at Headquarters Building, located between East Ave C & Ave D, at E end of parade ground. (Daily exc Mon; closed Jan 1, Thanksgiving, Dec 25) 213 E Avenue D, downtown near Concho River. Phone 915/657-4441 or -4444. ¢

O.C. Fisher Lake. Swimming, waterskiing; fishing; boating (ramps). Nature, bicycle, jogging trails; golf. Picnicking. Camping (tent & trailer sites) at Dry Creek & Red Arroyo. Two off-road vehicle areas. Fee for some activities. (Daily) Just W of town on US 67. Phone 915/949-4757 (headquarters). **Free.**

Annual Events

Frontier Days. Fort Concho National Historic Landmark. 3rd Sat June.

Fiestas Patrias. Fort Concho National Historic Landmark. Mid-Sept.

Motels

★★ **BEST WESTERN INN OF THE WEST.** *415 W Beauregard (76903). 915/653-2995; FAX 915/653-2995.* 75 rms, 3 story. S $40; D $45; each addl $6; under 12 free. Crib $6. Pet accepted, some restrictions. TV; cable (premium), VCR avail. Indoor pool. Restaurant 6 am-8 pm. Rm serv. Ck-out noon. Meeting rms. Business servs avail. In-rm modem link. Sun deck. Cr cds: A, C, D, DS, MC, V.

★★ **INN OF THE CONCHOS.** *2021 N Bryant (76903). 915/658-2811; FAX 915/653-7560.* 125 rms, 2 story. S $38-$42; D $42-$48; each addl $6; suites $65-$100; under 12 free. Crib free. Pet accepted, some restrictions. TV; cable (premium). Pool. Restaurant 6 am-2 pm. Rm serv. Bar 4 pm-2 am; dancing exc Sun. Ck-out noon. Meeting rms. Business servs avail. Sundries. Cr cds: A, C, D, DS, ER, JCB, MC, V.

★★ **LA QUINTA.** *2307 Loop 306 (76904). 915/949-0515; FAX 915/944-1187.* 170 rms, 2 story. S $54-$69; D $61-$76; each addl $7; suites $69; under 18 free. Crib free. Pet accepted, some restrictions. TV; cable (premium). Pool. Complimentary continental bkfst. Ck-out noon. Guest lndry. Meeting rms. Business servs avail. In-rm modem link. Some bathrm phones, Cr cds: A, C, D, DS, MC, V.

✓★ **OLE COACH.** *4205 S Bryant Blvd (76903). 915/653-6966; res: 800/227-6456 (TX); FAX 915/659-6456.* 82 rms, 2 story. S $29-$34; D $34-$39; each addl $5; under 12 free. Crib free. Pet accepted, some restrictions. TV; cable (premium). Pool. Bar 7 pm-2 am, closed Sun; entertainment. Ck-out 11:30 am. Business servs avail. Private patios, balconies. On river. Cr cds: A, C, D, DS, MC, V.

Hotel

★ ★ ★ **HOLIDAY INN CONVENTION CENTER.** *441 Rio Concho Dr (76903). 915/658-2828; FAX 915/658-8741.* 148 rms, 6 story. S, D $57-$80; each addl $8; suites $140-$160; under 12 free. Crib free. Pet accepted, some restrictions. TV; cable, VCR avail. Indoor pool; whirlpool, poolside serv. Restaurant 6:30 am-2 pm, 5:30-10 pm. Bar 4-11:30 pm. Ck-out noon. Meeting rms. Business servs avail. In-rm modem link. Airport, RR station, bus depot transportation. Some refrigerators. Cr cds: A, C, D, DS, JCB, MC, V.

Restaurants

★ ★ **CHINA GARDEN.** *4217 College Hill Blvd. 915/949-2838.* Hrs: 11 am-10:30 pm; Fri, Sat to 11:30 pm. Closed most major hols. Chinese, Amer menu. Bar. Semi-a la carte: lunch $4.75-$6.25, dinner $5.25-$27. Child's meals. Specializes in shrimp, steak, seafood. Parking. Chinese decor. Cr cds: A, D, DS, MC, V.

D

✔ ★ ★ **CRYSTAL'S.** *2216 Avenue N, at Avenue M. 915/949-1991.* Hrs: 11 am-10 pm; Fri, Sat to 11 pm. Closed major hols. Mexican, Amer menu. Bar. A la carte entrees: lunch, dinner $4.95-$12.95. Child's meals. Specializes in fajitas, quail, baby back ribs. Parking. Cr cds: A, C, D, DS, MC, V.

★ ★ **JOHN ZENTNER'S DAUGHTER.** *1901 Knickerbocker. 915/949-2821.* Hrs: 11 am-2 pm, 5-9:30 pm; Wed, Sun to 10 pm; Fri, Sat to 11 pm. Closed Dec 25. Bar. Semi-a la carte: lunch $4.95-$5.25, dinner $3.95-$18.95. Specializes in steak. Cr cds: A, C, D, DS, MC, V.

D SC

★ ★ **TASTE OF ITALY.** *3520 Knickerbocker Rd (76904), in shopping center. 915/944-3290.* Hrs: 11 am-2 pm, 5:30-10:30 pm; Fri & Sat to 11 pm. Closed Sun; Thanksgiving, Dec 25. Res accepted. Italian menu. Bar. A la carte entrees: lunch $4.95-$6.95, dinner $6.95-$12.95. Child's meals. Specializes in veal dishes. Wine cellar. Cr cds: A, C, D, DS, MC, V.

D SC

Unrated Dining Spot

LUBY'S CAFETERIA. *1226 Sunset Mall (76904). 915/944-4511.* Hrs: 10:45 am-2:30 pm, 4:15-8 pm; Fri-Sun 10:45 am-8 pm; summer to 8:30 pm. Closed Dec 25. Avg ck: lunch $4.90, dinner $5.50. Specializes in chicken-fried steak, roast beef, haddock. Cr cds: DS, MC, V.

San Antonio (D-6)

(See New Braunfels, Seguin)

Founded 1718 **Pop** 935,933 **Elev** 701 ft **Area code** 210

In the course of its colorful history, this beautiful old city has been under six flags: France, Spain, Mexico, the Republic of Texas, Confederate States of America and United States of America. Each has definitely left its mark.

The Mission San Antonio de Valero (the Alamo) was founded by Friar Antonio de San Buenaventura Olivares in May, 1718, near the tree-lined San Antonio River. Four more missions were built along the river during the next 13 years. All continued to operate until about 1794. In 1718, Don Martin de Alarcon, Captain General and Governor of the Province of Texas, established a military post here. San Antonio has been a military center ever since.

The Alamo is in the center of town. Here, from February 23 to March 6, 1836, Davy Crockett, Colonel James Bowie, Colonel William B. Travis and 186 other Texans stood off General Antonio López de Santa Anna, dictator-president of Mexico, and his 5,000 troops. Every defender died in the battle. Their heroic stand was the inspiration for Texas' famous battle cry "Remember the Alamo!" Three months after the Alamo tragedy, San Antonio was almost deserted. Within a few years, however, it became a great western outpost. In the 1840s there was a heavy influx of Germans whose descendants still add to the city's cosmopolitan air. In the 1870s, new settlers, adventurers and cowboys on long cattle drives made this a tough, hard-drinking, hard-fighting, gambling town. San Antonio has evolved into a modern, prosperous city, but it retains much of the flavor of its past.

Transportation

San Antonio Intl Airport: Information 210/821-3411; lost and found 210/821-3436; weather 210/828-0683; cash machines, Terminals 1 & 2; Crown Room (Delta), Terminal 1, mezzanine level.

Car Rental Agencies: See toll-free numbers under Introduction.

Public Transportation: Buses, trolleys (Metropolitan Transit Authority), phone 210/227-2020.

Rail Passenger Service: Amtrak 800/872-7245.

What to See and Do

Alamodome. New multipurpose dome boasts a cable suspended roof, which is anchored from four concrete towers. This sports, concert and convention center employs 160,000 gross square feet of exhibit space and 30,000 square feet of conference space with configurations for basketball, hockey, football and major concerts (max seating 73,200). Guided tours include executive suites, locker rooms, mechanical features and the playing field (phone for schedule). Just E of HemisFair Park, across I-35/37. Phone 210/207-3652. Tour ¢¢

Auto tour. San Antonio Missions National Historical Park. Four Spanish colonial missions in San Antonio are administered by the National Park Service. Exhibits, talks, cultural demonstrations. Parishes within the missions are still active. (Daily; closed Jan 1, Dec 25) Phone 210/229-5701. **Free.** From Alamo Plaza drive S on Alamo St about 14 blks to South St Mary's St. Turn left about 14 blks (St Mary's St becomes Roosevelt Ave) to Mission Rd.

Mission Concepcion. Established in 1731, this is one of the best preserved missions in Texas and the oldest unrestored stone mission church in the country. It is built of porous limestone found nearby. There are some fine 18th-century frescoes; the acoustics of the building are remarkable. (Daily) 807 Mission Rd. Phone 210/229-5732. **Free.** Turn left onto Mission Rd, follow Mission Parkway signs to

Mission San Jose (1720). One of the largest and most successful missions in the Southwest; the church, Indian quarters, granary and old mill have all been restored. Built of tufaceous limestone, the church is famous for its carvings and masonry. The sacristy window is sometimes referred to as "Rosa's Window." Follow Napier Ave, right on Padre Dr and through underpass to Espada park. (Daily) 6539 San Jose Dr. Phone 210/229-4770 **Free.** Here is

Espada Dam (1740). Constructed to divert river water into irrigation ditches. Waters flow into Espada Aqueduct (see), which carries water to Mission Espada. Continue on Padre Drive (through low-water crossing) through Villamain to

Mission San Juan (1731). A self-sufficient community was centered around this mission. Indian artisans and farmers established a trade network with their surplus. (Daily) 9101 Graf Rd. Phone 210/229-

5734 **Free.** Take Graf Rd back to Ashley Rd, turn right to Villamein Rd S, right on Camino Coahuilteca to

Mission Espada (1731). Southernmost of the San Antonio chain of missions. Unusual arched doorway. Friary & chapel (except for facade) are restored. (Daily) 10040 Espada Rd. Phone 210/627-2021. **Free.** Follow Espada Rd N to

Espada Aqueduct (1735). This 120-ft-long Spanish Colonial aqueduct carried water over Piedras Creek continuously for more than 200 years. Nearby farms still use water from this system. Return to Espada Road S, turn right to Ashley and right again on Roosevelt Ave to return to San Antonio.

Brackenridge Park. This 340-acre park has picnicking, playground, athletic fields, golf; carousel, miniature train, sky ride, pedal boats. Some fees. (Daily) N Broadway (US 81), 2 mi N of the Alamo. Also here are

Witte Museum. History, anthropology and natural science collections and exhibits. Special attractions: Ancient Texans: Rock Art and Lifeways Along the Lower Pecos; "Texas Wild: Ecology Illustrated." On museum grounds are four reconstructed early Texas houses. Changing exhibits. (Daily; closed Thanksgiving, Dec 25) Sr citizen rate. 3801 Broadway, at Tuleta St. Phone 210/829-7262. ¢¢

Pioneer Hall. Houses collections of Texas trail drivers, pioneers and the Texas Rangers. Saddles, guns, tools, furniture and other memorabilia illustrate lifestyle of early Texans. (Daily exc Mon; closed Jan 1-2, Thanksgiving, Dec 24-26) 3805 Broadway. Phone 210/822-9011. ¢

Zoological Gardens and Aquarium. Bird and antelope collections particularly notable; also children's zoo with boat ride. (Daily) 3903 N St Mary's St. Phone 210/734-7183. ¢¢¢

Japanese Tea Gardens. Floral displays on walls and floor of abandoned quarry. Outdoor Grecian theater is also here. (Daily) **Free.**

Cascade Caverns Park. Located on 105-acre park is a water-formed underground cavern with spectacular rock formations. Special feature of this natural attraction is a 100-foot underground waterfall, viewed as the grand finale of a 45-minute guided tour (daily). Park has picnic facilities. 14 mi NW on I-10, exit 543 Cascade Caverns Rd, then W & follow signs. Phone 210/755-8080. ¢¢¢

Fiesta Texas. A 200-acre amusement park dramatically set in a former limestone quarry. Four themed areas—Spassburg (German), Los Festivales (Hispanic), Crackaxle Canyon (Western) and Rockville (1950s)—arranged around central Texas Square, highlight live entertainment productions on seven theater stages. Features include the Rattler, said to be one of the world's tallest and fastest wooden roller coasters, the Gully Washer river rapid ride, *Dornröschen,* an early 1900s-style carousel and *Kinderspielplatz,* a major area devoted to children's rides and amusements. Many restaurants and shops. (Mid-late Mar & Memorial Day wkend-Labor Day wkend, daily; late Mar-late May & early Sept-early Nov, Fri-Sun) 17000 I-10W, at jct Loop 410. Phone 210/697-5050. ¢¢¢¢¢

Fort Sam Houston Museum and National Historic Landmark. Fort Sam Houston is headquarters for both the US Fifth Army and Brooke Army Medical Center. Museum depicts history of fort and US Army in this region from 1845 to the present. Exhibits of uniforms, equipment and photographs detail growth of the post and events that occurred here. Audiovisual exhibits. More than 900 historic structures on base represent the era 1876-1935; the historic quadrangle once detained Geronimo and his renegade Apaches; self-guided tours. (Wed-Sun; closed hols) Off I-35, N New Braunfels Ave exit. Phone 210/221-1886. **Free.**

Gray Line bus tours. Contact 1430 E Houston St, 78202; 210/226-1706.

Institute of Texan Cultures. Exhibits depicting lives and contributions of the people of Texas. Multimedia presentation (4 shows daily); part of the University of Texas at San Antonio. (Daily exc Mon; closed Thanksgiving, Dec 25) Parking (fee). Special tours for the handicapped avail. HemisFair Park. Phone 210/558-2300. **Free.**

Lone Star Buckhorn Museums. Buckhorn Hall of Horns vast collection of horns, animal trophies and memorabilia dating to 1881. Also Hall of Fins and Feathers, collection of birds, fish and marine life. Buckhorn Saloon and O. Henry House. Hall of Texas History depicts memorable periods from 1534-1898. (Daily; closed Thanksgiving, Dec 25) Complimentary beer or root beer. Sr citizen rate. 600 Lone Star Blvd, on grounds of Lone Star Brewing Co. Phone 210/270-9400. ¢¢

McNay Art Museum. Includes Gothic, medieval, late 19th- and 20th-century American and European paintings; sculpture, graphic arts; rare books on theater arts, architecture and fine arts; changing exhibits (some fees). Patio with fountains; gardens. (Tues-Sat, also Sun afternoons; closed some major hols) 6000 N New Braunfels, at Austin Hwy. Phone 210/824-5368. **Free.**

Natural Bridge Caverns. These caverns are still in their formative period; Sherwood Forest has totem pole formations; the Castle of the White Giants has 40-foot-high Kings Throne; 70°F. One-and-one-quarter-hour guided tours every half-hour. Picnicking. (Daily; closed Jan 1, Thanksgiving, Dec 25) 8 mi NE of I-35 exit 175, on FM 3009 (Natural Bridge Caverns Rd). Phone 210/651-6101. ¢¢¢

Plaza Theater of Wax/Ripley's Believe It or Not! Wax museum with more than 225 historical and entertainment figures; horror chamber. In same building, Ripley's museum with more than 500 exhibits of the strange and bizarre. (Daily) 301 Alamo Plaza. Phone 210/224-WAXX. ¢¢¢

San Antonio Botanical Gardens. Thirty-three acres include formal gardens, Japanese garden, rose garden, herb gardens, xeriscape gardens, garden for the visually impaired. Native Texas area features lake, native flora and 1800s dwellings. Lucile Halsell Conservatory is a complex of five glass exhibition greenhouses. Self-guided tours. (Daily exc Mon; closed Jan 1, Dec 25) Sr citizen rate. 555 Funston Pl, at N New Braunfels Ave. Phone 210/821-5115. ¢¢

San Antonio Museum of Art. Works include pre-Columbian and Latin American folk art; Spanish colonial and Asian galleries; contemporary art in the Cowden Gallery; Ewing Halsell Wing for Ancient Art, with Egyptian, Greek and Roman antiquities. On grounds are sculpture garden, rest areas. (Daily; closed Thanksgiving, Dec 25) Sr citizen rate. 200 W Jones Ave. Phone 210/829-7262. ¢¢

San Antonio Symphony. Season includes 16 pairs of classical concerts (Thurs & Sat) and 10 sets of 3 of pops concerts (Sept-May, Fri-Sun) Majestic Theatre, downtown. Phone 210/554-1010. ¢¢¢¢¢

Sea World of Texas. The world's largest marine life park (250 acres) offers more than 25 shows, exhibits and attractions. Killer whale shows at 4,500-seat, multimillion-gallon "Shamu Stadium"; 300,000-gallon coral reef aquarium features many species of sharks & thousands of Indo-Pacific fishes. Sea lion, beluga whale/dolphin and water-ski shows; penguin habitat; water rides, children's play area. (Memorial Day-Labor Day, daily; Mar-late May & early Sept-Oct, wkends & hols) 10500 Sea World Dr, 16 mi NW via TX 151, between Loop 410 & Loop 1604. Phone 210/523-3611. ¢¢¢¢¢

Southwest Craft Center. Programs include art school, two galleries, art workshops, lectures & tours. (Daily exc Sun; closed some hols) 300 Augusta, on grounds of Old Ursuline Academy and Convent (1848). Phone 210/224-1848. **Free.**

Splashtown. An 18-acre water recreation theme park with 17 rides and attractions, including wave pool, slide complexes and large children's play area. Changing rooms, showers, lockers, rafts avail. (Memorial Day-Labor Day, daily; May & Sept, wkends) I-35 at exit 160. Phone 210/227-1100. ¢¢¢¢

Steves Homestead (1876). Victorian-era mansion on banks of San Antonio River in the King William Historic District. Period furnishings; landscaped grounds have carriage house, stable; wash house. Tours (daily; closed Jan 1, Thanksgiving, Dec 25) 509 King William St. Phone 210/225-5924. ¢

Tower of the Americas. Stands 750 feet high; observation level at 579 feet; glass-walled elevators. Revolving restaurant at 550-foot level (see RESTAURANTS). (Daily) HemisFair Park. Elevator ¢¢

VIA San Antonio Streetcar. Reproduction of rail streetcar that traveled the streets of San Antonio during the 1920s. Route includes downtown, St Paul's Square, the King William District, El Mercado or Alamo Plaza. (Daily) Phone 210/227-2020.

Vietnam Veterans Memorial. Memorial depicts a scene from the Battle for Hill 881 South—a radioman calling for help for a wounded comrade. In front of Municipal Auditorium, corner of E Martin & Jefferson Sts.

★**Walking tour.** Start at E side of Alamo Plaza (south of E Houston St, north of Crockett St and east of N Alamo) and visit

The Alamo (1718). Defended by the Texas heroes in the 1836 battle. The former church (now the shrine) and the Long Barrack Museum (formerly the Convento) are all that remain of the original mission buildings. The Long Barracks Museum contains an exhibit on Alamo history. Also on the grounds is a research library and museum-souvenir building. (Daily; closed Dec 24-25 & Fri afternoon during Fiesta Week) Phone 210/225-1391. **Free.** The Coppini Cenotaph monument on Alamo Plaza shows carved figures of the heroes. It was installed to mark the Centennial of the Battle of the Alamo. Across the street and S is

Menger Hotel. A famous hostelry in which Robert E. Lee, Theodore Roosevelt and William Jennings Bryan stayed. Bar where Roosevelt recruited the "Rough Riders" is still in use. (See HOTELS) Continue S 2 blks to Market St. Adj is

HemisFair Park. Among HemisFair '68 buildings that remain are the Tower of the Americas and the Institute of Texan Cultures. Also here are Convention Center and Theater for the Performing Arts, urban water park, shops, restaurants. Turn left (W) on Market St to river. Turn left again and walk to the

Arneson River Theatre. 503 Villita St. The audience sits on one side of the river; the stage is on the other. (See SEASONAL EVENTS) Climb steps through the theater and go through the arch. To the left is

La Villita. South of Paseo de La Villita, west of S Alamo St, north of Nueva St and east of S Presa St. This 250-year-old Spanish settlement was reconstructed during 1939 to preserve its unique buildings. A haven in the midst of the city where the old arts and crafts continue to flourish, the area has three patios where various functions are held. (Daily; closed Jan 1, Thanksgiving, Dec 25) Phone 210/299-8610. **Free.** Includes

Cos House. Here, on December 10, 1835, General Perfecto de Cos signed Articles of Capitulation after Texans had taken the town. **Free.** Leave La Villita and walk N on Presa St, crossing the river to the

Hertzberg Circus Collection and Museum. Museum and library with more than 20,000 items of circus memorabilia and research material; Clown Alley, restored ticket wagon, Tom Thumb carriage, miniature circus model. Changing exhibits. (Daily exc Sun & major hols) 210 W Market St. Phone 210/207-7810. ¢¢ Adj is an entrance to

Paseo del Rio. This 21-block "River Walk" along the meandering San Antonio River is lined with colorful shops, hotels, popular nightspots and many sidewalk cafes. Water taxis provide transportation. Going west a short distance from the Tower Life Bldg exit is Main Plaza. Across the plaza is

San Fernando Cathedral. The original parish church of Canary Islands settlers. Walk W, on either side of this, one block to

Military Plaza. City Hall stands in the center; on the northwest corner is a statue of Moses Austin, often called the Father of Texas. Just behind City Hall is the

Spanish Governor's Palace (1749). Note date and Hapsburg crest in the keystone. This was the office and residence of Spanish administrators. (Daily; closed Jan 1, Thanksgiving, Dec 25; also Fiesta Fri & 2 weeks following) 105 Military Plaza. Phone 210/224-0601. ¢ From here it is a short distance S to Nueva St and the

José Antonio Navarro State Historical Park. Complex of 3 limestone and adobe houses built circa 1850; home of a Texas patriot. Period furnishings; exhibits and documents. Tours. (Wed-Sat) 228 S Laredo St. Phone 210/226-4801. ¢ Return to Commerce St and continue W to

Market Square. Begins a block W of the palace where you cross San Pedro Creek. The city market offers Mexican goods and food. Return to starting point E along Commerce St.

Annual Events

Livestock Exposition & Rodeo. Joe and Harry Freeman Coliseum, 3201 E Houston St. Phone 210/225-5851. Early-mid-Feb.

Texas Independence Day & Flag Celebration. The Alamo. Mar 2.

Alamo Memorial Service. The Alamo. Mar 6.

Fiesta San Antonio. Celebrating Texas heroes since 1891 with 3 major parades (one on the San Antonio River), sports & food. More than 150 events held throughout city. Phone 210/227-5191. Apr 19-28.

Pilgrimage to the Alamo. Mid-Apr.

Boerne Berges Fest. 30 mi NW on I-10, in Boerne. German Festival of the Hills; continuous German and country & western entertainment; arts & crafts; horse races; pig races; parade; 10K walk; special events. Father's Day wkend.

Texas Folklife Festival. HemisFair Park. Crafts, folk music & dancing, entertainment, food representing more than 30 ethnic groups in Texas. Phone 210/226-7651. Early Aug.

Great Country River Festival. River Walk. Country music. Phone 210/227-4262. Wkend late Sept.

Fiestas Navidenas. Market Square. Christmas festival; bands; Mexican folk dances; Christmas foods. Phone 210/299-8600. Mid-Dec.

Las Posadas. Paseo del Rio. Procession assembles at La Mansion del Rio Hotel (see HOTELS) Song & candlelight procession has been a tradition for more than 250 years. Held in conjunction with **Fiesta de las Luminarias**, the fiesta of lights, when the River Walk is lined with candles. Re-enactment of the Holy Family's search for an inn. Evening ends with piñata party in Plaza Juárez in La Villita. Phone 210/224-6163. Dec.

Seasonal Events

Summer Festival. Performances of Latin-flavored *Fiesta Noche del Rio, Fiesta Flamenca* and *Fandango* at Arneson River Theatre. June-Aug.

Professional sports. Spurs (basketball), Alamodome. Oct-late Apr.

Additional Visitor Information

The Visitor Information Center has many helpful leaflets; contact 317 Alamo Plaza, 78205; 210/299-8155. For further information contact the Convention & Visitors Bureau, PO Box 2277, 78298; 210/270-8700 or 800/447-3372. San Antonio Conservation Society, 107 King William St, 78204, 210/224-6163, provides brochures for a walking tour of the King William Historic District.

City Neighborhoods

Many of the restaurants, unrated dining establishments and some lodgings listed under San Antonio include neighborhoods as well as exact street addresses. Geographic descriptions of these areas are given, followed by a table of restaurants arranged by neighborhood.

Downtown: South of I-35, west of I-35/37, north of Durango St and east of I-10. **North of Downtown:** North of I-35. **South of Downtown:** South of Durango St. **West of Downtown:** West of I-10.

La Villita: Downtown area south of Paseo de la Villita, west of S Alamo St, north of Nueva St and east of S Presa St.

Riverwalk (*Paseo del Rio*): Downtown area along San Antonio River and along canal extending east from the river between E Commerce and Market Sts.

SAN ANTONIO RESTAURANTS
BY NEIGHBORHOOD AREAS

(For full description, see alphabetical listings under Restaurants)

DOWNTOWN

Babylon Grill. 910 S Alamo

Guenther House. 205 E Guenther St

Mi Tierra. 218 Produce Row

Paesano's. 1715 McCullough Ave

Tower Of The Americas. 222 HemisFair Plaza

NORTH OF DOWNTOWN

Aldo's Ristorante. 8539 Fredericksburg Rd

Biga. 206 E Locust St

Billy Blues. 330 E Grayson St

Brazier At Los Patios. 2015 NE Loop I-410

Cappy's. 5011 Broadway St

Cascabel (Sheraton Fiesta). 37 NE Loop 410

Chez Ardid. 1919 San Pedro Ave

Crumpet's. 5800 Broadway St

5050 Diner. 5050 Broadway St

Formosa Gardens. 1011 NE Loop 410

Gazebo At Los Patios. 2015 NE Loop I-410

L'Etoile. 6106 Broadway St

La Calesa. 2103 E Hildebrand Ave

La Fogata. 2427 Vance Jackson Rd

Los Barrios. 4223 Blanco Rd

Luby's Cafeteria. 9919 Colonial Dr

Mencius' Gourmet Hunan. 7959 Fredericksburg Rd

Old San Francisco Steak House. 10223 Sahara St

Romano's Macaroni Grill. 24116 I-10 West

Ruth's Chris Steakhouse. 7720 Jones Maltsberger Rd

SOUTH OF DOWNTOWN

Carranza Meat Market. 701 Austin St

El Mirador. 722 S St Mary's St

WEST OF DOWNTOWN

La Margarita. 120 Produce Row

Pico De Gallo. 111 S Leona Ave

LA VILLITA

Anaqua Grill (Plaza San Antonio Hotel). 555 S Alamo St

Fig Tree. 515 Villita St

Little Rhein Steak House. 231 S Alamo St

Polo's At The Fairmount (Fairmount Hotel). 401 S Alamo St

RIVERWALK

The Bayous. 517 N Presa St

Boudro's, A Texas Bistro. 314 E Commerce St

Casa Rio. 430 E Commerce St

Dick's Last Resort. 406 Navarro St

Lone Star. 237 Losoya

Michelino's. 521 Riverwalk

Pieca d'Italia. 502 Riverwalk

Rio Rio Cantina. 421 E Commerce St

Note: When a listing is located in a town that does not have its own city heading, it will appear under the city nearest to its location. In these cases, the address and town appear in parenthesis immediately following the name of the establishment.

Motels

✔★★★ **BEST WESTERN CONTINENTAL INN.** *9735 I-35N (78233), north of downtown.* 210/655-3510; FAX 210/655-0778. 161 rms, 2 story. S $46-$56; D $58-$68; each addl $4. Crib free. TV; cable (premium). 2 pools; wading pool, whirlpools. Playground. Restaurant 6 am-10 pm. Rm serv. Bar. Ck-out noon. Coin lndry. Meeting rms. Business servs avail. In-rm modem link. Sundries. Some refrigerators. Cr cds: A, C, D, DS, MC, V.

D ⛱ ⊠ 🐾 SC

★★ **COURTYARD BY MARRIOTT.** *8585 Marriott Dr (78229), at Fredericksburg Rd, north of downtown.* 210/614-7100; FAX 210/614-7110. 146 rms, 3 story. S, D $73-$89; each addl (after 4th person) $10; wkend rates. Crib avail. TV; cable (premium). Pool. Complimentary coffee in rms. Restaurant 6:30-10:30 am; Sat, Sun 7 am-noon. Bar 5-10 pm. Ck-out 1 pm. Coin lndry. Meeting rms. In-rm modem link. Valet serv. Exercise equipt; weights, bicycles, whirlpool. Game rm. Refrigerator in suites. Balconies. Cr cds: A, C, D, DS, MC, V.

D ⊠ 🏋 ⊠ 🐾 SC

★★ **HAWTHORN SUITES.** *4041 Bluemel Rd (78240), at I-10, north of downtown.* 210/561-9660; FAX 210/561-9663. 128 kit. suites, 2 story. S, D $89-$129; under 12 free; wkly, wkend rates. Crib free. Pet accepted, some restrictions; $50. TV; cable. Heated pool; whirlpool. Complimentary bkfst; evening refreshments. Ck-out noon. Coin lndry. Meeting rm. Business servs avail. In-rm modem link. Valet serv. Health club privileges. Private patios, balconies. Picnic table. Fireplace in some suites. Cr cds: A, C, D, DS, MC, V.

D 🐾 ⛱ ⊠ 🐾 SC

★★ **HOLIDAY INN EXPRESS AIRPORT.** *95 NE Loop I-410 (78216), near Intl Airport, north of downtown.* 210/308-6700. 154 rms, 10 story. S $75-$89; D $85-$99; under 19 free. Crib free. Pet accepted, some restrictions. TV; cable (premium). Pool. Complimentary continental bkfst. Restaurant adj 11 am-midnight. Ck-out noon. Meeting rms. Business servs avail. In-rm modem link. Coin lndry. Free airport transportation. Cr cds: A, C, D, DS, MC, V.

D 🐾 ⊠ 🐾 SC

★ **HOLIDAY INN EXPRESS SEA WORLD.** *7043 Culebra Rd (78238), west of downtown.* 210/521-1485; FAX 210/520-5924. 72 rms, 2 story. S $59-$99; D $64-$104; each addl $5; under 18 free. Crib free. TV; cable (premium). Pool. Complimentary continental bkfst. Restaurant adj open 24 hrs. Ck-out noon. Meeting rm. Business servs avail. In-rm modem link. Coin lndry. Health club privileges. Cr cds: A, C, D, DS, JCB, MC, V.

D ⛱ ⊠ 🐾 SC

★★ **LA QUINTA INGRAM PARK.** *7134 NW Loop I-410 (78238).* 210/680-8883; FAX 210/681-3877. 195 rms, 3 story. S $59-$76; D $69-$76; suites $76-$122; under 18 free. Crib free. Pet accepted, some restrictions. TV; cable (premium). Pool. Complimentary continental bkfst. Restaurant adj open 24 hrs. Ck-out noon. Meeting rms. Refrigerators in suites. Cr cds: A, C, D, DS, MC, V.

D 🐾 ⛱ ⊠ 🐾 SC

★★ **LA QUINTA-MARKET SQUARE.** *900 Dolorosa St (78207), downtown.* 210/271-0001; FAX 210/228-0663. 124 rms, 2 story. S, D $84-$91; each addl $10; suites $126; under 18 free; higher rates Fiesta wk. Crib free. Pet accepted, some restrictions. TV; cable. Pool. Continental bkfst. Complimentary coffee. Restaurant opp open

24 hrs. Ck-out noon. In-rm modem link. Valet serv. Cr cds: A, C, D, DS, MC, V.

D ⚡ ⤫ ☒ 🔥 SC

★ ★ **SIERRA ROYALE HOTEL.** *6300 Rue Marielyne (78238), north of downtown.* 210/647-0041; res: 800/289-2444; FAX 210/647-4442. 88 kit. suites, 1-2 story. May-Sept: S $89-$99; D $129; each addl $10; monthly rates; lower rates rest of yr. Crib free. TV; cable (premium). Pool; whirlpool. Complimentary continental bkfst; refreshments. Complimentary coffee in rms. Restaurant nearby. Bar. Ck-out noon. Lndry facilities. Meeting rm. Business servs avail. In-rm modem link. Valet serv. Balconies. Picnic tables. Cr cds: A, C, D, DS, MC, V.

D ☒ ☒ 🔥 SC

Motor Hotels

✔ ★ **COMFORT INN AIRPORT.** *2635 NE Loop 410 (78217).* 210/653-9110; FAX 210/653-8615. 203 rms, 6 story. S, D $47-$85. Crib free. Pet accepted; deposit required. TV; cable (premium). Pool. Complimentary continental bkfst. Ck-out noon. Meeting rms. Business servs avail. In-rm modem link. Bellhops. Free airport transportation. Health club privileges. Near airport. Cr cds: A, C, D, DS, MC, V.

☒ ☒ ☒ SC

★ ★ **DRURY INN.** *143 NE Loop 410 (78216), at I-410 & Airport Blvd, near Intl Airport, north of downtown.* 210/366-4300. 125 rms, 4 story. S $69-$79; D $79-$89; each addl $10; under 18 free. Crib free. Pet accepted, some restrictions. TV; cable (premium). Pool. Complimentary bkfst; evening refreshments. Restaurant adj open 24 hrs. Serv bar. Ck-out noon. Coin lndry. Meeting rms. In-rm modem link. Free airport transportation. Some refrigerators. Cr cds: A, C, D, DS, MC, V.

D ⚡ ✈ ☒ ☒ SC

★ ★ **DRURY SUITES.** *8811 Jones Maltzberger Rd (78216), near Intl Airport, north of downtown.* 210/308-8100; FAX 210/308-8100. 139 suites, 6 story. S $105-$115; D $115-$125; each addl $10; under 18 free. Crib free. TV; cable (premium). Pool; whirlpool. Complimentary continental bkfst; evening refreshments. Restaurant opp 6 am-midnight. Ck-out noon. Meeting rm. In-rm modem link. Free airport transportation. Refrigerators. Cr cds: A, C, D, DS, MC, V.

D ☒ ✈ ☒ 🔥 SC

✔ ★ **HAMPTON INN.** *11010 I-10W (78230), north of downtown.* 210/561-9058; FAX 210/690-5566. 122 rms, 6 story. S $54-$85; D $64-$95; each addl $10; suites $89-$129; under 18 free. Crib free. TV; cable (premium). Pool. Complimentary continental bkfst. Complimentary coffee in lobby. Restaurant adj open 24 hrs. Ck-out noon. Meeting rms. In-rm modem link. Valet serv. Health club privileges. Many refrigerators. Cr cds: A, C, D, DS, MC, V.

D ☒ ☒ 🔥 SC

★ ★ **HOLIDAY INN RIVERWALK NORTH.** *110 Lexington Ave (78205), downtown.* 210/223-9461; FAX 210/223-9267. 324 rms, 9 story. S, D $79-$139; suites $150-$450; under 18 free. Crib free. Pool. TV; cable (premium). Restaurant 6 am-2 pm, 5-10 pm. Rm serv. Bar 2 pm-midnight. Ck-out noon. Coin lndry. Meeting rms. Bellhops. Gift shop. Exercise equipt; weights, bicycles, stair machine. Game rm. Refrigerators in suites. On river. Cr cds: A, C, D, DS, JCB, MC, V.

D ☒ ☂ ☒ 🔥 SC

Hotels

★ ★ **EMBASSY SUITES.** *10110 US 281N (78216), near Intl Airport, north of downtown.* 210/525-9999; FAX 210/525-0626. 261 suites, 9 story. S $99-$139; D $109-$159; each addl $20; under 12 free; wkend rates. Crib free. TV; cable (premium). Indoor pool. Complimentary full bkfst. Restaurant 11:30 am-2:30 pm, 5:30-10 pm; Fri, Sat to 11

pm. Bar 11-1 am. Ck-out 1 pm. Meeting rms. Business center. In-rm modem link. Gift shop. Free airport transportation. Exercise equipt; weights, treadmill, whirlpool, sauna. Refrigerators. Cr cds: A, C, D, DS, MC, V.

D ☒ ☂ ✈ ☒ ☒ SC ⚓

★ **EXECUTIVE GUESTHOUSE.** *12828 US 281N (78216), 12 mi N on US 281, exit Bitters, north of downtown.* 210/494-7600; res: 800/362-8700; FAX 210/545-4314. 124 rms, 4 story. S $89-$170; D $99-$170; each addl $10; under 12 free; wkend rates. Crib free. Pet accepted, some restrictions; $100 ($50 refundable). TV; cable. Indoor pool. Complimentary full bkfst; evening refreshments. Complimentary coffee in rms. Ck-out noon. Meeting rms. In-rm modem link. Free airport transportation. Exercise equipt; weights, bicycles, sauna. Bathrm phones, refrigerators; some in-rm whirlpools. Atrium. Cr cds: A, C, D, DS, MC, V.

D ⚡ ☒ ☂ ☒ 🔥 SC

★ ★ **FAIRMOUNT.** *401 S Alamo St (78205), at La Villita.* 210/224-8800; res: 800/642-3363; FAX 210/224-2767. 37 rms, 3 story, 17 suites. S $165-$185; D $175-$195; suites $200-$475; under 12 free. Crib free. Valet parking $8. TV; cable (premium), VCR avail (movies avail). Restaurant (see POLO'S AT THE FAIRMOUNT). Bar 11:30-1 am; entertainment Wed-Sat. Ck-out noon. Meeting rms. Business servs avail. In-rm modem link. Concierge. Bathrm phones. Balconies. Garden courtyard. Offers casual elegance and Southwestern comfort. Near the Riverwalk. Cr cds: A, C, D, DS, MC, V.

D ☒ 🔥 SC

★ ★ **HILTON PALACIO DEL RIO.** *200 S Alamo St (78205), on Riverwalk.* 210/222-1400; FAX 210/270-0761. 481 rms, 22 story. S $155-$185; D $175-$205; each addl $20; suites $325-$550; package plans. Crib free. Pet accepted, some restrictions. Garage $8, valet $18. TV; cable (premium), VCR avail. Pool; poolside serv. Complimentary coffee in rms. Restaurant 6:30-1 am. Bars 11:30-1:30 am, wkends to 2 am; entertainment, dancing. Ck-out 11 am. Convention facilities. Business center. Concierge. Gift shop. Tennis, golf privileges. Exercise equipt; weights, bicycles, whirlpool. Some bathrm phones, refrigerators. Balconies. Luxury level. Cr cds: A, C, D, DS, ER, JCB, MC, V.

D ⚡ ⚓⚓ ☒ ✈ ☒ ☒ SC

★ ★ **HOLIDAY INN-RIVER WALK.** *217 N St Mary's St (78205), on Riverwalk.* 210/224-2500; FAX 210/223-1302. 313 rms, 23 story. S, D $135-$155; suites $225-$350; under 18 free. Crib free. Pet accepted, some restrictions. Valet parking $8; in/out $5. TV; cable (premium). Heated pool; poolside serv. Restaurant 6:30 am-2 pm, 5:30-10 pm. Rm serv 6 am-midnight. Bar noon-12:30 am; Fri, Sat to 2 am; entertainment, dancing exc Sun & Mon. Ck-out noon. Convention facilities. Business servs avail. Exercise equipt; bicycles, treadmill, whirlpool. Refrigerator in suites. Balconies. View of river. Cr cds: A, C, D, DS, JCB, MC, V.

D ⚡ ☒ ☂ 🔥 SC

★ **HOWARD JOHNSON RIVERWALK PLAZA.** *100 Villita St (78205), near La Villita.* 210/226-2271; FAX 210/226-9453. 133 rms, 6 story. S $89; D $95; each addl $10; under 18 free; higher rates Fiesta Wk, special events. Crib free. Garage parking $4.75 in/out. TV; cable (premium). Pool. Complimentary coffee in rms. Restaurant 6:30 am-2 pm, 4-11 pm. Bar 4-11 pm. Ck-out 11 am. Meeting rms. Gift shop. Some balconies. Overlooks river. Cr cds: A, C, D, DS, MC, V.

D ☒ ☒ 🔥 SC

★ ★ **HYATT REGENCY.** *123 Losoya St (78205), on Riverwalk.* 210/222-1234; FAX 210/227-4925. 631 rms, 11 story. S $119-$189; D $130-$214; each addl $20; suites $200-$665; under 18 free; wkend packages. Garage parking $9, valet $12. TV; cable (premium), VCR avail. Pool; poolside serv. Restaurants 6:30 am-11 pm. Bar 11-2 am; entertainment, dancing. Meeting rms. Business center. Concierge. Shopping arcade. Exercise equipt; weights, bicycles, whirlpool. Minibars; some refrigerators. Balconies. River flows through lobby; waterfalls, atrium. Cr cds: A, C, D, DS, JCB, MC, V.

[D] [icons] SC

★ ★ ★ ★ **LA MANSION DEL RIO.** *112 College St (78205), on River Walk.* 210/225-2581; FAX 210/226-0389. Beamed ceilings highlight rooms that overlook a courtyard or the San Antonio River. The property was built around a restored historic 19th-Century law school building. 337 rms, 7 story. S $120-$245; D $145-$270; each addl $25; suites $375-$1,500; under 18 free; wkend rates; Sea World packages. Crib free. Garage $8, valet parking $10. TV; cable, VCR avail. Pool; poolside serv. Supervised child's activities (mid-May-Aug); ages 5-12. Restaurants 6:30 am-10 pm. Rm serv 24 hrs. Bar 11-2 am; entertainment. Ck-out noon. Convention facilities. Business servs avail. In-rm modem link. Concierge. Gift shop. Airport transportation. Minibars. Private patios, balconies. Cr cds: A, C, D, DS, JCB, MC, V.

[D] [icons] SC

★ ★ ★ **MARRIOTT RIVERCENTER.** *101 Bowie St (78205), opp convention Center, on Riverwalk.* 210/223-1000; FAX 210/223-6239. 1,000 units, 38 story, 82 suites. S $172; D $192; each addl $20; suites $225-$950; under 18 free; honeymoon plan. Crib free. Pet accepted. Garage $8, valet $11. TV; cable, VCR avail. Indoor/outdoor pool; poolside serv. Coffee in rms. Restaurant 6 am-midnight. Rm serv 24 hrs. Bar. Ck-out noon. Free lndry facilities. Convention facilities. Business center. In-rm modem link. Concierge. Shopping arcade. Barber, beauty shop. 18-hole golf privileges, greens fee $55, pro, putting green, driving range. Exercise equipt; weight machine, bicycles, whirlpool, sauna. Some refrigerators, wet bars. Balconies. Located on the banks of the San Antonio River and adj to spectacular Rivercenter shopping complex. Luxury level. Cr cds: A, C, D, DS, MC, V.

[D] [icons] SC

★ ★ ★ **MARRIOTT RIVERWALK.** *711 E River Walk (78205), on Riverwalk.* 210/224-4555; FAX 210/224-2754. 500 rms, 30 story. S $139-$185; D $139-$205; each addl $20; suites $395; under 17 free; wkend rates. Crib free. Pet accepted. Garage parking $7, valet $9.95. TV; cable (premium), VCR avail. Indoor/outdoor pool. Restaurant 6:30 am-11 pm. Rm serv 24 hrs. Bar 11:30-2 am; entertainment Tues-Sat, dancing. Ck-out noon. Meeting rms. Business center. In-rm modem link. Gift shop. Golf privileges. Exercise equipt; weights, bicycles, whirlpool, sauna. Some bathrm phones, refrigerators. Balconies. Many rms overlook San Antonio River. Luxury level. Cr cds: A, C, D, DS, ER, JCB, MC, V.

[D] [icons] SC

★ ★ ★ **MENGER.** *204 Alamo Plaza (78205), downtown.* 210/223-4361; res: 800/345-9285; FAX 210/228-0022. 350 rms, 5 story. S $102-$122; D $112-$132; each addl $10; suites $182-$456; under 18 free; package plans. Crib free. Garage $4.95, valet $9.95. TV; cable (premium), VCR avail. Pool. Restaurant 6:30 am-10 pm; wkends to 11 pm. Rm serv 24 hrs. Bar 11 am-midnight; piano bar. Ck-out noon. Convention facilities. Business servs avail. In-rm modem link. Concierge. Shopping arcade. Exercise equipt; bicycle, stair machine, whirlpool, sauna. Balconies. Historic atmosphere. Alamo opp. Cr cds: A, C, D, DS, ER, JCB, MC, V.

[D] [icons] SC

★ ★ ★ **PLAZA SAN ANTONIO.** *555 S Alamo St (78205), in La Villita.* 210/229-1000; res: 800/421-1172; FAX 210/229-1418. This gracious hotel recalls another era, with its croquet lawn, strolling peacocks, and four 19th-century buildings. Guest rooms, decorated in muted colors with reproduction antiques, are elegant but understated. 252 rms, 5-7 story. S $160-$230; D $180-$250; each addl $20; suites $320-$700; under 18 free; wkend rates. Crib free. Pet accepted, some restrictions. Valet parking $8. TV; cable (premium), VCR avail. Pool; poolside serv. Restaurant (see ANAQUA GRILL). Rm serv 24 hrs. Bar noon-1 am; entertainment Thurs-Sat. Ck-out noon. Meeting rms. Business servs avail. In-rm modem link. Concierge. Lighted tennis. Golf privileges. Exercise equipt; weights, bicycles, whirlpool, sauna. Mas-

sage. Complimentary bicycles. Private patios. Balconies. Complimentary newspaper. Cr cds: A, C, D, DS, ER, MC, V.

[D] [icons] SC

★ ★ **RADISSON DOWNTOWN MARKET SQUARE.** *502 W Durango (78207), downtown.* 210/224-7155; FAX 210/224-9130. 250 rms, 6 story. S $69-$119; D $79-$129; each addl $10; suites $135-$195; under 12 free. Crib free. Pet accepted; $50 deposit. TV; cable (premium). Pool. Restaurant 6:30 am-10 pm. Bar noon-midnight. Ck-out noon. Coin lndry. Meeting rms. Free garage parking. Gift shop. Exercise equipt; weights, bicycles, whirlpool. Game rm. Refrigerator in suites. Balconies. Cr cds: A, C, D, DS, MC, V.

[D] [icons] SC

★ ★ **RAMADA EMILY MORGAN.** *705 E Houston St (78205), adj to the Alamo, downtown.* 210/225-8486; res: 800/824-6674; FAX 210/225-7227. 177 rms, 14 story. S $89-$135; D $94-$149; each addl $10; package plans. Crib free. Parking $7. TV; cable (premium). Pool. Complimentary coffee in rms. Restaurant 6:30 am-2 pm, 5-10 pm. Bar 4-11 pm. Ck-out noon. Meeting rms. Business servs avail. In-rm modem link. Exercise equipt; weights, bicycles, whirlpool, sauna. In-rm whirlpools; many refrigerators. Former medical arts bldg (1925); renovated; contemporary decor. Located adjacent to historic Alamo. Cr cds: A, C, D, DS, JCB, MC, V.

[D] [icons] SC

★ ★ **SHERATON FIESTA.** *37 NE Loop 410 (78216), near Intl Airport, north of downtown.* 210/366-2424; FAX 210/341-0410. 290 rms, 5 story. S $120-$140; D $130-$150; each addl $15; suites $220-$290; under 17 free; wkend rates. Crib free. TV; cable (premium). Pool. Restaurants 6:30 am-10 pm; dining rm 6-10:30 pm. Rm serv 24 hrs. Bar 11-2 am; pianist Mon-Thurs, jazz band Fri & Sat. Ck-out noon. Convention facilities. Business servs avail. Free airport transportation. Exercise equipt; weight machine, bicycles, whirlpool, sauna. Some refrigerators. Private patios, balconies. Luxury level. Cr cds: A, C, D, DS, ER, JCB, MC, V.

[D] [icons] SC

★ ★ ★ **SHERATON GUNTER.** *205 E Houston St (78205), downtown.* 210/227-3241; FAX 210/227-3299. 322 rms, 12 story. S $85-$125; D $95-$135; each addl $10; suites $195-$390; under 18 free. Crib free. Garage $9. TV; cable (premium). Heated pool. Coffee in rms. Restaurant 6 am-10 pm; Fri, Sat to 11 pm. Bar 4 pm-2 am; Fri, Sat noon-2 am; Sun to midnight. Ck-out noon. Convention facilities. Business servs avail. In-rm modem link. Barber. Exercise equipt; weights, bicycles, whirlpool. Refrigerators avail. Built 1909. Cr cds: A, C, D, DS, ER, JCB, MC, V.

[D] [icons] SC

★ ★ ★ **ST. ANTHONY.** *300 E Travis St (78205), downtown.* 210/227-4392; res: 800/338-1338; FAX 210/227-0915. 350 rms, 9 story, 42 suites. S $125-$171; D $142-$190; each addl $15; suites $300-$550; under 12 free; wkend rates. Crib free. Garage parking $7, valet $10. Pet accepted; $25 deposit. TV; cable (premium). Heated pool; poolside serv. Restaurant 6:30 am-10 pm. Bar 2 pm-2 am. Ck-out noon. Convention facilities. Business servs avail. Gift shop. Exercise equipt; weight machine, rowers. Game rm. Refrigerators avail. This landmark property, built in 1909, is famous for its elegant lobby. Cr cds: A, C, D, DS, ER, JCB, MC, V.

[D] [icons] SC

★ ★ ★ **WYNDHAM.** *9821 Colonnade Blvd (78230), north of downtown.* 210/691-8888; res: 800/822-4200; FAX 210/691-1128. 326 rms, 20 story. S $119-$150; D $129-$160; each addl $10; suites $275-$535; under 18 free; wkend rates. Crib free. TV; cable. 2 pools, 1 indoor; poolside serv. Restaurant 6:30 am-11 pm. Bar 3 pm-1 am, Sun noon-1 am; entertainment. Ck-out noon. Meeting rms. Business servs avail. In-rm modem link. Gift shop. Free airport transportation. Exercise equipt; weights, bicycles, whirlpools, sauna. Some refrigerators. Garden with fountain. Crystal chandelier, marble in lobby. Cr cds: A, C, D, DS, ER, JCB, MC, V.

Inns

★ **B & B ON THE RIVER.** *129 Woodward Place (78204), Riverwalk.* 210/225-6333; FAX 210/271-3077. 11 rms (5 with shower only), 3 story. S, D $99-$135; suite $150-$165; each addl $20; under 6 free. TV. Complimentary full bkfst. Ck-out 11 am, ck-in noon. Balconies. Victorian decor; antiques. Totally nonsmoking. Cr cds: A, DS, MC, V.

★ ★ **BEAUREGARD HOUSE.** *215 Beauregard St (78204), downtown.* 210/222-1198; res: 800/841-9377. 3 rms, 2 with shower only, 2 story. S $75; D $85; each addl $11; under 8 free; package plans. Crib avail. TV in sitting rm; cable. Complimentary full bkfst 7-9 am. Complimentary tea. Restaurant nearby. Ck-out 11 am, ck-in 1 pm. Lndry facilities. Restored Victorian house (1902) in King William District; Riverwalk 1 blk. Totally nonsmoking. Cr cds: MC, V.

★ ★ **BECKMANN.** *222 E Guenther St (78204), downtown.* 210/229-1449; res: 800/945-1449. 5 rms (4 with shower only), 2 story, 2 suites. S, D $80-$100; suites $115-$130. Children over 12 yrs only. TV; cable. Complimentary full bkfst. Restaurant opp 7 am-3 pm. Ck-out 11 am, ck-in 4-6 pm. Luggage handling. Victorian house (1886) with wrap-around porch. Many antiques. Totally nonsmoking. Cr cds: A, D, DS, MC, V.

★ ★ ★ **OGE HOUSE.** *209 Washington (78204), Riverwalk.* 210/223-2353; res: 800/242-2770; FAX 210/226-5812. 9 rms (1 with shower only), 3 story. S, D $110-$195. Children over 16 only. TV; cable. Complimentary continental bkfst. Ck-out 11 am, ck-in 3 pm. In-rm modem link. Luggage handling. Refrigerators, many fireplaces. Mansion built 1857 for prominent rancher; antiques. Smoking on veranda only. Cr cds: A, C, D, DS, MC, V.

★ ★ **RIVERWALK.** *329 Old Guilbeau (78204), on Riverwalk.* 210/212-8300; FAX 210/229-9422. 11 rms (shower only), 2 story. S, D $89-$145; each $20; higher rates hols (2-3 day min). TV; cable. Complimentary coffee in rms; continental bkfst. Ck-out 11 am, ck-in 3 pm. Refrigerators. Two authentic log cabins moved here from Tennessee. Totally nonsmoking. Cr cds: A, DS, MC, V.

Resort

★ ★ ★ **HYATT REGENCY HILL COUNTRY.** *9800 Hyatt Resort Dr (78251), north of downtown.* 210/647-1234; FAX 210/681-9681. A 56-foot-long wood-and-copper bar, the world's largest antler chandelier, and a man-made river for tubing are on this cushy Texas ranch-style property, spread out over 200 beautifully landscaped acres. 500 units, 4 story. Mid-Mar-Nov: S, D $220-$280; each addl $25; suites $405-$2,250; under 18 free; holiday, golf plans; lower rates rest of yr. Parking; valet $7. TV; cable. 2 heated pools; poolside serv. Supervised child's activities; ages 3-12. Restaurants 6:30 am-10 pm. Rm serv 6 am-midnight. Bar 4 pm-1 am; entertainment. Ck-out noon. Coin lndry. Convention facilities. Business center. In-rm modem link. Bellhops. Valet serv. Concierge. Shopping arcade. Sundries. Lighted tennis, pro. 18-hole golf, pro, greens fee $80-$90. Bicycle rentals. Exercise rm; instructor, weights, treadmill, whirlpool, sauna. Masseuse. Lawn games. Rec rm. Game rm. Refrigerators. Balconies. Luxury level. Cr cds: A, C, D, DS, JCB, MC, V.

Restaurants

★ ★ **ALDO'S RISTORANTE.** *8539 Fredericksburg Rd (78229), north of downtown.* 210/690-2536. Hrs: 11 am-10 pm; Fri to 11 pm; Sat 5-11 pm; Sun from 5 pm. Closed most major hols. Res accepted. Italian menu. Bar. Semi-a la carte: lunch $6.25-$9.95, dinner $8.95-$19.95. Specialty: salmone alla Pavarotti. Valet parking. Outdoor dining. Intimate dining in early 1900s house. Cr cds: A, C, D, DS, MC, V.

★ ★ ★ **ANAQUA GRILL.** *(See Plaza San Antonio Hotel)* 210/229-1000. Hrs: 7 am-2 pm, 6-10 pm; Fri & Sat to 11 pm; Sun brunch 10 am-2 pm. Res accepted. Bar. A la carte entrees: bkfst $4.25-$9.25, dinner $6.95-$17.95. Semi-a la carte: lunch $7.50-$12. Tapas $3.50-$9.95. Sun brunch $12.50-$17.95. Child's meals. Specializes in fresh seafood, Southwestern and Eurasian cuisine. Also dietary menu. Own baking. Valet parking. Outdoor dining. View of garden, courtyard, fountains. Cr cds: A, C, D, DS, ER, MC, V.

★ ★ **BABYLON GRILL.** *910 S Alamo (78205), downtown.* 210/229-9335. Hrs: 11 am-11 pm; Fri & Sat to midnight; Sun brunch to 3 pm. Closed July 4, Dec 25. Res accepted. Mediterranean menu. Bar. Semi-a la carte: lunch $4.95-$7.95, dinner $9.95-$17.95. Sun brunch $15.95. Child's meals. Specialties: roasted honey-comino pork loin, grilled lamb loin, paella. Flamenco guitarist Fri. Parking. In 1920s fruit market. Cr cds: A, DS, MC, V.

★ **THE BAYOUS.** *517 N Presa St, on Riverwalk.* 210/223-6403. Hrs: 11:30 am-11 pm; Fri, Sat to midnight; Sun brunch 11:30 am-3 pm. Res accepted. Cajun, Amer menu. Bar. Semi-a la carte: lunch $4.95-$9.95, dinner $7.95-$19.95. Sun brunch $10.95. Child's meals. Specialties: red snapper Valerie, shrimp Barataria, marinated crab claws. Oyster bar. Entertainment. Parking. Outdoor dining. Dining rm overlooks river. Cr cds: A, C, D, DS, MC, V.

★ ★ **BIGA.** *206 E Locust St, north of downtown.* 210/225-0722. Hrs: 11 am-2 pm, 6-10:30 pm; Mon from 6 pm; Fri 11 am-2 pm, 5:30-11 pm; Sat 5:30-11 pm. Closed Sun; some major hols. Wine, beer. Semi-a la carte: lunch $4.95-$8, dinner $11-$25. Entertainment Thurs. Specializes in Gulf seafood, breads, wild game. Parking. In converted old mansion. Extensive wine selection. Cr cds: A, C, D, DS, MC, V.

★ ★ **BOUDRO'S, A TEXAS BISTRO.** *314 E Commerce St, on Riverwalk.* 210/224-8484. Hrs: 11 am-11 pm; Fri, Sat to midnight. Res accepted. Southwestern menu. A la carte entrees: lunch $4-$9, dinner $12-$22. Specialties: blackened prime rib, smoked shrimp enchiladas, fresh Gulf red snapper. Outdoor dining. Historic building; pictographs on walls, original artwork. Cr cds: A, C, D, DS, MC, V.

★ ★ **CAPPY'S.** *5011 Broadway St, north of downtown.* 210/828-9669. Hrs: 11 am-10 pm; Fri, Sat to 11 pm; Sun 10:30 am-10 pm; Sun brunch to 3 pm. Closed July 4, Thanksgiving, Dec 25. Res accepted. Bar. Semi-a la carte: lunch $6.95-$8.95, dinner $10.95-$17.50. Sat, Sun brunch $7.50-$11.95. Child's meals. Specialties: chicken with artichoke hearts, snapper. Parking. Outdoor dining. Local artworks on display. Totally nonsmoking. Cr cds: A, C, D, MC, V.

★ **CARRANZA MEAT MARKET.** *701 Austin St, south of downtown.* 210/223-0903. Hrs: 11 am-2 pm, 5-10 pm; Fri to 11 pm; Sat 5-11 pm. Closed Sun; Thanksgiving, Dec 25. Amer menu. Wine, beer. Semi-a la carte: lunch $5.95-$28.95, dinner $7.95-$28.95. Specializes in steak, seafood, pasta. Parking. Originally a saloon and nightclub (1870). Family-owned. Cr cds: A.

✔★ **CASA RIO.** *430 E Commerce St, on Riverwalk.* 210/225-6718. Hrs: 11 am-11 pm. Closed Jan 1, Dec 25. Mexican menu. Serv bar. Semi-a la carte: lunch, dinner $3.95-$8.95. Child's meals. Specialties: green chicken enchiladas, fajitas, pollo asado. Parking. Outdoor dining. Riverboat dining by res. On San Antonio River. Family-owned. Cr cds: A, C, D, DS, MC, V.

★★ **CASCABEL.** *(See Sheraton Fiesta Hotel)* 210/366-2424. Hrs: 10:30 am-2 pm, 5:30-10 pm; Fri & Sat to 11 pm. Closed Sun; Thanksgiving, Dec 25. Res accepted. Southwestern menu. Bar. Semi-a la carte: lunch $9-$12, dinner $15-$25. Specialties: grilled salmon salad, sugar-cured black Angus tenderloin, achiote tempura shrimp. Parking. Cr cds: A, D, DS, MC, V.

★★★ **CHEZ ARDID.** *1919 San Pedro Ave, north of downtown.* 210/732-3203. Hrs: 6-10:30 pm. Closed Sun; Jan 1, Thanksgiving, Dec 25. Res accepted. French menu. Bar. Wine cellar. Semi-a la carte: dinner $17-$25. Specialties: grilled quail salad, crab meat Chez Ardid, rack of lamb, poached lobster. Valet parking. Pianist Fri & Sat. Chef-owned. Cr cds: A, C, D, MC, V.

★★ **CRUMPET'S.** *5800 Broadway St, north of downtown.* 210/821-5454. Hrs: 11 am-2:30 pm, 5:30-10 pm; Fri to 11 pm; Sat 11 am-3 pm, 5:30-11 pm; Sun 11 am-3 pm, 5-9 pm. Closed Jan 1, Dec 25. Res accepted. Bar. Wine list. Complete meals: lunch $6.95-$7.95, dinner $8.95-$16.50. Brunch $14.95. Specializes in beef, pasta, seafood. Own pasta, pastries. Classical musicians. Cr cds: A, C, D, DS, MC, V.

★★★ **FIG TREE.** *515 Villita St, in La Villita.* 210/224-1976. Hrs: 6-11 pm. Closed Jan 1, Thanksgiving, Dec 24, 25. Res accepted. Continental menu. Serv bar. Complete meal: dinner $45. Specializes in seafood, châteaubriand, rack of lamb. Outdoor dining. Elegant decor. Overlooks Riverwalk. Cr cds: A, C, D, DS, MC, V.

★★ **FORMOSA GARDENS.** *1011 NE Loop 410 (78209), north of downtown.* 210/828-9988. Hrs: 11 am-2:30 pm, 5-10 pm; early-bird dinner 5-6 pm. Closed Thanksgiving, Dec 25. Res accepted. Chinese menu. Bar. Semi-a la carte: lunch $4.75-$5.25, dinner $6.25-$25. Specializes in Hunan, Szechuan dishes. Valet parking. Outdoor dining. Dining room divided into small sections. Cr cds: A, C, D, DS, MC, V.

★★★ **L'ETOILE.** *6106 Broadway St, at Albany St, north of downtown.* 210/826-4551. Hrs: 11 am-2:30 pm, 5:30-10 pm; Fri, Sat to 11 pm; Sun 5-9:30 pm; early-bird dinner 5:30-6:30 pm. Res accepted. French menu. Bar. Wine list. Semi-a la carte: lunch $6.95-$14.95, dinner $9.95-$21.95. Specializes in pasta, fresh seafood, veal. Buffet (lunch). Own baking, pasta. Valet parking. Outdoor dining. French Provincial, garden-style dining rm. Cr cds: A, C, D, MC, V.

✔★ **LA CALESA.** *2103 E Hildebrand Ave, at Broadway St, north of downtown.* 210/822-4475. Hrs: 11 am-9:30 pm; Fri to 10:30 pm; Sat 9 am-10:30 pm; Sun 9 am-9 pm. Closed Easter, Thanksgiving, Dec 25. Mexican menu. Serv bar. Semi-a la carte: lunch, dinner $4.15-$11.95. Child's meals. Specialties: cochinita pibil, pollo en Escabeche. Parking. Outdoor dining. Authentic Mexican cuisine. Totally nonsmoking. Cr cds: A, C, D, DS, MC, V.

✔★ **LA FOGATA.** *2427 Vance Jackson Rd, 6 mi N on I-10, Vance Jackson exit, north of downtown.* 210/340-1337. Hrs: 11 am-11 pm; Fri to midnight; Sat & Sun 7:30 am-midnight. Closed Jan 1, Dec 25. Mexican menu. Bar. Semi-a la carte: bkfst $3.25-$4.25, lunch, dinner $5.25-$14.95. Child's meals. Specializes in enchilada verdes, Mexican bkfst. Own tortillas. Parking. Outdoor dining. Mexican decor. Cr cds: A, C, D, DS, MC, V.

✔★ **LA MARGARITA.** *120 Produce Row, west of downtown.* 210/227-7140. Hrs: 11 am-10 pm; Fri, Sat to midnight. Mexican menu. Bar. Semi-a la carte: lunch, dinner $4.95-$9.50. Child's meals. Specializes in fajitas, shrimp cocktail, oyster cocktail. Entertainment. Parking. Outdoor dining. Restored farmers market building (1910). Cr cds: A, C, D, DS, MC, V.

★★ **LITTLE RHEIN STEAK HOUSE.** *231 S Alamo St, in La Villita.* 210/225-2111. Hrs: 5-11 pm. Closed Jan 1, Thanksgiving, Dec 24-25. Res accepted. Bar. Semi-a la carte: dinner $13.75-$29.95. Child's meals. Specializes in steak, seafood, lamb chops. Terrace dining. Overlooks San Antonio River and Outdoor theater. First 2-story structure in San Antonio (1847). Cr cds: A, C, D, DS, MC, V.

★★ **LONE STAR.** *237 Losoya (78205), on Riverwalk.* 210/223-9374. Hrs: 11 am-10:30 pm; Fri, Sat to 11:30 pm. Closed Thanksgiving, Dec 24 & 25. Bar. Semi-a la carte: dinner $7.95-$19.95. Child's meals. Specializes in steak. Outdoor dining. Cr cds: A, DS, MC, V.

✔★ **LOS BARRIOS.** *4223 Blanco Rd (78212), north of downtown.* 210/732-6017. Hrs: 10 am-10 pm; Fri & Sat to midnight; Sun from 9 am. Closed Easter, Thanksgiving, Dec 25. Mexican menu. Bar. Semi-a la carte: lunch, dinner $5-$14. Child's meals. Specialties: enchilada verdes, cabrito, churrasco. Parking. Traditional Mexican dining. Cr cds: A, C, D, DS, MC, V.

★ **MENCIUS' GOURMET HUNAN.** *7959 Fredericksburg Rd, north of downtown.* 210/690-1848. Hrs: 11 am-2:15 pm, 5-10 pm; Sun-Tues to 9:30 pm. Closed Jan 1, Thanksgiving, Dec 25. Res accepted. Chinese menu. Bar. Semi-a la carte: lunch $4.75-$5.25, dinner $5.95-$14.95. Specialties: Mencius beef, shrimp & scallops, General Tso's chicken. Parking. Cr cds: A, C, D, MC, V.

✔★ **MI TIERRA.** *218 Produce Row, at Market Square, downtown.* 210/225-1262. Open 24 hrs. Mexican menu. Bar 5 pm-2 am; Sat, Sun from noon. Semi-a la carte: bkfst $2.50-$6.75, lunch, dinner $2.98-$9.95. Specializes in fajitas, cabrito, Mexican dinner combinations. Entertainment. Outdoor dining. Located in old farmers market building; built 1910. Family-owned. Cr cds: A, C, D, DS, MC, V.

★ **MICHELINO'S.** *521 Riverwalk, on Riverwalk.* 210/223-2939. Hrs: 11 am-11 pm; Fri, Sat to 11:30 pm. Northern Italian menu. Bar. Semi-a la carte: lunch $4.25-$12.25, dinner $7.95-$14.95. Child's meals. Specializes in fettucine verde, chicken Florentine, pizza. Outdoor dining. Cr cds: A, DS, MC, V.

★★ **OLD SAN FRANCISCO STEAK HOUSE.** *10223 Sahara St (10223), north of downtown.* 210/342-2321. Hrs: 11 am-2 pm (Mon-Fri), 5-11 pm; Fri, Sat to midnight; Sun 10:30 am-10 pm. Res accepted. Bar. A la carte: lunch $6.95-$13.95. Complete meals: dinner $10.95-$29.95. Sun brunch $7.95-$10.95. Child's meals. Specializes in steak, poultry, prime rib, seafood. Pianist; girl on red velvet swing. Valet parking. Victorian decor. Cr cds: A, C, D, DS, MC, V.

★★ **PAESANO'S.** *1715 McCullough Ave, downtown.* 210/226-9541. Hrs: 11 am-2 pm, 5-11 pm; Sat 5-11:30 pm; Sun 5-10 pm. Closed Mon; some major hols. Northern Italian menu. Bar. A la carte entrees: lunch $6.50-$7.95, dinner $6.95-$18.50. Specialties: shrimp Paesano, penne all'arrabbiata, veal Christina. Parking. Cr cds: A, C, D, MC, V.

⊡ ⤴

★ **PICO DE GALLO.** *111 S Leona Ave (78201), west of downtown.* 210/225-6060. Hrs: 7-10 am; Fri & Sat to 2 am; Sun from 8 am. Closed Thanksgiving. Mexican menu. Bar. Semi-a la carte: bkfst $3.95-$5.95, lunch, dinner $4.75-$8.95. Child's meals. Specializes in fajitas. Entertainment Wed-Sun. Mexican artifacts. Family-owned. Cr cds: A, C, D, DS, MC, V.

⤴

★ **PIECA D'ITALIA.** *502 Riverwalk (78205), on Riverwalk.* 210/227-5511. Hrs: 10:30 am-10:30 pm; Fri & Sat to midnight. Closed Thanksgiving, Dec 25. Res accepted. Italian menu. Wine, beer. Semi-a la carte: bkfst $1.99-$4.89, lunch, dinner $3.99-$15.95. Specializes in fresh pasta, pizza, orange roughy. Patio dining overlooking river, many tables under Crockett St Bridge. Cr cds: A, C, D, DS, MC, V.

⊡

★ ★ ★ **POLO'S AT THE FAIRMOUNT.** *(See Fairmount Hotel)* 210/224-8800. Hrs: 7-10:30 am, 11:30 am-2 pm, 6-10 pm; Fri to 10:30 pm; Sat 7-10:30 am, 6-10:30 pm; Sun 7 am-noon. Res accepted. Bar 11:30-1 am. A la carte entrees: bkfst $5-$8, lunch $5-$11.95, dinner $17-$35. Child's meals. Specialties: grilled game, Norwegian salmon, spinach salad with grilled quail. Valet parking. Outdoor dining. Cr cds: A, C, D, DS, MC, V.

⊡ ⤴

✔ ★ **RIO RIO CANTINA.** *421 E Commerce St, on Riverwalk.* 210/226-8462. Hrs: 11 am-11 pm; Fri & Sat to midnight. California, Tex-Mex menu. Bar. Semi-a la carte: lunch $4.95-$10, dinner $6.95-$15. Child's meals. Specialties: botano grande, carmones al mojo de ajo, enchiladas Rio Rio. Outdoor riverside dining. Cr cds: A, C, D, DS, MC, V.

⊡ ⤴

★ ★ **ROMANO'S MACARONI GRILL.** *24116 I-10 West (78257), 13 N on I-10W at Leon Springs exit, north of downtown.* 210/698-0003. Hrs: 11 am-10 pm; Fri, Sat to 11 pm. Closed Thanksgiving, Dec 25. Italian menu. Wine, beer. Semi-a la carte: lunch $5.95-$10.95, dinner $6.95-$16.50. Specializes in pasta, calamari fritti. Parking. No cr cds accepted.

⤴

★ ★ **RUTH'S CHRIS STEAKHOUSE.** *7720 Jones Maltsberger Rd, at Concord Plaza, north of downtown.* 210/821-5051. Hrs: 5-11 pm; Sun 4-10 pm. Closed Thanksgiving, Dec 25. Res accepted. Bar. A la carte entrees: dinner $17.95-$29.95. Specializes in steak, live Maine lobster, lamb. Parking. Upscale Southwestern decor. Cr cds: A, C, D, MC, V.

⊡ ⤴

★ ★ **TOWER OF THE AMERICAS.** *222 HemisFair Plaza, downtown.* 210/223-3101. Hrs: 11 am-2 pm, 5:30-10 pm; Fri to 10:30 pm; Sat 11 am-2:30 pm, 5:30-10:30 pm; Sun 11 am-2:30 pm. Closed Dec 25. Res accepted. Bar 5-11 pm; Fri, Sat 11-12:30 am. Complete meals: lunch $6.25-$12.95, dinner $11.95-$21.95. Child's meals. Specializes in lobster, steak, prime rib. Parking. Revolving tower; view of city. Elvtr fee is added to bill. Cr cds: A, C, D, DS, MC, V.

⊡ SC ⤴

Unrated Dining Spots

5050 DINER. *5050 Broadway St, north of downtown.* 210/828-4386. Hrs: 11-2 am. Res accepted. Mexican, Amer menu. Bar. Semi-a la carte: lunch, dinner $3.50-$7.50. Child's meals. Specialties: chicken-fried steak, Tex-Mex dishes. Parking. Neighborhood bistro atmosphere; art deco decor. Cr cds: A, D, DS, MC, V.

⊡ ⤴

BILLY BLUES. *330 E Grayson St, north of downtown.* 210/225-7409. Hrs: 11-1 am; wkends to 2 am. Closed some major hols. Res accepted. Bar. Semi-a la carte: lunch, dinner $4.25-$11.95. Child's meals. Specialties: smoked sausage, barbecued ribs, barbecued brisket. Own desserts. Entertainment. Parking. Outdoor dining. Features rock bands and dining in the "Billy Dome." Cr cds: A, D, DS, MC, V.

⊡ ⤴

BRAZIER AT LOS PATIOS. *2015 NE Loop I-410, Starcrest exit, north of downtown.* 210/655-9270. Hrs: 11:30 am-10 pm. Closed Mon; Nov-Feb. Southwestern menu. Bar. Semi-a la carte: lunch, dinner $5.95-$14.95. Specializes in mesquite-grilled steak, fish, chicken. Salad bar. Parking. Outdoor dining. On Salado Creek. Cr cds: A, D, DS, MC, V.

⤴

DICK'S LAST RESORT. *406 Navarro St, on Riverwalk.* 210/224-0026. Hrs: 11-2 am. Bar. Semi-a la carte: lunch $3.75-$8.95, dinner $8.95-$16.95. Specializes in barbecued ribs, fried catfish, honey-roasted chicken. Entertainment. Outdoor dining. Honky-tonk decor. Cr cds: A, C, D, DS, MC, V.

⊡ ⤴

EL MIRADOR. *722 S St Mary's St, south of downtown.* 210/225-9444. Hrs: 6:30 am-3 pm; Wed-Sat also 5:30-10 pm; Sun 9 am-3 pm. Closed some major hols. Mexican menu. Wine, beer. Semi-a la carte: bkfst $1.50-$4, lunch $2.50-$5.50, dinner $4.95-$11. Specialties: xochitl soup, Azteca soup. Parking. Cr cds: MC, V.

⊡ ⤴

GAZEBO AT LOS PATIOS. *2015 NE Loop I-410, Starcrest exit, north of downtown.* 210/655-6190. Hrs: 11:30 am-2:30 pm; Sat to 3 pm; Sun 11 am-3 pm. Closed Jan 1, Thanksgiving, Dec 25. Continental and Mexican menu. Bar 11:30 am-2:30 pm. Semi-a la carte: lunch $7.50-$9.95. Sun brunch $13.95. Specializes in crepes, chicken, quiche. Parking. Outdoor dining. Cr cds: A, DS, MC, V.

⤴

GUENTHER HOUSE. *205 E Guenther St (78204), downtown.* 210/227-1061. Hrs: 7 am-3 pm; Sun 8 am-2 pm. Closed Jan 1, Thanksgiving, Dec 25. Semi-a la carte: bkfst $2.50-$5.95, lunch $4.50-$6.25. Specializes in Belgian waffles, chicken salad, pastries. Parking. Outdoor dining. House built by founder of Pioneer Flour Mills (1860). Museum and gift shop on grounds. Cr cds: A, DS, MC, V.

LUBY'S CAFETERIA. *9919 Colonial Dr, north of downtown.* 210/696-2741. Hrs: 10:45 am-8:30 pm; winter to 8:15. Closed Dec 25. Avg ck: lunch $4.20, dinner $4.75. Specializes in fish, chicken-fried steak, fresh vegetables. Parking. Cr cds: DS, MC, V.

SC ⤴

San Jacinto Battleground (D-8)

(see Houston)

San Marcos (D-6)

(See New Braunfels, Seguin)

Founded 1851 **Pop** 28,743 **Elev** 578 ft **Area code** 512 **Zip** 78666
Information Convention & Visitors Bureau, PO Box 2310; 512/396-2495 or 800/782-7653, ext 177.

Fissures in the rocks of the Balcones escarpment pour out clear spring water to form the San Marcos River. A group of Franciscan monks are said to have discovered these springs on St Mark's Day in 1709, giving the river, and hence the town, its name. This is the center of farming and ranching for this part of the black lands. To the west above the Balcones escarpment lies scenic hill country with fine deer hunting.

What to See and Do

Aquarena Springs. Glass-bottom boats, from which aquatic plants, fish & spring formations can be seen; ferryboat or skyride to Hillside Gardens; 300-ft Sky Spiral; Texana Village; bird show. Submarine theater with underwater show. Restaurants. (Daily; closed Dec 25) 1 Aquarena Springs Dr. Phone 512/396-8900 or 800/999-9767. All-Adventure Pass ¢¢¢¢

Fishing from banks of the San Marcos River (license required); also scuba diving.

Lockhart State Park. Approx 260 acres. Pool (Memorial Day-Labor Day). 9-hole golf (fee). Picnicking. Improved camping. Standard fees. (Daily) Approx 20 mi NE via TX 80/142. Phone 512/398-3479. Per vehicle ¢¢

San Marcos Factory Shops. Over 100 outlet stores can be found in this outdoor shopping mall. Food court, winery. (Daily) 3939 I-35 S, at exit 200. Phone 512/396-2200.

Wonder World. Tours of cave formed by an earthquake. Cave temperature approx 70°F. Antigravity House, observation tower, train ride through wildlife park and waterfall. Picnic areas, snack bar. (Daily) 1000 Prospect St, W side of town. Phone 512/392-3760. ¢¢¢¢

Annual Events

Tours of Distinction. Spring tour of historic houses & restored building. Departs from old Mayor's house; docents & map/brochure. 1st wknd May.

Texas Water Safari. Five-day, 262-mile "world's toughest boat race." Canoe race starts in San Marcos at Aquarena Springs and ends in Seadrift. Contact Rte 1, Box 55R, Martindale 78655; 512/357-6113. 2nd Sat June.

Republic of Texas Chilympiad. Hays County Civic Center. Men's state chili championship cook-off (more than 500 entries); parade; 5K race; nightly concerts. Phone 512/396-5400. 3rd wknd Sept.

Motels

★ ★ **AQUARENA SPRINGS INN.** *1 Aquarena Springs Dr, 1 mi NW, off I-35 at Aquarena Springs Dr, in amusement park, on San Marcos River.* 512/396-8901. 24 rms, 2 story, 3 kits. S $59-$69, D $69-$79; each addl $10; kit. units $79-$99; under 15 free. Crib free. TV; cable (premium). Pool; wading pool, lifeguard. Complimentary continental bkfst. Restaurant adj 11 am-9:30 pm. Ck-out noon. Business servs avail. 9-hole golf. Garden trails. Some refrigerators. Balconies. Cr cds: A, C, D, DS, MC, V.

⊡ 🎿 ⋙ ⊠ 🔥 SC

★ **HOLIDAY INN.** *1635 Aquarena Springs Dr.* 512/353-8011; FAX 512/396-8062. 100 rms, 2 story. S $59-$79; D $69-$89; each addl (after 2nd person) $5; under 18 free. Pet accepted. TV; cable. Pool. Restaurant 6:30 am-2 pm, 5-10 pm. Rm serv. Bar 5 pm-midnight,

Sat to 1 am. Ck-out noon. Meeting rms. In-rm modem link. Valet serv. Cr cds: A, C, D, DS, JCB, MC, V.

⊡ 🚶 ⋙ ⊠ 🔥 SC

★ ★ **LA QUINTA.** *1619 I-35 N.* 512/392-8800; FAX 512/392-0324. 82 rms, 2 story. S $59-$89; D $69-$89; under 18 free. Crib free. Pet accepted, some restrictions. TV; cable. Heated pool; whirlpool. Complimentary continental bkfst. Restaurant adj open 24 hrs. Ck-out noon. Meeting rm. Some refrigerators. Cr cds: A, C, D, DS, MC, V.

⊡ 🚶 ⋙ ⊠ 🔥 SC

Inn

★ ★ ★ **CRYSTAL RIVER INN.** *326 W Hopkins.* 512/396-3739; FAX 512/353-3248. 12 rms in 3 bldgs, 2 story, 4 suites. Some rm phones. S $55-$95; D $60-$110; each addl $7.50-$10; suites $90-$130. Adults preferred. TV in some rms; cable. Complimentary full bkfst, tea/sherry. Catered meals avail on request. Restaurant nearby. Ck-out noon, ck-in 2 pm. Valet serv. Converted former homes of early settlers. Picnics, themed wknds; river trips avail. Formal gardens with fountain. Cr cds: A, C, D, DS, MC, V.

⊠ 🔥

Seguin (D-6)

(See New Braunfels, San Antonio, San Marcos)

Founded 1838 **Pop** 18,853 **Elev** 520 ft **Area code** 210 **Zip** 78155
Information Chamber of Commerce, 427 N Austin St, PO Box 710; 210/379-6382.

Seguin (pronounced se-GEEN), on the Guadalupe River, was first settled by Southern planters. The town later became a haven for German immigrants. Widely diversified crops, light manufacturing and oil contribute to its prosperity. Within the county, six power dams on the Guadalupe form lakes providing generous recreational facilities for water sports and fishing.

Annual Events

Youth Livestock Show. Feb.

Texas Ladies' State Chili Cookoff. Apr.

Guadalupe County Fair. 2nd wknd Oct.

Shamrock (F-3)

(See Amarillo)

Pop 2,286 **Elev** 2,310 ft **Area code** 806 **Zip** 79079
Information Chamber of Commerce, 121 N Main, PO Box 588; 806/256-3966.

Located in the eastern part of the Panhandle natural gas field, Shamrock has a gas pumping station and is also a farming center. The town's water tower on Main Street is said to be the tallest in the state.

What to See and Do

Pioneer West Museum. Renovated hotel furnished with items depicting pioneer days; kitchen, parlor and bedroom, doctor and dentist offices, Indian room, country store, school room, chapel, early barbershop, war room, Fort Elliot room and "Prairie-to-the-Moon" room honoring astronaut Alan Bean. Located on grounds is Justice of the Peace office and lawyer's office building. (Mon-Fri; wknds by appt; closed some hols) Donation. 204 N Madden St. Phone 806/256-3941.

Annual Event

St Patrick's Day Celebration. Parade, Miss Irish Rose Pageant, TRA team roping, entertainment, dances, 10K run, carnival, chili cookoff, banquet. Wkend nearest Mar 17.

Motels

★ ★ ★ **BEST WESTERN IRISH INN.** 301 I-40E. 806/256-2106. 157 rms, 2 story. S $40-$56; D $44-$58; each addl $4; under 12 free. Crib $3. TV; cable. Indoor pool; whirlpool. Restaurant open 24 hrs. Private club 5 pm-midnight. Ck-out 1 pm. Coin lndry. Meeting rm. Gift shop. Cr cds: A, C, D, DS, JCB, MC, V.

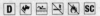

✔ ★ **WESTERN.** 104 E 12th St. 806/256-3244; FAX 806/256-3244, ext. 128. 24 rms, 2 story. S $25-$30; D $30-$35; each addl $5. Crib $2. Pet accepted. TV; cable (premium). Pool. Restaurant 6 am-9:30 pm. Ck-out 11 am. Cr cds: A, C, D, DS, MC, V.

Restaurant

✔ ★ **IRISH INN.** Frontage Rd, 303 I-40E. 806/256-2332. Open 24 hrs. Bar 5 pm-midnight. Semi-a la carte: bkfst $1.85-$4.75, lunch, dinner $1.75-$12.25. Sun brunch $5.95. Child's meals. Specializes in steak, fish, chicken. Salad bar. Parking. Cr cds: A, C, D, DS, MC, V.

Sherman (A-7)

(See Bonham, Denison, Gainesville, McKinney)

Pop 31,601 **Elev** 745 ft **Area code** 903 **Zip** 75090
Information Convention & Visitors Council, PO Box 1029; 903/893-1184.

Sherman is a major manufacturing and processing center, supplying a list of items ranging from wheat and pharmaceuticals to cotton gin machinery and truck bodies. This, along with Lake Texoma's tourism, contributes to a broad economic base.

What to See and Do

Hagerman National Wildlife Refuge. An 11,320-acre area on Lake Texoma provides food and rest for migratory waterfowl of the central flyway. Fishing. Boating (Apr-Sept). Trail, self-guided auto tour route. Picnicking. No camping. Visitor center. (Daily; closed some hols) NW via US 82, exit at FM 1417, go N to Refuge Rd, follow signs to HQ. Phone 903/786-2826.   **Free.**

Lake Texoma. 13 mi N (see LAKE TEXOMA, OK).

Red River Historical Museum. Quarterly exhibits; permanent exhibits include "Black Land, Red River," artifacts and furniture from Glen Eden, early plantation house whose site is now under Lake Texoma; country store, local history and farm and ranch room. (Tues-Fri, also Sat afternoons; closed major hols) Sr citizen rate. 301 S Walnut, in the historic Carnegie Library building (1914). Phone 903/893-7623.   ¢

Annual Events

Texoma Livestock Exposition. Loy Lake Park. 1st wk Apr.

Sherman Preservation League Tour of Homes. 3rd wkend Apr.

Motor Hotels

✔ ★ ★ **GRAYSON HOUSE.** 2105 Texoma Pkwy. 903/892-2161; res: 800/723-4194; FAX 903/893-3045. 146 rms, 2 story. S $49-$78; D $54-$82; each addl $8; under 18 free. Crib free. TV; cable (premium), VCR avail. Pool; whirlpool. Restaurant 6 am-2 pm, 5 pm-midnight; Sat to 1 am. Rm serv. Private club 4 pm-midnight. Ck-out 11 am. Business center. In-rm modem link. Sundries. Airport transportation. Health club privileges. Cr cds: A, C, D, DS, ER, JCB, MC, V.

★ ★ ★ **SHERATON INN-SHERMAN.** 3605 TX 75S, 3 mi S, exit 1417. 903/868-0555; FAX 903/892-9396. 142 rms, 2 story. S $59-$80; D $69-$89; each addl $10; suites $175-$225; under 18 free; wkend rates. Crib free. TV; cable. Pool; wading pool, whirlpool. Restaurant 6 am-2 pm, 5-10 pm. Rm serv. Private club 4 pm-midnight, Sat to 1 am; dancing. Ck-out noon. Coin lndry. Meeting rms. Valet serv. Some refrigerators. Cr cds: A, C, D, DS, MC, V.

Snyder (B-4)

(See Big Spring)

Founded 1876 **Pop** 12,195 **Elev** 2,316 ft **Area code** 915 **Zip** 79549
Information Chamber of Commerce, 2302 Avenue R, PO Box 840; 915/573-3558.

Snyder is the county seat for Scurry County, one of the nation's top oil producing counties. Its modern sports complex and public parks make it a center for recreational activities.

What to See and Do

Lake J.B. Thomas. Swimming; fishing; boating. Picnicking. 17 mi SW on TX 350.

Scurry County Museum. Local & county historical exhibits from prehistory to oil boom. Changing exhibits. (Daily exc Sat) ¼ mi E off TX 350 on Western Texas College campus. Phone 915/573-6107.   **Free.**

Annual Event

Scurry County Fair & White Buffalo Days. Mid-Sept.

Motels

✔ ★ **GREAT WESTERN.** 800 E Coliseum Dr. 915/573-1166; res: 800/496-6835; FAX 915/573-1166. 56 rms, 2 story. S $27; D $36; each addl $5; suites $45; under 12 free (max 1). Crib free. TV; cable (premium). Pool. Restaurant 5:30 am-2 pm, 6:30-9 pm; Sat & Sun to 2 pm. Bar 11:30 am-midnight, closed Sun. Ck-out noon. Cr cds: A, C, D, DS, MC, V.

★ ★ **PURPLE SAGE.** 1501 E Coliseum Dr, 1¾ mi E on US 84 Business, 180. 915/573-5491; res: 800/545-5792; FAX 915/573-9027. 45 rms, 2 kits. S $35-$45; D $38-$53; each addl $3-$5; suites $45-$53; kit. units $35-$48; under 15 free. Crib free. Pet accepted. TV; cable (premium), VCR avail (movies avail). Pool. Playground. Complimentary continental bkfst, coffee. Ck-out noon. Gift shop. Refrigerators. Picnic tables. Cr cds: A, C, D, DS, MC, V.

Restaurant

✔ ★ ★ **SHACK.** *1005 25th St. 915/573-4921.* Hrs: 11 am-2:30 pm, 5-10 pm; Sun to 2:30 pm. Closed most major hols. Semi-a la carte: lunch $3.50-$14.95, dinner $4.95-$14.95. Specializes in steak, seafood. Salad bar. Parking. Rustic. Old West decor. Cr cds: A, C, D, MC, V.

Sonora (C-4)

(See Ozona)

Settled 1890 **Pop** 2,751 **Elev** 2,120 ft **Area code** 915 **Zip** 76950
Information Chamber of Commerce, 705 N Crockett, PO Box 1172; 915/387-2880.

The longest fenced cattle trail in the world once stretched from Sonora to the town of Brady; it was 100 miles long, 250 feet wide and had holding pastures along the route. Today, the seat of Sutton County is a livestock and wool processing center.

What to See and Do

Caverns of Sonora. Unusually beautiful caverns with many rare and fine formations; guided tours within 30 min. Picnicking. Camping and RV park available (fee). (Daily) 8 mi W on I-10, then 7 mi S on FM 1989. Phone 915/387-3105. ¢¢¢

Annual Event

West Texas Championship. Chicken, brisket, goat & chili cook-offs. Includes horseshoe pitching, dance. Mid-Apr.

Motel

✔ ★ ★ **DEVIL'S RIVER.** *I-10 & Golf Course Rd/US 277, Sonora exit. 915/387-3516; FAX 915/387-2854.* 99 rms, 2 story. S $30-$38; D $41-$48; each addl $3. Crib $4. Pet accepted, some restrictions; $2. TV; cable, VCR avail. Pool. Restaurant 6 am-2 pm, 5-10 pm; Sun to 2 pm. Ck-out noon. Coin lndry. Meeting rm. Business servs avail. 9-hole golf privileges adj, greens fee $18. Cr cds: A, C, D, DS, MC, V.

South Padre Island (F-7)

(See Brownsville, Harlingen, Port Isabel)

Pop 1,677 **Elev** 0 ft **Area code** 210 **Zip** 78597
Information Convention & Visitors Bureau, 600 Padre Blvd; 210/761-6433 or 800/343-2368.

South Padre Island, located 2½ miles off Port Isabel, at the southern tip of Padre Island (see), has long been a favored vacationing spot; Karankawa Indians were known to have spent the winter months in this area as long as 400 years ago. The town, which averages only a half-mile wide, relies on tourism as its economic basis; activities from beachcombing to parasailing are popular, and numerous charter boat operators offer bay and deep-sea fishing excursions.

Annual Events

Miss USA Pageant. Phone 210/761-6433 or 800/343-2368. February.
Independence Day Celebration & Fireworks Extravaganza. July 4.

Island of Lights Festival. Late Nov-early Dec.

Motel

✔ ★ **DAYS INN.** *3913 Padre Blvd. 210/761-7831; FAX 210/761-2033.* 57 rms, 2 story. Mar-Labor Day: S, D $65-$70; each addl $10; under 12 free; higher rates Spring Break; lower rates rest of yr. Crib free. Pets accepted; $25. TV; cable. Pool; whirlpool. Ck-out noon. Coin lndry. Refrigerators. Opp ocean. Cr cds: A, C, D, DS, JCB, MC, V.

Motor Hotels

★ **BEST WESTERN FIESTA ISLES.** *5701 Padre Blvd. 210/761-4913; FAX 210/761-2719.* 58 rms, 3 story, 52 kits. Apr-Aug: S, D $84-$94; each addl $10; under 13 free; wkly rates; higher rates Mar; lower rates rest of yr. Crib free. Pet accepted. TV; cable. Pool; whirlpool. Complimentary coffee. Restaurant adj 7 am-3 pm. Ck-out noon. Meeting rm. Balconies. Beach 1½ blk. Cr cds: A, C, D, DS, MC, V.

★ ★ **HOLIDAY INN SUN SPREE.** *100 Padre Blvd, at Causeway. 210/761-5401; res: 800/531-7405 (exc TX), 800/292-7506 (TX); FAX 210/761-1560.* 227 rms, 6 story. S $79-$99; D $89-$109; suites $149; under 19 free; higher rates Mar. Crib free. TV; cable. Heated pool; wading pool, whirlpool, poolside serv. Restaurant 7 am-10 pm. Rm serv. Bar 5 pm-2 am. Ck-out noon. Coin lndry. Meeting rms. Bellhops. Valet serv. Gift shop. Balconies. Tennis court adj. Cr cds: A, C, D, DS, JCB, MC, V.

Hotels

★ ★ **BAHIA MAR.** *6300 Padre Blvd. 210/761-1343; res: 800/292-4502; FAX 210/761-6287.* 174 rms in main 12 story bldg, 26 cottages. Late May-early Sept: S, D $99-$160; each addl $10; kits. $104-$160; cottages $199-$230; wkend, wkly & hol rates; higher rates spring break, Dec hols; lower rates rest of yr. Crib free. TV; cable. Heated pool; whirlpool, poolside serv. Restaurant 8 am-2 pm. Bar 5 pm-2 am. Ck-out noon. Lighted tennis. Boats. Balconies. Picnic tables. Swimming beach. Cr cds: A, C, D, MC, V.

★ ★ **SHERATON.** *310 Padre Blvd. 210/761-6551; FAX 210/761-6570.* 250 units, 12 story. 56 kits. June-Aug: S, D $99-$150; each addl $10; suites $199-$270; under 17 free; lower rates rest of yr. Crib free. TV; cable. Pool; wading pool, poolside serv. Restaurants 6 am-10 pm. Bar 11-2 am; entertainment, dancing exc Sun. Ck-out noon. Coin lndry. Convention facilities. Gift shop. Tennis. Exercise equipt; weights, stair machine, whirlpool. Activities dir. Some refrigerators. Balconies. On beach. Cr cds: A, C, D, DS, MC, V.

Resort

★ ★ ★ **RADISSON.** *500 Padre Blvd. 210/761-6511; FAX 210/761-1602.* 182 rms, 2-12 story, 54 condominiums. Memorial Day-Labor Day: S, D $135-$155; each addl $10; condos (up to 6) $250; under 17 free; higher rates spring break; lower rates rest of yr. Crib free. TV; cable. 2 pools, 1 heated; whirlpools, poolside serv. Free supervised child's activities (Memorial Day-Labor Day). Dining rm 6:30 am-10 pm; Fri, Sat to 11 pm. Box lunches. Snack bar. Picnics. Rm serv. Bar 11-2 am; entertainment, dancing. Ck-out 11 am, ck-in 3 pm. Grocery 3 mi. Package store ½ mi. Meeting rms. Bellhops. Gift shop. Lighted tennis, pro. Golf privileges 25 mi. Swimming beach. Boating. Bicycle rentals. Lawn games. Soc dir. Health club privileges. Fishing guides avail.

Refrigerator in condos. Many balconies. Cr cds: A, C, D, DS, ER, MC, V.

Restaurants

✔★ BLACKBEARD'S. *103 E Saturn. 210/761-2962.* Hrs: 11 am-11 pm. Closed Thanksgiving, Dec 25. Bar. Semi-a la carte: lunch, dinner $4.50-$13. Specializes in seafood, steakburgers. Parking. Cr cds: A, C, D, DS, MC, V.
D

★★ GRILL ROOM. *708 Padre Blvd. 210/761-9331.* Hrs: 7-10 pm. Closed Mon, Tues; Easter, Thanksgiving, Dec 25; also 2 wks Dec. Res accepted. Continental menu. Bar. Semi-a la carte: dinner $13.95-$22.95. Specialties: red snapper Provence, grilled quail, baked shrimp Bubba. Cr cds: A, C, D, MC, V.
D

✔★ JESSE'S. *2700 Padre Blvd. 210/761-4500.* Hrs: 11 am-10 pm. Closed Dec 25. Mexican menu. Bar. Semi-a la carte: lunch & dinner $4-$12. Specializes in seafood, fajitas, enchiladas. Parking. Hunting lodge atmosphere; trophies displayed. Cr cds: A, C, D, DS, MC, V.

★★ JOSEPH'S. *210 S Padre Blvd. 210/761-4540.* Hrs: 5-10 pm. Closed Mon; Dec 25; also last 2 wks Nov. Res accepted. Bar. Semi-a la carte: dinner $9.95-$23. Specializes in prime rib, seafood, pasta. Parking. New England-style seafood house. Cr cds: A, C, D, DS, MC, V.
D

★ LA JAIBA. *2001 Padre Blvd. 210/761-9878.* Hrs: 11:30 am-2:30 pm, 5-9 pm. Closed Mon; Jan 1, Easter, Dec 25. Res accepted. Seafood menu. Bar. Semi-a la carte: lunch, dinner $4.95-$18.95. Child's meals. Specializes in Alaskan king crab, broiled baby snapper. Parking. Nautical atmosphere. Cr cds: A, C, DS, MC, V.
D

★★ SCAMPI'S. *206 W Aries St. 210/761-1755.* Hrs: 6-10 pm. Closed Dec 12-25. Res accepted. Bar 4:30-11 pm. Semi-a la carte: dinner $13.95-$23.95. Specialties: oysters Rockefeller, flounder Georgette, scampi Italiano. Own pasta. Parking. Outdoor dining. Casual bayside dining. Cr cds: A, DS, MC, V.
D

Stephenville (B-6)

(See Cleburne)

Settled 1850 **Pop** 13,502 **Elev** 1,277 ft **Area code** 817 **Zip** 76401

Information Chamber of Commerce, 187 W Washington; 817/965-5313 or -5323.

What to See and Do

Cross Timbers Country Opry. Family entertainment by country & western variety performers. (Sat evenings) Sr citizen rate. 1/2 mi E of US 281 via US 377 Bypass. Phone 817/965-4575. ¢¢¢

Dinosaur Valley State Park. 29 mi E on US 67. (See CLEBURNE)

Historical House Museum Complex. Rock English cottage (1869), two-story with bargeboards and vents with Pennsylvania hex signs. Church with fish-scaled steeple (1899); 3 log cabins; log corn crib (1861); 1890's 2-room schoolhouse; replica of carriage house containing museum of local history items. (Fri-Sun afternoons; closed hols) Contact Chamber of Commerce. 525 E Washington. **Free.**

Hoka Hey Fine Arts Gallery & Foundry. One of the foremost bronze foundries in the United States. Here stands Robert Summers' original 9-foot sculpture of John Wayne, among various other bronzes, paintings and prints. (Daily; closed hols) Foundry tours (by appt). 10 mi SW via US 377, in Dublin. Phone 817/445-2017. **Free.**

Tarleton State University (1899). (6,500 students) An affiliate of Texas A & M University. Clyde Wells Fine Arts Center. Horse breeding program is one of the finest in the nation; tours of campus farm. Phone 817/968-9000.

Motels

★★ BEST WESTERN CROSS TIMBERS. *1625 S Loop 377. 817/968-2114; FAX 817/968-2114, ext. 103.* 50 rms, 1-2 story. S $39-$43; D $44-$56; each addl $6; suites $55-$70; under 12 free. Crib $2. Pet accepted, some restrictions. TV; cable (premium). Pool. Complimentary continental bkfst, coffee. Restaurant adj open 24 hrs. Ck-out noon. Coin lndry. Business servs avail. In-rm modem link. Refrigerators. Cr cds: A, C, D, DS, JCB, MC, V.

✔★ DAYS INN. *701 S Loop, jct US 281 & 377. 817/968-3392; FAX 817/968-3527.* 65 rms, 2 story. S $33-$40; D $35-$60; each addl $5; under 12 free. Crib $5. Pet accepted. TV; cable (premium). Pool. Restaurant 6 am-8 pm; Sun 11 am-2 pm. Ck-out noon. Meeting rms. Business servs avail. Cr cds: A, C, D, DS, MC, V.

★★ HOLIDAY INN. *2865 W Washington. 817/968-5256; FAX 817/968-4255.* 100 rms, 2 story. S $50-$62; D $55-$67; each addl $5; suites $100-$150; under 19 free. Crib free. Pet accepted. TV; cable (premium), VCR avail. Pool. Restaurant 6 am-10 pm; Sun to 3 pm. Rm serv. Private club 5 pm-midnight, closed Sun. Ck-out noon. Meeting rms. Business servs avail. Valet serv. Sundries. Cr cds: A, C, D, DS, JCB, MC, V.

★ TEXAN MOTOR INN. *3030 W Washington. 817/968-5003; FAX 817/968-5060.* 30 rms. Mid-Apr-Sept: S $35; D $41; each addl $3; under 12 free; higher rates: rodeos, university events; lower rates rest of yr. Crib $3. Pet accepted, some restrictions: $3. TV; cable (premium). Complimentary continental bkfst, coffee. Restaurant nearby. Ck-out 11 am. Business servs avail. Bus station transportation. Cr cds: A, D, DS, MC, V.

Restaurant

✔★ JOSE'S. *1044 W Washington. 817/965-7400.* Hrs: 11 am-9:30 pm; Fri, Sat to 10 pm. Closed Jan 1, Thanksgiving, Dec 25. Mexican, Amer menu. Semi-a la carte: lunch, dinner $3.95-$11.40. Specializes in fajitas, enchiladas, breast of chicken. Parking. Cantina atmosphere. Cr cds: A, C, D, DS, MC, V.

Sulphur Springs (B-7)

(For accommodations see Greenville)

Pop 14,062 **Elev** 530 ft **Area code** 903 **Zip** 75482

Information Hopkins Co Chamber of Commerce, 1200 Houston St, PO Box 347; 903/885-6515.

Seat of Hopkins County with a Richardsonian Romanesque-style courthouse (1894), Sulphur Springs is the center of Texas' leading dairy region. The Leo St Clair music box collection, the Regional Livestock Exposition and Civic Center, Heritage Park and the Southwest Dairy Museum make this an interesting area to visit.

What to See and Do

Governor Hogg Shrine State Historical Park. Three museums with personal items of Governor J.S. Hogg and family (Wed-Sun; closed Jan 1, Dec 25). Nature, hiking trails. Picnicking, playground. (Daily) 25 mi SE; 518 S Main St, in Quitman. Phone 903/763-2701. ¢

Annual Events

Hopkins County Dairy Festival. Civic Center. 1 wk early June.

Fall Festival. Carnival, arts & crafts exhibits, special events. 2nd Sat-3rd Sat Sept.

CRA Finals Rodeo. Civic Center. Phone 903/885-8071. 2nd wkend Nov.

Sweetwater (B-5)

(See Abilene)

Founded 1881 **Pop** 11,967 **Elev** 2,164 ft **Area code** 915 **Zip** 79556
Information Chamber of Commerce, 810 E Broadway, PO Box 1148; 915/235-5488.

Sweetwater is a manufacturing center for electronics, wearing apparel and gypsum products. Hereford cattle, quarter horses and sheep are raised in large numbers in the area.

Hunting is good for deer, quail and turkey in south and central portions of the county.

What to See and Do

City-County Pioneer Museum. Historic house displays antique furniture, pioneer tools, early photographs of area; Indian artifacts; Women Air Force Service Pilots memorabilia. (Tues-Sat afternoons; closed hols) 610 E 3rd St. Phone 915/235-8547. **Free.**

Annual Events

Rattlesnake Roundup. Nolan County Coliseum, N end of Elm St. Also Gun & Coin Show. 2nd wkend Mar.

American Junior Rodeo National Finals. Nolan County Coliseum. 1st wk Aug.

Motels

★ ★ **HOLIDAY INN.** *Box 157, Georgia St at I-20.* 915/236-6887; FAX 915/236-6887, ext. 294. 107 rms, 2 story. S, D $46-$65; each addl $5; under 19 free. Crib free. Pet accepted. TV; cable (premium), VCR avail. Pool. Playground. Restaurant open 24 hrs. Rm serv. Private club 4 pm-midnight, Sat to 1 am; dancing. Ck-out 1 pm. Coin lndry. Meeting rms. Business servs avail. Some refrigerators. Cr cds: A, C, D, DS, JCB, MC, V.

[D] 🐾 ⛱ 🚫 🔥 SC

★ **MOTEL 6.** *510 NW Georgia, off I-20.* 915/235-4387. 121 rms, 2 story. S $25.95; D $29.99; each $4; under 17 free. Crib avail. Pet accepted. TV; cable (premium). Pool. Complimentary coffee in lobby. Restaurant opp open 24 hrs. Ck-out noon. Coin lndry. Cr cds: A, C, D, DS, MC, V.

🐾 ⛱ 🚫 🔥 SC

Temple (C-6)

(See Killeen, Salado, Waco)

Pop 46,109 **Elev** 736 ft **Area code** 817
Information Promotions & Tourism Dept, Municipal Bldg, Civic Center Box, 76501; 817/770-5720.

Temple is the principal commercial center for a large area of central Texas. Items manufactured here encompass industries as diverse as agriculture, plastics, machinery and electronics. Also in Temple are the Scott and White Clinic and Hospital, founded in 1904, and Texas A & M University School of Medicine.

What to See and Do

Belton Lake Swimming, waterskiing; fishing; boating (ramps). Picnicking, concession. Camping (tent & trailer sites, fee; hookups, dump station). (Daily) I-35S, exit W on FM 2305. Phone 817/939-1829. Per vehicle ¢¢ Also, **Stillhouse Hollow Lake.** 8 mi SW on I-35 to Belton, then 5 mi SW off US 190 (see SALADO). (Daily) **Free.**

Railroad & Pioneer Museum. Exhibits in restored Santa Fe Railroad depot (1907). Baldwin locomotive 3423, Santa Fe caboose. WWII troop sleeper and other pieces of rolling stock on grounds. Picnicking, playground. (Tues-Sat; closed major hols) S 31st St & W Ave H. Phone 817/778-6873. ¢

Recreation areas. The Recreation Dept maintains 26 parks, five of which have swimming, seven with tennis courts, three with 9-hole golf. Also 222-acre area on Belton Lake.

Annual Event

Independence Day Celebration & Belton PRCA Rodeo. 8 mi SW on I-35, in Belton. Carnival, fiddlers' contest, parade, rodeo. Phone 817/939-3551. 4 days early July.

Motels

★ ★ **BEST WESTERN- INN AT SCOTT & WHITE.** *2625 S 31st St (76504), I-35 at Loop 363 (exit 299).* 817/778-5511; res: 800/749-0318; FAX 817/773-3161. 129 rms, 1-2 story. S $49-$62; D $54-$63; each addl $8; suites $100-$125; under 18 free; wkly, wkend rates. Crib free. TV; cable. Pool. Restaurant 6 am-10 pm. Rm serv. Private club 4 pm-midnight. Ck-out noon. Meeting rms. Business servs avail. Bellhops. Valet serv. Sundries. Barber, beauty shop. Gift shop. Free airport, RR station, bus depot, hospital transportation. Health club privileges. Private patios, balconies. Near Scott & White Hospital. Cr cds: A, C, D, DS, MC, V.

[D] ⛱ 🚫 🔥

★ **HOLIDAY INN.** *802 N General Bruce Dr (76504-2337), I-35 exit 302.* 817/778-4411. 132 rms, 2 story. S $56-$65; $62-$71; each addl $6; under 12 free. Crib free. Pet accepted, some restrictions. TV; cable. Pool. Restaurant 6:30 am-2 pm, 5:30-10 pm; wkend hrs vary. Bar. Ck-out noon. Meeting rms. Business servs avail. In-rm modem link. Valet serv. Coin lndry. Picnic tables. Cr cds: A, C, D, DS, MC, V.

[D] 🐾 ⛱ 🚫 🔥

★ ★ **LA QUINTA.** *1604 W Barton Ave (76504).* 817/771-2980; FAX 817/778-7565. 106 rms, 3 story. S $52; D $59; each addl $7; under 18 free. Crib free. Pet accepted; some restrictions. TV; cable (premium), VCR avail. Pool. Continental bkfst. Complimentary coffee in lobby. Restaurant adj open 24 hrs. Ck-out noon. Meeting rm. Business servs avail. Sundries. Cr cds: A, C, D, DS, MC, V.

[D] 🐾 ⛱ 🚫 🔥 SC

Unrated Dining Spot

PICCADILLY CAFETERIA. *3111 S 31st St, in Temple Mall. 817/773-0590.* Hrs: 11 am-8:30 pm. Closed Dec 25. Avg ck: lunch, dinner $5.25. Specializes in seafood, roast beef, salad. Cr cds: A, C, D, DS, MC, V.

Texarkana (A-8)

Founded 1873 **Pop** Texarkana, TX, 31,656; Texarkana, AR, 22,631 **Elev** 336 ft **Area code** 903 (TX); 501 (AR)

Information Chamber of Commerce, 819 State Line Ave, PO Box 1464, 75504; 903/792-7191.

State Line Avenue divides this area into two separate cities, Texarkana, Arkansas, and Texarkana, Texas. The post office, which houses the Federal offices for both states, is centered on this line. The two civil governments cooperate closely. Texarkana is an agricultural, transportation, wholesale and manufacturing center serving four states and produces paper, tires, tank cars, furniture, food, metal and wood items. The army's Red River Depot and Lone Star Army Ammunition Plant are located just to the west of the city.

Fishing is good on many nearby lakes, and on the Sulphur, Red, Cossatot and Little rivers.

At the southeast corner of Third and Main Streets is a mural honoring one of Texarkana's most noted native sons, ragtime pioneer Scott Joplin.

What to See and Do

Perot Theatre (1924). Designed by Emil Weil to accommodate both live theater and films. This historic, 1,606-seat performing arts facility features professional and local amateur entertainment. 219 Main St. For tour and fee information phone 903/792-4992.

Texarkana Historical Museum. Local history displays include Caddo artifacts, Victorian parlor, doctor's office, 1885 kitchen; changing exhibits. (Tues-Sat; closed hols) 219 State Line Ave. Phone 903/793-4831. ¢

Wright Patman Dam & Lake Water sports (marina, ramps); hunting. Picnicking; playgrounds. Camping (Rocky Point, Clear Springs; hookups). Fee for some activities. (Daily) 12 mi SW on US 59. Phone 903/796-2419 (Rocky Point) or 903/838-8636 (Clear Springs).

Annual Event

Four States Fair & Rodeo. Fairgrounds. 3rd wkend Sept.

Motels

(All directions are given from the jct of US 67, 7th St, and the state line)

 ★ ★ **BEST WESTERN KINGS ROW INN.** *In AR (75502), 4200 State Line Ave (75502), at I-30 exit 223B. 501/774-3851; FAX 501/772-8440.* 160 rms, 2 story. S $36; D $46; each addl $5; under 12 free. Crib $2. Pet accepted, some restrictions. TV; cable (premium). Pool. Restaurant 6 am-9:30 pm. Ck-out noon. Lndry facilities. Meeting rms. Free airport transportation. Refrigerators. Balconies. Cr cds: A, C, D, DS, ER, JCB, MC, V.

★ **HOLIDAY INN EXPRESS.** *5401 N State Line Ave (75503). 903/792-3366; FAX 903/792-5649.* 112 rms, 3 story. S $49.50; D $54.50; suites $99; each addl $5; family rates. Crib free. Pet accepted, some restrictions. TV; cable (premium). Pool; whirlpool. Complimentary continental bkfst. Ck-out noon. Coin Indry. Meeting rms.

Free airport, RR station transportation. Some refrigerators. Cr cds: A, C, D, DS, ER, JCB, MC, V.

★ ★ **LA QUINTA.** *5201 State Line Ave (75503), at I-30 exit 223A/B. 903/794-1900; FAX 903/792-5506.* 130 rms, 2 story. S $49-$57, D $56-$64; each addl $7; suites $67; under 18 free. Crib free. Pet accepted. TV; cable (premium), VCR avail. Pool. Complimentary continental bkfst, coffee. Restaurant adj open 24 hrs. Ck-out noon. Meeting rms. Sundries. Free airport, RR station, bus depot transportation. Cr cds: A, C, D, DS, MC, V.

Motor Hotel

★ ★ ★ **HOLIDAY INN I-30.** *In AR (75502), 5100 State Line Ave (75502), just off I-30 exit 223B. 501/774-3521; FAX 501/772-3068.* 210 rms, 4 story. S $70-$76; D $80-$86; each addl $10; suite $140; under 18 free. Crib $5. TV; cable (premium). Heated pool; whirlpool, sauna. Complimentary coffee in rms. Restaurant 6 am-10 pm. Rm serv. Private club 11 am-10 pm; Fri, Sat to 11 pm; Sun 1-10 pm. Ck-out noon. Coin Indry. Meeting rms. Bellhops. Exercise rm. Holidome. Game rm. Private patios, balconies. Cr cds: A, C, D, DS, JCB, MC, V.

Inn

★ ★ **MANSION ON MAIN.** *802 Main St (75501). 903/792-1835.* 6 rms (2 with shower only), 2 story, 2 suites. S, D $60-$75; suites $99. TV; cable (premium). Complimentary full bkfst. Restaurant nearby. Ck-out 11 am. Built 1895; columns from St Louis World's Fair. Oak and cherry furnishings; many antiques. Totally nonsmoking. Cr cds: A, MC, V.

Unrated Dining Spots

BRYCE'S CAFETERIA. *2021 Mall Dr, at jct I-30 & Summerhill Rd. 903/792-1611.* Hrs: 11 am-2 pm; 5-8 pm. Closed Jan 1, Dec 25. Avg ck: lunch, dinner $5. Specializes in homemade pies. Menu changes daily. Colonial-style building. Family-owned. Cr cds: DS, MC, V.

LUBY'S CAFETERIA. *99 Central Mall (75503), I-30 Richmond Rd exit. 903/838-6661.* Hrs: 10:45 am-2:30 pm, 4:15-8 pm; Fri-Sun 10:45 am-8 pm. Closed Dec 25. Avg ck: lunch, dinner $5. Specializes in fried chicken, breaded cutlet, seafood. Cr cds: DS, MC, V.

Texas City (D-8)

(See Galveston, Houston)

Pop 40,822 **Elev** 12 ft **Area code** 409

Information Chamber of Commerce, 8419 Emmett F. Lowry Expy, Suite 105, PO Box 3330; 409/935-1408 or 713/280-3917.

Texas City is located on the mainland, opposite Galveston. A 40-foot ship channel connects to the gulf. Several large oil refineries and chemical plants are located here.

What to See and Do

Fishing. From three municipal fishing piers on dike extending five miles into Galveston Bay. Swimming; waterskiing. Boating (ramps free). Picnicking.

Annual Events

Funfest. Competition tennis, rugby, windsurfing, racquetball; fun run; barbecue cook-off. June.

Shrimp Boil. Rotary Pavilion, Nessler Park. Food, dancing. Aug.

Fair on the Square. Laurel & 1st Sts, in La Marque. Entertainment, food, arts & crafts, parade. Phone 409/938-0527. Last full wkend Sept.

Motel

★ ★ **LA QUINTA.** *1121 TX 146 N (77590). 409/948-3101; FAX 409/945-4412.* 121 rms, 2 story. S $51-$65; D $58-$72; each addl $7; under 18 free. Pet accepted. Crib free. TV; cable (premium). Pool. Complimentary continental bkfst. Retsaurant adj open 24 hrs. Ck-out noon. Meeting rms. Coin lndry. Cr cds: A, C, D, DS, ER, JCB, MC, V.

Tyler (B-8)

(See Athens, Longview)

Founded 1846 **Pop** 75,450 **Elev** 545 ft **Area code** 903

Information Convention & Visitors Bureau, 407 N Broadway, 75702; 903/592-1661 or 800/235-5712.

More than 30% of the field-grown rose bushes in the United States come from the Tyler area. An area of diversified resources such as livestock, crops, forest products and iron ore, Tyler is also a headquarters for the East Texas oilfield.

What to See and Do

Brookshire's World of Wildlife Museum & Country Store. More than 200 specimens of animals from all over the world, some in natural habitat exhibits. Replica 1920s country store stocked with authentic items. Res advised. (Tues-Sat; closed major hols) 1600 W SW Loop 323. Phone 903/534-2169. **Free.**

Caldwell Zoo. More than 120 acres; domestic & wild animals. (Daily; closed Jan 1, Thanksgiving, Dec 25) Gentry Pkwy & M.L. King Blvd, NW part of town. Phone 903/593-0121. **Free.**

Carnegie History Center. Exhibits cover history of Tyler and Smith County. (Tues-Sun afternoons; closed major hols) Tours by appt. 125 S College, in former Carnegie Public Library. Phone 903/593-7989. **Free.**

Goodman Museum. Antebellum artifacts, antiques, 19th-century medical instruments in house built ca 1860. (Mar-Oct, Wed-Sun; rest of yr, Mon-Fri; closed Dec 25) 624 N Broadway. Phone 903/531-1286. **Free.**

Hudnall Planetarium. Astronomy exhibits (Sept-mid-May, Mon-Thurs; closed college vacations). Shows (Sept-mid-May, Sun & Wed; closed college vacations). S Mahon, on Tyler Junior College campus, 2 mi SE, off TX 64. Phone 903/510-2312. ¢

⭐ **Tyler Rose Garden.** The formal garden has 500 varieties on 15 acres; museum, community center. Museum and visitors center displays photos, memorabilia, past Rose Festival gowns. (Tues-Sat, also Sun afternoons; closed hols) 1900 W Front St, 1¼ mi W on TX 31 at Fairgrounds. Phone 903/531-1212. ¢¢

Tyler State Park. Swimming; fishing; boating (ramp, rentals). Picnicking, concession. Improved campsites (hookups, dump station). Six lakes are within a few miles. Reservations advised. Standard fees. (Daily) 8 mi N on FM 14 from Loop 323. Phone 903/597-5338.

Annual Events

Azalea Trail. Late Mar-early Apr.

East Texas Fair. Late Sept.

Texas Rose Festival. Parade, pageantry; tours of rose fields. Rose show. Mid-Oct.

Motels

✔ ★ **DAYS INN.** *3300 Mineola (75702). 903/595-2451; FAX 903/595-2261.* 187 rms, 2 story. S $38-$48; D $40-$50; each addl $6; suites $65-$85; under 18 free. Crib free. Pet accepted. TV; cable (premium), VCR avail. Pool. Restaurant open 24 hrs. Rm serv 8 am-8 pm. Private club 4 pm-midnight. Ck-out noon. Coin lndry. Meeting rms. Business servs avail. Valet serv. Sundries. Barber, beauty shop. Airport transportation. Exercise equipt; weights, bicycles. Rec rm. Some refrigerators. Cr cds: A, C, D, DS, ER, MC, V.

✔ ★ **ECONO LODGE.** *3209 W Gentry Pkwy (75702). 903/593-0103.* 50 rms. S $31.95-$37.95; D $35.95-$39.95; each addl $5; under 18 free; higher rates: Canton Days, 1st wkend of month. Pet accepted; $2. TV; cable (premium), VCR avail, (movies avail $3.75). Pool. Complimentary coffee in lobby. Restaurant nearby. Ck-out noon. Cr cds: A, C, D, DS, MC, V.

★ ★ **HOLIDAY INN-SOUTHEAST CROSSING.** *3310 Troup Hwy (75701), jct TX 110, Loop 323. 903/593-3600; FAX 903/533-9571, ext. 350.* 160 rms, 2 story. S, D $69-$72; suites $125; under 18 free; wkend rates. Crib free. Pet accepted. TV; cable (premium), VCR avail. Pool; poolside serv. Coffee in rms. Restaurant 6 am-1 pm, 5:30-10 pm; Sat, Sun 7 am-1 pm. Rm serv. Private club 5-10 pm, closed Sun. Ck-out noon. Coin lndry. Meeting rms. Business servs avail. In-rm modem link. Valet serv. Sundries. Free airport transportation. Health club privileges. Cr cds: A, C, D, DS, JCB, MC, V.

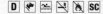

★ ★ **LA QUINTA.** *1601 W Southwest Loop 323 (75701). 903/561-2223; FAX 903/581-5708.* 130 rms, 2 story. S $57-$64; D $67-$74; each addl $10. Crib free. Pet accepted, some restrictions. TV; cable (premium). Pool. Complimentary continental bkfst, coffee. Restaurant adj open 24 hrs. Ck-out noon. Meeting rms. In-rm modem link. Valet serv. Sundries. Free airport transportation. Cr cds: A, C, D, DS, MC, V.

★ ★ **RESIDENCE INN BY MARRIOTT.** *3303 Troup Hwy (75701). 903/595-5188; FAX 903/595-5719.* 128 kit. suites, 2 story. Kit. suites $86-$114; wkend rates. Pet accepted; $50. TV; cable (premium). Heated pool; whirlpool. Complimentary continental bkfst, coffee. Ck-out noon. Coin lndry. Meeting rms. Business servs avail. In-rm modem link. Valet serv. Sundries. Free airport transportation. Health club privileges. Sport court. Balconies. Picnic tables, grills. Cr cds: A, C, D, DS, JCB, MC, V.

Hotels

★ **HOWARD JOHNSON.** *2843 NW Loop 323 (75702). 903/597-1301; FAX 903/597-9437.* 139 rms, 4 story. S $47-$49; D $53-$57; each addl $6; under 18 free. Crib free. Pet accepted, some restrictions. TV; cable (premium), VCR avail. Pool. Complimentary continental bkfst. Restaurant 5-10 pm. Private club 5-11 pm, Sat to midnight. Ck-out 1 pm. Meeting rms. Business servs avail. Free airport, RR station, bus depot transportation. Balconies. Cr cds: A, C, D, DS, MC, V.

★ ★ ★ **SHERATON.** *5701 S Broadway (75703). 903/561-5800; FAX 903/561-9916.* 186 rms, 8 story. S $80-$86; D $90-$96; each addl $10; suites $135-$250; under 17 free. Crib free. TV; cable (premium). Pool; wading pool, whirlpool, poolside serv. Complimentary coffee. Restaurant 6:30 am-10:30 pm. Private club 11 am-midnight, Sat to 1 am, Sun noon-10:30 pm; entertainment, dancing. Ck-out noon. Meeting rms. Business center. Free airport transportation. Health club privileges. Some refrigerators. Balconies. Cr cds: A, C, D, DS, JCB, MC, V.

D ⊠ ⊠ ⊠ SC ⊼

Restaurants

✔ ★ **LIANG'S.** *1828 E SE Loop 323 (75701). 903/593-7883.* Hrs: 11 am-10 pm; Fri & Sat to 11 pm. Closed Thanksgiving. Res accepted. Chinese menu. Bar. Semi-a la carte: lunch $3.95-$5.50, dinner $5.25-$10.95. Child's meals. Specialties: chicken Liang-style, Oriental beef. Parking. Large wood dragon sculpture. Cr cds: A, D, DS, MC, V.

D

★ ★ **POTPOURRI HOUSE.** *2301 S Broadway (75701). 903/592-4171.* Hrs: 11 am-3 pm; dessert menu 3-4 pm. Closed Sun; some major hols. Res accepted. Semi-a la carte: lunch $5.95-$7.25. Childs' meals. Specializes in marinated chicken breast, Heavenly Chicken Salad, turtle fudge cheesecake. Salad bar. Own baking, soups. Parking. Victorian garden decor. Totally nonsmoking. Cr cds: A, MC, V.

D

✔ ★ **SZECHUAN.** *6421 S Broadway (75703). 903/581-4310.* Hrs: 11 am-10 pm; Fri & Sat to 11 pm. Closed Thanksgiving. Res accepted. Chinese menu. Bar. Semi-a la carte: lunch $3.95-$4.50, dinner $6.95-$13.95. Specialties: General Tso's chicken, crispy shrimp. Parking. Modern decor. Cr cds: A, C, D, DS, MC, V.

D

Unrated Dining Spots

LUBY'S CAFETERIA. *1815 Roseland, in Bergfeld Shopping Ctr. 903/597-2901.* Hrs: 10:45 am-2:30 pm, 4:15-8 pm; Sat, Sun 10:45 am-8 pm. Closed Dec 24-25. Avg ck: lunch $4.45, dinner $4.60. Specializes in salads, homemade pastries. Cr cds: DS, MC, V.

D

TYLER SQUARE TEA ROOM. *117 S Broadway. 903/592-2433.* Hrs: 10 am-5 pm. Closed Sun; most major hols. Res accepted. Semi-a la carte: lunch $2.95-$6.55. Child's meals. Specializes in gem salad, banana split salad, quiche. Salad bar (exc Sat). Tea room on balcony above antique shop. Cr cds: A.

Uvalde (D-5)

(See Brackettville, Eagle Pass)

Founded 1855 **Pop** 14,729 **Elev** 913 ft **Area code** 210 **Zip** 78801
Information Chamber of Commerce, PO Box 706; 210/278-3361.

The Balcones escarpment divides Uvalde County into rugged upland hills and valleys to the north and low, flat mesquite country to the south. Livestock, cotton, vegetables, pecans and large quantities of honey from desert blossoms, called "Uvalde honey," come from the area.

What to See and Do

Garner Memorial Museum. Home of Vice President John Nance Garner; houses displays on the life and career of Garner, and Uvalde County history. (Daily exc Sun; closed major hols) 333 N Park St. Phone 210/278-5018. ¢

Garner State Park. Swimming; fishing. Hiking trail; birdwatching. Miniature golf (seasonal). Picnicking, concessions. Improved campsites, screened shelters, cabins (dump station). Standard fees. (Daily) 30 mi N on US 83, then 1 mi E on Park Rd 29. Phone 210/232-6132. Per vehicle ¢¢¢

Grand Opera House (1891) Used for plays, ballets, orchestra performances; also includes historical room. Tours (Mon-Fri; closed most hols). 104 W North St. Phone 210/278-4184.

Annual Events

Sahawe Indian Dance Ceremonials. 3 wkends Feb, 1 wk July.

Air Fiesta. Garner Field Rd. Soaring competitions. Aug.

Cactus Jack Festival. Art show, Native American dancers. 2nd wkend Oct.

Motel

★ **HOLIDAY INN.** *920 E Main. 210/278-4511.* 150 rms, 2 story. S $49-$52; D $57-$60; each addl $8; suites $78-$84; under 18 free. TV; cable (premium). Pool. Restaurant 6 am-2 pm, 5-10 pm. Rm serv. Bar 4:30-11:45 pm, closed Sun; dancing. Ck-out noon. Meeting rms. Valet serv. Cr cds: A, C, D, DS, JCB, MC, V.

D ⊁ ⊠ ⊠ ⊠ SC

Van Horn (C-2)

Pop 2,930 **Elev** 4,010 ft **Area code** 915 **Zip** 79855
Information Chamber of Commerce, 1801 W Broadway, PO Box 762; 915/283-2043.

The mountains surrounding Van Horn provide an exceptional setting for the town, which is a cattle and sheep market. It is also a center for cotton, vegetables and grain, first grown here in 1950 after discovery of a great underground water deposit. Milling talc and marble are equally important industries.

Just west of town in the Diablo Mountains roams the last remaining flock of bighorn sheep in Texas. These sheep are the subject of a successful breeding program. Deer, antelope, quail and dove are abundant in the rugged mountains of the area.

Annual Events

Livestock Show. Convention Center. Auction, barbecue. Mid-Jan.

Culberson County Fair. Late Sept.

Motels

★ ★ **BEST WESTERN INN OF VAN HORN.** *Box 1179, 6 blks W on US 80 Business. 915/283-2410; FAX 915/283-2143.* 60 rms. S $37-$43; D $44-$53; each addl $4; suites $60; under 12 free. Crib $2. Pet accepted, some restrictions. TV; cable (premium). Pool. Complimentary continental bkfst. Restaurant 6:15 am-10 pm. Private club 5-11 pm. Closed Sun. Ck-out noon. Lndry facilities. Business servs avail. 9-hole golf privileges. Cr cds: A, C, D, DS, ER, JCB, MC, V.

D ⊁ ⊼ ⊠ ⊠ ⊠ SC

✔ ★ **HOWARD JOHNSON.** *Box 776, 1 mi W on US 80 Business. 915/283-2780; res: 800/543-8831; FAX 915/283-2804.* 98 rms, 2 story. S $40-$47; D $47-$50; each addl $5; under 18 free. Crib free. Pet accepted, some restrictions. TV; cable (premium), VCR avail. Pool; wading pool. Restaurant 6 am-10 pm. Rm serv. Ck-out 1 pm. Bar;

entertainment. Coin lndry. Meeting rms. Business servs avail. Sundries. Cr cds: A, C, D, DS, MC, V.

Restaurant

✔★ **SMOKEHOUSE.** 905 Broadway, I-10 exit 138 (E), 140 (W). 915/283-2453. Hrs: 6 am-10:30 pm. Closed Dec 25. Res accepted. Mexican, Amer menu. A la carte entrees: bkfst $1.50-$5.95, lunch $2.95-$12.95, dinner $4-$12.95. Child's meals. Specializes in smoked meats, homemade bread. Parking. Three themed dining areas. Auto museum adj. Cr cds: A, D, DS, MC, V.

D

Vernon (A-5)

(See Wichita Falls)

Founded 1889 **Pop** 12,001 **Elev** 1,216 ft **Area code** 817 **Zip** 76384
Information Chamber of Commerce, 1725 Pease St, PO Box 1538; 817/552-2564.

Vernon is headquarters of the 500,000-acre W.T. Waggoner Ranch, one of the largest in the United States. In its early days it was a supply point for trail riders driving herds of cattle north. Doan's Crossing, 16 miles northeast, was a famous cattle trail crossing for the Red River.

What to See and Do

Lake Kemp. Swimming, waterskiing; fishing; boating. 25 mi S via US 183, 283.

Red River Valley Museum. Archaeological exhibits & Native American artifacts. Big game collection includes more than 130 trophies, including black rhino and polar bear; History of Texas Ranching Room includes a 10-by-20-foot Waggoner mural. Sculpture exhibit includes busts of famous people; traveling exhibits room. (Tues-Sun afternoons; closed some major hols) On US 70, just off US 287. Phone 817/553-1848. **Free.**

Annual Event

Santa Rosa Roundup. Rodeo, parade, specialty acts, Santa Rosa Palomino Club. Phone 817/552-6868. 3rd wkend May.

Motels

★ **DAYS INN.** 3110 Frontage Rd, off US 287 Bentley St exit. 817/552-9982; FAX 817/552-7851. 50 rms, 2 story. S $42; D $47. TV; VCR avail (movies avail). Pool. Restaurant adj 6 am-9 pm. Ck-out noon. Business servs avail. Cr cds: A, C, D, DS, MC, V.

✔★ **GREEN TREE INN.** 3029 Morton, off US 287, Bentley St exit. 817/552-5421; res: 800/600-5421; FAX 817/552-5421. 30 rms. S $30-$34; D $34-$42; each addl $4; under 12 free. TV; cable. Pool. Complimentary coffee, continental bkfst in lobby. Ck-out 11 am. Cr cds: A, C, D, DS, MC, V.

Restaurants

✔★ **GOLDEN CORRAL.** 4201 College Dr. 817/552-2901. Hrs: 7 am-10 pm; Fri-Sat to 11 pm. Closed Dec 25. Continental bkfst buffet: $2.99. A la carte entrees: lunch, dinner $4.29-$9.99. Child's meals. Specializes in steak. Parking. Cr cds: DS, MC, V.

D SC

★ **HUIE PALACE.** 2424 Wilbarger. 817/552-2573. Hrs: 11 am-2 pm, 5-9 pm. Closed Thanksgiving, Dec 25. Res accepted. Chinese, Mexican, Amer menu. A la carte entrees: lunch $4.25-$13.75, dinner $5.25-$13.75. Child's meals. Specializes in Chinese dinners, seafood. Parking. Oriental decor. Cr cds: A, C, D, DS, MC, V.

D

Victoria (D-7)

(See Goliad, Port Lavaca)

Founded 1824 **Pop** 55,076 **Elev** 93 ft **Area code** 512
Information Convention & Visitors Bureau, 700 Main Center, Suite 101, PO Box 2465, 77902; 512/573-5277 or 800/926-5774.

In 1685 Robert Cavelier, Sieur de La Salle, established a fort at the head of Lavaca Bay and claimed the area for France. The Spanish set up a fort and a mission in 1722. Victoria itself was settled by the Spanish, founded in 1824 by Martin DeLeon and named after a Mexican President, Guadalupe Victoria. Anglo-Americans soon moved in and were active in the Texas Revolution.

Victoria County is one of the leading cattle areas in Texas. Brahmans and crossbreeds are a big part of the economy. Victoria, with its oil and chemicals, is a part of the booming Texas Gulf Coast. Shipping is aided by the 35-mile-long Victoria Canal, connecting link to the Intracoastal Waterway.

What to See and Do

Coleto Creek Reservoir. Approx 3,100 acres of fresh water. Extensive lakefront; waterskiing, fishing (lighted pier); boating. Nature trail, pavilion. Picnicking, playground. Improved camping (fee). (Daily) 14 mi SW via US 59S. Phone 512/575-6366. Per vehicle ¢¢¢

Memorial Square. Oldest public burial ground in the city. Three monuments outline history of the area. A steam locomotive and Dutch windmill are also here. Commercial & Wheeler Sts.

Riverside Park. A 562-acre site on Guadalupe River. Picnic areas, barbecue pits; playgrounds; duck pond; rose garden; hiking/biking trail; boat ramp; 27-hole golf, baseball fields, RV campsites (fee). (Daily) Red River & Memorial Sts. **Free.** Within the park is

Texas Zoo. Indoor & outdoor exhibits of animals native to Texas include margays, ocelots, jaguarundis and a pair of rare red wolves. (Daily; closed Jan 1, Thanksgiving, Dec 25) 110 Memorial Dr. ¢

Annual Events

PRCA Rodeo. Victoria Community Center. Last wkend Feb.

Victoria Jaycees Stockshow. 2nd wkend Mar.

Bach Festival. June.

Motels

✔★★ **HAMPTON INN.** 3112 Houston Hwy (77901). 512/578-2030; FAX 512/573-1238. 102 rms, 2 story. S, D $42-$49; suites $52-$59; under 18 free. Crib free. Pet accepted. TV; cable. Pool. Complimentary continental bkfst. Restaurant nearby. Ck-out 1 pm. Meeting rms. Valet serv. Free airport transportation. Health club privileges. Cr cds: A, C, D, DS, MC, V.

★★ **HOLIDAY INN.** 2705 E Houston Hwy (77901). 512/575-0251; FAX 512/575-8362. 226 rms, 2 story. S $48-$64; D $55-$71;

each addl $7; suites $64-$71; under 18 free; wkend rates. Crib free. Pet accepted. TV; cable (premium). Indoor/outdoor pool. Restaurant 6 am-10 pm. Rm serv. Bar 3 pm-12:30 am, closed Sun; dancing. Ck-out 1 pm. Coin lndry. Meeting rms. Business servs avail. In-rm modem link. Bellhops. Valet serv. Sundries. Free airport transportation. Exercise equipt; weight machine, bicycle, whirlpool, sauna. Holidome. Game rm. Cr cds: A, C, D, DS, JCB, MC, V.

★ ★ LA QUINTA. 7603 N Navarro Hwy (77904). 512/572-3585; FAX 512/576-4617. 130 rms, 2 story. S $48-$55; D $56-$64; each addl $8; under 18 free. Crib free. TV. Pool. Complimentary continental bkfst. Restaurant adj open 24 hrs. Ck-out noon. Meeting rms. Cr cds: A, C, D, DS, MC, V.

✔ ★ ★ RAMADA INN. 3901 Houston Hwy (77901). 512/578-2723; FAX 512/578-2723, ext. 306. 126 rms, 2 story. S $42-$47; D $44-$49; each addl $10; family, wkend rates. Crib free. TV; cable. Pool; whirlpool, sauna, poolside serv. Restaurant 6 am-10 pm; Sun 7 am-3 pm. Rm serv to 9:30 pm. Bar 4 pm-midnight, closed Sun. Ck-out 1 pm. Meeting rms. Free airport, bus depot transportation. Cr cds: A, C, D, DS, JCB, MC, V.

Restaurant

★ OLDE VICTORIA. 207 N Navarro. 512/572-8840. Hrs: 11 am-2 pm, 5-10 pm; Sat from 5 pm. Closed Sun; Thanksgiving, Dec 25. Res accepted. French, Italian menu. Bar. Semi-a la carte: lunch $4.95-$9.95, dinner $8.95-$16.95. Child's meals. Specialties: tournedos Capri, veal & shrimp Milano. Outdoor dining. Old mansion in historic section of town. Cr cds: A, MC, V.

D

Unrated Dining Spot

LUBY'S CAFETERIA. 7800 N Avaro. 512/572-3023. Hrs: 10:45 am-2:30 pm, 4:15-8:30 pm; Sat, Sun 10:45 am-8:30 pm. Closed Dec 25. Avg ck: lunch, dinner $4.85. Specializes in roast beef, fried fish, fresh vegetables. Parking. Cr cds: DS, MC, V.

Waco (C-7)

(See Groesbeck, Temple)

Founded 1849 **Pop** 103,590 **Elev** 427 ft **Area code** 817
Information Waco Tourist Information Center, PO Box 2570, 76702; 817/750-8696 or 800/922-6386.

Named for the Huaco (WAY-co) Indians, this area has been a trade, distribution and travel center since the first permanent white settler, Captain Shapley P. Ross, ran a ferry across the Brazos River. The ferry put Waco on the main thoroughfare to the West.

From 1857 to 1865 the city was at the center of the Texas secessionist movement. Consequently it suffered considerable disruption of civic and business affairs, making a slow recovery after the Civil War. Waco is now alive with industries and modern businesses.

What to See and Do

Baylor University (1845). (12,000 students) Chartered by the Republic of Texas in 1845, Baylor University is the oldest university in continuous existence in the state. 1301 University Parks Dr. Phone 817/755-1921. On the 425-acre campus are

Strecker Museum. Biology, geology, archaeology and anthropology exhibits; "Man's Cultural Heritage in Central Texas"; 1835 log cabin. World's largest fossil sea turtle; exhibit of local reptiles. (Daily exc Mon; closed some major hols) Basement of Sid Richardson Science Bldg. Phone 817/755-1110. **Free.**

Armstrong Browning Library. World's largest collection of books, letters, manuscripts, memorabilia of Robert Browning and Elizabeth Barrett Browning. (Daily exc Sun; closed hols) 700 Speight St. Phone 817/755-3566. **Free.**

Gov. Bill & Vara Daniel Historic Village. A reconstructed 1890s Texas river town. (Daily exc Mon) University Parks Dr. Phone 817/755-1160. **¢¢**

Fort Fisher Park. Headquarters for Company F, Texas Rangers, Waco Tourist Information Center and the Texas Rangers Hall of Fame and Museum. Approx 30 acres. Picnicking. Camping (tent & trailer sites; 2-wk limit; fee). (Daily) I-35 & University Dr, exit 335B. Phone 817/750-5996. **Free.** Within the park is

Texas Ranger Hall of Fame & Museum. Texas Ranger memorabilia, firearms exhibits & dioramas with wax figures depict more than 170-year history of Texas Rangers; 20-min film, *Story of Texas Rangers;* Western art; library. (Daily; closed Jan 1, Dec 25) Phone 817/750-8631. **¢¢**

Lake Waco Swimming, waterskiing; fishing; boating (ramps). Nature trail. Picnicking. Camping (tent & trailer sites, dump station). Some fees. (Daily) Headquarters is 2 mi NW on FM 1637 (N 19th St), then approx 1½ mi W, follow signs. Phone 817/756-5379. Per vehicle **¢¢**

Restored houses. Earle-Napier-Kinnard House (1867). 814 S 4th St. Two-story Greek-revival home; furnished in 1860s style (summer tours Thurs-Mon). **East Terrace** (ca 1872). 100 Mill St. Two-story Italianate villa-style house built with bricks made from Brazos River clay; period furnishings. **Fort House** (1868). 503 S 4th St. Antiques and local historical exhibits in Greek-revival home. **Champe Carter McCulloch House** (1866). 407 Columbus Ave. Two-story Greek-revival home, period furnishings. (All houses: Sat & Sun; closed Easter & Thanksgiving weeks & Dec-Jan 2) Combination ticket avail. Phone 817/753-5166. Per house **¢**

The Art Center. Permanent and changing exhibits in renovated Mediterranean-style house. (Tues-Sat & Sun afternoon) Sr citizen rate. 1300 College Dr. Phone 817/752-4371. **¢**

Annual Events

Brazos River Festival & Pilgrimage. Cotton Palace Pageant; tours of homes; festival at Fort Fisher. Last full wkend Apr.

Heart o' Texas Fair & Rodeo. Coliseum & Fairgrounds, 46th & Bosque Blvd. Early Oct.

Christmas on the Brazos. 1st full wkend Dec.

Seasonal Event

Heart o' Texas Speedway. 203 Trailwood. Stock car racing. Phone 817/829-2294. Mar-Sept.

Motels

★ ★ BEST WESTERN OLD MAIN LODGE. *PO Box 174 (76703), I-35 at 4th St.* 817/753-0316; FAX 817/753-3811. 84 rms. S $50; D $56; each addl $6; under 18 free; higher rates special events. Crib free. Pool. TV; cable (premium). Complimentary coffee in lobby. Restaurant adj open 24 hrs. Ck-out 1 pm. Meeting rms. Business servs avail. Valet serv. Some refrigerators. Cr cds: A, C, D, DS, MC, V.

✔ ★ COMFORT INN. 1430 I-35S (76706). 817/752-1991. 53 rms, 2 story. S ,D $52-$89; each addl $5; suites $89; under 18 free; higher rates special events. Crib free. TV; cable (premium), VCR avail.

Pool. Complimentary continental bkfst. Ck-out 11 am. Meeting rms. Business servs avail. In-rm modem link. Cr cds: A, C, D, DS, MC, V.

[D] [≈] [⊠] [☂] [SC]

★ ★ **LA QUINTA MOTOR INN.** *1110 S 9th St (76706), I-35 exit 18th St.* 817/752-9741; FAX 817/757-1600. 102 rms, 2 story. S $52-$59; D $59-$66; each addl $7; suites $62-$72; under 18 free. Crib free. Pet accepted, some restrictions. TV; cable (premium), VCR avail. Pool. Complimentary continental bkfst. Complimentary coffee in lobby. Restaurant adj open 24 hrs. Ck-out noon. Meeting rm. Business servs avail. In-rm modem link. Valet serv. Sundries. Baylor Univ nearby. Cr cds: A, C, D, DS, MC, V.

[D] [✔] [≈] [⊠] [☂] [SC]

★ ★ **LEXINGTON INN.** *115 Jack Kultgen Frwy (76706).* 817/754-1266; FAX 817/755-8612. 113 rms, 3 story. S $55-$58; D $62-$67; addl $7; under 16 free. Crib free. TV; cable. Heated pool; whirlpool. Complimentary continental bkfst, coffee. Restaurant nearby. Ck-out noon. Meeting rm. Business servs avail. In-rm modem link. Valet serv. Free airport transportation. Adj Baylor Univ. Free Wed evening cookout. Cr cds: A, C, D, DS, MC, V.

[D] [≈] [⊠] [☂] [SC]

★ ★ **QUALITY INN.** *801 S 4th St (76706), I-35 4th & 5th St exit.* 817/757-2000; FAX 817/757-1110. 148 rms, 2 story. S $60-$70; D $66-$76; each addl $6; under 18 free. Crib free. TV; cable (premium). Indoor pool. Complimentary continental bkfst. Coffee in rms. Restaurant 6 am-2 pm, 5-9 pm; Sat from 7 am, Sun 7-10 am. Rm serv. Bar 5-9 pm, closed Sun. Ck-out noon. Coin lndry. Meeting rms. Business center. In-rm modem link. Valet serv. Airport, bus depot transportation. Exercise equipt; weight machine, stair machine, whirlpool. Game rm. Cr cds: A, C, D, DS, MC, V.

[D] [≈] [🏋] [⊠] [☂] [SC] [♿] [⚖]

Motor Hotels

★ ★ **HOLIDAY INN I-35.** *1001 Lake Brazos Dr (76704), I-35 Lake Brazos Dr exit.* 817/753-0261; FAX 817/753-0227. 171 rms, 4 story. S $65-$80; D $75-$85; each addl $6; suites $100-$164; under 19 free; higher rates Baylor Univ football, special event wkends. Crib free. Pet accepted. TV. Pool; wading pool. Restaurant 6 am-2 pm, 5-10 pm. Rm serv. Bar 5 pm-midnight. Ck-out noon. Coin lndry. Meeting rms. Business servs avail. In-rm modem link. Valet serv. Sundries. Health club privileges. Balconies. Near Brazos River. Cr cds: A, C, D, DS, JCB, MC, V.

[D] [✔] [≈] [⊠] [☂] [SC]

✔ ★ **RAMADA INN.** *4201 Franklin Ave (76710).* 817/772-9440; FAX 817/751-0020. 123 rms, 2 story. S, D $55-$65; each addl $8; under 18 free; higher rates special events. Crib free. Pet accepted, some restrictions. TV; cable (premium). Pool. Complimentary continental bkfst, coffee in rms. Restaurant 5:30 am-2 pm, 5-10 pm. Ck-out noon. Coin lndry. Meeting rms. Business servs avail. Free airport transportation. Refrigerators. Cr cds: A, C, D, DS, MC, V.

[✔] [≈] [⊠] [☂] [SC]

Hotel

★ ★ ★ **HILTON INN.** *113 S University Parks Dr (76701).* 817/754-8484; FAX 817/752-2214. 199 rms, 11 story. S $69-$89; D $79-$99; each addl $10; family rates; higher rates special events. TV; cable (premium), VCR avail. Pool; whirlpool, poolside serv. Restaurant 6:30 am-2 pm, 5-10 pm. Bar 4 pm-midnight, Sat to 1 am. Ck-out noon. Convention facilities. Business servs avail. Free airport, bus depot transportation. Tennis. On Brazos River, adj Convention Center and Indian Spring Park. Cr cds: A, C, D, DS, ER, MC, V.

[D] [🏋] [≈] [⊠] [☂] [SC]

Restaurants

★ ★ **BRAZOS QUEEN II.** *On Brazos River (76703), I-35 exit Fort Fisher Park.* 817/757-2332. Hrs: 5-10 pm. Closed Sun & Mon; some major hols. Res accepted. Bar. Semi-a la carte: dinner $7.95-$24. Child's meals. Specializes in New Orleans-style dishes, fresh seafood, beef. Parking. Reproduction of Victorian-era riverboat; grand staircase in dining salon similar to that of Delta Queen. Cr cds: A, DS, MC, V.

[D]

✔ ★ **ELITE CAFE.** *2132 S Valley Mills Dr (76632).* 817/754-4941. Hrs: 8-10 pm; Fri & Sat to 11 pm. Closed Dec 25. Bar 11:30 am-midnight. Semi-a la carte: bkfst $1.50-$3.95, lunch, dinner $3.95-$12.95. Child's meals. Specializes in steak, fajitas, cheese burgers. Parking. Art deco furnishings. Cr cds: A, C, D, DS, MC, V.

[D]

★ ★ **NICK'S.** *4508 W Waco Dr (76710).* 817/772-7790. Hrs: 11 am-9:30 pm; Fri to 10 pm; Sat 5-10 pm. Closed Sun; major hols; also Dec 24-Jan 2. Res accepted. Greek, Mexican, Amer menu. Bar. Semi-a la carte: lunch $5-$15, dinner $8-$27. Child's meals. Specializes in steak, seafood. Parking. Local artwork. Family-owned. Cr cds: A, C, D, DS, MC, V.

✔ ★ **TANGLEWOOD FARMS.** *221 I-35S, exit 335 B (76706).* 817/752-7221. Hrs: 6 am-9 pm; Fri, Sat to 11 pm. Semi-a la carte: bkfst $4.25-$7.95, lunch, dinner $4.95-$13. Child's meals. Specializes in country-fried steak, catfish, pork chops. Own biscuits. Cr cds: A, C, D, DS, MC, V.

[D] [SC]

★ **WATERWORKS.** *101 Martin Luther King Ave (76706), I-35 Lake Brazos Dr exit.* 817/756-2181. Hrs: 5-10:30 pm. Closed major hols. Bar. Semi-a la carte: dinner $14.95-$24.50. Child's meals. Specialties: veal Oscar, crab meat & shrimp-stuffed filet, steak Gabrielle. Entertainment Tues, Fri & Sat. Parking. Cr cds: A, DS, MC, V.

Unrated Dining Spots

LUBY'S CAFETERIA. *1520 N Valley Mills Dr, in Parkdale Shopping Center.* 817/776-0521. Hrs: 10:45 am-8:30 pm. Closed Dec 24 eve-Dec 25. Avg ck: lunch $5.50, dinner $6.50. Specializes in fried fish, okra, strawberry pie. Cr cds: DS, MC, V.

UNDERWOOD'S CAFETERIA. *1800 N Valley Mills Dr.* 817/776-9441. Hrs: 10:30 am-9 pm. Closed Wed; Thanksgiving, Dec 25. Avg ck: lunch, dinner $6. Specializes in barbecued beef, chicken, ribs. Parking. Cr cds: MC, V.

[D]

Weatherford (B-6)

(For accommodations see Fort Worth, also see Mineral Wells)

Pop 14,804 **Elev** 1,052 ft **Area code** 817 **Zip** 76086
Information Chamber of Commerce, 401 Ft Worth St, PO Box 310; 817/594-3801.

What to See and Do

Heritage Gallery. 1214 Charles St, in Weatherford Public Library. Memorabilia of famous Weatherford citizens including Mary Martin, Larry Hagman and Jim Wright, former Speaker of the House. (Mon-Fri, afternoons) Phone 817/598-4150. **Free.**

Holland Lake Park. Ten-acre municipal park; living museum of nature. An original dog-run log cabin, the first built in the county. Playground, picnicking. (Daily) Off Clear Lake Rd exit from I-20.

Lake Weatherford. Water sports, fishing; boating, Picnicking. (Daily) 8 mi NE on FM 1707.

Trinity Meadows Raceway. Parimutuel race track for both quarterhorse & Thoroughbred racing; stakes & futurity racing. (Mar-Dec, Thurs-Sun) 10 mi E on I-20 (US 80/180), between exits 415 & 418; N side of hwy, entrance from frontage road. Phone 817/441-9240. ¢¢

Annual Event

Peach Festival. 2nd Sat July.

Wichita Falls (A-6)

(See Vernon)

Founded 1882 **Pop** 96,259 **Elev** 946 ft **Area code** 817
Information Convention and Visitors Bureau, PO Box 630, 76307; 817/723-2741 or 800/799-6732.

Wichita Falls was named for the Wichita who lived on the Big Wichita River, near a waterfall that disappeared around the turn of the century. A re-creation of the falls was completed in 1987 and has become the symbol of a prosperous community. Wichita Falls is an industrial center for 150 manufacturing plants that produce a variety of products, such as fiberglass reinforcements, plate glass, gas turbine components, oil field equipment and electronic components. Livestock, wheat, oil and cotton also contribute to the economy. Sheppard AFB, one of the largest air force technical training centers in the nation, is five miles north on US 277/281.

The rebuilt falls can be seen from I-44 heading into town from the north. They are 54 feet high and recirculate the river's waters at a rate of 3,500 gallons per minute.

What to See and Do

Kell House (1909). Landmark with original family furnishings. High ceilings, oak floors, ornate woodwork, period pieces. Guided tour relates history of the early settlement of the area. Tours (Tues-Fri & Sun, afternoons; closed some major hols) 900 Bluff St. Phone 817/723-0623. ¢¢

Recreational facilities.

Lake Wichita. Swimming, waterskiing; fishing; boating. Off Fairway Blvd.

Lake Arrowhead State Park. Swimming, waterskiing; fishing; boating (ramp, rentals). Nature, bridle trails. Picnicking, playground. Improved camping (hookups, dump station). Standard fees. 15 mi SE of town via US 281 & FM 1954. Phone 817/528-2211.

Lake Kickapoo. Swimming, waterskiing; fishing; boating. 25 mi SW via US 82 to Mankins, then S off TX 25.

Diversion Reservoir. Swimming, waterskiing; fishing; boating. 25 mi W via US 82, TX 258.

Trails & Tales of Boomtown, USA. Displays, photographs and audiovisual presentations illustrate the famous 1918 Burkburnett oil boom and surrounding events. Guided bus tour (1³/₄ hr) of various sites relevant to the boom. (June-Oct, Fri & Sat; tour, Sat only) Sr citizen rate. 102 W 3rd St in Burkburnett; 15 mi N on I-44E to TX 240W, Burkburnett exit. Phone 817/569-0460. Tour and video ¢¢¢

Wichita Falls Museum & Art Center. Permanent & changing art and hands-on science exhibits; Children's Discovery Room. Planetarium shows (Sat & Sun afternoons, fee). Museum (daily exc Mon; closed hols). 2 Eureka Circle. Phone 817/692-0923. ¢¢

Annual Events

Texas Weapon Collectors Association Gun & Knife Shows. 350 exhibitors from 8-state area; antique and modern firearms. Activities Center. Wkends in Jan, Feb, Apr, Aug & Nov.

Spring Fling Festival. Wichita Falls Museum & Art Center. National arts and crafts fair, auction; entertainment, children's activities. Last full wkend Apr.

Texas Ranch Roundup. Team competition among 11 of the largest ranches in Texas. Phone 817/322-0771. 3rd wkend Aug.

Hotter 'n Hell Bicycle Ride. Trails varying in length from 6 miles to 100 miles; race. Music; homemade ice cream contest; food and beverages. Phone 817/322-3223. 9 days before Labor Day.

Fantasy of Lights. Midwestern State University. 3400 Taft Blvd, 2 mi SW. More than 30 magnificent Christmas diplays and 18,000 lights outlining campus buildings. Begun in 1920s. Dec.

Motels

★ **DAYS INN.** *1211 Central Frwy (76304), Maurine St exit.* 817/723-5541; FAX 817/723-6342. 101 rms, 2 story. S $48-$54; D $54-$60; each addl $6; under 15 free. TV; cable (premium). Pool. Playground. Ck-out 11 am. Meeting rms. Free airport transportation. Cr cds: A, C, D, DS, ER, MC, V.

⊠ ⊠ ⊠ ⊠ SC

✔ ★ **ECONO LODGE.** *1700 Fifth St (76301).* 817/761-1889; FAX 817/761-1505. 115 rms, 4 story. S $39; D $43; each addl $4; under 18 free. Crib free. TV; cable (premium). Pool. Complimentary continental bkfst, coffee. Restaurant nearby. Ck-out 11 am. Meeting rm. Business servs avail. Cr cds: A, C, D, DS, MC, V.

D ⊠ ⊠ ⊠ ⊠ SC

★ ★ **LA QUINTA.** *1128 Central Frwy N (76305).* 817/322-6971; FAX 817/723-2573. 139 rms, 2 story. S $45; D $53; each addl $8; suites $59-$63; under 18 free. Crib free. TV; cable. Pool. Complimentary continental bkfst 6:30-9:30 am. Restaurant adj open 24 hrs. Ck-out noon. Coin lndry. Meeting rm. Valet serv. Cr cds: A, C, D, DS, MC, V.

D ⊠ ⊠ ⊠ ⊠ SC

Motor Hotel

★ ★ **HOLIDAY INN.** *401 Broad St (76301).* 817/766-6000; FAX 817/766-5942. 248 rms, 4 story. S $58; D $68; each addl $10; suites $99-$200; under 17 free; higher rates wkend of Hotter 'n Hell Bicycle Ride. Crib free. TV. 2 pools, 1 indoor; wading pool, whirlpool, poolside serv. Restaurant 6 am-2 pm, 5-10 pm. Rm serv. Bar 4 pm-midnight. Ck-out noon. Meeting rms. Bellhops. Sundries. Gift shop. Putting green. Game rm. Bathrm phone, refrigerator, wet bar in suites. Cr cds: A, C, D, DS, MC, V.

D ⊠ ⊠ ⊠ SC

Hotel

★ ★ **SHERATON.** *100 Central Frwy (76307), 2 mi N on I-44.* 817/761-6000; FAX 817/766-1488. 167 units, 6 story. S $66-$76; D $70-$80; each addl $10; suites $85-$235; under 18 free. Crib free. TV; cable (premium), VCR avail. Indoor/outdoor pool; whirlpool, poolside serv. Restaurant 6 am-2 pm, 5-10 pm. Rm serv 6 am-10 pm. Bar 4 pm-2 am, closed Sun; entertainment, dancing. Ck-out noon. Meeting rms. Business servs avail. In-rm modem link. Airport transportation. Game rm. Refrigerators. Cr cds: A, C, D, DS, ER, MC, V.

D ⊠ ⊠ ⊠ ⊠ SC

Restaurants

★ **CHINA HOUSE.** *507 Beverly Dr, at jct Loop 11. 817/723-9290.* Hrs: 11 am-9:30 pm. Chinese, Amer menu. Bar. Semi-a la carte: lunch, dinner $3.75-$9.25. Chinese decor; lanterns; fish tank in lobby. Parking. Cr cds: A, DS, MC, V.

✔★ **EL CHICOS.** *1028 Central Frwy. 817/322-1455.* Hrs: 11 am-10 pm; Fri, Sat to 11 pm. Closed Thanksgiving, Dec 25. Res accepted. Tex-Mex menu. Bar. A la carte entrees: lunch, dinner $2-$8. Semi-a la carte: lunch $4-$8, dinner $5-$8. Child's meals. Specializes in fajitas. Parking. Mexican decor; murals, wall hangings, rugs. Cr cds: A, C, D, DS, MC, V.

Unrated Dining Spot

LUBY'S CAFETERIA. *1801 9th St (76301). 817/723-8233.* Hrs: 11 am-2:30 pm, 4:30-8:30 pm. Closed Dec 24 & 25. Avg ck: lunch, dinner $4-$6. Specializes in seafood, prime rib. Salad bar. Cr cds: D, DS, MC, V.

Index

Establishment names are listed in alphabetical order followed by a symbol identifying their classification, and then city, state and page number. Establishments affiliated with a chain appear alphabetically under their chain name, followed by the state, city and page number. The symbols for classification are: [H] for hotels; [I] for inns; [M] for motels; [L] for lodges; [MH] for motor hotels; [R] for restaurants; [RO] for resorts, guest ranches, and cottage colonies; [U] for unrated dining spots. States are arranged alphabetically as are the cities and towns within each state.

The right oil can save more than an expensive car.

Mobil Travel Guide

Order Form

If you would like other editions of the MOBIL TRAVEL GUIDES that might not be available at your local bookstore or Mobil dealer, please use this order form or call the toll-free number below.

Ship to:

Name _____

Address _____

City _____ State _____ Zip _____

☐ My check is enclosed.

☐ Please charge my credit card

    ☐ VISA ☐ MasterCard ☐ American Express

Credit Card # _____

Expiration _____

Signature _____

Please send me the following 1996 Mobil Travel Guides:

☐ 0-679-03042-5
California and the West (Arizona, California, Nevada, Utah)
$14.95 (Can $21)

☐ 0-679-03044-1
Great Lakes (Illinois, Indiana, Michigan, Ohio, Wisconsin, Canada: Ontario)
$14.95 (Can $21)

☐ 0-679-03045-X
Mid-Atlantic (Delaware, District of Columbia, Maryland, New Jersey, North Carolina, Pennsylvania, South Carolina, Virginia, West Virginia)
$14.95 (Can $21)

☐ 0-679-03046-8
Northeast (Connecticut, Maine, Massachusetts, New Hampshire, New York, Rhode Island, Vermont, Canada: New Brunswick, Nova Scotia, Ontario, Prince Edward Island, Québec)
$14.95 (Can $21)

☐ 0-679-03047-6
Northwest and Great Plains (Idaho, Iowa, Minnesota, Montana, Nebraska, North Dakota, Oregon, South Dakota, Washington, Wyoming, Canada: Alberta, British Columbia, Manitoba)
$14.95 (Can $21)

☐ 0-679-03048-4
Southeast (Alabama, Florida, Georgia, Kentucky, Mississippi, Tennessee)
$14.95 (Can $21)

☐ 0-679-03049-2
Southwest & South Central (Arkansas, Colorado, Kansas, Louisiana, Missouri, New Mexico, Oklahoma, Texas)
$14.95 (Can $21)

☐ 0-679-03043-3
Frequent Traveler's Guide to Major Cities (Detailed coverage of 46 major U.S. cities, plus airport maps)
$15.95 (Can $21.95)

Total cost of book(s) ordered $ _____

Shipping & Handling (please add $2 for first book, $.50 for each additional book) $ _____

Add applicable sales tax* $ _____

    TOTAL AMOUNT ENCLOSED $ _____

*To ensure that all orders are processed efficiently, please apply sales tax in Canada and in the following states: CA, CT, FL, IL, NJ, NY, TN and WA.

Please mail this form to:

Mobil Travel Guides
Random House
400 Hahn Rd.
Westminster, MD 21157
**or call toll-free, 24 hours
a day 1-800-533-6478**

Mobil Travel Guide

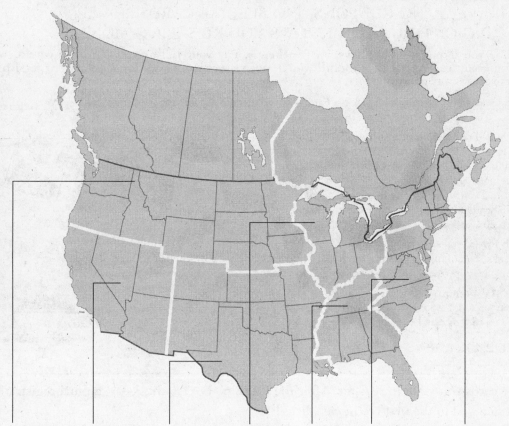

Northwest & Great Plains

Idaho
Iowa
Minnesota
Montana
Nebraska
North Dakota
Oregon
South Dakota
Washington
Wyoming

Canada:
Alberta
British Columbia
Manitoba

California & the West

Arizona
California
Nevada
Utah

Southwest & South Central

Arkansas
Colorado
Kansas
Louisiana
Missouri
New Mexico
Oklahoma
Texas

Great Lakes

Illinois
Indiana
Michigan
Ohio
Wisconsin

Canada:
Ontario

Southeast

Alabama
Florida
Georgia
Kentucky
Mississippi
Tennessee

Mid–Atlantic

Delaware
District of Columbia
Maryland
New Jersey
North Carolina
Pennsylvania
South Carolina
Virginia
West Virginia

Northeast

Connecticut
Maine
Massachusetts
New Hampshire
New York
Rhode Island
Vermont

Canada:
New Brunswick
Nova Scotia
Ontario
Prince Edward Island
Quebec

GET
20% CASH BACK
WHEN YOU DINE AT YOUR FAVORITE RESTAURANTS

NO COUPONS, NO SPECIAL CARDS...
NO ONE BUT YOU KNOWS YOU'RE SAVING MONEY!

Dine anytime you like – even holidays and weekends. Pay your bill as you normally would, with your existing credit cards. The next month, you'll receive a rebate check for 20% of your total bills, including beverages, tax and tip!

Simply register your credit cards with Dining à la Card, then use them to pay for your meals. It's that easy. *No one will know you're saving money* because your receipt shows the full amount and rebate checks are mailed directly to you.

More than 3,400 restaurants nationwide.

Hundreds of new restaurants are added each month. Try something new or choose your old favorites. At every participating restaurant, your first visit each month guarantees you a 20% cash rebate – up to $120 per visit. Whether you want to grab a quick bite or enjoy an intimate candlelight dinner, Dining à la Card will make the evening more attractive with 20% cash back.

Try it FREE for 60 days.

Enroll now and start earning 20% cash rebates today. If you're not satisfied with your savings, just call within 60 days to cancel your membership. Your credit card will not be charged and you keep the cash rebates you've earned.

REGISTER BY PHONE
800-833-3463
MOBIL GUIDE
SPECIAL ORDER CODE 027-312-009

TOLL FREE 24 HOURS

Dining à la Card™
Your Choice. Your Card. Your Business.

Choose the cards you want to register. After the FREE 60 DAYS, the $49.⁹⁵ annual registration fee will be charged to the first credit card listed.

❑ American Express ❑ VISA ❑ MasterCard ❑ Discover

Acct. # ☐☐☐☐☐☐☐☐☐☐☐☐☐☐☐☐☐☐☐

Exp. Date ☐☐☐☐

❑ American Express ❑ VISA ❑ MasterCard ❑ Discover

Acct. # ☐☐☐☐☐☐☐☐☐☐☐☐☐☐☐☐☐☐☐

Exp. Date ☐☐☐☐

❑ American Express ❑ VISA ❑ MasterCard ❑ Discover

Acct. # ☐☐☐☐☐☐☐☐☐☐☐☐☐☐☐☐☐☐☐

Exp. Date ☐☐☐☐

Name _____

Address _____

City _____

State _____ Zip _____

Home Phone ( ) _____

Bus. Phone ( ) _____

Signature X _____

027-312-009

Mail/Fax to: **Dining à la Card** - 200 N. Martingale Rd., Schaumburg, IL 60173 FAX 708–605–7149

951312(V5)

Product of The Signature Group, part of Montgomery Ward.

YOU CAN HELP MAKE THE *MOBIL TRAVEL GUIDES* MORE ACCURATE AND USEFUL

ALL INFORMATION WILL BE KEPT CONFIDENTIAL

Your Name_____
(Please Print)

Street_____

City, State, Zip_____

Were children with you on trip? ☐ Yes ☐ No

Number of people in your party _____

Your occupation_____

1.

Establishment name_____

Hotel ☐ Resort ☐ Cafeteria ☐
Motel ☐ Inn ☐ Restaurant ☐

Street_____ City_____ State _____

Do you agree with our description? ☐ Yes ☐ No If not, give reason_____

Please give us your opinion of the following:

ROOM DECOR	CLEANLINESS	SERVICE	FOOD
☐ Excellent	☐ Spotless	☐ Excellent	☐ Excellent
☐ Good	☐ Clean	☐ Good	☐ Good
☐ Fair	☐ Unclean	☐ Fair	☐ Fair
☐ Poor	☐ Dirty	☐ Poor	☐ Poor

1996 *GUIDE* RATING _____ ★

CHECK YOUR SUGGESTED RATING BELOW:
☐ ★ good, satisfactory ☐ ★★★★ outstanding
☐ ★★ very good ☐ ★★★★★ one of best
☐ ★★★ excellent in country
☐ ✓ unusually good value

Comments:_____

Date of visit_____

First visit? ☐ Yes ☐ No

2.

Establishment name_____

Hotel ☐ Resort ☐ Cafeteria ☐
Motel ☐ Inn ☐ Restaurant ☐

Street_____ City_____ State _____

Do you agree with our description? ☐ Yes ☐ No If not, give reason_____

Please give us your opinion of the following:

ROOM DECOR	CLEANLINESS	SERVICE	FOOD
☐ Excellent	☐ Spotless	☐ Excellent	☐ Excellent
☐ Good	☐ Clean	☐ Good	☐ Good
☐ Fair	☐ Unclean	☐ Fair	☐ Fair
☐ Poor	☐ Dirty	☐ Poor	☐ Poor

1996 *GUIDE* RATING _____ ★

CHECK YOUR SUGGESTED RATING BELOW:
☐ ★ good, satisfactory ☐ ★★★★ outstanding
☐ ★★ very good ☐ ★★★★★ one of best
☐ ★★★ excellent in country
☐ ✓ unusually good value

Comments:_____

Date of visit_____

First visit? ☐ Yes ☐ No

3.

Establishment name_____

Hotel ☐ Resort ☐ Cafeteria ☐
Motel ☐ Inn ☐ Restaurant ☐

Street_____ City_____ State _____

Do you agree with our description? ☐ Yes ☐ No If not, give reason_____

Please give us your opinion of the following:

ROOM DECOR	CLEANLINESS	SERVICE	FOOD
☐ Excellent	☐ Spotless	☐ Excellent	☐ Excellent
☐ Good	☐ Clean	☐ Good	☐ Good
☐ Fair	☐ Unclean	☐ Fair	☐ Fair
☐ Poor	☐ Dirty	☐ Poor	☐ Poor

1996 *GUIDE* RATING _____ ★

CHECK YOUR SUGGESTED RATING BELOW:
☐ ★ good, satisfactory ☐ ★★★★ outstanding
☐ ★★ very good ☐ ★★★★★ one of best
☐ ★★★ excellent in country
☐ ✓ unusually good value

Comments:_____

Date of visit_____

First visit? ☐ Yes ☐ No

FOLD AND TAPE (OR SEAL) FOR MAILING–DO NOT STAPLE

CUT ALONG DOTTED LINE

Revised editions are now being prepared for publication next year:

California and the West: Arizona, California, Nevada, Utah

Northeast: Connecticut, Maine, Massachusetts, New Hampshire, New York, Rhode Island, Vermont; Eastern Canada.

Mid-Atlantic: Delaware, District of Columbia, Maryland, New Jersey, North Carolina, Pennsylvania, South Carolina, Virginia, West Virginia.

Southeast: Alabama, Florida, Georgia, Kentucky, Mississippi, Tennessee.

Great Lakes: Illinois, Indiana, Michigan, Ohio, Wisconsin; Ontario, Canada.

Northwest: Idaho, Iowa, Minnesota, Montana, Nebraska, North Dakota, Oregon, South Dakota, Washington, Wyoming; Western Canada.

Southwest: Arkansas, Colorado, Kansas, Louisiana, Missouri, New Mexico, Oklahoma, Texas.

Frequent Traveler s Guide to Major Cities: Detailed coverage of 46 Major Cities, plus airport maps.

Mobil Travel Guides are available at Mobil Service Stations, bookstores, or by mail from Mobil Travel Guides, Random House, 400 Hahn Rd., Westminster, MD 21157, or call toll-free, 24 hours a day, 1-800-533-6478.

HOW CAN WE IMPROVE *MOBIL TRAVEL GUIDES*?

Mobil Travel Guides are constantly revising and improving. All attractions are updated and all listings are revised and evaluated annually. You can contribute to the accuracy and usefulness of the guides by sending us your reactions to the places you have visited. Your suggestions for improvement of the guides are also welcome. Just complete this prepaid mailing form or address letters to: *Mobil Travel Guide,* 4709 West Golf Rd., Suite 803, Skokie, IL 60076. The editors of the *Mobil Travel Guides* appreciate your useful comments.

Have you sent us one of these forms before?   ☐ Yes   ☐ No

Please make any general comment here. Thanks! _____

_____

_____

_____

★★★★★ Mobil Travel Guide®

The Guide That Saves You Money When You Travel.

AVIS — We try harder.®

$10.00-$20.00 OFF A WEEKEND RENTAL!

Rent an Intermediate through Full Size 4-Door car for a minimum of two consecutive weekend days and you can save $5.00 per day, up to a total of $20.00 off for four weekend rental days, when you present this coupon at a participating Avis location in the U.S.

Subject to complete Terms and Conditions on back. For information and reservations, call your travel consultant or an employee-owner of Avis at **1-800-831-8000**. And be sure to mention your Avis Worldwide Discount (AWD) number: **A291814**.

Rental Days	$ Off
2	$10
3	$15
4	$20

Coupon #MUGD717 for a 2 day rental
Coupon #MUGD718 for a 3 day rental
Coupon #MUGD719 for a 4 day rental

Offer expires December 31, 1996

CHOICE HOTELS INTERNATIONAL

Sleep · Comfort · Quality · Clarion · Friendship · Econo Lodge · Rodeway

10% OFF

The next time you're traveling, call **1-800-4-CHOICE** and request, **"Mobil Travelers' Discount."** You'll save 10% at participating Comfort, Quality, Clarion, Sleep, Econo Lodge, Rodeway and Friendship hotels. 1,400 Choice hotels will provide a free continental breakfast and children 18 and younger stay free when they share the same room as their parents.

Advance reservations are required through **1-800-4-CHOICE**. Discounts are based on availability at participating hotels and cannot be used in conjunction with any other discounts or promotions.

Offer expires December 31, 1996

Godfather's Pizza®

SPECIAL OFFER

Buy one large pizza for the price of a medium pizza.

Valid at participating locations. One coupon per visit, please. May not be used in conjunction with any other discount or promotion. Delivery charge extra. Limited delivery area and times.

Offer expires December 31, 1996

$5.00 OFF

This deluxe insulated cooler bag, perfect for camping, commuting, picnics or for taking along to your favorite sporting event. Measures 8 1/2" W x 6" D x 7" H. Retails for $9.99.

Offer expires December 31, 1996

Travel Discounters

UP TO $100.00 OFF

Receive up to $100.00 off when you buy an airline ticket from Travel Discounters. Call **1-800-355-1065** and mention code **MTG** in order to receive the discount.

Savings are subject to certain restrictions and availability. Valid for flights on most major airlines. See reverse for discount chart.

Offer expires December 31, 1996

General Cinema · LOEWS The Sony Theatres · UNITED ARTISTS

THEATRE DISCOUNT

Valid at all participating theatres. Please order all tickets in one order. Enclose 1 check for entire order. Please send me:

_____ Sony/Loews at $4.50 each = _____

_____ United Artists at $4.00 each = _____

_____ General Cinemas at $4.50 each = _____

Add $1.00 for handling. Allow 2-3 weeks for delivery. Make check payable to: Taste Publications International, 1031 Cromwell Bridge Road, Baltimore, MD 21286. Complete application on reverse side.

Offer expires December 31, 1996

Audio Diversions

SAVE UP TO 25%

Order three audiobooks from Audio Diversions 2,300 book collection and receive the fourth one (of similar value) with our compliments or receive 25% off on all purchases of 3 or more audiobooks (add $5.60 for shipping and handling). Call **1-800-628-6145** for more information. Ask for **CLUB 3B**.

Offer expires December 31, 1996

U.S. Express

SPECIAL OFFER

Get more than 100 rolls of Kodak film and 35mm camera for only $9.95.

Get a focus free 35mm Camtec Camera and special photo finishing package from U.S. EXPRESS, INC., a participating National KODAK Colorwatch System Lab that offers you FREE KODAK film (your choice) returned with your pictures. You'll also save 40% OFF on processing when dealing direct with our national lab.

© 1995 U.S. Express. Void where prohibited. Film offer valid with purchased processing. This offer not affiliated with Eastman Kodak Co.

Offer expires December 31, 1996

Please note: All offers may not be available in Canada.
Call (410) 825-3463 if you are unable to use an
800 number listed on the coupon.

CHOICE HOTELS
I N T E R N A T I O N A L

Friendship Econo Lodge RODEWAY

With your 10% **Mobil Travelers' Discount**,
the Choices - and savings - are better.
So, call **1-800-4-CHOICE** today!

TASTE PUBLICATIONS INTERNATIONAL

Terms and Conditions — Offer valid on an Intermediate (Group C) through a Full Size 4-Door (Group E) car for a 2-day minimum weekend rental. Coupon must be surrendered at time of rental; one per rental. May be used in conjunction with Taste Publications rates and discounts. May not be used in conjunction with any other coupon, promotion or offer. Coupon valid at Avis corporate and participating licensee locations in the continental U.S. Weekend rental period begins Thursday noon, and car must be returned by Monday 11:59 p.m. or coupon will not be valid. Offer not available during holiday and other blackout periods. Offer may not be available on all rates at all times. **An advance reservation is required.** Cars subject to availability. Taxes, local government surcharges and optional items, such as LDW, additional driver fee and refueling, are extra. Renter must meet Avis age, driver and credit requirements. Minimum age is 25. Offer expires December 31, 1996.
Rental Sales Agent Instructions At Checkout:
- In AWD, enter **A291814**.
- For a 3 day rental, enter **MUGD718** in CPN
- Complete this information: RA#_____ Rental Location_____
- For a 2 day rental, enter **MUGD717** in CPN
- For a 4 day rental, enter **MUGD719** in CPN
- Attach to COUPON tape.

©1995 Wizard Co., Inc.

TASTE PUBLICATIONS INTERNATIONAL

Yours for only $4.99 plus $3.95 shipping and handling.
Mail check or money order for $8.94 with coupon.
(IL residents add 8 3/4% sales tax) for each set to:
Joy International
3928 North Rockwell Street, Chicago, IL 60618

Name _____
Address _____
City _____
State _____ Zip _____

003A   109/82

TASTE PUBLICATIONS INTERNATIONAL

Godfather's Pizza ®

TASTE PUBLICATIONS INTERNATIONAL

General Cinema LOEWS The Sony Theatres

UNITED ARTISTS

A self-addressed stamped envelope must be enclosed to process your order. No refunds or exchanges. Mail order only, not redeemable at box office. Passes have expiration dates, generally one year from purchase.

Name _____
Address _____
City _____ State _____ Zip _____

TASTE PUBLICATIONS INTERNATIONAL

Travel Discounters

Minimum ticket price	Save
$200.00	$25.00
$250.00	$50.00
$350.00	$75.00
$450.00	$100.00

TASTE PUBLICATIONS INTERNATIONAL

Credit Card Orders Call
(615) 584-2626
Or enclose $9.95 (express shipping & handling) included.
RUSH MY 35mm CAMERA AND KODAK FILM OFFER TO:

_____
Name

_____
Address

_____
City/State/Zip

Mail $9.95 Payment of Check or Money Order to: **U.S. EXPRESS**
7035 Middlebrook Pike • P.O. Box 51730 • Knoxville, TN 37950

Auth. No. 347

TASTE PUBLICATIONS INTERNATIONAL

Audio Diversions

*Where Books
Talk and
People Listen.*

Audio Diversions offers one of the broadest collections of Literature for Listening currently available. With more than 2,300 titles carefully drawn from among the latest travelbooks and the best in adventure, mystery, biography, business, motivational, inspirational and self help books, Audio Diversions is sure to have what you need to purchase or rent. Rentals come with addressed and stamped packages for easy return. $5.60 for shipping and handling. Call **1-800-628-6145**. Ask for **CLUB 3B**.

TASTE PUBLICATIONS INTERNATIONAL

Read each coupon carefully before using. Discounts only apply to the items and terms specified in the offer at participating locations. Remove the coupon you wish to use.

DAYS INN
Follow the Sun℠

For reservations call:
1-800-DAYS INN

- Available at participating properties.
- This coupon cannot be combined with any other special discount offer.
- Limit one coupon per room, per stay.
- Offer expires December 31, 1996.

TASTE PUBLICATIONS INTERNATIONAL

Budget.
All The Difference In The World.™

Please note: Because of high competition in certain markets, occasionally promotional rates will be less than the discounted rate you are quoted. In those cases, it will be to your benefit to reserve at the promotional rate. Discount valid at participating locations only. Discounts apply to Economy through Luxury cars.

TASTE PUBLICATIONS INTERNATIONAL

❏ Yes! I want to preserve and protect our National Parks by becoming a National Parks and Conservation Association Member.
❏ I enclose a check for $15.00 for my one-year membership.
❏ Charge my annual dues to my ❏ Visa ❏ MasterCard ❏ Amex

Acct. #: _____ Exp. Date: _____
Signature: _____
Name: _____
Address: _____
City: _____ State: _____ Zip: _____
Phone: _____
Please allow 6-8 weeks for delivery of your fanny pack and first issue of National Parks Magazine.

Make checks payable and mail to:
NPCA, 1776 Massachusetts Ave. NW, Washington, DC 20036-1904

TASTE PUBLICATIONS INTERNATIONAL

The Place

Where Fresh is the Taste.™

TASTE PUBLICATIONS INTERNATIONAL

I Can't Believe It's **Yogurt!**®

TASTE PUBLICATIONS INTERNATIONAL

CPI Photo®
The 1-HR Photo Specialists
Over 600 locations nationwide

FOX PHOTO®

Call **1-800-366-3655**
for the location near you.

TASTE PUBLICATIONS INTERNATIONAL

BUSCH GARDENS
WILLIAMSBURG, VA.
An Anheuser-Busch Theme Park.

WATER COUNTRY USA
WILLIAMSBURG, VA.
An Anheuser-Busch Theme Park.

Present this coupon when purchasing your ticket at any Busch Gardens Williamsburg or Water Country USA general admission window to receive your discount on the regular one-day admission price. Children two and under are admitted FREE. Admission price includes all regularly scheduled rides, shows and attractions. This coupon has no cash value and cannot be used in conjunction with any other discount. Prices and schedule subject to change without notice. Busch Gardens Williamsburg and Water Country USA have a "no solicitation" policy. Limit six tickets per coupon.

1 2 3 4 5 6
Please circle number of admissions.
PLU# R364 C365

TASTE PUBLICATIONS INTERNATIONAL

Yours for only $19.95 plus $5.95 shipping and handling.
Mail check or money order for $25.90 with coupon
(IL residents add 8 3/4% sales tax) for each set to:

Joy International, 3928 North Rockwell Street, Chicago, IL 60618

Name _____
Address _____
City _____
State _____ Zip _____

003A   109/82

TASTE PUBLICATIONS INTERNATIONAL